MW00966808

As *Employee Benefits Answer Book, Te:* Departments of Labor, Treasury, and Health and Human Services issued interim final regulations addressing one *key* question: When will changes to a grandfathered group health plan after March 23, 2010, cause it to lose its grandfathered status?

The requirements of the 2010 Health Reform Act and their application to grandfathered plans are discussed extensively throughout *Employee Benefits Answer Book.* In this edition, you will find the answers to crucial questions about the 2010 Health Reform Act, including when a plan qualifies as a grandfathered plan (see Q 3:1). This update is written to help employers and benefit professionals assess how future changes to a group health plan will affect its grandfathered status and impact compliance with the 2010 Health Reform Act requirements.

The 2010 Health Reform Act [Patient Protection and Affordable Care Act, Pub L. No. 111-148 (Mar. 23, 2010)] as amended by the Health Care and Education Reconciliation Act of 2010 [Pub L. No. 111-152 (Mar. 30, 2010)] imposes new and extensive coverage and benefit mandates and restrictions on group health plans and health insurance issuers providing group health plan coverage. While some of these new requirements apply across the board, others do not apply to "grandfathered plans" in existence on March 23, 2010. For example, all plans, including grandfathered plans, must comply with the new prohibitions on preexisting-condition exclusions and lifetime and annual limits on coverage as well as coverage requirements for adult children. However, grandfathered plans are not required to comply with many new mandates and prohibitions, including first-dollar coverage of preventive care services and new nondiscrimination requirements for insured group health plans.

Basic Rules

Under the statute and the interim final regulations issued on June 14, 2010 [26 C.F.R. § 54.9815-1251T; 29 C.F.R. § 2590.715-1251; 45 C.F.R. § 147.140], a *grandfathered health plan* is defined as a plan in which an individual was enrolled on March 23, 2010. However, the interim final regulations emphasize that a plan need not continue to cover the same individual or individuals to maintain its grandfathered status. A group health plan or group health insurance coverage will not cease to be grandfathered health plan coverage merely because one or more (or even all) individuals enrolled on March 23, 2010, cease to be covered, provided the plan or group health insurance coverage has continuously covered someone since March 23, 2010 (not necessarily the same person, but at all times at least one person).

The regulations also make it clear that the determination of grandfathered status is to be made separately with respect to each benefit package made available under a group health plan or health insurance coverage.

To maintain its status as a grandfathered health plan, a plan or health insurance coverage must meet the following requirements.

Disclosure of grandfathered status. The plan must include a statement in any plan materials provided to a participant or beneficiary that the plan or coverage believes it is a grandfathered health plan within the meaning of the 2010 Health Reform Act and must provide contact information for questions and complaints. The regulations contain a model statement that will satisfy this disclosure requirement. The regulations can be found at *http://www.federalregister.gov/OFR Upload/OFRData/2010-14488_PI.pdf*

Documentation of plan or policy terms on March 23, 2010. The plan must maintain records documenting the terms of the plan or health insurance coverage in effect on March 23, 2010, and any other documents necessary to verify, explain, or clarify its status as a grandfathered health plan; and must make such records available for examination upon request.

Changes in Enrollees

As noted above, changes in the individuals enrolled in the plan generally will not cause a plan to lose its grandfathered status.

If an individual was enrolled in a group health plan or health insurance coverage on March 23, 2010, grandfathered health plan coverage includes coverage of family members of the individual who enroll after March 23, 2010 in the grandfathered health plan coverage of the individual.

In addition, a group health plan (including health insurance coverage provided in connection with the group health plan) that provided coverage on March 23, 2010 and has retained its status as a grandfathered health plan counts as grandfathered health plan coverage for new employees (whether newly hired or newly enrolled) and their families enrolling in the plan after March 23, 2010.

However, the interim final regulations contain two anti-abuse rules that are designed to prevent employers from circumventing the grandfather plan rules.

1. *Mergers and acquisitions.* If the principal purpose of a merger, acquisition, or similar business restructuring is to cover new individuals under a grandfathered health plan, the plan will cease to be a grandfathered health plan. According to the preamble to the regulations, the goal of this rule is to prevent grandfather status from being bought and sold as a commodity in commercial transactions.

2. *Plan to plan transfers.* As a general rule, transferring employees from one plan to another won't cause a loss of grandfather status. For example, routine changes during an open enrollment period are permitted. However, a loss of grandfather status will result where employees are transferred to a plan in order to make changes to their coverage that would result in a loss of grandfather status if made directly and there was no bona fide employment-based reason for the transfer. For this purpose, changing the terms or cost of coverage is not a bona fide employment-based reason. The transferee plan will lose its grandfather status if treating the transferee plan as an amendment of the transferor plan would cause a loss of grandfather status.

Example 1. As of March 23, 2010, a group health plan offers two benefit packages, Options F and G. During an open enrollment period, some of the employees who were enrolled in Option F on March 23, 2010 switch to Option G. *Result:* The group health coverage provided under Option G remains a grandfathered health plan because employees previously enrolled in Option F are treated as new enrollees in Option G.

Example 2. The facts are the same as those in Example 1, except that the employer eliminates Option F because of its cost and transfers employees covered under Option F to Option G. If instead of transferring employees from Option F to Option G, Option F was amended to match the terms of Option G, then Option F would cease to be a grandfathered health plan. *Result:* The employer did not have a bona fide employment-based reason to transfer employees from Option F to Option G. Therefore, Option G ceases to be a grandfathered health plan with respect to all employees.

Example 3. A group health plan offers two benefit packages on March 23, 2010, Options H and I. On March 23, 2010, Option H provides coverage only for employees in one manufacturing plant. Subsequently, the plant is closed, and some employees in the closed plant are moved to another plant. The employer eliminates Option H, and the employees that are moved are transferred to Option I. If, instead of transferring employees from Option H to Option I, Option H was amended to match the terms of Option I, then Option H would cease to be a grandfathered health plan. *Result:* Although treating the change as an amendment to Option I would cause a loss of grandfather status, the employer had a bona fide employment-based reason for transferring the employees. Therefore, Option I does not cease to be grandfathered health plan.

Changes in Benefits

Not surprisingly, an increase in plan benefits will not cause a plan to lose its grandfather status. However, the interim final regulations provide that the elimination of all or substantially all benefits to diagnose or treat a particular condition will cause a plan to cease to be a grandfathered health plan. For this purpose, the elimination of benefits for any necessary element to diagnose or treat a condition is considered the elimination of all or substantially all benefits to diagnose or treat the condition.

> **Example.** As of March 23, 2010, the terms of a group health plan provided benefits for a particular mental health condition, the treatment for which is a combination of counseling and prescription drugs. Subsequently, the plan eliminates benefits for counseling. *Result:* The plan ceases to be a grandfathered health plan. Because counseling is an element that is necessary to treat the mental condition, the plan is considered to have eliminated substantially all benefits for the treatment of the condition.

Changes in Cost-sharing

In the case of a *percentage* cost-sharing requirement (such as an individual's coinsurance requirement), any increase from March 23, 2010 will cause a loss of grandfathered status.

> **Example 1.** On March 23, 2010, a grandfathered health plan has a coinsurance requirement of 20% for inpatient surgery. The plan is subsequently amended to increase the coinsurance requirement to 25%. *Result*: The increase causes the plan to lose its grandfather status.

In the case of a *fixed-amount copayment*, a plan will lose grandfather status if the total increase in the copayment measured from March 23, 2010 exceeds the greater of (1) an amount equal to $5 increased by medical inflation (i.e., $5 times medical inflation, plus $5), or (2) a maximum percentage increase.

An increase in a *fixed-amount cost-sharing requirement other than a copayment* (for example, a deductible or out-of-pocket limit) will cause a plan to cease to be a grandfathered health plan, if the total percentage increase in the cost-sharing requirement measured from March 23, 2010 exceeds a maximum percentage increase.

For purposes of these rules, the maximum percentage increase equals medical inflation since March 2010, expressed as a percentage, plus 15 percentage points.

> **Example 2.** On March 23, 2010, a grandfathered health plan has a copayment of $30 per office visit for specialists. The plan is subsequently amended to increase the copayment to $40. The change represents a 33.33% increase in the copayment. Assuming medical inflation since March 2010, expressed as a percentage is 22.69%, the maximum percentage increase is 37.69% (22.69% + 15%). *Result*: Because 33.33% does not exceed the maximum percentage of 37.69%, the change in the copayment requirement at that time does not cause the plan to cease to be a grandfathered health plan.

Example 3. The facts are the same as those in Example 2, except that the grandfathered health plan increases the $40 copayment requirement to $45 for a later plan year. The change represents a percentage increase of 50% and a $15 total dollar increase in the copayment since March 23, 2010. At the time of the increase, medical inflation since March 2010 is 25.27%, so the maximum percentage increase is 40.27% (25.27% − 15%). In addition, $5 increased by medical inflation is $6.26. *Result*: Because the total increase since March 23, 2010 exceeds both the dollar limit and the maximum percentage limit, the plan ceases to be a grandfathered plan.

Changes in Employer Contributions

A plan will lose its grandfather status if the sponsoring employer or employee organization decreases its contribution rate for the cost of any tier of coverage for any class of similarly situated individuals by more than 5 percentage points below the contribution rate for the coverage period that includes March 23, 2010.

Example. On March 23, 2010, a self-insured group health plan provides two tiers of coverage—self-only and family. The employer contributes 80% of the total cost of self-only coverage and 60% of the total cost of family coverage for family. Subsequently, the employer reduces the contribution to 50% for family coverage, but keeps the same contribution rate for self-only coverage. *Result*: The 10 percentage point decrease in the contribution rate for family coverage causes the plan to cease to be a grandfathered health plan. The fact that the contribution rate for self-only coverage remains the same does not change the result.

Changes in Annual Limits

If, as of March 23, 2010, a plan imposed an overall annual limit on plan benefits, any decrease in the dollar value of the annual limit will cause the plan to lose its grandfather status.

If, as of March 23, 2010, a plan did not impose an overall annual or lifetime limit on benefits, the adoption of an annual limit will cause the plan to lose its grandfather status. However, if the plan in effect on March 23, 2010, imposed an overall lifetime limit but no overall annual limit, subsequent imposition of an annual limit will cost the plan its grandfather status only if the overall annual limit is *lower* than the lifetime limit in effect on March 23, 2010.

Note, however, that for plan years beginning on or after September 23, 2010, group health plans—including grandfathered plans—are prohibited from imposing lifetime limits on plan benefits. Plans—including grandfathered plans—may impose only "restricted" annual limits on essential benefits for plan years beginning before 2014, and are prohibited from imposing annual limits on essential benefits thereafter.

Changes in Insurance

Significantly, the interim final regulations provide that a change in insurers will cause a group health plan to lose its grandfather status. The regulations provide that if an employer or employee organization enters into a new policy, certificate, or contract of insurance after March 23, 2010 (because, for example, any previous policy, certificate, or contract of insurance is not being renewed), then that policy, certificate, or contract of insurance is not a grandfathered health plan with respect to the individuals in the group health plan.

Collectively Bargained Plans

An insured group health plan subject to a collective bargaining agreement ratified before March 23, 2010, is grandfathered at least until the date on which the last agreement relating to the coverage that was in effect on March 23, 2010, terminates. Collectively bargained plans may make changes to the benefit structure before the agreement terminates and remain grandfathered. After the termination date, grandfather status will be determined by comparing the plan, as it existed on March 23, 2010 to the changes that the plan made before termination under the rules established by the interim final regulations. However, this special grandfather treatment for collectively bargained plans applies only to *insured* plans. According to the preamble to the regulations, the statutory language of the special grandfather provision refers solely to "health insurance coverage" and does not refer to a group health plan; therefore, the interim final regulations apply the provision only to insured plans maintained pursuant to a collective bargaining agreement and not to self-insured plans. Thus, presumably, the grandfather status of a self-insured collectively bargained plan must be tested under the general rules discussed above.

The regulations also make it clear that the special grandfather rules for insured collectively bargained plans do not create a blanket exemption from the 2010 Health Reform Act requirements. Thus, the provisions that apply to grandfathered health plans apply to collectively bargained plans before and after termination of the last of the applicable collective bargaining agreement.

Transition Rules

The regulations writers acknowledge that group health plans are not set in stone. Group health plans and health insurance issuers often make routine changes from year to year, and some plans and issuers may have needed to implement such changes prior to the issuance of the interim final regulations. The interim final regulations provide a series of transition rules to deal with plan changes that might cause a plan to lose its grandfather status.

Changes made prior to March 23, 2010. The following changes will be considered part of the terms of a plan or health insurance coverage on

March 23, 2010 even though they were not effective at that time, and will not cause a loss of grandfather status:

- Changes effective after March 23, 2010, pursuant to a legally binding contract entered into on or before March 23, 2010;
- Changes effective after March 23, 2010, pursuant to a filing on or before March 23, 2010 with a State insurance department; or
- Changes effective after March 23, 2010, pursuant to written amendments to a plan that were adopted on or before March 23, 2010.

Changes made after March 23, 2010, and prior to regulations. If a group health plan or insurer made changes to the terms of a plan after March 23, 2010, and before June 14, 2010, the changes will not cause the plan or health insurance coverage to cease to be a grandfathered health plan if the changes are revoked or modified effective as of the first day of the first plan year beginning on or after September 23, 2010. For this purpose, changes will be considered to have been adopted prior to June 14, 2010 if:

- The changes are effective before that date;
- The changes are effective on or after that date pursuant to a legally binding contract entered into before that date;
- The changes are effective on or after that date pursuant to a filing before that date with a State insurance department; or
- The changes are effective on or after that date pursuant to written amendments to a plan that were adopted before that date.

Enforcement policy. Finally, for purposes of enforcement, the Departments of Treasury, Labor, and HHS will take into account good-faith efforts to comply with a reasonable interpretation of the statutory requirements and may disregard changes to plan and policy terms that were made before June 14, 2010, and that only modestly exceed those changes permitted under the regulations.

In the months and years ahead, employers with grandfathered plans will have some tough choices to make when it comes to plan changes. An employer can continue offering the plan or coverage in effect on March 23, 2010 with limited changes, and retain grandfather status, or it can significantly change the terms of the plan or coverage and be required to comply with the full panoply of 2010 Health Reform Act requirements. To determine the value of retaining the health plan's grandfather status, an employer will have to weigh the costs and benefits of grandfathered status against the costs and benefits of any proposed changes in the plan. This analysis will depend on such factors as the respective costs of grandfathered and non-grandfathered health plans, the plan's current level of compliance with the 2010 Health Act requirements, and the preferences of the plan's covered employees. In the Tenth Edition of *Employee Benefits Answer Book* readers will find comprehensive explanations of the 2010 Health Reform Act requirements to assist in making these important choices.

ASPEN PUBLISHERS

Employee Benefits Answer Book
Tenth Edition

by Dorinda D. DeScherer & Terence M. Myers

Employee Benefits Answer Book provides comprehensive guidance for employers and professionals involved in the design and administration of employee benefit plans. It starts with an informative overview of the regulatory framework governing employee benefits, then devotes individual chapters to detailed discussion of the myriad issues concerning different types of benefit arrangements. The question-and-answer format is ideal for probing key topics such as COBRA continuation coverage, retiree health care coverage, health coverage portability requirements, group long-term care insurance, dependent care assistance, adoption assistance, vacation and severance pay plans, death benefits, financing employee benefits, and financial accounting for employee benefits.

Employee Benefits Answer Book offers readers up-to-date information on various federal laws impacting employee benefits, including the Family and Medical Leave Act (FMLA), the Age Discrimination in Employment Act (ADEA), the Americans with Disabilities Act (ADA), the ADA Amendments Act (ADAAA), and the American Recovery and Reinvestment Act of 2009 (ARRA)—to name just a few. In addition, summaries of case law developments, practice pointers, and examples are included throughout the volume.

Highlights of the Tenth Edition

The past 12 months have seen the most significant new developments in employee benefits in almost four decades. Employers and benefits professionals have a great deal to digest, and this revised and expanded *Employee Benefits Answer Book* will help you every step of the way—explaining the what's, why's, and how's to keep your plans in compliance with the sweeping new changes.

First and foremost in terms of benefit changes is the mammoth 2010 Health Reform Act (technically, the Patient Protection and Affordable Care Act, Pub L. No. 111-148 (Mar. 23, 2010), amended by the Health Care and Education Reconciliation Act of 2010, Pub L. No. 111-152 (Mar. 30, 2010)). The Health Reform Act literally rewrites the book on group health plans. Whether an employer has an existing health plan, is setting up a new plan, or even has no current intention of providing employee health care coverage, the Health Reform Act can have an important impact.

The Tenth Edition provides the answers—and the crucial deadlines—for such Health Reform Act provisions as:

- Restrictions on lifetime and annual benefit limits;
- Restrictions on preexisting conditions;
- Prohibition on retroactive coverage cancellations;
- Prohibition on discrimination;
- Mandatory preventive care benefits;
- New employer reporting requirements;
- Automatic enrollment rules;
- Pay or play mandate for large employers;
- Restrictions on maximum waiting periods;
- Cap on flexible spending account contributions;
- New American Health Benefit Exchanges;
- New Small Business Health Opportunity Program (SHOP Exchanges) for small employers; and
- Excise tax on "Cadillac" health insurance coverage.

And there's more. The Health Reform Act came on the heels of a host of other major legal and regulatory developments during the past year. The Tenth Edition provides employers and benefits professionals with extensive and up-to-date guidance on:

- The new parity requirements for mental health and substance abuse disorder benefits under the Mental Health Parity and Addiction Equity Act of 2008 (MHPAEA);
- The Genetic Information Nondiscrimination Act of 2008 (GINA) and its impact on group health and welfare benefit plans;
- The comparability requirements for health savings accounts;
- The new disability nondiscrimination requirements of ADAAA;
- Updated rules under the FMLA, including the requirements for family military leave;
- New compliance hurdles for employee wellness programs;
- The COBRA premium subsidy for involuntarily terminated employees;

- New requirements under the HITECH Act to protect the privacy and security of employees' personal health information;

- The extended deadline for financial institutions and creditors to comply with the Red Flag Rules; and

- Expanded transportation fringe benefits, including the benefits for bicycle commuters.

7/10

For questions concerning this shipment, billing, or other customer service matters, call our Customer Service Department at 1-800-234-1660.

For toll-free ordering, please call 1-800-638-8437.

ASPEN PUBLISHERS

Employee Benefits Answer Book

Tenth Edition

Dorinda D. DeScherer
Terence M. Myers

 Wolters Kluwer
Law & Business

AUSTIN   BOSTON   CHICAGO   NEW YORK   THE NETHERLANDS

This publication is designed to provide accurate and authoritative information in regard to the subject matter covered. It is sold with the understanding that the publisher is not engaged in rendering legal, accounting, or other professional services. If legal advice or other professional assistance is required, the services of a competent professional person should be sought.

—From a *Declaration of Principles* jointly adopted by
a Committee of the American Bar Association and
a Committee of Publishers and Associations

Printed in the United States of America

ISBN 978-0-7355-9116-5

1 2 3 4 5 6 7 8 9 0

About Wolters Kluwer Law & Business

Wolters Kluwer Law & Business is a leading provider of research information and workflow solutions in key specialty areas. The strengths of the individual brands of Aspen Publishers, CCH, Kluwer Law International and Loislaw are aligned within Wolters Kluwer Law & Business to provide comprehensive, in-depth solutions and expert-authored content for the legal, professional and education markets.

CCH was founded in 1913 and has served more than four generations of business professionals and their clients. The CCH products in the Wolters Kluwer Law & Business group are highly regarded electronic and print resources for legal, securities, antitrust and trade regulation, government contracting, banking, pension, payroll, employment and labor, and healthcare reimbursement and compliance professionals.

Aspen Publishers is a leading information provider for attorneys, business professionals and law students. Written by preeminent authorities, Aspen products offer analytical and practical information in a range of specialty practice areas from securities law and intellectual property to mergers and acquisitions and pension/benefits. Aspen's trusted legal education resources provide professors and students with high-quality, up-to-date and effective resources for successful instruction and study in all areas of the law.

Kluwer Law International supplies the global business community with comprehensive English-language international legal information. Legal practitioners, corporate counsel and business executives around the world rely on the Kluwer Law International journals, loose-leafs, books and electronic products for authoritative information in many areas of international legal practice.

Loislaw is a premier provider of digitized legal content to small law firm practitioners of various specializations. Loislaw provides attorneys with the ability to quickly and efficiently find the necessary legal information they need, when and where they need it, by facilitating access to primary law as well as state-specific law, records, forms and treatises.

Wolters Kluwer Law & Business, a unit of Wolters Kluwer, is headquartered in New York and Riverwoods, Illinois. Wolters Kluwer is a leading multinational publisher and information services company.

ASPEN PUBLISHERS SUBSCRIPTION NOTICE

This Aspen Publishers product is updated on a periodic basis with supplements to reflect important changes in the subject matter. If you purchased this product directly from Aspen Publishers, we have already recorded your subscription for the update service.

If, however, you purchased this product from a bookstore and wish to receive future updates and revised or related volumes billed separately with a 30-day examination review, please contact our Customer Service Department at 1-800-234-1660 or send your name, company name (if applicable), address, and the title of the product to:

ASPEN PUBLISHERS
7201 McKinney Circle
Frederick, MD 21704

Important Aspen Publishers Contact Information

- To order any Aspen Publishers title, go to *www.aspenpublishers.com* or call 1-800-638-8437.

- To reinstate your manual update service, call 1-800-638-8437.

- To contact Customer Care, e-mail *customer.care@aspenpublishers .com*, call 1-800-234-1660, fax 1-800-901-9075, or mail correspondence to Order Department, Aspen Publishers, PO Box 990, Frederick, MD 21705.

- To review your account history or pay an invoice online, visit *www.aspenpublishers.com/payinvoices*.

Preface

Employee Benefits Answer Book is designed for professionals who need quick and authoritative answers to their clients' questions on whether to institute or continue medical plans, group term life insurance, cafeteria plans, or other employee welfare benefit plans; how to choose and implement the plans most suited to their needs; and how to comply with complex federal reporting and disclosure requirements.

Because employee benefits is one of the most rapidly changing areas of the law, professionals involved in the design and administration of employee benefits must stay on top of the new rules and regulations issued by various federal agencies and significant cases affecting employee benefit plans.

The authors use straightforward, nontechnical language to set forth their thoughtful overview of the basic concepts in each chapter and then delve into the details. The question-and-answer format enables readers to zoom right to the key information they are seeking, and cross-references remind them of other pertinent considerations.

Numbering System. The questions are numbered consecutively within each chapter (e.g., 2:1, 2:2, 2:3, etc.). In annual supplements, new questions may be inserted between existing questions of the main volume. For example, a new question inserted between Q 1:8 and Q 1:9 would be designated Q 1:8.1. When a question in the main volume is revised, it is reproduced in the supplement. When a chapter in the main volume is replaced, question numbers and cross-references within the chapter are renumbered and updated.

List of Questions. The List of Questions in the front of the book helps the reader locate areas of immediate interest. This list serves as a detailed table of contents. Within each chapter, the section headings group and organize questions by topic.

Examples. Numerous examples are provided throughout the chapters to illustrate important concepts.

Notes and Practice Pointers. Interspersed liberally throughout the text are paragraphs that underscore practical considerations and "tips" that are intended to help the practitioner design, implement, and administer effective employee benefit plans.

Citations. Citations to cases and references to statutes and authorities are included for readers who may wish to research specific topics.

Glossary. A glossary of technical terms and acronyms commonly used in the welfare benefits area is provided at the end of the book.

Tables of Statutes, Authorities, and Cases. Tables of statutes, authorities, and cases are finders' aids appreciated by readers who wish to research specific topics. The entries in these tables are referenced to question numbers.

Index. A topical index is provided as a further aid to locating specific information. All references in the index are to question numbers.

About the Authors

Dorinda D. DeScherer, J.D., is a graduate of Barnard College of Columbia University and the University of Maryland School of Law. A former associate managing editor for Prentice Hall Information Services, where she had primary responsibility for special projects, including explanatory materials on new tax laws, Ms. DeScherer has extensive experience writing and editing a wide range of tax and business publications.

Terence M. Myers, J.D., is a graduate of Georgetown University and the National Law Center, George Washington University. He is former managing editor of the Tax & Professional Practice unit of Prentice Hall, Inc. He has broad experience in launching, writing, and editing tax publications.

DeScherer and Myers are the chief editors of Editorial Resource Group, Inc. (ERG). Through ERG they create, write, edit, and market successful tax, financial, business, and management-related publications. ERG's products are directed at CPAs, tax lawyers, corporate officers, human resource professionals, tax return preparers, and small business owners. ERG's publications include *Wage Hour Compliance Handbook* and *Business Tax Answer Book*, published by Aspen Publishers. ERG has also contributed to a variety of tax and professional newsletters and authored continuing professional education courses.

Contents

CHAPTER 3
Group Health Plans: Structure and Administration 3-1

Contents

CHAPTER 4

Retiree Medical Benefits

Contents

Contents

CHAPTER **8**
Dependent Care Assistance and Adoption Assistance ... 8-1

CHAPTER **9**
Group Long-Term Care Insurance 9-1

CHAPTER **10**
Disability Income Plans 10-1

Contents

CHAPTER 17

Age Discrimination in Employment Act of 1967 17-1

Contents

List of Questions

Chapter 1 Introduction

Plan Development: Adoption, Amendment, and Termination

Plan Assets

Chapter 3   Group Health Plans: Structure and Administration

Tax Treatment of Participants

Health Reimbursement Arrangements

Medical Savings Accounts

Health Savings Accounts

Employee Assistance Programs

Chapter 4 Retiree Medical Benefits

Chapter 5 Group Health Plans: Mandated Benefits and Standards

Prohibition of Discrimination in Favor of Highly Compensated Employees

Medicare Secondary-Payer Rules

Children's Health Insurance Program

Chapter 6 COBRA Requirements for Continuation of Coverage Under Group Health Plans

Plan Year

Subsidized COBRA Coverage for Assistance-Eligible Individuals

Chapter 7 Cafeteria Plans

Elections

Chapter 8 Dependent Care Assistance and Adoption Assistance

Dependent Care Assistance Programs

Chapter 9 Group Long-Term Care Insurance

Chapter 10 Disability Income Plans

Chapter 11 Group Term Life Insurance Plans

Basic Concepts

General Death Benefit Requirement

"Group of Employees" Requirement

Chapter 12 Death Benefits Other Than Employee Group Term Life Insurance

Dependent Group Term Life Insurance

Group Universal Life Insurance

Uninsured Death Benefits

Split-Dollar Life Insurance

Chapter 13 Fringe Benefits

Overview

No-Additional-Cost Services

Employee Discounts

Qualified Moving Expense Reimbursements

Employee Gifts and Achievement Awards

Disaster Relief Assistance

Group Legal Services Plans

Chapter 15 Vacation and Severance Pay Plans

Chapter 16 Family and Medical Leave

Basic Concepts

Certification of FMLA Leave Eligibility

Chapter 17 Age Discrimination in Employment Act of 1967

Basic Concepts

Covered Employers

Covered Employees

Providing Lesser Benefits to Older Workers

Chapter 19 Other Federal Laws

Title VII of the Civil Rights Act of 1964

Genetic Information Nondiscrimination Act of 2008

Miscellaneous

Chapter 20 Funding and Financing Welfare Benefits

Overview of Funding Alternatives

Welfare Benefit Fund Rules

Financing Welfare Benefits with Life Insurance

Financial Accounting Rules for Nonpension Retiree and Postemployment Benefits

Postretirement Welfare Benefits

Disclosure Requirements

Reducing or Eliminating the Accounting Liability

Postemployment Benefits

Chapter 1

Introduction

In recent years, increasing attention has focused on "soft" employee benefits—those "other" benefits besides pensions and profit sharing plans. Medical coverage, life insurance, long-term disability benefits, severance pay, and other employee welfare benefits have assumed heightened importance as the safety net that protects employees now, on a day-to-day basis. Employees sue to get them. Former employees sue to keep from losing them. Congress regulates them more. Employers face higher and higher costs in providing them. Everybody is getting squeezed, and the result is far more scrutiny of how these benefits are designed and administered. Therein lie the headaches and the challenges.

Employee Benefits Answer Book, Tenth Edition, is designed to bring beginners from 0 to 60 miles an hour as painlessly as possible. Each chapter gives readers a solid grounding in the basic concepts first and then explores the all-important details. For advanced practitioners, this book reviews the key concepts and highlights the emerging legal issues that affect plan design and administration. The Q&A format lends itself to "dipping in" to check on an issue and dipping in again later to check on another. Readers zoom right to the key information, and cross-references remind them of other pertinent considerations. The numerous citations help readers verify a particular issue and/or research it further.

Since this book is about the law—what practitioners need to know, what they must do, and what options they may have—it isn't always easy reading. Some of the applicable statutes and regulations contain lengthy technical requirements. But we have tried hard to make it clear and understandable.

A Road Map to the Tenth Edition

Q 1:1   How do the individual chapters explain pieces of the employee welfare benefit law puzzle?

Chapter 2, The Regulatory Scheme: ERISA. The Employee Retirement Income Security Act of 1974 (ERISA) is the key building block. One simply cannot be an employee benefit professional without understanding the major requirements of this law. ERISA is such a huge law that it also cannot be understood all at once. Professionals will need to keep referring to it, exploring each part until they grasp the overall scheme and master its various requirements. Chapter 2 explains who is a fiduciary; what specific standards of conduct ERISA imposes on fiduciaries; and how plans must be written, communicated to participants, and filed with various different federal agencies. It covers ERISA's requirements for administering plan benefits, for handling plan money, and for participants and beneficiaries to claim benefits. Most important, it carefully walks readers through the concept of preemption of state law, one of ERISA's most powerful and far-reaching provisions. And, of course, chapter 2 contains a complete catalog of the numerous ERISA penalties that can apply when things go wrong.

Chapter 3, Group Health Plans: Structure and Administration. Year after year, health benefits rank as the most important benefit to employees—and as the most expensive for employers. Moreover, group health plans have become the target of increasing federal regulation, including the massive 2010 Health Reform Act. Consequently, properly structuring group health benefits and administering them in accordance with the law is one of the most important—and often daunting—tasks for benefits professionals. This chapter focuses on the nuts and bolts of group health plans, including types of medical plans and various methods of cost-effective design, and the requirements for administration of health benefits. The tax rules for employers and employees are also discussed in detail. Most importantly, this chapter contains comprehensive coverage of the 2010 Health Reform Act and its impact on the structure and administration of group health plans.

Chapter 4, Retiree Medical Benefits. Retiree medical benefits are desperately needed by retired individuals on fixed incomes and painfully costly for employers. Managing costs, cutting back benefits, and funding future liability are covered in this chapter.

Chapter 5, Group Health Plans: Mandated Benefits and Standards. Congress has set its sights on group health plans in recent years, imposing new and extensive coverage requirements. From the Health Insurance Portability and Accountability Act of 1996 (HIPAA) to the 2010 Health Reform Act, nearly every year has heralded in a new mandate or new restriction on employer-provided health coverage. These requirements and restrictions are explored in detail in this chapter.

Chapter 6, COBRA Requirements for Continuation of Coverage Under Group Health Plans. This chapter is a how-to guide to the Consolidated Omnibus Budget Reconciliation Act of 1985 (COBRA) that covers a wide range of issues, such as initial COBRA notices, qualified individuals, qualifying events, who must notify whom when a qualifying event occurs, electing COBRA coverage, type and duration of required group health plan coverage, when it can be cut off early, how much can be charged, divorce, retirement, termination for gross misconduct, and mergers and acquisitions.

Chapter 7, Cafeteria Plans. Cafeteria plans are creatures of the Internal Revenue Code. This chapter describes how they work, what is required to set them up correctly, and how to navigate the often complex administrative requirements. Key problem areas for employers considering or administering cafeteria plans are the extensive and labor-intensive nondiscrimination rules associated with these plans. For these employers, the new SIMPLE cafeteria plan introduced by the 2010 Health Reform Act may be the answer. Look no further than this chapter for details on this newest cafeteria plan option.

Chapter 8, Dependent Care Assistance and Adoption Assistance. This chapter deals with employee benefits for workers with children. It explains the special tax rules for dependent care assistance plans that enable working parents to obtain financial help for child care. Employer-provided adoption assistance programs provide an additional financial boost for both domestic and foreign adoptions. The special tax benefits for these programs—including expanded tax breaks under the 2010 Health Reform Act—are discussed in this chapter.

Chapter 9, Group Long-Term Care Insurance. Group long-term care insurance is a popular benefit. This chapter describes what it is, what it does, how it is taxed, and why it is so attractive.

Chapter 10, Disability Income Plans. Disability income plans replace income lost when an individual cannot work because of a disability. This chapter reviews the tax rules and spends considerable time on how to avoid fraudulent claims that run up the cost of the plan. Regulations regarding the processing of disability benefit claims are also included.

Chapter 11, Group Term Life Insurance Plans. Employer-provided group term life insurance is a bread-and-butter benefit that forms a crucial part of an employee's financial safety net. The tax rules are extensive and detailed, and giving more benefits to key employees can backfire spectacularly. This chapter covers the dos and don'ts of plan design, how discrimination testing must be performed, and the traps that can cause employee-pay-all group term life insurance to be treated and taxed as employer-paid.

Chapter 12, Death Benefits Other Than Employee Group Term Life Insurance. This chapter covers the many additional ways that employers provide or make available financial protection to employees in the event of death. Included are dependent group term life insurance, accidental death benefits, business travel accident insurance, group universal life insurance, uninsured death benefits, split-dollar life insurance, bonus life insurance, death benefits under qualified retirement plans, accelerated death benefits, and living benefits. (Corporate-owned life insurance, which protects the employer rather than the employee, is covered in chapter 19.)

Chapter 13, Fringe Benefits. This is the category of last resort for obtaining favorable tax treatment of employer-provided benefits. The rules are many and decidedly picky. This chapter covers no-additional-cost services, employee discounts, working condition fringe benefits, aircraft, cars and other vehicles, *de minimis* fringe benefits, employer-operated eating facilities, occasional meal money and local transportation fare, transportation benefits, on-premises athletic facilities, meals and lodging, employee gifts and achievement awards, and group legal services plans. This chapter also looks at the timely topic of employer-provided disaster relief assistance.

Chapter 14, Educational Assistance. A well-educated workforce can benefit an employer. Moreover, educational assistance receives several types of favorable tax treatment under the Internal Revenue Code. The confusing web of rules governing educational assistance is carefully delineated from the rules governing qualified scholarships and tuition assistance plans.

Chapter 15, Vacation and Severance Pay Plans. This is a chapter about money: when employees get it and when they don't. Severance pay, in particular, has generated an increasing amount of litigation, and the case law developments discussed here teach much about careful plan design and administration. Also included is the trend toward enlarging the fiduciary responsibility to disclose plans that are in the works but not yet adopted.

Chapter 16, Family and Medical Leave. The rules for this federally mandated benefit are only slightly less complicated than the blueprints for all of New York City. One editor suggested, tongue in cheek, "Try to sum up." We did.

Chapter 17, Age Discrimination in Employment Act of 1967. The Equal Employment Opportunity Commission's ADEA regulations are discussed in detail in this chapter. They dictate parameters within which group term life insurance and long-term disability plans, for example, must be designed and priced. Requirements for knowing waiver of ADEA rights are included.

Chapter 18, Americans with Disabilities Act of 1990. The ADA, amended in 2008, adds yet another layer of regulation for employee welfare benefit plans. This chapter discusses the ADA's definition of disability and the ways employers can and cannot limit welfare benefits for disabled individuals, particularly under long-term disability plans.

Chapter 19, Other Federal Laws. This chapter covers all the other somewhat unlikely places where even more rules applying to employee welfare benefit plans are located. It includes labor laws and collective bargaining, Titles VI and VII of the Civil Rights Act of 1964, the Equal Pay Act of 1963, the Rehabilitation Act of 1973, the Worker Adjustment and Retraining Notification Act of 1988, and federal law regarding retiree benefits of bankrupt companies. Of particular significance for an increasing number of employers are the rights of veterans and military retirees, and employer benefit and compensation obligations regarding employees who perform military service.

Chapter 20, Funding and Financing Welfare Benefits. This chapter covers the strategies employers use to pay for various benefits by insuring, self-insuring, setting up trusts, buying life insurance, and so forth, and what funding methods yield tax advantages. Besides the welfare benefit fund rules and voluntary employees' beneficiary association trusts, this chapter also discusses creative alternatives such as funding postretirement medical benefits under a pension plan. Of particular note are new restrictions on the use of corporate-owned life insurance as a benefit funding mechanism.

Chapter 21, Financial Accounting Rules for Nonpension Retiree and Postemployment Benefits. This chapter discusses required disclosures to shareholders and investors and the uniform rules employers must use when calculating their unfunded future liability for nonpension retiree benefits.

A Thumbnail Guide to Important Regulatory Goals

Q 1:2   Why are employee welfare benefit plans so heavily regulated?

Employee welfare benefit plans are heavily regulated for two reasons. First, fringe benefits have evolved into an important safety net of financial protection for employees. Second, because the majority of health and welfare benefits are provided through employer plans, social policy goals of increasing coverage or benefits can most readily be accomplished by requiring employers to amend their plans.

Q 1:3   Why are there so many different laws regulating employee welfare benefit plans?

There is no single law regulating employee welfare benefits because changes in the welfare benefits area tend to be smaller in scope and done in fits and starts rather than as part of a complete overhaul of the entire area. The result is a patchwork of requirements that welfare benefit plans must meet. Even the massive 2010 Health Reform Act builds on, rather than preempts, existing rules to a large extent.

In the tax area, former Section 89 of the Internal Revenue Code (Code; I.R.C.) attempted to overhaul and make uniform a whole series of tax rules with conflicting eligibility and coverage standards for welfare benefit plans. However, the proposed regulations were so gruesomely complicated and burdensome that employers put up a stiff resistance and had Section 89 repealed.

Q 1:4   Are employers required to offer employee welfare benefits to employees?

Currently, no federal law absolutely requires an employer to offer an employee welfare benefit plan, although new "pay or play' rules in the 2010 Health Reform Act require large employers to provide employee health benefits or pay a penalty. All of the federal laws discussed in this book do, however, place requirements, conditions, and limitations on plans that the employer may voluntarily offer.

Q 1:5   How is regulation of employee welfare benefits structured to accomplish the desired social policy goals?

By far the most popular vehicle for influencing employer-provided welfare benefit plans is the Internal Revenue Code. Congress can create a powerful economic push toward desired employer behavior by incorporating financial incentives or disincentives into the Code. Typically, one of four techniques is used:

1. Allowing or restricting the deductibility of employer contributions to plans;

2. Exempting from taxation or taxing the value of coverage provided to employees;

3. Exempting from taxation or taxing the benefits received from the plan by the employee or beneficiary; and

4. Imposing excise taxes on the employer for undesirable practices.

These methods are often used to ensure that the plan's eligibility provisions and covered benefits do not discriminate in favor of highly compensated employees. They are also used to encourage employers to extend plan coverage to a significant portion of rank-and-file employees. Occasionally, these methods are used to require benefits deemed socially desirable, such as continuation of medical plan coverage for a period of time after termination of employment, death, or divorce (COBRA excise tax); coverage of specific medical conditions, such as end-stage renal disease (Code Section 5000 excise tax); coverage of pediatric vaccines; or coverage of preexisting conditions (HIPAA). Occasionally, these techniques are used in combination to achieve the maximum desired behavior.

Other federal laws generally fall into two categories: those that seek to regulate employee benefit plans directly and those that do so more indirectly. For example, Section 701 of the Employee Retirement Income Security Act of 1974 (ERISA) restricts group health plans from imposing preexisting-condition limits or exclusions in excess of stated maximums; COBRA and the Family and Medical Leave Act of 1993 (FMLA) require that the right to continue group health plan coverage be granted in certain circumstances. Other federal laws prohibit broad categories of specified behavior, such as discrimination based on age, sex, race, color, religion, national origin, disability, or genetic information within specified contexts, such as in hiring, firing, and wage and compensation practices. For example, Title VII of the Civil Rights Act prohibits, among other things, discrimination on the basis of sex in a wide variety of employment contexts, including employer-provided fringe benefits plans, and has recently begun to be interpreted as barring discrimination on the basis of sexual orientation.

The statutes may impose civil fines for violations and criminal sanctions for intentional wrongdoing, allow private individuals to bring lawsuits, or empower governmental agencies to impose fines and penalties or to bring enforcement proceedings.

Q 1:6   Which federal agencies have jurisdiction over employee benefits?

A variety of federal agencies have jurisdiction over specific aspects of employee welfare benefit plans. The agencies with major responsibilities in the employee welfare benefit plan area include:

1. The Internal Revenue Service (IRS), which administers the Code provisions governing various types of welfare benefit plans;

2. The U.S. Department of Labor (DOL), which administers ERISA, the FMLA, and other federal labor laws;

3. The Equal Employment Opportunity Commission (EEOC), which administers the Civil Rights Act of 1964, the Age Discrimination in Employment Act (ADEA), and the Americans with Disabilities Act (ADA); and

4. The U.S. Department of Health and Human Services (DHHS), which administers the federal Health Maintenance Organizations Act and the Social Security Act, including the provisions affecting employer-provided medical plan treatment of Medicare-eligible individuals.

Q 1:7   When employers design their welfare benefit plans, must they duplicate various governmental benefits?

Employee welfare benefit plans frequently are structured to take into account the benefits available to employees under various kinds of governmental welfare benefit programs. Thus, an employee benefit plan may integrate its benefits with the governmental benefits (sometimes resulting in reduced benefits from the employer's plan) so the employees do not receive more total benefits than the employer considers appropriate. In recent years, the federal government has become more sensitive to employer attempts to achieve savings in this manner, and statutory changes have limited or forbidden integration in certain areas, particularly in the area of Medicare and Medicaid benefits.

Q 1:8   Do states impose another layer of regulation on employee welfare benefit plans?

States continue to be aggressive in attempting to regulate the scope and content of employee welfare benefit plans (requiring, for example, substance abuse coverage, hospice care, coverage of divorced spouses, and coverage of the services of various licensed professionals such as podiatrists, chiropractors, and midwives). States also continue attempting to define broadly when a plan is "insured" and thus subject to state insurance laws.

As discussed in detail in chapter 2, federal law (ERISA) generally preempts all state laws affecting employee welfare benefit plans; however, an exception is provided for insured plans because insurance policies or contracts issued to such plans remain subject to extensive state insurance laws and regulations. Accordingly, a multistate employer may find it difficult, if not impossible, to maintain a uniform nationwide welfare benefit plan unless the plan is uninsured. Moreover, there is constant debate about whether particular state laws relate to ERISA plans or fall into ERISA's insurance law exemption. As a result, the cases on whether ERISA preempts state law continue to proliferate.

Practical Plan Administration

Q 1:9   How, ideally, should an employer approach designing and administering employee welfare benefit plans?

Numerous practice pointers are provided throughout the following chapters. Underlying each is the core message: Taking simple steps now can save a lot of headaches later.

The key is preventive planning. The first step is to design and administer plans to meet, at minimum, the known requirements of the applicable laws. A surprising number of employers simply fail to do this. As several of the chapters in this book explain, however, mistakes can be costly. Each chapter sets forth the major issues that need to be considered and, where appropriate, the consequences of failing to comply or to take action. Second, if there are practical steps that can be taken to avoid costly administrative errors and potential future litigation, we try to point them out. Third, changes in the law, the regulations, and individual case decisions constantly affect plan design and administration. It is important to keep up with developments and incorporate them into welfare benefit programs.

There are no guarantees; sometimes there are no clear answers. But we have designed this edition of the *Employee Benefits Answer Book* to help provide a solid groundwork for wise benefit plan decisions.

Chapter 2

The Regulatory Scheme: ERISA

The Employee Retirement Income Security Act of 1974 (ERISA) is the main federal statute that provides the regulatory framework for employee welfare benefit plans. This chapter describes the ERISA rules that pertain to welfare benefit plans only; ERISA's pension plan rules are beyond the scope of this book.

Provisions of ERISA specifically affecting group health plans—including significant changes made by the 2010 Health Reform Act—are discussed in detail in other chapters of this book.

Basic Concepts and Definitions

Q 2:1   What does the Employee Retirement Income Security Act of 1974 cover?

Although ERISA is perhaps more frequently viewed in a retirement plan context and, in general, regulates retirement plans more heavily than welfare benefit plans, ERISA provides significant protections for participants in employee welfare benefit plans and their beneficiaries. To this end, ERISA imposes a variety of reporting and disclosure requirements on administrators of welfare benefit plans. These requirements mandate that certain financial and other plan information be reported to the Internal Revenue Service (IRS) and the Department of Labor (DOL) and be disclosed to plan participants and their beneficiaries. ERISA also mandates standards of conduct, responsibility, and obligation for fiduciaries of employee benefit plans and provides appropriate remedies, sanctions, and access to the federal courts when these responsibilities have been breached.

Preemption of state law. A major benefit of ERISA, particularly for multistate employers, comes from ERISA's preemption of most state laws. The ERISA preemption provisions (which are described in detail in this chapter) are intended to preserve flexibility for multistate employers that desire to offer a single, uniform benefit plan on a regional or nationwide basis. While the courts have given ERISA's preemption of state law a broad sweep, the exact limits of ERISA preemption continue to be heavily litigated.

Group health plan requirements. Since its enactment in 1974, ERISA has been repeatedly amended to impose an ever-increasing number of coverage standards and operational requirements on group health plans. The 2010 Health Reform Act (Patient Protection and Affordable Care Act) [Pub L. No. 111-148 (Mar. 23, 2010)] as amended by the Health Care and Education Affordability Reconciliation Act of 2010 [Pub L. No. 111-152 (Mar. 30, 2010)] has significantly added to these requirements. These requirements are discussed in detail in the following chapters:

- Chapter 3—Group Health Plans: Structure and Administration
- Chapter 5—Group Health Plans: Mandated Benefits and Standards
- Chapter 6—COBRA Requirements for Continuation of Coverage

Note. ERISA's extensive pension plan rules are beyond the scope of this book.

Q 2:2   How does ERISA regulate the structure or design of a welfare benefit plan?

A welfare benefit plan covered by ERISA must meet the following legal requirements:

1. The plan must be in writing and contain specified information (see Qs 2:22–2:27);

2. The assets of the plan must be held in trust by one or more trustees, unless certain exemptions are satisfied (see Qs 2:95–2:99);

3. The plan must establish, maintain, and inform participants and beneficiaries of the procedure for presenting claims for benefits, the basis for claim denials, and the procedure for appealing denials of claims. The appeal procedure must afford a reasonable opportunity for a full and fair review by the appropriate named fiduciary (see Qs 2:125–2:139); and

4. The plan must contain whatever benefit provisions may be required under ERISA (see Qs 2:44–2:45).

[ERISA §§ 402, 403, 503, 601–609, 701–734; 29 U.S.C. §§ 1102, 1103, 1133, 1161, 1169]

Q 2:3   Who is the plan sponsor?

Under ERISA, the plan sponsor is:

1. The employer, if the plan is established or maintained by a single employer;

2. The employee organization, if the plan is established or maintained by an employee organization; or

3. The association, committee, joint board of trustees, or other similar group of representatives of the parties that establish or maintain the plan, if the plan is established or maintained by two or more employers or jointly by one or more employers and one or more employee organizations.

[ERISA §3(16)(B); 29 U.S.C. §1002(16)(B)]

Q 2:4   Who is the plan administrator?

Under ERISA, the plan administrator is either:

1. The person whom the plan instrument specifically designates as plan administrator; or

2. In the absence of such a designation, the plan sponsor.

[ERISA 3(16)(A); 29 U.S.C. §1002(16)(A)]

Covered Employers

Q 2:5   Which employers and other entities are subject to ERISA?

ERISA generally covers employee welfare benefit plans established or maintained by:

1. Any employer engaged in interstate commerce or in any industry or activity affecting interstate commerce [ERISA §§3(5), 3(11), 3(12), 4(a)(1); 29 U.S.C. §§1002(5), 1002(11), 1002(12), 1003(a)(1)];

2. One or more employee organizations representing employees engaged in interstate commerce or in any industry or activity affecting interstate commerce [ERISA §§3(4), 3(11), 3(12), 4(a)(2), 4(a)(3); 29 U.S.C. §§1002(4), 1002(11), 1002(12), 1003(a)(2), 1003(a)(3); DOL Adv. Op. 90-11A (Apr. 25, 1990)]; or

3. Both of the above, jointly. [ERISA §4(a)(3); 29 U.S.C. §1003(a)(3)]

Employer. ERISA defines an employer as any person acting directly as an employer, or indirectly in the interest of an employer, in relation to an employee benefit plan and includes a group or association of employers acting for an employer in such capacity. [ERISA §3(5); 29 U.S.C. §1002(5)] The DOL has ruled that where a nonprofit trade association of small employers established a health benefit plan for its members and their employees and dependents, the plan was not an ERISA plan. The trade association that sponsored the plan was not "a group or association of employers acting for an employer" and therefore was not an employer for ERISA purposes. [DOL Adv. Op. 94-07A (Mar. 14, 1994); *see also* DOL Adv. Op. 93-32A (Dec. 16, 1993), DOL Adv. Op. 96-25A]

Note. While the trade association plan was held not to be an ERISA plan, those small employers that provided coverage to their common-law employees would have separate ERISA plans (see Q 2:18).

Where an employer furnished a surety bond to an employee benefit plan and then defaulted on its contributions and went bankrupt, the surety was held not to be an "employer" or acting "in the interest of an employer" under ERISA Section 3(5). [Greenblatt v. Delta Plumbing & Heating Corp., 63 F.3d 561 (2d Cir. 1995)]

A federal appellate court has held that a trust established to provide health benefits to small employers (those with 500 employees or less) was not an ERISA employee benefit plan. In order to be eligible for benefits, each employer was required to join a small-business association. The court found, however, that for an association to be considered "a group or association of employers acting for an employer," ERISA requires a bona fide organizational relationship between the members other than for the purpose of qualifying for benefits. Because the only purpose of the so-called association was to obtain benefit coverage, the association did not qualify as an employer for ERISA purposes. [Moideen v. Gillespie, 55 F.3d 1478 (9th Cir. 1995)]

Partnerships. For purposes of the group health plan standards set forth in Part 7 of Title I of ERISA, the term *employer* also includes a partnership in relation to any partner. [ERISA §732(d)]

Employee organizations. A union was held to qualify as an "employee organization" because the union members participated in the union's activities by voting in union elections. Also, the union represented its members in dealing with the members' employer over employment-related matters. [DOL Adv. Op. 95-03A (Apr. 3, 1995)]

Interstate commerce. One district court held that where an employer had two employees and was engaged in a business that did not affect interstate commerce, the employer's welfare benefit plan was not subject to ERISA. [Sheffield v. Allstate Life Ins. Co., 756 F. Supp. 309 (S.D. Tex. 1991)]

*Welfare benefit plan.*The definition of an ERISA welfare benefit plan is covered in Qs 2:10–2:20. Note that ERISA contains a special definition of *group health plan* applicable only to Part 6 of Title I of ERISA (continuation coverage and other standards) and a second special definition of group health plan applicable only to Part 7 of Title I of ERISA (portability and other group health plan standards).

Q 2:6   Is there a minimum number of employees required for ERISA coverage?

No. ERISA covers employers of any size and employee benefit plans of any size.

Covered Employees

Q 2:7   Who is considered to be an employee for ERISA purposes?

The United States Supreme Court has held that traditional agency law criteria (and not some broader standard) should be used to determine whether an individual is an employee or an independent contractor and that ERISA covers only employees. Thus, the normal common-law tests for employee status apply. [National Mut. Co. v. Darden, 112 S. Ct. 1344 (1992)] Despite this, a U.S. appellate court has held that a partner in a large accounting firm was an employee for ERISA (and Age Discrimination in Employment Act (ADEA)) purposes. In the court's view, the individual was not a "true" partner because his partnership interest lacked some, but not all, of the traditional partnership interest characteristics, such as making capital contributions, sharing in profits and losses, and exercising substantial management authority. [Simpson v. Ernst & Young, 20 Employee Benefits Cas. (BNA) 2088 (6th Cir. 1996)]

Special rules for partners and independent contractors. Despite the general rule that ERISA applies only to employees, ERISA's Consolidated Omnibus Budget Reconciliation Act (COBRA) provisions apply to independent contractors [ERISA §607(2)], and the group health plan standards contained in Part 7 of Title I of ERISA apply to partners and self-employed individuals. [ERISA §732(d)]

Q 2:8   When does an individual become a plan participant in a welfare benefit plan for ERISA purposes?

For purposes of ERISA, an individual becomes a participant in a welfare benefit plan on the earliest of the following dates:

1. The date designated by the plan as the date on which the individual begins participation in the plan;
2. The date on which the individual becomes eligible for a benefit under the plan, subject only to the occurrence of the contingency for which the benefit is provided; or
3. The date on which the individual makes a voluntary or mandatory contribution to the plan.

[DOL Reg. §2510.3-3(d)(1)(i)]

Q 2:9   When does an individual stop being a participant in a welfare benefit plan for ERISA purposes?

For purposes of ERISA, an individual ceases to be a participant in a welfare benefit plan on the earliest date on which (1) he or she becomes ineligible to receive any plan benefit even if the contingency for which the benefit is provided occurs and (2) the individual is not designated by the plan as a participant. [DOL Reg. §2510.3-3(d)(2)(i)]

> **Example.** The Third Circuit Court of Appeals concluded that a former company executive was not a "participant" in a company severance plan and, therefore, was not entitled to sue for benefits under ERISA. Although the executive was initially placed on a list of employees who would become eligible for severance benefits when and if they were laid off by the employer, the executive voluntarily terminated employment before being laid off. Therefore, the executive no longer qualified as a participant who could become eligible for benefits under the severance plan. [Miller v. Rite Aid Corp., 334 F.3d 335 (3d Cir. 2003)]

However, in actions brought by former participants for benefits or other ERISA relief, the federal courts in many cases have taken an expansive view of who constitutes a plan "participant" for purposes of standing to sue. A former employee who has a "colorable claim" to benefits or is within the "zone of interests" ERISA was designed to protect may be considered a participant for standing to sue purposes. [Sofo v. Pan Am. Life Ins. Co., 13 F.3d 239 (7th Cir. 1994); Vartanian v. Monsanto Co., 14 F.3d 697 (1st Cir. 1994)] Other federal circuit courts of appeal have taken a more restrictive view and have denied standing to sue where the former employee had received all the benefits to which he or she was entitled. [*See* Raymond v. Mobil Oil Corp., 983 F.2d 1528 (10th Cir. 1993) and cases cited therein.]

Following the addition of Section 732 to ERISA, which extends the protections of Part 7 of Title I of ERISA to partners and former partners, former partners appear to have standing to enforce the group health plan standards contained in Part 7 of Title I of ERISA.

Covered Plans

Q 2:10   What constitutes an employee welfare benefit plan for purposes of ERISA?

For purposes of ERISA, an *employee welfare benefit plan* (also called a welfare benefit plan) is any plan, fund, or program established or maintained by an employer, employee organization, or both, to the extent established or maintained for the purpose of providing participants or their beneficiaries, through the purchase of insurance or otherwise, any or all of the following:

- Medical, surgical, or hospital care or benefits
- Benefits in the event of sickness, accident, disability, death, or unemployment
- Vacation benefits
- Apprenticeship or other training programs
- Day care centers
- Scholarship funds
- Prepaid legal services
- Any benefit (other than pensions at retirement or death and insurance to provide such pensions) described in Section 302(c) of the Labor Management Relations Act of 1947 (LMRA). These include severance benefits and financial assistance for employee housing.

[ERISA §3(1); 29 U.S.C. §1002(1); DOL Reg. §2510.3-1(a)(2)]

ERISA plan found to exist. An employer plan that provided coverage for federally mandated medical examinations for employees who may have been exposed to asbestos was held to be an ERISA medical benefits plan. [DOL Adv. Op. 94-14A (Apr. 20, 1994)] Also, an employer plan providing coverage for medical examinations of airline pilots required by the Federal Aviation Administration was held to be a medical benefits plan for ERISA purposes. [Aloha Airlines, Inc. v. Ahue, 12 F.3d 1498 (9th Cir. 1993)]

An employer was held to have created an ERISA plan by telling its employees that it was contributing to a multiemployer pension and welfare plan and by distributing brochures of the plan, even though the employer never made the required contributions and kept the money for itself. The federal appeals court took the position that although the formalities of establishing a plan had not been followed, the totality of the circumstances surrounding the situation supported the conclusion that an ERISA plan had been created. [Kenney v. Roland Parson Contracting Corp., 28 F.3d 1254 (D.C. Cir. 1994)]

In some cases an employer may offer its employees "freebies" in the form of goods or services that it normally sells to the general public. An employer should not assume, however, that these perks do not constitute a plan under ERISA. For example, a grocery store chain was found to have established an ERISA plan when it offered monthly grocery vouchers to retirees who had at least 20 years of service, were at least age 60 at retirement, and had worked in a supervisory position for at least one year. [Musmeci v. Schwegmann Giant Super Mkts., Inc., 82 Fed. Appx. 144 (5th Cir. Aug. 15, 2003)]

ERISA plan found not to exist. DOL Advisory Opinion 91-25A (July 2, 1991) states that a dependent care spending account plan that was established by an employer solely to permit employees to contribute on a pretax basis for reimbursement of dependent care service provider expenses was not an employee welfare benefit plan subject to ERISA, because the plan allowed employees to choose the service providers, and the plan did not provide particular day care centers.

Another DOL advisory opinion held that a salary reduction plan providing employees with the ability to pay health plan contributions on a pretax basis did not create an ERISA plan separate from the group health plan but was merely a part of the group health plan. [DOL Adv. Op. 96-12A]

The DOL has ruled that a labor-management cooperation committee trust established by a union in order to improve communication between labor and management was not an ERISA welfare benefit plan, because the trust did not provide any of the categories of benefits listed above. [DOL Adv. Op. 94-33A (Sept. 16, 1994)] In a similar vein, the DOL held that an industry advancement and cooperative fund established jointly by an employer trade association and a union, for the purpose of improving relations between employers and employees and to support the industry in general, was not an ERISA plan, because the plan did not provide benefits of the type listed above. [DOL Adv. Op. 94-29A (July 21, 1994)] The DOL also ruled that a health and welfare plan established by a thoroughbred racing association was not an ERISA plan. The plan covered the owners of the thoroughbred horses and trainers and assistants of the owners as well. Since some owners were self-employed and had no common-law employees, the association was held not to be an association of employers eligible to establish an ERISA plan for its members. [DOL Adv. Op. 95-01A (Feb. 13, 1995)]

A federal appeals court ruled that an employer program that offered alternative positions to employees whose jobs were due to be eliminated did not constitute an ERISA plan. The court pointed out that the plan provided continued employment rather than unemployment benefits. A separate program that gave employees in the alternative job program the option to quit and receive a lump-sum benefit also was found not to be an ERISA plan, since the lump-sum payment required no ongoing administrative scheme. [Sherrod v. General Motors Corp., 33 F.3d 636 (6th Cir. 1994)] See Q 2:20 for a discussion of when an ongoing practice of providing benefits constitutes an ERISA plan.

Another federal appeals court held that a new layoff policy adopted by an employer did not constitute an ERISA plan. Under the layoff policy, employees meeting certain age and service requirements would be offered alternative employment before being laid off. Since the layoff policy did not provide the type of benefits described by ERISA, no ERISA plan was created. [Ritter v. Hughes Aircraft Co., 58 F.3d 454 (9th Cir. 1995)]

Q 2:11   Does ERISA cover employee benefit plans even if they are employee-pay-all plans?

Yes. Whether ERISA applies is a question of fact. As discussed in Q 2:5, a plan is governed by ERISA if it is established or maintained by an employer, an employee organization, or both. The DOL has issued a regulation for determining when a group or group-type insurance arrangement may be excluded from ERISA. [DOL Reg. §2510.3-1(j)] Group or group-type programs that an insurer offers to employees or members of an employee organization will be excluded from ERISA coverage if the following four requirements are met:

1. The employer or employee organization does not make any contributions;

2. Participation in the program is completely voluntary for employees or members;

3. The employer's or employee organization's sole functions with respect to the program are, without endorsing the program, (a) to permit the insurer to publicize the program to employees or members, (b) to collect premiums through payroll deductions or dues checkoffs, and (c) to remit the premiums to the insurer; and

4. The employer or employee organization receives no consideration (cash or otherwise) in connection with the program other than reasonable compensation, excluding any profit, for administrative services actually rendered in connection with payroll deductions or dues checkoffs.

Employer contributions. An employer was held to have established an ERISA plan where it subsidized the cost of health insurance policies for several of its employees. The fact that the employees were permitted to choose the insurers they wanted did not make the arrangement too loose to constitute a plan. [Madonia v. Blue Cross & Blue Shield of Va., 11 F.3d 444 (4th Cir. 1993)] The Court of Appeals for the Eleventh Circuit considered a group medical plan under which the employer paid the premium cost for its employees, but the employees were required to pay the entire premium cost for dependent coverage. When an employee lost his spouse's coverage because of nonpayment of premiums for dependent coverage, the employee and his wife sued under state law. Holding that state law was preempted by ERISA, the circuit court of appeals refused to sever the dependent coverage from the employee coverage under the plan. As a result, the preceding DOL regulation was held not to exclude the plan from ERISA coverage because the employer did make contributions to the overall plan. [Smith v. Jefferson Pilot Life Ins. Co., 14 F.3d 562 (11th Cir. 1994)] The Sixth Circuit rejected a similar "severing" argument in a case involving employer-paid premiums for long-term disability. In *Helfman v. GE Group Life Assurance Co.* [No. 08-2168, 2009 U.S. App. LEXIS 16816 (6th Cir. July 24, 2009)], the employer paid all the premiums for the insurance, except the premium for one employee who had reimbursed the employer for the premiums paid on his behalf. The employee, who wanted to sue the insurer under state law, claimed that since he paid his own premiums, there was no plan subject to ERISA, and hence his lawsuit was not preempted. However, the Sixth Circuit held that if an employer contributes to any employee's payment of premiums, ERISA must apply to the entirety of the insurance program, regardless of whether one employee pays his own premiums in full. According to the court, the ERISA policy of uniform regulation dictates a finding that a single plan may not be variously governed by ERISA and state law, depending on the particular employee in question. [Helfman v. GE Group Life Assurance Co., 2009 U.S. Dist. LEXIS 112889 (E.D. Mich. Dec. 4, 2009)]

Employer endorsement. Item 3 is especially important in determining whether an ERISA plan exists. Employer actions such as negotiating fees, processing claims, producing summary plan descriptions (SPDs), or selecting among options to be offered to its employees could constitute sufficient employer involvement to fall outside the exemption and cause an ERISA plan to exist.

The Court of Appeals for the Fifth Circuit has considered how limited the employer's involvement in an employee-pay-all group insurance plan must be to fall within the preceding regulatory exemption. The employer in question provided accidental death and dismemberment insurance to its employees on an employee-pay-all basis, and participation by employees was voluntary. The employer collected and remitted premiums to the insurance company, hired and employee benefits administrator to forward employee claims to the insurance company, presented the plan as a supplement to the rest of its benefit program, and distributed to employees a descriptive benefit booklet with the employer's own name and logo on it. The booklet encouraged employees to give participation in the plan careful consideration because it could be a valuable supplement to their existing coverage.

The appellate court concluded that the employer endorsed the plan and that its involvement in the plan was not limited to the activities specified in the regulation. It also found that, apart from the regulation, the employer clearly intended to establish an ERISA plan and had indeed "established" an ERISA plan, because there was a meaningful degree of employer participation in the creation and administration of the plan. [Hansen v. Continental Ins. Co., 940 F.2d 971 (5th Cir. 1991)]

Similarly, the Eleventh Circuit concluded that an employer's involvement with an employee-pay-all disability plan was governed by ERISA. The employer's employee handbook referenced the plan as an available benefit, the employer selected the plan and established a fund to pay benefits, and the employer involved itself in the benefit payment process by supplying claim forms. [Moorman v. Unum Provident Corp., 464 F.3d 1260 (11th Cir. 2006)]

On the other hand, an employer that made a group insurance program available to its employees was held not to have established an ERISA plan where the employer performed only ministerial functions under the plan. The employer did not become involved in plan design or operation and did not endorse the program or include it as part of its employee benefits package. [Johnson v. Watts Regulator Co., 63 F.3d 1129 (1st Cir. 1995)]

Q 2:12   Is an employee assistance program an ERISA plan?

Possibly. If the employee assistance program (EAP) offers more than referrals to health care providers and actually either provides or reimburses medical care services, it is an ERISA plan. An EAP that provided no initial evaluation or counseling or reimbursement for services and was limited to referrals only has been determined not to be an ERISA plan. [DOL Adv. Op. 91-26A (July 19, 1991)] (EAPs are discussed in detail in chapter 3.)

Q 2:13   Is a health savings account subject to ERISA?

According to the DOL, a health savings account (HSA) generally does not constitute an employee welfare benefit plan subject to ERISA where employer involvement is limited. Employer contributions to an HSA do not give rise to an ERISA-covered plan if all the following conditions are met:

1. The establishment of the HSA is completely voluntary on the part of an employee;

2. The employer does not limit the ability to move funds to another HSA;

3. The employer does not impose conditions on the use of HSA funds beyond those permitted by the Internal Revenue Code (Code);

4. The employer does not make or influence investment decisions regarding the HSA funds;

5. The employer does not represent that the HSA is an employee welfare benefit plan; and

6. The employer does not receive payment or compensation in connection with the HSA.

[DOL Field Assist. Bull. 2004-01, Apr. 7, 2004]

However, this does not mean an employer's involvement with an HSA must be strictly hands off. For example, the DOL says that an employer may open an HSA for an employee and make employer contributions without violating the requirement that establishment of an HSA be voluntary on the part of an employee. The "completely voluntary" requirement is designed to ensure that employee contributions are voluntary. In addition, the employer may select or limit the HSA providers that it allows to market products in the workplace without converting the HSA into an ERISA plan. On the other hand, if an employer receives a discount on other products in return for selecting an HSA vendor, the employer would be treated as receiving payment or compensation in connection with the HSA, which would subject the plan to ERISA and give rise to fiduciary responsibility and prohibited transaction issues. [DOL Field Assist. Bull. 2006-02, Oct. 21, 2006]

(HSAs are discussed in detail in chapter 3.)

Q 2:14　Is a plan covering only one employee subject to ERISA?

Yes. If the interstate commerce requirement is satisfied by the employer, then a plan maintained by the employer for only one employee can constitute an ERISA plan. Note, however, that an employee benefit plan covering only a self-employed individual and his or her spouse is excluded from ERISA coverage (see Q 2:18). A partner-only group health plan *is* subject to Part 7 of Title I of ERISA and must comply with the group health plan standards contained in Part 7.

Q 2:15　Can an individual's employment agreement constitute an ERISA plan?

Courts have generally taken the position that individuals' employment contracts are not ERISA plans. [*See* Lackey v. Whitehall Corp., 704 F. Supp. 201 (D. Kan. 1988); McQueen v. Salida Coca-Cola Bottling Co., 652 F. Supp. 1471 (D. Colo. 1987)] For example, where an employment contract with a company president provided that the president would receive no payments after termination if termination was for cause, and would continue to receive salary and insurance for a specified period if termination was without cause, the employment contract was held not to create an ERISA plan. Because the employer had no discretion concerning the time, amount, or form of payment, the employment contract did not require an ongoing administrative scheme and therefore did not constitute a plan for ERISA purposes. [Delaye v. Agripac Inc., 39 F.3d 235 (9th Cir. 1994)]

However, a series of employment contracts providing golden parachute payments upon a change in control has been held to constitute an ERISA severance pay plan. [Purser v. Enron Corp., 10 Employee Benefits Cas. (BNA) 1561 (W.D. Pa. 1988); DOL Adv. Op. 91-20A (July 2, 1991)]

Moreover, in the case of a postemployment agreement, the Court of Appeals for the Eleventh Circuit has held that a letter agreement between an employer and a general manager who agreed to retire in return for certain payments and benefits, including medical insurance, was an ERISA plan. [Williams v. Wright, 927 F.2d 1540 (11th Cir. 1991)]

Because disputes of this nature often arise when severance pay is involved, this topic is also discussed in detail in chapter 15, Vacation and Severance Pay Plans.

Q 2:16　What is a top-hat welfare benefit plan, and to what extent does ERISA regulate it?

A welfare benefit plan is considered a top-hat welfare benefit plan under the following conditions:

1. Benefits of the plan are provided

2. The plan is maintained by an employer primarily for the purpose of providing benefits for a select group of management or highly compensated employees; and

    a. Solely from the employer's general assets,

    b. Solely from insurance contracts, the premiums for which are paid from the employer's general assets, issued by an insurance company or similar organization qualified to do business in any state, or

    c. From a combination of (a) and (b).

An example of a top-hat plan would be an insured supplemental medical plan maintained by the employer for executives only and for which no employee contributions are charged.

Such a top-hat welfare benefit plan is exempt by regulation from all ERISA reporting and disclosure requirements except for the requirement to provide plan documents to the Secretary of Labor upon request. [ERISA §104(a)(3); 29 U.S.C. §1024(a)(3); DOL Reg. §2520.104-24; compare DOL Reg. §2520.104-23 for top-hat pension plans]

A U.S. district court has held that participants in a top-hat plan can sue under ERISA to enforce their rights under the plan. Although top-hat plans are exempt from most requirements of ERISA, they nevertheless are ERISA plans, and ERISA legal remedies are applicable. [Kemmerer v. ICI Americas Inc., 17 Employee Benefits Cas. (BNA) 2166 (E.D. Pa. 1994)] A federal appeals court held, however, that a plan administrator could not be held liable for breaches of fiduciary duty under ERISA because the plan involved constituted a top-hat plan. [Duggan v. Hobbs, 99 F.3d 307 (9th Cir. 1996)]

Q 2:17   Can a top-hat welfare benefit plan cover some employees who are not part of a select group of management or highly compensated employees?

Apparently not. The DOL takes the position that the word *primarily* (see Q 2:16) refers to the employer's purpose of providing benefits and not to the group of employees covered. Thus, it appears that to qualify for the regulatory exemption, the top-hat plan must be solely for the benefit of a select group of management or highly compensated employees. [DOL Adv. Op. 90-14A (May 8, 1990)]

While there are no DOL regulations defining what constitutes a "select group of management or highly compensated employees," the DOL has indicated informally that it views the group as smaller than the "highly compensated" classification used by the IRS in the tax-qualified pension plan context.

The U.S. Court of Appeals for the Second Circuit has held that a nonqualified deferred compensation plan covering up to 15 percent of a bank's workforce still qualified for ERISA top-hat exemption. This executive group consisted of 15.34 percent of the bank's workforce. [Demery v. Extebank Deferred Compensation Plan (B), 216 F.3d 283 (2d Cir. 2000)] Previously, the Fourth Circuit had rejected a group constituting 18 percent of a workforce, and the DOL had rejected a participant group constituting 7.5 percent of an employer's workforce. [DOL Adv. Op. 85-37]

Q 2:18 Which welfare benefit plans are not covered by ERISA?

The following types of employee welfare benefit plans are not covered by ERISA:

1. *Government plans.* Plans maintained by federal, state, and local governments or agencies thereof for their employees. [ERISA §§4(b)(1), 3(32); 29 U.S.C. §§1003(b)(1), 1002(32)] A welfare benefit plan sponsored by a police relief association was held to qualify as an exempt governmental plan, even though the plan was not sponsored by a governmental agency, because membership was conditioned on governmental employment. [DOL Adv. Op. 95-25A (Oct. 3, 1995)] A welfare benefit plan maintained for public school teachers was found to be a governmental plan even though it also covered some nongovernmental employees. The number of nongovernmental employees covered was insignificant, and their employers acted exclusively in representing the governmental employees in employment and benefit matters. [DOL Adv. Op. 95-15A (June 26, 1995)]

2. *Church plans.* Certain plans maintained by tax-exempt churches for their employees. [ERISA §§4(b)(2), 3(33); 29 U.S.C. §§1003(b)(2), 1002(33)]

3. *Plans required by state law.* Plans maintained solely for the purpose of complying with applicable workers' compensation laws or unemployment compensation or disability insurance laws. [ERISA §4(b)(3); 29 U.S.C. §1003(b)(4)]

4. *Foreign plans.* Plans maintained outside of the United States primarily for the benefit of persons substantially all of whom are nonresident aliens. [ERISA §4(b)(4)] The DOL has ruled that a plan of a foreign corporation under which slightly less than 10 percent of the participants were U.S. citizens or residents qualified as a foreign plan and therefore was exempt from ERISA. [DOL Adv. Op. 82-38A (Aug. 2, 1982)]

5. *Plans that cover only self-employed individuals.* Plans that cover no "common-law employees" generally are not subject to ERISA, although Part 7 of ERISA Title I (imposing portability and other standards on group health plans) expressly applies to plans covering partners. The definition of a common-law employee is too complex to explain in detail here, but one ground rule is that a common-law employee is someone who works under the control of another person or legal entity such as a corporation.

6. *Plans that cover only married sole shareholders of a corporation.* DOL regulations indicate that a plan covering only an individual and spouse who are the sole owners of a corporation, whether or not the individual's spouse is a common-law employee of the corporation, is not treated as an ERISA plan. [DOL Reg. §§2510.3-3(b), 2510.3-3(c)] If the plan covering the married sole shareholders also covers common-law employees of the corporation, the plan is an ERISA plan. In such a case, a federal appellate

court has held that the sole shareholders are beneficiaries under an ERISA plan, and their rights are governed by ERISA; therefore, their state-law claims against the plan's insurer are preempted by ERISA. [Robinson v. Sinomaz, 58 F.3d 365 (8th Cir. 1995)]

Certain other exclusions apply to welfare benefit plans that are subject to ERISA. For example, welfare benefit plans are generally subject to much simpler reporting and disclosure requirements than are pension plans and are entirely exempt from the participation, vesting, benefit accrual, and funding requirements of ERISA that apply to pension plans. [ERISA §§101, 105, 201(1), 301(a)(1); 29 U.S.C. §§1021, 1025, 1051(1), 1081(a)(2)] In the case of a so-called top-hat welfare benefit plan, almost all of the ERISA provisions are not applicable, either by statute or by regulation (see Qs 2:16–2:17). ERISA's mandated benefit provisions for group health plans also do not apply to certain plans (see chapter 5).

Q 2:19 Are there employee benefit practices and programs that are not considered employee welfare benefit plans under ERISA?

Yes. DOL regulations specify certain practices and programs providing benefits to employees that are not considered welfare benefit plans subject to ERISA. These include the following:

1. *Payroll practices.* The payment of an employee's normal compensation in full or in part out of the employer's general assets for periods when the employee is physically or mentally unable to work—that is, an unfunded short-term disability plan—is not a welfare benefit plan. [DOL Adv. Op. 93-20A (July 16, 1993); McGraw v. F.D. Servs. Inc., 811 F. Supp. 222 (D.S.C. 1993)] It appears that if a disability program provides more than an employee's normal compensation or is funded in any way—that is, it is provided through insurance or by a union welfare fund—the program will be a welfare benefit plan subject to ERISA. [DOL Reg. §§2510.3-1(b)(1), 2510.3-1(b)(2); Abella v. W.A. Foote Mem'l Hosp. Inc., 740 F.2d 4 (6th Cir. 1984); DOL Adv. Op. 85-23A (Apr. 16, 1985)] DOL regulations also list a number of other types of payroll practices that are not ERISA plans. These include compensation paid to an employee (a) while absent on active military duty, (b) while absent for the purpose of serving as a juror or as a witness in an official proceeding, (c) on account of periods of time during which the employee performs little or no productive work while engaged in training (whether or not subsidized by government funds), or (d) who is relieved of duties while on sabbatical leave or while pursuing further education. [DOL Reg. §2510.3-1(b)(3)]

2. *Group or group-type employee-pay-all insurance programs.* (See Q 2:11.)

3. *Unfunded scholarship programs.* These include tuition and educational expense reimbursement programs, under which payments are made solely from the employer's or employee organization's general assets. [DOL Reg. §2510.3-1(k)]

4. *On-premises facilities.* These include recreation, dining, first aid, or other facilities (other than day care centers) maintained on the premises of the employer or employee organization for use by employees or members of the employee organization. [DOL Reg. §2510.3-1(c)] Employer-provided day care centers are covered ERISA benefits.

5. *Holiday gifts and remembrance funds.* These include small gifts, such as turkeys, given by employers to employees at Christmas or other holidays or programs that provide remembrances such as flowers or a small gift for sickness, death, or termination of employment of employees or members of their families. [DOL Reg. §§2510.3-1(d), 2510.3-1(g)]

6. *Adoption benefits.* Although not mentioned in DOL regulations, adoption benefits under Code Section 137 are not covered by ERISA.

Q 2:20 When does a "practice" constitute a "plan" for the purposes of ERISA?

This issue has been the subject of case law developments in recent years. In addition to the discussion below, this issue is addressed further in chapter 15.

Funded practices, such as funded vacation pay and severance pay programs, are welfare benefit plans subject to ERISA. [Mackey v. Lanier Collection Agency & Serv. Inc., 486 U.S. 825 (1988); DOL Adv. Op. 89-06A (Apr. 7, 1989)]

Vacation pay plans that are unfunded are exempt from ERISA as "payroll practices." [Massachusetts v. Morash, 490 U.S. 107 (1989)] These include plans that pay a "premium" (extra compensation) to induce employees to take vacations at a time favorable to the employer for business reasons. [DOL Reg. §2510.3-1(b)(3)(i)] However, under DOL regulations, unfunded severance pay plans are generally considered welfare benefit plans and, in certain circumstances, may be considered pension plans for ERISA purposes. [ERISA §3(2)(B); 29 U.S.C. §1002(2)(B); DOL Reg. §§2510.3-1(a)(3), 2510.3-2(b); DOL Adv. Op. 83-47A (Sept. 13, 1983)]

In some cases, an employer's vacation pay setup can straddle the line between a funded welfare benefit plan and an unfunded payroll practice. For example, in an advisory opinion, the DOL considered a situation where an employer established a trust to pay vacation benefits. The trust document entitled the trust to receive actuarially determined contributions from the employer. However, the trust administrator never consulted an actuary or set a contribution rate. Instead, the employer made contributions to the trust as needed to fund vacation pay checks. The trust issued vacation pay checks on the same schedule as the employer's normal payroll and the vacation pay checks included the same general payroll information as employees' normal paychecks. In assessing the vacation pay setup, the DOL noted that an employer program of compensating employees for vacation benefits out of the employer's general assets is not a welfare plan covered by ERISA. However, it also noted that the rule does not apply when vacation benefits are paid from a source other than the employer's general assets, such as a trust. Nonetheless, the DOL determined that the employer's vacation pay trust did not constitute an ERISA plan. While, technically, the trust was a separate entity with a legal obligation to pay vacation benefits, in reality the trust was a mere pass-through vehicle for the employer's payment of ordinary vacation wages. [DOL Adv. Op. 2004-08A (July 2, 2004)]

A one-time, lump-sum payment triggered by a single event (such as a single payment of severance pay upon a plant closing) has been held insufficient to create a plan. However, an employer commitment to pay benefits systematically on a regular, ongoing basis does constitute an ERISA plan if such a commitment relies on a uniform administrative scheme, including a set of standard procedures for the processing of claims and the payment of benefits. [Fort Halifax Packing Co. v. Coyne, 482 U.S. 1 (1987)] For example, the Second Circuit held that there was no ERISA plan where an employer had an ongoing practice of providing payments in return for release agreements from terminated employees, but there was no communication or other evidence suggesting that a reasonable employee would perceive an ongoing commitment by the employer to provide such payments. [Kawski v. Johnson & Johnson, 347 Fed. Appx. 610 (2d Cir. 2009)]

The U.S. Court of Appeals for the Eighth Circuit held that a golden parachute severance pay arrangement was not an employee benefit plan subject to ERISA, because it did not require the establishment of an ongoing administrative scheme by the employer. Under the arrangement, the employee involved was entitled to a lump-sum payment if he terminated employment for good reason within one year of a hostile takeover. The determination of whether there was a good reason was solely in the employee's judgment. Since there was a single-sum payment and no discretionary determination of benefits to be made by the employer, the court concluded that no ERISA plan existed. [Kulinski v. Medtronic Bio-Medicus Inc., 21 F.3d 254 (58th Cir. 1994); see also Fontenot v. N.L. Indus., Inc., 953 F.2d 960 (5th Cir. 1992)]

An employer that made employees a series of early retirement offers over a four-year period was held not to have created an ERISA plan. Each offer involved one-time lump-sum payments that did not entail the creation of continuing administrative and financial obligations by the employer. [Belanger v. Wyman-Gordon Co., 71 F.3d 451 (1st Cir. 1995)]

An employer's severance program was held not to give rise to an ERISA plan where the president of the company exercised complete discretion in deciding who would be awarded severance payments and how much would be paid. The court found that though an ERISA plan need not be in writing, it must permit a reasonable person to determine the benefits, the source of financing, and the procedures for collecting the plan's benefit. Because, in this case, the payments were completely discretionary on the part of the company president, no ERISA plan existed. [Spanos v. Continental Publ'g Servs., 1994 U.S. Dist. LEXIS 6695 (N.D. Cal. May 17, 1994)]

Requirements for Plan Document

Q 2:21　Does an ERISA plan exist even if there is no written plan document?

Yes. If the plan's benefits include one or more of the benefits governed by ERISA, an ERISA plan exists. No written plan document or funding mechanism need exist for there to be a plan for ERISA purposes. A plan administrator's failure or refusal to put a plan in writing is merely a violation of ERISA and does not avoid coverage of the plan by ERISA. [Blau v. Del Monte Corp., 748 F.2d 1348 (9th Cir. 1984); Adams v. Avondale Indus. Inc., 905 F.2d 943 (6th Cir. 1990)]

When an employer had an unwritten severance pay policy for executives, which entitled terminated executives to a year's salary and coverage in the employer's benefits plans, it was held that an ERISA plan existed, and a terminated executive was entitled to benefits under the unwritten plan. [Warner v. J.P. Stevens & Co., Pens. Plan Guide (CCH) ¶ 23,840K (5th Cir. 1991)]

The Second Circuit Court of Appeals held that a benefits "summary" that was distributed to employees years before an official benefits plan was adopted constituted a "plan" within the meaning of ERISA. The summary, which was accompanied by a memorandum announcing the benefits plan, described the long-term disability (LTD) benefits available to employees, but did not specify that LTD benefits were subject to an offset for Social Security disability and workers' compensation payments received by employees. A "benefit booklet" distributed almost nine months later did describe the offsets, and the written plan document—which was finalized more than four years after the summary was distributed—also included the offsets. However, a group of employees, who became disabled during the period following the distribution of the summary and before the issuance of the benefits booklet, filed a lawsuit challenging the offsets. The Second Circuit concluded that the employer was bound by the terms of the plan as set forth in the summary, and was not entitled to offset the LTD benefits. According to the court, a plan is established under ERISA if a reasonable person can ascertain the intended benefits, a class of beneficiaries, the source of the financing, and the procedures for receiving benefits. "However slap-dash," said the court, "the program summary and the accompanying memorandum fulfill these requirements." The court acknowledged that the summary contained a disclaimer that it was not intended to cover all the details of the plan and that "the actual provisions of the plan will govern." However, the court specifically rejected the notion that the disclaimer rendered the summary a "non-plan" when it was the only written document describing the benefit. "Crediting such a disclaimer in this situation would allow an employer effectively to 'opt out' of ERISA's requirements despite the establishment of an employee benefits scheme that meets ERISA's definition of a plan," said the court. [Feifer v. Prudential Ins. Co. of Am., 306 F.3d 1202 (2d Cir. 2002)]

In another case, a Wal-Mart employee who was disabled as a result of a car accident challenged the right of the retailer's health plan to recoup benefits it had paid from the amount received by the employee in settlement of a lawsuit over the accident. The health plan relied on a provision in the summary plan description (SPD) that gave the plan the right to recoup benefits it paid from amounts received by an employee or beneficiary from a legal settlement or judgment. There was, however, no official health plan document. The employee argued that the reimbursement provision was unenforceable because it was not part of a formal plan document. The Eighth Circuit Court of Appeals sided with the Wal-Mart plan, ruling that where no other source of benefits exists, the SPD, regardless of its label, *is* the plan document. To bolster its opinion, the court pointed out that if a dispute had arisen over the amount of benefits payable to the employee, Wal-Mart would undoubtedly have had to pay benefits in accordance with the SPD. Moreover, the court pointed out that since the employee had in fact received medical benefits under the terms of the SPD, he could not be relieved of corresponding obligations imposed by the same document. "[W]hat is good for the goose is good for the gander," the court said. [Administrative Comm. of the Wal-Mart Stores, Inc. Assoc.'s Health & Welfare Plan v. Gamboa, 479 F.3d 538 (8th Cir. 2007)]

Because the issue of whether an ERISA plan exists has been heavily litigated with respect to severance pay plans, this issue is discussed in detail in chapter 15.

Q 2:22   What provisions must the written plan document contain?

The written plan document required by ERISA must contain the following information:

1. A designation (by name or pursuant to a procedure contained in the plan) of one or more fiduciaries (see Qs 2:27–2:35) with authority to control and manage the operation and administration of the plan;

2. A procedure for establishing and carrying out a funding policy and method consistent with the objectives of the plan and with ERISA requirements (but see Q 2:26);

3. A description of any procedure for allocating responsibilities for plan operation and administration;

4. A procedure for amending the plan and for identifying those persons with authority to amend the plan;

5. A statement of the basis on which payments are made to the plan (such as by contributions from the employer or from employees, or both); and

6. A statement of the basis on which the plan makes payments (for example, the covered benefits under the plan), including the elective COBRA continuation of group health plan coverage benefits specifically mandated by ERISA.

[ERISA §§402(a), 402(b); 29 U.S.C. §§1102(a), 1102(b)]

A federal appellate court has held that an employer's board resolution authorizing a life insurance plan and setting out a vesting schedule was not a part of the plan document. The court held that the life insurance policy constituted the plan document, and it permitted the employer to terminate the coverage at any time. Therefore, the employees had no vested rights in the coverage. [Cinelli v. Security Pacific Corp., 61 F.3d 1437 (9th Cir. 1995)]

Q 2:23 How specific must an amendment procedure be?

The U.S. Supreme Court has held, in *Curtiss-Wright Corp. v. Schoonejongen*, that an ERISA plan provision stating that the employer reserves the right to modify or amend the plan is sufficient to satisfy the ERISA requirement that the plan document contain a procedure for amending the plan and for identifying those persons with authority to amend the plan. The appellate court in *Curtiss-Wright Corp.* had held that the plan language was too vague, and therefore a plan amendment curtailing retiree health benefits was invalid. The lower court decision had caused great concern among employers, since many employer plans had similar provisions. Thus, the U.S. Supreme Court decision eliminated some major concerns over the possibility that past plan amendments could be held invalid. Pending the Supreme Court decision, many employers amended their plan provisions to spell out in detail the mechanics involved in a plan amendment. Presumably, those amendments will remain despite the Supreme Court reversal. [Curtiss-Wright Corp. v. Schoonejongen, 514 U.S. 73 (1995)]

Practice Pointer. The U.S. Supreme Court remanded the case for a determination as to whether the amendment in question had been properly adopted. Therefore, in addition to having a plan amendment procedure set forth in the plan document, the employer and employer's counsel should make sure that plan amendments are adopted with all the formalities that are required pursuant to the plan procedure.

Note. The various operational issues concerning amending a plan to cut back benefits, oral amendments, late amendments, and so on are discussed in Qs 2:46–2:54.

Q 2:24 May the plan document contain other provisions?

The plan document may, but is not required to, include provisions to the effect that:

1. Any person or group may serve in more than one fiduciary capacity concerning the plan;
2. A fiduciary may employ one or more persons to render advice with regard to any responsibility the fiduciary has under the plan; and
3. A named fiduciary (defined in Qs 2:27–2:28, 2:31) with respect to the control and management of the plan may appoint one or more investment managers to manage any assets of the plan.

[ERISA §402(c); 29 U.S.C. §1102]

Q 2:25   Must benefits under an ERISA welfare benefit plan be definitely determinable?

It appears that if the plan document specifically reserves the right to determine eligibility for benefits, or the amount of benefits, on a case-by-case basis, such a plan provision will be recognized. In contrast to the rules governing ERISA pension plans, there appears to be no requirement that welfare benefits be fixed and determinable. [Hamilton v. Air Jamaica Ltd., 945 F.2d 74 (3d Cir. 1991); *see also* Petrella v. NL Indus. Inc., 529 F. Supp. 1357 (D. N.J. 1982)] (Note that the proposed tax regulations under former Section 89 of the Internal Revenue Code, now repealed, would have added a requirement that benefits be definitely determinable.)

Q 2:26   If benefits are paid out of the employer's general assets, must the plan document contain a funding policy and procedure?

No. If the welfare benefit plan is unfunded, the plan need not provide such a procedure. [ERISA §301(a)(1); 29 U.S.C. §1081(a)(1); DOL Reg. §2509.75-5, Q&A FR-5] (See chapter 20 for a further discussion of funding.)

Fiduciaries

Q 2:27   Who is a plan fiduciary?

Under ERISA, any person, including an individual, partnership, joint venture, corporation, or the like, as defined in ERISA Section 3(9) [29 U.S.C. §1002(9)], is a fiduciary with respect to an employee welfare benefit plan to the extent that the person:

1. Exercises any discretionary authority or control over plan management, or exercises any authority or control (whether or not it is discretionary) over management or disposition of plan assets;
2. Renders investment advice for a fee or other compensation, direct or indirect, for any plan money or other plan property; or
3. Has any discretionary authority or responsibility for plan administration.

Only persons who perform one or more of the functions described above are plan fiduciaries. Thus, persons who have no authority or control over plan assets but who perform only administrative or nondiscretionary functions for a plan are not considered fiduciaries (see Q 2:31). [ERISA §3(21)(A); 29 U.S.C. §1002(21)(A); DOL Reg. §2509.75-8, Q&A D-2]

Practice Pointer. Under the above definition, a plan's fiduciaries ordinarily would include the plan's trustees, the plan administrator, the plan's investment manager, the members of the plan's investment committee, and the person who selects these individuals. Since a person's status as a fiduciary depends on his or her function rather than title, a person may be a fiduciary even though he or she does not hold a titled position with respect to a plan if he or she has authority over or performs the functions described above. [DOL Reg. §§2509.75-8, Qs&As D-3, D-4, FR-17, 2509.75-5, 2510.3-21]

Q 2:28   What is a *named fiduciary*?

Every plan covered under ERISA must specifically designate in the plan document at least one named fiduciary, identified by office (that is, title or position) or identified by name, who has the responsibility for the plan's operation and administration. This requirement enables employees and other interested parties to determine who is responsible for operating the plan. [ERISA §402(a); 29 U.S.C. §1102(a); DOL Reg. §§2509.75-8, Q&A FR-12, 2510.3-21]

Employer. The employer may designate itself as the named fiduciary. [DOL Reg. §2509.75-5, Q&A FR-3] A corporate employer may designate itself as the named fiduciary in order to shield its officers, employees, directors, and others from personal liability. The Court of Appeals for the Third Circuit noted that a corporation always exercises discretionary authority, control, or responsibility through its employees. However, when the plan names the corporation as a fiduciary, an officer of the corporation who exercises discretion on behalf of that corporation is not a fiduciary under ERISA unless it can be shown that the officer has an individual discretionary role with respect to plan administration. For example, if the corporation delegates some of its fiduciary responsibilities under the plan to an officer, then the officer would be an ERISA fiduciary. [Confer v. Custom Eng'g Co., 952 F.2d 34 (3d Cir. 1991)]

Plan committees and joint boards. The plan committee is the named fiduciary if the plan document (1) provides that a plan committee has the authority to control and manage the operation and administration of the plan and (2) specifies who constitutes the committee either by position or by naming individuals to the committee. A plan document may split these functions between two or more plan committees, such as an administrative committee and an investment committee. Similarly, in a union-negotiated employee welfare benefit plan, if the joint board on which employees and employers are equally represented is expressly given such authority, the persons designated as members of the joint board are named fiduciaries. [ERISA §402(a); DOL Reg. §2509.75-5, Qs&As FR-1–FR-2]

Q 2:29   Is the employer a fiduciary?

Generally, yes, if the plan is established and maintained by the employer (that is, a single-employer plan). In such a plan, the employer generally exercises discretionary authority, control, or responsibility acting through its employees and therefore is a fiduciary (even if not a named fiduciary in the plan documents).

In a federal appeals court decision, the court held that an employer that arranged for supplemental life insurance coverage for its employees from a life insurance company, announced the plan to employees in meetings, and printed and distributed plan booklets to employees was an ERISA fiduciary. The court found that the employer had exercised discretionary authority and responsibility in the administration of the plan. [Curcio v. John Hancock Mut. Life Ins. Co., 18 Employee Benefits Cas. (BNA) 1822 (3d Cir. 1994)]

Q 2:30   Are members of the employer's board of directors fiduciaries?

Yes, if the plan is established and maintained by the employer. The board members will be fiduciaries only to the extent that they perform fiduciary duties. If they select plan fiduciaries pursuant to authorization contained in the plan, they retain residual fiduciary responsibility for the prudent selection and retention of those individuals. If the directors are named fiduciaries in the plan document, their liability can be limited by allocating fiduciary responsibilities and delegating them according to procedures contained in the plan. However, they are still subject to cofiduciary liability. [ERISA §405; 29 U.S.C. §1105; DOL Reg. §2509.75-8, Qs&As D-4, FR-16]

Q 2:31   Is a person who performs purely ministerial functions a fiduciary?

No. A person who lacks the power to make any decisions about plan policy, interpretations, practices, or procedures and who performs certain administrative functions for an ERISA plan within a framework of policies, interpretations, rules, practices, and procedures made by others is not a fiduciary.

The administrative functions that are covered by this protective blanket are:

- Applying the rules for determining eligibility for participation or benefits
- Calculating service and compensation credits for benefits
- Preparing employee communications material
- Maintaining participants' service and employment records
- Preparing reports required by government agencies
- Calculating benefits
- Orienting new participants and advising participants of their rights and options under the plan
- Collecting and applying contributions as provided in the plan
- Preparing reports concerning participants' benefits
- Processing claims
- Making recommendations to others about decisions with respect to plan administration

[DOL Reg. §2509.75-8, Q&A D-2]

Practice Pointer. Even if individuals perform only ministerial duties and have none of the responsibilities listed in Q 2:27, they nonetheless may have to be bonded if they handle funds or other property of the plan. (See the discussion of bonding at Qs 2:118–2:124.)

The Ninth Circuit Court of Appeals has held that a third-party plan administrator (TPA) was not a fiduciary because it had performed only ministerial functions and did not exercise control over the plan. The TPA was sued by plan participants as a fiduciary to recover funds that had been embezzled from the plan by a plan trustee. The court upheld the district court's grant of summary judgment because the TPA was not a fiduciary of the plan. [CSA 401(k) Plan v. Pension Professionals Inc., 195 F.3d 1135 (9th Cir. 1999)] The court said that a person's actions, and not the agreed-upon contractual responsibilities, determine the person's status. TPAs are not fiduciaries if they merely perform ministerial functions, including preparing financial reports.

On the other hand, the Sixth Circuit held that a TPA can be considered an ERISA fiduciary if it exercises any authority or control over plan assets, even if it does not have discretionary control over the management or disposition of assets. The case involved plan participants' claims that the TPA improperly allocated plan assets to itself after the plan ceased operations. [Briscoe v. Fine, 444 F.3d 478 (6th Cir. 2006)]

Q 2:32 Is an attorney, accountant, actuary, or consultant a fiduciary?

Generally, no. An attorney, accountant, actuary, or consultant (other than an investment advisor to the plan) who renders legal, accounting, actuarial, or consulting services to an employee welfare benefit plan is not a fiduciary unless he or she also:

1. Exercises discretionary authority or control over plan management;
2. Exercises authority or control over management or disposition of plan assets;
3. Renders investment advice for plan assets for a direct or indirect fee; or
4. Possesses any discretionary authority or responsibility in plan administration.

[DOL Reg. §2509.75-5, Q&A D-1]

An insurance agent was held to be an ERISA fiduciary where the plan's trustees hired the insurance agent to advise them on insurance matters. The trustees were not knowledgeable about insurance matters and, as a result, the insurance agent in operation had discretionary authority and control over plan assets. [Reich v. Lancaster, 55 F.3d 1034 (5th Cir. 1995)]

Brokers who sold limited partnership interests to ERISA plans on a commission basis were held to be fiduciaries where the facts showed that the brokers had great influence and control over the plans' investment decisions. [Reich v. McManus, 883 F. Supp. 1144 (D. Ill. 1995)] However, a broker and benefits consultant who merely recommended an investment was held not to be a fiduciary. The consultant did not have discretionary authority over the plan's investments and did not receive a fee for providing investment advice. [Mid-Atlantic Perfusion Assocs. v. Professional Ass'n Consulting Servs., 60 F.3d 816 (3d Cir. 1995)]

Practice Pointer. If an advisor makes plan decisions on behalf of a client, instead of merely presenting alternatives for the client's decision, this exercise of discretion could make the advisor a fiduciary.

Q 2:33 Is a health maintenance organization an ERISA fiduciary?

No. In a landmark decision, the U.S. Supreme Court held that health maintenance organizations (HMOs) cannot be sued as fiduciaries for breaching their duties under ERISA.

Significantly, the lawsuit struck directly at the heart of the HMO—medical cost control. The suit claimed that an HMO's practice of rewarding physicians for limiting medical care entailed an inherent breach of ERISA's requirement that a plan fiduciary act solely in the interest of plan participants. According to the lawsuit, such incentives create a climate in which decisions are made in the physician's own self-interest, rather than in the plan participant's interest.

The Supreme Court held that an HMO is not acting as an ERISA fiduciary when it makes decisions about a patient's treatment. Moreover, the Court said that adopting the view that physician incentives are an automatic breach of ERISA would "be nothing less than the elimination of the for-profit HMO."

According to the Court, cost control is inherent to HMOs, and cost-controlling measures are commonly complemented by financial incentives to physicians, who are rewarded for decreasing utilization of services and penalized for excessive treatment. The basic check on these financial incentives and disincentives is the same as under fee-for-service plans: the physician's professional obligation to provide services with a reasonable degree of skill and judgment in the patient's interest. Moreover, the Court noted that the adequacy of professional obligations to counter financial self-interest is open to challenge under any setup. For example, HMOs initially became popular because fee-for-service physicians were thought to be providing unnecessary or useless services, while today many critics charge that HMOs often ignore the needs of patients in order to improve their own bottom lines. Whether either of those charges is true, the issue is one of medical malpractice, not fiduciary duty under ERISA. [Pegram v. Herdrich, 530 U.S. 211 (2000)]

Q 2:34 Is a plan required to have a specific number of fiduciaries?

No. Plans are not required to have a specific number of fiduciaries. However, at least one named fiduciary must serve as plan administrator, and there must be an appropriate named fiduciary for appeals of denied claims. If plan assets must be held in trust (see Qs 2:95–2:99), there must be at least one trustee. [DOL Reg. §2509.75-8, Q&A FR-12]

Q 2:35 May fiduciary duties be allocated among fiduciaries and delegated by fiduciaries to others?

Yes, they may, but only pursuant to authority contained in the plan. Delegation of the authority or discretion to manage or control plan assets is strictly circumscribed. Additionally, even a permissible allocation or delegation does not relieve a fiduciary of cofiduciary duties (see Q 2:109). [ERISA §§403(a) 405(b)(1), 405(b)(3)(B), 405(c), 405(d); 29 U.S.C. §§1103(a), 1105(b)(1), 1105(b)(3)(B), 1105(c), 1105(d); DOL Reg. §2509.75-8, Qs &As FR-13–FR-17]

Fiduciary Responsibility

Q 2:36 What are the standards an ERISA fiduciary must satisfy in discharging duties under the plan?

In discharging its duties under the plan, a fiduciary must adhere to four general rules of conduct:

1. The exclusive-benefit rule
2. The prudent man rule
3. The diversification rule
4. The adherence-to-plan-documents rule

[ERISA §404(a); 29 U.S.C. §1104(a)]

Q 2:37 What is the exclusive-benefit rule?

ERISA's *exclusive-benefit rule* requires a fiduciary to discharge his or her fiduciary duties with respect to a plan (1) solely in the interest of the participants and beneficiaries and (2) for the exclusive purpose of providing benefits to participants and their beneficiaries and defraying reasonable administrative expenses. [ERISA §404(a); 29 U.S.C. §1104(a)] Generally, this means that plan assets must never inure to the benefit of the employer. [ERISA §403(c); 29 U.S.C. §1103(c)]

Q 2:38 What is the prudent man rule?

ERISA's *prudent man rule* requires a fiduciary to act with the same care, skill, prudence, and diligence that a prudent man acting in a like capacity and familiar with such matters would use in the conduct of an enterprise of the same character and aims under the same circumstances. [ERISA §404(a)(1)(B); 29 U.S.C. §1104(a)(1)(B)]

The DOL ruled that, in certain circumstances, an ERISA plan fiduciary investing plan assets may take into consideration economically targeted investments (that is, investments designed to serve some economic or social purposes, such as providing jobs for plan participants) as long as the investments comply with the prudence and other fiduciary requirements of ERISA. However, if the economically targeted investment is expected to produce a lower investment return than comparable available investments, or involves greater risk than comparable available investments, such an investment would not be prudent. [DOL Int. Bull. 94-1, 59 Fed. Reg. 32,606 (June 23, 1994)]

> **Note.** DOL Interpretive Bulletin 94-1 is aimed at encouraging economically targeted investments. However, many of the investments being promoted as economically or socially desirable for ERISA plan investment seem to involve lower returns and/or greater risks than other available investments. The DOL provides no relief for such investments.

Q 2:39   What is the diversification rule?

ERISA's *diversification rule* requires a fiduciary with investment responsibilities to diversify the investments of the plan to minimize the risk of large losses unless, under the circumstances, it is clearly prudent not to do so. [ERISA §404(a)(1)(C); 29 U.S.C. §1104(a)(1)(C)]

The conference report issued under ERISA states that plans may invest all of their assets in a single bank or other pooled investment fund that has diversified investments within the pooled fund. The conference report indicates that the same rule is applied to investments in a mutual fund. The conference report also states that, generally, a plan can be invested wholly in insurance or annuity contracts without violating the diversification rules, because the insurance company's assets are usually invested in a diversified manner. [H. Rep. 93-1280, 93d Cong. 2d Sess., at 305 (1974)]

A federal district court held that a plan trustee who was experienced in real estate investing did not act imprudently by investing more than 70 percent of a plan's assets in real estate investments. The trustee was able to show that the investments were fairly safe, offered a competitive rate of return, and satisfied the plan's liquidity needs. The court also noted that the real estate mortgages involved were of short duration, carried a competitive rate of interest, and were made to creditworthy borrowers. Therefore, the court held that the heavy plan concentration in real estate was prudent in the circumstances involved. [Reich v. King, 18 Employee Benefits Cas. (BNA) 1801 (D.C. Md. 1994)] A later decision by the U.S. Court of Appeals for the Fifth Circuit held that an investment of 63 percent of a plan's assets in a single parcel of real estate was not imprudent under the facts of the case. [Metzler v. Graham, 112 F.3d 207 (5th Cir. 1997)]

Q 2:40   How must fiduciaries adhere to the plan documents?

ERISA fiduciaries are directed to discharge their duties in accordance with the documents and instruments governing the plan. For welfare benefit plans, they may do this only to the extent that the documents and instruments do not contravene ERISA Title I concerning reporting and disclosure, fiduciary responsibility, prohibited transactions, and the like. [ERISA §404(a)(1)(D); 29 U.S.C. §1104(a)(1)(D)]

Furthermore, ERISA restricts the manner in which the plan document may be used to limit the liability of fiduciaries. Provisions contained in a plan document, instrument, or agreement that attempt to relieve fiduciaries of responsibility or liability—other than an express allocation or delegation of responsibility that is permitted under ERISA (see Qs 2:35, 2:110) are void as against public policy. [ERISA §§403(a), 405(b)(1), 405(b)(3)(B), 405(c), 405(d), 410(a); 29 U.S.C. §§1103(a), 1105(b)(1), 1105(b)(3)(B), 1105(c), 1105(d), 1110(a)]

Compliance with other laws. If the plan document violates other applicable laws, or omits provisions required by other applicable laws, the plan administrator must ignore the illegal plan provision and administer the plan in compliance with applicable law. In an advisory opinion, the DOL has held that ERISA requires plan fiduciaries to comply not only with ERISA, but also other federal laws that are not preempted by ERISA. The DOL also stated that plans whose terms are not consistent with other federal laws and regulations should be amended to comply with those requirements. In that advisory opinion, the DOL concluded that an ERISA health plan fiduciary is obligated to comply with the Medicare secondary-payer provisions of the federal Medicare program. Also, if a Medicare reimbursement claim is not submitted to the plan in accordance with the plan's terms, the DOL stated that the fiduciary must disregard the plan's terms and process the claim. [DOL Adv. Op. 93-23A (Sept. 3, 1993)] The Balanced Budget Act of 1997 [Pub. L. No. 105-33, 111 Stat. 351 (1997)] amended the Social Security Act to permit recovery of overpayments by Medicare provided that it submits a request to the group health plan within three years from the date the item or service was furnished, regardless of any shorter claim-filing limit that may exist under the group health plan. [Social Security Act §1862(b)(2)(B)(v), added by §4632(a) of the Balanced Budget Act of 1997]

Q 2:41   What consequences may ensue if no written plan document exists?

A number of risks are present if the plan administrator fails to perform its fiduciary responsibility by preparing a written plan document. The chief risk incurred by maintaining an unwritten ERISA plan is that a court may disagree with the employer's characterization of what benefits the plan covers or excludes and rule against the employer and in favor of the employee(s) on coverage issues. This can be quite costly for the employer.

Q 2:42   Are there consequences if employees try to circumvent coverage limitations contained in a plan document, such as a copayment requirement?

At least one case has upheld an insurance company's right to deny plan benefits altogether when a health care provider agreed not to charge the plan participant the 20 percent copayment that the participant otherwise would have had to pay under the plan, in effect accepting the insurance company's reimbursement as full payment. The court in that case upheld complete denial of the claim. [Kennedy v. Connecticut Gen. Life Ins. Co., 924 F.2d 698 (7th Cir. 1991)]

Q 2:43   Does ERISA's fiduciary duty apply to selecting service providers for an employee benefit plan?

Yes, it does. Several years ago, the DOL issued an advisory opinion letter concerning a fiduciary's duty when selecting or determining to maintain health care service providers. Plan fiduciaries must balance cost and quality when selecting health care plans and health care providers. [DOL Adv. Op. to Diane Orantes Cerest (Feb. 19, 1998)]

More recently, the DOL made it clear that plan fiduciaries must act prudently in selecting service providers for an employee benefit plan and must ensure that no more than reasonable compensation is paid for services provided, taking into account the direct and indirect compensation received by the service providers.

However, to fulfill their duties, plan fiduciaries must have information about the fees and compensation received by the service provider and whether there are relationships or interests on the part of the service provider that may call into question the provider's objectivity in providing services to the plan. To address that issue, the DOL has proposed regulations that would require that contracts with service providers disclose the service providers' direct and indirect compensation and potential conflicts of interest that may affect their objectivity. During the term of the contract, a service provider would also be required to disclose any material changes in the information originally disclosed. [Prop. DOL Reg. § 2550.408b-2(c)]

The disclosure requirements would apply to:

- Fiduciary service providers;
- Providers of banking, consulting, custodial, insurance, investment advisory or management, recordkeeping, securities brokerage, or third-party administration services; and
- Providers who receive indirect compensation for accounting, actuarial, auditing, legal, or valuation services.

If a contract with a covered service provider does not contain the required disclosures, the plan fiduciary would technically be in violation of ERISA's restrictions on prohibited transactions and would be potentially subject to an excise tax for the violation. However, the DOL has also proposed an exemption from the prohibited transaction rules to provide relief for a plan fiduciary who enters into a service provider contract that is deficient because, unbeknownst to the fiduciary, the service provider did not make the required disclosures.

Mandated Benefit Provisions

Q 2:44   Does ERISA impose minimum benefit requirements on welfare benefit plans?

As originally drafted, ERISA contained extensive substantive requirements for pension plans but no mandatory benefit provisions affecting welfare benefit plans. However, starting with the COBRA continuation coverage requirements in 1985 and ending most recently with the 2010 Health Reform Act, Congress has grafted onto ERISA numerous mandates and requirements for group health plans. ERISA's broad applicability, its reporting and disclosure requirements, and its claims and enforcement provisions help to effectuate widespread employer compliance. The COBRA continuation coverage requirements are covered in chapter 6. Mandated benefit requirements and other group health plan standards are discussed in chapter 5.

Q 2:45   Are employers free to design welfare benefit plans covered by ERISA in any manner they choose?

No. A mosaic of requirements is imposed by both federal laws and state laws.

Federal laws. Even though ERISA allows broad flexibility of welfare benefit plan design (subject to specific requirements for group health plans discussed in chapter 5), ERISA does not preempt other federal laws. As a result, an employee welfare benefit plan may be subject to numerous minimum or mandatory benefit requirements, including nondiscrimination requirements, contained in other federal laws.

For example, the particular type of plan may have to meet nondiscrimination rules imposed by the Internal Revenue Code in order for the employer's contribution to be deductible and the coverage and benefit payments to be tax-free (or at least available on a tax-favored basis) to employees. Additional nondiscrimination rules that the Code imposes on particular methods of funding employee welfare benefits are discussed in chapter 20.

The employer's plan design flexibility is also limited by other federal laws prohibiting discrimination on the basis of age, sex, race, national origin, religion, disability, need for family or medical leave, or military service. (See chapters 16–19.) In addition, plan design may be affected by mental health and substance abuse disorder parity requirements (see chapter 5) and genetic information nondiscrimination rules (see chapters 5 and 19).

The DOL has issued an advisory opinion in which it held that ERISA requires plan fiduciaries to comply not only with ERISA, but also with other federal laws that are not preempted by ERISA. Further, the DOL advised that if a plan's terms were not consistent with the requirements of other federal laws, the plan should be amended to so comply. [DOL Adv. Op. 93-23A (Sept. 3, 1993)]

State laws. Whether state laws can validly impose additional conditions on ERISA-covered welfare benefit plans is examined in Qs 2:170–2:186.

Plan Development: Adoption, Amendment, and Termination

Q 2:46   When an employer adopts a new employee welfare benefit plan, is the adoption of the plan a fiduciary function?

No. Employers are free to offer welfare benefit plans, and the decision to have one is purely a management decision. The employer is under no duty to act solely in the interests of employees and potential plan participants and beneficiaries when determining whether to have a plan or what the content of the plan will be. [Belade v. ITT Corp., 909 F.2d 736 (2d Cir. 1990); Moore v. Metropolitan Life Ins. Co., 856 F.2d 488 (2d Cir. 1988)]

Q 2:47   Is an employer's decision to amend an existing employee welfare benefit plan a fiduciary function?

No. Under ERISA, decisions regarding what benefits are to be included in a welfare benefit plan and whether to increase or decrease welfare benefit plan benefits are corporate management decisions, not fiduciary decisions. An employer that is under no obligation to offer a plan at all also is under no obligation to offer any particular level of benefits under a voluntarily provided plan (other than those mandated by law for the particular type of plan at issue). [Chervin v. Sulzer Bingham Pumps, Inc., 1992 U.S. App. LEXIS 12627 (9th Cir. May 29, 1992)]

However, and most important, the ability of an employer to change a benefits plan will be affected if it fails to clearly and unambiguously reserve the right to alter or diminish benefits under the plan or engages in a course of conduct that a court may find to have effectively guaranteed a particular level of benefits. [Schalk v. Teledyne Inc., 751 F. Supp. 1261 (W.D. Mich. 1990); Alexander v. Primerica Holdings Inc., 967 F.2d 90 (3d Cir. 1992)] In addition, the employer may be barred from amending the plan if the plan amendment fails to comply with the amendment procedure set forth in the plan. [Curtiss-Wright Corp. v. Schoonejongen, 514 U.S. 73 (1995)]

Furthermore, the employer may have contractually agreed to maintain a particular level of benefits, such as in a collectively bargained plan, and later may be unable to unilaterally alter benefits without subjecting itself to a charge of engaging in an unfair labor practice.

In reversing the U.S. Court of Appeals for the Ninth Circuit, the U.S. Supreme Court held that Hughes Aircraft Company did not violate ERISA by amending a contributory retirement plan to establish a noncontributory plan, and by failing to distribute surplus plan assets from the contributory plan to the participants of that plan. [Hughes Aircraft Co. v. Jacobson, 525 U.S. 432 (1999); 26 Pens. & Ben. Rep. (BNA) 4 (Jan. 25, 1999)] The ruling of the lower court had permitted a class of participants in the contributory plan to sue the company under ERISA after it had created a noncontributory benefit structure and had transferred the over-funded plan's surplus—almost $1 billion—to this new noncontributory plan structure. The noncontributory plan included many new employees who had not contributed to the original plan. The Supreme Court ruled that "plan members lack claim to any particular asset held in plan's general asset pool, and instead merely have right to accrued benefits." In addition, the Court said that "the employer satisfied its continuing contractual and legal obligation to assure that the plan was adequately funded."

A federal district court held that where (1) employees had accepted a special early retirement offer, (2) the SPD was ambiguous as to whether the coverage could be changed, and (3) the written materials and other written and oral communications materials explaining the offer indicated that lifetime medical coverage would be provided at no additional cost, the employer was barred from amending the plan to reduce or eliminate the medical coverage. [Sprague v. General Motors Corp., 843 F. Supp. 266 (E.D. Mich. 1994)]

Q 2:48   Is an employer's decision to cut back or terminate an employee welfare benefit plan a fiduciary function?

No. The mere determination to do so is not a fiduciary function. [Moore v. Metropolitan Life Ins. Co., 856 F.2d 488 (2d Cir. 1988); Musto v. American Gen. Corp., 861 F.2d 897 (6th Cir. 1988)] Note, however, that the employer may be precluded from doing so by past communications and actions or by a collective bargaining agreement. [*See* Senn v. United Dominion Indus. Inc., 951 F.2d 806 (7th Cir. 1992)] A U.S. appellate court has held that an employer can modify its ERISA plan benefits even though treatment for specific conditions has already begun. [Owens v. Storehouse Inc., 984 F.2d 394 (11th Cir. 1993)] A federal district court in the Fourth Circuit held, however, that where a course of medical treatment had begun at a time when the treatment was covered by the health plan, the plan could not be amended with retroactive effect so as to eliminate coverage of the treatment. [Wheeler v. Dynamic Eng'g Inc., 850 F. Supp. 459 (E.D. Va. 1994)]

> **Note.** Special notification requirements apply to material reductions of covered services and benefits under group health plans. An extremely broad definition of *material* applies for this purpose. (See chapter 5.)

Moreover, a plan should be careful that all communications with employees clearly communicate the plan's reservation of rights to amend or terminate the plan. In a decision involving a dispute almost two decades long over termination of a retiree medical plan, the Third Circuit held that a company, as plan sponsor, breached its fiduciary duty under ERISA when company employees counseled a group of prospective retirees about the cost and duration of retiree health benefits without cautioning them that retiree benefits were subject to change. According to the Third Circuit, the fact that the company disclosed its reservation of rights in the summary plan description and other documentation was not enough because it did not present that information when counseling the employees on their retirement decisions. "In essence," said the court, "by failing to qualify its statements, . . . [the company] placed a period where it should have placed a comma in the course of explaining retiree medical benefits to . . . [the employees] and, in doing so, misrepresented the cost and duration of the benefits." [*In re* Unisys Corp. Ret. Med. Benefit ERISA Litig., 579 F.3d 220 (3d Cir. 2009)]

Q 2:49   Can a written plan document be amended orally?

No. Oral amendments do not modify the written terms of an ERISA plan. A company announced that its new medical plan would not cover motorcycle accidents, but the plan document failed to exclude them. The Court of Appeals for the Third Circuit held that the employer's oral statements were not plan amendments and that the employer's attempted retroactive amendment of the plan to correct the omission was not effective to exclude the employee's claims. The court affirmed a lower court's ruling that the employer displayed bad faith by backdating the plan to deprive the employee of benefits. The court also ruled that a formal plan amendment could be prospective only. [Confer v. Custom Eng'g Co., 952 F.2d 34, 41 (3d Cir. 1991); *see also* Hozier v. Midwest Fasteners Inc., 908 F. 2d 1155 (3d Cir. 1990)]

Where a welfare benefit plan had a formal amendment procedure, an oral modification of the plan was held to be ineffective. A written amendment to the plan had been prepared that had not been signed and formally adopted. [Breuer v. Protexall Inc., 50 F.3d 453 (7th Cir. 1995)] A complete cancellation of an ERISA plan is subject to the required amendment procedures of ERISA, a federal appellate court has held. The court observed that it would be illogical for ERISA to protect employees from changes in benefits but not from total elimination of their benefits. [Ackerman v. Warnaco Inc., 55 F.3d 117 (3d Cir. 1995)]

One question that has arisen is whether oral verification of the existence of medical insurance coverage takes priority over the actual terms of the plan (if different), such as when a hospital calls the employer's insurance carrier to verify coverage prior to admission or treatment. At least one court has held that the plan document's exclusions will apply even if an erroneous oral verification of coverage was previously made and that the plan is not estopped from denying coverage. [Rodriguez v. Western & Southern Life Ins. Co., 948 F.2d 969 (5th Cir. 1991); *see also* Owens v. Storehouse Inc., 984 F.2d 394 (11th Cir. 1993)] However, a health care provider, as an assignee of an employee's claims, was permitted to sue the employer's insurance carrier for coverage based on the insurance carrier's oral verification of coverage despite the prior cancellation of the employee's coverage. [Psychiatric Inst. of Washington, DC, Inc. v. Connecticut Gen. Life Ins. Co., 780 F. Supp. 24 (D.D.C. 1992)]

Q 2:50   Can a plan amendment be given retroactive effect?

ERISA contains provisions dealing with the retroactive amendment of pension plans and limiting the right to make such retroactive amendments if accrued benefits are sought to be reduced. [ERISA §302(c)(8); 29 U.S.C. §1082(c)] However, ERISA provides no statutory limitation on making welfare plan amendments retroactive, and many employers had assumed that reasonable retroactivity was permitted, especially where the changes had been communicated to employees in advance of or concurrently with the date of the plan changes. The case law on this issue, however, suggests otherwise.

Cutting back covered benefits after expenses have been incurred. The Court of Appeals for the Third Circuit has held that an employer that intended to exclude coverage for motorcycle accidents under its medical plan, but failed to do so, could not retroactively amend the plan to deprive employees of benefits. [Confer v. Custom Eng'g Co., 952 F.2d 34, 41 (3d Cir. 1991)]

Q 2:51   Can an employer implement plan cutbacks before "official" plan amendments have been adopted?

A federal appeals court decision strongly suggests that a welfare benefit plan amendment may not be given retroactive effect, at least to the extent it reduces employee contributions or benefits. In that case, an employer maintained both pension and welfare benefit plans subject to ERISA. The employer informed the employees in advance about changes in the plans, including the dates the changes would become effective. Counsel for the employer drafted plan amendments well after the changes were announced and well after they were scheduled to take effect. The amendments were formally executed with the effective dates as originally announced to the employees. The court held that informal and oral amendments are not permitted by ERISA and therefore that the plans were not amended until the formal amendments were properly executed. The court then went on to hold that the effective dates of the amendments were the dates they were executed and not the earlier effective dates that had been communicated to employees. [Smith v. National Credit Union Admin. Bd., 18 Employee Benefits Cas. (BNA) 2323 (11th Cir. 1994)]

Practice Pointer. While the Eleventh Circuit decision may not be followed in other circuits, it would be prudent for employers to execute formal plan amendments promptly and, if possible, before or at the same time the amendment is to take effect.

Q 2:52   What if the plan amendment is made but does not comply with the plan's amendment procedure?

This practice could backfire on an employer. In one case, an employer's human resources department circulated a description of new, reduced severance benefits to management, and the plan was administered in accordance with that description. However, several terminated employees successfully sued for the previous higher level of severance benefits because no written plan amendment had been adopted before the benefit cutbacks were implemented. [Hozier v. Midwest Fasteners Inc., 908 F.2d 1155 (3d Cir. 1990)] See also the discussion in Q 2:51 of the decision by the U.S. Court of Appeals for the Eleventh Circuit in *Smith v. National Credit Union Administrative Board.* In that case, the court held that plan amendments are effective only if formal plan amendments are executed and that, when executed, the formal plan amendments cannot be given retroactive effect.

Q 2:53   May an employer amend an ERISA welfare benefit plan to reduce benefits prospectively?

The Supreme Court has stated that "ERISA does not mandate that employers provide any particular [employee welfare] benefits, and does not itself proscribe discrimination in the provision of employee [welfare] benefits." [Shaw v. Delta Airlines Inc., 463 U.S. 85 (1983)] Accordingly, it appears that as long as the employer has expressly reserved the right to cut back benefits, ERISA permits an employer to do so prospectively. However, since the *Shaw* decision, several mandatory minimum benefit requirements affecting group health plans have been added to ERISA (see discussion in Qs 2:44–2:45). Employers should take care that any planned benefit cutback does not run afoul of these requirements.

Except for the ERISA requirements noted above, the right to prospectively cut back benefits appears to include expenses incurred in the future for conditions that preexist the date of the plan amendment. However, one court has held that health plan coverage cannot be terminated for a covered condition for which medical treatment had begun prior to the date of the amendment eliminating coverage (see Q 2:48). State insurance laws that fall outside of ERISA's preemption provisions may preclude reduction of particular insured benefits. However, general state labor laws prohibiting employment discrimination in the terms, conditions, and privileges of employment would probably be preempted from applying to ERISA welfare benefit plans. (ERISA preemption is discussed in detail in Qs 2:170–2:186.)

Q 2:54   Is the employer responsible if the written description of the plan's benefits contains an error?

An employer may be held to the obligation described in the erroneous document. An employer that intended to exclude coverage for motorcycle accidents under its medical plan, but failed to do so, was not permitted to retroactively amend the plan to deprive employees of benefits. [Confer v. Custom Eng'g Co., 952 F.2d 34, 41 (3d Cir. 1991)] A handbook that erroneously listed higher severance pay benefits than the company intended due to a printer's error was held to be an enforceable ERISA written plan. [Hamilton v. Air Jamaica Ltd., 945 F.2d 74 (3d Cir. 1991) (denying the employee's claim based on another provision in the handbook)]

> **Practice Pointer.** Although the cases cited above involve simple mistakes, coverage may be granted for failure to "tie up all the loose ends" in benefit documents. In view of the case law developments concerning ERISA plan documents, SPDs, and other employee communications, it is advisable to review carefully all such documents from a legal standpoint prior to implementing or publishing them. Prevention is crucial here. Once the document is out, employees may rely on it to their detriment or, if they are unhappy with a denial of benefit coverage, may be able to exploit its loopholes in a lawsuit. When an insurance contract is involved, the cases indicate that a separate plan document may be advisable, and it is extremely important that

the SPD fairly disclose all material terms, conditions, limitations, and exclusions contained in the insurance contract.

Because the awards in some cases have been extremely high relative to the cost of simple "preventive planning," it is advisable to perform an ERISA legal review periodically, to plug all the loopholes highlighted (or newly created) by case law developments. Such reviews may save a company from an embarrassing and expensive court case resulting in judgment for the employee on a point that easily could have been anticipated and dealt with in the planning stage. And, as highlighted by *Hamilton*, even if benefit communications are being handled by an outside consulting firm or printer, the employer should review the printer's proof to help catch any errors.

Plan Assets

Q 2:55 What are plan assets?

There is no ERISA definition of the term *plan assets*. In the ordinary sense of the words, plan assets are those amounts set aside in trust or otherwise in order to provide plan benefits and to pay for plan expenses. Plan assets generally are derived from employer and employee contributions and from investment earnings on such contributions.

Q 2:56 Why is it important to know if there are plan assets?

If there are plan assets under the plan, they must be maintained and administered in accordance with the fiduciary responsibility and prohibited transaction rules of ERISA (see Qs 2:36–2:41, 2:100–2:105).

Q 2:57 Are employee contributions for welfare benefit plan coverage considered to be plan assets?

Yes. [DOL Reg. §2510.3-102, 61 Fed. Reg. 41,220 (Aug. 7, 1996)] See Qs 2:95–2:99 for a discussion of when employee contributions must be held in trust.

Q 2:58 Are pretax contributions for welfare benefit plan coverage under a cafeteria plan considered to be plan assets?

Yes. The DOL takes the position that they are, regardless of how the IRS characterizes them for tax purposes. [Prop. DOL Reg. §2510.3-102, 60 Fed. Reg. 66,036 (Dec. 20, 1995)] (See Q 2:99 for a discussion of whether they must be held in trust.)

Q 2:59   Does an unfunded welfare benefit plan have plan assets?

No. If the welfare benefit plan is truly unfunded—that is, the welfare benefits are paid solely from the general assets of the employer—there are no plan assets.

Q 2:60   Are funds held in trust for the payment of benefits (and expenses) under a welfare benefit plan considered to be plan assets?

Yes, generally they are. However, the DOL ruled that funds held in an employer's revocable trust and subject to the claims of the employer's creditors, to be used by the employer as a discretionary source of employer premiums, are not plan assets. [DOL Adv. Op. 93-14A (May 5, 1993)]

Q 2:61   Is an insurance policy purchased by an employer or plan trustee for the purpose of providing plan benefits a plan asset?

Generally, yes. [ERISA §401(b)(2)] However, corporate-owned life insurance or stop-loss insurance purchased to finance plan benefits, if structured properly, should not be treated as a plan asset (see Qs 20:97–20:103).

The DOL has clarified that a stop-loss policy (see chapter 20) purchased directly by the employer, under which the proceeds are payable into the general assets of the employer and subject to the claims of the employer's general creditors, does not constitute a plan asset. [DOL Adv. Op. 92-02A (Jan. 17, 1992)] Advisory Opinion 92-02A specified that no representation would be made to plan participants or beneficiaries that the policy would provide plan benefits or be security for payment of plan benefits. In addition, the plan benefits would not be limited or controlled in any manner by the amount of stop-loss insurance proceeds received by the employer. The advisory opinion concluded that because the policy would not be an asset of the plan and would not provide benefits under the plan, it need not be reported (on Schedule A) or submitted with the Form 5500 annual report to the IRS.

A state's attempt to regulate stop-loss policies with liability triggers below specified levels was held to be invalid as applied to a policy issued to an ERISA health plan. [American Med. Sec. v. Bartlett, 111 F.3d 358 (4th Cir. 1997)]

Q 2:62   If an ERISA plan invests in another entity, such as a corporation or partnership, do the underlying assets of the other entity constitute plan assets?

Generally, when a plan invests in another entity, the plan's assets include its investment in the other entity but do not, solely because of such investment, include any of the underlying assets of the other entity.

However, if the plan's investment is an "equity interest" in an entity that is neither a publicly offered security nor a registered investment company (such as a mutual fund), the plan's investment includes the equity interest and an undivided interest in the underlying assets of the other entity, unless:

1. The entity is an operating company or
2. Equity participation in the entity by benefits plan investors is not significant.

[DOL Reg. §2510.3-101(a)]

Q 2:63　What is an equity interest?

An *equity interest* is any interest in an entity other than an investment that is treated as indebtedness under applicable local law and that has no substantial equity features. An equity interest includes a profits interest in a partnership, an undivided ownership interest in property, and a beneficial interest in a trust. [DOL Reg. §2510.3-101(b)(1)]

Q 2:64　What is an operating company?

An *operating company* is an entity that is primarily engaged, directly or through a majority-owned subsidiary or subsidiaries, in the production or sale of a product or service other than the investment of capital. For example, if a plan invests in the stock of an automobile manufacturer, the stock held by the plan will be plan assets, but the assets (plants, equipment) owned by the automobile manufacturer will not be, because the automobile manufacturer is an operating company. [DOL Reg. §2510.3-101(c)(1)]

If an entity does not qualify as an operating company under the above definition, it may still qualify as an operating company if it meets a detailed definition in the DOL regulations for either a venture capital operating company or a real estate operating company. [DOL Reg. §§2510.3-101(c)(1), 2510.3-101(d), 2510.3-101(e)]

Q 2:65　When is equity participation by benefit plan investors in an entity not "significant," so that the underlying assets of the entity will not be considered plan assets?

Equity participation in an entity by benefit plan investors is significant on any date if, immediately after the most recent acquisition, 25 percent or more of the value of any class of equity interests in the entity is held by benefit plan investors. Thus, it is necessary to keep equity participation of benefit plan investors below the 25 percent level in order for the assets of the entity not to be considered plan assets (assuming the entity is not an operating company). For this purpose, a benefit plan investor includes not only ERISA plans but non-ERISA employee benefit plans such as governmental plans and individual retirement accounts and annuities (IRAs). [DOL Reg. §2510.3-101(f)]

Q 2:66 If an employer or plan trustee purchases an insurance contract to provide welfare plan benefits, are the underlying assets of the insurance company considered plan assets?

ERISA provides that, in the case of a plan to which a guaranteed benefit policy is issued, the assets of the plan include the policy but not the underlying assets of the insurance company. The term *guaranteed benefit policy* is defined for this purpose as an insurance policy or contract to the extent that it provides benefits whose amount is guaranteed by the insurance company. The term's definition does not include amounts held in the insurance company's separate account (other than any of the insurance company's own funds held in the separate account, that is, separate account surplus). [ERISA §401(b)(2); 29 U.S.C. §1101(b)(2)] Most insurance policies purchased to provide employee welfare benefits (for example, group term life, medical, disability) appear to meet the definition of a guaranteed benefit policy, and thus the insurance company's underlying assets (other than employee benefit plan assets held in a separate account) should not be deemed plan assets.

In an ERISA pension plan case, the U.S. Supreme Court held that a pension plan contract issued by an insurance company that guaranteed some but not all pension benefits for plan participants was a guaranteed benefit policy only to the extent of the benefits guaranteed; therefore, with respect to the portion of the contract that was not guaranteed, the insurer's general account assets were plan assets and the insurer was a fiduciary of the ERISA plan. [John Hancock Mut. Life Ins. Co. v. Harris Trust & Sav. Bank, 114 S. Ct. 517 (1993)] Further developments regarding this issue are discussed in Q 2:69.

Q 2:67 What is the insurance company's "separate account"?

An insurance company's *separate account* is a designated pool of investment assets maintained by the company pursuant to policies under which the policyholders have agreed to have part or all of the contributions under the policies invested in the separate account. Generally, the benefits provided under the policies will vary depending wholly or partially on the investment experience of the separate account. A separate account may be established for one customer or for a number of customers (this latter type is known as a *pooled separate account*).

Generally, insurers maintain a number of separate accounts, some as pooled accounts and some as single-customer accounts. Each separate account ordinarily will be established with a specific type of investment portfolio involved—for example, a common stock account, a bond account, or a real estate account.

Separate account contracts of insurance companies are issued primarily for the purpose of funding pension and savings plans. However, they can be used in the welfare benefit plan area and have been used as a funding vehicle for reserves maintained to provide postretirement group life and medical benefits.

Q 2:68   Are the assets held in an insurance company's separate account in which an ERISA welfare benefit plan participates considered plan assets under ERISA?

Yes. The only exceptions are the following:

1. If the insurance company has its own funds in the separate account (that is, separate account surplus), such funds are not plan assets [ERISA §401(b)(2)(B); 29 U.S.C. §1101(b)(2)(B)] and

2. If the insurance company maintains the separate account solely in connection with fixed contractual obligations of the insurance company, under which the amounts payable or credited to the plan and to any participant or beneficiary of the plan are not affected in any manner by the investment performance of the separate account, the funds in the separate account are not plan assets. [DOL Reg. §2510.3-101(h)(1)(iii)]

For example, a plan may have a guaranteed interest contract that guarantees a fixed rate of interest, such as 8 percent. The insurance company may set up a separate account on its books that holds bonds providing it with an investment return of at least 8 percent. As long as the plan has the fixed obligation of the insurance company and does not have to rely on the investment return of the bonds in the separate account, the bonds in the separate account are not considered plan assets.

Q 2:69   Are insurance company assets not held for the benefit of separate account policies deemed to be plan assets because the insurance company insures welfare plan benefits?

Such assets are referred to as *general account assets.* An insurer's general account assets consist of all the assets held by the insurer to meet all of its policy and contractual liabilities (other than separate account assets held for liabilities to separate account policyholders) and all other liabilities, as well as the insurer's capital and surplus funds.

As previously discussed (see Q 2:66), ERISA provides that, to the extent a policy is a guaranteed benefit policy, the assets underlying the policy (that is, all the insurer's general account assets) are not deemed to be plan assets; however, to the extent the policy does not provide guaranteed benefits, the general account assets are deemed plan assets. The U.S. Supreme Court has stated that each component of the contract bears examination to determine whether it qualifies as a guaranteed benefit policy and that a component fits within the guaranteed benefit policy only if it allocates investment risk to the insurer. [John Hancock Mut. Life Ins. Co. v. Harris Trust & Sav. Bank, 114 S. Ct. 517, 520 (1993)]

Federal pension law generally does not consider assets of insurance company general accounts as including plan assets subject to ERISA. However, the 1993 Supreme Court ruling in *John Hancock* concluded that plan investments in certain insurance contracts could result in an insurer holding plan assets. In such cases, insurance companies become fiduciaries subject to ERISA's rules.

On July 12, 1995, the DOL granted a class exemption giving insurance companies conditional relief for transactions between their general account and companies that had preexisting relationships with investing plans. This class exemption will continue to provide limited relief for insurers that choose not to comply with the final rule.

A final rule provides a broad safe harbor by stating that insurance companies would not be deemed fiduciaries under ERISA by virtue of plan investments in certain general account policies that were issued by an insurer on or before December 31, 1998.

To come within the safe harbor, insurance companies must:

1. Disclose to plan clients the method by which expenses and income are allocated to the contract;

2. Allow plans to terminate or discontinue a policy upon 90 days' notice to the insurer and to elect either a lump-sum payout without penalty or annual installment payments over a ten-year period with interest; and

3. Give plans written notice of certain amendments 60 days before their taking effect.

[65 Fed. Reg. 613 (Jan. 5, 2000)]

Q 2:70 Are employee contributions to a welfare benefit plan considered to be plan assets?

Yes. [DOL Reg. §2510.3-102] See Qs 2:95–2:99 for a discussion of when employee contributions must be held in trust.

Q 2:71 Are group insurance policy dividends under a welfare benefit plan's group insurance policy plan assets?

The DOL takes the position that experience-rating dividends, refunds, and credits (hereafter referred to as dividends) under a group insurance policy attributable to employee contributions are plan assets. Determining whether policy dividends are attributable to employee contributions requires careful analysis of the language of the documents and instruments governing the welfare benefit plan. This includes the group insurance policy, the plan document, and the SPD given to plan participants.

A memorandum by the DOL's Office of the Solicitor sets out the DOL's position in a number of common situations involving group insurance policy dividends, as follows:

1. *Employer pays the entire cost.* If the employer is required to pay the entire cost, it is entitled to keep the entire amount of the group insurance policy dividends, and the dividends are not plan assets.

2. *Employees pay the entire cost.* If the plan documents require that the employees pay the entire cost of the group policy, any dividends are fully

attributable to employee contributions. The dividends are plan assets and have to be used for the exclusive benefit of the employees in the plan.

3. *Employer and employees each pay a fixed percentage of the entire cost.* The plan documents provide that the employer and employees each will pay a specified percentage of the entire cost of the group insurance coverage (for example, employer pays 75 percent, employees pay 25 percent). Any dividends must be allocated in direct proportion to the employer's and employees' contributions (for example, employer gets 75 percent and employees get 25 percent). The dividend portions allocated to employees are plan assets and must be used for the exclusive benefit of the employees in the plan.

4. *Employer pays a fixed amount of the entire cost and employees pay the balance.* The plan documents require the employer to pay a fixed amount. The employees are responsible for any cost in excess of that amount. Any dividends are considered to be attributable to the employees' contributions and are plan assets, except in the rare case where a dividend exceeds the employees' contributions, in which case the excess can be received by the employer. For example, if the employer is required to pay $75,000, the employees contribute $25,000, and a policy dividend of $10,000 is declared, the $10,000 dividend is attributable solely to the employees' contributions. If the dividend were $30,000, $25,000 would be attributable to the employees' contributions and $5,000 to the employer's contribution.

5. *Employees pay a fixed amount of the entire cost and employer pays the balance.* If the plan documents require the employees to pay a fixed amount for the cost of the insurance coverage and the employer is responsible for the remainder of the cost, the employer is entitled to retain the entire dividend as long as the dividend does not exceed the contribution paid by the employer. If the dividend does exceed the employer contribution, the excess is attributable to the employees' contributions and must be applied for their benefit.

Practice Pointer. It is essential that the plan documents (including the SPD) spell out how contributions and dividends are allocated. The DOL has forced employers to return millions of dollars in dividends because the plan documents failed to give the employer the right to receive them. Such clarity is especially important if multiple coverages are combined for dividend experience or if dividend experience is determined on a cumulative basis under the insurance policy rather than on a policy-year basis or both. Poor documentation can prove to be costly.

Note. The disposition of experience dividends can become an important issue when setting price tags under comprehensive cafeteria plans. If a dividend is paid on one benefit option, the employer may wish to use the excess to subsidize the cost of another benefit option under the cafeteria plan. Whether such a proposed use would violate the preceding guidelines may depend in part on whether the DOL would view the cafeteria plan as a single integrated plan or as a collection of separate plans. If the arrangement is viewed as a collection of separate plans, a fiduciary violation would occur if the cross-subsidization of price tags is viewed as diverting the assets of one plan for use by another plan.

IRS proposed cafeteria plan regulations issued in 2007 provide that experience gains can be retained by the employer, used to reduce salary reduction amounts for the next plan year, returned to employees, or used to defray administrative expenses of the plan. [Prop. Treas. Reg. § 1.125-5(o)] The proposed regulations provide rules for allocating experience gains among employees (see chapter 7).

Q 2:72   Can all expenses related to a plan be paid from plan assets?

No. While some expenses are properly payable from plan assets, other expenses must be paid by the sponsoring employer. The DOL's Pension and Welfare Benefits Administration (since renamed the Employee Benefits Security Administration) released an advisory opinion that explains the ground rules for allocating plan expenses between the plan and the employer. [Adv. Op. 2001-01A]

The opinion states that deciding whether to pay a particular expense out of plan assets is a fiduciary act governed by ERISA. In determining which expenses to pay from plan assets, a fiduciary must act prudently and solely in the interests of plan participants and their beneficiaries. As a general rule, expenses fall into three categories.

Administrative expenses. Reasonable expenses of administering a plan may be paid out of plan assets. Reasonable administrative expenses include direct expenses properly incurred in performing a fiduciary's duties to a plan.

Settlor expenses. On the other hand, some activities relate to the formation rather than the management of a plan. These so-called settlor functions, which include decisions relating to the establishment, design, and termination of a plan, are generally not fiduciary activities governed by ERISA. Therefore, expenses connected with settlor functions are not reasonable expenses of the plan. These expenses are incurred for the benefit of the employer and involve services for which the employer would reasonably be expected to pay in the normal course of business.

In an earlier advisory opinion, the DOL noted that a plan's tax-qualified status confers benefits on both the sponsoring employer and the plan. There-fore, in the case of a plan that is intended to be tax-qualified and that otherwise permits payment of expenses from plan assets, some tax-qualification expenses can reasonably be allocated to the plan. [Adv. Op. 97-03A] However, the more recent advisory opinion says that plan administrators have incorrectly inter-preted that opinion to mean that all tax-qualification expenses can be allocated between the employer and the plan. Instead, the DOL says that formation of a plan as a tax-qualified plan is a settlor activity for which the plan may not pay.

Implementation expenses. Nonetheless, the plan may pay reasonable expenses incurred in connection with implementation of a settlor decision. For example, once a settlor has determined that a plan is intended to be tax-qualified, implementation activities to maintain the plan's tax-qualified status might include drafting plan amendments required by changes in the tax law, discrimination testing, and requesting IRS determination letters. On the other hand, if maintaining the plan's tax-qualified status involves an analysis of options for amending the plan from which the sponsoring employer makes a choice, the expenses incurred in such an analysis would be settlor expenses that could not be paid by the plan.

Trustees and Investment Managers

Q 2:73   Must a trustee consent to being named or appointed?

Yes. The trustee must expressly accept the appointment or nomination in order for ERISA responsibility to attach. [ERISA §403(a); 29 U.S.C. §1103(a)]

Q 2:74   What responsibility does ERISA impose on a plan trustee?

Except for certain carefully drawn exceptions, the plan trustee or trustees have exclusive authority and discretion to manage and control the assets of the plan. This makes them ERISA fiduciaries. [ERISA §403(a); 29 U.S.C. §1103(a)] Although trustees are appointed by plan sponsors, ERISA imposes on them a duty of undivided loyalty to the trust fund beneficiaries, that is, the employees and their dependents. [*See* NLRB v. Amax Coal Co., 453 U.S. 322 (1981).]

Q 2:75   How is responsibility shared when there are multiple trustees?

When two or more trustees hold plan assets, the trustees must jointly manage and control the assets of the plan unless the trust instrument specifically provides otherwise. Additionally, each trustee must use reasonable care to prevent a co-trustee from committing a breach of fiduciary duty (see Q 2:108). [ERISA §405(b); 29 U.S.C. §1105(b)]

Q 2:76   What if the plan assets are held in more than one trust?

A trustee generally is responsible only for acts and omissions concerning the assets that the particular trustee holds in trust. [ERISA §405(b)(3); 29 U.S.C. §1105(b)(3)]

Q 2:77   Can a plan delegate investment authority over plan assets?

Yes. Under strictly limited circumstances investment authority can be delegated. Investment authority over plan assets may be delegated to a qualified investment manager (as defined in Q 2:78) if the plan expressly gives the named fiduciary responsible for control and management of plan assets the power to appoint an investment manager or managers to manage (including the power to acquire or dispose of) plan assets. In this case, the trustee or trustees generally are not liable for the acts or omissions of the investment manager and are not under an obligation to invest or otherwise to manage any plan assets that are subject to the management of the investment manager. [ERISA §§402(c)(3), 403(a)(2), 405(d)(1); 29 U.S.C. §§1102(c)(3), 1103(a)(2), 1105(d)(1)]

In addition, the DOL has issued a technical amendment to a prohibited transaction exemption (PTE 86-128) that allows employee benefit plan fiduciaries to use certain affiliated broker-dealers to execute securities transactions for their plans. Prior to the amendment, the prohibited transaction rules did not permit the receipt of a fee by a plan trustee having discretionary authority over plan assets. However, the amendment permits trustees of plans with at least $50 million in assets to receive a fee for the execution of securities transactions for their plans. The amendment is designed to address consolidation in the financial services industry that has resulted in more trustees having an affiliation with broker-dealers. The amendment essentially puts trustees on a level playing field with investment managers.

Q 2:78   What are the requirements for an investment manager?

An investment manager must be a person registered under the Investment Advisors Act of 1940, a bank or trust company, or an insurance company qualified under the laws of more than one state to manage, acquire, or dispose of plan assets.

In addition, the investment manager must acknowledge in writing that it is a fiduciary with respect to the plan. [ERISA §3(38); 29 U.S.C. §1002(38)]

Q 2:79   May trustees follow instructions from named plan fiduciaries?

Yes, they may, at least under limited circumstances. The plan document must expressly provide that the trustee is subject to the direction of a named fiduciary who is not a trustee. In that case, the investment manager is subject to any "proper" directions that the nontrustee named fiduciary makes, as long as those instructions are in accordance with the terms of the plan and are not otherwise contrary to ERISA. [ERISA §403(a)(1); 29 U.S.C. §1103(a)(1)]

Q 2:80   If the plan assets include corporate stock, is the voting of stock proxies a fiduciary duty?

The DOL has stated that the proxy voting of corporate stock held by an ERISA plan is part of the fiduciary act of managing plan assets. [DOL Int. Bull. 94-2, 59 Fed. Reg. 38,860 (July 29, 1994)] Therefore, if the fiduciary responsibility of voting proxies is not exercised, or is exercised blindly (such as by always voting with management), the responsible fiduciary may risk being charged with a breach of fiduciary duty.

Q 2:81   Which fiduciary has the responsibility for voting corporate stock proxies?

The responsibility for voting corporate stock proxies lies exclusively with the plan trustee unless the trustee is subject to the directions of a named fiduciary or unless the power to manage, acquire, or dispose of the corporate stock has been delegated to an investment manager. [DOL Int. Bull. 94-2, 59 Fed. Reg. 38,860 (July 29, 1994)]

Q 2:82   If the authority to manage the plan's corporate stock investments has been delegated to an investment manager, who has the responsibility for voting the corporate stock proxies?

Where the authority to manage the corporate stock investment has been delegated to an investment manager, the investment manager ordinarily has the sole authority to vote the corporate stock proxies. However, the named fiduciary making the delegation can reserve to itself or to another named fiduciary authorized by the plan document the right to direct the proxy voting. Such a reservation can cover all proxies or only those related to specific stock or to specific issues.

If the plan document or the investment management agreement says that the investment manager is not required to vote corporate stock proxies but does not preclude it, the investment manager has exclusive responsibility for voting the proxies. However, if the investment manager is expressly precluded from voting the corporate stock proxies, the responsibility lies with the plan trustee. In turn, the trustee may be subject to the directions of a named fiduciary if the plan so provides. [DOL Int. Bull. 94-2, 59 Fed. Reg. 38,860 (July 29, 1994)]

Q 2:83   What guidelines must the responsible fiduciary follow in exercising proxy voting?

In voting proxies for corporate stock investments of an ERISA plan, the responsible fiduciary must consider those factors that may affect the value of the plan's investments. The responsible fiduciary cannot subordinate the interests of the plan's participants and beneficiaries to other objectives. [DOL Int. Bull. 94-2, 59 Fed. Reg. 38,860 (July 29, 1994)]

Q 2:84   Is it necessary to monitor an investment manager's exercise of proxy voting?

Yes. A named fiduciary who has appointed an investment manager to manage corporate stock and has allowed the investment manager to exercise the corporate stock proxies must monitor the investment manager's proxy voting actions along with the other activities of the investment manager. Monitoring requires proper documentation of the investment manager's activities, including accurate records on proxy voting. The named fiduciary must be able to monitor not only the investment manager's proxy voting procedures, but also to review actions taken in individual proxy voting situations. [DOL Int. Bull. 94-2, 59 Fed. Reg. 38,860 (July 29, 1994)]

Q 2:85   Do the same fiduciary requirements apply to the proxy voting of stock of both domestic corporations and foreign corporations?

The DOL takes the view that the same rules generally apply whether domestic stock or foreign stock is involved. However, it points out that voting proxies for foreign stock can incur additional costs and that the responsible fiduciary can consider whether the effect of a proxy vote on the foreign stock's investment value outweighs the additional cost of voting. The DOL also points out that, in deciding whether to purchase the stock of a foreign corporation, the fiduciary should consider whether the difficulty and expenses involved in voting the stock are reflected in the market price of the foreign stock. [DOL Int. Bull. 94-2, 59 Fed. Reg. 38,860 (July 29, 1994)]

Q 2:86   What is a statement of investment policy?

The DOL defines a *statement of investment policy* as a written statement giving fiduciaries responsible for plan investments guidelines or general instructions on various types or categories of investment management decisions (it can include proxy voting decisions). However, a statement of investment policy does not contain directions on the purchase or sale of a specific investment at a specific time or direct the voting of specific plan proxies.

As part of the process of appointing an investment manager, the named fiduciary making the appointment may provide in the investment management agreement that the investment manager must comply with a statement of investment policy, including guidelines concerning permitted and prohibited investments and investment courses of action. [DOL Int. Bull. 94-2, 59 Fed. Reg. 38,860 (July 29, 1994)]

Q 2:87   Is a funded ERISA plan required to have one or more statements of investment policy?

There is no provision in ERISA that requires a funded plan to have one or more statements of investment policy. In the absence of a statement of investment policy, the investment manager has exclusive authority to manage the delegated plan assets. The investment manager is not relieved of its fiduciary responsibilities even if it follows directions on specific investment decisions from the named fiduciary or any other person. [DOL Int. Bull. 94-2, 59 Fed. Reg. 38,860 (July 29, 1994)]

Q 2:88   Is an investment manager obligated to follow a statement of investment policy?

An investment manager who has been provided with a statement of investment policy by the named fiduciary authorized to appoint the investment manager must comply with the statement of investment policy except to the extent it violates ERISA. For example, if following the guidelines would be imprudent or result in a prohibited transaction, the investment manager should not follow the guidelines. [DOL Int. Bull. 94-2, 59 Fed. Reg. 38,860 (July 29, 1994)]

Q 2:89   Does providing a statement of investment policy to an investment manager relieve the named fiduciary of its fiduciary duties?

In providing a statement of investment policy to the investment manager, the named fiduciary is exercising its fiduciary duties. However, the named fiduciary is not relieved of its duty to monitor the performance of the investment manager, nor of the need to maintain proper documentation of the investment manager's activities and of the monitoring activities of the named fiduciary. [DOL Int. Bull. 94-2, 59 Fed. Reg. 38,860 (July 29, 1994)]

Q 2:90   What factors should a named fiduciary take into account in drawing up a statement of investment policy?

As an ERISA fiduciary, the named fiduciary may need to take into account such factors as the plan's funding policy, liquidity needs, the ERISA fiduciary issues of prudence, diversification, and prohibited transactions, and other ERISA requirements. [DOL Int. Bull. 94-2, 59 Fed. Reg. 38,860 (July 29, 1994)]

Q 2:91   What rules apply where a pooled investment fund with many separate participating plans is involved?

The DOL states that the investment manager of a pooled investment fund may require plans wishing to participate in the pooled fund to accept the investment manager's own statement of investment policy as a condition of participation in the pooled fund. In the absence of such a requirement, the DOL points out that the investment manager of the pooled fund could be subject to conflicting proxy voting policies from its participating plans. The investment manager would have to try to reconcile the conflicting proxy voting policies of the participating plans (to the extent they did not conflict with ERISA). This could require, to the extent permitted by applicable law, voting the proxies in proportion to each plan's participation in the pooled fund. [DOL Int. Bull. 94-2, 59 Fed. Reg. 38,860 (July 29, 1994)]

Q 2:92 **May or must a plan take an active role in monitoring or influencing the management of corporations whose stock it holds?**

The DOL's view is that an ERISA plan that has an investment policy of monitoring or influencing the management of corporations in which the plan holds stock is being consistent with ERISA fiduciary duties, if the investment policy is reasonably likely to enhance the value of the stock. The DOL does not go so far as to take the position that an ERISA plan must take an active shareholder role, although the DOL clearly encourages it. [DOL Int. Bull. 94-2, 59 Fed. Reg. 38,860 (July 29, 1994)]

Q 2:93 **What types of issues are likely to affect the value of the corporate stock?**

The DOL indicates that the ERISA plan may wish to actively monitor and communicate with management on issues such as:

- The independence and expertise of the board of directors
- Assuring that the board of directors has sufficient information to monitor management
- The appropriateness of executive compensation
- Corporate policy on mergers and acquisitions
- Debt financing and capitalization
- Long-term business plans
- Job training and other workplace practices
- Financial and nonfinancial measures of corporate performance

[DOL Int. Bull. 94-2, 59 Fed. Reg. 38,860 (July 29, 1994)]

Q 2:94 **What methods can an ERISA plan use to influence corporate policy?**

The DOL points out that active monitoring and management communication can be carried on through a variety of methods, such as correspondence with management, meetings with management, and the exercise of all legal rights of a shareholder of the corporation. [DOL Int. Bull. 94-2, 59 Fed. Reg. 38,860 (July 29, 1994)]

Trust Requirement

Q 2:95 **Must plan assets always be in trust?**

The assets of ERISA plans must be held in trust unless they are held by an insurance company or consist of insurance contracts or policies issued by an insurance company qualified to do business in a state. [ERISA §§403(a), 403(b); 29 U.S.C. §§1103(a), 1103(b)]

Q 2:96   Are employee contributions always plan assets that must be held in trust?

Yes. Plan assets include amounts (other than union dues) that a participant or beneficiary pays to an employer, or amounts that a participant has had withheld from his or her wages by an employer, for contribution to the plan. These amounts must be held in trust (unless they are held by an insurance company). [DOL Reg. §2510.3-102]

Q 2:97   Are there any exemptions from the trust requirement for employee contributions?

Yes. The general rule is that employee contributions that become plan assets are subject to ERISA's trust requirement. [DOL Reg. §2510.3-102] The DOL has stated that it would consider the appropriateness of an exemption from the trust requirement for certain welfare benefit plans that could show that employee contributions constituted reimbursement to the employer for money expended in premium payments or benefits. [Preamble to Final Plan Asset Reg., 53 Fed. Reg. 17,628 (May 17, 1988)] It has also suspended enforcement of the trust requirement for employee contributions that are applied only to the payment of premiums for certain insured welfare benefit plans (provided that they are forwarded to the insurance company within 90 days) until the adoption of final regulations providing relief from the trust and reporting and disclosure requirements of Title I of ERISA. [ERISA Tech. Rel. 92-01, 57 Fed. Reg. 23,272 (June 2, 1992), as modified by DOL News Rel. 93-363 (Aug. 27, 1993)]

In the final plan asset regulations published on August 7, 1996, the DOL confirmed that ERISA Technical Release 92-01 is not affected by the new final regulations and remains in effect until further notice. [61 Fed. Reg. 41,220, 41,222]

Q 2:98   When must employee contributions be placed in trust?

Under the DOL final plan asset regulations effective generally on February 3, 1997, employee contributions to a welfare benefit plan must be placed in trust as of the earliest date on which they can reasonably be segregated from the employer's general assets. This period may in no event exceed 90 days from the date on which the contributions:

- Are received by the employer (if the participant or beneficiary pays them to the employer); or
- Would otherwise have been payable to the participant in cash (if the amounts are withheld by an employer from a participant's wages).

This regulatory provision allows great flexibility for accommodating individual employer payroll arrangements. It is important to note that the 90-day limit is an outside limit on when employee contributions must be deposited in trust, not a safe-harbor provision. [DOL Reg. §2510.3-102]

Practice Pointer. The point at which employee contributions to ERISA welfare benefit plans become "plan assets" that must be deposited in trust will vary by employer because of differing pay periods and the complexity of the payroll systems.

Q 2:99   Are elective contributions to cafeteria plans treated as employee contributions for purposes of the trust requirement?

The DOL has not adopted the tax concept of treating employee contributions made pursuant to elective salary reduction as employer contributions (see chapter 7). Accordingly, the DOL's final regulations on the trust requirement for employee contributions to ERISA welfare benefit plans, which contain no specific mention of cafeteria plans, apparently would require elective salary reduction contributions to medical flexible spending accounts under cafeteria plans to be held in trust. The DOL has confirmed this interpretation but suspended enforcement while it considers whether to grant a class exemption or individual exemptions from the trust requirement in these circumstances. The suspension is effective until the adoption of final regulations providing relief from the ERISA Title I trust and reporting and disclosure requirements. However, participant contributions may be used only for the payment of plan benefits and reasonable administrative expenses of the plan. [DOL Reg. §2510. 3-102; ERISA Tech. Rel. 92-01 (June 2, 1992), *as modified by* DOL News Rel. 93-363 (Aug. 27, 1993)] If the sole qualified benefit under the cafeteria plan is a dependent care assistance plan that does not fall within Section 2(1) of ERISA, then no trust is required in any event. [DOL Adv. Op. 91-25A (July 2, 1992)]

In the final plan asset regulations published on August 7, 1996, the DOL confirmed that ERISA Technical Release 92-01 is not affected by the new final regulations and remains in effect until further notice. [61 Fed. Reg. 41,220, 41,222]

Prohibited Transactions

Q 2:100   What is a *prohibited transaction* under ERISA?

ERISA prohibits certain transactions between the plan and a party in interest (see Q 2:101). The statute lists several broad classes of transactions that are prohibited unless permitted under a lengthy list of exceptions and exclusions (see Q 2:102). [ERISA §§406–408; 29 U.S.C. §§1106–1108] (A parallel set of rules concerning transactions between tax-qualified retirement plans and "disqualified persons," contained in Code Section 4975, does not apply to welfare benefit plans.)

ERISA also prohibits self-dealing by plan fiduciaries (see Q 2:103).

Q 2:101   What is a party in interest?

The term *party in interest* encompasses the following:

1. Any plan fiduciary (including any administrator, officer, trustee, or custodian), counsel, or employee of the employee welfare benefit plan;
2. Any person providing services to the plan;
3. An employer that has any employees covered by the plan;
4. Anyone having 50 percent or more control of an employer with employees covered by the plan;
5. A relative (spouse, ancestor, lineal descendant, or spouse of a lineal descendant) of anyone listed in items 1 through 4;
6. Any organization that is 50 percent or more owned by anyone in items 1 through 4; and
7. Any employee, officer, director, or 10-percent-or-more shareholder (or 10-percent-or-more partner or joint venturer) in items 2, 3, 5, or 6.

[ERISA §§3(14)–3(15); 29 U.S.C. §§1002(14)–1002(15)]

Q 2:102   What transactions between plans and parties in interest does ERISA prohibit?

ERISA generally prohibits any transaction that directly or indirectly constitutes:

- A sale, exchange, or lease of any property between the plan and a party in interest
- A loan of money or other extension of credit between the plan and a party in interest
- The furnishing of goods, services, or facilities between the plan and a party in interest
- The transfer or use of plan assets by or for the benefit of a party in interest
- The acquisition or holding of nonqualifying or excess qualifying employer securities or real property by the plan

Extensive exceptions and exemptions apply to these provisions. [ERISA §§406–408; 29 U.S.C. §§1106–1108]

Q 2:103   What acts by fiduciaries constitute prohibited self-dealing?

A fiduciary with respect to an ERISA plan cannot deal with the assets of the plan in his or her own interest or for his or her own account; receive any consideration for his or her own personal account from any party dealing with the plan in any transaction involving the plan; or act on behalf of a party whose interests are adverse to the plan, or of its participants or beneficiaries, in any transaction involving the plan. [ERISA §406(b); 29 U.S.C. §1106(b)]

The U.S. Supreme Court overturned a Seventh Circuit decision, unanimously determining that an HMO had not violated its ERISA fiduciary duties by giving its physicians financial incentives to limit the amount of care provided to patients. [Pegram v. Herdrich, 530 U.S. 211 (2000)] The Court said it is up to Congress, and not the courts, to decide whether to prohibit certain HMO incentives.

Q 2:104   Can a prohibited transaction be a continuing violation?

Yes. A prohibited transaction such as a loan or lease is viewed as continuing in nature. Accordingly, it is subject to multiple penalties. For example, a lease between a plan and a party in interest that constitutes a prohibited transaction will be subject to a separate penalty for each year that it continues. [DOL Reg. §2560.502i-1(e)]

Q 2:105   Are exemptions from ERISA's prohibited transaction provisions available?

In addition to the exemptions and exclusions it provides, ERISA authorizes the Secretary of Labor to exempt individual fiduciaries or transactions, or classes of fiduciaries or transactions, from ERISA's prohibited transaction provisions. The DOL has granted numerous individual and class exemptions pursuant to this authority. [ERISA §408(a); 29 U.S.C. §1108(a); Exemption Application Proc. 55 Fed. Reg. 32,836 (Aug. 10, 1990)]

Fiduciary Liability

Q 2:106   What liabilities does ERISA impose on fiduciaries?

ERISA imposes three types of liabilities on fiduciaries (including trustees):

1. Any fiduciary that breaches ERISA fiduciary duties is personally liable to the plan for any losses that result from a breach and must restore to the plan any profits made through use of plan assets. The fiduciary is also subject to other equitable and remedial relief, including being removed (that is, prohibited from ever serving as a plan fiduciary) and being required to pay interest and attorneys' fees. [ERISA §409(a); 29 U.S.C. §1109(a)]

2. If a judicial proceeding is brought by the Secretary of Labor, fiduciaries can be subject to a civil fine and a penalty (see Qs 2:190–2:191). [ERISA §502(l); 29 U.S.C. §1132(l)]

3. ERISA also imposes cofiduciary liability, that is, liability for the acts or omissions of other plan fiduciaries (see Q 2:109).

Q 2:107 May a fiduciary rely on information supplied by persons performing purely ministerial functions?

Generally, yes, the fiduciary may rely on information, data, analysis, and the like, furnished by persons who perform purely ministerial functions with respect to the plan, provided that the fiduciary has exercised prudence in selecting and in continuing to retain those persons. [DOL Reg. §2509.75-8, Q&A FR-11] (See Q 2:17.)

Q 2:108 If a fiduciary appoints trustees or other fiduciaries, does the appointing fiduciary retain any responsibility for the appointees' actions?

Provided that the power to make such appointments is expressly contained in the plan document (see Q 2:35), the appointing fiduciary generally will be responsible only for the selection and retention of such individuals. The appointing fiduciary should review the performance of trustees and other fiduciaries at reasonable intervals to ensure that their performance is in accordance with the plan documents and ERISA and that it satisfies the needs of the plan. No particular method or procedure for doing so is specified under ERISA. [DOL Reg. §2509.75-8, Q&A FR-17] However, the appointing fiduciary always remains subject to cofiduciary responsibility and to the attendant liabilities (see Q 2:109).

Practice Pointer. An appointment that was initially prudent and in the interests of the plan may cease to be so under later facts and circumstances. The appointing fiduciary is responsible for monitoring the appointee's acts and for removing and replacing an appointee as appropriate.

Q 2:109 How can a fiduciary be liable for the acts or omissions of another fiduciary?

A plan document may allocate or delegate fiduciary duties (including the duties of trusteeship). For example, the plan might designate a benefit committee as the named fiduciary for plan administration and an investment committee as the named fiduciary for the control and management of plan assets. However, even if the plan document carefully allocates or delegates fiduciary duties, a fiduciary nonetheless will be liable for another fiduciary's breach of fiduciary duty concerning the same plan (referred to as *cofiduciary responsibility*) if the fiduciary:

1. Knowingly participates in, or knowingly conceals, the act or omission of another fiduciary, knowing it to be a breach;
2. Fails to comply with its own fiduciary responsibilities and thereby enables the other fiduciary to commit a breach; or
3. Becomes aware of another fiduciary's breach and fails to make reasonable efforts under the circumstances to remedy it.

In other words, one fiduciary may become liable for the breach of another plan fiduciary if the first fiduciary's own performance is so inadequate that it creates an opportunity for the second fiduciary to commit a breach or if the first fiduciary discovers the second fiduciary's breach and fails to take appropriate remedial action. [ERISA §405(a); 29 U.S.C. §1105(a)]

Q 2:110 May the plan exculpate a fiduciary from violations of fiduciary duty?

No. Although ERISA permits plans to include express authority to allocate or delegate fiduciary responsibility or to appoint an investment manager, any other provision in an agreement or instrument that purports to relieve a fiduciary from responsibility or liability for any responsibility, obligation, or duty under ERISA's fiduciary provisions is void as against public policy. [ERISA §410(a); 29 U.S.C. §1110(a)]

Q 2:111 May a plan insure its fiduciaries, or itself, against liability or losses resulting from fiduciary breaches?

Yes. A plan may purchase insurance for its fiduciaries or for itself to cover liability or losses caused by a fiduciary act or omission. However, the insurance must permit the insurer recourse against a fiduciary that has breached its fiduciary duty. [ERISA §410(b)(1); 29 U.S.C. §1110(b)(1)]

Q 2:112 If fiduciary liability insurance is purchased by a fiduciary or plan sponsor rather than by the plan, must the policy allow recourse against the fiduciary?

No. If the fiduciary, the employer, or an employee organization purchases the policy, the insurance carrier need not be permitted recourse against the fiduciary. [ERISA §§410(b)(2), 410(b)(3); 29 U.S.C. §§1110(b)(2), 1110(b)(3)]

Q 2:113 May plan fiduciaries be indemnified out of plan assets?

They may not be indemnified for breaches of fiduciary duty. Indemnification would relieve the fiduciary from responsibility and liability to the plan because it would effectively forfeit the plan's right to recover from the fiduciary plan losses caused by a fiduciary breach. [DOL Reg. §2509.75-4] However, indemnification of a fiduciary for expenses incurred in defending against a wrongful charge of fiduciary violations was held not to be barred by ERISA. [Packer Eng'g Inc. v. Kratville, 965 F.2d 174 (7th Cir. 1992)]

Q 2:114 May the plan sponsor indemnify plan fiduciaries?

Yes. An employer or employee organization generally may indemnify a plan fiduciary out of its own assets. [DOL Reg. §2509.75-4, Ex. (1)]

Q 2:115   Will correction of an ERISA violation avoid penalties?

In some cases, correction of a fiduciary violation can be made without penalty. The DOL offers a Voluntary Fiduciary Correction Program (VFCP), which permits certain types of financial transactions to be voluntarily corrected. The VFCP covers 19 specific financial transactions:

1. Delinquent participant contributions and participant loan repayments to pension plans
2. Delinquent participant contributions to insured welfare plans
3. Delinquent participant contributions to welfare plan trusts
4. Fair market interest rate loans with parties in interest
5. Below-market interest rate loans with parties in interest
6. Below-market interest rate loans with nonparties in interest
7. Below-market interest rate loans due to delay in perfecting security interest
8. Participant loans failing to comply with plan provisions for amount, duration, or level amortization
9. Defaulted participant loans
10. Purchase of assets by plans from parties in interest
11. Sale of assets by plans to parties in interest
12. Sale and leaseback of property to sponsoring employers
13. Purchase of assets from nonparties in interest at more than fair market value
14. Sale of assets to nonparties in interest at less than fair market value
15. Holding of an illiquid asset previously purchased by plan
16. Benefit payments based on improper valuation of plan assets
17. Payment of duplicate, excessive, or unnecessary compensation
18. Improper payment of expenses by plan
19. Payment of dual compensation to plan fiduciaries

Anyone who may be liable for fiduciary violations under ERISA, including employee benefit plan sponsors, officials, and other parties in interest, may take advantage of the VFCP. Applicants do not have to consult or negotiate with the EBSA to use the program. To qualify for relief under the VFCP, a plan fiduciary must take the following four steps:

1. Identify any violations and determine whether they fall within the transactions listed;
2. Follow the process for correcting specific violations (e.g., improper loans, incorrect valuation of plan assets);
3. Calculate and restore any losses and profits with interest and distribute any supplemental benefits; and
4. File an application with the appropriate EBSA regional office that includes documentation providing evidence of corrected financial transactions.

Fiduciaries who fully comply with all terms and procedures of the VFCP will receive a no-action letter from the EBSA indicating that there will be no further enforcement action in connection with the transaction. The agency does, however, reserve the right to conduct an investigation to determine truthfulness, completeness, and full correction. In addition, full correction under the VFCP will not give a fiduciary relief from actions by other government agencies, including the IRS.

Acceptable corrections. The VFCP provides special rules for correcting the transactions. As a general rule, applicants must do the following:

1. Conduct valuations of plan assets using generally recognized markets for the assets or obtain written appraisal reports from qualified professionals that are based on generally accepted appraisal standards

2. Restore to the plan the principal amount involved, plus the greater of (1) lost earnings starting on the date of the loss and extending the recovery date or (2) profits resulting from the use of the principal amount for the same period

3. Pay the expenses associated with correcting the transactions, such as appraisal costs or cost of recalculating participant account balances

4. Make supplemental distributions to former employees, beneficiaries, or alternate payees when appropriate and provide proof of the payments

Applicants must restore the plan, participants, and beneficiaries to the condition they would have been in had the fiduciary breach not occurred. Plans must then file amended returns to reflect the corrected transactions or valuations.

Applicants must also provide proof of payments to participants and beneficiaries or segregate affected assets in cases where a plan is unable to locate a missing participant or beneficiary. However, payment of a correction amount may be made directly to the plan where distributions to separated plan participants would be less than $20 and the cost of correction exceeds the distributions owed.

Excise tax waiver. The tax law generally imposes a 15 percent excise tax on prohibited transactions. If a timely correction is not made, the tax jumps to 100 percent of the amount involved in the prohibited transaction. [I.R.C. §4975] However, the tax law permits the IRS, in conjunction with the DOL, to exempt certain classes of transactions from the excise tax.

To encourage use of the VFCP, the DOL has finalized tax exemptions for the following six transactions covered by the program:

1. Failure to timely remit participant contributions to plans;

2. Loans made at the fair market interest rate by plans with parties in interest;

3. Purchases or sales of assets between plans and parties in interest at fair market value;

4. Sales of real property to plans by employers at fair market value and leaseback of the property at fair rental value;

5. Prohibited transaction violations involved in the purchase of an asset by a plan when the asset has been determined to be illiquid, and/or the subsequent sale of the illiquid asset by the plan; and

6. Use of plan assets to pay expenses to a service provider for services that are characterized as "settlor expenses," provided such payments were not expressly prohibited in the plan documents.

To qualify for the exemption, applicants must repay delinquent contributions to plans no more than 180 days from the date the money was received by the employer or would be payable to participants in cash. Except in the case of delinquent contributions, the exemption applies only if no more than 10 percent of the fair market value of total plan assets was involved in the prohibited transaction. A transaction will not be covered by the exemption if it is part of an arrangement or understanding that benefits a related party or if an application for correction of a similar transaction was submitted under the VFCP within the prior three years. Notice of the transaction and the correction must be provided to interested parties.

Nonfiduciary Liability

Q 2:116   Can a person who is not an ERISA fiduciary be liable for a breach of fiduciary duty?

The Supreme Court has held that a nonfiduciary party in interest can be held liable when ERISA's prohibited transaction rules are violated. When ERISA provides that injured parties may seek "appropriate relief," that relief may be sought from any party in interest that participated in the prohibited transaction. In the case of prohibited transactions, ERISA's focus is on redressing the violation, not on who is liable. Other ERISA provisions specify who can be held liable for violations, but the prohibited transaction provisions do not specify such limits.

The Court noted that another section of ERISA permits the DOL to bring a lawsuit against a fiduciary or *other person* who knowingly participated in a fiduciary's ERISA violation. Therefore, it follows that plan fiduciaries and participants should also be allowed to sue those other persons. [Harris Trust & Savings Bank v. Salomon Smith Barney Inc., 530 U.S. 238 (2000)]

Q 2:117   Can a person who is not an ERISA fiduciary be liable for civil penalties under ERISA?

Yes. An ERISA nonfiduciary who knowingly participates in a breach of fiduciary responsibility may be subject to a civil penalty of 20 percent of the recovery amount in a judicial proceeding brought by the Secretary of Labor. [ERISA §502(l)(1); 29 U.S.C. §1132(l)(1); Interim DOL Reg. §2570.80] Also, if the ERISA nonfiduciary is a party in interest to the welfare benefit plan and participates in a prohibited transaction involving the plan, a civil penalty of up to 5 percent of the amount involved (and an additional 100 percent if the violation is not corrected within 90 days after a final agency action order) may be imposed on the ERISA nonfiduciary. [ERISA §502(i); 29 U.S.C. §1132(i); DOL Reg. §2560.502i-1] (See Qs 2:210–2:211.)

The U.S. Supreme Court has ruled that a nonfiduciary party in interest to a pension plan governed by ERISA may be sued for equitable relief under the civil enforcement provision in ERISA Section 502(a)(3) for participating in an ERISA prohibited transaction. [Harris Trust & Sav. Bank v. Salomon Smith Barney Inc., 530 U.S. 238 (2000)] The Court said that ERISA Section 502(1), which authorizes the Secretary of Labor to assess civil penalties against a plan fiduciary or "other person" who knowingly participates in a fiduciary's violation, "resolves the matter" by compelling the "conclusion that defendant status under 502(a)(3) may arise from duties imposed by 502(a)(3) itself, and does not turn on whether the defendant is expressly subject to a duty under one of ERISA's substantive provisions."

Bonding Requirement

Q 2:118   Who must be bonded?

Every fiduciary and every other person who handles funds or other property of the plan (as explained in Q 2:121) must be bonded. These individuals must be bonded to receive, handle, disburse, or otherwise exercise custody or control of plan funds or other plan property or to direct the performance of such functions. Certain exemptions may apply to banks, insurers, and other financial institutions. [ERISA §§412(a), 412(b); 29 U.S.C. §§1112(a), 1112(b)]

Q 2:119   Why is bonding required?

ERISA requires certain individuals who handle plan money to be bonded in order to provide protection against losses caused by their fraud or dishonesty, either directly or through collusion with others. Thus, bonding generally provides protection against losses from larceny, theft, embezzlement, forgery, misappropriation, wrongful conversion, willful misapplication, or other fraudulent or dishonest acts. The plan must be protected from loss, even though the person committing the act does not personally gain from the act. [ERISA §412(a); 29 U.S.C. §1112(a); Temp. DOL Reg. §§2580.412-6, 2580.412-9]

Q 2:120   Is bonding required for all plans?

No. If the only source from which benefits are paid is the general assets of an employer or employee organization, then the administrators, officers, and employees of such plans are exempt from the bonding requirement. [ERISA §412(a)(1); 29 U.S.C. §1112(a)(1)]

Q 2:121   When are funds and property "handled"?

Individuals are considered to "handle" funds whenever their duties or activities involve a risk that the funds could be lost in the event of fraud or dishonesty. The duties that constitute handling relate to receipt, safekeeping, and disbursement of; access to; or decision-making power with respect to plan funds. Any person with the power to sign or endorse checks is considered to be handling plan funds. Certain acts are considered ministerial and thus do not fall within the bonding requirements. [Temp. DOL Reg. §2580.412-6]

Q 2:122   What dollar amount is required for a bond?

The amount of the bond must be at least (1) $1,000 or (2) 10 percent of the amount of the funds handled, but in no case will the bond be less than $1,000 or more than $500,000, unless the Secretary of Labor prescribes a higher amount, subject to the 10 percent limitation. Further, the bond may not contain any deductible amount. [ERISA §412(a); 29 U.S.C. §1112(a); Temp. DOL Reg. §2580.412-11]

Q 2:123   What form or type of bond is acceptable?

The bond must be in a form or of a type approved by the Secretary of Labor. Permissible forms and types include individual bonds and schedule or blanket forms of bonds that cover a group or class. [ERISA §412(a); 29 U.S.C. §1112(a); Temp. DOL Reg. §2580.412-10]

Q 2:124   Which sureties can issue acceptable ERISA bonds?

Generally, a corporate surety holding a grant of authority from the Secretary of the Treasury must issue the ERISA bond. Bonds from certain companies authorized as reinsurers of federal bonds and certain arrangements with the underwriters at Lloyds, London, also qualify. [ERISA §412(a); 29 U.S.C. §1112(a); Temp. DOL Reg. §2580.412-21]

Claims Procedure Requirement

Q 2:125   What is a claim?

A claim for benefits is a request made by a plan participant in accordance with a plan's reasonable procedure for filing benefit claims. [DOL Reg. §2560. 503-1(c)]

Q 2:126   What are the requirements regarding reasonable claims procedures?

DOL regulations require every employee benefit plan to establish and maintain reasonable procedures governing the filing of benefit claims, notification of benefit determinations, and appeal of adverse benefit determinations.

A plan's claims procedures are considered reasonable only if:

1. A description of all claims procedures and applicable time frames is included in the plan's SPD (see Q 2:142);

2. The claims procedures do not contain any provision and are not administered in a way that unduly inhibits the filing or processing of plan claims, such as a provision or practice requiring the payment of a fee or costs as a condition for making a claim or appealing an adverse decision;

3. The procedures do not preclude an authorized representative from acting on behalf of a claimant in pursuing a benefit claim or appealing an adverse determination (although the plan may establish reasonable procedures for determining whether an individual has been authorized to act on behalf of a claimant); and

4. The procedures contain administrative processes and safeguards designed to ensure and to verify that benefit claim determinations are made in accordance with the governing plan documents and that the plan provisions are applied consistently with respect to similarly situated claimants.

[DOL Reg. §2560.503-1(b)]

In addition, a plan's claims procedures must meet specific requirements regarding notifications of benefit determinations and appeals of adverse determinations.

If a plan fails to establish and follow reasonable claims procedures, a claimant will be considered to have exhausted the administrative remedies available under the plan and will be entitled to sue for benefits under ERISA Section 501(a). [DOL Reg. §2560.503-1(l)]

> **Note.** Specific claims procedures apply to group health plans. The specific requirements for group health plans are discussed in chapter 3.

Q 2:127   If a claim is denied, how soon must the participant be informed?

As a general rule, a participant or beneficiary whose claim for plan benefits is partially or wholly denied must be notified in writing within a reasonable period of time after the plan receives the claim. This period ordinarily cannot exceed 90 days. If an extension of time for processing is required because of special circumstances, the claimant must receive written notice of the extension before the end of the initial 90-day period. The written notice must spell out the special circumstances necessitating the extension and the date by which the plan expects to render the final decision. The extension cannot exceed 90 days from the end of the initial 90-day period. [DOL Reg. §2560.503-1(f)]

Note. Shorter deadlines apply to group health plans and disability plans. The specific requirements for group health plans are discussed in chapter 3; the requirements for disability plans are discussed in chapter 10.

Q 2:128 What information must be given to a claimant if a claim for benefits is denied?

In the case of an adverse benefit determination, the plan administrator must provide the claimant with written or electronic notice setting forth the following information in a manner calculated to be understood by the claimant:

- The specific reason(s) for the adverse determination;
- Reference to the specific plan provision on which the determination is based;
- A description of any additional material or information necessary to perfect the claim and an explanation of why such material or information is necessary;
- A description of the plan's review procedures and the applicable time limits, including a statement of the claimant's right to bring a civil action under ERISA Section 502(a) following an adverse determination on review; and
- A copy of any rule, guideline, protocol, or other similar criterion that was relied on in making the adverse determination or a statement indicating that such a rule was relied on and that a copy will be provided free of charge upon request.

[DOL Reg. §2560.503-1(g)]

Note. Special rules apply to adverse determinations by group health plans. These rules are discussed in detail in chapter 3.

Q 2:129 How long does a claimant have to appeal a denied claim?

As a general rule, a plan must allow the claimant at least 60 days after receipt of written notification of a claim denial to file a request for review of the denied claim. [DOL Reg. §2560.503-1(h)]

Note. Longer time limits apply to appeals of adverse determinations by group health plans or disability plans. The claims procedures for group health plans are described in detail in chapter 3; the procedures for disability plans are discussed in chapter 10.

Q 2:130 What procedural rights does a claimant have on appeal?

The plan's appeal procedure must provide for a full and fair review of the claim and the adverse determination. Specifically, the procedure must provide a claimant with the opportunity to submit written comments, documents, records, and other information regarding the claim. In addition, the plan must provide the claimant, upon request and free of charge, with reasonable access to and copies of all documents, records, and other information relevant to the claim. [DOL Reg. §2560.503-1(h)]

> **Note.** Special appeal procedures apply to group health plans and disability plans. The claims procedures for group health plans are described in detail in chapter 3; the procedures for disability plans are described in chapter 10.

Q 2:131   Must a claimant be allowed to appear in person to appeal a claims denial?

No. ERISA imposes no such requirement. The plan may require that the appeals of denied claims be made solely by written submissions. [DOL Reg. §2560.503-1(h)]

Q 2:132   How soon after the appeal is the claimant entitled to a decision?

As a general rule, a decision must be rendered within 60 days after the plan receives the request for review of the claim. If special circumstances require an extension of time for processing, written notice of the extension must be furnished to the claimant during the initial 60-day period. The extension cannot exceed an additional 60 days.

If the appropriate named fiduciary that reviews claims denials is a committee or board of trustees that holds meetings at least quarterly, a claim must be heard at the next meeting unless the request for review is received within 30 days of that meeting. If the claim for review is received within 30 days of the next meeting, the benefit determination must be made no later than the second meeting following the request for review. If special circumstances require an extension of time for processing, the decision must be rendered by the third meeting after initial receipt of the claim, and the claimant must be given written notice describing the special circumstances and the date on which the benefit determination will be made. This notice must be provided before the beginning of the extension period.

The plan administrator must notify the claimant of the benefit determination as soon as possible, but not later than five days after the determination is made. [DOL Reg. §2560.503-1(i)]

> **Note.** Special time limits apply to appeals of adverse determinations regarding health and disability claims. The claims and appeals procedures for group health plans are described in chapter 3; the procedures for disability plans are described in chapter 10.

Q 2:133 What information must the decision on the appeal contain?

The plan administrator may provide either written or electronic notification of the review determination. In the case of an adverse determination, the notification must set forth all of the following information in a manner calculated to be understood by the claimant:

- The specific reasons for the adverse determination;
- Reference to the specific plan provisions on which the adverse determination is based;
- A statement that the claimant is entitled to receive, upon request and free of charge, reasonable access to, and copies of, all documents, records, and other information relevant to the claim;
- A statement describing any voluntary appeal procedures offered by the plan; and
- A statement of the claimant's right to bring a lawsuit under ERISA Section 501(a).

[DOL Reg. §2560.503-1(j)]

Q 2:134 Do special claims procedure provisions apply to collectively bargained plans?

Yes. Special rules apply to any plan established and maintained pursuant to a collective bargaining agreement (other than a plan covered by Section 302(c)(5) of the Labor Management Relations Act of 1947 (LMRA) concerning joint representation of the board of trustees). Such a plan is deemed to satisfy ERISA's initial claims procedure requirements if the collective bargaining agreement incorporates, by specific reference, provisions concerning (1) the filing of benefit claims and their initial disposition and (2) a grievance and arbitration procedure for denied claims. [DOL Reg. §2560.503-1(b)(2)]

Q 2:135 Are any covered plans exempt from ERISA's claims procedure requirements?

Yes. Employee welfare benefit plans that provide only apprenticeship training benefits need not provide claims procedures at all. [DOL Reg. §2560.503-1(n)]

Q 2:136 Can a claimant bring a lawsuit for benefits without first following the plan's claims and appeals procedures?

Ordinarily, no. The courts generally have held that when the plan provides reasonable claims and appeals procedures, a claimant must first exhaust his or her administrative remedies in order to bring a lawsuit for benefits. [Kross v. Western Elec. Co., 701 F.2d 1238 (7th Cir. 1983)]

An ERISA plan that did not provide a notice of claim denial in Spanish to a Spanish-speaking employee (but did provide the appeal procedures in Spanish) was held to have acted properly, because ERISA did not require the denial notice to be in Spanish or another foreign language. Therefore, the employee was not excused from the requirement to exhaust the plan's administrative remedies before a lawsuit could be brought. [Diaz v. United Agric. Employee Welfare Benefit Plan & Trust, 50 F.3d 1478 (9th Cir. 1995)]

In another case, a plan participant who was denied short-term disability benefits took her case directly to court rather than file an appeal as required under the plan's claim procedures. The plan sponsor argued that the lawsuit should be dismissed because of the failure to exhaust the plan's claims procedure. However, the employee argued that she had interpreted the plan's SPD as giving her a choice between filing an appeal with the plan or suing in court. In explaining the right to sue, the SPD, using model language from the DOL regulations stated: "If you have a claim for benefits which is denied or ignored, in whole or in part, you may file suit in a state or Federal court." Also in accordance with the DOL regulations, the SPD described the plan's claim procedure and stated that a claimant "may use this procedure" to appeal a denied claim. Based on the language in the SPD, the Eleventh Circuit ruled that the employee's lawsuit was not barred. The court concluded that, reading the two statements together, the employee reasonably interpreted the use of the word "may" in each statement to mean that she had a choice. The court noted that that was especially true because neither the SPD nor the letter she received denying her claim explained that the plan's claim procedure had to be followed before going to court. [Watts v. Bellsouth Telcomms., Inc., 316 F.3d 1203 (11th Cir. 2003)]

A court may waive the requirement to exhaust administrative remedies if pursuing those remedies would be an exercise in futility. For example, in a Sixth Circuit case, an employee was seeking long-term disability benefits and a waiver of his life insurance premiums on account of disability. To qualify for long-term disability benefits, the employee had to be unable to perform the duties of his own occupation. The test for a waiver of life insurance premiums was tougher; the employee had to be unable to perform the duties of any occupation for which he was reasonably qualified. When the employer's insurer denied the claim for long-term disability benefits on the grounds that the employee was able to perform the duties of his "sedentary" occupation, the employee sought administrative review, which proved futile. The employee did not seek administrative review of the insurer's denial of a premium waiver. Instead, he took both issues to court. A district court ruled in favor of the employee on the long-term disability claim. However, the district court dismissed the premium waiver claim on the grounds that the employee did not exhaust his administrative remedies and that the time for seeking administrative review had expired. On appeal, the Sixth Circuit held that the employee's lawsuit for a premium waiver could go forward. According to the court, the requirement to exhaust administrative remedies does not apply when the review process would be futile. In the employee's case, the insurer had determined that the employee was able to perform his own occupation. And, according to the court, that determination

Employee Benefits Answer Book

necessarily precluded him from arguing with a straight face to the same insurance company that he was unable to perform any occupation. [Dozier v. Sun Life Assurance Co. of Can., 466 F.3d 532 (6th Cir. 2006)]

Q 2:137   Is there a time limit for filing a lawsuit for benefits?

ERISA does not specify the statute of limitations for filing a lawsuit challenging the denial of a benefit claims. Therefore, the courts have generally applied analogous limitations periods under state laws. As a result, the time limit for filing a claim is often unclear and will vary from state to state.

To address this issue, a plan may impose a specific time limit for bringing suit in the plan document. However, to be enforceable, such a time limit must be clear and unambiguous.

In one court case, the spouse of a covered employee suffered from cystic fibrosis and received extensive treatment for her condition from the time of her marriage when her plan coverage began and her death a year later. However, the plan denied benefits for her treatment based on its preexisting-condition limitation, which excluded coverage for conditions for which treatment was received during the 90 days preceding the date coverage began under the plan. The plan's denial of benefits was upheld under the plan's internal appeals procedures. A year and a half after the internal appeal was completed, the covered employee filed suit against the plan complaining that the preexisting-condition exclusion did not apply because his spouse had not received treatment for her condition during the 90 days preceding their marriage. The plan moved to have the lawsuit dismissed on the grounds that the covered employee had not filed suit within the one-year limitations period specified in the plan's SPD.

The Tenth Circuit Court of Appeals held that the lawsuit could continue because the plan's SPD was ambiguous. The portion of the SPD dealing with benefits underwritten by the plan's insurer included a section entitled "Legal Action," which stated that no legal action for health benefits under the group policy could be commenced more than three years after the time for providing proof of loss under the plan. However, the portion of the SPD describing the plan's appeals procedure stated that a legal action must be brought within one year after the date of an internal decision on appeal. The Tenth Circuit noted that the two provisions were contradictory. Moreover, they did not cross reference each other and there was no explanation of how they could work together. In addition, there was no clear indication of which legal actions were subject to the one-year limitations period. The court concluded that the plan, as drafter of the SPD, should bear the consequences of the inaccuracies. Therefore, it held that the longer three-year limitations period should apply to the covered employee's lawsuit. [Haymond v. Eighth Dist. Elec. Benefit Fund, 36 Fed. Appx. 369 (10th Cir. May 28, 2002)]

Moreover, another case makes it clear that the plan participant must be alerted that the time period for filing a lawsuit has begun to run. An insured disability plan provided that no legal action for benefits could be commenced "more than 3 years after the time proof of claim is required." The plan also provided that "proof of continued disability" had to be provided within 30 days of a "request for proof." The plan's insurer informed a plan participant that his benefits were being terminated based on the medical information in its possession. However, the insurer advised the participant that he could submit any additional support for his claim for continued benefits. The participant appealed under the plan's claims procedures, but the denial of benefits was upheld. The participant filed a lawsuit more than three years after the claims procedures were completed. The insurer asked the court to dismiss the case on the grounds that it was not filed within the plan's three-year limitations period for filing suit. The Ninth Circuit Court of Appeals refused to apply the plan's limitation period. According to the court, neither the original notification letter from the insurer nor the letter denying the appeal constituted a "request for proof" that would trigger the running of the limitations period since neither letter specifically used the terms "proof," "request for proof," or "proof of claim." The court allowed the participant's lawsuit to continue because it was filed within the four-year statute of limitations period for ERISA claims in California. [Mogck v. UNUM Life Ins. Co. of Am., 292 F.3d 1025 (9th Cir. 2002)].

On the other hand, several recent appeals court cases have held that plan-imposed limitation periods for filing lawsuits were enforceable against plan participants. [*See, e.g.*, Scharff v. Raytheon Co. Short Term Disability Plan, No. 07-55951, 2009 WL 2871229 (9th Cir. Sept. 9, 2009) (one-year limitation on lawsuit was displayed prominently enough in SPD to be found and understood by the average plan participant despite claims that it was not placed in the proper section of the SPD in a sufficiently conspicuous manner; Salisbury v. Hartford Life & Accident Co., 2009 WL 3112411 (10th Cir. Sept. 30, 2009) (three-year limitations period enforceable despite claims that the starting point of the limitations period was ambiguous).]

Q 2:138   What standard of review do the courts use in deciding whether to uphold the fiduciary's decision denying an appeal of a denied claim?

If the plan document provides that the fiduciary has discretionary authority in determining eligibility, interpreting plan provisions, and ruling on appeals of denied claims, the courts generally will uphold the fiduciary's decision unless it is an abuse of discretion, an arbitrary and capricious decision, or a violation of the law. Under this very limited form of judicial review, the fiduciary's decision will be accepted and upheld if it is based on substantial evidence, even if the court would have decided the claim differently. However, if the fiduciary has a conflict of interest, the court might give somewhat less latitude to the fiduciary's exercise of his or her discretionary authority.

A federal appellate court considered a denial of severance benefits for an employee terminated because of gross misconduct. The employee argued that because the plan was unfunded and the plan's committee that denied benefits was composed of company officers, there was an automatic bias on the part of the committee. The court noted that the company was financially healthy and that payment of the benefits would have a negligible effect on the employer.

Also, ERISA specifically recognizes that corporate officers can serve in an ERISA fiduciary capacity. Therefore, the committee's exercise of its discretionary authority was upheld. [Chalmers v. Quaker Oats Co., 61 F.3d 1340 (7th Cir. 1995)]

If, however, the plan document does not provide for such discretionary authority, the courts apply a *de novo* standard and decide the merits of the claim without giving any special deference to the fiduciary's interpretations and reasons for denying the claim appeal. Under this broad standard of judicial review, a court could interpret the plan or the goals underlying the plan differently than the individuals who are charged with responsibility for administering the plan and differently than the plan sponsor may have intended. [Firestone Tire & Rubber Co. v. Bruch, 488 U.S. 809 (1989)]

> **Practice Pointer.** A plan fiduciary's determination is far more likely to be upheld in court if it is reviewed under the discretionary standard. However, the plan must make it crystal clear that the fiduciary has discretionary authority. In one case, for example, the Ninth Circuit Court of Appeals determined that the language of a disability benefit plan did not "unambiguously" state that the plan administrator had discretionary authority in making benefits decisions. The plan stated that the employer's insurance carrier "solely is responsible for providing benefits under this Plan." However, the court said that this language only made it clear that the carrier rather than the employer was responsible for providing benefits. The statement said nothing about how benefit determinations were made. In addition, the plan stated that "the carrier will make all decisions on claims" and that "operation and administration of claim procedures . . . including the review and payment or denial of claims . . . shall be vested in the carrier." However, the court said, those phrases did not grant discretionary authority either. According to the court, an allocation of decision-making authority is not, by itself, a grant of discretionary authority in making those decisions. [Ingram v. Martin Marietta Long Term Disability Income Plan, 244 F.3d 1109 (9th Cir. 2001)]

The Ninth Circuit opinion gives some hints as to how an employer plan can make it clear that the plan administrator had discretionary authority over benefit claims. The court pointed out that in some cases where it has applied the discretionary standard, the plans in question used the magic word "discretion" to describe the administrator's authority to award benefits. [McDaniel v. Chevron Corp., 203 F.3d 1099 (9th Cir. 2000); Friedrich v. Intel Corp., 181 F.3d 1105 (9th Cir. 1999)] In another case, the plan clearly and unmistakably conferred discretion by stating that the administrator's decision "shall not be overturned unless arbitrary and capricious or unless there is no rational basis for the decision." [Grosz-Salomon v. Paul Revere Life Ins. Co., 237 F.3d 1154 (9th Cir. 2001)]

In a 2008 decision, the Supreme Court acknowledged that even when a plan administrator has discretionary authority over benefit claims, an inherent conflict of interest exists if the plan administrator both evaluates and pays claims because the administrator stands to gain financially by denying the claims. For example, in the case before the Court, the Court concluded that an insurance company that both reviewed a participant's claim for benefits under an ERISA plan and was responsible for paying the benefits was operating under a conflict of interest. Moreover, the same would hold true for an employer that operated as plan administrator under a self-insured plan. [Metropolitan Life Ins. Co. v. Glenn, 128 S. Ct. 2343 (2008)]

However, the Court did not go so far as to say that any case involving such a conflict of interest should be reviewed *de novo*. Instead, the Court made it clear that the conflict of interest is a "factor" that must be considered in determining whether there was an abuse of discretion in denying the claim. The Court did not specify the weight to be given to the conflict of interest in any given case, indicating that the conflict will be more important where there is a higher likelihood that it influenced the benefits decision (where the administrator has a history of biased claims administration) and less important "where the administrator has taken active steps to reduce potential bias and to promote accuracy, for example, by walling off claims administrators from those interested in firms finances." [Metropolitan Life Ins. Co. v. Glenn, 128 S. Ct. 2343 (2008)]

In the wake of the decision in *Metropolitan Life*, a number of circuit courts addressed the standard of review in similar conflict of interest cases. In three of those cases, the Second, Fourth, and Eleventh Circuits concluded that the heightened standard of review they had previously applied in such cases is no longer appropriate in light of the Supreme Court decision. Instead, the courts concluded that a conflict of interest should be analyzed as a factor in determining whether there was an abuse of discretion in denying benefits. [*See* McCauley v. First Unum Life Ins. Co. 551 F.3d 126 (2d Cir. 2008); Champion v. Black & Decker (USA), Inc., 550 F.3d 353 (4th Cir. 2008); Doyle v. Liberty Life Assurance Co. of Boston, 542 F.3d 1352 (11th Cir. 2008).]

Following the Supreme Court decision in *Metropolitan Life,* the Ninth Circuit specifically held that a conflict of interest exists where an employer pays benefits under a self-funded plan, even if the benefits are paid from a trust administered by the employer's benefits committee. According to the court, even through the benefits are not paid directly by the employer, the employer still has a financial incentive to keep claims' experience as low as possible, since the less the trust pays out as benefits, the less the employer will need to contribute to the trust. [Burke v. Pitney Bowes Inc. Long-Term Disability Plan, 544 F.3d 1016 (9th Cir. 2008)]

Q 2:139   Must an ERISA welfare benefit plan establish procedures for complying with state domestic relations orders?

The question of whether welfare benefit plans must have procedures for complying with state domestic relations orders is a live issue.

A *domestic relations order* (DRO) is a judgment, decree, or order (including the approval of a property settlement) that is made pursuant to state domestic relations law (including community property law) and that relates to the provision of child support, alimony payments, or marital property rights for the benefit of a spouse, former spouse, child, or other dependent of a participant.

DROs frequently award a share of an employee's retirement benefits to a former spouse or child in connection with a divorce. Therefore ERISA specifically provides that a retirement plan must establish procedures for determining if a domestic relations order is a qualified domestic relations order (QDRO) and for administering distributions under such orders. A domestic relations order can be a QDRO only if it creates or recognizes the existence of an alternate payee's right to receive, or assigns to an alternate payee the right to receive, all or a part of a participant's benefits. For purposes of the QDRO provisions, an alternate payee cannot be anyone other than a spouse, former spouse, child, or other dependent of a participant. In addition, the order must meet a number of technical requirements. A retirement plan is not required to and is not permitted to honor a domestic relations order unless it is a QDRO.

The mandate for QDRO procedures is found in Title I, Part 2 of ERISA (Section 206(d)(3)(G)(ii)), which by its terms applies to "any employee benefit plan . . . other than . . . an employee welfare benefit plan." [ERISA Section 201(1)] Therefore, the QDRO rules technically do not apply to welfare benefits plans.

Nonetheless, five of the twelve federal circuit courts have concluded that the QDRO rules do apply to welfare benefit plans.

In one case, the Court of Appeals for the Seventh Circuit has held that ERISA, read literally, does not preempt the application of a QDRO to employer-provided life insurance. In that case, a husband and wife who divorced were obligated by the divorce decree to name their children as beneficiaries under each one's employer-provided life insurance. The father then died without having done so; instead, he had named his new wife as sole beneficiary of his employer-provided life insurance. The Seventh Circuit upheld the allocation of benefits specified in the divorce decree. [Metropolitan Life Ins. Co. v. Wheaton, 42 F.3d 1080 (7th Cir. 1994)] The Seventh Circuit has jurisdiction in Illinois, Indiana, and Wisconsin.

In addition, four other circuit courts have held that the QDRO rules apply to welfare benefits plans. Those circuits are the Second (Connecticut, New York, Vermont), the Fourth (Maryland, North Carolina, South Carolina, Virginia, West Virginia), the Sixth (Kentucky, Michigan, Ohio, Tennessee), and the Tenth (Colorado, Kansas, New Mexico, Oklahoma, Utah, Wisconsin). Therefore, a large number of employers across the country are faced with the question of how to handle DROs relating to welfare benefits.

Of course, plans that do not involve survivor benefits are not likely to be faced with DROs concerning benefit payments. However, other plans are likely to encounter DROs. For example, each of the cases in which it has been held that the QDRO rules do apply to welfare benefit plans involved a court order requiring payment of life insurance benefits under an ERISA plan to someone other than the designated beneficiary under the plan.

Practice Pointer. Plan administrators in all jurisdictions may want to consult legal counsel on the best way to handle competing claims between an employee's named beneficiary and a party named in a DRO. One option is to establish plan procedures modeled on the retirement plan QDRO rules to handle such claims. Alternatively, a plan may want to leave the decision-making to the courts by means of a judicial proceeding known as interpleader. In an interpleader action, the plan administrator deposits the contested benefits with the court and notifies the claimants that they must resolve their dispute in court. In this manner, the plan admits liability for the benefit, but the court assumes responsibility for the funds until payment can be made. The plan is thereby relieved of the responsibility of seeing to any further application of the funds, and the court, in effect, "holds the bag" until the dispute is resolved.

Reporting and Disclosure Requirements

Q 2:140   What are an employer's reporting and disclosure obligations under ERISA?

ERISA mandates that an employer communicate certain information about employee benefit plans to plan participants, the DOL, the IRS, the Health Care Financing Administration (HCFA) and, for certain retirement plans only, the Pension Benefit Guaranty Corporation (PBGC).

ERISA also requires retention of records relating to employee benefit plans and relating to the benefits of participants and beneficiaries. As used in ERISA, the term *employee benefit plan* refers to pension plans (single-employer and multiemployer defined benefits plans and defined contribution plans) as well as welfare benefit plans (plans that provide medical, accident, disability, death, and other nonretirement benefits). Generally, the plan administrator is responsible for compliance with ERISA reporting and disclosure requirements.

Q 2:141   Are all ERISA welfare benefit plans subject to all the reporting and disclosure requirements of ERISA?

No. The DOL regulations provide exemptions for some (but not all) of the reporting and disclosure requirements within the following categories of welfare benefit plans:

1. Unfunded (see Q 2:161) or fully insured welfare benefit plans with fewer than 100 participants at the beginning of the plan year [DOL Reg. §2520.104-20];

2. Welfare benefit plans with fewer than 100 participants at the beginning of the plan year that are part of a group insurance arrangement providing benefits to the employees of two or more unaffiliated employers [DOL Reg. §2520.104-21];

3. Apprenticeship and training benefit programs [DOL Reg. §2520.104-22];

4. Unfunded or fully insured welfare benefit plans providing benefits for a select group of management or highly compensated employees (commonly referred to as "top-hat plans") [DOL Reg. 2520.104-24];

5. Day care centers [DOL Reg. §2520.104-25]; and

6. Dues-financed welfare benefit plans maintained by employee organizations. [DOL Reg. §2520.104-26]

Plans that do not meet the definition of *group health plan* under Part 7 of Title I of ERISA are excluded from the various disclosure requirements mandated in Part 7.

Q 2:142   What is a summary plan description?

The *summary plan description* (SPD) is a written summary of the benefits under the plan and a statement of participant rights under ERISA. The plan administrator of a welfare benefit plan is required to provide an SPD to active and retired plan participants. [ERISA §104(b)]

Q 2:143   Must the SPD be a single booklet?

No. The SPD may consist of several documents. For example, some versions or inserts may apply only in certain geographic areas or to certain classes of employees. [DOL Reg. §2520.102-4]

Under current DOL regulations, a plan's claim procedures may be in a separate document, but the SPD must contain a description of all claims procedures and applicable time frames. [DOL Reg. §2560.503-1(b)(2)]

Q 2:144   Must the SPD be written in a particular style?

Yes. The format of an SPD must satisfy two general standards: (1) it must be written in a manner calculated to be understood by the average plan participant, and (2) it must be comprehensive enough to inform participants and beneficiaries of their rights and obligations under the plan. In preparing the SPD, the plan administrator must take into account the level of comprehension and education of typical plan participants and the complexity of the plan's terms. Technical jargon and long, complex sentences must be limited or eliminated entirely, and the use of clarifying examples, illustrations, cross-references, and a table of contents may be necessary.

The SPD cannot have the effect of misleading, misinforming, or failing to inform participants and beneficiaries. The advantages and disadvantages of the plan must be presented without either exaggerating the benefits or minimizing the limitations.

The descriptions of exceptions, limitations, reductions, and other restrictions of plan benefits cannot be minimized, rendered obscure, or otherwise made to appear unimportant. In addition, the exceptions, limitations, reductions, or restrictions of plan benefits cannot be summarized or described in a manner less prominent than the style, captions, printing type, and prominence used to describe or summarize plan benefits.

Foreign-language notice requirement. If the English-language SPD would fail to adequately inform foreign-language-speaking participants of their rights and obligations under the plan, the SPD must be made available to plan participants in languages other than English under the following circumstances:

1. If 25 percent of the plan's participants are literate only in the same non-English language and the plan covers fewer than 100 participants at the beginning of the year or

2. If the lesser of 500 participants or 10 percent or more of all plan participants are literate only in the same non-English language and the plan covers 100 or more participants at the beginning of the plan year.

The SPD must prominently display a notice in the non-English language offering assistance to participants and detailing the procedures they must follow in order to obtain assistance. The assistance, which need not be written, must be given in the non-English language and be calculated to provide the participants with a reasonable opportunity to become informed about their rights and obligations under the plan. [DOL Reg. §§2520.102-2, 2520.102-3(t)]

Note. The 2010 Health Reform Act mandates the use of uniform explanation of coverage documents for group health plans. See discussion in chapter 3.

Q 2:145   Must any particular information be included in the SPD?

Yes. The DOL regulations list the information that must be included in the SPD and written in the style described in Q 2:144. The required information concerns plan benefits and other technical information.

Information regarding plan benefits. Currently, the SPD must set forth at least the following information regarding plan benefits:

1. Requirements for eligibility to participate, including any age or service requirements.

2. A description or summary of benefits and, for welfare benefit plans, conditions for eligibility to receive them. If the plan has extensive schedules of benefits, only a general description is required if reference is made to detailed schedules of benefits that are available without cost to any participant or beneficiary who so requests.

3. A clear statement of circumstances that could result in disqualification, ineligibility, or denial, loss, forfeiture, or suspension of benefits that might otherwise reasonably be expected to be covered by the plan based on the rest of the booklet's description.

4. The authority of the plan sponsors or others to amend, cut back, or terminate the plan and the circumstances under which these acts may be done, plus the benefits, rights, and obligations of participants and beneficiaries on termination or amendment that reduces plan benefits. A description of procedures for filing claim forms, notifications of benefit

determinations, review of denied claims, applicable time limits, and ERISA remedies for denials. Claim procedures can be furnished as a separate document accompanying the plan's SPD, provided that the document also satisfies the SPD style and format requirements and that the SPD itself includes a statement that the plan's claims procedures are furnished, without charge, as a separate document.

Other required technical information. The SPD must also contain certain technical information intended to facilitate the individual's ability to obtain plan rights and benefits and, if necessary, to sue to obtain them. This technical information includes:

1. Name and address of the plan (and, if different, the name of the plan as it is commonly known to participants and beneficiaries).

2. Name and address of the sponsoring employer or sponsoring employee organization. For a collectively bargained plan, this would be the association, committee, joint board of trustees, parent, or most significant employer of an employer group contributing to the same plan, or other similar representative of the parties that established or maintained the plan, plus (a) a statement that a complete list of the sponsoring employers and employee organizations may be obtained by participants and beneficiaries upon written request to the plan administrator and is available for examination or (b) a statement that participants and beneficiaries may obtain, upon written request to the plan administrator, information regarding whether a particular employer is a sponsor of the plan and, if so, its address.

3. If the plan is established or maintained by two or more employers, the identity of the association, committee, joint board of trustees, parent or most significant employer of the employer group contributing to the plan, or other representative of the parties who established or maintain the plan, plus (a) a statement that a complete list of the sponsoring employers and employee organizations may be obtained by participants and beneficiaries upon written request to the plan administrator and is available for examination or (b) a statement that participants and beneficiaries may obtain, upon written request to the plan administrator, information regarding whether a particular employer is a sponsor of the plan and, if so, its address.

4. The employer identification number assigned by the IRS to the plan sponsor.

5. The plan number assigned by the plan sponsor.

6. The type of pension or welfare benefit plan (e.g., group health plan, disability plan).

7. The type of administration of the plan (e.g., contract administration or insurer administration). If a health insurance issuer (such as an insurance company or HMO) is responsible, in whole or in part, for the financing or administration of a group health plan, the SPD must indicate the name and address of the issuer, whether and to what extent benefits under the

plan are guaranteed under a contract or policy of insurance issued by the issuer, and the nature of any administrative services (e.g., payment of claims) provided by the issuer.

8. The name, business address, and business telephone number of the plan administrator as that term is defined by ERISA Section 3(16).

9. The name of the person designated as agent for service of legal process and the address at which process may be served on such person. Additionally, the SPD must include a statement that service of legal process may be made on a plan trustee or the plan administrator.

10. The name, title, and address of the principal place of business of each trustee of the plan.

11. For collectively bargained plans, a statement that the plan is maintained pursuant to one or more collective bargaining agreements and that a copy of any such agreement may be obtained by participants and beneficiaries upon written request to the plan administrator and is also available for examination by participants and beneficiaries as required by DOL regulations.

12. The sources of contributions for the plan (e.g., employer, employees) and the method by which the amount of contribution is calculated.

13. The identity of any funding medium used to accumulate assets to provide benefits. Any insurance company, trust fund, or any other institution, organization, or other entity that maintains a fund on behalf of the plan or through which the plan is funded or benefits are provided must be identified in the SPD.

14. The date of the end of the year used to maintain the plan's records.

15. The procedures to be followed in presenting claims for benefits under the plan and the remedies available under the plan for the redress of claims that are denied in whole or in part (including procedures required by ERISA Section 503).

16. A statement of ERISA rights, including the office at the DOL through which participants and beneficiaries may seek assistance or information.

[DOL Reg. §2520.102-3; as amended, 65 Fed. Reg. 70,225 (Nov. 21, 2000); ERISA §102(b), as amended by HIPAA §101(b)] (Additional requirements apply to SPDs for employee pension plans.)

Group health plan SPDs must also include the following information:

1. Procedures for making qualified medical child support (QMCSO) determinations or a statement that a copy of the procedure can be obtained from the plan administrator without charge. In addition, the notice of ERISA rights must state that individuals who disagree with the plan's decision or lack thereof concerning a QMCSO can sue the plan.

2. Cost-sharing provisions, including premiums, deductibles, coinsurance, and copayment amounts to be borne by the beneficiary.

3. Annual or lifetime caps or other limits on plan benefits.

4. The extent of coverage for preventive services.

5. Whether, and under what circumstances, existing and new drugs are covered.

6. Whether, and under what circumstances, medical tests, devices, and procedures are covered.

7. Provisions governing use of network providers, the composition of the provider network, and whether, and under what circumstances, out-of-network services are covered. Also, a listing of providers must be furnished and can be furnished as a separate document if the SPD contains a general description of the provider network and indicates that provider lists are furnished automatically, without charge, as a separate document.

8. Conditions or limits on selecting primary care or specialty providers.

9. Conditions or limits on obtaining emergency medical care.

10. Preauthorization or utilization requirements that are a condition to obtaining a benefit or service under the plan, plus the procedures for obtaining preauthorizations, approvals, or utilization review decisions.

11. A description of COBRA continuation rights and the obligations of participants and beneficiaries, including qualifying events, premiums, notice and election requirements and procedures, and duration of coverage. Additionally an expanded notice of ERISA rights must include a three-sentence description of COBRA rights.

12. The notice of ERISA rights must include required text disclosing the right to obtain a certificate of creditable coverage from the plan and the effect on the preexisting-condition exclusion applicable to the individual who fails to submit evidence of creditable coverage.

13. The funding arrangements for the plan. The DOL says disclosure is intended to ensure that SPDs clearly inform participants about the role of health insurance issuers in their group health plan, particularly in those cases where the plan is self-funded and the insurer is serving only as a contract administrator or claims payer rather than an insurer. If a health insurance issuer is responsible for financing or administration (including payment of claims), the SPD must include the name and address of such issuer.

14. If the group health plan provides maternity or newborn infant coverage, disclosure of federal or state-law requirements regarding maternity and newborn hospital stays. The Newborns' and Mothers' Health Protection Act (NMHPA) provides that federal requirements do not apply to health insurance coverage in a state if state law provides for hospital stays that are at least as long as those required under federal law (i.e., 48 hours following vaginal delivery or 96 hours following a cesarean section) or meets certain other requirements.

For required disclosure of material reductions to group health plans, see Q 2:150.

Note. The 2010 Health Reform Act mandates the use of uniform explanation of coverage documents for group health plans. See discussion in chapter 3.

Q 2:146 Does the full range of SPD requirements apply to federally qualified HMOs offered by the employer?

In the past, DOL regulations contained a limited exemption for federally qualified HMOs. Under current regulations, HMOs must comply with the full range of SPD requirements.

Q 2:147 When must the SPD be distributed?

The SPD (other than a summary description of a material reduction in covered services or benefits provided under a group health plan) must be furnished no later than 90 days after the individual becomes a plan participant or begins receiving benefits, or, if later, 120 days after the plan is established. Thereafter, it must be distributed every ten years if there are no material modifications and every five years if there have been material modifications that must, at that point, be incorporated into it (see Q 2:150). [ERISA §104(b)(1)(B); DOL Reg. §§2520.104a-3, 2520.104b-2]

Material reduction of care or services under a group health plan. A summary description of material reduction in covered services or benefits provided under a group health plan is required to be provided not later than 60 days after the date the modification or change is adopted. Alternatively, plan sponsors may provide such description at regular intervals of not more that 90 days. [ERISA §104(b), amended by HIPAA §101]

For this purpose, a "material reduction in covered services or benefits" is any modification to the plan or change in the information required to be included in the SPD that, independently or in conjunction with other contemporaneous modification, *would be considered by the average plan participant* to be an important reduction in covered services or benefits under the plan. Such reductions include any change that reduces or eliminates benefits payable under the plan (including, as a result of a change in formulas, methodologies, or schedules that serve as the basis for making benefit determinations); increases deductibles, copayments, or other amount to be paid by a participant or beneficiary; reduces the service area of an HMO; or establishes new conditions or requirements (e.g., preauthorization requirements) to obtaining services or benefits under the plan. [DOL Reg. §2520.104b-3 (Jan. 7, 2002)]

Q 2:148 Must the SPD be filed with the Department of Labor?

The Taxpayer Relief Act of 1997 (TRA '97) [Pub. L. No. 105-34] eliminated the requirement that employee benefit plan administrators automatically file SPDs and summaries of material modifications (SMMs) with the DOL. However, TRA '97 also amended ERISA to require an administrator to furnish any documents relating to an employee benefit plan to the DOL upon request.

[ERISA §104(a); 29 U.S.C. §1024(a)] Requested documents may include, but are not limited to, the latest SPD (including any summaries of plan changes not included in the SPD) and the bargaining agreement, trust agreement, contract, or other instrument under which the plan is established or operated. TRA '97 also added a new ERISA provision giving the DOL the authority to assess civil penalties for a plan administrator's failure to furnish requested materials within 30 days. [ERISA §502(c)(6); 29 U.S.C. §1132(c)(6)] The maximum penalty is $110 per day, but in no event more than $1,100 per request. No penalty is imposed for failures resulting from matters reasonably beyond the control of the plan administrator.

DOL regulations make it clear that the DOL will limit the exercise of its authority to requests for SPDs (and SMMs) on behalf of plan participants and beneficiaries and requests for other documents that a participant or beneficiary has requested, in writing, and that the plan administrator had failed or refused to furnish. [DOL Reg. §2520.104a-8] For this purpose, participants or beneficiaries will include individuals who are deemed participants or beneficiaries under ERISA Sections 3(7) and 3(8) [29 U.S.C. §§1002(7), 1002(8)] alternate payees under a QDRO or prospective alternate payees, current or prospective qualified COBRA beneficiaries, current or prospective alternate recipients or representatives under a QMCSO, or their representatives.

The ERISA statement of rights included in SPDs must explain the right of participants or beneficiaries to request certain documents from the plan and the availability of assistance from the DOL. [DOL Reg. §2520.102-3(t)]

Penalties, up to the maximum of $110 per day or $1,100 per request, will begin to accrue if a requested document is not received by the 30th day following the DOL's request. A document sent by certified mail will be treated as received by the DOL on the mailing date; if certified mail is not used, the document will be treated as delivered on the date it is actually received by the DOL. Multiple requests for the same or similar documents will be considered separate requests for purposes of calculating penalties. Penalties will be calculated taking into account the degree of willfulness of the failure. The DOL may waive all or part of a penalty on a showing by the administrator that the failure or refusal to furnish a document was the result of matters reasonably beyond the administrator's control. The penalty is the responsibility of the plan administrator; it may not be paid out of plan funds. [DOL Reg. §2560.502c-6]

Q 2:149   What methods can the employer use to distribute SPDs?

The plan administrator is required to use measures reasonably calculated to ensure actual receipt of the SPD by participants and beneficiaries, and the method or methods of delivery used must be likely to result in full distribution.

Workplace distribution. In-hand distribution to the employee at his or her workplace is permitted; however, it is not acceptable merely to leave copies in locations frequented by employees, such as in the reception area or cafeteria.

In one case, however, the Second Circuit concluded that an employer that distributed SPDs at a mass meeting did not do enough to ensure that each employee received a copy. AlliedSignal acquired all the assets of Textron and hired former Textron employees, including Mr. Leyda. AlliedSignal invited the former Textron employees to attend a meeting about the company's benefits. The company distributed SPDs, enrollment forms, and beneficiary designation forms at the meeting, and left additional copies for employees who did not attend. AlliedSignal directed supervisors to track employees who were on leave or traveling on the day of the meeting, so that it could send the materials to those employees. Mr. Leyda did not attend the meeting (apparently because he was too busy). However, because he was not identified as on leave or traveling, he was not sent the SPD or other materials. As a result, Mr. Leyda did not learn about the differences between AlliedSignal's and Textron's life insurance benefits. Mr. Leyda assumed that AlliedSignal automatically provided $120,000 of coverage (equal to three times his salary) as Textron had and opted to buy an additional $40,000 of coverage through the AlliedSignal plan, for what he assumed was a total of $160,000. In fact, AlliedSignal provided automatic coverage for only one-and-one-half times his salary. Therefore, when Mr. Leyda died, his widow received $100,000 in life insurance proceeds, instead of the $160,000 she had expected. Mrs. Leyda sued AlliedSignal in its capacity as plan administrator for failure to provide an SPD. A district court awarded Mrs. Leyda $62,250 in damages, and the Second Circuit upheld the award. According to the Second Circuit, AlliedSignal was wrong to assume that the only employees not attending the meeting would be those on trips or on leave. Moreover, the court said AlliedSignal would have known that Mr. Leyda did not attend if someone had taken attendance at the meeting. [Leyda v. AlliedSignal Inc., 322 F.3d 199 (2d Cir. 2003)]

Newsletter articles. Printing the SPD or an update to it as an insert in a periodical (such as a union newspaper or internal company newsletter) is acceptable only if the periodical is comprehensive and up to date. The front page must display a prominent notice advising readers that the issue contains an insert with important information about rights under the plan and ERISA that should be read and retained for future reference. If some employees are not on the mailing list, other methods of distribution must be used in conjunction with the periodical so that the methods taken together are reasonably calculated to ensure actual receipt.

Mailing. SPDs may be mailed to employees, but SPDs not sent by first-class mail must have return and forwarding postage guaranteed and address correction requested. [DOL Reg. §2520.104b-1]

An employee's claim that an ERISA plan had failed to provide the employee with an SPD was rejected. The plan showed that, based on its records and regular business practices, SPDs and updates had been mailed by first-class mail to the employee's last known address. The plan must prove that SPDs were sent but need not prove that they were actually received. [Campbell v. Emery Air Freight Corp., 1995 U.S. Dist. LEXIS 6529 (E.D. Pa. 1995)]

Distribution through electronic media. Provided that certain requirements are met, SPDs and other communications with plan participants may be furnished electronically (see Q 2:159). [DOL Reg. §2520.104b-1]

Q 2:150   Must SPDs be updated periodically?

Yes. In general, participants must be given an update summarizing material modifications to the plan no later than 210 days after the close of the plan year in which the modification or change is adopted, regardless of when the modification or change becomes effective. A revised SPD incorporating these changes must be issued no later than 210 days after the end of the plan year that includes the fifth anniversary of the date on which the SPD was distributed. [ERISA §104(b)(1); 29 U.S.C. §1024(b)(1); DOL Reg. §2520.104b-2] If no plan changes have been made since the prior SPD was distributed, ten years is substituted for five years.

Special rule for material reduction of group health plan coverage. Section 104(b) of ERISA requires that if covered services or benefits under a group health plan are materially reduced, a summary description of that change must be distributed to participants and beneficiaries within 60 days after the date of adoption of the change or notification.

Q 2:151   Must plan participants be notified when an employee benefit plan is terminated?

Although ERISA specifically requires plan participants to be notified of material modifications to an employee benefit plan (see Q 2:147), there is no specific requirement that participants be notified of termination of a plan. However, two appellate courts have held that the broad fiduciary responsibilities imposed by ERISA require a plan administrator to provide timely notification to employees of termination of their benefits. [Willet v. Blue Cross & Blue Shield of Ala., 953 F.2d 1335 (11th Cir. 1992); Peralta v. Hispanic Bus. Inc., 419 F.3d 1064 (9th Cir. 2005)]

In *Peralta,* a company provided long-term disability (LTD) benefits for its employees. At some point, the LTD policy was cancelled, although it was unclear whether the cancellation was intentional or inadvertent. The employees were not notified of the cancellation until a new employee benefits manager discovered a memo indicating that someone had cancelled the coverage. In the interim, an employee suffered serious injuries in an automobile accident. Believing she had LTD coverage, the employee attempted to file a claim, but no benefits were ultimately paid because of the cancellation of the coverage. The employee filed suit, claiming she had relied on the employer's LTD coverage and had not purchased private insurance. She asked the court to order reinstatement of her LTD benefits or equitable relief equivalent to those benefits. The Ninth Circuit held that the employer's failure to notify the employee of the cancellation of her LTD coverage was a breach of fiduciary duty under ERISA. However, the court declined to provide a remedy to the employee. According to the court, it was impossible to reinstate the employee's LTD benefits because the LTD plan no longer existed. Moreover, no equitable relief was available to the employee. The court noted that in the case of a procedural breach, such as failure to give notice, equitable relief is available only if the employer's action amounted to bad faith, concealment, or fraud. Although the employer in this case was clearly negligent in not communicating the policy cancellation, there was no evidence of bad faith. The court also pointed out that the relief requested by the employee amounted to money damages equal to the LTD benefits she would have received if the policy had not been cancelled, and that remedy was simply not available in equity.

Q 2:152 If the SPD and the official plan document contents differ, which governs the rights of employees?

There are court decisions on both sides of the issue. However, a number of federal courts of appeals have held that the SPD overrules the formal plan document, at least when it can be shown that the participant or beneficiary relied on the SPD to his or her detriment or was prejudiced by it. [Aiken v. Policy Mgmt. Sys. Corp., 13 F.3d 138 (4th Cir. 1994), and cases cited therein]

The Third Circuit Court of Appeals considered the case of an employer that provided its employees with basic group life and accidental death and dismemberment (AD&D) insurance coverage. The employer added supplemental group life insurance as an option, and the SPD stated that it would include supplemental AD&D coverage as well. However, the group insurance policy did not provide for AD&D coverage under the supplemental coverage. When an employee died by accident and the insurance company refused to pay supplemental AD&D benefits, the beneficiary sued the insurer and the employer. The appellate court held that the employer was responsible for the misrepresentation of the coverage in the SPD and that there had been reliance on the part of the employee and beneficiary. The employer, and not the insurer, was required to pay the supplemental AD&D amounts. The court also ruled that the employer had breached its fiduciary duties by making the misrepresentations in the SPD. [Curcio v. John Hancock Mut. Life. Ins. Co., 18 Employee Benefits Cas. (BNA) 1822 (3d Cir. 1994)]

However, not all courts require a showing that the employee relied on or was prejudiced by the SPD. For example, the Fifth Circuit analogized the plan document and SPD to a contract. The Fifth Circuit said, if an SPD conflicts with a plan document, a court should read the terms of the "contract" to include the terms of the plan document as modified by any conflicting language in the SPD. The court also noted that just as enforcement of a contract generally does not require that the parties actually read and rely on the terms, enforcement of an SPD's terms does not require a showing of reliance. [Washington v. Murphy Oil USA, Inc., 497 F.3d 453 (5th Cir. 2007)]

On the other hand, the document in question must rise to the level of an SPD in order to override the official terms of the plan. A district court held that a document that appeared to be a series of PowerPoint slides showing highlights of the employer's benefits program was so lacking in detail that it could not be deemed an SPD. "Because the . . . document is not a summary plan description, the maxim that the summary plan description governs when it conflicts with the plan . . . is inapplicable here," the court wrote. [Louderback v. Litton Indus., 504 F. Supp. 2d 1145 (D. Kan. 2007)]

Q 2:153   What COBRA continuation of group health plan coverage notices does ERISA require?

For group health plans, the plan administrator is responsible for the following three separate disclosures to employees regarding COBRA continuation of general health plan coverage:

1. When the plan first becomes subject to COBRA or, if later, when plan coverage begins, active employees and their spouses must be notified, within a specified time limit, of their right to elect continuation of group health plan coverage. [ERISA §606(1); 29 U.S.C. §1166(1); I.R.C. §4980B(f)(6)(A)]

2. When a COBRA-qualifying event occurs, qualified beneficiaries must be notified, within a specified time limit, of their right to elect continuation of group health plan coverage. [ERISA §606(4); 29 U.S.C. §1166(4); I.R.C. §4980B(f)(6)(D)]

3. When the COBRA continuation of group health coverage ends, qualified beneficiaries must be notified of their right to elect to convert to individual coverage, if conversion rights are otherwise available under the group health plan. [Treas. Reg. §54.4980B-7 Q&A-8]

A DOL regulation requires health plan SPDs to provide detailed information on COBRA rights. [DOL Reg. §2520.102-3(o), 65 Fed. Reg. 70,225 (Nov. 21, 2000)] The DOL says that furnishing a copy of an SPD containing complete COBRA information will satisfy the initial COBRA notice requirement, provided the SPD is furnished at the time an employee first becomes covered by the plan (rather than within 90 days of the commencement of participation as permitted under the SPD regulations).

Employers and plan administrators may comply with COBRA's election notice rules by sending a single, first-class mailing to qualified beneficiaries who reside at the same address. Such mailings should include a separate election notice for each qualified beneficiary; if a single notice is sent, the mailing should clearly identify the qualified beneficiaries covered by the notice and clearly explain the separate and independent right each has to elect COBRA coverage. [ERISA Op. Ltr. 99-14A (Nov. 10, 1999)]

In a somewhat questionable decision, the U.S. Court of Appeals for the Third Circuit held that a plan administrator could be sued for violation of his fiduciary duties by failing to volunteer to provide COBRA information. The COBRA-eligible employee died during the COBRA election period, after the proper COBRA notices had been sent. The decedent's widow called the plan administrator and asked for information about a death benefit. The plan administrator provided the requested information but did not volunteer any information about the spouse's right to elect COBRA continuation coverage. [Bixler v. Central Pa. Teamsters Health & Welfare Fund, 12 F.3d 1292 (3d Cir. 1993)]

See chapter 6 for further discussion of required COBRA notices.

Q 2:154   What notice regarding QMCSOs does ERISA require?

Upon receipt of a medical child support court order, the plan administrator of a group health plan is responsible for immediately notifying the participant and each alternate recipient described in that court order of the plan's procedure for determining whether the court order is a QMCSO within the meaning of ERISA Section 609. Then, within a reasonable period after receiving the court order, the plan administrator must determine whether the court order is in fact a QMCSO and notify the plan participant and each alternate recipient of its determination. [ERISA §609; 29 U.S.C. §1169, as added by OBRA '93 §4301] (QMCSOs are discussed in detail in chapter 5.)

Current DOL regulations require SPDs of health plans to provide specific disclosure concerning QMCSOs (see Q 2:145).

Q 2:155   Are plan participants entitled to detailed notice of a partial or total claim denial?

Yes. For a detailed discussion of the claims process, see Qs 2:125–2:139.

Q 2:156   Are plan participants entitled to an annual statement of their plan benefits?

No. ERISA's annual benefit statement notice requirements apply only to pension plans. [ERISA §§105, 209] However, many employers voluntarily include welfare benefit plans in their annual benefit statements as a way of publicizing their comprehensive benefit programs.

Q 2:157   What is a summary annual report?

A *summary annual report* (SAR) is a brief version of the Form 5500 series financial information filed with the IRS. The SAR must be distributed annually to participants on or before the last day of the ninth month after the close of the plan year or two months after the close of the period for which the extension of the due date for filing the annual report with the IRS was granted. Prescribed form language is provided for this purpose, and foreign-language notice requirements apply. [ERISA §104(b); 29 U.S.C. §1024(b); DOL Reg. §§2520.104b-1, 2520.104b-10] SARs are subject to the same method of distribution requirements as are SPDs.

Employers are required to disclose in the SPD the participant's right to obtain a copy of the SAR.

Certain plans are exempt from having to provide SARs (see Q 2:161). [DOL Reg. §§2520.104-20–2520.104-26]

Q 2:158   What information must be provided upon request to a participant or beneficiary?

The plan administrator of a welfare benefit plan must furnish or make available for inspection and copying, within 30 days of a request from a participant or beneficiary, a copy of any of the following:

- The latest Form 5500 series annual report;
- The plan document, including any related collective bargaining agreement, trust agreement, contract, or other instrument under which the plan is established or operated;
- The most recent updated SPD; or
- Any plan termination report.

Several limited exemptions are available (see Q 2:141). DOL regulations clarify that insurance contracts and SARs are included in documents that are required to be disclosed (see Q 2:145).

A federal district court has held that a plan participant was entitled to know the source of his pension benefits and to receive detailed information on the calculation of his benefits. [Maiuro v. Federal Express Corp., 17 Employee Benefits Cas. (BNA) 2425 (D.N.J. 1994)] The same principles would appear to apply in the case of welfare benefits where the benefits may be derived from differing sources (such as an insurer, a trust, or the employer's general assets), and the determination of the benefits may require detailed calculation (such as in the case of disability benefits based on compensation and years of service).

A decision by the Court of Appeals for the Ninth Circuit held that a retirement plan administrator was required to provide a list of participants and beneficiaries to a group of retirees. The retirees wanted the list in order to inform the participants and beneficiaries of the employer's alleged improper use of plan assets, to gain support for benefit negotiations with the employer, and to sue for increased benefits. The court held that the list was a document under which the plan was established or operated and must therefore be disclosed. The court decision is based on an expansive interpretation of the statutory wording, and it appears that the decision may not necessarily be followed in other circuits. [Hughes Salaried Retirees Action Comm. v. Administrator of the Hughes Non-Bargaining Ret. Plan, 18 Employee Benefits Cas. (BNA) 2497 (9th Cir. 1994), *cert. denied*, 20 Employee Benefits Cas. (BNA) 1352 (S. Ct. 1996)]

Moreover, a plan fiduciary must give accurate information to plan participants. The Sixth Circuit Court of Appeals held that an employer breached its fiduciary duties under ERISA when it gave false and misleading information to employees about the status of their health benefits following early retirement under an early retirement incentive program. During exit interviews, the company's human resources representative told employees that their health benefits would not change during retirement. In fact, shortly after the employees accepted early retirement, the company amended the plan to increase premiums, deductibles, and copayments under the retiree health plan. [James v. Pirelli Armstrong Tire Corp., 305 F.3d 439 (6th Cir. 2002)]

On the other hand, at least one court has held that the employer or plan administrator does not have a duty to volunteer information about the status of a participant's or beneficiary's individual plan benefits. For example, the First Circuit held that an employer did not breach its fiduciary duties under ERISA when it failed to inform an employee that he would lose eligibility for long-term disability benefits when he switched from full-time to part-time status. [Watson v. Deaconess Waltham Hosp., 298 F.3d 102 (1st Cir. 2002)]

In addition, the First Circuit concluded that an employer did not have a duty to inform an employee's ex-wife about changes in his life insurance coverage. When the couple divorced, the court ordered the employee to designate his ex-wife as irrevocable beneficiary of two employer-sponsored life insurance policies, a basic policy and an optional policy. The employer was informed of the order, and the ex-wife was duly designated as beneficiary. At the time, the employer promised in a letter to the ex-wife that it would notify her by registered mail within 24 hours of the employee's termination of employment. The employer subsequently replaced the option policy with one issued by a different insurer. The employee applied for the new policy and named his new wife as beneficiary. The ex-wife was not informed of the change. When the employee terminated employment, he continued the optional policy, but not the basic policy that named his ex-wife as beneficiary. The employer promptly sent a certified letter to the ex-wife notifying her of the employee's termination of employment and informing her that she could convert the basic policy to an individual policy. However, the ex-wife never received the letter because she had moved. When she learned of the employee's termination of employment, he assured her that he had continued both the basic and optional policies naming her as beneficiary. However, when the employee later died, she discovered she was not entitled to any insurance benefit. The ex-wife sued the employer, claiming that the employer had breached its fiduciary duty by failing to inform her of the replacement of the optional policy and by failing to give her notice of the employee's termination. As to the optional policy, the court held that employer did not have a fiduciary duty to give individualized information to a plan beneficiary. Moreover, the employer had substantially complied with its obligation to inform her of the employee's termination, even though it sent the letter by certified rather than registered mail. The company's agreement with the ex-wife merely required it to give notice, not to ensure that the notice was received. [Barrs v. Lockheed Martin Corp., 287 F.3d 202 (1st Cir. 2002)]

Q 2:159   May employee benefit plan communications be delivered electronically?

The DOL issued a safe harbor rule that permits the electronic delivery of ERISA notices and employee benefit plan disclosures. [DOL Reg. §2520.104b-1] As originally proposed, the safe harbor rule would have permitted electronic delivery of SPDs, SMMs, and SARs to plan participants at work site locations. In addition to expanding the types of documents that may be provided electronically, the final rule authorizes electronic disclosure to participants, beneficiaries, and other persons entitled to ERISA disclosures at off-site locations. *Work site disclosures to plan participants.* Notices and other communications may be delivered electronically to a plan participant if (1) he or she has the ability to effectively access documents in electronic form at the work site or at another work location (e.g., a travel location or home office) and (2) access to the employer's or plan sponsor's electronic information system is an integral part of the participant's job duties. Commentators suggested that electronic delivery should be permitted if a participant has access to the information system in a common area of the workplace. However, the DOL rejected that suggestion, concluding that only those participants who regularly access the employer's system are likely to receive timely communications. So, for example, delivery of COBRA or other notices through a computer kiosk located in the common area of a workplace is not permitted under the final regulations.

The original safe harbor proposal would have required that participants have the ability to readily convert electronic documents to paper form free of charge. The final safe harbor does not include that requirement. However, participants must be given the right to request and obtain paper versions of electronic documents. Paper documents must be furnished free of charge if ERISA or DOL regulations require the document to be furnished without charge. However, if the plan is permitted to impose a reasonable charge for a document, a reasonable charge may be imposed for furnishing a paper version of an electronic document.

Off-site disclosures. Notices and other communications may also be delivered electronically to participants, beneficiaries, and other persons entitled to plan disclosures under ERISA if they have consented to receiving documents electronically.

Prior to giving consent to electronic delivery of communications, an individual must receive a clear and conspicuous statement identifying the documents or categories of documents to which the consent will apply. The statement must also explain that the consent may be withdrawn at any time without charge; describe the procedures for withdrawing consent and for updating address or other information required for delivery; explain the right to obtain a paper document, including whether a paper document will be furnished without charge; and identify any software or hardware requirements for accessing the electronic documents.

In the case of documents furnished through the Internet or another electronic communication network, the individual must provide an address for the receipt of documents and must consent or confirm consent in a manner that reasonably demonstrates his or her ability to access electronic communications. If there are changes in hardware or software that may create a material risk that an individual may be unable to access documents electronically, the individual must be provided with a statement of the revised hardware or software requirements and must be given the right to withdraw consent for electronic delivery without charge. Following notification of a hardware or software change, an individual must again affirmatively consent to receive documents electronically.

The requirements for an e-mail address and electronic confirmation of consent do not apply where the electronic delivery is made via CD, DVD, or similar media that are not dependent on electronic transmission.

Requirements for electronic documents. The plan administrator must take appropriate and necessary measures to ensure that the system used for furnishing documents results in actual receipt of the transmitted information. Such measures may include return-receipt electronic mail features or periodic reviews or surveys to confirm receipt of transmitted information.

Electronic documents must be prepared and furnished in a manner consistent with the style, content, and format requirements for paper documents. This does not mean that electronic documents must be identical to their paper counterparts, however. For example, the DOL says that the rules do not preclude the use of interactive technologies, multimedia components, or hyperlink technologies in furnishing electronic documents.

IRS requirements. Certain welfare benefit notices, elections, and consent forms are required by the Internal Revenue Code and are governed by the IRS. The IRS has issued regulations governing the use of electronic media for notices and other documents within its jurisdiction. [Treas. Reg. §1.401(a)-21] In the case of welfare benefits, the IRS regulations apply to notices, elections, and other disclosures related to:

- Accident and health plans or arrangements [I.R.C. §§104, 105],
- Cafeteria plans [I.R.C. §125],
- Educational assistance plans [I.R.C. §127],
- Qualified transportation fringe benefits [I.R.C. §132],
- Archer medical savings accounts [I.R.C. §220], and
- Health savings accounts [I.R.C. §223].

The regulations do *not* apply to notices, consents, or disclosures required by ERISA that fall under the jurisdiction of the DOL. For example, the regulations do not apply to furnishing of SPDs, which are governed by the DOL regulations discussed above (see Q 2:149).

In addition, the rules for the use of electronic media apply in addition to all other general requirements for particular notices and elections. Any communication provided electronically must satisfy all the other Code and regulatory requirements for that communication.

The content of an electronic communication and the delivery method must be reasonably designed to provide information in a way that is no less understandable than if provided in a paper document. Moreover, the electronic transmission must alert the recipient to the significance of the electronic document (including the subject matter) and provide instructions for accessing the document. [Treas. Reg. §1.401(a)-21(a)(5)]

The regulations provide two options:

1. *Consent method.* Under the general rules, a plan must obtain a participant's consent before providing a notice using electronically. The participant's consent must be given in a way that reasonably demonstrates that the participant can access the notice electronically. Consent can be given in writing on paper or by some other nonelectronic means, but only if the participant confirms the consent in a way that reasonably demonstrates that he or she can access the notice electronically. Before providing consent, the participant must be given a disclosure statement that outlines the scope of the consent, the participant's right to withdraw the consent (including any conditions, consequences, or fees), and the right to receive the communication on paper. The disclosure must specify the hardware and software requirements for electronic documents and the procedures for updating the participant's electronic contact information. If the hardware or software requirements change, a new consent must be obtained from the participant. [Treas. Reg. §1.401(a)-21(b)]

2. *Automatic method.* Under this method, an electronic notice can be provided automatically if the recipient is advised that a paper copy may be requested and will be provided at no charge. However, to use this method, the recipient of the notice must be "effectively able" to access the electronic medium used to provide the notice. [Treas. Reg. §1.401(a)-21(c)])

Electronic elections. A benefit election can be made electronically if all of the following requirements are met:

1. The participant is effectively able to access the electronic system.
2. The electronic system is reasonably designed to prevent any person other than the participant from making the election.
3. The electronic system must provide the participant with a reasonable opportunity to review, confirm, modify, or rescind the election before it becomes effective.
4. The participant must receive a confirmation of the election through either a written paper document or electronic medium that meets the regulatory requirements within a reasonable time period.
5. In the case of an election that must be witnessed by a plan representative or a notary public, the individual's signature must be witnessed in the physical presence of a plan representative or a notary.

[Treas. Reg. §1.401(a)-21(d)]

The regulations are effective for applicable notices and elections on or after January 1, 2007.

Q 2:160   What documents regarding welfare benefit plans must be filed with the DOL?

The plan administrator must file a Form 5500 series annual report for each ERISA Title I welfare benefit plan unless an exemption applies. [ERISA §104; 29 U.S.C. §1024] The Form 5500 is designed to provide detailed information on the qualification, financial condition, bonding, party-in-interest transactions, and other operations of the plan. The form is filed with the EBSA, which furnishes the IRS (and, for certain pension plans, the PBGC) with a copy of the report. The annual report form must be filed no later than the end of the seventh month following the end of the plan year, although the plan administrator may file for an additional two-and-a-half-month extension. The plan administrator also must notify the DOL of a change in plan name, change in the name or address of the plan administrator, merger or consolidation of the plan with another plan, or termination of the plan. (Welfare benefit plans generally use the Form 5500 series annual report for such notifications.) [ERISA §§103, 104; 29 U.S.C. §§1023, 1024; 2006 Instructions for Form 5500]

Late filings. The DOL has implemented the Delinquent Filer Voluntary Compliance program for voluntarily making late filings of Form 5500 and paying a reduced penalty. This program is described in detail in Q 2:189.

Q 2:161   What welfare benefit plans are exempt from the requirement of filing a Form 5500?

Several exemptions from the Form 5500 annual reporting requirements are available, as follows:

- *Small plans.* The Form 5500 filing is not required in the case of a welfare benefit plan that covers fewer than 100 participants as of the beginning of the plan year and is fully insured, unfunded, or a combination of fully insured and unfunded. For this purpose, an unfunded welfare benefit plan is one that has its benefits paid as needed directly from the general assets of the employer. In order to be considered a fully insured welfare benefit plan, the benefits must be provided exclusively through insurance policies, the premiums of which must be paid directly by the employer from its general assets or partly from its general assets and partly from employee contributions (which the employer forwards within three months of receipt). [DOL Reg. §2520.104-20; 2006 Instructions for Form 5500]

- *Foreign plans.* Form 5500 is not required for a plan maintained outside the United States primarily for persons substantially all of whom are nonresident aliens. [2006 Instructions for Form 5500]

- *Top-hat plans.* An unfunded or insured welfare benefit plan for a select group of management or highly compensated employees is not required to file Form 5500. [DOL Reg. §2520.104-24; 2006 Instructions for Form 5500]

- *State-mandated plans.* No Form 5500 filing is required for plans maintained solely to comply with workers' compensation, unemployment compensation, or disability insurance laws, since those plans are exempt from ERISA. [ERISA §4(b)(3); 29 U.S.C. §1003(b)(3); 2006 Instructions for Form 5500]

- *Governmental plans.* Plans maintained by federal, state, and local government or agencies thereof for their employees. [2006 Instructions for Form 5500]

- *Group insurance plans.* A welfare benefit plan that participates in a group insurance arrangement that files a Form 5500 on behalf of the plan is not required to file its own form. [DOL Reg. §2520.103-2; 2006 Instructions for Form 5500]

- *Apprenticeship or training plans.* [DOL Reg. §2520.104-22; 2006 Instructions for Form 5500]

- *An unfunded dues-financed welfare benefit plan.* [DOL Reg. §2520.104-26; 2006 Instructions for Form 5500]

- *Church plans.* [ERISA §3(33); 2006 Instructions for Form 5500]

- *Individual and partnership plans.* A welfare benefit plan solely for an individual (and spouse) who wholly owns a trade or business or a plan or partners (and spouses) in a partnership. [DOL Reg. §2510.3-3(b); 2006 Instructions for Form 5500]

Fringe benefit plans. The Code technically requires reporting by certain fringe benefit plans, including cafeteria plans [I.R.C. §125], educational assistance programs [I.R.C. §127], and adoption assistance programs. [I.R.C. §§137, 6039D] In the past, the IRS required these plans to file an annual information return on a special Schedule F, Fringe Benefit Plan Annual Information Return, attached to Form 5500. However, the IRS suspended that requirement as of April 4, 2002, effective for all plan years, for all unfiled returns, including those for years before 2001. [Notice 2002-24, 2002-16 I.R.B. 785]

Other fringe benefit plans, including group term life insurance plans [I.R.C. §79], accident and health plans [I.R.C. §§105 and 106], and dependent care assistance plans I.R.C. §129] are technically subject to the IRS reporting requirement. However, these other fringe benefit plans have been exempt from filing under a long-standing IRS rule. [Notice 90-24, 1990-1 C.B. 335]

The IRS says that it is evaluating the reporting requirements for all fringe benefit plans. Any future reporting obligations will apply only to plan years beginning on or after the date of publication of future guidance.

Q 2:162 When is an accountant's report required to be filed with Form 5500 for a welfare benefit plan?

An independent qualified public accountant's opinion must be attached to the Form 5500 unless the plan is an employee welfare benefit plan that is unfunded, fully insured, or a combination of unfunded and fully insured. [DOL Reg. §2520.104-44; 2006 Instructions for Form 5500; ERISA Tech. Rel. 92-01, 57 Fed. Reg. 23,272 (June 2, 1992)] If the plan is funded by a voluntary employers' beneficiary association (VEBA) trust, an independent qualified public accountant's opinion is required. [2006 Instructions for Form 5500] Note that if the plan falls within the suspension of trust requirement (see Q 2:97), the accountant's opinion is waived.

Q 2:163   Can Form 5500 be filed electronically?

Yes, in fact, it must be so filed. DOL regulations require electronic filing of Form 5500. [DOL Reg. § 2520.104a-2] Beginning January 2010, an all-electronic system called EFAST-2 receives the electronic annual returns/reports. Filers can register for electronic credentials through the EFAST-2 Web site (*www.efast.dol. gov*).

Q 2:164   What is the penalty if a Form 5500 is late or was never filed?

The statutory penalty for failure to file a Form 5500 annual report is $1,000 per day. However, the DOL has implemented the Delinquent Filer Voluntary Compliance (DFVC) program, which can significantly reduce an employer's penalty. For a one-time payment, each overdue annual report can be filed. This program is described in detail in Q 2:189.

Q 2:165   What documents regarding welfare benefit plans must be filed with the DOL?

Under current rules, there is no requirement for mandatory filing of plan documents with the DOL.

However, a copy of the SPD or SMM is required to be furnished to the Secretary of Labor upon request. [ERISA §104(a)(6), added by §1503 of Pub. L. No. 105-34]

Certain types of investments. Common or collective trusts and pooled separate accounts, master trusts, and certain other investment entities can file certain financial information concerning their investments directly with the DOL. Such entities must file no later than the date on which the plan's annual Form 5500 report is due. If the financial information is filed directly with the DOL, the plan is relieved from filing the same information as part of the Form 5500 annual report filing.

Top-hat plans. An employer maintaining a top-hat welfare benefit plan primarily for the purpose of providing benefits for a select group of management or highly compensated employees (see Q 2:16) must provide plan documents to the Secretary of Labor upon request. [ERISA §104(a)(3); 29 U.S.C. §1024(a)(3); DOL Reg. §2520.104-24] In contrast, the ERISA exemption for top-hat pension plans requires affirmative action. [DOL Reg. §2520.104-23]

Q 2:166   What recordkeeping requirements does ERISA impose on employers?

ERISA requires employers to retain certain benefit records and copies of various plan documents and backup information (see Qs 2:167–2:168).

Q 2:167 What records relating to various plan documents must be kept and for how long?

ERISA has a blanket record retention requirement of six years for information relating to plan documents, SPDs, annual reports, SARs, individual benefit statements, and all other certifications and reports that are required to be filed under ERISA's reporting and disclosure rules (or would be required to be filed but for an exemption). Employers are required to keep sufficiently detailed information and data necessary to verify, explain, clarify, or check such documents for accuracy and completeness, including vouchers, worksheets, receipts, and applicable resolutions. [ERISA §107; 29 U.S.C. §1027]

Note that other laws may require record retention for longer periods.

Q 2:168 May employee benefit plan records be maintained electronically?

DOL regulations permit the use of electronic media to comply with ERISA's rules regarding the maintenance and retention of plan records. An electronic record keeping system must meet all the following requirements:

1. The system has reasonable controls to ensure the integrity, accuracy, authenticity, and reliability of the records kept in electronic form.

2. The electronic records are maintained in reasonable order, in a safe and accessible place, and in such a manner that they may be readily inspected or examined. For example, the record keeping system should be capable of indexing, retaining, preserving, and reproducing the records.

3. The electronic records can be readily converted into legible and readable paper copy as may be needed to satisfy reporting and disclosure requirements or any other obligations under ERISA.

4. Adequate records management practices are established and implemented, such as procedures for labeling electronically maintained records, providing a secure storage environment, creating backups, observing quality assurance through regular evaluations, and retaining paper copies of records that cannot be adequately transferred to the electronic system.

The regulations provide that paper original records generally may be discarded once they have been transferred to an electronic system that complies with all record maintenance requirements unless the electronic record would not constitute a duplicate or substitute record under the terms of the plan and federal or state law. [DOL Reg. §2520.107-1]

Q 2:169 Does the DOL have a program that reduces fines for plan administrators who voluntarily correct employee benefit plans?

Yes. The DOL's Voluntary Fiduciary Correction Program (VFCP) permits certain types of financial transactions to be voluntarily corrected.

The VFCP covers 19 specific financial transactions:

1. Delinquent participant contributions and loan repayments to pension plans
2. Delinquent participant contributions to insured welfare plans
3. Delinquent participant contributions to welfare plan trusts
4. Fair market interest rate loans with parties in interest
5. Below-market interest rate loans with parties in interest
6. Below-market interest rate loans with non-parties in interest
7. Below-market interest rate loans due to delay in perfecting security interest
8. Participant loans failing to comply with plan provisions for amount, duration, or level of amortization
9. Defaulted participant loans Purchase of assets from parties in interest
10. Sale of assets by plans to parties in interest. Sale and leaseback of property to sponsoring employer
11. Purchase of assets from non-parties in interest at more than market value
12. Sale of assets to non-parties in interest at below market value
13. Holding of an illiquid asset previously purchased by plan
14. Benefit payments based on improper valuation of plan assets
15. Payment of duplicate, excessive, or unnecessary compensation
16. Improper payment of expenses by plan
17. Payment of dual compensation to plan fiduciaries

Anyone who may be liable for fiduciary violations under ERISA, including employee benefit plan sponsors, officials, and other parties in interest, may take advantage of the VFCP. Applicants do not have to consult or negotiate with the PWBA to use the program. To qualify for relief under the VFCP, a plan fiduciary must take the following four steps:

1. Identify any violations and determine whether they fall within the transactions listed;
2. Follow the process for correcting specific violations (e.g., improper loans, incorrect valuation of plan assets);
3. Calculate and restore any losses and profits with interest and distribute any supplemental benefits; and
4. File an application with the appropriate PWBA regional office that includes documentation providing evidence of corrected financial transactions.

Fiduciaries who comply fully with all terms and procedures of the VFCP will receive a no-action letter from the ESBA indicating that there will be no further enforcement action in connection with the transaction. The agency does, however, reserve the right to conduct an investigation to determine truthfulness, completeness, and full correction. In addition, full correction under the

VFCP will not give a fiduciary relief from actions by other government agencies, including the IRS.

Acceptable corrections. The VFCP provides special rules for correcting the transactions. As a general rule, applicants must do the following:

- Conduct valuations of plan assets using generally recognized markets for the assets or obtain written appraisal reports from qualified professionals that are based on generally accepted appraisal standards
- Restore to the plan the principal amount involved, plus the greater of (1) lost earnings starting on the date of the loss and extending to the recovery date or (2) profits resulting from the use of the principal amount for the same period
- Pay the expenses associated with correcting the transactions, such as appraisal costs or cost of recalculating participant account balances
- Make supplemental distributions to former employees, beneficiaries, or alternate payees when appropriate and provide proof of the payments

Applicants must restore the plan, participants, and beneficiaries to the condition they would have been in had the fiduciary breach not occurred. Plans must then file amended returns to reflect the corrected transactions or valuations.

Under the VFCP, applicants must also provide proof of payments to participants and beneficiaries or *segregate* affected assets in cases where a plan is unable to locate a missing participant or beneficiary. However, payment of a correction amount may be made directly to the plan where distributions to separated plan participants would be less than $20 and the cost of correction exceeds the distributions owed.

Excise tax waiver. The tax law generally imposes a 15 percent excise tax on prohibited transactions. If a timely correction is not made, the tax jumps to 100 percent of the amount involved in the prohibited transaction. [I.R.C. §4975] However, the tax law permits the exemption of certain classes of transactions from the excise tax.

To encourage the use of the VFCP, the DOL has finalized an excise tax exemption for the following six specific transactions covered by the program:

1. Failure to timely remit participant contributions to plans;
2. Loans made at fair market interest rate by plans with parties in interest;
3. Purchases or sales of assets between plans and parties in interest at fair market value;
4. Sales of real property to plans by employers at fair market value and leaseback of the property at fair value;
5. Prohibited transaction violations involved in the purchase of an asset by a plan when the asset has been determined to be illiquid, and/or the subsequent sale of the illiquid asset by the plan; and

6. Use of plan assets to pay a service provider for services that are characterized as "settlor expenses," provided such payments were not expressly prohibited in the plan documents.

To qualify for the exemption, applicants must repay delinquent contributions to plans no more than 180 days from the date the money was received by the employer or would be payable to participants in cash. Except in the case of delinquent contributions, the exemption applies only if no more than 10 percent of the fair market value of total plan assets was involved in the prohibited transaction. A transaction will not be covered by the exemption if it is part of an arrangement or understanding that benefits a related party or if an application for correction of a similar transaction was submitted under the VFCP within the prior three years. Notice of the transaction and the correction must be provided to interested parties.

Preemption of State Law

Q 2:170   What is preemption of state law?

Preemption of state law is a legal principle under which federal law nullifies, in whole or in part, state laws on the same or a similar subject because federal law has "occupied the field." Preemption is not to be implied automatically; rather, it requires a clear and affirmative congressional command either explicitly stated in the statute itself or implicitly contained in its structure and purpose. [Jones v. Rath Packing Co., 430 U.S. 519, 525 (1977); Shaw v. Delta Airlines, 463 U.S. 85, 95 (1983)]

Q 2:171   Does ERISA supersede and preempt state laws affecting welfare benefit plans?

Generally, yes. Section 514(a) of ERISA broadly preempts virtually all state laws that "relate to" employee welfare benefit plans subject to ERISA. For this purpose, state laws include state regulations, administrative interpretations, court decisions, and other state actions. "State" includes a state, any political subdivision thereof, or any agency or instrumentality of either, that purports to regulate, directly or indirectly, the terms and conditions of employee benefit plans covered by Title I of ERISA. [ERISA §§514(c)(1), 514(c)(2); 29 U.S.C §§1144(c)(1), 1144(c)(2)]

The Supreme Court has held that a state law "relates to" an ERISA plan if it has a connection with or refers to such a plan. [Shaw v. Delta Airlines, 463 U.S. 85, 95 (1983)] (For a discussion of whether a state law "relates to" an ERISA plan, see Qs 2:170, 2:172–2:175.)

Note. ERISA does not preempt other federal laws from applying to ERISA-covered plans.

Q 2:172 When does a state law involve but not "relate to" an ERISA plan and therefore avoid preemption?

This is a heavily litigated issue, and it is difficult to find a consistent pattern in the decided cases. Generally, a state law is considered not to "relate to" an ERISA plan when its impact on the plan is tenuous, remote, and peripheral. Among the factors the courts have looked at are whether the state law:

1. Involves an area traditionally left to state regulation (such as domestic relations law or malpractice);
2. Involves an area comprehensively regulated by ERISA (such as disclosure to employees or claims procedures); and
3. Directly or indirectly affects the terms and conditions of the ERISA plan.

The U.S. Supreme Court initially took a broad interpretation of the scope of ERISA preemption. The Court seems to have retrenched somewhat, and is now more reluctant to find that state laws not directly aimed at ERISA plans are preempted, particularly where the state law involves an area of traditional state regulation. [*See* California Div. of Labor Stds. Enforcement v. Dillingham Constr., 519 U.S. 316 (1997); De Buono v. NYSA-ILA Med. & Clinical Servs. Fund, 520 U.S. 806 (1997); Boggs v. Boggs, 520 U.S. 833 (1997)]

However, in its most recent decision on this issue, the Court held that ERISA preempted a state law providing that designation of a spouse as beneficiary of certain assets, including life insurance and employee benefits, is automatically revoked on divorce. According to the Court, ERISA preempts any state laws that "have a connection with or reference to" an ERISA plan. The Court concluded that the state law conflicted with ERISA because it interfered with nationally uniform plan administration. [Egelhoff v. Egelhoff, 121 S. Ct. 1322 (2001)] (See also Q 2:173.)

Q 2:173 Do state laws imposing charges or taxes on hospital bills "relate to" ERISA plans?

In an ERISA preemption decision of major importance, the Supreme Court resolved a split between two federal courts of appeal and unanimously ruled that general state laws imposing charges or taxes on hospital and other medical service providers do not "relate to" ERISA plans, even though such charges and taxes may have a substantial indirect economic effect on the costs of ERISA plans. [New York State Conference of Blue Cross & Blue Shield Plans v. Travelers Ins. Co., 19 Employee Benefits Cas. (BNA) 1137 (S. Ct. 1995)] The case involved a New York law imposing hospital surcharges that were passed on to commercial insurers, HMOs, and self-insured plans. Blue Cross and Blue Shield was exempt from the surcharges. The law was intended to encourage coverage with the "Blues," which were considered to have greater risks because of their open enrollment practices.

Looking to the legislative history of ERISA, the Court concluded that preemption was intended to permit uniform nationwide administration and uniform interstate benefit programs. However, the New York hospital surcharge law was not aimed at uniformity, and the Court noted that differences in cost are common even without any state action. The Court was careful to state that it was not saying that all state laws with an indirect economic effect on ERISA plans are valid. The opinion indicates that such a law might impose such acute and onerous burdens on ERISA plans that ERISA preemption would apply. Following the Supreme Court's decision, a number of federal appellate court decisions have upheld state taxes or charges affecting ERISA plans. The Second Circuit Court of Appeals upheld a surcharge imposed on health insurers other than Blue Cross/Blue Shield, because the surcharge was considered to have too tenuous and remote a relationship to ERISA plans. [New York State Health Maintenance Org. Conference v. Curiale, 64 F.3d 794 (2d Cir. 1995)] In another case, the Second Circuit held not to be preempted a surcharge on medical bills designed to subsidize medical care for the poor. [New England Health Care Union Dist. 1199 v. Mt. Sinai Hosp., 65 F.3d 1024 (2d Cir. 1995)] Also, the Eighth Circuit Court of Appeals held that a Minnesota law imposing a 2 percent gross receipts tax on hospitals and health care providers was not preempted by ERISA, even though it indirectly increased ERISA health plan costs. [Boyle v. Anderson, 68 F.3d 1093 (8th Cir. 1995)] The Second Circuit Court of Appeals, on remand from the Supreme Court, affirmed its earlier finding that a hospital tax imposed directly on hospital services provided by an ERISA plan was preempted by ERISA because the tax had a direct economic impact on the ERISA plan. [NYSA-ILA Med. & Clinical Servs. Fund v. Axelrod, 19 Employee Benefits Cas. (BNA) 2361 (2d Cir. 1996)] However, the U.S. Supreme Court reversed on the ground that the New York law was a law of general application and involved an area of traditional state regulation, health and safety. The Court rejected the idea of drawing a clear distinction between the direct or indirect effect of state law on ERISA plans. [De Buono v. NYSA-ILA Med. & Clinical Servs. Fund, 520 U.S. 806 (1997)]

Q 2:174   Does ERISA preempt state labor laws affecting employee welfare benefit plans?

The answer depends on how the state labor law is structured.

The Supreme Court affirmed an appeals court ruling that held that ERISA preempted a state "prevailing wage" law (that mandated a certain level of contributions to employee welfare benefit plans for employers engaged in public works project). [Local Union 598 Plumbers & Pipefitters Indus. Journeymen & Apprentices Training Fund v. J. A. Jones Constr. Co., 846 F.2d 1213 (9th Cir. 1988), *aff'd without opinion*, 498 U.S. 881 (1988)] In another context, a federal appellate court held that ERISA preempts a state wage payment law as applied to severance pay benefits. [General Elec. Co. v. NYS Dep't of Labor, 891 F.2d 25 (2d Cir. 1989)] ERISA has also been held to preempt the application of New York's age discrimination law to an ERISA severance plan [Barbagallo v. General Motors Corp., 818 F. Supp. 573 (S.D.N.Y. 1993)] and the application of an Indiana civil rights law to an ERISA plan in an AIDS case. [Westhoven v. Lincoln Foodservice Prods. Inc., 616 N.E. 2d 778 (Ind. Ct. App. 1993)]

A Puerto Rican law mandating vacation leave was held to be preempted by ERISA even though it was a law of general application that affected employers whether or not they had an ERISA plan. The law imposed different requirements from those benefits provided by an ERISA plan and thus had a substantial impact on the ERISA plan. [Rosario-Cordero v. Crowley Towing & Transp. Co., 46 F.3d 120 (1st Cir. 1995)]

The U.S. Supreme Court has held that ERISA did not preempt a state prevailing wage law where the state law did not dictate the choices that were available to employers to comply with the state law and thus did not necessarily affect the operation of ERISA plans. [California Div. of Labor Stds. Enforcement v. Dillingham Constr., 519 U.S. 316 (1997)]

Q 2:175 What are the exceptions to ERISA's preemption of state laws purporting to regulate employee benefit plans?

There are a number of exceptions to ERISA's preemption provisions:

Saving clause. ERISA contains a "saving clause" that keeps certain state laws free from preemption (see Q 2:176). Generally, whether attempted state regulation of the content of an employee benefit plan is preempted under the saving clause depends on the type of plan at issue (that is, insured or self-insured).

Medicaid laws. ERISA also does not preempt state laws that bar any employee welfare benefit plan provisions with the effect of limiting or excluding coverage or payment for health care, because an individual is provided, or eligible for, Medicaid benefits or services. The preemption exception applies to the extent that the law is necessary for the state to be eligible to receive Medicaid reimbursement. [ERISA §514(b)(8); 29 U.S.C. §1144(b)(8)]

Hawaii Prepaid Health Care Act. ERISA does not preempt the Hawaii Prepaid Health Care Act as its substantive provisions existed on September 2, 1974. [ERISA §514(b)(5); 29 U.S.C. §1144(b)(5)] The 2010 Health Reform Act [Patient Protection and Affordable Care Act, Pub. L. No. 111-148 (Mar. 23, 2010), as amended by the Health Care and Education Affordability Reconciliation Act, Pub. L. No. 111-152 (Mar. 30, 2010)] specifically provides that the law does not modify or limit the application of the exemption for Hawaii's Prepaid Health Care Act. [PPACA § 1560(b)]

State criminal laws. ERISA does not preempt the general criminal laws of a state. [ERISA §514(b)(4); 29 U.S.C. §1144(b)(4)] However, a criminal law that is limited in application to employee welfare benefit plans (e.g., a state law providing that employee welfare benefit plan fiduciaries are criminally liable for breaches of fiduciary duty) is apparently preempted.

Workers' compensation laws. ERISA does not preempt plans maintained solely to comply with state workers' compensation laws. However, because this issue frequently arises in the context of a multi-benefit plan that provides both workers' compensation benefits and group medical benefits, this issue and the relevant cases are discussed in detail in chapter 3.

Q 2:176   What state laws are saved from preemption under ERISA's saving clause?

ERISA generally does not preempt state laws regulating insurance, banking, or securities—that is, they are saved from preemption. [ERISA §514(b)(2)(A); 29 U.S.C. §1144(2)(A)]

The most significant exemption for welfare benefit plan is the insurance law exemption, and the precise scope of this exemption has been a matter of broad debate and much litigation. The U.S. Supreme Court has held that a state insurance law falls within the scope of this exemption if the law regulates the "business of insurance." For this purpose, a state law is considered to regulate the business of insurance if the practice that it regulates satisfies a three-part test:

1. The practice has the effect of transferring or spreading a policyholder's risk;

2. The practice is an integral part of the policy relationship between the insurer and the insured; and

3. The practice is limited to entities within the insurance industry.

[Metropolitan Life Ins. Co. v. Massachusetts, 471 U.S. 724, 743 (1985), *citing* Union Labor Life Ins. Co. v. Pireno, 458 U.S. 119, 129 (1982)]

Practice Pointer. As a general rule, a state law (including a state law denominated as an "insurance law") that is phrased as "an employer shall do such and such" is very likely to be preempted by ERISA from applying to an ERISA-covered employee benefit plan. Such a law would not fall within the scope of ERISA's saving clause, because the term *employer* is not limited to entities within the insurance industry.

Note, however, that even if a law is saved from preemption under ERISA's saving clause, ERISA's deemer clause, discussed in Q 2:177, provides an exception to this exception.

Q 2:177   What is ERISA's "deemer clause"?

Section 514 of ERISA also provides that a state may not deem an employee benefit plan (other than one established primarily for the purpose of providing death benefits), nor any trust established under such a plan, to be an insurance company or other insurer, bank, trust company, or investment company or to be engaged in the business of insurance or banking for purposes of any law of any state purporting to regulate insurance companies, insurance contracts, banks, trust companies, or investment companies. [ERISA §514(b)(2)(B); 29 U.S.C. §1144(b)(2)(B)] For example, a state may not treat a self-insured medical plan as an "insurance company" and attempt to regulate it as such. [FMC Corp. v. Holliday, 498 U.S. 52 (1990)] Accordingly, a self-insured plan is exempt from state insurance laws to the extent that they "relate to" the plan.

Claims practices. ERISA also preempts state laws that regulate insurance companies providing claims and other administrative services to self-insured plans. Because entities other than insurance companies can process the claims and perform other administrative services, and there is no transferring or spreading of risk between the plan and the insurance company in such instances, the exception to ERISA preemption for laws regulating insurance has been held inapplicable. [Insurance Bd. Under Social Ins. Plan of Bethlehem Steel Corp. v. Muir, 819 F.2d 408 (3d Cir. 1987)] (See also Q 2:179.)

Q 2:178   If an ERISA plan is fully insured, can state law regulate the content of the policy purchased to provide benefits under the plan?

In general, yes. State insurance law is not preempted with respect to fully insured welfare benefit plans, because, although a state may not regulate the plan or the trust, it can regulate the content of the insurance policy. However, the applicable state law must regulate a practice that is the "business of insurance." Thus, for example, the Supreme Court upheld the application of a state-mandated benefit law to a policy under a fully insured medical plan. [Metropolitan Life Ins. Co. v. Massachusetts, 471 U.S. 724 (1985)] Similarly, the Court of Appeals for the Sixth Circuit held that a state law requiring a successor insurer under a medical plan to provide a substantially similar policy to the previous one was not preempted by ERISA. [International Resources, Inc. v. New York Life Ins. Co., 950 F.2d 294 (6th Cir. 1991)] In contrast, the Court of Appeals for the Tenth Circuit refused to uphold the application of a state insurance law to an ERISA life insurance plan when the law, which invalidated a life insurance beneficiary designation of a spouse who divorced the insured before his or her death, also applied to retirement and compensation arrangements (and hence was not limited to the policyholder/insured relationship) and did not alter or spread policyholder risk. [Metropolitan Life Ins. Co. v. Hanslip, 939 F.2d 904 (10th Cir. 1991)] Thus, it is important to be aware that not all state laws that are physically located within the state's insurance code will automatically be treated as "insurance" laws for ERISA preemption purposes. Each must be examined under the Supreme Court's three-prong test for the "business of insurance" (see Q 2:176).

A state law requiring life insurance companies to pay interest on death proceeds from the date of death was held not to be preempted as applied to life insurance under an ERISA plan on the ground that it was a law regulating insurance and thus was not preempted by virtue of the saving clause. [Franklin H. Williams Ins. Trust v. Travelers Ins. Co., 50 F.3d 144 (2d Cir. 1995)] To the contrary, a federal district court found that a state law mandating payment of interest on delayed payment of insurance proceeds was preempted as it applied to an ERISA insurance plan. However, the court then went on to find that, under federal common law, payment of interest was appropriate. [Hizer v. General Motors Corp., Allison Gas Turbine Div., 888 F. Supp. 1453 (S.D. Ind. 1995)]

Mandated providers. There is also a variety of state laws that purport to mandate the types of remedial care providers that the plan must cover (for example, chiropractors, acupuncturists, and certified nurse midwives). A number of courts have found that ERISA preempts these laws regardless of whether the plan is insured, because the law does not relate to the business of insurance. [Taylor v. Blue Cross/Blue Shield of NY, 684 F. Supp. 1352 (E.D. La. 1988)] Another federal district court has held that state laws setting time limits for adjudicating claims, requiring that noncontracting health care providers be paid at the same rate as contracting health care providers, and containing any-willing-provider requirements for dental and drug plans, were preempted by ERISA. While the laws were in the state's insurance code, they were not limited to insurance companies, but also applied to self-funded ERISA plans and other uninsured plans. The court found that the state laws also failed the three-prong test for the "business of insurance."[Texas Pharmacy Ass'n v. Prudential Ins. Co., 105 F.3d 1035 (5th Cir. 1997); CIGNA Health Plan of La., 82 F.3d 642 (5th Cir. 1996); Blue Cross & Blue Shield of Ala. v. Nielsen, 20 Employee Benefits Cas. (BNA) 1019 (N.D. Ala. 1996)]

Q 2:179   Does ERISA preempt state administration of claims laws?

The weight of court decisions supports the position that ERISA's provisions for administration of claims provide an exclusive remedy and that state laws regulating claims practices of insurers are thus preempted when the insurance is provided pursuant to an ERISA employee welfare benefit plan. [Pilot Life Ins. Co. v. Dedeaux, 481 U.S. 41 (1987); In re Life Ins. Co. of North Am., 857 F.2d 1190 (8th Cir. 1988); Ramirez v. Inter-Continental Hotels, 890 F.2d 760 (5th Cir. 1989)] Because the U.S. Supreme Court construed the remedies provision contained in Section 502 rather than the preemption provision contained in Section 514 of ERISA, it found a separate implied preemption of state law in Section 502. As a result, no "saving clause" or "deemer clause" analysis (see Qs 2:176–2:177) applies in this instance.

Medical malpractice claims. Medical malpractice claims against health care providers associated with ERISA plans involve additional interpretive issues concerning whether the claim truly relates to the ERISA plan or only to the practice of medicine.

Q 2:180   Does ERISA preempt state laws that attempt to require employer contributions to welfare benefit plans?

Yes. [Stone & Webster Eng'g Corp. v. Ilsley, 690 F.2d 323 (2d Cir. 1982), *aff'd on appeal without opinion, sub nom.* Arcudi v. Stone & Webster Eng'g Corp., 463 U.S. 1220 (1983)]

Q 2:181   Does ERISA preempt state laws that regulate insurance companies and third-party administrators providing claims and other administrative services to self-insured plans?

Yes. Since entities other than insurance companies can process the claims and perform other administrative services, and there is no transferring or spreading of insurance risk between the plan and the insurance company in such instances, the exception to ERISA preemption for laws regulating insurance has been held inapplicable. [Insurance Bd. Under Social Ins. Plan of Bethlehem Steel Corp. v. Muir, 819 F.2d 408 (3d Cir. 1987)]

ERISA has also been held to preempt a state statute that attempted to regulate and tax third-party administrators of ERISA plans. The appellate court found that the state law's reporting requirements imposed significant burdens on the ERISA plans and held that the statute was not an insurance law saved from preemption, because it did not involve the spreading of insurance risk. [NGS American Inc. v. Barnes, 998 F.2d 296 (5th Cir. 1993)]

Q 2:182 Does ERISA preempt state laws taxing employee welfare benefit plans?

Yes, ERISA does preempt these laws. [ERISA §514(b)(5)(B)(i); 29 U.S.C. §1144(b)(5)(B)(i); National Carriers Conference Comm. v. Heffernan, 454 F. Supp. 914 (D. Conn. 1978)] However, a state value-added tax imposed on an employer was held not to be preempted even though ERISA plan contributions became a part of the compensation component of the value-added tax base. The tax was found to have only a tenuous, remote, or peripheral effect on ERISA plans. The tax is imposed on the employer, not the plan, and thus does not affect the relationship between the plan and the employer and employees. [Thiokol Corp. v. Roberts, 19 Employee Benefits Cas. (BNA) 2871 (6th Cir. 1996)]

Q 2:183 Does ERISA preempt state laws taxing insurance policy premiums paid with respect to employee welfare benefit plans?

No, it does not, because the tax is imposed on the insurance company and not on the plan, even though the insurer generally passes on the tax cost to the plan. In addition, one federal appeals court has held that ERISA does not bar a California premium tax on a minimum premium plan insurer where the state calculates the tax using not only the premiums paid to the insurer, but also the benefits paid by the employer, as the base for the tax. [General Motors Corp. v. California State Bd. of Equalization, 815 F.2d 1305 (9th Cir. 1987), *cert. denied*, 485 U.S. 941 (1988)] California has not extended its tax position to tax benefits paid by an employer under self-insured plans that purchase stop-loss insurance coverage.

Q 2:184 May a state use its garnishment laws to attach an employee's interest in a welfare benefit plan?

Yes. The U.S. Supreme Court has overturned a state law barring garnishment of ERISA plans. The Supreme Court noted that Congress has specifically barred alienation of pension benefits but not of welfare benefits. The Court went on to hold that ERISA does not preempt a general garnishment statute. [Mackey v. Lanier Collection Agency & Serv. Inc., 486 U.S. 825 (1988)]

Q 2:185   Can states regulate the benefits provided by multiple-employer welfare arrangements?

Multiple-employer welfare arrangements (MEWAs) are multiple-employer arrangements that are not maintained or established pursuant to a collective bargaining agreement and that offer health benefit coverage. In many cases, the coverage is offered to small employers that might not be able to obtain group insurance from commercial carriers. [ERISA §3(40)(A); 29 U.S.C. §1002(40)(A)]

States can regulate the benefits provided by a MEWA to varying degrees, depending on whether the MEWA is fully insured and whether it is an "employee welfare benefit plan" covered under ERISA:

1. If a MEWA is covered by ERISA (see Q 2:5) and is fully insured, state law regulating insurance applies only to the extent of standards regulating reserves and contributions and their enforcement; [ERISA §514(b)(6); 29 U.S.C. §1144(b)(6)]

2. If the MEWA is covered by ERISA (see Q 2:5) but is not fully insured, state law regulating insurance applies to the extent that the law is not inconsistent with ERISA; [ERISA §514(b)(6); 29 U.S.C. §1144(b)(6)]

3. If the MEWA is not subject to ERISA (that is, it is not sponsored by one or more employers or employee organizations), it is entirely subject to state law and regulation. This is the case, for example, if an insurance company sponsors the MEWA; [DOL Adv. Op. Ltrs. 84-47A (Dec. 5, 1984), 84-43A (Nov. 6, 1984), 84-41A (Oct. 26, 1984), 92-21A (Oct. 19, 1992)] or

4. If the MEWA is not itself an employee welfare benefit plan covered under ERISA, each employer participating in the MEWA is considered to have its own ERISA plan. [ERISA §514(b)(6); 29 U.S.C. §1144(b)(6); DOL Adv. Ops. 90-07A (Apr. 6, 1990) and 90-10A (May 3, 1990)]

The 2010 Health Reform Act amends ERISA in authorizing the Secretary of Labor to adopt regulatory standards, or issue specific orders establishing that a person engaged in the business of providing insurance through a MEWA is subject to the state laws regulating insurance, regardless of whether state law is otherwise preempted. [ERISA § 520 as added by PPACA § 6602] Employees and agents of MEWAs are prohibited, subject to criminal penalties, from making false statements in marketing materials regarding the plan's solvency or benefits or the status of the plan regarding exemption from state regulatory authority. [ERISA § 519 as added by PPACA §6601]

In addition, the 2010 Health Reform Act directs the Secretary of Labor to require MEWAs that are not group health plans to register with the DOL before operating in a state. [ERISA § 101(g) as amended by PPACA § 6606] The Secretary of Labor is authorized to issue cease-and-desist orders to temporarily shut down MEWAs conducting fraudulent activities or posing a serious threat to the public and to seize the plan's assets if it appears that the plan is in financially hazardous condition. [ERISA § 521 as added by PPACA § 6605]

Q 2:186   If the MEWA is covered by ERISA and is not fully insured, can a state regulate the MEWA under its laws applicable to commercial insurance companies?

Yes. The DOL has held that nothing in ERISA precludes the application of the same state insurance laws that apply to any insurer to an ERISA-covered MEWA that is not fully insured. In addition, a state insurance law will be deemed consistent with ERISA even if the law requires an ERISA-covered MEWA that is not fully insured to meet more stringent standards of conduct or because the law requires that it provide more or greater protections to plan participants and beneficiaries than those required by ERISA. Such protective measures may include a state's authorization to require and enforce registration, licensing, reporting, and similar requirements necessary to establish and monitor compliance with general state insurance laws or insurance laws specifically regulating MEWAs. [DOL Adv. Op. 90-18A (July 2, 1990)]

ERISA authorizes the Secretary of Labor to exempt from state insurance regulation ERISA-covered MEWAs that are not fully insured, either individually or by class. [ERISA §514(b)(6)(B); 29 U.S.C. §1144(b)(6)(B)] In view of DOL concerns over lack of adequate regulation of such MEWAs, it appears unlikely that the DOL will exercise its authority to grant exemptions. In contrast, the 2010 Health Reform Act amends ERISA by authorizing the Secretary of Labor to adopt regulatory standards, or issue specific orders, establishing that a person engaged in the business of providing insurance through a MEWA is subject to the state laws regulating insurance, regardless of whether state law is otherwise preempted. [ERISA §520 as added by PPACA §6602]

The definition of a MEWA [ERISA §3(40)(A)] does not include a collectively bargained multiemployer plan. DOL regulations provide that in order to be a collective bargaining agreement, the agreement must be in writing, must be executed on behalf of an employer and representatives of an employee labor organization, and must be the result of good-faith, arm's-length bargaining. In addition, generally 85 percent of the plan participants must be present or former employees in one or more groups or bargaining units covered by the collective bargaining agreement. [DOL Reg. §2510.3-40]

Penalties and Enforcement

Q 2:187   What civil penalty applies to a failure to provide participants with information?

ERISA grants courts the discretion to impose a $100-per-day penalty on plan administrators who fail or refuse to comply with a request for certain information that ERISA requires the plan administrator to provide to participants and beneficiaries within 30 days after they request it. [ERISA §502(c); 29 U.S.C. §1132(c); DOL Reg. §2560.502c-1] The plan administrator is personally liable if such a penalty is imposed, and the penalty is payable to the plan participant or beneficiary who requested the information. The Court of Appeals for the First

Circuit upheld a lower court's assessment of $12,600 against an employer for its late response to a retirement plan participant's request for information concerning the plan. [Law v. Ernst & Young, 956 F. 2d 364 (1st Cir. 1992)]

DOL request for documents. If the Secretary of Labor has requested information from the plan administrator (see Q 2:165) and the plan administrator fails to furnish the information, the DOL may impose a $110-per-day penalty, capped at $1,100 per request. Further, no penalty is imposed for any failure resulting from matters reasonably beyond the control of the plan administrator. [ERISA §502(c)(6), added by TRA '97 §1503; DOL Reg. §2560.502c-6]

If a pension plan is making a qualified transfer of excess pension assets to a health benefits account, a $100-per-day penalty applies for each day the required notice to participants is late. [ERISA §§502(c)(1), 101(e)(1); 29 U.S.C. §§1132(c)(1), 1021(e)(1)]

Q 2:188   What ERISA penalty applies to failure to give the required notice of the right to COBRA continuation of group health plan coverage?

The $110-per-day penalty contained in ERISA Section 502(c) [29 U.S.C. §1132(c)] also applies to a failure or refusal to provide an initial COBRA notice and notice of COBRA rights when group health coverage is lost. Excise tax penalties may also apply. [I.R.C. §4980B] (See chapter 6 for a discussion of the COBRA excise tax.)

Q 2:189   What is the civil penalty for failing to file annual reports?

ERISA Section 502 [29 U.S.C. §1132] grants the DOL authority to impose up to a $1,100-per-day penalty on the plan administrator (see Q 2:4) for failure or refusal to file annual reports. Plans required to file under Code Section 6039D are also subject to a penalty of $25 per day, up to a maximum of $15,000, for late or incomplete filings. [I.R.C. §6652(e); DOL Reg. §2560.502c-2]

The DOL has adopted enforcement procedures for assessing civil penalties (1) against parties in interest that engage in prohibited transactions with welfare benefit plans and (2) for failure to file annual reports. [ERISA §502; 29 U.S.C §1132; DOL Reg. §§2560.502c-2, 2560.502i-1, 2570.60–2570.71, 2570.80–2570.87]

Delinquent Filer Voluntary Compliance (DFVC) Program. The DFVC Program is designed to encourage delinquent plan administrators to comply with their annual reporting obligations by assessing reduced civil penalties against those who take advantage of the program.

Eligibility for the DFVC Program is limited to plan administrators with outstanding filing obligations under Title I of ERISA who have not been notified in writing by the DOL of a failure to file.

Participation in the DFVC Program is a two-part process. First, a plan administrator must file a complete Form 5500 series annual return/report, including all schedules and attachments, for each year for which relief is requested. To complete these filings, plan administrators may use the Form 5500 for the year for which relief is sought or the most current form available. Second, the plan administrator must submit the required documentation and penalty amounts to the DFVC Program. The plan administrator is personally liable for the penalty; amounts paid under the DFVC Program cannot be paid from plan assets. Under the DFVC Program, the basic per-day penalty for delinquent filings is $10 (reduced from $50).

The maximum penalty for a single late annual report is $750 for a small plan (and $2,000 for a large plan). A small plan is generally one with fewer than 100 participants at the beginning of the plan year.

The DFVC Program includes a per-plan cap that is designed to encourage compliance by plan administrators that have failed to file annual reports for multiple years. The per-plan cap limits the penalty to $1,500 for a small plan and $4,000 for a large plan, regardless of the number of late annual reports filed for the plan at the same time. The DOL cautions that there is no per-administrator cap. If the same person is the administrator or sponsor or several plans with delinquent reports, the maximum penalty amounts apply to each plan.

Q 2:190   What are the penalties for a failure to comply with the fiduciary responsibility provisions of ERISA?

The fiduciary can be required to reimburse the plan for any losses caused by a fiduciary breach. The fiduciary may also be barred from serving as a fiduciary. Finally, if a judicial proceeding is brought by the Secretary of Labor for a breach of fiduciary responsibility, the Secretary may assess a civil penalty of 20 percent of the recovery amount. [ERISA §§409, 502(e); 29 U.S.C. §§1109, 1132(e); Interim DOL Reg. §2570.80]

Q 2:191   What is the penalty for engaging in a prohibited transaction?

The Secretary of Labor may impose a penalty of up to 5 percent of the amount involved in the prohibited transaction relating to an ERISA welfare benefit plan. If the violation is not corrected within 90 days after a final agency action order, the Secretary may assess an additional penalty of up to 100 percent of the amount involved. If the prohibited transaction is a continuing one (see Q 2:104), the penalties will be assessed for each year that the transaction continues. However, the penalties are suspended during timely hearings before an administrative law judge and appeals to the Secretary of Labor. [ERISA §502(i); 29 U.S.C. §1132(i); DOL Reg. §§2560.502i-1, 2570.1–2570.12] (A similar penalty relating to tax-qualified retirement plans is contained in Code Section 4975.)

Q 2:192   How does ERISA protect participants and beneficiaries against interference with their rights?

ERISA makes it unlawful (1) to discharge, fine, suspend, expel, discipline, or discriminate against a participant or beneficiary for exercising any right to which he or she may become entitled under an ERISA plan or (2) to take such action against a participant or beneficiary for giving information or testifying in any inquiry or proceeding relating to ERISA. [ERISA §510] ERISA also provides for certain criminal penalties (see Q 2:193).

Note that an employee need not actually be participating in an employee benefit plan in order to fall within the scope of ERISA Section 510's protection. The Court of Appeals for the Sixth Circuit held that an individual who was discharged between her date of hire (when she was given orientation) and her starting date, because of the employer's concern about high medical costs associated with her infant's illness, was an employee and that her discharge therefore violated the provisions of ERISA Section 510. [Fleming v. Ayers & Assoc., 948 F.2d 993 (6th Cir. 1991)]

In a split decision by the full Fourth Circuit Court of Appeals, the majority held that an employer's threat to cut off free health benefits voluntarily provided by the employer unless the employee dropped a lawsuit claiming entitlement to long-term disability benefits was not a violation of Section 510 of ERISA. Because the employer provided the health benefits coverage even though not required to do so by its health plan, the benefits were purely gratuitous on the part of the employer, and the employer could revoke the coverage without its being considered retaliatory for purposes of Section 510 of ERISA. [Stiltner v. Beretta USA Corp., 74 F.3d 1473 (4th Cir. 1996)]

The U.S. Supreme Court, in a unanimous decision that resolved a split among the federal appeals courts, held that Section 510 of ERISA applies not only to pension plans but also to welfare benefit plans, without regard to whether the welfare benefits are vested or the fact that the employer could amend or cancel the welfare benefit plan. [Inter-Modal Rail Employees Ass'n v. Atchison, Topeka & Santa Fe Ry. Co., 520 U.S. 510 (1997)]

A key question, of course, is what remedies are available to an employee when an employer violates ERISA Section 510. In a case on point, the Tenth Circuit Court of Appeals held that an employer violated Section 510 when it closed one of its plants in order to prevent employees from attaining eligibility for pension and health care benefits. However, the court also determined that an award of back pay was not an allowable remedy for the employer's violation because back pay did not constitute "equitable relief" allowable under ERISA. Moreover, while reinstatement of the employees would have provided equitable relief, reinstatement was not possible by the time the legal proceedings were concluded. A strongly worded dissenting opinion chastised the majority of the court for denying any appropriate remedy to the employees. According to the dissenting justice, "Through no fault of their own, the class plaintiffs find themselves devoid of the undeniably appropriate equitable remedy of reinstatement. Back pay . . . provides an appropriate equitable alternative." [Millsap v. McDonnell Douglas Corp., 368 F.3d 1246 (10th Cir. 2004)]

Q 2:193   How might ERISA violations result in criminal penalties?

It is illegal to use, to threaten to use, or to attempt to use fraud, force, or violence to restrain, coerce, or intimidate any participant or beneficiary for the purpose of interfering with or preventing the exercise of any ERISA right. Willful violators can be fined $10,000 or imprisoned for one year, or both. [ERISA §511; 29 U.S.C. §1141]

In addition, any person who is convicted of a willful violation of Part 1 of Title I of ERISA or any regulation or order issued under any such provision can be fined not more than $5,000 ($10,000 for violations by persons who are not individuals) or imprisoned for not more than one year. This applies to failure to comply with ERISA's reporting and disclosure duties, including, but not limited to:

- Failure to prepare an SPD
- Failure to provide each participant (and certain beneficiaries) with copies of the SPD and all material modifications
- Failure to prepare and file an annual report with the IRS, including all required schedules thereto
- Failure to provide an SPD to the Secretary of Labor
- Failure to make certain documents relating to the plan available for inspection by any plan participant or beneficiary
- Failure to provide participants with an SAR
- Failure to furnish a participant who makes a written request with a copy (for which a reasonable charge may be made) of the latest updated SPD, plan document, annual report, terminal report (if any), collective bargaining agreement, trust agreement, or other instruments under which the plan is established or operated

[ERISA §501; 29 U.S.C. §1131]

Q 2:194   When does ERISA permit civil suits?

ERISA contains a comprehensive civil enforcement scheme. It allows civil suits by various parties to recover plan benefits, for breach of fiduciary duties, to enjoin acts or practices that violate ERISA or the terms of the plan, and to obtain other appropriate equitable relief.

Six main categories of civil action are expressly authorized under ERISA:

1. *Employee benefit and disclosure rights.* A participant or beneficiary may bring a civil action under ERISA in order to enforce ERISA's $110-per-day penalty provision for failure to provide certain plan materials upon request or to give required COBRA notices (see Q 2:210). [ERISA §502(a)(1)(A); 29 U.S.C. §1132(a)(1)(A)]

2. *Breach of fiduciary duty.* A participant, beneficiary, fiduciary, or the Secretary of Labor may bring a civil action for "appropriate relief" under Section 409 of ERISA. Under Section 409, any person who is a fiduciary under ERISA who breaches his or her duties under the plan is personally liable to make good to the plan any losses resulting from the breach and to restore any profits the fiduciary made through use of the plan's assets. Section 409 also permits a court to take "such other equitable or remedial relief as the court may deem appropriate." [ERISA §§502(a)(2), 409; 29 U.S.C. §§1132(a)(2), 1109]

3. *Injunctive or equitable relief.* A participant, beneficiary, or fiduciary may bring a civil action under ERISA in order to enjoin any action or practice that violates Title I of ERISA or the terms of the plan, obtain "other appropriate equitable relief," redress such violations, or enforce Title I of ERISA or the terms of the plan. [ERISA §502(a)(3); 29 U.S.C. §1132(a)(3)]

4. *Annual benefit statements.* A participant, beneficiary, or the Secretary of Labor may bring a civil action under ERISA to enforce the annual benefit statement provisions applicable to pension plans. [ERISA §502(a)(4); 29 U.S.C. §1132(a)(4)]

5. *Enforcement by Secretary of Labor.* The Secretary of Labor may also bring a civil action under ERISA in order to enjoin any act or practice violating Title I of ERISA, obtain "other appropriate equitable relief," redress such violations, or enforce the provisions of Title I of ERISA. [ERISA §502(a)(5); 29 U.S.C. §1132(a)(5)]

6. *Collection of monetary penalties.* The Secretary of Labor may bring a civil action under ERISA to collect the following penalties:

   a. The civil penalty of up to $1,100 per day (subject to increase for inflation) applicable to a plan administrator's failure or refusal to file an annual report (that is, the Form 5500 series annual report required to be filed with the DOL) or failure to provide material information in an annual report (which, because it is deficient, is treated as if it had not been filed) (see Q 2:189);

   b. The civil penalty against parties in interest engaging in a prohibited transaction (see Q 2:191);

   c. Civil penalties for violations by fiduciaries for prohibited transactions with ERISA plans (see Q 2:191); or

   d. The civil penalty for MEWA reporting violations (see chapter 5).

[ERISA §§502(a)(6), 502(c); 29 U.S.C. §§1132(a)(6), 1132(c)]

Q 2:195   May an employee benefit plan be sued as a separate entity?

Yes. However, any monetary judgment under Title I of ERISA against an employee benefit plan will be enforceable only against the plan as an entity and not against any other person unless his or her liability is established in an individual capacity under Title I of ERISA. [ERISA §502(d); 29 U.S.C. §1132(d)]

Q 2:196   Can an action under ERISA be brought in state court?

Generally not. ERISA provides that the U.S. district courts shall have exclusive jurisdiction of ERISA Title I actions brought by a participant, beneficiary, fiduciary, or the Secretary of Labor. Actions may be brought in a U.S. district court without regard to the amount in controversy or to the citizenship of the parties.

An exception is made for civil actions brought by a participant or beneficiary to recover benefits due him or her under the plan, to enforce his or her rights under the plan, or to clarify his or her rights to future benefits under the plan; actions can be brought either in a state court or a U.S. district court. [ERISA §502(e); 29 U.S.C. §1132(e)] However, an action to recover benefits brought in state court may be removed to federal court by the defendants (if done in a timely fashion). [Metropolitan Life Ins. Co. v. Taylor, 481 U.S. 58 (1987)]

Q 2:197   Can the exclusive jurisdiction of U.S. district courts under ERISA be defeated by filing, in a state court action, a complaint that asserts only state-law causes of action?

Ordinarily, plaintiffs can play these types of games to stay in state court by taking advantage of what is known as the "well-pleaded complaint" rule. However, ERISA has been interpreted to provide an exception to the general rule.

The general rule is that a cause of action arises under federal law for purposes of having federal question jurisdiction only when the plaintiff's well-pleaded complaint raises federal law issues. Since preemption of a state law by a federal law is ordinarily a defense raised by the defendant, the issue of federal preemption thus would not appear on the face of a well-pleaded complaint and would not authorize removal of the case to a federal court.

However, an exception to the well-pleaded complaint rule occurs when Congress has so completely preempted a particular area that all state-law causes of action are displaced and a complaint raising a claim in such area is necessarily federal in character. In Metropolitan Life Ins. Co. v. Taylor [481 U.S. 58 (1987)], the U.S. Supreme Court held that a suit that purports to raise only state-law claims but falls within the scope of Section 502(a) of ERISA is necessarily federal in character by virtue of the clearly manifested intent of Congress. Accordingly, such a suit arises under the laws of the United States and is removable to federal court by the defendants.

Q 2:198   What additional protection does ERISA provide to individuals seeking redress under the statute?

To deter violations of ERISA, and to notify the relevant enforcement agencies of suits in which they might wish to intervene, a copy of the complaint in any civil or criminal action under ERISA (except an action brought by one or more participants solely to recover benefits due to them under the terms of the plan) must be filed by certified mail with both the Secretary of Labor and the Secretary of the Treasury. Both secretaries may, at their discretion, intervene in any action (except that the Secretary of the Treasury may not intervene in an action under Part 4 of Title I relating to fiduciary duties). [ERISA §502(h); 29 U.S.C. §1132(h)]

Q 2:199   What other enforcement authority does ERISA provide to the Secretary of Labor?

ERISA grants the Secretary of Labor the express authority to make investigations, require production of books and records, and enter such places and question such individuals as the Secretary deems necessary to determine if an ERISA violation exists. This assumes that the Secretary has reasonable cause to believe a violation exists or the entry is pursuant to an agreement with the plan. The Secretary is also expressly authorized to share information with other governmental agencies. [ERISA §§504, 506; 29 U.S.C. §§1143, 1136]

The Secretary also has additional enforcement authority with respect to delinquent pension plan contributions. [ERISA §502(b); 29 U.S.C. §1132(b)] No parallel provisions are provided for contributions to welfare benefit plans.

Q 2:200   What is the effect of mandatory arbitration of claims on a participant's ability to bring an ERISA action?

When a participant signs an agreement containing an arbitration clause, the agreement appears to be enforceable under ERISA. The Court of Appeals for the Second Circuit held that Congress did not intend to preclude waiver of a judicial forum for claims for an ERISA violation and that arbitration is not inconsistent with ERISA's underlying purposes. The court noted that Congress's provision of exclusive federal jurisdiction of claims brought to enforce ERISA's substantive provisions concerns only which judicial forum is available, not whether an arbitral forum is available.

The court noted that no issue of possible inadequate union representation was present in the case under review, since no collective bargaining agreement existed. The employee signed the agreement containing the arbitration clause and thus could not complain that his rights were bargained away by a third party. Accordingly, statutory claims arising under ERISA may be the subject of compulsory arbitration. [Bird v. Shearson Lehman/American Express Inc., 926 F.2d 116 (2d Cir. 1991)] The dissent in that case protested that arbitration did not comport with the underlying purposes of ERISA, because there is no general requirement that arbitrators of commercial disputes explain the reasons for their decisions or that they follow legal precedent. The dissent pointed to testimony before Congress that arbitrators in the securities industry frequently ignored legal precedent in favor of "rough justice."

An arbitration agreement contained in an individual employment agreement was also upheld under ERISA. [Fox v. Merrill Lynch & Co., 453 F. Supp. 561 (S.D.N.Y. 1978)] Arbitration provisions in contracts with service providers to ERISA plans have also been upheld. [Fabian Fin. Servs. v. Kurt H Volk Inc. Profit-Sharing Plan, 768 F. Supp. 728 (C.D. Cal. 1991)]

When the extent of an employer's obligation or the terms of a benefits plan are incorporated into a collective bargaining agreement, different concerns come into play, and conflicts may be required to be submitted to compulsory arbitration under the collective bargaining agreement. Much of the case law in this area involves disputes over the extent of the issues falling within the scope of the contractual grievance or arbitration procedures. If the claim is subject to binding arbitration, the effect on the claimant's ERISA claim appeal may be dispositive. A U.S. district court opinion held that a denial of medical and long-term disability coverage by the board of trustees of a Taft-Hartley welfare benefit fund is final and binding and must be given *res judicata* effect in the claimant's ERISA claim appeal action. This meant that the court could not undertake any review of the arbitrator's decision. [Kravik v. Automotive Machinists Health & Welfare Fund, 13 Employee Benefits Cas. (BNA) 2269 (E.D. Mont. 1991)]

The Court of Appeals for the Ninth Circuit held that the doctrine of *res judicata* does not bar claims under ERISA Section 510 by employees who allege that they were laid off to prevent them from attaining the requisite service to qualify for pension benefits. The court held that an ERISA Section 510 claim concerns interference with attainment of rights under an ERISA benefit plan, not a collective bargaining agreement. The arbitrator therefore would have nothing to decide. In any event, participants are not required to exhaust grievance or arbitration remedies prior to bringing an action under Section 510 of ERISA. The court concluded that the participants were entitled to a *de novo* review of their ERISA Section 510 claims. [Amaro v. Continental Can Co., 724 F.2d 747 (9th Cir. 1984)]

Remedies for Breach of Fiduciary Duties

Q 2:201   What remedies are available against ERISA fiduciaries who breach their fiduciary duties?

A plan fiduciary who breaches any of the responsibilities, obligations, or duties imposed on fiduciaries by ERISA is personally liable to make good to the plan any losses resulting from the breach and to restore to the plan any profits that have been made by the fiduciary through his or her use of the plan assets.

A fiduciary is also subject to such other equitable or remedial relief as the court hearing the action may deem appropriate, including removal of the fiduciary. [ERISA §409(a); 29 U.S.C. §1109(a)]

Q 2:202   May an ERISA plan sue, in its own name, a fiduciary of the plan for breach of fiduciary duties?

No. An action for breach of fiduciary duty may be brought by the Secretary of Labor, or by a participant, beneficiary, or other plan fiduciary. However, the plan itself is not included among those entitled to sue to enforce ERISA Section

409. [ERISA §502(a)(2); 29 U.S.C. §1132(a)(2); Pressroom Unions–Printers League Income Sec. Fund v. Continental Assurance Co., 700 F.2d 889 (2d Cir. 1983)]

Q 2:203 May a plan participant, beneficiary, or fiduciary sue a breaching fiduciary of the plan under ERISA Section 409 and recover damages in his or her individual capacity?

The Supreme Court resolved a split among the lower federal courts on this issue by its decision in *Varity Corp. v. Howe.* [116 S. Ct. 1065 (1996)] In that case, the Court held that a former employee who had lost welfare plan coverage could bring an action on his own behalf for breach of fiduciary duty under Section 502(a)(3) of ERISA. [29 U.S.C. §1132(a)(3)] Under that provision, only equitable relief was available, and the Court held that compensatory damages could not be awarded. However, equitable relief in the form of restitution for past-due benefits and an injunction to reinstate the individual's coverage under the employer's plan was available.

Q 2:204 What kind of other equitable or remedial relief can a court require for a breach of fiduciary duty?

The statutory provision authorizing such other equitable or remedial relief "as the court may deem appropriate" gives the court very wide discretion in fashioning a remedy to address the particular fiduciary breach in the case before it. In addition to removal of the fiduciary, which is specifically authorized in ERISA Section 409 [29 U.S.C. §1109], the court has available the traditional equitable remedies of injunction and specific performance.

The U.S. Court of Appeals for the Second Circuit upheld a lower court order permanently barring certain investment advisors from acting as fiduciaries or providing services to ERISA plans. The court noted that such a broad-based injunctive remedy may be appropriate when fiduciaries engage in egregious self-dealing. [Beck v. Levering, 947 F.2d 639 (2d Cir. 1991)]

Q 2:205 Is a fiduciary of an ERISA plan who commits a fiduciary breach subject to extra contractual compensatory or punitive damages under ERISA?

No. In an action brought on behalf of the plan under ERISA Sections 409(a) and 502(a), the U.S. Supreme Court held that ERISA does not provide for or permit extra contractual compensatory or punitive damages. [Massachusetts Mut. Life Ins. Co. v. Russell, 473 U.S. 134 (1985)]

Note. The U.S. Supreme Court decision in *Massachusetts Mutual* is limited to an action brought under ERISA Sections 409(a) and 502(a)(2). Thus, the issue of whether extra contractual compensatory or punitive damages are allowable in actions brought under other provisions of ERISA is not yet finally settled, although most court decisions on this issue hold that extra contractual or punitive damages are not available (see Q 2:212).

Q 2:206 Can a plaintiff in an action for breach of fiduciary duty under ERISA Section 409(a) demand a jury trial?

It appears not. The remedies provided by ERISA Section 409(a) appear to be essentially equitable in nature, so that there is no constitutional entitlement to a trial by jury.

Q 2:207 What is the statute of limitations for an action for breach of fiduciary duty under ERISA?

An action against a fiduciary for breach of fiduciary duty must be commenced by the earlier of:

1. Six years after (a) the date of the last action that constituted a part of the breach or violation or (b) in the case of an omission, the latest date on which the fiduciary could have cured the breach or violation or

2. Three years after the earliest date on which the plaintiff had actual knowledge of the breach or violation.

Exception. In the case of fraud or concealment, the action may be commenced within six years after the date of discovery of such breach or violation. [ERISA §413; 29 U.S.C. §1113]

In a decision by the U.S. Court of Appeals for the Seventh Circuit, the court held that the reference in the statute to actual knowledge was to be strictly construed, so that actual knowledge did not include constructive knowledge—that is, notice of facts which, in the exercise of reasonable diligence, would lead to actual knowledge.

The court of appeals also addressed the issue of whether the reference in the exception above to "fraud or concealment" referred to the nature of the factual allegations supporting the claim of breach of fiduciary duty (in this case, securities fraud) or to the steps taken by the fiduciary to cover up the breach. While recognizing that there was a split of opinion among the courts on the issue, the court of appeals concluded that the better view is that the phrase "in case of fraud or concealment" refers to steps taken by the defendant to hide the fact of the breach rather than to the underlying nature of the plaintiff's claim. [Radiology Center, S.C. v. Stifel, Nicolaus & Co., 919 F.2d 1216 (7th Cir. 1990)]

Remedies of Plan Participants and Beneficiaries

Q 2:208   Can a plan participant or beneficiary bring suit to recover plan benefits or to enforce his or her rights under the plan?

Yes. ERISA provides that a civil action may be brought by a participant or beneficiary (1) to recover benefits due him or her; (2) to enforce his or her rights under the plan; or (3) to clarify his or her rights to future benefits under the plan. [ERISA §502(a)(1)(B); 29 U.S.C. §1132(a)(1)(B)]

Q 2:209   Can a plan participant or beneficiary bring suit if the plan administrator fails to provide plan information as required under ERISA?

Yes. If the plan administrator fails or refuses to furnish the requested information within 30 days (unless such failure or refusal results from matters reasonably beyond the control of the plan administrator), the plan participant or beneficiary may bring suit, and the court in its discretion may require the administrator to pay the plan participant or beneficiary up to $110 a day from the date of the failure or refusal.

A plan participant or beneficiary may also bring suit and in the court's discretion be awarded up to $110 a day for a plan administrator's failure to provide a required COBRA notice under ERISA Section 606. [ERISA §§502(a)(1)(A), 502(c); 29 U.S.C. §§1132(a)(1)(A), 1132(c)]

The duty to provide documents and other information falls on the plan administrator, not on third parties who provide services to the plan. [ERISA §104(b)(4)] In a recent case, for example, the Eighth Circuit refused to impose statutory penalties on a plan's insurer for failing to provide documents requested by a plan participant because the insurer was not the plan administrator. The plan's SPD clearly identified the employer as the plan administrator and the insurer's role in handling claims did not make it the plan administrator. [Ross v. Rail Car Am. Group Disability Income Plan, 285 F.3d 735 (8th Cir. 2002); *see also* Caffey v. UNUM Life Ins. Co., 302 F.3d 576 (6th Cir. 2002)] ERISA defines the plan administrator to be the plan sponsor unless some other person or entity is named as plan administrator in the plan documents. Because of the potential liability, third-party administrators and insurers will rarely agree to be named as plan administrator.

Q 2:210   Can a plan participant or beneficiary bring a civil action for any other reason under ERISA?

A participant or beneficiary can bring a suit (1) to enjoin any act or practice that violates ERISA or the terms of the plan or (2) to obtain other appropriate equitable relief to redress the violations or to enforce ERISA or the terms of the plan. [ERISA §502(a)(3); 29 U.S.C. §1132(a)(3)]

Q 2:211   Can a plan participant or beneficiary bring an action for plan benefits without exhausting the plan's administrative remedies?

Generally not. The great weight of case law supports the view that the plan's administrative remedies must be exhausted before the plan participant or beneficiary can begin a legal action to recover benefits.

A decision by the U.S. Court of Appeals for the Sixth Circuit held that administrative appeal of a denied claim was a prerequisite to the commencement of a lawsuit, even though the plan document was written in permissive language (that is, a participant "may request a review"). [Baxter v. C.A. Muer Corp., 941 F.2d 451 (6th Cir. 1991)]

In a more recent decision, the Eleventh Circuit concluded that a participant's lawsuit was not barred, even though she had not exhausted her administrative remedies under the plan's claim procedures. According to the court, the plan's use of the permissive term "may" could reasonably have led the participant to believe she had a choice between filing an appeal with the plan and taking her case to court. In explaining the right to sue, the plan's SPD, using model language from the DOL regulations, stated: "If you have a claim for benefits which is denied or ignored, in whole or in part, you may file suit in a state or Federal court." Also in accordance with the DOL regulations, the SPD described the plan's claim procedure and stated that a claimant "may use this procedure" to appeal a denied claim. However, neither the SPD nor other communications from the plan explained that the plan's claim procedure had to be followed before going to court. [Watts v. Bellsouth Telecomms., Inc., 316 F.3d 1203 (11th Cir. 2003)]

A federal appeals court has held that an employee could not be required to exhaust all administrative remedies before filing suit under ERISA where the employer denied a request for information pertinent to the employee's claim during the claim appeal period. [Wilczynski v. Lumbermens Mut. Cas. Co., 93 F.3d 397 (7th Cir. 1996)]

A court may waive the requirement to exhaust administrative remedies if pursuing those remedies would be an exercise in futility. For example, in a Sixth Circuit case, an employee was seeking long-term disability benefits and a waiver of his life insurance premiums on account of disability. To qualify for long-term disability benefits, the employee had to be unable to perform the duties of his own occupation. The test for a waiver of life insurance premiums was tougher; the employee had to be unable to perform the duties of any occupation for which he was reasonably qualified. When the employer's insurer denied the employee's claim for long-term disability benefits on the grounds that the employee was able to perform the duties of his "sedentary" occupation, the employee sought administrative review, which proved futile. The employee did not seek administrative review of the insurer's denial of a premium waiver. Instead, he took both issues to court. A district court ruled in favor of the employee on the long-term disability claim. However, the district court dismissed the premium waiver claim on the grounds that the employee did not exhaust his administrative remedies and that the time for seeking administrative review had expired.

On appeal, the Sixth Circuit held that the employee's lawsuit for a premium waiver could go forward. According to the court, the requirement to exhaust administrative remedies does not apply when the review process would futile. In the employee's case, the insurer had determined that the employee was able to perform his own occupation. And, according to the court, that determination necessarily precluded him from arguing with a straight face to the same insurance company that he was unable to perform any occupation. [Dozier v. Sun Life Assurance Co. of Can., 466 F.3d 532 (6th Cir. 2006)]

Exhaustion of administrative remedies is not required where only statutory violations or breaches of fiduciary duty are alleged. A former employee who signed a separation agreement that included a general waiver and who failed to exhaust the pension plan's administrative remedies was not precluded from filing suit challenging the employer's elimination of a special retirement benefit. [Bellas v. CBS Inc., 221 F.3d 517 (3d Cir. 2000)]

Q 2:212 May a plan participant or beneficiary suing for and receiving payment of plan benefits receive compensatory or punitive damages?

It appears not. The U.S. Court of Appeals for the Seventh Circuit held that neither compensatory nor punitive damages could be obtained in a suit by a participant or beneficiary under either Section 502(a)(1)(B) or Section 502(a)(3) of ERISA. The court relied heavily on the reasoning of the U.S. Supreme Court in *Massachusetts Mutual* (see Q 2:205) to the effect that Congress did not intend to authorize remedies beyond those it enacted in ERISA. [Harsch v. Eisenberg, 956 F.2d 651 (7th Cir. 1992); *see also* Reinking v. Philadelphia Am. Life Ins. Co., 910 F.2d 1210 (4th Cir. 1990) (extra-contractual damages for emotional distress not allowed under ERISA); Medina v. Anthem Life Ins. Co., 16 Employee Benefits Cas. (BNA) 1533 (5th Cir. 1993) (extracontractual and punitive damages not allowable against an insurer that denied a health benefit claim)]

The U.S. Court of Appeals for the Fourth Circuit considered the case of an employee who had been discharged on the grounds of poor performance. The employee sued, claiming that he had really been fired so the employer's medical plan would not have to pay his medical bills. He alleged that the firing had caused him great mental anguish. The court held that ERISA Sections 501(a)(1)(B) and 502(a)(3) do not permit a cause of action for mental anguish. [Garrett v. Merchant's Inc., CCH Pen. Plan Guide, ¶ 23, 897J (4th Cir. 1994)]

The U.S. Supreme Court let stand an appeals court decision that held that punitive damages are not available under ERISA. [Audet v. Prudential Health Care Plan Inc., 165 F.3d 40 (11th Cir. 1998), *cert. denied,* 526 U.S. 1087 (1999)] The U.S. District Court for the Southern District of Florida ruled that an HMO that was part of an employee welfare benefit plan covered under ERISA improperly denied medical coverage for therapy and awarded expenses of the therapy but did not award punitive damages to the participant. The U.S. Court of Appeals for the Eleventh Circuit affirmed the district court's decision holding that a plan beneficiary can sue to enforce her rights under the plan and under ERISA, and for equitable relief, but not for punitive or compensatory damages.

Q 2:213   Is a plan participant or beneficiary suing for plan benefits entitled to a jury trial?

Although the issue is not settled, the weight of appellate authority indicates that the courts view such actions as essentially equitable in nature and therefore not subject to the constitutional requirement under the Seventh Amendment to the Constitution that actions at law are generally entitled to a jury trial if the plaintiff so elects. [*See* Pane v. RCA Corp., 868 F.2d 631 (3d Cir. 1989) and cases cited therein.]

Note. Nevertheless, federal court decisions are split on this issue, and it may have to be resolved ultimately by the U.S. Supreme Court.

Q 2:214   Is a participant or beneficiary who wins a suit for benefits also entitled to attorneys' fees and costs?

A court may allow attorneys' fees and costs to either party in an ERISA action. [ERISA §502(g)(1)] The U.S. Court of Appeals for the Sixth Circuit has indicated that the following factors are to be taken into account by the trial court in deciding whether an award of attorneys' fees should be made:

1. The degree of the opposing party's culpability or bad faith;
2. The ability of the opposing party to satisfy an award of attorneys' fees;
3. The deterrent effect of an award on other persons under similar circumstances;
4. Whether the party requesting attorneys' fees sought to confer a common benefit on all plan participants and beneficiaries or to resolve significant ERISA legal questions; and
5. The relative merits of the parties' positions.

While all the circuit courts of appeal appear to follow this five-factor analysis, one line of cases creates a presumption that a prevailing individual participant or beneficiary should ordinarily be awarded attorneys' fees unless it would be unjust to do so. Another line of cases rejects such an assumption. [*See* Armistead v. Vernitron Corp., 944 F.2d 1287 (6th Cir. 1991) (no presumption in favor of prevailing plaintiff); Rodriguez v. MEBA Pension Trust, 956 F.2d 468 (4th Cir. 1992) (presumption in favor of prevailing plaintiff)] The Eighth Circuit, which had previously relied on a presumption in favor of a prevailing participant or beneficiary, changed sides on this issue. According to the Eighth Circuit, ERISA provides that attorneys' fees may be awarded at the discretion of the court, and a presumption in favor of an award of fees undermines that discretion. Instead, the Eighth Circuit concluded that courts in its jurisdiction should use the five-factor test as well as "other relevant considerations as general guidelines for determining when a fee is appropriate." [Martin v. Arkansas Blue Cross & Blue Shield, 299 F.3d 966 (8th Cir. 2002)]

Chapter 3

Group Health Plans: Structure and Administration

Group health plans—including medical, dental, and prescription drug plans; vision care plans; health care flexible spending accounts (FSAs); and employee assistance programs (EAPs)—are often the most valued employee welfare benefits, with employees consistently ranking health benefits as one of the most important benefits their employers provide. These plans, regulated chiefly by the Internal Revenue Code (Code) and the Employee Retirement Income Security Act of 1974 (ERISA), are also affected by a number of other federal and state laws.

This chapter discusses the ground rules for medical benefits, including such basic concepts as plan types and funding options, coordination of benefits, and federal tax rules governing health benefits. It includes comprehensive coverage of key elements of the 2010 Health Reform Act, including employer and employee responsibilities for health coverage, the implementation of state-based health insurance Exchanges, and new tax rules and regulations.

Medical benefits for retirees are covered in chapter 4. Mandated health benefits and other standards for group health plans, including new requirements in the 2010 Health Reform Act, are discussed in chapter 5.

Impact of 2010 Health Reform Act

Q 3:1   Does the 2010 Health Reform Act require an employer to adopt a new group health plan?

No. Group health plans in existence on March 23, 2010, the date of enactment of the 2010 Health Reform Act [Patient Protection and Affordable Care Act, Pub. L. No. 111-148 (Mar. 23, 2010)] (PPACA) as amended by the Health Care and Education Reconciliation Act of 2010 [Pub. L. No. 111-152 (Mar. 30, 2010)], are "grandfathered health plans." [PPACA § 1251(e)]

The 2010 Health Reform Act specifically provides that nothing in the law ". . . shall be construed to require that an individual terminate coverage under a group health plan or health insurance coverage in which such individual was enrolled on the date of enactment, . . ." [PPACA § 1251(a)(1)]

Grandfathered group health plans may enroll new employees and their family members in the plan. [PPACA § 1251(c)] Family members of employees covered by the plan on the date of enactment can join the plan, if such enrollment is permitted under the terms of the plan in effect on the date of enactment. [PPACA § 1251(b)]

As a general rule, the provisions of the 2010 Health Reform Act do not apply to grandfathered plans. [PPACA § 1251(a)(2)] However, this is not a blanket exception. Many of the new coverage requirements and other standards in the law do apply to grandfathered plans and will require changes in the terms and operations of existing plans.

In the case of health insurance coverage maintained pursuant to one or more collective bargaining agreements that were ratified before the date of enactment, the health reform law generally will not apply until the date on which the last collective bargaining agreement related to such coverage terminates. [PPACA § 1251(d)] The 2010 Health Reform Act provides that an amendment to a plan solely to comply with a requirement of the health reform law will not be treated as a termination of the collective bargaining agreement that causes the plan to lose its grandfathered status. However, here again, although these plans are grandfathered, many of the new coverage requirements and other standards do apply to grandfathered collectively bargained plans.

Q 3:2   How does the 2010 Health Reform Act affect group health plans?

The 2010 Health Reform Act is the most sweeping legislation affecting group health plans in decades with provisions ranging from the big-picture (new employer responsibility and health benefit requirements) to the mundane (whether over-the-counter drugs can be paid through a health flexible spending account or other reimbursement arrangement).

Key elements of the 2010 Health Reform Act fall into the following broad categories:

Employer Responsibility Requirements

- "Play or pay" mandates for large employers
- Automatic enrollment requirement for large employers
- Increased reporting requirements for group health plans

Health Insurance Exchanges and Insurance Market Reforms

- Creation of American Health Benefit Exchanges
- Small Business Health Opportunity Program (SHOP Exchanges) for small employers
- Insurance accessibility protections including guaranteed availability and renewability of coverage

Group Health Plan Coverage and Benefit Mandates (see chapter 5)

Tax Changes for Employers and Employees

- Small employer health insurance tax credit
- Premium tax credit for individuals
- Excise tax on high-cost group health plans
- Per capita fees on health insurance and self-insured plans

Of course, there are many more "hidden gems" in the 2010 Health Reform Act, including a reinsurance program for employers providing health benefits for early retirees (see chapter 4), a SIMPLE cafeteria plan for small employers (see chapter 7), and a new payroll deduction option for long-term care coverage (see chapter 8).

Q 3:3   When are group health plans required to comply with the 2010 Health Reform Act?

The precise deadline for complying with the 2010 Health Reform Act depends on a variety of factors—the effective date of the particular law change, the type of plan in question, whether the plan operates on a fiscal or calendar year, the size of the sponsoring employer, and the status of the plan as a "grandfathered plan."

While some provisions in the 2010 Health Reform Act take effect immediately, others have delayed effective dates—in some cases, as late as 2018. In addition, some provisions apply only to large employers, some only to small employers, some only to insured plans, and some only to group health insurance issuers. Finally, "grandfathered plans" in existence on the March 23, 2010 enactment date are exempted from some of the law's new requirements, while other requirements apply across the board regardless of a plan's status. Given those caveats, the following shows the capsule compliance deadlines for the major 2010 Health Reform Act provisions.

Compliance required by 2010

- Small business tax credit for costs of employee health coverage (chapter 3)
- Prohibition of preexisting-condition exclusions for children (chapter 5)
- Prohibition on rescission of health coverage (chapter 5)
- Prohibition of lifetime limits on coverage (chapter 5)
- Restrictions on annual coverage limits (chapter 5)
- First-dollar coverage of preventive health services (chapter 5)
- Extension of dependent coverage to adult children (chapter 5)
- Reinsurance program for employers providing health coverage to early retirees (chapter 4)
- Mandated appeals process for health plan coverage determinations and claims (chapter 3)
- Increased exclusion for employer-provided adoption assistance (chapter 8)
- Extension of prohibition on discrimination in favor of highly compensated employees (chapter 5)

Compliance required by 2011

- Cost accounting and rebate requirements for group health plan insurers (chapter 3)
- Reporting health coverage on Form W-2 (chapter 3)
- Ban on reimbursements from health reimbursement arrangements (HRAs, HSAs, MSAs, and FSAs) for over-the-counter drugs (chapters 3, 7)
- Increased penalty for nonqualified distributions from HSAs and MSAs (chapter 3)
- SIMPLE cafeteria plans for small employers (chapter 7)
- Payroll deduction long-term care program (chapter 9)

Compliance required by 2012

- Implementation of uniform standards for benefit and coverage explanations (chapter 3)

Compliance required by 2013

- Uniform standards for electronic health plan transactions (chapter 3)
- $2,500 annual limit on contributions to health FSAs (chapter 7)
- Elimination of deduction for employer Medicare Part D subsidy (chapter 4)

- Annual per-capita fees on group health insurers and self-insured plans for patient-centered outcomes research (chapter 3)

Compliance required by 2014

- Guaranteed availability and renewability of group health insurance (chapter 3)
- Restrictions on higher insurance premiums based on health status, age, or gender (chapter 3)
- Prohibition on all preexisting condition exclusions (chapter 5)
- Elimination of all annual limits on coverage (chapter 5)
- Prohibition of health coverage discrimination based on health status (chapter 5)
- Prohibition of excessive waiting periods for coverage (chapter 5)
- Establishment of American Health Benefit Exchanges and Small Business Health Options Programs (SHOP Exchanges) (chapter 3)
- Employer health coverage responsibility requirements for large employers (chapter 3)
- Employer-provided free choice vouchers for Exchange coverage (chapter 3)
- Individual health coverage responsibility requirements (chapter 3)
- Comprehensive coverage requirement for small group health insurance (chapter 3)
- Modified small business tax credit for employee health coverage (chapter 3)

Compliance required by 2018

- Excise tax on high-cost employer-provided health coverage (chapter 3)

Basic Concepts

Q 3:4   What is a group health plan?

In common parlance, a *group health plan* is a welfare benefit plan that provides medical care to participants and their beneficiaries.

However, each of the multiple laws regulating group health plans has its own nuanced definition of what constitutes a group health plan. The parameters of these laws and the significance of their varying definitions of a group health plan are explored throughout this book. The following is a capsule summary of the major laws regulating group health plans and their governing definitions.

Employee Retirement Income Security Act of 1974 (ERISA). ERISA is a multifaceted law, including both regulatory requirements for employee welfare benefit plans in general and for group health plans in particular.

The employee benefit protections contained in Title I of ERISA generally apply to an "employee welfare benefit plan," which is defined to include:

> any plan, fund, or program which was heretofore or is hereafter established or maintained by an employer or by an employee organization, or by both, to the extent that such plan, fund, or program was established or is maintained for the purpose of providing for its participants or their beneficiaries, through the purchase of insurance or otherwise, (A) medical, surgical, or hospital care or benefits, or benefits in the event of sickness, accident, disability, death or unemployment, or vacation benefits, apprenticeship or other training programs, or day care centers, scholarship funds, or prepaid legal services . . .

[ERISA § 3; 29 U.S.C. § 1002]

Part 6 of ERISA provides continuation coverage and other standards for group health plans, incorporating the requirements of the Consolidated Budget Reconciliation Act of 1985 (COBRA) and other mandates, including coverage for children pursuant to qualified medical child support orders, coverage for adopted children, pediatric vaccine coverage, and coverage for Medicaid-eligible individuals. For this purpose, a group health plan means

> an employee welfare benefit plan providing medical care (as defined in section 213(d) of . . . [the Internal Revenue Code] . . .) to participants or beneficiaries directly or through insurance, reimbursement, or otherwise.

Part 7 of ERISA also applies specifically to group health plans, incorporating requirements of the Health Insurance Portability and Accountability Act of 1996 (HIPAA), the Mental Health Parity and Addiction Equity Act of 2008 (MHPAEA), the Newborns' and Mothers' Health Protection Act of 1996 (NMHPA), and the Women's Health and Cancer Rights Act of 1998 (WHCA), the Genetic Information Nondiscrimination Act of 2008 (GINA), and other laws. For purposes of Part 7, a group health plan is defined as:

> an employee welfare benefit plan to the extent that the plan provides medical care (as defined in . . . [ERISA § 733(a)(2)] . . . and including items and services paid for as medical care) to employees or their dependents (as defined under the terms of the plan) directly or through insurance, reimbursement, or otherwise.

[ERISA § 733, 29 U.S.C. § 1191b]

The Department of Labor (DOL) has primary enforcement authority over the welfare benefit and group health plan requirements of ERISA.

Internal Revenue Code of 1986. The Internal Revenue Service (IRS) has parallel authority over the laws incorporated into ERISA, and the requirements of those laws (most notably, COBRA and HIPAA) are also incorporated into the Internal Revenue Code (Code; I.R.C.). Most significantly, this means that, in addition to the enforcement authority granted to the DOL under ERISA, the IRS can impose an excise tax under Code Section 4980D for violations of the Code requirements. For purposes of the Code, the term group health plan means:

> a plan (including a self-insured plan) of, or contributed to by, an employer (including a self-employed person) or employee organization to provide health care (directly or otherwise) to the employees, former employees, the employer, others associated or formerly associated with the employer in a business relationship, or their families.

[I.R.C. § 5000(b)]

Public Health Service Act (PHSA). The group health plan provisions of the PHSA generally do not apply to private sector employer plans; the law generally governs plans maintained by state and local governments that receive federal funding. However, the 2010 Health Reform Act adds new requirements and restrictions for group health plans to Part A of Title XXVII of the PHSA, including prohibitions and restrictions on benefit limits, preexisting-condition exclusions, waiting periods for coverage and rescissions of coverage as well as enhanced nondiscrimination requirements and coverage mandates. The 2010 Health Reform Act specifically provides that the provisions of Part A of Title XXVII as amended apply to group health plans and group health insurance issuers *as if included* in Part 7 of ERISA. [PPACA § 1562(e)] The 2010 Health Reform Law also adds to the Code new Section 9815, which provides that the PHSA provisions apply to group health plans and health insurance issuers *as if included* in the HIPAA provisions of the Code. [PPACA § 1562] As a result, the excise tax under Code Section 4980 applies to violations of the PHSA requirements.

The PHSA has its own operational definition of group health plan. However, because the new PHSA requirements are incorporated into Part 7 of ERISA and the Code, the Part 7 and Code definitions govern.

> **Practice Pointer.** There is broad overlap among these definitions—and the vast majority of employer-sponsored group health plans will fall within each of the operative definitions. Nonetheless, it is possible for a group health plan to be covered by some group health plan requirements but not by others. For example, a plan is not generally subject to ERISA unless it covers at least one common-law employee. However, the HIPAA portability requirements and other group health plan standards in Part 7 of Title I of ERISA are specifically extended to plans covering only partners in a partnership. [ERISA § 732, 29 U.S.C. § 1191a]

Q 3:5   What is medical care?

As with the term *group health plan* (see Q 3:1), the term *medical care* has more than one operating definition.

Internal Revenue Code. For federal income tax purposes, *medical care* is defined in Code Section 213. This definition is also incorporated by reference for purposes of the COBRA continuation coverage and other group health plan standards in Part 6 of ERISA.

Code Section 213 defines *medical care* to include amounts paid for

(1) the diagnosis, cure, mitigation, treatment, or prevention of disease or for the purpose of affecting any structure or function of the body;

(2) transportation primarily for and essential to such medical care; and

(3) insurance (including Medicare Part B premiums) covering medical care or for any qualified long-term care insurance contracts as defined in Code Section 7720B(b).

Under this Section 213 definition of medical care, the following definitions apply:

1. *Drugs.* A drug is considered to be a medical care expense only if it is a prescribed drug or insulin. [I.R.C. § 213(d)(3)]

   Note. Under pre-2010 Health Reform Act law, the IRS drew a distinction between expenses that qualified as deductible medical expenses for income tax purposes and expenses eligible for tax-free reimbursements from health savings accounts (HSAs), health flexible spending accounts (FSAs), and other reimbursement arrangements. The IRS ruled that amounts paid by an individual for over-the-counter (OTC) medicines or drugs that can be purchased without the prescription of a physician *cannot* be claimed as a medical expense deduction on the individual's income tax return. [Rev. Rul. 2003-58, 2003-22 I.R.B. 959] By contrast, the IRS concluded that amounts paid by an employee for medicines purchased without a physician's prescription to treat personal injuries or sickness nonetheless could be reimbursed on a tax-free basis by an employer health FSA. [Rev. Rul. 2003-102, 2003-38 I.R.B. 559] Effective for expenses incurred after December 31, 2010, the 2010 Health Reform Act generally bars health reimbursement arrangements (HRAs) from reimbursing expenses for OTC medicines or drugs, unless the medicine or drug is prescribed by a physician. [I.R.C. 106(f) as added by PPACA § 9003]

2. *Cosmetic surgery.* Cosmetic surgery or similar procedures are not considered medical care unless the surgery or procedure is necessary to ameliorate a deformity arising from, or directly related to, congenital abnormality, personal injury resulting from accident or trauma, or disfiguring disease. For this purpose, *cosmetic surgery* means any procedure that is directed at improving the patient's appearance and that does not meaningfully promote the proper function of the body or prevent or treat illness or disease. [I.R.C. § 213(d)(9)]

3. *Qualified long-term care services.* Qualified long-term care services as defined in Code Section 7702B(c) are treated as medical care unless the services are provided by a spouse or relative who is not a licensed professional with respect to such services or by certain related corporations. [I.R.C. §§ 213(d)(1), 213(d)(10); ERISA § 706(a)(2)]

ERISA purposes. For purposes of the continuation coverage standards and other standards in Part 6 of Title I of ERISA, the operating definition of *medical care* is drawn from Code Section 213.

Part 7 of ERISA has been repeatedly amended—including, most recently, by the 2010 Health Reform Act—to add various mandatory benefit provisions for group health plans. For the purpose of those provisions, *medical care* is specifically defined as:

a. Amounts paid for the diagnosis, cure, mitigation, treatment, or prevention of disease, or amounts paid for the purpose of affecting any structure or function of the body;

b. Amounts paid for transportation primarily for and essential to medical care referred to in item a; and

c. Amounts paid for insurance covering medical care referred to in items a and b.

[ERISA § 733(a)(2); 29 U.S.C. § 1191b(a)(2)]

Q 3:6   Do treatments or procedures that are cosmetic in nature or promote an individual's general well-being qualify as medical care?

Under both the Code and ERISA, medical care includes the diagnosis, cure, mitigation, treatment, or prevention of disease or procedures affecting a structure or function of the body. [I.R.C. § 213(d)(1); ERISA § 733(a)(2)] Thus, treatments or procedures that are cosmetic in nature or promote general well-being do not qualify as medical care. In the past, the IRS took a hard line on this issue. However, it has eased the rules somewhat in revenue rulings and other guidance issued in recent years.

Practice Pointer.   Although the IRS rulings and other guidance specifically deal with medical expense deductions, they also affect employer plans. To the extent expenses qualify as medical care, they qualify for reimbursement under a health care FSA or health reimbursement arrangement (HRA) and can be paid with funds in a medical savings account (MSA) or health savings account (HSA). Moreover, depending on the terms of the employer's group health plan, they may qualify as covered expenses.

For example, a long-standing IRS revenue ruling maintained that smoking-cessation programs did not qualify as medical care for individuals with no specific ailment or disease. [Rev. Rul. 79-162, 1979-1 C.B. 116] However, the IRS has ruled that the costs of smoking-cessation programs and prescription drugs to alleviate nicotine withdrawal (but not over-the-counter nicotine patches or gum) do qualify as medical expenses. [Rev. Rul. 99-28, 1999-1 C.B. 1269]

Another long-standing revenue ruling provided that a weight-reduction program qualified as medical care only if the program was connected with treating a specific ailment or disease. [Rev. Rul. 79-151, 1979-1 C.B. 116] Weight-reduction programs did not qualify as medical care for an individual who was simply trying to improve his or her appearance, general health, or sense of well-being. However, there is a substantial body of authority for treating obesity as a disease in and of itself. Therefore, according to a newer IRS ruling, the costs of weight-loss programs for the treatment of a specific illness, including obesity, qualify as expenses for medical care. [Rev. Rul. 2002-19, 2002-16 I.R.B. 779] Revenue Ruling 2002-19 notes that expenses for special diet food generally will not qualify as medical care expenses because such food is simply a substitute for what an individual would normally eat. The cost of special food is considered a medical care expense only if (1) the food alleviates or treats an illness, (2) it is not part of an individual's normal nutritional needs, and (3) the need for the special food is substantiated by a physician.

Health club membership fees that are incurred primarily for the purpose of preventing or alleviating obesity *may* be deductible as medical expenses. [IRS Information Ltr. 2002-0077 (June 28, 2002)] However, the IRS has cautioned that it will consider additional facts and circumstances in determining whether such fees qualify as medical expenses. The facts and circumstances include the location of the club, whether an alternative club is available closer to the taxpayer's home, the types of activities available, the services included in the health club membership fee, and whether the taxpayer would be able to safely fulfill his or her exercise need without joining a health club. The information letter mentions the tax law's prohibition on deductions for club dues [I.R.C. § 274(a)(3)], but does not address how that prohibition relates to the treatment of health club membership fees as medical expenses.

> **Note.** The information letter is not official IRS guidance. Moreover, it does not specifically state when club membership fees will—or will not—qualify as medical expenses. Therefore, employers should be wary about reimbursing such expenses.

The IRS has ruled that expenses for cosmetic surgery to correct disfigurement following an operation or to correct a defect caused by a disease or that interferes with the normal functioning of the body qualify as deductible expenses. [Rev. Rul. 2003-57, 293 I.R.B. 1] Revenue Ruling 2003-57 states that expenses for breast reconstruction following a mastectomy and eye surgery (LASIK and radial keratotomy surgery) to correct vision, for example, are deductible expenses. However, expenses for teeth whitening would not qualify, because the procedure does not correct a defect caused by disease or restore normal functioning of the body; the procedure merely improves a person's appearance.

In a reported decision, the Tax Court held that the costs of hormone therapy and sex reassignment surgery for an individual with gender identity disorder were deductible medical expenses for the treatment of a disease. However, because subsequent breast augmentation was directed at improving the individual's appearance and did not meaningfully promote the proper function of the body or treat a disease, the court ruled that breast augmentation surgery was cosmetic surgery that was excluded from the definition of medical care. [O'Donnabhain v. Commissioner, 134 T.C. No. 4, 2010 U.S. Tax Ct. LEXIS 4 (Feb. 2, 2010)]

In 2007, the IRS ruled that amounts paid for medical procedures can qualify as deductible medical expenses even if the procedures are not prescribed by a doctor. [Rev. Rul. 2007-72, 2007-50 I.R.B. 1154] According to the IRS, in determining whether an expense is for medical or personal reasons, the recommendation of a physician is important, but it is not crucial. Where expenses are for items that are wholly medical in nature and serve no other function in everyday life, a deduction can be claimed even if no doctor was involved.

The IRS ruling approved deductions for three types of expenses incurred by taxpayers without a doctor's order:

1. The cost of an annual physical,

2. The cost of a full-body scan to detect diseases or abnormalities, and

3. The cost of an at-home pregnancy test.

Note that deductions for such expenses may be approved even if the taxpayer is not suffering from any symptoms of a disease or illness. According to the IRS, deductible medical care includes amounts paid for diagnosis—and a diagnosis may include a finding that disease is absent or a test for changes in the function of the body, such as changes resulting from pregnancy, which are unrelated to a disease. [Rev. Rul. 2007-72, 2007-50 I.R.B. 1154]

Q 3:7 Is a group health plan required to cover all expenses that are considered medical care expenses?

Historically, employers have had broad latitude in designing group health plans. An employer-provided medical benefit plan generally does not cover all expenses that are considered medical care expenses for federal income tax purposes (although employers may choose to cover all such expenses). The chief reason for excluding certain types of expenses is cost. To control costs, employers must strike a balance between providing an attractive employee benefit package and providing a package that is simply too costly for the competitive and personnel relations advantages gained thereby.

This latitude in group health plan design has been increasingly narrowed in recent years, however. An ever-increasing number of federal laws require employers to provide coverage for specified benefits or to provide the coverage they do offer on a nondiscriminatory basis. The 2010 Health Reform Act imposes significant new mandates on group health plans and health insurance issuers offering group coverage. For example, going forward, plans offered by insurers operating in the small group market will be required to cover "minimum essential benefits" (see Q 3:24), whereas large employers will face penalties if they do not offer their employees "minimum essential coverage" (see Q 3:15). In addition, the 2010 Health Reform Act imposes new coverage requirements for preventive care and other services, as well as restrictions and prohibitions on preexisting-condition exclusions and annual and lifetime coverage limits. (See chapter 5 for more detailed discussion of these requirements.)

In addition, insured group health plans are subject to an increasing number of coverage requirements under state insurance laws.

Practice Pointer. Employers must carefully—and continually—review their plans to determine the extent to which coverage changes are required to comply with mandated benefits and other requirements.

One way to fill in any "gaps" in group health plan coverage is to offer employees some form of medical reimbursement arrangement for out-of-pocket medical expenses. These arrangements generally "wrap around" an employer-sponsored group health plan, and the types of expenses that can be reimbursed under such arrangements may be comprehensive enough to cover all or almost all expenses qualifying as medical care expenses for federal income tax purposes. These plans include employer-funded health reimbursement arrangements (HRAs), medical savings accounts (MSAs), and health savings accounts (HSAs) coupled with high-deductible health plans (HDHPs), and health flexible spending arrangements (FSAs) funded with employees' salary reduction contributions under a cafeteria plan.

Note. Health FSAs can be a particularly attractive option for employers because they are typically funded solely through employee salary reductions under a cafeteria plan. Moreover, employees have traditionally had unlimited flexibility in funding these plans, subject to the "use-it-or-lose-it" requirement that unspent amounts at year-end (or the end of a post-year end grace period) be forfeited. Beginning in 2013, however, the 2010 Health Reform Act imposes a $2,500 cap on annual FSA contributions. (See chapter 7 for a discussion of health care FSAs.)

Q 3:8   When does an employer have a medical plan?

For purposes of Code Section 106 (concerning the tax exclusion for the monthly value of employer-provided accident and health insurance coverage) and Code Section 105 (concerning the tax treatment of benefit payments or direct services received from employer-provided accident or health insurance), an *employer-sponsored medical plan* is an arrangement for the payment of amounts to employees in the event of personal injury or illness. Solely for the purpose of determining whether such a plan exists for tax purposes, such arrangements are not required to be in writing, and the employee's rights to benefits are not required to be enforceable. For tax purposes only, if the employee's rights are not enforceable, an employer-provided plan nonetheless will be considered to exist if, on the date the employee became ill or injured:

1. He or she was covered under a plan, or a program, policy, or custom having the effect of a plan, providing for the payment of amounts to the employee in the event of personal injuries or illness; and

2. Notice or knowledge of such plan was reasonably available to the employee.

[Treas. Reg. § 1.105-5(a)]

No minimum number of employees is required for a plan to exist for Code Section 105 purposes (see Q 3:13).

COBRA. The Code contains a separate definition of *group health plan* for COBRA purposes only. [I.R.C. §§ 4980B(g)(2), 5000(b)(1)] The IRS regulations explain how to determine when a group health plan exists for COBRA purposes. [Treas. Reg. § 54.4980B-2, Q&A-1(a)] Significantly, ERISA's COBRA provisions (Part 6 of Title I) also contain a separate definition of *group health plan,* but that definition differs from the Code's COBRA definition. [ERISA § 607(1), 29 U.S.C. § 1167(1)] Moreover, case law has interpreted ERISA's definition differently. (See chapter 6 for a discussion of COBRA's definitions of *group health plan* under the Code and ERISA.)

ERISA. Determining whether a plan exists for ERISA purposes is not always easy, and the issue has been and continues to be the subject of extensive litigation. This question is covered in chapter 2 and particularly in chapter 15, Vacation and Severance Pay Plans, because much of the litigation fleshing out this issue arises in the severance pay context. If a plan does exist for ERISA purposes, it may be required to comply with the plan document requirements of ERISA (see chapter 2). Although the general rule is that a plan does not exist under ERISA unless it covers at least one common-law employee, the group health plan requirements in Part 7 of Title I contain a special definition of *group health plan* that includes partner-only plans (see chapter 5 for details on these requirements).

Q 3:9 Is a health care FSA under a cafeteria plan considered a medical plan?

Yes, it is. A health care FSA under Code Section 105 is considered to be a self-insured medical plan and thus must satisfy the tax requirements of Code Section 105 and 106. In particular, a health care FSA must exhibit the risk-shifting and risk-distribution characteristics of insurance. [Prop. Treas. Reg. § 1.125-5(d)] (See chapter 7 for a detailed discussion of cafeteria plans.) As such it will be subject to COBRA, the Medicare secondary-payer rules, and other group health plans requirements. See chapters 5 and 7 for further details on how these requirements apply to health care FSAs.

Q 3:10 Is dread disease coverage or first occurrence coverage a medical plan?

Dread disease coverage is a limited form of medical coverage that typically covers all of the expenses associated with a particular dread disease or condition such as cancer. Sometimes these policies will pay a certain dollar amount upon the first occurrence or first diagnosis of the dread disease, over and above the expense of services (e.g., $2,000 upon the first occurrence, in addition to all other covered expenses). These benefits are considered medical coverage under Code Section 106. Any feature that carries over funds from year to year, such as a return of premium feature (under which a participant who incurs fewer covered expenses than the premiums he or she paid might get back the difference after, say, 20 years), would not, however, be part of Section 106 coverage because it is more akin to deferral of compensation. Similarly, a buildup benefit (e.g., upon first occurrence, the participant is also paid a cash lump sum equal to $500 for each year during which he or she was disease-free while covered under the policy) might not qualify as a Section 106 benefit, also because it is more akin to deferred compensation.

Q 3:11   Is a long-term care insurance plan considered to be a medical plan?

Long-term care insurance policies typically cover long-term nursing home care and other services not covered or not fully covered by Medicare or by the employer's regular medical plan. As a result, long-term care insurance plans are treated as medical plans for some purposes but not for others.

Treated as a medical plan. Previous confusion about whether long-term care insurance constituted deductible medical care under Code Section 213 has been resolved by the amendment of that section to include most qualified long-term care services as defined under Code Section 7702B. As a result, employer-provided coverage is excluded from income under Code Section 106 and benefits are nontaxable under Code Section 105. However, qualified long-term care services within the meaning of Code Section 7702B(c) cannot be offered through an FSA or similar arrangement. [I.R.C. § 106(c)]

Not treated as a medical plan. Under an express exception contained in Code Section 106(c), qualified long-term care services are not treated as employer-provided accident or health care (i.e., a qualified benefit) for purposes of Code Section 125 (concerning cafeteria plans) [I.R.C. § 125(f)] or for purposes of the COBRA continuation of coverage rules applicable to group health plans. [I.R.C. § 4980B(g)(2); ERISA § 607(1)]

Q 3:12   Is a Section 401(h) retiree medical account under a pension or annuity plan considered a medical plan?

No. A Section 401(h) retiree medical account under a pension or annuity plan is not considered to be a medical plan. Rather, the Section 401(h) provisions constitute a statutorily authorized method of setting aside funds in a pension or annuity plan before the plan participants retire in order to pay the cost of coverage under a medical plan in retirement. In effect, it is a "statutory holding tank" for funds that must be used for medical plan premiums or benefits and that cannot be used for pension benefits. Section 401(h) accounts are discussed in chapter 20 on funding and financing welfare benefits.

Q 3:13   Is a minimum number of employees a tax prerequisite for a medical plan?

No. The Code generally does not require a minimum number of employees in order for a medical plan to be deemed to exist. An employer-provided accident or health insurance plan may cover one or more employees [Treas. Reg. § 1.105-5(a)]

Comparison. For COBRA purposes, a "group health plan" under Code Sections 4980B and 5000(b)(1) must consist of at least two employees. ERISA's definition of a welfare benefit plan (which requires only one common-law employee) could potentially create interpretive difficulties because it is incorporated by reference into ERISA's COBRA provisions (see chapter 6).

Note. COBRA provides an exemption for small employers with fewer than 20 employees. That exemption is triggered by the size of an employer's workforce, not the size of any given health plan. Consequently, an employer with a workforce of 20 or more employees will be subject to COBRA regardless of the size of its group health plan.

Q 3:14   Is a self-employed individual considered an employee?

A self-employed individual is treated as an employee for some purposes but not for others. An individual who is self-employed is not considered an employee for purposes of Code Sections 105 and 106, concerning the taxability of employer-provided accident health plan coverage and the benefits paid under that coverage. [I.R.C. § 105(g); Treas. Reg. § 1.105-5(b)] Sole proprietors, partners, and more-than-2-percent S corporation shareholders are considered self-employed, while other shareholder-employees are not. [I.R.C. § 1372]

Note. Self-employed individuals are not absolutely barred from participating in medical plans, but they do not qualify for the same tax treatment as employees. As a result, the value of the coverage they receive is includable in gross income, and any medical benefits received do not automatically qualify for tax-free treatment under Code Section 105. [Treas. Reg. § 1.105-5(b)] However, self-employed individuals can deduct health insurance premiums paid and exclude the medical benefits they receive on their individual tax returns. The tax treatment of benefits provided to self-employed individuals is discussed later in this chapter.

Comparison. Under the special rules applicable to COBRA continuation of group health plan coverage, self-employed individuals are treated as employees for COBRA purposes only, and the rights and privileges conferred by COBRA do apply to them (see chapter 6). Partners are treated as employees for purposes of the group health plan requirements under Part 7 of ERISA (discussed in chapter 5).

Employer Responsibility for Health Coverage

Q 3:15   Does federal law require an employer to provide a group health plan?

There is no absolute federal mandate for private employers to provide a group health plan for employees. However, starting in 2014, under new "employer responsibility" provisions in the 2010 Health Reform Act, larger employers that do not offer *minimum essential coverage* under an employer-sponsored plan will do so at their peril.

Large employers not offering health coverage. The 2010 Health Reform Law provides that if:

- an *applicable large employer* fails to offer its full-time employees and their dependents the opportunity to enroll in *minimum essential coverage* under an *eligible employer-sponsored plan*, and

- at least one full-time employee is certified to the employer as having enrolled for a month in a qualified health plan through a state-based Exchange with respect to which a premium tax credit or cost-sharing reduction is allowed or paid to employee,

- the employer must pay an excise tax penalty based on the *total number of full-time employees* employed for that month.

[I.R.C. § 4980H(a) as added by PPACA § 1513 and amended by PPACA Reconciliation § 1003]

In other words, if a large employer does not offer health coverage and a single employee obtains federally subsidized coverage for any month, the employer will pay a penalty for all full-time employees.

Premium tax credits and cost sharing reductions. The employer responsibility penalty is tied to the refundable premium tax credits and cost sharing reductions available to lower-income individuals enrolling in a qualified health plan through a state-based health benefit Exchange starting in 2014. Individuals and qualified small businesses may purchase health coverage through an Exchange (see Qs 3:19–3:24.).

Individuals generally qualify for premium tax credits for health coverage purchased through an Exchange if their household income is between 100 percent and 400 percent of the federal poverty level and they are not eligible for minimum essential coverage under an employer plan (or Medicaid or other acceptable coverage). [I.R.C. § 36B as added by PPACA § 1401 and amended by PPACA § 10104 and PPACA Reconciliation §§ 1001, 1004] (Note: The federal poverty level depends on family size; for example, for 2010, 100 percent of the poverty level is approximately $10,830 for a single individual and $22,050 for a family of four.)

Employees who are eligible for minimum essential coverage under an employer plan qualify for premium tax credits if the coverage is unaffordable or does not provide minimum value and the employee declines the coverage. Coverage under an employer plan is considered unaffordable if the employee's required contribution for the coverage exceeds 9.5 percent of household income (indexed after 2014). Coverage does not provide minimum value if the employer pays less than 60 percent of the cost.

Individuals who obtain coverage through an Exchange and are eligible for premium tax credits may also qualify for cost sharing reductions (e.g., reductions of copayments, deductibles, or coinsurance), depending on household income level. [PPACA § 1402]

Applicable large employer. An *applicable large employer* is an employer that, for a calendar year, employed an average of at least 50 full-time employees on business days during the preceding year. If the employer was not in existence throughout the preceding calendar year, the determination of whether the employer is an applicable large employer will be based on the average number of employees that the employer is reasonably expected to employ on business days in the current calendar year. For purposes of determining whether an employer is an applicable large employer, both full-time employees and full-time equivalent employees must be counted.

A full-time employee for any month is an employee who is employed on average at least 30 hours per week. The IRS and the DOL are directed to issue necessary regulations, rules, and guidance for determining the hours of service of an employee, including rules for those employees who are not compensated on an hourly basis.

The number of an employer's full-time equivalent employees for a month is determined by dividing the total number of hours of service of all employees who are not full-time employees for the month by 120.

An employer *is not* treated as an applicable large employer for a calendar year if:

(1) the employer's workforce exceeds 50 full-time employees for 120 days or fewer during the calendar year, and

(2) the employees in excess of 50 employed during the 120-day period are seasonal workers (workers defined as seasonal under DOL Regulations Section 500.20(s)(1) and retail workers employed exclusively during holiday seasons).

Employers aggregated under the rules of Code Sections 414(b) (controlled groups of corporations), 414(c) (businesses under common control), 414(m) (affiliated service groups), and 414(o) (employee leasing and other arrangements treated as a single employer) are treated as a single employer for purposes of the penalty.

Minimum essential coverage. For purposes of the excise tax penalty, the law defines *minimum essential coverage* by reference to the "individual responsibility" provisions that require individuals to maintain such coverage. As such, the definition is cryptic at best.

An employer plan will qualify as minimum essential coverage if it is an "eligible-employer sponsored plan" offered in the large or small group market in a state or a "grandfathered plan." [I.R.C. § 4980H(a)(1); I.R.C. § 5000A(a)(f)(2) as added by PPACA § 1501 and amended by PPACA Reconciliation § 1002] An employer-provided group health plan is a "grandfathered plan" if it was in existence on March 23, 2010. [PPACA § 1251(e)] (See Q 3:1.)

The law specifies that "minimum essential coverage" *does not* include coverage for "excepted benefits," such as accident-only medical coverage or workers' compensation, or coverage that provides only limited benefits (e.g., dental or vision or coverage for a specific disease). (See chapter 5.)

Practice Pointer. The question as to when a plan will be deemed to provide "minimum essential coverage" will require further guidance. Presumably, that guidance will look to the essential benefits requirements for qualified health plans to be offered through the Exchanges (see Q 3:21). Under those rules, qualified plans are required to provide specified categories of coverage. Required coverage includes ambulatory care, emergency services, hospitalization, maternity and newborn care, mental health and substance use disorder services (including behavioral health treatment), prescription drugs, rehabilitative and habilitative services and devices), laboratory services, preventive and wellness services and chronic disease management, and pediatric services (including oral and vision care). [PPACA § 1302(b)]

Penalty amount. For a large employer not offering coverage, the penalty is $166.67 per month (1/12th of $2,000) per full-time employee (indexed after 2014). However, in calculating the penalty the number of full-time employees is reduced by 30.

Example 1. Big Co. does not offer a group health plan for its employees. Big Co. employs 100 full-time employees during each month in 2014. One of its full-time employees enrolls in a qualified health plan through an Exchange and receives a premium tax credit for each month in 2014. Big Co. must pay a penalty of $140,000 for 2014 ($2,000 per year x 70 employees (100 full-time employees – 30)).

Large employers offering coverage. As discussed above, employees who are eligible for minimum essential coverage under an employer plan can qualify for premium tax credits and cost sharing reductions for coverage purchased through an Exchange if the employer-provided coverage is unaffordable or does not provide minimum value.

The 2010 Health Reform Act provides that:

- If an *applicable large employer* offers its full-time employees and their dependents the opportunity to enroll in *minimum essential coverage* under an eligible employer-sponsored plan, and

- If at least one full-time employee is certified to the employer as having enrolled for a month in a qualified health plan with respect to which a premium tax credit or cost sharing reduction is allowed or paid to employee,

- the employer must pay an excise tax penalty based on the *total number of full-time employees who receive a tax credit or cost reduction* for that month. [I.R.C. § 4980H(a) as added by PPACA § 1513 and amended by PPACA Reconciliation § 1003]

Penalty amount. For employers who do offer minimum essential coverage but whose employees obtain subsidized coverage, the penalty is $250 per month (1/12th of $3,000) for each employee who receives a premium tax credit or cost reduction (indexed after 2014).

Example 2. In 2014, Maxi Co. offers minimum essential coverage to each of its 100 full-time employees for each month of the year. However, 10 of Maxi's employees decline the coverage because it is not affordable and instead purchase qualified coverage through an Exchange for which they receive premium tax credits and cost reductions. Maxi's penalty for the year is $20,000 ($2,000 x 10 employees receiving subsidies).

The maximum penalty for any employer for any month cannot exceed $166.67 times the number of full-time employees for that month reduced by 30 (i.e., the penalty for employers that do not offer coverage).

Practice Pointer. A grandfathered plan qualifies as minimum essential coverage, relieving the employer of liability for the penalty for an overall failure to provide coverage. However, an employer will be exposed to potential penalties if a grandfathered plan does not satisfy the affordability and minimum value requirements.

Employer notification. An employer will be notified if an employee is determined to be eligible for a premium tax credit or cost-sharing reduction because the employer does not offer minimum essential coverage or because the minimum essential coverage offered by the employer is unaffordable or does not provide minimum value. The notice will include information about the employer's potential liability for penalties under Code Section 4980HG. The employer will have an opportunity to appeal the determination. [PPACA § 1411]

Applicable employer reporting requirements. The 2010 Health Reform Act imposes a new information return requirement on applicable large employers subject to the employer responsibility provisions of Code Section 4980H.

Starting with the 2014 calendar year, an applicable large employer must report certain information to both the IRS and to each full-time employee. [I.R.C. § 6056 as added by PPACA § 1514 and amended by PPACA § 10108] Information returns are due to employees by January 31 of the year following the year for which the return is made and to the IRS as prescribed by the Secretary of the Treasury.

Information required to be reported to the IRS includes:

- The name, address, and tax identification number of the employer;
- A certification as to whether the employer offers its full-time employees and their dependents the opportunity to enroll in minimum essential coverage under an eligible employer-sponsored plan;
- The number of full-time employees of the employer for each month during the calendar year; and
- The name, address, and taxpayer identification number of each full-time employee employed by the employer during the calendar year and the

number of months, if any, during which the employee (and any dependents) was covered under a plan sponsored by the employer during the calendar year.

Employers that offer employees the opportunity to enroll in minimum essential coverage must also report:

- The months during the calendar year coverage was available;
- The monthly premium for the lowest cost option in each enrollment category; and
- The employer's share of the cost.

Information returns for each full-time employee must report the required information with respect to the employee.

Employee protections. The 2010 Health Reform Act amends the federal Fair Labor Standards Act (FLSA) to provide that and employer cannot discharge or discriminate against an employee with respect to compensation, terms, conditions, or other privilege of employment because the employee received a tax credit or cost reduction in connection with the purchase of health coverage through and exchange. [FLSA § 18C as added by PPACA § 1558] In addition, the Secretary of Labor is directed to conduct a study and report to Congress on whether employees' wages are reduced as a result of application of the employer responsibility penalty. [PPACA § 1513(c)]

Practice Pointer. A large employer must conduct a cost-benefit analysis to determine whether to "play or pay" under the employer responsibility rules. In conducting that analysis, employers should bear in mind that, while the employer responsibility penalty may be less costly than providing required coverage for employees, the penalty *is not* dedicated to providing coverage for the employer's employees. Employees must obtain their own coverage either through an Exchange or in the individual insurance market. Thus, an employer that chooses to pay the penalty will not get any "bang for its buck" in terms of employee goodwill. In addition, while excise taxes are generally deductible as business expenses, the 2010 Health Reform Act specifically provides that the employer responsibility penalty *is not* deductible for federal income tax purposes. [I.R.C. § 4980H(c)(7) as added by PPACA § 1513 and amended by PPACA Reconciliation § 1003; I.R.C. 275(a)(6)] By contrast, amounts expended to provide employee health benefits are deductible by the employer.

Q 3:16   Is an employer required to pay the cost of group health plan coverage for employees?

Technically, no. An employer is free to offer group health plan coverage on an employee-pay-all basis. However, under the "employer responsibility" provisions of the 2010 Health Reform Act, larger employers with 50 or more employees will be required to "play or pay" (see Q 3:15).

In addition, an employer of any size that pays any portion of the cost of employee coverage under a group health plan must contribute to the cost for certain employees to obtain alternative coverage through an Exchange.

Free choice vouchers. Starting in 2014, *offering employers* must provide free choice vouchers to *qualified employees* to be used to purchase health coverage through an Exchange. [PPACA § 10108]

Offering employer. An offering employer is any employer (regardless of size) that (1) offers minimum essential coverage through an eligible employer-sponsored plan and (2) pays any portion of the cost of the plan.

Qualified employee. A qualified employee is any employee

(1) whose required contribution (including any salary-reduction contribution) for the minimum essential coverage exceeds 8 percent but does not exceed 9.5 percent (indexed after 2014) of the employee's household income for the tax year that ends with or within the plan year;

(2) whose household income for the tax year is not greater than 400 percent of the federal poverty level; and

(3) who does not participate in the offering employee's health plan.

The amount of the free choice voucher must equal the monthly amount the employer would pay if the employee were covered under the employer's plan. If the employer sponsors multiple plans, the amount of the voucher must equal the amount the employer would pay if the employee were covered under the plan for which the employer pays the largest *percentage* of a covered employee's cost. The amount of a voucher is based on the cost of self-only coverage unless the employee purchases family coverage in an Exchange.

For example, if an employer offers plans that cost $200 and $300 per month and provides a 60 percent contribution for each plan, the value of the voucher must be 60 percent of the higher premium plan contribution (60 percent of $300), or $180. By contrast, if the employer provides a $150 contribution for the $200 plan (75 percent) and a $200 contribution for the $300 plan (67 percent), the value of the voucher must be equal to the employer's contribution for the $200 plan ($150), since that plan receives the greatest percentage contribution.

An Exchange must credit the amount of an employee's free choice voucher to the monthly premium for the employee's enrollment in any qualified health plan in the Exchange. The employer must pay the amount credited to the Exchange. If the amount of the free choice voucher exceeds the amount of the premium for the plan in which the employee is enrolled for the month, the excess must be paid to the employee.

The voucher amount credited toward coverage through an Exchange will be tax free to the employee; however, any excess paid to the employee will be included in gross income. [I.R.C. § 139D [sic] as added by PPACA § 10108 (duplicates § 139D Indian Health Care benefits added by PPACA § 9021)]

Employees who receive free choice vouchers are not eligible to receive a premium tax credit or cost reduction for the cost of coverage through an

Exchange. The employer is not subject to a penalty tax with respect to an employee who receives a free choice voucher. [I.R.C. § 4980H(b)(3)]

The amount of a free choice voucher is treated as a deductible compensation expense of the employer. [I.R.C. § 162(a) as amended by PPACA § 10108]

Offering employer reporting requirement. An offering employer is required to provide the same information returns in the same manner as applicable employers subject to the employer responsibility requirements (see Q 3:15), but only if the required employee contribution of any employee exceeds 8 percent of the wages paid by the employer to the employee. [I.R.C. § 6056 as added by PPACA § 1514 and amended by PPACA § 10108] In addition to the same information required of applicable employers, an offering employer must report the plan option for which the employer pays the largest portion of the cost of the plan and the portion of the cost paid by the employer in each of the enrollment categories under that option.

Note. The requirement to provide a free choice voucher is triggered if an employee's required contribution for coverage exceeds 8 percent of household income (total income of the employee and his or her spouse and dependents, if any); however, the reporting requirement is triggered if an employee's required contribution for coverage exceeds 8 percent of wages paid by the employer.

Q 3:17 Are employees required to enroll in an employer's group health plan?

No. However, the "individual responsibility" provisions of the 2010 Health Reform Act require every individual (with certain exceptions) to maintain minimum essential health coverage for any month beginning after 2013 or pay a tax penalty. [I.R.C. § 5000A as added by PPACA 1501 and amended by PPACA § 10106 and PPACA Reconciliation § 1002] Coverage under certain government-sponsored programs (e.g., Medicare and Medicaid), individual insurance, or employer-sponsored plans (including grandfathered group health plans in existence on March 23, 2010) satisfy the requirement to maintain health coverage.

For 2014, the maximum annual penalty for failure to maintain health coverage is $95 for an adult, rising to $325 for 2015, and to $695 for 2016 and later years. The maximum penalty for a minor under age 18 is one-half the adult amount. The maximum penalty per household is 300 percent of the adult penalty—$285 for 2014, increasing to $975 for 2015 and $2,085 for later years. Individuals must maintain coverage for their dependents or pay the penalty.

Individuals are exempt from the penalty if they cannot afford coverage because their required contribution (including salary reduction contributions) for employer-sponsored coverage or the lowest cost plan in their exchange exceeds 8 percent of household income for the year. Whether or not employer-sponsored coverage is affordable to an employee is based on the required contribution for self-only coverage. If self-only coverage is affordable to an employee, but family coverage is unaffordable, the employee is subject to the penalty if he or she does not maintain self-only coverage. However, the penalty does not apply to the employee's spouse or dependents if they do not maintain minimum essential coverage because family coverage is not affordable (i.e., the required contribution exceeds 8 percent of household income).

The penalty will not apply to short gaps in coverage of less than three months or in cases where failure to maintain coverage was due to hardship.

Health coverage reporting. Starting with the 2014 calendar year, the 2010 Health Reform Act requires insurers (including employers who self-insure) that provide minimum essential coverage to any individual during a calendar year to report certain health insurance coverage information to both the covered individual and to the IRS. [I.R.C. § 6055 as added by PPACA § 1502] Reports are due to covered individuals by January 31 following the year for which the information is reported.

Information required to be reported includes:

- the name, address, and taxpayer identification number (TIN) of the primary insured, and the name and TIN of each other individual covered under the policy;

- the dates during which the individual was covered under the policy during the calendar year;

- whether the coverage is a qualified health plan offered through an Exchange; and

- the amount of any premium tax credit or cost-sharing reduction received by the individual with respect to the coverage.

If coverage is through an employer-provided group health plan, the insurer is also required to report the name, address, and EIN of the employer; the portion of the premium, if any, required to be paid by the employer; and any other information the IRS may require to administer the health coverage tax credit for eligible small employers (see Q 3:99).

Note. For tax years beginning after 2010, employers must report the total cost of employer-sponsored health coverage on each employee's annual Form W-2, Wage and Tax Statement.

Automatic enrollment in large employer plans. The 2010 Health Reform Act amends the Fair Labor Standards Act (FLSA) to require *large employers* that offer group health plans to automatically enroll new employees and to automatically continue enrollment of current employees. [FLSA § 18A as added by PPACA § 1511; 29 U.S.C. § 218A]

The automatic enrollment requirement applies to an employer subject to the FLSA that (1) has more than 200 full-time employees and (2) offers employees coverage in one or more health plans.

New employees must be enrolled in one of the plans offered (subject to any waiting period authorized by law). Any automatic enrollment program must include adequate notice and the opportunity for an employee to opt out of any coverage.

The new requirement supersedes any state law that prevents an employer from complying with the requirement. The automatic enrollment requirement is effective as of the date of PPAPA's enactment (March 23, 2010), but specifies that automatic enrollment is to be implemented in accordance with regulations to be issued by the DOL.

Notice to employees of coverage options. The 2010 Health Reform Act also requires employers that are subject to the FLSA to provide written notice to employees informing them of coverage options, including the option to obtain coverage through an Exchange. [FLSA § 18b as added by PPACA § 1512; 29 U.S.C. § 218B]

The required notice must contain the following:

- Information about the Exchange, including a description of the services provided by the Exchange and how the employee may contact the Exchange to obtain assistance;
- If the employer's share of the cost of benefits under the employer's group health plan is less than 60 percent of the total, information about the premium tax credit and cost-sharing reductions that may be available if the employee purchases a qualified health plan through the Exchange.
- Notice that if the employee purchases a qualified health plan through the Exchange, the employee will lose the employer contribution (if any) to any health benefits plan offered by the employee and the opportunity to exclude such contribution from income for federal tax purposes.

Current employees must receive the notice no later than March 1, 2013. New employees hired on or after that date must receive notice at the time of hiring. (Although the state-based Exchanges are not required to be operational until January 1, 2014, the notice requirement assumes that sufficient information will be available as of March 1, 2013, to provide contact and other information to employees.)

Q 3:18   Does state law require an employer to provide group health plan coverage?

A number of states have laws mandating an employer to provide coverage, but ERISA generally preempts and thus invalidates them (see chapter 2). ERISA does not preempt the Hawaii Prepaid Health Care Act as in effect on the date ERISA was passed (not including any later amendments). The law was enacted two days before ERISA became effective, and Hawaii was so annoyed after all its work of bringing the law to fruition only to see it preempted two days later that it forcefully lobbied for a special exception (see chapter 2). The 2010 Health Reform Act specifically provides that the law does not modify or limit the application of the exemption for Hawaii's Prepaid Health Care Act. [PPACA § 1560(b)]

Massachusetts has enacted comprehensive health care legislation that includes "pay or play" provisions that impose surcharges on employers who do not provide a certain level of health benefits for employees. [H. 4850, An Act Providing Access to Affordable, Quality, Accountable Health Care] The requirements took effect on October 1, 2006.

Maryland's Fair Share Health Care Fund Act would have required certain employers either to spend at least 8 percent of payroll on employee health insurance or to pay the shortfall to the state. The Fourth Circuit, however, held that the Maryland law was preempted by ERISA. According to the Fourth Circuit Court of Appeals, because the law effectively would have required covered employers in Maryland to restructure their health insurance plans, it conflicted with ERISA's goal of permitting universal administration of such plans. [Retail Indus. Leaders Ass'n v. Fielder, 475 F.3d 180 (4th Cir. 2007)]

More recently, the city of San Francisco passed an ordinance requiring large and medium-sized employers to make quarterly health care expenditures to or on behalf of employees who work at least 10 hours per week in San Francisco and have been employed for at least 90 days. The expenditure requirement applies to large employers (100 or more employees) and medium-sized employers with 50 to 99 employees (as of January 1, 2008), and medium-sized employers with 20 to 49 employees (as of April 1, 2008). The ordinance does not require employers to pay for health care expenditures of employees who waive those expenditures because they receive health benefits from another employer, or to pay for the expenditures of managers or supervisors who earned more than $76,851 in 2008. The required expenditure for large employers is $1.76 per hour paid to each employee; the required expenditure for medium-sized employees is $1.17 per hour. Expenditures taken into account are contributions to health savings accounts (HSAs), reimbursements for out-of-pocket health care services, health care premiums to purchase coverage from a third party, the cost of self-insured health programs, or payments to the city. The city can use payments to fund a health access program for uninsured residents.

The San Francisco ordinance was challenged by a restaurant association on the grounds that the city ordinance was preempted by ERISA. However, a three-judge panel for the Ninth Circuit Court of Appeals ruled that the ordinance was not preempted by ERISA. [Golden Gate Rest. Ass'n v. City & County of San Francisco, No. 07-17370, 2009 U.S. App. LEXIS 5191 (9th Cir. Mar. 3, 2009)] The case is currently pending before the United States Supreme Court.

Practice Pointer. The precise interplay between the employer responsibility provision of the 2010 Health Reform Act and "pay or play" mandates under state or local law remains to be seen. Moreover, it is unclear whether the San Francisco ordinance (and, ultimately, the Massachusetts law) will withstand an ERISA preemption challenge. It is noteworthy that in the San Francisco case, the DOL filed an amicus brief with the Ninth Circuit in which it argued that the ordinance is preempted by ERISA. In addition, in February 2010, shortly before enactment of the 2010 Health Reform Act, the DOL filed notice that it plans issue regulations regarding when health care reform efforts on the part of state and local governments are subject to ERISA preemption.

Numerous state insurance laws require that insurance policies contain various minimum benefits, and such laws are not preempted by ERISA unless and to the extent that they attempt to regulate the employer, its plan, or the plan's trust. State insurance law is beyond the scope of this book, although the issue of whether a particular state law is preempted from applying to an ERISA plan is covered in chapter 2. Workers' compensation laws represent a special situation under ERISA and are discussed at Qs 3:194–3:195.

Health Insurance Exchanges and Group Health Insurance

Q 3:19   What is an American Health Benefit Exchange?

The 2010 Health Reform Act mandates that each state establish an American Health Benefit Exchange no later than January 1, 2014 through which individuals can purchase qualified health plans. Each state must also establish a Small Business Health Options Program (SHOP) Exchange through which qualified small employers can enroll their employees in qualified health plans (Q 3:22). [PPACA § 1311(b)] A state may establish a single Exchange offering both individual and SHOP services, provided the single Exchange has sufficient resources to assist individuals and employers. Multistate or regional exchanges are permitted if certain requirements are met.

Only qualified health plans (Q 3:20) will be offered through an Exchange. However, stand-alone dental plans providing only limited-scope dental benefits may be offered if they provide pediatric dental benefits.

The Secretary of Health and Human Services (HHS) is directed to develop a system for rating plans offered through an Exchange on the basis of relative quality and price. The Secretary is also directed to develop a system to evaluate enrollee satisfaction with qualified health plans offered through an Exchange. An Exchange must establish an Internet portal to provide rating and other comparative information on qualified plans offered through the exchange.

To facilitate "comparison shopping" for health plans, an Exchange must use a standardized format for presenting health benefit plan options in the Exchange, including the use of a uniform outline of coverage.

Q 3:20   What is a qualified health plan?

To be offered through an exchange, a *qualified health plan* must meet three requirements.

1. *Certification*. A qualified health plan must be certified by each Exchange through which it is offered. [PPACA § 1301(a)(1)(A)] An Exchange can certify a plan as a qualified health plan if (1) the plan meets the requirements for certification as promulgated by the Secretary of HHS and

(2) the Exchange determines that making the plan available through the Exchange is in the interest of qualified individuals and employers.

2. *Offering health insurance issuer.* To be qualified, a health plan must be offered by a health insurance issuer that is licensed and in good standing in each state where the plan is offered. In addition, the insurer must agree to offer at least one silver-level and one gold-level qualified health plan (Q 3:21) through the Exchange and must agree to charge the same premium for each qualified health plan, whether offered through the Exchange or directly from the insurer.

Essential health benefits. A qualified health plan must provide an essential health benefits package (Q 3:21).

[PPACA § 1301(a)]

Q 3:21   What is an essential health benefits package?

A plan that offers an *essential health benefits package* must (1) provide essential health benefits; (2) limit cost sharing; and (3) provide either bronze, silver, gold, or platinum level coverage. [PPACA § 1302(a)]

Essential health benefits. The Secretary of HHS is directed to define the essential health benefits. However, such benefits must include at least the following general categories of items and services:

- Ambulatory patient services
- Emergency services
- Hospitalization
- Maternity and newborn care
- Mental health and substance use disorder services, including behavioral health treatment
- Prescription drugs
- Rehabilitative and habilitative services and devices
- Laboratory services
- Preventive and wellness services and chronic disease management
- Pediatric services, including oral and vision care

[PPACA § 1302(b)]

In defining essential health benefits, HHS is directed to ensure that the scope of such benefits is equal to the scope of benefits provided under a typical employer plan. The Secretary of Labor is directed to conduct a survey of employer-sponsored coverage to determine the benefits typically covered and to provide a report to HHS.

A plan will not be treated as providing essential health benefits unless coverage for emergency services is provided without any requirement for prior authorization and is subject to the same cost-sharing requirements whether the services are provided in-network or out-of-network.

A qualified health plan cannot be required to include elective abortion services as part of its essential benefits package. If a plan does offer coverage for abortion services, premiums for such coverage must be paid separately, and benefits must be accounted for separately. A state can elect to prohibit abortion coverage in qualified plans offered through its Exchange if it enacts a law to provide such a prohibition. [PPACA § 1303 as amended by PPACA § 10104]

The requirement to provide essential health benefits does not prohibit a plan from providing benefits in excess of the required essential benefits. [PPACA § 1301(b)(5)] Moreover, states may require qualified health plans to offer benefits in addition to the essential health benefits. [PPACA § 1311(d)(3)] However, states that require additional benefits must defray the cost of those benefits for individuals who qualify for federal premium tax credits or cost-sharing reductions for coverage through the Exchange (Q 3:15).

Cost-sharing limits. A qualified plan must limit cost sharing, including deductibles, coinsurance, copayments or similar charges, and any other re-quired expenditure that is a qualified medical expense with respect to essential health benefits covered under the plan. Cost sharing does not include premiums, balance billing amounts for non-network providers, or expenditures for non-covered services. [PPACA § 1302(c)(3)]

Annual limit. The annual limits on cost sharing are tied to the annual out-of-pocket expense limits for high-deductible plans under the HSA rules. [PPACA § 1302(c)(1); I.R.C. § 223(c)(2)(A)(ii)]

For 2014, cost sharing under a qualified plan for self-only coverage cannot exceed the out-of-pocket limit for a self-only high-deductible plan as in effect for 2014. In the case of coverage other than self-only, cost sharing cannot exceed the out-of-pocket limit for a family high-deductible plan for 2014. (For 2011, the indexed limits are $5,950 for self-only coverage and $11,900 for family coverage.)

For 2015 and later years, cost sharing for self-only coverage cannot exceed the high-deductible plan limit in effect for 2014 (indexed based on premium cost increases) and cost sharing for other coverage cannot exceed twice the amount for self-only coverage.

Deductible limits for employer-sponsored plans. In the case of a plan offered in the small group market, the deductible under the plan cannot exceed $2,000 for self-only coverage or $4,000 for other coverage (indexed). The allowable deductible may be increased by the maximum amount of reimbursement that is reasonably expected to be available to a participant under a health FSA determined without regard to any salary-reduction arrangement. [PPACA § 1301(c)(2)] In other words, the deductible limit can be increased by *employer* contributions to an FSA, but not by employee salary-reduction contributions.

Coordination with other requirements. Notwithstanding the above cost-sharing requirements, a qualified plan must comply with the preventive coverage requirements that apply generally to group health plans and health insurance issuers. Under those rules, a plan may not impose any cost-sharing requirements for specified preventive services, including immunizations and preventive screenings. In addition, mental health parity requirements apply to qualified plans in the same manner as to group health plans and health insurers generally. See chapter 5 for a discussion of these requirement.

Levels of coverage. To meet the essential benefits requirement, a plan must provide one of four levels of coverage:

1. *Bronze level*—benefits equivalent to 60 percent of the full actuarial value of benefits provided under the plan.
2. *Silver level*—benefits equivalent to 70 percent of the full actuarial value of benefits provided under the plan.
3. *Gold level*—benefits equivalent to 80 percent of the full actuarial value of benefits provided under the plan.
4. *Platinum level*—benefits equivalent to 90 percent of the full actuarial value of benefits provided under the plan.

[PPACA § 1302(d)]

A plan's actuarial value is the share of costs for covered services that it would pay, on average, with a broadly representative group enrolled in the plan.

If a qualified health plan is offered through an Exchange at any level of coverage, the insurance issuer must also offer the plan *at that level* as a child-only plan in which the only enrollees are individuals who have not attained age 21 at the beginning of the plan year.

HHS may issue regulations under which employer contributions to an HSA can be taken into account in determining the level of coverage for an employer's plan.

Note. Plans offered through an Exchange may provide any of the four levels of coverage, including the minimum bronze level. However, insurers participating in the Exchange must offer at least one plan providing silver level and one plan providing gold level coverage. Premium subsidies and cost-sharing reductions for lower-income individuals (see Q 3:15) are tied to silver level plans.

Q 3:22   What is a SHOP Exchange?

A qualified employer may select coverage to be made available to employees through a state SHOP Exchange. Once the employer has selected a level of coverage, employees may choose to enroll in a qualified health plan that offers that level of coverage. [PPACA § 1312(a)(2)]

Qualified employer. A qualified employer is a small employer that elects to make all full-time employees eligible for one or more qualified health plans offered through an Exchange. [PPACA § 1312(f)(2)]

For this purpose, a small employer is an employer who (1) employed an average of at least one but not more than 100 employees on business days during the preceding calendar year and (2) employed at least one employee on the first day of the plan year. [PPACA § 1304(b)] For a plan year beginning before 2016, a state may limit qualified employers to small employers who employed not more than 50 employees on business days during the preceding year.

If an employer was not in existence throughout the preceding year, the determination of whether the employer is a small employer is based on the average number of employees that it is reasonably expected the employer will employ on business days in the current calendar year.

Once a small employer, always a small employer. The fact that an employer's workforce increases so that the employer no longer qualifies as a small employer will not make the employer ineligible for an Exchange. If a qualified small employer makes enrollment in qualified health plans available to employees through an Exchange, it will continue to be treated as a small employer until the first day it stops making such enrollment available to its employees.

Practice Pointer. The mechanics of a SHOP Exchange require further clarification. For example, the law does not specify how the premiums for Exchange-based coverage are to be paid.

Beginning in 2017, a state may allow issuers of health insurance coverage in the large group market to offer qualified health plans through its Exchange and may open the Exchange to large employers.

Q 3:23   Are qualified small employers required to purchase health coverage through an Exchange?

No. The Exchanges are strictly voluntary. Health insurance issuers may continue to offer health plans to qualified employers outside an Exchange and qualified employers may select health plan for their employees outside an Exchange. [PPACA § 1312(d)]

Q 3:24   Does federal law provide protections for employers seeking group health insurance coverage?

The Public Health Service Act (PHSA), as amended and expanded by the 2010 Health Reform Act, imposes a number of requirements and restrictions on health insurance issuers that are intended to ensure access to and affordability of coverage. [PHSA Title XXVII Part A] The 2010 Health Reform Act provides that these requirements and restrictions apply to health insurance issuers providing health insurance coverage in connection with group health plans as if included in ERISA and the Code. [ERISA § 715(a) as added by PPACA § 1562(e); I.R.C. § 9815(a)(1) as added by PPACA § 1562(f)] Consequently, violations are subject to ERISA's civil enforcement mechanisms. In addition, health insurance issuers are subject to civil monetary penalties for failure to meet the PHSA requirements. [PHSA § 2723] Except as noted, these requirements apply for plan years beginning on or after January 1, 2013 [PPACA § 12530]

Guaranteed availability of coverage. Beginning in 2014, an insurer that offers health insurance coverage in the group market in a state must accept every employer in the state that applies for coverage. [PHSA § 2702 as added by PPACA § 1201] Exceptions apply for denials of coverage based on the financial capacity of the insurer or network capacity in the case of network plans. Insurers may restrict enrollment to open or special enrollment periods, and may impose minimum employer contribution and group participation requirements.

Guaranteed renewability of coverage. Beginning in 2014, a health insurer that offers health insurance coverage in the group market must renew or continue in force coverage at the option of the plan sponsor. [PHSA § 2703 as added by PPACA § 1201]. Continuation of coverage may be denied for failure to pay required premiums or for fraud. Other situations in which coverage may be discontinued include failure on the part of the employer to meet minimum employer contribution and group participation requirements and the insurer's discontinuance of the particular coverage in question or discontinuance of all coverage. An insurer may modify coverage at the time of renewal, provided the modifications apply on a uniform basis to group health plans with that coverage.

Prohibition on rescission. A health insurance issuer offering group coverage may not rescind the coverage for an enrollee except in the case of fraud or misrepresentation. [PHSA § 2712 as added by PPACA § 1001] This requirement is effective for plan years beginning on or after September 23, 2010. [PPACA § 1004 as amended by PPACA Reconciliation § 2301]

Comprehensive coverage. A health insurance issuer that offers health insurance coverage in the *small group* market must provide coverage for the same essential health benefits package that is required to be provided by qualified plans offered in an Exchange (Q 3:21). [PHSA § 2707(a) as added by PPACA § 1201] This requirement is effective for plan years beginning after 2013. [PPACA § 1253] The requirement does not apply to grandfathered plans in existence as of the date of enactment (March 23, 2010) of the 2010 Health Reform Act.

See chapter 5 for other coverage requirements and standards applicable to group health plans and health insurance issuers offering group coverage.

Premium rating limitations. Effective for plan years beginning after 2013, the 2010 Health Reform Act imposes premium rating requirements for health insurance coverage offered in the *small group* market. Under these rules, the premium rates charged for a particular plan or coverage can vary only by (1) whether the coverage is for an individual or family, (2) rating area as established by the state in which the coverage is offered, (3) permissible age bands as set by the Secretary of HHS (limited to a variation of 3 to 1 for adults), and (4) tobacco usage (limited to a variation of 1.5 to 1). [PHSA § 2701 as added by PPACA § 1201]

The rating requirements do not apply to grandfathered plans. If a state permits health insurance issuers in the large group market to offer coverage through an Exchange (beginning in 2017), the requirements will apply to all coverage offered in the large group market in the state.

Accounting for costs. Starting with plan years beginning after March 23, 2010, each health insurer offering group of individual health insurance coverage—*including a grandfathered health plan*—must submit an annual cost report to HHS. The report must include the percentage of total premium revenue spent on (1) reimbursements for clinical services to plan enrollees, (2) activities that improve health care quality, and (3) all other non-claims costs (other than taxes and licensing or regulatory fees). These reports will be made available to the public on the HHS Web site. [PHSA § 2718 as added by PPACA § 1001 and amended by PPACA § 10101]

Rebates required. Beginning no later than January 1, 2011, a health insurer must provide rebates to plan enrollees, on a pro rata basis, for each plan year if the ratio premium revenue spent on reimbursements and quality improvement activities ((1) and (2) above) is less than:

- 85 percent in the case of coverage in the large group market, or
- 80 percent in the case of coverage in the small group or individual markets.

Types of Plans

Q 3:25   How does an employer make medical benefits available to employees?

Employer-provided medical plans generally fall into one of two broad categories: (1) indemnity plans and (2) managed care plans. However, health reimbursement arrangements have emerged as an alternative or add-on to traditional indemnity and managed care plans.

Traditional indemnity plans. Under medical care indemnity plans, also known as reimbursement plans and fee-for-service plans, the employee incurs a medical expense, and the employer's plan reimburses the expense after the fact either by paying the medical service provider (e.g., hospital or surgeon) directly or by reimbursing the employee after he or she has paid the medical service provider.

Managed care plans. Primarily as a result of efforts to control medical care costs, other types of medical care delivery systems have been developed and incorporated into employer-provided plans either as employee options or as mandated features. These include health maintenance organizations (HMOs), preferred provider organizations (PPOs), and point-of-service (POS) plans. These types of medical delivery systems contain mechanisms designed to "manage" (to a greater or lesser extent) the cost of care, type of care, or both. Many indemnity plans include a network of selected health care providers or a PPO combined with increased financial incentives to use those providers, but permit employees to go outside the network or use non-PPO providers. These hybrid plans are called point-of-service plans because they permit the employee to choose among several options each time he or she needs medical care (i.e., at the point of service).

Additionally, many of the cost-control features of HMOs and PPOs that provide incentives to choose more economical medical alternatives or limit care to what is medically necessary have, in many cases, been grafted onto the indemnity portion of medical plans, even if an HMO, PPO, or network option is not included. Features such as precertification and concurrent review of hospitalization and certain surgeries, second surgical opinions, case management, coverage of treatment in alternate settings such as hospices, home health care benefits, and judicious use of copayments have been incorporated, to a greater or lesser extent, into many indemnity-style medical insurance plans in order to control plan costs.

Note. DOL regulations lay down specific rules for processing and reviewing health care claims. These rules were prompted largely by the shift from traditional indemnity plans to plans with managed care features requiring preapproval of medical services. In addition, the 2010 Health Reform Act requires group health plans to implement an effective appeals process for appeals of coverage determinations and claims and sets forth minimum standards for an effective process. (See Qs 3:60–3:68.)

Q 3:26   What is an HMO?

An *HMO* is a health care organization, composed of medical care providers and affiliated health care institutions, that agrees to provide a specified range of medical care for a set fee (commonly referred to as a capitation fee) to individuals residing in its geographic service area. The fee (usually paid in monthly installments) covers the medical expenses incurred by the HMO member, regardless of the frequency or degree to which the HMO's medical services are used. The HMO member's primary care physician coordinates the member's care from other participating providers, health care institutions, and referral specialists. Because of this feature, HMOs have come to be referred to as "coordinated care" plans.

Example. An HMO agrees to provide specified medical care coverage for an employee and her family for a fee of $3,600 per year ($300 per month), regardless of whether their actual medical care expenses are more or less than that amount.

If an HMO is one of the options offered by the employer's medical benefit plan, the employer will pay part or all of the HMO fee. Any amount that the employer does not pay is paid by the employee via payroll deduction.

As originally conceived, HMOs generally required members to use the HMO's own physicians, affiliated hospitals, and other affiliated professionals in order to receive covered care, except in emergencies. In response to the problem of members who were on vacation or traveling on business outside the HMO's geographic service area when they needed medical care, HMOs developed various reciprocal agreements to provide out-of-service-area care for one another's members.

Note. One of the perceived disadvantages of traditional HMOs has been that members were "locked in" to the HMO providers. In recent years, many HMOs have begun to include an indemnity-type wraparound under which members can go outside the HMO's system for health care, even within the HMO's service area, and submit the bill to the HMO for reimbursement. When this indemnity option is exercised, the coverage for that service generally is at a lesser level (for example, 80 percent reimbursement rather than 100 percent coverage) than if the care were obtained directly from the HMO. Thus, the arrangement ceases to look like a traditional HMO and begins to look and function more like a point-of-service (POS) plan. (For a discussion of the requirements for federally qualified HMOs, see chapter 5.)

Q 3:27   How are traditional HMOs different from traditional medical plans?

The key features distinguishing HMOs from traditional (i.e., indemnity) medical plans are that they:

1. Provide care directly to members rather than reimbursing the cost of care obtained elsewhere; and
2. Exercise control over access to the medical care providers and health care institutions.

These features focus on the time when care is given, rather than after-the-fact determinations, and are thus designed to provide the HMO with greater control over cost, quality of care, and determinations regarding the medical necessity of care.

The U.S. Supreme Court struck a blow at what had traditionally been the economic underpinning of HMOs, which are designed to hold down health care costs by creating networks of providers who are willing to accept lower fees in return for a higher volume of business generated by the HMOs. In *Kentucky Association of Health Plans, Inc. v. Miller* [538 U.S. 329 (2003)], the Court held that Kentucky's "any willing provider" law was not preempted by ERISA. As a result, HMOs in that state and in other states with similar laws must accept any physician, pharmacist, or other health professional who meets the plan's contract criteria.

Opinions differ on the practical impact of the high court's ruling on HMOs because provider networks have expanded to include larger numbers of health care practitioners since the HMO concept originated. However, there is universal agreement that the Court's conclusion that ERISA does not automatically preempt state laws regulating insurance significantly impact HMOs and other insured health plans.

On the other hand, the Third Circuit Court of Appeals has ruled that ERISA does not require an HMO to disclose the financial incentives it pays to its physicians. In *Horvath v. Keystone Health Plan East, Inc.* [333 F.3d 450, 458 (3d Cir. 2003)], the benefits administrator of a law firm and a member of the HMO offered by the firm, sued the HMO. The administrator's lawsuit charged that, as an ERISA fiduciary, the HMO had a duty to disclosure to plan beneficiaries all material facts relating to the insurance benefits provided, including information on physician incentives. In reaching its conclusion, the Third Circuit noted that HMOs provide a variety of health care services for a fixed fee and in doing so attempt to control costs by carefully scrutinizing health care services. "These cost-controlling measures," said the court, "are commonly complemented by specific financial incentives to physicians, rewarding them for decreasing utilization of health care services and penalizing them for what may be found to be excessive treatment." [333 F.3d 450, 458 (3d Cir. 2003)] However, the court said, an HMO is under no duty to disclose information about such incentives unless a beneficiary would be harmed as a result of not having the information. [333 F.3d 450, 458 (3d Cir. 2003)]

Q 3:28   What is a federally qualified HMO?

HMOs that satisfy federal requirements regarding their structure and operation can apply for a designation of "federally qualified."

Although the federal Health Maintenance Organization Act of 1973 no longer requires employers to offer "federally qualified" HMOs as an alternative to their medical plans, the law continues to impose obligations on employers that do offer federally qualified HMOs.

The HMO Act's mandatory offering provisions expired in 1995. However, any employer or public entity (i.e., state or local government) that offers or continues to maintain a federally qualified HMO must satisfy certain requirements if it (1) had an average of 25 employees during any calendar quarter of the prior calendar year and (2) was covered under the minimum wage provisions of the Fair Labor Standards Act (FLSA) during any quarter in the prior calendar year or would have been but for Section 13a of the FLSA. [42 C.F.R. § 417.151, revised as of July 1, 1996] Those requirements include the following:

1. Offering the option of membership to its employees and their eligible dependents who reside in the HMO's federally qualified service area at the same time that a health benefits plan is offered to them. [42 C.F.R. § 417.153]

2. If an employer has employees who are represented by a bargaining representative, referring the option of membership in the federally qualified HMO to the bargaining representative and raising the issue in the collective bargaining process at certain designated times. [42 C.F.R. §§ 417.153(c), 417.156(a)]

3. Granting the HMO access to its employees and, depending on the circumstances, to its premises. [42 C.F.R. § 417.155(a)]

4. Reviewing the HMO's literature in advance to correct only "factual errors and misleading statements," unless the HMO agrees to more extensive

changes or more extensive changes are required by law. Furthermore, the employer must complete its review promptly so that it will not interfere with or delay the group enrollment period. [42 C.F.R. § 417.155(b)]

5. Permitting employees to select (which must be done in writing) from among the different alternatives in the employer's health benefit program (including HMO options) when they first become eligible for benefits, during the annual group open enrollment period, when they move into the service area of a federally qualified HMO for which they were not previously eligible, or when another alternative under which they are covered ceases operation. [42 C.F.R. §§ 417.155(c)(1), 417.155(e)(1)] For this purpose, employers generally must permit any eligible employee or dependent to enroll in an HMO, or transfer out of HMO coverage to a non-HMO alternative, during the group open enrollment period or upon the occurrence of any of the other circumstances described above, without imposing limitations based on health status, waiting periods, or exclusions as a condition either of enrollment in an HMO or of transfer from HMO to non-HMO coverage. [42 C.F.R. § 417.155(c)] Employers may, however, continue to impose conditions for the non-HMO alternative on individuals who are not switching out of an HMO, except to the extent prohibited by HIPAA.

6. Complying with the HMO Act's nondiscriminatory contribution requirement.

Required contributions. The HMO Act requires the employer to contribute toward the monthly cost of coverage under a federally qualified HMO if the employer contributes toward any of its other medical plan options. [42 U.S.C. § 300e-9(c)] Employers must contribute an amount toward the HMO's monthly premium that does not "financially discriminate" against an employee that enrolls in the HMO. The contribution will not discriminate financially if the method of determining the contribution is reasonable and is designed to ensure that employees have a fair choice among health benefit plan alternatives. [42 C.F.R. § 417.157] An employer need not, merely because it offers its employees the option of membership in a federally qualified HMO, pay more for health benefits than it would otherwise have to pay for them under a collective bargaining agreement or other contract (for example, health insurance contract) in effect at the time the employer includes the HMO in its health benefit plan. [42 U.S.C. § 300e-9(c); 42 C.F.R. § 417.157]

Examples of employer contributions for HMO coverage that will not be considered financially discriminatory include the following:

1. The per-employee contributions for the HMO and the non-HMO alternative are equal.

2. The employer contribution reflects the HMO's enrollment in terms of enrollee attributes that can reasonably be used to predict utilization, experience, costs, or risk. An employer using this method would contribute an equal amount for each enrollee in a given class established on the basis of those attributes, regardless of the health benefit option chosen by the employee.

3. The employer contribution is a fixed percentage of the premium for each of the alternatives offered.

4. The employer's HMO contribution is a negotiated amount that is mutually acceptable to the employer and the HMO. (The employer cannot insist on any contribution arrangement that would cause the HMO to violate any rules, such as the community rating requirement, to which it is subject.)

An employer contribution determined by an acceptable method can be adjusted by the employer if it would result in a nominal payment or no payment at all by HMO enrollees (because the HMO premium is lower than the premiums for the other alternatives offered). If the employer's policy is that all employees must contribute to their health care coverage, the employer can require HMO enrollees who would otherwise pay little or nothing to make a payment that does not exceed 50 percent of the required employee contribution to the principal non-HMO alternative. For this purpose, the principal non-HMO alternative is defined as the one that covers the largest number of enrollees from the particular employer. [42 C.F.R. § 417.157(a)(4)]

> **Note.** The final HMO regulation requires employers to retain for three years the data on which the HMO contribution calculations were based. [42 C.F.R. § 417.157(f)] Any amount by which the HMO's monthly premium charge exceeds the required monthly employer contribution may be charged to employees as the required employee contribution toward HMO coverage.

Inclusion in a cafeteria plan. When an employer permits employees to pay for medical coverage by salary reduction, after-tax employee contributions are converted into pretax employer contributions, thereby increasing the amount of employer contributions toward the coverage. This "premium conversion," which is governed by the Code Section 125 cafeteria plan rules, makes the coverage option for which it is available more financially attractive to employees by lowering their out-of-pocket premium cost. Accordingly, failure to offer this feature in connection with the HMO option could be viewed as financially discriminatory. In addition, if employer credits are allowable toward various options under the cafeteria plan, the credits should be equally available to be used toward HMO contributions as well.

Q 3:29   What is a PPO?

A *PPO* is a network of medical care providers that have agreed to provide various medical care services for specified fees. The network may be organized by the employer or by an outside entity such as an insurance company that either insures or administers the employer's plan. An employee who is covered by the PPO arrangement is generally required or encouraged to use a preferred provider. The expectation is that the cost to the plan will be less if the employee uses a preferred provider than if the employee uses a medical care provider that is not a preferred provider.

Q 3:30   How does a PPO differ from an HMO?

Generally, unless the PPO is the only option available, use of the PPO's preferred providers is voluntary. Employer medical plans often allow the participant to select either the PPO or the participant's own health care provider at any time on a service-by-service basis. In contrast, membership in a traditional HMO (generally for renewable one-year periods) restricts the employee to the use of the providers associated with that HMO for the duration of the membership period.

Q 3:31   What is a point-of-service plan?

Although generally thought of as a managed care plan, a *point-of-service plan* is actually a combination of traditional indemnity and network or participating provider coverage. The individual may choose each time he or she seeks medical care whether to go out of the network.

Typically, the plan will contain a financial incentive, such as a greater percentage reimbursement of claims, to encourage the member to use the participating provider. In addition, a higher copayment (the portion of each expense paid by the member, not the plan) may apply to expenses incurred when using nonparticipating providers so that the employee receives a lesser rate of reimbursement as the price for exercising his or her unfettered choice of health care providers.

The essence of a point-of-service plan is the preservation of the member's choice: he or she is never locked in to a particular set of health care providers and always has the option to select whatever health care provider he or she desires.

Q 3:32   What is a defined contribution health plan?

The *defined contribution health plan* is an emerging concept that is being touted as a way to rein in rising health care costs. Although defined contribution plans can take different forms, the basic concept is the same: The employer limits its contribution toward an employee's health coverage to a set sum, and if the cost of coverage exceeds that amount, the employee makes up the difference.

At the other end of the spectrum, an employer's defined contribution plan may offer employees prescreened and preselected health care options through either a single carrier or multiple carriers that are contracted for at group rates. Employees are given a set amount to spend on health coverage; if their coverage choices exceed that amount, they must pay the difference. Although this model also controls the employer's spending on health coverage, it does not take the employer out of the picture entirely. The employer remains responsible for choosing health care options and administering the plan and maintains accountability.

A defined contribution plan can also take the form of a health reimbursement arrangement that supplements other medical coverage. For example, an employer may offer health insurance coverage under a high-deductible plan and a maximum annual reimbursement for out-of-pocket medical expenses.

Tax treatment is a key issue with respect to defined contribution health plans. Group health insurance coverage is generally tax-free to employees and tax-deductible by the employer. In addition, benefits to employees are excludable from income. The IRS has ruled that health reimbursement arrangements (HRAs) that meet certain requirements also qualify for tax-favored treatment. The tax treatment of HRAs is discussed in detail in Qs 3:130–3:138.

Q 3:33   What is a dental maintenance organization?

A *dental maintenance organization* is a type of HMO offering only dental care benefits.

Q 3:34   What is a multiple-employer welfare arrangement?

A *multiple-employer welfare arrangement*, or MEWA, is a plan in which more than one unrelated employer participates. For this purpose, *unrelated* means that tax or other rules do not create a legal relationship such as parent-subsidiary between the employers that causes them to be treated as one employer for tax or other purposes. A MEWA cannot be collectively bargained. Each participating employer in a MEWA is generally considered to have its own plan for ERISA purposes. MEWA plans typically are developed to provide coverage to a group of employers with a common interest or bond, such as small banks or dentists. MEWAs are subject to state regulation under a special ERISA preemption rule even when they provide ERISA benefits. (See chapter 2 for a further discussion of MEWAs.)

In an Information Letter, the DOL concluded that a union-sponsored fund that provided medical and other benefits to employees of several participating employers was a MEWA and, thus, subject to state regulation. [DOL Information Letter (Aug. 23, 2002)] The DOL noted that it had never made a determination that the fund was a collectively bargained plan. Moreover, if asked to make such a determination, the plan was unlikely to qualify because many of the employees covered by the fund were "beneficial members" who were not represented by the union. Under DOL proposed regulations, a plan will not be deemed collectively bargained (and, therefore, exempt from state regulation) unless for any plan year 80 percent of the participants in the plan have a "nexus" to the collective bargaining relationship. [DOL Prop. Reg. § 2510.3-40(b)(2)]

All MEWAs (as well as entities claiming not to be MEWAs because of the exception for collectively bargained plans) are required to file Form M-1 with the DOL. [DOL Reg. § 2520.101-2] Form M-1 provides information about compliance with group health plan mandates. The annual Form M-1 is generally required to be filed by March 1 of the following year. The maximum penalty for failure to file Form M-1 is $1,100 per day.

Q 3:35   What is a collectively bargained medical plan?

A *collectively bargained medical plan* is a single plan in which more than one unrelated employer participates, and which is maintained pursuant to one or more collective bargaining agreements. This special characterization as a single collectively bargained plan has an impact on who has legal, administrative, and other duties regarding the plan's membership and whether the plan would qualify for any minimum-size exemptions under particular laws. In addition, ERISA preempts state regulation of a collectively bargained plan.

The DOL has proposed regulations that specify the criteria that must be met for a plan to be deemed a collectively bargained plan. [DOL Prop. Reg. § 2510.3-40] The regulations are intended to address "bogus" insurance products that are marketed as ERISA benefit plans that are exempt from state regulation.

Under final DOL regulations, all MEWAs (as well as entities claiming not to be MEWAs because of the exception for collectively bargained plans) are required to file Form M-1 with the DOL. [DOL Reg. § 2520.101-2] The form provides information about compliance with group health plan mandates. The annual Form M-1 is generally required to be filed by March 1 of the following year. The maximum penalty for failure to file Form M-1 is $1,100 per day.

Funding Types and Cost Sharing

Q 3:36   How is an employer-provided group health plan funded?

The employer has a wide choice of methods of funding a group health plan, including no funding (self-insurance), full insurance, partial insurance (a minimum-premium plan or stop-loss insurance), or funding through a trust. (See chapter 20 for additional discussion of these funding choices.) A prepaid health care plan such as an HMO is considered to be insured or similar to an insured plan for most purposes.

Q 3:37   May an employer share the cost of a group health plan with employees?

Yes. Employers can, and typically do, share the cost of a group health plan with employees. Note, however, that the 2010 Health Reform Act imposes new restrictions on group health plans and health insurance issuers offering group health plans that limit an employer's flexibility when it comes to cost sharing. Those rules include:

- Affordability and minimum value requirements for large employers under employer responsibility provisions (see Q 3:15);
- Minimum essential benefits requirements that limit cost sharing for insurance offered through state-based Exchanges and in the small group market (see Qs 3:21, 3:24); and

- Prohibitions on cost sharing for preventive services and restrictions on annual and lifetime limits for benefits under group health plans and group health insurance (see chapter 5).

Two common cost-sharing methods are sharing the cost of coverage and sharing the cost of covered services whenever they are incurred.

Sharing cost of coverage. The plan may be fully noncontributory (i.e., employees are not required to make a contribution from their pay in order to be covered) or only partly noncontributory (e.g., the employee's own coverage is noncontributory, but a contribution is required if the employee wishes to have dependent coverage). Alternatively, the plan may require the employee to pay a percentage of the cost of all coverage elected under the plan. Finally, the plan may be fully contributory, requiring the employee to contribute for all the coverage provided under the plan (employee-pay-all).

Sharing cost of covered services. Three common methods of sharing the cost of covered services as they are incurred are deductibles, coinsurance, and copayments.

(1) *Deductibles.* When the plan provides for an annual deductible (e.g., $250), the employee must pay for that amount of expenses with his or her own funds each year. The plan pays only for the expenses in excess of the deductible amount. The deductible need not be a fixed dollar amount applicable to all participants; increasingly, deductibles are tied to a nondiscriminatory measure such as by increasing the deductible according to compensation levels.

(2) *Coinsurance.* In a coinsurance arrangement, the plan pays a specified percentage of the covered medical expenses (for example, 80 percent), while the employee pays the remainder (in this example, 20 percent). The employee's portion is referred to as the coinsurance amount. (Hence, the employer and employee are coinsuring the benefits.) If the plan contains an in-network/out-of-network option or a PPO option, the coinsurance rate charged to the employee might be less for using the network or PPO providers and more for using other providers as a none too subtle encouragement to use the network or PPO. For example, the participant's coinsurance amount might be 10 percent for services provided by network or PPO providers and 30 percent when an out-of-network provider is used.

(3) *Copayments.* Copayments are single-service charges, such as $20 per doctor's office visit or $100 per hospitalization, that apply to particular services even after the annual deductible has been satisfied. These copayment charges must be paid by the participant; they are a way of sharing the cost of the particular service and encouraging the employee to consider carefully the frequency of his or her utilization of the medical services that are targeted in this manner.

Example. Sam participates in his employer's medical plan, which imposes a 20 percent coinsurance rate and a $15 copayment for each doctor's office visit. Sam gets the flu and goes to the doctor's office twice for treatment. For each office visit he pays a $15 copayment that is not reimbursed under the plan. His employer's plan will reimburse 80 percent of the remaining covered charges for each visit.

In a 2003 case, two plan participants brought a class action lawsuit against several health plans, challenging the copayments charged for prescription drugs. Each plan charged a fixed copayment ($5 per prescription), which in some cases exceeded the actual cost of the medication to the plan (although, in many other cases, the medications were far more expensive than the copayment). The plaintiffs argued that whenever a copayment exceeded the actual cost of the prescribed medication, the excess represented an amount wrongfully taken from the beneficiary and the excess charge constituted a breach of fiduciary duty. A U.S. district court concluded that the terms of the plan clearly specified the copayment amounts without making exception for cases where the copayment exceeded the plan's cost. Moreover, the court said, there can be no breach of fiduciary duty when an ERISA plan is implemented according to its written, nondiscretionary terms. The court also pointed out that the participants who brought the lawsuit actually came out ahead under the copayment plan—one paid $70 for 13 prescriptions that cost the plan $572.14, while the other paid $355 for 72 prescriptions for which the plan paid $2,181.84. The court noted that some participants may have experienced a "net loss" by paying more in copayments than the plan's cost for their prescriptions. However, the court said that would still not imply a breach of fiduciary duty, but rather the sort of reasonable "line-drawing" that is permitted under the law. In a brief opinion, the Ninth Circuit Court of Appeals affirmed the district court's decision. [Alves v. Harvard Pilgrim Health Care, Inc., 316 F.3d 290 (1st Cir. 2003), *aff'g* 204 F. Supp. 2d 198 (D. Mass. 2002)]

Combining cost-control techniques. To control plan costs, many employer-provided group health plans use a combination of cost-sharing features. Thus, a single plan may require employee contributions and contain both deductible and coinsurance features. Simple cost sharing often does not provide a sufficient incentive for the patient to be a more careful consumer of medical care services. In addition, many employers have added "managed care" features to their health care plans in order to better control plan costs.

Q 3:38   What is managed care?

Managed care refers to managing, overseeing, or channeling health care services under an employee benefit plan to provide cost-effective care and avoid unnecessary services. Although managed care is thought of as an arrangement whereby access to providers is controlled by a "gatekeeper," managed care is not that limited and encompasses a wide array of cost-control techniques that are increasingly being inserted into even traditional indemnity-type medical plans. Preferred providers are one feature of managed care. Another is utilization review, which includes preadmission certification, individual case management, and second surgical opinions.

DOL regulations impose time limits and requirements for the processing and review of health benefit claims, including preservice authorizations. The 2010

Health Reform Act requires group health plans to implement an effective appeals process for appeals of coverage determinations and claims and sets forth minimum standards for an effective process. (See Qs 3:70–3:78.)

Q 3:39   What is utilization review?

Utilization review (UR) is a process used to determine the need, extent, and effectiveness of health care services. The goal of UR is to help avoid unnecessarily lengthy or uneconomical care and to assure that the care is medically necessary and provided in the most appropriate setting.

Typically, a UR determination is made (1) before the services are provided (e.g., preadmission certification or second surgical opinion programs); (2) during the course of services (concurrent review); or (3) after the services have been rendered (retrospective review). When UR is performed, the UR entity uses medical practice guidelines for what is recommended or acceptable treatment for particular conditions to evaluate the medical care and services that are proposed to be given (prospective review), are currently being given (concurrent review), or were given (retrospective review). These medical practice guidelines have been developed (and, in many instances, are constantly being updated) by medical societies and research organizations, based in part on outcomes assessment; that is, after-the-fact review of how well various treatment alternatives have worked in actual practice in various circumstances. The earlier the review process is introduced, the more chance there is for affecting the course of treatment given and, as a result, the costs incurred for treatment.

Example. Prior to a hospitalization, UR might indicate that a one-week hospitalization is normal for a particular surgery. UR during that hospital stay might find that, because of complications, an additional four days in the hospital is medically necessary. At the end of the additional days, UR might find that the medically necessary follow-up care could be provided safely and cost-effectively in an extended care facility at a significantly lower daily rate, or at home with supplementary home health care services, instead of again extending the hospital stay.

UR may be obtained as a part of a benefits package offered by an insurance carrier or may be grafted onto an existing program by retaining a third-party firm specializing in review and monitoring of health care services and service providers.

Practice Pointer. The Newborns' and Mothers' Health Protection Act of 1996 expressly prohibits a plan from requiring precertification or authorizations for inpatient hospital stays for the statutory minimum number of hours following childbirth (see chapter 5). UR may also be limited by requirements of the 2010 Health Reform Act. For example, the minimum essential benefits requirements for insurance offered through state-based Exchanges and in the small group market prohibit prior authorization for emergency service (see Qs 3:21, 3:24)

DOL regulations impose time limits and requirements for the processing and review of health benefit claims, including preadmission certification and concurrent review. The 2010 Health Reform Act requires group health plans to implement an effective appeals process for appeals of coverage determinations and claims and sets forth minimum standards for an effective process. (See Qs 3:60–3:68.)

Q 3:40 What is preadmission certification?

Under a plan providing for *preadmission certification,* a participant normally is required to seek approval for nonemergency hospitalization in advance of admission to the hospital. The goal of this type of review is, first, to review whether the hospital is the most appropriate place in which to render the medical care and then if so, to evaluate how long a hospital stay is necessary and appropriate.

Failure to obtain preadmission certification may subject the participant to financial penalties in the form of lower benefit coverage or no coverage at all for the hospitalization in question. Plans that have a preadmission certification requirement typically exempt emergency care from this requirement but require prompt postadmission notification of any emergency admission. Under the 2010 Health Reform Act, the minimum essential benefits requirements for insurance offered through state-based Exchanges and in the small group market prohibit prior authorization for emergency service (see Qs 3:21, 3:24)

> **Practice Pointer.** It is important to note that requiring preadmission certification for hospital stays for a mother and newborn child following childbirth is expressly prohibited by the Newborns' and Mothers' Health Protection Act of 1996 (see chapter 5).

DOL regulations impose time limits and requirements for the processing and review of health benefit claims, including preadmission certification The 2010 Health Reform Act requires group health plans to implement an effective appeals process for appeals of coverage determinations and claims and sets forth minimum standards for an effective process. (See Qs 3:60–3:68.)

Q 3:41 What is concurrent review?

Concurrent review means monitoring a patient's care once he or she has been admitted to the hospital in order to better control the appropriateness and cost of medical care rendered and the duration of the hospital stay. The goal is to cut down on extra hospital days and excessive hospital tests and procedures, without adversely affecting the quality of the patient's medical care.

The UR entity determines whether the patient should be discharged or whether additional hospital days are warranted based on the patient's particular circumstances. Should the patient and the treating physician disagree with the UR determination, they generally may appeal.

Practice Pointer. A UR entity cannot cut short the hospital stay of a mother and newborn child following childbirth in violation of the minimum inpatient stay requirements of the Newborns' and Mothers' Health Protection Act of 1996. The portion of the hospital stay that exceeds the statutory minimum can, however, be made subject to the plan's concurrent review process.

DOL regulations impose time limits and requirements for the processing and review of health benefit claims, including concurrent review. The 2010 Health Reform Act requires group health plans to implement an effective appeals process for appeals of coverage determinations and claims and sets forth minimum standards for an effective process. (See Qs 3:60–3:68.)

Q 3:42   What is retrospective review?

Retrospective review is review of medical care services, typically hospitalization, after the fact—at the point when the plan is processing the claim for payment of the expenses for the care. As such, the review is advisory only; treatment alternatives are not proposed, and treatment is not modified or curtailed, because it already has been rendered.

Retrospective review includes confirming (1) that the patient was in fact covered under the plan on the date the services were rendered; (2) whether other coverage exists for coordination of benefits purposes; (3) whether the services actually were rendered to the patient; and (4) whether the charge was appropriate for the services rendered. The chief benefit of retrospective review is uncovering unnecessary services, unusual practice patterns, or fraudulent claims—information that may be used as a basis for plan design modifications in the future or for decisions regarding the continued inclusion of a particular health care provider in a program.

DOL regulations impose time limits and requirements for the processing and review of health benefit claims, including postservice claims. The 2010 Health Reform Act requires group health plans to implement an effective appeals process for appeals of coverage determinations and claims and sets forth minimum standards for an effective process. (See Qs 3:60–3:68.)

Q 3:43   What is a second surgical opinion procedure?

Under a *second surgical opinion procedure,* a participant is either required or encouraged to obtain a second opinion before obtaining certain specified nonemergency surgical procedures. To encourage the participant to do this, the plan typically covers the cost of a second surgical opinion in full and may also cover a third "tie-breaker" opinion. Failure to obtain a required second surgical opinion may result in a financial penalty such as reduced coverage (e.g., only 50 percent reimbursement) or no coverage at all for the surgical procedure. Increasingly, managed care plan design incorporates mandatory second surgical opinions for a rather lengthy list of specified nonemergency surgical procedures.

Usually, the participant is not obligated to abide by the results of the second surgical opinion, but it is hoped that advice not to have surgery will encourage the patient to consider alternate courses of treatment more seriously. Some employers have found, however, that the second surgical opinion usually agrees with the attending physician's recommendation, the surgery is performed anyway, and the plan does not achieve any savings; in fact, plan costs increase because the second surgical opinions are being paid for without any noticeable effect on the frequency or cost of surgery. This has led some benefit professionals to question whether second surgical opinion programs are worthwhile.

Q 3:44   What is individual case management?

Individual case management involves special handling for cases that are expected to have unusually high costs, such as catastrophic illness, AIDS, cancer, and traumatic head injuries. As soon as possible, case reviewers develop a proposed course of long-term treatment using cost-effective treatment alternatives and cost-effective settings (such as an extended care facility, a hospice, or home health care rather than hospitalization). Often, the medical plan covers treatments otherwise excluded if such treatment is recommended by the case management reviewers and agreed to by the patient and his or her physician. For example, the plan may not normally cover home health care or hospice care, but will provide it in an individual case management situation as an alternative to extended hospitalization.

Significantly, case management is almost always presented as a voluntary process that will be undertaken only with the agreement of the patient and treating physician. This is in part because case management takes the individual out of the usual covered benefits and designs a special set of targeted covered benefits for the particular individual. Most plans incorporating this feature give the patient the right to refuse it and simply take the plan's usual covered benefits instead; for example, if the patient prefers to reserve full freedom to consult any health care provider that he or she chooses or to try different courses of treatment from that recommended under the case management analysis.

Q 3:45   How are preferred providers incorporated into health care arrangements?

A panel of preferred providers (see Q 3:29) may be included in a health care arrangement in order to channel participants to preselected providers that will charge discounted fees as prearranged with the plan. The plan's benefit structure may include a financial incentive to encourage participants to use the preferred providers, such as waiver of copayments and/or deductibles. Alternatively, the plan may include a financial disincentive for failure to use the preferred provider, such as a reduced reimbursement level or no reimbursement at all.

Q 3:46   Does ERISA prevent employers from including managed care or cost containment features in their group health plans?

ERISA does not generally prevent employers from including managed care or cost-containment features (or both) in their group health plans. Employers sponsoring group health plans do not breach any ERISA fiduciary duties by incorporating managed care features into their plans. The decision to adopt or amend a plan is an employer/sponsor function under ERISA, not a fiduciary function. However, this employer prerogative must be exercised within the boundaries of the law.

Exceptions. ERISA does prohibit managed care or cost containment restrictions in some circumstance. The Newborns' and Mothers' Health Protection Act amended ERISA and the Code to require group health plans to provide a mandatory minimum hospital stay benefit for both the mother and the newborn child following birth. Moreover, this mandatory minimum benefit cannot be made subject to any precertification or authorization requirement. The 2010 Health Reform Act added a new prohibition on cost sharing for preventive services and restrictions on annual and lifetime limits for benefits under group health plans and group health insurance.

Moreover, group health plans are subject to other mandated benefit requirements and standards that employers must fulfill when implementing managed care features.

See chapter 5 for a completed discussion of these mandated benefit requirements and standards.

Practice Pointer. Once an employer decides to amend an ERISA plan, the manner in which the amendment is implemented is an area of fiduciary responsibility. Employers subject to ERISA should be mindful of the general ERISA duties regarding selection, monitoring, and retention of insurance carriers and other service providers to the plan and also should bear in mind the residual ERISA liability and cofiduciary liability. [*Compare* Corcoran v. United HealthCare Inc., 968 F.2d 1321 (5th Cir. 1992), *with* Salley v. E.I. DuPont de Nemours & Co., 966 F.2d 1011 (5th Cir. 1992).] In this regard, the DOL issued an advisory opinion letter specifically stating that selection, monitoring, and retention of vendors is a fiduciary function. The advisory opinion letter also sets forth some considerations for the plan regarding how often vendors should be changed or the function put out to bid. [DOL Adv. Op. Ltr. to Diane Orentes Cerest (Feb. 19, 1998)] (See chapter 2 for a detailed discussion of ERISA fiduciary responsibility and liability.)

Note. The employer's past course of conduct or the presence of a collective bargaining agreement may preclude the employer from unilaterally adopting or modifying a medical plan. The employer's ability to amend an ERISA-covered welfare benefit plan is discussed in detail in chapter 2.

Precertification of hospitalization. The Court of Appeals for the Third Circuit upheld a provision in an ERISA medical plan requiring that participants obtain precertification of hospitalization or suffer a 30 percent reduction in the level of reimbursement of covered expenses under the plan. A participant who experienced shortness of breath associated with heart disease and was hospitalized shortly thereafter was aware of his employer-provided medical plan's precertification provision but did not notify the hospital of it at the time he was admitted, and he carried an outdated medical plan ID card that did not contain the required information. The plan's precertification procedure also permitted an individual admitted to the hospital on an emergency basis to notify the plan within 48 hours of the admission, but the participant failed to do that as well. When the participant subsequently submitted a claim for expenses, the plan applied the 30 percent penalty for failure to obtain the required certification of hospitalization.

The appellate court drew a distinction between ERISA's concern with the administration of benefit plans and the design of such plans per se. It noted that ERISA does not impose a duty on employers to provide health care benefits to employees and held that ERISA's fiduciary responsibility provisions do not apply to the employer's design decisions and, hence, do not prohibit the inclusion of a penalty provision in the medical plan. Although the employee suffered significant economic deprivation, the employer did not violate ERISA by including a 30 percent penalty, even though the message conveyed by the precertification requirement could have been delivered by using a far lesser penalty. [Nazay v. Miller, 949 F.3d 1323, 14 Employee Benefit Cas. (BNA) 1953 (3d Cir. 1991)]

Note that the decision in *Nazay* was issued prior to the adoption of HIPAA, the Newborns' and Mothers' Health Protection Act of 1996, the Mental Health Parity Act of 1996 (and the Mental Health Parity and Addiction Equity Act of 2008), as well as the 2010 Health Reform Act, each of which amended ERISA expressly to incorporate limits on the employer's freedom of benefit design under group health plans. (These laws are discussed in detail in chapter 5.)

Participating providers and nonassignment clauses. Another method of encouraging employees to use a medical plan's managed care features is to incorporate participating providers and a nonassignment provision. Under such an arrangement, the employee is free to use either a participating or nonparticipating provider. The key mechanism for shifting utilization to the participating provider is the method of reimbursement. Typically, if the participant uses the participating provider, the plan pays the provider's fees directly to the provider, and the participant pays only the copayment (if any). If the participant uses a nonparticipating provider, the plan's nonassignment clause would force the participant to pay the entire bill first and then submit a claim for reimbursement, subject to the plan's copayment requirement. Thus, for example, if the plan pays 70 percent for a particular medical service, the employee who uses a participating provider would pay only the 30 percent copayment, but the employee who uses a nonparticipating provider first would have to pay 100 percent of the bill and then submit a claim for the 70 percent covered by the plan, accompanied by a copy of a bill marked "Paid." Sometimes the plan also is designed to reimburse the preferred provider's charges at a higher percentage or in full.

These nonassignment clauses have been challenged by nonparticipating providers. The Court of Appeals for the Ninth Circuit upheld such a plan design as not violating ERISA. Noting that Congress expressly incorporated in ERISA a prohibition against assignment of pension benefits but did not do so for welfare benefits, the appellate court held that Congress intended to allow the free marketplace to work out "competitive, cost effective, medical expense reducing structures as might evolve." [Davidowitz v. Delta Dental Plan of Cal., Inc., 946 F.2d 1476, 1481 (9th Cir. 1991)] The Court of Appeals for the Eighth Circuit has held that a general state law requiring free assignability of claims affects plan administration, including cost-control measures, and thus "relates to" an ERISA plan and is preempted by ERISA. [Arkansas Blue Cross & Blue Shield v. St. Mary's Hosp., 947 F.2d 1341 (8th Cir. 1991)]

Recovery from another source. Another cost-containment feature frequently incorporated into employer-sponsored group health plans is an offset for benefits recovered through legal action or claim settlement. Many plans require the participant to sign an agreement obligating him or her to reimburse the plan to the extent of any reimbursement of medical expenses (such as for settlement of an automobile accident claim for injuries). For further discussion of developments in this area, see Qs 3:85–3:86.

Plan Administration

Q 3:47 How does the 2010 Health Reform Act affect administration of a group health plan?

The 2010 Health Reform Act requires group health plans to develop and utilize uniform explanation of coverage documents and standardized definitions (Q 3:49) and implement an appeals process for review of coverage determinations and claims (Q 3:60).

Q 3:48 Are there specific requirements for health plan SPDs?

Yes. Under DOL regulations, health plan summary plan descriptions (SPDs) must describe:

- Any cost-sharing provisions, including premiums, deductibles, coinsurance, and copayments for which the participant or beneficiary will be responsible
- Any annual or lifetime caps or other limits on benefits
- The extent to which preventive services are covered
- Whether and under what circumstances existing and new drugs are covered under the plan
- Whether and under what circumstances coverage is provided for medical tests, devices, and procedures

- Provision governing the use of network providers, the composition of the provider network, and whether and under what circumstances coverage is provided for out-of-network services
- Any conditions or limits on the selection of primary care providers or providers of specialty medical care
- Any conditions or limits on obtaining emergency medical care
- Any provisions requiring preauthorization or utilization review as a condition of obtaining a benefit or service under the plan
- Procedures related to qualified medical child support orders
- The plan sponsor's authority to terminate the plan or eliminate benefits under the plan
- COBRA continuation coverage rights

[DOL Reg. § 2520.102-3]

In its preamble to the regulations, the DOL acknowledges that detailed lists of covered drugs, tests, procedures, and devices in the SPD could result in a lengthy tome. The DOL says the SPD is required only to adequately inform participants of their plan coverage and to direct them to a source where additional information about coverage for a specific item may be obtained free of charge. Similarly, the DOL says that a detailed list of network providers may be furnished in a separate document along with the SPD.

Q 3:49   What requirements does the 2010 Health Reform Act mandate for health plan benefit and coverage explanations?

The 2010 Health Reform Act directs the Secretary of HHS to develop standards for use by group health plans and health insurance issuers in compiling and providing to plan participants a summary of benefits and coverage explanation that accurately describes the benefits and coverage under the plan. The standards are required to be published no later than 12 months after the March 23 date of enactment of the 2010 Health Reform Act. [PHSA § 2715 as added by PPACA § 1001 as amended by PPACA § 10101]

Group health plans—including grandfathered plans—must comply with the new standards no later than 24 months after the date of enactment of the 2010 Health Reform Act. At that time, each employee must be provided with a compliant summary explanation prior to enrollment or reenrollment in the plan. The summary may be provided in electronic or paper form.

If a group health plan makes any material modification in any of the plan terms or coverage, the plan must provide notice of the modification to enrollees not later than 60 days before the modification will be effective.

A plan that willfully fails to provide the required information is subject to a fine of not more than $1,000 for each failure. For purposes of the penalty, failure to provide required information to each enrollee is treated as a separate violation.

The standards set by HHS must meet the following criteria in terms of appearance, language, and content:

- The standards must ensure that the summary of coverage and benefits is presented in a uniform format that does not exceed four pages in length and does not include print smaller than 12-point font.
- The standards must ensure the summary is presented in a culturally and linguistically appropriate manner and uses terminology understandable by the average plan enrollee.
- Content must include:
  - Uniform definitions of standard insurance and medical terms so that consumers can compare coverage and understand the terms of (or exceptions to) coverage. Insurance terms to be defined include premium, deductible, coinsurance, copayment, out-of-pocket limit, preferred provider, non-preferred provider, out-of-network copayments UCR (usual, customary, and reasonable) fees, excluded services, and grievance and appeals. Medical terms to be defined include hospitalization, hospital outpatient care, emergency room care, physician services, prescription drug coverage, durable medical equipment, home health care, skilled nursing care, and rehabilitation services.
  - Descriptions of coverage for each of the categories of essential health benefits (see Q 3:21) and other benefits specified by HHS.
  - Exceptions, reductions, or limitations on coverage.
  - Cost-sharing provisions, including deductible, coinsurance, and copayment obligations.
  - Renewability and continuation of coverage provisions.
  - Coverage facts information that includes examples illustrating common benefit scenarios, including pregnancy and serious or chronic medical conditions, and related cost sharing.
  - Disclosure of whether the plan provides minimum essential coverage and meets the minimum 60 percent value test under the employer responsibility requirements (see Q 3:15).
  - A statement that the document is a summary and that the coverage document for the plan should be consulted for the governing terms.
  - Contact information for additional information and a copy of the plan document.

Q 3:50   What requirements apply to the use of electronic media for health plan transactions?

The Health Insurance Portability and Accountability Act of 1996 (HIPAA) required the development of a nationally based electronic health information system. HIPAA directed the Secretary of HHS to develop standards for the electronic transfer and sharing of health information among health plans, health care clearinghouses, and health care providers that conduct transactions electronically.

> *Who is affected.* These requirements apply to group health plans that either have 50 or more participants or are administered by an entity other than the employer that established and maintains the plan. They also apply to employee welfare benefit plans or other arrangements established to offer or provide health care benefits to employees of two or more employers, health insurance issuers (including insurance carriers), HMOs, and long-term care policies, among others.

The regulations establish standards for eight types of electronic health transactions:

1. Health care claims and similar transactions
2. Health care eligibility transactions, including inquiries and responses concerning an individual's eligibility for benefits and coverage provided by the plan
3. Referral certification and similar transactions, such as a request by a health care provider to obtain authorization to refer an individual to another provider
4. Health care claim status inquiries and responses
5. Enrollment and disenrollment in a health plan
6. Health care payments and advice about the transfer of funds
7. Health plan premium payments
8. Coordination of benefits transactions to determine the relative payment responsibilities of two or more health plans or insurers covering an individual

The 2010 Health Reform Act mandates the development of further standards for electronic health transactions. The additional standards include:

1. Requirements for administrative and financial transactions to enable determination of an individual's eligibility and financial responsibility for specific services prior to or at the point of care
2. Operating rules for health claims and "encounter information," including enrollment and disenrollment in a plan, premium payments, and referral certification and authorization.

Beginning in 2014, health plans are required to certify compliance with the electronic standards. Noncompliant plans are subject to annual penalty of $1 per covered life (indexed) until certification is complete. [PPACA §§ 1104, 10109]

Medical privacy. In connection with this electronic system, Congress was required by HIPAA to develop final regulations pertaining to privacy standards for medical information by August 21, 1999. However, despite numerous proposals, Congress failed to enact these rules. On November 3, 1999, the HHS, acting on its authority under HIPAA, issued proposed regulations in the *Federal Register* on how private medical records are used, stored, and disclosed. Final regulations were issued in January 2001. While HIPAA mandated the development of privacy standards only for electronic transactions, the regulations apply broadly to personal medical information maintained in either electronic or paper form, as well as to oral communications. (See chapter 5.)

Electronic signatures. The Electronic Signatures in Global and National Commerce Act [Pub. L. No. 106-229, 114 Stat. 464 (2000)] gives agreements entered into through the use of electronic media the same legal status as paper versions. This Act significantly affected the way many transactions, including the administration of employee benefit plans, are conducted. For example, the law paved the way for electronic group health plan enrollment without the need for backup paper documentation to make an employee's agreement to pay plan premiums legally enforceable.

The Electronic Signatures in Global and National Commerce Act prohibits any state from denying legal effect to a signature, contract, or other record solely because it is in electronic form. If a law requires that a written agreement or other record of a transaction be retained, the Act provides that the requirement may be satisfied by retaining an accurate electronic record that is accessible for the prescribed period of time and in a form that is capable of being accurately reproduced.

The Electronic Signatures in Global and National Commerce Act includes protections for consumers entering into agreements electronically. To satisfy this requirement, an individual must agree to conduct the transaction, have records stored, have documents furnished electronically rather than on paper, and reasonably demonstrate that he or she can access electronic documents.

The electronic signature provisions of the Act took effect October 1, 2000. The electronic record keeping provisions became effective March 1, 2001.

Q 3:51   Is a health plan permitted to use electronic means to communicate with plan participants and maintain plan records?

Yes. Both the DOL and the IRS have approved the use of electronic media by plans for transactions under their jurisdiction.

DOL rules. The DOL regulations contain safe harbor rules under which an employer's use of electronic media for distributing plan documents and maintaining requirements will satisfy the requirements of ERISA. [DOL Reg. § 2520-104b-1(c)]

The regulations permit the use of electronic media to distribute the following health plan documents:

- HIPAA notices of creditable coverage
- COBRA notices
- Qualified medical child support order notices
- Benefit determination notices under the claim procedure regulations

The safe harbor applies only if the plan takes "appropriate and necessary" steps to ensure that the confidentiality of individual benefit and claims information is not compromised. That is, the electronic delivery system must contain features, such as the use of personal identification numbers (PINs) or passwords, to prevent individuals other than the intended recipient to access a notice.

The regulations permit electronic communication with plan participants who have access to the employer's electronic information system as an integral part of their jobs at any location where they are reasonably expected to perform their jobs.

The regulations also permit electronic communication with plan participants or beneficiaries who affirmatively consent to receiving documents electronically. Before consent is obtained, participants must be given notice (in either electronic or nonelectronic form) stating:

- The types of documents to be delivered electronically;
- The fact that consent can be withdrawn at any time without charge;
- The procedures for withdrawing consent and for updating the address for receiving electronic communications;
- The right to request and obtain paper versions of electronic documents and whether the paper version will be furnished free of charge; and
- The hardware or software requirements for accessing and storing the electronic documents.

If electronic documents will be sent via the Internet or another electronic communication network, a participant or beneficiary must give consent in a manner that reasonably demonstrates the ability to access the electronic documents and must provide an e-mail address. If documents will be distributed through some other type of electronic medium, such as a CD-ROM, all that is required is consent to receiving the documents in electronic form.

Consent to receive documents electronically will remain in effect until it is withdrawn. However, if there is a change in the hardware or software that is necessary to access or store electronic documents that makes it possible that participants or beneficiaries may not be able to access or store the documents, they must be given notice of the new requirements and must either give consent again or withdraw their consent without charge.

As noted above, an individual must have the right to obtain a paper version of a document on request. A plan may charge a reasonable fee for a paper document (unless the law otherwise prohibits such a fee). The electronic and paper documents do not have to be identical. However, both must meet the style, content, and format requirements applicable to the type of document.

Notice of the right to receive a paper document must be provided when a document is furnished electronically. In addition, if the significance of a document is not readily apparent, notice must be provided apprising the recipient of its significance. However, the preamble to the regulations makes it clear that this notice is not required if the document is attached to an e-mail that explains the document's significance. For example, a special notice would not be required if an e-mail accompanying a statement of material modifications states "The attached document describes changes in the benefits provided by your plan." Notice of the right to obtain a paper document and, if required, of the significance of a document must be given at the time the document is furnished. The notice may be provided electronically and may be provided along with other plan information, provided the notice is conspicuous enough to alert the recipient that a document has been furnished electronically.

The plan must take "appropriate and necessary" steps to ensure that documents that are furnished electronically are actually received by the intended recipients. These steps might include the use of a return receipt or an e-mail feature that provides notice of undelivered electronic documents.

The DOL regulations provide a safe harbor for using electronic media to satisfy certain recordkeeping requirements under ERISA. Those requirements generally provide that a plan must keep plan-related records for six years and must maintain records for each employee that can be used to determine the benefits due or to become due to the employee.

An electronic record keeping system will satisfy the requirements if:

- the system has reasonable controls to ensure the integrity, accuracy, authenticity, and reliability of the records;
- the records are maintained in reasonable order and in a safe and accessible plan so that they can be readily examined and inspected;
- the records are readily convertible into legible and readable paper documents if needed;
- the recordkeeping is not subject to an agreement or restriction that impairs the ability to comply with ERISA's requirements; and
- the plan establishes and follows adequate record management practices (such as labeling records, backing up records, and off-site storage).

If records are transferred to an electronic system that meets the requirements, the original paper records can be destroyed (unless the electronic record would not satisfy other federal or state law requirements).

IRS rules. IRS regulations govern the use of electronic media for benefit notices, elections, and other disclosures related to accident and health plans that are required by the Internal Revenue Code. [Treas. Reg. § 1.401(a)-21]

The regulations do *not* apply to notices, consents or disclosures required by ERISA that fall under the jurisdiction of the DOL. For example, the regulations do not apply to furnishing of SPDs, which are governed by the DOL regulations discussed above.

In addition, the rules for the use of electronic media apply in addition to all other general requirements for particular notices and elections. Any communication provided electronically must satisfy all the other Code and regulatory requirements for that communication.

The content of an electronic communication and the delivery method must be reasonably designed to provide information in a way that is no less understandable than if provided in a paper document. Moreover, the electronic transmission must alert the recipient to the significance of the electronic document (including the subject matter), and provide any instructions needed to access the document. [Treas. Reg. § 1.401(a)-21(a)(5)]

The IRS regulations provide two options:

1. *Consent method.* Under the general rules, a plan must obtain a participant's consent before providing a notice electronically. The participant's consent must be given in a way that reasonably demonstrates that the participant can access the notice electronically. Consent can be given on a written paper form or through some other nonelectronic means, but only if the participant confirms the consent in a way that reasonably demonstrates that he can access the notice electronically. Before consenting, the participant has to be given a disclosure statement that outlines the scope of the consent, the participant's right to withdraw the consent (including any conditions, consequences, or fees), and the right to receive the communication on paper. The disclosure must specify the hardware and software requirements for electronic documents and the procedures for updating the participant's electronic contact information. If the hardware or software requirements change, a new consent must be obtained from the participant. [Treas. Reg. § 1.401(a)-21(b)]

2. *Automatic method.* An electronic notice can be provided automatically if the recipient is advised that a paper copy of the notice may be requested and will be provided at no charge. However, to use this method, the recipient of the notice must be "effectively able" to access the electronic medium used to provide the notice. [Treas. Reg. § 1.401(a)-21(c)]

A benefit election can be made electronically if all of the following requirements are met:

1. The participant is effectively able to access the electronic system.
2. The electronic system is reasonably designed to prevent any person other than the participant from making the election.
3. The electronic system must provide the participant with a reasonable opportunity to review, confirm, modify, or rescind the election before it becomes effective.
4. The participant must receive a confirmation of the election through either a written paper document or an electronic medium that meets the regulatory requirements within a reasonable time.
5. In the case of an election that must be witnessed by a plan representative or a notary public, the individual's signature must be witnessed in the physical presence of a plan representative or a notary.

[Treas. Reg. § 1.401(a)-21(d)]

These regulations apply to applicable notices and elections on or after January 1, 2007.

Q 3:52   How do the federal medical privacy regulations affect the administration of group plans?

Regulations issued by the Department of Health and Human Services are designed to protect the privacy of personal medical records. [45 C.F.R. §§ 164. 102 *et seq.*] Although the regulations are aimed largely at health care providers, hospitals, health insurers, and health care clearinghouses, they also have significant implications for employers.

The medical privacy regulations generally prohibit the disclosure of personal medical records in any form without an individual's consent. Although the regulations were prompted by concerns about the privacy of electronic records, they also apply to disclosures of paper records and oral communications.

The regulations specifically provide that group health plans cannot disclose an employee's personal health information to a sponsoring employer for employment-related purposes such as hiring, firing, or determinations of promotions without the employee's authorization. Thus, an employer is required to obtain an employee's permission to access health information that is needed to determine reasonable accommodations under the ADA or to administer requests for leave under the FMLA. The regulations do, however, carve out exceptions for disclosures in connection with workers' compensation, the Occupational Safety and Health Act (OSH Act), and mine safety requirements.

The regulations also allow employees' health information to be disclosed to an employer without consent for certain limited purposes. For example, an employer may receive information from an on-site health care provider who provides care to an employee at the request of an employer. In addition, employers may be given information necessary to conduct an evaluation relating to medical surveillance of the workplace or to evaluate whether an employee has a work-related illness or injury.

A group health plan may also disclose summary health information to an employer for the purpose of obtaining premium bids for health insurance coverage or for the purpose of modifying, amending, or terminating a health plan.

Group health plans. The regulation establishes privacy safeguard standards that covered entities, including employer-sponsored group health plans, must meet, but leaves the detailed policies and procedures for meeting the standards to the discretion of each entity. The privacy safeguards must include the following:

1. *Written privacy procedures.* These must include procedures identifying who has access to protected medical information, how it will be used, and when information will or will not be disclosed to others.

2. *Training of employees and designation of a privacy officer.* All employees who have access to protected medical information must be given training so that they understand the privacy procedures. In addition, a privacy officer must be designated to be responsible for ensuring that the procedures are followed.

3. *Grievance procedures.* Procedures must be established to allow individuals to make inquiries or complaints regarding the privacy of their records.

Complying with the medical privacy requirements may be more onerous for employers with self-insured health plans than it is for employers whose plans are insured. In the case of insured plans, the employer may have little or no access to protected medical information. Nonetheless, all plans must provide for adequate separation between the plan and the employer. For example, the plan must do the following:

- Specify the circumstances in which employee health information will be disclosed to the sponsoring employer;
- Provide that the plan will disclose protected health information to the sponsoring employer only if the employer agrees to use the information only for purposes permitted by the regulations;
- Require the employer to return or destroy all protected health information that is in the employer's possession or, if that is not possible, limit further use or disclosure of the information to permitted purposes;
- Ensure adequate separation between the plan and the employer by describing those employees or classes of employee that may have access to employee health information that is disclosed to the employer; and
- Restrict access to health information that is submitted by a plan participant to those employees who handle plan administration functions that the employer performs for the plan, such as receiving and forwarding benefit claims.

The federal medical privacy regulations are discussed in detail in chapter 5.

Q 3:53   What fiduciary duty exists regarding the selection of health care providers or plans?

A DOL letter ruling addresses whether an employer can give quality of health care services priority over cost when contracting with or making choice from among various health care providers or plans. [DOL Adv. Op. Ltr. to Diane Orantes Cerest (Feb. 19, 1998)] The requester was concerned about whether ERISA would require fiduciaries to contract with the health care provider or plan that submits the lowest fee quote.

ERISA applies to selection of health care providers and plans. The DOL stated that the selection of a health care provider is subject to the general fiduciary standards and prohibited transaction provisions of ERISA when it involves the disposition of employee benefit plan assets. This is because it would constitute an exercise of authority or control with respect to the management and disposition of the plan's assets within the meaning of ERISA Section 3(21).

Applicable standard of care. In selecting a health care provider or plan, the fiduciary must discharge his or her duties with respect to the group health plan solely in the interest of the participants and beneficiaries and with the care and skill, prudence, and diligence under the circumstances then prevailing that a prudent person acting in a like capacity and familiar with such matters would use in the conduct of an enterprise of like character and like aims. The DOL notes that this is not a "man-in-the-street standard" and that some employers may have a need for consulting support in helping to make these decisions and in monitoring vendor performance. Also, ERISA's prohibited transaction rules, which permit the payment of no more than reasonable compensation for services necessary for the establishment or operation of the plan, apply.

Initial selection-objective process. The DOL's advisory opinion letter [DOL Adv. Op. Ltr. to Diane Orantes Cerest (Feb. 19, 1998)] states that an objective process is needed to elicit the appropriate decision-making information:

> In selecting a health care provider in this context, as with the selection of any service provider under ERISA, the responsible plan fiduciary must engage in an objective process designed to elicit information necessary to assess the qualifications of the provider, the quality of services offered, and the reasonableness of the fees charged in light of the services provided. In addition, the process should be designed to avoid self-dealing, conflicts of interest or other improper influence. What constitutes an appropriate method of selecting a health care provider, however, will depend upon the particular facts and circumstances. Soliciting bids among service providers at the outset is a means by which the fiduciary can obtain the necessary information relevant to the decision-making process.

Changing health care providers or plans. Whether the above process is appropriate in subsequent years may, according to the DOL, depend on, among other things, the fiduciary's knowledge of the service provider's work, the cost and quality of the services previously provided by the service provider, the fiduciary's knowledge of prevailing rates for similar services, as well as the cost to the plan of conducting a particular selection process. Regardless of the method used, however, the DOL states that the fiduciary must be able to demonstrate compliance with ERISA's fiduciary standards.

Cost as a factor. The DOL notes that, because numerous factors necessarily will be considered by the fiduciary when selecting health care service providers, the fiduciary need not select the lowest bidder when soliciting bids; however, the fiduciary must ensure that the compensation paid to a service provider is reasonable in light of the services provided to the plan.

Quality as a factor. In its advisory opinion letter, the DOL states its position that, because "quality of services" is a factor relevant to selection of a service provider, a plan fiduciary's failure to take quality of services into account in the selection process would constitute a breach of the fiduciary's duty under ERISA when the selection involves the disposition of plan assets. The DOL indicates that, in assessing "quality of services," a plan fiduciary may, among other things, consider the following factors:

1. The scope of choices and qualifications of medical providers and specialists available to participants;

2. Ease of access to medical providers;

3. Ease of access to information concerning the operations of the health care provider;

4. The extent to which internal procedures provide for timely consideration and resolution of patient questions and complaints;

5. The extent to which internal procedures provide for the confidentiality of patient records;

6. Enrollee satisfaction statistics; and

7. Rating or accreditation of health care services by independent services or state agencies.

While the advisory opinion letter is only binding on the individual or entity that requested it, it gives a clear picture of the DOL's thinking regarding the appropriate standards to apply when electing or changing health care providers and plans.

Q 3:54   When can health plans be sued by plan participants for a breach of fiduciary duty?

In the landmark decision *Pegram v. Herdrich* [530 U.S. 211 (2000)], the United States Supreme Court held that HMOs cannot be sued as fiduciaries for breaching their duties under ERISA.

Significantly, the lawsuit struck at the heart of the HMO—medical cost control. The suit claimed that an HMO's practice of rewarding physicians for limiting medical care entailed an inherent breach of ERISA's requirement that a plan fiduciary act solely in the interests of plan participants. According to the lawsuit, such incentives create a climate in which decisions are made in the physician's own self-interest rather than in the plan participant's interest.

The Court held that an HMO is not acting as an ERISA fiduciary when it makes decisions about a patient's treatment. Moreover, the Court said, adopting the view that physician incentives are an automatic breach of ERISA would "be nothing less than the elimination of the for-profit HMO."

According to the Court, cost control is inherent to HMOs—and cost-controlling measures are commonly complemented by financial incentives to physicians who are rewarded for decreasing utilization of services and penalized for excessive treatment. The basic check on these financial incentives and disincentives is the same under fee-for-service plans: the physician's professional obligation to provide services with a reasonable degree of skill and judgment in the patient's interest. Moreover, the Court noted that the adequacy of professional obligation to counter financial self-interest is open to challenge under any setup. For example, HMOs initially became popular because fee-for-service physicians were thought to be providing unnecessary or useless services, while today many critics charge that HMOs often ignore patients' individual needs to improve their own bottom lines. Whether either of those charges is true, however, the issue is one of medical malpractice, not fiduciary duty under ERISA.

In addition, in two related cases, the Supreme Court held that ERISA provides the exclusive remedy for plan participants to challenge health care coverage decisions. The Court struck down a Texas law that gave patients the right to sue their health plan for damages in state court. The cases involved one plan's refusal to provide coverage for an arthritis drug and another plan's refusal to authorize a continued hospital stay after surgery. The plan participants argued that their lawsuits should not be preempted by ERISA because these refusals were essentially health care treatment decisions, not merely coverage decisions. However, the Court rejected that argument, classifying the plan determinations as "pure eligibility decisions." Moreover, the Court also rejected the argument that the Texas law should not be preempted because it was a law regulating insurance. According to the Court, even if a law does regulate insurance, it is preempted by ERISA "if it provides a separate vehicle to assert a claim for benefits outside of, or in addition to, ERISA's remedial scheme." [Aetna Health Inc. v. Davila, 124 S. Ct. 2488 (2004); CIGNA HealthCare of Tex., Inc. v. Calad, 540 U.S. 1175 (2004)]

On the other hand, the Supreme Court has held that an employee could sue an HMO to compel compliance with the Illinois HMO Act, which requires independent medical review when a request for services is denied by an HMO and specifies that the HMO must provide the services if the reviewing physician determines the services to be medically necessary. The Court found that the HMO Act was not preempted by ERISA because it regulates insurance. [Rush Prudential HMO, Inc. v. Moran, 536 U.S. 355 (2002)] (See chapter 2 for a discussion of ERISA preemption.)

Q 3:55   Must employer contributions to group health plans be held in trust?

In 1988 the DOL issued final regulations under which it interpreted ERISA to provide that employer contributions to welfare benefit plans become plan assets for ERISA purposes when they reasonably can be segregated from the employer's assets. The DOL stated that it would consider the appropriateness of an exemption from the trust requirement for certain welfare benefit plans that could show that employee contributions constituted reimbursement to the employer for monies expended in premium payments or benefits. [Preamble to Final Plan Asset Reg., 53 Fed. Reg. 17,628 (May 17, 1988)] The DOL also suspended the enforcement of the trust requirement for employee contributions that represent payment of premiums for certain insured welfare benefit plans until the adoption of final regulations. [ERISA Tech. Rel. 92-01, 57 Fed. Reg. 23,272 (June 2, 1992), as modified by DOL News Rel. 93-363 (Aug. 27, 1993)] In revised final plan asset regulations published in 1996, the DOL confirmed that ERISA Technical Release 92-01 is not affected by the final regulations and remains in effect until further notice. [61 Fed. Reg. 41,220, 41,222]

Note. To qualify for this suspension of the trust requirement, employee contributions toward insured welfare benefit plans must be paid to the insurance company within 90 days.

Self-insured welfare benefit plans that require employee contributions do not fall within the suspension of enforcement.

Q 3:56 Are group insurance policy dividends under a group health plan's group insurance policy treated as plan assets?

In some cases, group insurance policy dividends can be plan assets in whole or in part for ERISA purposes. The DOL takes the position that experience-rating dividends, refunds, and credits (hereafter referred to as dividends) under a group insurance policy are plan assets to the extent they are attributable to employee contributions. Careful analysis of the language of the documents and instruments governing the welfare benefit plan is required to determine whether policy dividends are attributable to employee contributions. The documents and instruments to be analyzed include the group insurance policy, the plan document, and the SPD given to plan participants.

> **Note.** The issue of the appropriate use of dividends, refunds, or credits can arise, for example, where an employer with an employer-paid life insurance plan and employee-paid supplementary plan insured by the same policy receives a dividend or refund, or an employer that has received a refund on one plan wants to use the surplus to defray the price tag on another plan under a cafeteria plan arrangement. Each situation will need to be examined carefully to determine whether a breach of fiduciary duty would occur if the moneys are used or applied as proposed.

A memorandum by the DOL's Office of the Solicitor sets out the DOL's position in a number of common situations involving group insurance policy dividends, as follows:

1. *Employer pays the entire cost.* If the employer is required to pay the entire cost and is entitled to keep the entire amount of the group insurance policy dividends, the dividends are not plan assets.

2. *Employees pay the entire cost.* If the plan documents require that the employees pay the entire cost of the group policy, any dividends are fully attributable to employee contributions. The dividends are plan assets and have to be used for the exclusive benefit of the employees in the plan.

3. *Employer and employees each pay a fixed percentage of the entire cost.* If the plan documents provide that the employer and employees each will pay a specified percentage of the entire cost of the group insurance coverage (e.g., employer pays 75 percent and employees pay 25 percent), any dividends must be allocated in direct proportion to the employer's and employees' contributions (e.g., employer gets 75 percent and employees get 25 percent). The dividend portions allocated to employees are plan assets and must be used for the exclusive benefit of the employees in the plan.

4. *Employer pays a fixed amount of the entire cost, and employees pay the balance.* If the plan documents require the employer to pay a fixed amount and the employees are responsible for any cost in excess of that

amount, any dividends are attributable to the employees' contributions and are plan assets. However, in the rare case where a dividend exceeds the employees' contributions, the excess can be received by the employer. For example, if the employer is required to pay $75,000, the employees contribute $25,000, and a policy dividend of $10,000 is declared, the $10,000 dividend is attributable solely to the employees' contributions. If the dividend were $30,000, $25,000 would be attributable to employees' contributions and $5,000 to the employer's contributions.

5. *Employees pay a fixed amount of the entire cost, and the employer pays the balance.* If the plan documents require the employees to pay a fixed amount for the cost of the insurance coverage and the employer is responsible for the remainder of the cost, the employer is entitled to retain the entire dividend as long as the dividend does not exceed the contribution paid by the employer. If the dividend does exceed the employer's contribution, the excess is attributable to the employees' contributions and must be applied for their benefit.

Practice Pointer. The DOL has forced employers to return millions of dollars in dividends because the plan documents failed to give the employer the right to receive them. Therefore, it is essential that the plan documents (including the SPD) spell out exactly how contributions and dividends are allocated. Clarity is especially important if multiple coverages are combined for dividend experience or if dividend experience is determined on a cumulative years' basis under the insurance policy rather than on a single policy-year basis. Poor documentation can prove to be costly.

Note. If the group policy is held by an employee benefit trust or if the policy premiums are paid by such a trust, policy dividends apparently would be plan assets.

Q 3:57   Must managed care plans pass on their negotiated discounts to plan participants?

Not necessarily. Whether a managed care plan is required to pass through to participants discounts negotiated with participating providers and institutions apparently depends on the terms of the plan and insurance contract and the SPD distributed to employees.

In instances where a self-insured plan uses an insurance company as the administrator, the insurance company may be negotiating discounts with providers and pocketing the savings rather than passing them along to plan participants. The DOL has informally indicated that it is the obligation of all the parties involved to see that the plan gets the benefit of its bargain. [25 Pens. & Ben. Rep. (BNA) 14 (Apr. 6, 1998)] This would tend to indicate that the DOL views the sponsoring employer as having a duty of inquiry on this issue, although it has never issued any formal guidance in this area.

At least one court has held that negotiated discounts must be passed through where the documents in question can be fairly read to state that the employee's copayment amount is applied to the provider's charge after the application of the negotiated discount, rather than to the charge before the application of the negotiated discount. [Everson v. Blue Cross & Blue Shield of Ohio, 18 Employee Benefits Cas. (BNA) 2062 (D.C. Ohio 1994)] Careful coordination of the various documents describing the plan is necessary to avoid such a mistake, which is potentially costly for the managed care plan.

The failure to pass through negotiated discounts is increasingly coming under attack. A federal district court ruled that Blue Cross and Blue Shield of Ohio failed to pass along to employees the savings from secret discounts that it negotiated from hospitals. [McConocha v. Blue Cross & Blue Shield of Ohio, 898 F. Supp. 545 (N.D. Ohio 1995)] The DOL sued Blue Cross and Blue Shield of Massachusetts, claiming that it violated ERISA by failing to pass through millions of dollars in hospital rebates, thereby failing to act in the interests of the participants and beneficiaries. [Reich v. Blue Cross Blue Shield of Mass., No. 95-12522PBSS (D.C. Mass. 1995)] HMO Partners reached a settlement with the Arkansas Insurance Department, under which it agreed to refund approximately $1.4 million in savings from negotiated discounts that it failed to pass through to its members. As a result, the members paid more than the stated coinsurance share.

In addition to the various regulators, irate plan participants are pressing these claims. An individual participant filed a class action lawsuit against an insurance company that she claimed negotiated secret discounts with health care providers that were not reflected in the premiums charged to the policyholder. As a result, participants paid more than the 20 percent stated coinsurance rate. The participant also claimed that the insurance company's calculation of lifetime maximums was affected by this practice, and she asserted that the insurance company breached its ERISA fiduciary duties by these various actions. [Misch v. Community Mut. Ins. Co., 896 F. Supp. 724 (D. Ohio 1994)] A similar lawsuit was brought against Blue Cross and Blue Shield of Iowa. [Buris v. IASD Health Servs. Corp., 1995 U.S. Dist. LEXIS 15913 (D. Iowa Oct. 2, 1995)]

In another case, two plan participants brought a class action lawsuit against several health plans challenging the copayments charged for prescription drugs. Each of the plans charged a fixed copayment (e.g., $5 per prescription), which in some cases exceed the actual cost of the medication to the plan (although in many other cases, the medications were far more expensive than the copayment). The plan participants argued that whenever a copayment exceeded the actual cost of the prescribed medication, the excess represented an amount wrongfully taken from the beneficiary and the excess charge constituted a breach of fiduciary duty. A U.S. district court concluded that the terms of the plan clearly specified the copayment amounts without making exception for cases where the copayment exceeded the plan's cost. Moreover, the court said there can be no breach of fiduciary duty when an ERISA plan is implemented according to its written, nondiscretionary terms. The court also pointed out that the participants who brought the lawsuit actually came out ahead in the copayment plan—one paid $70 for 13 prescriptions that cost the plan $572.14, while the other paid $355 for 72 prescriptions for which the plan paid $2,181.84.

The court noted that it was possible some participants experienced a "net loss" by paying more in copayments than the plan's cost for their prescriptions. However, the court said that would still not imply a breach of fiduciary duty, but rather the sort of reasonable "line-drawing" that is permitted under the law. In a brief opinion, the Ninth Circuit Court of Appeals affirmed the district court's decision. [Alves v. Harvard Pilgrim Health Care, Inc., 204 F. Supp. 2d 198 (D. Mass. 2002), *aff'd*, 316 F.3d 290 (1st Cir. 2003)]

Q 3:58 Must an employer's determinations regarding its employees' eligibility for group health plan coverage always be given deference?

No. The Court of Appeals for the Third Circuit took to task an employer that repeatedly interpreted its medical plan eligibility requirements to exclude temporary employees even though no such exclusion was contained in the plan's language. "Simply because [the employer] has consistently misinterpreted the term 'full-time employee' doesn't mean that such misinterpretation should be deemed part of the Plan and sanctioned as lawful," the court held. It found that the employer had acted arbitrarily and capriciously by imposing a standard not required by the plan itself. [Epright v. Environmental Res. Mgmt., Inc. Health & Welfare Plan, 81 F.3d 335 (3d Cir. 1996)]

> **Practice Pointer.** In addition to interpreting the plan carefully, the employer can do much to set the stage for judicial deference to the plan fiduciary's interpretation of the plan. First, the plan document should clearly give the plan fiduciary the authority and responsibility to both interpret the terms of the plan and determine any facts relating to claims there under. Second, the plan document and the SPD should be reviewed to remove any conflicting or ambiguous provisions. Lastly, the employer should review the documents and its claims and administrative practice with legal counsel to assure that ERISA's standards are being met.

Q 3:59 Are employers acting in a fiduciary capacity when communicating about the likely future of plan benefits?

Yes. According to the United States Supreme Court [Varity Corp. v. Howe, 116 S. Ct. 1065 (1996)], employers act in a fiduciary capacity when communicating about the likely future of plan benefits. *Varity* held that an employer that both sponsors and administers an ERISA plan acts in a fiduciary capacity when making representations about the likely future of plan benefits. If the employer intentionally misrepresents information about the plan, it violates ERISA's fiduciary duty to act solely in the interests of the participants and beneficiaries. Although the employer might not have an affirmative duty to volunteer information about future plans, the disclosures that it does make must be truthful. Significantly, the Supreme Court also held that participants and beneficiaries have the right to obtain individual relief for such fiduciary breaches.

Additional case law developments have fleshed out this disclosure duty. Because the cases have concerned severance plans, they are discussed in chapter 15.

Health Benefit Claim Processing and Review

Q 3:60   Does federal law govern the processing and review of health benefit claims?

Yes. The DOL has issued regulations under ERISA governing the processing and review of health benefit claims. [DOL Reg. § 2560.503-1] A DOL fact sheet on the rules explains that they were prompted by changes in the health care industry. According to the DOL, the health care industry has shifted from a post-treatment system for paying medical claims to an integrated delivery system under which managed care organizations review and oversee doctors' medical decisions, often before care is provided. The regulations impose strict time limits for processing medical claims, require plans to establish and maintain claim procedures that meet specified requirements, and impose specific requirements and time limits for the review of adverse decisions.

The 2010 Health Reform Act requires group health plans and health insurance issuers to implement both internal and external appeals processes for review of coverage determinations and claims. [PHSA § 2719 as added by PPACA § 1001 and amended by PPACA § 10101] The requirement is generally effective for plan years beginning on or after September 23, 2010.

The plan or issuer must provide notice to enrollees, in a culturally and linguistically appropriate manner, of the available internal and external appeals processes and allow enrollees to review their files and present evidence and testimony as part of the appeals process. An enrollee must receive continued coverage pending the outcome of the appeals process.

Internal appeals processes must comply with the claims and appeals procedures set forth in the existing DOL regulations, and must be updated to comply with any additional standards established by the DOL.

External appeals processes must comply with any applicable state external review process, provided it includes the consumer protections set forth in the Uniform External Review Model Act promulgated by the National Association of Insurance Commissioners (NAIC). If no state external review process has been established or the plan is a self-insured plan not subject to state insurance regulation, the plan must implement an external review process that meets minimum standards similar to those in the Model Act. The Secretary of HHS may deem the external review process of a plan in operation on the date of enactment to be in compliance.

Q 3:61   What types of claims are subject to the claim procedure regulations?

The claim procedure rules apply to any "claim for benefits" under a covered health or disability plan. Guidance from the Employee Benefit Security Administration (EBSA) addresses what types of communications with a plan amount to a "claim for benefits." [DOL Frequently Asked Questions on the Benefit Claims Procedure Regulation (Dec. 15, 2001)]

According to the guidance, the claim procedures apply to a determination of whether an individual is eligible for coverage under a plan only if the determination is made as part of a claim for benefits. If an individual asks a question about eligibility for coverage under a plan without making a claim for benefits, the eligibility determination is not governed by the claim procedure rules. On the other hand, if an individual files a claim for benefits that is denied because he or she is not eligible for coverage under the plan, the coverage determination is part of a claim and must be handled in accordance with the claim procedures.

A request for prior approval is not a claim for benefits if the plan does not require prior approval. The claim procedures do apply to preservice claims. However, unless a plan requires prior approval, a mere request for advance information on the plan's possible coverage of items or services or advance approval of covered items or services does not constitute a preservice claim.

The rules do not apply to casual inquiries about benefits or the circumstances under which benefits might be paid by the plan. On the other hand, a group health plan that requires the submission of preservice claims is not entirely free to ignore preservice inquiries if it appears that an individual is attempting to make a claim, even if he or she is not acting in compliance with the plan's claim-filing procedures. In that case, the regulations require the plan to notify the individual of the proper claim procedures. For example, this type of notification is required if an individual or his or her authorized representative (for example, an attending physician) communicates with the individual or office that handles benefit matters about approval for a specific treatment, product, or service. Notice of the plan's claim procedures must be furnished as soon as possible, but no later than 24 hours in the case of urgent care claims or five days in the case of nonurgent claims. The notice may be given orally, unless written notification is requested.

In addition, the guidance makes it clear that the health plan claim procedures apply to dental or prescription drug benefits that are offered under a stand-alone plan or as part of a group health plan.

Both dental care and prescription drugs fall within the definition of medical care claims covered by the new claim procedures. The guidance makes it clear that the plan's procedures for filing benefit claims determine whether presenting a prescription to a pharmacy constitutes a claim for benefits. However, if it does not, the plan must have a reasonable procedure for submitting a claim for benefits for prescription drug coverage.

Q 3:62   What time limits apply to the processing of health benefit claims?

The DOL regulations significantly accelerate the processing of claims for health benefits under an ERISA plan.

Under long-standing regulations, the denial of any claim for benefits under an ERISA plan, including pension and welfare plans as well as health and disability plans, must be made "within a reasonable period of time." For this purpose, a period of more than 90 days is generally considered unreasonable. However, if special circumstances require a longer processing time, a plan can take an additional 90 days to process the claim, provided the plan participant is given notice describing the special circumstances before the end of the initial 90-day period. A plan may limit the period during which a plan participant can seek review of a claim denial, but the period may not be less than 30 days. A decision on review must be made within 60 days unless special circumstances warrant an additional 60-day extension.

However, the processing time limits for health benefit claims are shorter and depend on the type of claim.

Preservice claims. The regulations require claims requesting prior authorization for nonurgent care (*preservice claims*) to be handled within a "reasonable period of time appropriate to the medical circumstances," but not later than 15 days after the plan's receipt of the claim. A plan may extend its decision making for one additional 15-day period if the extension is necessary for reasons beyond the plan's control.

Postservice claims. Claims for payment for medical services that have already been provided (*postservice claims*) must be decided within a maximum period of 30 days from the date the plan receives the claim. Again, the plan is entitled to one 15-day extension if necessary for reasons beyond the plan's control.

Urgent care claims. Preservice claims for urgent medical care must be decided "as soon as possible, taking into account the medical exigencies," but not later than 72 hours after receipt of the claim. The 72-hour time limit does not apply if the claim does not provide enough information to make the determination. However, the plan must notify the participant of an incomplete claim within 24 hours and must give the participant at least 48 hours to complete the claim. The plan must make its determination within 48 hours of the time the claim is completed or the end of the period for completing the claim. No extensions are permitted in the case of urgent care claims.

A benefit claim involves urgent care if application of the normal processing times for preservice claims could seriously jeopardize the life or health of the patient or the patient's ability to regain maximum function. A claim is also considered urgent if, in the opinion of a physician with knowledge of the patient's condition, a longer processing period would subject the patient to severe pain that cannot be adequately managed without the requested care or treatment.

The determination of whether a claim involves urgent care can be made by a person acting on behalf of the plan "applying the judgment of a prudent layperson who possesses an average knowledge of health and medicine." However, a determination by a physician with knowledge of the patient's medical condition that a claim involves urgent care must be accepted by the plan.

Concurrent care claim. Special rules also apply to decisions regarding the termination or reduction of benefits for ongoing treatment. Before making this type of *concurrent care* decision, the plan administrator must notify the participant of a planned termination or reduction of benefits sufficiently in advance that the participant has time to appeal the decision before the benefit is reduced or terminated.

Concurrent care claims may also involve requests to extend a course of treatment beyond the time limits already authorized. Any such claim involving urgent care must be decided as soon as possible, taking into account the medical exigencies, but not later than 24 hours after receipt of the claim, provided the participant made the claim at least 24 hours prior to the expiration of the course of treatment.

The DOL emphasizes that these time limits are maximum periods, not automatic entitlements. If a specific claim presents no problems, it may be unreasonable to delay deciding the claim until the end of the maximum period. Similarly, an extended decision-making period is allowed only for reasons beyond the plan's control. The DOL says it will not view delays caused by cyclical or seasonal fluctuations in claims volume as matters beyond the plan's control that would justify an extension.

On the other hand, DOL guidance makes it clear that a claimant may *voluntarily* agree to an extension even if the plan would not be entitled to an extension under the regulations.

If an extension of time for making a benefit determination is necessary because the plan needs additional information from the claimant, the plan must give the claimant at least 45 days to supply the additional information. However, the extension notice may include a notice of adverse benefit determination that will apply if the claimant fails to provide the information within the time limit. The combined notice should make it clear that the period for the claimant to appeal the adverse determination will begin to run at the end of the period allowed for submitting the additional information (or from a later date if the plan terms give the claimant more time than required by law).

On the other hand, except in the case of urgent care claims, a plan is not required to extend the time for deciding a claim or to request additional information from a claimant. According to the DOL, "a plan may deny claims at any point in the administrative process on the basis that it does not have sufficient information." Such an adverse decision will allow the claimant to advance to the next stage of the claims process.

Q 3:63   Do the claim procedure regulations govern the time frame for paying claims?

No. The DOL regulations establish time frames for deciding claims, but they do not spell out when a decided claim must be paid or when approved services must be rendered. However, failure to provide services or benefit payments within a reasonable period of time following approval may be a breach of fiduciary responsibility under ERISA.

Q 3:64   Are group health plans required to follow specific procedures in processing health benefit claims?

DOL regulations require every employee benefit plan to establish and maintain reasonable procedures for processing claims and to include a description of those procedures in its SPD. In the case of group health plans, the regulations provide that the SPD must include a description of procedures for obtaining prior approval of a claim, such as preauthorization or utilization review procedures.

The regulations also specify that a plan's claim procedures may not contain any provision or be administered in any way that would inhibit or hamper a plan participant from making a claim. The DOL says that a provision or practice that requires payment of fees or costs as a condition of making a claim or appealing an adverse decision on a claim would be considered unduly inhibiting. In addition, the denial of health benefit claims because of failure to obtain prior approval would be unduly inhibiting if application of the prior approval process would seriously jeopardize the life or health of the patient—for example, if the patient is unconscious and in need of immediate medical treatment.

The claim procedures must permit an authorized representative to act on behalf of a plan participant in making a benefit claim or appealing an adverse benefit decision. The plan may establish reasonable procedures for deciding whether an individual has been authorized to act on behalf of a participant. However, in the case of a claim involving urgent medical care, a health care professional with knowledge of the participant's medical condition must be permitted to act as an authorized representative.

If a preservice claim for health benefits does not meet the plan requirements, the plan must notify the participant or authorized representative of the problem and the proper procedure for filing a claim. This notice must be provided as soon as possible, but not later than five days following the filing of the defective claim. In the case of a claim for urgent care, the notice must be provided within 24 hours. A plan is not required to provide notice of a defective postservice claim.

Q 3:65   Are group health plans subject to specific procedures and time limits for reviewing denied claims?

Regulations governing ERISA plans, including pension and welfare plans as well as health plans, provide that a plan may limit the period during which a plan participant can seek review of a claim denial, but the period may not be less than 30 days. A decision on review must be made within 60 days unless special circumstances warrant an additional 60-day extension.

However, the DOL provides special procedures and time limits for reviewing appeals of adverse health or disability benefit decisions.

Review procedures. An ERISA plan administrator must provide a participant with a written or electronic notice of any adverse benefit determination. The notice must specify the reason or reasons for denial of the claim and refer to the specific plan provisions on which the decision was based. The notice must also describe any additional material or information that is necessary to perfect the claim and the reason the material or information is necessary.

In the case of group health plans, the notice must contain information about any internal rules, guidelines, or protocols that were relied on in making the adverse decision. If the decision is based on a plan limit that excludes treatments that are experimental or not medically necessary, the notice must explain the scientific or clinical reasons for the decision. Alternatively, the notice may indicate that the information or explanation will be provided free of charge upon request.

The plan must provide a participant with a reasonable opportunity for a "full and fair" review of an adverse determination.

The process cannot give deference to the original adverse decision, and the decision on appeal must be made by someone other than the individual who made the original decision. If the appealed claim involves medical judgment, the plan must consult appropriate health care professionals before reaching a decision.

A plan may have no more than two mandatory levels of review. If a plan offers two levels of review, the second level may be arbitration. However, EBSA makes it clear that the arbitration must be nonbinding—that is, arbitration cannot limit the claimant's ability to challenge the decision in court. On the other hand, its guidance indicates that a plan can offer additional *voluntary* levels of review, including binding arbitration or some other form of alternative dispute resolution.

Time limits. The regulations lengthen the minimum time period for appealing an adverse health claim decision from 90 to 180 days. The 180-day rule applies to the first review level. The regulations do not specifically address the time frame for appealing to a second review level. However, they indicate that the procedure must be reasonable. According to the DOL, a plan must give a claimant a reasonable opportunity to pursue a full and fair review at the second level.

By contrast, the regulations substantially shorten the time period for making a decision on an appealed health claim. The time limit for review of a denied claim depends on the type of claim under review, as follows:

1. *Preservice claims* must be decided within a reasonable period of time appropriate to the medical circumstances, but not more than 30 days after the plan receives the request for review. If the plan provides for two levels of review, a decision on one level must be made within 15 days.

2. *Urgent care claims* must be decided as soon as possible, but not later than 72 hours after the review is requested.

3. *Postservice claims* must be decided not later than 60 days after receipt of the review request. If the plan has two levels of review, a decision on one level must be made within 30 days.

Q 3:66   When can a claimant take a claim to court?

A claimant generally must exhaust the plan's internal procedures before filing a civil action for benefits under ERISA Section 502(a)(1)(B). However, if a plan fails to establish or follow claims procedures consistent with the requirements of the regulation, a claimant will be treated as having exhausted the administrative remedies available under the plan and will be entitled to proceed to court. [DOL Reg. § 2560.503-1(1)]

On the other hand, DOL guidance makes it clear that the claimant will bear the burden of proving to the satisfaction of the court that the plan failed to establish or follow claims procedures consistent with the requirements of the regulation. Moreover, not every deviation by a plan from the requirements of the regulation will justify proceeding directly to court. The DOL points out that a plan that has established procedures that fully conform to the regulations might inadvertently deviate from those procedures in processing a particular claim. However, if the plan's procedures provide an opportunity to effectively remedy the error without hurting the claimant, the plan generally will not be treated as having failed to establish or follow reasonable procedures as contemplated by the regulations. Thus, for example, a plan that issues a notice of adverse benefit determination fully advising the claimant of the right to review and to request additional information from the plan may be able to correct an inadvertent failure to include in the notice the specific plan provision on which the denial was based. Ordinarily in that circumstance the plan will have provided access to a reasonable claims procedure consistent with the regulations. On the other hand, systematic deviations from the plan procedures, or deviations that cannot be corrected through plan procedures, such as the failure to include a description of the plan's review procedures in a notice of an adverse benefit determination, would justify a court determination that the plan failed to provide a reasonable procedure.

In addition, the DOL points out that filing a lawsuit without exhausting plan procedures could limit a claimant's appeal rights and cause the claimant to lose benefits under the plan. This could be the case when, during the time it takes for a court to dismiss the claimant's suit, the plan's deadline for filing an appeal expires. There is nothing in the regulation that would serve to toll internal plan deadlines for filing or appealing claims when a claimant files a premature lawsuit. [DOL FAQs on Claims Procedure Regulations are available online at *www.dol.gov/ebsa/Faqs/Faq_claims_proc_reg.html*]

As a general rule, lawsuits brought against an employer-provided health plan are governed by ERISA. Therefore, such suits must be brought in federal court, and remedies are limited to those permitted by ERISA (e.g., the benefits specified in the plan and other equitable relief). Other types of lawsuits, such as lawsuits seeking damages for negligence or breach of contract under state law, are generally preempted by ERISA.

One question that has arisen repeatedly in recent years is whether ERISA preempts a state-law medical malpractice claim against an HMO in connection with decisions by the HMO that involve both benefit eligibility and medical treatment (e.g., the choice of medication or length of a hospital stay). The Circuit Courts split on the issue, and the Supreme Court resolved the conflict in favor of preemption. [Aetna Health, Inc. v. Davila, 124 S. Ct. 2488 (2004)]

Q 3:67   Can a plan limit the time period for filing a lawsuit?

ERISA does not specify a statute of limitations for benefit claims, and limitations periods vary from state to state. Therefore, many plans specify the period for bringing a lawsuit in the plan document. There is nothing in the claim procedure regulations that prohibit a plan from imposing a time limit on filing a lawsuit regarding a claim for benefits. In addition, those courts that have addressed this issue have generally upheld reasonable time limits on filing suit. However, a recent decision makes it clear that a plan's SPD must clearly spell out the limitations period.

An individual was covered by a plan as the spouse of a covered employee. The employee's spouse suffered from cystic fibrosis and received extensive treatment for her condition from the time of her marriage when her plan coverage began and her death a year later. However, the plan denied benefits for her treatment based on its preexisting condition limitation, which excluded coverage for conditions for which treatment was received during the 90 days preceding the date coverage began under the plan. The plan's denial of benefits was upheld under the plan's internal appeals procedures. A year and a half after the internal appeal was completed, the covered employee filed suit against the plan complaining that the preexisting condition exclusion did not apply because his spouse had not received treatment for her condition during the 90 days preceding their marriage. The plan moved to have the lawsuit dismissed on the grounds that the covered employee had not filed suit within the one-year limitations period specified in the plan's SPD.

The Tenth Circuit Court of Appeals held that the lawsuit could continue because the plan's SPD was ambiguous. The portion of the SPD dealing with benefits underwritten by the plan's insurer included a section entitled "Legal Action," which stated that no legal action for health benefits under the group policy could be commenced more than three years after the time for providing proof of loss under the plan. However, the portion of the SPD describing the plan's appeals procedure stated that a legal action must be brought within one year after the date of an internal decision on appeal. The Tenth Circuit noted that the two provisions were contradictory. Moreover, they did not cross reference each other and there was no explanation of how they could work together. In addition, there was no clear indication of which legal actions were subject to the one-year limitations period. The court concluded that the plan, as drafter of the SPD, should bear the consequences of the inaccuracies. Therefore, it held that the longer three-year limitations period should apply to the covered employee's lawsuit. [Haymond v. Eighth Dist. Elec. Benefit Fund, 36 Fed. Appx. 369 (10th Cir. 2002)]

Q 3:68   Can a health care provider sue a plan to collect payment for medical expenses incurred by a plan participant?

The Fifth Circuit held that a hospital that had provided treatment to a plan participant could sue the plan because it had such a valid assignment. The plan argued that the plan document contained a general prohibition against benefit assignments. However, the hospital pointed out that the prohibition was qualified by language stating that assignments could be made to network providers, and there was no question that the hospital was a network provider. [Dallas County Hosp. Dist. v. Associates' Health & Welfare Plan, 293 F.3d 282 (5th Cir. 2002)]

In another case, the Fifth Circuit took assignment a step further. The court held that a collection agency could sue on behalf of a hospital to collect unpaid medical expenses incurred by a plan participant. The court noted that the employee, who had the right to sue as a plan participant, had assigned her rights to the hospital, which in turn assigned those rights to the collection agency. According to the court, ERISA does not prohibit the assignment of health care benefits to a hospital or other health care provider. Moreover, the court concluded that allowing a health care provider who has received such an assignment to use its own assignee to collect the benefits does not frustrate the goals and purposes of ERISA. "Denying derivative standing to health care providers would harm participants or beneficiaries because it would discourage providers from becoming assignees and possibly from helping beneficiaries who were unable to pay them up front. Likewise, granting derivative standing to the assignees of health care providers helps plan participants and beneficiaries by encouraging providers to accept participants who are unable to pay up front. Conversely, to bar health care providers from assigning their rights under ERISA, and shifting the risk of nonpayment to a third party, would chill health care providers' willingness to accept a patient. Third parties like [the collection agency] . . . will only be willing to purchase an assignment from a health care provider if they can be assured they will be afforded standing to sue for reimbursement." [Tango Transp. v. Healthcare Fin. Servs., LLC, 322 F.3d 888 (5th Cir. 2003)]

On the other hand, yet another Fifth Circuit decision makes it clear that a plan may limit a participant or beneficiary's ability to assign rights under the plan. Pamela Nichols' husband worked for Wal-Mart, and she was covered under Wal-Mart's health plan as a beneficiary. Wal-Mart's plan generally prohibited assignment of benefits under the plan. However, the plan did permit direct payment authorizations that directed the plan to pay benefits directly to a health care provider.

In December 1996, Nichols became a patient of LeTourneau Lifelike Orthotics & Prosthetics. At that time, she signed a form authorizing the plan to pay LeTourneau directly for all services she was entitled to under the plan. In early 1997, Nichols received a leg prosthesis that was covered by the plan. The plan paid $19,553 directly to LeTourneau for the prosthesis and related services. However, about a year and a half later, Nichols' doctor prescribed a new socket for the prosthesis. LeTourneau replaced the socket and submitted a claim to the Wal-Mart plan for $9,767. Neither Nichols nor LeTourneau had sought prior approval for replacement of the socket or verification that the procedure was covered by the plan. The Wal-Mart plan denied the claim based on a plan provision that limited coverage for prostheses to once every three years. LeTourneau filed a lawsuit against the plan seeking payment of the claim.

The Fifth Circuit threw out LeTourneau's lawsuit. The court acknowledged that the direct payment authorization Nichols signed did effectively assign her right to receive payment for covered claims. However, the direct payment authorization did not assign other rights under the plan, including the right to sue. Moreover, assignment of those rights was specifically prohibited by the plan. According to the court, "Any right that Nichols herself might have enjoyed as a beneficiary to challenge Wal-Mart's denial of coverage and to claim entitlement to socket replacement despite the passage of less than three years could not be assigned to any third party, including her provider of health care services; and, without an assignment, the provider, LeTourneau, could have no standing to pursue coverage." [LeTourneau Lifelike Orthotics & Prosthetics, Inc. v. Wal-Mart Stores, Inc., 298 F.3d 348 (5th Cir. 2002)]

Coordination of Benefits

Q 3:69   What is a coordination of benefits provision?

A *coordination of benefits (COB) provision* in a group health plan specifies the plan benefits that are payable from that plan if health care expenses are covered by more than one group or group-type health plan.

The COB rules are a series of rules that are applied in numerical order to help determine which plan is to be the primary payer (the plan that pays benefits first) and which plan will be the secondary payer (the plan that will pay benefits second). The significance of these characterizations is that the primary plan must pay benefits as if the secondary plan or plans did not exist. In other words, the primary plan pays the full amount of benefits covered under its terms. The secondary plan, in contrast, is allowed to take the benefits paid by the primary plan into account when calculating how much of the remaining unreimbursed expenses it will pay. [See NAIC Model COB Reg. 120-1, § 5.]

Q 3:70   What is the purpose of a COB provision?

The principal purpose of a COB provision is to limit excess coverage so that the employee will not receive reimbursements from more than one plan that in total exceed the actual amount of health care costs incurred. In other words, the purpose is to ensure that the employee does not receive a financial windfall from more than one medical plan for a single medical expense. The COB provision does this by permitting the secondary plan to reduce its benefit payments. [See NAIC Model COB Reg. 120-1, § 3. E.]

> **Note.** This coordination of payments with another plan generally is done for plans such as group insurance contracts, uninsured group or group-type coverage, group or group-type coverage through closed-panel plans (e.g., HMOs), the medical portion of group and individual "no-fault" and "fault" automobile insurance, Medicare (to the extent permitted by law), and group-type contracts not available to the general public that can be obtained and maintained because of membership in or connection with a particular organization or group, including franchise or blanket coverage. A group or group-type plan cannot coordinate with coverage such as individual insurance contracts or school accident-type coverages. [See NAIC Model COB Reg. 120-1, § 3. H.]

The COB provision also has a cost-control aspect, because it can significantly reduce the cost of the plan. In addition, the COB provision is designed to avoid claim-processing delays because it specifies which plan pays which benefits.

Q 3:71   Do all group health plans have COB provisions?

Most group health plans do contain COB provisions. If the plan provides benefits by means of an insurance contract, state insurance law may require the group health contract—and thus, indirectly, the plan—to contain a COB provision.

> **Note.** The National Association of Insurance Commissioners (NAIC), whose membership consists of the insurance commissioners from each state in the United States and the District of Columbia, has promulgated a group COB regulation that serves as a model for the states when they choose to adopt COB rules.

State insurance laws are preempted by ERISA from applying to self-insured medical plans; however, most self-insured plans contain COB provisions that voluntarily adhere to the basic structure of the NAIC's Group Coordination of Benefits Model Regulation.

Coordination with Medicare. ERISA does not preempt other federal laws. Accordingly, the Medicare secondary-payer (MSP) requirements of the Social Security Act, which Code Section 5000 requires group health plans to satisfy, must be adhered to as well. These separate MSP rules are discussed in chapter 5.

Q 3:72   What if only one plan has a COB provision?

Under the NAIC model COB regulation, the plan without a COB provision is primary, and the plan with a COB provision is secondary. [See NAIC Model COB Reg. 120-1, § 4. A.]

Q 3:73   Are COB provisions uniform?

No. COB provisions come in a variety of forms. As a practical matter, the COB provisions dealing with order of benefit determination (i.e., which plan pays first and which plan pays second) are generally uniform regardless of whether the plans are insured or uninsured and regardless of the state in which the insured plan is issued.

Most, but not all, states have adopted COB rules or regulations for group health insurance policies that are issued or delivered in the particular state; however, these rules may be based on different versions of the NAIC's model rule. Those states that have no formal COB rules generally will not permit insurance policy forms to be used in the state if they have COB provisions that do not conform to the more significant provisions of the NAIC model regulation.

Plans that are not subject to state regulation tend to use the model's order of benefit determination provisions primarily to avoid situations in which both plans can end up in a secondary position, thereby depriving a claimant covered under two plans of primary coverage.

Q 3:74   Does ERISA preempt state COB laws for self-insured and/or insured group health plans?

The answer to this question depends on the type of plan at issue.

Self-insured medical plans. ERISA preempts the application of state COB laws to self-insured group health plans. (See chapter 2 for further discussion of ERISA preemption principles.) However, when determining the federal common-law result under ERISA, courts may "borrow" from state COB principles or other federal laws to reach essentially the same result. [Reinforcing Iron Workers Local 426 Health & Welfare Fund v. Michigan Bell Tel. Co., 746 F. Supp. 668 (E.D. Mich. 1990) (Although ERISA preempted the Michigan COB Act with respect to self-insured plans, ERISA contains no language regarding which plan would be liable on a primary basis for the dependent child's medical expenses. The court determined that the self-insured plan's rule that the father's plan must pay before the mother's plan was sexually discriminatory in violation of state law and Title VII of the federal Civil Rights Act of 1964. Instead, the court used the rule contained in the father's plan that the primary plan is that of the parent whose birthday occurs first in the year.)]

The Court of Appeals for the Ninth Circuit has stated that the federal courts should develop uniform federal common-law COB rules that apply nationwide for plans not subject to state COB laws by virtue of ERISA preemption, rather than relying on particular state law rules. The court concluded, in accordance with the *Michigan Bell* decision, that the earliest-birthday rule was preferable to the father's-plan-primary rule because the earliest-birthday rule is gender neutral. The court also criticized the two plans for refusing to pay and thereby causing hardship to the beneficiaries, asserting that the plans should have found a way to pay the benefits and then work out the controversy between them. [PM Group Life Ins. Co. v. Western Growers Assurance Trust, 953 F.2d 543 (9th Cir. 1992)]

In a case involving conflicting COB clauses, a self-funded medical benefits plan covered by ERISA was found to be secondarily liable to a no-fault automobile insurer, where the ERISA-covered plan expressly disavowed its primary coverage responsibility. [CNA Ins. Co. v. Allstate Ins. Co., 36 F. Supp. 957 (E.D. Mich. 1999)] The case involved a five-year-old child who was seriously injured while a passenger in a car driven by her father. The father was insured by his employer's self-funded employee benefit plan and by a no-fault personal protection insurance policy from his auto insurance company. The child was a beneficiary under the benefit plan and was considered "insured" under her father's personal protection policy. The court pointed out that under the ERISA plan's COB provision, it had expressly disavowed the claims of the traditional insurer. According to the court, the ERISA plan coordinates health benefits with benefits payable under other plans, defines automobile no-fault policies such as the policy here at issue as "other plan," purports to eliminate duplicate coverage, and establishes rules for determining primary and secondary coverage.

Insured plans. ERISA does not preempt state COB laws with respect to insured plans.

Collectively bargained plans. ERISA preempts state COB laws from applying to collectively bargained plans if they are self-insured. [ERISA § 514]

MEWAs. A partially insured (but not a fully insured) MEWA apparently is subject to state COB laws. [ERISA § 514; 29 U.S.C. § 1144(b)(6)]

Q 3:75   What is the overall scheme of the COB rules?

COB rules impose an order of benefit determination. A series of rules is applied one by one, always in the same order, to the particular facts. The first rule to use is the first to clearly apply and describe which plan pays its benefits before another plan.

Order of benefit determination. The six order-of-benefit determination rules are:

1. Nondependent or dependent rule (see Qs 3:76–3:77);
2. Child covered under more than one plan rule (see Q 3:78);
3. Active or inactive employee rule (see Q 3:79);
4. Continuation coverage rule (see Q 3:80);

5. Longer or shorter length of coverage rule (see Q 3:81); and

6. Rule of last resort (see Q 3:82).

[NAIC Model COB Reg. 120-1, § 5.D]

> **Note.** See explanation of the rules for "true" coordination of benefits in Qs 3:76–3:84. Many health plans, simply subtract the amount paid under other coverage from the benefits otherwise due, which is an offset provision, and incorrectly refer to the offset as a COB provision.

Q 3:76 What are the general rules concerning coordination of insured plan benefits payable to an individual who is covered both as an employee or retiree and as a dependent under separate plans?

As previously noted (see Q 3:72), the NAIC model COB regulation provides that if an individual has coverage under two plans, and one plan has a COB provision whereas the other does not, the plan with no COB provision is primary plan, and the plan with the COB provision is the secondary plan. [NAIC Model COB Reg. 120-1, § 5.A]

If both plans have COB provisions, the first order of benefit determination rule that is applied is the "nondependent or dependent" rule. Under this rule, the plan that covers the person "other than as a dependent" (e.g., as an employee, member, subscriber, or retiree) is treated as the primary plan, and the plan that covers the person as a dependent is the secondary plan. Under a special exception to this rule, if the plan covering the individual as a dependent is primary to Medicare and the plan covering the individual as a retiree is secondary to Medicare, the order is reversed and the plan covering the individual as a dependent pays first (see Q 3:77).

> **Example.** Joan and Jack Smith work for different employers. Each spouse has coverage as an employee, and each has elected dependent coverage for the other. Both plans have COB provisions. Applying the "nondependent or dependent" rule, for Jack's health care expenses, Jack's plan is the primary plan; for Joan's health care expenses, Joan's plan is primary and Jack's plan is secondary. The primary plan pays benefits in the normal manner, without regard to the secondary plan. The secondary plan generally pays the difference between a maximum amount (not more than the total expenses actually incurred) and the amount paid by the primary plan. The secondary plan never pays more than it would have paid if it had been the primary plan.

Q 3:77 Which plan pays first when a retired individual is covered under a retiree medical plan and Medicare and is also covered as a dependent under a spouse's medical plan for active employees?

This special situation can create a vicious circle, with each plan asserting that it is the secondary payer, no plan being willing to be the primary payer, and the individual not getting paid. The NAIC model COB regulation addresses this situation by requiring that, as between the two group health plans, the plan covering the individual as a dependent of an active employee pays first and the plan covering the individual as a retiree pays second. [See NAIC Model COB Reg. 120-1, § 5. D(1).] Thus, in the situation described, the result under the "nondependent or dependent" rule is reversed. However, very few states have incorporated this exception into their COB rules.

The question remains: which plan is the primary payer in this situation? The Eleventh Circuit Court of Appeals has held that when self-insured ERISA plans do not include the so-called vicious circle exception in their COB provisions, the plan covering the person directly as a retiree will be primary. [Harris Corp. v. Humana, 253 F.3d 598 (11th Cir. 2001)] The Sixth Circuit Court of Appeals has also held that the retiree health plan is primary. [Baptist Mem'l Hosp. v. Pan Am. Life Ins. Co., 1995 U.S. App. LEXIS 7507 (6th Cir. Mar. 30, 1995)]

Q 3:78   What are the general rules for COB for dependent children when each parent has coverage?

Under the NAIC model COB regulation, this issue generally is resolved by the second order of benefit determination rule, the "child covered under more than one plan" rule. This rule is actually a series of three subrules that are applied in order until the primary plan is determined, as follows.

1. *Birthday rule.* If the parents are either (a) married or (b) not separated (whether or not they ever have been married), or if a court decree awards joint custody without specifying that one parent has the responsibility to provide health care coverage, then the plan covering the parent whose birthday falls earlier in the year is the primary plan. If both parents have the same birthday, the plan that has been in effect longer is primary. (Prior to the inclusion of the birthday rule in the NAIC model COB regulation, when both parents had dependent coverage, the father's plan was the primary plan.)

Note. Any default to a gender rule as a result of one or both plans retaining the old rule could be viewed as sexually discriminatory in violation of Title VII of the federal Civil Rights Act of 1964 (see Q 3:74) and therefore probably should be dropped from the plan.

2. *Court decree specifies responsibility.* If a court decree's terms specify that one of the parents is responsible for the child's health care expenses or health care coverage and that parent's plan has actual knowledge of those terms, then that plan is primary. If the parent with financial responsibility has no coverage for the child's health care services or expenses but the other parent does, then that parent's plan is primary. This subrule does not apply to any claim determination period or plan year during which benefits are paid or provided before the plan has actual knowledge of the decree.

3. *No court decree.* If the parents are not married or are separated (whether or not they were ever married) or divorced, and no court decree allocates

responsibility for the child's health care services or expenses, the following progression determines which plan from among the plans of the parents and their spouses (if any) is primary:

a. First, the plan of the custodial parent;

b. Second, if the parent with custody has remarried, the plan of that parent's new spouse;

c. Third, the plan of the noncustodial parent; and

d. Last, if the noncustodial parent has remarried, the plan of the noncustodial parent's new spouse.

[NAIC Model COB Reg. 120-1, § 5. D(2)(d)]

Example. Peter, who is divorced from Beth, has custody of his son but no plan coverage as an employee. Peter has remarried, and his new wife, Ann, has employee dependent coverage that includes Peter's son. Ann's plan is the primary plan for the child's health care expenses, and Beth's plan is secondary.

A case involving medical expenses for the child of divorced parents should be a wake-up call for plans covering divorced parents who switch custody arrangements without legal formalities. A court ruled that the father's plan was primary because he had legal custody of the child under the couple's divorce decree, even though the child had lived with the mother for several years. Each plan's COB provision stated that the plan of the parent with custody was primary. The father's plan argued that the mother's plan should have primary liability because the child lived with the mother and the mother claimed the child as a dependent for tax purposes. The court rejected that argument, ruling that the divorce decree granting custody to the father controlled. [Butler Mfg. Co. v. Blue Cross Blue Shield of Tex., 2006 U.S. Dist. LEXIS 85926 (W.D. Mo. Nov. 27, 2006)]

Q 3:79   How are insured plan benefits coordinated if an employee is laid off or retires?

The third order of benefit determination rule under the NAIC's model COB regulation, the "active or inactive employee" rule, provides that if the employee is covered under one plan as an active employee ("neither laid off nor retired") and under another plan as a laid-off or retired employee, the active-employee coverage is primary. This rule applies only if both plans have it in their COB provisions or if they agree to its application. [NAIC Model COB Reg. 120-1, § 5. D(3)]

Note. This rule applies only when both plans cover the individual as an employee, whether active or retired. The first COB rule governs when one of the two plans covers the individual as a dependent (see Q 3:86).

Q 3:80　How are insured plan benefits coordinated if an individual is covered under COBRA continuation coverage and is also covered under another plan?

The fourth order of benefit determination rule under the NAIC's model COB regulation, the "continuation coverage" rule, provides that if an individual who has continuation of group health plan coverage pursuant to COBRA or, pursuant to a state continuation law, is also covered under another plan, then the primary plan is the plan covering that person as an employee, member, subscriber, or retiree (or as that person's dependent). The continuation coverage is secondary. [NAIC Model COB Reg. 120-1, § 5. D(4)]

Because the COB rules are applied one by one, always in the same order, COBRA situations are frequently resolved by one of the earlier rules, and this rule comes into play less frequently than would be anticipated.

Q 3:81　If none of the previous rules determines which plan pays first, how is the determination made?

The NAIC model COB regulation's fifth order of benefit determination rule, the "longer or shorter length of coverage" rule, provides that if none of the previous rules determines which plan pays first, then the plan covering the individual for the longer period of time pays first.

To determine the length of time the individual has been covered under a plan, a "tacking" rule applies: two plans are treated as a single plan if the individual was eligible under the second one within 24 hours after the first ended. When making this determination, a new plan is not considered to have become effective upon a change in the amount or scope of a plan's benefits, a change in the insurer, direct care provider, or plan administrator, or a change from one type of plan to another (such as from a single-employer plan to a multiple-employer plan. [NAIC Model Reg. 120-1, § 5. D(5)]

Q 3:82　What if all of the order of determination rules fail to determine which plan pays first?

The NAIC model COB regulation's sixth and last COB rule is a fail-safe rule, here called the "rule of last resort," which provides that if none of the preceding five rules determines which plan is primary, the allowable expenses are to be shared equally between the plans. [NAIC Model Reg. 120-1, § 5. D(5)] Many summary plan descriptions (SPDs) erroneously leave this rule out.

Q 3:83　How much does a secondary plan pay?

The NAIC model COB regulation provides that the secondary plan pays the difference between "total allowable expenses" and whatever the primary plan pays, as long as the secondary plan does not pay more than it would have paid had it been the primary plan. "Total allowable expenses" are generally expenses that are covered in whole or in part under either of the coordinating plans. The determination of what the secondary plan would have paid had it been the primary plan is made on an aggregate basis over the plan year rather than on a claim-by-claim basis.

As a result, a secondary plan might have to pay benefits for expenses that it does not cover if (1) those expenses were covered (but not in full) by the other plan and (2) as a consequence of the operation of COB, it had savings (a credit balance) as a result of being the secondary plan during the current plan year. (This is different from an offset provision, under which the health plan with the offset provision would not pay for expenses that it does not cover.) The credit balance feature is rarely disclosed in certificates of coverage or SPDs, so participants are often unaware that additional potential reimbursement is available.

Example. A secondary plan does not cover mental and nervous conditions. As a result of previous claims during the year, it has achieved COB savings of $5,000 compared with what it would have paid if it had been the primary plan. A claim of $2,000 is now submitted for treatment relating to mental and nervous disorders, $1,000 of which is payable by the primary plan. The secondary plan must pay the other $1,000 even though it does not cover expenses incurred in the treatment of mental and nervous conditions. [NAIC Model COB Reg. 120-1, § 6. A]

The NAIC model COB regulation also contains model COB language for insurance contracts and required language to be inserted in the benefit summary materials that the insurance company prepares for employees. This model employee communication language details how the credit balance provision works, so that employees will be aware that they are entitled to use it. The model COB regulation allows this disclosure material to be changed to fit the style of the document in which it is to be included, but substantive changes are not permitted. Nonetheless, the possible use of credit balance savings by the participant is rarely disclosed in such benefit summary materials.

Less than 100 percent payment from both plans under COB. For a short time, the NAIC model COB regulation permitted plans to coordinate in ways that would allow them to preserve the deductibles and copayments inherent in their plans. For example, one permitted method would have allowed the secondary plan to pay the difference between what it would have paid on the claim had it been the primary plan and whatever the primary plan actually paid (essentially, an offset). Those rules were removed from the NAIC model regulation.

Uninsured plans and insured plans in the few states that adopted the rule before it was repealed by the NAIC may still use this method, although there is some doubt that it really results in cost-saving advantages to the plan. Plans that tend to favor this approach are often large employer plans that require little if any employee contribution for coverage. As employees covered by those plans realize that there is little advantage for their spouses to maintain their contributory employee health care coverage, they can be expected to have their spouses drop their own employee coverage and keep the dependent coverage. This migration away from duplicate coverage by a relatively small number of employees can erode any savings achieved by a more restrictive approach to what the secondary plan pays.

Preservation of managed care penalties. An amendment to the NAIC model regulation permits plans to take advantage of certain cost-containment penalties. Under this method of COB, if the primary plan limits or excludes benefits when the plan participant fails to abide by the plan's cost-containment programs (such as preadmission certification, PPO, or second surgical opinion), the amount of the penalty will not be considered an allowable expense. This feature is not available when a secondary plan's liability is generated by an HMO member seeking care outside the HMO, resulting in no liability to the primary HMO.

> **Example.** A plan pays 90 percent of covered hospital expenses if a preadmission review is performed for voluntary admissions, but pays only 70 percent if such a review is not performed. When the penalty is applied because the preadmission review was not performed, the secondary plan treats the 80 percent (the 10 percent copayment plus the 70 percent paid under the preadmission review penalty provision of the primary plan) as an allowable expense and pays only the 10 percent.

The above COB method is designed to protect the cost-containment features of the primary plan, not those of the secondary plan; therefore, if the secondary plan has a preadmission review provision, and if the primary plan paid 90 percent of such expenses, the secondary plan would have to pay the other 10 percent. [NAIC Model COB Reg. 120-1, § 23. A(40)(a)]

Q 3:84 Can state law prohibit a self-insured employee benefit plan from subtracting benefits payable under the state's no-fault law or require the plan to be the primary payer with the no-fault insurance carrier as the secondary payer only?

No. A state cannot regulate the terms of a self-insured group health plan. [FMC Corp. v. Holliday, 498 U.S. 52 (1990)]

Subrogation

Q 3:85 What is subrogation?

Group health plans typically contain provisions that give the plan the right to reimbursement of benefits paid if the employee receives another recovery for the same expenses. A subrogation provision, unlike COB provisions (see Q 3:69), gives the plan the right to reimbursement if the employee receives a recovery from any source, not just another health plan. For example, a subrogation provision may give a plan the right to recoup medical expenses paid in connection with an automobile accident if the employee subsequently receives a settlement in a lawsuit against the other driver.

Q 3:86   Are subrogation provisions enforceable by a group health plan?

Not always. In a significant decision, the U.S. Supreme Court held that a plan cannot sue to hold a participant or beneficiary personally liable for a reimbursement if the participant or beneficiary is not holding any specific funds that the plan would be entitled to recover under the reimbursement provision. [Great-West Life & Annuity Ins. Co. v. Knudson, 534 U.S. 204 (2002)]

Janette Knudson was involved in a car accident that rendered her quadriplegic. Knudson was covered under a self-insured health plan maintained by her husband's employer. She incurred $411,157.11 of medical expenses, most of which was paid by Great-West Life & Annuity Insurance Co., which provided stop-loss insurance to the self-insured plan. The plan contained a subrogation provision entitling it to reimbursement for benefits paid by the plan if a participant or beneficiary was entitled to recover from a third party. An agreement between the plan and Great-West assigned Great-West the right to reimbursements under the subrogation provision.

Following her accident, Knudson filed a lawsuit against the manufacturer of her car and others. The lawsuit was eventually settled for $650,000. The settlement allocated most of the recovery to attorneys' fees and a trust for Knudson's care, with about $14,000 going to Great-West as a reimbursement under the subrogation provision. Great-West sued Knudson to enforce its right to reimbursement for the remaining amount of medical expenses it had paid.

The Supreme Court held that the insurance company's lawsuit against Knudson was not permitted by ERISA. According to the Court, ERISA permits a plan to sue for "equitable relief" but bars "legal relief." A request for relief is "equitable" if one party has funds that the other claims. However, a simple claim for money due is "legal," and that is what the insurance company was asking for in Knudson's case.

In the wake of *Great-West,* the federal appeals courts split on the question of whether a plan is entitled to reimbursement when, unlike the situation in *Great-West,* the plan participant actually holds the funds received from a third party. The Supreme Court has resolved that issue in the affirmative. [Sereboff v. Mid Atl. Med. Servs., Inc., 126 S. Ct. 1869 (2006)]

The case involved a husband and wife—the Sereboffs—who were covered under a health plan maintained by the wife's employer. The couple was injured in a car accident and the plan paid about $75,000 for their medical expenses. However, the Sereboffs sued the driver of the other car involved in the accident and received a settlement of $750,000, which was placed in an investment account under the control of the Sereboffs. The plan sought recovery from the Sereboffs under a plan provision that required the Sereboffs to repay the plan if they should recover money from a third party as a result of an incident for which the plan provided benefits. The Supreme Court concluded that the plan's request was for equitable relief allowed by ERISA because the Sereboffs had possession of the settlement funds.

Legal Requirements Affecting Health Plans

Q 3:87   Are medical plans subject to ERISA?

Generally, an employer-sponsored medical plan is subject to ERISA and, as such, will be required to comply with the mandatory benefit provisions contained of ERISA.

Over the years, Congress has enacted a number of mandatory benefit requirements and other standards for group health plans and health insurance issuers providing coverage in connection with group health plans. These standards, which are incorporated into ERISA (Title I Parts 6 and 7) include:

- Limitations on exclusions from coverage based on preexisting conditions
- Special enrollment rights for employees and dependents
- Prohibition of discrimination on the basis of health status
- Genetic information nondiscrimination requirements
- Guaranteed renewability in multiemployer plans and certain welfare arrangements
- Standards relating to benefits for mothers and newborns
- Parity in mental health and substance abuse disorder benefits
- Required coverage for reconstructive surgery following mastectomies
- Coverage of dependent students on medically necessary leaves of absence
- Requirement to provide group health plan coverage pursuant to medical child support orders
- Required coverage for adoptive and pre-adoptive children
- Coverage for pediatric vaccines
- Coverage requirements for Medicaid-eligible individuals

The 2010 Health Reform Act builds on these requirements, imposing new mandates and new restrictions on group health plans and health insurance issuers providing group health plan coverage. These new rules include:

- Restriction of lifetime or annual benefit limits
- Prohibition of preexisting condition exclusions
- Prohibition on rescission of coverage
- Prohibition on excessive waiting periods for coverage
- Coverage of preventive services
- Extension of dependent coverage to adult children
- Enhanced prohibitions on discrimination based on health status
- Prohibition of discrimination in favor of highly compensated employees

These requirements are discussed in detail in chapter 5.

In addition, ERISA's reporting and disclosure, claims, and fiduciary responsibility provisions will apply. (See chapter 2 for a detailed discussion of ERISA.)

Q 3:88 Does federal law require continued health coverage for terminated and retired employees?

Yes. Under certain circumstances, terminated and retired employees are, by law, still eligible for benefits. Two federal laws, COBRA and the Retiree Benefits Bankruptcy Protection Act of 1988, require continuation of group health plan benefits and continuation of nonpension retiree benefits in bankruptcy, respectively. (See chapter 6 for further discussion of COBRA; see chapter 19 for nonpension retiree benefits in bankruptcy.)

Q 3:89 Must health coverage be provided to individuals who take family or medical leave?

An individual who takes a family or medical leave that qualifies under the Family and Medical Leave Act of 1993 (FMLA) is entitled to continue his or her group health plan coverage for the duration of the unpaid FMLA leave. If he or she does so, the employer is required to continue its portion of premium contributions, and provision must be made for the employee to continue his or her contributions in order to maintain group health coverage in force.

Whether the employee chooses to maintain coverage during the FMLA leave or to let the coverage lapse, coverage must resume upon return from FMLA leave. No special exclusions or waiting periods may be imposed on individuals who return to active employment at the conclusion of an FMLA leave (even if they did not maintain group health coverage or their group health coverage terminated because premium payments were untimely during the leave). However, the plan may impose exclusions or waiting periods to the extent that they would have applied had the individual not gone on FMLA leave. If the employee fails to return to employment at the conclusion of the FMLA leave, the employer may, in some circumstances, recover its portion of the premium payments.

Special FMLA provisions apply to cafeteria plans (see chapter 7) and with regard to COBRA continuation of coverage (see chapter 6). These and other FMLA issues also are discussed in detail in chapter 16.

Q 3:90 Must medical plan coverage be extended when an employee takes military leave?

Yes. Medical plan coverage generally must be extended when an employee takes military leave. The Uniformed Services Employment and Reemployment Rights Act of 1994 (USERRA) broadly prohibits employers from discriminating or taking acts of reprisal against persons who serve in the uniformed services. USERRA imposes COBRA-like extensions of coverage requirements on health plans for employees who perform service in the uniformed services, and these extensions of coverage requirements have no minimum employer size requirement. The USERRA requirements are discussed in detail in chapter 19.

Q 3:91   Must a medical plan cover care of veterans' non-service-connected disabilities in a Veterans Administration facility?

Yes. The Veterans' Health Care Amendments of 1986 invalidate provisions that exclude the coverage of care administered in a Veterans Administration (VA) hospital or nursing home that is related to treatment of a veteran's non-service-connected disability. The VA may recover the reasonable cost of any such care from any third-party payer, provided that the health plan contract would otherwise have covered the care or services if they had not been furnished by a department or agency of the United States. [38 U.S.C. § 629]

The reasonable cost is to be determined pursuant to VA regulations, reduced by any applicable plan deductible and copayment amounts that the third party can demonstrate would be payable under a comparable health plan contract to a nongovernmental facility. [38 U.S.C. § 629(c)(2)(b)]

Third-party payer. Third-party payers for these purposes generally include employers, employers' insurance carriers, and persons obligated to provide or pay expenses of health services under a health plan contract. [38 U.S.C. § 629(i)(3)]

Covered health plan contract. Covered health plan contracts generally include insurance policies or contracts, medical or hospital service agreements, membership or subscription contracts, and similar arrangements for paying expenses for health services provided to individuals or for providing services to individuals. [38 U.S.C. § 629(i)(1)(A)]

See chapter 19 for further details about veterans' rights regarding group health plan coverage.

Q 3:92   Must a medical plan cover inpatient care for military retirees and their dependents in military hospitals?

Yes. It should cover such care on much the same terms and for much the same reasons that it should cover veterans' non-service-connected disabilities (see Q 3:91). Title II of COBRA invalidates exclusions in health plan contracts for inpatient care received by military retirees and their dependents from military hospitals if the contract would otherwise cover such care. It authorizes the Secretary of Defense to recover the reasonable cost of any such services from third-party payers. Recovery is measured in the same way as for veterans' non-service-connected disabilities, except that it will be based on Department of Defense regulations.

The definitions of *third-party payer* and *covered health plan contract* for military retirees are the same as for veterans' non-service-connected disabilities. [10 U.S.C. § 1095; COBRA § 2001(b)]

See chapter 19 for further details about military retirees' rights regarding group health plan coverage.

Q 3:93   May a plan reduce or terminate medical coverage for an individual who is eligible for Medicare?

The Social Security Act and Code Section 5000 contain numerous provisions prohibiting an employer from reducing or terminating medical coverage once an individual becomes eligible for Medicare. As a result, an employer's group health plan is required to be primary to Medicare.

The Medicare-related restrictions on group health plans are as follows:

1. *Aged employees.* A group health plan of an employer with at least 20 employees may not take into account the age-based Medicare entitlement of individuals age 65 or older in current employment status and must provide coverage to such individuals on the same conditions as for younger employees.

2. *Aged spouses of employees.* A group health plan of an employer with at least 20 employees may not take into account the age-based Medicare entitlement of spouses age 65 or older of an employee of any age in current employment status, and the spouse must be covered under the plan under the same conditions as spouses under age 65.

3. *End-stage renal disease.* The group health plan of an employer or employee organization of any size may not take into account the Medicare eligibility or entitlement of individuals who have end-stage renal disease (ESRD) and who are covered or seek to be covered under the plan.

4. *Disability.* The group health plan of a large employer (having at least 100 employees) may not take into account the disability-based Medicare entitlement of any individual who is covered or seeks to be covered under the plan by virtue of current employment status.

These requirements are discussed in detail in chapter 5.

Q 3:94   Do state insurance laws or state laws mandating the coverage of particular benefits or health care providers apply to group health plans?

A state law (including a state law mandating coverage of particular benefits or health care providers) might apply to a group health plan if the plan is insured and the law is one that regulates insurance. However, ERISA's preemption provisions may, in some circumstances, bar the application of the state law to the particular group health plan. (ERISA preemption is discussed in detail in chapter 2 and in the state continuation of coverage laws section of chapter 6.)

Tax Treatment of Employers

Q 3:95   May an employer deduct its contributions to or payments under a medical benefit plan?

Yes. [Treas. Reg. § 1.162-10(a)] However, employer contributions to a welfare benefit fund such as a voluntary employees' beneficiary association (VEBA) must also satisfy the additional requirements imposed by Code Sections 419 and 419A. (See chapter 20 for a discussion of these funding requirements.)

As a general rule, an employer claims a deduction when the payment or contributions are made. However, an employer using the accrual method of accounting can deduct a business expense, including an expense for employee medical benefits, when all events have occurred that establish the fact of the liability, the amount of the liability can be determined with reasonable accuracy, and economic performance has occurred with respect to the liability. Thus, the IRS has ruled that, in the case of a self-insured medical reimbursement plan, an accrual method employer may deduct the cost of medical services provided to employees in the year the services are provided even though payments to the services providers are not made until the following year. The IRS concluded that the fact of liability and the amount of the liability are established in the taxable year the services are provided, so the liability for the medical expenses is incurred in the taxable year in which medical services are provided to the employees by the medical service provider because that is the time economic performance occurs. [IRS TAM 200846021 (July 23, 2008)]

Q 3:96   What is the small employer health insurance credit?

Under a provision added by the 2010 Health Reform Act , an eligible small employer can claim a tax credit for the cost of health insurance coverage for employees [I.R.C. § 45R as added by PPACA § 1421 and amended by PPACA § 10105; Notice 2010-44, 2010-22 I.R.B. 717]. The credit may be claimed for amounts paid or incurred in tax years beginning after 2009.

Eligible small employer. An employer qualifies for the credit if (1) it has no more than 25 full-time equivalent employees for the tax year; (2) its average annual wages do not exceed $50,000 per full-time equivalent employee; and (3) it pays health insurance premiums for employees under a qualifying contribution arrangement.

Members of a controlled group or an affiliated service group and other businesses under common control are treated as a single employer for purposes of the credit. The aggregation rules of Code Section 414(b), (c), (m), and (o) apply for this purpose.

Full-time equivalent employees. The number of full-time equivalent employees for a tax year is figured by dividing the total number of hours for which wages were paid (including paid time off) during the year by 2,080 (i.e., 40 hours a week for 52 weeks). However, if an employee is paid for more than 2,080 hours during the year, the extra hours are not counted in the calculation.

Finally, if result of the calculation is not a whole number, the number of employee is rounded down to the next whole number.

Example 1. Smallco has 22 full-time employees, and 7 part-time employees in 2010. Twenty of its full- time employees work exactly 2,080 hours in 2010. However, two full-time employees work a significant amount of overtime and put in 2,340 hours and 2,392 hours, respectively. Each part-timer works 1,040 hours during the year. Although two of Smallco's full-timers worked more than 2,080 hours, only the first 2,080 are taken into account, resulting in a total of 53,040 hours of service for the year ((22 x 2,080) + (7 x 1,040)). Dividing the total hours of service by 2,080 produces a full-time equivalent employee head count of 25.5, which is rounded down to 25. *Result:* Although Smallco employs a total of 29 individuals for 2010, it nonetheless can qualify for the credit because its full-time equivalent employees do not exceed 25 for the year.

An employer can count actual hours of service (including paid time off) or use a days-worked or weeks-worked equivalency whereby the employee is credited with 8 hours for any day or 40 hours for any week in which the employee would be credited with at least one hour of actual service.

Average annual wages. Wages are determined in the same way as for Social Security (FICA) tax, but without regard to the dollar limit for covered wages. The employer's average annual wage is figure by dividing total wages paid by the number of full-time equivalent employees (rounded down to the nearest $1,000).

Example 2. The facts are the same as those in Example 1. Assume that Smallco paid $1.25 million in wages for 2010. *Result:* Smallco meets the $50,000 test ($1,250,000 total wages / 25 full-time equivalent employees = $50,000 average annual wages) even if some of its employees earn far more than $50,000.

Disregarded employees. Hours worked by, and wages paid to, seasonal workers (such as agricultural workers and retail workers employed during holiday seasons) do not count in determining the number of full-time equivalent employees or average annual wages of the employer unless a worker works for the employer on more than 120 days during the taxable year.

Significantly, employee-owners are not factored into the equation when calculating employees or average wages. These include self-employed business owners, 2 percent shareholders of an S corporation, and 5 percent owners of a business (as well certain relatives and dependents).

Practice Pointer. Hours worked by and wages paid to these disregarded employees will not cause a business to lose the credit. On the other hand, premiums paid on behalf of disregarded employees are not taken into account in calculating the amount of the credit.

Qualifying contribution arrangement. A small employer qualifies for the credit only if the employer's health plan requires the employer to make nonelective contributions on behalf of each employee enrolled in the plan in an amount equal to not less than 50 percent of the premium cost of the coverage.

Transition rule for tax years beginning in 2010. The IRS announced that the following transition rules will apply for tax years beginning in 2010:

1. An employer that pays at least 50 percent of the premium for each enrolled employee will not fail to qualify merely because the employer does not pay a uniform percentage of the premium for each employee.

2. The requirement that the employer pay at least 50 percent of the premium for each enrolled employee applies to the premium for single employee-only coverage. Therefore, for an employee with single employee-only coverage, the requirement will be met if the employer pays at least 50 percent of the premium for that coverage. In the case of an employee with more expensive coverage (e.g., family or self-plus-one coverage, the requirement will be met if the employer pays an amount for the coverage that is no less than 50 percent of the premium for single coverage for that employee.

[Small Business Health Care Tax Credit: Frequently Asked Questions, Q/A-22; Notice 2010-44, 2010-22 I.R.B 717]

Amount of credit for tax years 2010–2013. For tax years beginning in 2010 through 2013, the maximum credit is 35 percent of the contributions made by the employer for health insurance premiums on behalf of employees (other than disregarded employees) for the tax year. So, for example, if an employer contributes one half the cost of family coverage that costs $20,000, the credit for that coverage will be $3,500 (35% x $10,000 employer contributions).

However, the amount of contributions taken into account is limited to the amount the employer would have contributed if an employee had enrolled in coverage with a so-called benchmark premium based on the average cost in the small group market for coverage in the employer's state. For example, if an employer contributes half the cost of family coverage that costs $20,000 per year, but the benchmark premium for family coverage is $15,000, only $7,500 of the employer's contribution will count when calculating the credit. Thus, the credit for that coverage will be $2,625 (35% x $7,500).

The amount of the benchmark premium is determined by HHS and published by the IRS. Benchmark premiums for 2010 can be found in Revenue Ruling 2010-13. [2010-21 I.R.B. 691]

Only nonelective employer contributions are taken into account in calculating the credit. An amount contributed pursuant to a salary-reduction arrangement under a cafeteria plan is not treated as an employer contribution for purposes of the credit.

Credit phaseout. The credit is reduced for employers with more than 10 full-time equivalent employees. The credit is also reduced for an employer with average annual wages of more than $25,000.

To figure the reduction for an employer with more than 10 full-time equivalent employees, the otherwise applicable credit is multiplied by a fraction, the numerator of which is the number of full-time equivalent employee over 10 and the denominator of which is 15.

For an employer paying average annual wages above $25,000, the amount of this reduction is equal to the amount of the otherwise allowable credit multiplied by a fraction, the numerator of which is the average annual wages of the employer in excess of $25,000 and the denominator of which is $25,000.

For an employer with more than 10 employees and paying average annual wages in excess of $25,000, the reduction is the sum of the amount of the two reductions.

Example. For the 2010 tax year, Mini Co. has 12 full-time equivalent employees (FTEs) and average annual wages of $30,000. Mini pays $96,000 in health care premiums for its employees. (The premiums do not exceed the benchmark premium for Mini's state.) Mini's credit is calculated as follows:

Initial credit amount before reduction	$33,600 (35% x $96,000)
Less	
Total credit reduction	$11,200 ($4,480 + $6,720)
Credit reduction for FTEs over 10	$ 4,480 ($33,600 x 2/15)
Credit reduction for wages in excess of $25,000	$ 6,720 ($33,600 x $5,000/$25,000)
2010 tax credit	$22,400

The credit is claimed on the employer's annual income tax return. The credit is nonrefundable; it is allowable only to the extent of the employer's income tax (or alternative minimum tax) liability for the year. As part of the general business credit, unused credit amounts can generally be carried back one year and carried forward 20 years. [I.R.C. § 38(b)(36) as added by PPACA § 1421; I.R.C. § 39(a)] However, because the small employer health insurance credit was not in effect prior to 2010, an unused credit for 2010 can only be carried forward. [I.R.C. § 39(d)]

No deduction is allowed for that portion of the premiums paid for by an employer that is equal to the amount of the credit allowed with respect to the premiums. [I.R.C. § 280C(h) as added by PPACA § 1421 and PPACA § 10105]

Tax-exempt employers. The credit may be claimed by a tax-exempt eligible small employer, subject to a reduced credit percentage and a special credit limit. For 2010 through 2013, the maximum credit for a tax-exempt employer is 25 percent of the employer's creditable expenses. The amount of the credit cannot exceed the amount of income and Medicare (HI) tax the employer is required to withhold from employee's wages plus the employer's share of Medicare tax on the employee's wages.

For a tax-exempt employer the credit is refundable.

Amount of credit for 2014 and later tax years. For tax years beginning in 2014 and later years, the credit percentage will rise to 50 percent (35 percent for tax-exempt employers). However, the credit will be available only to a qualified small employer that purchases health insurance coverage for its employees through a state Exchange and will be allowed only available for a maximum coverage period of two consecutive taxable years.

> **Practice Pointer.** The two-year limit does not apply before 2014, and tax years before 2014 do not count toward the maximum two-year period. Therefore, a qualified small employer can potentially claim the credit for six taxable years, starting with 2010.

Q 3:97   Are employers subject to any excise taxes based on the way a group health plan is structured?

Yes. A variety of excise taxes may be imposed on a group health plan.

Violations of the Medicare secondary-payer requirements are subject to an excise tax equal to 25 percent of the employer's expenses incurred during the calendar year for each group health plan to which it contributes. [I.R.C. § 5000(a)] See chapter 5 for a discussion of the Medicare secondary payer requirements.

An excise tax of $100 per day may be imposed for failure to comply with the mandated benefit requirements for group health plan requirements (see chapter 5), the pediatric vaccine coverage requirements (see chapter 5), or the COBRA continuation coverage requirements (see chapter 6) [I.R.C. §§ 4980B, 4980D]

Excise taxes may be imposed for failure to make comparable contributions to Archer MSAs and HSAs (see Qs 3:141, 3:171). [I.R.C. §§ 4980E, 4980G]

Excise tax reporting. Beginning January 1, 2010, excise tax liabilities for failure to meet certain health plan requirements must be self-reported by filing Form 8928, *Return of Certain Excise Taxes Under Chapter 43 of the Internal Revenue Code.* [Treas. Reg. § 54.6011-2]

2010 Health Reform Act. The 2010 Health Reform Act imposes additional excise taxes and fees and special assessments on group health coverage.

1. Large employers are subject to excise taxes for failure to meet the employer responsibility requirements for tax years beginning after 2013 (see Q 3:15).

2. Employers that provide high-cost "Cadillac" coverage are subject to an excise tax for tax years beginning after 2014 (see Q 3:98). [I.R.C. § 4980I as added by PPACA § 9001 and amended by PPACA § 10901 and PPACA Reconciliation § 1401]

3. Issuers of group health insurance policies and sponsors of self-insured plans are subject to per capita fees on covered lives for policy or plan years ending after September 30, 2012 (see Q 3:99). [I.R.C. §§ 4375–4377 as added by PPACA § 6301] [I.R.C. § 9511 as added by PPACA § 6301]

Q 3:98 What is the excise tax on high-cost employer-sponsored health coverage?

The 2010 Health Reform Act imposes a 40 percent excise tax on the *excess benefit* under an employer-sponsored plan. [I.R.C. § PPACA § 9001 as amended by PPACA § 10901 and PPACA Reconciliation § 1401] The tax is effective for tax years beginning after 2017.

Excess benefit. The excess benefit is the aggregate value of all employer-sponsored benefits for an employee over a threshold amount.

In determining the amount of excess benefit, all employer-sponsored coverage for an employee (including a former employee, surviving spouse, or other primary insured) that is excludable from income is taken into account, regardless of whether the employee or the employer pays for the coverage. Thus, employer-sponsored coverage includes reimbursements under a health flexible spending account (FSA) or health reimbursement arrangement (HRA) and contributions to a health savings account (HSA) or medical savings account (MSA).

Supplementary health insurance is included in determining excess coverage, with the exception of vision- or dental-only coverage and certain excepted coverage (as defined in Code Section 9832(c)(1) for purposes of the HIPAA portability requirements). Excepted coverage includes accident and disability income insurance, coverage issued as a supplement to liability insurance, general and automobile liability insurance, workers' compensation or similar insurance, automobile medical payment insurance, credit-only insurance, and similar coverage. Coverage for specified diseases and injuries and hospital indemnity or other indemnity insurance (as defined in Code Section 9832(c)(3)) *is not* included if the coverage is purchased exclusively by the employee with after-tax dollars, but *is* included if any portion of the coverage is employer-provided.

Employer-sponsored coverage includes both fully insured and self-insured health coverage, including on-site medical clinics that offer more than a de minimis amount of medical care and executive physical programs.

Valuation. The value of employer-sponsored coverage is generally determined in the same manner as the premiums for COBRA continuation coverage. In the case of a health FSA that limits reimbursements to the amount of an employee's salary reduction contributions, the value is the amount of salary reduction contributions for the year. If an FSA provides for employer contributions in excess of the employee's salary reduction contribution, those contributions are valued under the COBRA rules. The value of employer contributions to an HSA or MSA is the dollar amount of the contributions.

Benefit thresholds. For 2018, the law sets the threshold amount is at $10,200 for self-only coverage or $27,500 for family coverage. The family threshold generally applies to an employee only if the employee and at least one other beneficiary are enrolled in coverage other than self-only coverage that provides minimum essential coverage and under which benefits do not vary based on whether the covered individual is the employee or other beneficiary. However, in the case of a multiemployer plan, the family threshold applies regardless of whether an employee has individual or family coverage under the plan.

Higher thresholds apply to retirees (who have attained age 55 and who are not Medicare eligible) and to individuals in high-risk professions. High-risk professions include law enforcement, fire protection, emergency medical response, longshore work, construction, mining, agriculture, forestry, and fishing. For individuals in these professions, the threshold amounts are increased by $1,650 for self-only coverage or $3,450 for family coverage. Thus, the threshold amounts are $11,850 for self-only coverage or $30,950 for family coverage for 2018.

> **Practice Pointer.** The thresholds for 2018 are not set in stone. They will be increased if the actual growth in the cost of U.S. health care between 2010 and 2018 exceeds projected growth for that period. In addition, the thresholds will be adjusted for the age and gender of an employee.

Liability for excise tax. The tax on excess benefits is imposed pro rata on the coverage providers. To the extent coverage is provided through insurance, the tax is imposed on the issuers of the insurance. In the case of a self-insured group health plan or a health FSA or HRA, the tax is paid by the plan administrator. Where the employer acts as plan administrator of a self-insured plan, the tax is paid by the employer. If an employer contributes to an HSA or MSA on behalf of an employee, the employer is liable for the tax.

Employer responsibility. An employer is responsible for calculating the amount subject to the excise tax allocable to each insurer and plan administrator and reporting the amounts to each insurer and plan administrator and to the IRS. Each insurer or administrator is then responsible for calculating, reporting, and paying the excise tax to the IRS.

> **Example.** In 2018, Bill, an employee of XYZ Company, elects family coverage under a fully-insured group health policy with a value of $28,500 and contributes $2,500 to a health FSA that is administered by XYZ. The total value of Bill's coverage is $31,000. Assuming a coverage threshold of $27,500 for 2018, Bill's excess benefit is $3,500. Of that amount, XYZ reports $3,218 ($3,500 excess benefit × $28,500 insurance coverage / $31,000 total coverage) to the insurance company providing the group health policy. As administrator of the FSA, XYZ computes and reports the excise tax on $282 excess benefit allocable to Bill's FSA contribution ($3,500 excess benefit × $2,500 FSA contribution / $31,000 total coverage). The excise tax payable by the insurer is $1,287 (40% × $3,218); the excise tax payable by XYZ is $112.80 (40% × $282).

If an employer underreports the amount of excess benefit, the employer is subject to a penalty equal to the sum of the additional excise taxes (plus interest) that would have been owed by each insurer and administrator if the employer had reported correctly. No penalty will be imposed if the employer did not know of the underreporting and could not have discovered it using reasonable diligence. In addition, no penalty will be imposed if an employer corrects a reporting error within 30 days.

Q 3:99   What are the per capita fees on health insurance and self-insured group health plans?

The 2010 Health Reform Act establishes a Patient Centered Outcomes Research Trust Fund (PCORTF) to be funded through fees on health insurance policies and self-insured health plans. [I.R.C. § 9511 as added by PPACA § 6301; PPACA §§ 4375, 4376, 4377 as added by PPACA § 6301] Monies in the trust fund will be used to study the effectiveness and outcomes of medical treatments and services. The fees will take effect for policy or plan years ending after September 30, 2012, and will no longer apply for policy or plan years ending after September 30, 2019.

The fee is $2 multiplied by the average number of lives covered under the policy or plan. For policy or plan years ending in during fiscal year 2013, the fee is $1 per covered life. For any policy of plan year beginning after September 30, 2014, the $2 fee will be indexed based on the increase in national health expenditures.

In the case of a health insurance policy, the issuer of the policy is liable for the fee. In the case of a self-insured health plan, the plan sponsor is liable for the fee.

Practice Pointer. In the case of an insured group health plans, the fees are imposed on the insurer issuing the group health plan coverage. Nonetheless, the fees represent a cost of coverage that will ultimately be borne by the sponsoring employer.

Tax Treatment of Participants

Q 3:100   Are the employer's contributions to an employer-sponsored medical plan taxable to employees?

No. [Treas. Reg. § 1.106-1]

An employee's pretax contributions toward group health plan coverage or a health care FSA under a cafeteria plan are treated, for tax purposes only, as employer contributions that are excluded from income under Code Section 106. (See chapter 7.)

See Q 3:125 for a discussion of the special tax treatment applicable to more-than-2-percent shareholder-employees of a Subchapter S corporation.

Q 3:101 Are contributions made by an employer for health care for an employee's spouse or dependents taxable to the employee?

No, they are not. IRS regulations make it clear that the exclusion for employer-provided coverage under an accident or health plan applies to coverage for an employee's spouse or dependents. [Treas. Reg. § 1.106-1]

In the past, the definition of a *dependent* for this purpose was the same as the definition for other tax purposes (e.g., claiming dependency exemption). However, the Working Families Tax Relief Act of 2004 [Pub. L. No. 108-311, 118 Stat. 1166 (2004)] amended the definition of *dependent* and the amended definition led to some special rules for benefit purposes.

Under the new definition, an individual must be either a "qualifying child" or a "qualifying relative" to be a dependent. [I.R.C. § 152]

A qualifying child (1) must be under age 19 (or a student under age 24), (2) must live with the taxpayer for more than half the year, and (3) must not provide more than one half of his or her own support. In addition, a change made by the Fostering Connections to Success and Increasing Adoptions Act of 2008 [Pub. L. No. 110-351, 122 Stat. 3949 (Oct. 7, 2008)], which is effective for tax years beginning after 2008, provides that a qualifying child (other than a child who is permanently or totally disabled) must be younger than the claiming taxpayer. The "Adoptions Act" also makes it clear that a qualifying child must not have filed a joint return (other than to claim a refund) for the calendar year in which the taxable year of the taxpayer begins.

In the case of divorced or separated parents, a child is generally treated as the dependent of the noncustodial parent only if the custodial parent releases his or her claim to the tax exemption for the child. However, the IRS says that for purposes of health and certain other fringe benefits it will treat a child as the dependent of both parents (whether or not the custodial parent has released the claim to the exemption) if certain requirements are met. [Rev. Proc. 2008-48, 2008-36 I.R.B. 586] Assuming those requirements are met, the child will qualify for coverage as a dependent under the employer-provided health plan of either parent.

In some cases, a child will meet the requirements to be claimed as a qualifying child of both a parent and nonparent. For example, a minor child who lives in the same household as his mother and grandmother may meet the requirements to be a qualifying child of both of them. Under prior rules, the child could be treated only as a dependent of the parent. However, under a change made by the 2008 "Adoptions Act," effective for tax years beginning after 2008, where a parent does not claim a qualifying child as a dependent, another taxpayer may do so if that taxpayer's adjusted gross income is higher than the adjusted gross income of any parent of the child. Consequently, the nonparent will be able to treat the child as a dependent for health benefit purposes.

An individual who does not satisfy that definition may be a "qualifying relative" provided he or she (1) is related to the taxpayer (e.g., a child, parent, or sibling) or is a member of the taxpayer's household, (2) receives more than one half of his or her support from the taxpayer, *and* (3) does not have income in excess of the exemption amount for the year ($3,650 for 2010).

The addition of the third condition—the gross income limit—raised concerns that employer-provided health coverage for certain individuals would have to be treated as taxable income to an employee. For example, if a plan covered a 19-year-old child who was not a full-time student, the coverage would be taxable if the child earned more than the gross income limit for the year.

Fortunately, the IRS allayed these concerns. An IRS notice provides that the value of employer-provided coverage for an individual who meets the definition of a qualifying relative is excludable even if the individual's gross income exceeds the gross income limit. [IRS Notice 2004-79, 2004-49 I.R.B. 898]

Unfortunately, the IRS's quick fix did not address all the issues stemming from the change in the dependency definition. Absent legislative action, the general definition applies for purposes of withdrawals from health savings accounts (see Q 3:179) and for purposes of dependent care assistance plans (see chapter 8).

Another problem crops up in the case of a child who is a *qualifying relative* of one individual and is a *qualifying child* of another individual.

Example. Bob and Susan are not married, but live together along with Susan's son, Steve. Bob is not Steve's father. Bob supports the family. Susan has no income; she stays home to care for Steve. Under the rules described above, Steve is Susan's qualifying child. However, Steve also meets the requirements for being Bob's dependent as a qualifying relative.

Until recently, there was a catch: IRS rules provided that a qualifying child of an individual cannot also be a qualifying relative of someone else. Consequently, Bob could not claim Steve as a dependent for tax purposes. Moreover, coverage for Steve under Bob's employer-provided health plan could not qualify for tax-free treatment. Under new rules announced in January 2008, the IRS said a child will not be considered a qualifying child of an individual (e.g., a parent or any other individual for whom the child might otherwise be a qualified child) if that individual is (1) not required by law to file an income tax return and (2) either does not file a return or files an income tax return solely to obtain a refund of withheld income taxes. [IRS Notice 2008-5, 2008-2 I.R.B. 256] Thus, in the above example, Steve can be treated as Bob's dependent, and Bob's employer-provided coverage for Steve is eligible for tax-free treatment.

Practice Pointer. While the IRS notice eases the rules to some degree, it does not guarantee that health coverage provided to a child through a non-parent's health plan will qualify for tax-free treatment. If the child's parent is required to file a tax return (other than to obtain a refund), the child cannot be treated as a qualifying relative of an individual who is not a parent. Therefore, the child will not qualify as the non-parent's dependent, and coverage for the child provided by the non-parent's employer will not qualify for tax-free treatment.

Q 3:102   What is the tax treatment of coverage for an employee's adult child?

The 2010 Health Reform Act requires a group health plan (or a health insurance issuer offering group coverage) that provides dependent coverage of children to continue to make that coverage available for an adult child until the child turns 26 years of age. [I.R.C. § 9815 as added by PPACA § 1562; PHSA § 2714 as added by PPACA § 1001 and amended by PPACA Reconciliation § 2301(b); DOL Reg. § 54.9815-2714T(a)]

The 2010 Health Reform Act amends Code Section 105(b) to extend the general exclusion for reimbursements for medical care expenses under an employer-provided accident or health plan to any child of an employee who has not attained age 27 as of the end of the taxable year. [I.R.C. § 105(b) as amended by PPACA Reconciliation § 1004] This change also applies to the exclusion for employer-provided coverage under an accident or health plan for injuries or sickness for such a child. [Notice 2010-38, 2010-20 I.R.B. 682]

> **Note.** A parallel change is made for VEBAs and Section 401(h) accounts. [I.R.C. §§ 401(h), 501(c)(9) as amended by PPACA Reconciliation § 1004] The provision similarly amends Code Section 162(l) to permit self-employed individuals to take a deduction for the cost of medical coverage for any child of the taxpayer who has not attained age 27 as of the end of the taxable year. [I.R.C. § 162(l) as amended by PPACA Reconciliation § 1004]

Q 3:103   May an employer combine pretax salary reductions for premium costs with tax-free reimbursements for the same costs?

According to the IRS, double dipping is not allowed. One provision of the tax law states that employees owe no income tax on the cost of employer-provided health insurance. [I.R.C. § 106] Moreover, in 1961 the IRS ruled that if a company reimburses employees for the premiums they have paid for health insurance, the reimbursements qualify for tax-free treatment. [Rev. Rul. 61-46, 1961-1 C.B. 51] Thus, employers can pay premiums for employees' health insurance, either directly or through reimbursements, without the employees' having to pay tax on the amounts. In addition, if premium payments or reimbursements are tax-free, they are not subject to income tax withholding or Social Security and Medicare (FICA) taxes.

In a subsequent ruling, however, the IRS rejected an employer's efforts to combine these tax breaks. The employer had proposed two possible revisions to its health insurance plan. Under the first arrangement, the employer would simply cut employees' salaries and apply the savings to the premiums for their health insurance coverage. In other words, employees would exchange a portion of their salaries for health insurance coverage. Then the employer would make payments to the employees to reimburse them for their health insurance premium costs, as permitted by the 1961 ruling. Under the second arrangement, the salary cuts would be handled through a cafeteria plan. The employees could elect to take a lower salary in return for health insurance coverage. As with the first arrangement, the employer would reimburse the employees for their health insurance costs. Under either arrangement, the employer expected to save payroll taxes. According to the employer, there would be no FICA tax on the portion of the salaries the employees no longer received and no FICA tax on the reimbursements to the employees for their health insurance premiums.

However, the IRS ruled that the employer's analysis was incorrect: the reimbursement payments would be taxable to the employees and subject to income tax withholding and FICA taxes. According to the IRS, when the employer applies the pay reductions to the payment of employees' premium costs, the employer is making the payments, not the employees. As a result, the employees have not "paid" any health insurance premiums and there is nothing to reimburse them for. Therefore, the "reimbursement" payments to the employees will be treated as taxable compensation, not as tax-free premium reimbursements.

The IRS pointed out that the result would be different if the premium payments came out of the employees' after-tax salaries. In that case, the employees would have "paid" the premiums, and the reimbursement would be tax-free. However, having the employees pay the premiums with after-tax dollars would not produce any payroll tax savings. [Rev. Rul. 2002-3, 2002-2 I.R.B. 305]

Q 3:104   Are employer contributions for medical coverage for retired employees taxable to those individuals?

No. Employer contributions for retiree medical coverage are not taxable to the retirees. An employee who participates in an employer-funded accident or health plan is deemed to continue to be an employee for purposes of Code Sections 105 and 106. Accordingly, an employer's contributions to an accident or health plan that provides benefits for a retired employee are excludable from the retired employee's gross income. [Rev. Ruls. 62-119, 1992 C.B. 38; 75-539, 1975-2 C.B. 45; 82-196, 1982-2 C.B. 53]

Q 3:105   Are employer contributions for medical coverage for a deceased employee's surviving spouse and dependents taxable to those individuals?

No. Employer contributions to an accident or health plan that provides benefits for a deceased employee's surviving spouse and dependents are excludable from the gross income of the survivors under Code Section 106. [Rev. Rul. 82-196, 1982 C.B. 53]

Q 3:106   Are employer contributions for medical coverage for laid-off employees taxable to those individuals?

No. An employer's contributions to an accident or health plan on behalf of laid-off workers are based solely on the employment relationship. Accordingly, the laid-off worker is deemed to be an employee for purposes of Code Sections 105 and 106, and employer contributions to an accident or health plan that provides benefits for such individuals are excludable from their gross incomes under Code Section 106. [Rev. Rul. 85-121, 1985-2 C.B. 56]

Q 3:107   Are employer contributions for medical coverage under a severance plan taxable to terminated employees?

No. The IRS considered a severance plan that provided severance pay, medical coverage, and other benefits to eligible terminated employees. Under the plan, the employer agreed to pay the same portion of the cost of COBRA continuation coverage that it paid for active employees for the first 12 months of the COBRA continuation period. The IRS reasoned that the employer's contributions under the severance plan for medical coverage on behalf of the terminated employees was related solely to and based solely on the terminated employees' prior employment relationship with the employer. Accordingly, these individuals were employees for purposes of Code Sections 105 and 106, and the employer contributions toward their medical coverage were excludable from the terminated employees' gross incomes under Code Section 106. [Priv. Ltr. Rul. 9612008 (Dec. 18, 1995)]

Q 3:108   Are employer contributions toward premiums for COBRA continuation coverage taxable to qualified beneficiaries?

No. An employer contribution or subsidy toward the applicable premium for COBRA continuation coverage will not be taxable to the qualified beneficiary. Such a contribution qualifies as an employer contribution toward accident and health insurance within the meaning of Code Section 106, which excludes such employer contributions from the employee's gross income. [Priv. Ltr. Rul. 9612008 (Dec. 18, 1995)]

Q 3:109   What if the employer's plan covers nonspousal cohabitants or domestic partners?

If the employer-provided health plan covers an individual other than the employee, the employee's spouse, or the employee's dependent or adult child, then the fair market value of coverage must be included in income by the employee and reported by the employer as wages. The IRS has ruled that the value of the employer-provided coverage for the domestic partner in excess of the amount paid by the employee for such coverage is not excluded under Code Section 106 and is includable in income by the eligible employee under Code

Section 61 and subject to FICA and FUTA. For this purpose, fair market value is determined based on how much an individual would have to pay for such coverage in an arm's-length transaction; for group medical coverage, this amount is the fair market value of the group coverage. [Priv. Ltr. Rul. 9850011]

One way to provide a taxable benefit to an employee without increasing the employee's tax bill is to pick up the tax tab through a processing called "grossing up." Although grossing up a taxable benefit has received a stamp of approval from the IRS, a union welfare fund recently asked the DOL whether picking up the tax on domestic partner benefits was permissible under ERISA.

The union fund provides medical, surgical, hospital care, and similar health benefits to approximately 10,000 hotel and restaurant employees and their beneficiaries. Coverage is generally provided on a noncontributory basis. The covered employees are divided into separate plan units in different geographic areas, with each unit offering different benefits. Three units—in New York, Las Vegas, and Atlantic City—offer health benefits to employees' same-sex domestic partners. The New York unit also offers domestic partner benefits to opposite-sex couples who satisfy the definition of domestic partners. Approximately 109 employees in the three units have elected domestic partner coverage.

In connection with the provision of the domestic partner benefits, the fund adopted a plan amendment under which it will pay both the employer and the employee shares of FUTA and FICA taxes, as well as an additional gross-up amount representing the tax due on its payment of the employees' FICA tax.

According to the DOL, the fund's payment of the employer share of FICA taxes clearly will not run afoul of any ERISA rules. The fund is legally responsible for the employer share of the FICA taxes, so payment of those taxes would not be an improper expenditure of plan assets.

Furthermore, the DOL concluded that the fund's decision to pay the employee portion of FICA taxes for employees electing domestic partner coverage will not violate ERISA, provided the tax payments are clearly specified as additional plan benefits in the plan document. According to the DOL, such payments are an additional distribution from plan assets that must be provided as plan benefits; they cannot be justified as reasonable administrative expenses of the plan.

The same holds true for the additional gross-up amount. The fund's decision to pay the gross-up will not violate ERISA if the payments are clearly specified as plan benefits in the plan document. Again, these payments cannot be treated as reasonable administrative expenses of the plan. [DOL Adv. Op. 2001-05A (June 1, 2001)]

Domestic partner as "spouse." The marital status of an individual for tax purposes is generally determined by state law. Therefore, if an employee's opposite-sex domestic partner is recognized as a spouse under state law (e.g., in states that recognize common-law marriage), the value of employer-provided coverage for the domestic partner/spouse is excluded from the employee's income. However, the Defense of Marriage Act [Pub. L. No. 104-199, 110 Stat. 2419 (1996)], effective September 21, 1997, provides that for purposes of interpreting federal laws and regulations the word marriage means only a legal union between one man and one woman as husband and wife, and the word spouse refers only to a person of the opposite sex who is a husband or a wife. [1 U.S.C. § 7] Therefore, a same-sex domestic partner cannot qualify as a spouse for tax purposes, and employer-provided coverage for the partner is included in the employee's income.

In 2003, the Massachusetts Supreme Judicial Court held that the Massachusetts Constitution barred the state from denying an individual the "protections, benefits, and obligations of civil marriage" solely because the person chose to marry a person of the same sex. [Goodridge v. Department of Public Health, 440 Mass. 309 (Sup. Jud. Ct. 2003)]

According to guidance from the Massachusetts Department of Revenue, the value of employer-provided health benefits for a same-sex spouse is excludable from an employee's income for Massachusetts tax purposes. However, under the federal Defense of Marriage Act, a Massachusetts same-sex marriage is not recognized for federal tax purposes. Therefore, for federal tax purposes, the value of employer-provided health benefits for an employee's same-sex spouse are taxable to the employee, unless the spouse qualifies as a dependent (see below). [Massachusetts Tax Issues Associated with Same Sex Marriage, Technical IR 04-17]

In Connecticut, which officially authorized same-sex marriages effective October 28, 2008 [Kerrigan v. Commissioner of Pub. Health (SC 17716)], clarification of the status of same-sex spouses for health benefit purposes may require legislative action. The Connecticut Attorney General has opined that the state Supreme Court's opinion requiring same-sex marriage mandates that same-sex married couples be afforded the same tax treatment as other couples and specifically stated that same-sex couples must be allowed to file joint tax returns for state tax purposes. However, the Attorney General also noted that the rules for determining Connecticut personal income tax are largely dependent on a taxpayer's federal filing status. Therefore, the Attorney General recommended that "for the sake of clarity" state tax statutes be revised to conform the state Supreme Court's decision. [Connecticut Atty. Gen. Op. to Revenue Service, Oct. 28, 2008]

Iowa and Vermont, which legalized same-sex marriage in 2009, have not yet clarified the tax treatment of same-sex spouses.

Domestic partner as "dependent." For health benefit purposes, a dependent can include any individual who is a member of a taxpayer's household and receives more than half of his or her support from the taxpayer for a tax year, provided the relationship between the taxpayer and the individual is not in violation of local law. Therefore, an employee's domestic partner (whether same-sex or opposite-sex) can qualify as a dependent. If a domestic partner does qualify as an employee's dependent, employer-provided coverage for the domestic partner is excludable from the employee's income and is not subject to income tax withholding or employment taxes.

Note. The Working Families Tax Relief Act of 2004 [Pub. L. No. 108-311, 118 Stat. 1166 (2004)] revised the tax definition of a dependent to include a gross income limit, effective beginning in 2005. However, an IRS notice makes it clear that the gross income limit does not apply for purposes of the exclusion for employer-provided health coverage. [IRS Notice 2004-79, 2004-49 I.R.B. 898]

Of course, an employer is generally not privy to an employee's household and financial arrangements—and may be reluctant to inquire into such matters. So how does an employer determine if an employee's domestic partner qualifies as a dependent?

According to an IRS private letter ruling, an employer may be able to rely on an employee's certification of a domestic partner's dependent status. The employer requesting the private letter ruling established a certification process under which employees enrolling for domestic partner coverage were required to complete a notarized affidavit certifying the authenticity of the domestic partner relationship at the time of initial enrollment and annually thereafter. If an employee intended to claim the domestic partner as a dependent in order to exclude the domestic partner benefits from income, the employee was also required to certify that the tax law requirements for dependency status in Code Section 152 were met. According to the IRS, the employer could rely on these certifications to determine whether domestic partner benefits are subject to income and employment taxes because they include statements regarding the Section 152 requirements. [Priv. Ltr. Rul. 200339001 (Sept. 26, 2003)] Although a private letter ruling applies only to the taxpayer that requested it, a similar certification procedure would most likely be approved by the IRS.

Q 3:110   What is the tax treatment of employer-provided medical coverage for preadoptive children?

If a preadoptive child is placed with an employee by an authorized placement agency for legal adoption, the child is treated as the employee's son or daughter for tax purposes. Therefore, the child will qualify as a dependent of the employee if the employee provided more than half the support for the child for the year, and employer-provided medical coverage for the child will be excluded from the employee's income.

The IRS has ruled that the same rule does not apply to a privately placed preadoptive child. [Priv. Ltr. Rul. 9109060 (Dec. 6, 1990)] Note, however, that any individual will qualify as an employee's dependent—and employer-provided medical coverage for that individual will be excludable—if the employee provided more than half the individual's support for the year *and* the employee's home was the individual's principal place of abode for more than half the year.

For a discussion of when medical coverage must be extended to a preadoptive child, see chapter 5.

Q 3:111 Are benefits received under an employer-provided medical plan taxable to employees?

Non-highly compensated employees (NHCEs) are not taxed on benefits received under an employer-provided medical plan, regardless of whether the plan satisfies any applicable nondiscrimination requirements. However, if a *self-insured* group health plan discriminates in favor of highly compensated employees (HCEs), then all or a part of the benefits received by such HCEs will be included in their gross incomes (see Q 3:127). [I.R.C. § 105(h)]

> **Note.** The 2010 Health Reform Act expands the nondiscrimination tests in Code Section 105(h) to apply to group health plans other than self-insured plans effective for tax years beginning on or after September 23, 2010. However, the special tax treatment for HCEs in discriminatory plans continues to apply only to self-insured plans. Plans other than self-insured plans are subject to an excise tax penalty under Code Section 4980D for violations of the nondiscrimination requirements. [PHSA § 2716 as added by PPACA § 1001 and amended by PPACA § 10101] See chapter 5 for a discussion of when a group health plan discriminates in favor of HCEs. Also see Qs 3:133–3:136 for special rules applicable to partners and more-than- 2-percent shareholder-employees of S corporations.

To the extent that employer-provided coverage for an employee's domestic partner is included in the employee's gross income, the benefits payable to the domestic partner are treated as employee-paid and are excluded from income under Code Section 104(a)(3). If the value of the employer-provided coverage is excludable from the employee's income because the domestic partner qualifies as the employee's spouse or dependent, benefits payable to the domestic partner are excluded from income under Code Section 105. [Priv. Ltr. Rul. 9850011]

Q 3:112 How are highly compensated individuals taxed if a self-insured group health plan discriminates in favor of highly compensated employees?

Benefits paid to a highly compensated individual under a discriminatory self-insured plan are taxable to the extent they constitute an "excess reimbursement." [I.R.C. § 105(h)(1)] The amount of the excess reimbursement depends on whether the plan fails the eligibility test, the benefit test, or both. See chapter 5 for a discussion of the nondiscrimination tests.

Eligibility test failed. If the self-insured group health plan fails the eligibility test only, the taxable excess reimbursement to highly compensated individuals is calculated by taking the total reimbursements received by the highly compensated individual for the year and multiplying that total by a fraction, the numerator of which is the total plan year reimbursements to all highly compensated individuals and the denominator of which is the total plan year reimbursements to all plan participants.

Benefit test failed. If the self-insured group health plan fails the benefit test only, the taxable excess reimbursement is the portion of the reimbursement that is not available to all non-highly compensated individuals. For example, if the plan provides an annual maximum of $100,000 in reimbursements to highly compensated individuals and an annual maximum of only $50,000 to all other employees, a highly compensated individual who received $60,000 in benefits from the medical plan during that year would be taxed on $10,000 ($60,000 – $50,000), the portion that was not available to all non-highly compensated individuals.

Both tests failed. If the self-insured group health plan fails both the eligibility and the benefit tests, the excess reimbursement is calculated in two steps. First, the benefit test is applied. The amount of excess reimbursement under that test, having already been taken into consideration, is then subtracted out of the numerator and denominator when the eligibility test is subsequently calculated. An example of how this works is contained in Treasury Regulations Section 1.105-11(e)(3).

Q 3:113   If a self-insured group health plan is discriminatory, must the employer withhold taxes from the amount included in the gross income of highly compensated individuals?

No. Employers generally are not required to withhold taxes on the amount of any medical care reimbursement made to or for the benefit of an employee under a medical reimbursement plan (as defined in Code Section 105(h)(6)(b) [I.R.C. § 3121(a)(2); I.R.C. § 3401(a)(20) added by OBRA '90 § 11703(f)]

Q 3:114   Are benefits received by retired employees under an employer-provided medical plan taxable to those individuals?

No. The benefit payments received by retired employees under an employer-provided medical plan are excludable from income under Code Section 105 (subject to the nondiscrimination requirements). [Rev. Rul. 82-196, 1982-2 C.B. 53]

Q 3:115   Are benefits received under an employer-provided medical plan by the surviving spouse and dependents of a deceased employee taxable to those individuals?

No. The benefit payments received from an employer-provided medical plan by the surviving spouse and dependents of a deceased employee are excluded from income under Code Section 105 (subject to the nondiscrimination requirements). [Rev. Rul. 82-196, 1982-2 C.B. 53]

Q 3:116   Are benefits actually received by laid-off employees under an employer-provided medical plan taxable to those individuals?

No. The benefit payments received from an employer-provided medical plan by laid-off employees are excluded from income under Code Section 105 (subject to the nondiscrimination requirements). [Rev. Ruls. 62-119, 1962-2 C.B. 38; 75-539, 1975-2 C.B. 56]

Q 3:117   Is a health care bonus that covers a plan's annual insurance deductible excluded from income under Code Section 105?

No. In a private letter ruling, the IRS considered an arrangement under which a group health plan had an annual deductible of $1,000 per family per year. To compensate for this, the company paid each eligible employee a lump sum of $1,000 at the beginning of each year as a "health care bonus." The IRS ruled that the health care bonus was not being made in the event of personal injuries or sickness and therefore was not an amount referred to in Code Section 105. Even if the health care bonus were received through an accident or health plan, the employee still would be able to receive the bonus regardless of whether he or she incurred medical expenses. The bonus thus would not be excluded from income under Code Section 105. [Priv. Ltr. Rul. 9522030]

Q 3:118   What if the benefits are being received by terminated employees under a severance plan that provides medical coverage?

The IRS considered a severance plan that provided severance pay, medical coverage, and other benefits to eligible terminated employees. Under the plan, the employer agreed to pay the same portion of the cost of COBRA continuation coverage that it paid for active employees for the first 12 months of the COBRA continuation period. The IRS held that the recipients were employees for purposes of Code Sections 105 and 106. [Priv. Ltr. Rul. 9612008 (Dec. 18, 1995)] Accordingly, benefit payments received by terminated employees from employer-provided medical coverage under a severance plan are excluded from income under Code Section 105 (subject to the nondiscrimination requirements).

Q 3:119   Can a self-insured plan reimburse expenses incurred by an employee before the plan is adopted?

An IRS revenue ruling makes it clear that favorable tax treatment is not available for reimbursements made by a self-insured plan for expenses incurred by an employee before the plan is adopted. [Rev. Rul. 2002-58, 2002-38 I.R.B. 541] According to the IRS ruling, reimbursements for expenses incurred prior to the establishment of a plan are not excludable from an employee's gross income under Code Section 105(b) because they are not paid or received under an accident or health plan.

Example. Mini Corp. establishes a self-insured medical expense reimbursement plan on December 1, 2010. The plan document provides that the plan is effective as of January 1, 2010. The plan provides reimbursement for medical expenses incurred by a covered employee and the employee's spouse and dependents during the plan year. Employee Ann Anderson became a participant in the plan on December 1, 2010, and promptly submits claims for medical expenses incurred earlier in 2010. Mini reimburses Anderson's expenses in accordance with the terms of the plan. The IRS ruling makes it clear that those reimbursements are taxable income to Anderson.

In addition, at least two courts have held that reimbursements for expenses incurred prior to the establishment of a plan do not qualify for exclusion under Code Section 105(b). [American Family Mut. Ins. Co. v. United States, 815 F. Supp. 1206 (W.D. Wis. 1992); Wollenberg v. United States, 75 F. Supp. 2d 1032 (D. Neb. 1999)]

Q 3:120   Is an employer-provided advance reimbursement or loan to cover future medical expenses excludable from an employee's income?

The IRS has ruled that amounts an employer pays to an employee as advance reimbursements or loans for future medical expenses are not excludable from an employee's gross income under Code Section 105(b). Moreover, because the payments are not made on account of expenses incurred by the employee for medical care, the payments are subject to Social Security, Medicare, and federal unemployment tax. [Rev. Rul. 2002-80, 2002-49 I.R.B. 92]

Example 1. Midco provides health coverage for its employees through a group health insurance policy. The cost of the coverage is paid for through salary reductions, which are mandatory for highly compensated employees (HCEs) and elective for all other employees. For employees covered by the group health plan, Midco makes payments in amounts that cause the employee's after-tax pay to be approximately the same as it would have been if there were no salary reduction to pay the group health premiums. Midco characterizes these payments as "advance reimbursements" of uninsured medical expenses. During the year, employees submit claims to Midco for uninsured medical expenses. To the extent an employee submits claims during the year, Midco excludes the "advance reimbursement" payments from the employee's income and does not treat the amounts as wages for income tax withholding or payroll tax purposes. To the extent an employee does not have uninsured medical expenses equal to the "advance reimbursements" made to the employee, Midco treats the excess advances as additional compensation to the employee.

Result: Midco's "advance reimbursement" plan does not qualify as an accident or health plan for purposes of the Code Section 105(b) exclusion because payments are made to employees regardless of whether they incur medical expenses during the year. Therefore, none of the payments are excludable from employees' gross incomes.

Example 2. The facts are the same as those in Example 1, except that Midco characterizes the advance payments as "loans," which only become due and payable at the time and to the extent that employees submit claims for uninsured medical expenses. When an employee submits a claim, Midco reimburses the expenses and simultaneously offsets the amount of the reimbursement against the employee's "loan." Thus, to the extent an employee submits claims for uninsured expenses, Midco excludes his or her "loans" from gross income and from employment taxes. To the extent an employee does not have uninsured medical expenses equal to his or her "loans," Midco forgives the "loans."

Result: Although Midco characterizes the payments as "loans," it is understood that an employee will never become obligated to make payments. Therefore, the IRS says the arrangement does not constitute a loan for tax purposes. Instead, the "loans" are essentially advance reimbursements that are not excludable from employees' gross incomes and are subject to income tax withholding and payroll taxes.

Q 3:121   What is the income tax treatment of premiums paid for medical insurance coverage by a self-employed individual?

A self-employed individual generally may deduct 100 percent of the amounts paid for insurance providing medical coverage for the sole proprietor and his or her spouse and dependents. [I.R.C. § 162(*l*)] The deduction cannot exceed the earned income of the self-employed individual from the trade or business for which the plan providing the medical care coverage is established. The deduction is allowable as a deduction in calculating adjusted gross income, but it does not reduce net earnings from self-employment for purposes of the tax on self-employment income.

However, the deduction is not available if the self-employed individual is eligible for coverage under any subsidized health plan maintained by the employer of the individual or his or her spouse. [I.R.C. § 162(*l*) as amended by Pub. L. No. 104-7, § 1, 109 Stat. 93 (1995)]

Example. Joe, a sole proprietor, has a spouse with an employer-provided health plan that includes optional family coverage. Whether or not his spouse elects family coverage, Joe cannot deduct under Code Section 162(*l*) any part of the premiums he pays for medical insurance coverage, since he is eligible for coverage under his spouse's plan.

If no deduction is allowed, any medical benefits received under the medical insurance by the sole proprietor would qualify in full for exclusion from income under Code Section 104(a)(3).

Q 3:122   What is the income tax treatment of medical care coverage of a self-employed individual under a self-insured plan maintained by the individual?

If the self-insured plan has the characteristics of insurance (e.g., has adequate risk shifting) and is not merely a reimbursement arrangement, it will receive the same tax treatment as a commercially insured plan. If the self-insured plan does not have the characteristics of insurance, the deduction under Code Section 162(*l*) would not apply to the self-employed individual, and the benefits apparently would not be excludable from the individual's gross income under Code section 104(a)(3).

Q 3:123   What is the income tax treatment of premiums for medical insurance coverage paid by a partnership for coverage of its partners?

The IRS has ruled that when premium payments for medical insurance coverage are made without regard to partnership income, the premium payments are treated as guaranteed payments by the partnership under Code Section 707(c). Guaranteed payments are deductible by the partnership on the partnership tax return, and includable in each partner's gross income. Provided the conditions of Code Section 162(*l*) are met, the partner may deduct a percentage of the premium (see Q 3:121) and may treat the remainder as a medical expense for purposes of Code Section 213.

Because the partners are not employees, the guaranteed payments are not subject to withholding at source by the partnership. [Treas. Reg. § 1.707-1(c)] Alternatively, the partnership may choose to account for the payment of the medical insurance premiums as a reduction in distributions to the partners. In that case, the premiums are not deductible by the partnership, and distributable shares of partnership income and deductions and other items are not affected by payment of the premiums. Each partner may claim a deduction to the extent permitted under Code Section 162(*l*) (see Q 3:121). [Rev. Rul. 91-26, 1991-1 C.B. 184]

Q 3:124   What is the income tax treatment of medical care coverage provided to partners under a self-insured plan maintained by the partnership?

If the self-insured plan has the characteristics of insurance (e.g., has adequate risk-shifting) and is not merely a reimbursement arrangement, it will receive the same tax treatment as a commercially insured plan. The IRS has ruled that in cases where a self-funded plan covering partners in a partnership had the characteristics of insurance, partners could deduct premium payments under Code Section 162(*l*) and benefit payments from the plan were excludable from the partners' incomes under Code Section 104(a)(3). [Priv. Ltr. Rul. 200007025; Priv. Ltr. Rul. 200704017]

If the self-insured plan does not have the characteristics of insurance, the deduction under Code Section 162(l) would not apply to the partners, and the benefits apparently would not be excludable from the partners' gross income under Code Section 104(a)(3).

Q 3:125 What is the income tax treatment of premiums for medical insurance coverage for shareholder-employees of S corporations?

It depends on whether or not the shareholder-employee of the S corporation is a more-than-2-percent shareholder. If the shareholder-employee is not a more-than-2-percent shareholder-employee, medical insurance premiums paid by the employer on account of the shareholder employee's services as an employee normally will be excludable from the shareholder-employee's income under Code Section 106.

However, if the shareholder is a more-than-2-percent shareholder of the S corporation, Code Section 1373 provides that, for purposes of applying the fringe benefit rules, the Subchapter S corporation will be treated as a partnership, and a more-than-2-percent shareholder will be treated as a partner of the deemed partnership.

Applying this concept to premiums paid by an S corporation for medical insurance premiums for its more-than-2-percent shareholder-employees, the IRS has ruled that the S corporation can deduct the premiums paid as a business expense and, assuming the requirements of Code Section 162(*l*) are met, the shareholder-employees can claim a self-employed health insurance deduction, as provided in Q 3:131.

An IRS notice makes it clear that the self-employed health insurance deduction does not apply across the board to all health insurance premiums paid by or on behalf of owner-employees. The premiums must be paid or reimbursed by the S corporation and included in the owner-employee's gross income. According to the IRS, if those requirements are not met, a health plan providing coverage for the owner-employee has not been established by the S corporation and the owner-employee cannot claim the self-employed health insurance deduction. Instead, the premiums are treated as regular medical expenses subject to the 7.5 percent deduction floor. [IRS Notice 2008-1, 2008-2 I.R.B. 251]

It does not matter whether the health insurance policy is in the name of the S corporation or in the name of the S corporation owner-employee as long as the premiums are paid or reimbursed by the company and included in the employee-owner's gross income.

Example 1. ABC, Inc., an S corporation, obtains an accident and health insurance plan for employees in the name of the corporation. ABC makes all the premium payments directly to the insurance company. Ralph is a covered employee who owns one-third of the company's stock. ABC reports the amount of premiums paid for Ralph's coverage as wages on Ralph's W-2 and Ralph reports the payments as gross income on his tax return. *Result:* A plan for medical care for Ralph has been established by ABC, Inc., and Ralph can claim a self-employed health insurance deduction for the amount of ABC's payments.

Example 2. Don is a more-than-2-percent shareholder of DEF, Inc. He obtains an accident and health insurance policy in his own name. However, DEF makes all the premium payments to the insurance company. In addition, DEF reports the premiums paid as wages on Don's W-2 and Don reports the amount as gross income on his tax return. *Result:* DEF has established a plan for Don's medical care and Don can claim a self-employed health insurance deduction for DEF's premium payments.

It also does not matter whether the premiums are paid directly by the S corporation or reimbursed to the owner-employee.

Example 3. The facts are the same as those in Example 2, except that Don makes the premium payments to the insurer and is reimbursed by DEF after submitting proof of payment. DEF reports the reimbursements as wages on Don's W-2 and Don reports the reimbursements as gross income on his tax return. *Result:* Here again, a plan providing medical care to an owner-employee has been established by the corporation, and the owner-employee is allowed a self-employed health insurance deduction.

Amended returns. According to the IRS, S corporation owner-employees who did not claim self-employed health insurance deductions for health insurance premiums paid or reimbursed by the S corporation may file timely amended returns, provided they satisfy the requirements in new Notice 2008-1. Across the top of the amended return, the taxpayer should write "Filed Pursuant to Notice 2008-1."

An S corporation is required to file a Form W-2 for income tax purposes for each more-than-2-percent shareholder-employee having income from the premium payments. However, the income is not treated as wages for Social Security and Medicare tax purposes, as long as the premium payments are made under a plan or system for employees and their dependents generally, or for a class or classes of employees and their dependents. [Rev. Rul. 91-26, 1991-1 C.B. 184; IRS Ann. 92-16, 1992-5 I.R.B. 53]

Q 3:126 What is the income tax treatment of medical benefits received by a shareholder-employee of an S corporation under a self-insured medical plan?

If the shareholder-employee is not a more-than-2-percent shareholder, medical benefits received by the shareholder-employee in the capacity of employee should be treated in the same way as benefits received by other employees; namely, the exemptions provided by Code Section 105(b) should apply.

If the shareholder-employee is a more-than-2-percent shareholder, and if the IRS applies the same rules as in Revenue Ruling 91-26 for insured plans, the medical benefit payments by the Subchapter S corporation would be deductible by the corporation, but includable in the income of the more-than-2-percent shareholder-employee receiving the benefit.

In addition, if the self-insured plan has the characteristics of insurance, the deduction under Code Section 162(l) (see Q 3:121) apparently would be available to the more-than-2-percent shareholder-employee. [Rev. Rul. 91-26, 1991-1 C.B. 184]

Health Reimbursement Arrangements

Q 3:127   How are payments to an employee under a health reimbursement arrangement treated for tax purposes?

The IRS has given its stamp of approval to a type of defined contribution health plan, which it calls a health reimbursement arrangement (HRA) [Rev. Rul. 2002-41, 2002-28 I.R.B. 75; Notice 2002-45 (June 27, 2002); Rev. Rul. 2005-24, 2005-16 I.R.B. 892 (Apr. 5, 2005)]

According to the IRS, employer-provided contributions and medical care reimbursements made under a reimbursement arrangement that allows unused amounts to be carried forward are excludable from an employee's gross income under Code Sections 105 and 106.

An HRA is an arrangement that has the following characteristics:

1. It is paid for solely by the employer and not provided through a salary-reduction arrangement or cafeteria plan;

2. It reimburses the employee for medical care expenses incurred by the employee and the employee's spouse and dependents; and

3. It provides reimbursements up to a maximum dollar amount for a coverage period with any unused portion of the maximum dollar amount carried forward to increase the maximum reimbursement available in later coverage periods.

An HRA is also required to comply with a number of other rules that apply to health plans. These include:

- Compliance with COBRA health care continuation coverage requirements (see chapter 6);

- Compliance with the group health plan standards and nondiscrimination rules (see chapter 5);

- Compliance with the deduction limits for employer contributions [I.R.C. §§ 419, 419A]; and

- Compliance with ERISA's general requirements for welfare benefit plans (see chapter 2).

Q 3:128   Can contributions to an HRA be made through salary reductions or otherwise provided through a cafeteria plan?

No. Employer contributions to an HRA may not be attributable to employee salary reductions or otherwise provided under a cafeteria plan. [I.R.C. § 125] However, an HRA would not be treated as having been paid for through salary reductions merely because it is provided in conjunction with a cafeteria plan. Moreover, if an employer offers its employees a choice between employer-provided nontaxable benefits (e.g., coverage under an HRA or coverage under an HMO) with no cash or taxable benefits available, the choice is not a cafeteria plan election.

If employer contributions to an HRA are provided only if the employee makes a salary reduction election to receive other health coverage, then all of the facts and circumstances will be considered in determining whether the salary reduction election is attributable to the HRA. Assuming the terms of the salary reduction election indicate that the reduction will be used only to provide the other health coverage and not to pay for the HRA itself, the fact that the employee can participate in the HRA only if he or she elects the other coverage will not necessarily result in the salary reduction being attributed to the HRA.

On the other hand, if the salary reduction election exceeds the actual cost of coverage under the other plan, the reduction will be attributed to the HRA. For this purpose, the actual cost of the other coverage can be pegged to the cost of COBRA coverage for the period.

In addition, an arrangement will not be treated as an HRA if it interacts with a cafeteria plan in a way that permits employees to indirectly fund the HRA. For example, an employer offers an HRA and a health plan with an actual cost for coverage of $4,500. The employer gives the employees a choice of electing a $2,500 or a $3,500 salary reduction to fund the coverage, with employees electing a $2,500 reduction receiving a $1,000 maximum HRA reimbursement and employees electing a $3,500 reduction receiving a $2,000 maximum HRA reimbursement. In that case, the IRS says that, because the increase in the salary reduction is related to an increase in the maximum reimbursement, the plan will not qualify for tax-favored treatment.

Finally, the IRS says that a plan will not qualify as an HRA if the amount credited for reimbursements is directly or indirectly tied to amounts forfeited by an employee under a cafeteria plan's health flexible spending arrangement (FSA). (See chapter 7 for further discussion of cafeteria plans and FSAs.)

Q 3:129   What benefits can be provided through an HRA?

To qualify for the exclusions under Code Section 105 and Code Section 106, an HRA may provide only benefits that reimburse expenses for medical care (as defined in Code Section 213(d)) or for insurance covering qualifying medical care expenses.

Note. The 2010 Health Reform Act narrows the definition of medical care for purposes of HRAs and other reimbursement arrangements. Effective for expenses incurred after December 31, 2010, the 2010 Health Reform Act generally bars health reimbursement arrangements from reimbursing expenses for over-the-counter medicines or drugs, unless the medicine or drug is prescribed by a physician. [I.R.C. 106(f) as added by PPACA § 9003]

Each medical expense submitted for reimbursement must be substantiated. Moreover, an HRA cannot reimburse a medical expense that was deducted by the employee in a prior year or that was incurred before the first day the employee became enrolled in the HRA.

An HRA will not qualify if the employee or any other person has the right to receive cash or any other taxable or nontaxable benefit other than the reimbursement of medical care expenses. If an employee or other person has such a right either for the current year or a future year, all distributions made from the HRA for the current year will be included in gross income, even if the distributed amounts are used to pay medical expenses. For example, the IRS says that if an arrangement pays a death benefit without regard to medical expenses, no amounts paid under the arrangement will qualify as tax-free reimbursements for medical expenses.

The IRS notes that it will consider arrangements that are formally outside the HRA in determining whether benefits provided under an HRA qualify for the exclusion from gross income. If, for example, in the year an employee retires, he or she received a bonus that is tied to the maximum amount remaining in an HRA, the exclusion will not apply. Similarly, if an employer provides severance pay only to employees who have reimbursement amounts remaining in an HRA upon termination of employment, no amounts paid under the HRA will qualify for the exclusion.

Q 3:130   Can an HRA continue to reimburse former employees following retirement or termination of employment?

An HRA can continue to reimburse former employees and retired employees for medical expenses after termination of employment or retirement. For example, an HRA may provide for reimbursements to a former employee for medical expenses up to the remaining amount in that employee's account at the time of retirement or termination of employment. The plan may also provide that the maximum reimbursement available after retirement or termination of employment be reduced by the administrative cost of continuing the coverage. On the other hand, an HRA may provide additional employer contributions following an employee's retirement or termination of employment.

Note. HRAs are subject to the COBRA continuation coverage requirements. However, a plan may provide for continuation of coverage and additional contributions following retirement or termination even if the employee does not elect COBRA coverage.

Example 1. Alpha Company sponsors a major medical plan for its employees. The plan has a $2,000 annual deductible for employee-only coverage and a $4,000 annual deductible for family coverage. To participate in the major medical plan, an employee must make a salary reduction election under Alpha's cafeteria plan of $1,000 for employee-only coverage or $3,500 for family coverage. The election form provides that salary reduction elections are used only to pay for the major medical plan.

In addition to the major medical plan, Alpha sponsors an HRA that reimburses out-of-pocket medical expenses of employees and their spouses and dependents. The HRA is available only to employees who participate in the major medical plan. The HRA is paid for by Alpha, and employees do not make salary reduction elections to pay for the HRA. Employees do not have the right to receive any benefits other than reimbursements for medical expenses from the HRA.

Expenses eligible for reimbursement under the HRA are any medical expenses that would be covered by the major medical plan but for the plan's deductible or other dollar limits. Only substantiated expenses are reimbursed.

The maximum reimbursement for the first year an employee participates in the HRA is $1,000 for an employee with employee-only coverage under the major medical plan and $2,000 for an employee with family coverage. Unused amounts from one year are carried over for use in later years. Therefore, in each year after the first year, the maximum reimbursement is $1,000 for an employee with employee-only coverage or $2,000 for an employee with family coverage plus unused amounts from previous years.

When an employee retires or otherwise terminates employment, unused amounts in the HRA are no longer available unless the employee elects COBRA coverage. The COBRA premium for the major medical plan is $1,800 for employee-only coverage and $4,500 for family coverage.

Example 2. The facts are the same as those in Example 1, except that the plan provides that any reimbursement amounts that have not been used before an employee retires or terminates employment will continue to be available for medical expenses incurred by the employee, a spouse, or a dependent after the employee's retirement or termination of employment. The maximum reimbursement amount is not increased, however, unless the employee elects COBRA coverage (see below).

The IRS ruled that both plans described in these examples qualify as employer-provided accident and health plans used exclusively to reimburse expenses for medical care. Therefore, employer contributions to the plan and reimbursements for qualifying expenses will be tax free to employees. In particular, the IRS concluded that the employees' salary reductions were not attributable to the HRA because the plans specifically provided that the salary reductions were used only to pay for the major medical plan and the amount of the reductions did not exceed the actual cost of coverage under that plan as determined by the cost of COBRA coverage.

Moreover, in the case of the second plan, the IRS approved the continuation of HRA coverage for retirees and terminated employees, noting that coverage for former employees and their spouses and dependents qualifies for exclusion from income. [*See* Rev. Ruls. 82-196, 1982-47 I.R.B. 5; 85-121, 1986-42 I.R.B. 5.]

> **Practice Pointer.** HRAs are a close cousin of HSAs, which are available to employees of small employers and to the self-employed (see Qs 3:156–3:185). Both types of arrangements provide funds for reimbursement of an employee's medical expenses, and both types of arrangements permit carryover of unused amounts from year to year. However, there are some significant differences. HSAs are available only to employees or individuals with high-deductible health insurance and contributions to the account are limited. By contrast, HRA contributions are not limited and can be used to pay the cost of the employee's health insurance itself. In addition, amounts distributed from HSAs can be used for purposes other than medical expenses (although they are subject to tax and a 10 percent penalty if the account holder is under age 65). Amounts in an HRA cannot be distributed for purposes other than to pay medical expenses.

HRAs are also a close cousin of health FSAs, which permit employees to set aside salary on a pretax basis to pay out-of-pocket medical expenses incurred during the year. However, again, there are significant differences. Because HRAs are funded solely with employer contributions, they are not subject to a number of restrictions that apply to FSAs. Most notably, as can be seen from the above examples, HRAs are not subject to the use-it-or-lose-it rules that apply to FSAs. While FSA funds that are not used by year-end are forfeited (subject to a limited exception), unused HRA amounts can be carried over from year to year. In addition, unlike an FSA, the maximum reimbursement amount (other than carryover amounts) under an HRA for a coverage period need not be available at all times during the period. Also, an HRA may provide for a coverage period of less than one year, and expenses incurred during one coverage period may be reimbursed during a later year (provided the employee was covered by the HRA when the expense was incurred).

Q 3:131   Can an HRA reimburse medical expenses of a designated beneficiary following the death of the employee account holder?

An HRA can reimburse medical care expenses of an employee's spouse or dependents, including expenses incurred following the death of the employee. [Rev. Rul. 2005-24, 2005-16 I.R.B. 892] However, in a revenue ruling, the IRS made it clear that an HRA may not permit amounts to be paid as medical benefits to a beneficiary other than the deceased employee's spouse or dependent. [Rev. Rul. 2006-36, 2006-36 I.R.B. 353]

The plan described in Revenue Ruling 2006-36 provided for reimbursement of substantiated medical expenses of both current and former employees (including retired employees) and their spouses and dependents as well as expenses of the surviving spouse and dependents of a deceased employee. However, the plan also provided that, upon the death of a deceased employee's surviving spouse and last dependent or on the death of an employee with no surviving spouse or dependents, any unused reimbursement amount can be used to pay substantiated medical expenses of a beneficiary designated by the employee. This provision proved to be fatal to the plan.

The IRS concluded that the plan in question did not meet the tax law requirements because a beneficiary who is not an employee's spouse or dependent *could* receive reimbursements. Moreover, because of that fatal flaw, *none* of the payments made by the plan, including reimbursements of expenses of employee and their spouses or dependents, could be excluded from gross income.

Q 3:132   If an employee is covered by both a health FSA and an HRA, which plan pays first?

If an employee has coverage under both an FSA and an HRA for the same expenses, an IRS notice provides that amounts in the HRA must be exhausted before any reimbursement is made from the FSA. [Notice 2002-45, 2002-2 C.B. 93] However, an FSA can reimburse an expense that is not covered by the HRA. In no case can an employee be reimbursed by both an HRA and an FSA for the same expense.

Practice Pointer. Because of the use-it-or-lose-it feature of FSAs, an employer that chooses to offer both an FSA and an HRA may want to restrict HRA coverage to expenses that are not eligible for reimbursement under the FSA. For example, HRA reimbursements could be restricted to expenses that exceed the FSA contribution limit for the year.

Q 3:133   Can the value of unused vacation and sick leave be contributed to an HRA when the employee retires?

Yes. The IRS has ruled that employer contributions of the value of accumulated unused vacation and sick leave to HRAs for retirees are eligible for tax-free treatment, provided payments from the accounts are limited solely to reimbursements of substantiated medical care expenses incurred by the former employees and their spouses and dependents. [Rev. Rul. 2005-24, 2005-16 I.R.B. 892]

Example. Company A sponsors an HRA that reimburses employees solely for medical care expenses that are substantiated before the reimbursements are made. The plan reimburses expenses of both current and former employees, including retirees and their spouses and dependents. The plan also reimburses expenses of the surviving spouse and dependents of a deceased employee. On the death of a deceased employee's surviving spouse and last dependent, any unused reimbursement amount is forfeited.

Company A's plan is paid for solely by the employer. At the end of a plan year, a portion of each employee's unused reimbursement amount is forfeited and the remainder is carried forward. When an employee retires, Company A automatically contributes an amount to the retiree's account equal to the value of all or a portion of his or her unused vacation and sick leave. Such contributions are mandatory, and the retiree may not receive any of the designated amount in cash or other benefits. Result: The amount contributed to the plan, including the value of unused leave, as well as amounts paid from the plan are excludable from an employee's income.

Q 3:134   May an employee or retiree receive unused reimbursement amounts from an HRA in cash or other benefits?

No. If an HRA provides for the payment of unused reimbursement amounts in cash or other benefits, no amounts paid to an employee under the plan will be excludable from income. [I.R.C. § 105(b); Rev. Rul. 2005-24, 2005-16 I.R.B. 892] The following examples illustrate various reimbursement arrangements that will not qualify for tax-favored treatment.

Example 1. Company X sponsors an HRA that reimburses an employee solely for medical care expenses that are substantiated before the reimbursements are made. The plan is paid for solely by the employer. The plan provides that an employee will receive a cash payment equal to all or a portion of his or her unused reimbursement amount at the end of the plan year or on termination of employment, if earlier.

Example 2. Company Y sponsors an HRA that reimburses an employee solely for medical care expenses that are substantiated before the reimbursements are made. The plan, which is paid for solely by the employer, provides that on the death of an employee, all or a portion of the unused reimbursement amount will be paid in cash to a beneficiary or beneficiaries designated by the employee or, if no beneficiary is designated, to the employee's estate.

Example 3. Company Z sponsors an HRA that reimburses an employee solely for medical care expenses that are substantiated before the reimbursements are made. The plan is paid for solely by the employer. In addition, the employer sponsors an "option plan" that purports to be separate and apart from the HRA. If an employee elects to participate in the option plan, any used reimbursement amount in the HRA is forfeited at year-end. However, the employee may elect to transfer all or part of the "forfeited" amount to one of several retirement plans or to receive the amount in cash. If an employee does not elect to participate in the option plan, any unused reimbursement amount is carried forward for use in future plan years.

Q 3:135   Can an HRA make expense reimbursements using debit or credit cards?

Under a traditional HRA, employees pay for out-of-pocket medical expenses and then submit documentation to the employer to obtain reimbursements. However, the IRS has ruled that employees may be provided with debit or credit cards to tap their HRA funds. [Rev. Rul. 2003-43, 2003-21 I.R.B. 935] The IRS ruling gives two examples of such arrangements. In one case, the employer issues debit or stored-value cards to employees in amounts equal to each employee's HRA coverage amount. In the second case, the employer uses credit cards issued by a bank with individual credit limits equal to the amount of HRA coverage.

The IRS concluded that medical expense payments made under these arrangements are excludable from employees' incomes provided certain safeguards are in place to ensure that the cards are used only for eligible medical expenses. The plans examined by the IRS incorporated the following types of safeguards:

- Certification by each employee that (1) the health debit card will be used only for eligible medical expenses, (2) any medical expenses paid with the card has not been reimbursed from another source, (3) the employee will not seek reimbursement for the expense under any other health plan, and (4) the employee will maintain receipts or other documentation for any expense paid with the card.

- The card can be used only for payment to merchants or service providers that are authorized by the employer to provide health services and products.

- Card charges are treated as conditional pending documentation, unless they are for copayments, previously approved recurring expenses (such as prescription drug refills), or are verified as medical expenses at the time of sale.

- If an improper charge is made, the employee must repay the amount, have the amount withheld from his or her wages, or offset against other claims. If the amount is not fully recouped, the employee remains liable to the employer for the amount of the improper charge.

The IRS has ruled that another employer's debit card program did not satisfy the requirements because the employer did not require substantiation of all reimbursements made through the card but used sampling techniques to check up on employees' use of the cards. For example, the employer reviewed 20 percent of dental office transactions paid with the card, but only 5 percent of physician office charges. In addition, the employer did not review small charges and charges in whole dollar amounts, which were assumed to be for copayments. Only the charges sampled were required to be substantiated by submission of receipts. Because the employer did not require substantiation of all charges, the IRS concluded that all payments made with the debit cards—including charges for legitimate medical expenses—had to be included in employees' wages.

Practice Pointer. A debit or credit card program has distinct advantages for employees because they can pay medical expenses directly from their HRAs rather than pay the expenses with other funds and then seek reimbursement from the plan. However, Revenue Ruling 2003-43 makes it clear that *all* charges must be fully substantiated to ensure tax-free treatment for employees.

Revenue Ruling 2003-43 approving debit and credit card reimbursement arrangements contained a catch that could have significantly lessened the appeal of such arrangements. The ruling states:

Under the facts described, payments made to medical service providers through the use of debit, credit, and stored-value cards are reportable by the employer on Form 1099-MISC under I.R.C. Section 6041. Section 6041 provides for information reporting by persons engaged in a trade or business who make payments of fixed or determinable income to another person in the course of such trade or business of $600 or more in a taxable year.

Thus, under the terms of the IRS ruling, employers would have been faced with the administrative burden of reporting a plan participant's credit or debit card payments to a doctor or other health care provider if the annual total exceeded $600 per provider.

Note. Certain payments, including payments to pharmacies for prescription drugs and payments to not-for-profit hospitals, are not subject to the information reporting requirements.

Congress took action to eliminate this potential administrative hurdle when it enacted the Medicare Prescription Drug, Improvement, and Modernization Act [Pub. L. No. 108-173, 177 Stat. 2066 (2003)], which creates an exception to Form 1099 information reporting requirements for HRAs. The Act provides that the Code Section 6041 reporting requirements do not apply to any payment for medical care made under an HRA that is treated as employer-provided coverage under an accident or health plan. In a follow-up notice, the IRS provided additional details on acceptable substantiation methods. [Notice 2006-69, 2006-31 I.R.B. 107]

Direct third-party substantiation. If an employer receives information from an independent third party indicating the date of a medical service and the employee's responsibility for payment, the claim can be treated as fully substantiated without the need for further review. This might be the case, for example, when an employer receives an explanation of benefits (EOB) from an insurance company showing the amount of the employee's coinsurance payments for the service and the amount of the plan's deductible.

Copayment match substantiation. A debit or credit amount can be treated as substantiated if it exactly matches the plan's copayment amount for the particular product or services. For example, if an employee debits $10 for a doctor's visit under a plan with a $10 copayment for each doctor visit, the debit can be treated as automatically substantiated. Moreover, the IRS notice makes it clear that automatic substantiation applies if a debit or credit charge is an exact multiple of a plan copayment (e.g., a debit of $30 for three prescriptions under a plan with a $10 copayment for prescription drugs). The copayment match substantiation method can be used if a plan has multiple copayments for the same product or service (e.g., different copayments for generic and non-generic drugs). However, automatic substantiation applies only as long as the exact multiple does not exceed five times the maximum copayment. Moreover, copayment match substantiation can be used only for payments to service providers or merchants that have health care related merchant category codes. If the dollar amount of a debit or credit charge exceeds five times the copayment, the transaction must be treated as conditional pending additional confirmation.

Example 1. A plan requires a $5 copayment for generic drugs and a $10 copayment for non-generic drugs. An employee uses a debit card at a pharmacy to purchase five non-generic prescriptions, for a total debit of $50. Because the transaction is at a pharmacy, and the amount of the transaction is an exact multiple that does not exceed five times the maximum copayment for prescriptions, the debit can be treated as substantiated without further review or documentation.

Example 2. The facts are the same as those in Example 1, except that the employee uses the card at a pharmacy to pay for three generic prescriptions and three non-generic prescriptions for a total debit of $45. Because the transaction is at a pharmacy, and the amount of the transaction is an exact match of a combination of the plan's copayments that does not exceed five times the maximum copayment, the debit is automatically substantiated.

Example 3. The facts are the same as those in Example 1, except that the employee uses the card at a pharmacy to pay for six non-generic prescriptions, for a total charge of $60. Because the amount of the transaction exceeds five times the maximum $10 copayment for prescriptions, the debit must be substantiated by a receipt showing that the employee bought prescription drugs, the date of the purchase, and the amount of the purchase.

Example 4. The facts are the same as those in Example 1, except that the employee uses the card at a pharmacy to buy two non-generic prescriptions and a nonprescription medication for a total of $27. Because the debit is not an exact match of a multiple or combination of the copayments prescriptions, the transaction must be further substantiated.

Inventory information approval substantiation. If a company that provides debit or credit cards for a plan has a method for approving or rejecting transactions using inventory control information (such as SKUs) against a list of items that qualify as medical expenses, approved transactions can be treated as automatically substantiated. This method can be used for payments to merchants or service providers that do not have health care related merchant category codes, but only if the merchants or providers participate in the inventory information approval system.

Example. Employer B's HRA provides reimbursements for both prescription and nonprescription medications. The employer uses the inventory information approval system for debit card transactions, including transactions at participating stores that sell nonprescription medications but do not have health-related merchant codes. At one participating store, an employee goes to the counter stocked with aspirin, antacid, and cold medicines that cost $20.75, as well as $50 of items that do not qualify as medical expenses. The store's system compares the SKUs for all the items to a list of qualifying medical expenses. The debit for the $20.75 of medical expense items is approved, but the $50 debit for nonmedical items is rejected and the employee is asked for an additional payment for that amount. The $20.75 of medical items can be treated as automatically substantiated.

Caution. The 2010 Health Reform Act narrows the definition of medical care for purposes of HRAs and other reimbursement arrangements. Effective for expenses incurred after December 31, 2010, the 2010 Health Reform Act generally bars health reimbursement arrangements from reimbursing expenses for over-the-counter medicines or drugs, unless the medicine or drug is prescribed by a physician. [I.R.C. § 106(f) as added by PPACA § 9003]

Transition rule. The IRS provided transition relief to give non-health care merchants time to implement inventory systems. The relief provides that during the transition period a supermarket, grocery store, discount store, or wholesale club that does not have health care merchant codes will be treated as an "other medical care provider" with respect to debit card transactions. The same holds true for mail order vendors and web-based vendors that sell prescription drugs. Thus, debit cards can be used for purchases from such businesses. However, the IRS cautions that an employer must do follow-up substantiation of all charges incurred during the relief period and correct any unsubstantiated payments. The transition relief originally applied only to transactions occurring on or before December 31, 2008. [IRS Notice 2007-2, 2007-2 I.R.B. 254] However, the IRS extended the deadline for six months through June 30, 2009. [IRS Notice 2008-104, 2008-51 I.R.B. 1298]

After June 30, 2009, debit cards may not be used at any store, vendor, or merchant that does not have a health care merchant category code unless the store, vendor, or merchant has implemented an inventory information approval system.

Practice Pointer. IRS Notice 2007-2 makes it clear that "self-substantiation" by an employee will not satisfy the requirements. For example, an HSA will not satisfy the requirements if it reimburses expenses when an employee submits only a description, the amount, and the date of the expenses without a statement from an independent third party verifying the expenses. Moreover, *all* expenses paid under a plan that permits self-substantiation will be included in gross income, including reimbursements for legitimate medical expenses, whether or not they are substantiated.

The Federal Trade Commission (FTC) has issued new regulations to protect consumers from identity theft. [16 C.F.R. Pt. 681] The so-called Red Flag Rules were developed pursuant to the Fair and Accurate Credit Transactions (FACT) Act of 2003. [Pub. L. No. 108-159] The rules require financial institutions and creditors with covered accounts to implement theft prevention programs to identify, detect, and respond to patterns, practices, or specific activities that could indicate identity theft. Compliance is required by June 1, 2010. The FTC has made it clear that health care FSAs (and, presumably, HRAs) are not generally subject to the red flag rules. However, if an account includes a debit card feature, the issuer of the cards—typically, a third-party administrator acting on behalf of a sponsoring employer—will be considered a "financial institution" for purposes of the red flag rules and must implement identity theft protections. Consequently, employers that sponsor HRAs with a debit card feature should confirm that the card issuer is in compliance with the new rules.

Medical Savings Accounts

Q 3:136   What is a medical savings account?

A *medical savings account* (MSA) is a tax-exempt trust or custodial account that is set up to pay medical expenses in connection with a high-deductible health plan. Contributions to the account are deductible (or excludable from an employee's income if made by an employer), and amounts in the account can be withdrawn tax-free to pay for out-of-pocket medical expenses. Only self-employed individuals and employees for small employers (generally, those with 50 or fewer employees) are eligible to establish MSAs.

MSAs were a pilot project that was originally scheduled to expire at the end of 2000 but has been repeatedly extended. The last extension by the Tax Relief and Health Care Act of 2006 [Pub L. 109-433, 120 Stat. 3196 (2006)] expired on December 31, 2007. No new MSAs are currently permitted; however, qualifying MSAs remain eligible for tax benefits. [I.R.C. § 220; HIPAA § 301]

Q 3:137   Who is eligible for a medical savings account?

Employees covered under an employer-sponsored high-deductible plan (see Q 3:169) of a small employer and self-employed individuals are eligible individuals.

A small employer for this purpose is one that employed, on average, no more than 50 employees on the business days during either of the prior two years. A year is not taken into account unless the employer was in existence for the entire year, and special rules apply to small employers that have not yet been in existence for an entire year. The Section 414 controlled-group rules apply when determining if an employer is a small employer. If an employer with an existing MSA plan exceeds the 50-employee limit, it does continue to be treated as a small employer until the year in which it has more than 200 employees. [I.R.C. § 414; HIPAA § 301]

To be eligible to make an MSA contribution (or to have contributions made on his or her behalf), an employee of an eligible employer must be covered under an employer-sponsored high-deductible plan (see Q 3:138) and no other health plan (other than a plan providing certain permitted coverage) (see Q 3:139). For a self-employed individual to be eligible to make MSA contributions, he or she also must be covered under a high-deductible plan and no other health plan (other than a plan that provides certain permitted coverage).

Q 3:138   What is a high-deductible health plan for purposes of an MSA?

A *high-deductible health plan* (HDHP) is defined differently for persons with individual coverage and persons with family coverage. For individual coverage, an HDHP is a health plan with an annual deductible of at least $1,550 (indexed) and no more than $2,250 (indexed). For family coverage, an HDHP is a health plan with an annual deductible of at least $3,000 (indexed) and no more than

$5,500 (indexed). The maximum annual out-of-pocket expenses (e.g., deductibles and copayments) cannot exceed $3,000 (indexed) for individual coverage or $5,500 (indexed) for family coverage. After 1998, these dollar limits are indexed for inflation in $50 increments based on the consumer price index. A plan will not fail to qualify as an HDHP merely because state law prohibits it from having a deductible for preventive care. [I.R.C. § 220(c)(2), 220(g); HIPAA § 301]

For 2010, individual coverage must have a deductible of not less than $2,000 and not more than $3,000, with a maximum annual out-of-pocket expenditure of $4,050. For family coverage, the deductible must be at least $4,000 and not more than $6,050, with a cap on out-of-pocket expenditures of $7,400. [Rev. Proc. 2009-50, 2009-45 I.R.B. 617]

Some types of family plans do not meet the high-deductible rules. These plans have deductibles for individual family members that are less than the annual deductible for the plan as a whole. Under these plans, if the person meets the individual deductible for one family member, he or she does not have to meet the annual deductible amount for the family plan to receive a reimbursement.

> **Example.** Adam has health insurance with his employer in 2010. The annual deductible for the family plan is $4,000. This plan also has an individual deductible of $2,000 for each family member. Adam's wife, Betty, incurred $2,100 of covered medical expenses. The couple had no other medical expenses for 2010. The plan paid Adam $100 because Betty met the individual deductible of $2,000, even though the couple did not meet the $4,000 annual deductible for the family plan. The plan does not qualify as an HDHP.

Q 3:139　What other medical coverage can an MSA participant have?

An individual with coverage under an HDHP is still eligible for an MSA if he or she has certain other permitted coverage. Permitted coverage includes insurance or coverage (whether provided through insurance or otherwise) for accidents, disability, dental care, vision care, or long-term care. In addition, permitted insurance includes (1) Medicare supplemental insurance; (2) insurance for a specified disease or illness (insurance that provides a fixed payment for hospitalization); and (3) insurance in which substantially all of such coverage relates to any of the following:

- Liabilities incurred under a workers' compensation law
- Tort liabilities
- Liabilities relating to ownership or use of property (e.g., auto insurance)
- Such other similar liabilities as the Secretary of the Treasury may prescribe in regulations

[I.R.C. § 220(c)(3); HIPAA § 301]

Q 3:140   What is the maximum annual contribution that can be made to an MSA?

For persons with individual coverage, the maximum annual contribution for a year is 65 percent of the deductible under the HDHP. For persons with family coverage, the maximum annual contribution for a year is 75 percent of the deductible for the HDHP. This contribution limit is applied on a monthly basis. Contributions for any month cannot exceed one-twelfth of the applicable annual limit and cannot be made unless the person is an eligible individual as of the first day of the month. Special deduction rules apply for spouses having family coverage under two different plans. [I.R.C. § 220(b); HIPAA § 301]

An employee may make contributions to his or her MSA or contributions may be made by the employer sponsoring the HDHP, but not both. Thus, for example, if an employer makes less than the maximum annual contribution to an employee's MSA, the employee cannot make up the difference.

Q 3:141   Do any nondiscrimination rules apply to employer contributions made to MSAs?

Yes. An employer that provides employees with HDHP coverage coupled with an MSA and makes contributions to the MSAs must also make available during the same period a comparable contribution on behalf of all employees with comparable coverage. Controlled-group rules apply when making this determination.

If employer contributions violate the comparability rule during a period, the employer is subject to an excise tax equal to 35 percent of the aggregate amount contributed by the employer to its MSAs for that period. In cases of violations that are due to reasonable cause and not to willful neglect, the Secretary of the Treasury may waive part or all of this excise tax to the extent that payment of the tax would be excessive relative to the violation involved. [I.R.C. § 220(f); HIPAA § 301(c)(4)(A)]

Note. Beginning January 1, 2010, excise tax liabilities for failure to make comparable MSA contributions must be self-reported by filing Form 8928, *Return of Certain Excise Taxes Under Chapter 43 of the Internal Revenue Code.* [Treas. Reg. § 54.6011-2]

Q 3:142   How long does an employer or individual have to make MSA contributions?

Contributions to an MSA can be made until the due date for the individual's tax return for the year (determined without regard to extensions). [I.R.C. § 220(d)(4)(B); HIPAA § 301(a)]

Q 3:143   Do any tax reporting requirements apply with respect to MSAs?

Yes. Employers are required to report employer MSA contributions, and individuals are required to report the employer MSA contributions on their tax returns. [I.R.C. § 220(d)(4); HIPAA § 301]

Q 3:144   What can amounts in an MSA be used for?

MSA funds can be used to pay for the medical expenses of the individual and his or her spouse and dependents. Medical expenses are those expenses listed in Code Section 123, but they do not include expenses for insurance other than long-term care insurance, COBRA premiums, and premiums for health care coverage while an individual is receiving unemployment compensation. [I.R.C. § 220(d)(2); HIPAA § 301(a)]

> **Note.** The 2010 Health Reform Act narrows the definition of medical care for purposes of MSAs and other reimbursement arrangements. Effective for expenses incurred after December 31, 2010, the 2010 Health Reform Act generally bars tax-free reimbursements for expenses of over-the-counter medicines or drugs, unless the medicine or drug is prescribed by a physician. [I.R.C. § 106(f) as added by PPACA § 9003]

Q 3:145   Are earnings on amounts in an MSA taxable to the individual?

No, they are not. [I.R.C. § 220(e)(1); HIPAA § 301(a)]

Q 3:146   Are distributions from the MSA for payment of medical expenses taxable to the individual?

Generally not. However, any distributions that are not applied to permissible medical expenses are includable in the individual's gross income. In addition, a nonqualifying distribution is subject to penalty tax unless the distribution is made after the individual's Medicare eligibility (currently age 65), death, or disability. The penalty is 15 percent of the excess distribution for tax years beginning before 2011; the 2010 Health Reform Act increases the penalty to 20 percent of the excess distribution for tax years beginning after December 31, 2010. [I.R.C. 220 (f)(4) as amended by PPACA § 9004]

Q 3:147   What is the income tax treatment of MSAs at death?

The balance remaining in the decedent's account upon death is taxable unless the decedent's surviving spouse is the named beneficiary of the MSA. In that case, the surviving spouse is treated as the account holder. [I.R.C. § 220(f); HIPAA § 301]

If someone other than the spouse is the designated beneficiary, the account stops being an MSA on the date of death and the fair market value of the MSA becomes taxable to the designated beneficiary.

If there is no beneficiary, the fair market value of the MSA will be included on the deceased's final income tax return after death. [I.R.C. § 220(f)]

Health Savings Accounts

Q 3:148   What is a health savings account?

The Medicare Prescription Drug, Improvement, and Modernization Act of 2003 [Pub. L. No. 108-173, 117 Stat. 2066 (2003)] added Section 223 to the Internal Revenue Code to permit eligible individuals to establish health savings accounts (HSAs) for tax years beginning after December 31, 2003. HSAs are established to receive tax-favored contributions by or on behalf of eligible individuals, and amounts accumulated in an HSA may be distributed on a tax-free basis to pay or reimburse qualified medical expenses. HSA contributions may be made by an employer, by an employee, or by both.

The HSA is a tax-exempt trust or custodial account established exclusively for the purpose of paying qualified medical expenses of the account beneficiary who, for the months for which contributions are made to an HSA, is covered under a high-deductible health plan. [IRS Notice 2004-2, 2004-2 I.R.B. 269]

Q 3:149   Who may establish an HSA?

Anyone who is an "eligible individual" may establish an HSA. An *eligible individual* is an individual who (1) is covered under an HDHP; (2) is not also covered by any other health plan that is not an HDHP (with certain exceptions for plans providing limited types of coverage); (3) is not entitled to benefits under Medicare; and (4) cannot be claimed as a dependent on another person's tax return.

Eligibility is determined on a month-by-month basis as of the first day of the month.

IRS guidance makes it clear that an employee who has a choice between low-deductible coverage and a qualifying HDHP is an eligible individual for HSA purposes. The fact that the employee could have chosen low-deductible coverage does not affect HSA eligibility. [IRS Notice 2004-50, 2004-33 I.R.B. 196]

In the case of spouses, each spouse—if eligible—may have his or her own HSA. However, spouses may not have a joint HSA. [IRS Notice 2004-50, 2004-33 I.R.B. 196]

In Revenue Ruling 2005-25 [2005-18 I.R.B. 971], the IRS makes it clear that a married individual who otherwise qualifies can establish an HSA even if his or her spouse has low-deductible family coverage, provided the family plan does not cover the individual.

Medicare entitlement. Simply being eligible for Medicare will not generally render an individual ineligible for HSA purposes unless the individual has actually enrolled for Medicare benefits. The term "entitled to benefits under" Medicare means both eligibility and enrollment in Medicare. Thus, an otherwise eligible individual who is not actually enrolled in Medicare may contribute to an HSA until the month that individual is enrolled in Medicare. [Notice 2004-50 Q&A-2, 2004-33 I.R.B. 196; IRS Notice 2008-59 Q&A-5&6, 2008-59 I.R.B. 123]

> **Example 1.** Yolanda, age 66, is covered under her employer's HDHP. Although Yolanda is eligible for Medicare, she is not actually entitled to Medicare because she did not enroll in Medicare. Thus, Yolanda may contribute to an HSA.

> **Example 2.** In August 2010, Howard attains age 66 and applies for and begins receiving Social Security benefits. As a result of his application for Social Security benefits, Howard is automatically enrolled in Medicare Parts A and B. Thus, as of August 1, 2010, Howard is no longer an eligible individual and may not contribute to an HSA.

Q 3:150   What is a high-deductible health plan for purposes of an HSA?

A *high-deductible health plan* (HDHP) is a health plan that satisfies certain requirements with respect to deductibles and out-of-pocket expenses.

For 2010 or 2011, an HDHP providing self-only coverage must have an annual deductible of at least $1,200 and annual out-of-pocket expenses (deductibles, copayments and other amounts, but not premiums) of no more than $5,950. For family coverage, an HDHP must have an annual deductible of at least $2,400 and annual out-of-pocket expenses of no more than $11,900 for 2010. [Rev. Proc. 2009-29, 2009-22 I.R.B. 1050; Rev. Proc. 2010-22, 2010-23 I.R.B. 747] These amounts are indexed for inflation after 2007 under rules set by the 2006 Tax Relief and Health Care Act. [I.R.C. § 223(g)(1) as amended by the Tax Relief and Health Care Act, Pub. L. No. 109-433, 120 Stat. 3196 (2006)] In the case of family coverage, a health plan is an HDHP only if, under the terms of the plan and without regard to which family member or members incur expenses, no amounts are payable from the HDHP until the family as a whole has incurred annual covered medical expenses in excess of the minimum annual deductible. IRS guidance makes it clear, however, that benefits may be payable to an individual family member once the minimum HDHP deductible for family coverage has been reached even if the family as a whole is subject to a higher deductible. That is, an HDHP may have an embedded individual deductible as well as an umbrella family deductible. According to the IRS, an individual does not fail to be an eligible individual merely because of an embedded individual deductible that is no less than the minimum family HDHP deductible. [IRS Notice 2008-59 Q&A-4, 2008-59 I.R.B. 123]

> **Example.** In 2011, the Johnson family has health plan coverage with an umbrella deductible of $3,500, and an embedded individual deductible of $2,400. Thus, the plan will pay benefits for an individual family member once he or she has incurred covered expenses in excess of $2,400, and will pay benefits for any individual once the family's total expenses top $3,500.

The plan qualifies as an HDHP since embedded individual deductible is equal to the minimum required deductible for family coverage for 2011.

A plan will not fail to qualify as an HDHP merely because it does not have a deductible (or has a small deductible) for preventive care (e.g., the plan provides first dollar coverage for preventive care). However, except for preventive care, a plan cannot provide benefits for any year until the deductible for that year is met.

Example 1. Alpha Health Plan provides coverage for Jeremy and his family. The plan provides for the payment of covered medical expenses of any member of the family if the member has incurred covered medical expenses during the year in excess of $1,200 even if the family has not incurred covered medical expenses in excess of $2,400. If Jeremy incurs covered medical expenses of $1,500 in a year, the plan will pay $300. Thus, benefits are potentially available under the plan even if the family's covered medical expenses do not exceed $2,400. Because the plan provides family coverage with an annual deductible of less than $2,400, the plan is not an HDHP.

Example 2. The facts are the same as those in Example 1, except that the Alpha Health Plan has a $5,000 family deductible and provides payment for covered medical expenses if any member of Jeremy's family has incurred covered medical expenses during the year in excess of $2,400. The plan satisfies the requirements for an HDHP with respect to the deductibles.

In IRS Notice 2004-23 [2004-15 I.R.B. 725], the IRS issued a special safe harbor rule, which provides that *preventive care* includes (but is not limited to) the following:

- Periodic health evaluations, including tests and diagnostic procedures, in connection with routine examinations such as annual physicals;
- Routine prenatal and well-child care;
- Child and adult immunizations;
- Tobacco cessation programs;
- Obesity weight-loss programs; and
- Screening services (e.g., cancer screening).

Notice 2004-23 emphasizes that preventive care generally does not include any service to treat an existing illness, injury, or condition. The IRS notice makes it clear that the characterization of a service as preventive care is not dependent on state law. A plan will not qualify as an HDHP if it provides no-deductible or low-deductible coverage for services that do not qualify as preventive care under IRS rules, even if such coverage is required by state law.

Nonetheless, the IRS carved out a special transition rule for health plans that would have been disqualified as HDHPs solely because state law required first-dollar or low-deductible coverage for benefits that do not qualify as preventive care. Under the transition rule, a plan that would have been disqualified because of a state law in effect on January 1, 2004, was treated as an HDHP for all months before January 1, 2006. In announcing the transition rule, the IRS noted that the short period between the enactment of HSAs in late 2003 and the January 1, 2004, effective date gave states insufficient time to modify their laws to conform to the HSA rules. [IRS Notice 2004-43, 2004-27 I.R.B. 10] The IRS subsequently provided additional transitional relief for noncalendar-year plans. In announcing the relief, the IRS noted that a health plan generally may not reduce existing benefits before the plan's renewal date. Therefore, even though a state may have amended its laws before January 1, 2006, a plan with a renewal date other than January 1 had to retain state-mandated low-deductible coverage after that date. Consequently, the extended transitional relief provided that such plans qualified as HDHPs, even though they provided low-deductible state-mandated coverage after January 1. 2006. However, the transitional relief expired as of the earlier of the plan's renewal date or December 31, 2006. [IRS Notice 2005-83, 2005-49 I.R.B. 1075]

> **Note.** Effective for plan years beginning on or after September 23, 2010, the 2010 Health Reform Act requires group health plans (other than grandfathered plans in existence on March 23, 2010) to provide coverage for specified preventive care items or services and prohibits cost-sharing requirements for specified preventive care. [PHSA § 2713 as added by PPACA § 1001]

On the other hand, IRS guidance provides that even if a plan meets the minimum deductible requirement it will not qualify as an HDHP if limitations on plan benefits are such that the plan does not provide "significant benefits." Specifically, the IRS concluded that a plan meeting minimum deductible requirement that restricts benefits to in-patient or hospital care will not qualify as an HDHP. The restriction of benefits to medical services provided while the covered individual is admitted to a hospital or at an in-patient facility is not reasonable because significant other benefits do not remain available under the plan after application of the restriction. Thus, any expenses incurred by a covered individual for out-patient care or visits to physician's offices are treated as out-of-pocket expenses. And because the plan maximum for amounts paid by a covered individual does not restrict payments for those out-of-pocket expenses, the plan will not qualify as an HDHP. [IRS Notice 2008-59 Q&A-14, 2008-59 I.R.B. 123]

However, IRS guidance makes it clear that a plan may impose separate or higher deductibles for specific benefits and still qualify as an HDHP. So long as significant benefits remain available under the plan in addition to the benefits subject to the separate or higher deductible, amounts paid to satisfy the separate or higher deductible will not be treated as out-of-pocket expenses. [IRS Notice 2008-59 Q&A-13, 2008-59 I.R.B. 123] The IRS guidance gives the following example.

> **Example.** In 2011, a self-only health plan with a $3,000 deductible imposes a lifetime limit of $1,000,000 on reimbursements for covered benefits. The plan pays 100 percent of covered expenses after the $3,000 deductible is satisfied. Although the plan provides benefits for substance abuse treatment, the substance abuse treatment benefits are subject to a separate $5,000 deductible, and substance abuse benefits are limited to $10,000, after the

separate deductible is satisfied. The plan is an HDHP and no expense incurred by a covered individual other than the $3,000 general deductible is treated as an out-of-pocket expense.

Caution. Although the IRS guidance specifically approves a plan with a separate deductible and benefit limit for substance abuse benefits as an HDHP, employer plans that impose special limits on such benefits face another obstacle. The Paul Wellstone and Pete Domenici Mental Health Parity and Addiction Equity Act of 2008, which is effective for plan years beginning after October 3, 2009, requires that both the financial requirements (i.e., deductibles, copayments) and treatment limitations (i.e., number of visits, days of coverage) applied to mental health and substance use disorder benefits under a group health plan be no more restrictive than the financial requirements and treatment limitations applied to medical and surgical benefits. [I.R.C. § 9812, as amended by Pub. L. No. 110-343 (Oct. 3, 2008)] In addition, the 2010 Health Reform Act imposes new prohibitions on annual and lifetime limits on benefits. These requirements are discussed in detail in chapter 5.

Q 3:151 Are there special rules for determining whether a network plan qualifies as an HDHP?

Yes. A network plan generally provides more favorable benefits for services provided by its network of providers than for services provided outside of the network. A network plan will not fail to qualify as an HDHP (if it would otherwise meet the requirements of an HDHP) solely because the out-of-pocket expense limits for services provided outside of the network exceeds the maximum annual out-of-pocket expense limits allowed for an HDHP. In addition, the plan's annual deductible for out-of-network services is not taken into account in determining the annual contribution limit. The annual contribution limit is determined by reference to the deductible for services within the network.

Q 3:152 Can an individual qualify for HSA participation if he or she has other health coverage in addition to an HDHP?

No. An individual is ineligible for an HSA if he or she is covered under any health plan (whether as an individual, spouse, or dependent) that is not an HDHP. Thus, coverage under a traditional health care plan of a spouse's employer would disqualify an employee from HSA participation even if he or she is also covered by an HDHP offered by his or her own employer.

In Revenue Ruling 2005-25 [2005-18 I.R.B. 971], the IRS makes it clear that a married individual who otherwise qualifies may establish an HSA even if his or her spouse has low-deductible family coverage, provided the family plan does not cover the individual. Conversely, the IRS says that if an otherwise eligible individual has family HDHP coverage that covers dependents, the fact that the dependents have other non-HDHP coverage will not disqualify the individual from setting up an HSA. [IRS Notice 2008-59 Q&A-11, 2008-59 I.R.B. 123]

Moreover, an individual may have certain "permitted insurance" in addition to an HDHP and still qualify for HSA participation. *Permitted insurance* includes workers' compensation insurance, coverage for tort liabilities or liabilities relating to ownership or use of property (e.g., automobile insurance), insurance for a specified disease or illness, and insurance that pays a fixed amount per day (or other period) of hospitalization.

In addition to permitted insurance, an individual may also have coverage (whether through insurance or otherwise) for accidents, disability, dental care, vision care, or long-term care in addition to an HDHP.

IRS guidance makes it clear, however, that additional coverage that combines permitted insurance with other coverage that is not permitted insurance or disregarded coverage will disqualify an individual from HSA participation. [IRS Notice 2008-59 Q&A-2, 2008-59 I.R.B. 123]

Example. Jennifer is covered by an HDHP. In addition, Jennifer is covered by a "mini-med" plan that provides the following benefits: a fixed amount per day of hospitalization; a fixed amount per office visit with a physician; a fixed amount per out-patient treatment at a hospital; a fixed amount per ambulance use; and coverage for expenses relating to the treatment of a specified list of diseases. Although the fixed amount per day of hospitalization and specified disease benefits are allowed in addition to the HDHP as permitted insurance, the other benefits are not. Therefore, Jennifer is not an eligible individual who can contribute to an HSA.

Prescription drug coverage. An IRS revenue ruling makes it clear that prescription drug benefits are not "permitted" insurance or coverage for HSA purposes. Therefore, an individual who is covered by both an HDHP and a prescription drug plan is not an eligible individual for HSA purposes unless the drug plan is also an HDHP (i.e., the plan does not provide benefits until the required minimum annual benefit for an HDHP has been met). [Rev. Rul. 2004-38, 2004-15 I.R.B. 717]

The IRS provided some transition relief from this rule. For months before January 1, 2006, a separate prescription drug plan or rider that provided benefits before the minimum annual deductible of an HDHP did not disqualify an individual from making HSA contributions. [Rev. Proc. 2004-22, 2004-15 I.R.B. 727] However, plans must be in compliance with the IRS rule for 2006 and later years.

Health discount cards. A discount card that entitles an individual to discounts for health care services or products will not disqualify an individual from HSA eligibility as long as the individual is required to meet the regular HDHP deductible. The same holds true if a plan negotiates discounted prices from health care providers. [Notice 2004-50, 2004-33 I.R.B. 196]

Employee benefit programs. IRS guidance also makes it clear that coverage under an employee assistance program (EAP), disease management program, or wellness program will not affect HSA eligibility, provided the program does not provide significant benefits in the nature of medical care or treatment. Screening and other preventive care services are not treated as significant medical benefits. However, an employer generally cannot condition contributions to an employee's HSA on participation in such plans. [Notice 2004-50, 2004-33 I.R.B. 196]

On-site health care. According to the IRS, free health care or health care at charges below fair market value from a clinic on an employer's premises may or may not be disqualifying coverage depending on whether an employee receives significant benefits in the nature of medical care (in addition to disregarded coverage or preventive care). [IRS Notice 2008-59 Q&A-10, 2008-59 I.R.B. 123]

Example 1. A manufacturing plant operates an on-site clinic that provides the following free health care for employees: (1) physicals and immunizations; (2) injecting antigens provided by employees (e.g., performing allergy injections); (3) a variety of aspirin and other nonprescription pain relievers; and (4) treatment for injuries caused by accidents at the plant. The clinic does not provide significant benefits in the nature of medical care in addition to disregarded coverage or preventive care. Therefore, the benefits provided by the on-site clinic will not affect employees' eligibility for HSA participation.

Example 2. A hospital provides its employees with care at its facilities for all of their medical needs. For employees without health insurance, the hospital provides medical care at no charge. For employees who have health insurance, the hospital waives all deductibles and co-pays. Because the hospital provides significant care in the nature of medical services, the hospital's employees are not eligible individuals for HSA purposes.

Employer reimbursements. Reimbursements by an employer of medical expenses (other than expenses for preventive care or disregarded coverage) before an employee meets the minimum HDHP deductible for the year will taint an employee's HSA eligibility. [IRS Notice 2008-59 Q&A-3, 2008-59 I.R.B. 123]

Example 1. For 2011, an HDHP with self-only coverage has an annual deductible of $2,500. The employee pays the first $300 of covered medical expenses below the deductible. The employer reimburses the next $1,300 of covered medical expenses below the deductible. The employee is responsible for the last $900 of covered medical expenses below the deductible. Since $1,300 of medical expenses will be reimbursed by the employer before an employee has met the minimum self-only deductible of $1,200 for 2011, an employee covered by the plan is not eligible for an HSA because the employee has disqualifying coverage from a plan that is not an HDHP.

Note. The plan constitutes disqualifying coverage even though the total amount an employee must eventually pay ($1,200) is equal to the minimum required HDHP deductible of $1,200 for self-only coverage for the year.

Example 2. For 2011, an HDHP with self-only coverage has an annual deductible of $4,500. The employee pays the first $1,200 of covered medical expenses below the deductible. The employer reimburses the next $3,300 of covered medical expenses below the deductible. An employee covered by this type of plan is an eligible individual for HSA purposes because the employee is responsible for the minimum annual deductible of $1,200 before any employer reimbursements are made.

Other high-deductible coverage. An otherwise eligible individual covered by an HDHP will not be rendered ineligible because of coverage under another health plan so long as the other plan has a deductible equal to or greater than the statutory minimum HDHP deductible. [IRS Notice 2008-59 Q&A-7, 2008-59 I.R.B. 123]

> **Example.** Stephanie has self-only HDHP coverage for 2011 with a deductible of $2,500 and a life-time limit on benefits of $1,000,000. In addition to the HDHP, Stephanie has self-only catastrophic health plan coverage with a $1,000,000 deductible and a $2,000,000 life-time limit on benefits. Assuming Stephanie is otherwise eligible, the catastrophic coverage will not bar her from establishing an HSA.

Health FSAs and HRAs. For a discussion of the interplay between HSAs, health FSAs, and HRAs, see Q 3:153.

Q 3:153   Can an individual qualify for HSA participation if he or she is covered by a health FSA or an HRA?

As a general rule, an employee is ineligible for an HSA if he or she is covered by an employer-sponsored health FSA or HRA that pays or reimburses medical expenses incurred before the minimum annual HSA deductible has been satisfied. [Rev. Rul. 2004-45, 2004-22 I.R.B. 971]

However, coverage under the following types of FSAs or HRAs will not disqualify an employee from HSA participation:

- *Limited-purpose Health FSA or HRA.* A limited-purpose health FSA that pays or reimburses only benefits for "permitted coverage" (e.g., dental and vision, but not long-term care) or a limited-purpose HRA that pays or reimburses benefits for "permitted insurance" (for a specific disease or illness or that provides a fixed amount per day or other period of hospitalization) or "permitted coverage" (but not for long-term care services) can be offered in tandem with an HSA. A limited-purpose health FSA or HRA may pay or reimburse preventive care benefits.

- *Suspended HRA.* An employee covered by an HRA is eligible for HSA contributions if an election is made before the beginning of the HRA coverage period to suspend all reimbursements for medical expenses other than permitted insurance and permitted coverage (if otherwise allowed to be paid or reimbursed by the HRA). Eligibility for HSA contributions is limited to the period during which the HRA reimbursements are suspended. Moreover, if the HSA is funded through salary reduction under a cafeteria plan during the suspension period, the terms of the salary reduction election must indicate that the salary reduction is used only to pay for the HSA offered in conjunction with the HRA and not to pay for the HRA itself.

- *Post-Deductible Health FSA or HRA.* An employee covered by a post-deductible FSA or HRA is an eligible individual for the purpose of making contributions to an HSA. A post-deductible health FSA or HRA is one that does not pay or reimburse any medical expense incurred before the minimum annual HSA deductible is satisfied. The deductible for the HRA or health FSA need not be the same as the deductible for the HDHP, but in no event may any benefits be provided before the minimum annual HSA deductible has been met. Where the HDHP and the FSA or HSA do not have identical deductibles, contributions to the HSA are limited to the lower of the deductibles.

- *Retirement HRA.* A retirement HRA that pays or reimburses only those medical expenses incurred after retirement (and no expenses incurred before retirement) will not cause an employee to forego eligibility for HSA contributions. However, HSA contributions are limited to the period before retirement. After retirement, when payment or reimbursements can be made from the retirement HRA, no additional HSA contributions may be made.

Revenue Ruling 2004-45 also makes it clear that combinations of these arrangements are allowed. For example, if an employer offers a combined post-deductible health FSA and a limited-purpose health FSA, this would not disqualify an otherwise eligible employee from making or receiving HSA contributions.

An HRA may also reimburse an employee's premiums for HDHP coverage without disqualifying the employee from HSA participation. [IRS Notice 2008-59 Q&A-1, 2008-59 I.R.B. 123]

FSA and HRA rollovers. An option for an employee whose existing FSA or HRA is incompatible with the establishment of an HSA is to roll over the FSA or HRA funds to the HSA. Under a rule enacted by the Tax Relief and Health Care Act of 2006 [Pub. L. No. 109-433, 120 Stat. 3196 (2006)], employers have a limited opportunity to allow employees to make a one-time rollover of FSA or HRA funds by means of a qualified HSA distribution. [I.R.C. § 106(e) as amended by the 2006 Tax Relief and Health Care Act]

IRS Notice 2007-22 [2007-10 I.R.B. 670] makes it clear that if an employer wants to provide for qualified HSA distributions from an FSA or an HRA, the employer must amend the written FSA or HRA plan to allow rollovers.

A qualified HSA distribution is treated as a contribution by the employer to an employee's HSA that is excludable from gross income and is exempt from employment taxes. A qualified HSA distribution is permitted in addition to any regular HSA contributions for the year. Only one qualified HSA distribution is allowed with respect to any health FSA or HRA. Qualified distributions can be made from general-purpose FSAs and HRAs as well as from HSA-compatible FSAs and HRAs. [IRS Notice 2007-22, 2007-10 I.R.B. 670] On the other hand, a distribution that is not qualified is included in income and is subject to a 10 percent penalty tax. [I.R.C. § 106(e)(3)(A)]

A qualified HSA distribution cannot exceed the lesser of (a) the balance of the FSA or HRA on September 21, 2006, or (b) the balance on the date of the distribution. Thus, an individual who was not covered by an FSA or an HRA on September 21, 2006, cannot elect a qualified HSA distribution. Similarly, an individual who participated in an FSA with one employer on September 21, 2006, and, after that date, participates in an FSA with another employer cannot elect a qualified distribution from the second employer's FSA. [IRS Notice 2007-22, 2007-10 I.R.B. 670]

A qualified distribution can be made at any time before January 1, 2012. However, the IRS notice points out that not every distribution made before that date will qualify. For example, even if a distribution reduces the balance of an FSA or HSA to zero, the FSA or HRA coverage does not end. Therefore, if an FSA or HRA is not HSA-compatible, only transfers at the end of a plan year that result in termination of the FSA or HRA coverage or that result in disregarded coverage will be qualified distributions. For tax years beginning after December 31, 2006, coverage under a health FSA will be disregarded in determining an employee's eligibility for HSA purposes, provided that either (1) the balance in the FSA at the end of the plan year is zero or (2) the employee is making a qualified HSA distribution in an amount equal to the remaining balance in the FSA as of the end of the plan year. [I.R.C. § 223(c)(1)(B)(iii)] Thus, distributions from FSAs or HRAs that are not HSA-compatible and that take place at any time other than the end of a plan year will generally result in inclusion of the distribution in income and imposition of a 10 percent penalty tax.

On the other hand, not every year-end distribution will qualify. In the case of an FSA that does not provide for a grace period (see below), unused amounts remaining at year end must be forfeited. Thus, if an FSA does not provide for a grace period unused funds must be forfeited and cannot be transferred through a qualified distribution. Moreover, although the funds can be transferred before the end of the FSA plan year, such a distribution would not qualify because the individual would not be eligible for an HSA until the next year.

Employees who switch to HDHP coverage in mid-month must also be careful in timing their distributions. An employee who begins HDHP coverage after the first day of a month is not eligible to make a qualified distribution until the first day of the following month. If a distribution is made before the first day of the next month, it will be included in the employee's income and subject to a 10 percent penalty tax.

The balance in the health FSA or HRA is determined on a cash basis (i.e., expenses incurred that have not been reimbursed as of the date the determination is made are not taken into account).

The qualified HSA distribution rules are intended to assist employers and employees in switching to an HDHP/HSA from another type of health plan. Therefore, if, an employee is not an eligible individual for HSA purposes (e.g., is not covered by an HDHP) at any time during a testing period, the amount of the qualified HSA distribution must be included in the employee's gross income for the tax year that includes the first month in which the employee is not eligible.

In addition a 10 percent penalty tax applies to the included amount. [I.R.C. § 106(e)(3)(A)] Note, however, that if an employee ceases to be eligible because of death or disability, the addition to gross income and the penalty tax do not apply. [I.R.C. § 106(e)(3)(B)] The testing period is the 12 month period beginning with the month in which the qualified HSA distribution is made. [I.R.C. § 106(e)(4)(A)]

> **Example.** Jane has been covered by a traditional health plan and an HRA sponsored by her employer, Acme Co. Jane plans to switch to an HDHP and an HSA as of January 1, 2010. The balance in her HRA on September 21, 2007 was $2,000; the balance as of January 1, 2010 is $3,000. To facilitate Jane's switch in coverage, Acme can make a tax-free qualified HSA distribution from Jane's HRA to her HSA on January 1, 2010. The amount of the distribution is limited to $2,000 (the amount in the account as of September 21, 2007).

> **Practice Pointer.** Because the entire balance in the HRA in the example cannot be distributed to the employee's HSA, there might be a temptation to continue coverage under the HRA. However, that would be a bad move. The rule that an employee is not an eligible individual for HSA purposes if he or she has coverage under a general-purpose health FSA or HRA continues to apply. Therefore, if the employee in the example remains eligible under the HRA after the qualified distribution, she would not be an eligible individual for HSA purposes, and the amount of the qualified distribution would be subject to tax and penalty.

On the other hand, an employee with a zero balance in a general-purpose HRA as of the last day of a plan year will be HSA-eligible on the first day of the next plan year if one of the following conditions is met:

- The employee elects to waive HRA participation as of the first day of the next plan year;
- The employer terminates the general purpose HRA with respect to all employees as of the first day of the next plan year; or
- Effective on or before the first day of the next plan year, the employer converts the general-purpose HRA plan to an HSA-compatible plan.

[IRS Notice 2007-22, 2007-10 I.R.B. 670]

As a general rule, an employer must make comparable contributions to employees' HSAs (see Q 3:171).

The full range of comparability rules does not apply to qualified HSA distributions. However, if a qualified HSA distribution is offered to any employee covered under any HDHP, the employer must offer qualified HSA distributions to all eligible employees covered under any HDHP. However, if the employer offers HSA distributions only to employees covered under the employer's HDHP, the employer is not required to offer qualified HSA distributions to employees who are not covered under the employee's HDHP. [Treas. Reg. § 54.4980G-7] Failure to offer qualified HSA distributions to such employees will be treated as failure to meet the comparability requirements.

FSA grace period. Health FSAs used to operate on a strict "use-it-or-lose-it" basis. Any unspent funds remaining in an employee's FSA at the end of the plan year were forfeited to the plan. However, current IRS rules permit a health FSA to provide that expenses incurred during a grace period of up to 2 1/2 months immediately following the end of the plan year may be paid or reimbursed from funds remaining in an employee's FSA at the end of the prior plan year. [IRS Notice 2005-42, 2005-23 I.R.B. 1]

Overlapping coverage under an FSA and an HSA can arise if an employer's FSA provides for a grace period. For example, suppose an employee who was covered by an FSA for Year 1 wants to set up an HSA for Year 2. If the FSA has a grace period extending until March 15 of Year 2, the employee will not be eligible for HSA coverage until April 1 of Year 2—even if the employee is not covered by an FSA for Year 2.

The IRS suggests that one way to solve this problem for employees who are switching from FSA to HSA coverage is for the employer to amend its cafeteria plan document to provide for mandatory conversion of the general purpose FSA to a limited-purpose or post-deductible FSA during the grace period. [Rev. Rul. 2005-86, 2005-49 I.R.B. 1075]

However, the Tax Relief and Health Care Act of 2006 [Pub. L. No. 109-433, 120 Stat. 3196 (2006)] offers another option. For tax years beginning after December 31, 2006, coverage under a health FSA will be disregarded in determining an employee's eligibility for HSA purposes, provided that either (1) the balance in the FSA at the end of the plan year is zero or (2) the employee is making a qualified HSA distribution in an amount equal to the remaining balance in the FSA as of the end of the plan year. [I.R.C. § 223(c)(1)(B)(iii)]

In the committee reports on the Tax Relief and Health Care Act, Congress indicated that the IRS is expected to provide guidance to facilitate rollovers and the establishment of HSAs. For example, Congress expects the IRS guidance to provide that FSA coverage during a grace period will be disregarded if an employee elects HDHP coverage and a qualified HSA distribution before the end of a year, even if the transfer of the FSA funds cannot be completed until the following plan year. Moreover, Congress said similar rules should apply to any qualified HSA distributions in order to facilitate such distributions at the beginning of an employee's first year of HSA eligibility.

IRS Notice 2007-22 follows up on that mandate by providing that an employee with a year-end balance in a general-purpose FSA with a grace period or in a general-purpose HRA will be treated as an eligible individual for HSA purposes as of the first day of the first month of the following plan year that the employee has HDHP coverage, provided all of the following conditions are met:

1. The employer amends the health FSA or HRA effective by the last day of the plan year to allow qualified HSA distributions.

2. The employee has not previously made a qualified distribution from the FSA or HRA.

3. The employee has HDHP coverage as of the first day of the month in which a qualified distribution is made and the employee is otherwise eligible for an HSA.

4. The employee elects to have the employer make a qualified distribution from the health FSA or HRA by the last day of the plan year.

5. The FSA or HRA makes no reimbursements to the employee after the last day of the plan year.

6. The employer makes the qualified distribution directly to the HSA trustee by the fifteenth day of the third calendar month following the end of the year (March 15 in the case of calendar-year plans), but only after the employee becomes HSA-eligible.

7. The qualified distribution does not exceed the lesser of (a) the FSA or HRA balance on September 21, 2006 or (b) the date of the distribution.

8. Following the qualified distribution, either (a) there is a zero balance in the FSA or HRA and the employee is no longer a participant in any non-HSA-compatible plan or (b) the general-purpose FSA or HSA written plan is converted to an HSA-compatible FSA or HRA.

[IRS Notice 2007-22, 2007-10 I.R.B. 670]

Proposed cafeteria plan regulations issued in 2007 authorize Section 125 plans to offer HSA-compatible limited purpose FSAs and post-deductible FSAs (or a combination) and to provide for qualified HSA distributions from FSAs. [Prop. Treas. Reg. § 1.125-5(m), (n)] (See chapter 7.)

Q 3:154   Can a self-insured medical reimbursement plan sponsored by an employer be an HDHP?

Yes, it can, provided the minimum deductible and maximum out-of-pocket expense requirements are met.

Q 3:155   How are expenses applied against the HDHP deductible?

Only medical expenses that are described in Code Section 213(d) and that are covered by the HDHP may be taken into account in determining whether the HDHP deductible, or the minimum required deductible has been met. For example, if the HDHP does not cover chiropractic care, expenses incurred for chiropractic care do not count toward the HDHP deductible or the minimum required deductible. [IRS Notice 2008-59 Q&A-15, 2008-59 I.R.B. 123]

Example. In 2010, Hal and his wife and child have family HDHP coverage with a $2,500 deductible. The HDHP does not provide benefits for vision or dental care. In February 2009, the family incurs $2,500 in vision and dental expenses. In March 2010, the family incurs $400 in expenses covered by the HDHP (but for the deductible). The family must incur an additional $2,100 in covered medical expenses before the HDHP deductible is satisfied.

If an individual has self-only HDHP coverage, only medical expenses of the covered individual count toward satisfying the HDHP deductible or the minimum required deductible. [IRS Notice 2008-59 Q&A-15, 2008-59 I.R.B. 123] However, that is not necessarily the case if an individual switches from family coverage to self-only coverage during a plan year. According to the IRS, a plan can use any reasonable method to allocate covered expenses incurred during the period of family coverage to satisfy the deductible for self-only coverage. For example, subject to state law requirements, the plan can allocate to the self-only deductible only those expenses incurred by the covered individual. Alternatively, the plan can allocate the expenses incurred during family HDHP coverage on a per-capita basis according to the number of persons covered by the family HDHP. Moreover, if the family deductible was satisfied before the change to self-only coverage, the plan can treat the individual as having satisfied the self-only deductible for that plan year. In all cases, each expense must be allocated on a reasonable and consistent basis and each expense may be allocated to only one individual.

In the case of a switch from self-only HDHP coverage to family HDHP coverage, the family coverage plan may apply expenses incurred by the individual during the period of self-only coverage toward satisfying the family deductible. [IRS Notice 2004-50, 2004-33 I.R.B. 196]

Q 3:156   How and when is an HSA established?

An eligible individual can establish an HSA with a qualified HSA trustee or custodian in much the same way that the individual would establish an individual retirement account (IRA). Any insurance company or bank (or similar financial institution as defined in Code Section 408(n) can be an HSA trustee or custodian. In addition, any other person already approved by the IRS to be a trustee or custodian of IRAs or Archer MSAs is automatically approved to be an HSA trustee or custodian.

No permission or authorization from the IRS is necessary to establish an HSA. An eligible individual who is an employee may establish an HSA with or without the involvement of the employer.

Practice Pointer. Employers who wish to sponsor an HDHP in conjunction with HSAs can work with a bank or other custodian to establish HSAs for their employees.

Tax-free distributions from an HSA can be made only for qualified medical expenses that are incurred after the account is established.

An HSA is an exempt trust established through a written governing instrument under state law. Therefore, state trust law determines when an HSA is established. Most state trust laws require that for a trust to exist, an asset must be held in trust. Thus, in most states, an HSA must be funded to be established. Whether the account beneficiary's signature is required to establish the trust also depends on state law. [IRS Notice 2008-59 Q&A-38, 2008-59 I.R.B. 123]

A trustee treats an HSA as established before the date of establishment determined under state law, such as the date when HDHP coverage began. [IRS Notice 2008-59 Q&A-39, 2008-59 I.R.B. 123] However, an HSA that is funded by means of a rollover from a prior HSA or from an Archer MSA (but not a rollover from an IRA or from an FSA or HSA) is treated as established on the date the prior account was established. [IRS Notice 2008-59 Q&A-40, 2008-59 I.R.B. 123] (See Q 3:165 for discussion of the different types of rollover distributions.)

If an account beneficiary establishes an HSA, and later establishes another HSA, any later HSA is deemed to be established when the first HSA was established if the account beneficiary has an HSA with a balance greater than zero at any time during the 18-month period ending on the date the later HSA is established.

Example 1. An account beneficiary established an HSA on March 1, 2007. On June 15, 2007, he withdrew all the funds from the HSA, resulting in a zero balance. On November 21, 2008, he established a second HSA.

Because the second HSA was established within 18 months of June 15, 2007, the second HSA is deemed to be established on March 1, 2007.

Example 2. The facts are the same as those as Example 1, except that the account beneficiary establishes a third HSA on January 1, 2010. On that date, the second HSA has a balance greater than zero. The third HSA is deemed to be established on March 1, 2007.

Q 3:157   Who may contribute to an HSA?

An eligible individual may contribute to an HSA on his or her own behalf. In the case of an HSA established by an employee, either the employee or the employee's employer, or both, may contribute to the employee's HSA in a given year. For an HSA established by a self-employed (or unemployed) individual, the individual may contribute to the HSA. A family member may contribute to an HSA on behalf of another family member as long as that other family member is an eligible individual.

In Advisory Opinion 2004-09A, the DOL said that a bank or insurer can make cash contributions to an HSA as an incentive for a customer to establish an HSA. As stated in the opinion, an insurer planned to contract with a bank to provide HSA administration for employees of employers that purchased group HDHP coverage from the insurer. To promote HSA participation, the bank planned to provide new HSA customers with a $100 cash contribution. The DOL said such a contribution would be permissible because the tax law specifically provides that any person may make contributions to an individual's HSA.

Q 3:158   How much may be contributed to an HSA?

The maximum annual contribution to an HSA is the sum of the limits determined separately for each month as of the first day of the month.

For tax years beginning before 2007, the maximum monthly contribution was limited to one-twelfth of the lesser of (a) the maximum annual contribution or (b) the annual deductible under the HSA.

However, the 2006 Tax Relief and Health Care Act [Pub. L. No. 109-433, 120 Stat. 3196 (2006)] eliminates the plan deductible limit for tax years beginning after 2006. Therefore, employees or their employers (or a combination) can contribute one-twelfth of the maximum annual contribution for each month of eligibility. For 2010 or 2011, the maximum annual contribution for eligible individuals with self-only coverage under an HDHP is $3,050. For eligible individuals with family coverage, the 2010 maximum contribution is $6,150. [Rev. Proc. 2009-29, 2009-22 I.R.B. 1050; Rev. Proc. 2010-22, 2010-23 I.R.B. 747]

> **Practice Pointer.** The elimination of the plan deductible limit can significantly increase the maximum deduction, especially for individuals covered by an HDHP with a relatively low annual deductible.

> **Example.** Sam has self-only coverage under an HDHP and contributes to an HSA. The HDHP has the lowest permitted deductible—$1,200 for 2011. For 2010, Sam can contribute up to the maximum contribution limit of $3,050, even though that amount exceeds his deductible.

An individual is generally eligible for HSA contributions for a given month only if he or she is covered by an HDHP as of the first day of the month. [IRS Notice 2004-50, 2004-33 I.R.B. 196] However, here again, the 2006 Tax Relief and Health Care Act made a significant change. For tax years beginning after 2006, an individual who establishes an HSA part way through the year may contribute the full annual amount. For purposes of calculating the maximum annual contribution, an individual who is an eligible individual for the *last* month of the tax year is treated as (a) having been an eligible individual during *each* of the months in that tax year and (b) having been enrolled in the same HDHP in which he or she is enrolled for the last month of the tax year. [I.R.C. § 223(b)(8)(A)] (See Q 3:159 for further details on the full-contribution rule.)

> **Practice Pointer.** Only those part-year enrollees who begin HSA participation during the year and are covered by an HDHP at year-end are eligible to make the maximum annual contribution. Contributions by or for an individual who ceases to be eligible during the year continue to be limited to one-twelfth of the maximum contribution for each month of eligibility.

An individual who ceases to be an eligible individual may, until the date for filing the return (without extensions) for the year, make HSA contributions for the months of the year when he or she was an eligible individual. [IRS Notice 2008-59 Q&A-19, 2008-59 I.R.B. 123]

> **Example.** John has a self-only HDHP, and is an eligible individual for the first four months of 2011. He has until April 15, 2012 (the date for filing the 2010 return, without extensions) to contribute 4/12 × $3,050 ($1016.67) to an HSA for 2011.

All HSA contributions made by or on behalf of an eligible individual to an HSA are aggregated for purposes of applying the limit. The annual limit is decreased by total contributions to an Archer MSA (see Q 3:136). The same annual contribution limit applies whether the contributions are made by an employee, an employer, a self-employed person, or a family member. Unlike contributions to Archer MSAs, contributions to HSAs may be made by or on behalf of an eligible individual even if the individual has no compensation or if the contributions exceed the individual's compensation. If an individual has more than one HSA, the aggregate annual contributions to all his or her HSAs are subject to the limit.

Catch-up contributions. For individuals (and their spouses covered under the HDHP) between ages 55 and 65, the HSA contribution limit is increased by a separate catch-up contribution limit. The maximum catch-up contribution is $1,000 for 2009 and later years. As with the annual contribution limit, the catch-up contribution is also computed on a monthly basis.

An individual who is eligible to make catch-up contributions may only make such contributions to his or her own HSA. [IRS Notice 2004-50, Q&A-32; IRS Notice 2008-59 Q&A-22, 2008-59 I.R.B. 123] If both spouses are eligible for catch-up contributions, each spouse must make catch-up contributions to his or her own HSA.

No contributions after Medicare entitlement. Once an individual becomes entitled to benefits under Medicare, contributions, including catch-up contributions, cannot be made to an HSA.

The term "entitled to benefits under" Medicare means both eligibility and enrollment in Medicare. Thus, an otherwise eligible individual who is not actually enrolled in Medicare may contribute to an HSA until the month that individual is enrolled in Medicare. [IRS Notice 2004-50, 2004-33 I.R.B. 196; IRS Notice 2008-59 Q&A-5-Q&A-6, 2008-59 I.R.B. 123]

Example 1. Yolanda, age 66, is covered under her employer's HDHP. Although Yolanda is eligible for Medicare, she is not actually entitled to Medicare because she did not enroll in Medicare. Thus, Yolanda may contribute to an HSA.

Example 2. In August 2011, Howard Payne attains age 66 and applies for and begins receiving Social Security benefits. As a result of his application for Social Security benefits, Howard is automatically enrolled in Medicare. Thus, as of August 1, 2011, Howard is no longer an eligible individual and may not contribute to an HSA.

Family coverage rules. The maximum HSA contribution limit for a married couple where both spouses have family HDHP coverage is the statutory maximum for family coverage. This rule applies regardless of whether each spouse's family coverage covers the other spouse. The contribution limit is divided between the spouses by agreement. [IRS Notice 2008-59 Q&A-18, 2008-59 I.R.B. 123]

Example 1. In 2011, Henry, who is 37, and Wendy, who is 32, are married with two dependent children. Henry has HDHP family coverage for himself and their two children with an annual deductible of $3,000. Wendy has

HDHP family coverage for herself and their two children with a deductible of $3,500. The combined contribution limit for Henry and Wendy is $6,150, the maximum annual contribution limit. Henry and Wendy divide the $6,150 contribution limit between them by agreement.

The maximum annual HSA contribution limit for a married couple if one spouse has family HDHP coverage and the other spouse has self-only HDHP coverage is the statutory maximum for family coverage. The contribution limit is divided between the spouses by agreement. This is the result regardless of whether the family HDHP coverage includes the spouse with self-only HDHP coverage. [IRS Notice 2008-59 Q&A-18, 2008-59 I.R.B. 123]

Example 2. For 2011, Susan and Brad, both age 40, are married. Susan and Brad are otherwise eligible individuals. Brad has self-only HDHP coverage. Susan has an HDHP with family coverage for herself and their two children. The combined contribution limit for Susan and Brad is $6,150, the statutory contribution limit for family coverage for 2011. They divide the $6,150 contribution limit between them by agreement.

An IRS revenue ruling makes it clear that a married individual who otherwise qualifies can contribute to an HSA even if his or her spouse has low-deductible family coverage, provided the family plan does not cover the individual. [Rev. Rul. 2005-25, 2005-18 I.R.B. 971] The same holds true in cases where another dependent has coverage under a plan that is not an HDHP. The eligible individual may contribute the statutory maximum for family coverage. Other coverage of dependent children or spouses does not affect an individual's contribution limit, except that if the spouse is not an otherwise eligible individual, no part of the HSA contribution can be allocated to the spouse. [IRS Notice 2008-59 Q&A-18, 2008-59 I.R.B. 123]

Example. Jane and Victor are married. Jane has HDHP family coverage with an annual deductible of $5,000 for herself and one of the couple's two children. Victor has non-HDHP family coverage with a deductible of $200 for himself and the other child. Jane is excluded from Victor's non-HDHP coverage. Because the non-HDHP coverage does not cover Jane, the coverage does not affect Jane's eligibility to make HSA contributions up to the amount of her annual contribution limit. Therefore, Jane can contribute up to $6,150 to her HSA for 2011 (assuming she is not eligible for additional catch-up contributions).

Q 3:159   How does the full-contribution rule for part-year HSA eligible individuals work?

The full-contribution rule allows an individual who establishes an HSA part way through the year to contribute the full annual amount.

If an individual is an eligible individual on the first day of the last month of the individual's taxable year (December 1 for calendar year taxpayers), the individual's maximum HSA contribution for the year is the greater of the following:

The sum of the limits determined separately for each month based on eligibility and HDHP coverage on the first day of each month, plus catch-up contributions if applicable, or

The maximum annual HSA contribution based on the individual's HDHP coverage (self-only or family) on the first day of the last month of the individual's taxable year, plus catch-up contributions if applicable. [I.R.C. 223(b)(8)(A); Notice 2008-52, 2008-25 I.R.B. 1166]

If an individual is not an eligible individual on the first day of the last month of the individual's taxable year (December 1 for calendar year taxpayers), the individual's maximum HSA contribution for the year is determined under the sum of the monthly contribution limits rule under Code Section 223(b)(2).

Example 1. Aaron, age 53, enrolls in family HDHP coverage on December 1, 2011, and is eligible for an HSA as of that date. Aaron was not an eligible individual in any other month in 2010. His full contribution limit for 2011 is $6,150, the maximum contribution for an individual with family HDHP coverage. The sum of the monthly contribution limits is $512.50 (1/12 × $6,150). Therefore, Aaron's annual contribution limit for 2011 is $6,150, the greater of $6,150 or $512.50.

For purposes of computing the full-contribution amount, an eligible individual is treated as enrolled in the same HDHP coverage (i.e., self-only or family coverage) as he or she has on the first day of the last month of the year. On the other hand, the sum of the monthly contribution amounts is based on the individual's HDHP coverage as of the first day of each month.

Example 2. Betty, age 39, enrolls in self-only HDHP coverage on January 1, 2011, and is eligible to make HSA contributions as of that date. Betty's coverage changes to family HDHP coverage on November 1, 2011 and Betty retains family HDHP coverage through December 31, 2011. Because Betty had family HDHP coverage on December 1, 2011, her contribution limit under the full-contribution rule is $6,150 (the maximum contribution for an individual with family HDHP coverage). The sum of Betty's monthly contribution limits is $3,566.67 ((2/12 × $6,150 for two months of family coverage) + (10/12 × $3,050 for 10 months of self-only coverage)). Betty's annual contribution limit for 2010 is $6,150, the greater of $6,150 or $3,566.67.

Testing period rule. There is one catch to the full-contribution rule. An individual who takes advantage of the full-contribution rule must remain HSA-eligible during a testing period that begins on the first day of the last month of the current year and ends on the last day of the 12th month following that month. Thus, an individual who takes advantage of the full-contribution rule for 2010 must remain HSA-eligible through December 31, 2011. If an individual loses HSA eligibility during the testing period (for example, by switching to a low-deductible health plan), he or she must pay tax plus a 10 percent penalty on any contributions that would not have been allowable but for the full-contribution rule.

The amount that is included in income is computed by subtracting the sum of the monthly contribution limits that the individual would otherwise have been entitled to from the amount actually contributed. For example, a single employee who would have been allowed only one month's contribution for 2010 under the month-by-month rule, but contributed the maximum of $3,050 under the full-contribution rule, will owe tax plus a 10 percent penalty on 11/12ths of the contribution ($2,795.83) if the testing period requirement is not met.

Practice Pointer. It is not necessary to distribute the taxable amount from the HSA. A withdrawal will not prevent the inclusion of the amount in income or the additional 10 percent tax. Moreover, a withdrawal could result in a double tax whammy. The amount withdrawn will be treated like any other HSA distribution, even though the amount was included in gross income. Thus, if a distribution of the excess contributions is not used for qualified medical expenses, it will be included in gross income and will be subject to an additional 10 percent tax (unless an exception applies). See Q 3:166 for the tax treatment of distributions.

Example 3. Helen, age 25, enrolls in self-only HDHP coverage on July 1, 2011, and is eligible to make HSA contributions as of that date. She was not an eligible individual before July 1, 2011. Helen continues to be HSA-eligible as of December 1, 2011. Therefore, under the full-contribution rule, Helen contributes the $3,050 (the maximum 2011 contribution for individuals with self-only coverage) to her HSA for the year. However, Helen ceases to be an eligible individual on February 1, 2012. Because Helen does not meet the testing period requirement, Helen must include $1,270 in income for 2012 (the $3,050 contributed for 2011 under the full-contribution rule less $1,780 contributions she would have been allowed under the monthly contribution rule). That amount is also subject to a 10 percent penalty tax.

On February 2, 2012, Helen withdraws the $1,270 of taxable contributions from her HSA. The distribution is not used for qualified medical expenses. The $1,270 withdrawal is also included in Helen's gross income for 2012 and is also subject to another 10 percent additional tax. Bottom line: Helen must include a total of $3,560 in gross income for 2012 and pay an additional tax of $356.

Earnings on the taxable amount are not included in gross income or subject to the 10 percent additional tax for failure to meet the testing period requirement, so long as the earnings remain in the HSA or are used for qualified medical expenses.

Q 3:160   What kinds of contributions can be made to an HSA?

Contributions to an HSA must be made in cash. Contributions may not be made in the form of stock or other property. Payments for the HDHP and contributions to the HSA can be made through an employer's cafeteria plan.

Q 3:161   What is the tax treatment of an eligible individual's HSA contributions?

Contributions made by an eligible individual to an HSA (subject to the applicable contribution limit) are deductible above the line in determining adjusted gross income (AGI). Therefore, the contributions are deductible whether or not the eligible individual itemizes deductions. However, the individual cannot also deduct the contributions as medical expense deductions under Code Section 213. Contributions made by a family member on behalf of an eligible individual are deductible by the eligible individual in computing AGI. The contributions are deductible whether or not the eligible individual itemizes deductions. An individual who may be claimed as a dependent on another person's tax return is not an eligible individual and may not deduct contributions to an HSA.

Employer contributions. Employer contributions on behalf of an eligible employee are treated as employer-provided coverage for medical expenses under an accident or health plan and are excludable from the employee's gross income (subject to the applicable contribution limit). The employer contributions are not subject to income tax withholding or employment taxes. Contributions to an employee's HSA through a cafeteria plan are treated as employer contributions. The employee cannot deduct employer contributions on his or her federal income tax return as HSA contributions or as medical expense deductions under Code Section 213.

On the Form W-2, Code W is used to report an employer's contribution to an employee's HSA. HSA contributions are reported in box 12.

The exclusion for employer contributions is limited to contributions by an employer to the HSA of an employee who is an eligible individual. Any contribution by an employer to the HSA of a nonemployee (e.g., a spouse of an employee or any other individual), including salary reduction amounts made through a Code Section 125 cafeteria plan, must be included in the gross income and wages of the employee. [IRS Notice 2008-59 Q&A-26, 2008-59 I.R.B. 123]

Q 3:162   Is there a deadline for making contributions to an HSA for a tax year?

Yes. Contributions can be made in one or more payments, at the convenience of the individual or the employer, at any time from the beginning of the tax year until the due date (without extensions) for filing the individual's federal income tax return for that year. Thus, for most employees, contributions can be made up until April 15 following the end of the tax year.

When employer contributions (including salary reduction contributions) are made between January 1 and the date for filing the employees' returns without extension, the employer must notify the HSA trustee or custodian if the contributions relate to the prior year. The employer must also inform the employee of the designation. However, the contributions designated as made for the prior year are still reported in box 12 with code W on the employees' Form W-2 for the year in which the contributions are actually made.

> **Example.** In January 2011, Rizza Salon contributes $500 to each employee's HSA and notifies the HSA trustee (and provides a statement to the employees) that the contributions are for 2009. Subsequently, in 2011, Rizza contributes $250 to each employee's HSA on March 31, June 30, September 30, and December 31. For each employee whose HSA received these contributions, Rizza reports a total contribution of $1,500 in box 12 with code W on the Form W-2 for 2011.

However, for purposes of completing their individual income tax returns, the employees treat the post-year-end contributions as made in the year to which they relate. [IRS Notice 2008-59 Q&A-21, 2008-59 I.R.B. 123]

Although the annual contribution is generally determined monthly, the maximum contribution may be made on the first day of the year, subject to correction if it turns out to have been an excess amount.

> **Practice Pointer.** Employers may want to exercise caution in making up-front contributions to employees' HSAs. Once a contribution is made, it is nonforfeitable. For example, an employer that makes the maximum annual contribution to an employee's HSA at the beginning of the year cannot recoup any portion of the contribution, even if the employee terminates employment during the year. [I.R.C. § 223(d)(1)(e); IRS Notice 2004-50, 2004-33 I.R.B. 196; Treas. Reg. § 54.4980G-4]

Q 3:163   What happens if contributions to an individual's HSA exceed the annual contribution limit?

Contributions made by or on behalf of an individual to an HSA are not deductible to the extent they exceed the contribution limit. Contributions by an employer to an HSA for an employee are included in the gross income of the employee to the extent that they exceed the contribution limit or if they are made on behalf of an employee who is not an eligible individual. In addition, an annual excise tax of 6 percent for each taxable year is imposed on the HSA account holder for excess individual and employer contributions.

However, if the excess contributions for a taxable year and the net income attributable to the excess contributions are paid to the account holder before the due date (including extensions) for filing the account holder's federal income tax return for the tax year, the net income attributable to the excess contributions is included in the account holder's gross income for the taxable year in which the distribution is received but the excise tax is not imposed on the excess contribution and the distribution of the excess contribution is not taxed.

Excess employer contributions. An employer cannot recoup up-front contributions, even if the employee subsequently becomes ineligible for a portion of those contributions. Moreover, an employer cannot recoup amounts contributed after the employee ceases to be an eligible individual. [IRS Notice 2008-59 Q&A-25, 2008-59 I.R.B. 123]

Example. Nancy was an eligible individual for HSA purposes on January 1, 2011. On April 1, 2011, Nancy's spouse enrolled in a general purpose health FSA that covers all family members. Thus, Nancy became ineligible for HSA contributions as of that date. However, Nancy did not realize the FSA caused her to be ineligible until July 15, 2011, at which time she alerted her employer to cease HSA contributions. The employer's contributions to Nancy's HSA between April 1, 2011 and July 15, 2011 cannot be recouped by Nancy's employer because Nancy has a nonforfeitable interest in her HSA. Nancy is responsible for determining if the contributions exceed the maximum annual contribution limit and for withdrawing any excess contributions plus and including those amounts in gross income.

Certain erroneous contributions can be recouped.

If, due to an error, an employer contributes amounts to an employee's HSA that exceed the maximum annual contribution, the employer may correct the error. The employer may request that the financial institution return the excess amounts to the employer. Alternatively, if the employer does not recover the amounts, then the amounts must be included as gross income and wages on the employee's Form W-2 for the year during which the employer made contributions.

On the other hand, amounts contributed that are less than or equal to the maximum annual contribution may not be recouped from the employee's HSA. [IRS Notice 2008-59 Q&A-24, 2008-59 I.R.B. 123]

If an employer contributes to the account of an employee who was never an eligible individual, then no HSA ever existed and the employer may correct the error. At the employer's option, the employer may request that the financial institution return the amounts to the employer. However, if the employer does not recover the amounts by the end of the taxable year, then the amounts must be included as gross income and wages on the employee's Form W-2 for the year during which the employer made the contributions. [IRS Notice 2008-59 Q&A-23, 2008-59 I.R.B. 123]

Example 1. In February 2011, Mary's employer contributed $500 to Mary's HSA. However, in July 2011, the employer learned that Mary's account is not an HSA because Mary was never an eligible individual. The employer may either request that the financial institution holding Mary's account return the balance of the account ($500 plus earnings less administration fees directly paid from the account) to the employer. If the employer does not receive the balance of the account, the employer must include the contributions in Mary's gross income and wages on her Form W-2 for 2011.

Example 2. The facts are the same as those in Example 1, except that Mary's employer does not discover the mistake until July 2012. The employer must issue a corrected 2011 Form W-2 for Mary showing the contributions as wages, and Mary must file an amended income tax return for 2011.

Q 3:164   What is the tax treatment of an HSA?

An HSA is generally exempt from tax (like an IRA or Archer MSA) unless it has ceased to be an HSA. Earnings on amounts in an HSA are not includable in gross income while held in the HSA (i.e., inside buildup is not taxable). (See Q 3:166 regarding the taxation of distributions to the account beneficiary.)

Q 3:165   Can rollover contributions be made to an HSA?

The original HSA rules permitted rollover contributions from Archer MSAs and other HSAs. For tax years beginning before 2007, however, rollovers from other types of plans were not permitted. The 2006 Tax Relief and Health Care Act [Pub. L. No. 109-433, 120 Stat. 3196 (2006)] added new rules that permit individuals to make one-time rollovers from IRAs, health FSAs, or HSAs.

HSA rollovers. A rollover from one HSA to another does not affect an individual's contribution limit for the year and is not treated as a distribution from the account. [I.R.C. § 223(f)(5)] A contribution to an HSA is a rollover contribution if it is paid or distributed from an HSA to the account beneficiary, but only to the extent that the amount received is paid into an HSA for the benefit of the account beneficiary no later than the 60th day after the day on which the beneficiary received the payment or distribution. An amount will not be treated as a rollover contribution if, at any time during the one-year period ending on the day of receipt, the individual received another distribution from an HSA that was not includable in the individual's gross income because it was a rollover. [IRS Notice 2008-59, Q&A-20, 2008-59 I.R.B. 123]

One may make a rollover contribution from an HSA to a new HSA even if one is not otherwise eligible to make HSA contributions at the time of the rollover.

IRA rollovers. For tax years beginning after 2006, an individual who is eligible for an HSA can make one qualified HSA funding distribution from either a traditional IRA or a Roth IRA. Any amount that would otherwise be included in gross income on account of the distribution will be excluded if applicable requirements are met. [I.R.C. § 408(d)(9)(A), as amended by the 2006 Tax Relief and Health Care Act]

In addition a qualified HSA funding distribution is not subject to the 10 percent early withdrawal penalty tax applicable to IRA funds. [I.R.C. § 72(t)] However, no HSA deduction is allowed for the amount contributed to the HSA. Moreover, the annual limit on HSA contributions is reduced by the amount of a qualified HSA funding distribution. [I.R.C. § 223(b)(4)]

A qualified funding distribution may not be made from an ongoing SIMPLE IRA or an ongoing SEP IRA. For this purpose, a SEP IRA or SIMPLE IRA is treated as ongoing if an employer contribution is made for the plan year ending with or within the IRA owner's taxable year in which the qualified HSA funding distribution would be made. After the death of an IRA or Roth IRA account owner, a qualified HSA funding distribution may be made from an IRA or Roth IRA maintained for the benefit of an IRA or Roth IRA beneficiary. [Notice 2008-51, 2008-25 I.R.B. 1163]

A qualified HSA funding distribution must be made by means of a direct trustee-to-trustee transfer. [I.R.C. § 408(d)(9)(B)] If a check from an IRA or Roth IRA is made payable to an HSA trustee or custodian and delivered by the IRA or Roth IRA account owner to the HSA trustee or custodian, the payment to the HSA will be considered a direct payment by the IRA or Roth IRA trustee, custodian or issuer to the HSA. However, if an individual owns two or more IRAs, and wants to use amounts in multiple IRAs to make a qualified HSA funding distribution, the individual must first make an IRA-to-IRA transfer of the amounts to be distributed into a single IRA, and then make the one-time qualified HSA funding distribution from that IRA. [Notice 2008-51, 2008-25 I.R.B. 1163]

A qualified HSA funding distribution relates to the taxable year in which the distribution is actually made. The rules that allow contributions made before the deadline for filing an individual's federal income tax return to be treated as made on the last day of the preceding taxable year do not apply to qualified HSA funding distributions. [Notice 2008-51, 2008-25 I.R.B. 1163]

A qualified HSA funding distribution cannot exceed the IRA owner's maximum annual HSA contribution limit. The maximum annual HSA contribution is based on (1) the individual's age as of the end of the taxable year and (2) the individual's type of high deductible health plan (HDHP) coverage (self-only or family HDHP coverage) at the time of the distribution. For example, in 2010, an IRA owner who is an eligible individual with family HDHP coverage at the time of the distribution and who is age 55 or over by the end of the year is allowed a qualified HSA funding distribution of $6,050, plus a $1,000 catch-up contribution. An IRA or Roth IRA owner who is an eligible individual with self-only HDHP coverage, and who is under age 55 as of the end of the taxable year, is allowed a qualified HSA funding distribution of $3,050 for 2010. [Notice 2008-51, 2008-25 I.R.B. 1163]

As a general rule, an individual can make only one qualified HSA funding distribution during his or her lifetime. [I.R.C. § 408(d)(9)(C)(ii)(I)] However, if a qualified HSA funding distribution is made when an individual has self-only HDHP coverage, an additional distribution can be made later in the same tax year if the individual switches to family coverage. [I.R.C. § 408(d)(9)(C)(ii)(II); Notice 2008-51, 2008-25 I.R.B. 1163] The second distribution cannot exceed the HSA contribution limit for family coverage less the amount of the first distribution.

Once made, a qualified HSA funding distribution is irrevocable.

To ensure tax-free treatment for a qualified HSA funding distribution, an individual must remain eligible for HSA coverage during a 12-month testing period beginning with the month the qualified HSA funding distribution is made. [I.R.C. § 408(d)(9)(D)] If an individual is not eligible for HSA coverage (e.g., is not covered by an HDHP) at any time during a testing period, the amount of the qualified HSA funding distribution must be included in gross income for the tax year that includes the first month in which the individual is not eligible. In addition, a 10 percent penalty tax applies to the included amount.

Note, however, that if an individual ceases to be eligible because of death or disability, the addition to gross income and the penalty tax do not apply. For testing period purposes, an eligible individual who changes from family HDHP coverage to self-only HDHP coverage during the testing period remains an eligible individual. [Notice 2008-51, 2008-25 I.R.B. 1163]

FSA and HRA rollovers. Employers have a limited opportunity to allow employees to make a one-time rollover of FSA or HRA funds by means of a qualified HSA distribution. [I.R.C. § 106(e), as amended by the 2006 Tax Relief and Health Care Act] A qualified HSA distribution is treated as a contribution by the employer to an employee's HSA that is excludable from gross income and is exempt from employment taxes. A qualified HSA distribution from a health FSA or HRA does not affect the otherwise applicable limit on HSA contributions. For further details, see Q 3:154.

Q 3:166   When can an individual receive distributions from an HSA and how are distributions taxed?

The beneficiary of an HSA can receive distributions from the account at any time. However, the tax treatment of a distribution will depend on when it is received and how it is used.

Distributions from an HSA that are used exclusively to pay for qualified medical expenses of the account beneficiary and his or her spouse or dependents are excludable from gross income. In general, amounts in an HSA can be used for qualified medical expenses and will be excludable from gross income even if the individual is not currently eligible to make contributions to the HSA (e.g., the individual is over age 65 and enrolled in Medicare or is no longer covered by an HDHP). What's more, the exclusion applies to distributions for qualified expenses of a spouse or dependent who is not covered by the HDHP or is covered under another plan that is not an HDHP. [IRS Notice 2004-50, 2004-33 I.R.B. 196]

Any portion of a distribution that is not used exclusively to pay for qualified medical expenses of the account beneficiary and his or her spouse or dependents is includable in gross income of the account beneficiary and is subject to an additional tax on the amount includable, except in the case of distributions made after the account beneficiary's death, disability, or attainment of age 65. The additional tax is 10 percent of the excess distribution for tax years beginning before 2011; the 2010 Health Reform Act increases the additional tax to 20 percent for tax years beginning after December 31, 2010. [I.R.C. § 223(f)(4) as amended by PPACA § 9004]

HSA participants should be cautioned that a change in the tax definition of a dependent, effective starting in 2005, applies for purposes of determining the tax treatment of HSA distributions. Under this definition, a "qualifying relative" (other than a child under age 19 or a child under age 24 who is a full-time student) is treated as a dependent only if his or her gross income does not exceed the dependency exemption amount for the year ($3,650 for 2010). On the other hand, the IRS has made it clear that the gross income limit does not apply for purposes of the exclusion for employer-provided health coverage (see Q 3:101). Therefore, employer-provided health coverage for a relative who does not meet the gross income limit may be excludable from an employee's income; however, HSA distribution for that individual's medical expenses would be taxable.

Q 3:167   What are the qualified medical expenses that are eligible for tax-free distributions?

Qualified medical expenses are expenses paid by the account beneficiary or his or her spouse or dependents for medical care as defined in Code Section 213(d) but only to the extent the expenses are not covered by insurance or otherwise. For purposes of determining the itemized deduction for medical expenses, medical expenses paid or reimbursed by distributions from an HSA are not treated as expenses paid for medical care under Code Section 213.

Note. The 2010 Health Reform Act narrows the definition of medical care for purposes of HSAs and other reimbursement arrangements. Effective for expenses incurred after December 31, 2010, the 2010 Health Reform Act generally bars tax-free reimbursements for expenses for OTC medicines or drugs, unless the medicine or drug is prescribed by a physician. [I.R.C. § 106(f) as added by PPACA § 9003]

Health insurance premiums generally are not qualified medical expenses and cannot be paid with HSA funds on a tax-free basis. However, there are exceptions for qualified long-term care insurance, COBRA health care continuation coverage, and health care coverage while an individual is receiving unemployment compensation. In addition, for individuals over age 65, premiums for Medicare Parts A, B, or D; a Medicare HMO; and the employee share of premiums for employer-sponsored health insurance (including premiums for employer-sponsored retiree health insurance) can be paid from an HSA. [IRS Notice 2004-50, 2004-33 I.R.B. 196; IRS Notice 2008-59 Q&A-29 to Q&A-32, 2008-59 I.R.B. 123] Premiums for Medigap policies are not qualified medical expenses.

Medicare premiums. If an account beneficiary has attained age 65, premiums for Medicare for the account beneficiary, the account beneficiary's spouse, or the account beneficiary's dependents are qualified medical expenses. [IRS Notice 2004-50, 2004-33 I.R.B. 196; IRS Notice 2008-59 Q&A-29, 2008-59 I.R.B. 123] However, if the account beneficiary has not yet attained age 65, Medicare premiums for coverage of the account beneficiary's spouse (who has attained age 65) are not qualified medical expenses. [IRS Notice 2008-59, Q&A-30, 2008-59 I.R.B. 123]

The HSA rules provide that qualified expenses must be incurred after the HSA is established.

Q 3:168   Must employers who make contributions to an employee's HSA determine whether HSA distributions are used exclusively for qualified medical expenses?

No. It is the responsibility of each employee to make that determination. Employees should maintain records of their medical expenses sufficient to show that the distributions have been made exclusively for qualified medical expenses and are excludable from gross income.

Q 3:169   What happens to the money remaining in an HSA when the account holder dies?

Any balance remaining in the account holder's HSA at death becomes the property of the individual named in the HSA instrument as the beneficiary of the account. If the account holder's surviving spouse is the named beneficiary of the HSA, the HSA becomes the HSA of the surviving spouse. The surviving spouse is subject to income tax only to the extent distributions from the HSA are not used for qualified medical expenses.

If the HSA passes to a person other than the surviving spouse, the HSA ceases to be an HSA as of the date of the account holder's death, and that person is required to include in gross income the fair market value of the HSA assets as of the date of death. For a beneficiary other than the surviving spouse (except the decedent's estate), the includable amount is reduced by any payments from the HSA made for the decedent's qualified medical expenses, if paid within one year after death.

Q 3:170   Can an HSA be used to borrow or lend money?

No. An account beneficiary may not enter into "prohibited transactions" with an HSA (e.g., the account beneficiary may not sell, exchange, or lease property, borrow or lend money, pledge the HSA, furnish goods, services or facilities, transfer to or use by or for the benefit of himself/herself any assets of the HSA, etc.). If an account beneficiary engages in a prohibited transaction with his or her HSA, the sanction, in general, is disqualification of the account. Thus, the HSA stops being an HSA as of the first day of the taxable year of the prohibited transaction. The assets of the beneficiary's account are deemed distributed, and the appropriate taxes, including the 10 percent additional tax for distributions not used for qualified medical expenses, apply. If the employer sponsoring the account (or other disqualified person) is the party engaging in a prohibited transaction, then the employer (or other party) is liable for the excise tax, but the account beneficiary is not. [IRS Notice 2008-59 Q&A-37, 2008-59 I.R.B. 123]

Any direct or indirect extension of credit between the account beneficiary and his or her HSA is a prohibited transaction. Thus, an account beneficiary may not:

- Borrow money from his or her HSA [IRS Notice 2008-59 Q&A-34, 2008-59 I.R.B. 123]

- Use the HSA to borrow money, for example by obtaining a line of credit for the HSA [IRS Notice 2008-59 Q&A-35, 2008-59 I.R.B. 123]
- Pledge the HSA as security for a loan [IRS Notice 2008-59 Q&A-36, 2008-59 I.R.B. 123]

Q 3:171   Do any nondiscrimination rules apply if an employer makes contributions to HSAs for employees?

If an employer makes HSA contributions, the employer must make available comparable contributions on behalf of all "comparable participating employees" (i.e., eligible employees who are in the same category of employees and who have the same category of HDHP coverage) during the same period. Contributions are considered comparable if they are either the same amount or the same percentage of the deductible under the HDHP. [I.R.C. § 4980G; Treas. Reg. §§ 54.4980G-1 through 54.4980G-7]

Key exception. For tax years beginning after 2006, the 2006 Tax Relief and Health Care Act carves out an exception to the comparability rules enabling employers to make larger HSA contributions for NHCEs than for HCEs (as defined in Code Section 414(q)). Under this rule, HCEs are not treated as comparable participating employees for purposes of applying the comparability rules to an employer's contributions for NHCEs. [I.R.C. § 4980G(d)]

If employer contributions do not satisfy the comparability rules for a calendar year, the employer is subject to an excise tax equal to 35 percent of the aggregate amount contributed by the employer to HSAs for that period. However, if an employer's failure to satisfy the comparability rules is due to reasonable cause and not to willful neglect, all or part of the excise tax may be waived to the extent payment of the tax would be excessive relative to the failure involved.

Note. Beginning January 1, 2010, excise tax liabilities for failure to make comparable HSA contributions must be self-reported by filing Form 8928, *Return of Certain Excise Taxes Under Chapter 43 of the Internal Revenue Code.* [Treas. Reg. § 54.6011-2]

Q 3:172   Who are comparable participating employees for purposes of the comparability rules?

As a general rule, employees are divided into three categories for comparability testing: (1) current full-time employees; (2) current part-time employees; and (3) former employees (other than former employees with COBRA coverage).

Employees are considered part-time if they are customarily employed for fewer than 30 hours per week. Employees who are covered by a bona fide collective bargaining agreement are not comparable participating employees if health benefits were the subject of good-faith bargaining. Former employees covered by a collective bargaining agreement also are not comparable participating employees.

The three categories of employees are further broken down according to type of HDHP coverage. As a general rule, there are two categories of coverage: self-only HDHP coverage and family HDHP coverage.

So, for example, full-time employees with self-only HDHP coverage, part-time employees with self-only HDHP coverage, full-time employees with family coverage, and part-time employees with family coverage are all separate categories of employees, and different amounts can be contributed to the HSAs for each category.

However, IRS regulations allow a further breakdown of employees with family coverage into (1) self plus one, (2) self plus two, and (3) self plus three or more if the employer's plan different coverage options for such categories. Note, however, that if an HDHP has more than one coverage category that provides coverage for the same number of individuals, those categories must be treated as a single category for comparability testing. For example, employees covered under a category called "employee plus spouse" and employees covered under a category called "employee plus dependent" must be grouped together because both categories provide coverage for two individuals (i.e., self plus one coverage).

> **Example.** Mammoth Corp. maintains an HDHP and contributes to the HSAs of eligible employees who elect coverage under the HDHP. The HDHP has six coverage options: (1) self-only; (2) self plus spouse; (3) self plus dependent; (4) self plus spouse plus one dependent; (5) self plus two dependents; and (6) self plus spouse and two or more dependents. However, the plan provides only four categories of coverage for comparability testing:
>
> 1. Self only;
> 2. Self plus one (including employees with self plus spouse and self plus dependent coverage);
> 3. Self plus two (including employees with self plus spouse plus one dependent and self plus two dependents coverage); and
> 4. Self plus three or more (employees with self plus spouse and two or more dependents coverage).

Independent contractors, self-employed individuals, and partners in a partnership are not considered employees and are not subject to the comparability rules. Consequently, a self-employed individual may make contributions to his or her own HSA without making contributions for employees. Similarly, a partnership can make contributions to a partner's HSA without making comparable contributions for other partners or for non-partner employees. However, if contributions are made to any regular employee's HSA comparable contributions must be made for all comparable participating employees.

Non-employer provided HDHP coverage. An employer that contributes only to the HSAs of employees who are eligible individuals with coverage under an employer-provided HDHP is not required to make comparable contributions to

HSAs of employees who are covered under a non-employer provided HDHP, even if those employees are otherwise eligible for HSA contributions. However, if the employer contributes to the HSA of any employee who is an eligible individual with coverage under a non-employer provided HDHP, the employer must make comparable contributions to the HSAs of *all* comparable participating employees whether or not they are covered under the employer's HDHP. [Treas. Reg. § 54.4980G-3 Q&A-7]

> **Practice Pointer.** An employer is not necessarily privy to an employee's nonemployer-provided health care coverage. Therefore, the IRS says that an employer that is required to make comparable contributions for employees with nonemployer HDHP coverage will satisfy the comparability rule if it makes a reasonable good-faith effort to identify all comparable participating employees with nonemployer-provided HDHP coverage and makes comparable HSA contributions for those employees.

Contributions for spouses. If spouses work for the same employer but only one employee-spouse has family coverage under the employer's HDHP, the employer is required to contribute only to the HSA of the employee-spouse with coverage under the HDHP. The employer is not required to contribute to the HSA of the employee-spouse who is covered under the employer's HDHP because of his or her spouse's coverage. However, if the employer contributes to the HSA of any eligible employee with nonemployer-provided HDHP coverage, the employer must make comparable contributions to the HSAs of the employee-spouse who is covered under the employee's HDHP because of his or her spouse's coverage (assuming he or she is otherwise eligible).

> **Practice Pointer.** Bear in mind, however, that an employer's combined contributions for two employee-spouses are not required to exceed the annual contribution limit for individuals with family coverage.

Contributions for former employees. An employer that is required to make comparable contributions for former employees must take reasonable actions to locate any missing comparable participating former employees. In general, such actions include the use of certified mail, the Internal Revenue Service Letter Forwarding Program, or the Social Security Administration's Letter Forwarding Service.

Q 3:173   When are employer contributions considered comparable?

Contributions are comparable if, for each month in a calendar year, the contributions are either the same amount or the same percentage of the deductible under the HDHP for employees in the same group (i.e., full-time, part-time, and former employees) with the same category of coverage on the first day of that month.

An employer is not required to contribute the same amount or the same percentage of the deductible for employees with one category of HDHP coverage that it contributes for employees with a different category of HDHP coverage. For example, an employer that satisfies the comparability rules by contributing the same amount to the HSAs of all full-time employees with family HDHP coverage is not required to contribute any amount to the HSAs of full-time employees with self-only HDHP coverage, or to contribute the same percentage of deductible as it contributes for full-time employees with family HDHP coverage.

Example 1. Beta Corp. offers its employees an HDHP with a $3,000 deductible for self-only coverage and a $4,000 deductible for family coverage. Beta contributes $1,000 for the calendar year to the HSA of each full-time employee with self-only coverage and $2,000 for each full-time employee with family coverage. Beta's HSA contributions satisfy the comparability rules.

Example 2. Gamma Corp. maintains two HDHPs. Plan A has a $2,000 deductible for self-only coverage and a $4,000 deductible for family coverage. Plan B has a $2,500 deductible for self-only coverage and a $4,500 deductible for family coverage. Gamma makes contributions for each full-time employee covered under Plan A of $600 for self-only coverage and $1,000 for family coverage. Gamma will meet the comparability rules if it makes either the same amount of contributions for each full-time covered under Plan B (i.e., $600 for self-only coverage and $1,000 for family coverage) or contributions equal to the same percentage of the deductible (i.e., 30 percent of the deductible, or $750, for self-only coverage and 25 percent of the deductible, or $1,125, for family coverage).

Gamma also makes contributions to the HSA of each part-time employee covered under Plan A of $300 for self-only coverage and $500 for family coverage. Gamma will meet the comparability rules if it contributes the same amounts for employees covered under Plan B (i.e., $300 for self-only coverage and $500 for family coverage) or the same percentage of the deductible (i.e., 15 percent of the deductible, or $375, for self-only coverage) or 12.5 percent, or $563 for family coverage).

Employees with different categories of family HDHP coverage may be tested separately. However, the contribution for the self plus two category may not be less than the contribution for the self plus one category and the contribution for to the self plus three or more category may not be less than the contribution for the self plus two category.

Contributions under full-contribution rule. The full-contribution rule allows an employee who becomes eligible for an HSA part way through the year to make or receive contributions up to the maximum annual limit for his or her type of HDHP coverage (e.g., self-only or family) as of December 1 of that year.

An employer who makes the maximum calendar year HSA contribution, or who contributes more than a pro-rata amount, on behalf of employees who are mid-year eligible individuals will not fail to satisfy comparability merely because some employees will have received more contributions on a monthly basis than employees who worked the entire calendar year.

On the other hand, if an employer contributes more than the monthly pro-rata amount for the calendar year to the HSA of any employee who is a mid-year eligible individual, the employer must then contribute, on an equal and uniform basis, a greater than pro-rata amount to the HSAs of all comparable participating employees who are mid-year eligible individuals. Likewise, if the employer contributes the maximum annual contribution amount for the calendar year to the HSA of any employee who is a mid-year eligible individual, the employer must contribute the maximum amount to the HSAs of all comparable participating employees who are mid-year eligible individuals. [Treas. Reg. § 54.4980G-4 Q&A-2(h)]

> **Example 3.** On January 1, Quark Co. contributes $1,000 for the calendar year to the HSAs of employees who are eligible individuals with family HDHP coverage. In mid-March, Quark hires Ann, an eligible individual with family HDHP coverage. On April 1, Quark contributes $1,000 to Ann's HSA. In September, Bill becomes an eligible individual with HDHP coverage and on October 1, Quark contributes $1,000 to Bill's HSA. Quark does not make any other HSA contributions for the year. Quark's contributions satisfy the comparability rules.

Bear in mind, however, that an employer is not required to provide more than a pro-rata contribution based on the number of months an employee was an eligible individual and worked for the employer during the year.

> **Example 4.** For a calendar year, Rex Corp. has two employees, Carol and David. Carol, who is an eligible individual with family HDHP coverage, works for Rex for the entire year. David, who is also an eligible individual with family HDHP coverage, works for Rex from July 1 through December 31. Rex Corp. contributes $1,200 to Carol's HSA and $600 to David's HSA. Rex Corp. does not make any other HSA contributions for the year. Rex Corp.'s HSA contributions satisfy the comparability rules.

Qualified HSA distributions. An employer may permit employees to make qualified HSA distributions from a health FSA or HRA (see Q 3:153). The full range of comparability rules does not apply to qualified HSA distributions. However, if a qualified HSA distribution is offered to any employee covered under any HDHP, the employer must offer qualified HSA distributions to all eligible employees covered under any HDHP. However, if the employer offers HSA distributions only to employees covered under the employer's HDHP, the employer is not required to offer qualified HSA distributions to employees who are not covered under the employee's HDHP. [Treas. Reg. § 54.4980G-7]

Q 3:174   What are the special comparability rules for contributions to the HSAs of non-highly compensated employees?

Employers may make larger HSA contributions for NHCEs who are comparable participating employees than for HCEs who are comparable participating employees. In other words, HCEs are not taken into account for purposes of applying the comparability rules to an employer's contributions for NHCEs. [I.R.C. § 4980G(d); Treas. Reg. § 54.4980G-6 Q&A-1]

However, employer may not make larger contributions for HCEs than for NHCEs who are comparable participating employees. In other words, both HCEs and NHCEs are taken into account in determining whether contributions for HCEs meet the comparability rules. [Treas. Reg. § 54.4980G-6 Q&A-2]

Thus, an employer can make contributions for all comparable NHCEs without making any contributions (or making smaller, but not larger, contributions) for HCEs.

Example 1. Alpha Co. contributes $1,000 for the calendar year to the HSA of each full-time NHCE who is an eligible individual with self-only HDHP coverage. Alpha does not contribute to the HSA of any full-time HCE who is an eligible individual with self-only HDHP coverage. Alpha's contributions satisfy the comparability rules.

Example 2. Beta Corp. contributes $2,000 for the calendar year to the HSA of each full-time NHCE with self-only HDHP coverage and contributes $1,000 for the HSA of each full-time HCE with self-only HDHP coverage. Beta's contributions satisfy the comparability rules.

Example 3. Gamma Co. contributes $1,000 for the calendar year to the HSA of each full-time NHCE with self-only HDHP coverage. For the same calendar year, Gamma contributes $2,000 to the HSA of each full-time HCE with self-only HDHP coverage. Gamma's contributions do not satisfy the comparability rules.

Example 4. Delta Corp. contributes $1,000 for the calendar year to the HSA of each full-time non-management NHCE with family HDHP coverage. Delta contributes $500 for the calendar year to the HSA of each full-time management NHCE with family HDHP coverage. Delta's contributions do not satisfy the comparability rules because the NHCEs did not all receive comparable contributions.

The regulations make it clear that the special rules for NHCEs do not override the rule that an employer may break down employees into categories for comparability testing (see Q 3:172)—even if one of those categories is composed solely of HCEs. Under those rules an employer can make different contributions for employees with different level of family HDHP coverage so long as the contribution for the self-plus-two category is not less than the contributions for the self-plus-one category and the contribution for the self-plus-three-or-more category is not less than the contribution for the self-plus-two category. Thus, for example, the comparability rules will not be violated if an employer makes larger HSA contributions for the self-plus-two category than for the self-plus-one category, even if the employees in the self-plus-two category are all HCEs and the employees in the self-plus-one category are all NHCEs.

For comparability testing purposes, HCEs are defined in Code Section 414(q).

Q 3:175   How are comparable contributions made?

There are three ways to make comparable contributions:

1. Pay-as-you-go contributions—An employer makes periodic contributions during the calendar year to the HSAs of all employees who are eligible individuals as of the first day of the first month of period.

2. Look-back contributions—An employer makes contributions at the end of a period, taking into account all employees who were eligible individuals for any month during the period.

3. Prefunded contributions—An employer makes contributions for the entire calendar year to the HSAs of all employees who are eligible individuals at the beginning of the calendar year.

With both the pay-as you-go and look-back methods, an employer can set the periods for making contributions (e.g., a quarterly period covering three consecutive months in a calendar year) and the dates on which contributions will be made (e.g., the first day of the quarter or the last day of the quarter).

Given that HSA contributions are nonforfeitable, the employer cannot recoup pay-as-you go contributions if an employee terminates employment during the period. The IRS says an employer that makes contributions on a pay-as-you-go basis for a period covering more than one month will not violate the comparability rule because an employee who terminates employment before the end of the period receives more contributions on a monthly basis than employees who work the entire period. On the other hand, an employer that makes contributions on a pay-as-you-go basis for a period covering more than one month is not off the hook when it comes to contributions for employees who are hired after contributions for a period have been made. The employer must make HSA contributions for any comparable participating employees hired after the date of contribution for that period.

Example 1. Magma Corp. uses a quarterly period for making HSA contributions on a pay-as-you-go basis. It contributes $50 per month for each eligible employee. On January 1, Magma contributes $150 for Jason, who is an eligible employee on that date. On January 15, Jason terminates employment with Magma. In January, Magma hires Fred, who becomes an eligible individual as of February 1. Magma contributes $100 to Fred's HSA for the two months (February and March) in the quarter that Fred is an eligible employee. Magma's contributions of $150 for Jason and $100 for Fred satisfy the comparability rules.

Example 2. The facts are the same as those in Example 1, except that Magma makes contributions at the end of each quarter on a look-back basis. On March 31, Magma contributes $50 for Jason, who was eligible on the first day of one month in the quarter, and $100 for Fred, who was eligible on the first day of two months in the quarter. Magma's contributions satisfy the comparability rule.

As with pay-as-you-go contributions, an employer that prefunds employees' HSAs will not violate the comparability rules because an employee who terminates employment prior to the end of the calendar year has received more contributions on a monthly basis than the employees who work the entire calendar year. In addition, as with pay-as-you-go contributions, an employer must make comparable contributions for eligible employees who are hired after the initial funding. In this situation, the employer can make prefunded contributions for new hires or it can make contributions for new hires on a pay-as-you-go or look-back basis. However, the employer must use the same contribution method for all new hires.

> **Example.** On January 1, Delta Corp. makes prefunded contributions of $1,200 for the calendar year to the HSA of each employee who is an eligible individual on that date. In mid-May, Delta hires Ken, who becomes an eligible individual as of June 1. Delta is required to make comparable contributions to Ken's HSA beginning with June. Delta has three options for making Ken's contributions:
>
> 1. Prefunding Ken's HSA by contributing $700;
> 2. Contributing $100 per month to Ken's HSA on a pay-as-you-go basis; or
> 3. Making a look-back contribution of $100 per month to Ken's HSA for each month that Ken was an eligible individual and employed by Delta.

Accelerated contributions. Final regulations issued in 2008 give employers another option for funding employees' HSAs. The regulations provide that an employer can accelerate all or part of its annual contributions to the HSAs of employees who have incurred qualified medical expenses in excess of the employer's cumulative contributions up to that time. Accelerated contributions must be available on an equal and uniform basis to all employees throughout the calendar year. In addition, the employer must establish uniform requirements for the acceleration of contributions and determination of medical expenses. [Treas. Reg. § 54.4980G-4, Q&A-15]

Failure to establish an HSA. If an employee has not set up an HSA (or has established an HSA but not notified the employer) at the time the employer funds employees' HSAs, the employer will satisfy the comparability rule if it contributes required amounts plus reasonable interest to the employee's HSA when the employee establishes or notifies the employer of the HSA. The determination of whether an interest rate is reasonable will be based on all of the facts and circumstances. However, interest at the federal short-term rate will be deemed reasonable.

Final regulations issued in 2008 provide that an employer must comply with a notice requirement to meet the comparability rules for an employee who has not set up an HSA by year-end or who has not notified the employer of the establishment of an HSA. [Treas. Reg. § 54.4980G-4, Q&A-14] Specifically, the employer must provide written notice to the employee by January 15 of the year following the year for which contributions are to be made stating that the employee will receive comparable contributions if he or she establishes an HSA and so informs the employer by the last day of February. If the employee establishes the HSA and informs the employer by the last day of February, the employer must contribute the required amount plus reasonable interest to the employee's HSA by April 15.

Noncomparable contributions. The IRS regulations provide that the following contributions will *not* be considered comparable:

1. Matching contributions equal to the employee's HSA contribution or a percentage of the employee's HSA contribution;

2. Contributions conditioned on an employee's participation in health assessments, disease management programs, or wellness programs;

3. Additional contributions for employees who have attained a specified age or who have worked for the employer for a specified number of years; and

4. Additional contributions for employees who are eligible to make HSA catch-up contributions.

Q 3:176   Can an employer recoup excess noncomparable contributions from an employee's HSA?

No. An employee's interest in an HSA is nonforfeitable. Therefore, an employer cannot "fix" noncomparable contributions by recouping excess contributions from an employee's HSA. However, an employer can make *additional* HSA contributions to other employees' HSAs to satisfy the comparability rules. These contributions can be made up until April 15 following the calendar year in which the noncomparable contributions were made. An employer that makes additional HSA contributions to correct noncomparable contributions must also contribute reasonable interest. However, an employer is not required to contribute amounts in excess of the annual contribution limit for an employee's category of HDHP coverage.

Q 3:177   Do the comparability rules apply to HSA contributions made through a cafeteria plan?

The comparability rules do not apply to salary reduction HSA contributions made through a cafeteria plan if employees have the right to elect to receive cash or other taxable benefits in lieu of all or a portion of an HSA contribution. Moreover, an employer's cafeteria plan contributions to an HSA may be made on a matching basis or may be conditioned on participation in health assessments, disease management programs, or wellness programs.

Bear in mind, however, that nondiscrimination rules (including eligibility rules) under Code Section 125 do apply to HSA contributions made through cafeteria plans (see chapter 7). [Prop. Treas. Reg. § 1.125-7(n)]

Example 1. The Diebold Company written cafeteria plan permits employees to elect to receive cash or other benefits or to make pre-tax salary reduction contributions to their HSAs. Diebold automatically contributes a nonelective matching contribution to the HSA of each employee who makes a pretax HSA contribution. The Section 125 cafeteria plan nondiscrimination rules and not the comparability rules apply to Diebold's HSA contributions because the HSA contributions are made through the cafeteria plan.

Example 2. The facts are the same as those in Example 1, except that The Diebold Company makes nonelective contributions to HSAs only for employees who complete a health risk assessment and participate in a wellness program. The Section 125 cafeteria plan nondiscrimination rules and not the comparability rules apply to Diebold's HSA contributions because the HSA contributions are made through the cafeteria plan.

Q 3:178   What are the reporting rules for an HSA?

HSA trustees or custodians must report both contributions and distributions to account holders. In addition, employers must report contributions to an HSA in box 12 of an employee's Form W-2 using Code W (Employer's contribution to an employee's Health Savings Account (HSA). Employees must report annual contributions to and distributions from an HSA on their federal income tax returns.

Q 3:179   Are HSAs subject to COBRA continuation coverage under Code Section 4980B?

No. Like Archer MSAs, HSAs are not subject to COBRA continuation coverage.

Q 3:180   May eligible individuals use debit, credit, or stored-value cards to receive distributions from an HSA for qualified medical expenses?

Yes. The use of debit, credit, or stored-value cards are not subject to the substantiation requirements that apply to HRAs (see Q 3:163) or health FSAs (see chapter 7). Substantiation is not required because HSA funds can be used for nonmedical purposes. Funds used for nonmedical purposes must be reported as income on an employee's tax return and are subject to a penalty unless an exception applies.

> **Note.** The 2010 Health Reform Act narrows the definition of medical care for purposes of HSAs and other reimbursement arrangements. Effective for expenses incurred after December 31, 2010, the 2010 Health Reform Act generally bars tax-free treatment for reimbursements for OTC medicines or drugs, unless the medicine or drug is prescribed by a physician. [I.R.C. § 106(f), as added by PPACA § 9003] Consequently, HSA funds used for nonprescription drugs must be reported as income.

An HSA debit card may restrict payments to health care expenses, but only if the funds in the HSA are otherwise readily available. For example, in addition to the restricted debit card, the HSA account beneficiary must also be able to access the funds other than by purchasing health care with the debit card, such as through online transfers, withdrawals from automatic teller machines or check writing. An employer must notify employees that other access to the funds is available. [IRS Notice 2008-59 Q&A-27, 2008-59 I.R.B. 123]

The Federal Trade Commission (FTC) has issued new regulations to protect consumers from identity theft. [16 C.F.R. Pt. 681] The so-called Red Flag Rules were developed pursuant to the Fair and Accurate Credit Transactions (FACT) Act of 2003. [Pub. L. No. 108-159, 117 Stat. 1952] The rules require financial institutions and creditors with covered accounts to implement theft prevention programs to identify, detect, and respond to patterns, practices, or specific activities that could indicate identity theft. Compliance is required by June 1, 2010. As noted in Q 3:135, the FTC has made it clear that health care FSAs (and, presumably, HSAs) are not generally subject to the red flag rules. However, if an account includes a debit card feature, the issuer of the cards—typically, a third-party administrator acting on behalf of a sponsoring employer—will be considered a "financial institution" for purposes of the red flag rules and must implement identity theft protections. Consequently, employers that sponsor HSAs with a debit card feature should confirm that the card issuer is in compliance with the new rules.

Q 3:181   Can an HSA account holder authorize someone else to withdraw funds from his or her HSA?

Yes. Although an HSA is an individual account, an HSA account holder can designate other individuals (e.g., a spouse or dependents) to withdraw funds pursuant to the procedures of the trustee or custodian of the HSA. Distributions are subject to tax if they are not used to pay for qualified medical expenses for the HSA account holder, the account holder's spouse, or dependents. [IRS Notice 2008-59 Q&A-28, 2008-59 I.R.B. 123]

Q 3:182   Can a partnership or S corporation contribute to an HSA on behalf of a partner or S corporation shareholder-employee?

Yes. A partnership may contribute to a partner's HSA, and an S corporation may contribute to the HSA of a shareholder-employee. [IRS Notice 2005-8, 2005-4 I.R.B. 1] However, the contributions are subject to special tax rules.

Q 3:183   What is the tax treatment of a partnership's contributions to a partner's HSA?

Contributions by a partnership to a bona fide partner's HSA are not contributions by an employer to the HSA of an employee. [Rev. Rul. 69-184, 1969-1 C.B. 256] Instead, the partnership contributions may be treated either as distributions to the partner [I.R.C. § 731] or as guaranteed payments for services rendered to the partnership. [I.R.C. § 707(c); IRS Notice 2005-8, 2005-4 I.R.B. 1]

Contributions by a partnership to a partner's HSA that are treated as distributions to the partner are not deductible by the partnership and do not affect the distributive shares of partnership income and deductions. The contributions are reported as distributions of money on Schedule K-1 (Form 1065). However, the distributions are not included in the partner's net earnings from self-employment because the distributions do not affect a partner's distributive share of partnership income or loss. Assuming he or she meets the eligibility requirements, the partner can deduct the amount of the contributions made to his or her HSA during the taxable year as an adjustment to gross income on his or her federal income tax return under Code Sections 223(a) and 62(a)(19).

Contributions to a partner's HSA that are treated as guaranteed payments are deductible by the partnership as a trade or business expense [I.R.C. § 162] and are includable in the partner's gross income. The contributions are not excludable from the partner's gross income as employer-provided HSA contributions under Code Section 106(d) because the contributions are treated as a distributive share of partnership income. [Treas. Reg. § 1.707-1(c)] Contributions from a partnership to a partner's HSA that are treated as guaranteed payments are reported as guaranteed payments on Schedule K-1 (Form 1065). Because the contributions are guaranteed payments that are derived from the partnership's trade or business, and are for services rendered to the partnership, the contributions are included in the partner's net earnings from self-employment. Assuming the partner meets the eligibility requirements, he or she can deduct the amount of the contributions made to the HSA during the taxable year as an adjustment to gross income on his or her federal income tax return under Code Sections 223(a) and 62(a)(19).

Q 3:184   What is the tax treatment of an S corporation's contributions to the HSA of a shareholder-employee?

When it comes to fringe benefits, an S corporation is treated as a partnership, and any 2-percent shareholder of the S corporation is treated as a partner of such partnership. [I.R.C. § 1372] (A shareholder-employee owning less than 2 percent of the corporation is treated like any other employee.) Therefore, contributions by an S corporation to an HSA of a 2-percent shareholder-employee in consideration for services rendered are treated as guaranteed payments. [I.R.C. § 707(c)] The contributions are deductible by the S corporation and are includable in the 2-percent shareholder-employee's gross income. The 2-percent shareholder-employee cannot exclude the contribution from gross income as employer-provided HSA contributions under Code Section 106(d). [Rev. Rul. 91-26, 1991-1 C.B. 184]

For employment tax purposes, when contributions are made by an S corporation to an HSA of a 2-percent shareholder-employee, the 2-percent shareholder-employee is treated as an employee subject to regular Social Security and Medicare (FICA) tax and not as an individual subject to self-employment (SECA) tax. [IRS Ann. 92-16, 1992-5 I.R.B. 53] However, contributions to an HSA of a 2-percent shareholder-employee are not wages subject to FICA tax, even though the amounts must be included in wages for income tax withholding purposes. [I.R.C. § 3121(a)(2)(B)] Assuming he or she meets the eligibility requirements, the 2-percent shareholder-employee can deduct the amount of the contributions as an adjustment to gross income on his or her federal income tax return. [IRS Notice 2005-8, 2005-4 I.R.B. 1]

Q 3:185   Are HSAs subject to ERISA?

According to the DOL, HSAs generally do not constitute employee welfare benefit plans subject to ERISA where employer involvement is limited.

Employer contributions to an HSA do not give rise to an ERISA-covered plan if establishment of all of the following conditions are met:

1. Establishment of an HSA is completely voluntary on the part of an employee;
2. The employer does not limit the ability to move funds to another HSA;
3. The employer does not impose conditions on the use of HSA funds beyond those permitted by the Internal Revenue Code;
4. The employer does not make or influence investment decisions regarding the HSA funds;
5. The employer does not represent that the HSA is an employee welfare benefit plan; and
6. The employer does not receive payment or compensation in connection with the HSA.

[DOL Field Assist. Bull. 2004-01 (Apr. 7, 2004)]

This does not mean that an employer's involvement with an HSA must be strictly hands off. For example, the DOL says that an employer may open an HSA for an employee and make employer contributions without violating the requirement that establishment of an HSA be voluntary on the part of an employee. The "completely voluntary" requirement is designed to ensure that employee contributions are voluntary. In addition, the employer may select or limit the HSA providers that it allows to market products in the workplace without converting the HSA into an ERISA plan. On the other hand, if an employer receives a discount on other products in return for selecting an HSA vendor, the employer would be treated as receiving payment or compensation in connection with the HSA—and this would subject the plan to ERISA and give rise to fiduciary responsibility and prohibited transaction issues. [DOL Field Assist. Bull. 2006-02 (Oct. 21, 2006)]

Employee Assistance Programs

Q 3:186   What is an employee assistance program?

An *employee assistance program* (EAP) is an employer-provided benefit that may encompass counseling, referrals, and possibly treatment for a stated list of concerns, such as:

- Anxiety
- Stress
- Depression
- Drug abuse

- Alcoholism
- Work problems
- Family or marital problems
- Child care needs
- Adolescent problems
- Elder care needs (relating to a sick or elderly parent, parent-in-law, or other family member)
- Financial worries
- Legal concerns

EAPs run the gamut from being fairly limited in the scope of services covered to being broad-based programs designed to address numerous issues that affect workplace productivity. For example, a particular employer's EAP may focus solely on drug and alcohol abuse, while another employer's EAP may focus on everything from caring for a parent with Alzheimer's disease or a child with AIDS to marital counseling.

Q 3:187   Why do employers make EAPs available to their employees?

EAPs originally started as more or less informal programs to address lost workplace productivity due to excessive drinking and alcoholism. They have developed as a mechanism for an employer to help control the following situations that can result from substance abuse or other stressful personal and/or family circumstances:

- Absenteeism and tardiness
- Impaired workplace productivity
- Workplace accidents
- Increased health costs associated with employee impairment
- Emotional and financial distress

Q 3:188   What are the basic types of EAPs?

It has been said that no two EAPs are alike. Despite the variability among individual employers' programs, they can be roughly classified into a few groups.

First, EAPS may be internal or external. An internal EAP is an in-house program that may be affiliated with the employer's personnel department or medical department. An external EAP is a third-party organization that contracts with the employer to provide EAP services through its own network of professionals, counselors, and referral services in return for a monthly fee.

Second, EAPs may be roughly divided according to how comprehensive their services are. Full-service EAPs combine diagnosis, counseling, and referral for treatment or services. Often, a series of visits to a counselor or referral provider, such as two to seven visits, will be covered. Less comprehensive EAPs operate more like central clearinghouses for information and referral regarding services such as day care, elder care, community-based counseling programs, part-time nursing services, and companion services. Some EAPs consist of a telephone hotline to a trained counselor who makes an assessment and provides a referral to sources of professional help or community services, as indicated. To the extent the hotline is accompanied by a panoply of services, the hotline-type EAP will fall into the full-service or assessment and referral group.

If the EAP does not cover the cost of the referral services or covers only a certain number of visits, some of the referral services may qualify as covered medical expenses under the employer's medical plan.

Q 3:189   Is EAP participation voluntary?

EAP participation may be voluntary, through self-referral, or it may be suggested by the manager of an employee whose performance appears to be impaired. Some employer programs also make referral to an EAP mandatory upon identification of an employee as a substance abuser.

Q 3:190   Are EAP services always confidential?

EAPs generally are designed to provide a confidential source of help for employees. Some EAPs involve disclosure to the employer, such as to the employer's medical department or personnel department. Such disclosure may raise numerous employment law issues, including issues related to medical privacy. EAPs that offer medical services such as substance abuse or mental health counseling, fall within the definition of health plans subject to medical privacy regulations. By contrast, "referral-only" EAPs would not typically be considered health plans. (See chapter 5 for a detailed discussion of the privacy regulations.)

Q 3:191   Is an EAP an ERISA plan?

Although EAPs do not resemble conventional employee benefit programs, they may nonetheless fall within the scope of ERISA's definition of an employee welfare benefit plan. Under Section 3(1) of ERISA, an employee welfare plan includes plans that are established or maintained to provide, among other things, benefits in the event of sickness, accident, or disability. Although an EAP may cover various unconventional services, it may also cover benefits in the event of sickness or disability and thus constitute an ERISA plan.

The DOL has issued several advisory opinion letters on this issue, taking the position that benefits for the treatment of drug and alcohol abuse, stress, anxiety, depression, and similar health and medical problems constitute "medical" benefits or benefits "in the event of sickness, accident, or disability" within the meaning of Section 3(1) of ERISA. The medical privacy regulations reinforce this view by providing that EAPs that offer medical services such as substance abuse or mental health counseling fall within the definition of health plans subject to the privacy rules (see chapter 5).

A narrower question is presented by an EAP that provides only an initial evaluation and referral. If the initial assessment is performed by a trained health professional or counselor, it is possible that an ERISA plan will exist. The Court of Appeals for the Sixth Circuit found an EAP to be an ERISA plan. [*In re* General Motors Corp., 3 F.3d 980 (6th Cir. 1993)]

However, if the EAP coordinator has no special training and simply makes referrals from a published list of community resources, the EAP will not be considered an ERISA plan. The DOL found such a "bare-bones" program not to constitute an ERISA plan, because:

- The EAP provided only telephone referrals and not medical benefits or benefits in the event of sickness within the meaning of Section 3(1) of ERISA.
- The EAP toll-free number and hotline provided no more than generally available public information when making telephone referrals to employees. (Referrals were made to agencies selected from an annual publication of the Florida Department of Health and Rehabilitative Services.)
- The EAP coordinators had no special training in counseling or a related discipline.
- The EAP did not employ any counselors, on either an in-house or a contractual basis.
- Other than the initial referral, the EAP did not provide any other benefits free of charge.

[DOL Adv. Op. No. 91-26A (July 19, 1991); *see also* DOL Adv. Op. Nos. 92-12A (Apr. 20, 1992), 83-35A (June 27, 1993)]

Q 3:192   What are the consequences of an EAP being an ERISA plan?

If the EAP meets the definition of an ERISA welfare benefit plan, then all of the ERISA duties and responsibilities apply, including the reporting and disclosure requirements of Title I of ERISA.

The employer would be required, among other things, to take the following actions:

1. Prepare and distribute an SPD, updated as necessary via a summary of material modifications (SMM);
2. File the SPD and SMM with the DOL; and
3. File a Form 5500 annual report with the DOL unless an exemption applies (see chapter 2).

The DOL has not yet addressed how an employer is to provide full and fair review of an appeal of a denied claim under a confidential EAP.

Q 3:193   Is an EAP subject to COBRA?

Yes. If the EAP falls within the definition of an ERISA welfare benefit plan and it also provides "medical care" as defined in Code Section 213, then COBRA continuation rights must be offered. [ERISA § 607(1), 29 U.S.C. § 1167(1)] (COBRA is discussed in detail in chapter 6.)

Workers' Compensation

Q 3:194   Are employers required to provide employees with medical benefits under state workers' compensation laws?

Generally, yes. State workers' compensation laws require employers to provide benefits for job-related injuries and sickness. All such laws provide for reimbursement of medical expenses as one of the required benefits (disability income benefits and death benefits are also generally required benefits).

Q 3:195   Are medical benefit plans maintained in compliance with the requirements of state workers' compensation laws subject to ERISA?

A plan maintained solely for the purpose of complying with applicable state disability or workers' compensation laws is not subject to ERISA. [ERISA § 4(b)(3)]

However, rather than maintain a separately administered plan for workers' compensation benefits, some employers maintain a medical benefit plan for their employees that provides the medical benefits required by state workers' compensation laws as well as benefits for non-job-related injuries. The Supreme Court has held that such a multibenefit plan is subject to ERISA and that the application of a state workers' compensation law to the plan is preempted.

The first time the Supreme Court considered the issue, the state law in question concerned disability benefits (which presented the identical ERISA issues as would a state workers' compensation law). In reviewing the applicability of the ERISA workers' compensation plan exclusion to a multibenefit ERISA plan designed to satisfy a state's disability benefits law, the court reasoned that since the ERISA exclusion applies to plans, not portions of plans, a state cannot regulate the disability benefits portion of an employer's multibenefit ERISA plan. However, the court stated that a state can require an employer to maintain a separate plan solely to meet the state law requirements if, in the state's judgment, the disability benefits portion of the employer's multibenefit ERISA plan falls short of the state requirements. This latter holding stems from the court's concern that employers will attempt to combine benefits not meeting the state requirements with other benefits in multibenefit ERISA plans, thereby avoiding falling into the Section 4(b)(3) exclusion from ERISA, in order to invoke ERISA preemption. If the state is not satisfied that the multibenefit ERISA plan satisfies the state requirements, it may compel the employer to maintain a separate plan that does comply. [Shaw v. Delta Airlines, 463 U.S. 85 (1983)]

In the *Shaw* decision, significantly, the Supreme Court drew a distinction between a "front-end" analysis (whether the plan is an ERISA plan at all) and a "back-end" analysis (once it is determined that a plan is in fact an ERISA plan, ERISA Section 514 prevents states from regulating the plan directly under its disability and workers' compensation laws). The Court explained that it was not holding that Section 514 preempts state disability laws, evidently out of a concern that the front-end analysis would be skipped over too lightly. However, it should be noted that if a plan is an ERISA plan under the front-end analysis, then the result is precisely that; a state workers' compensation or disability benefits law cannot regulate the plan directly under the back-end analysis and is preempted. The Court's rather awkward explanation in *Shaw* has caused some confusion to persist. There have been attempts to hook various benefit requirements onto state workers' compensation laws and make them stick under the *Shaw* analysis.

The Supreme Court held such enlargements of state workers' compensation laws to be preempted by ERISA. [District of Columbia v. Greater Washington Bd. of Trade, 113 S. Ct. 580 (1992)] In the *Greater Washington* case, the Court considered whether ERISA preempted a provision of the workers' compensation law of the District of Columbia. Under the D.C. law provision, any employer providing plan coverage for an employee was required to provide health plan coverage equivalent to the existing health plan coverage during the period the employee received or was eligible to receive workers' compensation benefits (to a maximum of 52 weeks). The Court found that the D.C. law provision was preempted by ERISA because the benefits under the provision were tied to the level of benefits under the employer's ERISA plan, and the provision applied only to employers already providing benefits under ERISA plans.

The Supreme Court stated that the D.C. law specifically referred to welfare benefit plans regulated by ERISA and on that basis alone was preempted. Dismissing the District's argument that the law was part of its regulatory scheme for ERISA-exempt workers' compensation plans and its attempt to use *Shaw* to bolster its position, the Court stated:

> It makes no difference that [the extension of health coverage provisions] are part of the District's regulation of, and therefore also "relate to," ERISA-exempt workers' compensation plans. The exemptions from ERISA coverage set out in § 4(b), 29 U.S.C. § 1003(b), do not limit the preemptive sweep of § 514 once it is determined that the law in question relates to an ERISA-covered plan. See *Alessi v. Raybestos-Manhattan, Inc.*, 451 U.S. 504, 525 (1981) ("It is of no moment that New Jersey intrudes indirectly through a workers' compensation law, rather than directly, through a statute called 'pension regulation.'").

In *Greater Washington*, the Court attempted to clarify its *Shaw* analysis of when the ERISA Section 4(b)(3) front-end analysis is appropriate and when the ERISA Section 514 back-end analysis is appropriate. It pointed out that the statute in *Shaw* did not relate to ERISA plans, whereas the attempted extension of life and health insurance coverage at issue in *Greater Washington* did:

We held that . . . [New York's Disability Benefits Law] was not preempted by ERISA § 514(a) because it related exclusively to exempt employee benefit plans "maintained solely for the purpose of complying with applicable . . . disability insurance laws" within the meaning of § 4(b)(3). . . . [citation omitted] The fact that employers could comply with the New York law by administering the required disability benefits through a multibenefit ERISA plan did not mean that the law related to such ERISA plans for preemption purposes. [citation omitted] We simply held that as long as the employer's disability plan, "as an administrative unit, provide[d] only those benefits required by" the New York law, it could qualify as an exempt plan under ERISA § 4(b)(3). [citation omitted]. . . . As we have explained, the Disability Benefits Law upheld in *Shaw*—though mandating the creation of a "welfare plan" as defined in ERISA—did not relate to a welfare plan subject to ERISA regulation. [emphasis added] [The District of Columbia statute] does, and that is the end of the matter. [*Greater Washington*, 113 S. Ct. 580, 584]

The *Greater Washington* decision also overturned a contrary ruling by the Court of Appeals for the Second Circuit concerning a virtually identical Connecticut law. At issue in the Second Circuit case was a provision of the Connecticut workers' compensation statute that required employers that provide accident and health insurance or life insurance for employees to continue to do so for employees receiving or eligible to receive workers' compensation. The Connecticut law also provided that employers could do so by, among other alternatives, creating an injured employee's plan as an extension of any existing plan for working employees or by self-insurance. Seizing upon the language in *Shaw* concerning a state's ability to force the employer to choose between providing disability benefits in a separately administered plan and including the state-mandated benefits in its ERISA plan, a federal appellate court read it to mean that Connecticut could force the creation of a separate administrative unit within the ERISA plan to provide for this extension of health coverage. Accordingly, the appellate court held that the Connecticut statute was not preempted by ERISA Section 514, because it fell within the ERISA Section 4(b)(3) exception. The Supreme Court rejected this type of argument in *Greater Washington*, essentially stating that once the front-end ERISA coverage hurdle is cleared by a multibenefit ERISA plan, the back-end Section 514 preemption analysis is limited to whether the state law is preempted from applying to the employer's ERISA medical plan as it is presently constituted:

[P]etitioners argue that § 514(a) should be construed to require a two-step analysis: if the state law "relate[s] to" an ERISA-covered plan, it may still survive preemption if employers could comply with the [state workers' compensation] law through separately administered plans exempt under $4(b). . . . We cannot engraft a two-step analysis onto a one-step statute.

[R.R. Donnelley & Sons Co. v. Prevost, 915 F.2d 787 (2d Cir. 1990), *cert. denied*, 111 S. Ct. 1415 (1991), *overruled by*, District of Columbia v. Greater Washington Bd. of Trade, 113 S. Ct. 580 (1992)]

It now seems clear from several federal court decisions that ERISA does not preempt state workers' compensation laws (assuming, of course, that they do not attempt to regulate ERISA plans) and that a state may force an employer to maintain a separate workers' compensation plan meeting state requirements. [Employee Staffing Servs. Inc. v. Aubry, 18 Employee Benefits Cas. (BNA) 1033 (9th Cir. 1994); Barker v. Pick N Pull Auto Dismantlers Inc., Civ. S 91-1695, 819 F. Supp. 889 (E.D. Cal. 1993); Gomes v. Pick N Pull Auto Parts Inc., Civ. S 92-1722, 819 F. Supp. 889 (E.D. Cal. 1993)]

The *Aubry* case is particularly notable because of the state of California's aggressive approach. In *Aubry,* an ERISA-covered trust offering group health plan benefits, including workers' compensation benefits, was provided by a multiemployer trade and bargaining association to its employee-members. The state issued a stop-work order to one of the employers that employed some of the association's members, claiming that the association had failed to demonstrate that it complied with California's workers' compensation requirements. Although the association claimed that ERISA preempted the application of California's workers' compensation law to its plan, the Court of Appeals for the Ninth Circuit held that the state was not attempting to regulate or intrude upon the employer's trust and that the state's separate plan requirement was not preempted by ERISA.

A similar result was reached by the Court of Appeals for the Fourth Circuit in *Employers Resource Management Co. v. James.* [62 F.3d 627 (4th Cir. 1995)] In that case, the court upheld a Virginia workers' compensation law on the grounds that it only required employers to create separate workers' compensation plans. The ERISA preemption argument was also rejected by the Court of Appeals for the Tenth Circuit, which upheld an Oklahoma workers' compensation law that requires employers to provide workers' compensation insurance through approved insurance carriers or qualified self-insured plans. [Contract Servs. Employee Trust v. Davis, 55 F.3d 533 (10th Cir. 1995)]

Q 3:196   If an employer maintains a medical benefit plan subject to ERISA that provides coverage for job-related injuries or illnesses, are an employee's tort remedies against the employer under state law preempted?

Apparently not. In a U.S. district court decision, the court held that an employee's state court suit for personal injuries on the job, which were alleged to have been caused by the employer's negligence, was not preempted, even though the employer had an ERISA plan providing for medical and other benefits for such job-related injuries. The fact that the employee was covered under an ERISA of plan and could claim benefits for medical expenses arising from the job-related injuries was not considered to make the lawsuit sufficiently "related to" the plan to justify preemption of the state law action. [Eurine v. Wyatt Cafeterias Inc., 14 Employee Benefits Cas. (BNA) 1655 (N.D. Tex. 1991); *see also* Nunez v. Wyatt Cafeterias Inc., 14 Employee Benefits Cas. (BNA) 1388 (N.D. Tex. 1991)]

The Fifth Circuit Court of Appeals considered a case under Texas's workers' compensation statute. The statute, like those of many other states, made the benefits distributed under the Texas Workers' Compensation Act the employee's exclusive remedy for work-related injuries or death. The statute contained a feature that differs from many other states: Texas's scheme permits employers to opt out and not carry workers' compensation coverage under the statute. Employers can self-insure the risk, but Texas makes that alternative unattractive by vesting employees of nonsubscribing employers with the right to sue their employers for work-related injuries or death. In any such action, the nonsubscribing employer is also barred from using traditional common-law defenses such as contributory negligence and assumption of the risk.

The employer in this Texas case opted out of the statutory workers' compensation insurance and offered its own plan. The plan's terms also attempted to limit the participant's sole remedy for a workplace injury to the plan's benefits. The employee in question fell down a staircase and was injured. After she received her plan benefit for medical expenses and salary continuation, she sued for negligence. The employer claimed that the action was preempted by ERISA because it related to an ERISA plan. The Fifth Circuit disagreed, holding that the dispute regarding an unsafe workplace claim, standing alone, is not preempted by ERISA, because it affects only the employer/employee relationship and not the administrator/beneficiary relationship and is totally independent of the existence and administration of the ERISA plan. Notably, the employee was not seeking benefits under the plan nor claiming that the employer improperly processed her claim for benefits. Rather, the claim was related solely to damages for alleged negligent maintenance of the workplace.

Of major concern to the court was a plan sponsor's potential ability to nullify state law claims unrelated to an ERISA plan merely by asserting waivers in ERISA plans. The Fifth Circuit concluded that the waiver provision in the employer's workers' compensation plan does not invoke ERISA preemption; the proper inquiry for a preemption analysis is whether the state law in question relates to an ERISA plan. The Fifth Circuit then applied a traditional ERISA preemption analysis to the Texas statute and concluded that it did not relate to an ERISA plan and thus was not preempted, and the employee's negligence suit was permitted to proceed. [Hook v. Morrison Milling Co., 18 Employee Benefits Cas. (BNA) 2485 (5th Cir. 1994)]

Practice Pointer. In three states (New Jersey, South Carolina, and Texas) an employer is permitted to opt out of workers' compensation insurance coverage. In those states, or in any other state where an employer may be permitted to establish an ERISA plan not subject to the minimum requirements of the state workers' compensation law, the employer should carefully consider the effect of not subjecting itself to the state workers' compensation law coverage. The workers' compensation laws, while taking away from employers certain common-law defenses, can also provide advantages to employers by limiting the extent of employee recoveries.

Chapter 4

Retiree Medical Benefits

Retiree medical benefits have been the subject of intense interest and scrutiny for more than a decade. Employers faced with rising cost have taken steps to cut back or terminate retiree medical plans—while retirees faced with a loss of promised benefits have fought back vigorously.

The 2010 Health Reform Act is not likely to end these disputes—although it may significantly change the parameters of the debate.

2010 Health Reform Act

Q 4:1   How does the 2010 Health Reform Act affect retiree medical benefits?

The 2010 Health Reform Act (Patient Protection and Affordable Care Act) [Pub. L. No. 111-148 (Mar. 23, 2010)] as amended by the Health Care and Education Affordability Reconciliation Act of 2010 [H.R. 4872, Pub. L. No. 111-152 (Mar. 30, 2010)] makes three key changes that directly affect retiree medical benefits:

1. *Reinsurance for early retirees.* The 2010 Health Reform Act creates a temporary reinsurance program for employment-based plans that provide health benefits for early retirees who are age 55 or older but are not eligible for Medicare. The program will make payments to participating plans for a portion of retiree health benefit claims, with the payments used to lower the costs of the plan. This program will expire after 2013 (see Q 4:31).

2. *Elimination of "double dip" for subsidized retiree prescription drug costs.* When the Medicare prescription drug benefit was created by the Medicare Modernization Act of 2003 (MMA), the law intended the retiree prescription drug plan subsidy to be an incentive for employers to continue such benefits. The MMA essentially allowed employers to "double dip" by excluding the subsidies from income while taking a full deduction for the retiree drug costs. The 2010 Health Reform Act eliminates the double dip by requiring an employer's deduction for retiree drug costs to be reduced by the amount of any subsidy received, effective for tax years beginning after 2012 (see Q 4:45).

3. *Excise tax on high-cost health plans.* Starting in 2018, the 2010 Health Reform Act imposes an excise tax on high-cost health plans, sometimes referred to as "Cadillac" plans. The tax is payable by the insurer, in the case of an insured plan, or by the employer, in the case of a self-insured plan or reimbursement arrangement such as a health savings account (HSA) or other health reimbursement arrangement (HRA). The tax equals 40 percent of the "excess cost" of coverage for an employee (including a former employee) for a year (see Q 4:12).

To assess the impact of these changes going forward requires a brief look backward.

Retiree medical benefits have never been universal. Historically, retiree benefits have been offered by larger employers. However, rising health care costs, the country's growing retiree population, and a significant accounting change (see Qs 4:47–4:51) that requires employers to report retiree health liabilities on annual reports have prompted many employers to scale back retiree benefits significantly by (1) increasing premiums and cost-sharing for retirees, (2) tightening eligibility requirements, or (3) eliminating benefits for new hires and/or workers retiring after a certain date. Others have dropped coverage entirely.

Not surprisingly, cutbacks or elimination of retiree medical benefits have been met with vigorous resistance on the part of retirees. Most significantly, retirees and prospective retirees have increasingly challenged the employer's right to make any changes to a plan once it is in place.

The 2010 Health Reform Act is a work in progress. As the legislation unfolds, employers will need to review carefully their retiree medical plans from the perspective of both cost and coverage. For example:

- In the short term, the reinsurance program for early retirees offers a financial incentive for employers to provide health coverage for early retirees as a "bridge" to Medicare. As a temporary program, it also serves as a "bridge" to reforms taking effect in 2014. In the longer term, these reforms, which include guaranteed access to insurance coverage in the individual market and through state-based insurance exchanges coupled with underwriting reforms (including limited age rating), may make individual coverage more attractive to early retirees—and reduce the incentive for employer-provided coverage.

• The elimination of the double dip will clearly drive up costs for retiree prescription drug coverage and will require attendant accounting charges. However, the 2010 Health Reform Act also includes changes to the Medicare Part D prescription drug program, including filling the so-called donut hole (the gap between the initial coverage limit and the catastrophic coverage threshold), which may make Part D more attractive to retirees—and may make an employer subsidy for Part D benefits an attractive alternative to an employer-provided retiree drug plan.

• The excise tax on high-cost plans also has the potential to drive up retiree health costs, even with the more generous thresholds for retiree coverage. However, given its 2018 effective date, this tax does not present an immediate cost issue. Consequently, employers will have time to analyze their retiree health plans to determine potential tax exposure and to reduce costs as necessary.

Practice Pointer. Bear in mind that the rules and requirements generally applicable to group health plans—*including numerous new standards imposed by the 2010 Health Reform Act*—may apply to retiree medical plans. The precise application of these requirements will depend on a variety of factors, including whether the plan is a retiree-only plan or is part of a plan covering active employees, the nature of the particular requirement, and the plan's status as a grandfathered plan for purposes of the 2010 Health Reform Act. See chapters 3 and 5 for discussion of the structural and operational requirements for group health plans.

Obligation to Provide Retiree Medical Benefits

Q 4:2   Is an employer legally obligated to provide retiree medical benefits?

There is no law that requires a private employer to provide retiree medical benefits for its former employees. Employers are free, as a matter of corporate management discretion, to decide whether or not to adopt retiree medical benefit plans. In addition, the decision to adopt a plan is not an ERISA fiduciary function. [Belade v. ITT Corp., 909 F.2d 736 (2d Cir. 1990); Moore v. Metropolitan Life Ins. Co., 856 F.2d 488 (2d Cir. 1988)]

Q 4:3   What are the primary legal issues for retiree medical plans?

Although no law requires an employer to offer a medical plan to its employees, numerous laws regulate the manner in which such a plan, once offered, must be designed and administered.

A chief concern when developing a new plan or modifying an existing plan is whether the plan provisions comply with federal law directly or indirectly governing the content of employee benefit plans. In addition, state and local laws must be considered to the extent they are not preempted by the Employee Retirement Income Security Act of 1974 (ERISA).

A second concern is that group health plans covering retirees must be primary to Medicare in certain circumstances. This means that retiree medical plans cannot be pure "wraparound" plans vis-à-vis Medicare (see Qs 4:37–4:39).

A third concern is whether an employer has voluntarily assumed (either affirmatively in writing or through a course of conduct) a greater obligation to provide benefits than is required by such laws, in a manner that cannot be reversed or that can be reversed only with great difficulty (see Qs 4:20–4:30).

A fourth concern is whether an employer can use any tax-advantaged funding methods to lessen the burden of maintaining retiree medical benefits (see Qs 4:52–4:59).

Q 4:4   Once an employer decides to offer a retiree medical plan, does it have a duty to employees and potential plan participants to adopt the best plan it can afford?

No. An employer is under no duty to act solely in the interests of employees and potential plan participants and beneficiaries when determining what the content of a retiree medical plan will be. [Belade v. ITT Corp., 909 F.2d 736 (2d Cir. 1990); Moore v. Metropolitan Life Ins. Co., 856 F.2d 488 (2d Cir. 1988)]

Q 4:5   Are retiree medical benefits a form of deferred compensation that vests upon retirement?

No. Retiree medical benefits are not a form of deferred compensation that is "earned" incrementally over the course of an employee's service for the employer or that "vests" because the employee's service has been completed.

Q 4:6   Once an employer voluntarily offers retiree medical benefits, does ERISA require that retirees become vested in them?

Generally, no. ERISA does not contain any vesting provisions for welfare benefit plans. The U.S. Court of Appeals for the Sixth Circuit, in the benchmark case on the issue, held that there is no basis for finding mandatory vesting in ERISA of retiree welfare benefits. The appellate court noted that the legislature, rather than the courts, should determine whether mandatory vesting of retiree welfare benefits is appropriate. Absent such legislative action, the parties are free to set out by agreement or by private design, as set forth in the plan documents, whether retiree medical benefits vest or whether they can be terminated. [*In re* White Farm Equip. Co., 788 F.2d 1186 (6th Cir. 1986); *see also* Wise v. El Paso Natural Gas Co., 986 F.2d 929 (5th Cir. 1993)]

Although retiree medical benefits are not required to be vested as a matter of law, an employer may find that it has inadvertently created a "vested" benefit for retirees by plan document and other communications that fail to make it clear that the employer reserves the right to amend or terminate the benefits at any time. (See Qs 4:20–4:30 for a discussion of legal issues regarding plan cutbacks.)

Q 4:7 Once an employer voluntarily offers retiree medical benefits, does the Consolidated Omnibus Budget Reconciliation Act require that retirees become vested in them?

No. Rights under the Consolidated Omnibus Budget Reconciliation Act (COBRA) apply to full or partial loss of health benefits as the result of one of the statutory COBRA qualifying events (see chapter 6). COBRA continuation coverage, if elected, delays the termination date of retiree medical benefits but does not prohibit the employer from changing the benefit levels from time to time or from terminating the plan. In the case of a retired employee, however, the only qualifying event that can trigger COBRA coverage for the retiree is the bankruptcy of the employer (see chapter 6).

COBRA requires that a qualified beneficiary be given the right to elect COBRA continuation coverage that is (1) identical to that provided to similarly situated beneficiaries who have not undergone a qualifying event and (2) identical to the coverage the qualified beneficiaries themselves received immediately before the qualifying event, except for certain permitted differences (see chapter 6). The statute and the regulations define the required level of coverage at the time it is elected. Nothing in COBRA, however, prevents the employer from subsequently amending or modifying such coverage as to all participants or from terminating the plan. [I.R.C. § 4980B(f)(2); ERISA § 602(1); Public Health Service Act (PHSA) § 2102; Treas. Reg. 54.4980B-5 Q&A-1]

Q 4:8 Are retiree medical benefits a mandatory subject of collective bargaining?

Whether retiree medical benefits are a mandatory subject of collective bargaining depends on whether the individuals are currently employees or currently retired. An employer is required to bargain in good faith with a union representing its employees about the benefits active employees will receive when they retire. Retirees, however, are not considered to be "employees" under the National Labor Relations Act of 1935, as amended. Thus, an employer is not required to bargain over welfare benefits for already retired employees. Rather, benefits for current retirees are a permitted subject of bargaining; the employer may agree to bargain about them but is not required to do so. [Allied

Chem. & Alkali Workers of Am. Local Union No. 1 v. Pittsburgh Plate Glass Co. Chem. Div., 404 U.S. 157 (1971); Grown & Sharpe Mfg. Co., 299 N.L.R.B. 581 (1990)]

Q 4:9 If an employer offers retiree medical benefits pursuant to a collective bargaining agreement, do those employees who attain retirement age during the period of the agreement become vested in the retiree medical benefits?

Possibly. Although retiree medical benefits legally are not a form of deferred compensation, there is another layer of potential employer liability in the collective bargaining context resulting not from the retiree medical plan provisions but from the separate collective bargaining agreement. The theory underlying some of the case law construing collective bargaining agreements is that active employees who agree to forgo current wages in exchange for future benefits at retirement have, upon attaining retirement, an expectation of receiving those benefits throughout retirement. Under such a theory, the exchange is not characterized as the employer's receipt of the employee's current employment service in return for future deferred compensation, but rather as the employee's sacrifice of current compensation in return for promised future benefits upon retirement.

In the collective bargaining context, the Court of Appeals for the Sixth Circuit applied an "inference" that retiree medical benefits are "status benefits" that vest at retirement.

Thus, when the parties contract for benefits which accrue upon achievement of retiree status, there is an inference that the parties likely intended those benefits to continue as long as the beneficiary remains a retiree. This is not to say that retiree insurance benefits are necessarily interminable by their nature. Nor does any federal labor law policy identified to this court presumptively favor the finding of interminable rights to retiree insurance benefits when the collective bargaining agreement is silent. Rather, as a part of the context from which the collective bargaining agreement arose, the nature of such benefits simply provides another inference of intent. Standing alone, this factor would be insufficient to find an intent to create interminable benefits. In the present case, however, this contextual factor buttresses the already sufficient evidence of such intent in the language of this agreement itself.

[International Union, United Auto, Aerospace & Agric. Implement Workers of Am. v. Yard-Man Inc., 716 F.2d 1476, 1482 (6th Cir. 1983), *cert. denied*, 465 U.S. 1007 (1984)]

Numerous courts have used the status benefit theory to find that retiree medical benefits have vested where the provisions of the collective bargaining agreement (particularly ambiguous provisions) or other extrinsic evidence supports an inference of an intention to provide lifetime vesting. The absence of contract language limiting the duration of retiree health benefits or permitting the employer to modify or terminate them at will may also be found to create lifetime vesting. [Hinckley v. Kelsey-Hayes Co., 866 F. Supp. 1034 (E.D. Mich. 1994)]

However, where the contract language clearly limits the duration of retiree medical benefits to the term of the agreement, numerous courts have held that retiree medical benefits did not continue beyond the expiration of the collective bargaining agreement. [Arndt v. Wheelabrator Corp., 763 F. Supp. 396 (N.D. Ind. 1991); District 17, UMW v. Allied Corp., 765 F.2d 412 (4th Cir. 1985), *cert. denied*, 105 S. Ct. 3227 (1985); District 29, UMWA v. Royal Coal Co., 768 F.2d 588 (4th Cir. 1985); Turner v. Teamsters Local No. 302, 604 F.2d 1219 (9th Cir. 1979); Linville v. Teamsters Misc. & Indus. Workers Union, Local 284, 206 F.3d 648 (6th Cir. 2000)]

Other cases have rejected or simply ignored the status benefit theory on the basis that it is illogical to infer an intent to vest retiree benefits every time an employee is eligible to receive them on his or her retirement date, because ERISA explicitly exempts welfare benefits from its vesting requirements. [Anderson v. Alpha Portland Indus. Inc., 836 F.2d 1512 (8th Cir. 1988); *see also* Senn v. United Dominion Indus. Inc., 951 F.2d 806 (7th Cir. 1992)]

Practice Pointer. Because the inference of an intent to provide lifetime benefits might be applied by a court to an employer's conduct, employers desiring to avoid a commitment to lifetime retiree medical benefits at a particular level should attempt to carefully craft both plan and collective bargaining agreement provisions to clearly limit the duration of retiree medical benefits to the term of the collective bargaining agreement. It should be noted that an employer's particular collective bargaining situation may not afford enough latitude to achieve this result.

See also Qs 4:20–4:30 for a discussion of legal issues involving plan cutbacks.

Tax Treatment of Retiree Health Benefits

Q 4:10   Is a retiree taxed on employer-provided health benefits?

To qualify for favorable tax treatment, a health plan must be provided for the benefit of employees. [I.R.C. §§ 05, 106] The IRS has specifically ruled that employees for this purpose include retired employees and their spouses and dependents. [Rev. Rul. 62-199, 1962-2 C.B. 38; Rev. Rul. 75-539, 1975-2 C.B. 45]

As a result, an employer's contributions to an accident or health plan on behalf of retired employees are excluded from retirees' gross income, just as they are for current employees. [I.R.C. § 106; Treas. Reg. § 1.106-1]

Retirees also qualify for the exclusion for benefits paid from the plan to cover medical expenses. [I.R.C. § 105; Rev. Rul. 82-196, 182-2 C.B. 53] In limited circumstances, the IRS has extended the exclusion for retiree health benefits to cover benefits that have been converted from other taxable benefits. The issue here is constructive receipt—if the employees have the right to decide whether they receive retiree health benefits or a taxable benefit, then the exclusion will not apply even if they elect retiree health benefits.

For example, in one ruling a school district adopted a plan that converted retiring employees' sick leave into one of two benefits to be chosen by the school district: (1) additional medical coverage starting after the lapse of the district's regular retiree medical coverage, or (2) a qualified deferred compensation plan. The school district intended to base its choice for each retiree on several factors, including the retiree's access to other health insurance coverage, the value of the retiree's unused leave, and the willingness of the district's insurance carrier to cover retirees.

The IRS ruled that medical benefits provided under the plan to retirees would be tax-free. That's because the retirees did not have a choice at any time as to which of the two benefits they would receive. [Priv. Ltr. Rul. 200222019]

For further discussion of the tax treatment of employer-provided health benefits, see chapter 3.

Q 4:11 Can an employer deduct its contributions for retiree health benefits?

Employer contributions to or payments made under a medical plan, including a medical plan for retirees, are generally deductible as ordinary and necessary business expenses. [Treas. Reg.§ 1.162-10(a)] However, under the 2010 Health Reform Act, effective for tax years beginning after 2012, the deduction for retiree prescription drug expenses is limited for employers that received retiree prescription drug plan subsidies (Q 4:40).

Q 4:12 How does the tax on high-cost health plans affect retiree medical plans?

The 2010 Health Reform Act imposes a 40 percent excise tax on *excess coverage* under an employer-sponsored plan. [PPACA § 9001, as amended by PPACA § 10901 and PPACA Reconciliation § 1401] The tax is effective for tax years beginning after 2017.

The tax applies to any employer-sponsored coverage for an employee—including a former employee—that is excludable from income, regardless of whether the employee or the employer pays for the coverage.

For purposes of determining the amount of excess coverage, all employer-sponsored coverage is taken into account (other than certain excepted coverage, including vision- or dental-only coverage and long-term care coverage). The tax on excess coverage is imposed pro rata on the coverage providers. To the extent coverage is provided through insurance, the tax is imposed on the issuers of the insurance. In the case of a self-insured group health plan, the tax is paid by the plan administrator. Where the employer acts as plan administrator of a self-insured plan, the tax is paid by the employer.

Excess coverage. Excess coverage is the aggregate value of coverage over a threshold amount. For 2018, the law sets the threshold amount at $10,200 for self-only coverage and $27,500 for family coverage (employee plus one other beneficiary). However, for retirees who have attained age 55 and who are not Medicare-eligible, the threshold amounts are increased by $1,650 for self-only coverage and $3,450 for family coverage. Thus, the threshold amounts for those retirees will be $11,850 for self-only coverage and $30,950 for family coverage. These thresholds, however, may be increased if the actual growth in the cost of U.S. health care between 2010 and 2018 exceeds projected growth for that period.

For further details on the excise tax, see chapter 3.

Q 4:13   Can retiree health benefits be provided through a tax-qualified pension or annuity plan?

According to the IRS, amounts in a qualified retirement plan that are used to pay for accident or health insurance premiums are treated as a taxable distribution to the plan participant. The IRS has issued proposed regulations that make it clear that such a payment is taxable to the participant in the year the premium is paid. On the other hand, to the extent the premiums are treated as a taxable distribution, amounts received through the plan for personal injuries or sickness are excludable from gross income under Code Section 104(a)(3) and are not treated as plan distributions. [Prop. Treas. Reg. § 1.402(a)-1] The regulations are proposed to be effective for calendar years after they are published as final. However, the IRS says that no inference should be drawn that the payment of premiums from a qualified plan does not constitute a taxable distribution if made before the effective date of the regulations.

The proposed regulations do carve out an exception for a longstanding rule that permits health and accident benefits to be provided by a pension or annuity plan through a Section 401(h) account. [Prop. Treas. Reg. § 1.402(a)-1(e)(2)] A pension or annuity plan may provide health and accident benefits for retired employees and their spouses and dependents if all of the following requirements are satisfied:

1. The benefits are paid out of a separate account;
2. The employer's contributions to the account are reasonable and ascertainable;
3. The benefits provided are subordinate to the retirement benefits provided under the plan;
4. The terms of the plan require that any amount remaining in the plan be returned to the employer upon satisfaction of all liabilities under the plan to provide benefits; and
5. A separate account is established and maintained to provide benefits to key employees and their spouses and dependents.

[I.R.C. § 401(h); Treas. Reg. § 1.401-14(b), (c)]

Health and accident benefits are considered subordinate to the retirement benefits provided under the plan if the contributions made to provide medical benefits, plus any contributions made to provide life insurance, do not exceed 25 percent of the total contributions to the plan.

In addition, the proposed regulations reflect a new rule, added by the Pension Protection Act of 2006, that permits an exclusion from gross income of up to $3,000 per year for retirement plan distributions paid directly to an insurer to purchase accident or health insurance or qualified long-term care insurance for an eligible retired public safety officer and his or her spouse and dependents. [I.R.C. § 402(l); Prop. Reg. § 1.402(a)-1(e)(2)] In anticipation of a proposed technical correction, the IRS has made it clear that the exclusion for qualifying distributions from pension plans of public safety officers also applies to premiums paid to an accident or health plan that is self-insured. [Notice 2007-99, 2007-52 I.R.B. 1243]

Q 4:14   Can retirees use qualified retirement plan distributions to pay health insurance premiums or medical expenses on a tax-favored basis?

No. The IRS has ruled that qualified retirement plan distributions are includable in a retiree's gross income if they are used to pay health insurance premiums under a cafeteria plan or are applied directly to reimburse medical care expenses. [Rev. Rul. 2003-62, 2003-25 I.R.B. 1034; Prop. Treas. Reg. § 1.125-1(b)(3)]

Moreover, proposed regulations make it clear that amounts paid directly by the plan for accident or health insurance premiums are treated as taxable distributions (see Q 4:13).

Q 4:15   Can funds in a health reimbursement arrangement be used to reimburse a retired employee's postretirement medical expenses?

Yes. The IRS has specifically ruled that a health reimbursement arrangement (HRA) can continue to reimburse former employees or retired employees for medical expenses incurred after termination of employment or retirement. For example, an HRA may provide for reimbursements to a former employee for medical expenses up to the remaining amount in the employee's account at the time of retirement or termination of employment. The plan may also provide that the maximum reimbursement available after retirement or termination of employment be reduced by the administrative cost of continuing the coverage. On the other hand, an HRA may provide additional employer contributions following an employee's retirement or termination of employment. [Rev. Rul. 2002-41, 2002-28 I.R.B. 75; IRS Notice 2002-45, 2002-28 I.R.B. 93] (See chapter 3 for further information about HRAs.)

Q 4:16   Can an employer contribute the value of retiring employee's unused sick days to a health reimbursement arrangement on a tax-favored basis?

In an unofficial private letter ruling, the IRS considered an employer's plan to contribute the value of a retiring employee's unused sick days to an HRA to be used for postretirement medical expenses. Under the plan, employees would make no election with respect to the contribution of unused sick days and would have no right to receive the value of the sick days in cash or other benefits. The IRS ruled that nonelective contributions equal to the value of a retiring employee's unused sick leave would be excludable from the employee's income. [I.R.C.§ 106; Priv. Ltr. Rul. 200535015]

Cost Containment Design

Q 4:17   What options are available to an employer seeking to control retiree medical costs?

An employer has wide flexibility to achieve some control of retiree medical costs, subject to potential legal limits on its ability to change an existing plan (see Qs 4:20–4:30) and the requirements of federal or state law. Such control can be accomplished in a number of ways, including:

- Redefining the target group to incorporate pension-type goals, so that retiree medical benefit dollars are focused on the company's longer-service employees (see Q 4:18), and
- Reducing benefit costs through plan design (see Q 4:19).

Q 4:18   How can an employer incorporate pension-type goals into a retiree medical plan?

To incorporate pension-type goals into a retiree medical plan, an employer may consider formulating its contributions for retirees to reflect length of service. Under this type of design, employer contributions toward the premiums for retiree medical coverage would be more (and employee contributions would be less) for longer-service employees.

Q 4:19   How can an employer reduce retiree medical benefit costs through plan design?

An employer can help reduce retiree medical benefit costs through plan design in the following ways.

Shifting more of the risk of utilization and medical cost increases to retirees and to other plans. A number of mechanisms used singly or in combination can shift some of the risk, such as adding or increasing retiree contributions, deductibles, and copayments; adding or lowering annual or lifetime plan maximums (or both); or revising coordination of benefits provisions.

Changing the delivery mechanism. Costs can be reduced by offering one or more Medicare risk HMOs to retirees. By fixing its cost as a set dollar amount paid each month for coverage, an employer can significantly reduce estimated future costs of retiree medical benefits.

Capping the risk by offering a defined benefit or defined dollar plan. A retiree would be responsible for everything beyond the defined limits, creating a total shift of risk to retirees and other plans beyond the amount expressly assumed by the employer.

In addition to risk shifting, the plan design could focus on more cost-efficient options for the purchase of medical care and services by providing financial incentives for using them (and, often, financial penalties for not following the managed care procedures). The particular plan redesigns may vary considerably from employer to employer, depending on how aggressively the employer seeks to control plan costs. In particular, the basis of managed care is directing or monitoring access to care to ensure that the care provided or reimbursed under a plan is medically necessary and cost-efficient while providing incentives to health care providers to eliminate unnecessary or duplicative services and to reduce or contain the price charged for necessary care and services.

Plan Cutbacks—Legal Issues

Q 4:20   Can an employer reduce costs by increasing the premiums that retirees must pay for their medical benefits?

Possibly. As a general rule, an employer can unilaterally modify or terminate health and other welfare benefits at any time. However, health and welfare benefits may become vested, and thus unchangeable, if a promise to continue to provide the benefits without change is incorporated into the employer's plan. To determine whether health or other welfare benefits are vested, the courts look to the employer's formal written plan as well as the summary plan description (SPD) that is given to employees.

In one case, for example, a retired couple that had worked for the 3M Company argued that the company could not raise the premiums they paid for retiree health coverage. However, the Eighth Circuit Court of Appeals held that 3M was free to increase the premiums. The court pointed out that the SPD the couple received did not contain any explicit promises about the future of retiree health plans. The SPD did state that "the company fully intends to continue these plans indefinitely, but reserves the right to amend or discontinue them." However, the Eighth Circuit concluded that 3M's SPD language did not suggest an intent to vest retiree benefits. "It is plain and unambiguous," said the court, "that the word 'intends' does not indicate finality. To hold otherwise would render the words 'reserves the right to change or discontinue it if necessary' meaningless." Thus, the SPD did not specifically vest the retiree benefits and explicitly reserved the right to modify the retiree medical benefit plan at any time.

In reaching its decision, the Eighth Circuit noted that an SPD is not required to disclose that plan benefits are not vested. A health or other welfare plan SPD is required to disclose only those circumstances in which a plan beneficiary is not entitled to benefits otherwise provided by the terms of the plan. [Hughes v. 3M Retiree Med. Plan, 281 F.3d 786 (8th Cir. 2002)]

In another case involving a collectively bargained plan, the Sixth Circuit ruled that an employer could not require retirees to contribute a portion of health insurance premiums when the plan originally called for the premiums to be fully funded by the employer. The court concluded that the plan language, which was similar to language describing vested pension benefits, caused the fully funded health benefits to vest. [Yolton v. El Paso Tenn. Pipeline, 435 F.3d 571 (6th Cir. 2006)]

> **Practice Pointer.** Even if a plan document clearly reserves the right to terminate or change retiree medical benefits, it should avoid promissory language in the SPD that would lead former employees to believe that their benefits are vested. If there is any discrepancy between the formal plan and the SPD, the SPD, which is the document disclosed to employees, will generally control.

Q 4:21   Once an employer has adopted a retiree medical plan, must a particular level of benefits be maintained?

In general, an employer has broad design flexibility to reduce the future level of retiree medical benefits. Nonetheless, an employer must clearly and unambiguously reserve the right to alter or diminish benefits under the plan. [Dague v. Gencorp Inc., 875 F. Supp. 424 (N.D. Ohio 1994)] If an employer engages in a course of conduct that a court may find to have effectively guaranteed a particular level of benefits, the employer may find itself required to maintain that level of benefits even though it had not originally intended to do so. [Schalk v. Teledyne Inc., 751 F. Supp. 1261 (W.D. Mich. 1990); Chervin v. Sulzer Bingham Pumps Inc., 1990 U.S. Dist. LEXIS 18091 (D. Or. Nov. 6, 1990); *but see* Erdman v. Bethlehem Steel Corp. Employee Welfare Plans, 607 F. Supp. 196 (W.D.N.Y. 1985)]

In a U.S. district court case, the employer, in connection with a continuing workforce reduction program, had offered employees a variety of early retirement incentive programs. The SPDs did not expressly promise that retiree medical benefits would be continued for life with no changes. Still, the early retirement incentive program communications to eligible employees, which took a variety of forms (e.g., letters, memoranda, booklets, and oral statements), all indicated that the retiree medical benefits would be continued for life without any increased cost to the employees accepting the offer. Employees accepting an early retirement incentive offer signed a document of acceptance, which in some cases included a waiver of all legal claims against the employer.

The employer, relying on its right to amend under the plan document, increased deductibles and copayments for all its retirees. The district court held that the subclass of retirees who had accepted early retirement incentive offers had vested rights in their benefits at retirement. The court found the SPDs to be ambiguous and the representations of the employer as to lifetime retiree medical benefits coverage without change to have created a binding contract under ERISA common law for those retirees who accepted an early retirement incentive offer. [Sprague v. GMC, 92 F.3d 1425 (6th Cir. 1996)]

The Eighth Circuit Court of Appeals has held that an SPD that failed to disclose that retiree medical benefits could be amended or terminated created lifetime medical benefits for the retirees. Nonetheless, because neither ERISA nor the SPD regulations promulgated by the Department of Labor (DOL) require that a welfare plan SPD specifically disclose that its benefits are not vested, the appellate court refused to find that the SPD's silence on the issue of vesting constituted either a material misrepresentation or a breach of the plan administrator's duties. [Jensen v. Sipco Inc., 38 F. 3d 945 (8th Cir. 1994)]

Even if it has clearly reserved the right to reduce benefits, an employer cannot alter or diminish benefits under the plan in a way that violates federal law or, to the extent not preempted by ERISA, state insurance law. (ERISA probably would preempt the application to ERISA welfare benefit plans of general state labor laws prohibiting employment discrimination in the terms, conditions, and privileges of employment.)

Further, an employer cannot change plan coverage terms retroactively if employees thereby would be deprived of benefits for which they had already incurred expenses based on the coverage terms clearly communicated to them. The Court of Appeals for the Third Circuit has held that an employer that intended to exclude coverage for motorcycle accidents under its medical plan but failed to do so could not retroactively amend the plan to deprive employees of benefits for expenses from such accidents incurred before the amendment. [Confer v. Custom Eng'g Co., 952 F.2d 34 (3d Cir. 1991)] So long as an employer has expressly reserved the right to cut back benefits, however, nothing in ERISA prohibits an employer from doing so prospectively' including cutting back coverage for future expenses incurred for conditions that were first manifested or for which the employee first sought treatment before the date of the plan amendment. [McGann v. H & H Music Co., 946 F.2d 401 (5th Cir. 1991); *see also* Owens v. Storehouse Inc., 773 F. Supp. 416 (N.D. Ga. 1991)]

Q 4:22   Is an employer subject to a collective bargaining agreement free to amend, modify, or terminate a retiree medical plan before expiration of the collective bargaining agreement?

Not necessarily. The terms of the collective bargaining agreement and the plan will need to be examined to see whether an employer has the express authority to unilaterally change the plan before the expiration of the collective bargaining agreement without subjecting itself to an unfair labor practice charge.

In one case, the Seventh Circuit ruled that an employer that bought a manufacturing plant and hired its workers did not violate ERISA or the Labor-Management Relations Act of 1947 (LMRA) when it reduced and subsequently terminated retiree health care benefits in the mid-term of a collective bargaining agreement. [International Union, United Auto, Aerospace & Agric. Implement Workers of Am. v. Rockford Powertrain, Inc., 173 L.R.R.M. 2874 (N.D. Ill.), *aff'd*, 2003 U.S. App. LEXIS 24296 (7th Cir. Dec. 3, 2003)]

In 1988, Rockford Powertrain acquired a manufacturing plant from Borg-Warner Corporation. Following the acquisition, Rockford hired the majority of the plant's existing workers. Rockford assumed the obligations of the existing collective bargaining agreement with the workers. However, Rockford did not adopt Borg-Warner's retirement plan, which included subsidized health care benefits. Nor did Rockford agree to provide retirement benefits for any of Borg-Warner's retirees.

Rockford initially adopted a retirement benefit plan that provided retiree health care benefits. However, the SPD included a reservation of rights clause, which stated: "Although the company expects and intends to continue the plan indefinitely, it reserves the right to modify, suspend, or terminate them at any time." The SPD also stated that "in the event this group plan is terminated, coverage for you and your dependents will end immediately." The agreement between the union and Rockford included a statement specifying that the SPD was considered part of the agreement.

Rockford provided retiree health benefits for a time. However, it subsequently reduced its share of the premiums and then terminated the benefits entirely. The union and two Rockford retirees sued the company, alleging that Rockford had violated ERISA and the LMRA when it made unilateral changes to the retiree's health benefits in the mid-term of a collective bargaining agreement. The Seventh Circuit concluded that the health plan SPDs were incorporated into the collective bargaining agreement at the time Rockford acquired the plant and, therefore, the agreement included the reservation-of-rights clause that gave Rockford the authority to reduce or terminate retiree health benefits. In reaching its decision, the Seventh Circuit noted that under ERISA, welfare benefits do not vest automatically. According to the court, "Unless an employer contractually cedes its freedom, it is generally free under ERISA, for any reason at any time, to adopt, modify, or terminate its welfare plan."

Some collective bargaining agreements simply incorporate by reference employer-provided plans that clearly reserve the employer's right to amend or modify the plan at any time. In *Benedict v. United Intermountain Telephone Co.* [17 Employee Benefits Cas. (BNA) 1044 (E.D. Tenn. 1933)], a collective bargaining agreement did not prohibit charging retirees a premium. However, in *United Steelworkers v. Newman-Crosby Steel, Inc.* [822 F. Supp. 862 (D.R.I. 1993)] the court found that a collective bargaining agreement could not be modified by changes to the plan and SPD, both of which were amended to add the authority to make cutbacks.

Ambiguity in a collective bargaining agreement may create an opportunity for a court to consider extrinsic evidence concerning whether lifetime health benefits were promised. [Bidlack v. Wheelabrator Corp., 510 U.S. 909 (7th Cir.

1993)] Such extrinsic evidence might include summary plan descriptions that promise retiree life and health insurance "without cost to you." [Golden v. Kelsey-Hayes Co., 845 F. Supp. 410 (E.D. Mich. 1994)] Where two reasonable interpretations of the collective bargaining agreement were possible but the agreement did not indicate which was controlling, a federal district court was directed to admit extrinsic evidence on the issue of whether the employer had the right to unilaterally modify retiree medical benefits. [Stewart v. KHD Deutz of Am. Corp., 980 F. 2d 698 (11th Cir. 1993)]

Q 4:23   Is an employer subject to a collective bargaining agreement free to terminate retiree medical coverage upon expiration of the collective bargaining agreement?

The answer depends on the terms of the collective bargaining agreement, the plan, and applicable case law.

There is a substantial body of case law on the issue, and different courts have come to opposite conclusions based on their scrutiny of the underlying documents. In addition, some courts have applied an inference that retiree medical benefits are status benefits that vest upon attainment of retirement (see Q 4:9). An employer's ability to terminate retiree medical coverage upon the expiration of a collective bargaining agreement thus may come down to a facts-and-circumstances determination in each particular case.

In one case a federal jury found that the parties intended the scope and level of retiree medical benefits to continue beyond the expiration of the collective bargaining agreement. [Schalk v. Teledyne Indus. Inc., 751 F. Supp. 1261 (W.D. Mich. 1990)] A federal district court held that a contract provision, stating that retiree welfare benefits are to continue as long as an employee remains retired, indicated an intention that they become vested. [United Paper Workers v. Muskegon Paper Box Co., 704 F. Supp. 774 (W.D. Mich. 1988)] In another case, a federal district judge examined the language contained in both the insurance booklet and the SPD for a collectively bargained life insurance plan and, although the SPD contained a reservation of rights clause, found no clear statement in either document that the employer was entitled to unilaterally amend the plan. [United Steelworkers v. Newman-Crosby Steel Inc., 822 F. Supp. 862 (D.R.I. 1993)]

The Court of Appeals for the Seventh Circuit backed away from imposing a legal presumption that no vesting of retiree benefits exists absent clear contract language such as the term *vesting*. Instead, the court held that when a jury is determining whether an employer has committed itself to provide lifetime retiree benefits, the jury should be permitted to examine all the evidence surrounding the language of a collective bargaining agreement. In this case, vagueness in an expired collective bargaining agreement was supplemented by letters sent to retirees over a period of 22 years that promised that the employer would continue to pay the full cost of their Blue Cross Blue Shield coverage during their lifetimes. [Bidlack v. Wheelabrator Corp., 510 U.S. 909 (7th Cir. 1993)] On the other hand, the Seventh Circuit has also held that health benefits under a collective bargaining agreement were not vested even though the agreement referred to "lifetime" benefits. According to the court, health and welfare benefits, unlike pension benefits, do not automatically vest. Unless a contract provides for vesting, the presumption is that the benefits terminate when the collective bargaining agreement ends. Moreover, the fact that the agreement said benefits would last for a retiree's lifetime did not cause the benefits to vest. "Lifetime" benefits can be limited to the duration of a contract. Therefore, at the end of the collective bargaining agreement, the employer was free to revoke or modify the benefits. [Cherry v. Auburn Gear, Inc., 441 F.3d 476 (7th Cir. 2006)]

By contrast, the Sixth Circuit held that an automobile parts manufacturer violated a bargaining contract with the United Auto Workers by terminating retirees' lifetime health care benefits. The court found that the retirees' rights to health care benefits had vested and rejected the company's argument that the benefits did not extend past expiration of the last bargaining contract. [United Auto Workers v. BVR Liquidating Inc., 1999 U.S. App. LEXIS 29797 (6th Cir. Nov. 2, 1999)]

Also, in *Maurer v. Joy Techs. Inc.* [212 F.3d 907 (6th Cir. 2000)], the court held that a collective bargaining agreement's retiree medical benefits clause was sufficient to create a promise of lifetime benefits. In that case, the term of the initial collective bargaining agreement was three years. After that, the agreement was renegotiated a total of six times, and during the last renegotiation in 1991, the agreement incorporated a clause that expressly reserved the right of the company to amend or terminate the retiree medical plan. The retirees said that the preceding collective bargaining agreements created a promise of lifetime benefits for those retirees who were covered by the agreements. The court agreed with the retirees and held that the retirees who retired before the effective date of the 1991 collective bargaining agreement were entitled to lifetime benefits.

Q 4:24 Can an employer have a retiree medical plan with benefits based on age and length of service?

Basing benefits on the employee's age and length of service has been the subject of considerable discussion in recent years as employers attempt to redesign retiree medical plans to incorporate pension-type goals by rewarding longer-service employees.

The current regulations under Code Section 105 treat a self-insured medical plan as discriminatory unless the maximum benefit limit attributable to employer contributions is uniform for all participants and dependents and is not modified by reason of the participant's age or years of service. [Treas. Reg. § 1.105-11(c)(3)(i)] That means that if a self-insured retiree medical plan provides differing levels of benefits based on years of service, a Section 105(h) nondiscrimination issue exists. In addition, requiring greater contributions of younger participants in a self-insured retiree medical plan could raise a nondiscriminationissue under Code Section 105(h) because younger participants would receive fewer benefits per premium dollar.

The tax law rule applies only to self-insured plans. However, both insured and uninsured plans can run up against another nondiscrimination rule if retiree health benefits are based on age.

For example, employer contributions or the level of benefits provided may be structured to differentiate between retirees who are eligible for Medicare and those who are not. However, in a precedent-setting opinion, the Third Circuit Court of Appeals has held that a benefits package for retirees that discriminates on the basis of age will violate the Age Discrimination in Employment Act (ADEA).

In that case, the County of Erie, Pennsylvania, divided its retirees into two groups: (1) those who had reached age 65 and were eligible for Medicare and (2) those who had not yet reached age 65 and did not qualify for Medicare. Medicare-eligible retirees were enrolled in a plan that provided services through a health maintenance organization (HMO) and were required to enroll in and pay for Medicare Part B. Younger retirees were enrolled in a point-of-service (POS) plan that combined the features of an HMO with a traditional indemnity plan. A group of Medicare-eligible retirees brought a lawsuit claiming that the county had violated the ADEA by treating the Medicare-eligible retirees less favorably on account of their age.

The Third Circuit concluded that the language of the ADEA clearly applies to retirees as well as to active employees. According to the court, the law protects any "individuals" who have been treated differently by their "employer," including a former employer, because of age.

Moreover, while the county argued that the decision to place Medicare eligible employees in the HMO plan was motivated by factors other than age, the court concluded that the health plan choices were made on the basis of age. According to the court, Medicare eligibility "follows ineluctably upon attaining age 65. Thus, Medicare status is a direct proxy for age."

The court also rejected the county's argument that its health plan choices were not discriminatory because it simply placed each retiree in the least expensive plan for which he or she qualified. In addition, the court was unswayed by the county's contention that it could not have enrolled the Medicare-eligible retirees in the point-of-service plan because they were disqualified from that plan under the insurer's rules. The court acknowledged that there was no reason to believe that the county had malevolent motives in making the health plan choices. However, a policy based on age is illegal regardless of the underlying motive. Moreover, an employer cannot avoid responsibility for a discriminatory benefit plan merely because the discrimination arises from criteria imposed by an outside entity with whom the employer has contracted to provide the benefit. The Supreme Court refused to review the Third Circuit decision. [Erie County Retirees Ass'n v. County of Erie, 220 F.3d 193 (3d Cir. 2000), *cert. denied*, 121 S. Ct. 1247 (2001)]

Safe harbor. The ADEA does address the fact that benefits for older individuals may be more expensive. The law says that an employer must either provide equal benefits for older and younger individuals or incur the same costs on behalf of both. Thus, providing different benefits for Medicare-eligible retirees will not violate the ADEA if the benefits cost is the same as for younger retirees.

On the other hand, it may be impossible for an employer to satisfy the equal-cost safe harbor if its retiree health plan is integrated with Medicare. When a retiree has Medicare coverage, the employer will be able to shift a large portion of the cost of health care coverage to Medicare. Thus, the employer's cost will be less than for younger retirees.

For example, on remand from the Third Circuit, a district court ruled that the Erie County medical plan did not qualify for safe harbor protection. The court said that the fact that older retirees were required to pay Medicare Part B premiums, while younger retirees did not pay any premiums, resulted in lesser employer-provided benefits for the older retirees. In addition, it was undisputed that, without the costs incurred for Medicare coverage factored in, the county's cost of coverage for, the older retirees was less than that for younger retirees. [Erie County Retirees Ass'n v. County of Erie, 140 F. Supp. 2d 466 (W.D. Pa. 2001)]

Q 4:25   What is the government's enforcement position on retiree health plans that provide different benefits for older and younger retirees?

The Third Circuit's precedent-setting opinion regarding retiree health coverage (see Q 4:24) prompted the federal Equal Employment Opportunity Commission (EEOC) to make changes in its compliance manual. The revised manual stated that "if an employer eliminates health coverage for retirees who are eligible for Medicare—or if it refuses to cover its older retirees for the benefits it provides that are not offered by Medicare—older retirees will get less coverage than younger retirees on the basis of their age. Unless the employer can meet the equal cost defense, the law does not permit this age discrimination."

The revision of the compliance manual was short-lived, however. In August 2001, the EEOC rescinded section IV(B) of the manual chapter on employee benefits. The EEOC rescission notice stated that "Medicare carveout plans"—that is, those that simply deduct from the benefits provided to Medicare-eligible retirees those benefits that Medicare provides—do not violate the ADEA. However, the EEOC notice also states, "additional review is needed to assess other types of retiree health plan practices."

In 2003, the EEOC proposed regulations to allow employers to alter, reduce, or eliminate employer-sponsored retiree health benefits when an employee becomes eligible for Medicare or a comparable state-sponsored health plan. The EEOC derives its regulatory authority from an ADEA provision that allows the Commission to establish an exemption from any ADEA rule if it is "necessary and proper in the public interest." [ADEA § 9] According to the EEOC, "Because the *Erie County* decision was contributing to a continuing decline in the availability of employer-provided retiree health benefits, the Commission concluded that it would be in the best interest of employers, employees, and retirees to permit employers to offer these benefits to the greatest extent possible."

The regulations were scheduled to take effect when approved by the federal Office of Management and Budget and published in the *Federal Register*. However, the American Association of Retired Persons (AARP) challenged the EEOC's authority to grant the exemption. In the case brought by the AARP, the U.S. District Court for the Eastern District of Pennsylvania initially ruled that the EEOC did not have the authority to issue the regulations because they contravene the ADEA, and it issued an order blocking the regulations. [AARP v. EEOC, 383 F. Supp. 2d 705 (E.D. Pa. 2005)] The court subsequently withdrew that opinion and ruled that the EEOC regulations are not contrary to law. However, the court specifically barred the EEOC from finalizing the regulations pending review by the Third Circuit. In 2007, the Third Circuit affirmed the district court (and the Supreme Court declined to review that decision), allowing the regulations to proceed. [AARP v. EEOC, 390 F. Supp. 2d 437 (E.D. Pa. 2005, *aff'd*, 2007 App. LEXIS 12869 (3d Cir. 2007)]

The final EEOC regulations took effect on December 26, 2007. [29 C.F.R. § 1625.32] The final regulations permit employers to continue two practices that are commonly used to coordinate retiree health benefits with Medicare:

1. Provide health benefits only to retirees under age 65. These types of plans, called "Medicare bridge plans," are often used to provide health benefits to workers who retire before they become eligible for Medicare.

2. Provide supplemental health benefits to Medicare-eligible retirees (age 65 and older) without having to show that the benefits are identical to any benefits provided to early retirees who cannot receive Medicare benefits. In many cases, these plans, sometimes called "Medicare wraparound or supplement policies," provide retirees with prescription drug coverage.

Q 4:26   If an employer includes retiree medical benefits in an "early out" program, can it reduce or terminate those benefits later?

Whether benefits offered under an "early out" program can be reduced or terminated depends on how those benefits are included in the early retirement incentive program.

A federal appellate court upheld an employer's addition of deductible and copayment features to its medical plan for active and retired employees based on the employer's unambiguous reservation of the right to amend the plan stated in the SPD. It concluded that benefits generally did not vest at any particular level upon retirement. Before the addition of those changes, however, a group of employees had accepted the employer's offer of a special early retirement program in connection with a plant closing, workforce downsizing, and other employer-initiated actions. They signed written acceptance agreements that released the employer from liability for certain claims and stated that they had reviewed the benefits applicable to them and accepted them. The court concluded that, as to the employees who accepted the separate early retirement program, the employer entered into a bilateral contract to provide vested retiree medical benefits at a particular level in return for defined consideration (the release). [Sprague v. GMC, 92 F.3d 1425 (6th Cir. 1996)]

In a case before the Eighth Circuit Court of Appeals, certain employees who agreed to take early retirement received retiree health benefits in excess of those regularly provided to retirees by the employer. The regular retiree plan contained a provision permitting the employer to amend or cancel the plan. However, the releases employees signed in which they elected early retirement in exchange for enhanced benefits contained no such provision. Several years later, the employer made significant changes to the benefit plan that increased the early retirees' cost and reduced their benefits. The early retirees sued. They argued that they were vested in the enhanced retiree benefits plan because the releases they signed constituted a welfare benefit plan separate and apart from the regular retiree health plan. Since the employer did not reserve the right to change this separate plan, their benefits vested when they signed the releases.

The Eighth Circuit Court of Appeals ruled against the employees. The court said that the enhanced benefits plan for early retirees constituted an amendment to the existing regular retiree plan and did not represent a freestanding welfare benefit plan. The documents that the employer distributed in offering the early retirement benefits were not sufficient to explain retiree benefits without reference to the details contained in the regular retiree plan. Therefore, the employer's reservation of rights in the regular plan was sufficient to cover the enhanced benefits provided to early retirees [Stearns v. NCR Corp., 297 F.3d 706 (8th Cir. 2002)]

Note. An employer may be barred from amending its plan if the plan amendment fails to comply with the amendment procedure set forth in the plan. [Curtiss-Wright Corp. v. Schoonejongen, 514 U.S. 73 (1995)]

Q 4:27   Once an employer has offered an "early out" program promising lifetime medical benefits, what happens to those benefits if the company merges with another company?

In *DeBoard v. Sunshine Mining & Refining Co.* [208 F.3d 1228 (10th Cir. 2000)], the employer sent letters to eligible employees promising that if the employees took early retirement, the employer would provide them and their dependents with lifetime medical benefits. On the basis of that letter, several employees retired. Shortly before the letter was sent, the company merged. In the merger agreement, the new company agreed to not terminate or modify any existing employee welfare benefit plans for ten years. At the ten-year mark, the new company attempted to terminate dental and life insurance coverage and impose a $500 per month health insurance premium on retirees. The court held that the letters sent by the premerger company created a new and separate ERISA welfare benefit plan and that a reasonable person would have perceived an ongoing commitment by the employer to provide the benefits. The letters unambiguously guaranteed lifetime medical benefits to employees who participated in the early retirement plan—but they were entitled only to the same type of coverage as that provided to the company's current salaried employees.

While those former employees were entitled to lifetime benefits (albeit reduced ones), another case illustrates that "lifetime" benefits do not necessarily last for a lifetime.

In November 1991, Continental Insurance Company offered a voluntary special retirement program (VSRP) to certain employees. The VSRP included a monthly "health care allowance" (HCA). In describing the VSRP to eligible employees, Continental consistently described the HCA as a "lifetime" benefit. In the plan document, however, Continental reserved the right to amend the plan at any time.

In 1998, a few years after Continental was acquired by CNA Financial Corporation, CNA informed the employees who had accepted the VSRP that their HCA benefits would be eliminated as of January 1, 1999. A group of employees brought suit against CNA claiming that the company had violated ERISA by eliminating the HCA benefits.

The Seventh Circuit concluded that CNA had not violated ERISA when it terminated the HCA benefits. The court noted that CNA had conceded that the HCA benefit was a "lifetime benefit." However, according to the court, "'lifetime' may be construed as 'good for life unless revoked or modified'"— especially when the plan documents include a reservation of rights clause. According to the court, "the 'lifetime' nature of a welfare benefit does not operate to vest that benefit if the employer reserved the right to terminate the benefit."[Vallone v. CNA Fin. Corp., 375 F.3d 623 (7th Cir. 2004)]

Q 4:28   If an employer reduces severance pay by the value of retiree medical benefits as permitted under the ADEA, can the employer subsequently amend, modify, or terminate the retiree medical plan?

The answer depends on the level of retiree medical benefits that will be available after the amendment or modification. The Older Workers Benefits Protection Act (OWBPA) amendments to the ADEA require that the value of retiree health benefits that can be used to reduce severance pay and that is payable as a result of a contingent event unrelated to age meets minimum, specified standards. If an employer does make such a reduction, that minimum statutory level of retiree medical benefits must continue to be made available, or the employer will be subject to an action for specific performance by any "aggrieved individual" for failing to fulfill its obligation to provide retiree medical benefits. [ADEA § 4(l)(2)(F); 29 U.S.C. § 623(l)(2)(F)]

Practice Pointer. An employer contemplating reducing the level of retiree medical benefits to decrease its FAS 106 liability (see chapter 20) should consider whether coordinating severance pay and retiree medical benefits in this fashion effectively ties its hands regarding wholesale redesign of its retiree medical program.

Q 4:29 Do statements about "lifetime benefits" prevent an employer from amending or terminating its retiree medical plan?

Possibly. If a retiree medical plan and its SPD do not clearly reserve the right to amend the plan or are ambiguous on the issue of the intended duration of retiree medical benefits, a court might look to extrinsic evidence (i.e., evidence outside the governing document) to determine the employer's intent. When that happens, statements made in exit interviews or letters to retirees about lifetime benefits can harm an employer's position if the court cites such statements as evidence of the requisite intent to make the plan or its level of benefits permanent.

On the other hand, if a plan and its SPD are carefully drafted to include a clear and unambiguous reservation of the right to amend or terminate the plan, and the plan document allocates a discretionary power to interpret the plan to the employer, the plan administrator or trustee, or an authorized designee, the court will be required to enforce the plan's terms. In *In re Unisys Corp. Retiree Medical Benefit ERISA Litigation* [58 F.3d 896 (3d Cir. 1995)], for instance, the court held that where both the plan document and SPD contained a reservation of rights clause, retirees could not bring an action for breach of contract or equitable estoppel when the plan was changed.

> **Practice Pointer.** It is important that the employer protect itself on several fronts. First, the power to amend the plan should be carefully reserved. Second, the power to amend should not appear to be limited in scope, such as for "legislative changes" or other grounds that arguably would appear not to cover a simple decision to cut back coverage or increase cost sharing. Third, the employer or other plan fiduciary should be granted discretionary power to both interpret the terms of the plan and determine the facts thereunder.

Most significantly, the employer should be very careful not to undercut the plan terms by indicating in any way that the plan will not be changed. In a subsequent decision in an ongoing and protracted retiree medical benefit litigation, the Third Circuit held that the plan sponsor breached its fiduciary duty under ERISA when its employees counseled a group of prospective retirees about the cost and duration of retiree health benefits without cautioning them that retiree benefits were subject to change. According to the Third Circuit, the fact that the company disclosed its reservation of rights in the summary plan description and other documentation was not enough because it did not present that information when counseling the employees on their retirement decisions. "In essence," said the court, "by failing to qualify its statements, Unisys placed a period where it should have placed a comma in the course of explaining retiree medical benefits to these plaintiffs and, in doing so, misrepresented the cost and duration of the benefits." [*In re* Unisys Corp. Retiree Med. Benefit ERISA Litig., 579 F.3d 220 (3d Cir. 2009)]

Q 4:30　Can an employer mislead its employees about its intention to retain its retiree medical plan?

No. An employer may not affirmatively mislead employees about its retiree medical plan. Even if an employer has correctly included a reservation of rights clause in both the plan document and the summary plan description and could lawfully reduce or terminate benefits based on that clause, the employer nonetheless cannot effectively terminate the benefits through fraudulent means.

The United States Supreme Court has stated that an employer, when administering an employee benefit plan, cannot "participate knowingly and significantly in deceiving a plan's beneficiaries in order to save the employer money at the beneficiaries' expense." The employer, Varity Corporation, spun off a subsidiary that was significantly undercapitalized and encouraged employees to transfer to it. Subsequently, the subsidiary failed and went into receivership. Welfare benefits (including benefits to retirees that had been transferred to the subsidiary without their knowledge) were discontinued. In explaining the corporate transaction to employees, the company was less than forthright about the financial prospects of the subsidiary and the long-term prospects of health care and other benefits. The Supreme Court held that reasonable employees could have thought that the company was communicating with them both in its capacity as employer and in its capacity as plan administrator. It thus permitted individual workers to sue for breach of fiduciary duty under ERISA. [Varity Corp. v. Howe, 516 U.S. 911 (1995)] A case before the Sixth Circuit Court of Appeals addressed the issue of misleading employees about retiree health coverage. Pirelli Armstrong Tire Corporation purchased Armstrong's plant in Madison, Tenn. in 1988. In July 1990, Pirelli implemented a plan that provided various incentives to employees who elected to take early retirement. Pirelli provided written descriptions of the plan to its employees and required all employees to attend one of several mandatory meetings. At the meetings, employees were told that if they took early retirement, they would not be affected by upcoming changes to Pirelli's health care plan and their medical benefits would not change "during retirement." In addition, Pirelli's assistant employee relations manager responded to employees' questions by stating that their health care benefits would not change during their lifetimes. The plant manager also told employees that their medical benefits would not change during their retirement.

Three years later Pirelli changed the terms of the retiree health insurance plan. Under the new plan, retirees were subject to greater out-of-pocket expenses. Subsequently, Pirelli again amended the plan to increase premium contributions, deductibles, and maximum out-of-pocket amounts for retirees.

When the plan changes were challenged, a federal district ruled that Pirelli did not breach its fiduciary duties because there was no evidence that the assistant employee relations manager or the plant manager deliberately or negligently misled the retiring employees. However, the Sixth Circuit Court of Appeals reversed the district court. According to the appeals court, "Pirelli's breach of its fiduciary duty occurred when the company provided, on its own initiative, materially misleading and inaccurate information about the plan benefits to plaintiffs in group meetings and exit interviews. Pirelli's fiduciary duty to plaintiffs was triggered even though not all plaintiffs asked specific questions about the future benefits of the plan."[James v. Pirelli Armstrong Tire Corp., 305 F.3d 439 (6th Cir. 2002)]

Temporary Reinsurance Program for Early Retirees

Q 4:31   What is the temporary reinsurance program for early retirees?

The 2010 Health Reform Act directs the Secretary of Health and Human Services (HHS) to establish a temporary reinsurance program for retirees beginning in June 2010 and ending January 1, 2013. [PPACA § 1102 as amended by PPACA § 10102] The program will provide reimbursements to participating employment-based plans for a portion of the costs of providing health benefits to early retirees. HHS has issued interim final regulations implementing the program effective June 1, 2010. [45 C.F.R. §§ 149.1-149.160] Employers may participate in the program for plan years beginning before June 1, 2010, and ending after that date (e.g., 2010 calender year plans).

Q 4:32   What types of plans are eligible to participate in the temporary reinsurance program?

An employment-based group benefits plan that provides health benefits to early retirees is eligible to participate in the temporary reinsurance program. Eligible plans include private employer plans, state and local government plans, plans of employee organizations, voluntary employee beneficiary associations (VEBAs), and multiemployer plans. [PPACA § 1102(b)] Health benefits include medical, surgical, hospital, and other benefits to be determined by HHS, whether self-funded or provided through insurance.

To participate in the program, a plan must implement programs and procedures to generate cost savings for plan participants with chronic and high-cost conditions. Plans must apply for participation and be certified by the Secretary of HHS. The Secretary has the authority to stop taking applications for participation based on the available funding. [45 C.F.R. §§ 149.35-149.45]

Q 4:33   Who is an early retiree for purposes of the temporary reinsurance program?

Reimbursements under the temporary reinsurance program will be made for the costs of health benefits for early retirees, as well as spouses, surviving spouses, and dependents of early retirees who are covered under the group benefits plan.

Early retirees are individuals age 55 or older who do not qualify for Medicare and who are not active employees of an employer maintaining or currently contributing to the plan or of any employer who has made substantial contributions to the plan. [PPACA § 1102(a)(2)(C); 45 C.F.R. 149.2]

Q 4:34   How will reimbursements be provided under the temporary reinsurance program?

A participating employment-based plan must submit claims for reimbursement, including documentation of the actual costs of items and services for which the claim is being submitted. To be eligible for reimbursement, a claim may not be for less than $15,000 or more than $90,000 (as adjusted for inflation each fiscal year). If the claim is accepted, the program will reimburse the plan for 80 percent of the cost that exceeds $15,000. [PPACA § 1102(c)] In other words, if a plan submits the maximum $90,000 claim, the reimbursement will be $60,000 (80% × ($90,000 – $15,000)). Special transition rules apply for plan years beginning before June 1, 2010. [45 C.F.R. § 149.105]

Claims must be based on the actual amount expended by the plan within the plan year that health benefits are provided to an early retiree or a spouse, surviving spouse, or dependent of an early retiree. In determining the amount of a claim, the plan must take into account any negotiated price concessions (such as discounts, direct or indirect subsidies, rebates, and direct or indirect remunerations) obtained by the plan. Costs paid by the early retiree or by the early retiree's spouse, surviving spouse, or dependent in the form of deductibles, copayments, or coinsurance are included as amounts paid by the plan.

Q 4:35   Can reimbursements from the program be used for any purpose?

No. Amounts paid to a participating employment-based plan must be used to lower costs for the plan. [PPACA § 1102(c)(4)] Amounts may be used to reduce premium costs for the employer or other plan sponsor or to reduce premium contributions, copayments, deductible, coinsurance, or other out-of-pocket costs for plan participants. [45 C.F.R. § 149.200]

Program payments cannot be used as general revenues by the employer or plan sponsor.

Q 4:36   How are reimbursements from the program treated for tax purposes?

Payments from the temporary reinsurance program are not included in gross income of the employer or other plan sponsor. [PPACA § 1102(c))(5)]

The 2010 Health Reform Act does not specify the effect of the reimbursements on the employer's deduction for retiree health benefit costs. However, as a general rule no deduction is allowed for any expense allocable to tax-exempt income. [I.R.C. § 265(a); Treas. Reg. § 1.265-1(a)] Consequently, the employer's otherwise allowable deduction for retiree health plan costs should be reduced by the amount of any reimbursements.

Coordination with Medicare

Q 4:37 Can retiree medical plans be entirely secondary to Medicare?

As a general rule, Medicare is primary to retiree health coverage. However, retiree medical plans cannot be entirely secondary to Medicare. In certain cases involving end-stage renal disease (ESRD), a retiree medical plan is required to pay primary to Medicare. [42 U.S.C. § 1395y(b)(1)(C), as amended by § 13561 of OBRA'93]

Final regulations administered by the Centers for Medicare and Medicaid Services (CMS) provide that:

1. If the individual first becomes eligible for or entitled to Medicare based on ESRD and subsequently becomes entitled to Medicare based on age or disability during a 30-month coordination period, the group health plan, including a retiree medical plan, is obligated to pay primary to Medicare throughout the 30-month period.

2. The group health plan (including a retiree medical plan) must also pay primary for a 30-month coordination period when ESRD-based eligibility or entitlement occurs simultaneously with age-or disability-based entitlement.

3. If each of the following three conditions is satisfied, then Medicare continues to be primary after an aged or disabled beneficiary becomes eligible for Medicare on the basis of ESRD:

   a. Medicare entitlement based on age or disability occurs before entitlement due to ESRD;

   b. The Medicare secondary-payer prohibition against "taking into account" age- or disability-based entitlement does not apply because plan coverage is not "by virtue of current employment" or the employer has fewer than 20 employees (in the case of the aged) or fewer than 100 employees (in the case of the disabled); and

   c. The plan is already paying secondary to Medicare because the plan had justifiably taken into account the age- or disability-based entitlement.

Note that if the plan has failed to coordinate with Medicare before the individual becomes eligible for Medicare based on ESRD, the plan apparently forfeits this exemption and will have to pay primary to Medicare for the full 30-month period even though the coverage is retiree coverage.

If the individual elects a Medicare + Choice plan under Medicare Part C, Part C is also secondary to retiree group health plans on the same basis as for Parts A and B.

Q 4:38   Can an employer provide any financial incentive to encourage employees who are Medicare beneficiaries not to enroll in the employer's group health plan?

No. Employers and other entities such as insurers cannot offer Medicare beneficiaries any financial or other benefits as incentives not to enroll in, or to terminate enrollment in, a group health plan that is or would be primary to Medicare. An employer or other entity violating this prohibition is subject to a civil money penalty of up to $5,000 for each violation. [Social Security Act § 1862(b)(3); 29 U.S.C. § 1395y(b)(3); 42 C.F.R. § 411.103]

While this rule has limited applicability to retiree medical plans, it could be interpreted to bar an employer's practice of paying for Medicare Part B premiums as an alternative to enrollment in the employer's retiree medical plan for the limited ESRD group discussed in Q 4:37.

Q 4:39   What sanctions apply for violating the Medicare secondary-payer rules?

Stiff penalties apply to violations of the Medicare secondary-payer requirements, as follows.

Excise tax. The sponsoring employer or employee organization can be taxed in an amount equal to 25 percent of the employer's or employee organization's expenses incurred during the calendar year for each group health plan to which it contributes. [I.R.C.§ 5000(a); 42 U.S.C. § 1395y(a)(3)]

Double damages. The federal government also may bring an action against any entity, insurance policy, or plan to collect double damages for failure to pay as a primary payer. Individuals are also given a private right of action for double damages if the group health plan fails to pay benefits on a primary basis. [42 U.S.C. § 1395y(a)(2)(B)(ii)]

Retiree Prescription Drug Benefits

Q 4:40   What is the retiree prescription drug plan subsidy?

The Medicare Prescription Drug Improvement and Modernization Act of 2003 [Pub. L. No. 108-173, 117 Stat. 2066 (2003)] established a voluntary prescription drug benefit under Medicare Part D. In conjunction with that change, the Act provides for federal subsidy payments to employers and unions that sponsor qualified retiree prescription drug plans. Both the Medicare prescription drug benefit and the retiree prescription drug plan subsidies took effect in 2006.

Retiree prescription drug plan subsidies are provided for retirees who are eligible for Medicare prescription drug coverage, but who receive drug coverage through an employment-based plan. To receive the subsidy, a plan must offer benefits with an actuarial *value* equal to or greater than Medicare prescription drug benefits, although the benefits need not be identical to the benefits offered by Medicare.

For plan years ending in 2010, the subsidy covers 28 percent of prescription drug costs between $310 and $6,300 per eligible individual (i.e., up to $1,677.20 per individual). The dollar figures are indexed for inflation. The subsidy applies only to costs that are actually paid (net of discounts, chargebacks, and rebates) for prescription drugs; administrative costs are not included in calculating the subsidy. The subsidy is not included in the employer's gross income for federal income tax purposes and does not affect the deductibility of contributions by the employer to its retiree health plan.

Q 4:41 When is retiree prescription drug coverage considered actuarially equivalent to Medicare for purposes of the retiree prescription drug subsidy?

To qualify for the retiree prescription drug subsidy, an employer must show that its prescription drug coverage is actuarially equivalent to standard coverage under the Medicare prescription drug benefit. Regulations issued by the Health and Human Services Department's Centers for Medicare and Medicaid (CMS) lay down a two-part test for determining actuarial equivalence.

1. A "gross value" test in which the expected amount of paid claims for Medicare beneficiaries under the employer's plan must be at least equal to the expected amount of paid claims for the same beneficiaries under the defined standard prescription drug coverage, including catastrophic coverage available when an individual's out-of-pocket expenses exceed a specified threshold. [42 C.F.R. § 423.884(d)(1)(i)]

2. A "net value" test in which the net value of the sponsor's plan must be at least equal to the net value of the defined standard prescription drug coverage. [42 C.F.R. § 423.884(d)(1)(ii)] The net value of the sponsor's plan is calculated by subtracting retiree premiums or contributions from the gross value of the sponsor's plan. The net value of defined standard prescription drug coverage under Medicare Part D is calculated by subtracting the prescribed national beneficiary premium from the gross value of the defined standard prescription drug coverage.

In general, an employer must separately identify the various benefit options within its plan for which it wishes to claim the drug subsidy. Each option must satisfy the actuarial equivalence tests. For this purpose, a benefit option is a particular benefit design, category of benefits, or cost-sharing arrangement offered within a group health plan. If an employer offers retirees identical prescription drug coverage but charges them different premium amounts, the employer can treat the coverage as either a single benefit option (even though premiums charged differ among retirees), or as multiple benefit options, with each benefit option associated with a different premium level. An employer must be consistent in defining the benefit options. In other words, if an employer offering identical coverage at different premium levels treats the coverage as a single benefit option for purposes of determining actuarial equivalence, it must also treat the coverage as a single benefit option in other parts of the application and data submission process where the identification of benefit options is relevant.

Q 4:42   How does an employer claim the retiree prescription drug subsidy?

The application and payment process for the drug subsidy is handled electronically through the RDS Center's web site (*http://www.rds.cms.hhs.gov*). An employer seeking the subsidy must complete an electronic application through the RDS Center and submit the application 90 days before each plan year for which it intends to seek the subsidy. An application must be submitted for each group health plan. However, the application for a group health plan may include two or more benefit options in the plan (see Q 4:41), provided the options have the same benefit year start and end dates.

An employer may elect to receive subsidy payments on a monthly, quarterly, interim annual, or annual basis. Subsidy payments will be made by electronic funds transfer (EFT) to an account designated by the employer. An employer cannot choose to receive payments by check rather than EFT.

Q 4:43   What are the disclosure requirements for plans that provide prescription drug coverage?

All employers that offer prescription drug coverage—including employers who do not apply for the federal subsidy—must disclose to Medicare Part D-eligible plan participants whether or not the plan constitutes creditable coverage. This disclosure requirement applies to all Part D-eligible individuals covered by or applying for coverage under an employer's plan, including active and disabled employees, retirees, Medicare-eligible dependents, and eligible individuals receiving COBRA continuation coverage.

The purpose of the disclosure requirement is to provide Medicare-eligible individuals with important information necessary to decide whether and when to enroll for Medicare Part D prescription drug coverage. Individuals who do not have other creditable prescription drug coverage generally must enroll at the time they initially become eligible or they will face higher premiums when they enroll at a later date. If employer coverage is creditable, an individual may postpone enrolling in Part D without incurring a late enrollment penalty.

As a general rule, coverage is creditable if the actuarial value of the coverage equals or exceeds the actuarial value of standard Medicare using the gross value test that applies for purposes of the drug subsidy (see Q 4:41). [42 C.F.R. § 423.56(a)]

However, an employer that is *not* claiming the retiree prescription drug can use a simplified method based on plan design to determine if its plan constitutes creditable coverage. Under the simplified rules, a plan will be deemed to be creditable coverage if it provides:

1. Coverage for brand-name and generic prescriptions;
2. Reasonable access to retail drug providers and, optionally, access to mail order providers;
3. Benefit payments averaging at least 60 percent of a plan participant's prescription drug expenses; and
4. At least one of the following:
   a. No annual prescription drug benefit maximum limit or an annual maximum of at least $25,000, or
   b. Expected benefits of at least $2,000 per Medicare beneficiary, or
   c. An integrated plan design that covers both medical expenses and prescription drugs with an annual deductible of no more than $250, either no annual benefit maximum or an annual maximum of at least $25,000, and a lifetime combined maximum of at least $1 million.

An employer must also disclose to the CMS whether or not its coverage is creditable. However, this disclosure requirement does not apply to employers applying for the drug subsidy.

Integrated Plans. An *integrated plan* is a plan that combines a prescription drug benefit with other coverage (i.e., medical, dental, vision, and so forth). Such a plan must meet tests 1, 2, 3, and 4(c) above. A plan is considered integrated if it has a combined plan year deductible, a combined annual benefit maximum, and a combined lifetime benefit maximum for all benefits under the plan.

A nonintegrated plan must meet tests 1, 2, 3 and either 4(a) or 4(b). If a plan cannot use the simplified method, the employer must make an annual actuarial determination of whether the coverage is creditable.

Practice Pointer. The tests for creditable coverage are not identical to the actuarial equivalence tests required to claim the retiree prescription drug subsidy. Therefore, an employer plan that constitutes creditable coverage will not automatically qualify for the subsidy.

Model Notices. The CMS, which administers the retiree prescription drug subsidy, has issued model notices to inform retirees whether an employer's plan does or does not provide creditable coverage. The model notice can be found on the agency's web site (*www.cms.hhs.gov/Creditable Coverage*).

Notice timing. Creditable coverage disclosures to plan participants are required *prior to*:

1. The annual Part D election period, beginning November 15 and lasting through December 31 each year;
2. An individual participant's initial enrollment period for Part D;
3. The effective date of coverage for any Medicare eligible individual who joins the plan; and

4. The time the employer no longer offers prescription drug coverage or changes the coverage offered so that it is no longer creditable or becomes creditable.

Disclosure must also be made when requested by a plan participant. [42 C.F.R. § 423.56(f)]

Disclosure is considered to have been made prior to a triggering event only if it was provided within the previous 12 months. If a creditable coverage disclosure notice is provided to all plan participants annually, CMS will consider the first two disclosure requirements to be met.

Disclosure to CMS. Employers must disclose to the CMS whether or not their coverage is creditable. This requirement does not apply to employers that apply for the drug subsidy. A disclosure form can be found on the agency's web site (*www.cms.hhs.gov/Creditable Coverage*).

Disclosure to the CMS must be made no later than 60 days following the beginning of the employer's plan year.

Q 4:44   How does an employer apply for the prescription drug subsidy?

To apply for the prescription drug subsidy, an employer must submit an annual application through the RDS secure web site (*https://www.rds.cms.hhs.gov*). For calendar-year plans, applications are due by September 30. Non-calendar year plans must apply 90 days prior to the beginning of each plan year. The application must include an actuary's attestation that the plan meets the actuarial equivalence standard and certification that the creditable coverage status of the plan has or will be disclosed to plan participants.

The employer also must submit and periodically update enrollment information about retirees and dependents and drug costs incurred by the plan.

An employer may elect to receive the subsidy on a monthly, quarterly, or annual basis. All payments are made electronically.

Q 4:45   How is the retiree prescription drug subsidy treated for income tax purposes?

The amount of any qualified retiree prescription drug plan subsidy is excludable from the sponsoring employer's gross income for purposes of regular income tax and the alternative minimum tax. [I.R.C. § 139A]

For tax years beginning before January 1, 2013, the exclusion is not taken into account in determining the employer's deduction for retiree prescription drug costs. In other words, the employer can claim the full amount of retiree prescription drug costs as a business expense deduction unreduced by the amount of the excludable subsidy.

For tax years beginning after December 31, 2012, the 2010 Health Reform Act eliminates the rule that the exclusion for subsidy payments is not taken into account for purposes of determining an employer's deduction for retiree prescription drug costs. [I.R.C. § 139A, as amended by PPACA § 9012 and PPACA Reconciliation § 1407] Thus, the amount otherwise allowable as a deduction for retiree prescription drug costs would be reduced by the amount of the excludable subsidy payments received.

> **Practice Pointer.** Because of the delayed effective date, the law change will not have any effect on an employer's income tax liability until the first tax year beginning after 2012. However, it will have an *immediate* effect for accounting purposes (see Q 4:49).

Trust Requirement

Q 4:46   Are employee contributions to retiree medical plans considered plan assets subject to ERISA's trust requirement?

Yes. DOL regulations on the trust requirement for employee contributions to ERISA welfare benefit plans state that employee contributions are plan assets; however, the DOL has suspended enforcement (except for self-insured plans) while it considers whether to grant a class exemption or individual exemptions from the trust requirement to employee contributions to retiree medical plans. The suspension has been extended until final regulations are adopted or until further notice. [DOL Regs. § 2510.3-102; ERISA Tech. Rels. 88-1, 92-01; 52 Fed. Reg. 23,272 (June 2, 1992); DOL Notice, 58 Fed. Reg. 45,359 (Aug. 27, 1993)] As a condition of qualifying for this limited suspension, employee contributions for insured retiree medical plan coverage must be forwarded to the insurance company within 90 days.

In the final plan asset regulations published on August 7, 1996, the DOL confirmed that ERISA Technical Release 92-01 is not affected by the new final regulations and remains in effect until further notice. [61 Fed. Reg. 41,220, at 41,222 (Aug. 7, 1996)]

Financial Accounting Rules

Q 4:47   What financial accounting requirements apply to retiree welfare benefits?

In July 2009, the Financial Accounting Standards Board (FASB) reorganized its accounting standards into a topic-based FASB Accounting Standards Codification (ASC). For clarity, the references in this section are to the familiar FAS citations followed by the new ASC citations.

Statement of Financial Accounting Standards No. 106, *Employers' Accounting for Postretirement Benefits Other Than Pensions* (FAS 106, ASC 715) requires employers to estimate the future cost of their liability for future retiree medical benefits using specified assumptions and methodology and to recognize a portion of that amount as an expense on their financial statements each year.

The accounting treatment specified by FAS 106 (ASC 715) forces an awareness of the true cost of retiree benefit promises and a disclosure of the substantial future financial impact they can have.

Financial Accounting Series Report No. 129-B, "A Guide to Implementation of Statement 106 on Employers' Accounting for Postretirement Benefits Other Than Pensions: Questions and Answers" (Aug. 1993), provides further details about applying FAS 106 (ASC 715) and guidance about whether FAS 106 (ASC 715) or FAS 112 (ASC 712) on Employers' Accounting for Postemployment Benefits, which addresses benefits that are provided to former or inactive employees after employment but before retirement, applies.

FAS 132 (ASC 715) amended FAS 106 and FAS 112 to provide for more standardized reporting of financial information. The standards set forth in FAS 106 and FAS 132 have been codified in ASC Topic 715, Compensation— Retirement Benefits.

See chapter 21 for a detailed discussion of financial accounting rules.

Q 4:48 What are the financial accounting requirements if an employer is not legally obligated to provide retiree benefits?

FAS 106 (ASC 715) applies even if an employer is not legally obligated to provide retiree benefits. [FAS 106, Appendix A, Basis for Conclusions, § 156]

For FAS 106 (ASC 715) purposes, the ERISA status of a retiree welfare plan is irrelevant. FAS 106 (ASC 715) does not require a legally enforceable obligation; therefore, it does not matter that ERISA does not treat retiree medical plan benefits as "vested" and permits retiree medical plans to be amended or terminated under a reservation of rights clause.

FAS 106 (ASC 715) applies to any arrangement that is in substance a postretirement benefit plan, regardless of its form or the means or timing of its funding (and regardless of whether it is funded or unfunded). It also applies to written plans and to unwritten plans whose existence is based on a practice of paying postretirement benefits or on oral representations made to current or former employees. In the absence of evidence to the contrary, FAS 106 (ASC 715) presumes that an employer that has provided postretirement benefits in the past or is currently promising such benefits to employees will continue to provide retiree benefits. [FAS 106, § 8; ASC 715-10-15]

Q 4:49 How is the retiree prescription drug subsidy treated for financial accounting purposes?

Guidance from the FASB specifies how retiree health plan sponsors should reflect expected subsidies from the federal government under the Medicare Part D prescription drug program. According to FASB Staff Position 106-2 [FSP 106-2], employers must recognize the future expected subsidy payments as a reduction in the prescription drug plan costs and obligations that are computed under Statement of Financial Accounting Standards No. 106. [FAS 106, ASC 715]

In addition, the FASB rules require companies to treat future tax deductions for retiree drug costs as a deferred tax asset on their balance sheets. [FAS 109, ASC 740] The 2010 Health Reform Act mandates that, starting in 2013, income tax deductions for retiree drug costs must be reduced by federal subsidies received for those costs (see Q 4:45). Furthermore, under the FASB rules, the decrease in future tax deductions must be reported immediately for accounting purposes.

Q 4:50   What are the financial accounting requirements for retiree medical plans?

FAS 106 (ASC 715) requires that an employer's liability for postretirement medical benefits be shown on the employer's balance sheet and profit and loss statement. The liability must be accounted for on an accrual basis rather than on a cash (pay-as-you-go) basis. That means that the cost of the benefit must be shown when the employees are deemed to be "earning" the benefits, rather than later when the benefits are actually paid. FAS 106 (ASC 715) does not require that the liability for postretirement medical benefits be funded, however. (Details of these requirements are discussed in chapter 21.)

The FASB has published final guidance on how retiree health plan sponsors should reflect expected subsidies from the federal government under the Medicare Part D prescription drug program. According to FASB Staff Position 106-2 [FSP 106-2], employers must recognize the future expected subsidy payments as a reduction in the prescription drug plan costs and obligations that are computed under FAS 106.

Q 4:51   Is an employer to fund its postretirement welfare benefits?

No. FAS 106 (ASC 715) only requires that an employer recognize and disclose its liability for postretirement benefits on its financial statements, not that the employer fund such benefits.

Funding Options

Q 4:52   What options are available to an employer that wishes to reduce its accounting liability by prefunding retiree medical benefits on a tax-advantaged basis?

Employers have several options for prefunding retiree medical benefits, including the following:

- The welfare benefit fund rules of Code Sections 419 and 419A
- A Section 401(h) account under a pension or annuity plan
- Transfer of pension plan surplus

Each of the methods can be used alone or in conjunction with plan redesign techniques.

Q 4:53 How much of an employer's liability for retiree medical benefits can be funded under the welfare benefit fund rules of Code Sections 419 and 419A?

The welfare benefit fund rules found in Code Sections 419 and 419A allow tax-deductible funding of a reserve for postretirement medical insurance benefits if certain conditions are satisfied. The reserve must be funded over the working lives of the employees and be actuarially determined on a level basis, using assumptions that are reasonable in the aggregate.

The IRS has not issued formal guidance on how this funding limit applies to existing retirees, who have no remaining working lives. A question thus arises as to whether the permitted reserve for postretirement medical benefits could be funded all at once. The IRS has informally indicated that this cannot be done and issued a letter ruling approving a methodology for funding the retiree medical reserve over the working lives of active employees. [Priv. Ltr. Rul. 9710033] The amount that an employer contributes for retiree medical benefits cannot include any amount to cover anticipated inflation, and separate accounting is required for key employees. In addition, the income on the reserve for postretirement medical benefits accumulates on an after-tax basis unless certain exceptions apply.

(A more detailed discussion of the funding method under Code Sections 419 and 419A, including case law developments specifically affecting funding reserves for postretirement medical benefits, is contained in chapter 20.)

Q 4:54 How much of an employer's liability for retiree medical benefits can be funded using a Section 401(h) account under a pension or annuity plan?

An employer may establish and maintain a separate account, called a Section 401(h) account, under a pension or annuity plan, to pay for sickness, accident, hospitalization, and medical expenses of retired employees, their spouses, and their dependents. Various requirements must be met for the employer to do so.

One of those key requirements is that the retiree medical benefits must be subordinate to the retirement benefits under the plan and cannot exceed 25 percent of the total contributions (for pension, retiree medical, and life insurance) made to the pension or annuity plan since the date the Section 401(h) account was established under the pension plan. Within such limits, however, the total cost of retiree medical benefits (including anticipated inflation), can be prefunded, and earnings will accumulate in the Section 401(h) account tax-free. Because the flexibility to prefund in such a manner depends on the contributions made to the pension plan, the Section 401(h) method will be less useful for employers with well-funded pension plans.

(Section 401(h) accounts are discussed more fully in chapter 20.)

Q 4:55 Can an employer fund its liability for retiree medical benefits under a profit sharing retirement plan?

Although a Section 401(h) account cannot be maintained under a profit sharing plan because it is not a pension or annuity plan, an employer can always increase contributions under a profit sharing plan to cover part or all of the cost, later on, of retiree medical benefits. No special segregated account is necessary. By selecting a defined contribution plan to do so, an employer can use a retirement-type vehicle to obtain tax-free accumulation of earnings. On the other hand, when the benefits are paid out of the plan, they are taxable retirement benefits. The employer has no power to force an individual to use such funds for retiree medical benefits—although it can encourage such a choice.

However, the IRS has ruled that a profit-sharing plan that provided each participant with a separate profit sharing account and medical reimbursement account was not tax-qualified. The plan provided that payments from the medical reimbursement account could be used only to reimburse substantiated medical expenses of the plan participant, the participant's spouse, or the participant's dependent. Consequently, the plan violated the rule under Code Section 411 requiring that a participant's accrued benefit under a profit sharing plan be nonforfeitable. [Rev. Rul. 2005-55, 2005-2 C.B. 284]

On the other hand, the IRS ruling pointed out that if the plan provided that amounts in the medical reimbursement account could be distributed for any purpose on the same terms as amounts in the profit sharing account, the fact that those amounts could be used for medical expenses would not disqualify the plan.

Nonetheless, Revenue Ruling 2005-55 makes it clear that amounts distributed for medical expenses would not qualify as accident or health benefits eligible for exclusion from gross income under Code Section 105.

Q 4:56 Can an employer transfer any portion of a pension plan surplus to fund retiree medical benefits?

Yes. Code Section 420 provides a special mechanism for a "qualified transfer" of a part of the surplus under a defined benefit pension plan (other than a multiemployer plan) to a Section 401(h) account once each year, provided certain requirements are met. The employer does not incur tax or penalties on the transfer, as it would if the funds were withdrawn from the plan.

Code Section 420 is a temporary provision, which is currently set to expire after 2013.

Two of the applicable requirements may limit the attractiveness of this option. First, to be a qualified transfer, the pension plan must provide that the accrued benefits of any plan participant or beneficiary become nonforfeitable as if the plan had terminated immediately before the qualified transfer. This full vesting of accrued benefits may have a substantial cost impact on the employer. Second, under a "maintenance of effort" requirement, the applicable employer cost of the retiree medical benefits that are furnished must be at least as high, during the year of the qualified transfer and the four years after it, as during the two taxable years before the year of the qualified transfer.

The minimum cost requirement relates to the cost per individual covered by the plan for each year in the maintenance of effort period. Therefore, an employer could potentially reduce costs and still satisfy the maintenance of effort requirement by reducing the number of individuals covered by the plan. However, the IRS has issued final regulations under which the minimum cost requirement would not be met if the employer significantly reduces retiree health coverage during the maintenance of effort period. The regulations measure whether an employer has significantly reduced coverage by looking at the number of individuals (retirees, their spouses, and their dependents) who lose coverage during the period as a result of employer actions, measured on both an annual basis and a cumulative basis. Because of these restrictions and requirements, an employer contemplating a wholesale redesign and reduction of retiree medical benefits may not benefit from a transfer of excess pension assets.

(Section 420 qualified transfers are discussed in more detail in chapter 20.)

Q 4:57 Does financing with corporate-owned life insurance help reduce an employer's accounting liability?

A practice once popular was purchasing corporate-owned life insurance (COLI) on the lives of employees to cover the employer's liability for benefits under a retiree medical plan. COLI did not constitute a funding method for the welfare benefit plan, did not meet the requirements for creation of a plan asset under FAS 106 (ASC 715), and was not intended to create a plan asset for ERISA purposes. Thus, although it was a method for financing retiree medical liability, COLI did not reduce the amount of that liability for accounting purposes.

HIPAA, the Taxpayer Relief Act of 1997, and the Pension Protection Act of 2006 amended the Code to restrict severely the favorable tax treatment of COLI policies. In doing so, the amendments have effectively terminated COLI as a broad-based financing vehicle for retiree medical plans. (See further discussion of COLI in chapter 20.)

Q 4:58 Can retirement plan benefit payments be deferred and used as a pretax cafeteria plan contribution for retiree medical coverage?

One concept for financing the cost of retiree medical benefits was the use of pension plan payouts as a pretax cafeteria plan contribution toward retiree medical plan coverage. This technique, dubbed the *qualified cafeteria plan hybrid,* was described in detail in "New Cafeteria Plan Ideas—Qualified Cafeteria Plan Hybrid: Appetizing Addition to Retiree Funding Menu?" [Case & Colemen, 5 Benefits L.J. 533 (Winter 1992–93) and follow-up letters and articles in the same journal] Then commercial firms began marketing hybrid plans.

Under these plans, qualified plan distributions were reported as income on Form 1099-R, net of the cost of the accident and health coverage provided by the cafeteria plan. The amounts used to pay for accident and health coverage were treated as tax-free cafeteria plan contributions under Code Section 125. Marketers of the plan argued that retirees are specifically included as cafeteria plan participants because the term *employee* under Code Section 125 includes present and former employees of the employer. Thus, they contended that Congress must have intended that payments to former employees from retirement plans could be used to pay for accident and health benefits on a pretax basis. The marketers also argued that payments attributable to employer contributions to the retirement plan constituted "taxable benefits" or "cash" within the meaning of Code Section 125 that could be assigned, before receipt, as a pretax contribution to the plan.

Unfortunately, the IRS rejected this concept. In a Coordinated Issue Paper for All Industries, the IRS concluded that amounts distributed from a qualified plan and used to pay for benefits in a former employer's cafeteria plan must be included in a retiree's income and may not be treated as tax-free salary reductions under Code Section 125. [Coordinated Issue: All Industries Cafeteria Plan/Qualified Retirement Plan Hybrid Arrangement, Feb. 1, 2000] In follow-up settlement guidelines, the IRS has specifically stated that it will enforce that rule until further regulatory or judicial determinations are made. [Appeals Industry Specialization Program Coordinated Issue Settlement Guidelines: Cafeteria Plan/Qualified Retirement Plan Hybrid Arrangement, Mar. 6, 2001]

Code Section 402(a), which governs distributions from qualified retirement plans, states that, "except as otherwise provided in this section," any amount distributed from a plan is taxable to the plan participant in the year of the distribution. Code Section 402 contains only two exceptions. The first exception provides that if a distribution is made to a participant's spouse or former spouse under the terms of a qualified domestic relations order, the spouse or former spouse, rather than the participant, will be taxed on the distribution. [I.R.C. § 402(e)(1)(A)] The second exception provides that eligible rollover distributions that are properly rolled over into another qualified plan or individual retirement account (IRA) within 60 days are not included in income for the taxable year of the distribution. [I.R.C. § 402(c)]

According to the IRS, neither of those exceptions allows a participant to exclude distributions that are used to purchase benefits through the former employer's cafeteria plan. Because the "except as otherwise provided in this section" language in Code Section 402(a) does not encompass Code Section 125, the general rule applies and the distribution is includable in the retiree's gross income.

The IRS says this position is consistent with two long-standing revenue rulings concerning the use of retirement plan funds to purchase health and accident benefits. The first ruling states that while the purchase of accident and health insurance will not prevent qualification of a plan, the use of the funds to pay the cost of insurance for the employee or his or her beneficiaries is a taxable distribution within the meaning of Code Section 402. [Rev. Rul. 61-164, 1961-2

C.B. 99] The second ruling concluded that distributions from a qualified profit sharing plan to pay for a plan participant's medical care expenses are not excludable accident and health benefits but are taxable under Code Section 402 as previously earned deferred compensation. [Rev. Rul. 69-141, 1969-1 C.B. 48]

The IRS specifically rejected the marketers' arguments, stating that they do not overcome the fact that Code Section 402 contains specific rules for determining when a distribution from a qualified retirement plan is includable income and those rules do not include an exception for distributions paid through a cafeteria plan to an accident and health plan.

Proposed cafeteria plan regulations issued in 2007 specifically provide that amounts distributed from a qualified retirement plan that the former employees elect to have applied to pay health insurance premiums through a cafeteria plan are includable in the employees' gross income. [Prop. Treas. Reg. § 1.125-1(b)(3)]

Q 4:59   Can an employer fund retiree medical benefits using a rabbi trust or agency agreement?

The IRS has ruled privately on plans that fund retiree medical benefits using a rabbi trust or agency agreement.

Private Letter Ruling 9107031 upheld the use of an agency agreement to fund retiree medical benefits for retired key employees and their dependents, which fund was subject to the claims of the employer's general creditors. The arrangement would qualify as an accident and health plan for purposes of Code Sections 105 and 106, and the plan was held not to be a Section 419 welfare benefit fund.

Another employer's insured health plan arrangement, set up for 50 of its key employees, used a rabbi trust to fund the insurance premium payments. The trust remained revocable by the employer as long as a "special circumstance" (for example, a change in control) had not occurred. The premium trust was held not to be subject to the Section 419 funding rules unless and until the occurrence of a special circumstance. [Priv. Ltr. Rul. 9325050]

In its most recent ruling, the IRS considered an employer's plan to amend its rabbi trust arrangement to provide retiree health benefits for a new class of participants and their spouses, dependents, and survivors. To qualify for benefits, a participant must have retired, completed at least 15 years of active participation in a group health care plan maintained by the employer, have been enrolled in the plan on the day before retirement, and have received an immediate annuity from the employer's qualified pension plan. Health benefits may be paid either to the participant as reimbursements for covered expenses, to a service provider that renders health care, or to a voluntary employee beneficiary association (VEBA) that has paid or expects to pay the cost of covered health care.

The IRS ruled that the plan participants would not have to recognize income until amounts were actually paid or made available to them. In addition, the IRS ruled that:

- Amounts paid from the plan as reimbursements for medical care for a retired employee or his or her spouse or dependents would be excludable from gross income as amounts received under an accident or health plan [I.R.C.§ 105] and

- Premiums paid from the plan for accident or health insurance would be excludable from gross income as contributions by an employer to an accident or health plan.

[I.R.C.§ 106; Priv. Ltr. Rul. 200046012]

Caution. Under new tax law rules, compensation deferred under a nonqualified deferred compensation plan, including a rabbi trust, is includable in gross income to the extent it is not subject to a substantial risk of forfeiture unless the plan meets certain requirements. [I.R.C.§ 409A(a)]

Chapter 5

Group Health Plans: Mandated Benefits and Standards

The basic structural and operational requirements for employer-provided group health plans are contained in the Internal Revenue Code (Code) and the Employee Retirement Income Security Act of 1974 (ERISA), discussed in detail in chapter 3. However, a number of other federal laws affect the design and implementation of employee health benefits. The mandated benefits and other requirements of these laws—including the 2010 Health Reform Act—are discussed in this chapter.

Basic Rules

Q 5:1 How does federal law regulate the coverage and benefits provided by group health plans?

Federal regulation of the substantive content of group health plans has been an ongoing process. Beginning with the Employee Retirement Income Security Act of 1974 and culminating most recently in the 2010 Health Reform Act, Congress has repeatedly imposed mandatory requirements and restrictions on the content of group health plans.

The Employee Retirement Insurance Security Act of 1974 (ERISA) [Pub. L. No. 93-406] represents Congress' first foray into the regulation of employee benefit plans. Targeted largely at retirement plans, the law nonetheless encompasses employee welfare benefit plans, including group health plans, within the broad sweep of its employee protections. In its original incarnation, ERISA did not go directly to the heart of group health benefits—the coverage and benefits they provide for employees. Instead, the law set strict standards relating largely to plan administration and fiduciary responsibility. Nonetheless, ERISA is the building block for regulation of the substantive content of group health plans. In the more than 30 years since the passage of ERISA, Congress has grafted additional requirements onto ERISA (as well as the Internal Revenue Code and the Public Health Services Act (PHSA)) to address perceived abuses and to enhance protections for employees covered under employer-provided group health plans.

The Consolidated Omnibus Budget Reconciliation of 1985 (COBRA) [Pub L. No. 99-272] imposes a duty on employers to provide continuation of group health coverage to employees and their spouses and dependents who would otherwise lose coverage under the plan. (The COBRA continuation coverage requirements are discussed in chapter 6).

The Health Insurance Portability and Affordability Act of 1996 (HIPAA) [Pub. L. No. 104-191] added substantive benefit requirements to ERISA and the Internal Revenue Code (and, to a somewhat different extent, the PHSA). HIPAA imposes limits on plan exclusions for preexisting conditions, provides special enrollment rights to employees and their dependents under certain circumstances, and prohibits discrimination on the basis of health factors. HIPAA also requires health plans to implement safeguards to protect the privacy of individuals' personal health information.

The Mental Health Parity Act of 1996 (MHPA) [Pub. L. No. 104-204] and its more recent successor, the *Paul Wellstone and Pete Domenici Mental Health Parity and Addiction Equity Act of 2008* (MHPAEA) [Pub. L. No. 110-343] requires that mental health benefits (and under the MHPAEA substance use disorder benefits) provided under a group health plan must be provided on par with medical and surgical benefits under the plan.

The Newborns' and Mothers' Health Protection Act of 1996 (NHMPA) [Pub. L. No. 104-204] mandates that group health plans provide coverage for minimum hospital stays for mothers and newborns following childbirth.

The Women's Health and Cancer Right Act of 1998 (WHCRA) [Pub. L. No. 105-277] requires group health plans that provide coverage for mastectomies to provide coverage for breast reconstruction and other attendant medical services.

The Child Support Performance and Incentive Act of 1998 (CSPIA) [Pub. L. No. 105-200] requires group health plans that provide dependent coverage to provide such coverage pursuant to a qualified medical child support order (QMCSO).

The Genetic Information Nondiscrimination Act of 2008 (GINA) [Pub. L. No. 110-223] prohibits discrimination in health coverage based on genetic information.

The 2008 Student Health Insurance Act (Michelle's Law) [Pub. L. No. 110-381] requires group health plans to extend dependent coverage to college students on medically necessary leaves of absence from school.

2010 Health Reform Act. The Patient Protection and Affordable Care Act [Pub L. No. 111-148 (Mar. 23, 2010)], as amended by the Health Care and Education Reconciliation Act of 2010 [Pub L. No. 111-152 (Mar. 30, 2010)] builds on the earlier requirements, imposing extensive new coverage and benefit mandates and restrictions on group health plans and health insurance issuers providing group health plan coverage.

Technically, the 2010 Health Reform Act incorporates these requirements into Part A of Title XXVII of the Public Health Service Act (PHSA). [42 U.S.C. §§ 300gg *et seq.*] However, the law specifically provides that the provisions of the Part A of Title XXVII of the PHSA as amended apply to group health plans and group health insurance issuers as if included in Part 7 of ERISA. [ERISA § 715 as added by PPACA § 1562] The 2010 Health Reform Law also adds new Code Section 9815, which provides that the PHSA provisions apply to group health plans and health insurance issuers as if included in the Code. [I.R.C. § 9815 as added by PPACA § 1562]

Practice Pointer. The 2010 Health Reform Act does not negate the requirements of HIPAA or other laws as incorporated into ERISA and the Internal Revenue Code. However, the 2010 Health Reform Act provides that, to the extent there is a conflict between the existing provisions of ERISA or the Code and the 2010 Health Reform Act requirements, the 2010 Health Reform Act requirements apply. [ERISA § 715 as added by PPACA § 1562; I.R.C. § 9815 as added by PPACA § 1562]

Note. Unless otherwise noted, for purposes of this chapter the term "group health plan requirements" refers generally to those requirements included in Part 7 of Title I of ERISA and in Chapter 100 of the Internal Revenue Code. Certain group health plan requirements are included with the COBRA continuation coverage requirements in Part 6 of Title I of ERISA. These provisions include coverage for children pursuant to qualified medical child support orders, and requirements for coverage of pediatric vaccines.

Q 5:2   How does the 2010 Health Reform Act regulate group health plan coverage and benefits?

The 2010 Health Reform Act is the most sweeping legislation affecting group health plans in decades, with provisions ranging from the big-picture (new employer responsibility and health insurance market reforms) to the mundane (whether over-the-counter drugs can be paid through a health flexible spending account or other reimbursement arrangement).

The focus of this chapter is on the group health plan coverage and benefit mandates and restrictions imposed by the 2010 Health Reform Act. These requirements and restrictions include:

- Enhanced prohibitions on discrimination based on health status (Qs 5:17–5:39)
- Prohibition of discrimination in favor of highly compensated employees (Qs 5:40–5:46)
- Limitations on waiting periods for coverage (Q 5:50)
- Prohibition of coverage rescissions (Q 5:51)
- Prohibition of preexisting-condition exclusions (Qs 5:52–60)
- Prohibition of lifetime or annual benefit limits (Q 5:90)
- Cost-sharing limitations (Qs 5:91)
- Extension of dependent coverage to adult children (Q 5:93)
- Coverage of preventive services (Q 5:110)

Q 5:3   Which plans are subject to the group health plan requirements?

As a general rule, the group health plan requirements as incorporated into ERISA and the Code apply to covered plans.

Covered plans are defined differently under ERISA and the Code.

ERISA. The group health plan requirements in Part 7 of Title I apply to both group health plans and "health insurance coverage" (described below) issued in connection with a group health plan, except to the extent of any "exempted benefits" (see Q 5:6). Covered group health plans are employee welfare benefit plans (including partner-only plans) to the extent that they provide medical care (including items paid for as medical care) to employees or their dependents (as defined under the terms of the plan) directly or through insurance, reimbursement, or otherwise.

For this purpose, *medical care* is defined as amounts paid for:

1. The diagnosis, cure, mitigation, treatment, or prevention of disease or amounts paid for the purpose of affecting any structure or function of the body;

2. Transportation primarily for and essential to medical care described in item 1; and

3. Insurance covering medical care described in items 1 and 2.

[ERISA §§ 732(d), 733(a)]

Note. Part 7 incorporates most of the group health plans requirements, including provisions added by the 2010 Health Reform Act. A slightly different definition (which does not encompass partner-only plans) applies for purposes of Part 6 of Title I of ERISA, which includes the COBRA continuation coverage rules as well as requirements for coverage for children pursuant to qualified medical child support orders, coverage for adopted children, pediatric vaccine coverage, and coverage for Medicaid-eligible individuals.

Health insurance coverage. Under ERISA, *health insurance coverage* means benefits consisting of medical care (provided directly through insurance, reimbursement, or otherwise, including items and services paid for as medical care) under any hospital or medical service policy or certificate, hospital or medical service plan contract, or health maintenance contract offered by a health insurance issuer. A *health insurance issuer* is an insurance company, insurance service, or insurance organization (including a health maintenance organization (HMO) licensed by a state and subject to state law regulating insurance). Thus, ERISA directly regulates the content of insurance policies, HMO coverage, and the like, to the extent such coverage is provided in connection with ERISA group health plans. [ERISA § 706]

The Code. The parallel provisions of the Internal Revenue Code apply to "group health plans" as defined in Code Section 5000(b)(1). The Code's definitions of *health insurance coverage* and *health insurance issuer* track the ERISA definitions. [I.R.C. § 9832(b)]

Excluded plans. The group health plan requirements in ERISA and the Code generally do not apply to group health plans or coverage offered in connection with a group health plan (1) if the plan is a governmental plan or (2) for a plan year if, for that plan year, the group health plan has fewer than two participants who are current employees. [ERISA §§ 3(32), 705(a): I.R.C.§ 9804(a)] Certain state and local governmental plans are covered by similar group health plan provisions added to the Public Health Service Act.

Under final DOL and IRS regulations, the status of a group health plan as an excluded small plan is determined at the beginning of the plan year. A plan is an excluded plan only if, as of the first day of the plan year, it has fewer than two participants who are current employees. [DOL Final Reg. § 2590.732; Treas. Reg. § 54.9801-7] If the number of participants who are current employees drops below two during a plan year, the plan continues to be subject to the group health plan requirements for the remainder of the plan year.

The DOL has not officially addressed the question of how the group health plan requirements apply to retiree-only medical plans. However, in response to questions from the American Bar Association's Joint Committee on Employee

Benefits, the DOL stated that "the HIPAA requirements do not apply to a retiree only plan, with one exception." That exception is the Newborns' and Mothers' Health Protection Act (ERISA § 711), which applies to plans with fewer than two participants who are current employees. On the other hand, if the retiree medical plan is part of a medical plan that covers active employees then HIPAA will apply even to the retiree portion of the plan. [ABA Joint Comm. on Employee Benefits, Questions for the DOL (May 8, 2002); DOL Reg. § 2590.732; Treas. Reg. § 54.9831-1]

Proposed regulations issued under HIPAA include rules for determining the number of health plans maintained by an employer and the average number of employees employed by the employer. When finalized, these rules will apply in determining whether an employer is subject to group health plan requirements Part 7 of Title I of ERISA and how those rules apply to the employer's plan. [DOL Prop. Reg. § 2590.732; Prop. Treas. Reg. § 54.9831-1]

Q 5:4 Are all covered plans required to comply with the requirements of the 2010 Health Reform Act?

Group health plans in existence on the date of enactment (March 23, 2010) of the 2010 Health Reform Act are "grandfathered health plans." [PPACA § 1251(e)] As a general rule, the provisions of the 2010 Health Reform Act do not apply to grandfathered plans. [PPACA § 1251(a)(2)]

In the case of health insurance coverage maintained pursuant to one or more collective bargaining agreements that were ratified before the date of enactment, the 2010 Health Reform Act generally will not apply until the date on which the last collective bargaining agreement related to such coverage terminates. [PPACA § 1251(d)] The law provides that an amendment to a plan solely to comply with a requirement of the health reform law will not be treated as a termination of the collective bargaining agreement that causes the plan to lose its grandfathered status. However, here again, although these plans are grandfathered, many of the new coverage requirements and other standards do apply to grandfathered collectively bargained plans.

However, the treatment of a plan as a grandfathered plan is not a blanket exemption from the group health plan coverage and benefit requirements. The 2010 Health Reform Act provides that specified provisions do apply to the grandfathered plans. These provisions include:

- Prohibition of preexisting-condition exclusions (Q 5:52)
- Limitation of waiting periods for coverage (Q 5:50)
- Prohibition on rescission of coverage (Q 5:51)
- Prohibition on lifetime and annual limits (Q 5:90)
- Coverage requirements for adult children up to age 26 (Q 5:93)

Q 5:5   Are individual insurance policies subject to the group health plan requirements?

Regulations issued under HIPAA define a group health plan as "an employee welfare benefit plan to the extent that the plan provides medical care (including items and services paid for as medical care) to employees (including both current and former employees) or their dependents (as defined under the terms of the plan) directly or through insurance, reimbursement, or otherwise." [DOL Reg. § 2590.732; Treas. Reg. § 54.9831-1] This definition applies generally to the group health plan requirements incorporated into Part 7 of Title I of ERISA and the Internal Revenue Code.

If an employer provides coverage to its employees through two or more individual policies, the coverage may be considered coverage offered in connection with a group health plan that is subject to the group health requirements. According to the preamble to the regulations, the determination of whether there is a group health plan depends on the particular facts and circumstances surrounding the extent of the employer's involvement. For example, one significant factor in establishing whether there is a group health plan is the extent to which the employer makes contributions to health insurance premiums. The employer need not be a party to the insurance policy, or arrange or pay for it directly, in order for its coverage to be considered group health plan coverage. For example, if an employer's actions appear to endorse one or more policies offered by a health insurance issuer or issuers, the coverage might be group health plan coverage. On the other hand, the mere fact that an employer forwards employee payroll deductions to a health insurance issuer will not, alone, cause the coverage to become group health plan coverage. [Final Regulations for Health Coverage Portability, 69 Fed. Reg. 78,733 (Dec. 30, 2004)]

Q 5:6   Are any health benefits excepted from the group health plan requirements?

Yes. The group health plan requirements (as incorporated in Part 7 of Title I of ERISA and the Code) do not apply to four categories of "excepted benefits." The four categories of excepted (exempted) benefits are as follows:

1. *Benefits that are always exempted.* This category includes—
   a. Coverage only for accident, disability income insurance, or any combination thereof;
   b. Liability insurance, including general liability insurance and automobile liability insurance;
   c. Coverage issued as a supplement to liability insurance;
   d. Workers' compensation or similar insurance;
   e. Automobile medical payment insurance;
   f. Credit-only insurance;
   g. Coverage for on-site medical clinics; and

    h. Other similar insurance coverage, specified in the regulations, under which benefits for medical care are secondary or incidental to other insurance benefits.

The regulations do not currently specify other types of excepted benefits.

    2. *Limited-scope benefits.* Limited-scope dental or vision benefits and benefits for long-term care are exempted if they are (a) provided under a separate policy or rider or (b) otherwise not an integral part of the plan. [ERISA §§ 731(c)(1), 732(c)(2); I.R.C. § 9831(c)(1), 9832(c)(2)]

    DOL and IRS regulations provide that limited-scope benefits are not an integral part of a plan if participants have the right not to elect coverage for the benefits and if participants who do elect such benefits must pay additional premiums or contributions for the benefits.

    Under the final regulations, limited-scope dental benefits include those benefits substantially all of which are for treatment of the mouth (including any organ or structure within the mouth). Limited-scope vision benefits include benefits substantially all of which are for treatment of the eye. [DOL Reg. § 2590.732(c)(3)(iii); Treas. Reg. § 54.9831-1(c)(3)(iii)] Thus, under the final regulations, limited-scope dental benefits may include medical services, such as those associated with oral cancer or a mouth injury, while limited-scope vision benefits may include opthalmologic services such as treatment of an eye disease or injury.

    3. *Independent, noncoordinated benefits.* The following are excluded from the group health plan requirements if offered as independent, noncoordinated benefits—

    a. Coverage only for a specified disease or illness and

    b. Hospital indemnity or other fixed indemnity insurance.

    4. *Supplemental benefits.* The following are excluded from the group health plan requirements if provided under a separate policy, certificate, or contract of insurance: Medicare supplemental health insurance (as defined under Section 1882(g) of the Social Security Act (SSA)); coverage supplemental to the coverage provided under Chapter 22 of Title 10, United States Code (CHAMPUS supplemental programs); and similar supplemental coverage provided in addition to coverage under a group health plan. [ERISA §§ 705(c)(3), 706(c)(4); DOL Final Reg. § 2590.732; I.R.C. §§ 9831(c)(3), 9832(c)(4); Treas. Reg. § 54.9832-1]

The term "similar supplemental coverage" is not defined in the regulations. However, the regulations make it clear that for supplemental coverage to qualify as excepted benefits, the coverage must be specifically designed to fill in gaps in primary coverage, such as coinsurance or deductibles. Coverage that becomes secondary or supplemental only because of a coordination-of-benefits provision does not qualify as excepted supplemental benefits.

Nonetheless, the DOL (along with the Departments of Treasury and Health and Human Services, which jointly administer the group health plan requirements) became concerned that not all of the coverage that is being marketed as "similar supplemental coverage" actually qualifies. To address that issue, the DOL issued field assistance guidance that establishes safe harbor guidelines for "similar supplemental coverage." [DOL Field Assist. Bull. 2007-4] The IRS subsequently issued a notice that provides the same safe harbor guidelines. [Notice 2008-23, 2008-7 I.R.B. 433] The IRS anticipates that the safe harbor guidelines will be incorporated as requirements in future regulations.

Under the safe harbor guidelines, coverage will be treated as "similar supplemental coverage" if it is a separate policy, certificate, or contract of insurance that meets all of the following requirements:

1. *Independent of primary coverage.* The supplemental coverage is issued by an entity that does not provide the primary coverage under the group health plan. For this purpose all entities in the same controlled group of corporations or part of the same group of trades or businesses under common control (within the meaning of Code Section 52(a) or (b)) will be considered a single entity.

2. *Supplemental for gaps in primary coverage.* The supplemental coverage is specifically designed to supplement gaps in primary coverage, such as the payment of coinsurance or deductibles. As provided in the regulations, coverage that becomes secondary or supplemental to the primary plan under coordination of benefits rules will not be treated as specifically designed to fill gaps in coverage.

3. *Supplemental in value of coverage.* The cost of the supplemental coverage does not exceed 15 percent of the cost of primary coverage. Cost will be calculated in the same manner as cost is calculated for COBRA coverage purposes.

4. *Similar to Medicare supplemental coverage.* Supplemental coverage that is group health insurance does not differentiate among individuals in terms of eligibility, benefits, or any health factor.

[DOL Field Assist. Bull. 2007-04]

Q 5:7 Are health flexible spending arrangements subject to the group health plan requirements?

It depends. A health care flexible spending arrangement (FSA) is treated as exempt provided three conditions are met:

1. The employee has other group health plan coverage available to him or her from the employer for the year;

2. The other group health plan coverage does not consist solely of excepted benefits; and

3. The maximum benefit payable to the employee under the health care FSA for the year does not exceed the larger of:

   a. Two times the employee's salary reduction election or

   b. The amount of the employee's salary reduction election for the year plus $500.

For this purpose, any amount that an employee can elect to receive as taxable income but elects to apply to the health FSA is considered a salary reduction election (regardless of whether the amount is characterized as salary or as a credit under the arrangement). [DOL Reg. § 2590.732(c)(3)(v); Treas. Reg. § 54.9831-1(c)(3)(v)]

These conditions are sufficiently broad that many, but not all, health care FSAs will be eligible for this exemption. Assuming that the first two conditions are satisfied, the key to satisfying the third condition is how the health care FSA is funded.

Health care FSAs that are funded solely with salary reduction (pretax) contributions qualify for exemption if the benefits do not exceed the amount of the salary reduction amount. However, if benefits could exceed the amount of the salary reduction election (which could occur, for example, if forfeitures are reallocated under the plan), then whether the health care FSA is exempt from HIPAA is a fact-based inquiry. The FSA will be exempt only if the total amount allocated to the FSA does not exceed two times the amount of the employee's annual salary reduction election or, if greater, one times the amount of the employee's annual salary reduction election plus $500.

If a health care FSA is funded with nonelective employer contributions, application of the exemption will be a dollars-and-cents inquiry. When applying the exemption formula, nonelective employer contributions must be counted as additional employer contributions and not as salary reduction amounts. Nonelective employer contributions are amounts that the employee cannot elect to take in cash, including noncashable employer credits and employer matches.

Q 5:8 Are high-deductible health plans and health savings accounts subject to the group health plan requirements?

As a general rule, the DOL says that employer-sponsored high-deductible health plans (HDHPs) are employee welfare benefit plans. Moreover, because an employer-sponsored HDHP provides medical care, it is generally subject to the group health plan requirements.

On the other hand, the DOL has concluded that health savings accounts (HSAs) generally do not constitute employee welfare benefit plans. Therefore, the group health plan requirements generally will not apply. Moreover, the DOL has noted that many of the HIPAA portability requirements generally are not relevant for HSAs. For example, expense reimbursements from an HSA cannot be restricted by the employer. Therefore, HSAs cannot impose preexisting-condition exclusions. Similarly, special enrollment rules for dependent children or spouses are not relevant because once an HSA is established they are eligible for tax-free reimbursements immediately, regardless of whether they are covered by the supporting HDHP. Finally, HIPAA's comparability rules do not impact HSAs because the HSA rules themselves contain comparability requirements. [*See* DOL Field Assist. Bull. 2004-01, Apr. 7, 2004; Final Regulations for Health Coverage Portability, 69 Fed. Reg. 78,735 (Dec. 30, 2004)]

Practice Pointer. The DOL guidance deals specifically with the HIPAA requirements. However, the same reasoning would generally apply to the requirements in the 2010 Health Reform Act, including the prohibitions on preexisting-condition exclusions and lifetime and annual limits.

Q 5:9   Do the group health plan requirements apply to partners and self-employed individuals?

Despite the general rule that an ERISA plan must cover at least one common-law employee, the group health plan requirements expressly extend to partners and self-employed individuals.

Partnerships. For purposes of the group health plan requirements, any plan, fund, or program that would not otherwise be an ERISA welfare benefit plan and that is established or maintained by a partnership will be treated as an ERISA welfare benefit plan to the extent that it provides medical care to present or former partners in the partnership or to their dependents, directly or through insurance, reimbursement, or otherwise. For purposes of the group health plan requirements, the term *employer* also includes the partnership in relation to any partner, and the term *participant* includes an individual who is a partner in relation to the partnership and that individual's eligible dependents. [DOL Reg. § 2590.732(d); Treas. Reg. § 54.9831-1(d)]

Self-employed individuals. If a group health plan is maintained by a self-employed individual and at least one or more employees participate in the plan, the term *participant* also includes any self-employed individual who is or may become eligible to receive a benefit under the plan and the self-employed individual's eligible beneficiaries. [ERISA § 732(d)]

Q 5:10   What special requirements apply to multiemployer plans and multiple-employer welfare arrangements?

A multiemployer plan or a multiple-employer welfare arrangement (MEWA) may not deny an employer whose employees are covered under the plan continued access to the same or different coverage under the terms of the plan, except:

1. For nonpayment of contributions;
2. For fraud or other intentional misrepresentation of material fact by the employer;
3. For noncompliance with material plan provisions;
4. When the plan is ceasing to offer any coverage in a geographic area;
5. For failure to meet the terms of an applicable collective bargaining agreement, to renew a collective bargaining or other agreement requiring or authorizing contributions to the plan, or to employees covered by such an agreement; and
6. In the case of a plan offering benefits through a network plan, there is no longer any individual enrolled through the employer who lives, resides, or

works in the service area of the network plan and the plan applies this requirement uniformly without regard to the claims experience of employers or any health status–related factor of such individuals or their dependents (see Q 5:17).

[ERISA § 703; I.R.C. § 9803]

Network plan. For this purpose, a *network plan* is defined as health insurance coverage offered by a health insurance issuer under which the financing and delivery of medical care (including items and services paid for as medical care) are provided, in whole or in part, through a defined set of providers under contract with the issuer. [ERISA § 706(d)(3), added by HIPAA § 101(a); I.R.C. § 9805(d)(4), added by HIPAA § 401(a)]

The Secretary of Labor has issued regulations under ERISA requiring MEWAs providing benefits consisting of medical care that are not group health plans to report at least annually to the Secretary for the purpose of determining the extent to which ERISA's group health plan requirements are being carried out with respect to such benefits. Furthermore, the Secretary of Labor may assess a civil penalty against any person of up to $1,100 a day ($1,000 per day prior to March 25, 2003) from the date of such person's failure or refusal to file the information required by such regulations [HIPAA § 101(g); DOL Reg. § 2575.502c-5]

Q 5:11   Do any of the group health plan requirements undercut ERISA's preemption of state law provisions?

No, they do not. [ERISA § 713(a)(2)]

Q 5:12   If a state law imposes limits on group health plans, does ERISA or the state law control?

The answer depends on whether ERISA otherwise preempts the state law. If ERISA would otherwise preempt the application of the state law to the group health plan, then the group health plan requirements of ERISA (Sections 701 to 715) control. (See chapter 2 for a discussion of ERISA preemption provisions.)

If a state law establishes, implements, or continues in effect any standard or requirement solely relating to health insurance issuers (insurance companies, HMOs, and so forth) in connection with group health insurance coverage, the group health plan requirements do not supersede the application of such laws to health insurance issuers, with two important exceptions:

1. Any state law establishing, implementing, or continuing in effect any standard or requirement solely relating to health insurance issuers offering health insurance coverage in connection with a group health plan is superseded to the extent that such standard or requirement prevents the application of a requirement contained in Part 7 of ERISA; and

2. Any state law establishing, implementing, or continuing in effect a standard or requirement applicable to imposition of a preexisting-condition exclusion or limitation expressly governed by ERISA Section 701 (the HIPAA preexisting-condition requirements) that differs from the

standards or requirements specified by ERISA Section 701 is superseded except to the extent that such state law:

a. Requires a shorter look-back provision for preexisting-condition provisions;

b. Requires a shorter exclusion period than the 12-month and 18-month maximum exclusion/limitation periods specified by HIPAA;

c. Requires a more than 63-day break in creditable coverage before prior creditable coverage can be disregarded for purposes of the maximum exclusion period and for purposes of barring the application of preexisting exclusions and limitations to newborns, adopted children, and children placed for adoption;

d. Requires an enrollment period greater than 30 days for newborns;

e. Prohibits the imposition of any preexisting-condition exclusion in cases not described in HIPAA;

f. Requires special enrollment periods in addition to those required by the HIPAA; or

g. Reduces the maximum affiliation period for an HMO.

[ERISA § 731]

In other words, preexisting-condition exclusions are preempted except to the extent they provide *greater* rights for employees than apply under HIPAA.

Note. To the extent a preexisting-condition exclusion is prohibited under the requirements of the 2010 Health Reform Act (see Q 5:52), that prohibition supersedes the HIPAA preexisting-condition requirements. [ERISA § 715 as added by PPACA § 1562] Moreover, any state law permitting a preexisting-condition exclusion will be preempted under the general preemption rules.

ERISA's HIPAA requirements do not apply to health insurance issuers to the extent that they provide health insurance coverage in connection with a group health plan not itself subject to HIPAA. [HIPAA § 101(b)]

Q 5:13   What penalties are imposed for violations of the group health plan requirements?

Code Section 4980D imposes a COBRA-like excise tax on violations of the group health plan contained in Chapter 100 of the Internal Revenue Code (I.R.C. §§ 9801–9815). The excise tax is $100 per day per individual violation for each day of the noncompliance period, which begins on the date the violation first occurs and ends on the date the violation is corrected. This excise tax generally is imposed on the employer. If the plan is a multiemployer plan, the excise tax is imposed on the plan. If a MEWA violates the guaranteed renewability provisions described in Q 5:10, the excise tax is imposed on the MEWA.

Correction of violations. A violation is treated as corrected if it is retroactively undone to the extent possible, and the person to whom the violation relates is placed in a financial position that is as favorable as he or she would have been in had the violation not occurred.

Discovery rule. The excise tax will not apply if it is established to the satisfaction of the Secretary of the Treasury that the persons otherwise liable for the tax did not know and, exercising reasonable diligence, would not have known that such violation existed. This rule cannot be applied if the violation is not corrected before the date a notice of examination of income tax liability is sent to the employer.

30-day correction rule. The excise tax does not apply if the violation was due to reasonable cause and not willful neglect and was corrected within the 30-day period beginning on the first date the person otherwise liable for such tax knew, or exercising reasonable diligence would have known, that such violation existed. This rule cannot be applied if the violation is not corrected before the date a notice of examination of income tax liability is sent to the employer.

Mandatory minimum tax. If the violation is discovered after notice of examination of income tax liability is sent by the IRS to the employer, then the mandatory minimum amount of the tax is the lesser of $2,500 or the amount of the tax that would otherwise be applied. However, if the violations are more than *de minimis,* then the mandatory minimum tax is $15,000.

Maximum excise tax. A cap applies to the excise tax that can be imposed if the violation is due to reasonable cause and not to willful neglect. Otherwise, an unlimited excise tax penalty applies. The maximum excise tax (when the cap does apply) is as follows:

1. *Single-employer plans.* For violations concerning plans that are not multiemployer plans or MEWAs, the maximum excise tax applicable to violations that are due to reasonable cause and not to willful neglect is the lesser of (1) 10 percent of the aggregate amount paid or incurred by the employer (or predecessor employer) during the preceding taxable year for group health plans, or (2) $500,000.

2. *Multiemployer plans and MEWAs.* The maximum excise tax applicable to violations during the taxable year of the trust forming a part of such plan that are due to reasonable cause and not to willful neglect is the lesser of (1) 10 percent of the amount paid or incurred by such trust during such taxable year to provide medical care directly or through insurance, reimbursement, or otherwise, or (2) $500,000. For this purpose, all plans of which the same trust forms a part are treated as one plan.

If an employer is assessed the excise tax by reason of a violation concerning a multiemployer plan or a MEWA, the single-employer plan cap described in item 1 will apply to that employer.

Inadvertent-failure rule. If the violation is due to reasonable cause and not to willful neglect, the Secretary of the Treasury may waive all or part of the excise tax to the extent that the payment of such tax would be excessive relative to the failure involved.

Exception for small employers. If a group health plan of a small employer provides health insurance coverage solely through a contract with a health insurance issuer, no excise tax will be imposed on the small employer for a violation that is solely because of the health insurance coverage offered by such issuer. For this purpose, a small employer is an employer who employed at least two but not more than 50 employees on business days during the preceding calendar year and who employs at least two employees on the first day of the plan year. (A special rule applies if the employer was not in existence throughout the preceding calendar year.) The Section 414 controlled-group rules apply when making this determination of small-employer status.

Church plans. Several of the above provisions are somewhat different for church plans. [I.R.C. § 4980D]

Excise tax reporting. Beginning January 1, 2010, excise tax liabilities for failure to meet certain health plan requirements must be self-reported by filing Form 8928, *Return of Certain Excise Taxes Under Chapter 43 of the Internal Revenue Code.* [Treas. Reg. § 54.6011-2] In the case of excise taxes imposed by Code Section 4980D for failure to satisfy the HIPAA requirements, the form must be filed by the employer or other person responsible for providing or administering benefits under the plan (such as the insurer or third-party administrator). The form is due on or before the due date for filing the employer's or other person's federal income tax return for the year in which the failure occurred. If the failure is by a multiemployer plan, the form is due on or before the last day of the seventh month following the end of the plan year. [Treas. Reg. § 54.6071-1(a)] The tax due must be paid with the return. [Treas. Reg. § 54.6151-1]

Q 5:14   Do individuals have a right to bring a private lawsuit under the group health plan requirements?

Several U.S. district courts have held that individuals do not have the right to bring private lawsuits under the group health plan requirements. In one case, for example, an individual brought a private lawsuit claiming that her health insurer had improperly withheld payment for her surgery in violation of HIPAA's rules regarding preexisting conditions. [O'Donnell v. Blue Cross/Blue Shield of Wyo., 173 F. Supp. 2d 1176 (D. Wyo. 2001)] The court noted that HIPAA does not expressly provide for a private cause of action. Moreover, the court could find no congressional intent to create private rights or remedies under the law. According to the court, HIPAA specifically limits enforcement to the states or to the federal government in the absence of state enforcement. [*See also* Means v. Independent Life & Accident Ins. Co., 963 F. Supp. 1131 (M.D. Ala. 1997); Brock v. Provident Am. Ins. Co., 144 F. Supp. 2d 652 (N.D. Tex. 2001); Wright v. Combined Ins. Co. of Am., 959 F. Supp. 356 (N.D. Miss. 1997).]

Q 5:15   What are the disclosure requirements for group health plans?

HIPAA amended the ERISA technical requirements concerning (1) the content of summary plan descriptions (SPDs) and (2) both the timing and the permissible method of distribution to participants of a summary of material modifications (SMM).

Content of SPD. The SPD for a group health plan must include the following:

a. Identification of the DOL office through which participants and beneficiaries may seek assistance or information regarding their rights under ERISA and HIPAA. The Notice of ERISA rights contained in the regulations has been amended to accomplish this by providing a special address within the DOL for assistance.

b. Whether a health insurance issuer is responsible for the financing or administration (including payment of claims) of the plan and (if so) the name and address of such issuer. This means, for example, that if the plan includes the option of selecting from 50 different HMOs, the name and address of each such HMO would be required to be included in the SPD because the HMOs are responsible for financing part of the benefits of the group health plan. (Presumably, the employer is also submitting a Schedule A to the Form 5500 annual report to the IRS for each HMO so included.)

[ERISA § 102(b), as amended by HIPAA § 101(b)]

2010 Health Reform Act. The 2010 Health Reform Act directs the Secretary of Health and Human Services (HHS) to develop standards for use by group health plans and health insurance issuers in compiling and providing to plan participants a summary of benefits and coverage explanation that accurately describes the benefits and coverage under the plan. The standards are required to be published no later than 12 months after the date of enactment (March 23, 2010) of the 2010 Health Reform Act. [PHSA § 2715 as added by PPACA § 1001 as amended by PPACA § 10101] Group health plans—including grandfathered plans—must comply with the standards no later than 24 months after the date of enactment of the 2010 Health Reform Act.

Summary of material modifications. If a modification to group health plan benefits constitutes a material reduction in covered services or benefits, a summary description of that modification or change must be furnished to participants and beneficiaries within 60 days after the date the change or modification is adopted. Alternatively, the plan sponsors may provide that description at regular intervals of not more than 90 days.

MEWA reporting requirement. MEWAs are required to file annual HIPAA compliance reports. A MEWA must file Form M-1 once a year to demonstrate compliance with group health plan requirements. The reporting rule includes an exception to the reporting requirements for an *entity claiming exception* (ECE) that has been in existence for three years or longer. An ECE is defined as an entity that claims it is not a MEWA under the exception in Section 3(40)(A)(i) of ERISA for entities that are established or maintained under or pursuant to one or more agreements that the Secretary finds to be collective bargaining agreements. [DOL Reg. § 2520.101-2 (Apr. 9, 2003)]

Q 5:16   What is a material reduction in covered services or benefits?

For purposes of the required disclosure discussed in Q 5:15, a "material reduction in covered services or benefits" means any modification to the group health plan or change in the information required to be included in the SPD that, independently or together with other modifications or changes, would be considered *by the average plan participant* to be an important reduction in services or benefits and that:

1. Eliminates benefits payable under the plan;

2. Reduces benefits payable under the plan, including reductions resulting from a change in formulas, methodologies, or schedules that serve as the basis for making benefit determinations;

3. Increases deductibles, copayments, or other amounts to be paid by a participant or beneficiary;

4. Reduces an HMO's service area; or

5. Establishes new conditions or requirements (such as preauthorization requirements) for obtaining services or benefits under the plan.

[DOL Interim Final Rule, § 1520.104b-3]

Practice Pointer. If an employer is implementing a "total replacement" strategy that involves dropping its current medical coverage and implementing a comprehensive program with several medical care options (HMOs, point-of-service option, preferred provider organizations, and so forth), adopting the program well in advance of the annual enrollment period during which it is to be implemented could trigger an obligation on the employer's part to issue an SPD update long before it is ready to roll out the program. This has led to employers doing "everything but" officially adopting the changes until the last minute, because this rule literally requires that the changes be communicated via an SPD modification within eight weeks. The implications are the same for individual plan cutbacks, premium increases, and the like. Unless the employer is prepared to disclose bad news early, the change should not be officially adopted more than 60 days before the date the employer will be able to meet the disclosure deadline.

Nondiscrimination Based on Health Status

Q 5:17   Does federal law prohibit group health plans from discriminating based on health status?

HIPAA prohibits two types of discrimination by group health plans and health insurers offering group coverage:

1. *Discrimination in eligibility to enroll.* A group health plan may not establish any rule for eligibility or continued eligibility that discriminates based on a health factor of the enrolling individual or a dependent. [ERISA § 702(a); I.R.C. § 9802(a)]

2. *Discrimination in premiums or contributions.* A group health plan may not charge an individual a higher premium or contribution than other similarly situated individuals based on a health factor of the enrolling individual or a dependent. [ERISA § 702(b); I.R.C. § 9802(b)]

The Genetic Information Nondiscrimination Act of 2008 (GINA) [Pub. L. No. 110-223, 122 Stat. 881] amended ERISA and the Code to prohibit a third type of discrimination.

3. *Group based discrimination on the basis of genetic information.* Group health plans and health insurance issuers cannot base premiums for an employer or a group of similarly situated individuals on genetic information about any individual. [ERISA § 702(b)(3); I.R.C. § 9802(b)(3)] GINA also prohibits plans from requiring an individual or family member to undergo genetic tests and bars the collection of genetic information.

2010 Health Reform Act. The 2010 Health Reform Act includes health status nondiscrimination rules that are specifically incorporated into ERISA and the Code. [PHSA § 2705 as added by PPACA § 1201] The 2010 Health Reform Act rules apply to group health plans and to health insurers in the group or individual markets for plan years beginning on or after January 1, 2014. The rules do not apply to grandfathered plans. The 2010 Health Reform Act rules essentially parallel the existing ERISA and Code provisions with one key exception: the 2010 Health Reform Act adds specific statutory requirements for employee wellness programs (see Q 5:34).

Q 5:18   What is a health factor?

The nondiscrimination rules prohibit discrimination based on any of the following health factors:

- Health status
- Medical condition (including physical and mental illnesses)
- Claims experience
- Receipt of health care
- Medical history
- Genetic information
- Evidence of insurability (including conditions arising out of domestic violence)
- Disability

[Treas. Reg. § 54.9802-1(a)(1)]

For this purpose, evidence of insurability includes conditions arising out of domestic violence. [Treas. Reg. § 54.9802-1(a)(2)(i)] Evidence of insurability also includes participation in high-risk activities such as motorcycling, snowmobiling, all-terrain vehicle riding, horseback riding, or skiing. [Treas. Reg. § 54.9802-1(a)(2)(ii)]

2010 Health Reform Act. The 2010 Health Reform specifically authorizes the Secretary of Health and Human Services (HHS) to add to the list any other health-status related factor determined appropriate. [PHSA § 2705 as added by PPACA § 1201]

Q 5:19   What are eligibility rules?

Eligibility rules include, but are not limited to, rules relating to:

- Enrollment
- Effective date of coverage
- Waiting (or affiliation) periods
- Late and special enrollment
- Benefit packages, including rules for changing benefit package selections
- Benefits, including rules related to covered benefits, benefit restrictions, and cost-sharing mechanisms (e.g., coinsurance, copayments, and deductibles)
- Continued eligibility
- Termination of coverage or disenrollment of any individual

[Treas. Reg. § 54.9802-1(b)(ii)]

Q 5:20   Do the nondiscrimination rules require a group health plan to provide specific benefits?

The nondiscrimination rules do not require group health plans to provide any particular benefits. [Treas. Reg. § 54.9802-1(b)(2)(I)(A)] However, the benefits that are provided must be uniformly available to all similarly situated individuals. In addition, any restriction on a benefit or benefits must apply uniformly to all similarly situated individuals and must not be directed at any particular participant or beneficiary based on a health factor. [Treas. Reg. § 54.9802-1(b)(2)(I)(B)]

A plan may, for example, limit or exclude benefits for a specific disease or condition, for certain types of treatments or drugs, or for treatments that are determined to be experimental or medically unnecessary. However, any limitation or exclusion must apply uniformly to all similarly situated individuals and must not be directed at any particular participant or beneficiary.

A plan may also impose annual, lifetime, or other limits on benefits and may require the satisfaction of a deductible, copayment, coinsurance, or other cost-sharing requirement in order to obtain a benefit. Again, these limits or cost-sharing requirements must apply uniformly to all similarly situated individuals and must not be directed at any particular participant or beneficiary.

Example 1. A group health plan applies a $500,000 lifetime limit on all benefits to each participant or beneficiary covered under the plan. The lifetime limit is not discriminatory because it applies uniformly to all participants and beneficiaries and is not directed at any individual participant or beneficiary.

Example 2. A group health plan imposes a $2,000 lifetime limit for the treatment of temporomandibular joint syndrome (TMJ). The limit is not discriminatory because $2,000 of benefits for the treatment of TMJ is available uniformly to all similarly situated individuals. A plan may limit benefits for a specific disease or condition if the limit applies uniformly and is not directed at individual participants or beneficiaries.

Example 3. A group health plan limits benefits for prescription drugs to those listed on a drug formulary. The exclusion of coverage for drugs not listed on a drug formulary is not discriminatory because coverage for prescription drugs listed on the formulary is uniformly available to all similarly situated individuals and the exclusion is not directed at individual participants or beneficiaries.

Example 4. Under a group health plan, doctor visits are generally subject to a $250 annual deductible and a 20 percent coinsurance requirement. However, prenatal doctor visits are not subject to any deductible or coinsurance requirement. The plan does not violate the nondiscrimination requirements because a plan may establish different deductibles or coinsurance requirements for different services if they are applied uniformly and are not directed at individual participants and beneficiaries.

Example 5. A group health plan imposes a $2 million lifetime limit on all benefits. However, the $2 million limit is reduced to $10,000 for any participant or beneficiary who has a congenital heart defect. In this case, the plan is discriminatory because the lower limit applies only to participants or beneficiaries with congenital heat defects. It does not apply uniformly to all similarly situated individuals.

2010 Health Reform Act. Under the 2010 Health Reform Act, lifetime limits on essential benefits are prohibited for plan years beginning on or after September 23, 2010. Annual limits on essential benefits are restricted for plan years beginning on or after September 23, 2010, and are prohibited for plan years beginning on or after January 1, 2014. (See Q 5:90.) In addition, the 2010 Health Reform Act imposes limits on cost sharing (e.g., deductibles, copayments, coinsurance) effective for plan years beginning on or after January 1, 2014. (See Q 5:91.) Consequently, while a plan limit or cost-sharing requirement may pass the nondiscrimination tests, such limits and requirements must be vetted to determine whether they are prohibited or restricted under the 2010 Health Reform Act rules. Other laws, such as the Americans With Disabilities Act (ADA), may come into play as well. The HIPAA regulations make it clear that such laws are not superseded.

For this purpose, a plan amendment that is uniformly applicable to a group of similarly situated individuals and that is made effective no earlier than the first day of the first plan year after the amendment is adopted will not be considered to be directed at any individual participant or beneficiary. [Treas. Reg. § 54.9802-1(b)(2)(i)(C)]

Q 5:21   Can a plan apply different rules to different groups of employees?

The nondiscrimination rules apply only to groups of similarly situated individuals. A group health plan may apply different eligibility and payment requirements and provide different benefits to groups of individuals who are not similarly situated. [Treas. Reg. § 54.9802-1(d)] However, any distinctions among groups of individuals may not be based on a health factor.

A plan may treat participants as a separate group from beneficiaries. In addition, participants or beneficiaries may be divided into two or more distinct groups under the following rules.

Participants. A plan may treat participants as two or more groups of similarly situated individuals if the distinction is based on a bona fide employment-based classification that is consistent with the employer's usual business practice. Whether an employment-based classification is bona fide depends on all the relevant facts and circumstances. One particularly relevant factor is whether the employer uses the classification for purposes other than health care, such as determining eligibility for other employee benefits or determining other terms of employment.

For example, part-time and full-time employees, employees working in different geographic locations, or employees with different dates of hire or length of service could be treated as distinct groups of similarly situated employees, provided the distinction is consistent with the employer's usual business practice. Other permissible groups might include members of different collective bargaining units or employees in different occupations.

Beneficiaries. A plan may treat beneficiaries as two or more distinct groups of similarly situated individuals if the distinction is based on any of the following factors:

- A bona fide employment-based classification of the participant through whom the beneficiary is receiving coverage
- The beneficiary's relation to the participant (e.g., as a spouse or dependent)
- Marital status
- Age or student status of a beneficiary who is a child of a participant
- Any other factor that is not a health factor

Participants and their beneficiaries can also be treated as separate groups based on their health care choices. Thus, if the employer offers a choice of two or more benefit packages, individuals choosing one package may be treated as a separate group from individuals choosing another package.

In any event, creation or modification of a health benefit classification cannot be directed at individual participants or beneficiaries based on a health factor. So, for example, if an employer modifies an employment-based classification to single out individuals based on their health factors and to deny them health coverage, the classification would constitute prohibited discrimination.

Example. An employer sponsors a group health plan that provides the same benefit package to all employees. Six of the employer's seven employees have the same job title and responsibilities. One employee, George, has a different job title and responsibilities. After George files an expensive claim for benefits under the plan, the coverage is modified so that employees with George's job title received a different benefit package with a lower lifetime dollar limit. The new grouping is not permitted because creation of the new coverage classification is directed at George based on one or more health factors.

2010 Health Reform Act. Effective for plan years beginning on or after September 23, 2010, the 2010 Health Reform Act extends the Code Section 105(h) nondiscrimination requirements to group health plans other than self-insured plans (see Q 5:40). [PHSA § 2716 as added by PPACA § 1001 and amended by PPACA § 10101] Under those rules, a group health plan cannot discriminate in favor of highly compensated individuals as to either eligibility to participate or benefits provided under the plan. Consequently, any distinctions among groups of employees should be tested to determine if they satisfy the Code Section 105(h) requirements. Note, however, that this provision does not apply to group health plans that are grandfathered plans in existence on the date of enactment (March 23, 2010) of the 2010 Health Reform Act.

Q 5:22   May a group health plan require an individual to pass a physical exam or fill out a health questionnaire before enrolling in the plan?

A plan cannot require an individual to pass a physical exam before enrolling in the plan. This requirement applies both to individuals who enroll when they first become eligible for participation and to late enrollees. For example, a group health plan may not offer automatic enrollment to all employees who sign up within the first 30 days of employment but bar employees from enrolling after the 30-day period unless they pass a physical exam. Because the requirement to pass a physical is an eligibility rule that discriminates based on one or more health factors, it would violate HIPAA's nondiscrimination requirements. [Treas. Reg. § 54.9802-1(b)(1)(iii)]

The nondiscrimination rules do not automatically prohibit health questionnaires, but a questionnaire may violate the rules, depending on how the information is used. For example, scoring a questionnaire for "health points" as a condition for enrollment would constitute impermissible discrimination based on health factors.

Example. An employer applies for a group health policy from an insurer. As part of the application, the issuer receives health information about the individuals who will be covered under the plan. One employee, Anna, and her dependents have a history of high health claims. Based on this health information, the insurer excludes Anna and her dependents from the group policy it offers to the employer.

Under DOL regulations, the nondiscrimination rules also apply to health insurers. The insurer's exclusion of Anna and her dependents from coverage because of their history of high health claims imposes a condition for eligibility that discriminates based on one or more health factors, and thus violates the nondiscrimination rules. If the plan provides coverage through this policy and does not provide equivalent coverage for Anna and her dependents through other means, the plan will also violate the nondiscrimination rules. [DOL Reg. § 2590.702(b)(i)]

If the employer is a small employer (generally, an employer with 50 or fewer employees), the insurer also may violate rules that require issuers to offer all the policies they sell in the small group market on a guaranteed-available basis to all small employers and to accept every eligible individual in every small-employer group. [45 C.F.R. § 146.150] Beginning in 2014, a health insurer that offers health insurance coverage in either the large group or the small group market in a state must accept every employer in the state that applies for coverage and must enroll every eligible individual. [PHSA § 2702 as added by PPACA § 1201]

Practice Pointer. While a health questionnaire may not be barred by the general nondiscrimination requirements, it may nonetheless violate the ban on collection of genetic information under GINA (see Q 5:39).

Q 5:23   May a plan deny coverage to an otherwise eligible individual because he or she is hospitalized on the enrollment date?

In the past, many group health plans contained nonconfinement clauses that excluded coverage for individuals who were hospitalized on the date enrollment was scheduled to take effect. These clauses typically delayed enrollment until the individual was no longer an inpatient. These nonconfinement clauses are no longer permitted. They violate the nondiscrimination rules because they discriminate on the basis of health factors and improperly exclude coverage for preexisting conditions.

Under the nondiscrimination regulations, a plan may not establish a rule for eligibility or set any individual's premium or contribution rate based on whether the individual is confined to a hospital or other health care institution. In addition, a plan generally may not establish a rule for eligibility or set any individual's premium or contribution rate based on the individual's ability to engage in normal life activities. [Treas. Reg. § 54.9802-1(e)(1)]

Example. A group health plan provides that coverage for employees and their dependents generally takes effect on the first day of employment. However, coverage for a dependent who is confined to a hospital or other health care institution does not become effective until the confinement ends. The plan violates the rules because the nonconfinement clause delays coverage for dependents based on confinement to a hospital or other health care institution.

State continuation of coverage laws may require that a prior employer's plan continue to cover a hospitalized employee or dependent. The HIPAA regulations make it clear that the HIPAA rules do not affect any prior plan's requirement to provide coverage. If both employers are potentially liable for coverage, coordination of benefits (COB) rules would apply. See chapter 3 for a discussion of the COB rules.

Q 5:24   May a plan deny coverage for employees who are not actively at work on the enrollment date?

Many plans have so-called actively-at-work clauses that deny coverage for employees who are absent from work on the enrollment date. Enrollment is typically delayed until the first day the employee is actively at work. [Treas. Reg. § 54.9802-1(e)(2)(i)] Depending on how they are structured, these clauses may or may not violate the nondiscrimination rules.

The nondiscrimination regulations provide that a plan may not establish an eligibility rule or set an individual's premium rate based on whether the individual is actively at work, unless absence from work due to a health factor is treated as being actively at work. In other words, a plan can delay coverage for employees who are not actively at work for non-health-related reasons, but it may not delay coverage for employees who are absent for health reasons.

Key exceptions. A plan may, however, require an employee to actually begin work for the employer before coverage becomes effective, provided the same rule applies regardless of the reason for the employee's absence. [Treas. Reg. § 54.9802-1(e)(2)(ii)] In the case of a multiemployer plan, the plan may require the employee to begin a job in covered employment.

> **Example 1.** A group health plan provides that coverage for new employees begins on the first day the employee reports to work. Henry, a new hire, is scheduled to begin work on August 3. However, he is unable to begin work that day because of illness. Henry begins working on August 4, and his health coverage becomes effective on that date. Delaying Henry's coverage until he actually begins work does not violate the nondiscrimination rules. However, the plan would violate the rules if it delayed coverage only for employees who are absent for health reasons on the first day of work. For example, the plan would be discriminatory if it allowed coverage to take effect on the scheduled starting date for employees who were absent because of a death in the family but delayed coverage for employees who were absent for health reasons.

Bear in mind that a plan may impose different eligibility rules for different groups of similarly situated individuals provided those groupings are not made on the basis of health factors. [Treas. Reg. § 54.9802-1(e)(3)]

> **Example 2.** A group health plan provides that employees are eligible for coverage if they perform service for the employer for 30 or more hours per week or if they are on paid leave (such as annual, sick, or bereavement leave). Employees on unpaid leave are treated as a separate group of similarly situated individuals who are not eligible for coverage (except as required by laws such as COBRA and the FMLA). The treatment of employees on unpaid leave as a separate group of similarly situated individuals is not

discriminatory. However, if the plan carved out separate rules for individuals on sick leave, it would violate the rules because groups of similarly situated individuals cannot be treated differently based on a health factor.

Q 5:25   May a plan impose any enrollment restrictions on late enrollees?

A plan may not restrict enrollment of late enrollees based on a health factor. However, restrictions that are not based on health factors do not violate the nondiscrimination rules.

> **Example.** Under an employer's group health plan, employees who enroll during the first 30 days of employment may choose between two benefit packages: an indemnity option and an HMO option. Employees who enroll late are permitted to enroll in the HMO option only if they provide evidence of good health.

The requirement to provide evidence of good health to be eligible for late enrollment in the HMO option violates the nondiscrimination rules because it is a rule for eligibility that discriminates based on a health factor. However, if the plan limited late enrollees to only one option without requiring evidence of good health, it would not violate the nondiscrimination rules. The time an individual chooses to enroll is not a health factor.

Q 5:26   May a plan deny benefits for an injury because of how it occurred?

In some cases, a plan can deny benefits because of the source of an injury. However, if a plan provides benefits for a particular type of injury, it may not deny benefits for that type of injury because it results from an act of domestic violence or from a physical or mental health condition (regardless of whether the condition was diagnosed before the injury occurred). [Treas. Reg. § 54.9802-1(b)(2)(iii)]

> **Example.** A group health plan generally provides medical and surgical benefits, including coverage for hospital stays that are medically necessary. However, the plan excludes benefits for self-inflicted injuries or injuries sustained in connection with a suicide attempt. Don, who suffers from depression, attempts suicide and sustains injuries requiring hospitalization. The plan may not deny benefits for Don's hospitalization because the suicide attempt and resulting injuries resulted from a medical condition (depression).

Q 5:27   Can a group health plan deny enrollment or benefits to an individual who engages in a high-risk activity?

A plan *may not* deny enrollment to an individual because he or she engages in high-risk activities such as motorcycling, snowmobiling, all-terrain vehicle riding, horseback riding, or skiing. Denying participation because of such activities would be considered improper discrimination based on evidence of insurability (see Q 5:18). [Treas. Reg. § 54.9802-1(a)(2)(ii)]

A plan *may* exclude coverage for injuries sustained in high-risk activities, provided the exclusion applies uniformly to similarly situated individuals and is not directed at any particular individual or beneficiary.

> **Example 1.** An employer's group health plan generally allows all employees to enroll within the first 30 days of employment. However, individuals who participate in certain recreational activities such as motorcycling are excluded from coverage. This exclusion violates the nondiscrimination rules because it denies eligibility to enroll based on a health factor (evidence of insurability).

> **Example 2.** An employer's group health plan provides benefits for head injuries. However, the plan also has a general exclusion for any injury sustained while participating in a number of recreational activities, including bungee jumping. Ed sustains a head injury while bungee jumping. The plan may deny benefits for Ed's bungee-jumping injury. A plan may deny benefits based on the source of an injury, provided the injury did not result from an act of domestic violence or from a medical condition (see Q 5:18).

Q 5:28   May a group health plan deny benefits for a preexisting condition?

The 2010 Health Reform Act provides that a group health plan or health insurance issuer may not impose *any* preexisting-condition exclusion with respect to the plan or coverage. [PHSA § 2704 as added by PPACA § 1201]

The general prohibition on preexisting-condition exclusions applies for plan years beginning on or after January 1, 2014. However, the prohibition on preexisting-condition exclusion as it applies to plan enrollees who are under age 19 takes effect for plan years beginning on or after September 23, 2010. [PPACA § 1253 as amended by PPACA § 10103] The prohibitions apply to grandfathered group health plans [PPACA Reconciliation § 2301]

To the extent a preexisting-condition exclusion is not prohibited by the 2010 Health Reform Act, HIPAA imposes strict limits on preexisting-condition exclusions (see Qs 5:45–5:60). In addition, the HIPAA nondiscrimination rules provide that preexisting-condition exclusions must apply uniformly to all similarly situated individuals and must not be directed at individual participants or beneficiaries based on a health factor. [Treas. Reg. § 54.9802-1T(b)(3)]

> **Example.** A group health plan excludes coverage for conditions for which medical advice, diagnosis, care, or treatment was recommended or received within the six-month period ending on an individual's enrollment date. The preexisting-condition exclusion generally lasts for 12 months, offset by periods of creditable coverage. However, if an individual has no claims in the first six months following enrollment, the remainder of the exclusion period is waived.

> The plan's preexisting-condition exclusion violates the nondiscrimination rules because it does not apply uniformly to all similarly situated individuals. Individuals who have medical claims during the first six months following

enrollment are treated differently based on a health factor from similarly situated individuals who do not have such claims.

For this purpose, a plan amendment relating to a preexisting condition will not be considered directed at individual participants or beneficiaries if is made effective no earlier than the first day of the first plan year after adoption

Q 5:29 Can a group health plan charge higher premiums to some individuals because of health factors?

A group health plan may not require an individual as a condition of enrollment or continued enrollment to pay a higher premium or contribution based on a health factor. [Treas. Reg. § 54.9802-1(c)(1)(i)] A group rating based on individual health factors is not prohibited. [Treas. Reg. § 54.9802-1(c)(2)(i)] However, a health insurer may not charge an employer a different premium for an individual in a group of similarly situated individuals based on a health factor. [Treas. Reg. § 54.9802-1(c)(2)(ii)]

Example 1. An employer purchases group health plan coverage from an insurer. In order to determine the premium for the upcoming plan year, the insurer reviews the claims experience of individuals covered under the plan. The insurer finds that one participant, Frank, had significantly higher claims than other similarly situated individuals in the plan. The plan quotes the employer a higher per-participant rate because of Frank's claims experience. This type of rate setting is not prohibited by the nondiscrimination rules. The higher premium rate is not targeted at Frank because the employer is quoted the same rate for Frank as for other participants.

Example 2. The facts are the same as those in Example 1, except that the insurer quotes the employer a higher premium rate for Frank than for other plan participants. The insurer's rate-setting practice is discriminatory. However, the regulations say that the employer will be in violation of the rules only if it actually charges Frank a higher premium. The employer would not be in violation if it purchased the policy based on the quote but did not actually charge Frank more than similarly situated individuals.

Caution. The Genetic Information Nondiscrimination Act of 2008 [Pub. L. No. 110-223, 122 Stat. 881] (GINA) provides that group health plans and health insurance issuers cannot base premiums for an employer or a group of similarly situated individuals on genetic information about any individual (see Q 5:35). However, as indicated above, premiums may be increased for the group based upon the manifestation of a disease or disorder of an individual enrolled in the plan.

2010 Health Reform Act. Effective for plan years beginning after 2013, the 2010 Health Reform Act imposes premium rating requirements for health insurance coverage offered in the small group market. Under these rules, the premium rates charged for a particular plan or coverage can vary only by (1) whether the coverage is for an individual or family, (2) rating area as established by the state in which the coverage is offered, (3) permissible age bands as set by the

Secretary of HHS (limited to a variation of 3 to 1 for adults), and (4) tobacco usage (limited to a variation of 1.5 to 1). [PHSA § 2701 as added by PPACA § 1201] The rating requirements do not apply to grandfathered plans. If a state permits health insurance issuers in the large group market to offer coverage through an Exchange (beginning in 2017), the requirements will apply to all coverage offered in the large group market in the state.

Q 5:30   May a group health plan provide more favorable eligibility rules or premiums for individuals with adverse health factors?

The nondiscrimination rules permit "benign discrimination" in favor of individuals with adverse health factors. According to the regulations, nothing prevents a plan from establishing more favorable eligibility rules for individuals with an adverse health factor, such as disability, than for individuals without an adverse health factor. [Treas. Reg. § 54.9802-1(g)(1)] The regulations also make it clear that a plan may charge a higher contribution or premium to an individual who would not be eligible for coverage if it were not for the adverse health factor.

Example 1. An employer's group health plan is generally available to employees and their family members until the last day of the month in which the employee ceases to perform services for the employer. The plan generally charges employees $50 per month for employee-only coverage and $125 per month for family coverage. However, an employee who stops work because of a disability can remain in the plan for 12 months following the month in which he or she ceases to perform service for the employer. The plan charges $100 per month for employee-only coverage and $250 per month for family coverage during the extended period of coverage.

The plan provision allowing extended coverage for disabled employees and their families does not violate the nondiscrimination rules. In addition, the plan is permitted to charge disabled employees a higher premium during the extended coverage period.

The nondiscrimination rules also permit a group health plan to lower premiums or contributions for some individuals if the lower charge is based on an adverse health factor, such as disability.

Example 2. Under an employer's group health plan, employees are generally charged $50 per month for employee-only coverage and $125 per month for family coverage. However, employees who are disabled receive free coverage under the plan. Waiving the premium payments for disabled employees is permitted under the nondiscrimination rules.

Q 5:31   May a group health plan reward employees with discounts for good health or good health habits?

As a general rule, the health care nondiscrimination rules bar a plan from charging similarly situated individuals different premiums or contributions based on a health factor. For example, a plan is not permitted to charge smokers higher premiums than nonsmokers.

However, the nondiscrimination rules do not prevent a group health plan from lowering premiums, deductibles, copayments, or coinsurance as a reward for individuals who have complied with the requirements of a wellness program. [ERISA § 702(b)(2)(B); I.R.C. § 9802(b)(2)(b); PHSA § 2705(b)(2)(B); Treas. Reg. § 54.9802-1(b)(2)(ii)]

Caution. Employers should exercise particular care in crafting wellness programs. In addition to complying with the HIPAA nondiscrimination requirements, wellness programs must comply with a number of other rules, including the HIPAA medical privacy requirements, the ADA, and GINA. For example, the ADA requires that wellness programs be "voluntary," with the employer neither requiring participation nor penalizing employees who do not participate. Moreover, in an informal discussion letter, the Equal Employment Opportunity Commission (EEOC) opined that certain questions in a wellness questionnaire that was required for participation in an employer's health reimbursement arrangement (HRA) constituted impermissible "disability-related inquiries" under the ADA. [ADA: Health Risk Assessments] Similarly, although GINA permits the collection of genetic information in connection with some types of voluntary wellness programs, the use and disclosure of that information is subject to strict limitations. (See Qs 5:163–5:182 for information on the HIPAA privacy rules; see chapter 18 for the ADA requirements; see Qs 5:35–5:39 and chapter 19 for information on GINA.)

2010 Health Reform Act. The 2010 Health Reform Act establishes statutory safe-harbor requirements for wellness programs. [PHSA § 2705(j) as added by PPACA § 1201] (See Q 5:34.)

Q 5:32   What is a wellness program?

A *wellness program* is a program to promote health and prevent disease. However, such programs are not always labeled "wellness programs." According to the DOL, examples include:

- A program that reduces individuals' cost sharing for complying with a preventive care plan;
- A diagnostic testing program for health problems;
- Rewards for attending educational classes;
- Following healthy lifestyle recommendations, or
- Meeting certain biometric targets (e.g., weight, cholesterol, nicotine use, or blood pressure targets).

Q 5:33   What are the HIPAA nondiscrimination requirements for wellness programs?

The IRS, the DOL, and HHS have jointly issued regulations governing wellness programs under the HIPAA nondiscrimination rules. The DOL's guidance on wellness programs makes it clear that a wellness program is required to comply with the regulations if and *only if* it operates as part of a group health plan and not as an employment policy separate from a group health plan. [DOL Field Assist. Bull. No. 2008-02 (Feb. 14, 2008)] For example, the DOL says that if an employer implements a policy that an employee who smokes will be fired, the policy is not part of a group health plan and is not subject to the wellness program regulations (although it may be governed by other laws).

The regulations lay down four requirements for a wellness program:

1. The total reward for all wellness programs does not exceed 20 percent of the total cost of employee-only coverage under the plan (including both employer and employee contributions).

2. The program is reasonably designed to promote health or prevent disease and gives eligible individuals the opportunity to qualify for a reward at least once each year.

3. The reward program is available to all similarly situated individuals and offers a reasonable alternative standard for obtaining an award to any individual for whom it would be unreasonably difficult due to a medical condition or medically inadvisable to attempt to meet the normal standard.

4. The plan discloses the terms of the program and the availability of a reasonable alternative standard in all plan materials.

[Treas. Reg. § 54.9802-1(f)(2)]

The regulations suggest the following language to satisfy the requirement for disclosing a reasonable alternative standard:

If it is unreasonably difficult due to a medical condition for you to achieve the standards for the reward under this program, or it is medically inadvisable for you to attempt to achieve the standards for the reward under this program, call us at [insert telephone number] and we will work with you to develop another way to qualify for the reward.

Example 1. A group health plan offers an annual premium discount of 10 percent of the cost of employee-only coverage to participants who adhere to a wellness program, which consists solely of giving an annual cholesterol test to participants. Those who achieve a cholesterol count of less than 200 receive the premium discount for the year.

The program is not a bona fide wellness program because the reward is not available to all similarly situated individuals. Some individuals may be unable to achieve a cholesterol level reduction, and the program does not make a reasonable alternative standard available to individuals who cannot meet the normal standard because of a health condition. As a result, the premium discount discriminates on the basis of a health factor.

Example 2. A group health plan offers an annual premium discount to employees who certify that they have not used tobacco products in the past year. Edward, a plan participant, is addicted to nicotine (a medical condition) and finds it unreasonably difficult to stop smoking.

Although it may seem paradoxical, to qualify as a bona fide wellness program, the plan must offer Edward a reasonable alternative standard for earning the premium discount. The regulations suggest that the plan could do this by giving Edward the premium discount for participation in a smoking cessation program (even if he doesn't stop smoking).

The regulations make it clear that a plan can require substantiation, such as a statement from the employee's physician that meeting the normal standard would be inadvisable or impossible. Moreover, the regulations offer employer plans an option for sidestepping the burden of crafting a separate alternative standard for each employee who cannot meet the normal standard. The plan can simply provide that the employee must follow the advice of his or her physician with regard to the health factor at issue.

Key point. The requirements in the regulations apply only to a program that ties rewards to results. The requirements do not apply to programs providing rewards that are not contingent on satisfying a standard related to a health factor. Examples of such programs include reimbursements for smoking cessation programs that are made regardless of whether an employee quits smoking, payments for health club memberships, rewards for attending health education seminars, and programs that encourage preventive care by waiving copayments or deductibles for well-baby visits.

Practice Pointer. The DOL provides a checklist for determining whether a wellness program is required to comply with the regulations—and whether or not the program is in compliance. [DOL Field Assist. Bull. No. 2008-02 (Feb. 14, 2008)]

Q 5:34   How does the 2010 Health Reform Act regulate wellness programs?

The 2010 Health Reform Act includes *statutory* safe harbor requirements for wellness programs that will satisfy the group health plan nondiscrimination requirements. [PHSA § 2705(j) as added by PPACA § 1201] The law specifically provides that nothing in the 2010 Health Reform Act rules would prohibit a wellness program that was established under prior law and complies with the HIPAA regulations (Q 5:33) from continuing to operate as long as those regulations remain in effect.

The 2010 Health Reform Act divides wellness programs into two categories: (1) programs with no conditions based on a health status factor, and (2) programs with conditions based on health status factors.

Programs with no conditions based on a health status factor. If none of the conditions for obtaining a premium discount or other reward or rebate for participation in a wellness program is based on an individual satisfying a standard that is related to a health status factor, the wellness program will satisfy the nondiscrimination requirements if participation is available to all similarly situated individuals. The following programs automatically fall in this category:

- A program that reimburses all or part of the cost for memberships in a fitness center
- A diagnostic testing program that provides a reward for participation but does not base any part of the reward on outcomes
- A program that encourages preventive care related to a health condition by waiving copayment or deductible requirements for the costs of items or services related to the condition (e.g. prenatal care or well-baby visits)
- A program that reimburses individuals for the costs of smoking cessation programs without regard to whether an individual quits smoking
- A program that provides a reward to individuals for attending a periodic health education seminar

Programs with conditions based on health status factors. If any of the conditions for obtaining a premium discount or other rebate or reward is based on an individual satisfying a standard that is related to a health status factor, the following conditions must be met:

1. The total rewards for all wellness programs that require satisfaction of a standard related to a health status factor do not exceed 30 percent of the cost of employee-only coverage under the plan. If an employee's spouse or dependents can participate fully in the wellness program, total rewards cannot exceed 30 percent of the cost of the coverage in which the employee and any dependents are enrolled. The cap on total rewards can be increased to 50 percent if the Secretaries of Labor, HHS, and Treasury deem such an increase appropriate.

2. The wellness program must be reasonably designed to promote health or prevent disease. A program will meet this requirement if it has a reasonable chance of improving health or preventing disease in participating individuals, is not overly burdensome, is not a subterfuge for discrimination based on health status, and is not "highly suspect" in the method chosen to promote health or prevent disease.

3. Eligible individuals can qualify for a reward under the program at least once each year.

4. The full reward under the program is available to all similarly situated individuals. A program will not meet this requirement unless it provides a reasonable alternative standard (or a waiver of the applicable standard) if it is unreasonably difficult for an individual to meet the applicable standard for a reward due to a medical condition or it is medically inadvisable for the individual to attempt to meet the standard. A plan can seek verification from an individual's physician that a health status factor makes it unreasonably difficult or medically inadvisable for an individual to satisfy the applicable standard for a reward.

5. The plan discloses in all plan materials describing the wellness program the availability of an alternative standard (or waiver of the applicable standard) for qualifying for a reward.

The 2010 Health Reform Act requirements are strikingly similar to the requirements in the HIPAA regulations. However, the HIPAA regulations cap total rewards at 20 percent of the cost of coverage, whereas the 2010 Reform Act sets the cap at 30 percent (with the possibility of an increase to 50 percent).

Q 5:35   May a group health plan use genetic information when administering the plan?

The Genetic Information Nondiscrimination Act of 2008 [Pub. L. No. 110-223, 122 Stat. 881 (May 21, 2008)] (GINA) prohibits genetic discrimination in employment and in health insurance. Title I of GINA amends ERISA, the PHSA, the Code, and the Social Security Act (SSA) to prohibit discrimination in health coverage based on genetic information.

Specifically, GINA prohibits group health plans and group health insurance issuers from the following:

- Using genetic information to adjust premium or contribution amounts for the group covered under the plan [I.R.C. § 9802(b)(3), as added by Pub. L. No. 110-233, § 103; ERISA § 702(b)(3), as added by Pub. L. No. 110-223, § 101; 42 U.S.C.S. § 300gg-1(b)(3), as added by Pub. L. No. 110-233, § 102];

- Requesting or requiring an individual or family member of an individual to undergo a genetic test [I.R.C. § 9802(c); ERISA § 702(c); 42 U.S.C. § 300gg-1(c)]; and

- Requesting, requiring, or purchasing genetic information for underwriting purposes or prior to an individual's enrollment under the plan. [I.R.C. § 9802(d); ERISA § 702(d); 42 U.S.C.S. § 300gg-1(d)]

Genetic information includes information about an individual's genetic tests, the genetic tests of an individual's family members, and the manifestation of a disease or disorder in an individual's family members. Genetic information also includes an individual's request for, or receipt of, genetic services, but does not include information about the sex or age of any individual. Genetic information about an individual includes the genetic information about a fetus carried by a pregnant woman or an embryo legally held by an individual utilizing an assisted reproductive technology.

The provisions of GINA are effective for group health plans and health insurance issuers in the group market for plan years beginning after May 21, 2009. The Departments of Labor, Health and Human Services, and the Treasury have issued interim final regulations interpreting and clarifying GINA. [26 C.F.R. Pt. 54; 29 C.F.R. Pt. 2590; 45 C.F.R. Pts. 144, 146, and 148] The regulations apply to group health plans and group health insurance issuers for plan years beginning on or after December 7, 2009.

Q 5:36   What plans are covered by the genetic information nondiscrimination requirements?

GINA applies more broadly than the general HIPAA requirements. The HIPAA requirements generally do not apply to a group health plan that has fewer than two participants who are current employees. However, that exception for small group health plans does not apply for purposes of genetic information nondiscrimination requirements. [Treas. Reg. § 54.9831-1(b)(2); DOL Reg. § 2590.732(b)(2); HHS Reg. § 146.145(b)(2)]

> **Practice Pointer.** While the genetic nondiscrimination requirements apply broadly to all group health plans, many plans are not affected because they have not historically collected or used genetic information for underwriting purposes. According to the preamble to the interim final regulations, the DOL, HHS, and the Treasury anticipate that compliance with the new rules most directly impacts those plans that include wellness and disease management programs that offer rewards and incentives (e.g., premium rebates, lower deductibles, or cash bonus payments) to employees that complete health risk assessments.

Q 5:37   What is the prohibition on the use of genetic information to adjust group rates?

GINA and the interim final regulations expand the prohibitions against discrimination by prohibiting group health plans and health insurers that offer coverage in connection with a group plan from adjusting premium or contribution rates for the plan or a group of similarly situated individuals based on genetic information. [I.R.C. § 9802(b)(3), as added by Pub. L. No. 110-233, § 103; ERISA § 702(b)(3), as added by Pub. L. No. 110-223, § 101; 42 U.S.C.S. § 300gg-1(b)(3), as added by Pub. L. No. 110-233, § 102; Treas. Reg. § 54.9802-3T(b); DOL Reg. § 2590.702-1(b); HHS Reg. § 146.122(b)]

> **Practice Pointer.** GINA also prohibits group health plans and health insurers from requiring genetic tests or collecting genetic information for underwriting purposes. However, those prohibitions are separate from the prohibition on using genetic information to adjust group rates. Even if a plan or insurer has legitimately obtained genetic test results or other genetic information, it may not use the information to set rates.

The rules do not bar a plan or insurer from adjusting group premiums or contributions based on the actual manifestation of a disease in an individual enrolled in the plan. However, the manifestation of a disease or disorder in one plan participant cannot be used as genetic information about another plan participant to further increase the premiums or contributions under the plan. Sounds tricky? The regulations provide the following example.

> **Example.** In order to determine premiums for the coming year, a group health plan's insurer reviews the claims experience of individuals covered by the plan. The insurer finds that one employee has made claims for treatment of polycystic kidney disease. The employee in question has two dependent

children who are covered under the plan. The insurer quotes the plan a higher per-participant rate based on the employee's claims experience and the likelihood that the employee's two children may develop kidney disease. *Result:* The insurer has violated the prohibition on using genetic information to set rates. The insurer is using genetic information (family medical history) about a condition that has not been manifested in the employee's children to increase the plan premiums. Note, however, that the insurer would be permitted to increase the plan premiums based solely on the employee's claims experience.

2010 Health Reform Act. Effective for plan years beginning after 2013, the 2010 Health Reform Act imposes premium rating requirements for health insurance coverage offered in the small group market. Under these rules, the premium rates charged for a particular plan or coverage can vary only by (1) whether the coverage is for an individual or family, (2) rating area as established by the state in which the coverage is offered, (3) permissible age bands as set by the Secretary of HHS (limited to a variation of 3 to 1 for adults), and (4) tobacco usage (limited to a variation of 1.5 to 1). [PHSA § 2701, as added by PPACA § 1201] The rating requirements do not apply to grandfathered plans. If a state permits health insurance issuers in the large group market to offer coverage through an Exchange (beginning in 2017), the requirements will apply to all coverage offered in the large group market in the state.

Q 5:38   What is the prohibition on requesting or requiring genetic tests?

GINA and the interim regulations generally prohibit group health plans and insurers from requesting or requiring individuals or their family members to undergo genetic tests. [I.R.C. § 9802(c); ERISA § 702(c); 42 U.S.C.S. § 300gg-1(c); Treas. Reg. § 54.9802-3T(c); DOL Reg. § 2590.702-1(c); HHS Reg. § 146.122(c)] However, there are three exceptions to this prohibition:

1. *Health care professional exception.* A health care professional who is providing health care services to an individual can request that the individual undergo a genetic test. To qualify for this exception, the health care professional must actually be providing services to the individual, rather than services to the plan. For example, claims review by a health care professional would not qualify as providing health care services to an individual. On the other hand, the regulations make it clear that a treatment-related recommendation of genetic testing will qualify, even if the doctor is employed by the HMO covering the patient.

2. *Payment determination exception.* A plan or its insurer can obtain and use the results of a genetic test to make a determination regarding payment under the plan For example, if a plan conditions payment for an item or service on its medical appropriateness and appropriateness depends on the genetic makeup of the patient, the plan can condition payment on the results of a genetic test—and can refuse payment if the patient does not undergo the test. However, a plan or insurer can request only the

minimum amount of information necessary to make the payment determination.

Example 1. A group health plan generally covers yearly mammograms starting at age 40, but covers yearly mammograms starting at age 30 for individuals with certain gene mutations that increase their risk for breast cancer. Allison, age 33, a plan participant who has such a gene mutation, has an annual mammogram and submits a claim for payment. The plan, following an established policy, asks Allison to submit evidence that she has a gene mutation that increases her risk for breast cancer. *Result:* The plan does not violate the prohibition on requesting genetic tests because the appropriateness of the mammogram depends on Allison's genetic makeup and the minimum information necessary to determine the appropriateness includes the results of Allison's genetic test.

Example 2. A group health plan covers genetic testing for celiac disease in individuals who have family members with the disease. When Brian's son is diagnosed with celiac disease, Brian undergoes a genetic test for the disease and submits a claim for payment to the plan's insurer. The insurer asks Brian to submit the results of the test before the claim is paid. *Result:* The insurer has violated the prohibition on requesting genetic tests because the insurer does not need to know the *results* of Brian's test to make a determination about payment.

3. *Research exception.* A group health plan or insurer may request—*but not require*—a plan participant or beneficiary to undergo genetic testing as part of a research study, provided certain strict requirements are met. These requirements include providing notice and obtaining informed consent from the participant or beneficiary and providing notice to the Department of Labor.

Q 5:39   What is the prohibition on the collection of genetic information?

GINA and the interim regulations bar a group health plan or insurer from collecting genetic information for underwriting purposes as well as prior to or in connection with an individual's enrollment under the plan. [I.R.C. § 9802(d); ERISA § 702(d); 42 U.S.C.S. § 300gg-1(d); Treas. Reg. § 54.9802-3T(d); DOL Reg. § 2590.702-1(d); HHS Reg. § 146.122(d)] Collecting genetic information includes requesting, requiring, or purchasing such information.

Practice Pointer. The ban on collection of genetic information is the most far-reaching of the genetic nondiscrimination requirements, particularly for plans that include wellness programs, disease management programs, or health risk assessments. While commentators strongly urged that regulations implementing GINA contain a blanket exception for such programs, no such exception was included in the interim final regulations.

Collection of genetic information prior to or in connection with enrollment. A group health plan must not collect genetic information about an individual prior to the individual's effective date of coverage under the plan or in connection with the rules governing eligibility.

Collection for underwriting. For purposes of the genetic information nondiscrimination rules, underwriting encompasses far more than rating and pricing a group policy. Underwriting is defined broadly to include rules for eligibility for benefits and the computation of premium amounts. Consequently, wellness programs that provide rewards for completing health risk assessments that request genetic information (including family medical history) violate the prohibition against collecting genetic information for underwriting. Moreover, such programs violate the prohibition even if the rewards are not based on the outcome of the assessment—and even though such programs would not violate the general nondiscrimination requirements for wellness programs.

On the other hand, the regulations do not bar a plan or insurer from collecting genetic information through health risk assessments as long as no rewards are provided (and as long as the request is not made prior to or in connection with enrollment in the plan). Moreover, plans or insurers are permitted to offer rewards for completing a risk assessment as long as the risk assessment does not collect genetic information.

Example 1. A group health plan provides a premium reduction to enrollees who complete a health risk assessment that includes questions about family medical history. The assessment is requested after enrollment and whether or not the assessment is completed has no impact on the individual's enrollment. Nonetheless, this health risk assessment would violate the prohibition on collection of genetic information because it includes genetic information (family medical history) and is used for underwriting purposes (to provide a premium reduction).

Example 2. The facts are the same as those in Example 1, except that the plan does not provide a premium reduction or other reward for completing the HRA. Although the assessment asks for genetic information (family medical history), it does not violate the prohibition on the collection of such information because it is not used for underwriting purposes.

Example 3. A group health plan asks enrollees to complete a health risk assessment that includes questions about family medical history. The assessment is requested prior to enrollment in the plan, but there is no reward or penalty for completing or not completing the assessment. Although the health risk assessment is not used for underwriting, it violates the prohibition because it asks for genetic information prior to enrollment.

Example 4. A group health plan asks enrollees to complete two separate health risk assessments after enrollment; the assessments are unrelated to enrollment. The first assessment specifies that the individual should answer only for himself or herself and not for the family, and it does not ask about any genetic tests the individual has undergone or genetic services the individual has received. The second health risk assessment asks about family medical history and the results of genetic tests the individual has undergone. The plan offers a reward for completing the first assessment. There is no reward for completing the second assessment, and the instructions make it clear that the second assessment is strictly voluntary and will not affect the reward for the first assessment. Neither health risk assessment violates the prohibition on collection of genetic information. There is no collection of genetic information in connection with the first assessment, and the request for genetic information in the second assessment is not used for underwriting purposes because no reward is provided.

Exception for "incidental" collection. The regulations carve out an exception where the collection of genetic information is incidental to the collection of other information. This exception applies only if the information collected is not used for underwriting purposes. Moreover, the exception does not apply if it is reasonable for the plan or insurer to anticipate that genetic information may be received as part of the collection process unless the collection request specifically warns that genetic information should not be provided.

Exception for medical appropriateness. The regulations provide that where an individual is seeking a benefit or coverage under a plan, requesting family medical history or other genetic information to determine whether the benefit is medically appropriate for payment does not fall within the prohibition on collection of genetic information. In other words, the regulations extend the statutory exception for genetic tests in connection with the payment determinations to all types of genetic information. However, as with the payment determination, the plan may request only the minimum amount of information necessary to determine medical appropriateness.

The regulations also make it clear that the medical appropriateness exception applies only when an individual is seeking a benefit or coverage.

Example 5. A group health plan provides a premium reduction to enrollees who complete an assessment for health risks that includes questions about family medical history. The assessment is requested after enrollment and whether or not it is completed or whether responses are provided has no effect on enrollment. There is no premium reduction or other reward for completing the assessment. However, based on their answers to questions about family medical history, individuals may become eligible for additional benefits under the plan by being enrolled in a disease management program. *Result:* Because the questions about family medical history could result in an individual being eligible for additional benefits, the questions constitute a prohibited request for genetic information for underwriting purposes. Although the plan offers a disease management program based on the medical appropriateness, the exception does not apply because the individual enrollee is not seeking benefits.

Example 6. A group health plan offers a diabetes disease management program to individuals for whom it is medically appropriate. The plan sends out notices to all participants describing the program. Individuals interested in the program are advised to contact the plan to demonstrate that they have diabetes or are at risk for diabetes. For individuals who do not currently have diabetes, genetic information may be used to demonstrate that they are at risk. *Result:* In this case, the medical appropriateness exception applies to the collection of genetic information because individuals contact the plan to request the benefit.

Prohibition of Discrimination in Favor of Highly Compensated Employees

Q 5:40   Do the nondiscrimination rules of Code Section 105 apply to all employer-provided medical plans?

As originally enacted, Code Section 105, which provides a tax exclusion for employer-provided accident and health benefits, imposed nondiscrimination requirements on *self-insured plans only*. Under those rules, if a self-insured plan is discriminatory, all or part of the benefits provided to highly compensated employees are not eligible for exclusion and are includable in income (see chapter 3).

Effective for plan years beginning on or after September 23, 2010, the 2010 Health Reform Act extends the Code Section 105(h) nondiscrimination requirements to group health plans other than self-insured plans. [PHSA § 2716, as added by PPACA § 1001 and amended by PPACA § 10101] However, the special tax treatment for discriminatory self-insured plans is not extended to other group health plans. Instead, the excise tax under Code Section 4980D applies for violation of the nondiscrimination requirements. This provision does not apply group health plans that are grandfathered plans in existence on the date of enactment (March 23, 2010) of the 2010 Health Reform Act.

The questions that follow describe the plan design requirements for eligibility and benefits that a *self-insured* group health plan must, at a minimum, satisfy to receive favorable tax treatment for benefits paid to highly compensated employees (HCEs). The 2010 Health Reform Act provides that "similar" requirements apply to plans other than self-insured plans.

Q 5:41   What is a self-insured medical reimbursement plan?

A *self-insured medical reimbursement plan* is an employer plan that provides reimbursement to employees for medical care expenses other than reimbursement under a policy of accident and health insurance. [I.R.C. § 105(h)(6)]

Note. Effective for plan years beginning on or after September 23, 2010, the 2010 extends the Code Section 105(h) nondiscrimination requirements to group health plans other than self-insured plans. [PHSA § 2716, as added by PPACA § 1001 and amended by PPACA § 10101] However, the penalties for violations differ (see Q 5:49). In addition, extension of the nondiscrimination requirements does not apply to group health plans that are grandfathered plans in existence on the date of enactment (March 23, 2010) of the 2010 Health Reform Act. Consequently, the definition of a self-insured plan remains relevant.

A policy of accident and health insurance for this purpose is either (1) a policy issued by a licensed insurer or (2) a reimbursement arrangement in the nature of a prepaid health care plan (such as an HMO) that is regulated under federal or state law in a manner similar to the regulation of insurance companies. [Treas. Reg. § 1.105-11(b)(1)(i)]

Risk shifting. Even a plan underwritten by an insurance company, or a prepaid health care plan, will be considered self-insured unless risk is shifted to the insurer or prepaid health care plan. Thus, a cost-plus policy or a policy providing only administrative or bookkeeping services will be considered self-insured. A plan will not be considered self-insured merely because one factor the insurer uses to determine the premium is the employer's prior claims experience. [Treas. Reg. § 1.105(b)(1)(ii)]

Captive insurance companies. A plan insured with a captive insurance company (i.e., an insurance company that is fully or partially owned by the employer providing the plan) is considered insured only if, for the plan year, the premiums paid by unrelated companies are 50 percent or more of the total premiums received and the policy of insurance is similar to policies sold to unrelated companies. [Treas. Reg. § 1.105-11(b)(1)(iii)]

Q 5:42   When is a group health plan nondiscriminatory under Code Section 105(h)?

Under Code Section 105(h), a plan cannot discriminate in favor of highly compensated individuals as to either eligibility to participate or benefits provided under the plan. [I.R.C. § 105(h)(2)]

Employees. In applying these nondiscrimination rules, all employees treated as employed by a single employer under the qualified pension controlled-group rules spelled out in Code Sections 414(b), 414(c), and 414(m) will be treated as employed by a single employer. [I.R.C. § 105(h)(8)] The medical plans within the controlled group need not, however, be tested together. (See Q 5:47.)

Q 5:43   Who is a highly compensated individual?

For purposes of the nondiscrimination tests of Code Section 105(h), *highly compensated individuals* are defined as:

- The five highest-paid officers;
- Shareholders owning more than 10 percent of the value of the employer's stock; or
- The highest-paid 25 percent of employees, disregarding certain excludable employees who are not participating (those with less than three years of service at the start of the plan year, those under age 25 at the start of the plan year, part-time or seasonal employees, nonparticipants covered by a collective bargaining agreement, and nonresident aliens with no U.S.-source earned income from the employer).

[I.R.C. §§ 105(h)(3), 105(h)(4)]

Q 5:44   When does a group health plan discriminate as to eligibility?

Under Code Section 105(h), a plan discriminates in favor of highly compensated individuals with regard to eligibility to participate unless it benefits:

- 70 percent of all employees;
- 80 percent of all eligible employees, if at least 70 percent of all employees are eligible to benefit under the plan; or
- A nondiscriminatory classification of employees.

[I.R.C. § 105(h)(3)]

As noted, this discriminatory eligibility rule must be applied on a controlled-group basis.

The statute provides some relief for passing the eligibility test. When applying this discriminatory eligibility test, certain classes of employees may be excluded:

1. Employees with fewer than three years of service before the plan year started;
2. Employees who have not attained age 25 before the plan year started;
3. Part-time (generally, fewer than 25 hours per week) and seasonal (generally, less than seven months per year) employees;
4. Employees included in a unit of employees covered by a collective bargaining agreement, if accident and health benefits were the subject of good-faith bargaining; and
5. Nonresident aliens with no U.S.-source earned income from the employer.

If certain standards contained in the regulation are met, part-time employees whose customary employment is fewer than 35 hours per week may be excluded. [I.R.C. § 105(h); Treas. Reg. § 1.105-11(c)(2)(iii)]

Q 5:45   When does a group health plan discriminate with respect to benefits?

Under Code Section 105(h), a group health plan discriminates in favor of highly compensated individuals with regard to benefits unless all of the benefits provided to highly compensated individuals are provided on the same basis to all other individuals. This discrimination test is a "design" test rather than a "utilization" test: it measures benefit availability, not the amount of plan benefits actually received by participants. Significantly, the exclusions available for the discriminatory eligibility test (see Q 3:44) do not apply to this discriminatory benefits test. As a result, all participants within the controlled group must be counted when applying this discriminatory benefit test.

Practice Pointer. This benefit nondiscrimination rule is capable of being completely satisfied by the design of the group health plan (thus avoiding periodic testing for possible discrimination). If the employer has a single group health plan for all employees within its controlled group, and all of the benefits under the group health plan are uniformly available to all participants at the same cost without any different features (level of benefits, premiums, copayments, or different starting dates, for example) for any employee or subgroup of employees, the benefit discrimination test may be satisfied. However, the sponsoring employer could still be tripped up by the "discrimination in operation" subrule described below.

Proportionate to compensation. If the plan covers highly compensated individuals, it will be treated as discriminatory with respect to benefits if the type and amount of benefits under the medical plan are proportionate to compensation. [Treas. Reg. § 1.105-11(c)(3)(i)]

Related to age or service. The current regulations under Code Section 105 also treat a plan as discriminatory if it has a maximum benefit limit (attributable to employer contributions) for any single benefit or combination of benefits, unless such maximum benefit limit is uniform for all participants and dependents of the participating employees and is not modified by reason of the participant's age or years of service. [Treas. Reg. § 1.105-11(c)(3)(i)]

Discrimination in operation. Self-insured medical plans are also prohibited from discriminating in operation. This is a facts-and-circumstances inquiry, and the mere fact that highly compensated individuals use more benefits under the plan than other participants does not make the plan discriminatory in operation. [Treas. Reg. § 1.105-11(c)(3)(ii)] The duration of the benefit at issue is examined. If the benefit is added to the plan when a highly compensated individual needs it and then deleted, for example, discrimination in operation could occur. In general, unless a benefit is being added to address the needs of an executive, this pitfall should be relatively easy to avoid.

Q 5:46   Do the Section 105(h) nondiscrimination rules apply to executive-only physical examination programs?

No. The Section 105(h) nondiscrimination rules do not apply to executive-only physical examination programs. IRS regulations specifically exempt reimbursements paid under a plan for medical diagnostic procedures for an employee (but not for the employee's spouse or dependents), such as a self-insured executive-only physical examination plan. The allowable medical diagnostic procedures include routine medical examinations, blood tests, and X-rays. Further details are contained in IRS regulations. [Treas. Reg. § 1.105-11(g)]

Q 5:47   If an employer has multiple group health plans, are they tested separately under Code Section 105(h)?

That is entirely up to the sponsoring employer. Multiple group health plans are permitted to be tested separately under the Section 105(h) nondiscrimination rules. The employer may choose to designate two or more plans as a single plan for purposes of meeting the nondiscrimination rules. [Treas. Reg. § 1.105-11(c)(4)(i)] This rule is particularly useful where the employer offers numerous group health plans in its controlled group.

Q 5:48   If a discriminatory group health plan is included in a cafeteria plan, what is the effect on the cafeteria plan?

The cafeteria plan is not be adversely affected. A proposed Treasury regulation on cafeteria plans states that the mere failure of any "qualified benefit" to satisfy the nondiscrimination requirements of other applicable Code sections, such as Code Section 105(h), will not disqualify the entire cafeteria plan. [Prop. Treas. Reg. § 1.125-2(j)] However, highly compensated individuals will still face adverse tax consequences under Code Section 105(h).

Q 5:49   What are the consequences if a group health plan is discriminatory?

If a self-insured group health plan discriminates in favor of HCEs, then all or a part of the benefits received by such employees will be included in their gross incomes. [I.R.C. § 105(h)] See chapter 3 for a complete discussion of the tax treatment of HCEs under discriminatory plans.

The 2010 Health Reform Act does not specifically extend the special tax rules to plans other than self-insured plans. Instead, for plans other than self-insured plans, the law incorporates the nondiscrimination *requirements* as part of the Code's group health plan requirements. [I.R.C. § 9815, as added by PPACA § 1562(f)] Violations of the Code's group health plan requirements are subject to an excise tax under Code Section 4980D (see Q 5:13).

Waiting Periods and Preexisting-Condition Exclusions

Q 5:50   Can a group health plan impose a waiting period for coverage under the plan?

Yes. However, under the 2010 Health Reform Act, a group health plan or a health insurance issuer offering group coverage cannot impose a waiting period of more than 90 days. [PHSA § 2708, as added by PPACA § 1201 and amended by PPACA § 10103] This limitation of the waiting period applies for plan years beginning on or after January 1, 2014. The limitation applies to grandfathered plans. [PPACA § 1253; PPACA § 1251, as amended by PPACA Reconciliation § 2301]

Q 5:51   Can a group health plan rescind coverage for a participant or beneficiary once it has begun?

The 2010 Health Reform Act provides that a group health plan or health insurance issuer cannot rescind coverage for an enrollee, except in the case of fraud or an intentional misrepresentation of material fact as prohibited under the terms of the plan. [PHSA § 2712, as added by PPACA § 1001] This requirement applies to both new and grandfathered plans for plan years beginning on or after September 23, 2010. [PPACA § 1004; PPACA § 1251, as amended by PPACA Reconciliation § 2301]

Under prior law, the Eighth Circuit Court of Appeals held that an insurer that was the administrator of an employer's health plan did not abuse its discretionary power when it retroactively rescinded health insurance coverage for an employee who had misrepresented his medical history when he applied for coverage. [Shipley v. Arkansas Blue Cross & Blue Shield, 333 F.3d 898 (8th Cir. 2003)] When William Shipley applied for health insurance through his employer's health plan, which was administered by Arkansas Blue Cross and Blue Shield (ABCBS), he completed an enrollment form that asked questions about his medical history. Shipley answered "no" to a number of those questions, including questions as to whether he had ever been diagnosed with sinusitis, asthma, chronic obstructive pulmonary disease (COPD), or disorder of the lungs and whether he was taking any medication.

Soon after obtaining the health insurance coverage, Shipley paid a number of visits to a doctor for respiratory problems and was diagnosed with cancer and COPD. After investigating Shipley's medical history, ABCBS discovered that Shipley had, in fact, been treated for chest congestion and an upper respiratory infection, acute sinusitis, and asthmatic bronchitis, and was taking several medications. ABCBS rescinded Shipley's insurance coverage retroactive to its original effective date on the grounds that Shipley had made material misrepresentations on his application form.

In reaching its decision, the Eighth Circuit noted that the employer's plan was governed by ERISA. However, there is no provision in ERISA dealing with rescission of health benefits in response to misrepresentations in a health insurance application. Therefore, the court said federal common law controls. And the court concluded that federal common law allows for rescission of an ERISA-governed insurance policy that is procured through material misstatement or omissions of the insured. Moreover, the court determined that Shipley's misstatements on his application were material because truthful information on the application form would have caused ABCBS to rate the policy differently and would have affected Shipley's coverage for preexisting conditions.

In addition to the Eighth Circuit Court of Appeals, at least four other appellate courts have recognized a right of rescission by an ERISA plan. [Security Life Ins. Co. of Am. v. Meyling, 146 F.3d 1184 (9th Cir. 1998); Davies v. Centennial Life Ins. Co., 128 F.3d 934 (6th Cir. 1997); Hauser v. Life Gen. Sec. Ins. Co., 56 F.3d 1330 (11th Cir. 1995); Nash v. Trustees of Boston Univ., 946 F.2d 960 (1st Cir. 1991)]

Q 5:52 Can a group health plan impose any preexisting-condition exclusions on coverage under the plan?

HIPAA (as incorporated in ERISA and the Internal Revenue Code) restricts—but does not prohibit—a plan from imposing preexisting-condition exclusions. The HIPAA requirements limit (1) the "look-back period" a plan may use for determining whether a preexisting condition exists and (2) the period after coverage begins during which a plan can exclude or limit benefits for a preexisting condition. [ERISA § 701; I.R.C § 9801]

2010 Health Reform Act. The 2010 Health Reform Act provides that a group health plan or health insurance issuer may not impose *any* preexisting-condition exclusion with respect to the plan or coverage. [PHSA § 2704, as added by PPACA § 1201]

The general prohibition on preexisting-condition exclusions applies for plan years beginning on or after January 1, 2014. However, the prohibition on preexisting-condition exclusion as it applies to plan enrollees who are under age 19 takes effect for plan years beginning on or after September 23, 2010. [PPACA § 1253 as amended by PPACA § 10103] The prohibitions apply to grandfathered group health plans [PPACA Reconciliation § 2301]

Note. The 2010 Health Reform Act specifically adopts the same definition of "preexisting-condition exclusion" that applies for purposes of the HIPAA requirements (see Q 5:53). Under that definition, a "preexisting-condition exclusion" is "a limitation or exclusion of benefits relating to a condition based on the fact that the condition was present before the date of enrollment for such coverage, whether or not any medical advice, diagnosis, care, or treatment was recommended or received before such date." [PHSA § 2704(b)(1) as added by PPACA § 1201]

Despite that definition, there was some controversy following enactment of the 2010 Health Reform Act as to whether the law required health insurers to provide *coverage* to children with preexisting conditions or merely required that *benefits* be provided with respect to a preexisting condition once a child qualified for enrollment in the plan. In a strongly worded letter to America's Health Insurance Plans (AHIP), an industry group representing health insurance companies, Secretary of Health and Human Service Kathleen Sebelius responded to that controversy by indicating that HHS plans to issue regulations confirming that "the term 'pre-existing condition exclusion' applies both to a child's access to a plan and his or her benefits once he or she is in the plan." [Sebelius Letter to America's Health Insurance Plans, Mar. 29, 2010] In addition, the chairmen of the three committees with jurisdiction over health policy in the U.S. House of Representatives (Energy and Commerce, Ways and Means, and Education and Labor) issued a joint statement indicating that under the 2010 Health Reform Act "plans that include coverage of children cannot deny coverage to a child based on a pre-existing condition." [Tri-Committee Chairmen Statement, Mar. 24, 2010] The controversy was apparently resolved when Karen Ignani, President and CEO of AHIP, responded in a letter to Secretary Sebelius that "With respect to the provisions related to coverage for children, we await and will fully comply with regulations consistent with the principles described in your letter."

Practice Pointer. The 2010 Health Reform Act does not negate the HIPAA requirements for preexisting conditions. However, the 2010 Health Reform

Act provides that, to the extent there is a conflict between the existing provisions of ERISA or the Code and the 2010 Health Reform Act requirements, the 2010 Health Reform Act requirements apply. [ERISA § 715 as added by PPACA § 1562; I.R.C. § 9815 as added by PPACA § 1562] Consequently, to the extent a preexisting-condition exclusion is not prohibited under the 2010 Health Reform Act rules, any such exclusion must comply with the HIPAA requirements.

Q 5:53   What is a preexisting-condition exclusion?

A *preexisting-condition exclusion* includes any limitation or exclusion of benefits relating to a condition that was present before the effective date of coverage under a group health plan or group health insurance coverage, whether or not any medical advice, diagnosis, care, or treatment was recommended or received before that day. [DOL Reg. § 2590.701(-3(a); Treas. Reg. § 54.9801-3(a)]

A plan provision does not have to use the term *preexisting condition* to fall within the definition of a preexisting-condition exclusion. For example, if a plan provides that treatment for injuries in connection with an accident will be covered only if the accident occurred while the individual was covered by the plan, the plan provision operates as a preexisting-condition exclusion because it limits benefits for a condition that was present before the individual's enrollment in the plan. Similarly, HIPAA regulations make it clear that a plan provision that counts benefits received under prior health coverage against a life benefit limit or one that denies benefits for pregnancy until 12 months after an individual becomes eligible for other plan benefits will be treated as a preexisting-condition exclusion. The regulations also clarify that exclusions for congenital conditions are preexisting-condition exclusions unless the plan excludes benefits for all instances of a condition.

Q 5:54   How does HIPAA limit preexisting-condition exclusions?

HIPAA places outside limits on the ability to limit plan costs for medical conditions that the individual had prior to the effective date of new group health plan coverage. These federally mandated standards affect (1) the look-back period that can be used by the plan (see Q 5:56) and (2) the maximum period after coverage begins that the group health plan can exclude or limit benefits for the preexisting condition (see Q 5:57).

Alternative to preexisting-condition exclusion. HMOs may provide for an "affiliation period" as an alternative to the use of any preexisting-condition limitations or exclusions, provided that such period is uniformly applied without regard to any health status-related factors (see Q 5:18) and does not exceed two months (three months for late enrollees). [ERISA § 701(g)]

Under HIPAA regulations an affiliation period can be imposed if each of the following requirements is met:

1. No preexisting-condition exclusion is imposed for any coverage offered by the HMO in connection with the particular group health plan.

2. No premium is charged to a participant or beneficiary for the affiliation period.

3. The affiliation period for the HMO coverage is consistent with the HIPAA nondiscrimination provisions.

4. The affiliation period does not exceed two months (or three months for a late enrollee).

5. The affiliation period begins on the enrollment date (or, in the case of a late enrollee, the affiliation period begins on the day that would be the first day of coverage, but for the affiliation period).

6. The affiliation period for enrollment in the HMO under a plan runs concurrently with any waiting period.

[DOL Reg. § 2590.701-7]

The regulations make it clear that an affiliation period begins on an individual's plan enrollment, not when coverage under a particular benefit package option begins. Therefore, if a group health plan offers multiple benefit package options, the HMO option cannot impose an affiliation period on a plan participant who switches from another option to the HMO benefit package option (assuming the period of time that has elapsed since the individual's initial enrollment date exceeds the duration of the HMO affiliation period).

Q 5:55   Are there any preexisting-condition exclusions that are prohibited under HIPAA?

Yes. HIPAA prohibits group health plans from imposing preexisting-condition limits or exclusions with respect to (1) newborns, (2) adopted children and children placed for adoption, (3) pregnancy, and (4) genetic information unsupported by a related diagnosis.

Newborns. HIPAA prohibits group health plans from imposing any preexisting-condition limits or exclusions with respect to a newborn who is covered under creditable coverage as of the 30th day of the period beginning with the newborn's date of birth; however, an exclusion is not barred after the end of the first 63-day period during which the newborn child was not covered under any creditable coverage.

Adopted children and children placed for adoption. HIPAA prohibits group health plans from imposing preexisting-condition limits or exclusions on children who are adopted or placed for adoption prior to age 18 and who are covered under creditable coverage as of the 30th day of the period beginning with the date of adoption or placement for adoption; however, an exclusion is not barred after the end of the first 63-day period during which the adopted or placed child was not covered under any creditable coverage.

Pregnancy. HIPAA prohibits group health plans from imposing any preexisting-condition limits or exclusions relating to pregnancy.

Genetic information. HIPAA prohibits genetic information from being treated as a preexisting condition absent a diagnosis of a condition related to the information. Genetic information encompasses information about an individual's genetic tests, genetic tests of an individual's family members, the manifestation of a disease, or disorder in family members of an individual; any request for or receipt of genetic service by the individual or a family member. [ERISA §§ 701(b), 701(d); I.R.C. §§ 9801(b), 9801(d); DOL Reg. § 2590.701-3; Treas. Reg. § 54.9801-2]

> **Practice Pointer.** The Genetic Information Nondiscrimination Act of 2008 [Pub. L. No. 110-223, 112 Stat. 881 (May 21, 2008)] (GINA) expands the protections for genetic information provided in HIPAA by prohibiting group health plans from requiring or requesting genetic testing, collecting genetic information (including family medical history), or using genetic information for underwriting purposes (see Qs 5:35–5:39).

> The above definition of genetic information has been conformed to the definition for purposes of GINA. For further details on what constitutes genetic information, see Q 5:35.

Q 5:56 What is the maximum look-back period permitted by HIPAA for a preexisting-condition limit or exclusion?

The maximum look-back period for a preexisting-condition limit or exclusion is six months from the enrollment date in the group health plan. [ERISA § 701(a); DOL Final Reg. § 2590.701-3(a)(2); I.R.C. § 9801(a)(1); Treas. Reg. § 54.9801-3(a)(2)]

Enrollment date. HIPAA includes a special definition of *enrollment date*: the earliest of (1) the date coverage begins or (2) the first date of the group health plan's waiting period. For this purpose, *waiting period* means the period that must pass with respect to that individual before he or she is eligible to be covered for benefits under the terms of the plan. [ERISA § 701(b)(4); I.R.C. § 9801(b)(4)] For a new hire, the enrollment date is the date of hire, assuming that his or her employment status (e.g., full-time or part-time) also immediately satisfies any employment status requirement for eligibility under the plan.

Waiting period. For any potential participant or beneficiary in the plan, HIPAA defines *waiting period* as the period that must pass with respect to the individual before the individual is eligible to be covered for benefits under the terms of the plan. [ERISA § 701(b)(4); I.R.C. § 9801(b)(4)] There is no waiting period applicable to mandatory special enrollment periods or late enrollments.

> **Practice Pointer.** This rule continues to be misstated in SPDs, possibly indicating that it continues to be misunderstood and, presumably, is not being administered correctly. When a group health plan has a waiting period, it is not permitted to measure the preexisting-condition look-back period from the date coverage actually begins. That is because the statutory definition of the date from which the look-back period is to be measured is the earlier of the date coverage begins or the date the waiting period begins.

Thus, if a medical plan requires a six-month waiting period, an employee might not become covered until the seventh month, but the look-back period is measured backward from his or her date of hire. As a result, a condition that is first diagnosed or treated during the waiting period cannot be subject to the plan's preexisting-condition exclusion provision.

Note. Effective for plan years beginning after 2013, the 2010 Health Reform Act prohibits a group health plan from imposing a waiting period for coverage of more than 90 days. [PHSA § 2708, as added by PPACA § 1201] This requirement applies to grandfathered plans [PPACA § 1251 as amended by PPACA Reconciliation § 2301]

Example 1. John obtains a new job and immediately elects to join his new employer's group health plan. The plan contains a preexisting-condition limitation under which expenses for any condition diagnosed or treated within 12 months before coverage becomes effective will be excluded for the first year of coverage under the plan. Eleven months ago, John experienced pain in his hip and was seen by a doctor, who advised him that he had osteoporosis and would eventually need a hip replacement. John has not consulted any doctor, received any treatment, or taken any medication for that condition for the last 10 months; however, within days after he joins his new employer's health plan, John experiences excruciating pain in his hip and a few weeks later has hip replacement surgery. His employer's group health plan refuses to cover the expenses for the surgery, claiming that the osteoporosis in his hip was a preexisting condition under the terms of the plan because it was diagnosed within one year before his coverage began. Under HIPAA, the group health plan's 12-month look-back period is illegal because the maximum permitted look-back period is six months. The plan cannot refuse to provide otherwise covered benefits for this condition because John did not seek medical advice or receive (or have recommended to him) any diagnosis, care, or treatment within the six-month period prior to his enrollment date.

Example 2. The facts are the same as those in Example 1, except that John's osteoporosis was diagnosed five months before his date of hire. Because the diagnosis of the condition occurred within HIPAA's maximum permitted look-back period (six months), the group health plan can apply a preexisting-condition limitation to that condition.

Example 3. Mary obtains a new job and, on her first day of work, signs up for coverage under her new employer's group health plan. Under the plan's eligibility provisions, a newly hired employee's enrollment does not become effective (and coverage does not begin) until he or she has worked at least 90 consecutive days. The plan also contains a preexisting-condition limitation that excludes, for the first six months after coverage begins, expenses for any condition that is diagnosed or treated within three months before coverage begins.

Two weeks after Mary starts her new job, she is diagnosed as having leukemia and begins treatment. When her 90-day waiting period is up and her group health plan coverage becomes effective, she immediately begins submitting bills for her treatments after that date. The plan rejects the expenses on the grounds that they relate to a preexisting condition for which Mary sought treatment within three months before her coverage began. Under HIPAA, the group health plan's provision is illegal. HIPAA requires that the look-back period end with the enrollment date, which is defined under HIPAA as the earlier of the date coverage begins or the first day of the waiting period. Thus, the look-back period ended on Mary's date of hire (i.e., the first day of the plan's 90-day waiting period). Because Mary's condition was diagnosed after that date, it is not excludable as a preexisting condition.

If an individual's condition is diagnosed and treatment is recommended *before* the six-month look-back period, that individual can be subject to a preexisting-condition exclusion if the recommended treatment is received during the look-back period. If, however, the individual does not receive the recommended treatment during the look-back period, no exclusion may apply.

Example 4. Susan is diagnosed with a medical condition eight months before her enrollment date in her employer's group health plan. Susan's doctor recommends that she take a prescription drug for three months, and Susan dutifully follows the doctor's recommendation. Although Susan's diagnosis preceded the look-back period, her employer's plan may impose a preexisting-condition exclusion with respect to her condition. The exclusion is permissible because Susan received treatment (took the prescription medication) during the six-month period ending on her enrollment date in the plan.

Example 5. Doreen is treated for a medical condition seven months before her enrollment date in a group health plan. Her doctor recommends that, as part of her treatment, Doreen undergo a follow-up examination two months after treatment. Despite the doctor's recommendation, Doreen does not receive a follow-up examination. Nor does she receive any other medical advice, diagnosis, care, or treatment for her condition during the six-month period ending on her enrollment date. Doreen's employer cannot impose a preexisting-condition exclusion with respect to her condition because she only received treatment prior to the look-back period.

Q 5:57 What is the maximum period under HIPAA that a group health plan can exclude or limit covered benefits for a preexisting condition?

Under HIPAA, the exclusion period for expenses or treatment related to a preexisting condition cannot extend for more than 12 months after the enrollment date (or 18 months in the case of a late enrollee). For new hires, the enrollment date is the earlier of the date the individual's coverage begins or the first day of the plan's waiting period. [ERISA §§ 701(a)(2), 701(b)(2)]

If an employee or dependent is a late enrollee or special enrollee, any period before such late or special enrollment is not a waiting period. [DOL Final

Reg. § 2590.701-3(a)(3)(iii); Treas. Reg. § 54.9801-3(a)(3)(iii)] Therefore, the enrollment date for that individual is the date on which coverage begins.

Reduction of exclusion period. HIPAA requires that the 12- or 18-month exclusion or limitation period applicable to preexisting conditions be reduced by the individual's aggregate creditable coverage (see Q 5:58), excluding any period of creditable coverage prior to a break in coverage of at least 63 days.

> **Practice Pointer.** A participant's maximum exclusion period is reduced by two things. First, it is reduced by prior creditable coverage other than coverage prior to a 63-day break in coverage. Second, the 12-month exclusion period is further reduced by any applicable waiting period and the additional processing time before the individual's coverage actually begins. This is because HIPAA's definition of *enrollment date* requires that waiting periods and the preexisting-condition exclusion period run concurrently (and, as a result, one must be credited toward the other).

Alternate method of crediting coverage. Group health plans and health insurance issuers have the option to elect an alternate method of crediting coverage based on coverage of benefits within certain specified classes or categories of benefits rather than with respect to the plan as a whole. The creditable service then must be counted with respect to a class or category of benefits if any level of benefits is covered within such class or category. For example, if the dental portion of a plan contains a special preexisting-condition exclusion, the plan can require that only prior creditable coverage of the same type (i.e., prior dental coverage) may be used to reduce the dental preexisting-condition exclusion period.

To use this alternative, the group health plan or health insurance issuer must elect it on a uniform basis for all participants and beneficiaries. [ERISA §§ 701(a)(3), 701(c); I.R.C. § 9801(a)(3)]

For details on crediting coverage, see Qs 5:85–5:86.

Q 5:58   What is creditable coverage?

Creditable coverage includes, among other things, group health plan or health insurance coverage, coverage under Medicare Part A or B, state health benefit risk pools, and public health plans. Waiting periods do not count as creditable coverage. [ERISA § 701(c); I.R.C. § 9801(c)(3)]

The HIPAA regulations add two categories of creditable coverage. [DOL Reg. § 2590.701-4; Treas. Reg. § 54.9801-4] Under the regulations, creditable coverage includes coverage under the State Children's Health Insurance Program (SCHIP), which was created by Congress under the Balanced Budget Act of 1997. [Pub. L. No. 105-33, 111 Stat. 251 (Aug. 5, 1997)] (SCHIP was reauthorized, and renamed CHIP by the Children's Health Insurance Program Reauthorization Act of 2009 [Pub. L. No. 111-3, 123 Stat. 8 (Feb. 4, 2009)].) The regulations also expand the scope of creditable coverage under a public health plan to include any coverage provided by a governmental health plan, whether provided through insurance or otherwise. Interim regulations referred only to coverage provided through health insurance. Creditable public health coverage is also expanded to include coverage provided through plans maintained by the U.S. government or by foreign governments. Interim regulations defined creditable public health coverage to include only health coverage under a plan of a state, county or other political subdivision. For details regarding creditable coverage, see Qs 5:61–5:89.

Q 5:59 How does an individual establish creditable coverage under the HIPAA rules?

As a general rule, an individual establishes creditable coverage by presenting a certificate of creditable coverage from his or her former health plan or insurer. Group health plans and health insurance issuers must provide a written certification that includes (1) the period of creditable coverage of the individual under the plan, (2) the coverage (if any) under a COBRA continuation provision, and (3) any applicable waiting period or affiliation period. For details on a group health plan's obligation to issue certificates of creditable coverage, when and how they are to be issued, and the required content of such certificates, see Qs 5:61–5:89.

However, a plan may not consider an individual's inability to obtain a certificate to be evidence of the absence of creditable coverage. In the absence of a certificate, creditable coverage may be established by other documentary evidence, including:

- Explanations of benefits (EOBs) or other correspondence from a plan or issuer indicating coverage
- Pay stubs showing a payroll deduction for health coverage
- A health insurance identification card
- A certificate of coverage under a group health policy
- Records from medical care providers indicating health coverage
- Third-party statements verifying periods of coverage
- Other relevant documents that evidence periods of health coverage

In addition, creditable coverage may be corroborated through means other than documentation, such as by a telephone call from a plan or provider to a third party verifying creditable coverage [DOL Reg. § 2590.701-5; Treas. Reg. § 54.9801-5]

The HIPAA regulations make it clear that a plan may not impose any limit on the amount of time that an individual has to present a certificate or other evidence of creditable coverage. [DOL Reg. § 2590.701-3; Treas. Reg. § 54.9801-3]

Q 5:60 Is a group health plan required to give plan participants notice of a preexisting-condition exclusion?

Yes. The HIPAA regulations require two notices regarding a preexisting-condition exclusion.

General notice of preexisting-condition exclusion. A group health plan must give participants a written general notice before it can impose a preexisting-condition exclusion. [DOL Reg. § 2590.701-3©; Treas. Reg. § 54.9801-3(c)] This notice generally must be provided as part of any written application materials for enrollment in the plan. If the plan does not distribute such materials, the notice must be provided as soon as possible following a request for enrollment in the plan.

The general notice must contain the following information:

- The existence and terms of any preexisting-condition exclusion under the plan, including the length of the plan's look-back period, the maximum length of the exclusion period, and how the plan will reduce the maximum exclusion period by creditable coverage.

- A description of the right to demonstrate creditable coverage, including a description of an individual's right to request a certificate from a prior plan or issuer and a statement that the current plan or issuer will assist in obtaining a certificate from any prior plan or issuer, if necessary.

- A person to contact (including an address or telephone number) for additional information or assistance regarding the preexisting-condition exclusion.

Individual notice of preexisting-condition exclusion. Once an individual has presented evidence of creditable coverage, the plan or issuer must provide the individual with a written notice of the length of any preexisting-condition exclusion that remains after offsetting for prior creditable coverage. [DOL Reg. § 2590.701-3(c); Treas. Reg. § 54.9801-3(e)]

The individual notice must include the following information:

- The plan's determination of any preexisting-condition exclusion period that applies to the individual, including the last day on which the preexisting-condition exclusion will apply.

- The basis for the plan's determination, including the source and substance of any information on which the plan relied.

- An explanation of the individual's right to submit additional evidence of creditable coverage.

- A description of any applicable appeal procedures established by the plan.

This notice is not required to identify any specific medical conditions of the individual that could be subject to the exclusion. Moreover, no notice is required if the plan does not impose a preexisting-condition exclusion, or if the plan's preexisting-condition exclusion is completely offset by the individual's prior creditable coverage.

The individual notice of a preexisting-condition exclusion is not necessarily binding on the plan. The plan may modify an initial determination of creditable coverage if it determines that the individual did not have the creditable coverage he or she claimed. To make such a modification, however, the plan must provide a notice of the new determination to the individual. Moreover, until the new notice is provided, the plan must operate in a manner consistent with the original notice.

Certificates of Creditable Coverage

Q 5:61 Why do group health plans have to provide written certifications of coverage to participants and dependents?

Under HIPAA, certificates of creditable coverage permit new enrollees in group health plans to prove that they had prior "creditable coverage" and to have that prior creditable coverage taken into account for purposes of reducing or satisfying the new group health plan's preexisting-condition limit.

Certificates of creditable coverage can also be used to help obtain individual insurance coverage. HIPAA imposes guaranteed issue requirements on health insurance issuers (e.g., insurance carriers, HMOs, and Blue Cross/ Blue Shield organizations) participating in the individual health insurance market. Under these requirements, health insurance issuers in the individual health insurance market cannot decline to offer an individual health insurance policy to anyone who:

a. Has been covered under a group health plan, governmental plan, or church plan for at least 18 months without a break in coverage of more than 63 days;

b. Does not have other health insurance coverage; and

c. Is not eligible for any other group health insurance coverage or Medicare.

[I.R.C. § 9801; ERISA § 701; HIPAA § 111]

2010 Health Reform Act. The 2010 Health Reform Act provides that a group health plan or health insurance issuer may not impose *any* preexisting-condition exclusion with respect to the plan or coverage. [PHSA § 2704 as added by PPACA § 1201] The general prohibition on preexisting-condition exclusions applies for plan years beginning on or after January 1, 2014. However, the prohibition on preexisting-condition exclusion as it applies to plan enrollees who are under age 19 takes effect for plan years beginning on or after September 23, 2010. [PPACA § 1253 as amended by PPACA § 10103] The prohibitions apply to grandfathered group health plans [PPACA Reconciliation § 2301]. In addition, beginning in 2014, the 2010 Health Reform Act requires health insurers in the individual market to accept every individual that applies for coverage. [PHSA § 2702 as added by PPACA § 1201]

> **Practice Pointer.** The need for certificates of creditable coverage will essentially disappear once the 2010 Health Reform Act requirements become fully operational. Nonetheless, certificates of creditable coverage remain significant during the transition to full implementation of the 2010 Health Reform Act rules.

Q 5:62 Who is obligated to issue certificates of creditable coverage?

HIPAA imposes the obligation to issue certificates of creditable coverage on all "group health plans" with several specified exceptions (see Q 5:63) and on health insurance issuers (insurance companies, HMOs, etc.). The term *group health plan,* for this purpose, is defined differently under the Internal Revenue Code and ERISA due to differing terminology, but the definitions achieve essentially the same result, as follows:

Definition in Internal Revenue Code. The definition for this purpose is the same for COBRA and for the Code's Medicare secondary-payer provisions:

> The term *group health plan* means a plan (including a self-insured plan) of, or contributed to by, an employer (including a self-employed person) or employee organization to provide health care (directly or otherwise) to the employees, former employees, the employer, others associated with the employer in a business relationship, or their families. [I.R.C. § 9832(a), incorporating I.R.C. § 5000(b)(1)]

Definition in ERISA. HIPAA added a multipart definition to ERISA in order to expressly include partners and to include a definition of *medical care* similar to that contained in the Code.

> (1) In General.—The term "group health plan" means an employee welfare benefit plan to the extent that the plan provides medical care (as defined in paragraph (2) and including items and services paid for as medical care) to employees or their dependents (as defined under the terms of the plan) directly or through insurance, reimbursement, or otherwise. (2) Medical Care.—The term "medical care" means amounts paid for—(A) the diagnosis, cure, mitigation, treatment, or prevention of disease, or amounts paid for the purpose of affecting any structure or function of the body, (B) amounts paid for transportation primarily for and essential to medical care referred to in subparagraph (A), and (C) amounts paid for insurance covering medical care referred to in subparagraphs (A) and (B).

[ERISA § 734(a)]

Significantly, the HIPAA amendment to ERISA expressly and unmistakably includes partnerships and partners:

> (d) Treatment of Partnerships.—For purposes of this part—(1) Treatment as a group health plan.—Any plan, fund, or program which would not be (but for this subsection) an employee welfare benefit plan and which is established or maintained by a partnership, to the extent that such plan, fund, or program provides medical care (including items and services paid for as medical care) to present or former partners in the partnership or to their dependents (as defined under the terms of the plan, fund, or program), directly or through insurance, reimbursement, or otherwise, shall be treated (subject to paragraph (2)) as an employee welfare benefit plan which is a group health plan). (2) Employer. In the case of a group health plan, the term "employer" also includes the partnership in relation to any partner. (3) Participants of group health

plans.—In the case of a group health plan, the term "participant" also includes—(A) in connection with a group health plan maintained by a partnership, an individual who is a partner in relation to the partnership, or (B) in connection with a group health plan maintained by a self-employed individual (under which one or more employees are participants), the self-employed individual, if such individual is, or may become, eligible to receive a benefit under the plan or such individual's beneficiaries may be eligible to receive any such benefit.

Health insurance issuers are also required to provide certificates of coverage. For a discussion of how plans and issuers may divide the responsibility between them so as to avoid issuing duplicate certificates, see Q 5:65.

Q 5:63   Which health plans are exempt from the HIPAA certification requirements?

There are plans that are completely exempt from the requirement to issue creditable coverage certificates. For example, limited-scope dental and vision care plans are not required to issue certificates of coverage or to respond to inquiries regarding creditable coverage. [Treas. Reg. § 54.9801-4; DOL Reg. § 2590.732]

Obligation of non-HIPAA-covered health plan to provide certificates of coverage. Despite the general rule that a plan excluded from HIPAA will have no obligation to provide certificates of creditable coverage, special rules applicable to certain exempt plans require them to provide certificates consistent with the HIPAA regulations. Plans affected are Medicare, Medicaid, CHAMPUS, the Indian Health Service, nonfederal governmental plans generally, and nonfederal plans that opt out of certain parts of the Public Health Service Act. [Treas. Reg. § 54.9801-4; DOL Final Reg. § 2590.701-4]

Q 5:64   When is a health care FSA exempt from the HIPAA certification requirement?

A health care FSA that meets the requirements of Code Section 106(c)(2) (see chapter 7) is treated as exempt, provided three conditions are met:

1. The employee has other group health plan coverage available to him or her from the employer for the year;
2. The other group health plan coverage does not consist solely of excepted benefits; and
3. The maximum benefit payable to the employee under the health care FSA for the year does not exceed the larger of:
   a. Two times the employee's salary reduction election or
   b. The amount of the employee's salary reduction election for the year plus $500.

For this purpose, any amount that an employee can elect to receive as taxable income but elects to apply to the health FSA is considered a salary reduction election (regardless of whether the amount is characterized as salary or as a credit under the arrangement). [DOL Reg. § 2590.732(c)(3)(v); Treas. Reg. § 54.9831-1(c)(3)(v)]

These conditions are broad enough that many, but not all, health care FSAs are eligible for this exemption. Assuming that the first two conditions are satisfied, the key to satisfying the third condition will be how the health care FSA is funded.

Health care FSAs that are funded solely with salary reduction (pretax) contributions will qualify for exemption if benefits do not exceed the amount of the salary reduction amount. However, if benefits could exceed the amount of the salary reduction election (which could occur, for example, if forfeitures are reallocated under the plan), then whether the health care FSA is exempt from HIPAA is a fact-based inquiry. The FSA will be exempt only if the total amount allocated to the FSA does not exceed two times the amount of the employee's annual salary reduction election or, if greater, one times the amount of the employee's annual salary reduction election plus $500.

If a health care FSA is funded with nonelective employer contributions, application of the exemption will be a dollars-and-cents inquiry. When applying the exemption formula, nonelective employer contributions must be counted as additional employer contributions and not as salary reduction amounts. Non-elective employer contributions are amounts that the employee cannot elect to take in cash, including noncashable employer credits and employer matches.

Q 5:65   When is a plan relieved of the responsibility for providing certificates of creditable coverage?

HIPAA requires that certificates of creditable coverage be issued by two entities: (1) group health plans and (2) health insurance issuers (which include HMOs and insurance companies) that issue a contract or policy in connection with a covered group health plan. To forestall the issuance of duplicate certificates, the HIPAA regulations contain a series of rules for allocating this responsibility between plans and health insurance issuers, as follows:

1. *Certificate of creditable coverage provided by the other party.* An entity required to provide a certificate will be deemed to have satisfied the requirement if the certificate is provided by a second entity, as long as the certificate contains the information that the first entity is otherwise required to disclose.

2. *Agreement between the plan and the issuer.* An insured group health plan is permitted to enter into a written agreement with the insurance company or issuer under which the parties agree that the insurance company or issuer (and not the group health plan) will be responsible for issuing the certificates to individuals covered under the plan. When such an agreement exists and the insurance company or issuer fails to furnish a required certificate of creditable coverage, the insurance company or issuer (and not the group health plan) will be liable for the violation.

3. *No responsibility for another entity's coverage.* A health insurance company or other issuer is not responsible for certifying any portion of an individual's group health plan coverage that was provided by another party.

4. *Limited liability upon insurer or coverage option changes.* If an individual's coverage under the issuer's policy ceases before plan coverage does (e.g., due to the individual's election of another coverage option or due to termination or replacement of the insurance carrier or issuer), the insurance carrier or issuer can satisfy its obligation to issue a certificate of creditable coverage by providing sufficient information to the plan (or to another party designated by the plan) to enable the plan (or other party) to issue a certificate when the individual's plan coverage ceases. However, if the individual's plan coverage ceases at the same time coverage under the insurance carrier's or issuer's policy ceases, then this rule does not relieve the insurance carrier or issuer of its obligation to issue a certificate of creditable coverage.

[Treas. Reg. § 54.9801-5(a); DOL Reg. § 2590.701-5(a)]

Q 5:66   What types of coverage can be used as creditable coverage?

The law broadly defines the types of prior coverage that can be used to satisfy preexisting-condition exclusion periods under group health plans or for applying for individual health insurance coverage. Creditable coverage does not include waiting periods but does include coverage under the following:

1. A group health plan;

2. Health insurance coverage, whether or not the insurer is subject to HIPAA and without regard to whether the coverage is offered in the group market, the individual market, or otherwise. For this purpose, *health insurance coverage* means benefits consisting of medical care (provided directly, through insurance or reimbursement, or otherwise) under any hospital or medical service policy or certificate, hospital, or medical service contract offered by a health insurance issuer (an insurance company, insurance service, or insurance organization, including an HMO) that is—

   a. Required to be licensed to engage in the business of insurance in a state and

   b. Subject to state law that regulates insurance (within the meaning of ERISA Section 514(b));

3. Medicare;

4. Medicaid, except for coverage consisting solely of those benefits associated with the Social Security Act's program for distributing pediatric vaccines;

5. Medical and dental coverage for members and certain former members of the uniformed services (the armed forces and the Commissioned Corps of the National Oceanic and Atmospheric Administration and of the Public

Health Service) and their dependents under Title 10, Chapter 55, of the United States Code;

6. A medical care program of the Indian Health Service or of a tribal organization;

7. A "state health benefits risk pool," which includes—

   a. Any organization qualifying under Code Section 501(c)(26),

   b. A qualified high-risk pool described in Section 2744(c)(2) of the Public Health Service Act, or

   c. Any other arrangement sponsored by a state if the membership composition is specified by the state and the arrangement is established and maintained primarily to provide health insurance coverage for individuals who are residents of that state and who, because they have or have had a medical condition, cannot obtain medical coverage for that condition through insurance or from an HMO or are able to obtain such coverage only at a rate that is substantially higher than the rate for coverage through the membership organization;

8. A health plan offered under the Federal Employees Health Benefits Program;

9. A public health plan, which includes any plan established or maintained by a state, the U.S. government, a foreign country, or any political subdivision of a state, the U.S. government, or a foreign country that provides health insurance coverage to individuals who are enrolled in the plan;

10. A health benefits plan under Section 5(e) of the Peace Corps Act; and

11. A state Children's Health Insurance Program (CHIP) under Title XXI of the Social Security Act.

[ERISA § 701(c); I.R.C. § 9801(c)(3); DOL Reg. § 1290.701-4; Treas. Reg. §§ 54.9801-4, 54.9801-5]

Waiting periods. Waiting periods do not count as creditable coverage. DOL proposed regulations contain rules for determining creditable coverage when health plan coverage ends in connection with an employee taking leave under the Family and Medical Leave Act. [DOL Prop. Reg. § 2590.701-6; Prop. Treas. Reg. §§ 54.9801-4, 54.9801-5]

Q 5:67   What types of coverage cannot be used as creditable coverage?

Creditable coverage does not include coverage consisting solely of coverage of "excepted benefits." For this purpose, the excepted benefits that cannot be used as creditable coverage include the following:

1. The portion of any group health plan consisting of one or more of any of the other benefits in this list;

   a. Limited-scope dental benefits,

    b. Limited-scope vision benefits, or

    c. Long-term care benefits that satisfy certain conditions;

2. Coverage limited to a specific disease or illness (such as a cancer-only policy) or a fixed-dollar indemnity (e.g., $200 per day);

3. Long-term care benefits that are—

    a. Either subject to state long-term care insurance laws or for qualified long-term care services under Code Section 7702B(c)(1),

    b. Provided under a qualified long-term care insurance contract as defined under Code Section 7702B(b), or

    c. Based on cognitive impairment or a loss of functional capacity that is expected to be chronic.

4. Medigap or Medsupp insurance, CHAMPUS, and similar coverage to supplement coverage under a group health plan, if provided under a separate policy, certificate, or contract of insurance;

5. Accident-only coverage (including accidental death and dismemberment);

6. Disability income insurance;

7. Liability insurance, including general liability insurance and automobile liability insurance;

8. Coverage issued as a supplement to liability insurance;

9. Workers' compensation or similar insurance;

10. Automobile medical payment insurance;

11. Credit-only insurance (such as mortgage insurance);

12. Exempt FSA coverage; and

13. Health savings accounts (HSAs).

[I.R.C. § 9832; ERISA § 733(c); DOL Reg. § 2590.732(c); I.R.C. § 9832(c)(1); Treas. Reg. § 54.9831-1(c)]

Q 5:68   Is all coverage under a covered group health plan treated as creditable coverage?

Yes. The period of creditable coverage includes the period during which the individual was actually covered under the particular group health plan issuing the certificate of coverage. However, creditable coverage does not include any waiting period under the plan or any delay for processing the enrollment once the plan's waiting period has been satisfied. Thus, waiting periods and processing delays are disregarded when calculating the period of creditable coverage. [I.R.C. § 9801(c)(2)(B); ERISA § 701(c)(2)(B)]

Significant break in coverage. HIPAA draws a distinction between (1) creditable coverage and (2) how much of the individual's creditable coverage must be counted toward the next plan's preexisting-condition exclusion period. Creditable coverage includes coverage both before and after breaks in coverage (see Q 5:69). Whether all that pre- and post-break creditable coverage is required to be counted by the next plan toward its preexisting-condition exclusion is another issue entirely (see Q 5:85). [I.R.C. § 9801(c)(2)(A); ERISA § 701(c)(2)(A)]

Q 5:69   What is a significant break in coverage?

HIPAA generally defines a *significant break in coverage* as a period of at least 63 consecutive days during which the individual was not covered by any creditable coverage. [I.R.C. § 9801(c)(2); ERISA § 701(c)(2)] Waiting periods and affiliation periods are not counted as part of a break in coverage.

Proposed HIPAA regulations toll the beginning of the period that is used for determining whether a significant break in coverage has occurred if a certificate of creditable coverage is not provided on or before the day coverage ends. The significant-break-in-coverage period would be tolled until a certificate is provided, but not more than 44 days after the coverage ceases. [DOL Prop. Reg. § 2590.701-4; Prop. Treas. Reg. § 9801-4] This tolling rule is intended to address the inequity of individuals' losing coverage without being aware that coverage has ended.

Longer break in service required under state insurance law. If state insurance law applies to the policy or contract issued to an ERISA-covered group health plan, and a state insurance law that is not preempted by ERISA from applying to that particular group health plan requires a break longer than 63 days before coverage occurring prior to the break can be disregarded, then such longer break in service must be used. [ERISA § 731(b)(2)(iii)]

Q 5:70   What if the individual previously was covered under more than one plan?

Plan issuing the certificate. If the individual was previously covered under more than one plan or plan option of the same employer, the plan issuing the certificate of coverage may be required to aggregate the coverage under each of the prior plans for purposes of the required disclosures in the certificate of coverage (see Q 5:74) because creditable coverage is defined as *all* coverage under the plans listed in Q 5:66.

Plan crediting prior coverage. Whether a significant break in coverage has occurred is for the recipient of the creditable coverage information to determine. If an individual is submitting one or more certificates of creditable coverage documenting prior coverage under more than one group health plan, the recipient group health plan must aggregate the prior periods of coverage when determining (1) how much creditable coverage should be applied toward the recipient plan's preexisting-condition exclusion period and (2) whether there was a significant break in coverage that would allow it to disregard any portion of the prior coverage.

Q 5:71   When must a covered group health plan issue certificates of coverage to a particular individual?

Certificates of creditable coverage are required to be issued at three distinct times. The group health plan must issue two of the certificates automatically and must issue the third certificate only upon request.

1. *First automatic certificate.* The first certificate of creditable coverage must be provided automatically to any covered person:
   a. Who is a COBRA-qualified beneficiary who loses coverage because of a COBRA-qualifying event and
   b. Whose coverage under the group health plan ceases but who is not entitled to elect COBRA continuation coverage (e.g., the individual drops coverage but continues to work, or the employer has fewer than the 20 employees required for COBRA coverage, or the individual is terminated for gross misconduct).
2. *Second automatic certificate.* A second certificate of coverage must be provided automatically when a COBRA-qualified beneficiary's COBRA continuation coverage ceases.
3. *Third certificate, upon request.* A group health plan also must furnish a certificate of creditable coverage upon request of the plan participant, his or her covered dependents, or a designated representative of either. This request must be made within 24 months after coverage under the plan or COBRA continuation coverage ceases. This certificate must be provided regardless of whether the individual previously received one or more certificates of coverage.

[I.R.C. § 9801(e)(1); ERISA § 701(e)(1)]

The HIPAA regulations make it clear that an individual is entitled to request and receive a certificate of creditable coverage while their coverage under the employer's plan is still in effect. [DOL Reg. § 2590.701-5; Treas. Reg. § 701(e)(1)]

> **Practice Pointer.** The covered individual's right to a certificate of coverage at each of these times is material information that should be fully disclosed in the SPD. The final HIPAA regulations make it clear that procedures for requesting and receiving certificates must be in writing.

Q 5:72   What is the maximum number of certificates that a group health plan is required to issue to any individual?

Each individual will receive at least one certificate. Individuals who elect COBRA continuation coverage will receive a second certificate when that coverage expires. The real question is how many additional copies of certificates of creditable coverage the individual can request during the 24-month period after coverage under the plan ends. Significantly, neither the statute nor the HIPAA regulations place a limit on the number of requests. Moreover, the HIPAA regulations expressly state that a timely request for a certificate during the 24-month period must be honored even if the individual has previously received a certificate within that time period. [Treas. Reg. § 54.9801-5; DOL Reg. § 2590.701-5]

Accordingly, if an individual loses or misplaces his or her certificate of coverage several times, the plan will be obligated to issue replacements as long as each request is made within 24 months of the date the individual's coverage under the plan terminated. For example, a plan in which an individual enrolls may, if authorized by the individual, request a certificate of the individual's creditable coverage on behalf of the individual from a plan in which the individual was formerly enrolled. After the request is received, the former plan or issuer is required to provide the certificate by the earliest date that the plan, acting in a reasonable and prompt fashion, can provide the certificate.

Q 5:73   Who is entitled to receive a certificate of creditable coverage?

Automatic certificates. Employees and their covered dependents are entitled to receive the automatic certificates of creditable coverage described in Q 5:71. (For an explanation of when the plan is permitted to double up and send the information for various family members to a single individual, see Q 5:75.)

Certificates upon request. In addition to employees and their covered dependents, the designated representative of such individuals also is entitled to receive a certificate of coverage upon request as described in Q 5:72. [I.R.C. § 9801(e); ERISA § 701(e): Treas. Reg. § 54.9801-5; DOL Reg. § 2590.701-5]

Practice Pointer. Which individuals are entitled to receive a certificate of creditable coverage and when they are entitled to receive it is material information that should be fully disclosed in the group health plan's SPD. The final HIPAA regulations make it clear that procedures for requesting and receiving certificates must be in writing.

Q 5:74   What information must be set forth in a certificate of creditable coverage?

A certificate of creditable coverage must include the following information:

1. The date the certificate is issued;
2. The name of the group health plan providing the coverage described in the certificate;
3. The name of the participant or dependent with respect to whom the certificate applies, including any information necessary for the plan providing the coverage specified in the certificate to identify the covered person, such as the individual's plan identification number;
4. The name, address, and telephone number of the plan administrator or issuer required to provide the certificate;

5. If different from that in item 4 above, the telephone number to call for further information regarding the certificate;

6. If the individual has been covered under the plan for at least 18 months (546 days) disregarding creditable coverage before a significant break in coverage, a statement to that effect;

7. If the individual has been covered under the plan for less than 18 months, the date the plan's waiting period (if any) and affiliation period (if applicable) began and the date the creditable coverage began (i.e., the date the individual's coverage under the plan became effective); and

8. The date creditable coverage ended, unless creditable coverage is continuing as of the date of the certificate.

Coverage period reflected in the certificate. The period of coverage required to be reflected in the certificate might vary depending on whether the certificate is being provided automatically or upon request. An automatic certificate (see Q 5:71) must reflect the last period of continuous coverage ending on the date coverage ceased. A certificate provided upon request within 24 months after coverage ceases must include each period of continuous coverage ending within the 24-month period ending on the date of request (or continuing on the date of request). A separate certificate may be provided for each such period of continuous coverage. [Treas. Reg. § 54.9801-5; DOL Reg. § 2590.701-5]

The regulations provide that the certificate must also include an educational statement regarding HIPAA explaining (1) the restrictions on the ability of a plan or issuer to impose a preexisting-condition exclusion (including an individual's ability to reduce a preexisting-condition exclusion by creditable coverage); (2) special enrollment rights; (3) the prohibitions against discrimination based on any health factor; (4) the right to individual health coverage; (5) the fact that state law may require issuers to provide additional protections to individuals in that state; and (6) where to get more information. Proposed rules would add a requirement that the educational statement disclose information about the Family and Medical Leave Act. [DOL Prop. Reg. § 2590.701-5; Prop. Treas. Reg. § 54.9801-5]

Dependent coverage. A plan must use reasonable efforts to determine any information needed to certify dependent coverage. [Treas. Reg. § 54.9801-5; DOL Reg. § 2590.701-5]

Example. A group health plan covers employees and their dependents. The plan annually requests all employees to provide updated information regarding dependents, including the specific date on which an employee has a new dependent or on which a person ceases to be an employee's dependent. The plan has satisfied the requirement that it make reasonable efforts to determine the cessation of dependents' coverage and the related dependent coverage information.

Q 5:75   Can a single certificate of creditable coverage cover more than one individual?

Yes. A single certificate of creditable coverage form may include coverage information on more than one family member. However, if the information is not identical for each individual, the form must provide all the required information for each individual and must separately state the information that is not identical. [Treas. Reg. § 54.9801-5; DOL Reg. § 2590.701-5]

Q 5:76   Why must a certificate of creditable coverage distinguish between when the waiting period began and when coverage actually started?

The HIPAA regulations require that the certificate of creditable coverage break out any waiting period under the plan unless the individual has been continuously covered for at least 18 months. Presumably, this is so the new plan will have enough information to isolate and credit only actual coverage under the prior plan and to disregard any prior waiting period (which is not considered to be either creditable coverage or any part of a break in coverage). If the individual already has at least 18 months of prior group health plan coverage without a 63-day break in coverage, he or she will have enough creditable coverage to zero out the maximum preexisting-condition exclusion period that can be imposed (18 months for late enrollees), so any prior waiting period becomes irrelevant.

Q 5:77   What if the group health plan issuing the certificate switched insurance carriers or replaced a prior group health plan of the same employer?

The HIPAA regulations make the group health plan responsible for aggregating information regarding prior carriers, switches from one plan option to another, and replacement plans and reflecting it on the certificate of coverage.

If an insurance carrier is replaced with another or the individual switches from one plan option to another, the issuer is required to provide sufficient information to the plan (or to another party designated by the plan) to enable a certificate to be provided by the plan (or other party), once the individual's plan coverage ceases, that reflects the period of coverage under the prior carrier's policy or the previously elected option. This will satisfy the issuer's obligation to provide an automatic certificate of coverage to the individual. However, if the individual's group health plan coverage actually ceases when coverage under the issuer's policy does, the issuer is not relieved from issuing an automatic certificate. Also, an issuer is permitted to presume that an individual whose coverage ceases at a time other than the effective date for changing enrollment options has ceased to be covered under the plan. [Treas. Reg. § 54.9801-5; DOL Reg. § 2590.701-5]

Q 5:78   How quickly must a certificate of coverage be provided?

The required response time depends on which certificate of creditable coverage is being issued.

First automatic certificate of coverage. The first automatic certificate of coverage (see Q 5:71) must be issued at the time the individual would lose coverage under the plan in the absence of COBRA continuation coverage or any alternative coverage offered to the individual. A plan or issuer will satisfy this requirement if it provides the automatic certificate no later than the time the COBRA notice is required to be provided.

Second automatic certificate of coverage. The second automatic certificate of coverage (see Q 5:71) must be furnished within a reasonable time after COBRA continuation coverage ceases.

Certificate provided upon request. If a request is made by the participant, dependent, or authorized representative within 24 months after coverage under the plan or COBRA continuation coverage has ceased, a certificate of coverage must be provided by the earliest date that the plan, acting in a reasonable and prompt fashion, can provide it.

Example 1. Amy terminates her employment with Employer Q. Amy is a qualified beneficiary entitled to elect COBRA continuation coverage under Employer Q's group health plan. A notice of the rights provided under COBRA is typically furnished to a qualified beneficiary under the plan within 10 days after the covered employee terminates employment. The automatic certificate may be provided at the same time that Amy receives the COBRA notice.

Example 2. The facts are the same as those in Example 1, except that the automatic certificate for Amy is not completed by the time the COBRA notice is furnished. The automatic certificate may be provided within the period permitted by the law for the delivery of notices under COBRA.

Example 3. Employer R maintains an insured group health plan. R has never had as many as 20 employees, and R's plan is not subject to the COBRA continuation coverage provisions. However, R operates in a state that has a state program similar to COBRA. R is required to provide its employees who terminate employment and lose coverage under the plan with the automatic certificate no later than the time a notice is required to be furnished to the employee under the state program.

Example 4. Charlie terminates employment with Employer S and receives both a notice of his rights under COBRA and an automatic certificate. Charlie elects COBRA continuation coverage under S's group health plan. After four months of COBRA continuation coverage and the expiration of a 30-day grace period, Employer S's group health plan determines that Charlie's COBRA continuation coverage has ceased due to his failure to make a timely payment for continuation coverage. The plan must provide an updated automatic certificate to Charlie within a reasonable time after the end of the grace period.

Q 5:79   How is the certificate of creditable coverage required to be delivered?

The certificate must be in writing and may be sent by first-class mail. Delivery to the participant's (and his or her spouse's) last known address is treated as delivery to all individuals residing at that address. If, however, a dependent's last known address is different from the plan participant's, a certificate covering that dependent must be delivered to that address. [Treas. Reg. § 54.9801-5; DOL Reg. § 2590.701-5]

A covered person may designate another individual or entity to receive the certificate of creditable coverage on his or her behalf.

Q 5:80   Can the first automatic certificate of creditable coverage be combined with a notice of COBRA rights?

Yes. For those individuals who are entitled to receive both notices, there is no statutory restriction against combining the first automatic certificate of creditable coverage with the COBRA notice in a single document, as long as the information concerning the participant's creditable coverage is clear and understandable. This method would save on administrative and mailing costs.

Caution. Combining the two documents in a single form will not entirely satisfy the group health plan's HIPAA obligations regarding this first automatic certificate, because a certificate also is required to be issued to an individual who is not eligible to elect COBRA. For example, this combined notice would not suffice for an individual who quit the group health plan but keeps on working or an individual whose employment is terminated due to gross misconduct. If this method is chosen, it will be necessary to track these individuals separately from the COBRA mailing to make sure that they are given the proper HIPAA notices of creditable coverage.

Q 5:81   Does HIPAA authorize any alternate methods of delivery?

Yes. Under certain circumstances, creditable coverage information may be transferred by other means, such as by telephone. For example, creditable coverage may be transferred by a telephone call from a plan or provider to a third party verifying creditable coverage. [Treas. Reg. § 54.9801-5; DOL Reg. § 2590.701-5]

Certificates of creditable coverage may be provided electronically, provided certain requirements are met. [DOL Reg. § 2520.104b-1]

Q 5:82   When must a group health plan respond to another group health plan's request for information?

When a group health plan is determining how much of its preexisting-condition exclusion period is affected by the individual's certificate of creditable coverage, it may contact the prior plan for further information or clarification. If the prior plan is exempt from HIPAA, it is not obligated to respond *unless* it falls into a group of plans designated in the regulations as being required to respond. Thus, an ERISA-covered dental plan that is determined to be exempt from HIPAA as a limited-scope dental plan does not have to issue certificates of coverage or respond to requests for information concerning creditable coverage.

Obligation of non-covered health plan to provide certificates of coverage. Despite this general rule, special rules require exempt entities to provide certificates consistent with the HIPAA regulations. Plans affected are Medicare, Medicaid, CHAMPUS, the Indian Health Service, nonfederal governmental plans generally, and nonfederal plans that opt out of certain parts of the Public Health Service Act. [Treas. Reg. § 54.9801-5; DOL Reg. § 2590.701-5]

Q 5:83   If a group health plan receives a certificate of creditable coverage from an individual, how is it obligated (if at all) to respond?

If the group health plan does not contain a preexisting-condition exclusion period, the plan need do nothing with the certificate of coverage.

If the group health plan *does* have a preexisting-condition exclusion period, two things must happen.

First, the plan must notify the individual in advance and *in writing* of the existence and terms of the preexisting-condition exclusion, including the individual's right to demonstrate creditable coverage and to request a certificate of creditable coverage from a prior plan. This notice must also indicate that the plan will assist the individual in obtaining certificates of coverage from any prior plans.

Second, once the group health plan actually receives a certificate of creditable coverage from the individual, it must act within a reasonable time to:

1. Make a determination, based on the facts and circumstances, concerning whether the individual has qualifying creditable coverage;

2. Apply that creditable coverage toward the plan's preexisting-condition limitation; and

3. If the creditable coverage does not completely zero out the preexisting-condition exclusion period, notify the individual *in writing* of how much of the plan's preexisting-condition period will be applied to him or her and specify—

    a. The basis for the plan's determination;

    b. The source and substance of any information on which the plan relied; and

    c. The plan's procedures for the individual to appeal the decision regarding the preexisting-condition exclusion period.

[Treas. Reg. § 54.9801-5; DOL Reg. § 2590.701-5]

Note. If the group health plan is presented with a certificate of coverage from a health care FSA, there would appear to be nothing requiring the plan to take the certificate at face value. The plan administrator could make inquiries of the sponsor or administrator of the health care FSA to determine whether the FSA was, in fact, subject to HIPAA for the period covered by the certificate. If it was not actually subject to HIPAA at that time, the coverage is not creditable coverage and can be disregarded (see Q 5:64).

Q 5:84   What if the individual submits more than one certificate of coverage?

If the group health plan receiving several certificates of coverage from an individual has a preexisting-condition exclusion period, then it is required to aggregate the coverage periods and count all the days an individual has creditable coverage from each source. Where the individual was covered under two different plans on the same day, all coverage on that day is counted as one day. [Treas. Reg. § 54.9801-4; DOL Reg. § 2590.701-4]

Q 5:85   How is creditable coverage counted for purposes of reducing the new plan's preexisting-condition exclusion period?

The HIPAA regulations provide for two different methods of counting creditable coverage: the standard method and the alternate method.

Standard method. When determining whether a preexisting-condition exclusion period should be reduced, the amount of creditable coverage is determined without regard to specific benefits in the coverage.

First, all the days that the individual had coverage under one or more types of creditable coverage are counted. (Coverage from all sources on a particular day is counted as only one day.)

Second, all days in any waiting period are not counted as creditable coverage.

Third, whether a significant break in coverage (see Q 5:69) has occurred must be determined.

Fourth, creditable coverage occurring prior to a significant break in coverage may (but is not required to) be disregarded.

Fifth, the creditable coverage to be used is applied toward the group health plan's preexisting-condition exclusion period.

The plan is permitted to use any other counting method for reducing the preexisting-condition exclusion period (but not for issuing certificates), as long as the method used is at least as favorable to the individual as the above standard method.

Alternate method. If a plan has different preexisting-condition exclusion periods for any of five specified categories of benefits, the plan can require that only prior coverage of the same type be credited toward the preexisting-condition exclusion (e.g., that prior dental coverage only be permitted as a credit toward the dental preexisting-condition exclusion). This alternate method may be used for any or all of the categories. The five categories are (1) mental health, (2) substance abuse treatment, (3) prescription drugs, (4) dental care, and (5) vision care.

The plan is permitted to apply a different preexisting-condition exclusion period for each of these categories as well as a separate exclusion for the rest of the plan's benefits not within any of these categories. Creditable coverage determined for a particular category of benefits will apply only toward that category's preexisting-condition exclusion period. Creditable coverage for the preexisting-condition limit applicable to the plan benefits that do not fall into one of the preceding categories is determined under the standard method. [Treas. Reg. § 54.9801-4; DOL Reg. § 2590.701-4]

To be able to use this alternate method of crediting prior creditable coverage, several conditions must be met. The group health plan is required to:

1. State prominently that it is using the alternate method of counting creditable coverage in disclosure statements concerning the plan, and state this to each enrollee at the time of enrollment under the plan; and

2. Include in these statements a description of the effect of using the alternate method, including identifying the categories used.

[Treas. Reg. § 54.9801-4; DOL Reg. § 2590.701-4]

HIPAA imposes a special duty of cooperation and disclosure on plans issuing certificates of coverage so that a plan using this alternate method of counting creditable coverage can determine how to apply creditable coverage under a prior plan. When an individual enrolls in a plan using this alternate method of counting creditable coverage, the prior plan is obligated to respond promptly to a request of the current plan (the "requesting plan") for disclosure of information. The prior plan is required to identify to the requesting plan the categories of benefits (if any) contained in its certificate of coverage for which the requesting plan is using the alternate method of counting creditable coverage. For example, if the requesting plan is imposing a separate preexisting-condition exclusion on dental coverage and, under the alternate method, will credit only prior dental coverage toward that preexisting-condition exclusion period, then the prior plan must, upon request, break down the coverage indicated on the certificate of coverage that it had issued into dental (if any) and other coverage. The prior plan furnishing this information is permitted to charge the requesting plan for the reasonable cost of disclosing this information. [Treas. Reg. § 54.9801-5]

Q 5:86 What if the new plan has different exclusion periods for different categories of benefits?

If the categories fall within the list of permitted categories for using the alternate method of crediting coverage under HIPAA, then the plan can determine whether that limit has been satisfied independently of the plan's general preexisting-condition exclusion period by using the alternate method of crediting service as described in Q 5:85. [Treas. Reg. § 54.9801-4; DOL Reg. § 2590.701-4]

If the separate exclusion period is for a benefit that is not one of the five permitted categories for using the alternate method (see Q 5:85), only the standard method of crediting prior coverage may be used. Prior creditable coverage of *any* type (other than coverage prior to a 63-day break) must be used to reduce or eliminate the preexisting-condition exclusion period for that benefit.

Q 5:87　Must a group health plan accept other documentation in lieu of a certificate of creditable coverage?

Yes. A group health plan is required, under some circumstances, to accept other documentation in lieu of a certificate of creditable coverage. If the accuracy of a certificate is contested or a certificate is unavailable when the individual needs it, the individual has the right to demonstrate creditable coverage (and waiting or affiliation periods) by presenting alternative documents or by other means. For example, the individual may use this alternative means to demonstrate creditable coverage when

- An entity has failed to provide a certificate within the required time period;
- The individual has creditable coverage but the entity providing the coverage is exempt from the HIPAA requirement to provide a certificate of creditable coverage;
- The individual has an urgent medical condition that necessitates a determination before he or she can deliver a certificate to the plan; or
- The individual has lost his or her certificate of creditable coverage and cannot obtain another one.

Documents. In the absence of a certificate, the individual may establish creditable coverage (and waiting periods or affiliation periods) by providing any of the following:

- An explanation of benefit (EOB claim or other correspondence) from a plan or issuer indicating coverage;
- Pay stubs showing a payroll deduction for health coverage;
- A health insurance identification card;
- A certificate of coverage under a group health policy;
- Records from medical care providers indicating coverage; or
- Any other relevant documents that provide evidence of periods of health coverage.

Other evidence. An individual may also establish creditable coverage (and waiting period or affiliation period information) through means other than documents, such as by a telephone call from the plan or provider to a third party verifying creditable coverage.

Consideration of evidence. The plan must take into account all information that it obtains or that is presented on behalf of an individual to determine whether that individual has creditable coverage and is entitled to offset all or a portion of any preexisting-condition exclusion period. This determination must be made based on the relevant facts and circumstances. Furthermore, the plan is required to treat the individual as having furnished a certificate if:

- The individual attests to the period of creditable coverage;
- The individual also presents relevant corroborating evidence of some creditable coverage during the period; and
- The individual cooperates with the plan's efforts to verify the individual's coverage.

For this purpose, cooperation includes providing, upon the plan's or issuer's request, a written authorization for the plan to request a certificate on the individual's behalf and cooperating in efforts to determine the validity of the corroborating evidence and the dates of creditable coverage. The plan can refuse to credit coverage when the individual fails to cooperate with the plan's or issuer's efforts to verify coverage. However, the plan cannot consider the individual's inability to obtain a certificate to be evidence of the absence of creditable coverage. [Treas. Reg. § 54.9801-5; DOL Reg. § 2590.701-5]

Q 5:88   Who is liable for failures to issue certificates of creditable coverage?

The excise tax for violations of the group health plan requirements imposed by Code Section 4980D (see Q 5:13) generally is imposed on the employer (on a controlled-group basis). In the case of a multiemployer plan, the penalty is imposed on the plan. The ERISA penalty of up to $100 per day for failure to provide required notices is imposed on the plan administrator. Additional remedies are available under ERISA's general enforcement provisions.

Q 5:89   What is the penalty for failure to issue certificates of creditable coverage?

The penalty under the Internal Revenue Code for failure to issue a certificate of coverage is the same as for other violations of HIPAA's group health plan requirements (see Q 5:13). Note that HIPAA permits the parties to allocate the responsibility for issuing the certificates of creditable coverage.

Excise tax reporting. Beginning January 1, 2010, excise tax liabilities for failure to meet certain health plan requirements must be self-reported by filing Form 8928, *Return of Certain Excise Taxes Under Chapter 43 of the Internal Revenue Code.* [Treas. Reg. § 54.6011-2] In the case of excise taxes imposed by Code Section 4980D for failure to satisfy the HIPAA requirements, the form must be filed by the employer or other person responsible for providing or administering benefits under the plan (such as the insurer or third-party administrator). The form is due on or before the due date for filing the employer's or other person's federal income tax return for the year in which the failure occurred. If the failure is by a multiemployer plan, the form is due on or before the last day of the seventh month following the end of the plan year. [Treas. Reg. § 54.6071-1(a)] The tax due must be paid with the return. [Treas. Reg. § 54.6151-1]

Coverage Limits and Cost-Sharing Requirements

Q 5:90 Does federal law restrict or prohibit a group health plan from imposing lifetime and annual limits on covered services?

A lifetime limit is the maximum amount a plan will pay for health care services over the course of an insured's lifetime. An annual limit is the maximum amount a plan will pay for health care services each year. Depending on the terms of the plan, lifetime and annual limits may apply on an overall basis, on a per beneficiary basis, or with respect to specific covered services.

Historically, federal law has not imposed any overall restriction or prohibition on lifetime or annual limits. However, federal law has over time imposed requirements that limit the application of lifetime and annual limits. For example:

The Health Insurance Portability and Accountability Act of 1996 (HIPAA) prohibits group health plans from discriminating based on health status. Under those rules, any restriction on a benefit or benefits under the plan must apply uniformly to all similarly situated individuals and must not be directed at any particular participant or beneficiary based on a health factor.

The Mental Health Parity and Addiction Equity Act of 2008 (MHPAEA) requires that annual and lifetime limits for mental health coverage and substance use disorder benefits be no more restrictive than those for all medical and surgical coverage. (The MHPAEA's precursor, the Mental Health Parity Act of 1996 (MHPA), required parity in lifetime and annual limits for mental health benefits, but did not apply to coverage for substance use disorder benefits.)

The nondiscrimination provisions of HIPAA and the mental health parity rules are specifically incorporated into ERISA and the Internal Revenue Code. [ERISA §§ 702, 712; I.R.C. §§ 9801; 9812]

2010 Health Reform Act. The 2010 Health Reform Act generally prohibits a group health plan or health insurance issuer from establishing lifetime limits or annual limits on the dollar value of benefits for any participant or beneficiary. [PHSA § 2711(a)(1), as added by PPACA § 1005 and amended by PPACA § 10101]

The prohibitions on lifetime and annual limits extend only to "essential health benefits." The 2010 Health Reform Act does not prohibit a group health plan or health insurance issuer from placing annual or lifetime per beneficiary limits on specific covered benefits that are not essential health benefits, to the extent such limits are otherwise permitted under federal or state law. [PHSA § 2711(b), as added by PPACA § 1005 and amended by PPACA § 10101]

"Essential health benefits" are to be defined by the Secretary of Health and Human Services (HHS), but must include at least the following general categories of items and services:

- Ambulatory patient services
- Emergency services
- Hospitalization
- Maternity and newborn care
- Mental health and substance use disorder services, including behavioral health treatment
- Prescription drugs
- Rehabilitative and habilitative services and devices
- Laboratory services
- Preventive and wellness services and chronic disease management
- Pediatric services, including oral and vision care

[PPACA § 1302(b)]

Lifetime limits. The prohibition on lifetime limits is effective for plan years beginning on or after September 23, 2010 (six months after the date of enactment of the Health Reform Act). [PPACA § 1004] Moreover, the prohibition applies to grandfathered plans as well as new plans [PPACA § 1251 as amended by PPACA Reconciliation § 2301]

> **Practice Pointer.** The prohibition on lifetime limits will impact the majority of group health plans. It has been estimated that more than half the individuals with employer-provided health insurance are subject to lifetime limits, the most common limits being $1 million and $2 million.

Annual limits. Like the prohibition on lifetime limits, the ban on annual limits applies for plan years beginning on or after September 23, 2010, and applies to both grandfathered and new plans. [PPACA § 1251 as amended by PPACA Reconciliation § 2301] However, for plan years beginning before January 1, 2014, a group health plan or health insurance issuer may establish a "restricted annual limit" on the dollar value of benefits for any participant or beneficiary with respect to essential health benefits.

Here again, what constitutes a "restricted annual limit" is to be determined by the Secretary of HHS. In defining the term, the Secretary is directed to ensure that access to needed service is made available with a minimum impact on service.

Starting with the 2014 plan year, annual limits for essential benefits are prohibited entirely.

Like the HIPAA nondiscrimination and mental health parity requirements, the 2010 Health Reform Act requirements are incorporated into ERISA and the Internal Revenue Code [ERISA § 715 as added by PPACA § 1562; I.R.C. § 9815 as added by PPACA § 1562]

Practice Pointer. The 2010 Health Reform Act does not negate the restrictions on lifetime and annual limits imposed by HIPAA or the MHPAEA. It provides that, to the extent there is a conflict between the existing provisions of ERISA or the Code and the 2010 Health Reform Act requirements, the 2010 Health Reform Act requirements apply. On the other hand, to the extent a plan limit is permitted under the 2010 Health Reform Act rules (e.g., a "restricted" annual limit on essential benefits or a lifetime or annual limit on nonessential benefits), that limit must comply with the HIPAA nondiscrimination and mental health parity requirements.

Q 5:91   Are group health plans permitted to impose cost-sharing requirements on plan participants?

Yes. Cost-sharing requirements, including deductibles, copayments, and coinsurance, are permitted.

However, the 2010 Health Reform Act requires group health plans to comply with specified cost-sharing limits for plan years beginning after 2013. [PHSA § 2707(b) as added by PPACA § 1201] The cost-sharing limits do not apply to grandfathered plans.

A plan must limit cost sharing, including deductibles, coinsurance, copayments, or similar charges and any other required expenditure that is a qualified medical expense with respect to essential health benefits covered under the plan. Cost sharing does not include premiums, balance billing amounts for non-network providers, or expenditures for non-covered services. [PPACA § 1302(c)(3)]

The annual limits on cost sharing are tied to the annual out-of-pocket expense limits for high-deductible health plans (HDHPs) under the health savings account (HSA) rules. [PPACA § 1302(c)(1); I.R.C. 223(c)(2)(A)(ii)]

Out-of-pocket limits. For 2014, cost sharing for self-only coverage cannot exceed the out-of-pocket limit for a self-only high-deductible plan as in effect for 2014. In the case of coverage other than self-only, cost sharing cannot exceed the out-of-pocket limit for a family high-deductible plan for 2014. (For 2011, the indexed limits are $5,950 for self-only coverage and $11,900 for family coverage.)

For 2015 and later years, cost sharing for self-only coverage cannot exceed the HDHP limit in effect for 2014 (indexed based on premium cost increases) and cost-sharing for other coverage cannot exceed twice the amount for self-only coverage.

Deductible limits. The deductible under the plan cannot exceed $2,000 for self-only coverage or $4,000 for other coverage (indexed). The allowable deductible may be increased by the maximum amount of reimbursement that is reasonably expected to be available to a participant under an FSA determined without regard to any salary-reduction arrangement. [PPACA § 1302(c)(2)] In other words, the deductible limit can be increased by *employer* contributions to an FSA, but not by employee salary-reduction contributions.

Dependent Coverage Requirements

Q 5:92   Are group health plans required to provide coverage for spouses and dependent children?

No. A plan may provide coverage only for employees. However, to the extent a plan does provide coverage for dependents, specific requirements apply:

1. Under a provision added by the 2010 Health Reform Act, the plan must make coverage available for an adult child until the child turns 26 years of age (see Q 5:93).

2. The plan must provide special extended coverage to dependent college students on medically necessary leave of absence from school (see Q 5:94).

3. Adopted children and children placed for adoption must be covered under the same terms and conditions as natural children (see Q 5:95).

Practice Pointer. The IRS and the Departments of Labor and Health and Human Services have issued regulations implementing the adult child coverage requirements. [26 C.F.R. § 54.9815-2714; 29 C.F.R. § 2590.2714; 45 C.F.R. § 147.120] And those regulations make it clear that the law change will impact plan coverage for children of any age. Under prior law, plans often conditioned dependent coverage on factors in addition to the age of the child, such as student status, residency, and financial support. The regulations, however, provide that, for a child who has not attained age 26, a plan or issuer cannot define *eligible dependent* other than in terms of a relationship between a child and the participant.

Q 5:93   When is a group health plan required to provide dependent coverage for a participant's adult child?

The 2010 Health Reform Act requires a group health plan (or a health insurance issuer offering group coverage) that provides dependent coverage of children to continue to make that coverage available for an adult child until the child turns 26 years of age. [I.R.C. § 9815 as added by PPACA § 1562; PHSA § 2714, as added by PPACA § 1001 and amended by PPACA Reconciliation § 2301(b)]

The extended coverage requirement is generally effective for plan years beginning on or after September 23, 2010. [PPACA § 1004] However, before 2014, a "grandfathered health plan" is required to provide extended coverage to an adult child only if the child is not eligible to enroll in another employer-sponsored group health plan. [PPACA Reconciliation § 2301(a)(ii)] A grandfathered health plan generally includes a group health plan in existence on the effective date of the 2010 Health Reform Act (March 23, 2010), group health insurance covering an individual on that date, or coverage maintained pursuant to a collective bargaining agreement ratified before that date [PPACA § 1251].

Note. The 2010 Health Reform Act amends Code Section 105(b) to extend the general exclusion for reimbursements for medical care expenses under an employer-provided accident or health plan to any child of an employee who has not attained age 27 as of the end of the taxable year. [I.R.C. § 105(b) as amended by PPACA Reconciliation § 1004] This change also applies to the exclusion under Code Section 106 for employer-provided coverage under an accident or health plan for injuries or sickness for such a child. [Notice 2010-39, 2010-20 I.R.B. 682] See chapter 3 for a discussion of the tax treatment of employer-provided health coverage.

Q 5:94   What is the requirement to provide dependent coverage for college students on medically necessary leaves of absence?

The 2008 Student Health Insurance Act, also known as "Michelle's Law," requires group health plans that offer dependent coverage to provide special extended coverage to college students who take a leave of absence from school or reduce their schedules due to a severe illness or injury. [Pub. L. No. 110-381, 122 Stat. 4081 (Oct. 9, 2008)] The law provides that a group health plan may not terminate coverage of a dependent child due to a medically necessary leave of absence from college before the earlier of:

- The date that is one year after the first day of the medically necessary leave of absence; or
- The date on which the coverage would otherwise terminate under the plan's terms.

[I.R.C. § 9813(b)(1); ERISA § 714 as added by Pub. L. No. 110-381; PHSA § 2728 as added by Pub. L. No. 110-381 and redesignated by Pub. L. No.111-138]

Moreover, there can be no change in a child's benefits as a result of a medically necessary leave of absence. A dependent child whose benefits are continued is entitled to the same benefits during the leave as if the child continued to be a covered student and the leave was not a medically necessary leave. [I.R.C. § 9813(c) as added by Pub. L. No. 110-381]

The requirement applies to medically necessary leaves of absence during plan years beginning on or after October 9, 2009. Thus, in the case of calendar year plans, the rules apply starting in 2010.

A *medically necessary leave of absence* means a leave of absence from or any other change in enrollment at a postsecondary educational institution that:

- Commences while the child is suffering from a serious illness or injury;
- Is medically necessary; and
- Causes the child to lose student status for purposes of coverage under the group health plan.

[I.R.C. § 9813(a) as added by Pub. L. No. 110-381]

The prohibition on termination of a child's coverage applies only if the plan, or the issuer of health insurance in connection with the plan, receives written certification by a treating physician of the child stating that the child is suffering from a serious illness or injury and that the leave of absence or other change in enrollment is medically necessary. [I.R.C. § 9813(b)(3) as added by Pub. L. No. 110-381]

Notice requirement. Any notice regarding a requirement for certification of student status under the plan must include a description of the rules for continued coverage during medically necessary leaves of absence. The notice must be in language that is understandable to the typical plan participant.

> **Pratice Pointer.** It appears that Michelle's Law has been rendered largely redundant by the 2010 Health Reform Act provision requiring a group health plan to provide dependent coverage for a child up to age 26 (see Q 5:93).

Q 5:95   Does federal law permit a group health plan to exclude adopted children and children placed for adoption?

If the group health plan is an ERISA plan, it cannot exclude adopted children or children who are placed for adoption from the plan's eligibility provisions. ERISA Section 609(c) imposes two rules that essentially establish a minimum standard for group health plan treatment of adopted children and children placed for adoption.

1. *General requirement of coverage.* Under the first rule, group health plans must cover adopted children and children who are placed for adoption (whether or not the adoption has become final) under the same terms and conditions as apply to dependent children who are natural children of participants or beneficiaries under the plan. To qualify, the child who is adopted or placed for adoption must be under age 18 as of the date of adoption or placement. For this purpose, a child is considered to be "placed for adoption" if a person has assumed and retains a legal obligation for total or partial support of the child in anticipation of adoption (see Q 5:96). This protection applies only to children under the age of 18 as of the date of the adoption or placement. [ERISA § 609(c)(1)]

Example 1. Carol works for an insurance company and is covered under its group health plan, which offers dependent coverage. She and her husband adopt a baby girl. The plan must cover the adopted baby girl.

Example 2. Andrew is hired by a major manufacturer. He completes the 30-day waiting period for coverage and enrolls his family in the company's medical plan. Andrew wishes to enroll his wife's two sons from a previous marriage, whom he adopted two years ago. One of the boys is 17, and the other is a 19-year-old full-time college student. This ERISA provision requires that both of these adopted boys be covered under the company's plan to the same extent as natural children. While one of the boys is older than the age limit for adopted children protected by ERISA Section 609, both boys were adopted by Andrew while they were under age 18.

Plans are required to provide special enrollment rights to adoptive and preadoptive children (see chapter 5).

2. *Preexisting-condition restrictions.* Under the second rule, coverage for adopted and preadoptive children protected by ERISA Section 609 (i.e., those who have not yet attained age 18 as of the date of adoption or placement) cannot be restricted solely on the basis of a preexisting condition of the child at the time such a child would otherwise become eligible for coverage under the plan, if the adoption or placement for adoption occurs while the participant or beneficiary is eligible for coverage under the plan. [ERISA § 609(c)]

Note. Effective for plan years beginning on or after September 23, 2010, the 2010 Health Reform Act prohibits preexisting-condition exclusions for *all* children under age 19. [PHSA § 2704, as added by PPACA § 1201 and amended by PPACA § 10103] (See Q 5:52.)

Practice Pointer. Although ERISA requires that a group health plan cover preadoptive children, the child's coverage is not always nontaxable (see chapter 3).

Q 5:96   When is a child considered to be placed for adoption?

For purposes of all of ERISA's requirements concerning group health plan coverage of children who are adopted or placed for adoption, "placement" or "being placed" for adoption means that the participant or beneficiary assumes and retains a legal obligation for total or partial support of a child in anticipation of adopting that child. The placement terminates when this legal obligation terminates. [ERISA §§ 733(d)(4)] The same uniform provision applies to the parallel provisions under the Code.

Agreements to pay birth expenses. The DOL has taken the position that an agreement to pay the mother's birth expenses is not, by itself, an agreement to support the child. It is not, therefore, a legal obligation of the type contemplated by ERISA Section 609(c)(3)(B). An agreement to pay only the child's birth expenses also would not, in and of itself, be sufficient evidence of the assumption and retention of a legal obligation for support of a child in anticipation of adoption. [DOL Adv. Op. 95-18A (July 27, 1995)]

Foreign adoptions. Whether an agreement to provide full or partial support for a child born and residing outside the United States in anticipation of his or her adoption and immigration to the United States constitutes "a legal obligation for total or partial support of such child in anticipation of adoption" within the meaning of ERISA Section 609(c)(3)(B) is a question of the facts and circumstances associated with the agreement. The DOL has taken the position that, in the case of either a domestic or foreign adoption, the obligation that has been assumed or retained by a participant or beneficiary of the group health plan must be one that can be enforced in a court of competent jurisdiction. [DOL Adv. Op. 95-18A (July 27, 1995)]

For the standards specifically applicable to adoptions and foreign adoptions under employer-provided adoption benefit plans, see chapter 8.

Q 5:97   If the participant's or beneficiary's support obligation terminates, can the group health plan require reimbursement for expenses incurred on behalf of a child during the child's placement for adoption?

No. A group health plan cannot require reimbursement of expenses incurred on behalf of a child during the child's placement for adoption if the participant's or beneficiary's support obligation subsequently terminates. The DOL takes the position that nothing in ERISA Section 609(c) requires that the placement must ultimately result in an adoption. If an employer could require reimbursement of otherwise legitimate plan expenses incurred during the period that the child was placed for adoption merely because of the termination of the placement, that would be tantamount to a retroactive denial of coverage in violation of ERISA Section 609(c). [DOL Adv. Op. 95-18A (July 27, 1995)]

Q 5:98   Must a group health plan cover the birth expenses of a child adopted or placed for adoption to the same extent as birth expenses of a child born to the plan participant?

Yes. Section 609(c) of ERISA requires that if a group health plan provides dependent coverage, the group health plan must provide benefits to dependent children placed for adoption with participants or beneficiaries under the same terms and conditions as apply in the case of dependent children who are natural children of plan participants or beneficiaries. If certain expenses related to birth are covered expenses of a dependent child under the plan, then those expenses must also be covered by the plan when they are incurred by a child who is adopted by or placed for adoption with a participant or beneficiary. The terms of the particular group health plan must be consulted to determine whether any particular expense associated with the birth is to be attributed to the child rather than the mother. [DOL Adv. Op. 95-18A (July 27, 1995)]

Additionally, requirements concerning discrimination against individual participants and beneficiaries based on health status potentially apply to the extent an adopted child would be excluded because of health status and the need to receive health care (see Qs 5:17–5:39).

Q 5:99   Is a group health plan required to cover the expenses of the birth mother?

No. A group health plan is not required to cover the expenses of a birth mother (unless the birth mother is a participant or beneficiary under the group health plan and can claim such expenses in her own right). ERISA Section 609(c) does not require group health plans to cover expenses attributable to the birth mother of a child who has been placed for adoption with a participant or beneficiary. [DOL Adv. Op. 95-18A (July 27, 1995)]

Q 5:100   Must a group health plan cover birth and other expenses of a child incurred prior to placement for adoption if the plan participant or beneficiary must pay such expenses as a condition of the adoption?

No. Group health plans are obligated to cover children only upon placement for adoption—that is, once the participant or beneficiary has assumed a legal obligation for total or partial support of the child in anticipation of adoption of the child. Group health plans are not required to extend coverage to a child or reimburse the child's health care expenses incurred prior to the child's placement for adoption even when such payment is an express condition of the adoption. [DOL Adv. Op. 95-18A (July 27, 1995)]

Q 5:101   If the group health plan's coverage is being provided through an HMO, must the plan cover expenses for birth, illness, or accident outside the service area occurring prior to or during transit of an adoptive child to the HMO service area?

An HMO's coverage of expenses for birth, illness, or accident outside the service area occurring prior to or during transit to the HMO's service area will depend on the terms of the HMO's coverage. Whatever out-of-area benefits would be provided to natural children of participants and beneficiaries must be provided to children who are placed for adoption with participants or beneficiaries. [DOL Adv. Op. 95-18A (July 27, 1995)]

The Newborns' and Mothers' Health Protection Act of 1996 (NMHPA) may also require that a mandatory minimum hospital stay be provided. Although that act is silent on the interplay of the mandatory maternity hospital stay provisions and out-of-area penalties, it appears that whatever reductions in reimbursement may be applicable to out-of-area nonmaternity hospitalizations may also permissibly be applied to maternity situations because the statute specifically permits a group health plan to impose deductibles, coinsurance, or other cost sharing in relation to benefits for hospital lengths of stay in connection with childbirth. In view of the mandatory nature of the hospital benefit coverage under the act, it would appear that the HMO may be able to reduce, but not totally deny, such coverage.

Q 5:102   Do the adopted-child provisions of ERISA apply to children of retirees?

The answer to this question depends on the ERISA section at issue. ERISA Section 609's adopted-child provisions apply to children of retirees. Under ERISA Section 609(c), if the ERISA group health plan provides coverage for dependent children of retired participants, it cannot deny such coverage to children who are adopted by or placed for adoption with a retired participant solely on the grounds that the child has been adopted or placed for adoption. [DOL Adv. Op. 95-18A (July 27, 1995)] The adopted-child provisions in ERISA's special enrollment rights provisions (contained in Section 701(f)) will only apply to retiree medical coverage under a plan having at least two participants who are current employees on the first day of the plan year and then only if coverage for dependent children is provided in any manner.

Q 5:103   Are group health plans required to recognize same-sex domestic partners as spouses?

No. Group health plans are not required to recognize same-sex domestic partners for purposes of COBRA continuation of coverage, mandatory special open enrollment periods, or other federal law requirements. The Defense of Marriage Act [Pub. L. No. 104-199, 110 Stat. 2419 (1996)] (DOMA) provides that the word *marriage* means only a legal union between one man and one woman as husband and wife, and that the word *spouse* refers only to a person of the opposite sex who is a husband or a wife when determining the meaning of any act of Congress or of any ruling, regulation, or interpretation of the various administrative bureaus and agencies of the United States. [1 U.S.C. § 7]

But what if a same-sex couple is legally married under state law or the law of a foreign jurisdiction? Is an employer's plan required to provide health benefits to an employee's same-sex spouse if it provides spousal benefits to heterosexual married couples? This may become a live issue for employers in the near future.

In late 2003, the Massachusetts Supreme Judicial Court held that the Massachusetts Constitution barred the Commonwealth of Massachusetts from denying an individual the "protections, benefits, and obligations of civil marriage" solely because the person chose to marry a person of the same sex—thus paving the way for same-sex marriages. [Goodridge v. Department of Public Health, 440 Mass. 309 (Mass. Sup. Jud. Ct. 2003)] Significantly, in 2009, Massachusetts filed a lawsuit in the federal district court for Massachusetts challenging DOMA on the grounds that it interferes with the Commonwealth's sovereign authority to define and regulate marriage and constitutes an overreaching and discriminatory federal law. [Commonwealth of Mass. v. U.S. Department of Health & Human Servs., Case No. 1:2009cv11156 (U.S. Dist. Ct. D. Mass. (July 8, 2009)]

In 2008, California briefly became the second state to recognize same-sex marriage. In May 2008, the California Supreme Court ruled that barring gay and lesbian couples from marrying violated the state constitution. [*In re* Marriage Cases, 43 Cal. 4th 757 (2008)] The California Supreme Court's ruling took effect on June 16, 2008, allowing same-sex couples from California as well as from other jurisdictions to legally marry in California, but the ruling was short-lived. On November 4, 2008, California voters approved Proposition 8, to change the state constitution to restrict the definition of marriage to a union between one man and one woman and to eliminate the right of same-sex couples to marry in the state. The amendment took effect on November 5, 2008. Approximately 18,000 same-sex marriages performed in the state between June and November 2008 remain legally recognized.

2008 also marked the authorization of same-sex marriage in the state of Connecticut. On October 10, 2008, the Connecticut Supreme Court held that the Connecticut law limiting marriage to heterosexual couples violates the state constitutional guarantee of equal protection. The decision became effective October 28, 2008. [Kerrigan v. Commissioner of Pub. Health (SC 17716)]

More recently, the Iowa Supreme Court held the state's same-sex marriage ban to be unconstitutional and legalized same-sex marriage in that state effective April 27, 2009. [Varnum v. Brien, No. 07-1499, 2009 WL 874044 (Iowa Sup. Ct. Apr. 3, 2009)] In Vermont, the state legislature legalized same-sex marriage effective September 1, 2009. [S. 115] In 2009, voters in Maine approved Question 1, a "People's Veto" of legislation passed by the state legislature and signed by the governor that would have enabled any two persons otherwise qualified under state law to marry regardless of the sex of each person.

As a result of these developments, employers in all states are likely to be presented with benefit claims from same-sex couples who have tied the knot. The resolution of those claims will depend on state law as well as the terms of the employer's plan. For example, the New York State Supreme Court has held that a woman whose same-sex marriage took place in Canada was entitled to recognition in New York State. The case arose when the employer denied the woman's application for health benefits for her same-sex spouse even though the employer provided health benefits to the opposite-sex spouses of its employees. [Martinez v. Monroe Cmty Coll., 850 N.Y.S.2d 740, *app. denied,* 10 N.Y.3d (2008)] Following up on that case, New York State's Insurance Department issued an opinion and notice concluding that where an employer offers group health insurance to employees and their spouses, the same-sex spouse of a New York employee who enters into a marriage legally performed outside the state is entitled to health insurance coverage to the same extent as any opposite-sex spouse. [Circular Letter No. 27 (Nov. 21, 2008)] Similarly, the State of Connecticut Insurance Department issued a bulletin stating that a spouse in a same-sex marriage is to be treated the same as a spouse in a heterosexual marriage for all purposes, including insurance. [Bulletin IC-2 (Nov. 18, 2008)]

Another issue arises when a marriage follows a sex-change operation by one of the partners. The Supreme Court of Kansas rejected the spousal status of a male-to-female transsexual who married a male partner in another state. [*In re* Estate of Gardiner, 42 F.3d 120 (D. Kan. 2002)] The case involved the transsexual's right to a share of the partner's estate. However, the validity of a transsexual's marriage may also arise in terms of eligibility for health or other benefits that are provided to an employee's spouse.

The facts of the Kansas case showed that J'Noel Ball's original birth certificate, which was issued in Wisconsin, indicated that J'Noel was born a male. After J'Noel underwent sex reassignment surgery, the birth certificate was amended under Wisconsin law to indicate that J'Noel was female. J'Noel subsequently met Marshall Gardiner, and they were "married" in Kansas. When Marshall died intestate about a year later, J'Noel claimed that she was entitled to a spousal share of Marshall's estate. Marshall's son by his first marriage objected to J'Noel's claim on the grounds that J'Noel remained male despite the surgery, and therefore was not Marshall's legal spouse under Kansas law.

The Kansas Supreme Court noted that there are two distinct lines of cases on the question of the validity of the marriage of a post-operative transsexual. One line of cases determines a transsexual's sexual classification at the time of the marriage. Thus, a marriage between a male-to-female transsexual and a man would be valid in states adopting that view. The other line of cases judges the validity of the marriage based on the sexual classification of the transsexual at birth. Thus, a marriage between a man and a transsexual person who was born male would be invalid. The Kansas court adopted the latter view, noting that the Kansas legislature has declared that the state's public policy is to recognize only the traditional marriage between two parties born of opposite sexes and has declared all other marriages void. [*In re* Estate of Gardiner, 42 F.3d 120 (D. Kan. 2002)] To date, only a handful of other courts have addressed this issue. Courts in Texas and Ohio have taken the same position as the Kansas court. [*In re* Ladrach, 32 Ohio Misc. 2d 6 (1987); Littleton v. Prange, 9 S.W.3d 223 (Tex. Civ. App. 1999)] By contrast, a New Jersey court has ruled that a marriage between a man and a postoperative male-to-female transsexual was a lawful marriage under New Jersey state law. [MT v. JT, 140 N.J. Super. 77 (App. Div.), *cert. denied*, 71 N.J. 345 (1976)]

It should be noted, however, that employers are completely free to cover same-sex domestic partners under their group health plans voluntarily. Moreover, if an employee's transsexual partner does not qualify as a legal spouse under state law, he or she would qualify for coverage as a domestic partner.

Note. If coverage is extended to an employee's same-sex spouse or to a domestic partner of either sex, the value of the spouse's or domestic partner's coverage may be taxable to the employee (see chapter 3) unless it can be demonstrated that the spouse or domestic partner is a tax dependent within the meaning of Code Section 52.

Practice Pointer. When implementing domestic partner coverage, employers must determine whether to offer benefits to both same-sex and opposite-sex domestic partners or whether to cover only same-sex partners. Many employers have chosen the latter course on the theory that opposite-sex partners can marry if they wish to. However, it should be noted that this has prompted claims of discrimination from employees with opposite-sex partners—albeit so far unsuccessful ones. For example, the Seventh Circuit Court of Appeals upheld a school district's policy of providing domestic partner benefits only to same-sex partners. The court said it was rational for the district to refuse to extend domestic partner benefits to persons who can marry. Therefore, the school's policy did not violate employees' rights. [Irizzary v. Board of Educ., 251 F.3d 604 (7th Cir. 2001); FMC Corp. v. Holliday, 498 U.S. 52 (1990)] More recently, a Massachusetts federal district court ruled that the female domestic partner of an unmarried male employee was not entitled to health benefits even though the employer provided health benefits to employees' same-sex domestic partners. The employee claimed the denial of benefits was unlawful discrimination based on sexual orientation, which is prohibited under Massachusetts laws. The employer argued that the Massachusetts law was superseded by ERISA, which does not require coverage for domestic partners. The court agreed with the employer that ERISA, not state law, controlled. According to the court, because application of Massachusetts' law would have required the administration of the employer's plan in Massachusetts to differ from the administration of the plan in other states where the employer had employees, the state law was preempted by ERISA. [Partners Healthcare Sys., Inc. v. Sullivan, 497 F. Supp. 2d 42 (D. Mass. 2007)]

Q 5:104   Can a state or local governmental body compel a group health plan to cover domestic partners or same-sex partners?

An employer faced with such a requirement will need to consider its response carefully. Often, such state and local laws contain punitive features for employers that do not comply, such as restricting the employers' ability to conduct business in the state or with the local governmental entity in question.

In one case, an employer challenged a San Francisco ordinance that prohibits any city agency or department from contracting with a company that discriminates between employees with spouses and employees with domestic partners in providing various benefits, including health benefits. The ordinance applies to employees whose domestic partnerships have been registered under state or local law. A contractor that breaches the nondiscrimination requirement can be subject to a penalty of $50 per day for each employee affected by the discrimination. In addition, the city may terminate or suspend its contract with the contractor in whole or part and can deem the contractor to be an "irresponsible bidder" that is barred from contracting with the city for up to two years.

Shortly after the San Francisco ordinance was enacted, an Ohio-based corporation bid on a servicing contract for city-owned property. The city notified the contractor that it was the low bidder but that in order to be a "responsible bidder" it was required to certify its willingness to comply with the domestic partner ordinance. The contractor declined on the grounds that compliance with the ordinance was contrary to its religious and moral principles. The contractor's bid was subsequently rejected by the city, and the contractor filed suit, claiming that the ordinance was invalid under the Commerce and Due Process Clauses of the U.S. Constitution and under California law. The Ninth Circuit Court of Appeals upheld the ordinance, concluding that it did not violate either state or federal law. [S.D. Myers, Inc. v. City & County of San Francisco, 253 F.3d 461 (9th Cir. 2001)]

The San Francisco ordinance is likely to face continuing challenges. In another case, a U.S. district court held that the ordinance was entirely preempted insofar as it affects ERISA plans providing ERISA benefits, including health benefits. [Air Transport Ass'n of Am. v. City & County of San Francisco, 992 F. Supp. 1149 (N.D. Cal. 1998)] Although other portions of that decision were appealed to the Ninth Circuit, the ERISA preemption issue was not. The Ninth Circuit affirmed those portions of the district court decision.

Although San Francisco has pioneered legislation requiring city contractors to provide domestic partner benefits, it no longer stands alone on this issue. At least 10 U.S. cities have enacted similar domestic partner benefit legislation. Moreover, the state of California has enacted legislation requiring certain state contractors to provide domestic partner benefits.

These laws continue to be controversial and face continuing challenges in the courts.

Q 5:105   May employers require employees to provide documentation of their dependents' eligibility?

Yes. Employers may require employees to provide documentation of their dependents' eligibility (and carefully drafted language in the SPD can be a big help in educating employees as to the documentary requirements).

The Court of Appeals for the Fourth Circuit upheld a group health plan's determination that the employee's daughter was not a covered dependent, where the employee had failed to provide the plan with any documentation for his statement that he met the plan's requirement of providing more than half of his daughter's support. [HCA Health Servs. of Va. v. Amerihealth Inc., 19 Employee Benefits Cas. (BNA) 1997 (4th Cir. 1995)]

Practice Pointer. A continuing administrative problem is how to know when a dependent should be dropped off the eligibility rolls for the plan. Employees often forget to mention that their dependents no longer qualify under the plan, resulting in the plan's continuing to pay benefits for individuals who are no longer eligible. This can become expensive for the plan and constitutes a diversion of plan assets for nonplan purposes. One possible method of addressing this is to place a strong warning in the SPD that the employee must submit such documentation as may be required or face disciplinary action, including suspension of plan payments and possible termination of employment. In addition, health plan "audits" requiring documentation of a dependent's eligibility are becoming increasingly common as employers attempt to rein in health plan costs.

Special Enrollment Rights

Q 5:106   Are group health plans and health insurance issuers required to provide special enrollment periods for individuals or their dependents?

Yes. Group health plans and health insurance issuers issuing coverage in connection with a group health plan must provide mandatory open enrollment periods for two classes of individuals who are eligible but not enrolled: (1) certain individuals losing other coverage and (2) new dependents due to marriage, birth, adoption, or placement for adoption (and the spouse, if otherwise eligible for coverage), if certain requirements are met.

Effective April 1, 2009, the Children's Health Insurance Program Reauthorization Act of 2009 [Pub. L No. 111-3, 123 Stat. 8 (Feb. 4, 2009)] (CHIPRA) requires group health plans and group health insurance issuers to provide special enrollment rights for employees and their dependents who lose eligibility for coverage under a state Medicaid or Children's Health Insurance Program (CHIP), or become eligible for state premium assistance under Medicaid or CHIP. [I.R.C. § 9801(f)(3)(A); ERISA § 701(f)(3)(A); PHS Act § 2701(f)(3)(A) as amended by Pub. L. No. 111-3]

Q 5:107   Under what circumstances must a plan or issuer provide a special enrollment period for individuals who lose other coverage?

A mandatory special enrollment period must be provided for employees and dependents who are eligible for coverage but not enrolled and who lose other group health plan coverage if each of the following conditions is met:

1. The employee or dependent was covered under a group health plan or had health insurance coverage at the time coverage was previously offered to the employee or dependent;

2. The employee stated in writing at that time that the other coverage was the reason for declining enrollment, but only if that written statement was required at the time by the plan sponsor or issuer and the employee was provided with a notice of that requirement and the consequences of that requirement at that time;

3. The employee's or dependent's other coverage

   a. Was COBRA continuation that has been exhausted or

   b. Was not COBRA continuation, and either such coverage has been terminated as a result of loss of eligibility for the coverage (including as a result of legal separation, divorce, death, cessation of dependent status, termination of employment, reduction in the number of hours of employment, or operation of a lifetime limit on benefits), or employer contributions (including contributions by any current or former employer of the individual or another plan) toward such coverage for the individual have been terminated (even if plan coverage continues). Loss of eligibility does not, however, include a loss resulting from the failure to pay premiums on a timely basis or termination for cause (such as making a fraudulent claim or an intentional misrepresentation of a material fact in connection with the plan); and

4. Under the terms of the plan, the employee requests special enrollment for himself or herself or the dependent no later than 30 days after the date of exhaustion of coverage, termination of coverage, or termination of employer contributions.

Regulations issued under HIPAA make it clear that when an employee's spouse or dependent has special enrollment rights due to a loss of other health coverage, both the spouse or dependent and the employee may enroll in the plan. Moreover, if the employee is already enrolled he or she may change benefit options when a spouse or dependent becomes eligible for special enrollment. [DOL Reg. § 2590.701-6; Treas. Reg. § 54.9801-6]

Proposed regulations provide for tolling of the special enrollment period in those cases where the individual does not receive a certificate of creditable coverage before his or her other health plan coverage ceases. Under the proposed regulations, the special enrollment period would not terminate until the end of the 30-day period beginning on the first day after the earlier of the date that a certificate of creditable coverage is provided or the date that is 44 days after coverage ceases. [DOL Prop. Reg. § 2590.701-6; Prop. Treas. Reg. § 54.9801-6]

Effective date of enrollment. Enrollment must become effective no later than the first day of the calendar month beginning after the date the completed request for enrollment is received. [ERISA § 701(f); I.R.C. § 9801(f)]

The regulations make it clear that if special enrollment rights coincide with a late enrollment period, an individual who requests special enrollment cannot be treated as a late enrollee. [DOL Reg. § 2590.701-6; Treas. Reg. § 54.9801-6] This rule may, for example, affect the individual's effective date of enrollment as well as the length of any preexisting-condition exclusion.

Applicability to retiree medical coverage. If the plan's retiree medical coverage is subject to the group health plan requirements, the preceding rules do not apply because they are expressly limited to employees and dependents of employees.

Applicability to cafeteria plan coverage. Cafeteria plan regulations regarding changes in status reflect these special enrollment rights. Accordingly, an individual who is subject to a special enrollment right may revoke his or her cafeteria plan election regarding group health plan coverage midyear and modify it to correspond with the applicable special enrollment right and the resulting desired enrollment in the underlying group health plan. [Treas. Reg. § 1.125-4(b)]

The proposed regulations contain rules for determining special enrollment rights when health plan coverage ends in connection with an employee's taking leave under the Family and Medical Leave Act. [DOL Prop. Reg. § 2590.701-6; Prop. Treas. Reg. § 54.9801-6]

Q 5:108   Under what circumstances must a plan or issuer provide a special enrollment period for new dependents by reason of marriage, birth, adoption, or placement for adoption?

Special enrollment periods must be provided for new dependents if:

1. The group health plan includes coverage for dependents of an individual, and the individual either is a participant or has satisfied any applicable

waiting periods and would be eligible for enrollment but for failure to enroll during a previous enrollment period; or

2. A person becomes a dependent of the individual by marriage, birth, adoption, or placement for adoption.

Timing of special enrollment period. The dependent's special enrollment period must be a minimum of 30 days, beginning on the later of (1) the date dependent coverage is made available or (2) the date of the marriage, birth, adoption, or placement for adoption.

Who may be enrolled. During this time, the dependent child or new spouse may be enrolled. In addition, the individual's spouse may be enrolled as a dependent upon the birth, adoption, or placement for adoption, if the spouse is otherwise eligible for coverage. [ERISA §§ 701(f), 101(a); I.R.C. § 9801(f)] Moreover, the DOL has made it clear that an employee who is otherwise eligible, but not enrolled for coverage, may enroll when special enrollment rights of a dependent are triggered by marriage, birth, adoption, or placement for adoption. [DOL Compliance Guidance (Feb. 27, 2003); DOL Reg. § 2590.701-6(a)(2)(ii): Treas. Reg. § 54.9801-6(a)(2)(ii)]

Effective date of enrollment. Coverage must be effective retroactively to the date of birth, adoption, or placement for adoption. In the case of marriage, coverage must become effective no later than the first day of the first month beginning after the date the completed request for enrollment is received. [ERISA § 701(f)(2)(C); DOL Reg. § 2390.701-6; I.R.C. § 9802(a); Treas. Reg. § 54.9801-6]

The regulations make it clear that if special enrollment rights coincide with a late enrollment period, an individual who requests special enrollment cannot be treated as a late enrollee. [DOL Reg. § 2590.701-6; Treas. Reg. § 54.9801-6] This rule may, for example, affect the individual's effective date of enrollment as well as the length of any preexisting-condition exclusion.

Applicability to retiree coverage. If the plan's retiree medical coverage is subject to the group health plan requirements, this rule does apply because it refers to *participants* (a term not limited to employees that could include retirees) and dependents of participants. Thus, for example, if the retiree medical portion of a group health plan limited coverage to the retiree and his or her spouse who is covered on the date of retirement, such a limit would be invalid and the plan would also have to permit enrollment of new spouses under this rule.

Applicability to cafeteria plan coverage. Final cafeteria plan regulations recognize HIPAA special enrollment rights as a "change in status" event that would permit the employee to revoke his or her cafeteria plan election midyear and modify it to correspond with the applicable HIPAA special enrollment right. [Treas. Reg. § 1.125-4(b)]

Q 5:109   Are there notice and procedural rules applicable for purposes of special enrollment?

Yes. The HIPAA regulations state that a plan must provide a description of special enrollment to all employees—employees who decline enrollment as well as those who enroll in the plan. The notice must be provided at or before the time an employee is initially offered the opportunity to enroll in the plan. [DOL Reg. § 2590.701-6; Treas. Reg. § 54.9801-6]

Proposed HIPAA regulations make it clear that an individual's special enrollment rights are triggered if he or she makes an oral or written request for special enrollment during the 30-day special enrollment period. A plan may not require an individual to file a completed application for health coverage by the end of the special enrollment period. [DOL Prop. Reg. § 2590.701-6; Prop. Treas. Reg. § 54.980-1-6]

Once a timely request has been made, the plan may require the individual to complete all enrollment materials within a reasonable time after the end of the special enrollment period. A plan can impose a deadline for submitting the completed enrollment materials. However, the deadline must be extended for information that an individual making reasonable efforts cannot obtain within that deadline.

The introduction to the proposed regulations notes that some plans have imposed application requirements that could not reasonably be completed within the special enrollment period, such as requiring the Social Security number of a newborn within 30 days of birth. This practice effectively denies individuals their right to special enrollment of their dependents. Under the proposed regulations, a plan would be required to provide an extended deadline for receiving a newborn's Social Security number. In no event may a plan deny special enrollment for a newborn because the Social Security number for the newborn could not be provided within the special enrollment period.

When a special enrollment right is the result of loss of eligibility for other coverage or of marriage, coverage generally must begin no later than the first day of the first calendar month after the date the plan or issuer receives the request for special enrollment. However, under the proposed regulations, if the plan requires completion of additional enrollment materials, coverage must begin no later than the first day of the first calendar month after the plan receives enrollment materials that are substantially complete.

When the special enrollment right results from a birth, coverage must begin on the date of birth. In the case of adoption or placement for adoption, coverage must begin no later than the date of the adoption or placement for adoption. Under the proposed regulations, if a plan requires completion of additional enrollment materials, it is not required to provide benefits until substantially complete enrollment materials have been received. However, the benefits provided at that time must be retroactive to the date of birth, adoption, or placement for adoption.

Mandated Benefits

Q 5:110   Does federal law require group health plans to provide specific benefits?

Historically, federal law has not mandated that a group health plan provide specific benefits, although (as discussed throughout this chapter) once a particular type or level of coverage is offered, a number of nondiscrimination rules and other mandates regulate the manner in which that coverage must be provided.

The 2010 Health Reform Act breaks new ground by requiring group health plans and group health insurance to provide specified benefits.

Essential coverage requirements. Beginning in 2014, large employers are subject to employer responsibility requirements under which they must provide "minimum essential coverage" to employees or pay an excise tax for failure to do so. [I.R.C. § 4980H as added by PPACA § 1513 and amended by PPACA Reconciliation § 1003]

In addition, beginning in 2014, health insurance issuers offering coverage in the small group market must provide coverage for an essential health benefits package [PHSA § 2707(a) as added by PPACA § 1201] This requirement is effective for plan years beginning after 2013. [PPACA § 1253] The requirement does not apply to grandfathered plans in existence as of the date of enactment (March 23, 2010) of the 2010 Health Reform Act. See chapter 3 for a complete discussion of these requirements.

Preventive coverage requirement. Under the 2010 Health Reform Act, a group health plan or health insurance issuer offering group coverage must, at a minimum, provide coverage for specified preventive services. These services must be provided on a first-dollar basis without any cost-sharing requirement. [PHSA § 2713 as added by PPACA § 1001] This requirement is effective for plan years beginning on or after September 23, 2010, but does not apply to grandfathered health plans. [PPACA § 1004, PPACA § 1251]

Required preventive services are:

- Evidence-based items or services with a rating of "A" or "B" in the recommendations of the United States Preventive Services Task Force;
- Immunizations recommended by the Advisory Committee on Immunization Practices of the Centers for Disease Control and Prevention;
- Evidence-informed preventive care and screenings for infants, children, and adolescents provided for in the comprehensive guidelines supported by the Health and Human Services Administration; and
- Additional preventive care and screenings for women provided for in the comprehensive guidelines supported by the Health and Human Services Administration.

Plans must comply with future recommendations and guidelines as they are established. However, the law provides that the Secretary of Health and Human

Services is to establish a minimum interval of at least one-year between the date on which a preventive care recommendation or guideline is issued and the plan year for which such preventive care must be provided.

Mental Health and Substance Use Disorder Benefits

Q 5:111   How does federal law regulate mental health and substance use disorder benefits?

The Paul Wellstone and Pete Domenici Mental Health Parity and Addiction Equity Act of 2008 [Pub. L. No. 110-343, 122 Stat. 3765 (Oct. 3, 2008)] (MHPAEA) provides that annual and lifetime dollar limits for both mental health coverage and substance use disorder benefits be no more restrictive than those for all medical and surgical coverage. In addition, the law requires that other financial requirements (i.e., deductibles, copayments) and treatment limitations (i.e., number of visits, days of coverage) applied to mental health and substance use disorder benefits under a group health plan be no more restrictive than the financial requirements and treatment limitations that apply to medical and surgical benefits. [I.R.C. § 9812 as amended by Pub. L. No. 110-343 (Oct. 3, 2008)] The MHPAEA is effective for plan years beginning on or after October 3, 2009. Thus, for calendar year plans, the law applies beginning January 1, 2010. In the case of collectively bargained plans, the law applies for plan years beginning after the later of January 1, 2009, or the date on which the current agreement terminates. The mental health parity requirements enacted by the Mental Health Parity Act of 1996 (MHPA) [Pub. L. No. 104-204, 110 Stat. 2874 (1996)] apply until the new law takes effect. [Pub. L. No. 110-343 § 512(e)(1)]

Like the original MHPA, the MHPAEA requires parity in annual and lifetime limits dollar limits. However, by contrast with the original MHPA rules, the new law imposes those parity requirements for both mental health and substance use disorder benefits; the MHPA did not apply to coverage for substance abuse or chemical dependency. Moreover, the MHPAEA requires parity in other financial requirements as well as treatment limitations, whereas the MHPA did not prevent a plan from imposing more restrictive service limits (e.g., number of hospital days or outpatient visits covered) or cost-sharing requirements on mental health coverage. Finally, the MHPAEA is permanent, whereas the MHPA was a "temporary" provision that was repeatedly extended by Congress. [I.R.C. § 9812(f) repealed]

2010 Health Reform Act. The 2010 Health Reform Act generally prohibits a group health plan or health insurance issuer from establishing lifetime limits or annual limits on the dollar value of "essential health benefits" for any participant or beneficiary (Q 5:90). [PHSA § 2711(a)(1) as added by PPACA § 1005 as amended by PPACA § 10101] The prohibition on lifetime limits is effective for plan years beginning on or after September 23, 2010 (6 months after the date of enactment). [PPACA § 1004] Moreover, the prohibition applies to grandfathered plans as well as new plans [PPACA § 1251 as amended by PPACA Reconciliation § 2301] Like the prohibition on lifetime limits, the ban on annual limits applies for plan years beginning on or after September 23, 2010, and applies to both grandfathered and new plans. [PPACA § 1251 as amended by PPACA Reconciliation § 2301] However, for plan years beginning before January 1, 2014, a group health plan or health insurance issuer may establish a "restricted annual limit" on the dollar value of benefits for any participant or beneficiary with respect to essential health benefits.

In addition, the 2010 Health Reform Act requires group health plans to comply with specified cost-sharing limits for plan years beginning after 2013. [PHSA § 2707(b) as added by PPACA § 1201] The cost-sharing limits do not apply to grandfathered plans.

> **Practice Pointer.** The parity requirements for mental health and substance use disorder benefits will be rendered moot to the extent the 2010 Health Reform Act prohibits annual or lifetime benefit limits or restricts other financial limitations on benefits. However, the parity requirements are not negated entirely. To the extent a limit on benefits, a financial requirement, or a treatment limitation is permitted under the 2010 Health Reform Act rules, it must be tested for compliance with the parity requirements.

The Departments of Labor, Health and Human Services and the Treasury have issued interim final regulations implementing the MHPAEA. [26 C.F.R. § 54.9812-1T; 29 C.F.R. § 2590.712; 45 C.F.R. § 146.136]

In general, the requirements of the regulations apply for plan years beginning on or after July 1, 2010. In the case of collectively bargained plans, the requirements of the regulations do not apply to the plan or to health insurance coverage provided in connection with the plan until the date on which the MHPAEA applies to the plan if later. [26 C.F.R. § 54.9812-1T(i); 29 C.F.R. § 2590. 712(i); 45 C.F.R. § 146.136(i)]

Penalties for violations. The excise penalty tax under Code Section 4980D (see Q 5:13) applies to violations of the parity rules. ERISA's general enforcement provisions also apply.

[ERISA § 712; I.R.C. §§ 9812, 4980D]

Excise tax reporting. Beginning January 1, 2010, excise tax liabilities for failure to meet certain health plan requirements must be self-reported by filing Form 8928, *Return of Certain Excise Taxes Under Chapter 43 of the Internal Revenue Code.* [Treas. Reg. § 54.6011-2] In the case of excise taxes imposed by Code Section 4980D for failure to satisfy the parity requirements, the form must be filed by the employer or other person responsible for providing or administering benefits under the plan (such as the insurer or third-party administrator). The form is due on or before the due date for filing the employer's or other person's federal income tax return for the year in which the failure occurred. If the failure is by a multiemployer plan, the form is due on or before the last day of the seventh month following the end of the plan year. [Treas. Reg. § 54.6071-1(a)] The tax due must be paid with the return. [Treas. Reg. § 54.6151-1]

Q 5:112   What plans are required to comply with the parity requirements?

The MHPAEA parity requirements apply to a group health plan offering medical/surgical benefits and mental health or substance use disorder benefits. Most significantly, the interim final MHPAEA regulations provide that, for purposes of the parity requirements, all medical benefits provided by an employer or employee organization constitute a single group health plan. [26 C.F.R. § 54.9812-1T(e); 29 C.F.R. § 2590.712(e); 45 C.F.R. § 146.136(e)] Consequently, an employer cannot avoid the parity requirements by establishing separate plans for medical/surgical benefits and for mental health or substance use disorder benefits.

Health insurance issuers are subject to the parity requirements if the health insurance coverage is offered in connection with a group health plan. A health insurer may not sell to a plan a policy, certificate, or contract of insurance that fails to comply with the parity requirements except for a year in which the plan is exempt from the parity requirements (see below).

Practice Pointer. Neither the MHPAEA nor the implementing regulations require a group health plan to provide any mental health benefits or substance use disorder benefits. Nor does a plan's coverage of one or more mental health conditions or substance use disorders require it to provide benefits for any other mental health condition or substance use disorder.

Small-employer exemption. Under the MHPAEA, an employer is an exempt small employer for a plan year if it employed an average of at least 2 individuals (or 1 individual in the case of an employer residing in a state that permits small groups to include a single individual), but not more than 50 individuals, on business days during the preceding calendar year. [I.R.C. § 9812(c)(1), as amended]

If an employer was not in existence throughout the preceding calendar year, whether the employer is a small employer is determined based on the average number of employees the employer reasonably expects to employ on business days during the current calendar year.

Increased-cost exemption. The MHPAEA provides that if application of the parity rules results in a specified percentage increase in total plan costs for a plan year, the parity rules will not apply to the plan during the following plan year. The specified percentage is 2 percent for the first plan year the new parity rules apply (generally, 2010 for calendar year plans) and 1 percent for each subsequent year. [I.R.C. § 9812(c)(2)(A), as amended] However, the exemption will apply to the plan for only one plan year.

If a group health plan seeks an increased-cost exemption, the determination of the plan's increased cost must be made only after the plan has complied with the parity rules for the first six months of the plan year involved. Moreover, such determinations must be made and certified by a qualified and licensed actuary who is a member in good standing of the American Academy of Actuaries. [I.R.C. § 9812(c)(2), as amended]

A group health plan that qualifies for and elects to implement an increased-cost exemption must promptly notify the IRS, appropriate state agencies, and the plan's participants and beneficiaries.

By contrast, under the MHPA rules, the mental health parity rules do not apply to a group health plan if they would cause the plan's cost to increase by at least 1 percent. Moreover, once the requisite cost increase was demonstrated, the exemption applied for an unlimited period of time. [Treas. Reg. § 54.9806-1T; DOL Reg. § 2590.712; 62 Fed. Reg. 66,932 (Dec. 22, 1997)]

Q 5:113   What are the parity requirements for annual and lifetime dollar limits?

Under the MHPAEA annual and lifetime dollar limits for mental health and substance use disorder benefits are subject to the following rules:

Plans containing no lifetime limit and/or no annual limit or limits on less than one-third of all medical/surgical benefits. If a group health plan or insurance coverage does not contain an aggregate lifetime or annual dollar limit on any medical/surgical benefits or includes an aggregate lifetime or annual dollar limit that applies to less than one-third of all medical/surgical benefits, no aggregate lifetime dollar limit or annual dollar limit can be imposed on mental health or substance use disorder benefits.

Plans containing lifetime and/or annual limits on at least two-thirds of all medical surgical benefits. If a group health plan or insurance coverage contains an aggregate lifetime dollar limit or annual dollar limit on at least two-thirds of all medical/surgical benefits, then the group health plan has two choices:

1. Apply the aggregate lifetime or annual dollar limit both to the medical/surgical benefits and to mental health or substance use disorder benefits in a manner that does not distinguish between the two types of benefits; or

2. Apply a separate limit to mental health and substance use disorder benefits that is not less than the aggregate lifetime dollar limit or annual dollar limit that is imposed on medical/surgical benefits.

Example 1. A group health plan has no annual limit on medical/surgical benefits and a $10,000 annual limit on mental health and substance use disorder benefits. To comply with the MHPAEA requirements the plan sponsor is considering three options: (1) eliminating the dollar limit on mental health and substance use disorder benefits; (2) replacing the annual dollar limit on mental health and substance use disorder benefits with a $500,000 annual limit on all benefits, or (3) replacing the annual dollar limit on mental health and substance use disorder benefits with a $250,000 annual limit on medical/surgical benefits and a separate $250,000 annual limit on mental health and substance use disorder benefits. *Result:* Any of the three options will comply with the MHPAEA requirements.

Other plans. If a group health plan or insurance coverage does not fit into one of the above categories, it can satisfy the parity requirements by imposing no lifetime or annual dollar limit on mental health or substance use disorder benefits. Alternatively, the plan can impose an aggregate lifetime or annual dollar limit on mental health or substance use disorder benefits based on the weighted average limits that apply to the different categories of medical and surgical benefits.

> **Example 2.** A group health plan includes a $100,000 annual limit of medical/surgical benefits for cardiopulmonary diseases. The plan does not include an annual dollar limit for any other category of medical/surgical benefits. The plan calculates that 40 percent of plan payments for medical/surgical benefits are for cardiopulmonary diseases. The plan also calculates that $1 million is a reasonable estimate of the upper limit on the dollar amount the plan may incur for the other 60 percent of payments for medical surgical benefits. *Result:* The plan sponsor can choose to impose no limit on mental health or substance use disorder benefits or can impose a weighted average annual dollar limit on such benefits. In this case, the minimum weighted average annual dollar limit that can be applied to the mental health or substance use disorder benefits is $640,000 (40% x $100,000 + 60% x $1,000,000 = $640,000)

[26 C.F.R. § 54.9812-1T(b); 29 C.F.R. § 2590.712(b); 45 C.F.R. § 146.136(b)]

Q 5:114   What are the parity requirements for financial requirements and treatment limitations?

Under the MHPAEA, a group health plan that provides both medical and surgical benefits and mental health or substance use disorder benefits must ensure that the financial requirements that apply to the mental health or substance use disorder benefits are no more restrictive than the "predominant" financial requirements that are applied to substantially all medical and surgical benefits covered by the plan, and that there are no separate cost-sharing requirements that apply only to the mental health or substance abuse benefits. [I.R.C. § 9812(a)(3)(A)(i), as amended] Similarly, the treatment limitations that apply to the mental health or substance use disorder benefits must be no more restrictive than the "predominant" treatment limitations that apply to substantially all medical and surgical benefits covered by the plan, and no separate treatment limits may apply only to mental health or substance use disorder benefits. [I.R.C. § 9812(a)(3)(A)(ii)]

Financial requirements include deductibles, copayments, coinsurance, and out-of-pocket maximums (but not aggregate lifetime limits or annual limits subject to the rules discussed in Q 5:113). [26 C.F.R. § 54.9812-1T(a); 29 C.F.R. § 2590.712(a); 45 C.F.R. § 146.136(a)]

Treatment limitations include limits on the frequency of treatment, number of visits, days of coverage, or other similar limits on the scope or duration of treatment. Treatment limitations include both quantitative limitations that are expressed numerically (for example, an annual limit of 50 outpatient visits) and nonquantitative limitations that otherwise limit the scope or duration of benefits for treatment under the plan (e.g., prescription drug formularies). However, a permanent exclusion of all benefits for a specific condition or disorder is not a treatment limitation. [26 C.F.R. § 54.9812-1T(a); 29 C.F.R. § 2590.712(a); 45 C.F.R. § 146.136(a)]

A financial requirement or treatment limit is considered "predominant" if it is the most common or frequent type of limit or requirement. [I.R.C. § 9812(a)(3)(B)(ii)]

The MHPAEA interim final regulations lay down the following parity rules for financial requirements and treatment limitations. [26 C.F.R. § 54.9812-1T(c); 29 C.F.R. § 2590.712(c); 45 C.F.R. § 146.136(c)]

Basic rules. Group health plans often vary the financial requirements and treatment limitations imposed on benefits based on whether the treatment is provided on an inpatient, outpatient, or emergency basis; whether the provider is or is not a member of the plan's network; or whether the benefit is specifically for a prescription drug.

Under the MHPAEA regulations, the benefits provided under a plan are grouped into six classifications:

1. Inpatient, in-network
2. Inpatient, out-of-network
3. Outpatient, in-network
4. Outpatient, out-of-network
5. Emergency care
6. Prescription drugs

The parity requirements for financial requirements and treatment limitations are applied on a classification-by-classification basis. And the six classifications set forth in the regulations are the only classification that can be used for purposes of the parity requirements. For example, a plan may provide lower copayments (a financial requirement) for treatment by a primary care physician than for treatment by a specialist. However, the regulations do not allow the separate classification of generalists and specialists for purposes of applying the parity requirements.

Similarly, a plan may provide different types of financial requirements and treatment limitations. For example, these different types may include copayments, coinsurance, annual visit limits and episode visits. Moreover, plans often apply more than one financial requirement or treatment limitation to particular benefits. Under the MHPAEA regulations, in determining parity a financial requirement or treatment limitation must be compared only to financial requirements or treatment limitations of the same type within a benefit classification. For example, copayments are compared only to other copayments, annual visit limits to other annual visit limits, and so on; conversely, copayments are not compared to coinsurance, and annual visit limits are not compared to episode visit limits.

Financial requirements and treatment limitations may also vary by magnitude. For example, a plan may impose a $20 copayment or a $30 copayment depending on the benefit involved. Under the regulations, the "level" of a type of financial requirement or treatment limitation (such as a dollar percentage or day or visit amount) will also come into play in applying the parity requirements.

> **Practice Pointer.** Under the regulations, if a plan provides any benefits for a mental health condition or substance use disorder, benefits must be provided for that condition or disorder in each classification for which any medical/surgical benefits are provided. However, the regulations do not require an expansion of the range of mental health conditions or substance use disorders covered under the plan. If, for example, a plan does not offer benefits for medical/surgical benefits on an outpatient, out-of-network basis, there is no requirement to provide benefits for mental health conditions or substance use disorders on an outpatient, out-of-network basis.

Parity requirements for financial incentives and quantitative treatment limitations. The first step in applying the parity requirements to financial incentive and quantitative treatment limits is to determine whether a requirement or limitation applies to "substantially all" medical/surgical benefits in a classification. A financial requirement or quantitative treatment limit applies to substantially all medical/surgical benefits in a classification if it applies to two-thirds of the benefits in that classification.

If a type of financial requirement or quantitative treatment limit does not apply to at least two-thirds of medical/surgical benefits in a classification, that type of requirement or limit cannot apply to mental health or substance use disorder benefits in that classification.

The second step is to determine if a financial requirement or quantitative treatment limit is the "predominant" requirement or limitation for that classification.

If only a single level of a type of financial requirement or quantitative treatment limitation applies to at least two-thirds of medical/surgical benefits in a classification, this analysis is simple. That type and level is the predominant requirement or limit for the classification.

If, however, a financial requirement or quantitative treatment limitation has multiple levels and no single level applies to at least two-thirds of the medical/surgical benefits in the classification, the analysis is trickier.

If a single level of a financial requirement or quantitative treatment limitation applies to more than one-half the medical/surgical benefits subject to the requirement in a classification, that level is predominant. Consequently the plan cannot apply that requirement or limitation to mental health or substance use disorder benefits at a more restrictive level.

If no single level applies to more than one-half the medical/surgical requirements, the plan can combine levels (starting with the most restrictive level and working down) until it passes the one-half mark. The *least restrictive* level within the combined levels is then the predominant requirement or limit for the classification.

Example. For outpatient, in-network medical surgical benefits, a plan imposes five different copayment levels. Based on projected plan payments and costs, it determines that a $10 copayment applies to 25 percent of medical/surgical benefits, a $15 copayment to 25 percent, a $20 copayment to 37.5 percent, and a $50 copayment to 12.5 percent. Beginning with the highest $50 copayment levels, the plan combines levels and determines that the three highest levels—$50, $20, and $15—apply to more than one-half the medical/surgical benefits. Thus, the plan may not impose any copayment on outpatient, in-network mental health or substance use disorder benefits that is more than the least restrictive $15 copayment in the combined levels.

However, to simplify things, the plan can simply treat the *least restrictive* of all the levels as predominant. Thus, in the above example, the plan could skip the combination process and treat the least restrictive $10 copayment level as the maximum copayment for mental health or substance use disorder benefits.

If a plan provides benefits for more than one coverage unit with different levels of financial requirements or quantitative treatment limitations within a classification of benefits, the predominant level of a particular requirement or limitation must be determined separately for each coverage unit. For example, a plan with different deductibles for self-only and family coverage must determine the predominant level of the deductible for self-only coverage separately from the predominant level for family coverage.

Cumulative financial requirements or quantitative treatment limitations. Although copayments and coinsurance generally apply separately to each expense, other financial requirements (most notably, deductibles) accumulate as expenses are incurred.

The preamble to the MHPAEA regulations notes that the law itself is not clear on whether parity requires that medical/surgical and mental health or substance use disorder benefits must be subject to a single combined deductible or whether a plan can have separate but equal deductibles for each type of expense.

The regulations resolve this ambiguity in favor of single combined deductibles or other accumulating financial requirements or quantitative treatment limitations. For example, a plan cannot impose a $250 deductible on medical/surgical benefits and a separate $250 deductible on mental health or substance use disorder benefits. However, the plan can impose a combined $500 deductible on all benefits.

Prescription drug benefits. Plans that offer prescription drug benefits often impose different financial requirements for different tiers of drugs. The placement of a drug in a tier is generally based on factors that have nothing to do with whether the drug is usually prescribed for medical/surgical conditions or a mental health or substance use disorder. Consequently, the regulations provide that if a plan imposes different levels of financial requirements on different tiers of drugs based on reasonable factors (such as cost, efficacy, generic versus brand name, and mail order versus pharmacy), without regard to whether a drug is generally prescribed for medical/surgical or mental health or substance disorder, the plan will satisfy the parity requirements.

Parity requirements for nonquantitative treatment limitations. Plans typically impose a variety of limits that impact the scope or duration of benefits under the plan, but that are not expressed numerically. Under the MHPAEA regulations, these nonquantitative treatment limitations must also satisfy parity requirements. [26 C.F.R. § 54.9812-1T(c)(4); 29 C.F.R. § 2590.712(c)(4); 45 C.F.R. § 146.136(c)(4)]

Examples of nonquantitative treatment limitations include:

- Medical management standards limiting or excluding benefits based on medical necessity or medical appropriateness, or based on whether the treatment is experimental or investigative;
- Formulary design for prescription drugs;
- Standards for provider admission to participate in a network, including reimbursement rates;
- Plan methods for determining usual, customary, and reasonable charges;
- Refusal to pay for higher-cost therapies until it can be shown that a lower-cost therapy is not effective (also known as fail-first policies or step therapy protocols); and
- Exclusions based on failure to complete a course of treatment.

The regulations generally prohibit the imposition of any nonquantitative treatment limitation on mental health or substance use disorder benefits unless the factors used in applying the limitation to mental health or substance use disorder benefits are comparable to, and applied no more stringently than the factors used in applying the limitations to medical/surgical benefits.

Example. A plan requires prior approval that a course of treatment is medically necessary both in the case of medical/surgical and mental health and substance use disorders. If prior approval is not obtained for medical/surgical treatments, the plan reduces the otherwise applicable benefit by 25 percent. However, no benefits are paid for mental health or substance use disorder treatments that do not have prior approval. Result: The plan violates the parity requirements. Although the same nonquantitative treatment limitation—medical necessity—applies to both types of benefits, the penalty for failure to obtain prior approval for mental health or substance use disorder treatments is not comparable to the penalty for failure to obtain prior approval for medical/surgical treatments.

The preamble to the regulations emphasizes that this means the limitations must actually be applied in an even-handed manner. For example, if a claims administrator has discretion to approve benefits for treatment based on medical necessity, and that discretion is routinely used to approve medical/surgical benefits while denying mental health or substance use disorder benefits (and clinically approved standards of care do not justify the difference), the use of discretion violates the parity requirements. On the other hand, the preamble acknowledges that different illnesses and injuries require different review and different care. Therefore, the mere fact of different results does not mean that a limitation does not comply with parity.

In some cases, a plan may coordinate benefits under a group health plan with mental health or substance use disorder benefits offered through an employee assistance program (EAP). In general, the provision of mental health or substance use disorder benefits by an EAP in addition to benefits offered by a group health plan will not violate the parity requirements. However, requiring participants to exhaust their EAP benefits—making the EAP a gatekeeper—before they are eligible for benefits under the health plan is a nonquantitative treatment limitation subject to the parity requirements. Therefore, unless a comparable requirement applies to medical/surgical benefits (whether or not through an EAP), the requirement cannot be applied to mental health or substance use disorder benefits.

Disclosure requirements. The MHPAEA imposes two new disclosure requirements for group health plans and health insurance coverage offered in connection with a group health plan.

Medical necessity determinations. The criteria for medical necessity determinations with respect to mental health or substance use disorder benefits must be made available to any current or potential participant, beneficiary, or contracting provider on request.

Benefit denials. The reason for any denial of reimbursement or payment for services for mental health or substance use disorder benefits must be made available to the participant or beneficiary. For plans subject to ERISA, this disclosure must be made in a form and manner consistent with the ERISA claims procedure regulations for group health plans (see chapter 2). For plans not subject to ERISA, the disclosure must be provided within a reasonable time and in a reasonable manner. Compliance with the ERISA claims procedure regulations will satisfy that standard.

[26 C.F.R. § 54.9812-1T(d); 29 C.F.R. § 2590.712(d); 45 C.F.R. § 146.136(d)]

Benefits for Maternity, Newborns, and Mothers

Q 5:115   Does federal law require a medical plan to offer maternity benefits?

There is no federal requirement that group health plans cover maternity benefits; however, several federal laws do regulate the manner in which any maternity benefits contained in a group health plan may be structured, as follows.

1. Title VII of the Civil Rights Act of 1964, as amended by the Pregnancy Discrimination Act of 1978, mandates that covered employers treat pregnancy in the same way as all other conditions. If employees have a choice of several health plans or options, each option must comply with

this rule, regardless of who pays the premiums. Female employees cannot be forced to pay for more expensive dependent or family coverage to obtain maternity coverage. Equal treatment means that no separate deductibles may be allowed or maximum recoverable amounts imposed. Reimbursement must be provided for pregnancy-related conditions in the same way (for example, a fixed-dollar amount or a percentage of reasonable and customary charges) as for other conditions. Hospitalization and office visits (including prenatal and postnatal visits) must be covered on the same basis as for other conditions. However, plans are not required to cover expenses for abortions except where the life of the mother would be endangered if the fetus were carried to term and in cases where there are complications arising from an abortion (see Q 5:116).

2. Pregnancy-related conditions of nonspouse dependents are not required to be covered as long as the plan excludes the pregnancy-related conditions of nonspouse dependents of male and female employees equally. [42 U.S.C. § 2000e(k); EEOC Reg. Pt. 1604, App. Qs & As 21, 23–30]

3. HIPAA prohibits a group health plan from including pregnancy in any preexisting-condition exclusion period limit (see Q 5:55).

4. The Newborns' and Mothers' Health Protection Act of 1996 specifies a minimum hospital stay for newborns and mothers and invalidates pre-certification or authorization requirements for mandated minimum stays (see Q 5:118).

2010 Health Reform Act. Starting in 2014, large employers subject to the employer responsibility requirements must provide "minimum essential benefits" to their employees or pay and excise tax for failure to do so. In addition, starting in 2014, insurers in the small group market must provide coverage for minimum essential benefits. The Secretary of Health and Human Services is directed to define what constitutes essential benefits. However, such benefits must include maternity and newborn care. See chapter 3 for a discussion of these requirements, including their application to grandfathered group health plans.

Q 5:116   Does federal law require group health plans to cover abortions?

Yes, in some cases. Title VII of the Civil Rights Act of 1964, as amended by the Pregnancy Discrimination Act of 1978, does require that health insurance benefits be provided for abortions, but only when the pregnancy threatens the life of the mother if the fetus were carried to term. Medical complications arising from abortion, such as excessive hemorrhaging, must also be covered. (See chapter 19 for further discussion of Title VII.) [42 U.S.C. § 2000e(k); EEOC Reg. Pt. 1604, App. Qs & As 35–37]

2010 Health Reform Act. The 2010 Health Reform Act specifically provides that qualified plans to be offered through state-based health insurance exchanges (see chapter 3) cannot be required to cover abortions (except as discussed above). If a plan does offer coverage for abortion services, premiums for such coverage must be paid separately and benefits must be accounted for separately. A state can elect to prohibit abortion coverage in qualified plans offered through the state's exchange if the state enacts a law to provide such a prohibition. [PPACA § 1303 as amended by PPACA § 10104]

Q 5:117   Does federal law require group health plans to cover prescription contraceptives?

There is no federal mandate that group health plans cover prescription contraceptives or contraceptive devices. However, in an administrative decision, the Equal Employment Opportunity Commission (EEOC) held that an employer's failure to provide health insurance coverage for prescription contraceptives while covering a number of other preventive drugs, devices, and services violated Title VII of the Civil Rights Act of 1964, as amended by the Pregnancy Discrimination Act (PDA). [EEOC Decision (Dec. 14, 2000)]

According to the EEOC, the PDA requires equal treatment of women "affected by pregnancy, childbirth, or related medical conditions" in all aspects of employment, including the receipt of fringe benefits. Moreover, the Supreme Court has held that the PDA protects women from discrimination because they have the ability to become pregnant. [International Union, UAW v. Johnson Controls, 499 U.S. 187 (1991)] Contraception is a means by which a woman controls her ability to become pregnant. Therefore, the EEOC says, the PDA's prohibition on discrimination against women based on their ability to become pregnant necessarily includes a prohibition on discrimination related to a woman's use of contraception. Under the PDA, for example, an employer cannot discharge an employee from her job because she uses contraceptives. Similarly, an employer health insurance plan cannot discriminate by denying benefits for prescription contraceptives if it provides benefits for comparable drugs and devices.

The EEOC noted that the health plan at issue in its ruling provided coverage for a wide variety of preventive measures, including vaccinations, prescription drugs to prevent the development of medical conditions such as high blood pressure or cholesterol, preventive care for children and adults, and preventive dental care. In addition, it covered surgical sterilizations, as well as Viagra for patients who complained about decreased sexual interest or energy. Therefore, the EEOC concluded that the employer was required to cover prescription contraceptives in the same way.

Specifically, the EEOC said the employer must cover the expenses of prescription contraceptives to the same extent and on the same terms that it covers other types of drugs, devices, and preventive care. Moreover, the employer must also offer the same coverage for contraceptive-related outpatient services that is offered for other outpatient services. Thus, if a woman visits a doctor to obtain a prescription for contraceptives, she must be given the same coverage that would apply to a doctor visit for other preventive or health maintenance services. On the other hand, if the plan limits coverage for comparable drugs or services (for example, by imposing maximum benefit caps), those limits may also be applied to contraception.

Finally, the EEOC said the plan must cover the full range of prescription contraceptive choices. Because a woman's health needs may change—and because different women may need different prescription contraceptives—the plan must cover all of the available options for prescription contraception. Moreover, the employer must include contraception coverage in each health plan choice it offers to employees.

Since the EEOC ruling, at least two court cases have held that an employer's selective exclusion of contraceptives, while covering other preventive medications, violated the PDA. [Erickson v. Bartell Drug Co., 141 F. Supp. 2d 1266 (D. Wash. 2001); *In re* Union Pac. R.R. Employment Practices Litig., 378 F. Supp. 2d 1139 (D. Neb. 2005)] In addition, a U.S. district court denied an employer's motion to dismiss an employee's lawsuit, which claimed that the exclusion of coverage for prescription contraceptives under the employer's group health plan violated the PDA. According to the court, the employee's allegations were sufficient to state a claim for sex discrimination. Although the plan's exclusion was "facially neutral" in that it applied to all employees, it only burdened female employees because prescription contraceptives are available only to women. [Colley v. DaimlerChrysler Corp., 281 F. Supp. 979 (E.D. Mo. 2003)]

However, one of these cases has been overturned on appeal. The Eighth Circuit, which is the only appellate court to rule on this issue, held that a group health plan that excludes coverage for both male and female contraceptives (other than for medically necessary noncontraceptive purposes) does not violate the PDA.

According to the Eighth Circuit, the district court incorrectly characterized the plan's policy as denying prescription contraception for coverage only for women when, in fact, the plan excludes all types of contraceptives for both men and women. However, the court did acknowledge that prescription contraceptives are currently available only for women.

Moreover, the court said the PDA does not require contraceptive coverage because contraception is not related to pregnancy, being used only prior to pregnancy. The court dismissed the EEOC's position as "unpersuasive," noting that the EEOC administrative decision compared prescription contraceptives to a broad spectrum of other preventive measures without citing a basis for doing so. In addition, the court questioned the consistency of the EEOC's position inasmuch as the administrative decision came 22 years after enactment of the PDA. [Standridge v. Union Pac. R.R. Co., 479 F.3d 936 (8th Cir. 2007)]

Practice Pointer. While the Eighth Circuit's decision protects employers within its jurisdiction (North Dakota, South Dakota, Minnesota, Nebraska, Iowa, Missouri, and Arkansas), employers in other states that do not cover prescription contraception still face potential lawsuits. Therefore, they may want to gauge the cost of adding such coverage against the costs of litigation. In addition, employers should also check state law. At least 30 states have passed legislation mandating some level of coverage for contraceptives. Most of these states require health insurance policies that cover prescription drugs to also cover prescription contraceptives. A number of states include exemptions for employers who object to contraceptive coverage for religious reasons. Other states exempt "religious employers." However, religious employers do not necessarily include every organization with a religious connection.

California's Women's Contraception Equity Act, which requires group health plans that provide coverage for prescription drugs to also cover female contraceptives, exempts religious employers. Under the law, religious employers are defined as any entity that (1) includes religious values, (2) primarily employs persons who share the same religious tenets, (3) primarily serves persons who share the religious tenets of the entity, and (4) is a nonprofit organization. However, according to the California Supreme Court, that definition does not encompass Catholic Charities, which challenged the law. The court concluded that Catholic Charities of Sacramento, Inc. did not satisfy any of the exemption criteria and was essentially a "secular" organization. Most of the organization's employees were non-Catholic and their work primarily involved providing food, shelter, and clothing to the poor, rather than promoting religious tenets. The U.S. Supreme Court declined to review the state court decision. [Catholic Charities of Sacramento, Inc. v. Superior Court, 32 Cal. 4th 527 (Cal. Sup. Ct.), *cert. denied by* Catholic Charities of Sacramento, Inc. v. California, 125 S. Ct. 53 (2004)].

Q 5:118   Can a group health plan limit hospitalization benefits for newborns and mothers or require that such benefits be authorized or precertified as a condition of coverage?

No. The Newborns' and Mothers' Health Protection Act of 1996 (NMHPA), which amended ERISA to add a new Section 711 (TRA '97 subsequently amended the Code to add new Section 9811 containing parallel provisions), requires that group health plans and health insurance issuers (insurance carriers, HMOs, and so on) providing coverage that includes hospital lengths of stay cannot:

1. Restrict benefits for any hospital length of stay in connection with childbirth for the mother or newborn child to less than 48 hours following a normal vaginal delivery or to less than 96 hours following a cesarean section; or

2. Require that a provider obtain authorization from the plan or the issuer for prescribing any length of stay required by item 1 above.

These requirements do not apply in any case where the decision to discharge the mother or her newborn child prior to the otherwise applicable mandatory minimum length of stay is made by the attending provider in consultation with the mother.

Final regulations under the NMHPA issued in 2008 make it clear that the hospital stay begins at the time of delivery (or the time of the last delivery in the case of multiple births) if the delivery occurs in the hospital. In the case of a delivery outside the hospital, the hospital stay begins at the time of admittance as a hospital inpatient in connection with childbirth. Under the regulations, whether a hospital stay is in connection with childbirth is a medical decision to be made by the attending medical provider. For example, the regulations indicate the hospital admission of a woman who gives birth at home and subsequently begins bleeding excessively would be in connection with childbirth so that the hospital length of stay requirements would apply. By contrast, the hospital admission of a newborn who is born at home and subsequently develops pneumonia would not be in connection with childbirth and would not trigger the length of stay requirements. [29 C.F.R. § 2590.711]

The NMHPA also provides that a group health plan cannot:

1. Deny the mother or her newborn eligibility or continued eligibility to enroll in or renew coverage under the terms of the plan solely to avoid the act's requirements;

2. Make monetary rebates or payments to the mother to encourage her to accept less than the statutory minimum maternity hospital length-of-stay benefit;

3. Provide monetary or other incentives to the attending provider to induce him or her to provide care inconsistent with the act's requirements; or

4. Restrict benefits for any portion of a hospital length of stay required by the act in a manner that is less favorable than any preceding portion of such stay.

Notwithstanding the above restrictions, ERISA Section 711 and Code Section 9811 do not

1. Require that a participant or beneficiary give birth in a hospital or stay in a hospital for a fixed period of time following the birth of her child;

2. Prevent a group health plan or issuer from imposing deductibles, coinsurance, or other cost-sharing mechanisms in relation to benefits for hospital length of stay relating to childbirth for a mother or newborn child, except that cost sharing for the mandatory minimum hospital stay cannot be greater than for any preceding portion of such stay; or

3. Prevent a group health plan or health insurance issuer from negotiating the level and type of reimbursement for care provided in accordance with new ERISA Section 711 and Code Section 9811. *Covered group health plans.* Group health plans are covered regardless of the size of the sponsoring employer or the number of plan participants.

Exception for certain state insurance coverage. The law contains an exception for health insurance coverage offered by health insurance issuers (insurance companies, HMOs, and so forth) subject to certain state laws concerning health insurance coverage if (1) the state law requires at least the same minimum hospital stays; (2) such coverage is provided for maternity and pediatric care in accordance with guidelines established by the American College of Obstetricians and Gynecologists, the American Academy of Pediatrics, or other established professional medical associations; or (3) the law requires that hospital length of stay relating to maternity care be left to the decision of the provider in consultation with the mother.

Penalty for violations. The Code Section 4980D excise tax (see Q 5:13) applies to violations of these rules. ERISA's general enforcement provisions also apply to ERISA-covered plans. [ERISA § 711, added by the Newborns' and Mothers' Health Protection Act of 1996; I.R.C. § 9811, added by TRA '97]

Q 5:119   Does federal law permit group health plans to reduce or eliminate coverage for pediatric vaccines?

If the particular group health plan was in effect May 1, 1993, ERISA Section 609(d) and Code Section 4980B(f)(1) require that the plan may not reduce its coverage of the costs of pediatric vaccines below the level of coverage provided on May 1, 1993.

Note. Although anti-cutback provisions are common in the rules governing retirement plans, the pediatric vaccine provision represents the first time Congress elected to permanently vest medical coverage at a particular level. If the plan had coverage for pediatric vaccines on May 1, 1993, that coverage cannot be cut back or diminished during the life of the group health plan.

Penalty for noncompliance. The COBRA excise tax penalty of $110 per day applies to violations. A limit of the lesser of (1) 10 percent of the aggregate amount paid or incurred by the employer (or predecessor employer) during the preceding taxable year for group health plans or (2) $500,000 applies to violations that are due to reasonable cause and not to willful neglect. However, the excise tax apparently is unlimited if the violation was due to willful neglect or is not due to reasonable cause. (See chapter 6 for a detailed discussion of the COBRA excise tax.) [ERISA § 609(d)]

Benefits Under the Women's Health and Cancer Rights Act

Q 5:120   What is the Women's Health and Cancer Rights Act?

The Women's Health and Cancer Rights Act of 1998 (WHCRA) provides important protections for breast cancer patients who elect breast reconstruction in connection with a mastectomy. The WHCRA amends ERISA and requires all group health plans, insurance companies, individual insurance policies, and HMOs that provide coverage for medical and surgical benefits for mastectomies to provide coverage for the following:

1. All stages of reconstruction of the breast on which the mastectomy was performed;

2. Surgery for reconstruction of the other breast to produce a symmetrical appearance; and

3. Prostheses and treatment of physical complications at all stages of the mastectomy, including lymphedemas.

The DOL and the HHS have issued general guidance on WHCRA requirements in question-and-answer format. The guidance also includes a model annual notice that can be used to comply with the act.

Q 5:121   Under WHCRA, may group health plans, insurance companies, or HMOs impose deductibles or coinsurance requirements for reconstructive surgery in connection with a mastectomy?

Yes, but only if the deductibles and coinsurance are consistent with those established for other benefits under the plan or coverage.

Q 5:122   What are the notice requirements under the WHCRA?

All group health plans and their insurance issuers that offer mastectomy coverage are subject to two notice requirements under the WHCRA.

1. An initial notice describing the benefits required under the WHCRA must be provided upon enrollment in the plan.
2. An annual notice of WHCRA benefits must be furnished to plan participants. A plan or health insurance issuer satisfies the annual requirement if the plan delivers the annual notice any time during a plan year. The DOL guidance clarifies that a plan or health insurance issuer does not have to provide a participant with an annual notice for the plan year during which that participant enrolled if the participant was provided the appropriate notice when enrolling in the plan.

These notices must be delivered in accordance with the DOL's disclosure regulations applicable to furnishing SPDs (see chapter 2). [29 C.F.R. § 2520-104b-1] For example, the notices may be provided by first-class mail or any other means of delivery prescribed in the regulation. It is the view of the DOL that a separate notice would be required to be furnished to a group health plan beneficiary where the last known address of the beneficiary is different from the last known address of the covered participant.

The notices must describe the benefits that the WHCRA requires the group health plan and its insurance companies or HMOs to cover. The notice must indicate that, in the case of a participant or beneficiary who is receiving benefits under the plan in connection with a mastectomy and who elects breast reconstruction, the coverage will be provided in a manner determined in consultation with the attending physician and the patient for the following:

1. Reconstruction of the breast on which the mastectomy was performed;
2. Surgery and reconstruction of the other breast to produce a symmetrical appearance; and
3. Prostheses and treatment of physical complications at all stages of the mastectomy, including lymphedemas.

The notice must also describe any deductibles and coinsurance limitations applicable to such coverage. Under the WHCRA, coverage of breast reconstruction benefits may be subject only to deductibles and coinsurance limitations consistent with those established for other benefits under the plan or coverage.

Plans that do not use enrollment notices to meet the annual notice requirement may distribute annually a notice (1) informing participants of the availability of benefits for the treatment of mastectomy-related services, including reconstructive surgery, prosthesis, and lymphedema under the plan, and (2) containing information on how to obtain a detailed description of the mastectomy-related benefits available under the plan.

To avoid duplication of notices, a group health plan or its insurance companies or HMOs can satisfy the WHCRA's notice requirements by contracting with another party that provides the required notice. For example, in the case of a group health plan funded through an insurance policy, the group health plan will satisfy the notice requirements with respect to a participant or beneficiary if the insurance company or HMO actually provides the notice that includes the information required by the WHCRA. [ERISA § 713, 29 U.S.C. § 1185; 42 U.S.C. § 300 gg-51]

Qualified Medical Child Support Orders

Q 5:123 Does a group health plan have to honor a qualified medical child support order?

Yes. ERISA Section 609(a), as amended by the Child Support Performance and Incentive Act of 1998 (CSPIA), requires a group health plan to honor a qualified medical child support order (QMCSO) submitted to the plan and pay benefits to:

1. Any child who is an "alternate recipient" specified therein;
2. The child's custodial parent or guardian who incurs covered expenses on the child's behalf; or
3. An official of a state or political subdivision whose name and address has been substituted for that of any alternate payee in the order. [ERISA § 609(a); 29 U.S.C. § 1169(a), as amended by § 5613 of the Balanced Budget Act of 1997]

The HHS and the DOL have issued regulations on state implementation of the CSPIA. The regulations also govern the administration by employers and health plan administrators of QMCSOs. [65 Fed. Reg. 82,127 (Dec. 27, 2000)]

The rules incorporate a model national medical-support notice (NMSN) that provides a uniform method of informing employers about the need to enroll children of noncustodial parents in employer-sponsored health care plans. It includes instructions for employers that receive the notice but do not sponsor health plans. In addition to including the NMSN, the DOL rule implements an amendment to ERISA Section 609(a) made by Section 401 of the CSPIA. ERISA Section 609(a), as amended, provides that each ERISA-governed group plan shall provide benefits in accordance with the applicable requirements of any QMCSO.

The DOL's Employee Benefits Security Administration (EBSA) has also issued a Compliance Guide for Qualified Medical Support Orders, which provides information in the form of questions and answers about QMCSOs and NMSNs as well as other resources relating to medical care for children. The publication is available on EBSA's Web site at *www.dol.gov/ebsa* under Publications.

> **Practice Pointer.** The DOL regulations make it clear that a plan is required to provide only those benefits that it provides to any dependent of a participant who is enrolled in the plan and any benefits that are necessary to satisfy state law requirements. For example, a plan is not required to honor a QMCSO if it does not provide dependent coverage.

Q 5:124   When is a court order a QMCSO?

A medical child support order that meets certain statutory conditions is a QMCSO. A medical child support order is:

1. Any court judgment, decree, or order (including approval of a settlement agreement) issued by a court of competent jurisdiction under a state's domestic relations or community property law or

2. A judgment, decree, order, or administrative notice, issued through an administrative process established under state law and having the effect of law under the applicable state's law that (a) provides for child support or health benefit coverage for a child of a participant in a group health plan and (b) relates to benefits under such a plan.

The medical child support order is "qualified" (i.e., it is a QMCSO) if it (1) recognizes an existing right, creates a right, or assigns the child the right to receive (as an "alternate recipient") benefits for which a participant or beneficiary is eligible under the group health plan and (2) contains the additional information described in Q 5:125.

Court and administrative judgments, decrees, and orders, as well as administrative notices issued under certain state laws relating to medical child support, also are QMCSOs. [ERISA § 609(a)(2), 29 U.S.C. § 1169(a)(2), as amended by § 5612 of the Balanced Budget Act of 1997]

Q 5:125   What information will an employer receive in connection with a QMCSO?

A QMSCO will contain all of the following information:

- The name of the issuing agency
- The name and last known address of the participant
- The name and address of each alternate recipient (i.e., child of the participant for whom coverage is to be provided) or the name and address

of a state official or agency that has been substituted for the address of the alternative recipient

- A reasonable description of the type of coverage to be provided or an indication that all available coverage is to be provided
- The period to which the order applies

[ERISA § 609(a)(3), 29 U.S.C. § 1169(a)(3), as amended by § 5613 of the Balanced Budget Act of 1997]

> A QMCSO cannot require a group health plan to provide any type or form of benefit or option not otherwise available under the plan, except to the extent necessary to meet medical child support laws described in Section 1908 of the Social Security Act. [ERISA § 609(a)(4), 29 U.S.C. § 1169(a)(4)]

Practice Pointer. A properly completed NMSN, which will contain all of the above information, is deemed to be a QMCSO.

Q 5:126 To which group health plans does a QMCSO apply?

A QMCSO is treated as applying to each group health plan that has received the order and from which the participant or beneficiary is eligible to receive benefits. However, an order cannot require the plan to provide any type or form of benefit, or any option, not otherwise provided under the plan (except to the extent necessary to meet the requirements of a law relating to medical child support described in section 1908 of the Social Security Act). [ERISA § 609(a)(3), 29 U.S.C. § 1169(a)(3), as amended by § 5613 of the Balanced Budget Act of 1997]

Q 5:127 What are the plan administrator's responsibilities regarding a QMCSO?

ERISA requires a plan administrator to:

1. Adopt a written procedure for determining whether a court order meets the requirements of a QMCSO (the procedure must provide for the notification of each alternate recipient specified in the order to receive benefits and permit each such alternate recipient to designate a representative for receipt of notices);
2. Notify, immediately upon receipt of the court order, the participant and each alternate recipient listed in the order of the plan's procedure for determining whether the order is a QMCSO; and
3. Make the determination and notify the plan participant and each alternate recipient of its conclusion within a reasonable period after receiving the order.

[ERISA § 609(a)(5), 29 U.S.C. § 1169(a)(5), added by § 4301 of OBRA '93]

A plan fiduciary's responsibilities will be discharged to the extent of payments made pursuant to the fiduciary's determinations, provided that the fiduciary acts in accordance with ERISA's fiduciary standards in determining whether the court order is a valid QMCSO. [ERISA § 609(a)(6), 29 U.S.C. § 1169(a)(6), added by § 4301 of OBRA '93]

According to new compliance guidance from the DOL's Employee Benefits Security Administration (EBSA), plan administrators must determine whether a medical child support order is qualified within a reasonable period of time after receiving the order. What is a reasonable period will depend on the circumstances. For example, an order that is clear and complete when submitted should require less time to review than one that is incomplete or unclear. However, the national medical-support notice (NMSN) provisions contain separate, specific time limits on the processing of the Notice by employers and plan administrators (see Q 5:128). [DOL Compliance Guide for Qualified Medical Child Support Orders, which is available online at *http://www.dol.gov/ebsa/publications/qmcso.html*]

The DOL Compliance Guide also makes it clear that a plan administrator is *not* required to reject a medical child support order as not qualified simply because the order fails to include factual identifying information that is easily obtainable by the administrator. For example, the DOL points out that an order may misstate the names of the participant or alternate recipients, but the plan administrator can clearly determine the correct names; or an order may omit the addresses of the participant or alternate recipients, but the plan administrator's records include this information. In such a case, the plan administrator should supplement the order with the appropriate identifying information rather than reject the order as not qualified.

Practice Pointer. A properly completed NMSN is deemed to be a QMCSO.

Q 5:128　What must employers and plan administrators do upon receipt of a QMCSO?

The NMSN spells out the procedures to be followed by employers when an employee is subject to a QMCSO.

Part A of the NMSN, the Notice to Withhold for Health Care Coverage, identifies the employee and the child or children for whom coverage is to be provided. The first step is to determine whether the employee is eligible for dependent coverage under the plan. If so, the employer forwards Part B, the Medical Support Notice, to the plan administrator. If the employer does not offer dependent coverage or the employee is not eligible for such coverage, the employer must return the response portion of the form to the state agency with that information. The response portion of the form is also used to inform the agency if the employee no longer works for the employer or if the amounts required to be withheld for medical coverage exceed state or federal withholding limits.

Upon receipt of Part B from the employer, the plan administrator must enroll the child or children for the specified coverage. This enrollment must be made without regard to open enrollment restrictions.

If the employee is not currently enrolled in the plan and the plan offers various coverage options, a response portion of the form must be returned to inform the state agency of the options from which to elect coverage. The response portion is also used to inform the agency if the plan administrator determines that the NMSN is not a QMCSO. The plan administrator must specify the reasons for that determination.

The employer and plan administrator generally have 40 days to act after receiving an NMSN. However, they are required to respond more quickly, if reasonable.

Q 5:129   What if an order names an employee who is not enrolled in the plan?

According to the new DOL compliance guidance, an employee who is eligible to enroll is a participant in the plan and the order is a medical child support order. [ERISA §§ 3(7), 609(a)(1); DOL Compliance Guide for Qualified Medical Child Support Orders] The plan administrator must determine whether the order is qualified and, if so, provide coverage to the child. If the employee must be enrolled in the plan as a condition for covering his or her dependents, the plan must enroll both the employee and the child.

The DOL takes the position that once a determination is made that an order is qualified, the child (and the employee, if necessary) must be enrolled as of the earliest possible date following such determination. Thus, if an insured plan only adds new participants or beneficiaries as of the first day of each month, the plan would be required to provide coverage to an alternate recipient as of the first day of the first month following the determination that the order is qualified.

According to the DOL, an employee named in a medical child support order who has not yet satisfied a plan's waiting period for enrollment (e.g., a requirement that the employee be employed for a certain number of days, or work a certain number of hours before being eligible for benefits) is also a participant in the plan. [ERISA §§ 3(7), 609(a)(1)] Therefore, upon determining that a medical child support order is qualified, the plan administrator must implement procedures to ensure that the child will begin receiving benefits once the employee satisfies the waiting period.

If medical child support is being implemented by means of an NMSN, a waiting period will affect the procedures for enrollment of the child named in the notice. (See Q 5:128 for an explanation of the general procedures for handling an NMSN.) Assuming the NMSN otherwise meets the requirements of a QMCSO, the procedures are as follows:

- For short waiting periods (90 days or less remaining at the time the plan administrator receives Part B from the employer), the plan administrator should qualify the NMSN and wait until the expiration of the period to enroll the child and notify the employer of the need, if any, to begin withholding from the employee's wages to provide for the child's coverage.

- For waiting periods of more than 90 days or when the period is measured by other means (e.g., hours worked), the plan administrator should inform the employer of the waiting period and wait for notification from the employer of the employee's satisfaction of the waiting period before enrolling the child.

Q 5:130   If a plan provides benefits solely through an HMO or other managed care organization, is the plan required to provide comparable benefits to a child who lives outside the HMO's service area?

No. A medical child support order is not qualified if it requires a plan to provide a type or form of benefit that is not otherwise available under the plan. Requiring a plan that provides benefits solely through a limited-area HMO to provide benefits to a child residing outside the HMO's service area (i.e., on a fee-for-service basis or other basis) would be requiring the plan to provide a form of benefit that the plan does not ordinarily provide. On the other hand, if the child is able to travel to the HMO's service area for medical care, the plan would be required to provide benefits to the child. [DOL Compliance Guide for Qualified Medical Child Support Orders; ERISA § 609(a)(4)]

Q 5:131   May a plan provide benefits to a child of a participant pursuant to a medical child support order that is *not* a qualified order?

Yes. According to DOL compliance guidance, there is nothing in ERISA to prevent a plan from providing coverage pursuant to the terms of any medical child support order, regardless of whether the order satisfies the qualification requirements. However, the terms of the plan itself might prohibit coverage of the child for other reasons—for example, the child does not reside with the participant or is not claimed as a dependent on the participant's federal income tax return. Bear in mind, however, that those plan restrictions will not apply in the case of an order that *is* a qualified order. [ERISA §§ 609(a)(2), (a)(4)]

Q 5:132   What type of coverage must be provided to a child under a QMCSO?

According to the DOL, a QMCSO should provide a coverage description that enables the plan administrator to determine which of the available options and levels of coverage should be provided to the child. For instance, if an order requires that a child be provided any coverage available under the plan, the plan administrator would determine what types of coverage are available under the plan (e.g., major medical, hospitalization, dental) and provide that coverage to the alternate recipient. However, if the plan offers more than one type of coverage (e.g., both an HMO and a fee-for-service option), the order should make clear which type of coverage should be provided or how the choice is to be made. If the order is unclear, the plan's procedures may direct the administrator to contact the submitting party or may provide other selection methods, similar to those established for the processing of NMSNs (see Q 5:128). If no procedures are indicated in the order, the administrator may have to reject the order.

It is the view of the DOL that a child receiving coverage under a QMCSO should be treated as a dependent of the participant under the plan. Therefore, if a plan provides that a dependent of the participant must be enrolled under the same coverage and with the same options as the participant, a child receiving coverage under a QMCSO must generally be enrolled under the same coverage and with the same options as those of the participant. However, if the QMCSO specifies that a child is to receive a particular level of coverage or option, which is available under the plan, but the participant is not enrolled in that coverage or has not selected that option, the plan may be required to change the participant's enrollment to the extent necessary to provide the specified coverage to the child. [ERISA § 609(a)(7)(QA); DOL Compliance Guide for Qualified Medical Child Support Orders]

Q 5:133   Does a group health plan have to provide any information to a custodial parent or state child support enforcement agency before the plan receives a medical child support order?

According to the DOL's Compliance Guide, Congress intended custodial parents and state child support enforcement agencies to have access to plan and participant benefit information needed to prepare a QMCSO. Information necessary for that purpose would include the summary plan description (SPD), relevant plan documents, and a description of particular coverage options, if any, that have been selected by the participant.

The DOL believes that Congress did not intend to require parties seeking coverage of a child to first submit a medical child support order to the plan in order to establish rights to information in connection with a child support proceeding. However, a plan administrator may require such disclosures upon receiving information that reasonably establishes that the disclosure request is being made in connection with a child support proceeding. A disclosure request from a state child support enforcement agency should be assumed to be made in connection with a child support proceeding. [DOL Compliance Guide for Qualified Medical Child Support Orders]

Q 5:134   If the plan requires additional employee contributions for coverage of a child under a QMCSO, who is responsible for the payments?

The order will ordinarily establish the obligations of the parties for the child's support. In most cases, the non-custodial parent who is a participant in a group health plan will be responsible for the payment of any costs associated with the provision of the coverage. Thus, the additional contributions will ordinarily be withheld from the participant's paychecks like other employee contributions.

If Federal or State withholding limitations prevent withholding the additional contributions from the employee's paycheck, the employer should notify the custodial parent, and the child support enforcement agency, if the agency is involved. Unless the employer is able to withhold the necessary contribution from the participant's paycheck, the plan is not required to extend coverage to the child. However, the custodial parent or the agency may be able to modify the amount of cash support to be provided, in order to enable the employer to withhold the required contribution to the plan. The participant may also voluntarily consent to the withholding of an amount otherwise in excess of applicable withholding limitations. [DOL Compliance Guide for Qualified Medical Child Support Orders]

Q 5:135   How should benefits for a child receiving coverage under a QMCSO be paid?

The plan should pay benefits to the child, the custodial parent, or the provider of health services to the child even if the plan terms require benefit payments to be made to the participant. In some instances, payment will be required to be made to the state child support enforcement or a Medicaid agency. [DOL Compliance Guide for Qualified Medical Child Support Orders; ERISA §§ 609(a)(8), (a)(9), and (b)(3); § 1908(a)(5) of the Social Security Act]

Q 5:136   May a group health plan impose preexisting-condition restrictions or exclusions on a child named in a QMCSO?

Under the 2010 Health Reform Act, effective for plan years beginning on or after September 23, 2010, a group health plan—including a grandfathered plan—cannot impose any preexisting-condition exclusion with respect to a child under age 19 [PHSA § 2704 as added by PPACA § 1201; PPACA § 1253 as amended by PPACA § 10103 and PPACA Reconciliation § 2301]

For prior plan years, a child named in a QMCSO is subject to the plan's generally applicable preexisting-condition restrictions or exclusions as permitted under the HIPAA requirements. However, the DOL takes the position that a group health plan's receipt of a medical child support order tolls the running of the 63-day break-in-coverage period for determining the child's creditable coverage (see Q 5:69). The time taken by the plan administrator to determine whether the medical child support order is qualified would not count toward a 63-day break. In addition, if the child had been previously covered under the plan, and the child's coverage was dropped by the participant in anticipation of divorce or separation, the DOL says that the period between the date the child's coverage is terminated and the date the plan administrator determines that an order is qualified would also not count as part of the 63-day period. [DOL Compliance Guide for Qualified Medical Child Support Orders]

Q 5:137   When may a plan cancel coverage for a child under a QMCSO?

A plan may cancel coverage for a child under a QMCSO at the same time and under the same conditions as it may cancel coverage for other dependents of participants under the plan. For instance, if the plan normally terminates coverage when a participant terminates employment, it can terminate coverage for a child covered pursuant to a QMCSO when the participant through whom the child is receiving coverage terminates employment. [DOL Compliance Guide for Qualified Medical Child Support Orders] A child covered under a QMSCO may, however, have the right to elect continuation coverage under the Consolidated Omnibus Budget Reconciliation Act (COBRA).

Q 5:138   Does a child covered by a group health plan pursuant to a QMCSO have any right to COBRA continuation coverage?

Yes. The IRS (which has jurisdiction over COBRA) has informed the DOL that a child covered pursuant to a QMCSO has the right to elect continuation coverage under COBRA, if the plan is subject to COBRA and if the child loses coverage as a result of a qualifying event. [DOL Compliance Guide for Qualified Medical Child Support Orders, Q 1-22.]

Q 5:139   Must rights associated with QMCSOs be disclosed in the group health plan's SPD?

Yes. The alternate payee's right to obtain a copy of the plan's QMCSO procedure and the right to receive benefits as an alternate payee if the order is in fact found to be a valid QMCSO are material information that should be fully disclosed in the SPD.

Q 5:140   What rights does the alternate recipient named in a QMCSO have?

An alternate recipient must be treated as a group health plan beneficiary for all ERISA purposes except Title I reporting and disclosure. For Title I reporting and disclosure purposes, the alternate recipient must be treated as a plan participant. [ERISA § 609(a)(7), 29 U.S.C. § 1169(a)(7), added by § 4301 of OBRA '93]

Practice Pointer. This enhanced status for reporting and disclosure purposes means that the plan must set up a procedure to assure that all alternate payees receive benefit communications (including, for example, annual enrollment materials) normally provided only to employees and COBRA continuees.

Q 5:141   How is a QMCSO enforced?

ERISA's regular enforcement provisions (see chapter 2) apply. States are also given a right to enforce compliance, and ERISA's preemption provisions do not apply to such state actions. [ERISA § 502(b)(6), 29 U.S.C. § 1144(b)(6), as amended by § 4301 of OBRA '93]

Medicare Secondary-Payer Rules

Q 5:142   Can medical coverage be reduced or terminated if an individual is eligible for Medicare?

The Social Security Act and Code Section 5000 contain numerous provisions prohibiting an employer from reducing or terminating medical coverage once an individual becomes eligible for Medicare. As a result, an employer's group health plan is required to be primary to Medicare. Below are listed the various Medicare-related restrictions that the Medicare secondary-payer (MSP) provisions of the Social Security Act impose on group health plans. These provisions are enforced by the Centers for Medicare and Medicaid Services (CMS) of the U.S. Department of Health and Human Services (HHS). (See Qs 5:143–5:149 for the details of each of these restrictions.)

Note. Severe penalties apply to violations of the Medicare secondary-payer requirements (see Q 5:150).

Practice Pointer. The DOL has issued an advisory opinion stating that plan fiduciaries must comply with the Medicare secondary-payer statute even if to do so would violate the terms of the group health plan.

The Medicare-related restrictions on group health plans are as follows:

1. *Aged employees.* A group health plan of an employer with at least 20 employees may not take into account the age-based Medicare entitlement of individuals age 65 or older in current employment status and must provide coverage to such individuals on the same conditions as to younger employees.

2. *Aged spouses of employees.* A group health plan of an employer with at least 20 employees may not take into account the age-based Medicare entitlement of spouses age 65 or older of an employee of any age in current employment status, and the spouse must be covered under the plan under the same conditions as spouses under age 65.

3. *End-stage renal disease.* The group health plan of an employer or employee organization of any size may not take into account the Medicare eligibility or entitlement of individuals who have end-stage renal disease (ESRD) and who are covered or seek to be covered under the plan. In addition, the group health plan may not differentiate in the benefits provided to such individuals on the basis of (a) the existence of ESRD or (b) the need for dialysis, or in any other manner. Coverage for such individuals must be primary to Medicare for 30 months, after which the medical coverage may be reduced or terminated unless another of the

Medicare rules prohibiting such a reduction or termination of benefits would apply. Under an exception to this ESRD rule, COBRA continuation of group health coverage is permitted to be terminated if, after electing COBRA continuation, the individual becomes entitled to (not merely eligible for) Medicare because of ESRD.

4. *Disability.* An employer participating in a large group health plan (as defined below) may not take into account the disability-based Medicare entitlement of any individual who is covered or seeks to be covered under the plan by virtue of current employment status.

5. *Financial incentives prohibited.* An employer may not attempt to shift the coverage burden to Medicare by providing financial or other incentives for Medicare-eligible individuals not to enroll in its group health plan (see Q 5:146).

6. *Duty to notify Medicare.* If an employer, insurer, underwriter, or third-party administrator learns that Medicare has mistakenly been the primary payer for services for which the third-party payer should be the primary payer, that employer, insurer, underwriter, or third-party administrator must provide detailed information to the Medicare intermediary or carrier that paid the claim (see Qs 5:153–5:157).

7. *Documentation requirement.* The CMS has the power to require plans to demonstrate that they have complied with the Medicare secondary-payer provisions and to require the submission of supporting documentation under penalty of perjury. If the CMS determines that the plan has failed to provide acceptable evidence or documentation of compliance with the Medicare secondary-payer requirements, it may determine that the plan is not in conformance and assess the penalty provided for in Code Section 5000 (see Q 5:150).

[42 C.F.R. § 114.112]

Group health plan. For this purpose, a *group health plan* is any arrangement made by one or more employers or employee organizations to provide health care directly or through other methods such as insurance or reimbursement to current or former employees, the employer, others associated or formerly associated with the employer in a business relationship, or their families that:

1. Is of, or contributed to by, one or more employers or employee organizations;

2. Provides for common administration if it involves more than one employer or employee organization; and

3. Provides substantially the same benefits or benefit options to all those enrolled.

This definition includes self-insured plans; plans of federal, state, and local governmental entities; and employee organization plans (e.g., union plans or employee health and welfare funds). It also includes employee-pay-all plans (offered under the auspices of one or more employers or employee organizations but receiving no financial contributions from them).

[42 U.S.C. § 411.101]

Large group health plan. For the purposes of the Medicare secondary-payer provisions, a *large group health plan* is a group health plan covering employees of either:

1. A single employer or employee organization that employed at least 100 full-time or part-time employees on 50 percent or more of its regular business days during the previous calendar year or

2. Two or more employers or employee organizations, at least one of which employed at least 100 full-time or part-time employees on 50 percent or more of its regular business days during the previous calendar year.

[42 U.S.C. § 411.101]

When applying any of the above minimum employee rules, controlled-group rules apply. [42 C.F.R. § 411.106]

MSP reporting. Starting in 2009, group health plans are required to identify situations in which the plans are or have been primary to Medicare and to submit the information to CMS [Pub. L. No. 110-173 amending 42 U.S.C. § 1395y(b)(7)] In the case of an insured plan, either the insurer or third-party administrator must gather information from the plan sponsor and plan participants to satisfy the reporting requirement. In the case of a self-insured plan, the plan administrator must satisfy the reporting requirement. The law authorizes the Secretary of HHS to specify the exact information that must be submitted and the form and manner of required reports, including how often reports must be submitted. The law imposes a hefty fine for noncompliance: $1,000 per day for each day of noncompliance for each individual for whom information should have been submitted.

The law also authorizes HHS to share information on Medicare entitlement and enrollment with group health plan insurers, third-party administrators, and fiduciaries. HHS is also authorized to share information gathered under the new reporting system as necessary for proper coordination of benefits. In keeping with this authorization, CMS will provide the reporting entities with Medicare entitlement information for those individuals in a plan who can be identified as Medicare beneficiaries. This data exchange is intended to assure that claims will be paid by the appropriate organization at first billing

MSP reporting began the third quarter of 2009. At that time, group health plans had to report Social Security numbers (SSNs) for all individuals whose initial health plan coverage began on or after January 1, 2009. Starting with the first quarter of 2010, reporting of SSNs is required for individuals whose coverage began before 2009. In the case of covered individuals who are enrolled in Medicare, reporting requirements include the individual's Medicare Health Insurance Claim Number (HICN) from the individual's Medicare Card.

Practice Pointer. The SSN and HCIN reporting requirements apply not only to covered employees, but also to spouses and dependents who are enrolled in an employer's group health plan. Consequently, employers should take steps to ensure that health plan enrollment forms collect the required numbers from new enrollees.

Q 5:143   When does a plan take into account Medicare entitlement or eligibility?

The regulations under the Social Security Act emphasize that Medicare entitlement (and for ESRD, Medicare eligibility) must not be "taken into account" by the plan. Actions that would constitute taking the Medicare entitlement into account include:

1. Failing to pay primary benefits to the extent required by law;
2. Offering coverage that is secondary to Medicare to individuals who are entitled to Medicare;
3. Terminating coverage because the individual has become entitled to Medicare, except as permitted under COBRA continuation provisions;
4. For a large group health plan, denying or terminating coverage because an individual is entitled to Medicare on the basis of disability while providing coverage for similarly situated individuals who are not entitled to Medicare on the basis of disability;

   Note. An increasingly common practice is to offer a separate medical plan to individuals who are totally disabled. In addition to the impact of the HIPAA nondiscrimination in eligibility rules and the Americans with Disabilities Act implications, employers should also review such a proposed course of action in light of the Medicare secondary-payer rules. The employer may wish to limit such segregation to those individuals who are no longer in "current employment status" so that the Medicare secondary-payer rules in this list do not apply.

5. Imposing limitations on benefits for Medicare-entitled individuals that do not apply to others enrolled in the plan, such as providing less comprehensive health care coverage, excluding benefits, reducing benefits, charging higher deductibles or coinsurance, providing for lower annual or lifetime benefit limits, or using more restrictive preexisting-illness limitations;
6. Charging higher premiums to an individual entitled to Medicare;
7. Requiring a Medicare-entitled individual to wait longer for coverage to begin;
8. Paying providers and suppliers less for services furnished to a Medicare beneficiary than for the same services furnished to an enrollee who is not entitled to Medicare;
9. Providing misleading or incomplete information that would have the effect of inducing a Medicare-entitled individual to reject the employer's group health plan, thereby making Medicare the primary payer;

10. Including in health insurance cards, claim forms, or brochures distributed to beneficiaries, providers, and suppliers instructions to bill Medicare first for services furnished to Medicare beneficiaries without stipulating that such action may be taken only when Medicare is the primary payer; and

11. Refusing to enroll an individual for whom Medicare would be the secondary payer when enrollment is available to similarly situated individuals for whom Medicare would not be the secondary payer.

[42 C.F.R. § 411.111(a)]

On the other hand, permissible actions include the following:

1. If the group health plan or large group health plan makes benefit distinctions among various categories of individuals that are unrelated to the fact that the individual is aged or disabled, it may also do so for individuals entitled to Medicare whose plan coverage is based on current employment status. For example, the plan could permissibly include distinctions based on the individual's length of service, occupation, or marital status.

2. If an aged or disabled Medicare beneficiary is in current employment status but has COBRA continuation because of reduced hours of work, the plan may permissibly pay benefits secondary to Medicare (making Medicare the primary payer). This is because the plan coverage, according to the Medicare regulations, is by virtue of the COBRA law rather than by virtue of the individual's current employment status.

3. A group health plan can terminate COBRA coverage when an individual becomes entitled to Medicare on the basis of ESRD to the extent permitted under COBRA. This would mean that COBRA continuation coverage can be cut off if the individual first becomes entitled to Medicare on the basis of ESRD after the date COBRA is elected (provided that the authority to cut off coverage under such circumstances is contained in the plan document) without violating the Medicare secondary-payer rules. Note that this result occurs because the Medicare secondary-payer rules merely establish the order of payment between the plan and Medicare and do not address the duration of the group health plan's coverage.

[42 C.F.R. § 411.111(b)]

Q 5:144   What is the additional prohibition against differentiating benefits based on either eligibility for or entitlement to Medicare on the basis of ESRD?

In addition to the activities listed in Q 5:143 that would constitute prohibited "taking into account" Medicare entitlement—and, in the case of ESRD, eligibility—a group health plan may not differentiate, in the benefits it provides, between individuals who have ESRD and other enrollees on the basis of the existence of ESRD or the need for renal dialysis, or in any other manner.

Actions that may constitute differentiation in plan benefits (which may also constitute "taking into account" Medicare eligibility or entitlement) include but are not limited to the following actions:

1. Terminating coverage of individuals with ESRD when there is no basis for the termination unrelated to ESRD (such as failure to pay plan premiums) that would result in termination for others who do not have ESRD;

2. Imposing only on persons who have ESRD benefit limitations such as less comprehensive health plan coverage, reductions in benefits, exclusions of benefits, a higher deductible or coinsurance, a longer waiting period, a lower annual or lifetime benefit limit, or more restrictive preexisting-illness limitations;

3. Charging individuals with ESRD higher premiums;

4. Paying providers and suppliers less for services furnished to individuals who have ESRD than for the same services furnished to those who do not have ESRD, such as paying 80 percent of the Medicare rate for renal dialysis on behalf of a plan enrollee who has ESRD and the usual, reasonable, and customary charge for renal dialysis on behalf of an enrollee who does not have ESRD; or

5. Failing to cover routine maintenance dialysis or kidney transplants, when a plan covers other dialysis services or other organ transplants.

Permitted activities, on the other hand, include the following:

1. Limiting covered utilization of a particular service as long as the limitation applies uniformly to all plan enrollees and

2. Paying benefits secondary to Medicare after the expiration of the 30 month coordination period, so long as the plan does not otherwise differentiate in the benefits it provides as described above.

[42 C.F.R. § 411.161(b)]

Q 5:145   For purposes of applying the MSP rules, when is the individual deemed to be in current employment status?

For purposes of the MSP rules, individuals are deemed to be in current employment status when they are actively at work and also in certain circumstances when they are not actively working.

Actively at work. The individual is in current employment status if he or she is actively working as an employee, is the employer (including a self-employed person), or is associated with the employer in a business relationship.

Not actively working. An individual who is not actively working can nonetheless be in current employment status for MSP rule purposes if he or she:

1. Is receiving disability benefits from an employer for up to six months (the first six months of employer disability benefits are subject to FICA taxes) or

2. Satisfies all of the following requirements—

a. Retains employment rights in the industry and has not had his or her employment terminated by the employer, if the employer provides the group health plan coverage (or has not had his or her membership in the employee organization terminated, if the employee organization provides the group health plan coverage). For this purpose, persons retaining employment rights include, but are not limited to, individuals on furlough, temporary layoff, or sick leave; teachers and seasonal workers who normally do not work through the year; and persons who have health coverage that extends beyond or between active employment periods (for example, based on an hours-bank arrangement). Whether or not the individual is receiving pay during the period of nonwork is not a factor;

b. Is not receiving disability benefits from an employer for more than six months;

c. Is not receiving disability benefits from Social Security; and

d. Has group health plan coverage that is not COBRA continuation coverage.

[42 C.F.R. §§ 411.104(a), 411.104(b)]

Q 5:146   Can an employer provide any financial incentive for employees who are Medicare beneficiaries not to enroll in the employer's group health plan?

No. Employers and other entities such as insurers are prohibited from offering Medicare beneficiaries any financial or other benefits as incentives not to enroll in, or to terminate enrollment in, a group health plan that is or would be primary to Medicare. If the employer or other entity violates this prohibition, it is subject to a civil money penalty of up to $5,000 for each violation. [Social Security Act § 1862(b)(3), 29 U.S.C. § 1395y(b)(3); 42 C.F.R. § 411.103]

Practice Pointer. Theoretically, this could encompass an employer's practice of paying Medicare Part B premiums as an alternative to enrollment in the retiree medical plan.

Q 5:147   Can an employer refuse to cover, or provide less medical coverage for, older employees or older spouses who are entitled to Medicare?

Generally not. Individuals age 65 or older in "current employment status" must be allowed to remain covered under the employer's group health plan under the same conditions, and receive the same benefits, as younger employees. A spouse (age 65 or older) of an individual in current employment status (regardless of his or her age) must also be covered under the employer's plan under the same conditions, and receive the same benefits, as employees' spouses under age 65. This provision, formerly contained in the Age Discrimination in Employment Act of 1967 (ADEA), has been recodified as Section

1862(b)(1) of the Social Security Act [42 U.S.C. § 1395y] and as Code Section 5000(c). [*See also* 42 C.F.R. § 411.102(b).]

No affirmative election required. It is important to understand that group health plans are absolutely required to be primary to Medicare for this working-aged group (including any enrolled spouse age 65 or older of an employee of any age). The employee or spouse need not make any special written affirmation of the desire to have the employer's plan pay primary and Medicare pay secondary. The employee chooses to have the employer's plan as primary payer simply by staying in it or chooses to have Medicare as primary payer by dropping out of the employer's plan; that is, Medicare becomes the primary payer when it is the employee's only available coverage.

> **Practice Pointer.** The regulations require that the employer refrain from providing misleading or incomplete information that would have the effect of inducing a Medicare-entitled individual to reject the employer plan, thereby making Medicare the primary carrier. Although the employer need not obtain an affirmative election against employer plan coverage, the employer must inform the individual that if he or she rejects the employer's group health plan, the plan will not be permitted to provide or pay for secondary benefits. [42 C.F.R. § 411.108(a)(9)]

Retirees. With one exception, the age-65-or-older provisions do not apply to former employees. An employer generally may provide that plan coverage of retired or terminated employees and their spouses and dependents who are eligible for Medicare will be secondary to Medicare, and the use of wraparound or Medicare supplemental coverage generally is not prohibited in these instances. (See Q 5:144 for the special exception regarding retirees with ESRD.) However, the employer needs to be mindful of the second prong of the "current employment status" definition. If the terminated employee retains employment rights in the industry and certain other requirements are met, that individual is subject to the same Medicare secondary-payer rules as is an active employee.

Small-employer exclusion. A single-employer group health plan is exempt from the age-65-or-older provisions of Code Section 5000 and the Social Security Act as long as it has fewer than 20 employees for each working day in each of 20 or more calendar weeks in the current calendar year. In addition, if a multiemployer or multiple-employer group health plan expressly elects the statutory exemption, then an employer participating in the plan and having fewer than 20 employees for each working day in each of 20 or more calendar weeks in the current calendar year also is exempt. The number of employers with current employment status is determined using the Code's controlled-group, affiliated-service group, and leased-employee rules. [Social Security Act § 1862(b)(1)(A), 42 U.S.C. § 1395y]

Q 5:148   Can retiree medical plans be entirely secondary to Medicare?

No. Retiree medical plans cannot be entirely secondary to Medicare. In certain cases involving end-stage renal disease, a retiree medical plan is required to pay primary to Medicare. [42 U.S.C. § 1395y(b)(1)(C), as amended by § 13561 of OBRA '93]

Final regulations administered by the Centers for Medicare and Medicaid Services provide the following rules:

1. If the individual first becomes eligible for or entitled to Medicare based on ESRD and subsequently becomes entitled to Medicare based on age or disability during the 18-month (now 30-month) coordination period, the group health plan, including a retiree medical plan, is obligated to pay primary to Medicare throughout the entire 18-month (now 30-month) period.

2. The group health plan (including a retiree medical plan) must also pay primary for a 30-month coordination period when ESRD-based eligibility or entitlement occurs simultaneously with age-based or disability-based entitlement.

3. If each of the following three conditions is satisfied, then Medicare continues to be primary after an aged or disabled beneficiary becomes eligible for Medicare on the basis of ESRD

   a. Medicare entitlement based on age or disability occurs before entitlement due to ESRD;

   b. The MSP prohibition against taking into account age-based or disability-based entitlement does not apply because plan coverage is not "by virtue of current employment" or the employer has fewer than 20 employees (in the case of the aged) or fewer than 100 employees (in the case of the disabled); and

   c. The plan is already paying secondary to Medicare because the plan had justifiably taken into account the age-based or disability-based entitlement.

Note that if the plan has failed to coordinate with Medicare before the individual becomes eligible for Medicare based on ESRD, the plan apparently forfeits this exemption and will have to pay primary to Medicare for the full 30-month period even though the coverage is retiree coverage.

Q 5:149   May a group health care plan refuse to pay expenses that are subject to Medicare private contracting?

Yes, it can if the expenses are paid pursuant to a Medicare private contract and the group health plan has been specifically amended to exclude such charges. The Balanced Budget Act of 1997 amended the Social Security Act to permit Medicare beneficiaries and physicians to enter into private contracts for health care services that will not be limited by the Medicare system reimbursement and balance billing limits. The physician must file a signed affidavit with the Secretary of Health and Human Services that, for the next two years, he or she will neither submit any claims to Medicare nor receive any payment from Medicare for items or services provided to any Medicare beneficiary. In other words, this is a "freedom of choice" provision under which the private contract accommodates the physician who does not wish to be limited to the Medicare rates (and is willing to forgo payment from Medicare) and the patient who is willing to pay whatever it takes to receive specified care and services from that physician. The price is, however, that the physician or practitioner will be barred from the Medicare program for two years. For those willing to enter into these private contracts, such expenses are then "outside" of Medicare, and the group health plan does not violate the Medicare secondary-payer rules by excluding them from coverage.

Private contracts must meet specific requirements spelled out in the law. First, the contract must be in writing and signed by the Medicare beneficiary before any item or service is provided under the contract, the contract must contain required content, and the contract must not be entered into at a time when the Medicare beneficiary is facing an emergency or urgent health care situation. Regarding the required content, the private contract between the physician and the Medicare beneficiary must clearly indicate to the Medicare beneficiary that, by signing such contract, the beneficiary agrees:

1. Not to submit a claim (or to request that the physician or practitioner submit a claim) to Medicare for such items or services even if they are otherwise covered by Medicare;

2. To be responsible, whether through insurance or otherwise, for payment of such items or services and understands that no reimbursement will be provided by Medicare;

3. That no Medicare limits apply to amounts that may be charged for such items and services;

4. That Medigap does not pay for such items and services because they will not be covered under Medicare and that other supplemental insurance plans may elect not to pay for them; and

5. That the Medicare beneficiary has the right to have the items or services provided by other physicians or practitioners who would be paid by Medicare.

The contract also must clearly indicate whether the physician or practitioner is excluded from participation under the Medicare program. The written affidavit must identify the physician or practitioner and be signed by him or her and provide that he or she will not submit any claim under Medicare for any item or service provided to any Medicare beneficiary and will not receive any reimbursement under Medicare during the two-year period beginning on the date the affidavit is signed, and a copy of it be filed with the Secretary no later than ten days after the private contract is entered into. [Social Security Act §§ 1802, 1862(a)(19)]

Q 5:150   What sanctions apply for violating the Medicare secondary-payer rules?

Stiff penalties apply to violations of the Medicare secondary-payer requirements.

Excise tax. If a group health plan of any size violates one of these provisions, then the sponsoring employer or employee organization can be taxed in an amount equal to 25 percent of the employer's or employee organization's expenses incurred during the calendar year for each group health plan to which it contributes. [I.R.C. § 5000(a); 42 U.S.C. § 1395y(a)(3)]

Double damages. The federal government also may bring an action against any entity, insurance policy, or plan to collect double damages for failure to pay as a primary payer. Individuals are also given a private right of action for double damages if the group health plan fails to pay benefits on a primary basis. [42 U.S.C. § 1395y(a)(2)(B)(ii)]

ERISA fiduciary violations. All of the ERISA remedies for a breach of fiduciary duty, including unlimited personal liability of the fiduciary for losses to the plan, would apply to the plan's failure to administer the Medicare secondary-payer rules correctly.

> **Practice Pointer.** Failing to pay a service rendered pursuant to a Medicare private contract (see Q 5:149) would violate the MSP rules unless a valid private contract exists; therefore, plan administrators need to consider how to administer a group health plan provision that excludes services rendered pursuant to Medicare private contracts. It might be prudent, for example, to request a copy of the contract and keep it on file. Also of concern is requiring the individual to disclose when such a contract exists.

Q 5:151   Can CMS force employers or plans to repay Medicare overpayments?

Yes. The CMS can force employers or plans to repay Medicare overpayments. It is authorized by statute to recover Medicare overpayments if another insurer is or should be the primary payer.

Regulatory scheme for recovery of Medicare overpayments. The CMS has both a direct right of action and a subrogated right of action (that is, deriving from the participant's right under the plan) to recover mistaken or conditional Medicare overpayments from any entity responsible for making a primary payment, including employers, insurance carriers, plans, or programs. The CMS may recover the primary payment it made from the third-party payer if the third-party payer was, or should have been, aware that Medicare has made a conditional primary payment but nonetheless proceeded to pay another entity (such as a doctor or hospital) for such services on a primary basis. [42 C.F.R. § 411.24(i)]

Partial invalidation of enforcement scheme. The regulations contained two disputed provisions. Under one such provision, collection was authorized from third-party administrators (TPAs). [42 C.F.R. § 411.24(e)] The second provision authorized recovery from an employer group health plan even if the plan's time limit for notifying the plan of a claim or for filing a claim for reimbursement has expired. [42 C.F.R. § 411.24(f)]

The Court of Appeals for the District of Columbia invalidated the portion of the regulation that permitted the recovery of conditional Medicare payments from TPAs. [Health Ins. Ass'n of Am. Inc. v. Shalala, 306 U.S. App. D.C. 104 (1994)]

The court narrowly interpreted the Medicare secondary-payer statute to apply only to the entities that bear the financial risk under a plan, not to the entities that merely fulfill the requirements imposed by a plan. It noted that TPAs (including an insurance carrier acting in the capacity of a TPA) perform administrative services for self-insuring employers, such as adjudicating claims and writing benefit checks drawn on the employer's funds, but do not use their own funds to pay claims. As a result of this decision, the government must proceed against individual employers and plans rather than against a TPA servicing multiple employers and plans.

The court also invalidated the portion of the regulation that authorized the recovery of conditional payments from a group health plan even if the plan's time limit for submitting a claim has already expired. [42 C.F.R. § 411.24(f)] However, subsequent to the court's decision, the Balanced Budget Act of 1997 authorized claims for repayments if the CMS files for reimbursement within three years of the date the expense was incurred, regardless of the plan's time limit for submitting a claim. [Social Security Act § 1862(b)(2)(B)(v), added by BBA § 4632(a)]

Q 5:152   Will a breach of fiduciary duty occur if the plan administrator's cooperation with the CMS Medicare overpayment enforcement scheme would violate the terms of the plan or the requirements of ERISA?

No, it will not. The DOL has issued an advisory opinion concerning how ERISA plan fiduciaries should respond to claims submitted to ERISA plans for recovery, pursuant to the Medicare secondary-payer statute, of mistaken primary payments made by Medicare. In that advisory opinion, the DOL took the position that group health plan fiduciaries are responsible for administering their plans to assure compliance with both ERISA and other applicable federal laws because other federal laws are not preempted by ERISA. [DOL Adv. Op. 93-23A (Sept. 3, 1993)]

Practice Pointer. The advisory opinion is binding only on the party that requested it, but it nonetheless provides guidance regarding the DOL's enforcement posture on Medicare secondary-payment issues. Significantly, it indicates the DOL's view that failure to include MSP provisions in the plan document or SPD might not be an acceptable excuse for failing to coordinate properly with Medicare.

The advisory opinion addressed several issues.

Conflict between terms of an ERISA plan and Medicare secondary-payer statute. If the terms of the group health plan comply with ERISA but do not comply with the requirements of other applicable federal laws or regulations, plan fiduciaries should take appropriate steps to assure that the plan is amended to comply with all applicable legal requirements. When a group health plan is covered both by the MSP statute and by Title I of ERISA, noncompliance with the Medicare statute and any regulations issued thereunder is not excused on the basis that the plan complies with ERISA.

Practice Pointer. This advisory opinion clearly warns of the DOL's position that plans must comply with all federal laws. This is particularly important for self-insured plans, where often the SPD performs dual duty as the portion of the official plan document with respect to benefits. It would be prudent to include the federal MSP rules for both active employees and retired employees, if the medical plan also includes retiree coverage. Additionally, separate retiree medical plans will need to reflect the MSP rules applicable to retirees.

Conflicting deadlines for claims. The main concern in the advisory opinion letter was the "claims override" provision in the Medicare regulation permitting Medicare to make a claim for a Medicare overpayment even after the group health plan's time limit for submission of claims and claim appeals has expired. The DOL indicated in the advisory opinion that the regulation must be followed and, as a result, plan fiduciaries would be required to disregard the plan's claims-filing requirements and allow such late claims. [42 C.F.R. § 411.24(f)] The DOL's enforcement position on this point was briefly affected by the subsequent invalidation of that portion of the regulation. [Health Ins. Ass'n of Am. Inc. v. Shalala, 306 U.S. App. D.C. 104 (1994)] The three-year statute of limitations enacted by the Balanced Budget Act of 1997 for recovery of Medicare overpayments, regardless of any time limits contained in the group health plan, breathed new life into the DOL's enforcement position on this issue when there is conflict between the plan's claims provisions and the MSP rules.

Refusal to acknowledge plan's primary status. The DOL took the position that a violation of ERISA's prudence requirement may arise if a fiduciary has no reasonable basis to believe that the plan should not be the primary payer but nonetheless refuses to acknowledge the plan's responsibility as primary payer under the Medicare secondary-payer statutes.

Unnecessarily causing plan to pay primary. The DOL took the position that if a fiduciary unnecessarily causes a plan to act as the primary payer when the plan clearly should not be the primary payer, the fiduciary would not be acting in a prudent manner and solely in the interests of the plan's participants and beneficiaries.

Practice Pointer. One important implication of this position is that group health plans will need to be diligent in coordinating correctly with Medicare for disabled individuals. Group health plans subject to the Medicare secondary-payer rule regarding disability-based Medicare entitlement are required to pay primary only for as long as the individual is in "current employment status." For those plans that provide extended coverage of disabled individuals, there will come a point where the disabled individual is no longer listed in the employer's records as an employee and is reclassified as a former employee. At that point, current employment status ceases, and, assuming that the individual is enrolled in Medicare at that point, the group health plan should begin paying secondary to Medicare. Continuing to pay primary once an individual with disability-based Medicare is no longer in current employment status would violate ERISA's prudence requirement, according to this advisory opinion.

Reasonable doubt as to plan's primary status. If there is reasonable doubt as to whether the plan is the primary payer, the appropriate plan fiduciary who is faced with a request from the CMS to recover a Medicare payment must make a prudent decision, based on all of the facts and circumstances available, whether to honor or to dispute the recovery request.

Inability to determine that claim is covered by plan. Significantly, the DOL noted that if the information provided by Medicare is not sufficient to enable plan fiduciaries to determine whether the claim relates to a service covered by the plan, it is incumbent upon the fiduciaries to take all reasonable action to ascertain the necessary information, including requesting additional information from the provider, the policyholder, the patient, and the Medicare contractor. This requirement is in strong contrast to the usual rule under ERISA, under which it generally is up to the participant or beneficiary to document to the plan's satisfaction that he or she incurred a covered expense under the plan.

Fiduciary's possible liability for double payment. The advisory opinion also took the position that if a plan fiduciary has permitted the payment of a claim to an entity other than Medicare when the fiduciary was aware, or should have been aware, that Medicare had already made a conditional payment of that claim, the CMS may seek recovery under its regulations. In that case, the DOL concluded, the fiduciary could be liable under ERISA to the plan for any losses incurred from having improperly permitted a double payment. The DOL noted, however, that if the plan fiduciary submits evidence to the CMS that the plan in fact made such full primary payment and provides information on who received the payment, Medicare would typically seek recovery directly from that entity.

Q 5:153   Is an employer or group health plan required to do anything if Medicare has mistakenly paid primary rather than secondary?

Yes. An employer or group health plan is required to take action if Medicare has mistakenly paid primary rather than secondary. The Medicare statute and regulations contain detailed requirements applicable to situations where it has paid a claim on a primary basis but another plan is the primary payer. [42 U.S.C. § 1395y(b)(1)(A)(i); 42 C.F.R. § 411] In such situations, the Medicare payment is considered to be "conditional." The key to the CMS's scheme for recovering conditional Medicare payments is obtaining sufficient information to document that another plan should have been the primary payer. The Medicare regulations place the burden of gathering and reporting this information on employers, plans, insurers, underwriters, and third-party administrators (collectively referred to as third-party payers). [42 C.F.R. § 411.25(a)] If a third-party payer learns that the CMS has made a Medicare primary payment for services for which the third-party payer has or should have made primary payment, special notice rules apply.

Q 5:154　When does the obligation to report a potential Medicare overpayment arise?

A DOL notice imposes a reporting obligation on the employer, plan, or other third-party payer when it has sufficient information to conclude that Medicare mistakenly or conditionally paid on a primary basis. [59 Fed. Reg. 4,285 (Jan. 31, 1994)] The notice gives three examples of when sufficient information is considered to have been received by the employer, plan, or other third-party payer:

1. Whenever it receives an Explanation of Medicare Benefits for the individual showing that Medicare made a primary payment for services for which the plan has also made, or should have made, a primary payment;

2. Whenever it receives a letter from the Medicare beneficiary indicating that Medicare made a primary payment for the item or service; or

3. Whenever the Medicare beneficiary files a claim under the group health plan that is initially denied, appeals it, and obtains a reversal of the denial (the plan must assume that Medicare made a primary payment in the interim).

This list is not all-inclusive, and the employer, plan, or third-party payer should be aware that it may obtain enough information through other means to trigger the Medicare notice obligation.

Q 5:155　Once the employer, plan, or other third-party payer has sufficient information to infer that a Medicare overpayment may have occurred, who must be notified?

Detailed information concerning the potential Medicare overpayment must be reported to the Medicare Secondary Payer Coordinator at the Medicare intermediary or carrier that processed the Medicare claim. If the identity of that Medicare intermediary or carrier is not apparent, the CMS regional office serving the state in which the health care provider is located must be contacted to obtain the identity of the appropriate intermediary or carrier.

Q 5:156　What party is obligated to make the report of a possible Medicare overpayment?

The answer depends on the type of group health plan at issue and how it is administered.

Self-insured and self-administered plans. If the group health plan is both self-insured and self-administered, the required information concerning the possible Medicare overpayment must be given by the employer to the Medicare intermediary or carrier (or CMS regional office).

Insured plans. If the plan is insured, the required information concerning the possible Medicare overpayment must be given by the insurer, underwriter, or third-party administrator to the Medicare intermediary or carrier (or CMS regional office).

Third-party administrators. If the plan is administered by a third party, the required information concerning the possible Medicare overpayment must be given by the insurer, underwriter, or third-party administrator. [59 Fed. Reg. 4,285 (Jan. 31, 1994)] As a result, the notice burden falls on the third-party payer most likely to have the relevant information at hand.

Note that TPAs still must adhere to this reporting requirement even though Medicare's regulatory authorization to make financial recovery of Medicare overpayments from TPAs has been invalidated (see Q 5:151).

Q 5:157   What specific details about a possible Medicare overpayment must be reported?

The following three categories of information concerning the mistaken or conditional Medicare payment must be reported to the Medicare intermediary or carrier that paid the claim:

Medicare beneficiary information:

- Beneficiary name, address, sex, and date of birth
- Beneficiary health insurance claim number (Medicare beneficiary number or health insurance claim number)
- Social Security number (if known)

Medicare information:

- Date of accident, injury, or illness
- Provider of service
- Amount of Medicare payment (if known)
- Date of service
- Date of Medicare payment (if known)

Employer health plan information:

- Policyholder name and address, usually the employee
- Beneficiary's relationship to policyholder (self, spouse, other)
- Insurer, underwriter, or third-party administrator name and address
- Sponsoring employer or employee organization name and address
- Group identifying number or other identifier
- Policy identification number or other identifier
- Individual beneficiary identifier (if a unique identifier is used by the employer group health plan)
- Name and phone number of contact person

- Period during which individual was covered under the group health plan (If coverage is still in effect, this fact must be stated.)
- Date and amount of payment
- Payee name and address

Deficiencies in information. If all of the above information is not available, the appropriate third-party payer (see Q 5:153) must report as much information as it has and certify that no further information is available. If the third-party payer subsequently obtains a previously unreported item of information, it must report the additional information unless it knows that Medicare has recovered the full amount of the primary payment the plan was obligated to pay (or the actual payment, if less). [59 Fed. Reg. 4,285 (Jan. 31, 1994)]

Identifying the appropriate Medicare carrier or intermediary. If the third-party payer cannot determine the identity of the Medicare intermediary or carrier that paid the claim, the CMS regional office serving the state in which the health care provider is located must be contacted to obtain the identity of the appropriate intermediary or carrier.

Children's Health Insurance Program

Q 5:158   What is the Children's Health Insurance Program?

In 1997, Congress established the State Children's Health Insurance Program (SCHIP) under Title XXI of the Social Security Act, enabling states to provide health insurance to targeted low-income children in families with incomes above the level of eligibility for Medicaid. All states and the District of Columbia have Title XXI programs.

In 2009, President Obama signed the Children's Health Insurance Program Reauthorization Act of 2009 [Pub. L. No. 111-3, 123 Stat. 8 (Feb. 4, 2009)], which provided continued funding for the program, redubbed CHIP, and made certain changes affecting employer-sponsored group health coverage. Those changes include:

- Authorization for states to offer premium assistance for qualified employer-sponsored coverage (QESC) of targeted low-income children;
- Special enrollment rights under a group health plan for employees and dependents;
- Employee notice and reporting requirements; and
- Penalties for violations of the special enrollment, employee notice, and reporting requirements.

The 2010 Health Reform Act extends funding for CHIP through 2015. [PPACA § 10203]

Q 5:159 When do employees qualify for group health plan premium assistance under CHIP?

Effective April 1, 2009, the CHIP Reauthorization Act permits states to offer a premium assistance subsidy for qualified employer-sponsored coverage (QESC) to targeted low-income children. [42 U.S.C. 1397ee(c)]

QESC is health coverage offered through an employer (1) that qualifies as creditable coverage (see Q 5:58); (2) for which the employer contribution toward any premium for such coverage is at least 40 percent; and (3) that is offered to all individuals in a manner that would be considered a nondiscriminatory eligibility classification under the rules of Code Section 105(h) governing self-insured employer health plans (see chapter 3). QESC does not include benefits provided under a flexible spending arrangement or a high-deductible health plan.

In general, the amount of the subsidy will be the difference between the employee contribution required for enrollment of the employee under the QESC, and the employee contribution required for enrollment of both the employee and the child.

A state may provide a premium assistance subsidy either directly to the employer or as a reimbursement to an employee for out-of-pocket expenditures. However, the employer may notify a state that it elects to opt out of being directly paid a premium assistance subsidy on behalf of an employee. If the employer opts out, it will withhold the total amount of the employee contribution required for enrollment of the employee and the child in the QESC, and the state will then pay the premium assistance subsidy directly to the employee.

States are required to establish a process for permitting the parent of a targeted low-income child receiving a premium assistance subsidy to unenroll the child from the QESC and to enroll the child in the state's CHIP effective on the first day of any month for which the child is eligible for the state CHIP.

The specific rules governing eligibility for and provision of group health plan premium assistance are determined by each state's CHIP program.

Q 5:160 What special enrollment rights are permitted in connection with CHIP?

Effective April 1, 2009, group health plans and group health insurance issuers must permit employees and dependents who are eligible for, but not enrolled in, a group health plan to enroll in the plan upon

- losing eligibility for coverage under a state Medicaid or Children's Health Insurance Program (CHIP), or
- becoming eligible for state premium assistance under Medicaid or CHIP.

The employee or dependent must request coverage within 60 days of being terminated from Medicaid or CHIP coverage or within 60 days of being determined to be eligible for premium assistance. [I.R.C. § 9801(f)(3)(A); ERISA § 701(f)(3)(A); PHSA § 2701(f)(3)(A) as amended by Pub. L. Law 111-3]

Q 5:161   What notices are employers required to provide to employees in connection with CHIP?

The Children's Health Insurance Program Reauthorization Act of 2009 [Pub. L. No. 111-3] requires employers to provide notices to employees of their potential eligibility for subsidies under Medicaid or CHIP. [I.R.C. § 9801(f)(3)(B); ERISA § 701(f)(3)(B); PHS Act § 2701(f)(3)(B) as amended by Pub. L. No. 111-3]

As required by the CHIP Reauthorization Act, the DOL released a model employer CHIP notice on February 4, 2010. CHIP notices are required annually. However, employers are not required to provide the first annual CHIP notices until the first plan year after the model notices are issued (January 1, 2011 for calendar-year plans). In conjunction with the model notice, the DOL released guidance on application of the CHIP notice requirement. [Publication of Model Notice for Employers to Use Regarding Eligibility for Premium Assistance Under Medicaid or the Children's Health Insurance Program, Notice, 75 Fed. Reg. 5,808 (Feb. 4, 2010)]

An employer that "maintains" a group health plan in a state must provide employees who are residents of the state with notice of opportunities available in the state for premium assistance under Medicaid and CHIP for health coverage of the employee or the employee's dependents. The notice is required to include information on how an employee may contact the state in which the employee resides for additional information regarding potential opportunities for premium assistance, including how to apply for such assistance. An employer may provide the CHIP Notice at the time it furnishes materials notifying the employee of health plan eligibility, at the time materials are provided to the employee in connection with open enrollment (or other coverage election process under the plan), or at the time the summary plan description (SPD) is provided to the employee. CHIP notices must be provided automatically, free of charge.

For purposes of the Employer CHIP Notice requirement, an employer providing benefits (directly or through insurance, reimbursement, or otherwise) for medical care in a state is considered to maintain a group health plan in that state. If that state provides premium assistance for the purchase of group health plan coverage under a state Medicaid plan CHIP, the employer must provide CHIP notices.

A group health plan that provides benefits for medical care directly (such as through an HMO) or through insurance, reimbursement or some other means to participants, beneficiaries, or providers in a state offering such premium assistance is required to provide Employer CHIP Notices, regardless of the employer's location or principal place of business (or the location or principal place of business of the group health plan, its administrator, its insurer, or any other service provider affiliated with the employer or the plan).

As of January 22, 2010, the following states offer one or more programs subject to the CHIP notice requirement:

- Alabama
- Alaska
- Arizona
- Arkansas
- California
- Colorado
- Florida
- Georgia
- Idaho
- Indiana
- Iowa
- Kansas
- Kentucky
- Louisiana
- Maine
- Massachusetts
- Minnesota
- Missouri
- Montana
- Nebraska
- Nevada
- New Hampshire
- New Jersey
- New Mexico
- New York
- North Carolina
- North Dakota
- Oklahoma
- Oregon
- Pennsylvania
- Rhode Island
- South Carolina
- Texas
- Utah
- Vermont
- Virginia
- Washington
- West Virginia
- Wisconsin, and
- Wyoming

However, employers should check the availability of such programs in all states in which they "maintain" a group health plan as of the required date for any CHIP notice. The DOL plans to update its Web site annually to reflect changes in the number of states offering premium assistance programs (and the contact information for those states), to help employers meet the CHIP notice requirements.

A CHIP Notice must inform each employee, regardless of enrollment status, of potential opportunities for premium assistance in the state in which the employee resides and state contact information. The state in which the employee resides may or may not be the same as the state in which the employer, the employer's principal place of business, the health plan, its insurer, or other service providers are located.

Example. An employer in the District of Columbia sponsors a group health plan that provides reimbursement for medical care to plan participants or their beneficiaries residing in the District of Columbia, Virginia, Maryland, West Virginia, Delaware, and Pennsylvania. The plan is considered to be maintained in all six states. Because at least one of those states (see list above) offers a premium assistance program, the employer is subject to the CHIP notice requirement. A CHIP notice must be provided to each employee residing in either Virginia, West Virginia, or Pennsylvania because those three states offer premium assistance programs (see list above).

Practice Pointer. Although CHIP notices are required to be provided only to those employees residing in states with premium assistance programs, the DOL acknowledges that it may be administratively easier to send CHIP notices to all employees than to distinguish between employees based on residency. The DOL permits employers to do so if they so choose. Employers may use the DOL's Model Employer CHIP Notice as a template for a national notice to fulfill the employer notice requirement.

Employers face civil penalties of up to $100 a day from the date of any failure to meet the CHIP notice requirement.

Q 5:162   Are employers subject to disclosure or reporting requirements in connection with CHIP?

In order for states to evaluate an employment-based plan to determine whether premium reimbursement is a cost-effective way to provide medical or child health assistance to an individual, plans are required to provide, upon request, information about their benefits to state Medicaid or CHIP programs. A model disclosure form will be released by August 4, 2010. States may begin requesting information from plans beginning with the first plan year after the model disclosure form is issued (January 1, 2011 for calendar-year plans). [I.R.C. § 9801(f)(3)(B); ERISA § 701(f)(3)(B); PHS Act § 2701(f)(3)(B) as amended by Pub. L. No. 111-3]

A penalty of up to $100 a day may be imposed for failure to timely provide any state with required information.

Privacy and Security Requirements

Q 5:163   What is the HIPAA privacy rule?

When it enacted HIPAA in 1996, Congress was concerned that, in an age of electronic health care transactions, additional safeguards were needed to protect individuals' medical privacy. As a result, HIPAA included "administrative simplification" provisions requiring the Secretary of Health and Human Services (HHS) to publish standards for the electronic exchange, privacy, and security of health information. [HIPAA §§ 261–264] HIPAA specifically directed HHS to issue privacy regulations governing individually identifiable health information if Congress did not enact privacy legislation within three years of HIPAA's enactment. Congress did not enact such legislation, and the HIPAA privacy regulations became a reality.

The privacy rules are not limited to electronic transactions, however. The regulations protect medical records or other individually identifiable health information, whether on paper, in computerized form, or communicated orally.

Although many of the privacy rules are aimed at doctors and other health care providers, a number of rules impact group health plans and their sponsoring employers. For example, the privacy rules generally require group health plans to establish policies and procedures to protect the confidentiality of protected health information (PHI) about plan participants and beneficiaries, to train employees in their privacy practices, and to provide notice of those practices to plan participants. Moreover, the rules limit the circumstances in which a group health plan may disclose PHI to the employer sponsoring the plan.

Q 5:164   Who is covered by the privacy rules?

The privacy rules apply to "covered entities," which include health plans, health care clearing houses, and any health care provider who transmits health care information in electronic form. [45 C.F.R. §§ 160.102, 160.103]

Most employer-sponsored group health plans are covered entities. However, there is one key exception: A group health plan with less than 50 participants that is administered solely by the employer that established and maintains the plan is not a covered entity.

Although an employer that sponsors a group health plan is not technically a covered entity, many of the privacy rule requirements will apply to the sponsoring employer if its employees have access to any PHI. For example, health plan enrollment information is considered PHI. Therefore, if the company employees handle health plan enrollment, the privacy rules must be followed to protect that information.

Because an employer's on-site medical clinic provides health care services, it may be classified as a health care provider. However, to be deemed a covered entity it must transmit certain types of data, such as claims for payment, electronically.

An on-site clinic that does fall within the ambit of the privacy rules may be part and parcel of the sponsoring employer. The privacy regulations permit a single legal entity that conducts both transactions that are covered by the privacy rule and transactions that are not covered to be classified as a hybrid entity. [45 C.F.R. §§ 164.103, 164.105] To be a hybrid entity, the employer must designate in writing those health care components (e.g., the clinic) that perform covered functions. Once the designation is made, the privacy rules will apply directly only to the health care components. If the designation is not made, all of the employer's operations will be technically subject to the privacy rules.

Q 5:165   What is a health plan for purposes of the privacy rules?

Health plans are defined broadly to include medical, dental, vision, prescription drug, health flexible spending account, and long-term care plans. In addition, employee assistance plans (EAPs) that offer medical services, such as substance abuse or mental health counseling, fall within the definition of health plans. By contrast, "referral-only" EAPs would not typically be considered health plans.

Because of this broad definition, a typical employer may sponsor several separate plans that are covered entities for purposes of the privacy rules.

Q 5:166   What is protected health information?

Protected health information (PHI) includes all *individually identifiable health* information that is held or transmitted by a covered entity or its business associates (see Q 5:167) in any form, whether electronic, paper, or oral. [45 C.F.R. § 160.103] PHI includes any information that identifies an individual or which it is reasonable to believe can be used to identify the individual that relates to:

- the individual's past, present, or future physical or mental health or condition;
- the provision of health care to the individual; or
- the past, present, or future payment for the provision of health care to the individual.

PHI does not include employment records that a covered entity maintains in its capacity as an employer.

As required by the Genetic Information Nondiscrimination Act of 2008 [Pub. L. No. 110-223, 122 Stat. 881] (GINA), the Department of Health and Human Services (HHS) has issued proposed regulations specifically providing that protected health information includes genetic information. [Prop. Reg. § 160. 103] In its preamble to the proposed regulation, HHS notes that while GINA requires an updated definition, the department has always taken the position that PHI includes genetic information. [HIPAA—Frequently Asked Questions, Q 354]

De-identified health information is not protected by the privacy rules, and there are no restrictions on the use or disclosure of such information. Information is considered de-identified if it does not identify the individual and provides no reasonable basis to identify the individual.

Q 5:167   What is a health plan's business associate?

A *business associate* is a person or organization other than a member of the health plan's workforce that performs certain functions or activities on behalf of the plan or provides services to the plan. [45 C.F.R. § 106.103] Business associate functions include claims processing, data analysis, utilization review, and billing. Business associate services include legal, actuarial, accounting, consulting, management, administrative, and financial services. The Health Information Technology for Economic and Clinical Health (HITECH) Act, which was enacted as part of the American Recovery and Reinvestment Act of 2009 [Pub. L. No. 111-5, 123 Stat. 115 (Feb. 17, 2009)] (ARRA), expands the definition of *business associate* to include any organization that provides data transmission services to a covered entity or to another business associate or requires access to PHI on a routine basis. This expanded definition includes a vendor who contracts with a covered entity to offer personal electronic health records.

A person or organization is not a business associate if functions performed for or services provided to the plan do not involve the disclosure or use of PHI and any access to PHI by the person or organization would be incidental. In a guidance document, HHS made it clear that business associates do not include service technicians, janitors, or couriers because they do not need PHI to perform their jobs. According to HHS, "Any disclosure of protected health information to janitorial personnel that occurs in the performance of their duties (such as may occur while emptying trash cans) is limited in nature, occurs as a by-product of their janitorial duties, and could not reasonably be prevented." However, HHS noted that a janitorial service might be considered a business associate if it was hired to handle records or shred documents containing PHI. [HHS Guidance Document (Oct. 8, 2002)]

Q 5:168 Can a group health plan disclose PHI to a business associate?

Obviously, disclosure of PHI to certain business associates such as third-party administrators is essential. However, the privacy rules provide that a plan cannot disclose PHI to a business associate without a *business associate contract* that imposes specified written safeguards on the business associate's use and disclosure of PHI. [45 C.F.R. § 164.532]

Q 5:169 What provisions must be included in a business associate contract?

A business associate contract must:

- List the permitted and required uses and disclosures of PHI by the business associate.

- Prohibit the use and disclosure of PHI other than as permitted or required by the contract or as required by law.

- Require the business associate to use appropriate safeguards to prevent uses and disclosures of PHI other than as allowed by the contract.

- Obligate the business associate to report to the plan any uses and disclosures in violation of the contract.

- Require the business associate to ensure that its agents and subcontractors who are given plan PHI agree to follow the restrictions and conditions imposed by the contract.

- Require the business associate to make the PHI available for participant access and disclosure purposes.

- Require the business associate to make its internal practices, books, and records relating to plan PHI available to HHS for purposes of determining the plan's compliance with the privacy rules.

- Require the business associate, if feasible, to return or destroy all plan PHI on termination of the contract or, if return or destruction is not feasible, to extend the protection of the contract and limit further use and disclosure of the PHI to those purposes that make return or destruction unfeasible.

- Authorize termination of the contract if the business violates a material term of the contract.

Q 5:170   When is disclosure of PHI required or permitted?

A plan (or its business associate) *must* make disclosure:

1. to an individual (or his or her personal representative) who requests access to or an accounting of disclosures of his or her PHI , and

2. to HHS when it is undertaking a compliance review or enforcement action. [45 C.F.R. § 164.502(a)]

A plan *may* make disclosure:

1. to an individual who requests access to his or her PHI when disclosure is not required, and

2. for purposes of treatment, payment, and health care operations. [45 C.F.R. § 164.502(a)]

Most disclosures of PHI in the day-to-day operations of group health plans will fall within the ambit of payment and health care operations. Payment activities include obtaining premiums, determining and fulfilling responsibilities for coverage and benefits, and furnishing or obtaining reimbursement for health care delivered to an individual. Health care operations include quality assessment and improvement operations; competency assurance; audits or legal services, including fraud and abuse detection and compliance programs; insurance functions; business planning, development, management and administration; and general administrative activities.

Note. There are numerous other circumstances in which disclosure is permitted, most of which will not come into play in the day-to-day operation of an employer-sponsored health plan. For example, disclosure may be made if it is required by law, for law enforcement purposes, or to comply with workers' compensation laws. Plan administrators who are unsure whether a particular disclosure is permitted may want to consult legal counsel.

The Genetic Information Nondiscrimination Act of 2008 (GINA) specifically prohibits the use of genetic information for underwriting purposes. The Department of Health and Human Services has proposed regulations reflecting this prohibition. The proposed regulations make it clear that the ban on disclosure of genetic information applies notwithstanding any other rule that would permit the disclosure and use of PHI. [HHS Prop. Reg. § 164.502(a)(3)]

Minimum necessary standard. Even if a disclosure is permitted under the privacy rules, a plan must make reasonable efforts to use, disclose, and request only the minimum amount of PHI needed to accomplish its intended purpose. [45 C.F.R. § 164.502(b), 164.514(d)] A plan must develop and implement policies and procedures to reasonably limit uses and disclosures to the minimum necessary.

The minimum necessary standard does not apply to disclosure of an individual's PHI to the individual or a personal representative, disclosure to HHS for compliance or enforcement purposes, disclosure required by law, or disclosure required for compliance with HIPAA.

Access and use. A plan must also develop and implement policies and procedures that restrict access and use of PHI only to those employees who need the information. These policies and procedures must identify employees or classes of employees who need access to PHI to carry out their duties, the categories of PHI to which access is needed, and any conditions under which they need the information to do their jobs.

Q 5:171   Must a plan obtain an individual's consent before disclosing PHI?

Obtaining written consent from an individual to disclose PHI for treatment, payment, and health care operations is generally optional. [45 C.F.R. § 164. 506(b)] However, new rules included in the Health Information Technology for Economic and Clinical Health (HITECH) Act, which was enacted as part of the American Recovery and Reinvestment Act of 2009 (ARRA), require covered entities to comply with individual requests to restrict disclosure of PHI to a plan for payment or health care operations (but not treatment) in situations where the health care provider has been paid by the individual in full out of pocket.

Practice Pointer. Although consent is not required for such disclosures, an employer may wish to include language in the plan enrollment form indicating that the participant acknowledges that he or she is consenting to use and disclosure of PHI for plan administration purposes.

Authorizations required. A plan must generally obtain an individual's written authorization for uses and disclosures of PHI that do not relate to treatment, payment, and health care operations or disclosures otherwise permitted or required by the privacy rules. [45 C.F.R. § 164.514(e)] A plan cannot condition treatment, payment, enrollment, or benefits eligibility on such authorizations except in limited circumstances when authorization is needed for pre-enrollment underwriting purposes.

Examples of disclosures that would require authorization include disclosures to a life insurer for coverage purposes or disclosure to an employer of the results of a pre-employment physical. Note, however, that there is nothing to prevent an employer from conditioning employment on an individual providing authorization for disclosure of a pre-employment physical.

Q 5:172   May a group health plan disclose PHI to the sponsoring employer?

A group health plan and the health insurer or HMO offered by the plan may disclose the following health information to the plan sponsor:

- Enrollment or disenrollment information with respect to the plan or an insurer or HMO offered by the plan.

- Summary health information requested by the plan sponsor to be used to obtain premium bids for providing health insurance coverage through the plan or to modify, terminate, or amend the plan. Summary health information is information that summarizes claims history, claims expenses, or types of claims experience of the individuals covered by the plan that is stripped of all individual identifiers other than zip codes.

- PHI of individuals enrolled in the plan for the plan sponsor to perform plan administration functions. Before providing the information, the plan must obtain certification from the sponsor that the group health plan document has been amended to impose restrictions on the sponsor's use and disclosure of the PHI, which must include a representation that the sponsor will not use or disclose the PHI for any employment-related action or decision or in connection with any other benefit plan. [45 C.F.R. § 164.504(f)]

- Bear in mind, however, that genetic information may not be used or disclosed for underwriting purposes (see Q 5:37).

Q 5:173   May a group health plan disclose PHI to a friend, relative, or other individual who is assisting a plan participant with health care matters?

According to HHS, the privacy rule permits a health plan to disclose to an individual's family member, relative, or close personal friend, PHI that is directly relevant to that person's involvement with the individual's care or payment for care. Disclosure can also be made to persons who are not family members, relatives, or close personal friends of the individual, provided the covered entity has reasonable assurance that the person has been identified by the individual as being involved in his or her care or payment for care.

PHI may be disclosed to such persons only if the individual does not object or if the plan can reasonably infer from the circumstances that the individual does not object to the disclosure. When the individual is not present or is incapacitated, the plan can disclose PHI if, in the exercise of professional judgment, it believes the disclosure is in the best interests of the individual.

HHS gives the following examples of permitted disclosures:

- A health plan may disclose relevant PHI to a beneficiary's daughter who has called to assist her hospitalized, elderly mother in resolving a claims or other payment issue.

- A health plan may disclose relevant PHI to a human resources representative who has called the plan with the beneficiary also on the line, or who could turn the phone over to the beneficiary to confirm for the plan that the representative calling is assisting the beneficiary.

- A health plan may disclose relevant PHI to a congressional office or staffer that has faxed to the plan a letter or e-mail it received from the beneficiary requesting intervention with respect to a health care claim, which assures the plan that the beneficiary has requested the congressional office's assistance.

[Privacy of Health Information/HIPAA Disclosures to Family and Friends, Mar. 14, 2006]

Q 5:174   What if PHI is disclosed in violation of the privacy rules?

The Health Information Technology for Economic and Clinical Health (HITECH) Act imposes new notification requirements on covered entities when an individual's unsecured PHI is breached. The Department of Health and Human Services (HHS) has issued interim final regulations implementing the breach notification requirements [45 C.F.R. Pt. D] The regulations, which were published on August 24, 2009, generally apply to security breaches occurring on or after September 23, 2009. However, HHS stated that it would use its enforcement discretion and not impose sanctions for failure to comply with the required notifications for breaches occurring during the 180-day period following publication of the regulations (i.e., until February 22, 2010).

Under the new regulations, a covered entity is required to notify an individual whose unsecured PHI has been, or is reasonably believed to have been, breached. Business associates must notify the covered entity of a breach of unsecured PHI. In extreme cases, where a breach involves more than 500 individuals, notice must be given to HHS. If a breach involves more than 500 residents of a state or jurisdiction, the covered entity must notify "prominent media outlets" of the breach. In the case of breaches involving fewer than 500 individuals, the covered entity must maintain a log of such breaches and submit the log annually to HHS.

The notification requirements apply only to a breach of unsecured PHI that has not been rendered unusable, unreadable, or indecipherable to unauthorized individuals through the use of a technology or methodology specified in HHS guidance.

Breach. A breach is defined as the unauthorized acquisition, access, use, or disclosure of PHI that compromises the security or privacy of the PHI such that the use or disclosure poses a significant risk of financial, reputational, or other harm to the affected individual.

There are three exceptions to the definition of a breach:

1. Unintentional acquisition, access, or use of PHI by a workforce member acting under the authority of a covered entity or business associate is not a breach if the acquisition, access or use was made in good faith, within the scope of the employment or other business relationship, and does not result in any further use or disclosure of the PHI. For example, the HHS says the breach notification requirements would not be triggered where a billing employee receives and opens an e-mail containing PHI about a patient that a nurse mistakenly sent to the billing employee, provided the employee alerts the nurse of the misdirected e-mail and then deletes it.

2. Inadvertent disclosure of PHI by one person authorized to access PHI at a covered entity or a business associate of another person at the covered entity or a business associate who is also authorized to access PHI at the covered entity or business associate is not a breach, provided there is not further disclosure of the PHI.

3. No breach has occurred if the covered entity or business associate has a good-faith belief that the unauthorized individual to whom the impermissible disclosure was made would not have been able to retain the PHI. For example, if a group health plan inadvertently sends an estimate of benefits to the wrong person and the envelope is returned as undeliverable. On the other hand, if the envelope is not returned, the incident must be treated as a potential breach.

If none of the exceptions applies, the covered entity must conduct a risk assessment to determine if the unauthorized access, use or disclosure will pose a significant risk of harm to the individual involved. The covered entity has the burden of proof and must document its risk assessment.

HHS says this risk assessment should take into account the type and amount of PHI involved. If the nature of the PHI does not pose a significant risk of financial, reputational, or other harm, then the violation is not a breach. For example, if a covered entity improperly discloses PHI that merely includes the name of an individual and the fact that the individual received services at a hospital, the disclosure would violate the HIPAA privacy rules but may not trigger the breach notification rules if it there is not significant risk of harm to the individual. On the other hand, if the information indicates the type of services the individual received (such as oncology services) or that the individual received services from a specialized facility (such as a substance abuse treatment facility), there is higher likelihood of potential harm, especially in light of fears of employment discrimination. The same holds true if the PHI includes information that increases the risk of identity theft, such as a Social Security number or mother's maiden name.

Individual breach notification. If a disclosure of PHI triggers the breach notification requirement, the covered entity must notify each individual whose unsecured PHI was (or is reasonably believed to have been) affected by the breach.

Notification to individuals must be made "without unreasonable delay," but no later than 60 calendar days after discovery of the breach.

The notice must be in plain language and include:

- A brief description of what happened, including the date of the breach and the date of discovery if known;
- A description of the types of unsecured PHI involved in the breach;
- Steps individuals should take to protect themselves from potential harm resulting from the breach;

- A brief description of the steps the covered entity is taking to investigate the breach, mitigate harm, and protect against future breaches;
- Contact procedures for additional information.

A breach notification must be sent to an affected individual's last known address via first class mail (or by e-mail if the individual has previously agreed to e-mail notification). Special notification procedures apply if contact information for affected individuals is outdated or insufficient.

Q 5:175 What other privacy requirements must a group health plan comply with?

If a plan is fully insured and maintains only enrollment data and summary health information, the plan is subject to two requirements:

Retaliation and waiver. The plan may not retaliate against an individual for exercising rights provided by the privacy rule or require an individual to waive any rights under the privacy rules as a condition for obtaining treatment, payment, enrollment, or benefits eligibility.

Amendment certification. The plan must obtain certification from the employer if the plan has been amended to permit disclosure of PHI to the plan sponsor by the health insurance issuer or HMO that services the plan. [45 C.F.R. § 164.530(k)]

In addition to those requirements, plans that are not fully insured or that have access to more extensive health information must:

- Develop and implement written privacy policies and procedures consistent with the privacy rule.
- Designate a privacy official responsible for developing and implementing privacy policy procedures.
- Designate a contact person or contact office responsible for receiving privacy complaints and providing information on the plan's privacy practices.
- Train all employees on its privacy policies and procedures to the extent necessary for them to carry out their function.
- Have and apply sanctions against employees who violate privacy policies and procedures.
- Mitigate, to the extent practicable, any harmful effect caused by use or disclosure of PHI by its employees or business associates in violation of privacy policies and procedures or the privacy rules.
- Maintain reasonable and appropriate administrative, technical, and physical safeguards to prevent intentional or unintentional use or disclosure of PHI in violation of the privacy rules.
- Implement procedures for individuals to complain about compliance with the privacy rules or privacy policies or procedures.

- Retain all privacy policies and procedures, privacy practices notices, dispositions of complaints, and other documents required by the privacy rules for six years after the later of the date of their creation or the last effective date. [45 C.F.R. § 164.530]

Q 5:176   How do the privacy rules affect administration of other workplace laws, such as the FMLA and the ADA?

Employers routinely request medical certifications under the FMLA to verify the existence of a serious health condition of the employee, a spouse, or a dependent that qualifies for job-protected leave. DOL regulations under the FMLA specifically authorize employers to ask for such medical certification (see chapter 16).

Employers also frequently request medical information from employees in connection with requests for accommodation under the ADA (see chapter 18).

If medical information in connection with an ADA or FMLA request is provided directly by an individual's physician, the individual must authorize the disclosure. Therefore, employers may want to furnish employees who request ADA accommodation or FMLA with a HIPAA-compliant authorization form to be used for this purpose. Alternatively, the employer can require that the health care provider give the information directly to the individual who, in turn, supplies it to the employer. Under this approach, authorization is not required because the information is supplied directly by the individual.

Practice Pointer. Employees will generally agree to comply with an employer's request for medical information in order to expedite processing of their ADA or FMLA requests. However, if an employee declines to authorize release of medical information, an employer would be well within its right to deny the requested accommodation or leave.

Q 5:177   May a group health plan disclose PHI to the employer for use in administering other benefit plans, such as sick leave or disability plans?

The privacy rules strictly prohibit an employer from using PHI that is disclosed in connection with plan administration for other purposes, including administration of other employee benefit plans. [45 C.F.R. § 164.504(f)] Therefore, an employee's authorization is required before information can be disclosed by the plan or by a health care provider for this purpose. However, an employee's refusal to authorize disclosure needed to process a benefit claim could be used as a basis for denying the claim.

Practice Pointer. Employers may want to amend their plans to provide for the required authorizations as a condition of receiving benefits.

Q 5:178   Do plan participants have to be notified about the privacy rules?

A fully insured plan is generally not required to provide privacy notices; such notices will be provided by the health insurance issuer or HMO offered by the plan.

Other plans must provide a privacy notice to plan participants. This notice must describe the ways the plan may use and disclose PHI, state the plan's duties to protect privacy, and provide information on its privacy practices. The notice must also describe an individual's rights with respect to PHI, including the right to complain to HHS and to the plan about privacy violations and must identify a point of contact for further information and for making complaints. If the plan (or an insurer or HMO, in the case of an insured plan) will disclose PHI to the sponsoring employer, that fact must be stated in the notice. [45 C.F.R. § 164.520]

A health plan must give notice to each new enrollee at the time of enrollment and send a reminder to every enrollee at least every three years that the notice is available upon request. A plan will satisfy the notice distribution requirement if notice is provided to the "named insured" who enrolled for coverage that also applies to a spouse and dependents.

According to HHS, a health plan can satisfy this requirement by:

- Sending the enrollee a copy of the notice;
- Mailing a reminder concerning availability of the notice with information on how to obtain a copy; or
- Including information about the notice and how to obtain a copy in a plan newsletter or other publication.

[Privacy of Health Information/HIPAA Group Health Plans Notice of Privacy Practices (Mar. 6, 2006)]

Q 5:179   What special rights do plan participants have with respect to PHI?

The privacy rules give plan participants three basic rights: the right to *access* PHI, the right to *amend* PHI, and the right to an *accounting* of disclosures of PHI. [45 C.F.R. §§ 164.524, 164.526, 164.528]

Access. With limited exceptions, a participant has the right to access and copy his or her PHI. A plan must respond to a participant's request for access within 30 days. One 30-day extension is allowed if the plan needs additional time to respond and notifies the participant in writing of the reason for the delay and the date by which the plan will respond.

Amendment. A participant also has the right to have the plan amend his or her PHI if the information is inaccurate or incomplete. A plan must respond to an amendment request within 60 days; although, here again, a 30-day extension is allowed if the plan needs additional time. A plan may deny an amendment request under certain circumstances, including its determination that the information is accurate and complete.

Accounting of disclosures. A plan participant has the right to receive an accounting of disclosures of his or her PHI. The maximum disclosure accounting period is the six years immediately preceding the accounting request. However, a plan is not required to account for disclosures made before its privacy rule compliance date.

Accounting is generally not required for disclosures made for treatment, payment, or health care operations, or for disclosures that are authorized by the participant.

Practice Pointer. Both self-insured and insured plans are required to comply with access, amendment, and accounting requests. However, insured plans will generally find the rules less burdensome because their insurers or HMOs will generally maintain PHI records and handle such requests.

Q 5:180   Are there penalties for violations of the privacy rules?

Yes. Moreover, the penalties for HIPAA violations were significantly increased by the Health Information Technology for Economic and Clinical Health (HITECH) Act, which was enacted as part of the American Recovery and Reinvestment Act of 2009 [Pub. L. No. 111-5, 123 Stat. 115] (ARRA). The increased penalties for HIPAA violations took effect on or after February 18, 2009

Under the HITECH Act, penalties are based on a tiered penalty structure that depends on the severity of the violation:

- If the covered entity did not know of the violation (and would not have known of the violation by exercising reasonable diligence), the Secretary of Health and Human Services can impose a penalty of no less than $100 and no more than $50,000, subject to an overall penalty limit of $1.5 million for identical violations during a calendar year.
- If the violation was due to reasonable cause and not to willful neglect, the penalty can be no less than $1,000 and no more than $50,000 per violation, subject to an overall limit of $1.5 million for identical violations during the calendar year.
- If the violation was due to willful neglect but was corrected within a 30-day period beginning on the date the covered entity first knew (or, exercising reasonable diligence, would have known) of the violation, the penalty can be no less than $10,000 and no more than $50,000 per violation, subject to an overall limit of $1.5 million for identical violations during the calendar year.
- If the violation was due to willful neglect and was not corrected, the minimum penalty is $50,000 per violation, subject to an overall limit of $1.5 million for identical violations during the calendar year.

[45 C.F.R. § 160.404(b)(2)]

For violations occurring before February 18, 2009, the maximum penalty was $100 for each failure to comply with a privacy rule requirement, and did not exceed $25,000 for multiple violations of the same privacy requirement in a calendar year.

Q 5:181   What is the HIPAA security rule?

Like the HIPAA privacy rule, the HIPAA security rule is designed to safeguard PHI of plan participants and beneficiaries. However, unlike the privacy rule, the security rule applies only to PHI that is transmitted by or maintained in "electronic media" such as a computer hard drive or magnetic tape or disks and tools used in transmitting information over the Internet and private networks. The security rule requires covered entities, including group health plans, to develop and implement administrative, technical, and physical safeguards to protect PHI when it is maintained or transmitted electronically. For example, a plan will be required to designate a security official responsible for compliance with the security rule.

Final regulations issued by the Department of Health and Human Services (HHS) make it clear that the security rule applies only to the group health plan itself, not to the sponsoring employer. Therefore, an employer with a fully insured plan generally will not be affected by the security rule. However, a self-insured plan that is administered by the sponsoring employer will have a compliance obligation.

[45 C.F.R. Parts 160, 162, and 164 Health Insurance Reform: Security Standards, Final Rule; 68 Fed. Reg. 8,297-299 (Feb. 20, 2003)]

Q 5:182   May an employer access medical information about an employee in connection with a credit investigation?

No. The Fair and Accurate Credit Transactions Act of 2003 [Pub. L. No. 108-159, 111 Stat. 1952] (FACTA), which became effective June 1, 2004, prohibits consumer reporting agencies from furnishing a report to an employer for employment purposes containing medical information about an individual unless the information furnished is "relevant to process or effect" the individual's employment, and the individual provides specific written consent that describes in clear and conspicuous language the use for which the information will be furnished. An employer who receives medical information in a consumer report is prohibited from disclosing that information to another person except to the extent necessary to accomplish the purpose for which the employer was authorized to receive the information.

Chapter 6

COBRA Requirements for Continuation of Coverage Under Group Health Plans

The Consolidated Omnibus Budget Reconciliation Act of 1985 (COBRA) imposes a duty on employers to provide continuation of group health coverage to employees, spouses, and dependents under certain circumstances. Employers must permit "qualified beneficiaries" to elect to continue their health insurance under the plan for 18, 29, or 36 months, depending on the "qualifying event" that entitles the person to coverage. Employees may be required to pay premiums for the continuation coverage, but employers generally are not permitted to charge more than 100 percent of the plan's cost for the coverage plus a 2 percent administrative service charge. Employers must be careful to observe the COBRA continuation of coverage provisions: there are strict and far-reaching sanctions for violations, and case law developments have expanded the type and extent of possible COBRA violations.

Overview

Q 6:1   What is the purpose of the COBRA continuation of coverage rules?

The COBRA continuation of coverage rules are intended to provide access to affordable health insurance when an employee or an employee's spouse or dependents lose coverage under an employer's plan. Because there is a real risk that the employee or spouse and his or her dependents will be left without access to affordable health insurance, Congress acted in 1985 to reduce this risk. A portion of the COBRA statute requires employers to provide continuation coverage at group rates to employees, their spouses, and their dependents.

Q 6:2   Where can the COBRA continuation of coverage requirements be found?

Virtually identical COBRA continuation coverage provisions are included in the following federal laws:

- The Internal Revenue Code [26 U.S.C. §4980B]
- The Employee Retirement Income Security Act of 1974 (ERISA), Sections 601 through 608 [29 U.S.C. §§1161–1168]
- The Public Health Service Act (PHSA), Sections 2201–2209 [42 U.S.C. §§300bb-1–300bb-8]

Final Treasury regulations are codified as Treasury Regulations Section 54.4980B through B-10. In addition, regulations interpreting the COBRA provisions in the Medicare secondary-payer provisions of the Social Security Act can be found in the Centers for Medicare and Medicaid Services (CMS) regulations at 42 C.F.R. Sections 411.160 through 411.165.

Q 6:3   When must the option of continuing group health plan coverage be provided?

The COBRA continuation of coverage rules mandate that individuals have the option of continuing coverage whenever all four of the following elements are present:

1. The employer is not exempt under COBRA (see Q 6:20);
2. The employer or employee organization maintains or contributes to a group health plan (including a self-insured plan) to provide health care (directly or indirectly) to employees, former employees, the employer, others associated or formerly associated with the employer in a business relationship, or their families (see Qs 6:4–6:19);

3. The individual is a qualified beneficiary (see Qs 6:33–6:40) and;

4. A qualifying event occurs that causes the qualified beneficiary to lose coverage under the group health plan (see Qs 6:41–6:69). This fourth and last point does not apply to one subset of qualified beneficiaries: children who are born to or adopted by the employee during his or her COBRA continuation period.

[I.R.C. §§4980B(f), 4980B(g)(2), 5000(b)(1); ERISA §601(a); PHSA §2101(a); Q&A-18(e); Treas. Reg. §54.4980B-3, Q&A-1(a)(3) (Feb. 3, 1999)]

Covered Plans

Q 6:4   What is a "group health plan" for COBRA continuation of coverage purposes?

The definition of *covered group health plan* contained in the Internal Revenue Code's COBRA provisions differs from that contained in ERISA's COBRA provisions.

Tax purposes. Under Code Sections 4980B(g)(2) and 5000(b)(1), a group health plan for COBRA purposes is defined as follows:

> The term *group health plan* means a plan (including a self-insured plan) of, or contributed to by, an employer (including a self-employed person) or employee organization to provide health care (directly or otherwise) to the employees, former employees, the employer, others associated or formerly associated with the employer in a business relationship, or their families. [I.R.C. §§4980B(g)(2), 5000(b)(1)]

The COBRA regulations require that the group health plan provide medical care as defined in Code Section 213(d) (see Q 6:7). In addition to group insurance arrangements, one or more individual insurance policies in any arrangement that involves the provision of medical care to two or more employees are also group health plans for this purpose. [Treas. Reg. §54. 4980B-2, Q&A-1(a) (Feb. 3, 1999)] (For COBRA's definition of "plan," see Qs 6:18–6:19.)

ERISA purposes. ERISA defines "group health plan" for COBRA purposes as follows:

> The term "group health plan" means an employee welfare benefit plan providing medical care (as defined in Section 213(d) of the Internal Revenue Code of 1986), to participants or beneficiaries directly or through insurance, reimbursement, or otherwise. [ERISA §607(1); 29 U.S.C. §1167(1)]

The ERISA definition of *group health plan* is also important because a significant proportion of COBRA claims are brought under ERISA. Accordingly, to succeed on an ERISA claim, it apparently also would be necessary for the plan to satisfy ERISA's separate definition of an employee welfare benefit plan. (See chapter 2.)

> **Practice Pointer.** ERISA contains two definitions of group health plans, which can be confusing. The mandated benefit provisions of Part 6 of Title I (including COBRA and qualified medical child support orders) use one definition, and the mandated benefit provisions of Part 7 of Title I (including the Health Insurance Portability and Accountability Act of 1996 (HIPAA) maternity hospital stays, and mental health parity) use a different definition. Thus, it is possible for a group health plan to be exempt from HIPAA but still be required to comply with COBRA.

Medicare secondary-payer rules. For purposes of the interplay between COBRA and the Social Security Act's Medicare secondary-payer rules, a separate definition of *group health plan* is provided that generally tracks the tax definition. [42 C.F.R. §411.101]

Q 6:5   What is a plan that is "maintained or contributed to by an employer or employee organization" for COBRA purposes?

The COBRA regulations use a "but for" test. They state that a plan is maintained by an employer or employee organization if the employee would not have been able to receive coverage at the same cost "but for" an employment-related connection to the employer or employee organization. Therefore, even if the employee pays the entire cost of plan coverage, the employer or employee organization will be obligated to follow COBRA's continuation of coverage rules as long as the employee receives a favorable rate because of the employment relationship. [Treas. Reg. §54.4980B-2, Q&A-1 (Feb. 3, 1999)]

Q 6:6   Can individual health policies provided by an employer constitute a group health plan subject to COBRA?

Whether individual health policies constitute a group health plan subject to COBRA depends on the extent of the employer's involvement in acquiring and maintaining the coverage.

COBRA defines the term *group health plan* to mean "an employee welfare benefit plan providing medical care . . . to participants or beneficiaries directly or through insurance, reimbursement, or otherwise." [29 U.S.C. §1167(l)] ERISA defines an employee welfare benefit plan to include any plan established or maintained by an employer for the purpose of providing medical, surgical, or hospital care benefits for its participants or their beneficiaries, through the purchase of insurance or otherwise. [29 U.S.C. §1002(1)] Department of Labor (DOL) regulations interpreting ERISA provide that a plan is generally considered not to be maintained by an employer or employee organization if the employer or organization does not contribute to, endorse, or perform any functions with respect to the plan. [DOL Reg. §2510.3-1(j)]

Thus, if an employer does not offer a specific plan to its employees, but leaves each employee free to shop around for his or her own health insurance,

ERISA and COBRA do not apply. In addition, under the DOL regulations, an employer can go a bit further—for example, by distributing advertising brochures from insurance providers, answering employee questions about insurance, or even deducting insurance premiums from employees' paychecks and remitting them to the insurer—without establishing a formal plan.

On the other hand, more extensive involvement on the part of the employer can cause individual policies to be treated as a group health plan. In one case, an employee sued her employer for failure to provide COBRA coverage when her employment was terminated and she lost her coverage under an individual health insurance policy that had been paid for by the employer. The employer asked the court to dismiss her lawsuit on the grounds that her health insurance policy did not constitute a group health plan subject to the COBRA coverage requirements. However, a U.S. district court refused to throw out the case. While the employer's paying for the coverage was not dispositive, that fact coupled with other factors, such as the employer's involvement in selecting the insurance carrier, raised questions about whether the employer had established a plan. [Stange v. Plaza Excavating, Inc. 2001 U.S. Dist. LEXIS 1190 (N.D. Ill. Feb. 7, 2001)]

Q 6:7 What is "medical care"?

A COBRA group health plan is one that provides "medical care" within the meaning of Code Section 213(d). Code Section 213(d) defines *medical care* to include "the diagnosis, cure, mitigation, treatment, or prevention of disease" and "any other undertaking for the purpose of affecting any structure or function of the body." Transportation that is "primarily for and essential to" medical care is also included in the Code's definition. [I.R.C. §§4980B(g)(2), 5000(b)(1); Treas. Reg. §54.4980B-2, Q&A-1(b) (Feb. 3, 1999)]

> **Note.** The Code's definition of a *group health plan* provides that a covered group health plan is one that provides health care while the ERISA definition refers to "medical care" as defined under Code Section 213. The COBRA regulations state that the term *health care* for COBRA purposes is the same as Code Section 213's medical care. [Treas. Reg. §54.4980B-2, Q&A-1(b) (Feb. 3, 1999)]

However, the COBRA regulations exclude programs that further general good health but do not relieve or alleviate health or medical problems and are generally accessible to and used by employees, whatever their state of health. For example, a fitness program or swimming pool used generally by employees would not qualify as a program of health care. [Treas. Reg. §54.4980B-2, Q&A-1(b) (Feb. 3, 1999)]

An employer's on-site health clinic may constitute a covered plan for COBRA purposes. However, first-aid treatment available only to current employees, at an on-site facility, during the employees' working hours is not considered medical care if the employees are not charged for the treatment and the care is limited to illness and injury occurring during working hours. [Treas. Reg. §54.4980B-2, Q&A-1(d)(1) (Feb. 3, 1999)]

Employer-maintained drug and alcohol treatment programs are considered to be medical care. [Treas. Reg. §54.4980B-2, Q&A-1(b) (Feb. 3, 1999)]

The fact that a benefit provided to employees is health-related does not automatically make it medical care subject to COBRA. For example, suppose a department store provides its employees with discounted prices on all merchandise, including health care items such as drugs or eyeglasses. The fact that the discount applies to health items does not make the program a medical care plan as long as the discount program is used by employees without regard to health needs or physical condition. On the other hand, if the employer maintaining the discount program is a health clinic, so that the program is used exclusively by employees with health or medical needs, the program would be considered a group health plan that provides medical care. [Treas. Reg. §54.4980B-2, Q&A-1(b)]

"Medical care" under Code Section 213 does not include cosmetic surgery or similar procedures, unless the surgery or procedure is necessary to ameliorate a deformity arising from or directly related to a congenital abnormality, personal injury resulting from an accident or trauma, or disfiguring disease. The term *cosmetic surgery* means any procedure that is directed at improving the patient's appearance and does not meaningfully promote the proper function of the body or prevent or treat illness or disease. [I.R.C. §213(d)(9), added by OBRA '90 §11342(a)] However, some procedures, such as weight-loss programs and cosmetic surgery, that may seem to be aimed at improving an individual's appearance may qualify as medical care. The IRS has ruled that the costs of weight-loss programs for the treatment of a specific illness, including obesity, qualify as expenses for medical care. [Rev. Rul. 2002-19, 2002-16 I.R.B. 779] The same holds true for cosmetic surgery to correct disfigurement following an operation (e.g., breast reconstruction following a mastectomy) or to correct a defect caused by a disease or a defect that interferes with the normal functioning of the body (e.g., laser surgery to correct vision, but not teeth whitening). [Rev. Rul. 2003-57, 293 I.R.B. 1] In addition, the IRS has ruled that the costs of smoking-cessation programs and prescription drugs to alleviate nicotine withdrawal (but not over-the-counter nicotine patches or gum) do qualify as medical expenses. [Rev. Rul. 99-28, 1999-1 C.B. 1269]

Long-term care. Although HIPAA amended Code Section 213 to include qualified long-term care services within the definition of medical care, COBRA was correspondingly amended to provide that COBRA rights and obligations do not apply to such plans. (See Q 6:14.)

Q 6:8 Is a medical plan of a governmental entity considered a group health plan for COBRA purposes?

The definition of *group health plan* used for COBRA purposes under the Code specifically excludes a plan of the federal government or other governmental entity. [I.R.C. §5000(d)] This would include the federal government's CHAMPUS health program for the armed services. [IRS Notice 90-58, 1990-2 C.B. 345

(Oct. 1, 1990)] However, parallel provisions of the PHSA apply COBRA continuation requirements generally to state and local government employers that receive funding under that act. [PHSA §2201 *et seq.*]

Q 6:9   Are self-insured plans subject to COBRA?

Yes. Group health plans are not exempt from COBRA solely by reason of being self-insured. [I.R.C. §§4980B(g)(2), 5000(b)(1); 42 C.F.R. §411.102] This would include health care flexible spending arrangements (FSAs), which are self-insured medical plans. (See Q 6:11.)

Q 6:10   Is a plan maintained by a voluntary employees' beneficiary association subject to COBRA?

Yes. A group health plan maintained by a voluntary employees' beneficiary association (VEBA) that is organized in whole or in part to maintain such a plan is subject to COBRA. [ERISA §§607(1)]

Q 6:11   Are cafeteria plans subject to COBRA?

Yes. If any option under a cafeteria plan, standing alone, would meet COBRA's definition of a covered group health plan, COBRA will apply to that option. Thus, for example, health care FSAs, group medical coverage options, dental options, and prescription drug options under cafeteria plans are subject to COBRA. [Treas. Reg. §54.4980B-2, Q&A-1(a) (Feb. 3, 1999)] For details on how the COBRA coverage requirements apply to cafeteria plans and health care FSAs, see Q 6:118.

Q 6:12   Are employee assistance programs subject to COBRA?

It depends. An employee assistance program (EAP) will be subject to COBRA if it is "maintained by an employer or employee organization" and provides "medical care" (see Q 6:7) such as coverage of psychiatric or mental health visits and not merely information and referrals only to noncovered professional counselors. The IRS has not issued specific guidance regarding the applicability of COBRA continuation of group health plan requirements to EAPs. The Department of Labor (DOL) has issued advisory opinion letters under ERISA concerning when an EAP is considered to provide medical care for ERISA coverage purposes. DOL Advisory Opinions may serve as a useful starting point for an analysis of the characterization of EAPs for tax purposes. See chapter 3 for further discussion of EAPs.

Q 6:13   Are medical savings accounts or health savings accounts subject to COBRA?

Medical savings accounts (known as Archer MSAs) and health savings accounts (HSAs) are tax-favored accounts that can be used to pay medical expenses in conjunction with a high-deductible health plan (HDHP) (see chapter 3). MSAs are available only to self-employed individuals and employees of small employers (generally, employers with no more than 50 employees). Contributions to an MSA may be made by either the employer or the employee, but not both. By contrast, any eligible individual with high-deductible health plan coverage may establish an HSA; contributions to an HSA may be made by both the employer and the employee.

MSAs are not subject to the COBRA continuation coverage requirements. Thus, a plan is not required to make COBRA continuation coverage available with respect to amounts contributed by an employer to a medical savings account. However, a high-deductible group health plan that covers MSA account holders will be subject to the COBRA coverage requirements. [Treas. Reg. §54.4980B-2, Q&A-1(f)] Presumably, the same holds true for health savings accounts (HSAs), although the regulations do not specifically address those arrangements.

Q 6:14 Are long-term care plans subject to COBRA?

HIPAA specifies that COBRA rules do not apply to qualified long-term care insurance contract plans. [I.R.C. §4980B(g)(2); ERISA §607(1); PHSA §2208(1), as added by HIPAA §321(d)]

In addition, Treasury regulations provide that a plan is not a group health plan subject to COBRA if substantially all of the coverage provided under the plan is for qualified long-term care services. An employer is permitted to use any reasonable method to determine if substantially all of the coverage provided under the plan is for qualified services. [Treas. Reg. §54.4980B-2, Q&A-1(e)]

Qualified long-term care services include necessary diagnostic, preventive, therapeutic, curing, treating, and rehabilitative services and personal care services required by a chronically ill individual. The services must be provided pursuant to a plan of care prescribed by a licensed practitioner. [I.R.C §7702B(c)]

Q 6:15 Are plans maintained solely for corporate directors, independent contractors, and the self-employed subject to COBRA?

A plan maintained solely for corporate directors, agents, independent contractors, and self-employed individuals is subject to the Code's COBRA requirements. The definition of *covered employee* in Code Section 4980B includes any individual who is, or was, provided coverage under a group health plan by virtue of the performance of services by the individual for one or more persons maintaining the plan, including a self-employed individual under Code Section 401(c)(1). [I.R.C. §4980B(f)(7)]

ERISA's definition of *covered employee* for COBRA purposes is identical. However, because ERISA plans must cover at least one common law employee, it appears that one such plan participant may be necessary in order to succeed on any ERISA claims.

In addition, a plan covering only directors, independent contractors, or self-employed individuals may qualify for exemption from the COBRA requirements as a small-employer plan. The small-employer exemption applies to a plan maintained by an employer that normally employed fewer than 20 employees during the preceding year. For this purpose, self-employed individuals, directors, independent contractors, or other individuals who are not common-law employees of the employer are not taken into account. [Treas. Reg. §54.4980B-2, Q&A-5(c)] Therefore, a plan covering only directors, independent contractors, or self-employed individuals will be exempt if the employer normally employs fewer than 20 common-law employees. (For details on the small-employer exemption, see Q 6:23.)

Q 6:16   How are multiple-employer welfare arrangements treated under COBRA?

Proposed regulations issued in 1987 provided that each employer participating in a multiple-employer welfare arrangement (MEWA) is considered to be maintaining a separate group health plan for COBRA purposes. [Prop. Treas. Reg. §1.162-26, Q&A-10(b)] Under that rule, COBRA's small-employer exemption would apply individually to each employer. Additionally, COBRA violations committed by one participating employer would not affect any other participating employer that is not in the same controlled group. However, neither the final COBRA regulations issued in 1999 nor those issued in 2001 specifically address MEWAs.

The final regulations provide that, as a general rule, all health benefits provided by one entity or trade or business are treated as a single plan. This default rule applies unless (1) it is clear from the instruments governing an arrangement or arrangements to provide health care benefits that the benefits are being provided under separate plans and (2) the arrangement or arrangements are actually operated as separate plans. The final regulations also provide that if the principal purpose of establishing separate plans is to evade any requirement of law, the separate plans will be considered a single plan to the extent necessary to prevent the evasion. [Treas. Reg. §54.4980B-2 Q&A-6]

Q 6:17   Are multiemployer plans subject to COBRA?

Yes. Generally, a multiemployer group health plan has two or more participating employers, and participation is pursuant to one or more collective bargaining agreements. For COBRA purposes, a multiemployer plan is treated as a single group health plan unless certain special rules require it to be treated as more than one plan (see Qs 6:18–6:19). The multiemployer plan will not qualify for the small-employer exemption from COBRA unless each participating employer separately qualifies for it. Furthermore, a single participating employer's failure to qualify for the small-employer exemption will subject the entire multiemployer group health plan to COBRA (see Qs 6:28–6:30 for further discussion of the small-employer exemption as applied to multiemployer plans).

Definition of "Plan" for COBRA Purposes

Q 6:18   Is a medical plan ever considered to be two or more separate group health plans, not a single plan, for COBRA purposes?

The 1987 proposed COBRA regulations contained a scheme for disaggregating, or breaking down, plans in order to break arrangements into their constituent group health plans. The smaller units were treated as separate plans for COBRA compliance purposes, even if the aggregate had traditionally been referred to as a single plan or was reported on Form 5500 as a single plan. [Prop. Treas. Reg. §1.162-26, Q&A-10(a) (June 15, 1987)] This scheme was unwieldy. It occasionally could produce more "plans" than the employer intended in its plan documents. [Prop. Treas. Reg. §1.162-26, Q&A-10(b)]

The current COBRA regulations, in contrast, eliminate the former scheme entirely in favor of a largely commonsense approach. [Treas. Reg. §54.4980B-2, Qs&As-1(a), 6(a) (Jan. 10, 2001)] As a general rule, all health benefits provided by a corporation, partnership, or other entity or trade or business, or by an employee organization, constitute one group health plan unless (1) it is clear from the governing instruments that the benefits are being provided under separate plans and (2) the arrangements are actually operated as a single plan.

However, a plan that is a multiemployer plan and a plan that is not a multiemployer plan are always treated as separate plans for COBRA purposes. [Treas. Reg. §54.4980B-2, Q&A-6(b) (Jan. 10, 2001)] Additionally, if the principal purpose of establishing separate plans is to evade any legal requirement, then they will be considered a single plan to the extent necessary to prevent the evasion. [Treas. Reg. §54.4980B-2, Q&A-6 (Jan. 10, 2001)]

This scheme grants employers broad discretion to determine the number of group health plans they maintain. Group health benefits can either be combined into a single plan or divided into separate plans, and the COBRA responsibilities will follow from the structure reflected in the plan documents.

Q 6:19   What is the significance of the number of plans?

The number of group health plans maintained by an employer is significant for several determinations, including:

- Cost of COBRA continuation coverage
- Beneficiaries' rights to elect separate coverage

Example. Employer X maintains a single group health plan, which provides major medical and prescription drug benefits. Employer Y maintains two separate plans, one providing major medical benefits and the other providing prescription drug benefits. Employer X can comply with the COBRA continuation coverage requirements by offering a qualifying beneficiary the choice of electing both major medical and prescription drug benefits or not receiving COBRA coverage under the plan. By contrast, Employer Y must offer a qualified beneficiary a choice of electing COBRA coverage under either the major medical plan or the prescription drug plan or both.

The number of group health plans can also be significant in determining whether a multiemployer plan will qualify for the COBRA exception for small employers with fewer than 20 employees (see Q 6:23). For a multiemployer plan to qualify for the exception, each of the employers in the plan must have normally employed fewer than 20 employees during the preceding calendar year. Therefore, if a joint board of trustees administers a single-employer plan, the plan will fail to qualify if any one of the employers in the plan employed 20 or more employees in the prior year. However, if the joint board of trustees maintains two or more multiemployer plans, one plan would not fail to qualify because an employer participating in another plan employed 20 or more employees in the prior year. [Treas. Reg. §54.4980B-2, Q&A-6(d)]

Covered Employers

Q 6:20   Are all employers subject to COBRA?

Although most employers are obligated to follow COBRA's rules if they provide group health plans, certain employers are exempt:

- Federal, state, and local governments (although the PHSA imposes similar COBRA requirements for state and local governments receiving funds under that act); and
- Churches, conventions and associations of churches, and certain church controlled organizations.

There is also an exemption for small employers (see Qs 6:23–6:30). [I.R.C. §4980B(d); ERISA §601(a); PHSA §2101(b)(2)]

Q 6:21   How is an employer defined for COBRA purposes?

COBRA's definition of *employer* uses the controlled-group rules of Code Section 414(b), (c), (m), and (o). [I.R.C. §414(t)(2); ERISA §607(4); Treas. Reg. §54.4980B-2, Q&A-2(a), (b), (c) (Feb. 3, 1999)] The controlled-group rules are intended to prevent an employer from structuring itself as two or more supposedly separate employers (whether or not incorporated) in order to avoid the application of various tax rules. These rules examine the degree of common ownership between two or more entities (including those having a parent subsidiary relationship or a prescribed percentage of common ownership) that are acting as a single employer.

These rules affect the employer's eligibility for COBRA's small-employer exemption (see Q 6:32).

COBRA's definition of *employer* also specifically includes a successor employer. An employer is a successor employer if it results from a consolidation, merger, or similar restructuring of the employer or if it is a mere continuation of the employer. [Treas. Reg. §54.4980B-2, Q&A-2] Under certain circumstances a purchaser of substantial assets is a successor employer to the employer selling the assets (see Q 6:158).

Q 6:22   Does COBRA cover the domestic subsidiary of a foreign corporation and/or the foreign parent of a domestic corporation?

This issue is not resolved by referring to the COBRA statute. First, COBRA does not apply at all to any employer that is immune from jurisdiction pursuant to the Foreign Sovereign Immunities Act (FSIA) because it is a foreign state or an instrumentality of that state. Second, COBRA may apply if an exception to FSIA applies, such as the act's commercial activities exception.

This thorny issue was addressed by the Ninth Circuit in *Gates v. Victor Fine Foods*. [54 F.3d 1457 (9th Cir. 1995)] In that case, a California pork-processing plant terminated its group health plan and shortly thereafter shut down its plant and terminated all of its employees. The employees sued, seeking to hold the plant, its parent, a British Columbia plant, and the parent of the British Columbia plant liable for violating COBRA. The Ninth Circuit held that applying COBRA's controlled-group rules was "placing the jurisdictional cart before the substantive horse." The court further held that before a federal court may apply corporate law, the controlled-group provisions of ERISA, or any other rule of law in a case involving a foreign state or instrumentality of that state, it must, as a threshold matter, find an exception to FSIA's grant of sovereign immunity. The court first examined the parent of the British Columbia plant and found that parent to be an agency or instrumentality of the province of Alberta because it was actually a governmental marketing board of sorts. It did not engage in any activities that would cause FSIA's commercial activities exception to apply, so it was thus immune from jurisdiction and could not be sued under COBRA. The British Columbia plant, on the other hand, was found not to fall within the protection of FSIA. The Ninth Circuit concluded that it and the processing plant were subject to COBRA, but that the Alberta parent was immune from jurisdiction.

Q 6:23   Are any employers too small to be subject to COBRA?

Yes, some are. Exempt employers are those that normally employed fewer than 20 employees on a "typical business day" in the year preceding the year for which exemption is sought (see Q 6:24). [I.R.C. § 4980B(d)(1); ERISA § 601(b); PHSA § 2201(b)(1)] However, because the controlled-group rules apply (see Q 6:21), an employer should carefully examine its business structure and relationships when determining whether it qualifies for this small-employer exemption.

Example. Corporation S employs 12 employees, all of whom work and reside in the United States. S maintains a group health plan for its employees and their families. S is a wholly owned subsidiary of Corporation P. In the previous calendar year, the controlled group of corporations consisting of P and S employed more than 19 employees, although the only employees in the United States were the employees of S.

Under the controlled-group rules, foreign corporations are not excluded from membership in a controlled group of corporations. [Treas. Reg. § 1. 414(b)-1] Therefore, the group health plan maintained by S does not qualify as a small-employer plan because the controlled group of P and S normally employed at least 20 employees in the preceding year.

Additionally, if the employer has in the past satisfied the small-employer exemption and then becomes too big, the employer should take care to notify its plan administrator so that the plan administrator can comply with the COBRA notice and coverage requirements. In one case, the employer pointed to its monthly insurance premium statement listing more than 20 employees as evidence that it had notified the plan administrator that COBRA now applied to the plan. The court in that case held such notice to be insufficient notice to the plan administrator. [Kidder v. H&B Marine, Inc., 932 F.2d 347 (5th Cir. 1991)]

Caution. Employers qualifying for the small-employer exception should avoid any words or actions that would lead an employee to believe that he or she is entitled to COBRA coverage. The Sixth Circuit Court of Appeals held that the doctrine of equitable estoppel may bar an employer from claiming that it does not meet the 20-employee threshold for providing COBRA coverage. [Thomas v. Miller, No. 05-2404, 2007 U.S. App. LEXIS 23635 (6th Cir. Sept. 27, 2007)] Significantly, the Sixth Circuit relied on a Supreme Court decision, which held that an employee could sue an employer for sex discrimination under Title VII of the Civil Rights Act of 1964 even though the employer moved to dismiss the case on the grounds that it did not meet the 15-employee threshold for application of that law. [Arbaugh v. Y&H Corp., 546 U.S. 500 (2006)]. According to the Court, a numerical employee threshold is only an element of a claim rather than a jurisdictional requirement. Thus, the Sixth Circuit reasoned that a numerical threshold should be treated like any other part of a claim that parties may concede, may be ordered by a court to admit—or can be equitably estopped from contesting. In light of the Sixth Circuit's reliance on a Supreme Court precedent, other federal circuits may well follow the same course.

The doctrine of equitable estoppel may bar a party to a lawsuit from asserting a certain claim in a lawsuit. However, for equitable estoppel to apply, five requirements must be met:

1. The party to be estopped must have used conduct or language that amounted to a representation of a material fact.

2. The party to be estopped must have been aware of the true facts.

3. The party to be estopped must have intended that the representation be relied on or acted in such a way that the other party had a right to believe that the representation was intended to be relied on.

4. The other party must have been unaware of the true facts.

5. The other party must have relied on the representation to its detriment.

Although it held that equitable estoppel could bar an employer from asserting the small-employer COBRA limit, the Sixth Circuit concluded that equitable estoppel *did not* apply in the case before the court. The employee in the case based her claim for COBRA coverage on the fact that she overheard company managers discussing the provision of COBRA coverage. The court concluded that that was not enough to satisfy the first and third elements required for equitable estoppel. According to the court, nothing in the discussion amounted to a representation that the employee in the case would receive COBRA coverage. Moreover, there was nothing to indicate that the managers intended said employee to rely on the conversation she overheard or on the provision of COBRA coverage to another employee.

Q 6:24   How is the typical-business-day standard satisfied?

The typical business-day standard is satisfied if, and only if, the employer had fewer than 20 employees (as defined in Q 6:25) on at least 50 percent of its typical business days during the preceding calendar year. [Treas. Reg. §54. 4989B-2, Q&A-5(c) (Feb. 3, 1999)]

For this purpose, the entire 12-month period must be considered. At least one court has rejected the use of a shorter period (such as a single month or a period of months smaller than the entire year) on the grounds that selecting a period shorter than 12 months could skew the employee count. [Martinez v. Dodge Printing Ctrs., Inc., 13 Employee Benefits Cas. (BNA) 1348 (D. Colo. 1991)]

Q 6:25   Which individuals are counted as employees in deciding whether an employer is too small for its group health plans to be subject to COBRA?

Both part-time and full-time employees are counted, although part-timers count only as a fraction of an employee. Additionally, at least one court has held that temporary employees should also be counted. [Martinez v. Dodge Printing Ctrs., Inc., 13 Employee Benefits Cas. (BNA) 1348 (D. Colo. 1991)]

Nonresident aliens with no income from U.S. sources apparently also must be counted for the purposes of the small-employer exemption.

An individual who is not a common-law employee of the employer is not counted for purposes of determining whether the employer has fewer than 20 employees. The COBRA regulations specifically provide that self-employed individuals, independent contractors, and directors are not counted. [Treas. Reg. §54.4980B-2, Q&A-5(c)]

In one case, a corporation located in Puerto Rico claimed that it was an exempt small employer even though 27 people worked in the business. The corporation argued that the company's two owners and seven of their relatives should not be counted because they did not fall within the definition of an employee in a Puerto Rican labor relations statute. However, the court held that Puerto Rico's definition did not apply for COBRA purposes. Instead, the court applied ERISA's definition of employee, which includes "any individual employed by an employer." Therefore, the court held that the corporation was subject to the COBRA continuation coverage requirements. [Jiminez v. Mueblerias Delgado, Inc., 196 F. Supp. 2d 125 (D.P.R. 2002)]

Note that once it is determined that a plan is subject to COBRA, the statute uses a separate definition of *covered employees* for purposes of determining who is entitled to COBRA rights under such a plan (see Q 6:34).

Q 6:26   How does an employer count employees?

In determining the number of employees, each full-time employee is counted as one employee. However, each part-timer is counted as a fraction of an employee equal to the number of hours the employee works divided by the number of hours he or she would have to work to be considered full-time. [Treas. Reg. §54.4980B-2, Q&A-5(d), (e)] The number of hours required to be full-time depends on the employer's normal business practice, but may be no more than 8 hours a day or 40 hours a week.

An employer may count employees on a daily basis or on a pay-period basis. The same counting method chosen must be used for all employees and must be used consistently throughout the year.

Counting employees on a daily basis. The employer must determine (1) the actual number of full-time employees on each typical business day and (2) the actual number of part-time employees and the hours worked by each part-time employee on each typical business day. Each full-time employee counts as one employee on each business day; each part-timer counts as a fraction equal to the number of hours worked on a given day divided by the number of hours necessary to be considered full-time.

Counting employees on a pay-period basis. The employer must determine (1) the actual number of full-time employees employed during each pay period and (2) the actual number of part-time employees and the hours worked by each part-time employee during the pay period. For each payday in the period, each full-time employee counts as one employee and each part-timer counts as a fraction equal to the number of hours worked in the pay period divided by the number of hours necessary to be considered full-time.

Q 6:27   Are entities under common control aggregated to determine eligibility for the small-employer exemption?

Yes. For purposes of the minimum-size requirement, the employer and all other entities under common control with it are considered to be a single employer. [I.R.C §414(t)] (The controlled-group rules are discussed in Q 6:21.) As a result, even if an employer has fewer than 20 employees, it will not qualify for COBRA's small-employer exemption if, together with all other related companies in the same controlled group, there are more than 20 employees. [*See* Kidder v. H&B Marine Inc., 932 F.2d 347 (5th Cir. 1991); Granger v. AAMCO Automatic Transmission Inc., 1992 U.S. Dist. LEXIS 14246 (D.N.J. Sept. 9, 1992)]

Q 6:28 How does the small-employer exemption apply to multiemployer plans?

A multiemployer plan, which is a plan maintained by at least two unrelated employers (that is, not in the same controlled group) pursuant to one or more collective bargaining agreements, is treated as a single group health plan for COBRA purposes. [ERISA §3(37)(A); Treas. Reg. §54.4908B-2, Q&A-5(a) (Feb. 3, 1999)] Accordingly, for the small-employer exemption to apply, every participating employer (determined under the controlled-group rules) must have fewer than 20 employees on a typical working day.

Q 6:29 What happens if an employer in an exempt small-employer plan increases its workforce?

The answer depends on the type of plan that is being affected by the workforce increase.

Single-employer plan. An increase in the sponsoring employer's workforce to 20 employees or more will eventually subject a single-employer plan to COBRA, but not immediately. The plan becomes subject to COBRA on the first day (January 1) of the calendar year immediately following the calendar year in which the employer's workforce normally exceeded 20 employees on a typical business day. This rule applies even if the plan year is not on a calendar year. [Treas. Reg. §54.4980B-2, Q&A-5(a)] By contrast, if an unrelated employer were to be added to a single-employer plan, no workforce increase would occur; instead, a multiple-employer welfare arrangement (MEWA) would be created.

Multiemployer plan. If any employer participating in the multiemployer plan reaches the 20-employee threshold midyear due to a workforce increase (i.e., by hiring more employees or adding another employer within the same controlled group), then all participating employers lose the exemption effective January 1 of the next calendar year. [Treas. Reg. §54.4980-2, Q&A-5(f)]

By contrast, if a new, unrelated employer with 20 or more employees joins a multiemployer plan, the entire plan and all participating employers become subject to COBRA immediately. [Treas. Reg. §54.4980B-2, Q&A-5(f)]

The IRS has issued guidance on applying the small-employer exception when an employer increases its workforce to 20 or more through a stock or asset acquisition. [*See* Rev. Rul. 2003-70, 2003-27 I.R.B. 3.] The IRS guidance gives two examples.

Example 1. Alpha Company maintains a group health plan for its employees. As of the beginning of the current year, Alpha qualified for the small-employer exception because it normally employed fewer than 20 employees in the prior year. During the current year, Alpha acquired all of the stock of Beta Company so that following the transfer Alpha and Beta are considered to be a single employer. The combined number of employees normally employed by Alpha and Beta during the prior year was at least 20.

According to the IRS, in applying the small-employer exception to a combined entity following a *stock transfer*, employees of each of the combined entities during any month must be taken into account. Therefore, because the employers in Example 1 combined employed at least 20 employees during the previous calendar year, a group health plan maintained by the combined entity becomes subject to COBRA as of the date of the stock transfer.

Example 2. Gamma Corporation maintains a group health plan for its employees. Because Gamma normally employed fewer than 20 employees during the prior year, Gamma qualified for the small-employer exception as of the beginning of the current year. During the current year, Gamma Corporation acquired all of the assets of Delta Company and continued the business operations associated with those assets without interruption or substantial changes. Gamma and Delta together employed at least 20 employees during the prior year.

According to the IRS, the *acquisition* of one company's assets by another does not cause the two companies to be treated as a single employer. Therefore, Gamma's group health plan will continue to be excepted from the COBRA coverage requirements until January 1 of the year following the year in which Gamma normally employs at least 20 employees (as determined under the normal application of the rules for determining whether a plan is a small-employer health plan).

Q 6:30 What happens if an employer covered by COBRA reduces its workforce below 20 employees?

In the year of the workforce reduction, the COBRA requirements continue to apply to qualifying events occurring in that year. If, as a result of the reduction, the employer qualifies for the small-employer exemption for the next calendar year, the employer will not be subject to COBRA with respect to qualifying events occurring in that year. However, the employer must continue to meet its COBRA responsibilities to individuals who became qualified beneficiaries (1) in the year the employer's workforce dropped below 20 and (2) in prior calendar years. [I.R.C. §4980B(d)(1); Treas. Reg. §54.4980B-2, Q&A-5(g)]

Multiemployer plans. If a multiemployer plan is subject to COBRA, the decrease in the size of a single participating employer below the 20-employee threshold does not cause either that employer or the multiemployer plan to become exempt from COBRA; all participating employers (determined under the controlled-group rules) must individually satisfy the small-employer exemption in order for the multiemployer plan (and all participating employers) to be exempt from the COBRA continuation of coverage rules. [Treas. Reg. §54. 4980B-2, Q&A-5(a) (Feb. 3, 1999)]

Q 6:31   What special COBRA requirements apply if an employer goes bankrupt?

If an employer files for protection under Title 11 of the United States Code, a broad group of retirees, their spouses or surviving spouses, and their dependents become qualified beneficiaries. The group is unusually broad because the statute picks up individuals whose coverage is lost or diminished because of a bankruptcy proceeding within one year before or after the qualifying event. Moreover, lifetime COBRA continuation coverage is extended to retirees and those who were surviving spouses at the time they became qualified beneficiaries. (See Qs 6:33–6:40.)

Q 6:32   When a business reorganization occurs, which employer must provide COBRA continuation coverage?

The COBRA regulations define a business reorganization to include both stock sales and asset sales. A stock sale is a transfer of stock that causes a corporation to become a different employer or a member of a different employer. An asset sale is a transfer of substantial assets, such as a plant or division, or substantially all of the assets of a trade or business. [Treas. Reg. §54-4980B-9, Q&A-1]

As a general rule, in the case of either a stock or an asset sale, the seller or selling group has the obligation to provide COBRA coverage to "M&A qualified beneficiaries." [Treas. Reg. §54.4980B-9, Q&A-8(a)] However, if the seller or selling group ceases to provide group health coverage to any employee in connection with the sale, the buyer or buying group must provide COBRA coverage to M&A qualified beneficiaries. [Treas. Reg. §54.4980B-9, Q&A-8(b)]

M&A qualified beneficiaries include existing qualified beneficiaries of the business being sold as well as beneficiaries whose COBRA-qualifying events are connected with the sale. [Treas. Reg. §54.4980B-9, Q&A-4]

Practice Pointer. The COBRA regulations make it clear that the buyer and the seller are free to allocate the responsibility for providing COBRA coverage by contract, even if the contract imposes responsibility on a party different from the party that would be responsible under the regulations. As long as the party to whom the contract allocates responsibility follows through, the other party is relieved of liability. However, if the party with responsibility under the contract does not perform, the party responsible under the COBRA regulations must provide the coverage. [Treas. Reg. §54.4980B-9, Q&A-7] (See Q 6:158.)

Qualified Beneficiaries

Q 6:33   Who is a qualified beneficiary?

Four classes of individuals are defined as *qualified beneficiaries,* based on their status on the day before the qualifying event (see Q 6:41):

1. A person who is a covered employee under a group health plan;
2. A covered employee's covered spouse;
3. A covered employee's covered dependent child; and
4. In bankruptcy situations, certain retirees and their spouses (including widows and widowers) and dependents.

[I.R.C. §4980B(g); ERISA §607; PHSA §2208; Treas. Reg. §54.4980B-3, Q&A-1(a)(i)(ii), Q&A-1(a)(2) (Feb. 3, 1999)]

The term "qualified beneficiaries" also includes children born to an employee, or children who are placed with the employee for adoption, during the employee's continuation coverage period. [I.R.C. §4980B(g)(1)(A); ERISA §602(2); PHSA §2202(2), all as amended by HIPAA §421] The law unintentionally omits children who are actually adopted (rather than placed for adoption) during the employee's continuation coverage period. However, the IRS has corrected this technical error in the regulations by defining "placed for adoption" as including children who are immediately adopted by the employee without prior placement for adoption. [Treas. Reg. §54.4980B-3, Q&A-1(g) (Feb. 3, 1999)]

Who is not a qualified beneficiary. With the exception of children who are born or placed for adoption with a covered employee, new family members who were not covered under the plan on the day before a qualifying event do not become qualified beneficiaries. [Treas. Reg. §54.4980B-3, Q&A-1(b)] For example, an individual who marries a qualified beneficiary during a period of continuation coverage is not a qualified beneficiary. Similarly, a child who is born to or placed for adoption with a qualified beneficiary (other than a covered employee) is not a qualified beneficiary. However, a new spouse or newborn or adopted child may have special enrollment rights under HIPAA during the COBRA continuation coverage period (see Q 6:39).

An individual who is covered under the plan on the day before a qualifying event by reason of another individual's election of COBRA coverage is not a qualifying beneficiary. [Treas. Reg. §54.4980B-3, Q&A-1(c)]

Example. Bob, a single employee, terminated employment with Alpha Co. and elected COBRA coverage under Alpha's plan. During the COBRA coverage period, Bob marries and elects to have his new spouse covered by the plan (under special enrollment rights). Bob's spouse is not a qualified beneficiary. Therefore, Alpha's plan is not required to offer Bob's spouse COBRA coverage if there is a subsequent qualifying event (e. g., Bob dies or the couple divorces) during Bob's COBRA coverage period.

A qualified beneficiary who does not elect COBRA continuation coverage in connection with a qualifying event ceases to be a qualified beneficiary at the end of the election period. [Treas. Reg. §54.4980B-3, Q&A-1(f)] For example, if a covered employee's spouse initially declined COBRA coverage but is later added to a covered employee's coverage during an open enrollment period, the spouse will not be a qualified beneficiary with respect to a second qualifying event.

Q 6:34   Who is a covered employee?

A *covered employee* is any individual who has, or had, coverage under a group health plan subject to COBRA, by reason of the performance of service by the individual for one or more persons maintaining the plan. This broad definition also includes individuals such as independent contractors and partners (see Q 6:35). Note that retirees and former employees receiving group health coverage because of their previous employment are considered covered employees. [I.R.C. §4980B(f)(7); ERISA §607(2); PHSA §2208(2); Treas. Reg. §54.4980B-3, Q&A-1(a)(1) (Feb. 3, 1999)]

Mere eligibility for coverage, without actual coverage, does not make a person a covered employee. Generally, the reason for the employee's (or former employee's) lack of actual coverage (such as having declined participation or having failed to satisfy requirements for participation) is irrelevant. However, if the plan's failure to provide or offer coverage was in violation of a law such as the Americans with Disabilities Act (ADA) or HIPAA, the employee (or former employee) will be treated as having the coverage that was denied or not offered. [Treas. Reg. §54.4980B-3, Q&A-2(b)]

A covered employee is a qualified beneficiary only with respect to three qualifying events:

1. Termination of employment
2. Reduction of hours of employment
3. Bankruptcy of the employer

Q 6:35   Can a self-employed individual be a covered employee?

Yes. A self-employed individual who actually participates in a group health plan subject to COBRA is a covered employee. This rule applies to individuals such as partners and sole proprietors, who are self-employed under the definition of Code Section 401(c)(1); it also applies to independent contractors and corporate directors. [I.R.C. §4980B(f)(7); ERISA §607(2); PHSA §2208(2); Treas. Reg. §54.4980B-3, Q&A-2(a), Q&A-2(b) (Feb. 3, 1999)]

Q 6:36   Are there special rules for nonresident aliens?

Yes. A person whose status as a covered employee is attributable to a period of time in which he or she was a nonresident alien without U.S.–source income cannot become a qualified beneficiary. The person's spouse and dependents also cannot become qualified beneficiaries by reason of their relationship to the alien employee. [Treas. Reg. §54.4908B-3, Q&A-1(c) (Feb. 3, 1999)]

Note. Nonresident aliens without U.S.-source income are counted for purposes of applying COBRA's small-employer exemption, as discussed in Q 6:25, because the statute does not contain a similar exclusion for that purpose.

Q 6:37 Can a dependent child be a qualified beneficiary when the event is the parents' divorce?

At least one court has stated, possibly erroneously, that a dependent child cannot be a qualified beneficiary when the statutory event is the parents' divorce. [Smith v. Borden, 1995 U.S. Dist. LEXIS 19728 (W.D. Mo. Oct. 23, 1995)] In that case, the employee had dropped his stepdaughter from his group health plan coverage at the time he obtained a divorce from her mother. The stepdaughter claimed that her loss of coverage was caused by the divorce and that she was a qualified beneficiary entitled to COBRA. The court disagreed, finding that her termination was due to the employee/stepfather's voluntary act, not due to the divorce. However, the court then went on to say that because the stepdaughter had not reached the limiting age under the plan, she had not experienced a qualifying event. The court further opined that "the right to continuation coverage . . . vests in the divorced spouse and not . . . in the dependent child." Although this court evidently could not imagine any scenario under which the child would lose coverage as a result of the parents' divorce, nothing in the statute appears to bar a child from being a qualified beneficiary if the child's loss of dependent status and corresponding loss of plan coverage was caused by the divorce rather than a voluntary action of one of the parents.

Q 6:38 Is a domestic partner covered under a group health plan required to be recognized as a qualified beneficiary?

No, the law does not require that domestic partners be treated as qualified beneficiaries. COBRA rights apply only to spouses and dependent children. [I.R.C. §4980(g)(1)] Under the Defense of Marriage Act [Pub. L. No. 104-199, 110 Stat. 2419 (1996)], no federal law, rule, or regulation is to be interpreted to include same-sex domestic partners as spouses. Furthermore, domestic partners, while they may be dependents, are not children.

The IRS has ruled privately that same-sex domestic partners may qualify as dependents for purposes of the tax exclusion for employer-provided health coverage. [Priv. Ltr. Rul. 985001] (See chapter 3.)

Practice Pointer. Bear in mind that COBRA provides the minimum standards for continuation coverage. It does not prohibit a company from offering additional continuation coverage, including coverage for domestic partners. However, companies with insured plans should obtain the approval of their insurer before extending such coverage.

Q 6:39　If a qualified beneficiary who is receiving COBRA coverage subsequently acquires a new family member, does that new family member also become a qualified beneficiary?

The answer depends on the type of new family member. Generally, only one measuring date—the day before the qualifying event—is used to determine who is a qualified beneficiary. On that date, the class of qualified beneficiaries entitled to elect COBRA overage is closed, with one exception. Children who are born to or placed for adoption with the covered employee during the COBRA continuation period are qualified beneficiaries as well. [I.R.C. §4980B(g)(1)(A), ERISA §607(3)(A), PHSA §2208(3), all as amended by §421of HIPAA]

Q 6:40　Can a retiree be a qualified beneficiary?

Generally not. Although COBRA's definition of a covered employee clearly includes retired and former employees, a retired or former employee generally cannot satisfy the remaining elements for COBRA eligibility: loss of coverage as a result of a qualifying event (retirees cannot terminate employment or reduce hours of employment). Retirees can, however, lose coverage and become qualified beneficiaries as a result of a bankruptcy filing (see Qs 6:41, 6:48). [Treas. Reg. §54.4980B-3, Q&A-2(b) (Feb. 3, 1999)]

Qualifying Events

Q 6:41　What is a qualifying event?

A *qualifying event* is any one of the following events (but only if the event results in a loss of group health plan coverage):

1. The death of a covered employee;
2. Termination of a covered employee's employment for any reason other than gross misconduct;
3. Reduction in the number of hours a covered employee is employed;
4. Divorce or separation of a covered employee and his or her spouse;
5. Medicare entitlement of a covered employee;
6. A child of the covered employee ceasing to meet the group health plan's definition of a dependent child; or
7. Commencement of a bankruptcy proceeding concerning an employer from whose employment the covered employee retired.

[I.R.C. §4980B(f)(3); ERISA §603; PHSA §2203; Treas. Reg. §54-49803-4, Q&A-1 (Feb. 3, 1999)]

Failure to return from FMLA leave. Taking leave under the Family and Medical Leave Act of 1993 (FMLA) is not a qualifying event. However, an employee's failure to return to work at the end of a period of qualifying FMLA leave (see chapter 16) may be a qualifying event (see Q 6:64).

Loss of coverage due to an event other than the ones listed above will not be a qualifying event. For example, plan amendments and cutbacks may cause a loss of coverage but are not the kind of events that COBRA addresses. Similarly, an employer's switch from one insurance policy to another with the same insurer or to a successor insurance carrier may cause a loss in coverage if the covered benefits under the replacement policy are less comprehensive, but the switch itself is not one of the qualifying events that trigger COBRA rights. [Kraft v. Northbrook Ins. Co. & Med. Plans, 813 F. Supp. 464, 475 n.19 (S.D. Miss. 1993)] A federal district court has held that an employee was not entitled to COBRA because her loss of group health plan coverage was due to her failure to pay premiums, not her termination of employment. [Aguilera v. Landmark Hotel-Metairie, 16 Employee Benefits Cas. (BNA) 1466 (E.D. La. 1992)]

Q 6:42   Why are the qualifying-event provisions included in COBRA?

COBRA is intended to provide a "bridge" in coverage for a limited period of time, so that the individual can get other group or individual health care coverage. For this reason, events that do not result in loss of group health plan coverage are not within the scope of COBRA. For example, if a plan covers spouses who are legally separated from employees covered by the plan, legal separation would not mean a loss of coverage; therefore, the employer sponsoring such a plan would not be required to offer continuation coverage to the estranged spouse of the employee.

Although it might seem that the purpose of COBRA is to protect the worker, in fact, there are only two situations in which an active covered employee can have the status of a qualified beneficiary under COBRA: termination, for reasons other than gross misconduct, and reduction of hours of employment. [Treas. Reg. §54.4980B-4, Q&A-1(c) (Feb. 3, 1999)]

Q 6:43   Must group health plan coverage actually cease in order to be considered "lost" for COBRA purposes?

Group health plan coverage need not cease entirely in order for a COBRA qualifying event to occur. For COBRA purposes, a loss of coverage is considered to occur when the covered individual ceases to be covered under the same terms and conditions as were in effect immediately before the qualifying event. Thus, a loss would occur if benefits decrease or are cut back due to a qualifying event. For example, suppose that an employee goes from full-time to half-time employment and, as a result, the employee's health plan coverage is reduced by half. In that instance, a loss of coverage would occur due to a reduction in hours, so COBRA rights are triggered. [Treas. Reg. §54.4980 B-4, Q&A-1(c) (Feb. 3, 1999)]

In addition, any increase in the premium or contribution that must be paid by a covered employee (or a spouse or dependent child) for coverage under the plan that results from a qualifying event is a loss of coverage.

Example. Betty retires after 30 years with Beta Corp. As a retiree, Betty is required to pay a higher premium for the same group health coverage she had before retirement. Betty's retirement is a qualifying event—termination of her employment—and she has lost coverage as a result of that event. Therefore, Beta must offer Betty COBRA continuation coverage.

Practice Pointer. The above rule may seem somewhat paradoxical. After all, a company may charge 102 percent of its cost for COBRA coverage and can cut off coverage at the end of the coverage period. A retiree may get a better deal in terms of both price and time if he or she sticks with retiree coverage. However, to comply with the rules, an employer must offer the COBRA coverage.

Q 6:44   Can a reduction in coverage trigger COBRA rights?

Yes, if the covered employee, spouse, or dependent child is no longer covered under the terms and conditions in effect immediately before the qualifying event, and the loss of coverage results from the occurrence of one of the specified events, such as termination of employment. If an employer merely amends its group health plan to cut back coverage generally, but the cutback is not related to one of the specified COBRA events, a qualifying event does not occur. [Treas. Reg. §54.4980 B-4, Q&A-1(c) (Feb. 3, 1999)]

Q 6:45   What if the individual loses coverage due to total disability?

If an individual becomes totally and permanently disabled but maintains his or her status as an employee, this would be a reduction in hours. A qualifying event therefore will occur if group health plan coverage is lost due to the individual's having become disabled. [United of Omaha v. Business Men's Assurance Co. of Am., 104 F.3d 1034 (8th Cir. 1996)]

Q 6:46   What if the loss of coverage is not simultaneous with the event?

General rule. Unless the plan provides otherwise, a qualifying event that results in a loss of group health plan coverage is deemed to occur when the event takes place, not when coverage is lost. For instance, if a terminated employee is entitled to a six-month extension of coverage (for whatever reason), the actual loss of coverage does not occur until the end of the six-month extension period. However, the date of an employee's termination will be treated as the date of the qualifying event, unless the plan provides otherwise. Thus, the maximum required COBRA coverage period will run from the date of the qualifying event, not from the date of the loss of coverage. [Gaskell v. Harvard Cooperative Soc'y, 17 Employee Benefits Cas. (BNA) 1152 (1st Cir. 1993); Treas. Reg. §54.4980B-4, Q&A-1(c) (Feb. 3, 1999); Treas. Reg. §54.4980B-7, Q&A-7]

If a loss of coverage does not occur before the end of the maximum coverage period, the event will not be considered a qualifying event. [Treas. Reg. §54.4980B-4, Q&A-1(c)]

Special plan provision rule. A group health plan may provide that the qualifying event occurs on the date coverage is actually lost, provided that the plan also provides that the notice period (see Q 6:70) also begins on the date coverage is actually lost. [I.R.C. §4980B(f)(8); ERISA §607(5)]

Special rule for FMLA leave. When an employee's failure to return from FMLA leave triggers COBRA coverage (see Q 6:65), the COBRA-qualifying event is deemed to occur on the last day of the FMLA leave, even if the employee actually lost coverage earlier due to failure to pay premiums during the period of the FMLA leave. [Treas. Reg. §54.4980B-7, Q&A-2] If the loss of coverage occurs at a later date, the plan may provide that qualifying event occurs on the date coverage is lost.

Q 6:47   What if an individual's coverage is reduced in anticipation of a qualifying event?

In a nonbankruptcy situation, the employer's anticipatory elimination or reduction of coverage is disregarded in determining whether the qualifying event causes a loss of coverage. In other words, the loss of coverage is measured from the level of coverage in force before the employer's anticipatory cutback. [Treas. Reg. §54.4980B-4, Q&A-1(c) (Feb. 3, 1999)] The COBRA regulations do not give any specific time period during which the cutback must occur to be treated as an anticipatory cutoff of benefits (see Q 6:106). Under prior law, an unresolved interpretive issue was whether anticipatory cutbacks that are disregarded under this COBRA rule are limited to those initiated by employers or whether they also include anticipatory cutbacks made by employees. The final COBRA regulations provided that a reduction or elimination of coverage in anticipation of an event includes an employee's eliminating the coverage of his or her spouse in anticipation of a divorce or legal separation. [Treas. Reg. §54.4980B-4, Q&A-1(c) (Feb. 3, 1999)]

In Revenue Ruling 2002-88 [2002-52 I.R.B. 995], the IRS makes it clear that a plan is not required to make COBRA coverage available from the date of the employee's anticipatory elimination of coverage for a soon-to-be ex-spouse. Instead, the plan is required to make COBRA coverage available to the spouse as of the date of the divorce.

Practice Pointer. All the facts and circumstances must be assessed in deciding whether the employer cut back benefits in anticipation of a qualified event. Presumably, the amount of time involved will be relevant.

Q 6:48   When is coverage "lost" in an employer bankruptcy?

In an employer bankruptcy, a "substantial elimination" of coverage of a qualified beneficiary who is a retiree or a spouse or surviving spouse of a retiree or a dependent child of a retiree that occurs within one year before or after the date the bankruptcy proceeding was begun is treated as a loss of coverage. In other words, COBRA's bankruptcy provisions pickup any substantial loss of coverage over a two-year period. [I.R.C. §4980B(f)(3); ERISA §603(6)]

Substantial elimination of coverage. COBRA does not define the term *substantial elimination of coverage,* and the final COBRA regulations are silent on

COBRA's bankruptcy provisions. As a result, an employer will be confronted with a number of interpretive issues when trying to determine how many individuals would become qualified beneficiaries in a bankruptcy situation. For example, how significant must an elimination of coverage be for it to be deemed substantial for COBRA purposes?

Based on the language of COBRA, it appears that an employer that terminates its retiree medical plan within one year of filing a bankruptcy petition must reinstate the plan benefits for such retirees who retired on or before the date of the substantial elimination of coverage for the duration of the COBRA period (assuming that the bankrupt entity continues to sponsor a group health plan). [I.R.C. §4980B(f)(3)(F); ERISA §603(6); Treas. Reg. §54.4908B-4, Q&A-1(c) (Feb. 3, 1999)]

Q 6:49 Is the Federal Deposit Insurance Corporation or a bank that takes over the assets and employees of a failed bank obligated to continue COBRA coverage for the failed bank's employees?

In a decision by the U.S. Court of Appeals for the Tenth Circuit, the court considered the situation in which a state bank failed and went into receivership and the Federal Deposit Insurance Corporation (FDIC) was appointed receiver and liquidating agent. At the same time, the bank ceased operations and terminated its health plan. Another bank then purchased some of the failed bank's assets and assumed depositor liability. The purchasing bank also hired some of the failed bank's employees and operated a branch at the failed bank's location. The purchase agreement explicitly provided that the purchasing bank had no obligation under the failed bank's employee benefit plans. The court concluded that the failed bank ceased doing business when it went into receivership, and that neither the FDIC nor the purchasing bank was a successor employer required to provide COBRA continuation coverage to the employees of the failed bank. [Leiding v. FDIC, No. 90-5078, 1991 U.S. App. LEXIS 19044 (10th Cir. Aug. 12, 1991)]

Subsequently, federal banking legislation was enacted and provides that the FDIC, in its capacity as a successor of a failed depository institution (whether acting directly or through a bridge bank), has the same obligation to provide COBRA continuation coverage as the failed institution would have had if it had not failed. The same requirement applies to any successor to the failed depository institution.

An entity is considered a successor to the failed depository institution during any period if:

1. The entity holds substantially all of the assets or liabilities of the failed institution; and

2. The entity is any of the following:

    a. The FDIC,

    b. A bridge bank, or

c. An entity that acquired the assets or liabilities of the failed institution from the FDIC or a bridge bank.

[Pub. L. No. 102-242, §451, 105 Stat. 2236 (1978)]

Q 6:50   Can a voluntary termination, such as quitting or abandoning a job, constitute a qualifying event?

Yes, if the voluntary termination occurs while the plan is subject to COBRA and it results in a loss of group health plan coverage. Unless the employee was guilty of gross misconduct, it is irrelevant whether a termination of employment or reduction in hours was voluntary or involuntary. [Treas. Reg. §54.4908B-4, Q&A-2 (Feb. 3, 1999)] An employee's resignation from his or her union has been held not to be a termination of employment for COBRA purposes. [Devoll v. Burdick Painting Inc., 18 Employee Benefits Cas. (BNA) 2107 (9th Cir. 1994)]

If the covered employee is not a common-law employee (for example, he or she is a partner in a partnership or a corporate director), termination of employment means termination of the relationship that gave rise to the individual's status as a covered employee for COBRA purposes. [Treas. Reg. §54.4908B-4, Q&A-2 (a) (2) (Feb. 3, 1999)]

Q 6:51   Is involuntary termination, for example, firing, a qualifying event?

Yes. Involuntary termination is a qualifying event (if it occurs while the plan is subject to COBRA and it results in a loss of group health plan coverage) unless the employee is guilty of gross misconduct. [I.R.C. §4980B(f)(3)(B); ERISA §603(2); Treas. Reg. §54.4908 B-4, Q&A-1(b)(2), Q&A-1(c) (Feb. 3, 1999)]

Resignation in lieu of firing. In one case, a company president who had allegedly embezzled the company's funds was permitted to resign in lieu of being fired. The court held that the termination of employment was a voluntary termination (rather than being a termination due to gross misconduct) and therefore COBRA coverage was required to be offered. [Conery v. Bath Assocs., 803 F. Supp. 1388 (N.D. Ind. 1992)]

Q 6:52   What behavior qualifies as gross misconduct that would make a terminated employee ineligible for COBRA coverage?

Employers are not required to provide COBRA coverage to an employee who is terminated as a result of his or her gross misconduct; however, neither the statute nor the COBRA regulations define the term *gross misconduct.* The IRS has also indicated that employers must make their own determinations about what constitutes gross misconduct. [Rev. Proc. 87-28, 1987-1 C.B. 770]

Because of this lack of definition, employers have been wary of invoking the gross misconduct exception on an ad hoc basis except in extreme situations.

However, one employer decided to craft its own definition and communicate it to employees in advance.

In 1986, when Food Lion, Inc., a supermarket chain, first became subject to the COBRA coverage requirement, the company's insurance department employees sought assistance in determining how to define gross misconduct for COBRA purposes. They requested advice, but the answer from every source was that Congress had simply left the matter to each employer to determine for itself.

Food Lion's human resources department decided to define gross misconduct by reference to a list of eight rules that Food Lion considered serious enough for immediate discharge without warning. These eight "rules of conduct" had been in effect at Food Lion for many years; employees were familiar with them, and managers and supervisors were experienced in their application.

Whenever an employee was terminated, Food Lion would assign a "term code" indicating the reason for the termination. If the term code indicated that an employee voluntarily quit or was dismissed because no work was available, he or she was sent a COBRA notice. If the term code indicated any other reason for the dismissal, an insurance department employee would ask the employee's manager or supervisor about the reasons for and circumstances of the termination. If it was determined that the employee was fired for gross misconduct, he or she would not be sent a COBRA notice. In questionable cases, the employee received the benefit of the doubt and was sent a COBRA notice.

Rickey Bryant and Stephen Bannister were terminated by Food Lion under its rule of conduct number 3, which provided for immediate discharge upon an employee's insubordination or refusal to comply with the instructions of a supervisor. Bryant was discharged for repeatedly refusing to obey direct instructions from his store manager and his area grocery supervisor. Several of the assigned tasks that he failed to perform involved cleanliness, which was important to Food Lion. Bannister also was fired for failing to obey instructions. He regularly failed to clean the dairy case as instructed, despite repeated warnings. He had also been previously reprimanded in writing for violating rule of conduct number 3.

Following its usual procedures, Food Lion determined that Bryant and Bannister were discharged for gross misconduct and did not send them COBRA notices. The employees sued.

A U.S. district court held that Food Lion's procedures constituted a good-faith effort to comply with COBRA and to develop a definition of gross misconduct consistent with the company's needs. The court also found that Bryant and Bannister were terminated for gross misconduct in accordance with that definition and thus were not entitled to COBRA coverage. In a terse opinion, the Fourth Circuit concluded that, based on its findings of fact, the district court did not err in finding that the employees' conduct constituted gross misconduct for COBRA purposes. [Bryant v. Food Lion Inc., 100 F. Supp. 2d 346 (D. S.C. 2000), *aff'd,* 8 Fed. Appx. 194 (4th Cir. 2001), *cert. denied,* 122 S. Ct. 459 (2001)]

Practice Pointer. Food Lion's approach of specifying what types of behavior will be deemed gross misconduct may serve as a useful model. However, companies may want to limit the "gross misconduct" label to serious offenses that can be identified through objective evidence—e.g., theft, embezzlement, violence in the workplace, or alcohol- or drug-related violations. In a borderline case, the safest course of action is to offer an employee COBRA coverage. An excise tax of $100 per day (or $200 per day per family) can be imposed on an employer for failure to provide required COBRA coverage. A court may award a penalty of up to $110 per day to an employee or family member who is not provided with a required COBRA notice. Moreover, a company that wrongfully denied COBRA coverage can be held liable for medical expenses incurred during the COBRA coverage period.

The case law provides some guidance on the types of situations that are likely to qualify for the gross misconduct exception to COBRA rights. A California case looked to the definition of *gross misconduct* contained in that state's unemployment insurance law (even though it was not required to) because of the similarity in purpose between the two laws. [Paris v. F. Korbel & Bros., Inc., 751 F. Supp. 834 (N.D. Cal. 1990)] The court in that case found that a single incident in which an employee disclosed confidential information was not gross misconduct for purposes of determining the employee's entitlement to COBRA continuation of group health plan coverage. This case probably would have reached the opposite conclusion had the single piece of confidential information been of vital importance to the employer's business, such as disclosure of a heavily guarded secret formula or recipe for the company's main product or of the code for the company's main vault.

Violent conduct on the job can be the basis for a finding of gross misconduct. In one case, a flight attendant became involved in an altercation with a coworker while cleaning an airplane between flights. In the course of the dispute, the flight attendant, who was white, threw an apple and called the coworker "nigger." The dispute then became physical, with the coworker attacking the flight attendant and holding her in a choke hold as passengers began to board the plane. The airline fired both employees. The flight attendant sued the airline for failure to provide COBRA coverage. The court found that the airline was not liable for COBRA coverage because the flight attendant's actions constituted gross misconduct. The court said that by throwing the apple and audibly uttering a racial epithet she had provoked the confrontation, and therefore she could not claim that she had played no part in the physical altercation. [Nakisa v. Continental Airlines, 2001 U.S. Dist. LEXIS 8952 (S.D. Tex. May 10, 2001)]

A number of other courts have also held that a termination of employment for violent conduct off the job can be a discharge for gross misconduct within the meaning of COBRA. In *Zickafoose v. UB Servs., Inc.* [23 F. Supp. 2d 652 (S.D. W.Va. 1998)], a male manager, whose relationship with a female coworker evidently extended beyond the employment setting, had a violent argument with her during her evening visit to his home and savagely beat her. The female coworker required hospitalization for five days as a result of severe pelvic injuries. The manager was charged with a felony offense of unlawful assault and pled no contest. One week later, the employer terminated the manager for gross misconduct stemming from the assault and canceled his insurance benefits. The court concluded that gross misconduct for purposes of COBRA includes non-work-related outrageous behavior if there is a substantial nexus between the behavior and the working environment such that the effects of the intolerable behavior extend into the employment arena. The court found that the employee's role as a supervisor coupled with an assault on a coworker, provided a logical nexus between the gross misconduct and the workplace to justify the disallowance of COBRA continuation rights.

In a later decision, the same court held that the conduct of an employee who savagely beat a coworker amounted to gross misconduct, even though it occurred off the job, because the nature of the conduct was outrageous and because there was a substantial nexus between the behavior and the working environment such that the effects of the intolerable behavior extended into the employment arena. [UB Servs., Inc. v. Gatson, 207 W.Va. 365 (2000)]

McKnight v. School District of Philadelphia [171 F. Supp. 2d 446 (E.D. Pa. 2001)], which also involved conduct outside the workplace, raises another interesting question: What happens if later events indicate that an employee's conduct may not have been as egregious as first believed? A school teacher was arrested and charged with assault and other crimes allegedly committed in his home against an 18-year-old male who was his student. After an investigatory hearing by the school district, the teacher was fired for "immorality." The criminal charges against the teacher were later dropped because of lack of evidence. The school district did not offer the teacher COBRA coverage at the time of his dismissal, and he sued. The school district argued that it was not required to offer COBRA coverage because the teacher was dismissed for gross misconduct. The teacher countered that his arrest could not be the basis of a finding of gross misconduct because the charges were later dropped. The court said that the inquiry as to the propriety of the employer's determination of gross misconduct should be limited to the evidence available to the employer at the time of the employee's termination. Moreover, the court concluded that the school district acted reasonably in using the information available to it at the time of the discharge to determine whether a COBRA notice was required. "Under this approach," the court said, "the court avoids serving as a 'super personnel department' engaged in second-guessing employment decisions based on information which was not available to the employer."

Other cases have upheld the employer's determination of gross misconduct where the behavior at issue involved mishandling of employer funds or stealing employer property. [*See, e,g.,* Burke v. American Stores Employee Benefit Plan, 818 F. Supp. 1131 (N.D. Ill. 1993) (stealing company property: 28 free turkeys impermissibly obtained with promotional coupons); Karby v. Standard Prods. Co., 7 Employee Benefits Cas. (BNA) 1235 (D. S.C. 1992) (conversion of company property to private use and failure to disclose receipt of an interest-free loan from the employer's supplier); Avina v. Texas Pig Stands Inc., 1991 U.S. Dist. LEXIS 13957 (W.D. Tex. Feb. 1, 1991) (cash handling and invoice irregularities, failure to improve store performance).]

When the initial reason for the termination of employment is subsequently changed, the determination of COBRA entitlement apparently can be based on the revised reason for the termination if the revision is supported by the facts and conforms to the employer's policies. Thus, for example, an employer was permitted to deny COBRA continuation of coverage to an employee who initially was fired for reasons other than gross misconduct but whose separation from service was reclassified as resulting from gross misconduct several months later when the employer discovered acts of misconduct. [Karby v. Standard Prods. Co., 7 Employee Benefits Cas. (BNA) 1235 (D.S.C. 1992)]

Resignation in lieu of firing because of gross misconduct. A similar issue regarding a change in the reason for employment termination is presented when an employee is permitted to resign in lieu of being fired. A company president who allegedly embezzled the company's funds was permitted to resign in lieu of being fired. When he was denied COBRA coverage because of his gross misconduct, the executive sued. The court in that case found that embezzlement of company funds by the company's president did constitute misconduct, but that the executive was nonetheless entitled to COBRA because his termination of employment was voluntary (a resignation) rather than because of the misconduct. [Conery v. Bath Assocs., 803 F. Supp. 1388 (N.D. Ind. 1992)]

Standard of proof. The question of the appropriate standard of proof for establishing an employee's gross misconduct was raised in *Conery* as well. The executive argued that the company should be required to prove beyond a reasonable doubt that gross misconduct occurred. The employer argued that a different inquiry was more appropriate: whether the company acted on a good-faith belief that the executive had engaged in gross misconduct. The court indicated that it favored the test proposed by the company but concluded that it did not need to resolve that issue because of the facts of the case (permitted resignation in lieu of firing). In another case, *Kariotis v. Navistar International Transportation Corp.* [131 F.3d 672 (7th Cir. 1997)], the court concluded that actual misconduct need not be shown. Rather, the employer's good-faith belief at the time of employment termination that the employee committed gross misconduct was sufficient. In *Kariotis*, the employee was terminated for cause because the employer believed that the employee had made a fraudulent claim for disability benefits after viewing a 17-minute surveillance videotape of her walking, driving, and performing other acts inconsistent with her claim of disability.

Spouses and dependents. If the employee's termination is for gross misconduct, the spouse and dependents also do not experience a loss of coverage resulting from a qualifying event (termination for gross misconduct is expressly excluded from the statutory list of qualifying events). The Seventh Circuit Court of Appeals has confirmed that COBRA explicitly excludes the employee's termination for gross misconduct from the list of qualifying events. When the employee is terminated for gross misconduct, the employer is relieved of its duty to provide the employee's spouse with COBRA notification. [Mlsna v. Unitel Commc'ns, Inc., 41 F.3d 1124 (7th Cir. 1994)]

Q 6:53   Is a strike or walkout a qualifying event?

If a strike or walkout that occurs while the plan is subject to COBRA results in a loss of group health plan coverage, it is a qualifying event. [Treas. Reg. §54.4980B-4, Q&A-2 (Feb. 3, 1999); Communications Workers of Am. v. NYNEX Corp., 898 F.2d 887 (2d Cir. 1990)]

Q 6:54   Is a layoff a qualifying event?

Yes, if the layoff occurs while the plan is subject to COBRA and it results in a loss of group health plan coverage. [Treas. Reg. §54.4980B-4, Q&A-2 (Feb. 3, 1999)]

Q 6:55   Is a call to active duty in the armed forces a qualifying event?

Assuming that the employee called to active duty either is terminated from employment or is placed on leave of absence or otherwise can be said to suffer a reduction in hours, the call to active duty constitutes a COBRA qualifying event will occur if, as a result, he or she loses group health plan coverage. [IRS News Rel. 90-142 (Nov. 21, 1990); IRS Notice 90-58, 1990-2 C.B. 345 (Oct. 1, 1990)]

However, under the Uniformed Services Employment and Reemployment Rights Act of 1994 (USERRA), which was enacted in the wake of the Persian Gulf war, an employer is required to hold an employee's job open for at least five years (or longer, in unusual circumstance) if the employee is called up for active duty. In addition, an employer must continue health coverage for the employee and his or her dependents during the employee's period of military service. The right to continued coverage ends on the earlier of (1) 18 months after the military service began or (2) the deadline for the employee to apply for reemployment with the employer. The employee and dependents are entitled to immediate reinstatement of health benefits when the employee returns to work. The plan cannot impose a waiting period for coverage.

If the employee's military service lasts 31 to 180 days, the employee must apply for reemploy men no later than 14 days after the completion of the period of service. If the employee's military service lasts 181 days or longer, the employee must apply for reemployment no later than 90 days after completion of the period of service. These deadlines can be extended if the employee is hospitalized or convalescing from an injury or illness that occurred or was aggravated during the period of service.

For periods of service up to 30 days, the employer can require the employee to pay the normal employee share of health coverage costs. For longer periods of service, the employer is permitted to charge up to 102 percent of the cost of coverage. [USERRA §4317(a)(2)].

Q 6:56   When does termination of employment occur for individuals other than common-law employees?

Termination occurs, for COBRA purposes, with the termination of the relationship (for example, a corporate directorship) that gave rise to the individual's treatment as an employee for COBRA purposes (see Q 6:15). [Treas. Reg. §54.4980B-4, Q&A-2(a)(2) (Feb. 3, 1999)]

Q 6:57   Can a qualifying event ever occur with regard to an employee's spouse or dependent even if the employee remains covered?

Yes. For example, a new retiree's spouse receiving coverage without cost might lose coverage six months after the employee's retirement because the spouse elects not to pay a premium that is required to retain coverage; in this case, the employee's retirement is a qualifying event, and the retiree's spouse is a qualified beneficiary. The same rule would apply if coverage were lost because of a divorce. [Treas. Reg. §54.4980B-4, Q&A-1(g), Ex. 3 (Feb. 3, 1999)]

Q 6:58   Can placing a disabled employee on inactive-employee status be a qualifying event?

Yes. However, even if there is a reduction in hours because of placement on inactive status, there will be a qualifying event only if there is also a loss of group health plan coverage within the maximum applicable COBRA continuation period. [Treas. Reg. §54.4980B-4, Q&A-1(e) (Feb. 3, 1999)]

Q 6:59   What if the employee becomes entitled to Medicare?

A covered employee's entitlement to Medicare (i.e., actual application for Medicare, not just eligibility for Medicare) is one of the events that possibly could trigger COBRA rights if it causes other covered family members to lose group health plan coverage.

> **Practice Pointer.** The IRS has yet to indicate whether the employee must be enrolled in both Medicare Part A and Medicare Part B in order to trigger COBRA rights, or whether enrollment in Medicare Part A is sufficient. Because enrollment in Medicare Part B is optional with the participant and requires the payment of a special premium for that additional coverage, it would seem that the employer should not be able to defeat COBRA rights by insisting that the participant enroll in Medicare Part B first.

Employees. An employee's own entitlement to Medicare cannot be a qualifying event for the employee, even if it results in a full or partial loss of group health plan coverage. [I.R.C. §4980B(g)(1)(B); ERISA §607(3)(B)]

Spouses and dependents. The covered employee's entitlement to Medicare could potentially result in a loss of group health plan coverage for his or her covered spouse or dependents. The employee's or retiree's family members will experience a qualifying event if they lose coverage because of the employee's or retiree's entitlement to Medicare.

Employee's entitlement to Medicare before a qualifying event. For the situation in which an employee becomes entitled to Medicare and subsequently has a termination of employment or reduction in hours resulting in a loss of coverage for his or her dependents, see Qs 6:119, 6:122.

Q 6:60 What if the employee and his or her spouse separate prior to divorce without a court order granting a legal separation?

An informal separation is not a COBRA-qualifying event; a divorce or legal separation is required. At least one court has interpreted this statutory requirement strictly. Where an employer's group health plan required that an employee's spouse must "share a permanent residence" in order to be covered, the spouse lost coverage under the plan when the employee and spouse informally separated without obtaining a court order granting a legal separation. In that case, the spouse lost coverage under the plan, but the loss was determined not to have resulted from a COBRA-qualifying event. [Goodall v. Gates Corp., 39 F.3d 1191 (10th Cir. 1994)]

Q 6:61 Does a protective order issued against an estranged spouse constitute a legal separation that triggers COBRA continuation coverage?

According to at least one appellate court, a protective order does not amount to a legal separation. In the case before the court, an employee and his wife were covered by his employer's group health plan. The employee's wife filed for divorce, and while the divorce was pending, the divorce court issued a series of protective orders directing the employee to stay away from his wife and the marital residence. When the employer learned of the protective orders, it concluded that the couple had entered into a "legal separation," which is a qualifying event under COBRA. Therefore, the employer terminated the wife's coverage under the plan and sent her a notice informing her that she could elect continued coverage under COBRA. The wife objected to the employer's characterization of the protective orders as a qualifying event, but nonetheless elected COBRA coverage. However, the wife did not pay the COBRA premiums, and the employer terminated her health coverage.

One month later, the wife informed the employer that the couple's divorce had become final and she was requesting COBRA coverage as a result of that qualifying event. The employer informed her that her COBRA rights had expired under her prior election due to nonpayment of premiums and could not be reinstated. The wife sued the employer for violating her COBRA rights.

The U.S. Court of Appeals for the Tenth Circuit concluded that the protective orders issued during the pendency of the divorce action did not amount to a "legal separation." Therefore, the wife's group health coverage did not terminate, and there was no qualifying event for COBRA purposes until the divorce became final. Although COBRA does not define a legal separation, the court determined that such a separation occurs when there is a final court decree determining the parties' legal rights and obligations but preserving the marriage bond. A decree of legal separation directs the parties to live apart *and* defines the parties' legal rights and obligations in regard to custody, support, property division, and/or maintenance. A temporary protective order does not meet that test. [Simpson v. T.D. Williamson, Inc., 414 F.3d 1203 (10th Cir. 2005)]

Q 6:62   What if the employee and his or her spouse obtain a court order granting a legal separation, but the group health plan coverage does not terminate when the spouses are separated?

No COBRA rights will be triggered. The statutory event of legal separation or divorce must result in a loss of coverage in order for COBRA rights to be triggered.

Q 6:63   Can an event that occurs before a plan is subject to COBRA serve as a qualifying event?

No. COBRA does not obligate group health plans to offer continuation coverage to individuals who lost coverage because of events that took place when the plan was excepted from the COBRA requirements. This is true even if the individual is entitled to an extension of plan coverage that lasts until a date after the plan becomes subject to COBRA. However, the COBRA regulations do require that COBRA continuation coverage be extended to anyone who experiences, after the group health plan becomes subject to COBRA, what would otherwise be a "second qualifying event" if COBRA had been in effect at the time of the first event (see Q 6:119). [Treas. Reg. §54.4980B-4, Q&A-1(d) (Feb. 3, 1999)]

> **Example.** Peter leaves his job at the end of a year when his employer's plan is an exempt small-employer plan. Peter and his wife, Laura, are given an extension of coverage for the first three months of the following calendar year. Even if the plan is not exempt in the following year, Peter's loss of coverage at the end of the extension would not be a qualifying event for COBRA purposes. However, if Peter and Laura divorce before the end of the extension and Laura loses coverage as a result of the divorce, the divorce would be a qualifying event entitling Laura to COBRA coverage.

Q 6:64   Is FMLA leave a qualifying event?

FMLA leave is a reduction in hours of employment, a COBRA statutory event. However, because an employer must provide continued group health benefits during FMLA leave, no loss of coverage occurs as a result of the leave. Therefore, the FMLA leave itself is not a qualifying event. [Treas. Reg. §54. 4980B-4, Q&A-1(a) (Feb. 3, 1999)] This is true even if, during the FMLA leave, the employee either failed to pay his or her portion of the premiums for coverage or declined coverage under the employer's group health plan. These employee acts are disregarded in determining whether a loss for COBRA purposes has occurred. [IRS Notice 94-103, 1994-51 I.R.B. 10, Q&A-3; Treas. Reg. §54.4980B-10, Q&A-3 (Jan. 10, 2001)]

A qualifying event will occur in the FMLA context when:

1. The employee (or the spouse or dependent child of the employee) is covered under the employer's group health plan on the day before the first day of FMLA leave (or becomes covered during the FMLA leave)

2. The employee does not return to employment with the employer at the end of the FMLA leave; and

3. The employee (or the spouse or dependent child of the employee) would, in the absence of COBRA coverage, lose group health plan coverage before the end of the maximum coverage period.

[Treas. Reg. §54.4980B-10, Q&A-1(a) (Jan. 10, 2001)] For this purpose, any termination of group health coverage during the FMLA leave for failure to pay premiums is disregarded. [IRS Notice 94-103, 1994-51 I.R.B. 10, Q&A-3; Treas. Reg. §54.4980B-10, Q&A-3 (Jan. 10, 2001)]

Q 6:65   When does the COBRA-qualifying event occur for an employee who fails to return to work at the end of his or her FMLA leave?

The issue of when the qualifying event occurs in the context of an FMLA leave is particularly important to a determination of the required duration of COBRA coverage because the applicable period of coverage begins on the date of the qualifying event. As a general rule, the COBRA-qualifying event for an employee who fails to return to work at the conclusion of his or her FMLA leave occurs on the last day of FMLA leave. [IRS Notice 94-103, 1994-51 I.R.B. 10, Q&A-2; Treas. Reg. §54.4980B-10, Q&A-2 (Jan. 10, 2001)] Based on the legislative history under the FMLA and the interim regulations issued by the DOL and the IRS interpreting the FMLA, the last day of FMLA leave is "when it becomes known that an employee is not returning to work and therefore ceases to be entitled to leave" under the FMLA. [139 Cong. Rec. S978 (1993); 29 C.F.R. §825.209(f)]

If coverage is not lost until a later date, the plan may provide that the maximum period of COBRA coverage will be measured from the date coverage is lost, rather than from the last day of family leave.

Practice Pointer. An employer cannot condition COBRA coverage on reimbursement of premiums it paid to continue health coverage during FMLA leave. The DOL has published rules describing the circumstances in which an employer may recover premiums it pays to maintain coverage, including family coverage, from an employee who fails to return from leave [29 C.F.R. §825.213] However, even if recovery of premiums is permitted, the right to COBRA coverage cannot be conditioned upon the employee's reimbursement. [Treas. Reg. §54.4980B-10, Q&A-5]

Q 6:66   What if the employer eliminates group health coverage during an employee's family leave?

An employee's failure to return from FMLA leave is not a qualifying event if the employer eliminates group health coverage for the class of employees to which the employee would have belonged if he or she had not taken leave. The employer must continue to employ that class of employees and the elimination of coverage must occur before the last day of the employee's FMLA leave. [Treas. Reg. §54.4980B-10]

Q 6:67   Is an employer's cessation of contributions to a multiemployer plan a qualifying event?

Cessation of contributions by an employer to a multiemployer group health plan is not itself a qualifying event, even though the cessation of contributions may cause employees and their family members to lose coverage under the plan. However, an event coinciding with the employer's cessation of contributions (e.g., a reduction of hours of employment in the case of striking employees) may be a qualifying event if it otherwise satisfies the requirements. [Treas. Reg. §54.4980B-9, Q&A-9]

Q 6:68   Who provides COBRA coverage for qualified beneficiaries when an employer stops contributing to a multiemployer plan?

As a general rule, the multiemployer plan has the obligation to make COBRA coverage available to qualifying beneficiaries of the noncontributing employer. However, if the employer makes other group health plan coverage available to the class of employees formerly covered by the multiemployer plan or begins contribution to another multiemployer plan for those employees, the employer must take over the COBRA coverage obligation from that date forward. [Treas. Reg. § 54.4980B-9, Q&A-10]

Q 6:69   Is a dependent child's loss of student status a qualifying event?

As a general rule, employer-provided health plans require an employee's child over age 18 to be a full-time student in order to qualify as a dependent eligible for coverage under the plan. Consequently, when a college student reduces his or her schedule to part-time, drops out of school, or graduates, he or she will generally no longer qualify for dependent coverage. Under the COBRA rules, a child of a covered employee ceasing to meet the plan's definition of a dependent is a qualifying event that will trigger COBRA coverage for the child. [I.R.C. § 4980B(f)(3); ERISA § 603; PHSA § 2203; Treas. Reg. § 54-49803-4, Q&A-1 (Feb. 3, 1999)] (See Q 6:41.) The child will be entitled to up to 36 weeks of COBRA coverage. [I.R.C. § 4980B(f)(2)(B)(i)(IV); ERISA § 602(2)(A)(iv)] (See Q 6:118.)

However, legislation enacted in 2008 and the 2010 Health Reform Act require group health plans to provide extended coverage for college students and other adult children.

Coverage of dependent students during medically necessary leaves of absence. Congress enacted a new law in 2008 that requires group health plans to provide special extended coverage to college students who take a leave of absence from school or reduce their schedules due to a severe illness or injury. On October 9, 2008, President George W. Bush signed into law the 2008 Student Health Insurance Act [Pub. L. No. 110-381] (also known as "Michelle's Law"), which provides that a group health plan may not terminate coverage of a dependent child due to a medically necessary leave of absence from college before the earlier of:

1. The date that is one year after the first day of the medically necessary leave of absence; or

2. The date on which the coverage would otherwise terminate under the plan's terms.

[I.R.C. § 9813(b)(1), ERISA § 714 as added by Pub. L. No. 110-381; PHSA § 2728 as added by Pub. L. No. 110-381 and redesignated by Pub. L. No. 111-138]

Moreover, there can be no change in a child's benefits as a result of a medically necessary leave of absence. A dependent child whose benefits are continued is entitled to the same benefit during the leave as if the child continued to be a covered student and the leave was not a medically necessary leave. [I.R.C. § 9813(c) as added by Pub. L. No. 110-381]

The new requirement applies to medically necessary leaves of absence during plan years beginning on or after October 9, 2009. Thus, in the case of calendar year plans, the rules apply starting in 2010.

A *medically necessary leave of absence* means a leave of absence from or any other change in enrollment at a postsecondary educational institution that:

1. Commences while the child is suffering from a serious illness or injury;

2. Is medically necessary; and

3. Causes the child to lose student status for purposes of coverage under the group health plan.

[I.R.C. § 9813(a) as added by Pub. L. No. 110-381]

The prohibition on termination of a child's coverage applies only if the plan, or the issuer of health insurance in connection with the plan, receives written certification by a treating physician of the child stating that the child is suffering from a serious illness or injury and that the leave of absence or other change in enrollment is medically necessary. [I.R.C. § 9813(b)(3) as added by Pub. L. No. 110-381]

Notice requirement. Any notice regarding a requirement for certification of student status under the plan must include a description of the rules for continued coverage during medically necessary leaves of absence. The notice must be in language that is understandable to the typical plan participant.

Coverage for adult children. The 2010 Health Reform Act requires a group health plan (or a health insurance issuer offering group coverage) that provides dependent coverage of children to continue to make that coverage available for children until they attain age 26. [I.R.C. § 9815 as added by PPACA § 1562; PHSA § 2714 as added by PPACA § 1001 and amended by PPACA Reconciliation § 2301(b)] The extended coverage requirement is generally effective for plan years beginning on or after September 23, 2010. [PPACA § 1004] However, before 2014, a "grandfathered health plan" is required to provide extended coverage to an adult child only if the child is not eligible to enroll in another employer-sponsored group health plan. [PPACA Reconciliation § 2301(a)(ii)] A grandfathered health plan generally includes a group health plan in existence on the effective date of the 2010 Health Reform Act (March 23, 2010), group health insurance covering an individual on that date, or coverage maintained pursuant to a collective bargaining agreement ratified before that date. [PPACA § 1251]

Practice Pointer. A group health plan may charge a COBRA beneficiary 102 percent of the cost of his or her coverage. [I.R.C. §§ 4980B(f)(2)(C), 4980B(f)(4)(A); ERISA §§ 601, 602(3); PHSA §§ 2202(3), 2204; Treas. Reg. § 54.4980B-8, Q&A-1(a)] (See Q 6:133.) By contrast, there is no provision in Michelle's Law for charging any special premium for continuation of a college student's coverage during a medically necessary leave. Consequently, it appears that plans must continue coverage on the same financial terms as before the leave. Similarly, it appears that coverage for an adult child required by the 2010 Health Reform Act must be provided on the same financial terms as coverage for a dependent child. In addition, the precise interplay between the new laws and the COBRA continuation coverage rules is not specified. However, because both laws extend *eligibility* for coverage under the plan itself, it appears that COBRA coverage would be triggered only if and when a student or adult child loses coverage under the plan as the result of a qualifying event.

Notice to Participants

Q 6:70 Must the summary plan description for a group health plan explain the COBRA continuation coverage rules?

DOL regulations provide that the summary plan description (SPD) for a group health plan that is subject to COBRA must include a description of the rights and obligations of participants and beneficiaries with respect to continuation coverage. [DOL Reg. §2520.102-3(o)] This description should include, among other things, information concerning:

- Qualifying events and qualified beneficiaries;
- Premiums;
- Notice and election requirements and procedures; and

- Duration of coverage.

Q 6:71　Must the plan notify employees and spouses of the existence of COBRA continuation rights before a qualifying event occurs?

Yes. The group health plan must notify all covered employees and spouses of their COBRA rights when the plan first comes under COBRA or when employees and spouses first become eligible to participate in the plan. [I.R.C. §4980B(f)(6); ERISA §§606(a)(1), 606(a)(3); PHSA §§2206(1), 2208(c); ERISA Tech. Rel. 86-2] This is known as the initial COBRA notice, and it is separate from the COBRA notice that is given later upon the occurrence of a qualifying event.

In DOL Advisory Opinion 94-17A [Apr. 29, 1994], the DOL took the position that the initial notice must be given to a covered employee's spouse only if and when the spouse becomes covered under the plan. Because the purpose of the initial notice is to alert a person to the possibility of future COBRA entitlement, that purpose would not be served by requiring the notice to be given to a spouse who is not covered by the plan (see also Q 6:75).

The COBRA regulations confirm this opinion by providing that a covered employee and the spouse of a covered employee must each be given notice of their COBRA rights when they individually become covered by the plan. The regulations provide a 90-day window for delivery of the initial COBRA notice beginning with the date on which a covered employee or spouse first becomes covered under the plan (or, if later, the date on which the plan first becomes subject to the COBRA requirements). [DOL Reg. §2590.606-1; 69 Fed. Reg. 30,083 (May 26, 2004)]

The regulations provide that the general notice must be provided earlier if an employee or an employee's spouse or dependent becomes eligible for COBRA coverage during the 90-day window. However, the regulations also make it clear that timely provision of a COBRA election notice satisfies the initial notice requirement.

There is no requirement to furnish a general notice to dependent children, even if the general notice requirement is triggered early by the occurrence of a qualifying event involving a dependent.

Practice Pointer. The regulations make it clear that it is not sufficient to give the initial COBRA notice to the employee when he or she joins the plan. The employer's COBRA administration program must also be able to track late enrollment of spouses and the addition of newly eligible spouses (newly-weds), so that the initial COBRA notice can be provided to the spouse at that time.

Some cases have interpreted the initial notice requirement to mean that the duty of providing it falls on all the parties to a plan, which include the employer, the trustees, the insurer, and others. [Kidder v. H&B Marine Inc., 925 F.2d 857 (5th Cir. 1991); Lawrence v. Jackson Mack Sales Inc., 837 F. Supp. 771 (S.D. Miss. 1992)] The statute, however, places sole responsibility on the plan administrator. The COBRA regulations also specifically require the initial CO-BRA notice to be provided by the plan administrator.

> **Caution.** In the case of some qualifying events, notably divorce, it is the employee's or qualified beneficiary's responsibility to notify the employer of the occurrence of a qualifying event. If the individual does not give this notice, COBRA rights are not triggered. The problem is that the individual has to be sufficiently well informed to know that he or she has to act in order to preserve the right to elect COBRA continuation coverage. If the employer fails to provide the initial COBRA notice, and the employee later becomes divorced, the employee's spouse might be totally unaware of the need to notify the employer that a qualifying event has occurred. Nonetheless, the employer could assert the spouse's failure to notify it of the divorce as an affirmative defense to an action for COBRA continuation coverage. However, at least one court has noted the unfairness of such a scenario and has refused to hold the employer faultless where the employer's initial failure to provide a notice of COBRA continuation rights may have contributed to the spouse's ignorance of her duty to notify the employer of her divorce. In *Crawford v. Pennsylvania Employees Benefit Trust Fund* [18 Employee Benefits Cas. (BNA) 1392 (E.D. Pa. 1994)], the court held that the wife was excused from her obligation to notify the plan of her divorce from the employee if the plan failed to provide her with a proper initial COBRA notice.

Q 6:72   Must plan administrators use any particular language for required COBRA notices?

No particular language is required. However, the final COBRA notice regulations provide that the notice must be written in a manner calculated to be understood by the average plan participant. Moreover, the regulations specify that the notice must contain the following information:

1. The name of the plan and the name, address and telephone number of a party or parties from whom additional information about the plan and continuation coverage can be obtained;

2. A general description of the continuation coverage under the plan, including:

   - Identification of the classes of individuals who may become qualified beneficiaries,

   - The types of qualifying events that may give rise to the right to continuation coverage,

   - The obligation of the employer to notify the plan administrator of the occurrence of certain qualifying events,

   - The maximum period for which continuation coverage may be available,

   - When and under what circumstances continuation coverage may be extended beyond the maximum period, and

   - The plan's premium requirements for continuation coverage;

3. An explanation of the responsibility of a qualified beneficiary to notify the plan administrator of a qualifying event that is a divorce, legal separation, or a child's ceasing to be a dependent under the terms of the plan, and a description of the plan's procedures for providing notice;

4. An explanation of the responsibility of qualified beneficiaries who are receiving continuation coverage to provide notice to the administrator of a Social Security disability determination and a description of the plan's procedures for providing notice;

5. An explanation of the importance of keeping the administrator informed of the current addresses of all participants or beneficiaries under the plan who are or may become qualified beneficiaries; and

6. A statement that the notice does not fully describe continuation coverage or other rights under the plan and that more complete information is available from the plan administrator and in the plan's SPD.

[DOL Reg. §2590.606-1; 69 Fed. Reg. 30,083 (May 26, 2004)]

The regulations include a model general notice. Use of an appropriately completed model notice will comply with the COBRA requirements, although the DOL does not require its use and anticipates that a variety of other notices will satisfy those requirements.

Q 6:73   Is there a prescribed method for distributing initial notices?

Yes. Sending a single notice by first-class mail to the last known address of covered employees and their spouses is generally deemed a good-faith effort at compliance under DOL rules, provided the plan's latest information indicates that both reside at that address. A single notice would not be permitted if a spouse's coverage under the plan begins at a different time from the covered employee's coverage unless the spouse's coverage begins before the date on which the notice must be provided to the covered employee. Further, in-hand furnishing of the initial notice at the workplace to the covered employee is deemed adequate delivery to the employee, but would not constitute adequate delivery to the employee's spouse. [DOL Reg. §2590.606-1] An initial notice may be delivered electronically provided specific requirements are met. [DOL Reg. §§2520.104b-1, 2590.606-1]

The COBRA notice regulations permit plans to satisfy the general notice requirement by including the required information in the plan's SPD and providing the SPD at a time that complies with the timing requirements for the general notice.

Q 6:74   May COBRA notices be sent electronically?

The DOL issued a safe harbor rule that permits the electronic delivery of ERISA notices and employee benefit plan disclosures, including COBRA notices (see chapter 2). [DOL Reg. §2520.104b-1]

Practice Pointer. Electronic delivery of COBRA and other notices is still in its infancy. Moreover, the use of electronic communications for COBRA purposes raises some logistical problems. For example, although it may be a simple matter to provide an initial COBRA notice to an employee at the workplace when the employee first becomes covered by a group health plan, an initial notice must also be provided to an employee's spouse when he or she first becomes covered by the plan—and to provide that notice electronically would require the spouse's consent.

Q 6:75   Must separate notices be sent to the employee and his or her spouse?

A single notice is sufficient if the employee and spouse become covered at the same time and the spouse's last known address is the same as the covered employee's. However, if the employer or plan administrator is aware that the spouses have different addresses, separate notices must be mailed. [ERISA Tech. Rel. 86-2] If a single employee who has already received the initial COBRA notice gets married and adds his or her new spouse to the health coverage, the spouse must be given a separate notice. [DOL Reg. §2590.606-1; DOL Adv. Op. 94-17A (Apr. 24, 1994)]

In general, a notice addressed to the covered spouse is a valid notice to all other qualified beneficiaries living with the spouse, such as the children. If the employee and spouse are living together, notice addressed to both of them will be treated as notice to all qualified beneficiaries residing with them at the time the notice is given. [I.R.C. §4980B(f)(6); DOL Reg. §2590.606-1; Preamble to ERISA Tech. Rel. 86-2]

Q 6:76   What happens if the dependent is covered under the plan due to a qualified medical child support order?

A child who is enrolled in the group health plan pursuant to the terms of a qualified medical child support order (QMCSO) is required to be treated as a plan participant for purposes of ERISA's reporting and disclosure rules and as a plan beneficiary for all other purposes. As a result, plan administrators should provide these children with separate copies of the group health plan's documents, including the SPD and COBRA notices. [ERISA §609(a)(7)]

Q 6:77   Who must notify the plan administrator when a qualifying event occurs?

The answer depends on the nature of the qualifying event.

When employer is required to give notice. The employer must give notice to the plan administrator within 30 days of the occurrence of a qualifying event concerning (1) the employee's or ex-employee's death, (2) the employee's termination of employment or reduction in hours, (3) the employee's becoming eligible for Medicare, or (4) the commencement of a bankruptcy proceeding by the employer. The 30-day notice period is counted from the date of loss of coverage if the plan provides that the COBRA continuation period will start on the date coverage is lost rather than on the date of the qualifying event. [DOL Reg. §2590.606-2] The final COBRA notice regulations require the employer to provide the plan administrator with enough information to enable the administrator to determine the identity of the plan, the identity of the covered employee, the nature of qualifying event, and the date of the qualifying event.

Special rule for multiemployer plans. In the case of a multiemployer plan, the plan document may provide for a notice period that is longer than 30 days, regardless of when the qualifying event occurs. [I.R.C. §4980B(f)(6)(B); ERISA §606(a)(2); 29 U.S.C. §1166(a)(2); DOL Reg. §2590.606-2] Multiemployer plan documents may also provide that the plan administrator will determine when an employee's termination of employment or reduction in hours has occurred, rather than requiring notice of those qualifying events from the employer. [I.R.C. §4980B(f)(6); ERISA §606(b); 29 U.S.C. §1166(b)] The employer's notice to the plan administrator must provide sufficient information to enable the administrator to determine the identity of the plan, the covered employee, the qualifying event, and the date of the qualifying event. [Prop. DOL Reg. §2590. 606-2(c)]

When employee or beneficiary is required to give notice. In order to secure continuation of coverage, the covered employee or qualified beneficiary must first provide notice to the plan administrator of divorce, legal separation, a dependent child's loss of dependent status under the plan's definition of dependency, or a second qualifying event. The notice must be given within 60 days of the later of (1) the date of the qualifying event, (2) the date that coverage would be lost because of the qualifying event, or (3) the date on which the employee or qualified beneficiary is informed of the notice requirement through the plan's SPD or the initial COBRA notice. [I.R.C. §4980B(f)(6)(C); ERISA §606(a)(3); 29 U.S.C. §1166(a)(3); PHSA §2206(3); Treas. Reg. §54.4980B-6, Q&A-2; DOL Reg. §2590.606-3] However, the COBRA notice regulations make it clear that a plan cannot automatically reject a late or incomplete notice.

The regulations provide that a plan must establish reasonable procedures for covered employees and beneficiaries to furnish notices of qualifying events. According to the regulations, a plan's procedures generally will be deemed reasonable if they are described in the plan's SPD, specify who is to receive notices, and specify the means for giving notice and the required content of the notice. If a plan does not have a reasonable procedure for giving notices, a notice will be deemed to have been provided if information adequately identifying a qualifying event is communicated to any of the parties who would customarily be considered in charge of the plan. In the case of a single-employer plan that failed to adopt reasonable notice procedures, notice will be deemed to have been provided if it is communicated to the person who customarily handles employee benefit matters for the employer.

A plan may require notices to be submitted by means of a specific form if the form is readily available without cost. Moreover, a plan may require specific information to be provided. However, a plan may not reject an incomplete notice as untimely if the notice is provided within the plan's time limits and contains enough information to enable the plan administrator to identify the plan, the covered employee and qualified beneficiary or beneficiaries, the qualifying event, and the date of the qualifying event. If a timely notice fails to supply all of the information required under the plan's procedures, the plan administrator can require the employee or beneficiary to supply the missing information. The DOL emphasizes that there is nothing in the regulations to preclude a plan from rejecting a notice when an employee or qualified beneficiary fails to supply the missing information within some reasonable time period. However, the DOL suggests that both the plan and its participants would benefit from a procedure that specifically defines when and under what circumstances a notice will be rejected for failure to provide additional information.

Employers should also bear in mind that the notice time limits are statutory minimums. A plan can provide for longer notice periods.

If the employer never provides the employee with the initial COBRA notice, the employee or covered family member may not be aware of the obligation to notify the employer of certain qualifying events. When this happens, courts have held that the employer cannot withhold COBRA benefits on the grounds that the qualified beneficiary did not give notice of the qualifying event. The DOL makes it clear that a plan's time limit for providing notice of a qualifying event cannot begin to run unless and until the plan has satisfied the initial notice requirement. [DOL Reg. §2590.606-3] On the other hand, where the employer has complied with the initial notice requirement, a beneficiary's failure to give notice of a qualifying event will cut off his or her COBRA rights (see Q 6:84).

Failure to notify the plan of a qualifying event can have other consequences for an employee. The Seventh Circuit Court of Appeals held that an employee committed fraud when he did not notify his employer's health plan of his divorce and allowed his ex-spouse to remain covered by the plan for five years following the divorce. The employee was ordered to repay the plan for $122,793 in medical expenses paid on behalf of his ex-spouse and to pay the plan $118,007 in damages. The court rejected the employee's argument that the plan's state-law fraud claim was preempted by ERISA. According to the court, the primary objective of ERISA is to protect the plan participants and their beneficiaries. "Thus," said the court, "far from thwarting ERISA's stated statutory objectives, the trustees' common law fraud claim is an attempt to protect the financial integrity of the fund, which is certainly in the plan participants' and beneficiaries' best interests, as well as being consistent with the trustees' fiduciary obligations under ERISA." [Trustees of the AFTRA Health Fund v. Biondi, 2002 U.S. App. LEXIS 21044 (7th Cir. Oct. 4, 2002)]

Notice of disability. Any qualified beneficiary who has been determined to be disabled for Social Security purposes at any time during the first 60 days of continuation coverage because of a qualifying event that was either a termination of employment or a reduction in hours is entitled to a total of up to 29 months of COBRA continuation coverage rather than 18 months (see Q 6:120). A qualified beneficiary who was determined to be disabled *before* COBRA coverage began and who remains disabled when COBRA coverage begins is also entitled to a disability extension. The coverage extension applies to the disabled beneficiary and to all other qualified beneficiaries who became entitled to COBRA coverage as a result of the same qualifying event.

To qualify for the extension, an individual must notify the plan administrator of the disability determination after the determination is made and before the end of the first 18 months of COBRA continuation coverage.

The COBRA notice regulations provide that a plan may require a beneficiary to provide disability notice within 60 days after the latest of (1) the date of the disability determination, (2) the date of the qualifying event, (3) the date on which the qualified beneficiary loses coverage under the plan, or (4) the date on which the qualified beneficiary is informed of the obligation to provide notice. Thus, under the regulations, a beneficiary who previously received a disability determination and has not received a subsequent determination that he or she is no longer disabled will have at least 60 days after a qualifying event to provide a disability notice. The regulations provide that failure to give the disability notice within those time limits could be a basis for denying the disability extension; however, the regulations also make it clear that plans may not decline to provide the disability extension unless the affected qualified beneficiaries were adequately notified, in advance, of the notice obligation. Again, the regulations specify that plans may adopt more generous notice requirements. [DOL Reg. §2590.606-3]

A disability extension is cut off if a qualified beneficiary is determined to no longer be disabled. Therefore, a qualified beneficiary who receives a determination from the Social Security Administration (SSA) that he or she is no longer disabled must so notify the plan. Under the COBRA notice regulations, the plan's time period for providing this notice may not end before the date that is at least 30 days after the later of (1) the date of the SSA determination or (2) the date the beneficiary is informed of the requirement to provide notice.

Q 6:78   Must each affected qualified beneficiary give notice of a qualifying event that will cause more than one qualified beneficiary to lose coverage?

No. Separate notices are not necessary. A timely notice of a qualifying event sent by a covered employee or by any affected qualified beneficiary will preserve the COBRA election rights of all qualified beneficiaries affected by the qualifying event. [Treas. Reg. §54.4980B-6, Q&A-2(b)]

The COBRA regulations specifically provide that the notice obligation can be satisfied for all qualified beneficiaries affected by a qualifying event through a single notice. Moreover, any individual representing the qualified beneficiaries can provide the notice. [DOL Reg. §2590.606-3]

Q 6:79   Must the employer provide specialized counseling with regard to COBRA rights?

No. When a qualifying event occurs, COBRA does not require anything beyond a simple notification that the employee has a right to continued coverage. The employer does not breach any fiduciary duties by failing to provide personalized counseling by a personnel officer to help a spouse or beneficiary understand his or her COBRA rights. The cases and the legislative history require only that they be given good-faith notification of the ability to elect continued coverage. However, no part of the notice can be false or deceptive, and plan administrators do act as fiduciaries in handling inquiries from eligible parties during the COBRA election period. [Hummer v. Sears Roebuck, 1994 U.S. Dist. LEXIS 3659 (E.D. Pa. Mar. 21, 1994)]

Q 6:80   What must the plan administrator do after being notified of a qualifying event?

On receiving timely notice of a qualifying event, a plan administrator has 14 days to notify each qualified beneficiary of his or her COBRA rights. [I.R.C. §4980B(f)(6); ERISA §606; PHSA §2206] For some qualifying events (such as the employee's termination of employment), the employer rather than the qualified beneficiary has 30 days to notify the plan administrator of the occurrence of the qualifying event. If the employer is also the plan administrator, an interpretive issue arises as to whether the employer should also have the additional 14 days that the plan administrator has to provide the COBRA notices to qualified beneficiaries. The final COBRA notice regulations resolve this issue in the employer's favor by providing that the notice must be furnished not later than 44 days after the date of the qualifying event (or, if the plan provides that COBRA coverage starts on the date of the loss of coverage, 44 days after the date of the loss of coverage). [DOL Reg. §2590.606-4]

Getting the notice to all qualified beneficiaries. The case law makes clear that this COBRA notice following the qualifying event must be provided to all qualified beneficiaries and not just to the employee. [Burgess v. Adams Tool & Eng'g Inc., 908 F. Supp. 473 (W.D. Mich. 1995)] In reviewing whether an employee's spouse received adequate notice of her COBRA rights, the court found that the notice that the plan administrator provided to the employee did not adequately notify the spouse because the letter was not addressed to her, only one copy of the letter was enclosed, it described only the rights of the employee and did not suggest that it was designed to notify the spouse of her rights, and there were no instructions that the employee should share the contents of the notice with his spouse.

On this issue, the COBRA notice regulations provide that a plan administrator can provide notice to a covered employee and the covered employee's spouse by furnishing a single notice *addressed to both the covered employee and the covered employee's spouse*, provided the most recent information available to the plan indicates that the employee and spouse reside at the same location. Notice to each qualified beneficiary who is a dependent child can be provided by furnishing a single notice to the covered employee or the covered employee's spouse, again provided the most recent information available to the plan indicates that the dependent child resides at the same location as the individual to whom the notice is provided.

Contents of COBRA election notice. The COBRA notice regulations specify the content of COBRA election notices. According to the DOL, in addition to providing significant pertinent facts, such as the names and contact information for the plan administrator and (if different) the COBRA administrator, and identification of the qualified beneficiaries and the qualifying event, the notice must describe the COBRA continuation coverage being made available and the manner in which the beneficiaries' COBRA rights must be exercised. In particular, the DOL says, the notice must make it clear that each beneficiary has an independent right to elect continuation coverage.

Under the regulations, the notice must be written in a manner calculated to be understood by the average plan participant and must contain all the following information:

- The name of the plan under which continuation coverage is available;
- The name, address and telephone number of the person responsible for the administration of COBRA benefits;
- Identification of the qualifying event;
- Identification, either by status (e.g., employee, spouse, dependent child) or name, of the qualified beneficiaries who are recognized by the plan as being entitled to continuation coverage with respect to the qualifying event;
- The date on which coverage under the plan will terminate (or has terminated) unless continuation coverage is elected;
- A statement that each qualified beneficiary has an independent right to elect continuation coverage;
- A statement that a covered employee or a qualified beneficiary who is the spouse of the covered employee (or was the spouse of the covered employee on the day before the qualifying event occurred) may elect continuation coverage on behalf of all other qualified beneficiaries and that a parent or legal guardian may elect continuation coverage on behalf of a minor child;
- An explanation of the plan's procedures for electing continuation coverage, including the time period during which the election must be made and the final date for making the election;
- An explanation of the consequences of failing to elect or waiving continuation coverage, including an explanation that the decision will affect future portability and special enrollment rights under HIPAA (and information on where to obtain additional information about those rights);
- A description of the plan's procedures for revoking a waiver of the right to continuation coverage before the date by which the election must be made;

- A description of the continuation coverage that will be made available under the plan if elected, including the date coverage will commence (either by providing a description of the coverage or by reference to the plan's SPD);

- An explanation of the maximum period of continuation coverage, if elected, and the continuation coverage termination date (including an explanation of any events that might cause continuation coverage to be terminated early);

- A description of the circumstances (if any) under which the maximum period may be extended due to a second qualifying event or a disability determination and the length of any extension;

- A description of the plan's requirements, procedures, and time limits for providing notice of a second qualifying event or disability determination and the consequences of failing to provide notice (required only in the case of a notice that offers COBRA coverage for less than 36 months);

- An explanation of the responsibility of qualified beneficiaries to provide notice if a disabled qualified beneficiary is determined to no longer be disabled (if applicable);

- The amount, if any, that each qualified beneficiary will be required to pay for continuation coverage;

- A description of the due dates for payments, the right to pay on a monthly basis, grace periods for payment, the address to which payments should be sent, and the consequences of delayed payment and non-payment; and

- An explanation of the importance of keeping the plan administrator informed of the current addresses of all qualified beneficiaries.

Although the list of required information is a lengthy one, the notice must also contain a statement indicating that it does not fully describe continuation coverage or other rights under the plan, and that more complete information is available in the plan's SPD or from the plan administrator. [DOL Reg. §2590. 606-4]

The regulations include a model notice that can be tailored to include plan-specific information. Although the model notice is not mandatory, the DOL says that use of an appropriately completed model notice will be considered good-faith compliance with the contents requirements of the regulations.

Notice of unavailability. The COBRA regulations also impose a notice require-ment on plan administrators who receive notice of a qualifying event from a plan participant or beneficiary who is not eligible for COBRA coverage under the plan. The regulations require the administrator to provide a notice to the individual explaining why he or she is not entitled to coverage. This notice is subject to the same timing requirement as the COBRA election notice—that is, it must be provided within 14 days following the plan administrator's receipt of notice of a qualifying event. [DOL Reg. §2590.606-4]

The regulations make it clear that a notice of unavailability must be furnished whenever the plan administrator denies coverage after receiving notice from a qualified beneficiary regardless of the reason for the denial and regardless of whether the notice involves a first qualifying event, a second qualifying event, or a request for a disability extension. For example, an unavailability notice would be required if the plan administrator denies coverage because of a determination that no qualifying event has occurred or because the qualified beneficiary did not provide notice in a timely manner or did not provide complete information.

In its preamble to the final regulations, the DOL explains, that when a participant or beneficiary submits a notice of a qualifying event, there is an expectation of COBRA coverage. Therefore, providing notice of ineligibility is intended to avoid problems stemming from misunderstandings in this area.

Q 6:81   Must a plan administrator notify a COBRA beneficiary when COBRA coverage is terminated?

In the past, there were no notice requirements upon termination of COBRA coverage. However, COBRA notice regulations issued by the DOL in 2004 require a plan administrator to provide specific notice in the event COBRA coverage is terminated before the end of the maximum coverage period (e.g., if the employer ceases to offer group health coverage to its employees or the COBRA premium is not timely paid). The notice must be provided as soon as administratively practicable after the termination decision is made, must explain why and when COBRA coverage is being terminated, and must describe any rights to other coverage the qualified beneficiaries will have upon termination. [DOL Reg. §2590.606-4]

The early termination notice is not required to be furnished *before* COBRA coverage can be terminated. However, the DOL says that there may be instances when a plan administrator is able to furnish the notice in advance and would be required to do so under the "as soon as reasonably practicable" standard.

On the other hand, the DOL says that plans can combine furnishing of the early termination notice with the certificate of creditable coverage required under HIPAA. That certificate is generally required to be provided within a reasonable time following the cessation of COBRA coverage (see Q 5:67). Plans must comply with the final COBRA notice regulations for the first plan year beginning on or after November 26, 2004.

Q 6:82   Is the COBRA notice following a qualifying event required to be in writing?

It has been widely assumed that a written notice of COBRA rights (whether on paper or in electronic form) must be provided following a qualifying event. However, at least one court has held that an employer that also served as the plan administrator met the notice requirement by orally explaining COBRA rights to a qualified beneficiary. The court noted that the law provides that the initial COBRA notice must be in writing. However, the law only provides that the plan administrator must "notify" a beneficiary of COBRA rights following a qualifying event; it does not specify that the notice must be in writing. [Chestnut v. Montgomery, 307 F.3d 698 (8th Cir. 2002)]

Practice Pointer. Although oral notification may be permitted, it may be unwise. A plan administrator may have difficulty proving that a conversation regarding COBRA rights actually took place. Moreover, without a written record, it may be difficult to prove that all the required COBRA information was properly communicated to the beneficiary.

DOL regulations clearly contemplate that the notice of COBRA rights be provided in writing and include a model notice. [DOL Reg. §2590.606-4]

Q 6:83   What happens if a qualified beneficiary turns down COBRA continuation coverage?

Each person has only the 60-day election period to elect coverage as, and receive the rights of, a qualified beneficiary. Turning down COBRA continuation coverage terminates a person's status as a qualified beneficiary at the end of the election period (defined in Q 6:92).

Note. While the 60-day election period is still in effect, the qualified beneficiary can change his or her mind as many times as he or she desires (see Q 6:97).

The COBRA notice regulations require the notice of COBRA rights to include information on the consequences of not electing COBRA coverage, including an explanation that the decision will affect future portability and special enrollment rights under HIPAA (and information on where to obtain additional information about those rights). [DOL Reg. §2590.606-4]

Q 6:84   What happens if the plan administrator is not notified of a qualifying event?

If the covered employee or qualified beneficiary fails to notify the plan administrator of a divorce, separation, or child's loss of dependency status, the group health plan is not required to offer the qualified beneficiary the option of COBRA continuation of coverage. [Treas. Reg. §54-4980B-6, Q&A-2] (See Q 6:89 for the special issues associated with qualified beneficiaries who are incapacitated.)

Caution. If the employer's own conduct caused or contributed to the qualified beneficiary's failure to provide notice of a qualifying event, the answer to this question could well be different.

The COBRA notice regulations make it clear that a qualified beneficiary cannot be required to give notice until he or she has been informed of the notice requirement. The regulations provide that notice must be given within 60 days of the *later of* (1) the date of the qualifying event, (2) the date that coverage would be lost because of the qualifying event, or (3) *the date on which the employee or qualified beneficiary is informed of the notice requirement through the plan's SPD or the initial COBRA notice.* [DOL Reg. §2590.606-3]

On the other hand, when an employer has complied with the initial notice requirements, failure to give notice of the qualifying event will cut off a beneficiary's COBRA rights. In one case, the court found that an employer's initial COBRA notice clearly and unambiguously informed an employee's spouse of her COBRA rights and obligations on the occurrence of a qualifying event. Moreover, that notice was properly sent to the only address the employer had on record. However, the spouse failed to notify the employer after her legal separation from the employee. As a result, she could not recover from the employer for failure to provide her with COBRA coverage. [Johnson v. Northwest Airlines, Inc., 2001 U.S. Dist. LEXIS 2160 (N.D. Cal. Feb. 23, 2001)]

Q 6:85 Is the plan administrator relieved of the duty to notify qualified beneficiaries of their COBRA rights if it hires others to perform that duty?

No. According to the DOL, the plan administrator's duty to notify qualified beneficiaries of their COBRA rights is a statutory duty that cannot be transferred to others. That is, although the plan administrator can delegate the COBRA function, it continues to retain the legal responsibility for it. Accordingly, the DOL has held that a plan administrator that enters into an arrangement or agreement with a service provider or other party to provide COBRA notices must take steps to ensure that the qualified beneficiaries are in fact properly notified. [DOL Adv. Op. 90-16A (May 31, 1990)]

In addition, the Eleventh Circuit Court of Appeals held that, although an employer may outsource its COBRA notice responsibility to a third party, it remains liable for COBRA notice violations committed by the third party. "Simply hiring an agent and then instructing the agent to send notice is not sufficient to satisfy the statute, where there is no evidence that the agent sent out a notice to the plaintiff, nor any evidence that the principal took the necessary steps to ensure that the agent would, in all cases, make such notification." The court upheld the lower court's imposition of $10,800 in penalties against the employer for failure to provide the required COBRA notice [Scott v. Suncoast Beverage Sales, Ltd., 295 F.3d 1223 (11th Cir. 2002)]

Q 6:86 What happens if the plan administrator fails to notify qualified beneficiaries of their COBRA rights?

A plan administrator that fails to provide a required COBRA notice to a qualified beneficiary can incur substantial excise tax liability and ERISA penalties (see Qs 6:166–6:179).

In addition, failure to give notice or failure to provide adequate notice in a timely manner may subject the plan administrator to liability for COBRA benefits for which it might not have been liable if timely adequate notice had been given.

In one case, for example, an employer argued that an employee was not harmed by its failure to send her timely notice of her COBRA rights because she could not have afforded to pay for COBRA coverage. In deposition testimony, the employee admitted that she did not have money to pay the COBRA premiums when she became unemployed. Moreover, when she was informed of her COBRA rights eight months later, the employee declined COBRA coverage. Nonetheless, a federal district court ordered the employer to pay the employee's attorneys' fees and her medical expenses from the beginning of the COBRA coverage period until the date she was informed of her rights. In addition, the court ordered the employer to pay the employee a penalty of $5 per day for the period the COBRA notice was delayed. The court said the sole purpose of the notice requirement is to ensure that qualified beneficiaries are fully informed of their rights and have the opportunity to elect coverage if they so choose. According to the court, COBRA beneficiaries should not have to establish after the fact that they would have found a way to afford COBRA insurance had they been informed of their rights. [Chenoweth v. Wal-Mart Stores, Inc., 159 F. Supp. 20 1032 (S.D. Ohio 2001)]

> **Note.** Courts have held that a plan administrator is required to provide notice even if the qualified beneficiary is already familiar with COBRA and has personal knowledge of his or her COBRA rights. [*See* Underwood v. Fluor Daniel Inc., 1997 U.S. App. LEXIS 1410 (4th Cir. Jan. 28, 1997) (spouse's "knowledge" of her COBRA rights is not the equivalent to "notice," and the employer was therefore liable for its failure to timely provide notice of COBRA rights to spouse)]

In a U.S. district court case, under the terms of a medical plan a dependent would lose coverage at age 19 unless the dependent was a full-time student. The dependent in the case had a serious accident shortly after his 19th birthday. The employee provided the plan administrator with information that, upon due inquiry, would have revealed that the dependent was not a full-time student. However, the plan administrator erroneously determined that plan coverage continued and failed to give a COBRA notice. Some time later, it was determined that coverage in fact had been lost at age 19, and the employee was asked to refund benefits paid erroneously. The court held that the plan administrator had failed to fulfill its fiduciary duties in determining whether coverage was in force and in failing to give a COBRA notice. The court assumed that if notice had been given, the dependent would have elected COBRA coverage in view of the serious injuries he had suffered, and thus COBRA continuation coverage was held to be in effect. [Swint v. Protective Life Ins. Co., 779 F. Supp. 532 (S.D. Ala. 1991)]

In another case, an employee was terminated, and she filed a COBRA claim asserting that the employer did not provide her with a COBRA election notice when she lost her coverage immediately after the termination. The employee was not notified of her loss of coverage until two months later, when she sought medical treatment. The employee's lawyer contacted the employer, which immediately acknowledged its mistake, reinstated coverage, and paid for coverage at its own expense for approximately five additional months. The employee sought penalties of $100 per day and attorneys' fees.

The court held that the employer admitted liability under COBRA but balanced the nature of the employer's conduct against the prejudice to the employee. The court ordered the employer to pay a penalty of $10 per day running from the deadline for providing the COBRA election notice through the date the employer corrected the mistake. The court also awarded attorneys' fees but limited the award to the value of the work the attorney performed up until reinstatement of coverage. [Cooper v. Harbour Inns of Baltimore Inc., 2000 U.S. Dist. LEXIS 4284 (D. Md. Mar. 20, 2000)]

In another decision on this issue, an employee was hired by the City of Pass Christian—subject to the COBRA provisions of the PHSA, not ERISA. At that time, Pass Christian maintained for its employees a medical benefits plan that was underwritten by Anthem Life Insurance Co. The employee joined the plan when she was hired by the city and received a booklet informing her that if she left her job she would have the right to continued healthcare coverage for 18 months. When she left her job four years later, she elected to continue her health care coverage.

Under the terms of the city's plan, the former employee was entitled to receive continuation coverage for 18 months. Just one day before the termination of her 18-month continued health care coverage, the City of Pass Christian switched insurers. The former employee was permitted to complete new coverage forms that day and received an insurance booklet that included an explanation of COBRA. She admitted she did not read the notice.

By error, the new insurer continued accepting premium payments for the ex-employee's coverage for approximately six weeks after her coverage was set to expire. The insurer then realized that she was not entitled to continued coverage and canceled her coverage effective for the following month.

According to the court, the former employee did not learn that her insurance was canceled until her insurance card was refused by a pharmacist. That same day, she was admitted to the hospital and underwent open-heart surgery, incurring medical expenses of $218,000. She sued both her employer and the new insurer.

The court ruled in favor of the city and its insurer. It concluded that any failure on the city's part to provide the employee with COBRA notice at the time her employment terminated was harmless because she in fact elected and received all the continuation coverage that she was entitled to under COBRA and the express terms of the group health plan. The court ruled that the new insurer, which started providing coverage after the expiration of the employee's 18-month continuation term, never had a duty to notify her of her continuation rights, and accordingly dismissed the insurer from the suit.

The court noted that while the city failed to give the employee adequate notice at the time her employment terminated, the notice she received from the insurer was more than adequate to put her on notice that her continuation coverage would expire 18 months after her employment termination. According to the court, the employee's failure to obtain an alternate source of health insurance coverage was attributable not so much to the inadequacy of notice as to her own failure adequately to read and heed the documents that were furnished to her. [Bigelow v. United Healthcare of Miss., Inc., 220 F.3d 339 (5th Cir. 2000)]

In one important decision on this issue, an employee became disabled and did not return to his job. He had coverage under the employer's group health insurance policy, which said disabled persons could continue their coverage on a self-pay basis for six months and then COBRA would be offered for 18 months. The employer mistakenly advised the employee that he could self-pay for coverage indefinitely and never provided him with a COBRA election notice.

Upon learning that the employee had been self-paying for coverage for more than 24 months, the insurer cut off his health coverage. The employee then sued his former employer for unpaid medical expenses. He alleged a failure to provide the COBRA election notice.

The employee claimed that by not notifying him of his COBRA rights, the employer deprived him of the opportunity to make arrangements for other coverage before his COBRA benefits ran out. The court said that the employee had received more than the 18 months of COBRA coverage to which he was entitled and therefore had no claim to additional coverage—even if the employer had failed to provide the COBRA election notice.

However, the court concluded the employer was not entitled to summary judgment on the employee's statutory penalty claim. It rejected the employer's argument that the SPD had adequately apprised the employee of his election rights; the statute specifically requires that a COBRA election notice be provided after a qualifying event. [Rittenhouse v. Professional Micro Sys. Inc., 1999 U.S. Dist. LEXIS 21695 (S.D. Ohio July 21, 1999)]

Q 6:87 Does the plan administrator have to guarantee that the qualified beneficiary actually receives the COBRA notice?

No. According to a case decided by the Fifth Circuit, the law requires employers to make a good-faith attempt to comply with COBRA's notice requirements. "This does not mean, however, that employers are required to ensure that plan participants actually receive notice," said the court. "Rather, it merely obligates employers to use means 'reasonably calculated to reach plan participants.'" [Degruise v. Sprint Corp., 279 F.3d 333 (5th Cir. 2002)]

The employer in this case sent a terminated employee's COBRA notice to the employee's last known address by certified mail with return receipt requested. The U.S. Postal Service twice attempted to deliver the notice, but the employee was out of town on a three-week honeymoon. The Postal Service left a notice in his mailbox that a certified letter was waiting for him at the post office. When the employee returned to town, he went to the post office to retrieve the letter, but the postal workers couldn't locate it and advised him to return in a couple of days to see if the letter had been found. He returned as directed, but the letter still had not been found. He had no way of knowing what the letter contained or who had sent it. The Postal Service finally located the letter and returned it to the employer with an indication that it had never been claimed by the employee.

Meanwhile, the employee had started a job with a new employer that offered health coverage. However, the new employer's plan denied certain of the employee's benefit claims because they related to a preexisting medical condition. Therefore, the employee filed a lawsuit against the old employer for failure to properly notify him of his COBRA coverage rights and demanding payment for his medical expenses.

The Fifth Circuit concluded that the employer's use of certified mail to send the COBRA notice to the address provided by the employee constituted a good-faith effort to notify the employee of his COBRA rights. The fact that the employer later learned that the notice had not been delivered did not change that result. The employer was not responsible for the letter's going undelivered and had no knowledge of why it had not been delivered.

On the other hand, a U.S. district court concluded that an employer's single mailing of a COBRA notice did not amount to a good-faith effort to notify a qualified beneficiary of his COBRA rights where the beneficiary promptly notified the employer that he had not received the notice. According to the court, the employer's failure to send a second mailing constituted a lack of good faith in notifying the beneficiary of his rights. The court specifically contrasted the Fifth Circuit decision, noting that in that case the employer knew only that the notice had not been delivered but had no idea why. Thus, the employer could reasonably have assumed that the delivery failure was the employee's fault, and thus its good faith was preserved. By contrast, the employer in the district court case had actual notice that its method of delivery had failed, belying a claim of good faith. [Wooderson v. American Airlines, Inc., 2001 U.S. Dist. LEXIS 3721 (N.D. Tex. Mar. 23, 2001)]

Although the DOL has addressed the requirements for providing initial COBRA notices (see Qs 6:73–6:75), it has not issued regulations or other guidance specifying what constitutes a good-faith effort to provide notice to a qualifying beneficiary on the occurrence of a qualifying event. Therefore, the courts have developed their own ground rules.

Presumption of receipt. The federal courts have held that a COBRA notice is presumed to have been received if it was properly addressed, stamped, and mailed. [Phillips v. Riverside Inc., 796 F. Supp. 403 (E.D. Ark. 1992)] When this presumption is applied, the employee's mere denial of receipt is not sufficient to rebut it. [Mercado-Garcia v. Ponce Fed. Bank, 979 F.2d 890 (1st Cir. 1992); *see also* Jachim v. KUTV Inc., 783 F. Supp. 1328 (D. Utah 1992); Truesdale v. Pacific Holding Co., 778 F. Supp. 77 (D.D.C. 1991); Ramos v. SEIU Local 74 Welfare Fund, 2002 U.S. Dist LEXIS 5849 (S.D.N.Y. Apr. 3, 2002)]

Employer's ability to prove proper mailing procedure. As a result of the presumption of receipt discussed above, disputes about whether the COBRA notice was received have focused in particular on the facts of the employer's procedure for sending it. In some cases, the employer was unable to establish the presumption of receipt because it could not prove that sufficient procedures were in place or were used in the particular instance and, as a result, lost the COBRA case. For example, in *DeSimone v. Siena College* [1991 U.S. Dist. LEXIS

5529 (N.D.N.Y. Apr. 24, 1991)], the employer presented testimony concerning its COBRA procedure but did not present testimony from anyone who had personally mailed the notice, directed another to do so, or observed another doing so. In other words, the employer failed to demonstrate that anyone had actually followed its COBRA procedure. In another case, testimony given by an individual without personal knowledge of what had been done with regard to the particular COBRA notice at issue also failed to convince the court. [Phillips v. Riverside Inc., 796 F. Supp. 403 (E.D. Ark. 1992); *see also* Lawrence v. Jackson Mack Sales Inc., 837 F. Supp. 771 (S.D. Miss. 1992)] In other cases, in contrast, convincing testimony regarding the employer's standard office procedures and whether they were followed in the particular circumstance was presented to the court. [Jachim v. KUTV Inc., 783 F. Supp. 1328 (D. Utah 1992); Ellis v. Ford Motor Co., 1996 U.S. App. LEXIS 22458 (6th Cir. Aug. 1, 1996)]

In one case, a terminated employee claimed that neither he nor his wife received any notices with regard to their COBRA rights. However, a district court held that the employee's claim was not supported by the evidence. The court noted that the key issue is not whether an employee actually receives a COBRA notice but whether the employer sent the notice in a good-faith manner and by means reasonably calculated to reach the employee. The court concluded that the employer had met that standard. The employer's benefits administrator testified that the employer's computer records confirmed that a COBRA notice was generated for the former employee and that she specifically recalled mailing the notice in accordance with the employer's standard procedures. The administrator's testimony, coupled with the fact that the notice was sent by first-class mail to the former employee's last known address, convinced the court that the employer had made a good-faith effort to notify the employee. [Gibbs v. A. Finkl & Sons Co., 27 Employee Benefits Cas. (BNA) 2477 (N.D. Ill. Feb. 25, 2002)]

Method of delivery. With regard to the method of delivery used, hand delivery directly to the employee has been upheld in one case. [Dehner v. Kansas City So. Indus. Inc., 713 F. Supp. 1397 (D. Kan. 1989)] In another, delivery of the notice to the employee's attorney was upheld. [Dixon v. Philadelphia Elec. Co., 1992 U.S. Dist. LEXIS 16047 (E.D. Pa. Sept. 23, 1992)]

Last known address. The address on the employer's records can be a critical concern. In one case, the employer had sent the COBRA notice to the employee's former address, which was the only address it had for COBRA notice purposes; however, the employee had notified her immediate supervisor of her new address and demonstrated knowledge on the company's part by providing other letters that the company had sent to her new address. [Martin v. Marriott Corp., 15 Employee Benefits Cas. (BNA) 1217 (D.D.C. 1992)] In a more recent case, an employee claimed that her former employer had not satisfied the notice requirement because it had sent her COBRA notice to the address she had used when she worked for the company, even though she claimed she called to inform the company of her new Puerto Rico address. Noting that the employee admitted to having her mail forwarded from her old address to her new Puerto Rico address, the district court dismissed the COBRA claim, holding that the employer had substantially complied with COBRA's notification requirements because the notice it sent was reasonably calculated to reach the former employee. The First Circuit Court of Appeals disagreed with the district court. Looking at the facts in the light most favorable to the employee, the First Circuit could not say as a matter of law that the company complied with the notice requirement because there was a factual dispute as to whether the company sent the notice to the employee's last known address. The court therefore said the employee's claim could not be dismissed without a trial on the merits. [Torres-Negron v. Merck & Co., 488 F.3d 34 (1st Cir. 2007)]

> **Practice Pointer.** These cases point up the importance of making supervisors aware of the need to communicate to the appropriate benefits administration personnel pertinent personnel-change information that supervisors receive informally.

On the other hand, if the company has been given an incomplete or incorrect address by the employee, the employer will not be held liable for the employee's mistake or failure to correct the information. [Truesdale v. Pacific Holding Co., 778 F. Supp. 77 (D.D.C. 1991)] In one case in which the employer realized that it did not have the employee's current address, the employer sent the COBRA materials to the employee's attorney, and the court concluded that that was a valid COBRA notice. [Dixon v. Philadelphia Elec. Co., 1992 U.S. Dist. LEXIS 16047 (E.D. Pa. Sept. 23, 1992)]

In an unusual case, the Eighth Circuit Court of Appeals held that an employer that also served as the plan administrator met the notice requirement by orally explaining COBRA rights to a qualified beneficiary. The court noted that the law provides that the initial COBRA notice must be in writing. However, the law only provides that the plan administer must "notify" a beneficiary of COBRA rights following a qualifying event; it does not specify that the notice must be in writing. [Chestnut v. Montgomery, 307 F.3d 698 (8th Cir. 2002)]

Notice to disabled employees. The ADA also affects the manner in which COBRA notices must be provided. Under the ADA, employers must, among other things, provide disabled employees with equal access to the terms, conditions, and privileges of employment through "reasonable accommodation," unless doing so would impose an undue hardship on the business operations of the employer. Neither the EEOC nor the IRS has provided any guidance yet on what this requirement means in the COBRA context; however, the regulations issued by the EEOC under the ADA indicate that the employer may be required to reasonably accommodate the disabled employee, such as by reading the COBRA notice to the employee and assisting with filling out the required forms. The form of accommodation is to be worked out on a case-by-case basis, and there is no single right answer or prescribed method of furnishing assistance in this instance. [29 C.F.R. §§ 1630.2(o), 1630.9(a), 1630.15(d)]

Computerized issuance. The procedure for issuing the notice is not required to be computerized to be reliable. [Southern Md. Hosp. Ctr. v. Corley, 6 F. Supp. 461 (D. Md. 1998)] However, delivery of COBRA notices via computer or other electronic means may become increasingly commonplace. The DOL has issued a safe harbor rule that permits the electronic delivery of ERISA notices and employee benefit plan disclosures, including COBRA notices (see chapter 2). [DOL Reg. § 2520.104b-1]

Q 6:88   Are COBRA notices required in connection with leave under the FMLA?

Yes, if a qualifying event occurs during the FMLA leave. A leave of absence taken under FMLA does not constitute a COBRA qualifying event, because no loss of coverage occurs as a result of the FMLA leave. [Notice 94-103, 1994-51 I.R.B. 10; Treas. Reg. §54.4980B-10, Q&A-1] FMLA requires employers to continue group health plan coverage during the period of leave "at the same level and under the conditions coverage would have been provided if the employee had continued in employment continuously for the duration of such leave." [FMLA §104(c)(1); 29 C.F.R. §825.209] Accordingly, it appears that the COBRA notice should not be distributed at the beginning of the leave period, because no qualifying event will have occurred at that time.

However, a qualifying event may occur on the last day of the FMLA leave, if the employee is not returning to employment. [Notice 94-103, 1994-51 I.R.B. 10; Treas. Reg. §54.4980B-10, Q&A-1, 2] The last day of the FMLA leave is the last day for which the leave is scheduled or when it becomes known that an employee is not returning to employment and therefore ceases to be entitled to leave under FMLA, whichever is earlier. [139 Cong. Rec. §978 (1993)] Thus, in the case of an employee who takes a leave under FMLA and notifies his or her employer that he or she will not be returning to work upon expiration of the leave period, the COBRA notice should be provided after the employer learns that the employee will not be returning to work. Specifically, the employer must notify the plan administrator within 30 days of being notified that the employee will not be returning to work, and the plan administrator must then provide the employee with a notice of COBRA rights within 14 days. [Notice 94-103, 1994-51 I.R.B. 10, Q&A-6]

Q 6:89   Is special treatment of COBRA notices required where the person entitled to elect COBRA coverage is mentally incapacitated?

Two court decisions indicate that a plan administrator may have to take extraordinary steps in providing notice where the person entitled to elect COBRA continuation coverage is not mentally able to make an informed decision. In a decision by the U.S. Court of Appeals for the Eleventh Circuit, the facts involved an employee who was in a persistent vegetative state as a result of strokes. After being kept on the payroll for a time, the employee became entitled to either 12 months of continuation coverage at no cost or 18 months of COBRA coverage. A proper COBRA notice was given, and the employee's spouse asked for further information, including an SPD that was not provided. No COBRA election was made, and the 12-month continuation coverage took effect. Shortly before the expiration of the 12-month period, the spouse was appointed legal guardian of the employee and attempted to elect COBRA coverage. The Court of Appeals held that a COBRA notice to an incompetent beneficiary is not effective unless it is accompanied by plan documents that allow the person acting on behalf of the incompetent beneficiary to make an informed and intelligent decision. Because the spouse had not been provided with an SPD, the COBRA notice was held to be ineffective, and the spouse guardian's election of COBRA continuation coverage was allowed. [Meadows v. Cagle's Inc., 954 F.2d 686 (11th Cir. 1992)]

In a U.S. district court case, an employee was given a timely COBRA notice; the employee elected coverage and paid the first COBRA premium. The employee then became mentally incompetent and failed to pay the next premium due, resulting in cancellation of the COBRA coverage. Some months later, a guardian for the incompetent employee was appointed, who attempted to reinstate the coverage by paying the delinquent premiums. The court ruled that the employer was required to reinstate the COBRA coverage. The court held that where a COBRA beneficiary misses a premium payment due to mental incapacity, the deadline for payment is tolled (frozen) for a reasonable period of time until the beneficiary or legally appointed guardian is able to cure the deficiency. [Sirkin v. Phillips Colls., Inc., 14 Employee Benefit Cas. 2193 (D.N.J. 1991); *see also* Branch v. G. Bernd Co., 955 F.2d 1574 (11th Cir. 1992)]

> **Practice Pointer.** If the plan administrator is aware that a COBRA beneficiary is mentally incompetent, it would be prudent to provide the COBRA election notice and premium payment notices to the legal representative (if any), spouse, or other person handling the incompetent person's affairs, as well as to the incompetent person.

Q 6:90 Can an employer or plan administrator be held liable for a COBRA continuation notice sent in error?

It appears that in some situations there could be liability.

A U.S. district court considered a situation where an employer erroneously advised the plan administrator to send out a COBRA notice and election form, even though the former employee receiving the notice was not entitled to COBRA continuation coverage. The former employee completed the election of coverage form and returned it to the plan administrator. The court held that the administrative error in sending out the COBRA notice and election form could not be construed as a binding offer of coverage because the statute and the terms of the plan did not provide for such coverage. [Smith v. Genelco, Inc., 777 F. Supp. 750 (E.D. Mo. 1991)]

In a decision by the U.S. Court of Appeals for the Eleventh Circuit, however, an employer was held to be estopped from retroactively denying COBRA benefits after first approving coverage, even though the former employee was not entitled to COBRA continuation for himself and his dependents under the then-current version of the COBRA statute because he was covered under his wife's health benefit plan. The court applied a federal common-law theory of equitable estoppel, which consists of the following five elements:

1. The party to be estopped misrepresented material facts;

2. The party to be estopped was aware of the true facts;

3. The party to be estopped intended that the misrepresentation be acted on or had reason to believe the party asserting the estoppel would rely upon it;

4. The party asserting the estoppel did not know, nor should it have known, the true facts; and

5. The party asserting the estoppel reasonably and detrimentally relied on the misrepresentation.

The appellate court concluded that all five elements of equitable estoppel had been met in the case and held that COBRA coverage applied. [National Cos. Health Benefit Plan v. St. Joseph's Hosp., 929 F.2d 1558 (11th Cir. 1991)]

COBRA Election and Enrollment

Q 6:91   Who is entitled to make a COBRA election?

Any qualified beneficiary who would otherwise lose coverage under a group health plan must be given an opportunity to elect to continue his or her group health plan coverage. (See Qs 6:106–6:117 for a discussion of the type of coverage that must be provided.)

Q 6:92   What is the minimum permitted election period?

Every qualified beneficiary must be given an election period of at least 60 days to decide whether to elect COBRA continuation coverage. [I.R.C. §4980B(f)(5)(A)(i)]

Q 6:93   When does the COBRA election period begin?

The COBRA election period begins on the later of (1) the date the qualified beneficiary would lose coverage because of a qualifying event or (2) the date the qualified beneficiary is notified of the right to elect continuation coverage. [I.R.C. §4980B(f)(5)(A)] (See Qs 6:43–6:48 for a discussion of when and under which conditions loss of coverage occurs.)

Q 6:94   Is the COBRA election period always limited to 60 days?

Not necessarily. The law provides for a *minimum* 60-day election period; it does not specify a *maximum* period. [I.R.C. §4980B(f)(5)(A)(i)] Therefore, an employer is free to give COBRA beneficiaries additional time to make the election.

Furthermore, as an appellate court case illustrates, an employer may inadvertently obligate itself to provide COBRA coverage even when an election is significantly overdue. The employee in the case became seriously ill and was expected to die shortly. His spouse contacted the employer about the employee's life insurance benefits. At that time, the spouse was informed that the employer planned to terminate the employee because of his disability. The spouse was informed of the employee's COBRA continuation coverage rights and given a COBRA enrollment form—but no COBRA election was made. More than 60 days following the employee's termination, the employer was contacted by a hospital about the employee's health coverage. Surprised to discover that the employee was still alive, the employer sent out an election notice and a new enrollment form. This time, the COBRA election form was duly completed. However, the employer's insurer declined to pay the employee's hospital bills on the grounds that the COBRA election was made too late. The Fifth Circuit Court of Appeals disagreed, holding that the COBRA election was valid. According to the court, the COBRA statute specifies only a minimum election period; it does not set a maximum period. Thus, unless a plan specifies otherwise, a COBRA beneficiary can elect COBRA coverage at any time within the continuation coverage period specified in the plan. [Lifecare Hosp., Inc. v. Health Plus of La., Inc., 418 F.3d 436 (5th Cir. 2005)]

> **Practice Pointer.** To avoid such unintended results, an employer's health plan document and COBRA election notice should specify both the *minimum* and *maximum* COBRA election period.

Q 6:95   What would happen if the notice is not sent on time?

The courts are divided on this issue. There is a question about whether a delay in providing this notice will result in the delayed commencement of the continuation coverage period. One court has held that if an employer has failed to notify a qualified beneficiary of COBRA rights, the continuation period has not as yet begun. [Ryan v. Policy Mgmt. Sys. Corp., 1993 U.S. Dist. LEXIS 13949, at *7 (N.D. Ill. Oct. 4, 1993)] However, in support of its conclusion, that court relied on the district court's decision in *Gaskell v. Harvard Cooperative Society*, which was subsequently vacated by the Court of Appeals for the First Circuit. [762 F. Supp. 1539 (D. Mass. 1991), *vacated and remanded*, 3 F.3d 495 (1st Cir. 1993)] The other courts that have addressed this issue have concluded that an employer's defective COBRA notice (or lack of notice entirely) to a qualified beneficiary is not a basis for extending the period of COBRA coverage. [*See, e. g.,* Burgess v. Adams Tool & Eng'g, Inc., 908 F. Supp. 473 (W.D. Mich. 1995); DiSabatino v. DiSabatino Bros., Inc., 894 F. Supp. 810 (D. Del. 1995); Smith v. Borden Inc., 1995 U.S. Dist. LEXIS 19728 (W.D. Mo. Oct. 23, 1995)]

In another case, an employee who was terminated filed a COBRA claim asserting that the employer did not provide her with a COBRA election notice when she lost her coverage immediately after the termination of her employment. The employee was not notified of her loss of coverage until two months later, when she sought medical treatment. The employee's lawyer contacted the employer, which immediately acknowledged its mistake, reinstated coverage, and paid for coverage at its own expense for approximately five additional months. The employee sought penalties of $100 per day and attorneys' fees.

The court held that the employer admitted liability under COBRA but balanced the nature of the employer's conduct against the prejudice to the employee. The court ordered the employer to pay a penalty of $10 per day running from the deadline for providing the COBRA election notice through the date that the employer corrected the mistake. The court also awarded attorneys' fees but limited the award to the value of the work the attorney performed up until reinstatement of coverage. [Cooper v. Harbour Inns of Baltimore Inc., 2000 U.S. Dist. LEXIS 4284 (D. Md. Mar. 20, 2000)]

In *Carter v. General Elec. Co.* [2000 U.S. Dist. LEXIS 3875 (N.D. Ill. Mar. 21, 2000)], the court ruled that a former employee's motion for violations of COBRA's notice requirements was untimely. Four years after being terminated, the employee brought suit against her former employer for violating the COBRA notice requirements. Even though COBRA does not contain an express statute of limitations period, the court followed analogous state law for determining the appropriate statute of limitations. The court held that the most analogous Illinois law was a two-year statute of limitations period for actions against insurance producers, limited insurance representatives, and registered firms. Based on that two-year period, the court barred the former employee's claims.

By contrast, in a case involving an employee who brought suit for COBRA violations four years after his employment terminated, the U.S. District Court for the District of Vermont concluded that an employee's claim was subject to a six-year statute of limitations. The court rejected the employer's argument that the most analogous limitations periods under state law were Vermont's two-year limitations period for wage disputes, three-year limitations period for personal injury or property damage claims, or three-year-and-90-day period for insurance claims. Instead, the court said, the employee's claim was not time-barred because it was most analogous to a claim for "economic damages," governed by Vermont's six-year statute of limitations. [Mattson v. Farrell Distrib. Corp., 163 F. Supp. 2d 411 (D. Vt. 2001)]

Q 6:96   Is the COBRA continuation election considered made when it is sent or when it is received?

Qualified beneficiaries must make their elections regarding COBRA coverage on or before the last day of the 60-day election period. The COBRA regulations provide that a qualified beneficiary's election is treated as made on the date that it is sent to the plan administrator. [Treas. Reg. §54.4980B-6, Q&A-1(b) (Feb. 3, 1999)] Accordingly, it appears that an election that is received after expiration of the 60-day election period but is postmarked (or otherwise sent) on or before the 60th day would be timely.

Q 6:97   Are qualified beneficiaries who waive COBRA continuation coverage allowed to change their minds?

Yes. A change is permitted under certain circumstances. A waiver of COBRA continuation coverage can be revoked at any time before the end of the election period. A waiver or revocation of a waiver is treated as made on the date it is sent to the employer or plan administrator. [Treas. Reg. §54-4980B-6, Q&A-4 (Feb. 3, 1999)]

Q 6:98   Must group health plan coverage be provided during the interim period when the qualified beneficiary is deciding whether to elect COBRA coverage?

Yes. After a qualified beneficiary elects COBRA continuation coverage, coverage generally must be provided retroactively to the date when it would have been lost. Indemnity or reimbursement arrangements have two alternatives: (1) coverage can be extended during the election period, or (2) if the plan permits retroactive reinstatement, the qualified beneficiary can be dropped from the plan and reinstated when an affirmative election is made. [Treas. Reg. §54-4980B-6, Q&A-3(a) (Feb. 3, 1999)]

However, if a qualified beneficiary waives COBRA coverage during the election period and later revokes the waiver, coverage need not be provided retroactively (that is, from the date of loss of coverage until the waiver is revoked). [Treas. Reg. §54.4980B-6, Q&A-4]

Q 6:99   What happens to claims incurred by the qualified beneficiary before making a decision about COBRA continuation coverage?

The group health plan is under no obligation to pay claims for covered plan expenses incurred during the election period until COBRA continuation coverage is actually elected and, if applicable, until premium payments have been made. [Treas. Reg. §54-4980B-6, Q&A-3(b) (Feb. 3, 1999)]

If a health care provider (e.g., a physician, hospital, or pharmacy) contacts a plan to confirm a qualified beneficiary's coverage during the election period, the plan must give a complete response about the beneficiary's COBRA continuation coverage rights. For example, if the plan provides coverage during the election period but cancels coverage retroactively if COBRA coverage is not elected, the plan must inform the provider that the qualified beneficiary is covered but the coverage is subject to retroactive termination. If the plan cancels coverage but retroactively reinstates it once an election is made, the plan must inform the provider that the beneficiary does not currently have coverage but will have retroactive coverage if the election is made.

Q 6:100   How do direct service plans, such as health maintenance organizations handle payment for services rendered during the election period but before an election is made?

Direct service plans and walk-in clinics have two options during the election period for dealing with a qualified beneficiary who has not made an election and paid the initial premium. The first option is to require the qualified beneficiary to choose between (1) electing and paying for the coverage or (2) paying the reasonable and customary charge for the plan's services on a fee-for-service basis. Qualified beneficiaries who take the fee-for-service option must be reimbursed for their payments within 30 days of making the election and paying the required initial premium.

The other option is for the plan to treat the qualified beneficiary's use of the facility as a constructive election of COBRA continuation coverage, requiring him or her to pay any applicable charge for coverage; however, the qualified beneficiary must be notified of the meaning of the constructive election before using the facility. [Treas. Reg. §54-4980B-6, Q&A-3(c)(i), (ii) (Feb. 3, 1999)]

Q 6:101   Can an employer speed up the decision by withholding money or benefits?

No. Employers are specifically forbidden to withhold benefits otherwise available to the qualified beneficiary, including payment for claims relating to covered expenses incurred before the qualifying event, to force a quicker decision about COBRA rights. A waiver of COBRA rights obtained by threats to withhold any benefit is invalid. [Treas. Reg. §54-4980B-6, Q&A-5 (Feb. 3, 1999)]

Potential breach of ERISA fiduciary duty. In one case, an employee convinced the court that the employer's attempt to force him to make an immediate decision as to whether to continue his group health plan coverage by electing COBRA also constituted a breach of fiduciary duty under ERISA. [Powell v. Bob Downes Chrysler-Plymouth, Inc., 763 F. Supp. 1023 (E.D. Mo. 1991)]

Q 6:102   Must a plan provide coverage once a qualified beneficiary elects COBRA coverage but before he or she forwards the initial premium payment?

Qualified beneficiaries must be given a 45-day grace period after election to forward the initial premium payment (which may include all outstanding premiums due). [Treas. Reg. §54.4980B-8, Q&A-5] The COBRA coverage regulations make it clear that a plan can provide coverage during this grace period and cancel it retroactively if payment is not made. Alternatively, the plan may cancel a qualified beneficiary's coverage if payment is not received at the time of the election and restore it retroactively once payment is received. [Treas. Reg. §54.4980B-8, Q&A-5(c)]

This retroactive coverage requirement will also impact the coverage representations that the employer, plan administrator, or third-party administrator makes in response to questions from providers during the election period and before the initial COBRA premium has been paid. If the plan opts to provide coverage but cancel it retroactively for nonpayment, the provider must be informed that the beneficiary is covered but that coverage is subject to retroactive termination if timely payment is not made. If the plan elects to cancel coverage and restore it retroactively, the provider must be told that the qualified beneficiary does not currently have coverage but will have coverage retroactively if payment is made. [Treas. Reg. §54.4980B-8, Q&A-5(c)]

Claims incurred after election but prior to premium payment. The COBRA regulations permit the employer to hold off paying claims incurred by the qualified beneficiary during the election period and pay them if, and only if, the COBRA beneficiary both elects and pays for COBRA coverage in a timely manner. For example, once an individual elects COBRA coverage, he or she is covered under the plan retroactive to the date coverage would otherwise have been lost. However, the employer can continue to hold off paying claims for covered expenses incurred during the period coverage otherwise would be lost until the qualified beneficiary actually forwards the COBRA premium. [Treas. Reg. §54-4980B-6, Q&A-3(b) (Feb. 3, 1999)] Thus, the qualified beneficiary is permitted to take a wait-and-see stance and only elect and pay for COBRA coverage (and obtain the resulting retroactive continuation coverage) if it appears that he or she will have substantial medical expenses. The employer, on the other hand, must grant retroactive coverage but is not required to bear the financial burden of claims for such coverage until the required premiums have been received.

Waiver and revocation of the waiver. In the case of a waiver followed by a revocation of the waiver, the group health plan is not required to provide retroactive coverage for the period from the loss of coverage until the date the waiver is revoked. [Treas. Reg. §54-4980B-6, Q&A-4 (Feb. 3, 1999)]

Q 6:103 Must each qualified beneficiary be allowed to make an independent election?

Yes. Each qualified beneficiary must be allowed to make an independent election concerning COBRA continuation coverage. The individual qualified beneficiary's right to make an independent election includes the right to switch to another group health plan during an open enrollment period. [Treas. Reg. §54-4980B-6, Q&A-6 (Feb. 3, 1999)]

The employee cannot reject COBRA coverage on behalf of his or her spouse and covered children, although the employee can elect COBRA coverage on their behalf (see Qs 6:104–6:105). [Treas. Reg. §54-4980B-6, Ex. 1 (Feb. 3, 1999)]

Q 6:104   Can the employee elect COBRA coverage on behalf of family members?

Yes. An employee may elect, both on his or her own behalf and on behalf of his or her covered spouse and dependents, to receive COBRA coverage. Such an affirmative election will be binding on the spouse and dependents.

If a covered employee or the spouse of a covered employee makes a COBRA coverage election that does not specify self-only coverage, the election will be deemed to include an election of COBRA coverage on behalf of all other qualified beneficiaries affected by the qualifying event. [Treas. Reg. §54.4980B-6, Q&A-6]

Q 6:105   Can a covered employee decline coverage on behalf of his or her spouse and dependents?

No. An employee cannot decline COBRA coverage on behalf of his or her covered spouse and dependents. If the covered employee turns down COBRA coverage, the covered spouse must be given an opportunity to elect it. Similarly, only the covered employee's affirmative election of coverage is binding on covered dependents; if both the employee and the spouse reject COBRA continuation coverage, each covered dependent child must also be given an opportunity to elect it. [I.R.C. §4980B(f)(5); ERISA §605; PHSA §2205; Treas. Reg. §54.4980B-6, Ex. 1]

The only exception is for minor children, on whose behalf elections to either continue or reject coverage can be made by their parents or legal guardians (regardless of whether the parent or guardian is a qualified beneficiary). With respect to an incapacitated or deceased qualified beneficiary, an election can be made by the legal representative of the qualified beneficiary or the qualified beneficiary's estate (as determined under applicable state law) or by the spouse of the qualified beneficiary. [Treas. Reg. §54.4980B-6, Q&A-6]

Type and Extent of Required Coverage

Q 6:106   What type of coverage must be offered to qualified beneficiaries?

When coverage is lost because of a qualifying event, COBRA gives qualified beneficiaries the right to elect group health plan coverage that is identical to the coverage provided to similarly situated non-COBRA beneficiaries who have not undergone a qualifying event.

This is ordinarily the same coverage the qualified beneficiaries received immediately before the qualifying event. However, if group health coverage is modified for similarly situated beneficiaries, the coverage made available to COBRA beneficiaries may be modified in the same way.

For this purpose, similarly situated non-COBRA beneficiaries are those covered employees and their spouses and dependents who are receiving coverage under the employer's plan (other than COBRA coverage) and who, based on all the facts and circumstances, are situated most similarly to the qualified beneficiary immediately before the qualifying event. [Treas. Reg. §54.4980B-3, Q&A-3]

If the continuation coverage offered differs from the coverage made available to similarly situated non-COBRA beneficiaries, the group health plan will not be in compliance with COBRA requirements unless other complying coverage is offered. Coverage limitations introduced in anticipation of a qualifying event are disregarded in assessing the adequacy of continuation coverage (see Q 6:47). [I.R.C. §4980B(f)(2); ERISA §602(1); PHSA §2102; Treas. Reg. §54.4980B-5, Q&A-1(a) (Feb. 3, 1999)]

An employer's promise that it would "work with" the plaintiff regarding coverage for her illness, when her illness was covered under the insurance provided to her prior to the qualifying event, did not satisfy COBRA. [Zemko v. Muntz Indus. Inc., 1995 U.S. Dist. LEXIS 6152 (N.D. Ill. May 8, 1995)]

A newborn or adopted child who becomes a qualified beneficiary during a period of COBRA coverage is generally entitled to elect the same coverage that dependent children of active employees receive under the benefit package in which the covered employee is enrolled at the time of the birth or placement for adoption. However, the child may elect different coverage during the next available open enrollment period under the plan. [Treas. Reg. §54.4980B-5, Q&A-1(a)]

Q 6:107 Must qualified beneficiaries demonstrate insurability in order to qualify for continuation coverage?

No. Continuation coverage cannot be conditioned on evidence of insurability, and employers are not allowed to discriminate against qualified beneficiaries who lack this evidence. [I.R.C. §4980B(f)(2); ERISA §602(4); PHSA §2102; Treas. Reg. §54.4980B-5, Q&A-1(a) (Feb. 3, 1999)]

Q 6:108 What is the effect on continuation coverage if the employer changes the coverage available to employees who have not undergone a qualifying event?

Employees do not vest in, and are not guaranteed, the level of benefits the plan offered on the day before the qualifying event. If coverage is modified for similarly situated active employees, COBRA coverage may be similarly modified.

However, if the employer eliminates the plan in which a COBRA beneficiary is enrolled but continues to maintain one or more plans for similarly situated non-COBRA beneficiaries, the beneficiary must be offered the option of enrolling in another plan. This is the case even if active employees in the terminated plan are not given that option. [I.R.C. §4980B(f)(2)(B)(ii); ERISA §602(4); PHSA §2202; Treas. Reg. §54.4980B-5, Q&A-1(a) (Feb. 3, 1999)]

Q 6:109   Must a plan permit qualified beneficiaries to participate in an open enrollment period?

Yes. An open enrollment period is the time in which an employee covered by a group health plan can select a different group health plan or add or eliminate coverage of family members. Any open enrollment period available to active employees must be made available to qualified beneficiaries; for instance, qualified beneficiaries must be permitted to add newly eligible dependents not previously enrolled if the plan otherwise permits it. Each qualified beneficiary in a family must be given the same opportunity to change plans as is given to an active employee. [Prop. Treas. Reg. §1.162-26, Q&A-30; Treas. Reg. §54. 4980B-5, Q&A-4(c) (Feb. 3, 1999)]

Practice Pointer. To ensure that the qualified beneficiaries are provided with the opportunity to exercise their open enrollment rights, it would be advisable to send enrollment forms and related information to the qualified beneficiaries at the same time that active employees are provided with the forms and information.

Q 6:110   Can a qualified beneficiary pick up coverage for family members outside of an open enrollment period?

Yes. HIPAA provides special enrollment rights for certain family members who lose other group health plan coverage as well as for new spouses and newborn and newly adopted children (see chapter 5). A qualified beneficiary who has timely elected and made timely payment for COBRA coverage has the same right to enroll family members under the special enrollment rules as do other plan participants. In addition to special enrollment rights, if the plan provides that new family members of active employees can become covered (either automatically or by election) before the next open enrollment period, the same rights apply to family members of a qualified COBRA beneficiary. [Treas. Reg. §54.4980B-5, Q&A-5]

If the addition of a new family member will result in a higher premium (for example, if the beneficiary previously had individual coverage or the premium for family coverage depends on family size), the plan can require payment of a higher amount for the COBRA coverage.

Newborn and adopted children also have special rights as qualified beneficiaries (see Q 6:39).

Q 6:111   Can a COBRA beneficiary change his or her coverage other than during an open enrollment period?

As a general rule, a qualified beneficiary need only be given an opportunity to continue the coverage he or she was receiving immediately before the qualifying event, even if that coverage is no longer of value to the beneficiary.

However, there is one exception. A qualified beneficiary who moves outside the area served by a region-specific benefits package must be given the opportunity to elect alternative coverage that the employer makes available to active employees. This alternative coverage must be made available within a reasonable period of time upon request, regardless of the reason for the relocation. [Treas. Reg. §54.4980B-5, Q&A-4]

If the employer or employee organization makes group health coverage available to similarly situated non-COBRA beneficiaries that can be extended in the area where the qualified beneficiary is relocating, then that is the coverage that must be made available to the relocating beneficiary. If the employer or organization does not offer coverage to similarly situated non-COBRA beneficiaries in the beneficiary's new area but does make coverage available to other employees in that area, then that coverage must be offered to the qualified beneficiary. An employer or employee organization is not required to provide alternative coverage if the only coverage offered to active employees is not available in the qualified beneficiary's new location (e.g., because all coverage is region-specific and does not service the beneficiary's new location).

The effective date of the alternative coverage must be no later than the date of the qualified beneficiary's relocation or, if later, the first day of the month following the month in which the qualified beneficiary requests alternative coverage.

Q 6:112   When COBRA continuation coverage is elected, how are deductibles handled?

Qualified beneficiaries electing COBRA coverage are generally subject to the same deductibles as similarly situated non-COBRA beneficiaries.

Of course, the commencement date of continuation coverage seldom falls on the first day of the period used to compute deductibles. COBRA recognizes this fact and requires that the qualified beneficiary be given credit for expenses incurred toward the group health plan's deductibles during the time before the continuation period began. Credit must be given as if the qualifying event had never occurred. [Treas. Reg. §54.4980b-5, Q&A-2(a)(b) (Feb. 3, 1999)]

If a deductible is computed separately for each individual, each individual's remaining deductible on the date COBRA coverage begins is the same as his or her remaining deductible immediately before that date. [Treas. Reg. §54. 4980B-5, Q&A-2(b)] If the deductible is computed on a family basis, the remaining deductible for the family depends on which family members elect COBRA coverage. In computing the remaining deductible for the family, only the expenses of family members receiving COBRA coverage must be taken into account. [Treas. Reg. §54.4980B-5, Q&A-2(c)]

If the group health plan's deductible is not a fixed amount but is based on the covered employee's compensation, the plan can treat the employee's compensation as frozen at the level used to compute the deductible immediately before COBRA continuation coverage began or it may take the employee's actual compensation into account. So, for example, if the COBRA qualifying event was a reduction of hours, the plan may take the employee's reduced compensation into account in applying the deductible. If the employee no longer works for the employer, the deductible must be applied using either the compensation used to compute the deductible immediately before COBRA coverage began or the compensation used to compute the deductible immediately before the employee's employment was terminated. [Treas. Reg. §54.4980b-5, Q&A-2(e) (Feb. 3, 1999)]

Q 6:113   If family members select different continuation options, how is the remaining deductible amount computed?

Under the COBRA regulations, each qualified beneficiary is required to be credited only with the expenses attributable to him or her. [Treas. Reg. §54.4980B-5, Q&A-2(c) (Feb. 3, 1999)]

Example. A group health plan has a $500 annual family deductible. The plan provides that when a covered employer divorces, coverage terminates immediately for the employee's spouse and any dependent children who do not remain in the employee's custody. George, a covered employee with two children, divorces. George's ex-wife obtains custody of the younger child, while George retains custody of the older child. George's ex-wife and the younger child elect COBRA coverage. At the time of the divorce, the family had accumulated $420 of covered expenses, including $70 of expenses incurred by George, $70 by George's ex-wife, $200 by the younger child, and $80 by the older child.

The family unit consisting of George' s ex-wife and the younger child had accumulated a total of $270 of covered expenses. Therefore, the remaining deductible for that family unit is $230. The plan does not have to credit that family unit with the $150 of expenses incurred by George and the older child. However, the remaining deductible for George and the older child is not affected because their coverage is not COBRA coverage.

Q 6:114   How are annual plan limits handled for COBRA coverage?

Plan limits, including copayment limits, annual catastrophic limits on out-of-pocket expenses, limits on specific benefits (such as maximum days of hospitalization), and annual or lifetime limits on the total dollar amount of expenses reimbursable under the plan, must be treated in the same way as deductibles (see Qs 6:112–6:113). [Treas. Reg. §54.4980B-5, Q&A-2(a) (Feb. 3, 1999)]

Example 1. A group health plan pays for a maximum of 150 days of hospital confinement per individual per calendar year. A covered employee, Ann, who has had 20 days of hospital confinement as of May 1, terminates her employment and elects COBRA coverage as of that date. During the remainder of the year, the plan must pay for a maximum of 130 days of hospital confinement for Ann.

Example 2. A group health plan reimburses a maximum of $20,000 of covered expenses per family per year. The same $20,000 limit applies to unmarried covered employees. An employee, Frank, and his wife divorce on May 1. Frank's ex-wife elects COBRA coverage as of that date. As of May 1, Frank had incurred $5,000 of covered expenses and his ex-wife had incurred $8,000 of expenses. The plan can limit reimbursements for Frank's ex-wife to $12,000 for the remainder of the year ($20,000 maximum limit − $8,000 of covered expenses). The remaining benefit limit for Frank is not affected because his coverage is not COBRA coverage.

Q 6:115   If an individual on COBRA continuation has other group health insurance, how are benefits coordinated?

If a COBRA continuee has other coverage that does not cut off his or her COBRA continuation coverage (see Qs 6:126–6:127), the coordination of benefits (COB) rules contained in each plan will determine which plan pays on a primary basis and which plan pays on a secondary basis. The NAIC's model COB rule (see chapter 3) has been adopted by most states, although not all states have adopted the most recent version. (Self-insured plans generally contain the standard COB rules, even though such plans are not subject to regulation by the state's insurance department.)

The model COB rule provides that the plan extending COBRA continuation coverage to the individual is secondary to another group health plan covering the individual as an employee, if that plan also contains the special COB rule for continuation coverage. However, the model COB rule contains several rules that are to be applied in order, until a solution is reached; the COBRA continuation rule is number four out of six and functions as a tiebreaker. Therefore, if the two plans at issue contain the standard COB rules, it is likely that the majority of COB issues will be resolved by the application of rules one through three and that the special COBRA rule will come into play infrequently.

Coordination of COBRA and Medicare. Usually, Medicare entitlement is a cutoff event for COBRA continuation, so the issue of which plan is primary and which is secondary does not often arise. However, if the qualifying event is bankruptcy of the employer, retirees have lifetime coverage, and spouses and dependents get an extra 36 months from the date of the employee's death. It thus is possible for Medicare-entitled individuals to continue to receive COBRA continuation coverage in this instance. Regulations under the Medicare secondary-payer provisions of the Social Security Act provide that the COBRA coverage is to be primary and Medicare is to be secondary. [42 C.F.R. §411. 162(a)(3)]

Q 6:116   How do the COBRA continuation coverage requirements apply to cafeteria plans?

Health benefits provided under a cafeteria plan or other flexible benefits arrangement are subject to COBRA. However, COBRA applies only to the type and level of coverage that the qualifying beneficiary was receiving on the day before a qualifying event. [Treas. Reg. §54.4980B-2, Q&A-8]

> **Example.** Under Magna Corp.'s cafeteria plan, employees can choose among life insurance coverage, membership in an HMO, traditional indemnity health coverage, and cash compensation. Of these choices, the HMO and the traditional indemnity plan are health plans subject to the COBRA requirements. Ken and Susan are unmarried employees of Magna. For a calendar year, Ken chose life insurance under the cafeteria plan, while Susan chose the traditional indemnity health plan. Both employees terminate their employment with Magna during the year.
>
> Magna does not have to offer Ken COBRA coverage upon termination of employment. However, Magna must offer Susan continued coverage under the indemnity plan. In addition, if Susan is still receiving COBRA continuation coverage at the time of the next open enrollment period for active employees, she must be offered the opportunity to switch from the indemnity plan to the HMO (but not to the life insurance coverage).

Q 6:117   Are there COBRA requirements for health care flexible spending accounts?

Health care flexible spending accounts (FSAs) allow employees to make salary reduction contributions on a pretax basis, which can be withdrawn from the account to pay out-of-pocket medical expenses. In some plans, the employer also makes contributions to employees' accounts.

Health care FSAs are considered health plans for COBRA purposes. [Treas. Reg. §54.4980B-2, Q&A-1] However, the obligation of a health care FSA to provide continued coverage may be limited if it meets two conditions:

1. Benefits provided under the health care FSA are "excepted benefits" [I.R.C. §§9831, 9832]; and

2. The maximum amount the employee can be required to pay for a year of COBRA coverage equals or exceeds the maximum benefit available under the FSA for the year. [Treas. Reg. §54.4980B-2, Q&A-8]

The IRS says that health care FSAs qualify as excepted benefits if (1) the maximum benefit payable to the employee for the year does not exceed two times the employee's salary reduction election for the year (or, if greater, the amount of the employee's salary reduction election plus $500) and (2) the employer offers other group health plan coverage for the year that is not limited to excepted benefits.

If both of the above conditions are met for a plan year, the health care FSA is not required to make COBRA coverage available for any *subsequent* plan year. In other words, the health care FSA can cut off an employee's coverage at the end of the plan year even if that is short of the normal COBRA coverage period.

In addition, the health care FSA is not required to make COBRA coverage available for the *current* plan year unless the benefits available during the remainder of the year will exceed the amount the FSA can charge for the coverage. In other words, COBRA coverage is not required if the plan will simply pay out an amount equal to (or even less than) it collects from the employee.

Example. Omega Corp. offers its employees a major medical plan and a health care FSA. The plans operate on a calendar-year basis. Before the beginning of each year, employees can elect to reduce their compensation by up to $1,200 and have that amount contributed to the health care FSA. Omega matches each employee's FSA contribution. Thus, the annual benefit available to an employee is two times his or her salary reduction election for the year. Omega has determined that a reasonable estimated cost of providing the coverage is equal to two times an employee's salary reduction for the year. Therefore, Omega can charge 102 percent of that amount as a COBRA premium. This premium is charged on a monthly basis. So, for an employee who makes the maximum $1,200 salary reduction election, the annual charge is $2,448 (102% × $2,400) and the monthly premium is $204.

Arnold, an Omega employee, has elected to make $1,200 of salary reduction contributions to the FSA for the year. Thus, Arnold's maximum benefit for the year is $2,400. Arnold terminates employment with Omega on May 31. As of that date, Arnold had received reimbursements of $300 for health care expenses from the FSA.

Omega's health care FSA meets both of the above conditions. The health care FSA is an excepted benefit because employees have other group health coverage available and the maximum benefit payable for the year is not greater than two times an employee's salary reduction election for the year. In addition, the maximum amount that can be charged for COBRA coverage exceeds the maximum benefit available for the year. Therefore, Omega's healthcare FSA is not required to make COBRA coverage available to Arnold for any year *after* the current year.

Omega's health care FSA is, however, required to offer Arnold COBRA coverage for the current year. After deducting his $300 of reimbursements, Arnold is eligible for an additional $2,100 of benefits for the year. However, the FSA can charge him only $1,428 for his COBRA coverage for the remainder of the year (7 months × $204). COBRA coverage is required because Arnold's remaining benefits will exceed the cost of his COBRA coverage.

If Arnold had received $1,000 of reimbursements as of the date he terminated employment, the plan would not be required to offer COBRA coverage for the current year. Arnold's remaining benefit of $1,400 would be less than the $1,428 the plan could charge for the coverage.

Duration of Coverage

Q 6:118   What is the maximum required COBRA continuation period?

The maximum period for which group health plan coverage is required to be continued under COBRA differs depending on which qualifying event has occurred. In general, if the qualifying event is termination of the covered employee's employment or reduction in his or her hours of employment, the applicable COBRA continuation period runs for a maximum of 18 months from the date of the qualifying event. For all other qualifying events, except for an employer's bankruptcy, the applicable COBRA continuation period is a maximum of 36 months from the date of the qualifying event. [I.R.C. §4980B(f)(2)(B)(i)(IV); ERISA §602(2)(A)(iv)]

If the qualifying event is the employer's filing of a bankruptcy petition under Title 11 of the United States Code, the maximum applicable COBRA continuation period is as follows:

1. For covered employees who retired on or before the date of a substantial elimination of coverage, coverage continues until their date of death (in other words, retirees receive lifetime coverage)

2. For individuals who are widows or widowers of such retirees on the day before the petition is filed, coverage continues until their date of death (in other words, widows and widowers of retirees also receive lifetime COBRA coverage)

3. In the case of the spouse and dependent children of a retiree, coverage continues until 36 months after the retiree's date of death.

[I.R.C. §§4980B(f)(2)(B)(i)(III), 4980(g)(1)(D); ERISA §§602(2)(A)(iii), 607(3)(C)]

Q 6:119   Is the maximum COBRA continuation coverage period ever extended?

Yes. There are three situations in which a maximum 18-month coverage period will be extended.

First, an initial 18-month maximum continuation coverage period will be extended to 29 months if a qualified beneficiary is disabled as of the date of the qualifying event or within 60 days after such date (see Q 6:120). The disability extension applies to the disabled qualified beneficiary and to all other family members who are entitled to COBRA coverage because of the same qualifying event.

Second, an initial 18-month coverage period (or a 29-month disability coverage period) will be extended to a maximum of 36 months if a second qualifying event occurs within the 18-month continuation period. The extension applies to all qualifying beneficiaries who became qualified beneficiaries because of the first qualifying event and were still covered under the plan when the second qualifying event occurred. [I.R.C. §4980B(f)(2); ERISA §603; PHSA §2202(2); Treas. Reg. §54.4980B-7, Q&A-6 (Feb. 3, 1999)]

> **Example 1.** Jon terminates employment and elects COBRA continuation coverage for himself, his spouse, and his two children. Two months later, he dies. The original 18-month continuation period is automatically extended to 36 months for his survivors who are still enrolled on the date of the second qualifying event.

The COBRA regulations clarify an important interpretive point: The extension of the 18-month coverage period to 36 months applies only in the case of a second qualifying event (such as death or divorce) that would normally give rise to an initial 36-month coverage period. Thus, an individual's reduction in hours of work that is a qualifying event (because it results in an immediate or delayed full or partial loss of group health plan coverage) followed by his or her termination of employment will not expand the coverage period beyond 18 months. [Treas. Reg. §5.4980B-4, Q&A-1(e) and Preamble (Feb. 3, 1999)]

Third, if an employee becomes entitled to Medicare and subsequently, within 18 months, experiences a termination of employment or reduction of hours resulting in a loss of plan coverage, the employee's covered spouse and children who are qualified beneficiaries are entitled to COBRA coverage for the period ending 36 months after the date of the employee's Medicare entitlement.

> **Example 2.** Sara becomes entitled to Medicare coverage on January 1, 2010. On April 1, 2010, Sara terminates employment. She and her spouse and children lose medical coverage. Sara is entitled to 18 months of COBRA coverage, to October 1 of 2011; however, her covered spouse and children are entitled to 21 months of COBRA coverage. [I.R.C. §4980B(f)(2)(B); ERISA §602(2)(A); PHSA §2202(2)(A) as amended retroactively to plan years beginning after 1989 by §1704(g) of the Small Business Job Protection Act of 1996, Pub. L. No. 104-188; Treas. Reg. §54.4980B-7, Q&A-4(d)]

Q 6:120   When is a qualified beneficiary entitled to a disability extension?

The Social Security disability rule provides that any qualified beneficiary who is determined to have been disabled at any time during the first 60 days of continuation coverage because of a qualifying event that was either a termination of employment or a reduction in hours is entitled to a total of up to 29 months of COBRA continuation coverage rather than 18 months. The disability extension applies to the disabled beneficiary and to all other qualified beneficiaries who became entitled to COBRA coverage as a result of the same qualifying event. [Treas. Reg. §54.4980B-7, Q&A-1, Q&A-5]

To qualify for the disability extension the beneficiary must be determined to be disabled under Title II or XVI of the Social Security Act. [42 U.S.C. 401-433 or 1381–1385] The extension applies if a qualified beneficiary is determined to be disabled at any time during the first 60 days of COBRA continuation coverage. As a general rule, the 60-day period is measured from the date of the qualifying event. If coverage is lost at a later date, the 60-day period is measured from that date if the plan provides for an extension of the required periods (see Q 6:124). In the case of a child who is born to or placed for adoption with a covered employee during the period of COBRA continuation coverage, the 60-day period is measured from the date of birth or placement for adoption.

A qualified beneficiary is considered to be disabled within the first 60 days of COBRA coverage if he or she was determined to be disabled before the first day of COBRA coverage and continues to be disabled when COBRA coverage begins.

To qualify for the extension, an individual must notify the plan administrator of the determination of disability under the Social Security Act within 60 days after the determination and before the end of the first 18 months of COBRA continuation. The qualified beneficiary also must notify the plan administrator within 30 days of a final determination that the qualified beneficiary is no longer disabled, and the special extension of continuation coverage will terminate as of the month that begins more than 30 days after the date of such final determination. [I.R.C. §§4980B(f)(2)(B)(i)(IV), 4980B(f)(6)(C); ERISA §§602(2), 602(3); PHSA §§2202(2)(A), 2202(3) as amended effective January 1, 1997, by HIPPA, Pub. L. No. 104-191]

The Eighth Circuit ruled that a printing company properly refused to extend a former employee's health benefits beyond 18 months when an official determination that the former employee was disabled was not made within the 18-month period. [Marsh v. Omaha Printing Co., 218 F.3d 854 (8th Cir. 2000); BNA 137 DLR A-3 (2000)] When the employee quit his employment, he opted to continue his health care through COBRA. The former employee became disabled shortly before the expiration of his 18-month continuation of coverage, but he did not receive a determination from Social Security that he was disabled until after the 18-month period had expired. His employer denied his request for a disability extension. The court said that because the former employee's Social Security disability determination was not made until after the expiration of his initial 18-month period of coverage, he was not entitled to the 11-month extension.

On the other hand, the Fifth Circuit held that an employer plan was required to provide a disability extension to two qualified beneficiaries even though they did not receive a disability determination before the end of the initial 18-month COBRA coverage period. The plan document reflected the COBRA requirement that a disability determination must be obtained before the end of the 18-month period. However, the plan's SPD did not reflect that rule. The court concluded that if the SPD conflicts with the plan document, the SPD controls and any ambiguities must be resolved in favor of qualified beneficiaries. Therefore, the court held that the two qualified beneficiaries were entitled to disability extensions despite the delayed disability determinations. The Supreme Court refused to review the Fifth Circuit's decision. [Fallo v. Piccadilly Cafeterias, Inc., 141 F.3d 580 (5th Cir. 1998), *cert. denied,* 123 S. Ct. 487 (U.S. 2002)]

The plan may charge up to 150 percent of the applicable premium for coverage during the disability extension period (see Q 6:121).

Q 6:121   What if a qualified beneficiary qualifies for both a disability extension and an extension because of a second qualifying event?

The COBRA regulations address what happens if an individual qualifies for both an 18-month extension (to 36 months) under the multiple qualifying event rule and an 11-month extension (to 29 months) under the disability extension rule. The regulations resolve this interpretive issue as follows:

1. If the second qualifying event occurs during the first 18 months of COBRA continuation coverage, coverage must be extended to up to 36 months from the original qualifying event. The second qualifying event rule takes priority over the disability extension rule, so coverage cannot be terminated after 29 months. In addition, the qualified beneficiary cannot be charged more than 102 percent of the applicable premium for any portion of the 36-month period, even if the individual otherwise meets all of the requirements for the COBRA disability extension.

2. If the second qualifying event occurs during the disability extension (that is, during the 19th through the 29th months of COBRA coverage), coverage must be extended up to 36 months from the original qualifying event. However, the plan is permitted to charge the disabled individual 150 percent of the applicable premium for the remainder of the COBRA continuation period—that is, from the 19th month to the 36th month.

[Treas. Reg. §54.4980B-8, Q&A-1(b), (Feb. 3, 1999)]

Q 6:122   Can an employee ever have the 18-month period extended due to the multiple qualifying event rule?

The COBRA regulations provide that the multiple qualifying event rule does not apply to an individual's reduction in hours of employment that is a qualifying event followed by a termination of employment. The preamble to the COBRA regulations states that treating a reduction of hours of employment that is a qualifying event, followed by a termination of employment, as variations of a single qualifying event rather than as two distinct qualifying events is consistent with the overall design of the statute. [I.R.C. §4980B(f)(2)(B)(i)(II); Treas. Reg. §54.4980B-4, Q&A-1(e) (Feb. 3, 1999)]

Q 6:123   Are any special extensions of the maximum COBRA coverage period applicable to individuals whose qualifying event is a termination of employment or reduction in hours of employment?

Under the American Recovery and Reinvestment Act of 2009 (ARRA) [Pub. L. No. 111-5, 123 Stat. 115 (Feb. 17, 2009)], the maximum required COBRA continuation period is modified for certain individuals whose qualifying event is a termination of employment or a reduction in hours.

PBGC recipients. For a covered employee (1) whose qualifying event was termination of employment or a reduction in hours of employment, and (2) who, as of the date of that qualifying event, has a nonforfeitable right to a pension benefit, any portion of which is to be paid by the Pension Benefit Guaranty Corporation (PBGC), the period of COBRA continuation coverage must extend at least to (i) the date of death of the covered employee, or (ii) for the covered employee's surviving spouse or dependent children, 24 months after the covered employee's date of death. [I.R.C. § 4980B(f)(2)(B)(i)(V), as amended by ARRA § 1899F(b)(2)]

However, the extension of the maximum COBRA continuation coverage period does not require any period of coverage to extend beyond December 31, 2010. [I.R.C. § 4980B(f)(2)(B)(i)(V)]

TAA-eligible individuals. For a covered employee (1) whose qualifying event was a termination of employment or a reduction in hours of employment, and (2) who is a TAA-eligible individual as of the date that the COBRA continuation coverage period would otherwise terminate, the period of COBRA continuation coverage will not terminate before the later of (i) 18 months after the qualifying event or (ii) 36 months, when if another qualifying event occurs within 18 months of the first qualifying event, or (iii) the date on which the covered employee ceases to be a TAA-eligible individual. [I.R.C. § 4980B(f)(2)(B)(i)(VI)]

However, the extension of the maximum COBRA continuation coverage period described above does not require any period of coverage to extend beyond December 31, 2010. [I.R.C. § 4980B(f)(2)(B)(i)(VI)]

These extensions apply to coverage periods that would otherwise end on or after the date of enactment (February 17, 2009) through December 31, 2010. [ARRA § 1899F(d)]

TAA-eligible individuals are workers who have lost their jobs due to increased imports from, or a shift in production to, foreign countries, and are eligible for certain benefits under the Trade Act of 1974.

Q 6:124 From what date is the maximum COBRA continuation period counted?

The general rule is that the COBRA coverage period begins on the date of the qualifying event, regardless of whether the loss of coverage occurs then or later. Accordingly, any "tail" or extension of full health coverage (for example, for three months after termination of employment) would count toward the COBRA continuation period as long as the coverage is identical to that offered to the employee immediately prior to the qualifying event (see Qs 6:41–6:58, 6:63).

However, the COBRA continuation period can be counted beginning with the date coverage is actually lost, provided that:

1. The plan document expressly provides for counting the COBRA continuation period from the date of loss; and

2. The plan document expressly provides that the employer's period for notifying the plan administrator of certain qualifying events (the employee's death, termination, reduction of hours, or becoming eligible for Medicare, or the employer's commencement of a bankruptcy proceeding involving certain retirees) will begin with the date of the loss of coverage. (See Q 6:76 for a discussion of how long the employer has for notifying the plan administrator of these events.)

[I.R.C. §4980B(f)(8)] (See Qs 6:43 and 6:46 for a discussion of when and under what conditions coverage is considered to be lost for COBRA purposes.)

Q 6:125   Can a plan terminate the coverage of a qualified beneficiary for cause during the COBRA continuation period?

COBRA continuation coverage may be terminated if the qualified beneficiary fails to timely pay any required premium for coverage under the plan. However, coverage may be terminated only if payment is not timely under the rules specified in the IRS regulations, even if different payment rules apply to non-COBRA beneficiaries. [Treas. Reg. §54.4980B-7, Q&A-1 (b)]

In general, qualified beneficiaries have a 30-day grace period (45 days for the initial premium payment) in which to submit premium payments. [I.R.C. §4980B(f)(2)(B)(iii); ERISA §602(2)(C)] Premium payments made after the grace period will also be considered timely if:

- Under the terms of the group health plan, covered employees and qualified beneficiaries have until such later date to pay for their coverage; or
- Under the terms of an arrangement between the employer and an insurance company, HMO, or other organization providing plan benefits on the employer's behalf, the employer permits a longer grace period within which to pay for coverage of similarly situated employees. [Treas. Reg. §54.4980B-8, Q&A-5(a)(2) (Feb. 3, 1999)]

If the qualified beneficiary's premium is not paid by the expiration of the grace period, coverage terminates retroactively to the first day of the period for which timely premium payment has not been made. [Treas. Reg. §54.4980B-8, Q&A-1]

In other situations, a plan may terminate a qualified beneficiary's coverage for cause on the same basis that the plan terminates coverage for similarly situated non-COBRA beneficiaries. For example, if a group health plan terminates the coverage of active employees for the submission of a fraudulent claim, coverage of a qualified COBRA beneficiary may also be terminated for submission of a fraudulent claim.

Q 6:126   Is early termination of the COBRA continuation period ever permitted?

Yes. COBRA continuation coverage terminates on the earliest of the following six dates:

1. The date on which the employer ceases to provide any group health plan to any employee (including successor plans).

2. The date on which plan coverage ceases because any premium required under the plan with respect to the qualified beneficiary has not been paid (see Q 6:153).

3. The date on which qualified beneficiary first becomes, *after* the date he or she elects COBRA continuation, covered under any other group health plan, as an employee or otherwise. Prior case law had split on the issue of whether preexisting health care coverage also "becomes effective" after the date of the COBRA election, thus permitting termination of COBRA coverage. The U.S. Supreme Court has resolved the split, ruling that the statute is unambiguous and permits cutoff of COBRA coverage only because of group health plan coverage that is first obtained after the date of the COBRA election. [Geissal v. Moore Med. Corp., 524 U.S. 74 (1998)]

4. The date on which a qualified beneficiary first becomes, after the date he or she elects COBRA continuation, entitled to Medicare benefits (that is, he or she has actually enrolled in Medicare). The date on which the qualified beneficiary reaches age 65 is irrelevant; entitlement to benefits, not mere eligibility, is required. Medicare entitlement does not, however, terminate the COBRA continuation period for individuals who become qualified beneficiaries because their employer filed for Title 11 protection. HHS originally had taken the position that employers may not cut off the COBRA coverage of employees who become entitled to Medicare because of end-stage renal disease (ESRD). This position was rejected by the Court of Appeals for the Fifth Circuit, which held that the Social Security law's ESRD provisions mandated the order of payment by requiring that employer-provided group health plans be the primary payer and Medicare the secondary payer for the first 18 months (now 30 months) of an individual's Medicare entitlement solely because of ESRD and that the Social Security law does not apply to a health plan's decision to terminate coverage. [Blue Cross & Blue Shield of Tex. Inc. v. Shalala, 995 F.2d 70 (5th Cir. 1993)] HHS has since conceded that the Medicare secondary-payer law merely affects the coordination of payments from the employer's group health plan and from Medicare and has issued a final regulation under the Social Security Act's Medicare secondary-payer provisions confirming that individuals who become entitled to Medicare because of ESRD can have their COBRA continuation coverage cut off. [42 C.F.R. § 411.162(a)(3)]

5. In case of an extension of the 18-month period because of Social Security disability, the date on which a qualified beneficiary loses Social Security disability status (see Q 6:120).

6. The last day of the maximum coverage period. [Treas. Reg. § 54.4980B-7, Q&A-1(a)]

[I.R.C. § 4980B(f)(2)(B); ERISA § 602(2); 29 U.S.C. § 1162(2); PHSA § 2202(2); Treas. Reg. § 54.4980B-7, Q&A-1(a)(3)]

In addition, a plan may terminate a qualified beneficiary's coverage for cause (see Q 6:125).

> **Practice Pointer.** If the employer intends to use any of these early cutoff provisions, they must be written into the particular group health plan. If the employer puts a full COBRA notice in the SPD, including notice that COBRA continuation coverage will terminate earlier if any of the above-listed events occurs, that will not be enough unless the SPD also functions as the ERISA plan document with respect to benefits. If it does not, the prudent employer will add these cutoff rights to the plan document for the group health plan as well. [Youngstown Aluminum Prods. Inc. v. Mid-West Benefits Servs. Inc., 91 F.3d 22 (6th Cir. 1996) (employer prohibited from terminating COBRA coverage early because of Medicare entitlement where the plan failed to specify that Medicare entitlement was an event resulting in the termination of COBRA coverage)]

DOL regulations require notice to qualified beneficiaries when COBRA coverage is terminated before the end of the maximum COBRA coverage period.

Nonpayment of premiums. At least one court has held that the plan administrator is not legally bound to advise a qualified beneficiary that he or she is late in paying a COBRA premium. [Fleury v. Bloom FCA! Inc., 1995 U.S. Dist. LEXIS 11738 (S.D.N.Y. Aug. 15, 1995)] If the plan administrator gratuitously communicates with the participant regarding the extension of premium due dates, the administrator must do so in a manner calculated to avoid confusion and misunderstanding. [Switzer v. Wal-Mart Stores Inc., 52 F.3d 1294 (5th Cir. 1995)]

CHAMPUS coverage. Coverage under the federal government's CHAMPUS program for individuals in military service does not constitute "coverage under any other group health plan" for purposes of this cutoff rule. [McGee v. Funderberg, 17 F.3d 112 (8th Cir. 1994); Notice 90-58, 1990-2 C.B. 345]

Terminated plan. In one case, a terminated employee was notified by his employer that he had a right to COBRA coverage. The employee elected COBRA coverage and made three months of premium payments to the employer on the assumption that he was securing COBRA benefits. However, the employee was then informed by the employer's insurance carrier that he was not eligible for coverage because the employer had allowed its health plan to lapse prior to his termination of employment. At the time of the employee's termination, the employer was unaware that its coverage had lapsed for failure to pay premiums; the employer did not learn of the lapse of coverage until shortly before the employee was informed by the insurer. The employer subsequently obtained new health insurance through another carrier and retroactively paid all health claims incurred by current employees during the interim period.

The terminated employee argued that he was entitled to COBRA coverage despite the lapse of the employer's health plan. Alternatively, he argued that the employer had self-insured its employees during the period between insured plans and was required to provide the employee with COBRA coverage under that plan.

Although it expressed sympathy with the employee, the court held that he was not entitled to COBRA coverage under either an insured or a self-insured plan. The evidence clearly established that the employer did not have an insured plan in place on the date of the employee's termination because its insurance had lapsed. Moreover, the employer could not have established a self-insured plan as of that date because it was not yet aware of the lapse of the insurance plan. [Glandorf v. W.G. Prod. Co., 2002 U.S. App. LEXIS 3724 (3d Cir. Mar. 8, 2002)]

Failure to re-enroll. A U.S. district court held that a COBRA beneficiary's coverage could be cut off because the beneficiary failed to re-enroll during the plan's opt-in enrollment period. [White v. Kroger Co., 2007 U.S. Dist. LEXIS 81470 (D. Utah 2007)] The employer's group health plan required all participants, including active participants as well as COBRA beneficiaries, to re-enroll in the plan each year during a two-week open enrollment period. The employer sent enrollment materials to COBRA beneficiaries along with a notice of the open enrollment dates. The materials warned that coverage would terminate if a beneficiary did not enroll during open enrollment. Nonetheless, the COBRA beneficiary in the case did not re-enroll. The employer sent a second notice to the beneficiary, indicating that no coverage had been elected and advising the beneficiary that she had until the end of a correction period to change her coverage choice. The beneficiary still did not re-enroll, and her coverage was terminated. When the COBRA beneficiary was later injured in a fall, she filed a lawsuit claiming that the plan had violated the COBRA rules by terminating her COBRA coverage before the end of her 18-month COBRA coverage period. The district court ruled, however, that the plan's actions did not violate COBRA rules. The court noted that COBRA regulations permit termination of COBRA coverage on the same grounds that coverage would terminate for active participants. Thus, since the plan provided for termination of coverage for active participants who failed to re-enroll, it was acceptable to terminate coverage for a COBRA beneficiary who did not re-enroll.

Q 6:127 Exactly when can coverage under another group health plan cut off COBRA continuation coverage?

Prior to the United States Supreme Court's decision in *Geissal v. Moore Medical Corp.* [524 U.S. 74 (1998)], the cases expressed contradictory views as to the circumstances in which other group health plan coverage could be used as the reason to cut off COBRA coverage.

The majority of the cases prior to the Supreme Court's decision held that the existence of other coverage was sufficient to terminate the qualified beneficiary's right to COBRA continuation coverage if the qualified beneficiary would not suffer a "significant gap" in coverage upon termination of COBRA coverage. In addition, some courts held that coverage that existed prior to the COBRA could justify a cutoff, while others concluded that only coverage taking effect during the COBRA period could be taken into account.

This split among the circuits was resolved by the Supreme Court's decision in *Geissal*, which rejected the "significant gap" theory and stated that the statute was clear on its face that only group health plan coverage obtained after the date of the COBRA election can be used as a cutoff event. In anticipation of the Supreme Court's decision, the IRS issued Notice 98-22 (1998-17 I.R.B. 5), reversing its position on this issue effective as of the date of the Court's decision but waiving excise tax liability for employers who relied on the IRS's prior position, as expressed in its regulations, prior to that date.

Current IRS regulations provide that a plan may cut off a qualified beneficiary's COBRA coverage only if a beneficiary first becomes covered by another group health plan (including a group health plan of a governmental employer or employee organization) after the date on which COBRA continuation coverage is elected. [Treas. Reg. §54.4980B-7, Q&A-2] To justify a cutoff, the other coverage must meet the following conditions:

1. The qualified beneficiary is actually covered, rather than merely eligible to be covered, under the other group health plan.

2. The other group health plan is not maintained by the employer or employee organization that maintains the plan under which COBRA coverage must be provided.

3. The other group health plan does not contain any exclusion or limitation with respect to any preexisting condition of the qualified beneficiary (other than an exclusion or limitation that does not apply to or is satisfied by the qualified beneficiary under the HIPAA requirements relating to preexisting-condition exclusions).

The regulations make it clear that if those conditions are satisfied, COBRA coverage may be cut off even if the other health coverage is less valuable to the qualified beneficiary.

Example 1. Charles is covered under a plan maintained by his employer, Alpha Company. He is also covered under a plan maintained by his spouse's employer. Charles terminates employment with Alpha and elects COBRA coverage under Alpha's plan. Alpha cannot terminate Charles's COBRA coverage on the basis of his coverage under his spouse's plan.

Example 2. Donald is covered by a plan maintained by his employer, Beta Corp. Donald terminates his employment with Beta and elects COBRA coverage under Beta's plan. Donald subsequently takes a job with Gamma Corp. and becomes covered under Gamma's plan. Gamma's plan does not contain any preexisting-condition exclusion or limitation that applies to Donald. Beta Corp. can terminate Donald's COBRA coverage on the date Donald becomes covered under Gamma's plan.

Example 3. The facts are the same as those in Example 2, except that Donald takes the job with Gamma and becomes covered under Gamma's plan before he elects COBRA coverage under Beta's plan. Because Donald became covered by Gamma's plan before he elected COBRA coverage under Beta's plan, Beta must offer COBRA coverage to Donald and cannot terminate that coverage because of Donald's coverage under Gamma's plan.

Q 6:128   Can COBRA coverage for existing qualified beneficiaries be cut off if the employer's workforce drops below 20 employees?

No. The small-employer exception for employers with fewer than 20 employees applies prospectively only. Therefore, an employer remains subject to the COBRA requirements in the year its workforce drops below the 20-employee mark. The exemption will apply only in the following year. Therefore, any individual who has a qualifying event in the calendar year of the workforce reduction (plus any COBRA continuees from prior calendar years) cannot have COBRA continuation coverage rights cut off. If the employer qualifies as an exempt small employer in the following calendar year, no additional individuals become qualified beneficiaries entitled to COBRA continuation rights. Again, however, coverage for preexisting COBRA beneficiaries must be continued (see Q 6:23). [I.R.C. §4980B(d)(1), as amended by COBRA '89 §11702(f)]

Q 6:129   After the COBRA continuation period ends, must the qualified beneficiary be given a chance to enroll in an individual conversion health plan?

If the plan does not contain a conversion privilege, continuees have no right to convert. However, continuees must be allowed to exercise any conversion privilege existing under the plan when their continuation coverage ends at the expiration of the maximum continuation period. [Treas. Reg. §54.4980B-7, Q&A-8 (Feb. 3, 1999)]

However, one court has held that COBRA does not obligate employers to send a specific individual notice to employees of their right to convert to individual coverage (although it would be prudent to disclose it in the SPD). The statute requires that the "option" of conversion be provided, not "notice" of the option to convert. [O'Brien v. Rivkin, Radler & Kremer, 1996 U.S. Dist. LEXIS 1047 (N.D. Ill. Feb. 2, 1996)]

In another case, a qualified beneficiary whose COBRA coverage was due to terminate called the insurer to inquire about alternative coverage. The insurer told him that if he continued paying the premiums, he would automatically become covered by an individual conversion policy when COBRA expired. The insurer continued to accept premiums. However, when the qualified beneficiary made a claim for reimbursement of significant medical expenses, the insurer said that the COBRA plan did not provide a conversion right for the qualified beneficiary.

The court said that the insurer's representations and acceptance of premiums should bind the insurer. It concluded that the insurer could be equitably estopped from denying the coverage because the COBRA plan's description of the conversion coverage option was ambiguous, and this allowed the qualified beneficiary to rely on the insurer's interpretation of the provision. [Wright v. Anthem Life Ins. Co., 2000 U.S. Dist. LEXIS 8899 (N.D. Miss. June 14, 2000)]

In another case, a group health plan provided an option to enroll in a conversion policy upon expiration of COBRA coverage. One month before the qualified beneficiary's COBRA coverage was to expire, the beneficiary and the plan administrator asked the insurer about post-COBRA health insurance coverage. The insurer provided the telephone number of a representative, who described individual policies to the beneficiary but did not offer a conversion policy. The beneficiary bought a policy that excluded preexisting conditions instead of the conversion policy that did not. The beneficiary was diagnosed with cancer and the insurer denied coverage, claiming a preexisting condition. The beneficiary sued the insurer, claiming breach of contract and bad faith.

The appeals court ruled that the insurer had made an honest mistake when the beneficiary was not told about the conversion policy option. However, the court ruled in favor of the beneficiary on the breach of contract claim because the beneficiary's doctor testified that he had not been diagnosed or treated for cancer before the effective date of the individual policy. [Wiedmeyer v. Blue Cross & Blue Shield United of Wis., 2000 Wis. App. LEXIS 509 (Wis. Ct. App. May 31, 2000)]

Q 6:130　　How much time must a qualified beneficiary be given to elect the conversion plan?

The qualified beneficiary must be given the option to exercise the conversion privilege during the 180-day period that ends on the date that the COBRA continuation period expires. [I.R.C. §4980B(f)(2)(E); ERISA §602(5); PHSA §2202; Treas. Reg. §54.4980B-7, Q&A-8 (Feb. 3, 1999)]

Premiums

Q 6:131　　Who pays for COBRA continuation coverage?

The employer may, if it wishes, pay all or part of the cost of COBRA continuation coverage. However, the employer is not required to pay for the coverage; a group health plan can charge a qualified beneficiary up to the full amount of the "applicable premium" (see Q 6:133).

Q 6:132　　When can a state pay COBRA premiums on behalf of a qualified beneficiary?

A state Medicaid program may pay the COBRA premiums for individuals whose income does not exceed the federal poverty level and whose resources do not exceed twice the maximum amount that an individual may have and obtain Supplemental Security Income (SSI) benefits in that state, if the state determines that the savings in expenditures under Medicaid resulting from such enrollment is likely to exceed the amount of COBRA premiums. This rule applies only if the COBRA continuation coverage is under a group health plan provided by an employer with 75 or more employees. [Social Security Act §§1902(a)(10)(F), 1902(u); 42 U.S.C. §1396a, added by OBRA '90 §4713]

Furthermore, if the state determines that enrollment in a group health plan would be more cost-effective than Medicaid coverage, it can compel enrollment in a group health plan provided that it pays any applicable COBRA premiums and all deductibles, coinsurance, and other cost sharing for services otherwise covered by Medicaid. [Social Security Act §1906; 42 U.S.C. §1396b, added by OBRA '90 §4713]

Q 6:133   How is the applicable premium that the qualified beneficiary can be required to pay calculated?

The applicable premium generally equals 100 percent of the cost of the coverage provided to similarly situated beneficiaries who have not experienced a qualifying event, plus an additional 2 percent for administrative expenses. For this calculation, it is irrelevant whether the employer, the employee, or both pay the premiums for the group health coverage of active employees who have not suffered a qualifying event. [I.R.C. §§4980B(f)(2)(C), 4980B(f)(4)(A); ERISA §§601, 602(3); PHSA §§2202(3), 2204; Treas. Reg. §54.4980B-8, Q&A-1(a)]

If coverage is extended because of Social Security disability (see Q 6:120), the employer may charge an applicable premium for the 19th month through the 29th month of up to 150 percent of the cost of coverage provided to similarly situated employees who have not experienced a qualifying event. However, if the individual first qualifies for a full 18-month extension under the second qualifying event rule, the 150 percent amount cannot be charged at any time during the entire 36-month COBRA continuation period. If the individual first qualified for the disability extension and then experienced a second qualifying event at any time during the 11-month extension period, he or she is entitled to an additional 7 months of coverage (for a total of 36 months). However, the plan can charge 150 percent during the entire 18-month extension (11 months plus 7 more months). [I.R.C. §4980B(f)(2)(C); Treas. Reg. §54.4980B-8, Q&A-1(b)]

Q 6:134   Which individuals are similarly situated for purposes of determining the applicable premium?

The legislative history of COBRA defines "similarly situated" individuals as those defined in the plan who have not suffered a qualifying event. Their medical conditions need not be similar to those of the qualified beneficiaries. Group health plans are not permitted to use a definition of *similarly situated* that violates the Equal Pay Act of 1963, Title VII of the Civil Rights Act of 1964, or other similar laws prohibiting discrimination in employment. (See chapter 19 for a discussion of these laws.) Nor may categories be created that would inappropriately increase the cost of COBRA continuation coverage to non-highly compensated employees.

It may not be acceptable to divide similarly situated individuals by region or by other subgroups of the entire pool of group health plan participants. In *Draper v. Baker Hughes, Inc.* [892 F. Supp. 1287, 1295 (E.D. Cal. 1995)], the employer billed each of its subsidiaries based upon the cost and claims experience of that particular subsidiary rather than based upon the claims experience of the entire company. Consequently, qualified beneficiaries from different divisions paid differing rates for identical COBRA coverage. In the plaintiff's case, the COBRA cost was more than three times the "blended rate" that the company paid to the insurance company based upon the entire company's claims experience. The court applied a three-prong analysis, as follows:

1. What is the plan?
2. What is the cost to the plan?
3. Who are the similarly situated beneficiaries?

The court found that the employer had a single, nationwide plan because benefits were provided to all employees under a single insurance contract. As a result, the court concluded that the cost to the plan is the applicable premium and that this amount is to be determined with reference to the average cost of insuring all of the plan's participants. The court found no statutory language to support the employer's contention that it could pass on the cost of insuring a subset of beneficiaries rather than the proportionate share of the net cost of insuring all beneficiaries under the plan.

Q 6:135   How is the cost of an insured plan calculated for applicable premium purposes?

Promised regulations on cost determinations under COBRA have not been issued, so it is unclear whether an employer that has traditionally taken administrative expenses into account when setting the premiums for active employee plans can continue to do so, given the 2 percent administrative surcharge permitted under COBRA.

Q 6:136   How is the cost of a self-insured plan calculated?

The statute provides two alternative methods for calculating the cost of a self-insured plan. Under the first, a self-insured plan's cost of providing continuation coverage for any period is equal to a reasonable estimate of the cost of providing coverage for the same period for similarly situated beneficiaries. The reasonable estimate must be actuarially determined, taking into account any factors prescribed by regulations. Apparently, healthcare cost inflation can be taken into account.

The second alternative permits the employer to define the cost as the applicable premium for similarly situated beneficiaries for the previous determination period, adjusted for cost-of-living changes by using the gross national product implicit price deflator for the 12-month period ending on the last day of the sixth month of that prior determination period. However, this method cannot be used for a self-insured plan if there is any significant difference in either the coverage under the plan or the employees covered under the plan since the prior determination period. [I.R.C. §4980B(f); ERISA §604(2); PHSA §2204(2)]

Presumably, when the COBRA cost regulations are issued, they will include guidelines for identifying a "significant difference."

Q 6:137   What is the time period used to calculate COBRA premiums?

COBRA premiums are calculated in advance for a fixed period of time, called the *determination period.* For any applicable premium, the determination period is 12 consecutive months. [I.R.C. §4980B(f); ERISA §604(2); PHSA §2204(3)]

The determination period is a single period for any benefit package. Thus, each qualified beneficiary does not have separate determination periods based on the date that his or her COBRA coverage began.

Q 6:138   When can a group health plan change the COBRA premium rate during a premium period?

A plan can increase the amount it requires a beneficiary to pay for COBRA coverage during a premium determination period only in three cases:

1. The plan has previously charged less than the maximum permitted premium and the increased amount does not exceed the maximum permitted premium (i.e., 102 percent of the cost of providing coverage to similarly situated non-COBRA beneficiaries for regular COBRA coverage or 150 percent during a disability extension).

2. The increase occurs during a disability extension period and the increased amount does not exceed the maximum permitted premium (i.e., 150 percent of the cost of providing coverage to similarly situated non-COBRA beneficiaries).

3. A qualified beneficiary changes the coverage being received.

[Treas. Reg. §54.4980-8, Q&A-2(b)]

Q 6:139   Can the employee direct the employer to credit his or her premium payment to a particular month or months?

No. The participant cannot direct an employer to apply a premium payment to a specified period. In *Kytle v. Stewart Title Co.* [788 F. Supp. 321 (S.D. Tex. 1992)], the employee lost coverage as of September 1. However, she noted on her first premium check that she intended the payment to cover the months of October and November because she erroneously thought that her COBRA coverage started in October. The court refused to honor the notation on her premium check, holding that notations on checks do not override the COBRA statute, which provides that continuation coverage starts immediately after group health plan coverage would otherwise end.

The Court of Appeals for the Fifth Circuit similarly refused to effectuate the intention of the participant in *Switzer v. Wal-Mart Stores, Inc.* [52 F.3d 1294 (5th Cir. 1995)] In the *Switzer* case, the employee, who had a heart condition, was rehired by his former employer, Wal-Mart. The Wal-Mart group health plan contained a preexisting-condition limitation that excluded such conditions until the participant had been continuously covered under the plan for 12 consecutive months. The participant recognized that he might suffer a lapse in coverage due to this preexisting-condition limit and that he needed to keep his COBRA continuation coverage in effect until the 12-month period elapsed. However, Switzer erroneously assumed that his final COBRA payment could be a partial payment that would cover only a part of the month. Wal-Mart sent him a letter stating he would need to make an additional COBRA premium payment to keep his COBRA coverage from expiring prior to the date he wished. The Court of Appeals held that the employer had no obligation under COBRA to inform the participant that his COBRA continuation coverage was about to be canceled for lack of premium payment. The Fifth Circuit acknowledged that an employer like Wal-Mart could not possibly give personalized attention to each employee and could not have known without an inquiry from the participant that he did not want his COBRA coverage to expire before a certain date. The court found that the communications that Wal-Mart did make to him were clear and unambiguous and held that its refusal to reinstate his COBRA continuation coverage was not arbitrary and capricious.

IRS regulations specifically provide that a qualified beneficiary cannot choose to have the first payment for COBRA coverage applied prospectively only. A plan is permitted to apply the first payment for COBRA coverage to the period beginning immediately after the date on which coverage under the plan would have been lost on account of the qualifying event. However, if the plan permits the beneficiary to waive coverage for any period before electing COBRA coverage, the first payment cannot be applied to the period of the waiver. [Treas. Reg. §54.4980B-8, Q&A-4]

Q 6:140   What is the premium determination period for an employer with several group health plans?

The 12-month period chosen as the determination period need not coincide with the plan year or other significant date for any of the employer's group health plans. Therefore, several plans with different plan years or policy anniversary dates can use a single, uniform determination period. [Treas. Reg. §54.4980B-8, Q&A-2(a) (Feb. 3, 1999)]

Q 6:141   Does each qualified beneficiary have a separate determination period?

No. A group health plan may choose a single, uniform determination period for calculating the premium for all COBRA beneficiaries, provided that the plan uses this period consistently from year to year. Each qualified beneficiary is not entitled to have a personal determination date based on the date his or her

COBRA continuation coverage begins. [Treas. Reg. §54.4980B-8, Q&A-2(a) (Feb. 3, 1999)]

Q 6:142   Can the employer charge all COBRA qualified beneficiaries a single, blended rate when active employees are charged either a single or a family rate?

No. [Rev. Rul. 96-8, 1996-4 I.R.B. 62 (Jan. 22, 1996)]

Q 6:143   Can the employer charge an individual premium rate to each family member who enrolls?

Not necessarily. A family rate should be charged if:

1. The employee, spouse, and child(ren) elect COBRA;
2. The employee and child(ren) elect COBRA; or
3. The spouse and child(ren) elect COBRA.

Thus, if the employee had six children and the entire family elected COBRA coverage, the employee would pay a family premium rather than eight premiums for individual coverage.

However, if the employee has family coverage and only the spouse elects COBRA or only one child elects COBRA, it would be appropriate to charge the single rate to the COBRA continuee. [Rev. Rul. 96-8, 1996-4 I.R.B. 62 (Jan. 22, 1996)]

Q 6:144   Can a plan increase the premium charged to a COBRA continuee who adds new dependents?

Yes. A premium increase is permitted if the increased family size causes a change in the coverage classification under the terms of the plan. The plan can charge the applicable premium for the new coverage classification.

Example. George, who is single, terminates employment and elects COBRA continuation coverage. His premium for individual enrollment is $45 a month. A few months later, George marries and enrolls his wife, Linda, during the plan's election of coverage period for newly eligible dependents. For the relevant determination period, the plan's premium is $70 per month for an individual plus one dependent. The plan can charge George the higher premium immediately.

[Treas. Reg. §54.4980B-8, Q&A-2(b)(3) (Feb. 3, 1999)]

Q 6:145   Can a COBRA continuee who chooses a different plan during an open enrollment period be charged the premium for the new coverage?

Yes. The plan can charge the qualified beneficiary the applicable premium for the newly selected coverage option, even if the qualified beneficiary must pay more than under the prior COBRA continuation coverage. On the other hand, if the beneficiary changes to a benefit package or coverage unit(e.g., a change from family to individual coverage) with a lower applicable premium, the plan cannot charge more than the applicable premium for the new coverage. [Treas. Reg. §54.4980B-8, Q&A-2(c) (Feb. 3, 1999)]

Q 6:146   Must COBRA continuees pay the same increases in the premium charged by a group health plan to similarly situated individuals who have not undergone a qualifying event?

The statute and regulations mandate predetermined, fixed COBRA rates for each 12-month determination period. Once an employer sets a determination date for a group health plan that becomes the only date on which rates for COBRA continuation coverage can change. [Treas. Reg. §54.4980B-8, Q&A-2(a) (Feb. 3, 1999)]

It is not clear from the regulations whether an exception to this rule is made when a plan amendment increasing or decreasing coverage leads to a premium increase or decrease for active-employee coverage. It is also unclear whether an employer that adds significant new health benefits to a group health plan in the middle of a determination period and consequently raises the rates for active employees may also raise rates for qualified beneficiaries.

Practice Pointer. In practice, a conservative approach would be to "batch" all benefit increases and make them effective on the annual determination date, so that their cost can be factored into the COBRA continuees' premium for the ensuing 12-month period.

Q 6:147   When determining COBRA cost, must an employer take into account experience refunds and policy dividends received from an insurance company?

The COBRA regulations do not deal with the proper handling of experience refunds and policy dividends paid by an insurance company as a result of favorable (i.e., lower than expected) claims experience for the policy year. Until regulations are issued, employers presumably will be held to a good-faith standard provided that their interpretation of the statute is reasonable and not applied in a discriminatory manner.

Q 6:148   When is the first payment for COBRA continuation coverage due?

The group health plan may not require payment of any premium due for the period beginning with the date coverage would otherwise be lost until 45 days after the individual makes his or her COBRA election. [I.R.C. §4980B(f)(2); ERISA §602(3); PHSA §2202(3); Treas. Reg. §54.4980B-8, Q&A-5(b)]

There is a 60-day election period, so the group health plan may have to wait up to 105 days (60 plus 45) before it gets the premium for such period (see Q 6:92). If the loss of coverage is not simultaneous with the qualifying event, this waiting period could be even longer. Additionally, because the election period must last 60 days after the later of the date coverage is lost or the plan administrator sends notification to the beneficiary that the qualifying event has occurred, a late notice automatically extends the permitted period for paying the batch of premiums. In such a case, the first payment will be for three or four months of coverage. [I.R.C. §4980B(f); ERISA §602(3); PHSA §2202(3); Treas. Reg. §54.4980B-8, Q&A-5 (a)(b)(c) (Feb. 3, 1999)]

Q 6:149   Can the employer take any steps to speed up the payment of the initial premium?

No. The employer is not allowed to withhold money or other benefits owed to a qualified beneficiary until the beneficiary pays for COBRA continuation coverage. For example, the employer cannot withhold a final paycheck or payment for medical claims incurred prior to an employee's termination of coverage as a means of speeding up the employee's payment of the initial COBRA premium. Nor can the plan withhold COBRA coverage once it is elected but before the initial premium is paid (see Q 6:102). However, the plan can delay payment of claims incurred during the election period and the initial 45-day grace period until the qualified beneficiary makes a timely election to get COBRA continuation coverage and actually pays the initial premium during the 45-day grace period. Special rules are provided for HMOs and other direct service providers. [Treas. Reg. §54.4980B-6, Q&A-5 (Feb. 3, 1999)]

Q 6:150   How must the first payment be credited?

The COBRA continuee's first payment must be applied toward continuation coverage retroactive to the date that coverage would have been lost because of a qualifying event. [Communications Workers of Am. v. NYNEX Corp., 898 F.2d 887 (2d Cir. 1990)]

However, if the qualified beneficiary first waived coverage, then revoked the waiver and made a timely election of COBRA continuation coverage, the first premium payment is not used to pay for the period covered by the waiver. [Treas. Reg. §54.4980B-8, Q&A-4 (Feb. 3, 1999)]

Q 6:151　After the initial payment, can the qualified beneficiaries be required to pay premiums quarterly or semiannually?

No. They must be given the option of paying premiums for COBRA continuation coverage in monthly installments. Other payment options can also be made available. [I.R.C. §4980B(f); ERISA §604(2)(C); PHSA §2202(3); Treas. Reg. §54.4980B-8, Q&A-3]

Q 6:152　When are premium payments deemed made?

The COBRA regulations make it clear that payment is considered made on the date on which it is sent to the plan. [Treas. Reg. §54.4980B-8, Q&A-5(e)] Thus, it is recommended that plans use the postmark date for determining whether a premium payment has been timely made.

Practice Pointer. If a plan administrator intends to require strict adherence to the time periods for premium payments, it would be advisable to specify in the SPD, in the COBRA notice, and, if applicable, on the premium coupons the manner in which premium payments will be considered made on a timely basis.

Prior to the final 1999 COBRA regulations, at least one court held that the issue of whether payment was made is to be determined by the intent of the parties. In a case in which the documents were not clear as to when payment was deemed made, the court looked to general contract principles to find that payment was made when mailed because a course of conduct had grown between the parties. [Barry v. Videojet Sys. Int'l, 1995 U.S. Dist. LEXIS 13421 (N.D. Ill. Sept 13, 1995)]

Although the final COBRA regulations (issued after *Videojet*) clarify that a premium payment is considered made when sent to the plan, *Videojet* may nevertheless remain instructive, inasmuch as the court appears to accept the underlying principle that the manner of payment and what constitutes timely payment are determined by the intent of the parties. Employers and plan administrators should be particularly careful when drafting plan documents and COBRA notices to clearly and unambiguously set forth the manner in which COBRA payments may be made and the definition of timely payment. In this way, an employer should be able to ensure that qualified beneficiaries understand and are subject to certain rules with respect to whether payments are timely made and thereby to avoid having a court divine the intent of the parties.

Q 6:153　What is the grace period, if any, for making premium payments?

A special grace period is required for the first payment (see Q 6:148). For other payments, the qualified beneficiary must be allowed a grace period of 30 days after the first day of each period of COBRA continuation coverage. COBRA beneficiaries are entitled to a longer period for payment if the plan specifies a later due date for payments by covered employees or qualified beneficiaries. COBRA beneficiaries are also entitled to a longer payment period if the contract between the employer and an insurer, HMO, or other entity that provides the coverage allows the employer a longer period to pay for coverage for similarly situated non-COBRA beneficiaries. For example, an employer that contracts with its health insurer for a 90-day grace period to forward overdue premiums must provide at least a 90-day grace period to qualified beneficiaries. [I.R.C. §4980B(f); ERISA §604(2)(C); PHSA §2202(2); Treas. Reg. §54.4980B-8, Q&A-5(b) (Feb. 3, 1999)]

Assuming that the COBRA notice given to the employee satisfies the statutory requirements, the employer has no further duty to remind the employee to pay overdue premiums in order to avoid the loss of COBRA continuation coverage. [Herrmann v. CenCom Cable Assoc. Inc., 15 Employee Benefits Cas. (BNA) 2810 (7th Cir. 1992)]

Q 6:154   What if the initial COBRA premium is not paid on time?

If the initial premium for COBRA coverage is not received by the beginning of the COBRA period, the plan has a choice. IRS regulations permit a plan to cancel coverage and reinstate it retroactively if payment is made by the end of the grace period. Alternatively, the plan may extend coverage during the grace period and cancel it retroactively if payment is not received by the end of the period. [Treas. Reg. §54.4980B-8, Q&A-5(c)].

In one case, the Tenth Circuit Court of Appeals upheld a health plan's retroactive termination of COBRA coverage when an employee failed to pay required COBRA premiums. The employee timely elected COBRA coverage but did not pay the initial COBRA premium by the end of the grace period. In the interim, she incurred approximately $8,000 of medical expenses. However, the plan denied her claim for payment of those expenses on the grounds that she was not covered by the plan at the time the expenses were incurred. The Tenth Circuit concluded that COBRA coverage retroactively terminates as of the date of the qualifying event if payment is not made during the grace period. Therefore, the plan had properly denied the employee's claim for benefits. [Goletto v. W.H. Braum, Inc., 2001 U.S. App. LEXIS 13676 (10th Cir. Feb. 1, 2001)]

Q 6:155   Can the employer cancel coverage during the grace period and then reinstate it if the qualified beneficiary pays the overdue premium?

The IRS regulations permit a plan to cancel COBRA coverage if payment is not received by the first day of a COBRA period and then reinstate coverage retroactively if payment is made by the end of the grace period. Alternatively, the plan may extend coverage during the grace period and cancel it retroactively if payment is not received. [Treas. Reg. §54.4980B-8, Q&A-5(c) (Feb. 3, 1999)]

Q 6:156　What happens if a COBRA payment is not made in full?

If the amount of the payment is not significantly less than the required amount, the payment will be treated as made in full unless the plan notifies the qualified beneficiary of the amount of the shortfall and grants a reasonable time for payment of the remaining amount.

A shortfall of no more than $50 (or 10 percent of the required payment, if less) will not be considered significant. As a safe-harbor rule, a period of 30 days after notice of the shortfall is provided will be considered a reasonable period for payment. [Treas. Reg. §54.4980B-8, Q&A-5(d)]

Q 6:157　How are COBRA premiums treated for income tax purposes?

An individual taxpayer may claim an itemized deduction for health insurance premiums, including COBRA premiums, and other out-of-pocket medical expenses. However, medical expenses are deductible only to the extent they exceed 7.5 percent of the taxpayer's adjusted gross income. [I.R.C. §213] Therefore, many taxpayers do not actually get a deduction. In addition, a taxpayer who claims the standard deduction and does not itemize deductions, cannot claim a medical expense deduction.

However, a self-employed taxpayer can claim an above-the-line deduction for health insurance costs. [I.R.C. §162(l)]

In addition, under rules included in the Trade Act of 2002 [Pub. L. No. 107-210, 116 Stat. 933 (2002)] and amended by ARRA [Pub. L. No. 111-5, 123 Stat. 115 (Feb. 17, 2009)], a limited group of COBRA beneficiaries may claim a refundable health coverage tax credit (HCTC) for a portion of their COBRA premiums. The HCTC is generally 65 percent of the amount paid for qualified health insurance for an eligible individual and for qualifying family members. However, the credit is temporarily increased to 80 percent for periods of coverage from May 1, 2009 to December 31, 2010.

The HCTC may be claimed by an individual who is certified as eligible for trade adjustment assistance under the Trade Act of 1974 as a result of losing his or her job because of import competition or shifts of production to other countries. The credit may also be claimed by an individual who is at least age 55 and is receiving pension benefits paid by the Pension Benefit Guaranty Corporation (PBGC).

The credit may be claimed for premiums paid for COBRA coverage for the eligible individual and his or her spouse and dependents. [I.R.C. §35]

The credit may also be claimed for premiums paid for other "qualified health insurance," including coverage provided by any employer or former employer of the individual or the individual's spouse. However, the credit may not be claimed if the employer pays at least 50 percent of the cost of coverage. For this purpose, coverage elected under a cafeteria plan is treated as paid by the employer. Therefore, if an employer picks up the tab for a former employee's COBRA coverage, the credit may not be claimed by the employee. Amounts distributed from a medical savings account (MSA) or health savings account (HSA) are not eligible for the credit. Amounts taken into account for purposes of the credit are not included in determining the regular medical expense deduction or the deduction for self-employed health insurance costs. [I.R.C. §35(g)]

Assistance eligible individuals (AEIs) receiving the COBRA premium subsidy (see Qs 6:186–6:193) are not eligible individuals for purposes of the IRS's HCTC. [I.R.C. § 35(g)(9)]

Beginning in January 2010, after a PBGC payee or Tax Adjustment Act (TAA) recipient enrolls in Medicare, dies, or finalizes a divorce, his or her family members may be eligible to continue receiving the HCTC for up to 24 months. [I.R.C. § 35(g)(9)]

The HCTC Program's transaction center issues payments for 65 percent (80 percent for periods of coverage from May 1, 2009 to December 31, 2010) of health coverage costs to the health insurance providers on behalf of eligible taxpayers claiming the credit in advance. Therefore, these eligible taxpayers are only responsible for payment of the remainder of the health coverage costs.

Mergers and Acquisitions

Q 6:158   When does a buyer become responsible for a seller's COBRA responsibilities and liabilities?

Generally, businesses (or parts of businesses) are purchased and sold in either stock transactions or asset transactions. These two types of transactions are fundamentally different. However, notwithstanding the common-law rules, the COBRA regulations apply basically the same rules to both asset sales and stock sales.

Under the final COBRA regulations, whether a business reorganization involves a stock or an asset sale, a group health plan maintained by the selling group involved in a merger or acquisition has the obligation to make COBRA continuation coverage available to so-called M&A beneficiaries with respect to that sale as long as the selling group maintains a group health plan after the sale. Neither a stock sale nor an asset sale has any effect on the COBRA continuation coverage requirements applicable to any group health plan for any period before the sale. [Treas. Reg. §54.4980B-9, Q&A-8(a)] The question of the regulatory allocation of responsibility for COBRA in a business reorganization arises when the selling group ceases to provide any group health plan to any employee in connection with the sale.

If the selling group ceases to provide any group health plan to any employee in connection with the sale, a group health plan of the buying group must make COBRA continuation coverage available to M&A qualified beneficiaries. The buying group's obligation begins on the later of (1) the date the selling group ceases to provide any group health plan to any employee or (2) the date of the asset or stock sale.

In the case of an asset sale, M&A qualified beneficiaries include covered employees and their family members whose qualifying event occurred prior to or in connection with the sale, provided the covered employee's last employment before the sale was connected with the assets being sold. In the case of a stock sale, M&A qualified beneficiaries include covered employees and their family members whose qualifying event occurred prior to or in connection with the sale, provided the covered employee's last employment was with the acquired organization. [Treas. Reg. §54.4980B-9, Q&A-4]

The buying group does not, however, have an obligation to make COBRA continuation coverage available to qualified beneficiaries of the selling group who are not M&A qualified beneficiaries with respect to the sale.

Example. A selling group consists of three corporations, Alpha, Beta, and Gamma. A buying group consists of two corporations, Delta and Epsilon. Each group maintains a single health plan for all employees of their respective corporations. The buying group enters into a contract to buy all of the stock of Gamma from the selling group. Immediately before the sale there are 25 qualified beneficiaries receiving COBRA coverage under the selling group's plan. Of those beneficiaries, 20 are qualified M&A beneficiaries with respect to the sale of Gamma because they had qualifying events connected with a covered employee whose last employment before the event was with Gamma. The other 5 COBRA beneficiaries had qualifying events in connection with an employee whose last employment before the event was with Alpha or Beta. At the time of the sale of Gamma, the selling group terminates its group health plan and begins to liquidate the assets of Alpha and Beta and lay off the employees of those corporations.

Because the selling group ceased to provide group health coverage to any employee in connection with the sale, the buying group has the obligation to make COBRA coverage available to the 20 M&A beneficiaries. However, the buying group is not obligated to make COBRA coverage available to the other 5 qualified beneficiaries of the selling group or to any of the Alpha and Beta employees whose employment is terminated.

Although the rules for allocating COBRA coverage responsibility are the same, there is one key difference between an asset sale and a stock sale. In the case of a stock sale, the sale is not a qualifying event with respect to an employee who continues to be employed by the acquired organization after the sale. However, an asset sale is a qualifying event with respect to a covered employee whose employment was associated with the assets being sold unless (1) the employee is employed by the buyer immediately after the sale and the buyer is a successor employer or (2) the employee does not lose coverage under the seller's group health plan after the sale. Thus, unless one of these two conditions is met, a covered employee and his or her family members who lose coverage under the seller's plan because of an asset sale must be offered COBRA coverage, even if the employee is employed by the buyer following the sale. COBRA coverage may be cut off, however, if the employee and family members become covered under the buyer's plan, provided the necessary conditions are met (see Q 6:127). [Treas. Reg. §54.4980B-9, Q&A-5, Q&A-6]

Q 6:159 Can the buyer and seller allocate the responsibility for providing COBRA coverage by contract?

Yes. A buyer and seller may allocate the responsibility for providing COBRA coverage by contract, even if the contract allocates responsibility to a different party than the party that would be responsible under the regulations. However, if the party responsible under the contract fails to perform, the party obligated under the regulations will continue to be held responsible for providing the coverage. [Treas. Reg. §54.4980B-9, Q&A-7]

Q 6:160 Is COBRA coverage required to be offered if employees continue health FSA participation under either the seller's or buyer's plan following a sale of business assets?

Assuming COBRA coverage is otherwise required (see Q 6:117), the seller's plan will generally have to offer COBRA coverage. However, the point at which COBRA coverage must be made available will depend on how the deal is structured. [Rev. Rul. 2002-32, 2002-23 I.R.B. 1069]

Example 1. Employer S maintains a cafeteria plan that includes a health FSA. To participate in the health FSA, employees elect pre-tax salary reductions in return for the right to receive medical care expense reimbursements up to the amount of the reduction election for the year. During the plan year, S enters into an agreement under which Employer B acquires a portion of S's assets. In connections with the sale, employees of S who work with the acquired assets terminate employment with S and become employees of B. Employer B agrees to create a cafeteria plan with a health FSA that offers pre-tax salary reductions. However, S and B arrange for the transferred employees to continue to participate in S's FSA for an agreed upon-period. They also agree that salary reductions made under S's plan will continue as if made under B's plan.

According to the IRS the transferred employees do not suffer a loss of coverage under S's FSA during the plan year. Therefore, S has no obligation to make COBRA coverage available at the time of the sale. However, it will be obligated to make COBRA coverage available on the first day of the plan year after the current plan year.

Example 2. The facts are the same as those in Example 1, except that, as part of the sale, B agrees to cover the transferred employees under B's health FSA. Under B's plan the transferred employees will have the same level of coverage as under S's health FSA and will be treated as if their participation had been continuous from the beginning of S's plan year. The transferred employees' existing salary reduction elections will be taken into account for the remainder of B's plan year as if made under B's health FSA. In addition, B's plan will reimburse medical care expenses incurred by the transferred employees up to the amount of the employees' elections reduced by amounts previously reimbursed by S. Thus, medical expenses incurred before the closing date of the sale but not previously reimbursed, as well as medical expenses incurred after the closing date of the sale, will be reimbursed by B's plan.

According to the IRS, S's obligation to offer COBRA coverage to the transferred employees is not affected by the coverage provided by B. Therefore, assuming COBRA coverage is otherwise required, S must offer COBRA coverage for the current plan year.

Preemption of State Continuation Laws

Q 6:161　Why are state continuation coverage laws important?

If a group health plan is subject to state continuation of coverage laws in addition to the federal COBRA statute, the employer's obligations will be defined by state and federal law taken together. The employer must determine how to handle situations in which the state law imposes more stringent requirements, such as shorter notice periods, an employer contribution requirement, or a longer continuation period, than under federal law. If, however, the state continuation law is preempted by ERISA from applying to the particular group health plan, the employer's obligations will be defined solely by federal law.

State continuation of coverage laws are of particular concern to insured group health plans, which generally are not able to take advantage of ERISA's preemption of state law. Self-insured plans subject to ERISA are, on the other hand, not subject to state insurance laws and most other state laws (see chapter 2). See Q 6:164 for a further discussion of ERISA preemption.

Q 6:162　How do state continuation of coverage laws differ from federal COBRA requirements?

A state's continuation of coverage laws may not precisely match the federal COBRA requirements. Typical areas of difference include the following:

Application to small employers. COBRA's continuation of coverage requirements contain an exemption for group health plans of small employers with fewer than 20 employees. State continuation laws may have a lower minimum employee requirement or might not contain any minimum employee or group size requirement at all.

Required minimum period of participation in the group health plan. COBRA's continuation of coverage requirements imposes a minimum participation requirement of only one day as a condition of becoming a qualified beneficiary, and COBRA rights must be extended to anyone covered under the plan on the day before the date of a qualifying event who loses coverage as a result of that event. Some state continuation of coverage laws, in contrast, apply only to individuals who satisfy a more lengthy statutory minimum participation requirement. Thus, although the state law might impose more stringent continuation requirements, it would apply to a smaller group of individuals.

Additional qualifying events. State continuation of coverage laws may add additional qualifying events. For example, the state might mandate continuation of coverage upon termination of coverage for any reason, thus creating a continuation right even if group health plan coverage is lost due to failure to pay premiums or termination of employment due to gross misconduct, for example.

Additional qualified beneficiaries. Under COBRA, a qualified beneficiary is an employee, spouse, or child who loses group health plan coverage as a result of a COBRA qualifying event plus any child born to or placed for adoption with the covered employee during the period of COBRA continuation coverage. [HIPAA §421(b), amending COBRA definition of "qualified beneficiary"] State continuation of coverage laws that include additional categories of qualifying events, therefore, correspondingly expand the classes of qualified beneficiaries. An individual who is a qualified beneficiary for state, but not federal, continuation law purposes would be entitled only to state-law continuation rights, assuming it is also determined that the state law in question applies to the group health plan.

Coordinating maximum continuation periods. COBRA contains various maximum duration limits on continuation coverage. The longest mandated duration (other than in bankruptcy situations) is 36 months. State continuation of coverage laws may require a longer duration. An issue thus arises as to whether the one continuation period runs after the other (referred to as "stacking" the continuation periods) or whether they run concurrently (referred to as "blending" the continuation periods). Assuming that the state continuation law applies to the plan, the legislative history under COBRA, quoted with approval in *Gaskell v. Harvard Cooperative Soc'y* [17 Employee Benefit Cas. (BNA) 1152 (1st Cir. 1993)], rejects the "stacking" theory and clarifies that the two periods are intended to run concurrently. In other words, the 18-month or 36-month COBRA continuation period includes, and is not in addition to, a continuation period permitted under state law. (The legislative history did not, however, contemplate the issues presented by a state continuation law that, by its terms, expressly runs after any period of federal continuation coverage.)

Certain benefits excluded from state continuation requirement. A number of state mini-COBRA laws exclude dental care, vision care, and prescription drug coverage from coverage that is required to be continued.

Additional cutoff events. COBRA permits continuation coverage to be cut short upon the occurrence of certain events (see Q 6:126). State continuation of coverage laws may contain additional categories of permitted cutoff events, such as early termination of continuation coverage if a surviving spouse remarries.

Employer contribution requirements. COBRA permits employers to require qualified beneficiaries to pay the full cost of continuation coverage, plus a 2 percent administrative charge, even if the employer pays part or all of the premium cost for individuals who have not experienced a qualifying event. Some state mini-COBRA statutes, however, require employers to pay part or all of the cost of the continuation coverage.

Different notice requirements. A number of state continuation of coverage laws contain shorter notice and election periods than does COBRA. A state continuation of coverage law may also require that the employees and their dependents notify the employer of all qualifying events. (COBRA, in contrast, splits this responsibility between qualified beneficiaries and the employer, depending upon the particular event.)

Conversion privileges. COBRA does not require that a group health plan make its conversion privilege available if the COBRA continuation period terminates early. State laws concerning conversion rights may require that conversion rights be provided whenever group health plan coverage terminates except for one or two events (typically, if the insurance policy is canceled or the plan terminates).

Q 6:163   Does ERISA preempt state continuation laws?

Yes. ERISA could possibly preempt the application of state continuation of coverage laws to a group health plan in certain circumstances.

In general, ERISA preempts any state law relating to ERISA-covered employee benefit plans. However, ERISA's preemption provisions do not apply to properly drafted state insurance laws. To qualify for this exception from ERISA preemption (which is referred to as the "saving clause"), the state law must be confined to regulating the "business of insurance." The Supreme Court has held that a state law will be treated as regulating the business of insurance, and thus be "saved" from ERISA preemption, if it regulates a practice that (1) has the effect of transferring or spreading a policyholder's risk, (2) is an integral part of the policy relationship between the insurer and the insured, and (3) is limited to entities within the insurance industry. [ERISA §514; Metropolitan Life Ins. Co. v. Massachusetts, 471 U.S. 724 (1985)] Thus, a law that is nominally a state insurance law nonetheless could be preempted from applying to an ERISA-covered plan if it exceeds these boundaries. For example, a law contained in a state's insurance code that requires employers to provide a particular benefit to employees would be preempted because it is not limited to entities within the insurance industry and instead attempts to regulate an employer's relationship with its employees. On the other hand, a similar law requiring all insurers licensed to do business in that state to include the benefit in any group health insurance policy they issue would be more likely to pass muster and not be preempted by ERISA.

ERISA also contains an exception to the exception. Even though state insurance laws that are confined to regulating the business of insurance are saved from being preempted by ERISA, a state insurance law cannot attempt to regulate a self-insured plan or its trust by deeming it to be an insurer or engaged in the business of insurance. Thus, ERISA preempts state insurance laws from applying to self-insured plans. If the employer has a self-insured group health plan, its continuation of coverage responsibility thus will be defined by reference only to the federal COBRA provisions. [*See, e.g.,* Bergin v. Wausau Ins. Cos., 18 Employee Benefits Cas. (BNA) 2580 (D. Mass. 1994).]

Caution. The preceding description of ERISA preemption principles is greatly simplified. Before determining that ERISA preempts a state continuation law from applying to a particular group health plan, an employer should consult ERISA counsel. First, if the plan has a stop-loss or other risk-sharing arrangement, the case law is conflicting concerning whether the plan is self-insured for ERISA preemption purposes. Second, the question of whether a law "relates to" an ERISA plan and other issues are not always as obvious as they might at first seem, and much conflicting case law exists.

ERISA preemption of state laws is discussed in more detail in chapter 2.

Q 6:164   Does ERISA preempt state law bad-faith claims relating to COBRA?

In two decisions, federal district courts ruled that state-law bad-faith claims relating to COBRA coverage were preempted by ERISA.

In the first case, an employee, Joan Audrey Coggins, worked for Wagner Hopkins, Inc., a company that operated two bowling alleys in Wisconsin. Coggins was insured under Wagner's group health insurance policy, which provided coverage for medical and prescription drug expenses. In June 1999, Coggins was diagnosed with cancer. Her condition worsened, and in September 1999 she resigned from Wagner after learning that her cancer was terminal. Coggins notified Wagner and its insurer that she wanted to continue her health insurance under COBRA, and she remained current on her health insurance premiums, which she paid directly to Wagner's health insurer.

Coggin's condition continued to deteriorate and in March 2000, she was prescribed a medication that slows the growth of cancerous tumors and which cost approximately $1,000 per month for the peak dosage. Her condition stabilized when she began taking the medication, but in May 2000, when Coggins was nearing the recommended peak dosage, the insurer's plan administrator sent her a letter stating that it had terminated her health insurance coverage as of the end of April. After receiving the letter, Coggins instructed her doctors to discontinue the medication because she could no longer afford it. At her doctor's urging, she agreed to continue the medication at half the peak dosage to conserve the pills she had on hand. Because of her concern that she could no longer afford medication without health insurance benefits, Coggins also took less pain medication, even though her pain was acute.

Coggins eventually obtained coverage under a state plan in June 2000. However, during the period she was without coverage, she had difficulty eating and sleeping, lost weight, and expressed deep anxiety to her family regarding her inability to pay her medical bills.

In a letter to Coggins dated October 6, 2000, the third-party administrator acknowledged that it had acted improperly in terminating her COBRA continuation coverage. Coggins died on November 4, 2000. Coggins's daughter subsequently brought a state court action on behalf of her mother's estate against Wagner, its insurer, and the plan administrator, for damages for bad-faith denial of health insurance coverage, negligent infliction of emotional distress, and violations of state law. The case was removed to a federal district court, which determined that the claims were preempted by ERISA because they all turned on the question of whether the defendants had improperly terminated Coggins's COBRA coverage. [Estate of Coggins v. Wagner Hopkins, Inc., 174 F. Supp. 2d 883 (W.D. Wis. 2001)] The district court permitted Coggins's daughter to amend her complaint to state a claim under ERISA. On the second action, the court determined that the plan administrator had improperly terminated Coggins's COBRA coverage. However, the estate's recovery was limited to the amount of out-of-pocket medical expenses that Coggins actually incurred during the period she was without health coverage less the amount of premiums she would have paid during that period. [Estate of Coggins v. Wagner Hopkins, Inc., 183 F. Supp. 2d 1126 (W.D. Wis. 2001)]

In a second case, an individual who had COBRA coverage under her former employer's health plan was diagnosed as suffering from serious hip problems. She was scheduled to undergo surgery as soon as possible in order to prevent the need for a total hip replacement. The insurer initially denied her claim for benefits, but after numerous requests, finally approved the surgery about five months later. However, when the doctor took an X-ray, he determined that her condition had deteriorated and that she required a total hip replacement. Before the surgery could take place, the insurer informed the individual that her COBRA coverage had expired. The insurer offered her two other plans under which she could elect coverage. The individual elected one of the two plans and had both her hips totally replaced. She subsequently filed a lawsuit in state court for bad faith for delaying approval of her claim for benefits. The insurer had the lawsuit moved to a federal district court, which determined that the employee's claim was preempted by ERISA because it related to COBRA health care coverage. Again, it should be noted that the court did not dismiss the lawsuit; it gave the employee an opportunity to amend her complaint to state a claim under ERISA. [Harrelson v. Blue Cross & Blue Shield of Ala., 150 F. Supp. 2d 1290 (M.D. Ala. 2001)]

Q 6:165   Does the Public Health Service Act preempt state continuation of coverage laws?

The Public Health Service Act (PHSA) is the third federal law containing COBRA provisions (the other two are the Internal Revenue Code and ERISA). The PHSA's COBRA provisions apply to group health plans maintained by any state or local government that receives federal funds under the PHSA. The PHSA does not contain a preemption scheme similar to Section 514 of ERISA. Moreover, the only appellate court to rule on the issue of PHSA preemption held that, because of this lack of a preemptive provision, there is no basis for finding a non conflicting state law to be preempted. [Radici v. Associated Ins. Cos., 217 F.3d 737 (9th Cir. 2000)]

COBRA Enforcement and Sanctions

Q 6:166   Which agencies have the power to enforce COBRA?

COBRA divides enforcement authority among three agencies: the IRS, Department of Health and Human Services (HHS), and the DOL. According to the Conference Report issued for COBRA, the Secretary of Labor issues the regulations dealing with disclosure and reporting; the Secretary of the Treasury (i.e., the IRS) makes rules for required coverage, deductions, and income inclusions; and the Secretary of Health and Human Services issues the regulations for continuation coverage provided by state and local governments. The HHS regulations must conform to those issued by the other two agencies. [H.R. Rep. No. 453, 99th Cong., 1st Sess. 562–563 (1985), quoted in ERISA Tech. Rel. 86-2]

In addition, because of the interplay of COBRA with the Medicare secondary-payer requirements of the Social Security Act, the CMS has limited jurisdiction on this issue.

Q 6:167   How are COBRA violations penalized?

COBRA violations are penalized by an excise tax that may be assessed against an employer or a multiemployer plan. The tax may also be assessed against a person, such as an insurer or third-party administrator, responsible for administering or providing benefits under a plan (other than in that person's capacity as an employee). In general, such a person will be liable for the excise tax if he or she assumes responsibility, under a legally enforceable written agreement, for performing the act to which the COBRA violation relates. [Treas. Reg. §54. 4980B-2, Q&A-10]

Q 6:168   How much is the excise tax imposed for COBRA violations?

The excise tax is $100 per day per qualified beneficiary for the duration of the noncompliance period (see Qs 6:169, 6:170), with a maximum of $200 per day per family, regardless of the number of qualified beneficiaries affected by the violation. [I.R.C. §§4980B(b)(1), 4980B(c)(3)]

Note. The COBRA excise tax may also be assessed if group health plan coverage for pediatric vaccines is reduced below the level in effect on May 1, 1993. This separate provision is discussed in chapter 3, which covers medical care in general.

Q 6:169   When does the noncompliance period used to calculate the excise tax begin?

The noncompliance period begins on the date the COBRA violation first occurs. However, for failure to provide coverage, the noncompliance period does not begin until 45 days after a written request for coverage is made.

An "inadvertent failure" rule exempts from excise taxation any part of the period for which it is established (to the satisfaction of the Secretary of the Treasury) that no potentially liable person knew, or should have known by exercising reasonable diligence, that the violation existed. However, this rule does not apply in situations in which a special audit rule applies (see Q 6:174). [I.R.C. §§4980B(b)(2)(A), 4980B(b)(3), 4980B(c)(1)]

Q 6:170   When does the noncompliance period end?

The period of noncompliance ends on the earlier of (1) the date on which the violation is corrected or (2) six months after the last day of the maximum applicable COBRA continuation period (excluding a failure to make timely premium payments). [I.R.C. §4980B(b)(2)(B)]

Q 6:171   When is a COBRA violation considered "corrected"?

A COBRA violation is considered corrected if (1) it is retroactively removed to the extent possible and (2) the financial position of the qualified beneficiary, or beneficiary's estate, is as good as it would have been if the violation had not occurred. For this purpose, it is assumed that the beneficiary would have elected the coverage that was most favorable in light of the expenses he or she had incurred since the beginning of the violation. [I.R.C. §4980B(g)(4); Conf. Rep. to accompany H.R. 4333, H.R. Rep. No. 1104, 100th Cong., 2d Sess. Vol. II, at 24 (1988)]

Q 6:172   Is there a grace period before the excise tax applies?

Yes. No excise tax applies to COBRA violations corrected during the first 30 days after any potentially liable person knows (or should have known by the exercise of reasonable diligence) of the violation. The violation must have had a reasonable cause. The grace period is unavailable for cases of willful neglect and violations that were not corrected before the special audit rule (see Q 6:174) is applied. [I.R.C. §§4980B(c)(1), 4980B(b)(3)]

Q 6:173   Does an audit of the employer affect the excise tax?

Yes. The special audit rule imposes a minimum excise tax on COBRA violations that are not corrected before the date when a notice of examination of income tax liability is sent to the employer, if the violations occurred or continue to occur during the period under examination. [I.R.C. §4980B(b)(3)]

Q 6:174   What is the excise tax under the special audit rule?

Under the special audit rule, the minimum excise tax per affected qualified beneficiary is either $2,500 or the otherwise applicable excise tax, whichever is less. But if an employer's (or multiemployer plan's) violations for any year are more than *de minimis,* the minimum excise tax imposed is the smaller of the otherwise applicable excise tax or $15,000. [I.R.C. §4980B(b)(3)] The Code does not define *de minimis.*

Q 6:175   Is there a maximum excise tax that can be imposed with respect to a single-employer plan?

There is no limit on the excise tax that can be assessed for a willful violation. However, if the violation was not willful, and the employer had reasonable cause for its actions, the maximum excise tax with respect to a single-employer plan for any taxable year is generally the lesser of (1) $500,000 or (2) 10 percent of the aggregate amount paid or incurred by the employer (or predecessor employer) during the preceding taxable year for group health plans. [I.R.C. §§4980B(c)(4)(A), 4980B(e)(1)(A)(i)]

Q 6:176   Is there a maximum excise tax that can be imposed for a violation committed by a multiemployer plan?

There is no limit on the excise tax that can be assessed for a willful violation. Otherwise, the maximum tax in any taxable year on the trust forming a part of the plan is the lesser of $500,000 or 10 percent of the amount paid or incurred during the taxable year to provide medical care (directly or through insurance, reimbursement, or otherwise). [I.R.C. §4980B(e)(1)(A)(ii)] In addition, if an employer participating in a multiemployer plan is assessed the excise tax, the single-employer plan maximum (see Q 6:175) applies to that employer. [I.R.C. §4980B(c)(4)(B)]

Q 6:177   Is there a maximum excise tax that can be imposed on persons other than employers or multiemployer plans?

For COBRA violations that are not willful and are due to reasonable cause, the maximum aggregate amount of tax that may be imposed on persons other than employers or multiemployer plans for COBRA violations concerning all plans during the taxable year is $2 million. There is no maximum excise tax for willful violations. [I.R.C. §4980B(c)(4)(C)]

Q 6:178   Who—other than employers or multiemployer plans—can be liable for excise tax?

Individuals responsible for administering benefits or making benefits available under the plan can be held liable if their actions or failures to act wholly or partially caused a COBRA violation. [I.R.C. §4980B(e)(1)(B)]

Benefit providers or administrators that are bound by a legally enforceable agreement to make COBRA coverage available are fully liable for a failure to make COBRA coverage available, but they are not liable for other violations unless they took responsibility for performing the act to which the failure relates. [I.R.C. §4980B(e)(2)(A)]

Benefit providers are liable for failure to comply with a written request for COBRA coverage sent by the qualified beneficiary if the qualifying event is a divorce, legal separation, or child's loss of dependency status or by the employer or plan administrator for all other qualifying events. [I.R.C. §4980B(e)(2)(B)]But liability will not be imposed if the employer's act or failure to act made it impossible for the person to make COBRA coverage available. [Conf. Rep. to accompany H.R. 4333, H.R. Rep. No. 1104, 100th Cong. 2d Sess., Vol. II, at 26 (1988)] A person providing coverage under the plan will not be liable for failure to comply with a written request to make COBRA coverage available sooner than 45 days after the date the notice is provided to such person. [I.R.C. §4980B(b)(2)] The legislative history indicates that this provision will not override a written agreement between an employer and a third party that obligates the third party to provide continuation coverage. [Conf. Rep. to accompany H.R. 4333, H.R. Rep. No. 1104, 100th Cong., 2d Sess., Vol. II, at 27 (1988)]

Q 6:179   May the IRS waive the excise tax penalty for a COBRA violation?

Yes. Part or all of the excise tax may be waived if failure to comply was due to reasonable cause and not to willful neglect, with the result that the payment of such tax would be excessive in proportion to the failure involved. The legislative history of COBRA states that excessiveness is judged by the seriousness of the failure to comply with COBRA, not by the taxpayer's ability to pay. [I.R.C. §4980B(c)(5); Conf. Rep. to accompany H.R. 4333, H.R. Rep. No. 1104, 100th Cong., 2d Sess., Vol. II, at 27 (1988)]

Q 6:180   How is the excise tax penalty for COBRA violations reported and collected?

Beginning January 1, 2010, excise tax liabilities for failure to meet certain health plan requirements must be self-reported by filing Form 8928, *Return of Certain Excise Taxes Under Chapter 43 of the Internal Revenue Code.* [Treas. Reg. § 54.6011-2] In the case of excise taxes imposed by Code Section 4980B for failure to satisfy the COBRA continuation coverage requirements, the form must be filed by the employer or other person responsible for providing or administering benefits under the plan (such as the insurer or third-party administrator). The form is due on or before the due date for filing the person's federal income tax return for the year in which the failure occurred. If the failure is by a multiemployer plan, the form is due on or before the last day of the seventh month following the end of the plan year. [Treas. Reg. § 54.6071-1(a)] The tax due must be paid with the return. [Treas. Reg. § 54.6151-1]

Q 6:181   What is the penalty for failure to notify employees and qualified beneficiaries of their COBRA rights?

A penalty of up to $110 per day applies to the plan administrator's failure to provide:

1. Written notice to each covered employee and his or her spouse of COBRA continuation rights at the time their group health care coverage commences (see Q 6:71); and

2. Notice of COBRA continuation rights to each qualified beneficiary who would lose coverage under the plan as a result of a qualifying event (see Qs 6:41–6:58, 6:63, 6:79).

[ERISA § 502(c)(1); U.S.C. § 1132(c)(1)]

In one case, the Eleventh Circuit Court of Appeals concluded that only a single penalty applies when a plan fails to give notice to a plan participant and to other beneficiaries in connection with a qualifying event.

The employee in the case, Daniel Wright, worked for Hanna Steel Corp. Wright, his wife, and their two minor children were covered by Hanna's self-funded group health plan. When Wright voluntarily terminated employment, the company failed to provide Wright, his wife, or the children with notice of their COBRA continuation rights. When Wright successfully sued the company for failing to provide COBRA notice, a U.S. district court ordered Hanna to pay Wright a penalty of $75 per day for each day of the maximum 18-month COBRA coverage period that applies in the case of termination of employment. The district court also ordered the company to pay penalties of $75 per day for failure to provide notice to Mrs. Wright and $10 per day for each of the children. On appeal, the Eleventh Circuit upheld the $75 per day penalty for Wright, but not the penalties for his wife and children. According to the appellate court, the penalty provision clearly states that when a plan fails to give notice in connection with a qualifying event, a court may assess a penalty only as to a single participant; penalties for beneficiaries are not available. [Wright v. Hanna Steel Corp., 270 F.3d 1336 (11th Cir. 2001)]

Note. The Eleventh Circuit's interpretation of the penalty provision makes sense when an entire family loses coverage as a result of a qualifying event. On the other hand, in the case of some qualifying events, the only individual to lose coverage is a beneficiary. For example, when a plan participant divorces, a COBRA notice must be sent to the spouse, not to the participant. Similarly, when a child reaches an age when he or she is no longer eligible for dependent coverage, a COBRA notice must be issued to the child, not the participant parent. However, the Eleventh Circuit's literal reading of the law would appear to preclude the imposition of penalties if those notices are not forthcoming.

Q 6:182   Are penalties for violations of the notice requirements imposed automatically?

No. Courts have the discretion to determine whether a penalty should be imposed and the amount of the penalty.

In one case, an employee who quit her job was not provided with a COBRA notice because of problems with the employer's computerized human resource information systems. When the employee learned of the loss of her health coverage, she wrote to the employer demanding coverage and threatening to file complaints with the EEOC, the DOL, the IRS, and various state agencies. She also retained a lawyer. After several months of back and forth exchanges, the company sent the employee a COBRA packet providing her with retroactive health benefits, with one full year of premiums paid for by the company. Nonetheless, the employee brought suit, asking the court to award her the maximum $110-per-day penalty for failure to provide timely notice of her COBRA rights. The court, however, refused to impose any penalties on the employer. According to the court, a penalty is warranted only when an employer acted in bad faith, and there was no evidence of bad faith in this case. While acknowledging that it took the employer considerable time to resolve the problem, the court did not attribute the delay to bad faith. According to the court, the delay was almost certainly exacerbated by the "overly shrill and adversarial" approach of the employee's lawyer. [Thompson v. Safeway, Inc., 2002 U.S. Dist. LEXIS 5707 (N.D. Ill. Mar 29, 2002)]

In another case, a district court refused to award penalties where an employer was delinquent in providing a terminated employee with notice of her COBRA rights, but permitted her to elect retroactive COBRA coverage. In view of the retroactive coverage, the court determined that the employee was not injured by the delay in providing notice and hence no penalties were justified. [Gigliotti v. Sprint Spectrum, L.P., 2001 U.S. Dist. LEXIS 20221 (N.D.N.Y. Dec. 7, 2001)]

Similarly, the First Circuit Court of Appeals upheld a district court's decision not to impose penalties on an employer that was "quite late" in providing a COBRA notice. According to the district court, penalties were not justified because the employer's failure to provide timely notice was not in bad faith and did not harm the employee. Although it was unclear why the notice was sent late, the district court noted that the company gave the employee the full 60 days to elect COBRA coverage, which she declined. On appeal, the employee argued that the district court did not properly exercise discretion in deciding whether to award penalties; instead, it relied on a per se rule that no penalties would be awarded absent harm to the employee or bad faith on the part of the employer. However, the First Circuit said that refusing to award penalties absent harm or bad faith was a proper exercise of the district court's discretion. "[A]lthough the district court *need* not find bad faith or prejudice to impose penalties," said the court, "it *may* give weight—even dispositive weight—to these factors in the exercise of its discretion."

On the other hand, the Eighth Circuit Court of Appeals upheld a lower court's award of the maximum allowable penalty—which came to $8,030—to an employee whose employer (who also served as plan administrator) failed to provide a COBRA election notice for several months following her termination of employment. The employee made repeated phone calls in an attempt to obtain the information and eventually hired an attorney to pursue the matter. After receiving two letters from the attorney, the company acknowledged its error and provided the employee with health coverage retroactive to her date of termination. The court acknowledged that the employer's failure to provide the COBRA notice was due to an administrative error "ostensibly caused by the company moving its offices," and that the employee did not suffer any loss of health benefits because of the retroactive provision of coverage. However, the court noted that the employee "was forced to invest time, effort, and money in hiring an attorney to gain access to information that she was legally entitled to." Therefore, the Eighth Circuit concluded that it was proper for the lower court to award the maximum penalty. [Brown v. Aventis Pharm., Inc., 341 F.3d 822 (8th Cir. 2003)]

Q 6:183   Does the $110-per-day penalty apply in the case of breaches of COBRA provisions other than the notice requirement?

Yes. The penalty also applies in the case of a plan administrator's failure or refusal to provide information requested by a plan participant. However, it does not apply to other violations of the COBRA rules. For example, a district court held that the penalty did not apply in a case involving wrongful denial of benefit claims. [Moreno v. St. Francis Hosp. & Health Ctr., 2001 U.S. Dist. LEXIS 17206 (N.D. Ill. Oct. 17, 2001)].

Plan Year

Q 6:184   What is a group health plan's plan year?

The plan year designated in the plan document is determinative, not the plan year shown on the Form 5500 annual report to the IRS. [Treas. Reg. §54. 4980B-2, Q&A-7(a)(b) (Feb. 3, 1999)]

Q 6:185   What is the plan year if the plan document does not specify a plan year or there is no plan document?

Many group health plans still operate without a plan document, even though ERISA may require one (see chapter 2). If the plan year is not spelled out in a plan document, the plan year is determined as follows:

1. If the plan imposes yearly deductibles and/or limits, the plan year is the year used for that purpose.

2. If the plan does not impose annual deductibles or limits, the plan year is the policy year.

3. If the plan is not insured or the insurance policy is not renewed on an annual basis, the plan year is the employer's tax year.

4. If none of the above applies, the plan year is the calendar year.

[Treas. Reg. §54.4980B-2, Q&A-7(b)(1)(2)(3)(4) (Feb. 3, 1999)]

Subsidized COBRA Coverage for Assistance-Eligible Individuals

Q 6:186   What is subsidized COBRA coverage?

The American Recovery and Reinvestment Act of 2009 (ARRA) [Pub. L. No. 111-5, 123 Stat. 115 (Feb. 17, 2009)] created a COBRA premium subsidy for individuals who become entitled to COBRA coverage because of an involuntary termination of employment. The subsidy is equal to 65 percent of the amount of the COBRA premium. [ARRA § 3001(a)(1)(A)] As originally enacted, the subsidy applied only to individuals who became eligible for COBRA coverage as a result of an involuntary termination of employment during the period beginning September 8, 2008 and ending December 31, 2008, and the subsidy was limited to a period of not more than nine months. However, the Department of Defense Appropriations Act of 2010 [Pub. L. No. 111-118, 123 Stat. 3409 (Dec. 19, 2009)] extended the subsidy to apply to individuals who became eligible for COBRA coverage as a result of an involuntary termination during the period beginning September 8, 2008 and ending February 28, 2010, and extended the duration of the subsidy to 15 months. The 15-month subsidy was subsequently extended to terminations through March 31, 2010, by the Temporary Extension Act of 2010 [Pub. L. No. 111-144] and through May 31, 2010, by the Continuing Extension Act of 2010. [Pub. L. No. 111-157] Pending legislation would extend the subsidy through December 31, 2010.

For purposes of the subsidy, COBRA continuation coverage includes continuation coverage provided under ERISA Sections 601 *et seq.* (other than § 609); Title XXII of the Public Health Service Act (PHSA); Internal Revenue Code Section 4980B; the Federal Employees Health Benefit Plan (FEHBP); or under a state program that provides comparable continuation coverage. [ARRA § 3001(a)(10)(B)]

The subsidy does not apply to coverage under a health FSA under a cafeteria plan. However, it does apply to COBRA coverage of any other group health plans, including a vision-only or dental-only plan and "mini-med plans," whether or not the employer pays a portion of the cost for active employees. The premium reduction does not apply to continuation coverage for non-health benefits that are not subject to COBRA continuation coverage, such as group life insurance. [Notice 2009-27, 2009-16 I.R.B. 838]

The subsidy applies to premiums for periods of coverage beginning on or after February 17, 2009, the date of enactment of ARRA. [ARRA § 2001(a)(1)(A)]

State continuation coverage. The subsidy applies to state-mandated continuation coverage only if the coverage is "comparable" to COBRA coverage. Comparable coverage does not include every state-law right to continuation coverage. To be comparable, the state-mandated coverage generally must allow an individual to continue coverage that is substantially similar to the coverage provided prior to the termination of employment at a monthly premium that is based on a specified percentage of the group health plan's cost for the coverage. A right to continue coverage with no rule limiting the maximum premium that can be charged for the coverage is not comparable to COBRA coverage. On the other hand, IRS guidance makes it clear that some differences are permitted. For example, a different period of continuation coverage under state law will not disqualify the coverage from being comparable. Similarly, the IRS says that state programs providing for different qualifying events, different qualified beneficiaries, or different maximum premiums generally will not fail to be comparable solely for those reasons. [Notice 2009-27, 2009-16 I.R.B. 838]

Q 6:187   Which individuals are eligible for the COBRA premium subsidy?

The COBRA premium subsidy is available to any AEI. An AEI includes any qualified beneficiary who is eligible for and elects COBRA coverage as a result of an the involuntary termination of employment that occurred during the subsidy eligibility period (see Q 6:186). [ARRA § 3001(a)(3) as amended]

Practice Pointer. An AEI can be any qualified beneficiary who is associated with the relevant covered employee (e.g., a dependent of an employee who is covered immediately before a qualifying event that is the involuntary termination of the covered employee's employment). As under the normal COBRA rules, the qualified beneficiary can independently elect COBRA, and under the Act can independently receive a subsidy.

The law includes an expedited 15-day review process under which an individual may request review of a group health plan's denial of treatment as an AEI.

Involuntary termination requirement. An individual qualifies as an AEI only if his or her COBRA coverage was triggered by an involuntary termination of employment during the subsidy eligibility period.

As a general rule, involuntary termination means severance from employment due to the independent exercise by the employer of its unilateral authority to terminate employment when the employee was willing and able to continue to work. [Notice 2009-27, 2009-16 I.R.B. 838] A firing for cause will qualify an employee for the subsidy unless the employer can deny COBRA coverage entirely on the grounds of gross misconduct (see Q 6:52).

However, IRS guidance makes it clear that an outright firing is not required. Involuntary termination may include the employer's failure to renew an employment contract where the employee was willing and able to execute a new contract on terms and conditions similar to those in the expiring contract.

The IRS guidance also provides that an *employee-initiated* termination may constitute an involuntary termination for purposes of the subsidy if the termination is for good reason due to an *employer* action that causes a material negative change in the employment relationship for the employee. For example, an involuntary termination includes a resignation prompted by a material change in the geographic location of the employee's employment.

A termination that is designated as a voluntary resignation may qualify as an involuntary termination if the employer would have terminated the employee's services in any event and the employee had knowledge of the employer's intent. Similarly, an employee's retirement may be an involuntary termination if the facts and circumstances indicate that it was prompted by imminent termination. A "buyout" elected by an employee in return for a severance package will be treated as an involuntary termination if the employer indicates that, after the offer period for the severance package, a certain number of remaining employees will be terminated.

Under the traditional COBRA rules, a reduction in an employee's hours or a temporary layoff or furlough is not treated as a termination of employment. Instead, a reduction in hours or layoff is a separate qualifying event if it causes the employee to lose health coverage. However, a reduction in hours or layoff can qualify as a termination of employment for purposes of the COBRA subsidy. According to the IRS, an involuntary reduction to zero hours, such as a layoff, furlough, or other suspension of employment that results in the employee's loss of health coverage is an involuntary termination of employment for purposes of the subsidy. On the other hand, if the employee's hours are simply cut back but not reduced to zero, the reduction is generally not an involuntary termination. However, the employee's voluntary termination of employment in response to the cutback may be an involuntary termination if the reduction in hours is a material negative change in the employment relationship for the employee.

The Temporary Extension Act 2010 [Pub. L. No. 111-144] expands eligibility for the subsidy to individuals who become eligible for COBRA coverage as a result of a reduction in hours and subsequently suffer an involuntary termination of employment. Under prior law, the subsidy applied only if the original COBRA-triggering event was an involuntary termination. This expansion of the eligibility rules applies only to individuals who became eligible for COBRA as a result of a reduction in hours on or after September 1, 2008, and were involuntarily terminated on or after March 2, 2010, and only for periods of coverage on or after March 2, 2010.

A strike or work stoppage initiated by *employees* is not an involuntary termination; however, a lockout initiated by the *employer* is an involuntary termination.

An employee's death or absence from work due to illness or disability does not constitute an involuntary termination.

To meet the involuntary termination requirement, there must be an *involuntary termination of employment,* not an involuntary termination of health coverage. Thus, COBRA-qualifying events, such as divorce or a child ceasing to be a dependent, are not involuntary terminations that qualify for the subsidy.

COBRA eligibility requirement. To qualify for the subsidy, *both* the involuntary termination of employment and the resulting loss of health care coverage triggering COBRA eligibility must occur during the subsidy eligibility period. If an employee's termination of employment occurs during the eligibility period, but the employee does not lose health coverage until a later date, the subsidy does not apply.

If an employer extends an employee's health coverage for a period of time following a termination of employment, the date of the loss of coverage will depend on how the employer treats the extended period of health coverage.

Example 1. Jason is involuntarily terminated from employment on February 15, 2010. Normally, his health coverage under his employer's plan would terminate on February 28, 2010. However, Jason's severance package includes six months of employer-paid health coverage, from March 1, 2010 through August 31, 2010. Jason's employer treats the six months of health coverage as a deferral of the employee's loss of coverage under the plan. As a result, Jason's loss of coverage will not be deemed to occur until August 31, 2010. Consequently, Jason will not be eligible for the COBRA subsidy because loss of coverage does not occur on or before May 31, 2010.

Example 2. The facts are the same as those in Example 1, except that Jason's employer treats the six months of paid health coverage as a provision of COBRA coverage on behalf of the employee. In this case, Jason would be eligible for the subsidy because loss of coverage will be deemed to have occurred on February 28, 2010.

Note. In Example 2, Jason would technically qualify as an AEI as of February 28, 2010; however, the actual subsidy would not be available until September 2010, when Jason must begin paying for COBRA coverage. The subsidy is based on the amount of premium actually charged to the employee for COBRA coverage. Where the employer provides coverage at no cost to the employee, there is no premium charge to which the subsidy applies (see Q 6:188).

Note. The above examples assume a May 31, 2010 cut-off date for the subsidy. However, pending legislation would extend the eligibility period through December 31, 2010.

An individual's COBRA eligibility must be triggered by the termination of employment in order to qualify for the subsidy. If COBRA continuation coverage is based on a qualifying event that occurred before the termination of employment, the later involuntary termination does not cause a qualified COBRA beneficiary to become an AEI.

Example 3. Ted is divorced on April 30, 2009. The divorce results in a loss of health coverage for his spouse, Lily. Lily is eligible for and timely elects COBRA continuation coverage. Following the divorce, Ted is involuntarily terminated and loses health coverage on October 30, 2009. He elects COBRA continuation coverage that begins November 30, 2009. Lily is not an AEI because the qualifying event with respect to her COBRA continuation coverage is not an involuntary termination. Ted is an AEI.

A termination with loss of health coverage must qualify the individual for COBRA continuation coverage (including certain federal or state coverage, as defined above) in order for the premium subsidy to apply. For example, if an employer that is not subject to the COBRA continuation requirements voluntarily offers continuation coverage to involuntarily terminated employees, those employees are *not* AEIs.

The *election* of COBRA coverage is *not* required to be made during the subsidy eligibility period as long as the continuation coverage itself begins during that period.

Practice Pointer. A qualified beneficiary must be given at least 60 days to elect COBRA coverage, beginning as of the later of the date of the loss of coverage or the date the beneficiary is notified of the right to elect COBRA coverage (see Qs 6:92, 6:93).

Q 6:188   What is the amount of the subsidy?

An AEI must be treated as having paid in full for COBRA coverage if he or she pays 35 percent of the premium. [ARRA § 3001(a)(1)(A)] Thus, the individual is effectively entitled to a "subsidy" for 65 percent of the premium.

The amount of the premium used to calculate the reduced premium is the premium amount that the employee would be required to pay for COBRA continuation coverage (e.g., 102 percent of the "applicable premium" for the period).

The law specifically provides that if a person other than the individual's employer pays on the individual's behalf, then the individual is treated as paying 35 percent of the premium, as is required to be entitled to the premium subsidy. Thus, the AEI's payment for COBRA premiums may be made on behalf of the AEI by another individual (e.g., a parent or guardian) or an entity (e.g., a state agency or a charity). Payment of COBRA premiums by the employer does not count as payment by an AEI for purposes of obtaining the subsidy.

If the amount charged to the AEI is less than the maximum COBRA premium, the amount actually charged is used to determine the AEI's 35 percent share and the subsidized amount. [Notice 2009-27, 2009-16 I.R.B. 838]

Example 1. Janet is an AEI who is charged $500 a month for COBRA continuation coverage under her employer's group health plan. She is entitled to COBRA continuation coverage upon the timely payment of $175 (35 percent × $500). The COBRA subsidy is $325 ($500 – $175).

Example 2. The facts are the same as those in Example 1, except that Janet's employer pays half of Janet's COBRA premium on her behalf and Janet is charged only $250 per month. Janet is entitled to COBRA continuation coverage upon the timely payment of $87.50 (35 percent × $250). The COBRA subsidy is $162.50 ($250 – $87.50).

Under the COBRA rules, an individual receiving COBRA coverage must have the same rights as active employees to change coverage during an open enrollment period (see Q 6:109). However, except in the case of a newborn or newly adopted child, a spouse or dependent who was not covered before a qualifying event is not a qualified beneficiary. The subsidy does not apply to any portion of a COBRA premium that is attributable to coverage for an individual who is not a qualified beneficiary, because such an individual is not an AEI.

When allocating the premium payment between coverage for an AEI and coverage for a non-AEI, the premium is allocated first to the cost of coverage for the AEI. Therefore, if coverage for the non-AEI does not add to the overall cost, the subsidy applies to the full amount paid for the coverage. However, if coverage for the non-AEI adds to the overall cost, the incremental cost is not eligible for the subsidy.

Example 3. Bob is an AEI with COBRA coverage for himself and his two dependent children, who are also AEIs. The COBRA coverage also covers Anne, Bob's niece, who is not an AEI. The premium for COBRA coverage for two or more dependents is $1,000 per month. Thus, the premium for coverage of the AEIs (Bob and the two children) would be $1,000 per month, regardless of the coverage for the non-AEI (Anne). The incremental cost of the coverage for Anne is $0. Therefore, the subsidy applies to the entire $1,000 premium. Bob is entitled to COBRA coverage upon timely payment of $350 (35 percent × $1,000), and the amount of the subsidy is $650 ($1,000 – $350).

Example 4. Mike has self-only COBRA continuation coverage. The premium for self-only COBRA coverage is $450 per month. Therefore, Mike must pay $157.50 (35 percent x $450) per month and is eligible for a subsidy of $292.50 (65 percent × $450) per month. However, during the subsidy period, the plan has an open enrollment period and Mike adds his wife, Betsy, and his dependent daughter, Liz (non-AEIs), to the coverage. The additional coverage raises the premium to $1,000 per month. The $550 incremental cost for the additional coverage is not eligible for the subsidy. Therefore, Mike's subsidy remains at $292.50 (65 percent x $450). Mike must pay $157.50 (35 percent x $450) plus $550 for the additional coverage, or a total of $707.50.

Q 6:189   How is the amount of the COBRA premium subsidy reimbursed to the employer or group health plan?

The amount of the COBRA premium subsidy (i.e., the premiums not paid by the COBRA beneficiary) will be reimbursed to the person to whom premiums arepayable under COBRA continuation coverage. [I.R.C. § 6432 as added by ARRA § 3001(a)(12)(A)] The mechanism for making the reimbursement is treatment of the amount of the unpaid premiums as a payment of the person's payroll taxes. If the amount treated as paid exceeds the amount of the person's liability for payroll taxes, the excess will be treated as an overpayment of payroll taxes.

The person to whom the reimbursement is payable is either (1) the multi-employer group health plan, (2) the employer maintaining a group health plan that is subject to federal COBRA continuation coverage requirements or that is self-insured, or (3) the insurer providing coverage under a plan not included in (1) or (2). Only this person is eligible to offset its payroll taxes by the amount of the subsidy. [I.R.C. § 6432(b)]

In the typical case where the employer maintaining a group health plan is eligible for reimbursement, the employer may recover the subsidy provided to assistance-eligible individuals by taking the subsidy amount as a credit on its quarterly Form 941 employment tax return. The employer may provide the subsidy—and take the credit on its employment tax return—only after it has received the 35 percent premium payment from the individual. [IR-2009-15; COBRA: Answers for Employers]

In the case of an insured plan, the subsidy is the amount of premiums paid by the employer to the insurer on behalf of the AEI. In the case of a self-insured plan, once the AEI has paid 35 percent of the otherwise required COBRA premium, the remaining 65 percent is treated as a premium subsidy to be reimbursed to the employer.

The law provides that the person entitled to reimbursement must file a claim for reimbursement at such time and in such manner as required by the IRS and must submit reports, including: (1) an attestation of the involuntary termination of employment of each covered employee on the basis of whose termination reimbursement is claimed; (2) a report of the amount of payroll taxes offset for a reporting period and estimated offsets for the subsequent reporting period; and (3) a report containing the TINs of all covered employees, the amount of subsidy reimbursed with respect to each covered employee and qualified beneficiaries, and a designation with respect to each covered employee as to whether the subsidy reimbursement is for coverage of one individual or of two or more individuals. [I.R.C. § 6432(e)]

Nonetheless, under the reimbursement mechanism specified by the IRS, the Form 941 filed by the person seeking reimbursement is required to include only the amount of the subsidy reimbursement and the number of assistance-eligible individuals to whom premium assistance was provided. However, the IRS indicates that the person seeking reimbursement is required to maintain documentation for the reimbursement claim. Such documentation includes, but is not limited to:

- Information on the receipt, including dates and amounts, of the AEIs' 35 percent shares of the premium.
- In the case of an insured plan, copy of an invoice or other supporting statement from the insurance carrier and proof of timely payment of the full premium to the insurance carrier required under COBRA.

- In the case of a self-insured plan, proof of the premium amount and proof of the coverage provided to the AEIs.

- Attestation of involuntary termination, including the date of the involuntary termination, for each covered employee whose involuntary termination is the basis for eligibility for the subsidy.

- Proof of each AEI's eligibility for COBRA coverage at any time during the subsidy eligibility period and election of COBRA coverage.

- A record of the Social Security numbers of all covered employees, the amount of the subsidy reimbursed with respect to each covered employee, and whether the subsidy was for one individual or two or more individuals.

- Other documents necessary to verify the correct amount of reimbursement.

Q 6:190   How long does the COBRA premium subsidy last?

Under the law as amended, an AEI is eligible for the premium subsidy for a period of not more than 15 months. The subsidy will end on:

- The first date the AEI is eligible for coverage under any other group health plan (other than limited coverage for dental, vision, counseling, or referral services; coverage under a flexible spending arrangement; or coverage of treatment at an on-site medical facility maintained by an employer and that consists primarily of first-aid services, prevention and wellness care, or similar care) or is eligible for Medicare benefits; or

- The earliest of (a) the date that is 15 months after the first day of the first month that the subsidy applies to the AEI, or (b) the date following the expiration of the maximum period of COBRA continuation coverage.

[ARRA § 3001(a)(2)(A) as amended by DOD Appropriations Act § 1010(b)]

An AEI who is no longer eligible for the subsidized COBRA premium either because of eligibility for coverage under another group health plan (other than limited coverage described above) or Medicare must notify the group health plan providing the subsidized COBRA coverage. The notice must be in writing and be provided in the time and manner that DOL may specify. [ARRA § 3001(a)(2)(C)] An AEI who fails to provide the required notice must pay a penalty equal to 110 percent of the premium subsidy received after termination of eligibility. [I.R.C. § 6720C(a) as added by ARRA § 3001(a)(13)(A)] No penalty will be imposed if failure to provide the required notice was due to reasonable cause and not to willful neglect. [I.R.C. § 6720C(b) as added by ARRA § 3001(a)(13)(A)]

The Department of Labor's Model COBRA Continuation Coverage Election Notice has been updated to reflect the COBRA premium subsidy and includes a model form that employers may provide to employees for this purpose.

The subsidy cut-off is triggered by *eligibility* for other health coverage even if the individual does not actually enroll for such coverage. [Notice 2009-27, 2009-16 I.R.B. 838]

Example 1. Zoe, an AEI, begins employment with a new employer on July 15, 2010 and is eligible to enroll in the new employer's plan with coverage effective August 1. However, Zoe declines the coverage and continues COBRA coverage. Although the eligibility for other coverage does not terminate Zoe's right to COBRA continuation coverage, the premium subsidy does not apply as of August 1, 2010.

Example 2. Carol and her husband, Bill, both AEIs, have COBRA coverage under the plan of Carol's former employer. Bill begins working for a new employer and is eligible to enroll for either self-only or family coverage under his new employer's plan. Bill opts for self-only coverage, while Carol remains covered by COBRA coverage. Although Carol is allowed to continue COBRA coverage, the premium subsidy is no longer available as of the date she became eligible for coverage under the plan of Bill's new employer.

Eligibility for retiree health coverage in lieu of COBRA coverage may or may not affect an AEI's eligibility for the subsidy. Eligibility for retiree health coverage will have no effect on the subsidy if the retiree health coverage is offered under the *same* group health plan as the COBRA coverage. However, if an AEI is eligible for retiree coverage under a *different* plan the subsidy will not apply.

Q 6:191   How is the COBRA premium subsidy treated for income tax purposes?

The COBRA premium subsidy is excluded from the gross income of an assistance-eligible individual (AEI). [I.R.C. § 139C as added by ARRA § 3001(a)(15)(A)]

However, the American Recovery and Reinvestment Act of 2009 provides a recapture rule for premium assistance provided to higher-income taxpayers. Under the recapture rule, if: (a) premium assistance is provided for any COBRA continuation coverage for the taxpayer, the taxpayer's spouse, or any dependent of the taxpayer during any portion of the tax year, and (b) the taxpayer's modified adjusted gross income (MAGI) for the tax year is more than $145,000 on a single return or $290,000 on a joint return, the taxpayer's income tax for the tax year will be increased by the amount of the premium assistance. A portion of the assistance is recaptured for taxpayers with MAGI between $125,000 and $145,000 on a single return or $250,000 and $290,000 on a joint return. [ARRA § 3001(b)(1)]

To avoid recapture, an individual can make a permanent election to waive the right to premium assistance. [ARRA § 3001(b)(3)] To waive the subsidy, an AEI must provide a signed and dated notification—which must make reference to a "permanent waiver"—to the employer or other person entitled to reimbursement for the COBRA subsidy (see Q 6:189). No notice is required to be given to the IRS or other government agency. If an AEI elects to waive the subsidy, the election may not be reversed and the individual may not receive the subsidy. [Notice 2009-27, 2009-16 I.R.B. 838]

On the other hand, the IRS notice makes it clear that an employer cannot effectively "waive" the subsidy for an AEI by refusing to provide the subsidy because the individual's income is too high. Even if an AEI's income is high enough that recapture would apply, COBRA coverage must be provided upon payment of 35 percent of the premium unless the AEI has notified the plan that he or she has elected to waive the subsidy.

For purposes of determining the gross income of the employer, the premium reduction is intended to be treated as an *employee* contribution to the group health plan. [Notice 2009-27, 2009-16 I.R.B. 838]

Q 6:192 Can an assistance-eligible individual change his or her health coverage election?

As a general rule, a COBRA beneficiary is only entitled to continue the coverage he or she had immediately prior to the COBRA qualifying event (see Q 6:111). However, the ARRA provides that an AEI may be given a special opportunity to change coverage options in conjunction with electing COBRA coverage.

The AEI may elect to enroll in different coverage only if the following conditions are met:

- The employer involved has determined that it will permit AEIs to enroll in different coverage;
- The premium for the different coverage is not more than the premium for coverage in which the individual was enrolled at the time of the qualifying event;
- The different coverage elected is also offered to active employees of the employer at the time the election is made; and
- The different coverage is not limited coverage

[ARRA § 3001(a)(1)(B)(ii)]

An AEI must make the election for different coverage not later than 90 days after the date of notice of the plan enrollment option, which must be provided as part of the notice of COBRA continuation coverage rights (see Q 6:193). Once an election of different coverage is made, it becomes COBRA continuation coverage, and must be continued for the entire COBRA period (generally 18 or 36 months) unless a change is otherwise permitted under the normal COBRA rules.

Q 6:193 What notices are required in connection with the COBRA premium subsidy?

The American Recovery and Reinvestment Act (ARRA) provides that the requirement to provide a notice of COBRA continuation coverage rights (see Qs

6:70–6:90) is not met unless the notice includes an additional notification about the availability of the premium reduction subsidy with respect to that COBRA coverage and a description of the option to enroll in different coverage if permitted by the employer (see Q: 6:192). [ARRA § 3001(a)(7)(A)(i)] A violation of this additional notice provision is also a violation of the notice requirements of the underlying COBRA provision.

The additional notification requirement may be met either by amending existing notice forms, or by including a separate document with the notice otherwise required. [ARRA § 3001(a)(7)(A)(iii)]

The additional notification must include:

- The forms necessary for establishing eligibility for the premium subsidy;
- The name, address, and telephone number of the plan administrator and any other person maintaining relevant information in connection with the premium subsidy;
- A description of the AEI's obligation to notify the plan providing continuation coverage of the AEI's eligibility for subsequent coverage under another group health plan or Medicare, and the penalty for failure to do so (see Q 6:190);
- A description, displayed in a prominent manner, of the qualified beneficiary's right to a reduced premium and any conditions on entitlement to the reduced premium; and
- A description of the qualified beneficiary's option to enroll in different coverage offered, if so permitted by the employer (see Q 6:192).

[ARRA § 3001(a)(7)(B)]

Chapter 7

Cafeteria Plans

Because the benefit needs of employees differ, cafeteria plans have become quite popular for the choices they offer from a menu of welfare benefit options. They can be a valuable benefit planning tool, allowing employers to add additional benefits on a subsidized basis. Cafeteria plans nevertheless entail unique and complex structural and operational requirements.

For smaller employers, the cafeteria plan nondiscrimination requirements, which require separate annual testing of both the plan as a whole and individual qualified benefits offered under the plan, can be particularly burdensome. To address this problem, the 2010 Health Reform Act creates a new SIMPLE cafeteria plan that provides a "safe harbor" from the nondiscrimination requirements.

This chapter reviews the basic concepts and tax requirements of cafeteria plans, as well as plan design considerations. The new SIMPLE cafeteria plan option is described in detail in this chapter.

The chapter reflects new proposed cafeteria plan regulations, which replace earlier proposed regulations that have been withdrawn. Although the new regulations are in proposed form, the IRS says employers can rely on them pending the issuance of final guidance.

2010 Health Reform Act

Q 7:1   How does the 2010 Health Reform Act affect cafeteria plans?

The provisions of the 2010 Health Reform Act—or the Patient Protection and Affordable Care Act [Pub L. No. 111-148 (Mar. 23, 2010)] (PPACA) as amended by the Health Care and Education Reconciliation Act of 2010 [Pub L. No. 111-152, 124 Stat. 1029 (Mar. 30, 2010)] (PPACA Reconciliation)—that *directly* affect health benefits provided through a cafeteria plan are not numerous, but they are significant.

The 2010 Health Reform Act:

- Requires group health plans offering dependent coverage—including plans offered under a cafeteria plan—to make coverage available for an adult child until the child turns age 26 (Q 7:13).
- Allows small employers to offer qualified health coverage through a health coverage Exchange as a qualified benefit under a cafeteria plan (Q 7:25).
- Imposes a $2,500 cap on contributions to a health care flexible spending arrangement (FSA) (Q 7:67).
- Prohibits health care FSAs from reimbursing expenses for over-the-counter (OTC) medicines or drugs (Q 7:68)
- Creates a SIMPLE cafeteria plan for small employers (Qs 7:96–7:99).

Bear in mind, however, that health coverage offered through a cafeteria plan must comply with the 2010 Health Reform Act provisions that apply to group health plans generally.

Basic Concepts

Q 7:2   What is a cafeteria plan?

A *cafeteria plan* is a written employer-provided plan that offers participants the opportunity to choose between at least one permitted taxable benefit (including cash) and at least one qualified employee benefit. [I.R.C. § 125(d); Prop. Treas. Reg. § 1.125-1(a)] Such a plan enables employees to have the opportunity to personalize their benefits to best suit their individual needs. The cafeteria plan must satisfy two types of requirements imposed by Section 125 of the Internal Revenue Code (Code).

The first set of requirements is structural, and violations will disqualify the entire plan so that no employee obtains the favorable tax benefits of Code Section 125. The second set of requirements pertains to nondiscrimination rules. Violations of these rules have adverse consequences only on the group (e.g., highly compensated employees or key employees) in whose favor discrimination is prohibited.

Q 7:3   Is an employer required to establish a cafeteria plan?

Although a cafeteria plan is the only way to offer employees a choice between taxable benefits or cash and tax-favored benefits for federal tax purposes, there is no federal law mandating that employers establish such plans. However, employers should check state law. A number of states have enacted legislation requiring employers to set up cafeteria plans for employees to pay for health insurance on a pre-tax basis. As we go to press, Massachusetts, Connecticut, Rhode Island, and Missouri have such laws on the books.

Q 7:4   What is the key requirement for having a Section 125 cafeteria plan?

The most important structural requirement and the defining characteristic of a tax-qualified cafeteria plan is that it must offer participants the choice between at least one permitted taxable benefit and at least one employer-provided qualified benefit. Qualified benefits generally are nontaxable benefits such as medical or dental coverage (see Q 7:18).

Permitted taxable benefits include cash and taxable benefits that are treated like cash. Taxable benefits that are treated like cash include property, employer-provided benefits that are taxable when received by the employee, and benefits purchased with after-tax employee contributions. [I.R.C. § 125(d)(1); Prop. Treas. Reg. § 1.125-1(a)] For example, long-term disability coverage is treated as cash if the cafeteria plan provides that an employee may purchase the coverage through the cafeteria plan with after-tax employee contributions or provides that the employee receiving such coverage is treated as having received cash compensation equal to the value of the coverage and then as having purchased the coverage with after-tax employee contributions. Other benefits that can be offered to employees on an after-tax basis include group-term life insurance, accident and health plan coverage, and dependent care assistance. [Prop. Treas. Reg. § 1.125-1(h)(1)]

A plan that offers taxable benefits other than permitted taxable benefits (called prohibited taxable benefits) will not qualify as a cafeteria plan. [Prop. Treas. Reg. § 1.125-1(i)]

A plan that offers employees only a choice between one or more qualified benefits is not a cafeteria plan. Similarly, a plan that offers only a choice of salary and permitted taxable benefits is not a cafeteria plan. [Prop. Treas. Reg. § 1.125-1(b)(4)]

Example 1. ABC Company offers its employees a medical plan with a high option and a low option. ABC employees who participate in either option must pay the applicable monthly employee portion of the premium on an after-tax basis. This is not a cafeteria plan. Employees are only being given a choice between two nontaxable benefits (the medical options).

Example 2. HLM Company offers its employees a medical plan and $50,000 of life insurance coverage. HLM employees who participate in either option obtain the coverage at no charge because the premium is entirely employer-paid. This is not a cafeteria plan because it provides only two nontaxable benefits (medical and life insurance coverage).

Example 3. Big Company offers its employees a plan under which they have the opportunity to have medical coverage if they reduce their salary by the amount of the employee premiums. This is a cafeteria plan. Employees have the choice of receiving salary only or reduced salary plus medical coverage.

Note. Under the IRS's proposed regulations, a plan such as Big Company's that offers as its sole benefit an election between cash and payment of the employee share of the employer-provided accident and health insurance premium (excludable from the employee's gross income under Section 106) is called a premium-only plan. [Prop. Treas. Reg. § 1.125-1(a)(5)]

To be valid, a cafeteria plan must also satisfy the plan format and nondiscrimination requirements of Code Section 125.

Q 7:5 Is a choice between cash and a qualified benefit available through pretax salary reductions enough to qualify as a cafeteria plan?

Yes. Salary reduction contributions are treated, for tax purposes, as employer contributions toward qualified benefits. [Prop. Treas. Reg. § 1.125-1(r)(2)] Thus, an employee's choice between (1) salary or (2) reduced salary plus one or more qualified benefits (see Qs 7:18–7:27) meets the criteria for a cafeteria plan. Of course, the plan must also meet all of the other structural requirements imposed by Code Section 125 to qualify as a cafeteria plan.

Under proposed regulations, a cafeteria plan is permitted to require employees to elect to pay the employees' share of any qualified benefit through salary reduction and not with after-tax employee contributions. A cafeteria plan is also permitted to pay reasonable cafeteria plan administrative fees through salary reduction amounts, and these salary reduction amounts are excludable from an employee's gross income. [Prop. Treas. Reg. § 1.125-1(r)(1)]

Q 7:6 May an employer make cafeteria plan contributions over and above employee salary reduction contributions?

Yes. A cafeteria plan may also provide that the employer contributions will or may be made on behalf of employees equal to (or up to) specified amounts (or specified percentages of compensation) and that these nonelective contributions can be used by employees to elect of benefits through the plan.

Nonelective employer contributions may take the form of "employer flex-credits" that can be used only for one or more qualified benefits (but not for cash or a taxable benefit). [Prop. Treas. Reg. §§ 1.125-1(r)(3); 1.125-5(b)]

> **Practice Pointer.** Because a key requirement of a cafeteria plan is that an employee must be offered an election between at least one taxable benefit (including cash) and one qualified benefit, a plan would not qualify as a cafeteria plan if contributions are limited to flex-credits that can only be used for qualified benefits.

> **Example.** XYZ, Inc. offers its employees an election between an employer flex-credit and qualified benefits. If an employee does not elect to apply the entire employer flex-credit to qualified benefits, he or she will receive no cash or other taxable benefit for the unused employer flex-credit. The XYZ plan is not a cafeteria plan because it does not offer an election between at least one taxable benefit and at least one nontaxable qualified benefit.

Q 7:7   What is the importance of complying with Code Section 125?

Under the Code, the unrestricted ability to receive compensation generally is taxable whether or not an employee in fact takes it: the employee is considered to be in "constructive receipt" of income. Code Section 125 provides a statutory exception to the doctrine of constructive receipt of income. It permits employers to make benefit choices available to employees as an alternative to cash without subjecting the employees to automatic taxation of cash or currently taxable benefits—even if not elected—just because they were made available to employees.

How Code Section 125 shelters employees from constructive receipt of income can be illustrated by comparing what happens when a valid cafeteria plan does not exist to what happens when one does.

Without a cafeteria plan. Generally, an employee who is offered a choice between cash (including taxable benefits) and nontaxable benefits will be treated, for tax purposes, as having received the cash. This is true even if the employee declines the cash and elects the nontaxable benefits before the year in which the cash would have been received. The employee is required to include the cash in gross income at the time he or she could have received it. [Prop. Treas. Reg. § 1.125-1, Q&A-9; Treas. Reg. § 1.451-2]

In a technical advice memorandum, the Internal Revenue Service (IRS) considered the case of an employer that did not have a formal cafeteria plan under Code Section 125. The employer did, however, give its new employees the option of receiving or declining health insurance coverage. If a new employee declined the coverage, he or she received higher compensation than he or she would have if the health insurance coverage had been chosen. The difference between the compensation paid if the employee elected health insurance coverage and the compensation paid if the employee declined health insurance coverage was not necessarily the actual cost of the health insurance coverage offered.

The IRS's decision in this matter illustrates that merely having a nondiscriminatory plan is not enough; the plan must meet all of the structural requirements of Code Section 125, including the written plan requirement, in order to be a valid cafeteria plan. Because no written plan existed in this instance, the IRS held that an employee who elected to receive the health insurance coverage would be taxed as if he or she had received the cash compensation that he or she would have received if the health insurance coverage had been refused. In the IRS's view, the election of health insurance coverage was, in effect, an assignment of future income. The employee therefore should be treated as if he or she had received the additional compensation and then paid for the health insurance coverage.

In addition, the IRS noted that in enacting the Section 125 rules, including nondiscrimination standards, Congress provided a specified method for giving employees a choice between cash and tax-free benefits. To permit tax-free treatment without any cafeteria plan in effect would violate congressional intent.

The IRS concluded that the additional income, based on the difference in compensation between electing and not electing health insurance coverage, was subject to income tax withholding and to FICA (Social Security and Medicare) and FUTA (federal unemployment) taxes. [Priv. Ltr. Rul. 9406002]

> **Practice Pointer.** Because the health coverage is treated as having been paid for with after-tax dollars, an employee in this situation may be able to claim the payments as a medical expense deduction. However, medical expenses are deductible only to the extent that they exceed 7.5 percent of adjusted gross income. [I.R.C. § 213]. Moreover, even if an employee's health premium costs exceed that threshold, a deduction is available only if the employee itemizes deductions rather than claiming the standard deduction for the year. Therefore, employees are likely to obtain little or no tax benefit from their payments.

> **Note.** Starting in 2013, the 2010 Health Reform Act increases the medical expense deduction threshold to 10 percent of adjusted gross income. However, for tax years beginning in 2013 through 2016, the 7.5 percent threshold will continue to apply if either the taxpayer or the taxpayer's spouse has reached age 65 before the end of the year. [I.R.C. § 213 as amended by PPACA § 9013]

With a cafeteria plan. If a choice is made available under a cafeteria plan that satisfies all of the structural and nondiscrimination requirements of Code Section 125, the result will be entirely different. Code Section 125 protects participants from being treated as having constructively received the cash or currently taxable benefits. It is an exception to the general income tax rules governing constructive receipt of income. As a result, a participant will not be required to include the cash (or currently taxable benefits) in gross income before the cash actually becomes currently available to the participant merely because he or she has the opportunity to choose between cash and the qualified benefits under the cafeteria plan. [Prop. Treas. Reg. §§ 1.125-1, Q&A-9, 1.125-2, Q&A-2]

Zero-tolerance enforcement. The proposed regulations take a hard line on cafeteria plan compliance. According to the regulations, Code Section 125 is the sole means by which an employer can offer employees an election between taxable and nontaxable benefits without the election resulting in inclusion in gross income by employees. Therefore, if a plan offering employees an election been taxable benefits (including cash) and nontaxable benefits does not meet the Code Section 125 requirements, the employee will have gross income regardless of what benefit was elected and when the election was made. The regulations provide that the employee must include in gross income the value of the taxable benefit with the greatest value the employee could have elected to receive, even if the employee actually elected only nontaxable benefits. The amount of the taxable benefit is includable in the employee's income in the year in which the employee would have actually received the taxable benefit if elected. Moreover, the regulations make it clear that this result applies even if the employee's election between the nontaxable benefits and taxable benefits was made prior to the year in which the employee would actually have received the taxable benefits. [Prop. Treas. Reg. § 1.125-1(b)]

The proposed regulations contain detailed requirements for what must be included in a written cafeteria plan document. And here again, noncompliance carries a heavy price tag. If there is no written plan document or the plan document fails to satisfy the written plan requirements, the plan will not qualify as a cafeteria plan resulting in gross income to employees. [Prop. Treas. Reg. § 1.125-1(c)(6)] What's more, even if the plan document is in order, failure to operate in compliance with the plan document and the regulations will disqualify the plan and result in gross income to employees. [Prop. Treas. Reg. § 1.125-1(b)(7)]

> **Practice Pointer.** It is significant that the proposed regulations do not offer relief for small problems with a plan document or operation of a plan. This zero-tolerance approach has been roundly criticized in the employer community. For example, in its comments to the IRS on the proposed regulations, the Employer's Council on Flexible Compensation recommends revising the regulations to provide that written plan defects or operational defects of a *de minimis* nature will not disqualify a plan or result in adverse tax consequences to employees if the plan sponsor takes appropriate action to correct the defect or prevent the defect from recurring.

Q 7:8 Why are cafeteria plans economically attractive to employers and employees?

Cafeteria plans can generate significant tax savings for both employers and employees. Such plans typically are structured to permit employees to pay for covered benefits on a pretax basis by electing to reduce their salaries by the corresponding contribution amount. As a result, compensation reported on

Form W-2 is less, and employees may achieve savings in federal income, FICA, and FUTA taxes. In most jurisdictions, state and local taxes are also reduced. In fact, numerical examples included in summary plan descriptions for these plans often will illustrate that the participant may possibly achieve a slight increase in take-home pay as a result of pretax payment of premiums.

Correspondingly, the taxable compensation paid by the employer is reduced. Thus, the employer's aggregate FICA and FUTA savings on salary reduction amounts make cafeteria plans economically attractive to employers.

Written Plan Requirement

Q 7:9   Must a cafeteria plan be in writing?

Yes. Code Section 125 requires that a cafeteria plan be a separate written benefit plan. [I.R.C. § 125(d)(1); Prop. Treas. Reg. § 1.125-1, Q&A-2]

This requirement is contained in the statute and therefore constitutes a structural requirement. That is, a written plan is one of several absolute statutory requirements for having a valid cafeteria plan. Failure to commit the plan to writing means that a cafeteria plan as defined in Code Section 125 does not exist, and all participants lose the benefit of Code Section 125's protection from constructive receipt of income. (See Q 7:7.)

The IRS proposed regulations contain detailed requirements for what must be included in a written cafeteria plan document. Noncompliance carries a heavy price tag. If there is no written plan document or if the plan document fails to satisfy the written plan requirements, the plan will not qualify as a cafeteria plan, resulting in gross income to employees. [Prop. Treas. Reg. § 1.125-1(c)(6)]

Q 7:10   What must the plan document of a cafeteria plan contain?

The proposed cafeteria plan regulations expand on the written plan requirement to specify certain content that must be included in the plan document. [Prop. Treas. Reg. § 1.125-1(c)] Under the proposed regulations, a written plan, which may comprise multiple documents, must contain all of the following information:

1. A specific description of each of the benefits available through the plan, including the periods during which the benefits are provided (the periods of coverage);

2. The plan's rules governing participation, and specifically requiring that all participants in the plan be employees;

3. The procedures governing employees' elections under the plan, including the period when elections may be made, the periods for which elections are effective, and a provision specifying that elections are irrevocable, except to the extent that optional change in status rules (see Q 7:52) are included in the plan;

4. The manner in which employer contributions may be made under the plan (for example, through an employee's salary reduction election or by nonelective contributions or both);

5. The maximum amount of elective salary reduction contributions available to an employee through the plan expressed as a maximum dollar amount or a maximum percentage of compensation, or the method for determining the maximum dollar amount;

6. For contributions to section 401(k) retirement plans, the maximum amount of elective contributions available to any employee through the plan, expressed as a maximum dollar amount or maximum percentage of compensation that may be contributed;

7. The plan year of the cafeteria plan;

8. If the plan offers paid time off, the required ordering rule for using nonelective and elective paid time off;

9. If the plan includes flexible spending arrangements (FSAs), provisions complying with special FSA requirements such as uniform coverage rule and use-or-lose rules (see Qs 7:29, 7:73);

10. If the plan includes a grace period for using FSA contributions, provisions complying with the grace period requirements (see Q 7:30); and

11. If the plan allows distributions from a health flexible spending arrangement (FSA) to an employee's health savings account (HSA), provisions complying with the distribution requirements (see Q 7:79).

Q 7:11   Can a written cafeteria plan be amended?

Yes. A cafeteria plan may be amended at any time during a plan year. However, the amendment can apply only for periods after the later of the adoption date or the effective date of the amendment. For an amendment adding a new benefit, the cafeteria plan must pay or reimburse only those expenses for the new benefit that are incurred after the later of the amendment's adoption date or effective date. [Prop. Treas. Reg. § 1.125-1(c)(5)]

If a cafeteria plan includes the choice of receiving benefits contained in other separate written plans, such as a group term life insurance plan or a medical plan, the benefits under those other plans need not be fully described in the cafeteria plan document as well. Instead, an employer is permitted to incorporate them by reference. If, however, the cafeteria plan offers different maximum levels of coverage, for example, those differences must be described in the cafeteria plan document. [Prop. Treas. Reg. § 1.125-1(c)(4)]

Thus, the proposed cafeteria plan regulations clearly recognize two forms of cafeteria plans: (1) an integrated plan, in which all of the benefits are described, and (2) a "spider-type" plan that refers to other, freestanding plans (the name comes from the fact that a diagram of this type of plan would look like a spider's legs reaching out from a main body).

Eligible Employees

Q 7:12   Who can participate in a cafeteria plan?

All participants in a Section 125 cafeteria plan must be employees. [I.R.C. § 125(d)(1)(A); Prop. Treas. Reg. § 1.125-1(a)(1)] A cafeteria plan cannot cover self-employed individuals or more-than-2-percent shareholders in S corporations (see Q 7:16). It should be noted, however, that full-time, nonemployee life insurance salespeople are considered employees. [I.R.C. § 7701(a)(20)] For cafeteria plan purposes, employees include both common-law and leased employees. [Prop. Treas. Reg. § 1.125-1(g)(1)]

A dual status individual who is an employee of an employer and also provides services to the employer as an independent contractor or director may participate in a cafeteria plan solely in his or her capacity as an employee. [Prop. Treas. Reg. § 1.125-1(g)(2)]

> **Example.** Blake is an employee as well as a director of the Lance Corporation. Blake's compensation as an employee is $50,000, and he receives $3,000 per year in director's fees. Blake wants to acquire health care coverage with a price tag of $5,000 through Lance Corporation's cafeteria plan. Blake can elect to reduce his employee compensation by $5,000 to acquire the health care coverage, but may not make any election with respect to the director's fees.

Former employees may participate in an employer's cafeteria plan. However a plan that is maintained primarily for the benefit of former employees will not qualify as a cafeteria plan. [Prop. Treas. Reg. § 1.125-1(g)(3)]

The requirement that all cafeteria plan participants be employees is a structural requirement because it is stated in the statute. It is thus one of several absolute statutory requirements for having a valid cafeteria plan. As a result, inclusion in a cafeteria plan of non-employees such as more-than-2-percent shareholders in an S corporation would cause it to be invalid, and the favorable tax treatment of Code Section 125 would be unavailable to any participant.

Q 7:13   May a cafeteria plan cover a participant's spouse, dependents, or other beneficiaries?

Yes. Although spouses and dependents cannot be active participants and cannot be given the opportunity to select among cafeteria plan benefits or to purchase specific alternatives offered under the plan, a qualified cafeteria plan may provide benefits to the spouses and dependents of participants. In other words, an employee's spouse and dependents can benefit from the employee's selection of an option for them, such as family medical insurance coverage. If a participant dies, his or her spouse will not be treated as an active participant merely because he or she may have to choose among various death benefit settlement options or distribution options. [Prop. Treas. Reg. § 1.125-1(g)(4)]

The proposed regulations make it clear that a cafeteria plan may allow an employee to elect accident and health coverage for an individual who is not the employee's spouse or dependent. However, the coverage will be treated as a taxable benefit. [Prop. Treas. Reg. § 1.125-1(h)(2)] On the other hand, payments or reimbursements received under the accident or health coverage will be tax free.

The 2010 Health Reform Act requires group health plans offering coverage of dependent children to make that coverage available until the children attain age 26. (See chapter 5 for a complete discussion of the application and effective date of this new requirement.) The 2010 Health Reform Act specifically extends the general exclusion under Code Section 105 for reimbursements of medical care expenses under an employer-provided accident or health plan to an employee's child who has not attained age 27 as of the end of the taxable year. [I.R.C. § 105(b) as amended by PPACA Reconciliation § 1004] This change also applies to Code Section 106, the exclusion for employer-provided coverage under an accident or health plan. [Notice 2010-38, 2010-20 I.R.B. 682] Consequently, coverage for an adult child provided through a cafeteria plan qualifies as a nontaxable qualified benefit.

Q 7:14 May a Section 125 cafeteria plan cover former employees?

Yes. Former employees are considered to be employees for purposes of a cafeteria plan. Still, a Section 125 cafeteria plan cannot be established predominantly for the benefit of an employer's former employees. An employer could not, for instance, maintain a retiree-only cafeteria plan. [Prop. Treas. Reg. § 1.125-1(g)(3)]

Q 7:15 Must a cafeteria plan cover former employees who elected COBRA continuation coverage?

Yes. To the extent that any benefit option under a cafeteria plan is a group health plan within the meaning of Code Section 4980B or ERISA Sections 601 *et seq.*, COBRA will apply to that health benefit option. As a result, any individual who satisfies the requirements of a COBRA qualified beneficiary has the right to elect COBRA continuation of that health benefit option (see Q 6:110).

The proposed regulations specifically allow a cafeteria plan to provide for payment of COBRA premiums (see Q 7:24).

For the effect of after-tax COBRA contributions on the cafeteria plan exemption from the ERISA trust requirement, see Q 7:86.

Q 7:16   May a cafeteria plan cover partners, sole proprietors, or S corporation shareholders?

No. A specific statutory requirement of Code Section 125 is that only employees may participate in a cafeteria plan. Partners and sole proprietors, who are self-employed, may not be treated as employees for cafeteria plan purposes. [I.R.C. §§ 125(d)(1)(A), 401(c); Prop. Treas. Reg. § 1.125-1(g)(2)] Additionally, an employee who is a more-than-2-percent shareholder in an S corporation on any day during the taxable year cannot participate in a cafeteria plan maintained by the S corporation. [I.R.C. § 1372; Prop. Treas. Reg. § 1.125-1(g)(2)]

However, a sole proprietorship can maintain a cafeteria plan covering employees of the business, but not the sole proprietor. Similarly, a partnership or S corporation can maintain a cafeteria plan covering employees, but not a partner or more-than-2-percent shareholder.

> **Practice Pointer.** The rule that only employees may participate in a cafeteria plan can be quite significant for benefit design in the dependent care area. If an employer maintains a dependent care program as an independent benefit, a partner, a sole proprietor, or a more-than-2-percent S corporation shareholder is eligible; however, if the program is offered under a cafeteria plan, any of those persons must be excluded.

Permitted Benefit Choices

Q 7:17   When can a benefit be treated as cash?

As noted above (see Q 7:4), the key requirement for a Section 125 cafeteria plan is that it must offer a choice between permitted taxable benefits (including cash) and one or more employer-provided qualified benefits. Benefits other than cash are permitted if they are treated like cash for tax purposes. Taxable benefits that are treated like cash include property, employer-provided benefits that are taxable when received by the employee, and benefits purchased with after-tax employee contributions. [I.R.C. § 125(d)(1); Prop. Treas. Reg. § 1.125-1(a)]

Thus, for example, if long-term disability insurance is included in the cafeteria plan and employees are required to pay applicable employee premiums on an after-tax basis, the long-term disability coverage will be treated as a currently taxable benefit or cash. (See Q 7:21 for the tax effect of offering disability benefits on an after-tax basis through a cafeteria plan.)

Q 7:18   Which benefits are qualified benefits?

The IRS proposed regulations provide that the following specific benefits are qualified benefits and can be provided on a pretax basis under a cafeteria plan:

- Accident or health insurance coverage that is excludable from income under Code Section 105 or Code Section 106, including self-insured medical reimbursement plan such as FSAs (see chapter 3 and Qs 7:66–7:84)

- Adoption assistance excludable under Code Section 137 (see chapter 8)

- Group term life insurance coverage for benefits of up to $50,000 that are excludable from gross income under Code Section 79 (see chapter 11 and Q 7:19)

- Dependent care assistance plan coverage that qualifies under Code Section 129 (see chapter 8)

- Participation in a qualified cash-or-deferred arrangement that is part of a profit sharing or stock bonus plan under Code Section 401(k)

- An accidental death and dismemberment policy that is excludable under Code Section 106 (see chapter 12)

- Long- or short-term disability coverage that is excludable under Code Section 106 (see chapter 10)

- Certain plans maintained by educational organizations to provide post-retirement group term life insurance as provided in Code Section 125(d)(2)(C)

- Contributions to health savings accounts (see chapter 3)

- Premiums for COBRA continuation coverage (see chapter 6 and Q 7:24)

[I.R.C. § 125(f); Prop. Treas. Reg. §§ 1.125-1(a)(3)]

Long-term care insurance. The Health Insurance Portability and Accountability Act of 1996 (HIPAA) [Pub. L. No. 104-191, 110 Stat. 1936 (1996)] expressly prohibits the inclusion of group long-term care insurance as a qualified benefit under cafeteria plans. [I.R.C. §§ 106(c), 125(f), as amended by HIPAA § 321(c)]

Q 7:19 Can a cafeteria plan offer group term life insurance coverage in excess of $50,000?

Yes, it can. However, special rules apply.

As indicated above (see Q 7:18), group term life insurance in an amount up to $50,000 that is excludable under Code Section 79 is a qualified benefit. As such, the benefit can be paid for with pretax salary reduction amounts or employer flex-credits. Thus, nothing is included in an employee's income with respect to coverage up to $50,000.

If a cafeteria plan offers group term life insurance in excess of $50,000, the proposed regulations provide that the premium for that coverage can also be paid for with pretax salary reductions or employer flex-credits. However, the *cost* of coverage exceeding coverage of $50,000 must be included in the employee's gross income. For this purpose, the cost of group-term life insurance is shown in Treasury Regulations Section 1.79-3(d)(2), Table I (Table I). [Prop. Treas. Reg. § 1.125-1(k)]

Example 1. Nell participates in a cafeteria plan that allows employees to elect salary reduction contributions for group term life insurance. Nell, who is age 42, elected salary reduction of $200 for $150,000 of group-term life insurance. Result: Nell's $200 salary reduction is excludable from income. However, because Nell's life insurance coverage exceeds $50,000, the Table I cost of the excess coverage must be included her income. The Table I cost is $120 for $100,000 of group-term life insurance for an individual between ages 40 to 44. Therefore, $120 is included in Nell's income.

The rule in the new proposed regulations differs from a longstanding IRS notice [Notice 89-110, 1989-2 C.B. 447], which provides that an employee electing group-term life insurance coverage in excess of $50,000 must include in income the greater of the Table I cost or the salary reduction amount or employer flex-credit used for the coverage. Under that rule, Nell's $200 salary reduction would be included in income because it exceeds the Table I cost of the excess coverage.

Practice Pointer. Although the new regulations are in proposed form, the IRS says they may be relied on pending the issuance of final regulations.

A cafeteria plan may also allow employees to pay for group-term life insurance on an after-tax basis. In that case, the cost of coverage in excess $50,000 that is included in income is reduced by the after-tax contributions.

Example 2. The facts are the same as those in Example 1, except that Nell elects a salary reduction of $100 and makes an after-tax contribution of $100 toward the purchase of group-term life insurance coverage. Result: Nell's $100 salary reduction is excludable from income. In addition, the $120 Table 1 cost for Nell's excess coverage is reduced by Nell's $100 of after-tax contributions. Therefore, $20 is includable in Nell's gross income on account of the $100,000 of excess group-term life insurance coverage.

In addition to offering group-term life insurance through a cafeteria plan, an employer may provide employees with group-term life insurance coverage outside of the plan. In determining the amount of coverage in excess of $50,000, coverage both inside and outside the cafeteria plan is taken into account.

Q 7:20   Is group term life insurance on the lives of a participant's spouse and children a qualified benefit?

Generally, no. Group term life insurance on the lives of a participant's spouse and children is not considered to be a qualified benefit because it is not excludable from income under Code Section 79. Moreover, even it is treated as a *de minimis* excludable fringe benefit under Code Section 132, it is not permitted to be included in the cafeteria plan as a qualified benefit.

The IRS proposed regulations specifically provide that group-term life insurance on the life of anyone other than an employee is a nonqualified benefit that may not be offered by a cafeteria plan. And that is true whether the benefit is or is not includable in the employee's gross income. [Prop. Treas. Reg. § 1.125-1(q)]

Q 7:21 Is long-term disability insurance a qualified benefit, and are there any special considerations in including such coverage in a cafeteria plan?

Employer-provided long-term disability (LTD) coverage meets the definition of a qualified benefit because it is accident or health insurance under Code Section 106 and the monthly value of coverage is excluded from income under Code Section 106. The IRS proposed regulations make it clear that both long- and short-term disability coverage are qualified benefits that may be offered under a cafeteria plan. [Prop. Treas. Reg. § 1.125-1(a)(3)(E)] Moreover, the proposed regulations provide that an LTD policy paying disability benefits over more than one year does not violate the prohibition against deferring compensation through a cafeteria plan. [Prop. Treas. Reg. § 1.125-1(p)(2)]

The *benefits* payable under an LTD plan are taxable to employees, however, if the benefits are employer-provided under Code Section 105. Although Code Section 105 excludes employer-provided payments for LTD coverage from gross income, the income benefit payments from employer-provided coverage are included in gross income. As a result, taxation of disability benefits paid through a cafeteria plan will occur, for example, if employees are permitted to make pretax payments for LTD coverage. This is because pretax payments are, for tax purposes only, treated as employer contributions; therefore, LTD coverage paid for in such a manner is treated as employer-provided.

Practice Pointer. Although benefits under an LTD plan are taxable to the employee if the coverage is paid for by the employer, they are excluded from the employee's gross income if the employee pays for the coverage. The employer may wish to provide LTD coverage under the cafeteria plan on both a pretax and after-tax basis. If participants in a cafeteria plan elect to purchase LTD coverage with after-tax dollars, that benefit will be treated as cash for purposes of the cash-or-qualified-benefit choice under the cafeteria plan. However, any disability benefits paid to the employee will be excluded from tax.

Q 7:22 Is a group legal services plan a qualified benefit?

No. Coverage under a group legal services plan that qualified under Code Section 120 previously was a qualified benefit for cafeteria plan purposes. The income exclusion for such services expired on June 30, 1992, however, and has not been reinstated by Congress. Group legal services therefore are no longer a qualified benefit under a cafeteria plan, but a fringe benefit (see chapter 13).

Q 7:23 Are there any tax-favored benefits that are not qualified benefits?

Yes, some tax-favored benefits are not qualified benefits. The IRS proposed regulations list the following nonqualified benefits that cannot be included in a cafeteria plan:

- Scholarships and fellowships described in Code Section 117 (see chapter 14)
- Employer-provided meals and lodging described in Code Section 119 (see chapter 13)
- Educational assistance described in Code Section 127 (see chapter 14);
- Fringe benefits described in Code Section 132 (see chapter 13);
- Long-term care insurance, or any product that is advertised, marketed, or offered as long-term care insurance (see chapter 9);
- Long-term care services (see chapter 9);
- Group-term life insurance on the life of any individual other than an employee whether includable in or excludable from the employee's gross income (see chapter 13);
- Health reimbursement arrangements (HRAs) that provide for carryover of unused reimbursement amounts (see chapter 3);
- Contributions to Archer medical savings accounts (MSAs) (see chapter 3); and
- Elective deferrals to a Section 403(b) plan

The proposed regulations make it clear that a plan that offers a nonqualified benefit is not a cafeteria plan. Employees' elections between taxable and nontaxable benefits through such a plan will result in the elected benefit being included in gross income. [Prop. Treas. Reg. § 1.125-1(q)]

Practice Pointer. Although long-term care insurance or services are non-qualified benefits that cannot be provided directly by a cafeteria plan, they can nonetheless be acquired indirectly through a plan. The proposed regulations make it clear that if a cafeteria plan offers HSA contributions as an option, funds from the HSA may be used to pay for long-term care insurance premiums or for long-term care services. [Prop. Treas. Reg. § 1.125-1(q)(3)]

Q 7:24 When can premiums for COBRA health care continuation coverage be paid through a cafeteria plan?

COBRA premiums are qualified benefits that can be offered by a cafeteria plan if the following conditions are met:

1. The premiums are excludable from an employee's income under Code Section 106 (see Q 3:129) or
2. The premiums are for the accident and health plan of the employer sponsoring the cafeteria plan, even if the fair market value of the premiums is included in an employee's income. [Prop. Treas. Reg. § 1.125-1(l)]

Example 1. Omega Corporation's cafeteria plan offers employees the option of electing cash, employer-provided accident and health benefits, or other qualified benefits. Omega's plan allows employees to make midyear election changes on account of certain changes in status (see Q 7:52), including a switch from full-time to part-time work. Abe, an Omega employee, switches from full-time to part-time status and loses coverage under Omega's health plan. He elects COBRA continuation coverage and changes his cafeteria plan election to reduce his salary in order to pay the COBRA premiums as permitted by Omega's plan. Abe's COBRA premiums are qualified benefits that are excludable from income under Code Section 125.

Example 2. Billy just started working for Omega. When he quit his previous job, he elected COBRA coverage under his former employer's plan. Billy will not be eligible to participate in Omega's health care plan for several months. Therefore, Billy elects to reduce his salary so as to pay his COBRA premiums through Omega's cafeteria plan. Billy's COBRA premiums are qualified benefits that are excludable from income under Code Section 125.

Example 3. Omega employee Charlie and his wife were both covered by Omega's health plan until their divorce became final in midyear. As of the date of the divorce, Charlie's ex-wife elects COBRA coverage under Omega's plan. Charlie changes his cafeteria plan election to pay his ex-wife's COBRA premiums. Accident and health coverage for a former spouse is a permitted cafeteria plan benefit. However, the premium payments must be made with after-tax dollars.

Q 7:25 Can payment or reimbursement of an employee's premiums for individual accident and health insurance be included as a cafeteria plan option?

Yes. Under the IRS proposed regulations, the payment or reimbursement of employees' substantiated individual health insurance premiums is excludable from employees' gross income under Code Section 106 and is a qualified benefit for purposes of Code Section 125. [Prop. Treas. Reg. § 1.125-1(m)]

Payments or reimbursements may be made in the following ways:

1. The cafeteria plan reimburses each employee directly for the amount of the employee's substantiated health insurance premium;

2. The cafeteria plan issues the employee a check payable to the health insurance company for the amount of the employee's health insurance premium, which the employee is obligated to tender to the insurance company; or

3. The cafeteria plan issues a check for the amount of the employee's health insurance premium that is payable jointly to the employee and the insurance company.

These reimbursements must be made directly by the cafeteria plan. A health FSA may not reimburse the employee's premiums for accident and health insurance.

Starting in 2014, the 2010 Health Reform Act provides for the establishment of Exchanges in each state through which individuals and qualified small employers with up to 100 employees can purchase coverage under a qualified health plan (QHP) that provides certain essential benefits (see chapter 3).

[PPACA § 1311(b)] The Health Reform Act provides that reimbursement of premiums for coverage under a QHP offered through an Exchange will be treated as a qualified benefit under a cafeteria plan if the sponsoring employer is a qualified small employer for purposes of the Exchange. Otherwise, reimbursement (or direct payment) of premiums for coverage under a QHP offered through an Exchange will not be treated as a qualified benefit under a cafeteria plan. [I.R.C. § 125(f)(3) as added by PPACA § 1515]

Q 7:26   Can a cafeteria plan ever offer deferred compensation as a qualified benefit?

As a general rule, a plan that offers a benefit that defers the receipt of compensation is not a cafeteria plan. [Prop. Treas. Reg. § 1.125-1(o)(1)] A plan that permits employees to carry over unused elective contributions, after-tax contributions, or plan benefits from one plan year to another defers compensation. This is the case regardless of how the contributions or benefits are used by the employee in the subsequent plan year (for example, whether they are automatically or electively converted into another taxable or nontaxable benefit in the subsequent plan year or used to provide additional benefits of the same type). Similarly, a cafeteria plan defers compensation if the plan permits employees to use contributions for one plan year to purchase a benefit that will be provided in a subsequent plan year.

Prohibited deferral of compensation also includes offering insurance with a savings or investment feature, such as whole life insurance or group universal life insurance.

If a plan defers compensation, any election between taxable and nontaxable benefits will result in gross income to the employees. [Prop. Treas. Reg. § 1.125-1(o)(2)]

There are, however, important exceptions to the no-deferral rule.

401(k) plans. A cafeteria plan can offer deferred compensation as a qualified benefit if the plan offers an option to make elective contributions under a cash-or-deferred arrangement that qualifies as a 401(k) plan. [I.R.C. § 125(d)(2); Prop. Treas. Reg. § 1.125-1(o)(3)(ii)]

Educational organization life insurance plans. There is a special exception for certain postretirement group life insurance plans maintained by educational institutions. [I.R.C. § 125(d)(2)(C); Prop. Reg. § 1.125-1(o)(iii)]

HSA contributions. Contributions to HSAs (but not Archer MSAs) are permitted to be made through a cafeteria plan even though unused amounts can be carried over from year to year. [I.R.C. § 125(d)(2)(D); Prop. Reg. § 1.125-1(o)(3)(iv)]

Accident and health insurance benefits relating to more than one year. The IRS proposed regulations provide that an accident and health insurance policy may include certain benefits that relate to more than one year without violating the prohibition against deferred compensation. [Prop. Treas. Reg. § 1.125-1(p)(1)] Permitted benefits include:

- Credit toward the deductible for unreimbursed covered expenses incurred in prior periods;
- Reasonable lifetime maximum limit on benefits;
- Level premiums;
- Premium waiver during disability;
- Guaranteed renewability of coverage without further evidence of insurability (but not guaranty of the amount of premium upon renewal);
- Coverage for a specified accidental injury;
- Coverage for a specified disease or illness, including payments at initial diagnosis of the specified disease or illness, and progressive payments of a set amount per month following the initial diagnosis (sometimes referred to as *progressive diagnosis payments*); and
- Payment of a fixed amount per day (or other period) of hospitalization.

These benefits are permitted only if no part of any benefit is used in one plan year to purchase a benefit in a subsequent plan year; the policy remains in effect only as long as premiums are timely paid on a current basis; there is no investment fund or cash value available for premium payments; and no part of any premium payment is held in a separate account for a participant or beneficiary.

Long-term disability benefits relating to more than one year. Under the proposed regulations, a long-term disability policy paying disability benefits over more than one year does not violate the prohibition against deferred compensation. [Prop. Treas. Reg. § 1.125-1(p)(2)]

Reasonable premium rebates or policy dividends. The proposed regulations also provide that reasonable premium rebates or policy dividends relating to cafeteria plan benefits won't be treated as prohibited deferred compensation so long as the rebates or dividends are paid before the close of the 12-month period following the close of the plan year to which the rebates or dividends relate. [Prop. Treas. Reg. § 1.125-1(p)(3)]

Two-year vision or dental insurance coverage. Under the proposed regulations, a cafeteria plan can require employees to make a two-year coverage election for vision or dental insurance (called a two-year "lock-in") provided premiums for each plan year are paid at least annually and salary reduction or flex credits from the first year cannot be used to pay for the second year. [Prop. Treas. Reg. § 1.125-1(p)(4)]

Advance payments for orthodontia. A health flexible spending arrangement (FSA) in a cafeteria plan is permitted, but not required, to reimburse employees for orthodontia services before the services are provided but only to the extent that the employee has actually made the payments in advance of the orthodontia services in order to receive the services. These orthodontia services are deemed to be incurred when the employee makes the advance payment. Reimbursing advance payments does not violate the prohibition against deferring compensation. [Prop. Treas. Reg. § 1.125-5(k)(3)(i)]

Reimbursement for durable medical equipment. A health FSA in a cafeteria plan that reimburses employees for medical equipment with a useful life extending beyond the period of coverage during which the expense is incurred does not provide deferred compensation. For example, a health FSA is permitted to reimburse the cost of a wheelchair for an employee. [Prop. Treas. Reg. § 1.125-5(k)(3)(ii)]

Payment of accident and health insurance premiums for the first month of the following plan year. Finally the proposed regulations provide that salary reduction amounts for the last month of a cafeteria plan year can be used to pay accident and health insurance premiums for the first month of the following plan year if such prepayment is done consistently for all plan participants. [Prop. Treas. Reg. § 1.125-1(p)(5)]

Example. Sigma Corporation maintains a calendar-year cafeteria plan for its employees, who are paid biweekly. The plan allows employees to pay for accident and health insurance through salary reductions. The plan provides that salary reduction amounts for the last pay period in December are applied to insurance premiums for the immediately following January. For 2010, Karen elects a salary reduction of $3,250 for accident and health insurance, which reduces each of her biweekly paychecks by $125 ($3,250 ÷ 26). For the last pay period in December, Karen's $125 salary reduction is applied to her accident and health insurance premium for January 2011.

Note. A special rule permits a limited deferral of contributions to a flexible spending account (FSA). Current IRS rules permit an FSA to provide that expenses incurred during a grace period of up to 2½ months immediately following the end of the year may be paid or reimbursed from funds remaining in the employee's FSA at the end of the prior plan year. [IRS Notice 2005-42, 2005-23 I.R.B. 1; Prop. Reg. § 1.125-1(e)] (See Q 7:29.)

Q 7:27 Is paid time off includable in a cafeteria plan?

Yes. Elective paid time off (PTO) (vacation days, sick days or personal days) is a "permitted benefit" under Treasury regulations; however, PTO is not a "qualified benefit." [Prop. Treas. Reg. § 1.125-1(a)(3); Prop. Treas. Reg. § 1.125-1(o)(4)] Thus, a plan that only offers employees choice between cash and PTO is not a cafeteria plan because it does not offer a choice between at least one qualified benefit and one permitted taxable benefit.

A cafeteria plan may permit participants to receive either additional or fewer paid vacation days on an elective basis. For example, if a plan sponsor gives employees two core weeks of vacation and the cafeteria plan permits employees to purchase one additional week, then the two core weeks are *nonelective paid time off* and the additional week that the employee may purchase constitutes *elective paid time off.* If a plan sponsor gives employees three weeks of vacation and, under the cafeteria plan, employees may elect to sell back one week and receive cash or other benefits instead, the week that they can sell back constitutes elective PTO. The vacation days that are not subject to any employee election are nonelective PTO.

Elective PTO can be included in a cafeteria plan only if there is no deferral of compensation. To avoid deferral of compensation, the cafeteria plan must preclude any employee from using elective PTO in a subsequent plan year or receiving cash for unused time off in a later year. However, unused PTO can be cashed out during the same plan year (see below).

To determine whether there has been a prohibited deferral of compensation a special ordering rule applies. Under that rule, all nonelective PTO is deemed to be used before any elective PTO. For example, if the employee is given two core weeks of vacation and purchases a third week of elective days under the cafeteria plan, but subsequently takes only two weeks of vacation days, the employee is treated as having one week of elective PTO remaining at year end.

A cafeteria plan must provide that all elective PTO remaining at the end of a plan year be either forfeited or cashed out. Whichever method is chosen must apply uniformly to all participants. If the plan provides for a cash-out of unused PTO, the employee must receive the cash on or before the last day of the plan year. The grace period rule (see Q 7:29) does not apply to PTO.

Practice Pointer. Any carryover of unused PTO into the next plan year will be treated as an operational failure that will disqualify a cafeteria plan under Code Section 125 and result in gross income to all employees (see Q 7:33).

Q 7:28 Can a cafeteria plan offer the choice between a qualified benefit or nothing?

Yes. If the plan offers a qualified benefit on a pretax basis, it would be a valid cafeteria plan because the choice of a qualified benefit or cash is presented. The qualified benefit does not also have to be available on an after-tax basis in order for a valid cafeteria plan to exist.

Use-It-or-Lose-It Rule

Q 7:29 What is the use-it-or-lose-it rule?

As a general rule, using a cafeteria plan to defer compensation is strictly forbidden. A cafeteria plan cannot offer participants the opportunity simply to defer or delay compensation they have earned and thus delay the resulting tax liability.

A qualified cafeteria plan cannot be used to defer compensation by indirect means either. Any available benefits that are not used during the period of coverage must be forfeited at the end of the period of coverage; this is referred to as the *use-it-or-lose-it rule*. [Prop. Treas. Reg. §§ 1.125-1(e), 1.125-5(c)(3)]

Exceptions. Permitted exceptions to the use-it-or-lose-it rule are (1) the 401(k) plan option, (2) a special exception for certain postretirement group life insurance plans maintained by educational institutions, (3) the special cashout in lieu of forfeiture option for elective PTO; and (4) contributions to an HSA (see Qs 7:25, 7:26, 7:32). [I.R.C. § 125(d)(2)(A); Prop. Treas. Reg. §§ 1.125-1(o), 1.125-1(o)(4)] In addition, a cafeteria plan is permitted to provide certain benefits that will last beyond the plan year and make advance reimbursements for certain expenses (see Q 7:26).

2¹/₂–month grace period. A cafeteria plan may also allow a grace period of up to 2¹/₂ months for employees to tap unused benefits from the prior plan year. [Notice 2005-42, 2005-23 I.R.B. 1; Prop. Treas. Reg. § 1.125-1(e)] The grace period option typically applies to health and dependent care FSAs. However, the IRS proposed regulations specifically provide that a grace period can be provided for any qualified benefit other than 401(k) plan contributions. In no event may a grace period be provided for elective PTO. [Prop. Treas. Reg. §§ 1.125-1(e)(1), 1.125-1(o)(4)(iv)]

If a grace period is adopted, qualified expenses incurred during the grace period may be paid or reimbursed from funds remaining in an employee's FSA at the end of the prior plan year.

Run-out period. Employers may also provide for a "run-out" period following the end of the plan year or following the end of a grace period, if adopted. During a run-out period participants can submit claims for reimbursement of qualified expenses incurred during the plan year and the grace period, if adopted. Any run-out period must be provided on a uniform and consistent basis to all participants. [Prop. Treas. Reg. § 1.125-1(F)]

Qualified reservist distributions. The Heroes Earnings Assistance and Relief Tax Act of 2008 [Pub. L. No. 110-245] creates another exception to the "use-it-or-lose-it" rule for employees who are called to active military duty. Such employees, as soon as they are activated, may pull their funds out of a health FSA—even if they do not have qualifying medical expenses.

Under the new law, a health FSA is permitted to make a qualified reservist distribution (QRD) of all or a portion of the participant's FSA balance if:

1. The participant is a reservist called to active duty for a period of at least 180 days (or is called for an indefinite period), and

2. The distribution is made during the period beginning with the call to active duty and ending on the last day of the coverage period of the FSA that includes the date of the call to active duty.

[I.R.C. § 125(h) as added by Pub. L. No. 110-245]

Note. QRDs are not treated as excludable medical expense reimbursements. A QRD is included in the gross income and wages of the employee and is subject to employment taxes. (See Q 7:85 for details on qualified reservist distributions.)

Q 7:30   What special rules apply if an employer adopts a grace period?

The proposed cafeteria plan regulations specify requirements that any grace period provision must satisfy. [Prop. Treas. Reg. § 1.125-1(e)] In addition, the proposed regulations describe optional features that may be included in a grace period provision.

A grace period may apply to some qualified benefits, but not to others. [Prop. Treas. Reg. § 1.125-1(e)(2)(ii)]

Any grace period provision must satisfy the written plan requirements (see Q 7:9). In addition, a grace period provision must satisfy all of the following requirements:

- The grace period must apply uniformly to all participants in the cafeteria plan, determined as of the last day of the plan year. Participants in the cafeteria plan through COBRA and participants who were participants as of the last day of the plan year but terminate during the grace period are treated as participants for purposes of a grace period.

- A grace period provision must state that unused benefits or contributions relating to a particular qualified benefit may only be used to pay or reimburse expenses incurred with respect to the same qualified benefit. (For example, unused amounts in a health FSA may not be used to pay or reimburse dependent care expenses incurred during the grace period.)

- A grace period provision must state that if unused benefits or contributions from the immediately preceding plan year exceed the expenses incurred during the grace period, the remaining unused benefits or contributions may not be carried forward to any subsequent period, cannot be cashed out, and must be forfeited under the use-or-lose rule.

[Prop. Treas. Reg. § 1.125-5(e)(3)]

Employers adopting a grace period have some options. The employer may place a limit on the amount of unused benefits or contributions available during the grace period. A limit must be uniform and apply to all participants and cannot be based on a percentage of the amount of the unused benefits or contributions remaining at the end of the immediately prior plan year. [Prop. Treas. Reg. § 1.125-5(e)(2)(ii)] A grace period may be shorter than 2½ months. [Prop. Treas. Reg. § 1.125-5(e)(2)(iii)]

Expenses for qualified benefits incurred during the grace period may be treated either as expenses incurred during the immediately preceding plan year or as expenses incurred during the current plan year. For example, the plan may first apply the unused contributions or benefits from the prior year to pay or reimburse grace period expenses and then, when the unused contributions and benefits from the prior year are exhausted, pay or reimburse grace period expenses from current-year contributions and benefits. [Prop. Treas. Reg. § 1.125-5(e)(2)(iv)]

In addition, the grace period provision may permit the employer to defer the allocation of expenses between prior year and current year until after the end of the grace period. [Prop. Treas. Reg. § 1.125-5(e)(2)(v)]

Reporting requirements. An employer is required to report cash reimbursements to an employee for dependent care assistance in Box 10 on the employee's Form W-2. If the employer does not know the actual amount of cash reimbursement at the time an employee's W-2 form is prepared, the employer can report a reasonable estimate of the total amount. In the case of a dependent care FSA, the amount contributed by the employee for the year (plus any employer matching contributions) will be considered a reasonable estimate. [Notice 89-111, 1989-2 C.B. 449; Notice 90-66, 1990-2 C.B. 350] If an employer adopts a grace period for a dependent care FSA, the employer should continue to report the amount elected by the employee for the year (plus matching contributions)—even if a portion of that amount will be used to reimburse expenses incurred in the following year. [Notice 2005-61, 2005 I.R.B. 1]

> **Example.** Concordia Corp. amends its calendar-year cafeteria plan to provide a grace period for the use of dependent care assistance until March 15 of the following year. Carl elects a salary reduction of $5,000 for dependent care assistance for Year 1, but has $500 of unused contributions remaining at the end of the year. In Year 2 Carl again elects $5,000 for dependent care assistance. Concordia's plan does not call for matching contributions. For Year 1, Concordia may report in Box 10 of Carl's Form W-2 the full $5,000 salary reduction amount elected for the year. Similarly, in Year 2, Concordia may report the $5,000 salary reduction amount that Carl elected for that year.

Contributions to and reimbursements from a health FSA are not required to be reported on the employee's Form W-2.

Q 7:31   May an employer make up forfeited benefits outside the qualified cafeteria plan?

No. An employer cannot take actions outside a cafeteria plan that it is prohibited from taking within the plan. Thus, an employer may not make cafeteria plan participants whole by providing them with a bonus outside the plan equal to the amount of unused reimbursement account benefits forfeited at the end of the plan year. Conversely, if an employee has drawn down greater benefits from a health care FSA than his or her pretax contributions thus far for the plan year, the employer cannot require the employee to refund the difference to the plan if he or she terminates participation in the cafeteria plan for any reason, including termination of employment. [Prop. Treas. Reg. § 1.125-1, Q&A-17]

Q 7:32 What cafeteria plan provisions could violate the ban on indirect deferred compensation?

Permitting employees to carry over unused benefits from one period of coverage to the next violates the prohibition against having deferred compensation in a cafeteria plan. It does not matter whether the benefits or contributions carried over are converted, automatically or electively, into another taxable or nontaxable benefit or are used to purchase additional benefits of the same type.

Permitting participants to use contributions for one plan year to purchase benefits to be provided in a subsequent year also violates the prohibition against indirect deferred compensation. (See Q 7:120 for how this rule applies to contributions in the case of a Family and Medical Leave Act (FMLA) leave spanning two plan years.) Including life, health, disability, or long-term care insurance coverage having a savings or investment feature, such as whole life insurance or group universal life insurance, would operate to permit the deferral of compensation in violation of the limitation on such action. [Prop. Treas. Reg. § 1.125-1(o)(1)]

However, a special rule permits a limited deferral of contributions to an FSA. Current IRS rules permit an FSA to provide that expenses incurred during a grace period of up to 2½ months immediately following the end of the year may be paid or reimbursed from funds remaining in an employee's FSA at the end of the prior plan year. [IRS Notice 2005-42, 2005-23 I.R.B. 1; Prop. Treas. Reg. § 1.125-1(e)] (See Q 7:29.)

Q 7:33 How does the forfeiture rule affect the way vacation pay options must be structured?

As indicated above (see Q 7:27), nonelective PTO must be used before elective PTO, and any unused elective time off cannot be carried over to another plan year.

Cashout of unused elective paid time off. The cafeteria plan may contain a provision permitting unused elective PTO to be cashed out. Under the proposed regulations, the participant must receive the cash by the last day of the cafeteria plan year. [Prop. Treas. Reg. § 1.125-1(o)(4)] Under prior rules, the cash was required to be received by the earlier of (1) the last day of the cafeteria plan's year or (2) the last day of the employee's taxable year to which pretax contributions used to purchase the unused days relate.

Forfeiture of unused elective vacation days. If unused elective vacation days are not cashed out, they must be forfeited. [Prop. Treas. Reg. § 1.125-1(o)(4)]

Practice Pointer. Any carryover of unused vacation days to the next plan year will disqualify a cafeteria plan under Code Section 125.

Q 7:34   Does the prohibition against using a cafeteria plan to defer compensation affect insurance-type benefits?

Yes. A cafeteria plan may not permit participants to purchase insurance (life, health, disability, or long-term care) that has a savings or investment feature, such as whole life insurance or group universal life insurance. Such a plan may, however, pay a reasonable premium rebate or policy dividend if the rebate or dividend is paid before the close of the 12-month period immediately following the plan year to which the rebate or dividend relates. [Prop. Treas. Reg. §§ 1.125-1(o)(1); 1.125-1(p)(3)]

Q 7:35   What happens to amounts that are forfeited under the use-it-or-lose-it rule?

When the amount of employee contributions and employer contributions to an FSA exceed the FSA's total claim reimbursements for the year, the excess must be forfeited by the employees under the use-it-or-lose it rule. The excess is known as an *experience gain*. [Prop. Treas. Reg. § 1.125-5(o)(1)]

The IRS proposed regulations provide several options for handling experience gains. Most notably, the proposed regulations make it clear that experience gains may be retained by the employer sponsoring the cafeteria plan. [Prop. Treas. Reg. § 1.125-5(o)(1)(i)]

If not retained by the employer, experience gains can be:

- Used to reduce employee salary reduction contributions for the following plan year on a reasonable and uniform basis,
- Returned to employees on a reasonable and uniform basis, or
- Used to defray administrative expenses of the cafeteria plan.

[Prop. Treas. Reg. § 1.125-5(o)(10(ii)]

Experience gains may not be used as contributions directly or indirectly to any deferred compensation benefit plan. [Prop. Treas. Reg. § 1.125-5(o)(2)]

If experience gains are used to reduce employee salary reduction contributions or returned to employees, the gains can be allocated based on the different coverage levels of employees under the FSA. However, experience gains may not be allocated among employees based (directly or indirectly) on their individual claims experience. [Prop. Treas. Reg. 1.125-5(o)(2)]

Example. Lyon Company has 1,200 employees. Lyon maintains a cafeteria plan under which employees can elect annual coverage under a health FSA in $100 increments from $500 to $2,000. For Year 1, 1,000 employees elect coverage under the health FSA. The health FSA has an experience gain of $5,000 for Year 1. Lyon Company can return the $5,000 to the employees who participated in the FSA for Year 1 on a per capita basis weighted to reflect their elected levels of coverage. Alternatively, the company can use the $5,000 to reduce the required Year 2 salary reduction contributions to the health FSA for all Year 1 participants (e.g., pricing a $500 health FSA for

Year 2 at $480) or to reimburse claims incurred above the elective limit in Year 2 as long as such reimbursements are made on a reasonable and uniform level.

Salary Reduction

Q 7:36   What is a salary reduction contribution?

A *salary reduction contribution* is an elective contribution made pursuant to a salary reduction agreement between an employer and a participant. Under a salary reduction agreement made before the salary becomes currently available (see Qs 7:41–7:44), required participant contributions for qualified benefits are made on a pretax basis (i.e., they are not included in the employee's taxable income). [Prop. Treas. Reg. § 1.125-1(r)(1)]

Generally, an employee contribution made on a pretax basis is, for tax purposes, considered to be an employer contribution that is made by the employer on the participant's behalf. That means that salary reduction contributions are generally treated as employer contributions for applicable nondiscrimination tests. [Prop. Treas. Reg. § 1.125-1(r)(2)]

Salary reduction contributions are treated as *employee* contributions for ERISA purposes and are, therefore, subject to ERISA's trust requirement. As discussed in Q 7:86, however, the DOL has suspended enforcement of the trust requirement for cafeteria plans until further notice.

> **Practice Pointer.** Because salary reduction payments are treated for tax purposes as employer-paid, payment of premiums using salary reduction could cause otherwise nontaxable benefits to become taxable to employees. That could be the result if salary reduction payments are used to pay for long-term disability coverage (see Q 7:21) or group term life insurance coverage exceeding $50,000 (see Q 7:19).

The IRS proposed regulations provide that cafeteria plan may offer employees the option to purchase benefits such as disability or group-term life insurance with after-tax employee contributions. [Prop. Treas. Reg. § 1.125-1(h)(1)] If an employee elects that option, the premiums will be treated as employee paid. However, the proposed regulations also provide that a plan can require employees to pay the employees' share of any qualified benefit through salary reduction and not with after-tax employee contributions. [Prop. Treas. Reg. § 1.125-1(r)(1)]

Q 7:37   Can retirement plan distributions be used as employer contributions to a retiree medical cafeteria plan?

No. In a Coordinated Issue Paper for All Industries, the IRS concluded that amounts distributed from a qualified plan and used to pay for benefits in a former employer's cafeteria plan must be included in a retiree's income and may not be treated as tax-free salary reductions under Code Section 125. [Coordinated Issue: All Industries Cafeteria Plan/Qualified Retirement Plan Hybrid

Arrangement, Feb. 1, 2000]. In follow-up settlement guidelines, the IRS has specifically stated that it will enforce that rule until further regulatory or judicial determinations are made. [Appeals Industry Specialization Program Coordinated Issue Settlement Guidelines: Cafeteria Plan/Qualified Retirement Plan Hybrid Arrangement, Mar. 6, 2001]

Code Section 402(a), which governs distributions from qualified retirement plans, states that "except as otherwise provided in this section" any amount distributed from a plan is taxable to the plan participant in the year of the distribution. Code Section 402 contains only two exceptions. The first exception provides that if a distribution is made to a participant's spouse or former spouse under the terms of a qualified domestic relations order, the spouse or former spouse, rather than the participant, will be taxed on the distribution. [I.R.C. § 402(e)(1)(A)] The second exception provides that eligible rollover distributions that are properly rolled over into another qualified plan or individual retirement account (IRA) within 60 days are not included in income for the taxable year of the distribution. [I.R.C. § 402(c)]

According to the IRS, neither of those exceptions allows a participant to exclude distributions that are used to purchase benefits through the former employer's cafeteria plan. Because the "except as otherwise provided in this section" language in Code Section 402(a) does not encompass Code Section 125, the general rule applies and the distribution is includable in the retiree's gross income. The IRS says this position is consistent with two long-standing revenue rulings concerning the use of retirement plan funds to purchase health and accident benefits. The first ruling states that while the purchase of accident and health insurance will not prevent qualification of a plan, the use of the funds to pay the cost of insurance for the employee or his or her beneficiaries is a taxable distribution within the meaning of Code Section 402. [Rev. Rul. 61-164, 1961-2 C.B. 99] The second ruling concluded that distributions from a qualified profit sharing plan to pay for a plan participant's medical care expenses are not excludable accident and health benefits but are taxable under Code Section 402 as previously earned deferred compensation. [Rev. Rul. 69-141, 1969-1 C.B. 48]

In addition, the proposed regulations provide that distributions from a qualified retirement plan that former employees elect to have applied to pay health insurance premiums through a cafeteria plan are includable in their gross incomes. These distributions are not cash for purposes of Section 125. Moreover, the plan is not a cafeteria plan with respect to the former employees. [Prop. Treas. Reg. § 1.125-1(b)(3)]

Period of Coverage

Q 7:38   What period must a cafeteria plan election cover?

The plan year generally is the coverage period for benefits provided through a cafeteria plan. Benefits elected for a plan year generally may not be carried forward to subsequent plan years. [Prop. Treas. Reg. § 1.125-1(d)(5)] Coverage cannot be elected on a month-by-month or expense-by-expense basis. [Prop. Treas. Reg. § 1.125-5(f)]

The plan year must be specified in the cafeteria plan. The plan year of a cafeteria plan must be 12 consecutive months, unless a short plan year is allowed. A plan year can begin on any day of any month and must end on the preceding day in the immediately following year. For example, a plan year that begins on October 15, 2010 must end on October 14, 2011. The plan year of a calendar-year plan begins on January 1 and ends on December 31 of the same calendar year. A plan year can be changed only for a valid business purpose.

A short plan year of less than 12 consecutive months is permitted for a valid business purpose. For example, if an employer establishes a cafeteria plan in midyear, but wants to use a calendar plan year, a short year will be allowed for the first plan year. A short plan year may also be allowed if a plan's year must be changed—for example, if the plan changes to a benefit provider with a benefit year that does not match the plan's year. [Prop. Treas. Reg. § 1.125-1(d)]

Q 7:39 Why is the period of coverage for a cafeteria plan important?

Several items hinge on the period of coverage of a cafeteria plan.

Election to participate. To avoid constructive receipt of income, an election to participate in a cafeteria plan must be made before the earlier of the date when taxable benefits are currently available or the first day of the plan year (or other coverage period). [Prop. Treas. Reg. § 1.125-2(a)(2)] If elections to participate are permitted to be retroactive, the cafeteria plan will be disqualified. [American Mut. Ins. Co. v. United States, 815 F. Supp. 1206 (W.D. Wis. 1992)] A key exception to this bar on retroactivity is the HIPAA rule permitting retroactive enrollment of newborns and children who are adopted or placed for adoption (see Q 7:46). In addition, the IRS proposed regulations provide for an election window for new employees (see Q 7:47).

Covered benefits. A cafeteria plan is permitted to pay only those expenses that are incurred during the period of coverage (and any grace period). Expenses incurred before the date the plan is in existence or the date the participant is covered under the plan, whichever is later, cannot be reimbursed by the cafeteria plan. Paying or reimbursing expenses for qualified benefits incurred before the later of the adoption date or effective date of the cafeteria plan or before the beginning of a period of coverage is an operational failure that will disqualify the plan. [Prop. Treas. Reg. § 1.125-1(c)(7)]

Exclusion from gross income. Because paying or reimbursing expenses incurred prior to a period of coverage is an operational failure that will disqualify the plan, employees' elections between taxable and nontaxable benefits result in gross income to the employees. [Prop. Treas. Reg. § 1.125-1(c)(7)(i)]

Elections

Q 7:40   How must cafeteria plan elections be structured to ensure that qualified benefits do not lose their favorable tax treatment?

An employer must adopt certain procedures for benefit elections to ensure that cafeteria plan participants are not deemed to have constructively received—and therefore are not taxed on—taxable benefits (including cash) that they have elected not to receive. To do this, the employer plan must make certain that the choice of benefits is made before the taxable benefits become currently available. [Prop. Treas. Reg. §§ 1.125-2(a)(2)]

Cash or another taxable benefit is currently available to the employee if it has been paid to the employee or if the employee is able currently to receive the cash or other taxable benefit at the employee's discretion.

A benefit will not be treated as currently available if there is a significant limitation or restriction on the employee's right to receive the benefit currently. Similarly, a benefit is not currently available if the employee may under no circumstances receive the benefit before a particular time in the future. [Prop. Treas. Reg. § 1.125-2(a)(3)]

No particular form of election is mandated.

Retroactive elections. HIPAA and its implementing regulations mandate that newborns and children under the age of 18 who are adopted or placed for adoption must be permitted to be enrolled retroactively to the date of birth, adoption, or placement if certain special enrollment circumstances are met. A temporary cafeteria plan regulation recognizes this mandatory retroactive enrollment. [Temp. Treas. Reg. § 1.125-4T(b)] (See Q 7:52 for permitted changes in status, including under this HIPAA rule.)

In addition, a new rule in the proposed regulations provides that new hires may be given 30 days after their hire date to make cafeteria plan elections that are effective as of the date of hire. [Prop. Treas. Reg. § 1.125-2(d)] (See Q 7:47.)

Q 7:41   When is a benefit considered currently available and therefore taxable?

A benefit is treated as *currently available* to a participant if the participant is free to receive it either (1) at his or her discretion or (2) by making an election or giving notice of intent to receive it. Thus, if the participant could freely decide during the plan year to change his or her mind about taking coverage on a pretax or after-tax basis, the benefit would be treated as currently available and therefore taxable. However, the mere ability to elect to receive a benefit at some future date does not in itself make the benefit currently available and therefore taxable, provided there is a substantial risk of forfeiture of the benefit (see Q 7:42).

Q 7:42   Is a benefit currently available if its receipt is limited or restricted?

A benefit will not be treated as currently available if there is a significant limitation or restriction on the employee's right to receive the benefit currently. Similarly, a benefit is not currently available if the employee may under no circumstances receive the benefit before a particular time in the future. [Prop. Treas. Reg. § 1.125-2(a)(3)]

Q 7:43   Must the cafeteria plan provide an annual enrollment period?

Nothing in the proposed cafeteria plan regulations actually requires an annual enrollment period. Offering an annual enrollment period to participants has developed as an administrative practice in response to the requirement in the proposed cafeteria plan regulations that the individual make an election prior to the period of coverage. [Prop. Treas. Reg. § 1.125-2(a)(2)]

On the other hand, the IRS proposed regulations make it clear that the annual election requirement is not as hard and fast as employers may have believed. For example, the proposed regulations specifically authorize two-year coverage elections for vision or dental insurance (called a two-year "lock-in") as well as long-term disability policies that provide benefits over more than one year. [Prop. Treas. Reg. § 1.125-1(p)(2), (4)] In addition, accident and health insurance policies may include certain benefits that relate to more than one year, such as guaranteed renewability. [Prop. Treas. Reg. § 1.125-1(p)(1)] (See Q 7:26.)

Q 7:44   Must an individual make an affirmative election to participate in a cafeteria plan?

An individual generally must *make* an election to participate in a cafeteria plan. [Prop. Treas. Reg. § 1.125-2(a)] In the past, many practitioners construed this requirement as requiring an affirmative election of qualified benefits, with cash compensation as the default option if the individual does not make an affirmative election. However, an IRS ruling made it clear that a cafeteria plan may provide that a particular benefit is the default option and require employees to affirmatively elect to receive cash compensation. [Rev. Rul. 2002-27, 2002-20 I.R.B. 925] The ruling dealt specifically with "opt-out" health coverage. However, the same principles would apply to any qualified benefits offered under a cafeteria plan.

> **Example.** Acme Corporation maintains a calendar-year cafeteria plan. The plan offers group health insurance with employee-only and family coverage options. The plan is in writing and is available to all employees immediately upon being hired.

Under the plan, each new employee is automatically enrolled for employee-only health coverage, with the employee's salary reduced on a pretax basis to pay for a portion of the cost, unless the employee affirmatively elects to receive cash. Alternatively, an employee with a spouse or child can elect family coverage. Automatic enrollment also applies to current employees in the first plan year that automatic enrollment takes effect.

At the time an employee is hired, he or she receives a notice explaining the automatic enrollment process and the employee's right to decline coverage and have no salary reduction. The notice spells out the salary reduction amounts for employee-only and family coverage, the procedure for opting out, the time by which an election must be made, and the period for which the election will be effective. Each current employee receives the same notice before the beginning of each plan year along with a description of the employee's existing coverage, if any.

For a new hire, an election to receive cash or to have family coverage is effective before the compensation for the first pay period is available. For current employees, an election is effective at the start of the calendar year. An election for a prior year carries over to the next year unless it is changed.

Result. The IRS says that the cafeteria plan rules apply if an employee can choose between cash and qualified benefits. Moreover, an employee's choice can be either in the form of an affirmative election to receive qualified benefits in lieu of cash or an affirmative election to receive cash in lieu of benefits. Therefore, Acme's automatic enrollment process, which gives employees the option of electing cash in lieu of health benefits, passes muster under the cafeteria plan rules. Contributions used to purchase health coverage will not be taxable to employees who do not elect to receive cash.

Example. Gamma Corporation's plan works much like Acme's plan with one key difference. Under Gamma's automatic enrollment process, an employee can affirmatively elect to receive cash in lieu of health benefits only if the employee certifies that he or she has other health coverage. Gamma does not, however, request or collect any other information from employees regarding other health coverage.

Result. According to the IRS, the cafeteria plan rules apply only to those employees who can elect between health coverage and cash (i.e., those employees who have other health coverage). Thus, for those employees, contributions to purchase group health insurance can be made on a pretax basis. On the other hand, the cafeteria plan rules do not apply to employee-only coverage for employees who cannot certify other health coverage because those employees do not have the ability to elect cash in lieu of coverage. However, coverage provided to those employees can qualify for tax-free treatment as employer-provided health coverage. [I.R.C. § 106(a)]

Retirement plan angle. The tax law imposes various limits on retirement plan contributions and benefits, many of which are based on an employee's compensation. [I.R.C. § 415] As a general rule, premiums for group health insurance are not treated as compensation for retirement plan purposes. However, compensation does include amounts contributed by the employer at the election of the employee that are excluded from the employee's income under the cafeteria plan rules. [Treas. Reg. § 1.415-2(d)(3)(iv)]

Thus, where employees have a choice between health benefits and cash, amounts contributed for the benefits are included in compensation. However, where employees do not have a choice between cash and benefits—as is the case with Gamma employees who cannot certify other health coverage—amounts paid for the health benefits do not technically qualify as compensation.

Nonetheless, the IRS says that in determining an employee's compensation for retirement plan purposes an employer can choose to include "deemed Section 125 compensation." For this purpose, deemed Section 125 compensation is an excludable amount that is not available to an employee in cash in lieu of group health coverage because the employee is not able to certify that he or she has other health coverage. The IRS cautions, however, that an amount can be treated as deemed Section 125 compensation only if the employer does not otherwise request or collect information about an employee's other health coverage as part of the plan enrollment process.

Practice Pointer. An opt-out health plan may boost enrollment by overcoming employee inertia. Moreover, it may prove to be a time-saver for a company's employee benefits personnel. Processing the paperwork for those employees who opt out or who switch to family coverage may prove less cumbersome than processing applications from all employees who choose to be covered by the plan.

Proposed regulations. The proposed regulations incorporate the rules laid down in the earlier revenue ruling. The regulations provide that for new employees or current employees who fail to make a timely election, a plan may (but is not required to) provide default elections for one or more qualified benefits. For example, the regulations say that a default provision may provide that an election made for any prior year is deemed to continue for every succeeding year unless changed. [Prop. Treas. Reg. § 1.125-2(b)(1)] The proposed regulations also make it clear that Code Section 125 applies only to employees who can elect between cash and a qualified benefit. Thus, in the situation described in Revenue Ruling 2002-27 and reiterated in the proposed regulations, where an employee with no other health coverage must be enrolled in the employer's health plan, the cafeteria plan rules do not apply. [Prop. Treas. Reg. § 1.125-1(b)(4)] It is significant, however, that there is no indication in the proposed regulations that such a mandatory coverage requirement would disqualify an employer's cafeteria plan.

There was some question as to whether the automatic payroll deduction under opt-out plans violated state laws requiring specific written authorizations from employees before making deductions from their paychecks. However, in an advisory opinion concerning a company benefit plan, the DOL concluded that ERISA preempts state laws that require an employer to obtain written consent before withholding amounts from an employee's wages for contribution to a group health plan or other welfare benefit plan covered by ERISA. [DOL Adv. Op. 2008-02A (Feb. 8, 2008)]

Q 7:45   Can an election to participate in a cafeteria plan be made electronically?

The proposed cafeteria plan regulations provide that cafeteria plan elections are not required to be on written paper documents; a plan may use electronic media for such elections. [Prop. Treas. Reg. § 1.125-2(a)(5)] The IRS has issued regulations governing the use of electronic media for notices and other documents within its jurisdiction. [Treas. Reg. § 1.401(a)-21] The proposed cafeteria plan regulations make it clear that those rules apply to electronic elections and changes in elections under Code Section 125.

The regulations do *not* apply to notices, consents, or disclosures required by ERISA that fall under the jurisdiction of the DOL. For example, the regulations do not apply to furnishing of summary plan descriptions (SPDs), which are governed by the DOL regulations (see chapter 2). In addition, the rules for the use of electronic media apply in addition to all other general requirements for particular notices and elections. Any communication provided electronically must satisfy all the other Code and regulatory requirements for that communication.

The content of an electronic communication and the delivery method must be reasonably designed to provide information in a way that is no less understandable than if provided in a paper document. Moreover, the electronic transmission must alert the recipient to the significance of the electronic document (including the subject matter), and provide any instructions needed to access the document. [Treas. Reg. § 1.401(a)-21(a)(5)]

The regulations provide for two options:

1. *Consent method.* Under the general rules, a plan must obtain a participant's consent before providing a notice electronically. The participant's consent must be given in a way that reasonably demonstrates that the participant can access the notice electronically. Consent can be given on a written paper form or through some other nonelectronic means, but only if the participant confirms the consent in a way that reasonably demonstrates that he can access the notice electronically. Before consenting, the participant is given a disclosure statement that outlines the scope of the consent, the participant's right to withdraw the consent (including any conditions, consequences, or fees), and the right to receive the communication on paper. The disclosure must specify the hardware and software requirements for electronic documents and the procedures for updating the participant's electronic contact information. If the hardware or software requirements change, a new consent must be obtained from the participant. [Treas. Reg. § 1.401(a)-21(b)]

2. *Automatic method.* An electronic notice can be provided automatically if the recipient is advised that a paper copy of the notice may be requested and will be provided at no charge. However, to use this method, the recipient of the notice must be "effectively able" to access the electronic medium used to provide the notice. [Treas. Reg. § 1.401(a)-21(c)]

Electronic elections. A benefit election can be made electronically if all of the following requirements are met:

1. The participant is effectively able to access the electronic system.

2. The electronic system is reasonably designed to prevent any person other than the participant from making the election.

3. The electronic system must provide the participant with a reasonable opportunity to review, confirm, modify, or rescind the election before it becomes effective.

4. The participant must receive a confirmation of the election through either a written paper document or an electronic medium that meets the regulation's requirements within a reasonable time period.

5. In the case of an election that must be witnessed by a plan representative or a notary public, the individual's signature must be witnessed in the physical presence of a plan representative or a notary.

[Treas. Reg. § 1.401(a)-21(d)]

The regulations apply to applicable notices and elections on or after January 1, 2007.

Q 7:46 Can a cafeteria plan election be retroactive?

As a general rule, no. An election to participate in a cafeteria plan is required to be made before the period of coverage to which it applies begins. [Prop. Treas. Reg. § 1.125-2(a)(2)] Retroactive elections can result in a cafeteria plan's disqualification. [Prop. Treas. Reg. § 1.125-1(c)(7)(ii)(A); American Mut. Ins. Co. v. United States, 815 F. Supp. 1206 (W.D. Wis. 1992)]

There are, however, two key exceptions:

1. HIPAA affects the prohibition against retroactive elections. The act mandates that group health plans provide a 30-day special open enrollment period in certain circumstances, including one for newborn children and children under the age of 18 who are adopted or placed for adoption. For those new dependents, coverage is required to be retroactive to the date of birth, adoption, or placement. Temporary cafeteria plan regulations expressly permit retroactive enrollment in these limited circumstances in recognition of HIPAA's clear statutory mandate. [Temp. Treas. Reg. § 1.125-4T] (See Q 7:52.)

2. A new rule in the proposed regulations provides that new hires may be given 30 days after their hire date to make cafeteria plan elections that are effective as of the date of hire. [Prop. Treas. Reg. § 1.125-2(d)] (See Q 7:47.)

Q 7:47   Do new employees have to make cafeteria plan elections immediately at the time of hire?

The proposed cafeteria plan regulations specifically provide that a plan may give employees 30 days after their date of hire to make elections between cash and qualified benefits. Once made, an election is effective as of the date of hire. However, salary reduction amounts used to pay for such an election must be from compensation not yet currently available on the date of the election. [Prop. Treas. Reg. § 1.125-2(d)]

The written cafeteria plan must provide that any employee who terminates employment and is rehired within 30 days after terminating employment (or who returns to employment following an unpaid leave of absence of fewer than 30 days) is not a new employee eligible for purposes of this election rule

Q 7:48   May a cafeteria plan use a one-time election that renews automatically unless a participant revokes it?

Yes. An initial affirmative election followed by a negative option reenrollment that automatically renews and extends the initial written election for succeeding periods of coverage is referred to as an *evergreen election*. In other words, once made, the affirmative election to participate in a cafeteria plan stays in force indefinitely unless it is affirmatively revoked. The proposed cafeteria plan regulations expressly authorize the evergreen approach. The proposed regulations provide that a plan can provide default elections for new hires and current employees who do not make timely elections—including a rule providing that an election made for any prior year is deemed to continue for every succeeding year unless changed. [Prop. Treas. Reg. § .125-2(b)(1)] Moreover, an IRS revenue ruling makes it clear that negative option elections are permitted under the cafeteria plan rules (see Q 7:44).

Q 7:49   What happens if an employee is permitted to change his or her mind after the election becomes effective?

The general rule is that all elections made under a cafeteria plan must be irrevocable as of the earlier of (1) the date when taxable benefits become currently available or (2) the first day of the plan year (or other coverage period). An election is not irrevocable if, after the earlier of those dates, employees have the right to revoke their elections of qualified benefits and instead receive the taxable benefits, even if employees do not actually revoke their elections. [Prop. Treas. Reg. § 1.125-2(a)(1)]

> **Example 1.** Argus Corporation's cafeteria plan offers employees a choice between $5,000 in cash for the plan year or up to $5,000 of dependent care assistance for the year. Employees must make their elections before the beginning of the plan year. Once the plan year has begun, they cannot revoke their elections. As a result, employees who elect dependent care assistance do not include the $5,000 of cash in gross income.

Example 2. The facts are the same as those in Example 1, except that Argus Corporation's plan permits employees to revoke their dependent care assistance elections at any time during the plan year and receive the unused amount of dependent care assistance in cash. The plan would not qualify as a cafeteria plan. All the employees are treated as receiving $5,000 in cash, even if they do not revoke their elections.

Although participant elections must be irrevocable during the period of coverage, the cafeteria plan rules contain numerous exceptions to this general rule. The Swiss cheese-like nature of the exceptions provides significant latitude for participants to revoke their elections and make new elections midyear in many circumstances (see Q 7:50).

Q 7:50 Are there any exceptions to the prohibitions against revocation of an election to participate in a cafeteria plan?

Yes. Exceptions to the prohibition against revocation of an election to participate in a cafeteria plan are as follows:

- Special enrollment rights (see Q 7:51)
- Changes in status (see Q 7:52)
- Separation from service (see Q 7:56)
- Changes in health plan costs and coverage (see Qs 7:57, 7:58)
- Addition of a new plan option (see Q 7:59)
- Changes in coverage under another health plan (see Q 7:60)
- Elective contributions under cash-or-deferred (i.e., 401(k)) arrangements (see Q 7:61)
- Employees taking FMLA leave (see Q 7:114)
- Salary reduction contributions to HSAs (see Q 7:62)

Practice Pointer. The change in status rules generally are permissive; that is, the employer may, but is not required to, include them in the cafeteria plan. Accordingly, if the employer wishes to permit changes in any of the above circumstances, then specific authority to do so must be included in the cafeteria plan document. [Prop. Treas. Reg. §§ 1.125-2(a)(4), 1.125-1(c)(1)(iii)]

Q 7:51 May a plan permit an employee to revoke an election for health coverage when enrollment in a health plan is permitted because of special enrollment rights?

The Health Insurance Portability and Accountability Act (HIPAA) requires a group health plan to allow special enrollment of an eligible employee or dependents who lose other group health coverage. In addition, a group health plan must provide special enrollment rights to an employee's new spouse or dependents (see Q 3:82). The cafeteria plan regulations provide that a plan may permit an employee to revoke a group health coverage election and make a new election that corresponds to the special enrollment rights. [Treas. Reg. § 1.125-4(b)]

> **Example.** An employer's group health plan permits employees to elect either employee-only group health coverage or family coverage. An employee's cost for group health coverage may be funded through salary reduction contributions under the employer's cafeteria plan, which operates on a calendar year. Arnold, who is married and has one child, elects employee-only coverage before the beginning of a calendar year. During that year, Arnold and his spouse adopt a second child. Because the newly adopted child is entitled to special enrollment rights under the group health plan, Arnold is entitled to enroll for family coverage under the employer's group health plan as of the date of the adoption. In addition, the employer's cafeteria plan may permit Arnold to prospectively change his salary reduction election to cover the cost of family coverage.

Q 7:52   May a revocation of a cafeteria plan election be permitted because of a change in status?

Yes, it may be. A participant may be (but is not required to be) permitted to revoke an election under the cafeteria plan for the remainder of the period of coverage (and, if the plan permits, to make a new election for the remainder of the period of coverage) on account of certain changes in status, provided the election change is consistent with the change in status.

The 2007 proposed regulations make it clear that if a plan adopts the change in status rules, an employee who experiences a change in status is permitted to revoke an election and make a new election for the remaining period of coverage—but only with respect to cash or other taxable benefits that are not yet currently available. [Prop. Treas. Reg. § 1.125-2(a)(4)]

Final IRS regulations address all of the changes in status for which a cafeteria plan may permit election changes, including changes with respect to accident or health coverage, group term life insurance coverage, dependent care assistance, and adoption assistance. [Treas. Reg. § 1.125-4(c)] In addition, the regulations contain guidance concerning election changes that are permitted because of changes in cost or coverage of a qualified benefits plan.

The following events are considered changes in status:

1. Events that change an employee's *legal marital status*, including marriage, spouse's death, divorce, legal separation, or annulment;

2. Events that change an employee's *number of dependents* (as defined in Code Section 152), including birth, adoption, placement for adoption, or death of a dependent;

3. Events that change the *employment status* of the employee, the employee's spouse, or the employee's dependent, including a termination or commencement of employment, a strike or lockout, a commencement of or return from an unpaid leave of absence, or a change in worksite. In

addition, if the eligibility conditions of the cafeteria plan or other benefit plan of the employee, spouse, or dependent depend on the employment status of that individual and there is a change in that individual's employment status, with the consequence that the individual becomes (or ceases to be) eligible under the plan, then that change constitutes a change in employment status. For example, a change in employment status would occur if a plan applies only to salaried employees and an employee switches from salaried to hourly paid employment, with the consequence that the employee ceases to be eligible for the plan.

4. Events that change an employee's *dependency status,* causing a dependent to satisfy or cease to satisfy eligibility requirements for coverage on account of attainment of age, student status, or any similar circumstance;

5. A change in the place of *residence* of the employee, the employee's spouse, or a dependent; and

6. For purposes of *adoption assistance* provided through a cafeteria plan, the commencement or termination of an adoption proceeding.

Consistency rule. As noted, it is not sufficient that one of the listed changes in status has occurred. The employee may revoke his or her election midyear and make a new election for the remainder of the plan year only if the election also satisfies the applicable consistency rule.

Q 7:53   What types of health coverage changes may be permitted when a change of status event occurs?

The employee's revocation and change of election is consistent with a change in status if and only if (1) the change in status results in the employee, spouse, or dependent gaining or losing eligibility for accident or health coverage under either the employer's plan or an accident or health plan of the spouse's or dependent's employer, and (2) the election change corresponds with that gain or loss of coverage. A change in status that affects eligibility under an employer's plan includes a change in status that results in an increase or decrease in the number of an employee's family members that may benefit from coverage under the plan.

Marriage. When an employee marries, the new spouse may be eligible for special enrollment in the employer's plan. In addition, the employee may be eligible to enroll in the spouse's plan. Thus, the employee may be permitted to drop coverage under the employer's plan or to add coverage for his or her new spouse.

Example. Magnum, Inc. provides health coverage (including a health care FSA) for its employees through its cafeteria plan. Before the beginning of the calendar year, Bob elects employee-only health coverage under Magnum's cafeteria plan and elects salary reduction contributions to fund coverage under the health care FSA. Bob marries Kathy during the year. Kathy's employer, Newland Corp., offers health coverage to its employees (but does not include any health care FSA). Before the marriage, Kathy had elected employee-only coverage under Newland's plan. Bob wants to revoke the election for employee-only coverage and is considering electing family health coverage under Magnum's plan or obtaining family health coverage under Newland's plan. Bob's marriage to Kathy is a change in status as defined under the new rules. Kathy has become eligible for coverage under Magnum's health plan. There are two possible election changes to correspond with the change in status: (1) Bob may elect family health coverage under Magnum's plan to cover himself and Kathy or (2) Bob may cancel coverage under Magnum's plan if Kathy elects family health coverage under Newland's plan to cover them both. Magnum's cafeteria plan may permit Bob to make either election change. Bob may also increase his salary reduction contributions to fund coverage for Kathy under Magnum's health care FSA.

Note. An employee who wants to decrease or cancel health coverage under an employer's plan because he or she becomes eligible for coverage under a spouse's plan may do so only if he or she actually becomes covered under the other plan. The IRS does not require an employer to obtain proof of such coverage. An employer can generally rely on an employee's certification that he or she has obtained or will obtain coverage under a spouse's plan (assuming the employer has no reason to believe the certification is incorrect).

Divorce, death, or dependency status. If the change in status event is an employee's divorce, annulment, or legal separation, the death of a spouse or dependent, or a dependent's ceasing to satisfy the eligibility requirements for coverage, the employee may be permitted to cancel health coverage for his or her ex-spouse or dependent.

Example. Cheryl, a single parent, elects family health coverage under a calendar-year cafeteria plan maintained by her employer. Cheryl and her 21-year-old son, Kevin, are covered under Cheryl's company health plan. In mid-year, Kevin graduates from college. Under the terms of the health plan, dependents over age 19 must be full-time students to receive coverage. Cheryl wants to revoke her election for family health coverage and obtain employee-only coverage under her company's cafeteria plan. Kevin's loss of eligibility for coverage under the terms of the health plan is a change in status. A revocation of Cheryl's election for family coverage and new election for employee-only coverage corresponds with the change in status. Thus, the company's cafeteria plan permits Cheryl to elect employee-only coverage.

Bear in mind, however, that cancellation of coverage for any individual other than the former spouse or dependent would not satisfy the consistency rule. Thus, if a dependent dies or ceases to be eligible for coverage under the plan, the employee may drop coverage only for that dependent. An election to drop the employee's own coverage or coverage for a spouse or another dependent would not correspond to the change in status. So, if Cheryl had a second child who remained eligible for coverage, Cheryl would not be permitted to drop coverage for that child and switch to employee-only coverage.

Judgment, decree, or order. If a judgment, decree, or order resulting from a divorce, legal separation, annulment, or change in legal custody (including a qualified medical child support order as defined in ERISA Section 609) requires accident or health coverage for an employee's child, the cafeteria plan may change the employee's election to provide coverage for the child if the order requires coverage under the employer's plan. The plan may also permit the employee to make an election to cancel coverage for the child if the order requires the former spouse to provide coverage. However, an election to cancel coverage may be permitted only if the former spouse actually provides coverage for the child. [Treas. Reg. § 1.125-4(d)]

Entitlement to Medicare or Medicaid. If the employee or his or her spouse or dependent who is enrolled in the employer's accident or health plan becomes entitled to Medicare or Medicaid coverage, other than coverage consisting solely of benefits under the program for distribution of pediatric vaccines, then the cafeteria plan may permit the employee to make an election change to cancel or reduce coverage of that individual under the accident or health plan.

In addition, if an employee, spouse, or dependent who has been entitled to such coverage under Medicare or Medicaid loses eligibility for such coverage, the cafeteria plan may permit the employee to make a prospective election to commence or increase coverage of that employee, spouse, or dependent under the accident or health plan. [Treas. Reg. § 1.125-4(e)]

Q 7:54 What types of changes in group-term life and disability coverage are permitted when an employee experiences a change in status?

The final cafeteria plan regulations provide that an election to increase group term life or disability coverage or an election to decrease such coverage is consistent with a change in status event.

> **Example.** Mike's employer provides group term life insurance coverage. Under the plan, an employee may elect life insurance coverage in an amount up to $50,000. Mike's employer also maintains a calendar-year cafeteria plan under which qualified benefits, including the group term life insurance coverage, are funded through salary reduction. Mike has a wife and a child. Before the beginning of the year, Mike elects $10,000 of group term life insurance coverage. In the course of the year, Mike and his wife divorce. The divorce is a change in status. Either an increase or a decrease in coverage is consistent with this change in status. His employer's cafeteria plan may permit Mike to increase or to decrease his group term life insurance coverage.

Q 7:55 How do the change in status rules apply to dependent care assistance and adoption assistance benefits?

The change in status rules for dependent care assistance and adoption assistance parallel the change in status rules for accident or health coverage and group term life insurance coverage with some additional rules specific to dependent care and adoption assistance. For example, whereas a change in the number of dependents is a status change for other types of qualified benefits, a change in the number of qualifying individuals (i.e., children under 13) is a change in status for purposes of dependent care assistance. In addition, the regulations specifically provide that commencement or termination of an adoption proceeding is a change in status event for adoption assistance.

As with other benefits, a change of election with respect to dependent care or adoption assistance must be on account of and correspond to the change in status. [Treas. Reg. § 1.125-4(c)(3)(ii)]

Example. Meg's employer maintains a calendar-year cafeteria plan that allows employees to elect coverage under a dependent care FSA. Meg has a daughter, Julia. Before the beginning of the calendar year, Meg elects salary reduction contributions of $4,000 during the year to fund coverage under the dependent care FSA for up to $4,000 of reimbursements for the year. During the year, Julia turns 13 and ceases to satisfy the definition of qualifying individual under the Code. Meg wishes to cancel coverage under the dependent care FSA. Julia's attainment of age 13 is a change in status that affects Meg's employment-related expenses. Meg may make a corresponding change to cancel coverage under the dependent care FSA.

Q 7:56　Is revocation of an election to participate in a cafeteria plan permitted if an employee separates from service?

Yes. Termination of employment is a change in status permitting cancellation of coverage. [Treas. Reg. § 1.125-4 (c)(4) Ex. 8] However, the regulations make it clear that terminating and rehiring an employee simply to permit a cafeteria plan election change will not be permitted.

Example. Before the beginning of the year, Howard elected to participate in his employer's cafeteria plan. Halfway through the year, Howard wants to cancel his coverage. With the prior understanding of his employer, Howard terminates employment and resumes employment one week later. Under the facts and circumstances, the principal purpose of Howard's termination was to alter his cafeteria plan election, and his reinstatement was understood at the time of the termination. Howard does not have a change in status that would permit a cafeteria plan election change.

On the other hand, the regulations state that Howard's termination would constitute a change in status permitting cancellation of coverage during his period of unemployment if the plan automatically reinstated his original election when he resumed employment (e.g., if the plan contained a provision requiring an employee who resumes employment within 30 days to return to the election in effect prior to the termination).

In addition, the regulations indicate that an unemployment period of more than 30 days will constitute a change in status. Thus, if Howard returned to work more than 30 days following his termination of employment, the plan could permit him to return to his original election or to make a new election.

Alternatively, the plan could prohibit Howard from participation in the plan for the remainder of the plan year.

The proposed regulations make it clear that a cafeteria plan may permit a terminating employee who is eligible for severance pay to elect between receiving the severance pay and using the severance pay to pay the COBRA premiums for accident and health insurance under the cafeteria plan. [Prop. Treas. Reg. § 1.125-1(b)(3)]

The same does not hold true for retirement plan distributions to terminating employees. The proposed regulations provide that distributions from a qualified retirement plan that a former employee elects to apply to payment of premiums for health insurance through the employer's cafeteria plan are includable in the former employee's gross income. These distributions are not cash for purposes of Code Section 125. The plan is not a cafeteria plan with respect to the former employees. [Prop. Treas. Reg. § 1.125-1(b)(3)] (See Q 7:37.)

Q 7:57 May a cafeteria plan permit revocation of an election to participate because of changes in the cost of a particular benefit?

Yes. The regulations permit election changes when there are significant changes in the cost of a particular cafeteria plan benefit. [Treas. Reg. § 1.125-4(f)]

Automatic changes. Adjustments for cost changes can be made automatically in some cases. If the costs of a qualified benefits plan increases (or decreases) during a period of coverage and, under the terms of the plan, employees are required to make a corresponding change in their payments, the cafeteria plan may, on a reasonable and consistent basis, automatically make a prospective increase (or decrease) in an employee's elective contributions to the plan. For example, if the cost of a self-insured accident or health plan increases, a plan may automatically make a corresponding change in the salary reduction charge.

Significant cost changes. If the cost charged to an employee for a benefit package option significantly increases or decreases during a period of coverage, the plan may permit the employee to make a corresponding election change. In the case of a cost decrease, employees who initially chose a different option may be permitted to make a midyear change to the less costly option. In addition, employees who initially passed up the benefit can be permitted to enroll in midyear. In the case of a cost increase, affected employees may be permitted to increase their contributions to cover the higher cost, switch to another coverage option, or drop that type of benefit if no option providing similar coverage is available.

For example, if the cost of an indemnity option under an accident or health plan increases significantly during a period of coverage, employees covered by the indemnity option may increase their contributions to pay the higher cost. Alternatively, the employees may be permitted to revoke their election of the indemnity option and elect coverage under another option, such as an HMO, or drop coverage entirely if no other option is offered.

Covered cost changes. The cost change rules apply to any increase or decrease in the amount of elective employee contributions under the plan, regardless of whether the cost change results from an action taken by the employee (such as a switch from full-time to part-time status) or from an action taken by the employer (such as a reduction in employer contributions). On the other hand, a purely elective switch to a different, more expensive benefit option is not a covered cost change.

> **Example.** Randy's employer maintains a cafeteria plan under which employees may elect accident or health coverage under either an indemnity plan or an HMO. Before the beginning of the year, Randy elects coverage under the HMO, paying a premium of $100 every month. During the year, Randy decides to switch to the indemnity plan, which charges a premium of $140 per month. Switching from the HMO to the indemnity plan is not a change in cost or coverage under the proposed rules. Even though his health plan may permit Randy to switch from the HMO to the indemnity plan, the cafeteria plan may not permit Randy to make an election change to reflect the increased premium. Accordingly, if Randy switches from the HMO to the indemnity plan, he may pay the additional $40 per month on an after-tax basis.

Dependent care coverage. In the case of a dependent care assistance plan, the cost change rules apply only if the cost change is imposed by a dependent care provider who is not a relative of the employee. However, the availability of a relative to provide child care services may constitute a coverage change that will justify a change in an employee's election.

> **Example.** Anita's employer maintains a calendar-year cafeteria plan that allows employees to elect coverage under a dependent care FSA. Anita's son, Sebastian, attends the employer's on-site child care center at an annual cost of $3,000. Before the beginning of the year, Anita elects salary reduction contributions of $3,000 during the year to fund coverage under the dependent care FSA for up to $3,000 of reimbursement for the year. Halfway through the year, Anita finds a new child care provider and wants to revoke her election of coverage under the dependent care FSA. The availability of dependent care services from the new child care provider—whether the provider is a household employee, a family member, or an independent person—is a significant change in coverage similar to a benefit package option becoming available. Anita's employer's cafeteria plan may permit Anita to elect to revoke her previous election of coverage under the dependent care FSA and make a new election to reflect the cost of the new child care provider.

Q 7:58   May a cafeteria plan permit an employee to make an election change if there is change in the coverage provided for a particular benefit?

If an employee or an employee's spouse or dependent experiences a significant curtailment of coverage (but not a loss of coverage), the plan may permit the employee to switch to a different benefit package providing similar coverage (but not drop coverage entirely). An election change may be permitted, for example, if there is a significant increase in the deductible, the copayment, or the out-of-pocket cost-sharing limit under a health plan. However, coverage under a plan is considered to be significantly curtailed only if there is an overall reduction in the coverage provided under the plan. Thus, in most cases, the loss of one particular physician in a network would not be considered a significant curtailment. [Treas. Reg. § 1.125-4(f)(3)]

If an employee (or the employee's spouse or dependent) has a significant curtailment of coverage that amounts to a loss of coverage, the plan may permit the employee to switch to a different benefit option providing similar coverage or drop coverage entirely if no similar option is available.

A loss of coverage generally means a complete loss of coverage. For example, a loss of coverage occurs if the benefit option an employee elected is eliminated, if an HMO ceases to be available in the area where an individual resides, or if an individual is no longer eligible for coverage because of an overall lifetime or annual limitation. In addition, a cafeteria plan may, in its discretion, treat the following as a loss of coverage:

- A substantial decrease in medical care providers available under a health option (such as a major hospital ceasing to be a member of a preferred provider network or a substantial decrease in the number of physicians participating in a preferred provider network or HMO);
- A reduction in the benefits for a specific type of medical condition for which an employee (or an employee's spouse or dependent) is currently undergoing treatment; or
- Any other similar fundamental loss of coverage.

Q 7:59   May a cafeteria plan permit a new election because of a new plan option for coverage added during the plan year or the improvement of an existing option?

Yes. If during a period of coverage a plan adds a new benefit package option or other coverage option, the cafeteria plan may permit affected employees to elect the newly added option prospectively on a pretax basis and make corresponding election changes with respect to other benefit package options providing similar coverage. [Treas. Reg. § 1.125-4(f)(3)(iii)]

Similarly, if a benefit option is significantly improved, the plan may allow employees to revoke their prior elections and make a new, prospective election for coverage under the improved option. In addition, the plan may permit eligible employees who had not previously made a cafeteria plan election to enroll in the plan and elect the new or improved option.

Q 7:60   May a cafeteria plan permit revocation of an election to participate because of changes in coverage under another health care plan?

Yes. A cafeteria plan may permit an employee to make a prospective election change that is on account of and corresponds to a change in coverage under another employer plan. A cafeteria plan may permit an employee to make an election change if coverage under the other plan changes because of a status change or because of an election change during an open enrollment period. [Treas. Reg. § 1.125-4(f)(4)]

In addition, a cafeteria plan may permit an employee to elect coverage under another health care plan if the employee (or the employee's spouse or dependent) loses coverage under a group health plan sponsored by a governmental or educational institution, such as a state children's health insurance program.

Note that if coverage under a HIPAA-covered health plan option under the cafeteria plan was previously declined in favor of another group health plan and the spouse now loses eligibility for that other coverage or the employer contributions toward that coverage cease, the temporary cafeteria plan regulations would require the cafeteria plan to honor a HIPAA special enrollment right (see Q 5:25).

Q 7:61 Do the Section 125 irrevocable election rules apply to a 401(k) option that is included in the cafeteria plan?

No. Instead, a cafeteria plan must follow the rules of Code Sections 401(k) and 401(m) that apply to 401(k) plans. [Treas. Reg. § 1.125-4(h)] Thus, the cafeteria plan may permit an employee to modify or revoke elections in accordance with Code Sections 401(k) and 401(m) and the regulations thereunder.

Q 7:62 May a cafeteria plan permit midyear changes in an employee's salary reduction contributions to a health savings account?

Yes. In fact, a plan is required to allow changes in HSA salary reduction contributions.

The IRS proposed regulations provide that a cafeteria plan offering HSA contributions as a qualified benefit, the plan *must*:

- Specifically describe the HSA contribution benefit;
- Allow employees to prospectively change salary reduction elections for HSA contributions on a monthly basis (or more frequently); and
- Allow employees who becomes ineligible to make HSA contributions to prospectively revoke salary reduction election for HSA contributions.

A cafeteria plan offering HSA contributions through salary reduction may permit employees to make prospective salary reductions at any time during the plan year. In addition, employees may be permitted to change or revoke existing salary reduction elections for HSA contributions at any time. Changes may either increase or decrease HSA contributions. A new election applies only to salary that is not yet currently available. [Prop. Treas. Reg. § 1.125-2(c)]

Premium Conversion Plans

Q 7:63 What is a premium conversion plan?

In a *premium conversion plan*, an employee is offered a choice of cash or pretax payment of employee contributions, typically for medical coverage. The employee elects to reduce his or her compensation or to forgo increases in compensation and to have such amounts contributed, as employer contributions, by the employer on his or her behalf. In other words, the contributions are "converted" from after-tax employee contributions to pretax employer contributions.

> **Note.** The choice of pretax participation in a benefit such as medical coverage or no benefit at all qualifies as a cafeteria plan under Code Section 125 because the required choice between cash or a qualified benefit is present. It is not necessary to offer the qualified benefit on an after-tax basis in order for a valid cafeteria plan to exist.

> **Caution.** Pretax contributions are considered to be employer contributions only for tax purposes. The DOL considers them to be employee contributions for ERISA purposes (see Q 7:86).

A premium conversion plan offering employees a choice between cash (e.g., salary) and payment of the employee share of the employer-provided accident and health insurance premium (excludable from the employee's gross income under Section 106) is referred to as a premium-only plan in the proposed cafeteria plan regulations. [Prop. Treas. Reg. § 1.125-1(a)(5)] The proposed regulations specifically provide that a cafeteria plan may be a premium-only plan. [Prop. Treas. Reg.§ 1.125-1(b)(4)(ii)] A special safe-harbor nondiscrimination test applies to premium-only plans. [Prop. Treas. Reg. § 1.125-7(f)] (See Q 7:92.)

Q 7:64 Is a premium conversion plan a cafeteria plan?

Yes. A premium conversion plan can be one of several choices under a cafeteria plan or a freestanding cafeteria plan, or it can be a feature within the plan to which it applies. The IRS proposed regulations provide that a cafeteria plan may be a premium-only plan that offers employees a choice between cash and payment of the employee share of accident and health insurance premiums. [Prop. Treas. Reg. §§ 1.125-1(a)(5), (b)(4)]

> **Caution.** Some employers simply add a pretax payment feature to an existing medical plan and fail to realize that they have created a combination Section 106 accident and health plan and Section 125 cafeteria plan. This combination status, once created, must be disclosed on the Form 5500 annual report that is filed with the DOL. Moreover, the plan will be subject to the written plan requirement and operational compliance requirements spelled out in the 2007 proposed IRS regulations. [Prop. Treas. Reg. § 1.125-1]

Regardless of how the premium conversion is structured, the plan document must provide that the employer will make employee contributions pursuant to salary reduction agreements under which participants elect to reduce their compensation or to forgo increases in compensation and to have such amounts contributed, as employer contributions, by the employer on their behalf. For purposes of Code Section 125, such amounts contributed are treated as employer contributions to the cafeteria plan to the extent that the agreement relates to salary that has not actually or constructively been received and that does not subsequently become available to the participant. [Prop. Treas. Reg. § 1.125-1(r)(2)]

Q 7:65   Is a premium conversion feature always beneficial to plan participants?

Not necessarily. Disability income benefits under an employee-pay-all disability plan are excludable from income under Code Section 104. If an employee pays for disability income coverage on a salary reduction basis, the coverage is converted to employer-provided accident and health insurance under Code Section 106. Any disability income benefits payable under an employer-provided disability plan become taxable to the disabled participant under Code Section 105 to the extent that they are attributable to employer contributions that were not included in gross income. Accordingly, an employer may wish to consider whether the premium conversion option for disability income coverage should be offered to employees and, if offered, whether the tax effect of selecting (or not selecting) the salary reduction option should be spelled out in employee communications.

> **Practice Pointer.** Many employers offer disability benefits on both a pretax and an after-tax basis through the cafeteria plan so that the participant can choose between current and future tax benefits associated with the type of payment involved.

A similar concern arises with group term life insurance coverage in excess of $50,000. Because such coverage may be taxable to employees under Code Section 79 if it is treated as provided directly or indirectly by the employer (see Qs 11:34–11:35), it may be more advantageous to employees if offered on an after-tax, employee-pay-all basis.

Flexible Spending Arrangements

Q 7:66   What is a flexible spending arrangement?

A *flexible spending arrangement* is an account credited with a certain level of contributions (either employer-paid or employee-paid or both) to reimburse specified expenses up to a specified maximum reimbursement level. The account generally is an unfunded book account of the employer. [Prop. Treas. Reg. § 1.125-5(a)(1)] An FSA is generally used for health or dependent care expenses. An FSA may also be used for adoption assistance. [Prop. Treas. Reg. § 1.125-5(h)] At the employer's option, a cafeteria plan can provide that only those employees who participate in one or more specified employer-provided accident and health plans may participate in a health FSA. [Prop. Treas. Reg. § 1.125-5(g)(1)]

Under the typical FSA, an employee designates an amount of salary reduction contribution for the plan year and directs his or her employer to credit that amount to the FSA. If the amount designated by the employee also represents the amount of dollars that can be drawn out of the FSA as benefits, the FSA is said to take a "contribution equals benefits" approach because a one-to-one relationship exists between the amount of salary reduction contributions and the maximum available benefits under the FSA.

A one-to-one relationship is not required, however. An FSA may also include "employer flex-credits," which are nonelective contributions that the employer makes for every employee eligible to participate in the employer's cafeteria plan, to be used at the employee's election only for one or more qualified benefits. [Prop. Treas. Reg. § 1.125-5(b)(1)] However, the maximum amount of reimbursement available to an employee cannot be substantially in excess of the total of the employee's salary reduction contribution and employer flex-credits. The maximum amount of reimbursement available under an FSA will satisfy the rule if it is less than 500 percent of that total. [Prop. Treas. Reg. § 1.125-5(a)(2)]

An FSA's coverage period must be 12 months (except in the case of a short plan year). [Prop. Treas. Reg. § 1.125-5(e)] However, FSAs for health, dependent care, and adoption assistance are each permitted to have a separate period of coverage, which may be different from the cafeteria plan's plan year.

A cafeteria plan is permitted to specify any interval for employees' salary reduction contributions; however, the specified interval must be uniform for all employees. [Prop. Treas. Reg. § 1.125-5(g)(2)]

Use-it-or-lose-it rule. FSAs must operate on a use-it-or-lose-it basis—that is, unused amounts remaining at the end of the period of coverage (plus any grace period) must be forfeited. [Prop. Treas. Reg. § 1.125-5(c)]

Example. Henry plans to have eye surgery in 2011. For the 2011 plan year, he elects to make $3,000 of salary reduction contributions to a health FSA to pay out-of-pocket expenses for the surgery. During the year, Howard learns that he cannot have the eye surgery performed. However, he does incur $1,000 of medical expenses that he submits to the FSA for reimbursement. As of December 31, 2011, there is $2,000 remaining in Howard's FSA, which will be forfeited under the use-it-or-lose it rule.

Forfeited amounts, called *experience gains*, may be retained by the employer, returned to employees, or used to defray administrative expenses of the cafeteria plan. [Prop. Treas. Reg. § 1.125-5(o)] (See Q 7:35.)

Q 7:67   Is there a dollar cap on the amount that can be contributed to a health FSA?

Historically, there has been no dollar limit on the amount that can be contributed to an employee's health FSA for a plan year, although overfunding of an FSA is discouraged by the use-it-or-lose it rule that requires forfeiture of unspent amounts remaining at year end (or at the end of a grace period, if applicable) (see Q 7:66).

Effective for tax years beginning after 2012, the 2010 Health Reform Act imposes a $2,500 limit on annual salary reduction contributions to a health FSA. [I.R.C. § 125(i) as added by PPACA § 9005 as amended by PPACA § 10902 and PPACA Reconciliation § 1403]

The $2,500 limit is a structural requirement. A cafeteria plan that does not include this limitation starting in 2013 will not qualify as a cafeteria plan within the meaning of Section 125.

Q 7:68   What types of expenses may be reimbursed under a health care FSA?

Reimbursements under a health care FSA must be specifically for medical expenses as defined in Code Section 213(d) (other than premium payments for accident or health insurance, disability insurance or long-term care insurance). [Prop. Treas. Reg. §§ 1.125-5(k)(1), (k)(4)]

Practice Pointer. As a group health plan covering Section 213 medical care, the health care FSA will be secondary to Medicare (see Q 7:71).

A health care FSA cannot reimburse premium payments for other health insurance coverage, such as for other coverage purchased by the employee or coverage maintained by an employer for the employee's spouse. Thus, although a health care FSA may be adopted to supplement or "wrap around" an existing medical plan, the FSA cannot be used to make pretax premium payments for that medical plan. Nonetheless, employee premiums for such a medical plan may be paid on a salary reduction basis through the ordinary operation of the cafeteria plan. A premium conversion option for the medical plan that the FSA supplements can be offered as a separate option under the cafeteria plan or as a second premium-only-plan. [Prop. Treas. Reg. §§ 1.125-1(a)(5), (b)(4)(2)] The bar on premium payments for other health insurance coverage also means that the FSA cannot be used to pay Medicare Part B premiums.

Example. Big Company makes medical plan coverage available to its employees, who are required to contribute toward the monthly premium cost. The plan pays 80 percent of covered benefits, and employees must pay the remaining 20 percent of such expenses. Big Company would like to establish a cafeteria plan to pay for the premiums and copayments. It establishes a health care FSA under which employees can elect salary reduction of up to $5,000 per year to be used to pay for medical expenses (including the 20 percent copayment) that are not covered under the Big Company medical plan. Employees cannot, however, use any portion of the $5,000 FSA amount to pay the monthly premium cost of their medical plan coverage.

If Big Company wishes to permit employees to pay their medical plan premiums on a pretax basis, it must have an additional salary reduction authorization for the premium conversion feature. The cafeteria plan would then have two parts: a health care FSA and a premium conversion option. Alternatively, the medical plan could be amended to add a premium conversion feature, thus creating a combination medical plan/cafeteria plan. In that case, the $5,000 FSA would be a separate cafeteria plan.

Q 7:69   Can a health FSA reimburse expenses for nonprescription medicines or drugs?

Effective for expenses incurred after December 31, 2010, a law change made by the 2010 Health Reform Act generally bars an FSA from reimbursing expenses for over-the-counter (OTC) medicines or drugs. The law change provides that an expense incurred for a medicine or drug will be treated as a medical expense only if the medicine or drug is a prescribed drug or insulin. [I.R.C. § 106(f) as added by PPACA § 9003] There is some wiggle room, however. The law specifically provides that what constitutes a prescribed drug is to be determined without regard to whether such drug is available without a prescription. Thus, under the provision, the cost of OTC medicines may not be reimbursed with excludable income through a health FSA, *unless the medicine is prescribed by a physician.*

Under prior law, the IRS drew a distinction between expenses that qualified as deductible medical expenses for income tax purposes and expenses eligible for tax-free reimbursements from an FSA. The IRS ruled that amounts paid by an individual for OTC medicines or drugs that can be purchased without the prescription of a physician *cannot* be claimed as a medical expense deduction on the individual's income tax return. [Rev. Rul. 2003-58, 2003-22 I.R.B. 959]

By contrast, the IRS concluded that amounts paid by an employee for medicines purchased without a physician's prescription to treat personal injuries or sickness nonetheless could be reimbursed on a tax-free basis by an employer health FSA. [Rev. Rul. 2003-102, 2003-38 I.R.B. 559]

Q 7:70   Is a health care FSA required to qualify as a Section 105 accident or health plan?

Yes. A health care FSA must be a bona fide accident or health plan under Code Sections 105 and 106. [Prop. Treas. Reg. § 1.125-5(k)(l)] As a result, it will be subject to the requirements of HIPAA (see chapters 3 and 5) unless it qualifies for the regulatory exemption adopted by the IRS (see Q 7:109).

Q 7:71   Must a health care FSA be the primary payer and Medicare a secondary payer?

Yes. It appears that a health care FSA, as a Section 105 medical plan, is subject to the requirements of Code Section 5000. Accordingly, the Section 5000 provisions requiring the medical plan to be the primary payer and Medicare to be the secondary payer under certain circumstances will apply to the health care FSA. [42 C.F.R. § 411.100, added by 60 Fed. Reg. 45,362 (Aug. 31, 1995)] (See Qs 5:133–5:151 for a discussion of Medicare secondary-payer rules.)

Characterization as a group health plan also means that a health care FSA would have to meet the additional requirements for group health plans contained in ERISA Section 609 dealing with coverage of pediatric vaccines, coverage of adopted children, and qualified medical child support orders and the HIPAA requirements (see chapters 3 and 5 for a detailed discussion of these requirements), unless the particular FSA qualifies for the regulatory exemption from HIPAA coverage (see Q 7:109).

Q 7:72   What insurance-type characteristics must a health care FSA exhibit?

A health care FSA is a self-insured medical plan. As a result, it must satisfy the following requirements:

1. Coverage need not be provided through a commercial insurance contract, but the FSA must exhibit the risk-shifting and risk distribution characteristics of insurance.
2. The reimbursement arrangement cannot have the effect of eliminating all, or substantially all, risk of loss to the employer maintaining the plan.
3. Reimbursements must be paid specifically to reimburse the participant for medical expenses incurred previously during the period of coverage.
4. Reimbursements cannot be paid to the participant in the form of cash or any other taxable or nontaxable benefit (including health coverage for an additional period) without regard to whether the employee in fact incurs medical expenses during the period of coverage.
5. The maximum amount of coverage must be available at all times during the period of coverage (reduced by prior reimbursements for the same period of coverage). Proration is required, however, when an employee did not continue his or her FSA coverage during an FMLA leave (see Q 7:119). [Prop. Treas. Reg. § 1.125-5(d)(1)]

If the risk of loss for an employer maintaining a plan or other insurer is negated, either under the arrangement itself or by some other means outside the plan, the arrangement does not shift and redistribute risk. Thus, for example, if an employee quits his or her job after submitting huge covered claims to a health care FSA, but after paying only a few salary reduction contributions to the FSA and leaving the FSA in a deficit position, the employer cannot require the employee to repay the excess of the FSA benefits paid over the salary reduction contributions actually made. Similarly, an employee's salary reduction contributions cannot be accelerated based on incurred claims and reimbursements. [Prop. Treas. Reg. § 1.125-5(d)(1)]

A health care FSA must also meet the general requirements for an FSA (see Qs 7:77–7:82).

Q 7:73 Why must health care FSA coverage be uniform throughout the period of coverage?

Coverage under a health care FSA must be uniform throughout the period of coverage in order to shift risk to the employer. The maximum amount of reimbursement under the FSA must be available at all times during the period of coverage and cannot hinge on how much the participant has contributed to the FSA to date in the coverage period. [Prop. Treas. Reg. § 1.125-5(d)(1)]

> **Example.** Little Company establishes a health care FSA to cover all medical expenses not covered under its group medical plan. Julia elects an annual reimbursable amount of $3,600 under the FSA. As a result, her monthly salary reduction contribution to the FSA is $300 ($3,600 ÷ 12). As of the second month of the period of coverage, Julia has contributed $600 via salary reduction. During the second month, she incurs a medical expense of $2,000 that is not covered by Little Company's medical plan and submits it to the FSA for reimbursement. Assuming that the expense is otherwise covered under the terms of the FSA, Little Company must pay the full $2,000 claim even though Julia has not yet contributed that much to her FSA. The book account for a particular participant must be credited at the start of the plan year with the full amount of reimbursement elected for the full period of coverage, and the participant must be given the right to receive the full amount of covered benefits at any time during the period of coverage.

Employers must make benefit payments on at least a monthly basis but are permitted to hold claims until the total amount submitted is at least a specified, reasonable minimum amount, such as $50. [Prop. Treas. Reg. § 1.125-5(d)(2)]

Permitted reduction in benefits. An employer is permitted to reduce the maximum amount of reimbursement available under the FSA at any time during the period of coverage by the amount of prior reimbursements attributable to the same period of coverage. [Prop. Treas. Reg. § 1.125-5(d)(1)]

Q 7:74 Is there a limit on the amount of expenses that can be reimbursed by a health care FSA?

Yes. The maximum amount of reimbursement by a health care FSA to a participant for a period of coverage must be less than 500 percent of the total contributions to the participant's FSA (employee salary reductions and employer flex credits). [Prop. Treas. Reg. § 1.125-5(a)(2)]

Q 7:75 How does a plan ensure that a participant cannot manipulate the amount of coverage under a health FSA?

A benefit under a cafeteria plan cannot be operated in a manner that allows a participant to purchase coverage under an accident or health plan only for periods for which he or she expects to incur expenses. Thus, for example, if a participant is allowed to elect coverage on a month-by-month or expense-by-expense basis, reimbursements will not be considered to flow from a qualified benefit and will not qualify for the Code Section 105(b) exclusion from gross income. On the other hand, if the period of coverage is 12 months and the cafeteria plan does not permit an employee to elect specific amounts of coverage, reimbursement, or salary reduction for less than 12 months, the cafeteria plan does not operate to enable participants to purchase coverage only for periods during which medical care will be incurred. [Prop. Treas. Reg. §§ 1.125-1, Q&A-17, 1.125-5(f)]

Q 7:76   When must an expense be incurred in order to be reimbursable by a health care FSA?

For an expense to be reimbursed under a health care FSA, it generally must be incurred during a participant's period of coverage under the FSA. However, a special rule permits an FSA to provide that expenses incurred during a grace period of up to 2½ months immediately following the end of the year may be paid or reimbursed from funds remaining in an employee's FSA at the end of the prior plan year. [IRS Notice 2005-42, 2005-23 I.R.B. 1; Prop. Treas. Reg. § 1.125-1(e)] (See Q 7:29.)

For FSA purposes, an expense is incurred when the medical care is received; other dates, such as the date on which the employee is formally billed or charged, the date he or she pays for the expense, or the date proof of expense is submitted, are not controlling. An FSA, it should be noted, cannot make advance reimbursements of projected expenses. [Prop. Treas. Reg. § 1.125-6(a)(2)(ii)]

An expense is not treated as incurred during a period of FSA coverage if it is incurred before the later of (1) the date on which the FSA is first in existence or (2) the date on which the participant first becomes covered under the FSA. [Prop. Treas. Reg. § 1.125-6(a)(2)] Paying or reimbursing expenses incurred before the later of the adoption date or effective date of the cafeteria plan or before the beginning of a period of coverage is an operational failure that will disqualify the plan. [Prop. Treas. Reg. § 1.125-1(c)(7)]

> **Note.** A key exception to this bar on retroactivity is the HIPAA rule permitting retroactive enrollment of newborns and children who are adopted or placed for adoption (see Q 7:51). In addition, the proposed regulations provide for an election window for new employees (see Q 7:47).

Delayed reimbursement. A cafeteria plan may provide a run-out period for covered medical care expenses to be reimbursed after the close of the period of coverage (or grace period, if any) in which they were incurred. [Prop. Treas. Reg. §§ 1.125-1(f), 1.125-6(a)(2)]

Multiyear expenses. As noted above, a health care FSA cannot make advance reimbursements for future or projected expenses. However, when it comes to certain types of health care expenses, the IRS takes a flexible approach.

The proposed cafeteria plan regulations specifically provide that a health FSA is permitted, but not required, to reimburse employees for orthodontia services before the services are performed, but only to the extent an employee has actually made advance payments for the orthodontia. The orthodontia services are deemed to be incurred when the advance payments are made. [Prop. Treas. Reg. § 1.125-5(k)(3)(i)]

In an unofficial information letter to a taxpayer several years ago, the IRS acknowledged that expenses like orthodontia are billed differently from other medical expenses, and the costs do not necessarily match up with the date the services are provided. In these cases, a patient is routinely charged an initial amount up front and thereafter is required to make periodic payments for services that will be provided over a lengthy period. Therefore, the IRS said it would be reasonable for a health care FSA to reimburse an employee for the full amount of expenses actually paid. On the other hand, the IRS said it would not be unreasonable for the plan administrator to request a breakdown of the bill and to reimburse only those expenses for which services have been provided. [IRS Information Letter (Feb. 19, 1997)]

Practice Pointer. Regardless of which reimbursement method a health care FSA selects, the policy should be clearly communicated to the employees. Employees must forfeit amounts contributed to a health care FSA that are not used for covered expenses by year end (or within a 2½-month grace period after year end, if permitted by the plan). Therefore, an employee who contributes to an FSA to cover up-front payments for orthodontia or similar treatments may be subject to a forfeiture if the plan's policy is to reimburse only for services actually rendered.

Special rules are applicable to expenses incurred during FMLA leave (see Q 7:119).

The proposed regulations also provide that a health FSA can reimburse expenses for durable medical equipment that will last beyond the end of the coverage period. For example, a health FSA is permitted to reimburse the cost of wheelchair for an employee. [Prop. Treas. Reg. § 1.125-5(k)(3)(iii)]

Terminated participants. If a health FSA participant terminates employment, expenses incurred after his or coverage ends are not reimbursable, unless the employee elects COBRA coverage for the FSA. [Prop. Treas. Reg. § 1.125-6(a)(ii)(iii)].

Example. Jill works for McGregor Company and participates in a health FSA under her employer's cafeteria plan. The cafeteria plan provides that participation terminates when an individual is no longer employed by McGregor, unless the former employee elects COBRA coverage for the FSA. Jill elected to make salary reduction contributions of $1,200 to the health FSA for the plan year. As of June 30, Jill has contributed $600 toward the health FSA but incurred no medical expenses. On June 30, Jill terminates employment with McGregor and she elects COBRA coverage. On July 15, Jill incurs a medical expense of $500. The cafeteria plan cannot reimburse Jill for any portion of the $500 because, at the time the expense was incurred, Jill was not a participant in the cafeteria plan.

Note. See chapter 6 for a discussion of how the COBRA coverage rules apply to health FSAs.

Q 7:77 What type of substantiation must a cafeteria plan require for claims for reimbursement from a health care FSA?

As a general rule, all expenses must be substantiated by information from an independent third-party describing the service or product, the date of the service or sale, and the amount. Self-substantiation or self-certification of an expense by an employee is not good enough. [Prop. Treas. Reg. § 1.125-6(b)(3)(i)]

However, a special rule applies when employees submit claims for reimbursement of health insurance deductibles or copayments. If the employer is provided with information from an independent third-party (such as an *explanation of benefits* (EOB) from an insurance company) that shows the date of medical care and the amount the employee is responsible for paying, the claim can be treated as fully substantiated provided the employee certifies that the amount has not been reimbursed and that the employee will not seek reimbursement from any other plan. [Prop. Treas. Reg. § 1.125-6(b)(3)(ii)]

Practice Pointer. "Self-substantiation" by an employee will not satisfy the requirements. Thus, an FSA will not satisfy the requirements if it reimburses expenses when an employee submits only a description, the amount, and the date of the expenses without a statement from an independent third party verifying the expenses. Moreover, *all* expenses paid under a plan that permits self-substantiation will be included in gross income, including reimbursements for legitimate medical expenses, whether or not they are substantiated.

Because the proposed cafeteria plan regulations make these requirements an absolute precondition to receiving benefits from the plan, they should be reflected in the plan document for the cafeteria plan.

Q 7:78 Can a health FSA make expense reimbursements using debit and credit cards?

Yes. Under a traditional FSA, employees pay for out-of-pocket medical expenses and then submit documentation to the employer to obtain reimbursements. However, a few years ago the IRS has ruled that employees covered by health FSAs can be provided with debit and/or credit cards to tap their FSA funds. [Rev. Rul. 2003-43, 2003-21 I.R.B. 935]

The IRS ruling approving debit and credit card reimbursement arrangements contained a catch that could have significantly lessened the appeal of such arrangements. The ruling stated: "Under the facts described, payments made to medical service providers through the use of debit, credit, and stored-value cards are reportable by the employer on Form 1099-MISC under Code Section 6041. Section 6041 provides for information reporting by persons engaged in a trade or business who make payments of fixed or determinable income to another person in the course of such trade or business of $600 or more in a taxable year." Thus, under the terms of the IRS rulings, employers would have been faced with the administrative burden of reporting a plan participant's credit or debit card payments to a doctor or other health care provider if annual total exceeded $600 per provider. (*Note:* Certain payments, including payments to pharmacies for prescription drugs and payments to not-for-profit hospitals, are not subject to the information reporting requirements.)

Fortunately, Congress took action to eliminate this potential administrative hurdle. The Medicare Prescription Drug Improvement and Modernization Act of 2003 [Pub. L. No. 108-173, 117 Stat. 2066 (2003)] creates an exception to Form 1099 information reporting requirements for health reimbursement arrangements. The law provides that the Code Section 6041 reporting requirements do not apply to any payment for medical care made under an FSA that is treated as employer-provided coverage under an accident or health plan.

Practice Pointer. A debit card or credit card program has distinct advantages for employees because they can pay medical expenses directly from their FSA accounts rather than paying the expenses with other funds and then seeking reimbursement from the plan. However, the IRS ruling makes it clear that *all* charges must be fully substantiated to ensure tax-free treatment for employees.

In a follow-up notice, the IRS provided additional details on acceptable substantiation methods for the use of debit and credit cards. [Notice 2006-69, 2006-31 I.R.B. 107]

The proposed regulations also spell out the ground rules for using debit, credit, or stored value cards (collectively referred to as debit cards) in connection with a health FSA. [Prop. Treas. Reg. § 1.125-6(d), (e), (f)] The proposed regulations incorporate previously issued guidance on the use of debit cards. [*See* Rev. Rul. 2003-43, 2003-1 C.B. 935, amplified; Notice 2006-69, 2006-31 I.R.B. 107, Notice 2007-2, 2007-2 I.R.B. 254; Rev. Proc. 98-25, 1998-1 C.B. 689.]

Debit card requirements. Before an employee participating in a health FSA is issued a debit card, the employee must sign a written agreement. The written agreement must provide that the employee:

- *Will* only use the card to pay for medical expenses of the employee or his or her spouse or dependents
- *Will not* use the debit card for any medical expense that has already been reimbursed
- *Will not* seek reimbursement under any other health plan for an expense paid for with the debit card, and
- *Will* acquire and retain documentation (including invoices and receipts) for any expense paid with the debit card.

The debit card must bear a statement providing that the agreements are reaffirmed each time the employee uses the card.

The debit card must be automatically cancelled when the employee ceases participation in the health FSA. Use of the debit card must be limited to:

- Physicians, dentists, vision care offices, hospitals, or other medical care providers with health care-related merchant category codes;

- Stores with the merchant category code for drugstores and pharmacies if, on a location by location basis, 90 percent of the store's gross receipts during the prior taxable year consisted of items that qualify as expenses for medical care; and

- Other stores that have implemented an inventory information approval system (see below).

Substantiation. The employer must require substantiation of all payments made with debit cards.

Permissible point-of-sale substantiation methods for payments to health care providers and to drugstores and pharmacies that meet the 90 percent gross receipts test are copayment matches, recurring expenses, and real-time substantiation. In the case of other charges, point-of-sale substantiation is done by matching inventory information with a list of allowable medical expenses. All other charges to a debit card must be treated as conditional until the plan receives information from an independent third party describing the goods or services, the date of the service or sale, and the amount of the transaction.

Copayment match substantiation. A debit or credit amount can be treated as substantiated if it exactly matches the plan's copayment amount for the particular product or services. For example, if an employee debits $10 for a doctor visit under a plan with a $10 copayment for each doctor visit, the debit can be treated as automatically substantiated. Moreover, automatic substantiation applies if a debit or credit charge is an exact multiple of a plan copayment (e.g., a debit of $30 for three prescriptions under a plan with a $10 copayment for prescription drugs). The copayment match substantiation method can be used if a plan has multiple copayments for the same product or service (e.g., different copayments for generic and nongeneric drugs). However, automatic substantiation applies only as long as the exact multiple does not exceed five times the maximum copayment. If the dollar amount of a debit or credit charge exceeds five times the copayment, the transaction must be treated as conditional pending additional confirmation.

Example 1. Plan X requires a $5 copayment for generic drugs and a $10 copayment for nongeneric drugs. Amy uses a debit card at a pharmacy to purchase five nongeneric prescriptions, for a total debit of $50. Because the transaction is at a pharmacy, and the amount of the transaction is an exact multiple that does not exceed five times the maximum copayment for prescriptions, the debit can be treated as substantiated without further review or documentation.

Example 2. The facts are the same as those in Example 1, except that Amy uses the card at a pharmacy to purchase three generic prescriptions and three nongeneric prescriptions for a total debit of $45. Because the transaction is at a pharmacy, and the amount of the transaction is an exact match of a combination of the plan's copayments that does not exceed five times the maximum copayment, the debit is automatically substantiated.

Example 3. The facts are the same as those in Example 1, except that Amy uses the card at a pharmacy to buy six nongeneric prescriptions for a total charge of $60. Because the amount of the transaction exceeds five times the maximum $10 copayment for prescriptions, the debit must be substantiated by a receipt showing that Amy bought prescription drugs, the date of the purchase, and the amount of the purchase.

Example 4. The facts are the same as those in Example 1, except that Amy uses the card at a pharmacy to buy two nongeneric prescriptions and a nonprescription medication for a total of $27. Because the debit is not an exact match of a multiple or combination of the copayments prescriptions, the transaction must be further substantiated.

Recurring expenses. Recurring expenses that match expenses previously approved as to amount, medical care provider and time period (for example, for an employee who refills a prescription drug on a regular basis at the same provider and in the same amount) can be treated as automatically substantiated without submission of a receipt or further review.

Real-time substantiation. If a independent third party (for example, medical care provider, merchant, or pharmacy benefit manager) provides information at the time and point of sale (by email, the internet, intranet or telephone) to verify that the charge is for a medical expense, the expense can be treated as substantiated.

Inventory information approval substantiation. Under an inventory information approval system, debit card transactions are approved or rejected by the card processor's or participating merchant's system using inventory control information (such as stock keeping units, or SKUs) against a list of items that qualify as medical expenses (including nonprescription drugs), approved transactions can be treated as automatically substantiated. If, after matching inventory information, it is determined that only some of the items purchased are medical expenses, the transaction is approved only as to the qualified medical expenses. In that case, the merchant or service-provider must ask for additional payment from the employee for the items that do not qualify. This method can be used for payments to merchants or service providers that do not have health care-related merchant category codes, but only if the merchants or providers participate in the inventory information approval system.

Example. Employer D's FSA provides reimbursements for both prescription and nonprescription medications. D uses the inventory information approval system for debit card transactions, including transactions at participating stores that sell nonprescription medications but do not have health-related merchant codes. At one participating store, D's employee, Bernie, goes to the counter with aspirin, antacid, and cold medicines that cost $20.75, as well as $50 of items that do not qualify as medical expenses. The store's system compares the SKUs for all the times to a list of qualifying medical expenses. The debit for the $20.75 of medical expense items is approved, but the $50 debit for nonmedical items is rejected and Bernie is asked for an additional payment for that amount. The $20.75 of medical items can be treated as automatically substantiated.

Transition rule. The IRS provided transition relief to give merchants of non-health care products time to implement inventory systems. However, as of July 1, 2009, debit cards cannot be used at any store, vendor, or merchant that did not have a health care merchant category code unless the store, vendor, or merchant had implemented an inventory information approval system. [IRS Notice 2007-2, 2007-2 I.R.B. 254; IRS Notice 2008-104, 2008-51 I.R.B. 1298]

Identity theft protection rules. The Federal Trade Commission (FTC) has issued new regulations called "Red Flag Rules" to protect consumers from identity theft. [16 C.F.R. pt. 681] These Red Flag Rules were developed pursuant to the Fair and Accurate Credit Transactions (FACT) Act of 2003. [Pub. L. No. 108-159, 117 Stat. 1952 (Dec. 4, 2003)] The rules require financial institutions and creditors with covered accounts to implement theft-prevention programs to identify, detect, and respond to patterns, practices, or specific activities that could indicate identity theft. Compliance was required by June 1, 2010.

The FTC has made it clear that health care FSAs are not generally subject to the Red Flag Rules. According to the FTC, neither offering employees health care FSAs nor maintaining those accounts for employers makes a business subject to the Red Flag Rules. However, if an FSA includes a debit card feature, the issuer of the cards—typically, a third-party administrator acting on behalf of a sponsoring employer—will be considered a "financial institution" for purposes of the Red Flag Rules and must implement identity-theft protections. Consequently, employers that sponsor FSAs with a debit card feature should confirm that the card issuer is in compliance with the new rules.

Q 7:79 May an employee who has an HSA elect a health FSA?

A health savings account (HSA) is a tax-exempt trust or custodial account established exclusively for the purpose of paying qualified medical expenses of the account beneficiary who, for the months for which contributions are made to an HSA, is covered under a high-deductible health plan (HDHP). [IRS Notice 2004-2, 2004-2 I.R.B. 269] (See chapter 3 for fuller discussion of HSAs.) As a general rule, an employee is ineligible for an HSA if he or she is covered by an employer-sponsored health FSA that pays or reimburses medical expenses incurred before the minimum annual deductible for the HDHP has been satisfied. [Rev. Rul. 2004-45, 2004-22 I.R.B. 971]

However, coverage under an HSA-compatible *limited-purpose health FSA* or *post-deductible health FSA* will not disqualify an employee from HSA participation. Limited-purpose health FSAs *and* post-deductible health FSAs that meet all the requirements of Code Section 125 can be offered through a cafeteria plan. [Prop. Treas. Reg. § 1.125-2(m)(1)]

Limited-purpose health FSA. A limited-purpose health FSA is one that pays or reimburses only benefits for "permitted coverage" (i.e., preventive, vision or dental coverage). A limited-purpose health FSA may pay or reimburse preventive care benefits. [Prop. Treas. Reg. § 1.125-2(m)(3)]

Post-deductible health FSA. A post-deductible health FSA or HRA is one that does not pay or reimburse any medical expense incurred before the minimum annual deductible is satisfied. No medical expenses incurred before the annual HDHP deductible is satisfied may be reimbursed by a post-deductible FSA, regardless of whether the HDHP covers the expense or whether the deductible is later satisfied. For example, even if chiropractic care is not covered under the HDHP, expenses for chiropractic care incurred before the HDHP deductible is satisfied are not reimbursable at any time by a post-deductible health FSA. The deductible for a post-deductible health FSA need not be the same as the deductible for the HDHP, but in no event may any benefits be provided before the minimum annual HDHP deductible has been met even if the deductible can be satisfied by different expenses. [Prop. Treas. Reg. § 1.125-2(m)(4)]

Combination limited-purpose and post-deductible FSA. The 2007 proposed regulations authorize a limited-purpose post-deductible FSA combo. An FSA is a combination of a limited-purpose health FSA and post-deductible health FSA if each of the benefits and reimbursements provided under the FSA are permitted under either a limited-purpose health FSA or post-deductible health FSA. For example, before the HDHP deductible is satisfied, a combination limited-purpose and post-deductible health FSA may reimburse only preventive, vision or dental expenses. A combination limited-purpose and post-deductible health FSA may also reimburse any medical expense that may otherwise be paid by an FSA (that is, no insurance premiums or long-term care benefits) that is incurred after the HDHP deductible is satisfied. [Prop. Treas. Reg. § 1.125-2(m)(4)]

Substantiation requirements. In addition to providing third-party substantiation of medical expenses (see Q 7:77), a participant in a post-deductible health FSA must provide information from an independent third party that the HDHP deductible has been satisfied. A participant in a limited-purpose health FSA must provide information from an independent third-party that the medical expenses are for vision care, dental care or preventive care. [Prop. Treas. Reg. § 1.125-2(m)(6)]

Q 7:80 Are there any special considerations if an employee wants to switch from a health FSA for one plan year to an HSA for the next year?

There may be. If the employer's cafeteria plan provides that health FSAs operate on a strict "use-it-or-lose-it" basis, any unspent funds remaining in an employee's FSA at the end of the plan year are forfeited to the plan. Therefore, an employee will no longer be covered by the FSA when HSA participation commences.

However, overlapping coverage under an FSA and an HSA can arise if an employer's FSA provides for a grace period. For example, suppose an employee who was covered by an FSA for Year 1 wants to set up an HSA for Year 2. If the FSA has a grace period extending until March 15 of Year 2, the employee will not be eligible for HSA coverage until April 1 of Year 2—even if the employee is not covered by an FSA for Year 2.

The IRS has suggested that one way to solve this problem for employees who are switching from FSA to HSA coverage is for the employer to amend its cafeteria plan document to provide for mandatory conversion of the general purpose FSA to a limited-purpose or post-deductible FSA during the grace period. [Rev. Rul. 2005-86, 2005-49 I.R.B. 1075]

However, the Tax Relief and Health Care Act of 2006 [Pub. L. No. 109-433, 120 Stat. 3196 (2006)] created another option. For tax years beginning after December 31, 2006, coverage under a health FSA is disregarded in determining an employee's eligibility for HSA purposes, provided that either (1) the balance in the FSA at the end of the plan year is zero or (2) the employee is making a qualified HSA distribution in an amount equal to the remaining balance in the FSA as of the end of the plan year. [I.R.C. § 223(c)(1)(B)(iii)]

In the committee reports on the Tax Relief and Health Care Act, Congress indicated that the IRS is expected to provide guidance to facilitate rollovers and the establishment of HSAs. For example, Congress expects the IRS guidance to provide that FSA coverage during a grace period will be disregarded if an employee elects HDHP coverage and a qualified HSA distribution before the end of a year, even if the transfer of the FSA funds cannot be completed until the following plan year. Moreover, Congress said similar rules should apply to any qualified HSA distributions in order to facilitate such distributions at the beginning of an employee's first year of HSA eligibility.

An IRS notice followed up on that mandate by providing that an employee with a year-end balance in a general purpose FSA with a grace period will be treated as an eligible individual for HSA purposes as of the first day of the first month of the following plan year that the employee has HDHP coverage if all of the following conditions are met:

- The employer amends the health FSA effective by the last day of the plan year to allow qualified HSA distributions.
- The employee has not previously made a qualified distribution from the FSA.
- The employee has HDHP coverage as of the first day of the month in which a qualified distribution is made and the employee is otherwise eligible for an HSA.
- The employee elects to have the employer make a qualified distribution from the health FSA by the last day of the plan year.
- The FSA makes no reimbursements to the employee after the last day of the plan year.
- The employer makes the qualified distribution directly to the HSA trustee by the 15th day of the third calendar month following the end of the year (March 15 in the case of calendar year plans), but only after the employee becomes HSA-eligible.
- The qualified distribution does not exceed the lesser of (a) the FSA balance on September 21, 2006, or (b) the date of the distribution.

Following the qualified distribution, either (a) there is a zero balance in the FSA and the employee is no longer a participant in any non-HSA-compatible plan or (b) the general purpose FSA is converted to an HSA-compatible FSA. [IRS Notice 2007-22, 2007-10 I.R.B. 670]

The proposed cafeteria plan regulations provide that a cafeteria plan can offer employees the right to elect qualified HSA distributions. [Prop. Treas. Reg. § 1.125-2(n)]

Practice Pointer. Although a qualified HSA distribution can be made for any year through 2011, there is a potential catch for some employees. An individual who was not covered by an FSA on September 21, 2006, cannot elect a qualified HSA distribution. Similarly, an individual who participated in an FSA with one employer on September 21, 2006, and subsequently participates in an FSA with another employer after that date cannot elect a qualified distribution from the second employer's FSA. [IRS Notice 2007-32, 2007-10 I.R.B. 670] So an employee who signed up for a health FSA for the first time in 2010 but wants to elect an HSA for 2011 cannot make a qualified HSA distribution of funds remaining in the FSA at the end of 2010. The employee's only option to avoid overlapping coverage during the FSA grace period is to convert the FSA to a limited purpose or post-deductible FSA if permitted by the cafeteria plan (see Q 7:79).

Q 7:81   What design restrictions are applicable to dependent care FSAs under cafeteria plans?

Dependent care FSAs must comply with the incurred expense, timing, and anti-manipulation principles similar to those that apply to health care FSAs, as well as with claim substantiation standards. [Prop. Treas. Reg. §§ 1.125-5(h)(3); 1.125-6(d)(4)] Dependent care FSAs, however, are not required to provide uniform coverage throughout the coverage period, as is required for health care FSAs (see Q 7:73). [Prop. Treas. Reg. § 1.125-5(d)(4)]

Example. The Biddle Company adopts a dependent care FSA. Brian, a Biddle employee, elects an annual reimbursable amount of $1,200 under the dependent care FSA. As a result, his monthly salary reduction contribution to the dependent care FSA is $100 ($1,200 ÷ 12). In the second month of the period of coverage, Brian has contributed $200 via salary reduction. During the second month, he incurs a covered dependent care expense in the amount of $400 and submits the bill to the dependent care FSA for reimbursement. The Biddle Company is not required to pay the full $400 claim because the dependent care FSA is not subject to any risk-shifting requirement. Biddle can pay $200 of the claim and hold the remainder pending additional salary reduction contributions.

A dependent care assistance FSA can only reimburse expenses incurred while an employee is covered by the plan. Moreover, the FSA cannot reimburse dependent care expenses until the expenses are incurred. For this purpose, dependent care expenses are treated as incurred when the care is provided, not when the employee is billed, charged for, or pays for the dependent care. [Prop. Treas. Reg. § 1.125-6(a)(4)]

> **Example 1.** Mary works for Finney Corporation where she participates in a cafeteria plan. Mary has a one-year-old son and elects $5,000 of coverage under the plan's dependent care FSA. On February 1, Mary reserves a place for her son at a child care center and pays a nonrefundable $500 fee, which will be applied against the center's $1,200 monthly charge for the first month of care. On March 1, the child care center begins caring for Mary's son. On that date, Mary pays the center $700 (the $1,200 charge for March less the $500 fee). On April 1, Mary pays the center $1,200 for the care to be provided in April. Since the dependent care expenses are incurred when the services are provided, the $500 fee Mary paid on February 1 and the $700 paid on March 1 may not be reimbursed until April 1 (or, if later, when the amounts are substantiated). For dependent care services provided in April, the $1,200 paid on April 1 may be reimbursed as of May 1 (or when substantiated).

> **Example 2.** The facts are the same as those in Example 1, except that Mary made other child care arrangements and did not use the center's services. Consequently, she forfeited the nonrefundable $500 fee. Because the child care center provided no services to Mary, the $500 fee is not eligible for reimbursement.

Optional spend-down. Under the IRS proposed regulations, a cafeteria plan may provide that dependent care expenses incurred after the date an employee stops participation in the cafeteria plan (for example, after termination) and through the last day of that plan year (and any grace period) may be reimbursed from unused benefits. [Prop. Treas. Reg. § 1.125-6(a)(4)(v)]

> **Example 3.** For a calendar year, Joe elects to make $5,000 of salary reduction contributions to a dependent care assistance FSA through his company's cafeteria plan. Joe leaves the company on June 30. As of that date, Joe has made $2,500 in salary reduction contributions. However, he incurred and was reimbursed for only $2,000 of child care expenses, leaving $500 remaining in the plan. After Joe starts work with another company, he incurs more than $500 of child expenses for the remainder of the year. Because Joe's former employer's cafeteria plan allows terminated employees to "spend down" unused salary reduction amounts for dependent care assistance, Joe can claim reimbursement for $500 of child care expenses incurred after his termination of employment.

> **Note.** There is no similar spend-down provision for health FSAs. However, terminated participants in a health FSA can elect COBRA continuation coverage. Presumably, this spend-down provision is intended to parallel the COBRA option for health FSAs.

Substantiation. Dependent care expenses are subject to the general substantiation rules. Expenses must be substantiated by information from an independent third party describing the services, the date of the services, and the amount. Self-substantiation or self-certification of an expense by an employee is not good enough. [Prop. Treas. Reg. § 1.125-6(b)(3)(i)]

Q 7:82   Can unused contributions under a health care FSA be used to reimburse excess expenses under a dependent care FSA and vice versa?

No. A health care FSA cannot reimburse dependent care expenses, nor can a dependent care FSA reimburse health care expenses. If any contributions remain unused in an FSA at the close of the period of coverage (plus a grace period, if permitted by the plan), they must be forfeited under the use-it-or-lose-it rule (see Q 7:29). The proposed Treasury regulations do, however, permit an FSA that has experience gain for a period of coverage to return the excess of employer- and employee-paid premiums paid plus income, if any, over total claim reimbursement and reasonable administrative expenses to the premium payers as dividends or premium refunds. In no case may that be done based directly or indirectly on individual claims experience. [Prop. Treas. Reg. § 1.125-5(o)]

Q 7:83   Can debit, credit or stored-value cards be provided to participants in a dependent care FSA?

An employer may use a debit or other payment card program to provide benefits under a dependent care FSA. However, dependent care expenses may not be reimbursed before the expenses are incurred. Dependent care expenses are treated as having been incurred when the dependent care services are provided, not when the expenses are formally billed or charged, or paid by the participant. [Prop. Treas. Reg. § 1.125-6(a)(4)(i)] Therefore, if a dependent care provider requires payment before the dependent care services are provided, those expenses cannot be reimbursed at the time of payment, even through the use of a payment card program. [Prop. Treas. Reg. § 1.125-6(g)]

Nonetheless, the IRS says that an employer may use a special method to provide reimbursements for dependent care expenses through a payment card program. [Notice 2006-69, 2006-31 I.R.B. 107; Prop. Treas. Reg. § 1.125-6(g)]

Under the special method, the employee pays initial expenses to the dependent care provider at the beginning of the plan year or on enrollment in the dependent care FSA. The employee then submits to the employer or plan administrator a statement from the dependent care provider substantiating the dates and amounts for the services. After the statement is received, but *not before the date the services are provided as indicated on the statement*, the plan makes available through the payment card an amount equal to the lesser of (1) the previously incurred and substantiated expense, or (2) the employee's total salary reduction amount to date. The amount available through the card can be increased in the amount of any additional dependent care expenses only after the additional expenses have been incurred. The amount on the card may then be used to pay for later dependent care expenses. These later card transactions may be treated as substantiated without further review if the transactions are for an amount equal to or less than the previously substantiated amount.

If there is an increase to the previously substantiated amount or a change in the dependent care provider, the employee must submit a statement or receipt from the dependent care provider substantiating the new claimed expense before amounts relating to the increased amount or new provider may be added to the card.

> **Example.** Zeta Corp. sponsors a dependent care FSA through its cafeteria plan. Salary reduction amounts for participating employees are made on a weekly payroll basis. Thus, at any given time, the amount of available dependent care coverage equals the employee's salary reduction amount to date minus claims previously paid from the plan. Zeta has adopted a payment card program for its dependent care FSA. Stella, a participant in the dependent care FSA, has elected $5,000 of dependent care coverage. Zeta reduces Stella's weekly salary by $96.15 to pay for coverage under the dependent care FSA. At the beginning of the plan year, Stella is issued a debit card with a balance of zero. Stella's childcare provider, ABC Daycare Center, requires a $250 advance payment at the beginning of each week for dependent care services that will be provided during the week. The dependent care services qualify for reimbursement under the dependent care FSA. However, Stella cannot be reimbursed for any amounts until the end of the first week after the services have been provided. She submits a claim for reimbursement that includes a statement from ABC Daycare with a description of the services, the amount charged, and the dates of the services to be provided. Once services have been provided for the first week, Zeta increases the balance of Stella's payment card to $96.15 (i.e., the lesser of her salary reduction to date or the incurred dependent care expenses). Stella uses the card to pay ABC $96.15 on the first day of the next week and pays ABC the balance due for the week ($153.85) by check.

To the extent that this card transaction and each subsequent transaction is with ABC and is for an amount equal to or less than the previously substantiated amount, the charges are fully substantiated without the need for the submission of a statement by Stella or further review by the employer. However, additional amounts may not be made available on the card until the end of each week when the services have been provided.

Q 7:84 May transferred employees continue FSA participation after part of a business is sold?

The IRS has ruled that following the sale of a business's assets, transferred employees who elected to participate in a health FSA under the seller's cafeteria plan may continue to exclude salary reduction amounts and medical expense reimbursements from gross income without interruption and at the same level of coverage after becoming employees of the buyer if one of the following conditions is met:

1. The seller agrees to continue its existing health FSA for the transferred employees; or

2. The buyer agrees to adopt a continuation of the seller's FSA for the transferred employees.

[Rev. Rul. 2002-32, 2002-23 I.R.B. 1069]

Example 1. Employer A maintains a cafeteria plan that includes a health FSA. To participate in the health FSA, employees elect pretax salary reductions in return for the right to receive medical care expense reimbursements up to the amount of the reduction election for the year. During the plan year, A enters into an agreement under which Employer B acquires a portion of A's assets. In connection with the sale, employees of A who work with the acquired assets terminate employment with A and become employees of B. Employer B agrees to create a cafeteria plan that offers a health FSA that offers pretax salary reductions. However, A and B agree that the transferred employees will continue to participate in A's FSA for an agreed-upon period. They also agree that salary reductions made under A's plan will continue as if made under B's plan.

Example 2. The facts are the same as those in Example 1, except that, as part of the sale, B agrees to cover the transferred employees under its own health FSA. Under B's plan, the transferred employees will have the same level of coverage as under A's health FSA and will be treated as if their participation had been continuous from the beginning of A's plan year. The transferred employee's existing salary reduction elections will be taken into account for the remainder of B's plan year as if made under B's health FSA. In addition, B's plan will reimburse medical care expenses incurred by the transferred employees up to the amount of the employees' elections reduced by amounts previously reimbursed by A. Thus, medical expenses incurred before the closing date of the sale but not previously reimbursed as well as medical expenses incurred after the closing date of the sale will be reimbursed by B's plan.

In addition to approving both B's plan and A's plan, the IRS noted that neither plan involves a loss of eligibility for FSA coverage or other change in status. Therefore, transferred employees continue to be subject to their existing FSA elections and may not change those elections unless a change in status event occurs.

Q 7:85   What is a qualified reservist distribution?

The Heroes Earnings Assistance and Relief Tax Act of 2008 [Pub. L. No. 110-245, 122 Stat. 1624] permits a health FSA to make special distributions to employees who are called to active military duty. Such employees, as soon as they are activated, may pull their funds out of an FSA—even if they do not have qualifying medical expenses.

A health FSA is permitted to make a qualified reservist distribution (QRD) of all or a portion of the participant's FSA balance if:

- The participant is a reservist called to active duty for a period of at least 180 days (or is called for an indefinite period), and

- The distribution is made during the period beginning with the call to active duty and ending on the last day of the coverage period of the FSA that includes the date of the call to active duty.

[I.R.C. § 125(h) as added by Pub. L. No. 110-245]

According to IRS guidance, if an employee requests a QRD, the employer must receive a copy of the order or call to active duty before making any distribution. An employer may rely on the order or call to determine the period of the employee's active duty. If the order or call specifies that the period of duty is for 180 days or more or is indefinite, the employee is eligible for a QRD. The employee's eligibility for a QRD will not be affected if the actual period of active duty lasts for less than 180 days or is otherwise changed. If the period specified in the order or call is less than 180 days, a QRD is not allowed. However, subsequent orders or calls to duty that increase the total period to 180 days or more will qualify the employee for a QRD. For example, if an employee is called to active duty for 120 days, but his or her duty is subsequently extended for an additional 60 days, the employee qualifies for a QRD. [IRS Notice 2008-82, 2008-41 I.R.B. 853]

The IRS guidance provides that the cafeteria plan should specify how the plan will determine an employee's health FSA balance for purposes of making a QRD. The plan may provide that the amount available as a QRD will be:

- The entire amount elected for the health FSA for the plan year minus health FSA reimbursements received as of the date of the QRD request;
- The amount contributed to the health FSA as of the date of the QRD request minus health FSA reimbursements received as of the date of the QRD request; or
- Some other amount not exceeding the entire amount elected for FSA for the plan year less reimbursements.

If the plan does not specify how the plan will determine the amount available as a QRD, then the amount available will be the amount contributed as of the date of the QRD request minus health FSA reimbursements received as of that date.

> **Practice Pointer.** A health FSA is generally required to provide uniform coverage throughout the plan year. That is, the maximum amount of reimbursement must be available at all times regardless of how much the employee has actually contributed to the FSA as of the time of the reimbursement. However, the IRS guidance permits a QRD to be limited to the amount of an employee's actual contributions (less prior reimbursements).

IRS guidance makes it clear that a plan is not required to provide for QRDs. The decision whether to allow a QRD from a health FSA is optional with the employer. However, if permitted, QRDs must be uniformly available to all plan participants.

The plan may specify a process for employees to request QRDs. These rules may specify how many QRDs can be made to an employee during the same plan year. A plan must permit an employee to submit health FSA claims for medical expenses incurred before the date a QRD is requested and must reimburse the employee for those claims. However, in the case of medical expenses incurred after the QRD is requested, the plan may either: (1) permit the employee to submit claims incurred before the end of the plan year (and grace period, if applicable) or (2) terminate an employee's right to submit claims.

An employee must request a QRD on or after the date of his or her order or call to active duty and before the last day of the plan year (or grace period, if applicable) in which the call order occurs. An employer must pay the QRD to the employee within a reasonable time, but not more than 60 days after the request is made.

> **Practice Pointer.** QRDs are generally permitted only if the plan is amended to allow QRDs. A plan amendment may be made to allow QRDs prospectively only. Thus, a QRD can generally be made only on or after the effective date of the plan amendment providing for QRDs. However, the IRS guidance makes it clear that a plan may be retroactively amended to allow QRDs on or after June 18, 2008, so long as the amendment is in place by December 31, 2009.

A QRD is included in the employee's gross income and wages and is subject to employment taxes. The employer must report the QRD as wages on the employee's Form W-2 for the year in which the QRD is paid to the employee. The amount reported as wages is reduced by an amount in the health FSA representing after-tax contributions.

Trust Requirement

Q 7:86 Are salary reduction contributions to a cafeteria plan required to be held in trust?

Although the IRS views salary reduction contributions, or elective contributions, as employer contributions for tax purposes because they are not considered to be constructively received by cafeteria plan participants, the DOL views them as employee contributions for ERISA purposes. The DOL's former final regulation on the trust requirement for employee contributions to ERISA welfare benefit plans [60 Fed. Reg. 66,036 (Dec. 20, 1995)] contained no specific mention of cafeteria plans and apparently would have required elective contributions for cafeteria plan benefit options, including medical reimbursement accounts, to be deposited in trust.

The DOL confirmed that interpretation but suspended enforcement while it considered whether to grant a class exemption or individual exemptions from the trust requirement in such circumstances. The suspension was extended until final regulations are adopted or until further notice. Certain conditions must be met in order to qualify for this suspension, including payment of employee contributions toward insured plan options over to the insurer within 90 days. [DOL Reg. § 2510.3-102; ERISA Tech. Rel. Nos. 88-1, 92-01; 57 Fed. Reg. 23,272 (June 2, 1992); DOL News Rel. 93-363 (Aug. 27, 1993)] In the final plan asset regulations published on August 7, 1996, the DOL confirmed that ERISA Technical Release 92-01 is not affected by the new final regulations and remains in effect until further notice. [61 Fed. Reg. 41,220, 41,222 (Aug. 7, 1996)]

The DOL also confirmed that the mere receipt of after-tax contributions (e.g., COBRA contributions) by a cafeteria plan would not by itself affect the availability of the relief provided for cafeteria plans in ERISA Technical Release 92-01. [61 Fed. Reg. 41,220, 41,223 (Aug. 7, 1996)]

The Fourth Circuit Court of Appeals has affirmed the DOL's position that cafeteria plan contributions do not have to be held in trust as long as they are treated as plan assets and handled in accordance with ERISA's fiduciary standards. In the case before the court, an employer routinely remitted employees' pretax health plan contributions to the plan administrator on a weekly basis. However, when the employer began experiencing financial difficulties, the employer stopped making its own contributions to the plan. Moreover, the employees' contributions were remitted less frequently. The employer eventually shut down the plan, leaving claims unpaid. Disgruntled employees sued the employer, arguing among other things that it had breached its fiduciary duty by failing to remit the employee contributions to the plan administrator in a timely manner. The Fourth Circuit rejected the employees' argument. According to the court, the employer had forwarded all employee contributions to the plan administrator within 90 days of withholding from weekly paychecks, as required by DOL regulations, and there was no evidence that employee contributions were misused for general business expenses of the company. The court concluded that the fact that the employer slowed down the timing of its payment of employee contributions was not a breach of fiduciary duty. According to the court, the contributions were forwarded to the plan administrator as soon as practicable in light of the financial situation of the company. [Phelps v. C.T. Enters., 194 Fed Appx. 120 (4th Cir. Aug. 9, 2006)]

Section 125 Nondiscrimination Rules

Q 7:87   Must cafeteria plans satisfy any nondiscrimination rules?

Yes. A cafeteria plan must pass an eligibility test (see Qs 7:89–7:90), a contributions and benefits test (see Qs 7:91–7:92), and a concentration test (see Q 7:93) in order for highly compensated individuals to receive the tax benefits of Code Section 125. Failure to meet these nondiscrimination requirements has no effect on non-highly compensated cafeteria plan participants.

Certain qualified benefits offered under a cafeteria plan, including group term life insurance and dependent care assistance programs, are subject to their own nondiscrimination rules. The plan must independently satisfy these requirements.

The proposed cafeteria plan regulations make it clear that, in addition to meeting the nondiscrimination tests, a cafeteria plan must not discriminate in favor of highly compensated participants in actual operation. A plan may be discriminatory in actual operation if the duration of the plan (or of a particular nontaxable benefit offered through the plan) is for a period during which only highly compensated participants use the plan or benefit. [Prop. Treas. Reg.

§ 1.125-7(k)] For example, a plan might be considered discriminatory if adoption assistance is added to the plan when the company president is in the process of adopting a child and dropped from the plan when the adoption is final.

Nondiscrimination testing. Nondiscrimination testing must be performed as of the last day of the plan year, taking into account all non-excludable employees (or former employees) who were employees on any day during the plan year. [Prop. Treas. Reg. § 1.125-7(j)]

Any employee who has completed three years of employment (and satisfies any other conditions for participation that are not related to length of service) must be allowed to participate in a cafeteria plan no later than the first day of the first plan year beginning after the date the employee completed three years of employment. [Prop. Treas. Reg. § 1.125-7(b)(2)] Employees who have not completed three years of employment can be excluded from participation. If an employer limits participation to employees who have completed three years of employment, employees who have not completed three years of employment do not have to be taken into account for eligibility testing. [Prop. Treas. Reg. § 1.125-7(b)(3)]

Moreover, even if a cafeteria plan benefits employees who have not completed three years of employment, the cafeteria plan has the option of testing for nondiscrimination as if the plan were two separate plans—one plan benefiting the employees with fewer than three years of employment; and another plan benefiting the employees who have completed three years of employment. [Prop. Treas. Reg. § 1.125-7(g)]

Conversely, an employer that sponsors more than one cafeteria plan can combine the plans for purposes of nondiscrimination testing. However, the proposed regulations caution that if a principal purpose of combining the plans is to manipulate the nondiscrimination testing requirements or to otherwise discriminate in favor of highly compensated individuals or participants, the combination will not be allowed. [Prop. Treas. Reg. § 1.125-7(h)]

Effective for tax years beginning after 2010, the 2010 Health Reform Act offers small employers a simple alternative to nondiscrimination testing—a SIMPLE cafeteria plan. Under a special safe-harbor rule, a SIMPLE cafeteria plan that meets minimum eligibility, participation, and contribution requirements will automatically satisfy the cafeteria plan nondiscrimination requirements (see Qs 7:96–7:99).

Q 7:88   Who are highly compensated individuals?

The proposed cafeteria plan regulations provide much-needed guidance on the cafeteria plan nondiscrimination rules—including definitions of key terms such as *highly compensated individual.*

Under Code Section 125, *highly compensated individuals* are defined as

- Officers
- 5-percent shareholders
- Highly compensated employees (HCEs)
- Spouses or dependents of any of the preceding individuals

Officers. The proposed regulations provide that officers include any individual who was an officer for the prior plan year (or the current plan year in the case of the first year of employment). Whether an individual is an officer is determined based on all the facts and circumstances. Generally, the term *officer* means an administrative executive who is in regular and continued service. An individual who has the title of an officer but not the authority of an officer is not an officer. On the other hand, an individual without the title of an officer but who has the authority of an officer is an officer. [Prop. Treas. Reg. § 1.125-7(a)(7)]

5-percent shareholders. A 5-percent shareholder is an individual who in either the preceding plan year or current plan year owns *more than* 5 percent of the voting power or value of all classes of stock of the employer, determined without attribution. [Prop. Treas. Reg. § 1.125-7(a)(8)]

Highly compensated employees. HCEs include any individuals who for the prior plan year (or the current plan year in the case of the first year of employment) had compensation from the employer in excess of the compensation amount specified in Code Section 414(q)(1)(B), and, if elected by the employer, was also in the top-paid group of employees (determined by reference to Code Section 414(q)(3)) for the year. [Prop. Treas. Reg. § 1.125-7(a)(9)] For 2010, the applicable compensation amount is $110,000.

Q 7:89　What is the nondiscriminatory eligibility test imposed by Code Section 125?

A Section 125 cafeteria plan cannot discriminate in favor of highly compensated individuals as to eligibility to participate in the plan. If it does discriminate, the favorable tax treatment of Code Section 125 is denied to highly compensated individuals, but there is no effect on non-highly compensated participants. [I.R.C. § 125(b)(1)(A)]

The proposed cafeteria plan regulations provide examples of plans that do—and do not—meet the eligibility test. [Prop. Treas. Reg. § 1.125-7(b)]

Example 1. Alpha Company has one employer-provided accident and health insurance plan. The cost to participants electing the accident and health plan is $10,000 per year for single coverage. All employees have the same opportunity to salary reduce $10,000 for accident and health plan. The cafeteria plan satisfies the eligibility test.

Example 2. The facts are the same as those in Example 1, except that the cafeteria plan offers non-highly compensated employees an election to reduce their salary by $10,000 to pay premiums for single coverage. The cafeteria plan provides an $8,000 employer flex-credit to highly compensated employees to pay a portion of the premium, and provides an election to those employees to reduce their salary by $2,000 to pay the balance of the premium. The cafeteria plan fails the eligibility test.

Example 3. Beta Company's cafeteria plan offers two employer-provided accident and health insurance plans: Plan X, available only to highly compensated participants, is a low-deductible plan. Plan Y, available only to non-highly compensated participants, is a high-deductible plan. The annual premium for single coverage under Plan X is $15,000 per year, and $8,000 per year for Plan Y. Employer B's cafeteria plan provides that highly compensated participants may elect salary reduction of $15,000 for coverage under Plan X, and that non-highly compensated participants may elect salary reduction of $8,000 for coverage under Plan Y. The cafeteria plan fails the eligibility test.

Example 4. The facts are the same as those in Example 3, except that the amount of salary reduction for both highly compensated participants and non-highly compensated participants is $8,000. Nonetheless, the cafeteria plan fails the eligibility test.

Q 7:90 How does a cafeteria plan meet the eligibility test?

A plan's eligibility requirements are not deemed to favor highly compensated individuals if the plan satisfies the following four statutory safe harbor criteria:

1. It meets the nondiscriminatory classification test contained in Code Section 410(b)(2)(A)(i), a section that deals with minimum coverage requirements for qualified retirement plans.
2. It does not require more than three years of service as a precondition for participation.
3. It imposes a uniform minimum service requirement for all employees.
4. Employees who satisfy the uniform participation requirement commence plan participation no later than the first day of the first plan year beginning after the condition is satisfied.

[I.R.C. § 125(g)(3)]

The proposed cafeteria plan regulations provide guidance on the eligibility test by incorporating some of the rules that apply for retirement plan nondiscrimination purposes. These rules are found in Treasury Regulations Section 1.410(b)-4(b) and (c) dealing with reasonable classification of employees and the percentages of highly and non-highly compensated employees benefiting.

Under the proposed regulations, a cafeteria plan does not discriminate in favor of highly compensated individuals if the plan benefits a group of employees who qualify under a reasonable classification established by the employer [Treas. Reg. § 1.410(b)-4(b)] and the group of employees included in the classification satisfies either a safe harbor percentage test or an unsafe harbor percentage test. [Treas. Reg. § 1.410(b)-4(c); Prop. Treas. Reg. § 1.125-7(b)]

Under those rules a classification of employees is reasonable if it is established under objective business criteria that identify the employees who benefit under the plan. Reasonable classifications generally include specified job categories, nature of compensation (for example, salaried or hourly), geographic location, and similar criteria. Identification of employees by name or other criteria that has the effect of naming employees is not reasonable.

To apply the percentage tests, the percentage of non-highly compensated individuals who benefit under the plan is divided by the percentage of highly compensated individuals who benefit. The exact ratio required for a particular employer to meet the tests depends on the concentration of non-highly compensated individuals in the plan—the higher the concentration, the lower ratio. Acceptable minimum ratios range from 50 percent down to 20 percent.

Q 7:91　What is the nondiscriminatory contributions and benefits test imposed on cafeteria plans by Code Section 125?

A Section 125 cafeteria plan cannot discriminate in favor of highly compensated participants with regard to contributions and benefits. [I.R.C. § 125(b)(1)(B)] For that purpose, a cafeteria plan will not be considered discriminatory with regard to contributions and benefits if qualified benefits and total benefits (or the employer contributions allocable to each) do not discriminate in favor of highly compensated participants. [I.R.C. § 125(c)]

The proposed cafeteria plan regulations provide an objective test to determine when the actual election of benefits is discriminatory. Specifically, the new proposed regulations provide that a cafeteria plan must give each similarly situated participant a uniform opportunity to elect qualified benefits, and that highly compensated participants must not actually disproportionately elect qualified benefits. [Prop. Treas. Reg. § 1.125-7(c)]

Qualified benefits are disproportionately elected by highly compensated participants if the total qualified benefits elected by highly compensated participants measured as a percentage of the total compensation of highly compensated participants is more than the total qualified benefits elected by non-highly compensated participants measured as a percentage of the total compensation of non-highly compensated participants.

A plan must also give each similarly situated participant a uniform election with respect to employer contributions, and the highly compensated individuals must not disproportionately elect employer contributions for qualified benefits. Here again, this is measured by comparing employer contributions elected by highly compensated participants measured as a percentage of compensation to employer contributions elected by non-highly compensated individuals measured as a percentage of compensation.

Example. Beta Company's cafeteria plan satisfies the eligibility test. In addition, highly compensated participants in the plan elect total qualified benefits equaling 5 percent of total compensation, while non-highly compensated participants elect total qualified benefits equaling 10 percent of total compensation. Beta's cafeteria plan passes the contribution and benefits test.

Q 7:92   Are there any safe harbor nondiscrimination tests for cafeteria plans?

Yes, there is one statutory safe harbor that applies to health benefits. In addition, the proposed cafeteria plan regulations carve out a safe harbor for premium-only health plans.

Health plan safe harbor. Health benefits eligible for the safe harbor are limited to major medical coverage. The safe harbor does not apply to dental coverage or health FSAs. [Prop. Treas. Reg. § 1.125-7(e)(3)]

Health benefits will be treated as nondiscriminatory if

1. Contributions on behalf of each participant equal either—
   a. 100 percent of the cost of the coverage of the majority of similarly situated highly compensated participants or
   b. At least 75 percent of the cost of the coverage of the similarly situated participants having the highest-cost health benefit under the plan; and
2. Contributions or benefits that exceed those described in (1) bear a uniform relationship to compensation.

[I.R.C. § 125(g)(2)]

The proposed regulations provide that in determining which participants are similarly situated, reasonable differences in plan benefits may be taken into account (for example, variations in plan benefits offered to employees working in different geographic locations or to employees with family coverage versus employee-only coverage). [Prop. Treas. Reg. § 1.125-7(e)(2)]

Safe harbor test for premium-only-plans. A premium-only plan that offers employees a choice between cash compensation and health insurance premium payments will satisfy the nondiscrimination rules if, for that plan year, the plan satisfies the safe harbor percentage test for eligibility (see Q 7:90) regardless of the actual benefits chosen by employees. [Prop. Treas. Reg. § 1.125-7(f)] Thus, a premium-only-plan that passes the safe harbor percentage test will be treated as nondiscriminatory even if it would not meet the nondiscriminatory benefits test (see Q 7:91) because highly compensated employees disproportionately elect qualified benefits.

Example. Gamma Corporation's cafeteria plan is a premium-only plan. The written cafeteria plan offers one employer-provided accident and health plan and offers all employees the election to make salary reduction contributions of the same amount or the same percentage of the premium for self-only or family coverage. All key employees and all highly compensated employees elect salary reduction for the accident and health plan, but only 20 percent of non-highly compensated employees elect the accident and health plan.

Because all are eligible to benefit under the plan, Gamma's ratio percentage is 100 percent, far more than the maximum 50 percent needed to meet the safe harbor. Therefore, Gamma's premium-only plan satisfies the nondiscrimination rules.

Q 7:93   What is the nondiscriminatory 25 percent concentration test imposed on cafeteria plans by Code Section 125?

If a Section 125 cafeteria plan provides more than 25 percent of its nontaxable benefits (excluding group term life insurance in excess of $50,000) to key employees, the key employees are not eligible for cafeteria plan tax treatment. [I.R.C. § 125(b)(2)]

For Section 125 purposes, a *key employee* is any individual who, at any time during the plan year or any of the prior four years, is one of the following:

1. An officer with annual compensation greater than an indexed amount ($160,000 for 2009 and 2010);

2. A 5-percent owner of the employer; or

3. A 1-percent owner having compensation in excess of $150,000.

[I.R.C. § 416(i)(1)]

Q 7:94   Are collectively bargained plans subject to the nondiscrimination rules of Code Section 125?

No. Collectively bargained plans are not subject to the nondiscrimination rules of Code Section 125. [I.R.C. § 125(g)(1)]

Q 7:95   What are the plan limits for collectively bargained benefits?

The plan limits set forth in Q 7:93 do not apply to certain collectively bargained plans. Plan limits for collectively bargained plans are one half of the indexed dollar limit (50% of $195,000 for 2010) for defined benefit plans. This applies to participants in defined plans that

1. Are maintained under a collective bargaining agreement;

2. Have at least 100 participants at all times during the year;

3. Determine benefits solely by reference to length of service, which year the service was rendered, age at retirement, and date of retirement;

4. Provide that employees who have at least four years of service have a nonforfeitable right to 100 percent of their accrued benefit derived from employer contributions; and

5. Require, as a condition of participation, that employees complete a period of not more than 60 consecutive days of service with the employer or employers maintaining the plan.

[I.R.C. § 415(b)(7)(A)–(E)]

SIMPLE Cafeteria Plan

Q 7:96   What is a SIMPLE cafeteria plan?

A SIMPLE cafeteria plan is a safe-harbor plan, created by the 2010 Health Reform Act, that will automatically satisfy the overall cafeteria plan nondiscrimination rules as well as the nondiscrimination rules that apply separately to certain specified qualified benefits provided under the plan. [I.R.C. § 125(j) as added by PPACA § 9022] An eligible small employer (Q 7:97) may establish a SIMPLE cafeteria plan for plan years beginning after December 31, 2010. [PPACA § 9022(b)]

A SIMPLE cafeteria plan must meet two requirements:

1. A minimum eligibility and participation requirement (Q 7:98), and

2. A minimum contribution requirement (Q 7:99).

A plan that satisfies both requirements for a plan year will be treated as meeting the following applicable nondiscrimination requirements for the year:

- The cafeteria plan nondiscrimination requirements specified in Code Section 125(b) (see Qs 7:87–7:94);

- The nondiscrimination requirements for employer-provided group term life insurance specified in Code Section 79(d) (see chapter 11);

- The nondiscrimination requirements for dependent care assistance programs under Code Section 129(d) (see chapter 8); and

- The health benefit nondiscrimination requirements in Code Section 105(h) (see chapter 5).

Note. The Code Section 105(h) nondiscrimination requirements have historically applied only to self-insured medical reimbursement plans. However, the 2010 Health Reform Act broadens the scope of Section 105(h) to apply to group health plans other than self-insured plans (see chapter 5).

Q 7:97   Which employers are eligible to maintain a SIMPLE cafeteria plan?

An employer qualifies to establish a SIMPLE cafeteria plan for a year if the employer employed an average of 100 or fewer employees on business days during either of the two preceding years. [I.R.C. § 125(j)(5)]

A year may only be taken into account if the employer was in existence throughout the year. If an employer was not in existence throughout the preceding year, the eligibility determination is based on the average number of employees that the employer is reasonably expected to employ on business days in the current year.

Once an employer qualifies as an eligible small employer and maintains a SIMPLE cafeteria plan for any year, the employer can continue to maintain a SIMPLE cafeteria plan for employees (including new employees) of the same trade or business until the year following the year in which the employer employs an average of 200 or more employees.

The determination of whether an employer is an eligible small employer is made by applying the controlled group rules of Code Sections 52(a) and 52(b) under which all members of the controlled group are treated as a single employer. In addition, the definition of employee includes leased employees within the meaning of Code Sections 414(n) and 414(o).

Q 7:98   What is the minimum eligibility and participation requirement for a SIMPLE cafeteria plan?

An employer satisfies the minimum eligibility and participation requirement of a SIMPLE cafeteria plan if:

- All employees with at least 1,000 hours of service for the preceding plan year are eligible to participate; and
- Each employee eligible to participate may elect any benefit available under the plan (subject to terms and conditions that apply to all participants). [I.R.C. § 125(j)(4)]

A SIMPLE cafeteria plan may exclude employees who:

- Have not attained age 21 before the close of a plan year;
- Have not completed one year of service with the employer as of any day during the plan year;
- Are covered under a collective bargaining agreement pursuant to which benefits provided by the cafeteria plan were the subject of good-faith bargaining between employee representatives and the employer; or
- Are nonresident aliens working outside the United States (described in Code Section 410(b)(3)(C)).

An employer may prescribe age or service requirements that differ from those described above if those requirements apply to all employees.

Q 7:99   What is the minimum contribution requirement for a SIMPLE cafeteria plan?

To qualify as a SIMPLE cafeteria plan, the plan must require the employer to make a minimum contribution to provide benefits under the plan on behalf of each qualified employee, whether or not the employee makes salary reduction contributions to the plan. [I.R.C. § 125(j)(3)] A *qualified employee* is any employee who is not a highly compensated employee (HCE) (within the meaning of Code Section 414(q)) or a key employee (as defined in Code Section 416(i)).

The minimum contribution on behalf of each qualified employee may be calculated under either a nonelective contribution method or a matching contribution method, but the same method must be used for all qualified employees.

Nonelective contribution method. Under this method, the minimum contribution on behalf of each qualified employee must equal a uniform percentage (not less than 2 percent) of the eligible employee's compensation for the plan year, determined without regard to whether the employee makes any salary reduction contribution under the cafeteria plan.

Matching contribution method. The minimum matching contribution is the lesser of (1) 100 percent of the amount of the salary reduction contributions elected to be made by the qualified employee for the plan year or (2) 6 percent of the qualified employee's compensation for the plan year.

A SIMPLE cafeteria plan can provide matching contributions in addition to the minimum required contributions, but only if matching contributions with respect to salary reduction contributions for any HCE or key employee are not made at a greater rate than matching contributions for any non-highly compensated employee (NHCE). An employer may provide qualified benefits under the plan in addition to required contributions.

An HCE is an employee who: (1) was a 5 percent owner at any time during the year or the preceding year, or (2) for the preceding year, received compensation from the employer in excess of an indexed amount ($110,000 for 2009 and 2010), and, if the employer elects, was in the top-paid 20 percent of employees for the preceding year. [I.R.C. §§ 125(2)(D)(iv), 414(q)]

A *key employee* is an employee who, at any time during the plan year, is: (1) an officer of the employer and received more than an indexed amount ($160,000 for 2009 and 2010) of compensation from the employer; (2) a 5-percent owner of the employer; or (3) a 1-percent owner of the employer and received annual compensation from the employer in excess of $150,000. [I.R.C. §§ 125(2)(D)(iii), 416(i)]

Tax Treatment of Cafeteria Plan Benefits

Q 7:100   Can a benefit ever become taxable because it is offered through a cafeteria plan?

Yes. For example, if disability insurance is included in a cafeteria plan on an employer-paid basis or on a pretax contribution basis, disability income insurance benefit payments will be taxable. This is true even if the coverage is funded entirely or partially with employee salary reduction contributions, because salary reduction contributions are treated as employer contributions. [I.R.C. § 105(d); Prop. Treas. Reg. § 1.125-1, (r)(2)]

A similar concern arises with group term life insurance coverage in excess of $50,000, which may be taxable under Code Section 79 if it is treated as employer-provided (see Q 7:65).

Q 7:101　What are the tax consequences of a cafeteria plan that is discriminatory under Code Section 125?

A highly compensated participant or key employee in a discriminatory cafeteria plan is taxed on the combination of the taxable benefits with the greatest aggregate value that the employee could have selected under the cafeteria plan, regardless of whether he or she in fact selected that particular benefit combination. The amounts are first allocated to the taxable benefits actually selected and then on a pro rata basis to the nontaxable benefits in fact selected. [Prop. Treas. Reg. § 1.125-7(m)(2)]

The amounts are treated as having been received by the highly compensated participant in his or her taxable year "within which ends the plan year with respect to which an election was or could have been made."[Prop. Treas. Reg. § 1.125-7(m)(2)]

There are no adverse tax consequences for participants in a discriminatory cafeteria plan who are not highly compensated.

Practice Pointer. Note that this limited adverse effect applies only to failure to satisfy the nondiscrimination rules of Code Section 125. In contrast, if the plan violates one of the structural requirements of Code Section 125, it will not be a valid cafeteria plan, and nobody will be entitled to favorable tax treatment under Code Section 125.

Q 7:102　What happens if a qualified benefit fails a nondiscrimination test of a Code Section other than Code Section 125?

A qualified benefit is excludable from gross income only if both the rules under Code Section 125 and the specific rules providing for the exclusion of the benefit from gross income are satisfied. Thus, if the nondiscrimination rules for specific qualified benefits are not satisfied, those qualified benefits are includable in gross income. For example, if $50,000 in group-term life insurance is offered through a cafeteria plan, the nondiscrimination rules in Section 79(d) must be satisfied in order to exclude the coverage from gross income. [Prop. Treas. Reg. § 1.125-1(j)]

Q 7:103　What happens if the plan violates a structural requirement of Code Section 125?

Unlike violations of the nondiscrimination rules, which affect only the group in whose favor discrimination is prohibited, violation of a Section 125 structural requirement invalidates the cafeteria plan for all participants. An example of such a structural requirement is the requirement that the cafeteria plan be in writing. Thus, the 2007 proposed regulations provide that if there is no written plan or the written plan fails to satisfy any of the regulatory requirements, the plan is not a cafeteria plan and each employee's election between taxable and nontaxable benefits results in gross income to the employee. [Prop. Treas. Reg. § 1.125-1(c)(6)]

However, having a written plan that meets all the regulatory requirements is not enough to safeguard the plan. The plan must operate in accordance with the Code Section 125 requirements and the written plan document. If a cafeteria plan fails to operate according to its written plan or otherwise fails to operate in accordance with Code Section 125 and its regulations, the plan will be disqualified resulting in gross income to employees. [Prop. Treas. Reg. § 1.125-1(c)(7)]

The proposed cafeteria plan regulations give the following examples of operational failures that will disqualify a cafeteria plan:

- Paying or reimbursing expenses for qualified benefits incurred before the later of the adoption date or effective date of the cafeteria plan, before the beginning of a period of coverage or before the later of the date of adoption or effective date of a plan amendment adding a new benefit;
- Offering benefits other than permitted taxable benefits and qualified benefits;
- Operating to defer compensation (except as permitted by Code Section 125 or the regulations);
- Failing to comply with the uniform coverage rule for a health FSA;
- Failing to comply with the use-or-lose rule;
- Allowing employees to revoke elections or make new elections (except as permitted by Code Section 125 or the regulations)
- Failing to comply with substantiation requirements;
- Paying or reimbursing nonqualified expenses from an FSA;
- Making improper allocations of experience gains;
- Failing to comply with the grace period rules; or
- Failing to comply with the qualified HSA distribution rules.

Q 7:104 Are cafeteria plan benefits subject to payroll taxes?

Qualified nontaxable benefits provided through a cafeteria plan are generally also exempt from FICA and FUTA taxes. There is, however, one key exception: qualified adoption assistance benefits are excludable from income and are not subject to income tax withholding. However, these benefits are subject to FICA and FUTA taxes. [I.R.S. Notice 97-9, 1997-1 C.B. 365]

An employer-provided benefit that is subject to FICA taxes when provided outside a cafeteria plan does not become nontaxable when offered under a qualified cafeteria plan as a qualified benefit. Thus, for example, the cost of employer-provided group term life insurance coverage amounts over $50,000, which is includable in an employee's income and is subject to FICA tax when provided outside of a cafeteria plan, will not escape such taxes merely because it is offered as a benefit under a cafeteria plan. The IRS has issued a notice clarifying this interpretation. [I.R.S. Notice 88-82, 1988-2 C.B. 398]

In the case of group term life insurance coverage, an employer is not required to withhold and pay over the employee's share of the FICA tax with respect to coverage for periods during which an employment relationship no longer exists between the employee and the employer. The employer is nonetheless required to include on the W-2 statement provided to the former employee the portion of the compensation applicable to the imputed value of the group term life insurance and the amount of FICA tax due on such value. The former employee is required to pay his or her portion of the FICA tax directly to the IRS. (See Q 11:80 as to how the tax is to be taken into account on the former employee's Form 1040.) [I.R.C. § 3102(d), as added by OBRA '90 § 5124(a)]

Q 7:105   Is the amount of salary reduction used to "purchase" qualified benefits subject to FICA tax or federal unemployment tax?

No. The exemption from tax can produce significant employee and employer savings if the salary reduction applies to compensation below the FICA wage base ($106,800 for the 6.2 percent Old Age, Survivors, and Disability Insurance (OASDI) tax for 2010). Moreover, even if the salary reduction applies to income above the FICA wage base, both the employee and the employer will save on Medicare taxes (the 1.45 percent Hospital Insurance (HI) tax applies to all wages). Note, however, that these tax savings will be realized only if the salary reduction is used to purchase benefits that are themselves exempt from FICA and FUTA tax (see Q 7:104).

Practice Pointer. Employers and employees should be aware that the FICA savings may reduce the ultimate Social Security benefit slightly.

Q 7:106   Does receipt of dependent care assistance benefits under a cafeteria plan reduce the child care tax credit otherwise available to an employee?

Yes. There is a dollar-for-dollar reduction in the child care tax credit for benefits paid under an employer-provided dependent care assistance program. (For a discussion of the interplay between Section 129 dependent care assistance plan benefits, which can be offered as a qualified benefit under a cafeteria plan, and the dependent care tax credit, see Qs 8:21–8:22.)

Reporting and Disclosure Requirements

Q 7:107   Must the plan administrator file a Form 5500 for a cafeteria plan?

Yes. The reporting requirements for cafeteria plans come from Code Section 6039D, which requires every employer that maintains a cafeteria plan, including agencies of a state, to file certain information with the IRS annually. Annual reporting to the DOL is also required by ERISA. The IRS and DOL coordinate the reporting requirements by requiring plans to file a Form 5500, *Annual Return/ Report for Employee Benefit Plans,* with the DOL.

Effect of Other Laws

Q 7:108   Is a cafeteria plan subject to ERISA?

Yes. Cafeteria plans containing ERISA-governed benefits, such as a medical plan option, are subject to ERISA. A plan is covered by ERISA "to the extent" that it offers benefits described in ERISA Section 3(1). The DOL apparently has taken the position that the inclusion of an ERISA-covered benefit as a component of a cafeteria plan subjects the entire plan to Title I of ERISA (concerning reporting, disclosure, group health plan provisions, and fiduciary responsibility and claims). [DOL Inf. Ltr. to Erwin A. Peterson (Jan. 10, 1990)]

It should be noted that a health care FSA, as a group health plan, would also be required to meet the additional requirements for group health plans contained in ERISA's COBRA provisions (see chapter 2 and Q 7:110) and in ERISA Section 609 concerning coverage of pediatric vaccines, coverage of adopted children, and qualified medical child support orders. As well, the maternity, mental health, and mastectomy requirements contained in new ERISA Sections 711, 712, and 713 would apply (see chapter 3).

Note. Under a "regulatory clarification," some health care FSAs are exempt from ERISA's HIPAA provisions (including the requirement to issue certificates of creditable coverage), while others are subject to them, depending on the facts and circumstances of the particular FSA's design. (See Q 7:109.)

Q 7:109   Is a health care FSA subject to HIPAA?

Because HIPAA's definition of group health plan was broad enough to encompass health care FSAs, an interpretive issue arose as to whether HIPAA was really intended to apply to them. FSAs typically are provided as a supplement to the employer's primary coverage and are designed to cover the cost of copayments, deductibles, and medical care expenses that are excluded from such coverage. Coverage under a health care FSA is minimal (e.g., up to $3,000 or so per year), and individuals frequently are permitted to elect varying amounts, as long as the cap is not exceeded. Applying HIPAA's rules to this type of coverage is awkward at best, and providing certificates of coverage (and hence credit under another plan's preexisting-condition exclusion) seemed unfair in light of the minimal nature of FSA coverage.

Under a "regulatory clarification," a health care FSA is permitted to be treated as exempt for all HIPAA purposes provided each of three conditions is met. Many health care FSAs are eligible for this exemption.

1. The employee must have other group health plan coverage available to him or her for the year;

2. The other group health plan coverage cannot consist solely of benefits that are exempt from HIPAA; and

3. The maximum benefit payable to the employee under the particular health care FSA for the year cannot exceed the larger of

   (a) Two times the employee's salary reduction election or

   (b) The amount of the employee's salary reduction election for the year plus $500.

[Application of HIPAA Group Market Portability Rules to Health Flexible Spending Arrangements; Final Rule, 62 Fed. Reg. 67,688 (Dec. 29, 1997)]

Assuming that the first two conditions are satisfied, the key to satisfying the third condition will be how the health care FSA is funded.

Salary reduction only health care FSAs. Health care FSAs that are funded solely with salary reduction (pretax) contributions will qualify for this exemption if benefits do not exceed the amount of the salary reduction election. However, if benefits may exceed the amount of the salary reduction election (which could occur, for example, if forfeitures from the prior year had been reallocated under the plan), then whether the FSA is exempt from HIPAA is a fact-based inquiry. The FSA will be exempt only if the total amount allocated does not exceed two times the amount of the employee's annual salary reduction election or, if greater, one times the amount of the employee's annual salary reduction election plus $500.

Nonelective employer contributions. When applying the preceding exemption formula, nonelective employer contributions must be counted as additional employer contributions and not as salary reduction amounts. Nonelective employer contributions are amounts that the employee cannot elect to take in cash, including noncashable employer credits and employer matches.

Cashable employer credits. When applying the exemption formula, an interpretive issue arises concerning the proper characterization of cashable employer credits. These are amounts that the employee can choose either to receive as cash or to have applied as employer contributions. The issue is whether these cashable credits are "salary reduction" or should be counted toward the $500 in additional employer contributions. The IRS has informally indicated that cashable credits that are taken as employer contributions are viewed as salary reductions, a favorable interpretation for purposes of qualifying for the HIPAA exemption. For plans that contain a provision that would cause a default contribution to the health care FSA when the employee has failed to specify how the cashable credit is to be used, the existence of the default feature should not change this analysis because the exemption looks at the maximum benefit "available." [Application of HIPAA Group Market Portability Rules to Health Flexible Spending Arrangements; Final Rule, 62 Fed. Reg. 67,688 (Dec. 29, 1997)]

Q 7:110   Is a cafeteria plan subject to COBRA?

Yes. A cafeteria plan is affected by the COBRA continuation of coverage requirements to the extent it includes group health benefits. Employees electing health benefits made available under the cafeteria plan have a right to COBRA protection (see chapter 6) to the same extent as beneficiaries of other group health plans.

Practice Pointer. It is important to remember that a health care FSA that is exempt from HIPAA under the "regulatory clarification" is still subject to COBRA. However, the obligation of such plans to provide COBRA coverage may be limited (see chapter 6).

The proposed cafeteria plan regulations specifically authorize the payment of COBRA premiums through a cafeteria plan (see Q 7:24).

Q 7:111   Is a cafeteria plan subject to the Medicare secondary-payer rules?

Yes. A cafeteria plan is affected by the Medicare secondary-payer (MSP) rules contained in the Social Security Act [42 U.S.C. § 1395] to the extent the plan includes group health benefits, including a health care FSA or reimbursement account. [I.R.C. § 5000, incorporating the MSP rules by reference] Regulations administered by the Centers for Medicare and Medicaid Services (CMS) describe when a group health plan (including a health care FSA) must pay primary (that is, first), leaving Medicare as the secondary payer. [See "Medicare Program; Medicare Secondary Payer for Individuals Entitled to Medicare and Also Covered Under Group Health Plans," 60 Fed. Reg. 45,344 (Aug. 31, 1995).]

At one time there was concern that one provision of the MSP law conflicted with the typical workings of a cafeteria plan. Under the MSP provision, it is illegal for an employer or other entity such as an insurer to offer Medicare beneficiaries financial incentives or other benefits not to enroll in, or to terminate enrollment in, a group health plan (including a health care FSA) that would be primary to Medicare. A $5,000 penalty attaches to each violation. Thus, for example, a provision in a cafeteria plan that allows employees to take flex credits and spend them on something other than health care, or to take cash instead, could technically violate the financial incentives provision. However, in a letter to the American Bar Association's Joint Committee on Employee Benefits, the CMS allayed those concerns. According to the CMS, as long as any cash payment to an employee is made based on the employee's election under the employer's Code Section 125 cafeteria plan, the cash payment would not violate the prohibition on financial incentives under the MSP rules.

In 2009, new MSP reporting rules requiring group health plans to furnish certain information regarding Medicare-eligible beneficiaries to CMS became effective. [Pub. L. No. 110-173, amending 42 U.S.C. § 1395y(b)(7)] For details on the reporting requirements, see chapter 5.

Q 7:112   How does the Americans with Disabilities Act of 1990 affect health care FSAs?

Because health care FSAs are self-insured medical plans, they are prohibited from including any disability-based distinction that would be treated as a "subterfuge to evade the purposes of the [ADA]4." (See Q 18:29.)

Q 7:113　How does the Family and Medical Leave Act of 1993 affect cafeteria plans?

The Family and Medical Leave Act (FMLA) requires covered employers to provide eligible employees with up to 12 weeks of leave to care for a newborn or newly adopted child, to care for an immediate family member who is ill, or to attend to the employee's own serious health condition. In addition, a new provision enacted in 2008 requires covered employers to allow family members to take up to 26 weeks of unpaid leave to care for wounded military personnel or up to 12 weeks for "any qualifying exigency" related to a family member's call-up to active duty or deployment.

The FMLA generally applies to employers with 50 or more employees. (The FMLA is discussed in detail in chapter 16.)

The FMLA also requires covered employers to maintain an employee's health coverage during FMLA leave or, if the employee chooses to drop coverage, to restore benefits when the employee returns from leave.

If health coverage is provided under a company cafeteria plan, which permits employees to pick and choose between cash compensation and taxable and nontaxable compensation, the employer must comply with both the FMLA and the tax law rules governing cafeteria plans. For example, IRS regulations make it clear that an employee on FMLA leave has the same cafeteria plan rights as employees participating in the cafeteria plan who are not on FMLA leave. Therefore, employees on leave must be given the same opportunities as active employees to enroll in the plan or change their health coverage elections. In addition, employees on FMLA leave have the right to discontinue health coverage during the period of FMLA leave and reinstate coverage upon returning from leave (see Qs 7:114–7:122, 16:37).

Q 7:114　Must an employee taking FMLA leave be permitted to revoke an existing election of group health plan coverage under a cafeteria plan?

Under final IRS regulations, an employer must either allow an employee on unpaid FMLA leave to revoke his or her health coverage, including coverage under a health care flexible spending arrangement (FSA), or continue the employee's coverage but allow the employee to discontinue payment of his or her share of the premiums. According to the final regulations, the FMLA does not require an employer to allow an employee to revoke coverage if the employer pays the employee's share of the premiums. [29 C.F.R. § 825.209(e); Treas. Reg. § 1.125-3, Q&A-1] If the employer continues an employee's coverage during FMLA leave, the employer can recover the employee's share of the premiums when the employee returns to work (see Q 7:118).

Practice Pointer. The best option for an employer may depend on a number of factors. For example, depending on the terms of the plan, it may be administratively easier to continue an employee's coverage than to reinstate coverage once an employee has dropped it. On the other hand, if the employer pays the employee's share of the premiums, it may be difficult to recoup those premium payments from an employee who does not return from FMLA leave.

DOL regulations permit an employer to recover its cost of the premiums, including both the employer and the employee shares, through deduction from any sums due the employee (e.g., unpaid wages or vacation pay), provided the deductions do not otherwise violate applicable federal or state wage payment or other laws. Alternatively, the employer may sue the employee to recover such costs. However, DOL regulations preclude recovery if the employee fails to return to work because of his or her own serious health condition or circumstances beyond the employee's control. Such circumstances might include the serious health condition of a newborn, a spouse's job transfer, the serious health condition of a relative other than an immediate family member, or a layoff during FMLA leave. [29 C.F.R. § 825.213]

Q 7:115 Must an employee returning from FMLA leave be permitted to be reinstated if his or her group health plan coverage under a cafeteria plan terminated during the FMLA leave?

Yes. An employee returning from FMLA leave must be permitted to be reinstated if the employee's group health plan coverage under a cafeteria plan (including a health care FSA) terminated during the FMLA leave, either by the employee's revocation or as a result of nonpayment of employee premiums. Generally, reinstatement must be on the same terms as before the leave (including family or dependent coverage), subject to any changes in benefit levels that may have taken place during the period of FMLA leave. In addition, an employee has the right to revoke or change elections (e.g., because of changes in status or cost or coverage changes) under the same terms and conditions as active employees participating in the cafeteria plan. Thus, an employee reinstated after FMLA leave could change elections based on a change in family status to the same extent as other employees. There are, however, special rules applicable to reinstatement in a health care FSA (see Q 7:119). [29 C.F.R. §§ 825.209(e), 825.215(d); Treas. Reg. § 1.125-3, Q&A-1; Prop. Treas. Reg. § 1.125-3, Q&A-1]

Q 7:116 Who is responsible for making premium payments under a cafeteria plan when an employee on FMLA leave elects to continue group health plan coverage?

An employee who chooses to continue group health plan coverage (including a health care FSA) while on FMLA leave may be required by an employer to pay the share of the premiums he or she was paying while at work. The employer must continue to pay the share of the premium cost that it was paying while the employee was working. [29 C.F.R. §§ 825.100(b), 825.210(a); Treas. Reg. § 1.125-3, Q&A-2]

Q 7:117   What payment options are required or permitted in the case of an employee on FMLA leave who elects to continue group health plan coverage under a cafeteria plan?

A cafeteria plan may offer three types of payment options, or a combination of options, to an employee who elects to continue group health plan coverage under a cafeteria plan. They are referred to as the prepay option, the pay-as-you-go option, and the catch-up option. [Treas. Reg. § 1.125-3, Q&A-3]

Prepay option. Under this option, the cafeteria plan may allow employees going on FMLA leave to prepay their premiums for the FMLA leave period. Prepayment can be made on either a pretax or an after-tax basis. Pretax contributions can be made from any taxable compensation the employee receives, such as cashed-out vacation or sick days. However, the use of pretax salary reduction contributions is restricted if an employee's FMLA leave spans two cafeteria plan years (see Q 7:120).

Pay-as-you-go option. Under this option, an employee can choose to pay FMLA leave premiums while on leave. This can be done by following a COBRA premium-type schedule, by using the same method as employees on a non-FMLA leave, or by any other method agreed to by the employer and employee. Generally, such contributions will have to be made on an after-tax basis, unless the employee on FMLA leave has taxable compensation during the FMLA leave period from which pretax reductions can be taken.

Catch-up option. This option is available only if the employer and employee agree before the FMLA leave that the employer will pay the employee's premiums for health coverage that the employee elects to continue during the leave period, and the employee will repay the employer for the FMLA leave premiums when the employee returns to work. The catch-up contributions can be made on either a pretax or an after-tax basis, but contributions on a pretax basis must comply with all cafeteria plan requirements.

The catch-up option can be the sole FMLA premium payment option if it is also the sole payment option for employees on unpaid non-FMLA leave.

Payment ground rules. The final IRS regulations lay down the following ground rules for payment options:

1. Whatever payment options are offered to employees on non-FMLA leave must be offered to employees on FMLA leave. However, a cafeteria plan may include prepayment as an option for employees on FMLA leave even if that option is not offered to employees on unpaid non-FMLA leave.

2. The catch-up option may be the sole option offered to employees on FMLA leave if and only if it is the only option offered to employees on unpaid non-FMLA leave.

3. If the pay-as-you-go option is offered to employees on unpaid non-FMLA leave, that option must also be offered to employees on FMLA leave. In this situation, the employer may also offer employees on FMLA leave the prepay or catch-up option.

No-pay alternative. In lieu of offering any of the above three options, an employer can choose to waive the employee's contributions for FMLA leave health plan coverage, provided the employer does so on a nondiscriminatory basis.

Q 7:118   What happens if an employee chooses to continue health coverage on a pay-as-you-go basis but does not make the required premium payments?

If an employee fails to make payments under the pay-as-you-go option (see Q 7:117), the employer has two choices: (1) terminate the employee's coverage or (2) continue the employee's coverage by paying both the employer's and the employee's shares of the premiums. Under final IRS regulations, an employee on FMLA leave cannot require the employer to terminate coverage. However, an employee who chooses to discontinue premium payments cannot be required to make contributions until the FMLA leave ends.

If an employer continues coverage despite the employee's nonpayment of premiums, the employer can use the catch-up option to recover the employee's share of the premiums when the employee returns from leave.

No prior agreement with the employee is required in order to use the catch-up option in this situation.

Q 7:119   What rules apply to health care FSA coverage for employees on FMLA leave?

Generally, health care FSAs are subject to the same rules as other group health plans for employees on FMLA leave. An employer must permit an employee taking FMLA leave to continue coverage under a health care FSA. In the case of an employee on unpaid FMLA leave, the employer must either allow the employee to terminate coverage or continue the coverage but allow the employee to discontinue payment of his or her share of the premiums. An employee returning from FMLA leave must be permitted to resume FSA coverage that had terminated or lapsed during the FMLA leave. In addition, under final IRS regulations, an employer may require an employee to resume FSA coverage on returning from FMLA leave, provided employees who return from unpaid non-FMLA leave are required to resume coverage.

An employee who continues health care FSA coverage while on FMLA leave is subject to the normal uniform coverage rules regardless of the premium payment method selected. The full FSA coverage amount, less reimbursements, must be available at all times during the FMLA leave period.

An employee who terminates health care FSA coverage during an FMLA leave cannot be reimbursed for any expenses incurred during the period of termination. If an employee who terminated coverage elects to rejoin the health care FSA when the FMLA leave is over, or if the employer requires the employee to resume coverage, the employee may not retroactively elect health care FSA coverage for claims incurred while the coverage was terminated. Under the final

FMLA regulations, an employee must be given the choice of either (1) resuming his or her original level of coverage and making up any unpaid premium payments or (2) resuming coverage at a reduced level without making up the unpaid premiums. If the employee chooses the second option, the employer cannot require the employee to pay any more than the remaining amounts due, even if the plan has already paid out an amount to the employee that exceeds the total premium payments that will be made for the year.

> **Example 1.** Ned, an employee of Megacorp, elects an annual $1,200 health care FSA benefit and makes pretax contributions of $100 a month. On April 1, Ned takes a three-month FMLA leave of absence and elects to terminate health care FSA coverage. Ned has had no medical expenses at that point but has made three months of FSA contributions totaling $300. Ned's FSA coverage ceases during the FMLA leave, and he makes no premium payments for April, May, or June. On July 1, Ned returns to work and requests reinstatement in the health care FSA. Ned must be given the option of resuming coverage at the $1,200 level in effect before his leave and making up the $300 of premiums due during his three-month leave. Alternatively, Ned may choose to resume FSA coverage at a level that is reduced to reflect the period during which no premiums were paid. [Treas. Reg. § 1.125-3, Q&A-6]

If Ned chooses the first option, his coverage for the remainder of the year will be $1,200, and his premiums for the remaining six months of the year will be increased to $150 per month to make up the $300 of missed premiums. If Ned chooses prorated coverage, his coverage for the remainder of the plan year will be $900, and he will resume making premium payments of $100 per month for the remainder of the plan year. In neither case will Ned be entitled to submit claims or receive reimbursements for expenses incurred during his three-month FMLA leave.

> **Example 2.** The facts are the same as those in Example 1, except that Ned incurred medical expenses totaling $200 in February and obtained reimbursement of those expenses. If Ned chooses to resume coverage at the level in effect before his FMLA leave, Ned's coverage for the remainder of the year will be $1,000 ($1,200 less the $200 of reimbursements), and his premiums for the remainder of the year will increase to $150 per month to make up the $300 of missed premiums. If Ned chooses prorated coverage, his coverage for the remainder of the year will be $700 ($1,200 prorated for three months, reduced by $200 of reimbursements), and his monthly premiums for the remainder of the year will be $100.

Q 7:120   What restrictions apply to employee contributions during an FMLA leave that spans two cafeteria plan years?

A cafeteria plan cannot operate in a way that permits a participant to defer compensation from one plan year to a later plan year. Therefore, if an FMLA leave spans two cafeteria plan years, a participant cannot use the prepay option on a pretax basis to pay the later year's employee contributions.

Example. Maria, an employee of Artz, Inc., contributes $100 a month to a cafeteria plan on a pretax basis. Maria takes a three-month FMLA leave for the last two months of the current plan year and the first month of the next plan year and elects to continue plan participation. Although Maria can prepay the first two months' contributions on a pretax basis, she cannot prepay the third month's contribution on a pretax basis because it falls in a later plan year. Maria must either prepay for the third month on an after-tax basis or use another plan option, such as pay-as-you-go or catch-up, to pay the third month's contribution. [Treas. Reg. § 1.125-3, Q&A-5]

Q 7:121 What payment options are available to an employee who is on paid FMLA leave?

If an employee is on paid FMLA leave and the employer mandates that the employee continue group health plan coverage during the leave, the employee's share of the premiums must be paid by the method normally used during any paid leave. Thus, if the employee is contributing from salary on a pretax basis, that method normally would be continued during the paid FMLA leave period. If the FMLA leave period extends beyond the paid leave period and becomes unpaid leave, the options described in Q 7:117 would become applicable (to the extent provided under the cafeteria plan). [29 C.F.R. § 825.207; Treas. Reg. § 1.125-3, Q&A-4]

Q 7:122 What requirements apply to non-health benefit plan coverage during FMLA leave?

The FMLA does not require an employer to continue an employee's non-health benefits (for example, group life insurance) during an employee's FMLA leave period. An employee's entitlement to benefits other than group health coverage during FMLA leave is determined by the employer's established policy for providing such benefits when an employee is on non-FMLA leave. Therefore, an employee who takes FMLA leave is entitled to revoke an election of non-health benefits under a cafeteria plan to the same extent as employees taking non-FMLA leave. However, the FMLA provides that, in certain cases, an employer may continue an employee's non-health cafeteria plan benefits during FMLA leave to ensure that the employer can meet its responsibility to provide equivalent benefits when the employee returns from leave. If an employer continues an employee's non-health benefits during FMLA leave, the employer may recover costs it incurs in paying the employee's share of the contributions during the FMLA leave period. These repayments by the employee may be made on a pretax basis. [29 C.F.R. § 825.213(b); Treas. Reg. § 1.125-3, Q&A-7]

The employer must permit an employee whose non-health benefit plan coverage terminated while on FMLA leave to be reinstated in the coverage upon return to work following the FMLA leave. [29 C.F.R. § 825.214(a); Treas. Reg. § 1.125-3, Q&A-7]

Chapter 8

Dependent Care Assistance and Adoption Assistance

A popular form of fringe benefit that employers frequently provide to their employees is dependent care assistance, either through a cafeteria or flexible benefits plan or as a separate benefits plan. In addition, employers can provide tax-free financial assistance to employees who adopt a child—whether from a foreign country or within the United States. The 2010 Health Reform Act, which was signed into law on March 23, 2010, enhances this valuable fringe benefit.

Dependent Care Assistance Programs

Q 8:1 What is a dependent care assistance program?

A *dependent care assistance program* (DCAP) is an employer-provided program of benefits for employees' dependents. Benefits may take the form of employer-maintained dependent care centers, cash reimbursement of dependent care expenses incurred by the employee, or both. (See Q 8:15 for a detailed description of the dependent care assistance that can be reimbursed by a tax-qualified DCAP under Section 129 of the Internal Revenue Code (Code).

Q 8:2 Does the Employee Retirement Income Security Act apply to dependent care assistance programs?

No, generally DCAPs are not subject to the Employee Retirement Income Security Act of 1974 (ERISA); however, if the employer provides or sponsors a day care center, ERISA does apply. [ERISA § 3(1); DOL Adv. Op. 88-10A (Aug. 12, 1988)] (See chapter 2 for a discussion of ERISA.)

Dependent care FSAs. The Department of Labor (DOL) has issued an advisory opinion letter that examines whether a dependent care flexible spending arrangement (FSA) under a cafeteria plan is an ERISA welfare plan. It concluded that if the employer has no day care facilities, and the employees may select any eligible day care center or other dependent care provider for which the FSA provides reimbursement, the FSA will not be an ERISA welfare benefit plan. [DOL Adv. Op. 91-25A (July 2, 1991)]

> **Note.** This means that state wage payment laws requiring written authorization before deductions may be taken from paychecks would not be preempted by ERISA. These laws therefore will need to be considered when structuring the methodology for making elections regarding the FSA. (See chapter 7.)

Q 8:3   Are employees taxed on benefits received from an employer-provided dependent care assistance program?

If the DCAP satisfies the requirements of Code Section 129, the employee can exclude the reimbursements or the value of the services from income up to specified limits. [I.R.C. § 129] These limits are discussed in Q 8:12.

Q 8:4   Are there tax advantages for employers that contribute to dependent care assistance programs?

Yes. Employers generally may deduct amounts paid or incurred under a DCAP as an "ordinary and necessary" business expense under Code Section 162. For employer-sponsored day care centers, this applies to operating expenses rather than capital expenditures. Capital expenditures, such as the costs of constructing a facility, are included in the employer's tax basis, which is used to compute gain or loss if the facility is sold. [I.R.C. §§ 129, 162; Treas. Reg. § 1.162-10; Rev. Rul. 73-348, 1973-2 C.B. 31]

The Economic Growth and Tax Relief Reconciliation Act of 2001 (EGTRRA) created a tax credit for employers that provide child care assistance to employees. An employer can claim a tax credit equal to 25 percent of qualified child care expenses (see Q 8:5) and 10 percent of qualified child care resource and referral expenses (see Q 8:6). The maximum credit that may be claimed cannot exceed $150,000 per year. [I.R.C. § 45F] The credit is included along with certain other tax credits in determining an employer's general business credit for the tax year. The general business credit is subject to an overall limitation based on an employer's tax liability for the year. [I.R.C. § 38]

An employer's deduction for dependent care assistance expenses is reduced by the amount claimed as a tax credit. If a credit is claimed for capital expenses of acquiring, constructing, rehabilitating, or expanding a facility, the employer's tax basis in the facility is reduced by the amount of the credit.

Credits claimed in connection with a facility are subject to recapture if the employer ceases operation of the facility or transfers its interest in the facility during the first ten years after the facility is placed in service. Recaptured credits are treated as additional taxable income to the employer in the year of recapture. The amount of credits subject to recapture is gradually reduced during the ten-year recapture period. For example, if an employer ceases operation of a child care facility within the first three years after it is placed in service, 100 percent of the credits will be recaptured. On the other hand, if the employer shuts down the facility in the ninth or tenth year of operation, only 10 percent of the credits will be recaptured.

Absent congressional action, tax changes made by EGTRRA, including the tax credit for employer-provided child care assistance, are scheduled to sunset for tax years beginning after 2010.

Q 8:5   What are qualified child care expenses for purposes of the tax credit for employer-provided child care expenses?

An employer may claim the 25 percent tax credit for qualified child care expenses for amounts paid to acquire, construct, rehabilitate, or expand property that is to be used as part of the employer's child care facility. The 25 percent credit may also be claimed for expenses of operating the facility, including certain costs incurred for employee training and compensation.

Employers that contract with an outside child care facility to provide child care services for employees may claim the 25 percent credit for their costs.

To qualify for the credit, a child care facility must meet all applicable state and local laws, including any licensing laws. In addition, a facility will not qualify unless it offers open enrollment to employees and does not discriminate in favor of highly compensated employees. [I.R.C. §§ 45F(c)(1), 45F(c)(2)]

Q 8:6   What are qualified child care resource and referral expenses for purposes of the tax credit for employer-provided child care expenses?

A 10 percent credit may be claimed for amounts paid or incurred under a contract to provide child care resource or referral services to employees. Again, the services must be available to employees generally and must not discriminate in favor of highly compensated employees. [I.R.C. § 45F(c)(3)]

Q 8:7   May partners, S corporation shareholders, and sole proprietors receive tax-favored dependent care assistance benefits under an employer-provided program?

The answer to this question depends on whether the DCAP is part of a Section 125 cafeteria plan.

No cafeteria plan. If the employer-provided dependent care assistance benefits are not associated with a cafeteria plan, partners, S corporation shareholders, and sole proprietors may participate. The term "employee" as used in Code Section 129 includes a self-employed individual. A sole proprietor is treated as his or her own employer, and a partnership is treated as the employer of each of its partners. [I.R.C. §§ 129(e)(3), 129(e)(4)]

Dependent care assistance as part of a cafeteria plan. If the DCAP is part of a cafeteria plan, the answer is different (see Q 8:21). All participants in a cafeteria plan must be employees. Partners and sole proprietors who are self-employed cannot be treated as employees for cafeteria plan purposes. [I.R.C. §§ 125(d)(1)(A), 401(c); Prop. Treas. Reg. § 1.125-1(g)(4)] Additionally, an employee who is a more-than-2-percent shareholder in an S corporation on any day during the taxable year cannot participate in a cafeteria plan maintained by the S corporation. [I.R.C. § 1372] Because the limitation of cafeteria plan participants to employees is an express statutory requirement, the inclusion of these individuals would cause the plan not to be a valid cafeteria plan under Code Section 125 and all participants to lose the Section 125 protection against constructive receipt of income.

Q 8:8   May an employee who receives dependent care assistance benefits under an employer-provided program also claim the Section 21 tax credit for dependent care?

An employee who receives employer-provided dependent care assistance is not automatically barred from claiming an individual tax credit for dependent care expenses. However, benefit payments received under a Section 129 employer-provided DCAP reduce the amount of expenses that may be taken into account in computing the federal income tax credit for dependent care expenses under Code Section 21 on a dollar-for-dollar basis. [I.R.C. § 21(c)] (See Qs 8:22–8:24 for a detailed discussion of this tax credit.)

Under current rules, more employees may qualify for both tax breaks. Prior to 2003, the amount of dependent care expenses that could be taken into account in computing the dependent care credit was capped at $2,400 for one qualifying individual and $4,800 for two or more individuals. Therefore, if an employee received the maximum $5,000 of employer-provided assistance (see Q 8:12), he or she could not claim a dependent care tax credit. Beginning in 2003, EGTRRA increased the maximum amount of creditable dependent care expenses to $3,000 for one individual and $6,000 for two or more individuals. However, EGTRRA did not increase the limit on employer-provided assistance. As a result, an employee who receives the maximum of $5,000 of DCAP benefits for the care of two or more individuals will be eligible to claim a tax credit for up to $1,000 of additional expenses ($6,000 maximum creditable expenses less $5,000 DCAP benefits).

Tax changes made by EGTRRA are scheduled to sunset for tax years beginning after 2010. Thus, absent congressional action, the maximum amount of creditable expenses for purposes of the dependent care credit will drop to pre-EGTRRA levels.

Q 8:9   Does the dependent care assistance program have to be in writing?

Yes. Even though ERISA may not always apply to these programs (see Q 8:2), a separate provision contained in Code Section 129 requires that the employer-provided DCAP be set out in a separate written plan. [I.R.C. § 129(d)(1)]

This express structural requirement means that an unwritten DCAP possibly might not qualify for the favorable tax treatment available under Code Section 129. (See Q 8:19.)

Q 8:10   What is the exclusive-benefit requirement for employer-provided dependent care assistance programs?

Code Section 129 requires that an employer-provided DCAP be for the exclusive benefit of employees. [I.R.C. § 129(d)(1)]

Q 8:11   What disclosure of program benefits is required to be made to eligible employees?

Code Section 129 imposes two disclosure requirements. First, the sponsoring employer must provide reasonable notification of the availability and terms of its program to eligible employees. [I.R.C. § 129(d)(6)] Second, the plan must furnish each employee who has received benefits in the preceding calendar year with a written statement by January 31 showing the amounts paid or expenses incurred by the employer in providing dependent care assistance to the employee. [I.R.C. § 129(d)(7)] Reporting the amount of dependent care assistance to each employee on the employee's annual W-2 statement satisfies this second requirement. [I.R.C. §§ 129(d), 6051(a)(9)]

> **Note.** ERISA does not apply to a DCAP unless the plan includes an employer-provided or employer-sponsored day care center; therefore, a summary plan description (SPD) is not required. Nonetheless, employers typically provide participants with an ERISA-type SPD to parallel the level of disclosure made for other components of a cafeteria plan and to facilitate enrollment in and administration of the program.

Q 8:12   What is the maximum amount of tax-favored benefits that may be provided by a dependent care assistance program?

Code Section 129 provides a four-part annual limit for allowable employer-provided dependent care assistance benefits. The applicable limit for a particular employee will depend on the employee's marital status, tax filing status, and earned income, and the spouse's earned income. The maximum aggregate dollar amount of excludable employer-provided dependent care assistance benefits under Code Section 129 is the lesser of:

1. $5,000 if the participant is single or is married and files a joint tax return; or

2. $2,500 if the participant is married and files a separate tax return; or

3. The earned income of the participant, if single; or

4. If the participant is married, the earned income of the spouse who earned the lesser amount during the calendar year. (See the special spousal earned income rule that follows.)

[I.R.C. §§ 129(a)(2), 129(b)]

The earned income limitation may reduce Code Section 129's overall dollar limit on the permissible amount of employer-provided dependent care assistance benefits and may further reduce (or completely eliminate) the dollar amount allowable.

Spousal earned income. A spouse who is incapacitated or who is a full-time student for at least five months during the calendar year is treated as having earned income of not less than $250 per month if there is one qualifying dependent and not less than $500 per month if there are two or more qualifying dependents. [I.R.C. §§ 121(d), 129(b)(2), 129(e)(2)]

On-site care. Dependent care assistance received from the employer's on-site facility is to be valued based on the use of the on-site facility by the employee's dependent(s) and the value of the services provided by the facility with respect to such dependent(s). [I.R.C. § 129(e)(8)]

Note. It is important that each of these limits be set forth in the written plan document and in employee communication materials.

Q 8:13 If the employee's spouse does not work and is neither disabled nor a full-time student, can the employee receive any reimbursements under the employer's dependent care assistance program?

No. Under these circumstances, the earned income limitation discussed in Q 8:12 would reduce the amount of benefits available under the employer's plan to zero. [I.R.C. §§ 121(d), 129(b)]

This result occurs because of the underlying purpose of Code Section 129. Only dependent care assistance expenses incurred to enable the employee to be gainfully employed are permissible. The underlying assumption of the statute seems to be that an employee with a nonworking spouse does not need dependent care assistance in order to work; however, as can be seen from the limits set forth in Q 8:12, the statute does recognize the need for some dependent care assistance when the nonworking spouse is either incapacitated or a full-time student.

Q 8:14 Under the employer's plan, who can be a qualifying dependent?

To be excludable under Code Section 129, the dependent care expenses must be incurred in caring for a *qualifying individual*. This individual must fall into one of the following three categories:

1. A dependent of the employee who is under the age of 13 and for whom the employee can claim a dependency exemption;

2. A dependent of the employee who is physically or mentally incapable of caring for himself or herself and who has the same principal abode as the employee for more than half the year; or

3. The spouse of the employee who is physically or mentally incapable of caring for himself or herself and who has the same principal abode as the employee for more than half the year.

[I.R.C. §§ 129(e)(1); 21(b)(1)]

According to final IRS regulations implementing the dependent care tax credit, a person is considered to be physically or mentally incapable of self-care if, as a result of a physical or mental defect, the person is incapable of caring for personal hygienic or nutritional needs or requires the full-time attention of other people for his or her safety or the safety of others. The inability to engage in any substantial gainful activity or to perform the normal household functions of a homemaker or to care for minor children does not of itself establish that a person is incapable of self-care. [I.R.C. §§ 21(b)(1), 21(b)(2)(A), 129(e)(1); Treas. Reg. § 1.21-1(b)(3)]) In regard to the first category, the IRS has established a uniform method for determining when a child attains a specific age for various tax purposes, including dependent care assistance programs. [Rev. Rul. 2003-72, 2003-33 I.R.B. 346] Under the uniform method, a child attains a given age on the anniversary of the date he or she was born. For example, a child born on January 1, 1995, attains age 13 on January 1, 2008, and no longer qualifies as an eligible dependent for dependent care assistance purposes.

> **Practice Pointer.** The above categories provide employers with flexibility in designing a DCAP. The program's benefits can be limited to child care or can be broadened to include care of incapacitated adult dependents, such as parents, who qualify as tax dependents under Code Section 152. If the DCAP covers adult care outside the home, then the adult in question must regularly spend at least eight hours a day in the employee's household. (See Q 8:15.)

Q 8:15 What types of dependent care expenses can the employer's program cover?

The expenses must be for household services and care of qualifying dependents. The expenses must be incurred to enable the employee to be gainfully employed. According to IRS final regulations dealing with the dependent care credit, an expense is not employment related merely because it is paid or incurred while the taxpayer is gainfully employed—the *purpose* of the expense must be to permit gainful employment. [Treas. Reg. § 1.21-1(a), (c)]

Examples of expenses that may be paid for or reimbursed under a Section 129 plan include:

- At-home care for a child or other qualifying dependent
- The cost of a housekeeper who cares for a dependent and also performs household services
- Dependent care centers that meet state or local government requirements and provide day care for more than six individuals
- Transportation furnished by a dependent care provider
- Employment tax paid on wages of a care provider
- Room and board expenses for a caregiver over and above normal household expenses
- Indirect expenses such as agency fees, application fees, or deposits to obtain care

If the qualifying individual (see Q 8:14) is not a dependent under the age of 13, dependent care expenses that are incurred outside the home can be taken into account only if the qualifying individual regularly spends at least eight hours a day in the employee's household. [I.R.C. § 21(b)(2)(B)]

Schools and camps. The final IRS regulations specifically provide that the full amount paid to a preschool in which a qualifying child is enrolled is considered to be for the care of the child, even though the school also furnishes educational services. By contrast, the proposed regulations make it clear that expenses for kindergarten or higher grades are not dependent care expenses because they are primarily for education. However, the cost of before- or after-school care for a child in kindergarten or a higher grade may qualify. [Treas. Reg. § 1.21-1(d)(5)]

In addition, the regulations provide that the cost of a day camp or similar program can qualify, even if the camp specializes in a particular activity. Expenses for overnight camps, however, are not employment-related expenses. [Treas. Reg. § 1.21-1(d)(6), (7)]

Amounts paid for food, lodging and clothing are generally not qualifying expenses for dependent care. According to the proposed regulations, however, these expenses can count if they are inseparable from the care of an individual. For example, lunch and snacks at a preschool are deemed to be for care because the expenses are incidental and inseparable from the care provided by the school. On the other hand, the regulations make it clear that the cost of a boarding school must be allocated between expense for care and expenses for education, meals, and housing.

Qualifying caregivers. The services cannot be provided by an individual for whom the employee or the employee's spouse can claim a dependency exemption or by the employee's child under age 19 (determined as of the close of the taxable year). [I.R.C. §§ 21(b)(2), 21(e)(6), 129(e)]

Requirement of tax identification information. In order to be reimbursed under a Section 129 employer-provided DCAP, the employee must provide the name, address, and taxpayer identification number (TIN) of the person performing the services (or, if the service provider is a tax-exempt organization such as an educational organization, the name and address of such person or entity). [I.R.C. § 129(e)(9)]

> **Practice Pointer.** As a result of this requirement, an employee generally cannot obtain reimbursement for a nanny or housekeeper who is an illegal alien and/or who does not have a Social Security number. In addition, reimbursement cannot be claimed for a caregiver whom the employee is paying "under the table" without withholding or paying Social Security taxes. To avoid employee misunderstanding, it would be advisable to include the requirement of a TIN in the descriptive materials relating to the employer's DCAP. This requirement may help to explain why employers sometimes experience difficulty in encouraging non-highly compensated employees to enroll in a seemingly attractive benefit program and thus have difficulty satisfying the nondiscrimination rules imposed by Code Section 129.

Q 8:16   Are employer-provided dependent care assistance programs subject to nondiscrimination rules?

Yes. The plan may not discriminate in favor of highly compensated employees (as defined in Code Section 414(q)) or their dependents. To be nondiscriminatory, the plan must pass an eligibility test, a benefit test, a 25 percent concentration test, and a 55 percent concentration test. Failure to satisfy these rules does not affect employees who are not highly compensated, but favorable tax benefits are not available to highly compensated employees if the plan is discriminatory. [I.R.C. §§ 129(d)(1), 129(d)(2), 129(d)(3), 129(d)(4), 129(d)(8)]

Q 8:17   What are the nondiscrimination tests?

Code Section 129 imposes the following four nondiscrimination requirements on employer-provided DCAPs:

1. *Eligibility test.* The program must benefit employees who qualify under a classification set up by the employer and found by the Internal Revenue Service not to discriminate in favor of highly compensated employees (as defined in Code Section 414(q)) or their dependents.

2. *Benefit test.* The contributions or benefits under the program cannot discriminate in favor of highly compensated employees (as defined in Code Section 414(q)) or their dependents.

3. *25 percent concentration test.* Not more than 25 percent of the amounts the employer pays or incurs for dependent care assistance during the year may be provided for more-than-5-percent owners (or their spouses or dependents) of the stock or the capital or profits interest in the employer at any time during the year.

4. *55 percent concentration test.* The average benefits provided to non-highly compensated employees under all such plans of the employer must be at

least 55 percent of the average benefits provided to highly compensated employees. In the case of any benefits provided through a salary reduction agreement, employees whose compensation is less than $25,000 may be disregarded when applying this test.

[I.R.C. §§ 129(d)(2), 129(d)(3), 129(d)(4), 129(d)(8)]

Controlled group basis. The preceding tests are to be performed on a controlled group basis. Test 4 may be applied separately to each of the employer's separate lines of business. [I.R.C. § 414(r)(1)]

Permitted exclusions when performing the tests. When performing tests 1 and 4, the employer need not take into account employees who are under age 21, employees who have not completed a year of service, or employees who are covered by an agreement that the IRS finds to be a collective bargaining agreement, if there is evidence that dependent care benefits were the subject of good-faith bargaining between the employee representatives and the employer(s). [I.R.C. § 129(d)(9)]

Effect of utilization rates. Tests 1 and 2 are not affected by the actual utilization rates under the DCAP. Tests 3 and 4 measure how much of the program's benefits are actually received by participants. [I.R.C. § 125(e)(6)]

Q 8:18 What are the tax consequences if the employer's written dependent care assistance program fails the Section 129(d) nondiscrimination requirements?

The answer to this question depends on whether the written DCAP is a part of a cafeteria plan.

DCAP not part of a cafeteria plan. If the employer's DCAP fails any of the nondiscrimination requirements or other requirements (such as the separate written plan requirement) imposed by Code Section 129, only highly compensated employees (HCEs) will be taxed on the benefits received from the program. Non-highly compensated employees (NHCEs) will not be affected, and their plan benefits will continue to be excludable from federal income taxes up to the applicable limit under Code Section 129.

DCAP as part of a cafeteria plan. If the DCAP is a part of a cafeteria plan, then any failure under Code Section 129 has the consequences described in the preceding paragraph; however, failing the nondiscrimination requirements of Code Section 129 will not disqualify the cafeteria plan.

Q 8:19 What are the tax consequences if the employer's dependent care assistance program fails the Section 129 written plan requirement?

The answer to this question is not clear. Although Code Section 129(d) imposes adverse tax consequences only on HCEs for violations of the nondiscrimination rules of the plan, it is not entirely clear whether such a limited fallout would also apply if the plan is unwritten.

One possible interpretation is that an unwritten plan does not affect the tax consequences for NHCEs. Code Section 129(d) states that a DCAP is a written plan "for the purposes of this section" but discusses tax consequences only for failure to meet the nondiscrimination requirements "of this subsection." It would appear then that Code Section 129(d) defines a DCAP at the outset as a separate written plan, and the IRS could take the interpretive position that an unwritten plan is not a valid dependent care assistance program under Code Section 129.

Practice Pointer. If the DCAP is included in a fully integrated cafeteria plan, Code Section 125 will require that the entire cafeteria plan be in writing (see Q 7:8).

Q 8:20   Is the employer required to pay Federal Insurance Contribution Act (FICA) tax or Federal Unemployment Tax Act (FUTA) tax on, or withhold taxes from, dependent care assistance program payments?

As long as it is reasonable for the employer to believe that payments from its Section 129 DCAP are excludable from the employee's gross income, such program payments are not subject to FICA tax, FUTA tax, or federal income tax withholding requirements. [I.R.C. §§ 3121(a)(18), 3306(b)(13), 3401(a)(18)]

Q 8:21   Can a dependent care assistance program be made a part of a cafeteria plan?

Yes. The Code Section 125 cafeteria plan rules permit a DCAP meeting the requirements of Code Section 129 to be included as a "qualified benefit" under a cafeteria plan. A DCAP can be included as an FSA option and paid for by employee salary reduction or by employer contributions, or both. However, partners, sole proprietors, and more-than-2-percent shareholders in an S corporation would not be eligible to participate in the DCAP because only employees may participate in cafeteria plans. See chapter 7 for a discussion of the cafeteria plan rules, including the additional Section 125 nondiscrimination rules that would apply to such an arrangement. [I.R.C. § 125(f); Prop. Treas. Reg. §§ 1.125-1(a)(3)(F), 1.125-5(h)]

Q 8:22   What is the dependent care tax credit?

Code Section 21 contains a tax credit for certain dependent care assistance expenses incurred by the taxpayer to enable him or her to be gainfully employed. An employee is entitled to a tax credit for amounts paid for the care of dependents under the age of 13, disabled dependents, or a disabled spouse (qualified dependents). The credit is equal to 35 percent of eligible dependent care expenses for taxpayers with adjusted gross income (AGI) of $15,000 or less, phased down to 20 percent for taxpayers with AGI in excess of $43,000. [I.R.C. § 21(a)(2)] The maximum amount of credit eligible expenses is $3,000 for one dependent and $6,000 for two or more. [I.R.C. § 21(c)] So for taxpayers with

AGI over $43,000, the maximum credit will be $600 for one child and $1,200 for two or more children. The credit cannot exceed the individual's income tax liability, and married couples generally must file joint returns in order to claim the credit. [I.R.C. §§ 21(a), 21(e)(2)]

Note that benefit payments received under a Section 129 employer-provided DCAP will reduce the amount of expenses that may be taken into consideration under the federal income tax credit for dependent care assistance under Code Section 21 on a dollar-for-dollar basis. [I.R.C. § 21(c)]

> **Practice Pointer.** Typically, the employer's communications and distributed materials regarding the DCAP will include a brief mention of the availability of the tax credit and the effect of plan benefits on the amount of the credit available. The income level of the employee and his or her spouse will determine whether the employer-provided program benefit exclusion or the tax credit is more favorable.

Q 8:23   Does the employer have any obligation to help the employee determine which tax benefit—the exclusion or the credit—is more advantageous?

No. Currently, applicable tax rules do not require such disclosure. The requirement that an employer with a DCAP disclose to its employees that both the exclusion and the credit are available to them, and outline the circumstances under which one may be more advantageous than the other, was contained in the proposed Treasury regulations under former Code Section 89, both of which were repealed. Employers are, however, free to provide such information.

Q 8:24   Is there any information that the employee must provide the IRS?

Yes. An employee claiming a dependent care credit or exclusion must provide the name, address, and TIN of each dependent care provider. Failure to provide this information will result in loss of the credit or exclusion unless the employee can show to the IRS's satisfaction that he or she exercised due diligence in attempting to provide the information. If the dependent care provider is a tax-exempt organization, the requirement of a TIN does not apply, but the name and address of the tax-exempt organization must be provided on the tax return. [I.R.C. §§ 21(e)(9), 129(e)(9), 6109(a)(3)]

Q 8:25   Is an employer required to report any dependent care assistance program information to the IRS?

Although DCAPs are technically subject to IRS reporting requirements, they have been exempt from filing under a long-standing IRS rule. [IRS Notice 90-24, 1990-1 C.B. 335] In the past, cafeteria plans (including those that provide dependent care assistance) were required to file an annual information return. However, the IRS suspended that requirement as of April 4, 2002, effective for all plan years, for all unfiled returns, including years before 2001. [IRS Notice 2002-24, 2002-16 I.R.B. 785]

W-2 reporting. An employer that provides dependent care assistance is required to report cash reimbursements to an employee for dependent care assistance in box 10 of the employee's Form W-2. If the employer does not know the actual amount of cash reimbursement at the time the W-2 form is prepared, it may report a reasonable estimate of the total amount. In the case of a dependent care FSA, the amount contributed by the employee for the year (plus any employer matching contributions) will be considered a reasonable estimate. [IRS Notice 89-111, 1989-2 C.B. 449; IRS Notice 90-66, 1990-2 C.B. 350] If an employer adopts a grace period for a dependent care FSA (see Q 7:28), the employer should continue to report the amount elected by the employee for the year (plus matching contributions)—even if a portion of that amount will be used to reimburse expenses incurred in the following year. [IRS Notice 2005-61, 2005 I.R.B. 1]

Q 8:26   Can an employer use a debit or other payment card to provide benefits under a dependent care assistance program?

Yes. However, dependent care expenses cannot be reimbursed before the expenses are incurred. For this reason, dependent care expenses are treated as having been incurred at the time dependent care services are provided, not at the time the expenses are formally billed, charged for, or paid by the participant. Therefore, if a dependent care provider requires payment before the dependent care services are provided, those expenses cannot be reimbursed at the time of payment, even through the use of a payment card program. [Notice 2006-69, 2006-31 I.R.B. 107] Employers may also use debit cards to reimburse expenses under a dependent care FSA (see chapter 7).

Adoption Assistance Programs

Q 8:27   Are adoption assistance programs subject to ERISA?

No, they are not.

Q 8:28   Can an adoption assistance program be included in a cafeteria plan?

Yes, an adoption assistance program meeting the requirements of Code Section 137 is a qualified benefit for purposes of Code Section 125. Accordingly, this benefit may be offered through a cafeteria plan. [Notice 97-9, 1997-2 I.R.B. 35; Prop. Treas. Reg. § 1.125-1(a)(3)(G)]

Q 8:29   What are the requirements for an adoption assistance program under Code Section 137?

The following requirements apply to an adoption assistance program under Code Section 137:

1. An absolute structural requirement is that the adoption assistance program be a separate written plan of the employer for the exclusive benefit of its employees. The Section 137 exclusion is not available unless, *before adoption expenses are incurred by either the employer or the employee,* the written plan is in existence and the employee receives notification of the existence of the plan.

2. The plan does not have to be funded.

3. Reasonable notification of the availability and terms of the program must be provided to eligible employees.

4. The program must benefit employees under a classification set up by the employer and found by the IRS not to discriminate in favor of highly compensated employees (as defined in Code Section 414(q)) or their spouses or dependents.

5. No more than 5 percent of the amounts paid or incurred by the employer during the year may be provided for the class of individuals who are shareholders or owners owning more than 5 percent of the stock or the capital or profits interest in the employer.

6. An employee receiving payments under an adoption assistance program must provide the employer reasonable substantiation that payments or reimbursements made under the program constitute qualified adoption expenses.

[I.R.C. §§ 137(b)(2), 137(b)(3), 137(b)(5), 137(b)(6), 137(c); Notice 97-9, 1997-2 I.R.B. 35]

Note. An employer is not required to apply to the IRS for a determination that the plan is a qualified program. [Notice 97-9, 1997-2 I.R.B. 35]

Q 8:30   What are qualified adoption expenses?

Qualified adoption expenses are reasonable and necessary adoption fees, court costs, attorneys' fees, and other expenses that are directly related to, and the principal purpose of which is for, the legal adoption of an "eligible child" (see Q 8:31) by the employee. They include such amounts paid or expenses incurred in connection with any unsuccessful attempt to adopt an eligible child before successfully finalizing the adoption of another eligible child. [Notice 97-9, 1997-2 I.R.B. 35]

Qualified adoption expenses do not include expenses that are incurred (1) in violation of state or federal law, (2) in carrying out a surrogate parenting arrangement, or (3) in adopting a child of the employee's spouse. [I.R.C. §§137(d), 36C] Also excluded is any expense for which a deduction or credit is allowed under any other provision of the Code or for which funds are received under any federal, state, or local program. [Notice 97-9, 1997-2 I.R.B. 35]

Q 8:31   Who is an eligible child?

An *eligible child* is an individual who either (1) has not attained age 18 or (2) is physically or mentally incapable of caring for himself or herself. [I.R.C. § 36C]

An IRS revenue ruling establishes a uniform method for determining when a child attains a specific age for various tax purposes, including adoption assistance programs. [Rev. Rul. 2003-72, 2003-33 I.R.B. 346] Under the uniform method, a child attains a given age on the anniversary of the date he or she was born. For example, a child born on March 1, 1989, attains age 18 on March 1, 2007, and would no longer qualify as an eligible child for adoption assistance purposes (unless he or she is incapable of self-care).

Q 8:32   What is the income tax treatment of payments or reimbursements made to an employee for qualified adoption expenses?

Employer-provided adoption assistance is excludable from gross income up to a maximum amount per eligible child, including a child with "special needs" (see Q 8:33). The maximum exclusion was originally capped at $5,000 ($6,000 for special-needs adoptions), but was increased to $10,000, subject to inflation adjustments for tax years beginning after 2002 by EGTRRA. Thus, for 2010, the maximum exclusion was scheduled to be $12,170 per eligible child. [Rev. Proc. 2009-50, 2009-45 I.R.B. 617] However, the 2010 Health Reform Act increases the maximum exclusion to $13,170 for tax years beginning after 2009, subject to inflation adjustments in taxable years beginning after 2010. [I.R.C. § 137(b)(1), as amended by the Patient Protection and Affordable Care Act, Pub. L. No. 111-148 (Mar. 23, 2010) (PPACA)]

In the case of most adoptions, the exclusion is limited to the amount of qualified adoption expenses actually paid or incurred by the employee. However, the maximum exclusion is available to an employee who adopts a special-needs child, regardless of the amount of the employee's qualified adoption expenses. [I.R.C. §§ 137(a), 137(b)(1)]

The exclusion for employer-provided adoption assistance was originally scheduled to expire after 2001. EGTRRA made the exclusion "permanent." However, under a special "sunset" provision, tax changes made by EGTRRA are scheduled to expire after 2010. The 2010 Health Reform Act delays the sunset of the adoption exclusion for one year. [PPACA § 10909] Thus, absent further congressional action, the exclusion will expire for tax years beginning after December 31, 2011.

The exclusion for employer-provided adoption assistance is not an annual exclusion but a per-adoptee exclusion. According to the IRS, if an employee makes an unsuccessful adoption attempt and then successfully adopts an eligible child, the expenses of the unsuccessful adoption are included in the maximum exclusion limit for the successful adoption. [Notice 97-9, 1997-2 I.R.B. 35]

> **Note.** The IRS notice does not address the treatment of employees who make an unsuccessful adoption attempt and then give up. However, the IRS has made it clear that the exclusion is available for expenses connected with a domestic adoption even if the adoption never becomes final. [IRS Publication 968, Tax Benefits for Adoption] In the case of a foreign adoption, the tax exclusion for adoption assistance is available only if and when the adoption becomes final (see Q 8:35).

Reduction of maximum exclusion. The maximum per-adoptee exclusion is reduced for employees with higher incomes and is eliminated entirely for employees with incomes above a specified point (see Q 8:34 for details about this income-based limit).

Timing of exclusion. Generally, the exclusion is available for the year in which the employee pays the qualified adoption expenses in connection with the adoption of an eligible child who is a citizen or resident of the United States at the time the adoption commenced. In the case of a foreign adoption, employer-provided assistance is excludable from income only if and when the adoption becomes final (see Q 8:35).

A married couple must file a joint return to qualify for the exclusion unless they lived apart from each other for the last six months of the taxable year and the individual claiming the exclusion (1) maintained as his or her home a household for the eligible child for more than half of the taxable year and (2) furnished over half of the cost of maintaining that household in that taxable year. For this purpose, an individual legally separated from his or her spouse under a decree of divorce or separate maintenance will not be considered married. [I.R.C. § 137(e)]

Q 8:33   Who is a child with special needs?

A child has special needs if:

1. A state has determined that the child cannot or should not be returned to the home of his or her parents;

2. The same state has determined that a specific factor (such as ethnic background, age, membership in a minority or sibling group, a medical condition, or a handicap) makes it reasonable to conclude that the child cannot be placed with adoptive parents without providing adoption assistance; and

3. The child with special needs is a citizen or resident of the United States, including any possession of the United States.

[I.R.C. §36C (formerly § 23); Notice 97-9, 1997-2 I.R.B. 35]

Q 8:34   What is the income limitation on the amount of employer-provided adoption expense benefits that may be excluded from income?

The amount otherwise excludable under Code Section 137 (see Q 8:32) is reduced for employees with higher incomes and is eliminated entirely for employees with incomes above a certain level. [I.R.C. § 137(b)(2)] These income limitations are subject to annual inflation adjustments. For 2010, the exclusion begins to phase out for taxpayers with modified adjusted gross income (MAGI) in excess of $182,520 and is completely phased out for taxpayers with MAGI of $222,520 or more. [Rev. Proc. 2009-50, 2009-45 I.R.B. 619] The employer can treat amounts up to the maximum per adoptee limit as excludable adoption assistance on an employee's Form W-2. The employee is responsible for calculating the income limit and making appropriate adjustments on his or her income tax return. In addition, if the employee is not eligible for the exclusion or is eligible for only a partial exclusion, the employee should make necessary adjustments to income tax withholding or estimated tax payments to account for the tax on the adoption assistance payments.

Q 8:35   For foreign adoptions, what additional limitations apply to the Section 137 exclusion from income?

In the case of a foreign adoption, the exclusion does not apply until the adoption becomes final. [I.R.C. §§ 36C (formerly § 23), 137(e)]

Special rule for foreign adoptions. If the eligible child being adopted is not a citizen or resident of the United States at the time the adoption is commenced, the exclusion is not available until the adoption becomes final. Amounts paid or incurred by the employer for qualified adoption expenses prior to the year in which the adoption becomes final are includable in the employee's gross income for that year and excludable in the taxable year in which the adoption becomes final. Accordingly, if the employer reimburses qualified adoption expenses (which are not subject to income tax withholding but are subject to FICA and FUTA withholding) in a year prior to the year in which the foreign adoption becomes final, the employee is responsible for making an adjustment on his or her Form 1040 to include in gross income the taxable portion of the reimbursement. For the year in which the foreign adoption becomes final, the employee is responsible for claiming the exclusion by adjusting his or her Form 1040 accordingly. Expenses paid or incurred prior to the 1997 taxable year do not qualify for the exclusion. [Notice 97-9, 1997-2 I.R.B. 35]

When is a foreign adoption final? The IRS has issued a revenue procedure to establish safe harbor rules for determining the finality of a foreign adoption. [Rev. Proc. 2005-31, 2005-26 I.R.B. 1374]

The revenue procedure applies to qualified adoption expenses paid or incurred in connection with the adoption of a foreign-born child who has received an "immediate relative" (IR) visa from the Department of State. An IR visa is issued only to a foreign-born child who enters the United States pursuant to a decree of adoption or guardianship granted by a court or other government agency (competent authority) with jurisdiction over child welfare matters in the foreign country. The revenue procedure does not apply to the adoption of a child who is already a citizen or resident of the United States when the adoption proceedings begin. In addition, the revenue procedure will not apply to the adoption of a foreign child that is governed by the Intercountry Adoption Act of 2000, when it takes effect in the United States (see below).

IR visas come in three varieties:

1. An IR-2 visa issued to a foreign-born child under age 16 who has been in the legal custody of, and has resided with, the adoptive parent or parents for at least two years.

2. An IR-3 visa issued to a foreign-born child after a full and final adoption has occurred in a foreign country.

3. An IR-4 visa issued to a child if a foreign country grants legal guardianship or custody to the prospective adoptive parent or parents or to an individual or agency acting on their behalf. An IR-4 visa is also issued if the foreign country grants a simple adoption (in which one or both of the adoptive parents do not see the child before or during the proceedings).

Under Revenue Procedure 2005-31, a taxpayer may treat the adoption of a foreign-born child, who receives an IR-2 visa, an IR-3 visa, or an IR-4 visa under a decree of simple adoption, as final either (1) in the taxable year in which the foreign court or competent authority enters a decree of adoption or (2) in the taxable year in which a home state court enters a decree of re-adoption or otherwise recognizes the foreign decree, if that taxable year is one of the next two taxable years after the taxable year in which the foreign decree was entered.

In the case of a child who is issued an IR-4 visa under a grant of legal guardianship or custody (as opposed to simple adoption), the adoption may be treated as final in the taxable year in which a home state court enters an adoption decree. [Rev. Proc. 2005-31, 2005-26 I.R.B. 1374]

The Intercountry Adoption Act of 2000 (IAA) [Pub. L. 106-279, 114 Stat. 825 (2000)] will implement the Hague Convention on Protection of Children and Co-operation in Respect of Intercountry Adoption. When IAA enters into force in the United States, it generally will apply to adoptions in which both the sending and the receiving countries are parties to the convention. A convention adoption subject to the IAA will be final for federal income tax purposes (1) in the taxable year for which the Secretary of State certifies an adoption as final or (2) in the year in which the state court enters a final decree of adoption.

Q 8:36   Are there other tax breaks for adoption expenses?

Yes. Taxpayers may claim a tax credit for eligible adoption expenses. [I.R.C. § 36C (formerly § 23), as amended by PPACA] As with the adoption exclusion (see Q 8:32), the 2010 Health Reform Act increases the maximum credit to $13,150 for tax years beginning after 2009. [I.R.C. § 36C(b)(1)] Moreover, the law makes the credit refundable after 2009. Thus, taxpayers whose adoption credit exceeds their tax liability for the year will receive the benefit in the form of a refund.

In the case of most adoptions, the credit is limited to the amount of qualified adoption expenses actually paid or incurred by the taxpayer. However, the maximum credit is available to a taxpayer who adopts a special-needs child, regardless of the amount of qualified adoption expenses. The maximum credit is phased out for taxpayers with MAGI above a certain level. The phase-out range is subject to inflation adjustments. For 2010, the credit phases out for taxpayers with MAGI between $182,520 and $222,520. The credit for expenses incurred in connection with the domestic adoption of a child who does not have special needs can be claimed in the year *following* the year in which the expenses are paid. However, expenses paid or incurred in the year the adoption becomes final can be claimed as a credit in that year. The credit for adoption of a child with special needs can be claimed only in the year the adoption becomes final. Expenses for a foreign adoption can also be claimed as a credit in the year the adoption becomes final. The credit is nonrefundable, but unused credits can be carried over for five years.

Like the exclusion for employer-provided adoption assistance, the adoption tax credit was increased and made "permanent" by EGTRRA. However, under EGTRRA's sunset provision, the adoption credit was scheduled to expire after 2010. The 2010 Health Reform Act delays the sunset of the adoption credit for one year until 2012. [PPACA § 10909] Note that the tax credit for special-needs adoptions is permanent, but it will revert to pre-EGTRRA levels (maximum of $6,000 or actual adoption expenses, subject to a phaseout once the taxpayer's modified adjusted gross income reaches $75,000) under the sunset. The adoption tax credit and the exclusion for employer-provided assistance are not mutually exclusive. An individual may claim both the maximum allowable credit and the maximum allowable exclusion in connection with a single adoption.

> **Example.** Tom and his wife, Susan, adopted a child in 2010. The adoption was not a foreign adoption and the child was not a special-needs child. Tom's employer reimbursed $10,000 of eligible adoption expenses under its adoption assistance plan. Tom and Susan paid another $5,000 of eligible expenses out of their own pockets in 2010. The couple's adjusted gross income is below the phase-out range for the exclusion and credit.
>
> Tom and Susan may exclude the $10,000 of employer-provided adoption assistance from their income for 2010. In addition, they can claim an adoption credit in 2010 for the $5,000 of expenses they paid themselves.

> **Note.** An individual cannot claim both the credit and the exclusion for the same expenses. In addition, an employee cannot claim the credit for any expense reimbursed by his or her employer, whether or not the amount is reimbursed under an adoption assistance plan.

Q 8:37   Is an employer that offers an adoption assistance program required to file an annual report with the IRS?

Yes. An employer offering an adoption assistance program is required by Code Section 6039D to file a Form 5500 annual report for the program. [I.R.C. § 6039D(d), as amended by the Taxpayer Relief Act of 1997, § 1601(j)]

Q 8:38   Are employer-provided adoption expense benefits subject to withholding, FICA, and FUTA?

Amounts paid or expenses incurred by an employer for qualified adoption expenses under a Section 137 adoption assistance program are not subject to income tax withholding; however, they are subject to FICA, FUTA, and railroad retirement tax. [Notice 97-9, 1997-2 I.R.B. 35]

Q 8:39   Do any special reporting requirements apply to an employee claiming the exclusion?

Yes. The employee is required to provide available information about the name, age, and TIN of each adopted child as well as other information required by the IRS. [I.R.C. §§ 36C, 137(e)]

In lieu of such information, the employee may be required to furnish other information, including the identity of the agent assisting with the adoption.

Additionally, individuals who are married at the end of the taxable year must file a joint federal income tax return to claim the adoption credit or exclusion unless they lived apart from each other and the individual claiming the credit or exclusion (1) maintained as his or her home a household for the eligible child for more than half of the taxable year and (2) furnished over half of the cost of maintaining that household in that taxable year. For this purpose, an individual is not considered to be married if he or she is legally separated from his or her spouse under a decree of divorce or separate maintenance. [Notice 97-9, 1997-2 I.R.B. 35]

Child's identification number. The adopted child's identification number is one of the following:

- The child's Social Security number (SSN) if the child has one or one can be obtained before the return for the year must be filed
- The child's individual TIN if the child is a resident alien or nonresident alien and is not eligible for an SSN
- An adoption TIN if the child is a U.S. citizen or resident who is in the process of being adopted and an SSN cannot be obtained until the adoption becomes final

[I.R.S. Publication 968, *Tax Benefits for Adoption*]

Q 8:40   Does the Section 137 exclusion for employer-provided adoption assistance expire at some point?

The exclusion was scheduled to expire for amounts paid or expenses incurred after December 31, 2001. EGTRRA made the exclusion permanent—with a catch. All EGTRRA provisions are scheduled to sunset for tax years beginning after 2010, unless extended by Congress. The 2010 Health Reform Law delays the sunset of the adoption assistance exclusion for one year, until tax years beginning after 2011. [PPACA § 10909]

Chapter 9

Group Long-Term Care Insurance

Group long-term care insurance is a benefit designed to provide
financial assistance to, or on behalf of, individuals (usually older
individuals) whose ability to care for themselves has become
significantly diminished or impaired. This chapter discusses what
group long-term care insurance is and how it is taxed.

Basic Concepts

Q 9:1   What is long-term care insurance?

Long-term care insurance generally provides financial protection against
potentially devastating costs associated with long-term care for functionally
disabled individuals who are unable to care for themselves because of a chronic
or irremediable physical or mental condition. Long-term care covers both
medical and nonmedical support services provided in a setting other than an
acute care unit of a hospital. In the Health Insurance Portability and Accountability Act of 1996 (HIPAA), Congress provided favorable tax treatment for
long-term care insurance. To receive favorable tax treatment, long-term care
insurance must meet specific requirements contained in the Internal Revenue
Code (see Qs 9:5–9:11).

Q 9:2   What types of care and services are typically covered by group
long-term care insurance?

Group long-term care insurance policies typically cover the following services, usually for employees and spouses, retirees and spouses, and in some
cases also the employee's parents and parents-in-law:

1. Nursing home care;

2. Home health care;

3. Adult day care; and

4. Respite care (temporary care provided to allow the caregiver some time away from the patient).

Group long-term care insurance policies frequently incorporate managed care features, such as individual case management, to control costs. Long-term care encompasses more than just medical care; it can include a broad range of nonrehabilitative personal and social services, such as transportation, meal preparation, housekeeping services, and help with activities of daily living (ADLs) such as eating, dressing, and bathing. Such additional nonmedical services are custodial in nature and generally are not covered, or are covered only for a strictly limited duration, under traditional medical insurance. (For the particular features that must be included in a tax-qualified long-term care insurance contract, see Qs 9:5–9:11.)

Note that long-term care benefits may also be provided as an accelerated death benefit feature of a life insurance policy. Accelerated death benefits are discussed in chapter 12.

Q 9:3   What additional features are typically included in group long-term care insurance?

Group long-term care insurance policies may contain various additional features that make the coverage attractive to employees. Such features might include:

- An inflation protection option
- Guaranteed renewability
- Waiver of premiums
- Unlimited nursing home care benefit period
- Portability

Q 9:4   Is group long-term care insurance considered accident and health insurance?

Group long-term care insurance is a hybrid product—one that combines various features of (1) life insurance (through buildup of individual reserves sometimes characterized as similar to group universal life insurance); (2) medical insurance; and (3) other coverage not falling under either of those two general categories, such as custodial care, certain adult day care services, and respite care.

Despite the hybrid nature of long-term care insurance, HIPAA makes it clear that long-term care coverage meeting certain specified statutory requirements will receive favorable tax treatment similar to that accorded to accident and health insurance. [*See* HIPAA, Title III, Subtitle C.]

Q 9:5   What are the tax requirements for a qualified long-term care insurance contract?

In order to be treated as a qualified long-term care insurance contract for tax purposes, the contract must meet all of the following requirements:

1. The only insurance protection provided under the contract is coverage of "qualified long-term care services" (see Q 9:6);

2. The contract does not pay or reimburse expenses covered by Medicare (including Medicare deductibles or coinsurance amounts) except where Medicare is secondary or the contract makes per diem or other periodic payments without regard to expenses;

3. The contract is guaranteed renewable;

4. The contract does not provide for a cash surrender value or other money that can be borrowed or paid, pledged, or assigned as collateral for a loan (this does not prohibit a refund on the death of the insured or on a complete surrender or cancellation of the contract if the refund does not exceed the premiums paid under the contract);

5. All premium refunds and policyholder dividends must be applied as a reduction in future premiums or to increase future benefits; and

6. The contract complies with a number of consumer protection provisions.

[I.R.C. § 7702B, as added by HIPAA §§ 321(a), 325]

Grandfathered contracts. A long-term care policy issued prior to 1997 is treated as a qualified long-term care contract regardless of whether it satisfies the above requirements. In the case of a group contract, the issue date of the contract is the date it was issued. Thus, individuals added on or after January 1, 1997, to a grandfathered group contract are entitled to grandfathered contract treatment. For an individual contract, the issue date generally is the date assigned to the contract by the insurance company, but in no event is it earlier than the date the application is signed. [Treas. Reg. § 1.7702B-2]

However, Treasury Regulations Section 1.7702B-2(b)(4) treats a change to a long-term care insurance contract issued prior to 1997 as a new contract. A change includes any change in the terms of the contract altering the amount or timing of any item payable by the policyholder, the insured, or the insurance company. The following changes are not to be treated as a new contract:

- A policyholder's exercise of any right provided under the terms of the contract as in effect on December 31, 1996, or a right required by applicable state law to be provided to the policyholder;

- A change in the mode of premium payment (for example, a change from monthly to quarterly premiums);

- In the case of a policy that is guaranteed renewable or noncancellable, a classwide increase or decrease in premiums;

- A reduction in premiums due to the purchase of a long-term care insurance contract by a family member of the policyholder;

- A reduction in coverage made at the request of a policyholder;

- A reduction in premiums as a result of extending to an individual policyholder a discount applicable to similar categories of individuals pursuant to a premium rate structure that was in effect on December 31, 1996, for the issuer's pre-1997 long-term care insurance contracts of the same type;
- The purchase of a rider to increase benefits under a pre-1997 contract, if the rider would constitute a qualified long-term care insurance contract if it were a separate contract;
- The deletion of a rider or provision of a contract that prohibited coordination of benefits with Medicare; and
- The substitution of one insurer for another insurer in an assumption reinsurance transaction.

[Treas. Reg. § 1.7702B-2(b)(4)]

Q 9:6   What are qualified long-term care services?

Qualified long-term care services are necessary diagnostic, preventive, therapeutic, curing, treating, mitigating, rehabilitative, maintenance, and personal care services that are:

1. Required by a chronically ill individual (see Q 9:7) and
2. Provided pursuant to a plan of care prescribed by a licensed health care practitioner (see Q 9:10).

[I.R.C. § 7702B(c)(1)]

Q 9:7   Who is a chronically ill individual?

A *chronically ill individual* is one who has been certified by a licensed health care practitioner (see Q 9:10) as:

1. Being unable to perform (without substantial assistance from another person) at least two activities of daily living (see Q 9:8) for at least 90 days due to a loss of functional capacity (the IRS refers to this as the *ADL trigger*);
2. Having a level of disability similar to the above (as prescribed by regulations) (the *similar level trigger*); or
3. Requiring substantial supervision to protect the individual from threats to health and safety due to severe cognitive impairment (the *cognitive impairment trigger*) (see Q 9:13).

A person satisfying one of these tests will not qualify as a chronically ill individual unless a licensed health care practitioner has certified the person's status within the preceding 12 months. [I.R.C. § 7702B(c)(2)(A); IRS Notice 97-31, 1997-21 I.R.B. 1]

Q 9:8   What are activities of daily living?

In order to meet the first test of a chronically ill individual (i.e., the ADL trigger), the person must be unable to perform without "substantial assistance" (see Q 9:11) at least two activities of daily living (ADLs) for at least 90 days. For this purpose, ADLs comprise: (1) eating, (2) toileting, (3) transferring, (4) bathing, (5) dressing, and (6) continence. The long-term care contract must take into account at least five of these six ADLs in order to qualify for favorable tax treatment. [I.R.C. § 7702B(c)(2)(B)]

> **Note.** The 90-day period is not a waiting period. The certification can provide that the person will be unable to perform at least two ADLs for at least 90 days in the future.

Q 9:9   What is a plan of care prescribed by a licensed health care practitioner?

Neither the statute nor IRS Notice 97-31 [1997-21 I.R.B. 1] provides any guidance on this issue.

Q 9:10   Who is a licensed health care practitioner?

A *licensed health care practitioner* is a physician as defined in the Social Security Act or any registered professional nurse, licensed social worker, or other persons meeting requirements in IRS regulations that may be issued. [I.R.C. § 7702B(c)(4)]

Q 9:11   What constitutes substantial assistance under the ADL trigger?

For purposes of the ADL trigger, the IRS has provided the following safe-harbor definitions:

1. *Substantial assistance* means either hands-on assistance or standby assistance.

2. *Hands-on assistance* means the physical assistance of another person without which the individual would be unable to perform the ADL.

3. *Standby assistance* means the presence of another person within arm's reach of the individual that is necessary to prevent, by physical intervention, injury to the individual while he or she is performing the ADL (such as being ready to catch the individual if he or she falls while getting into or out of the bathtub or shower, or being ready to remove food from the individual's throat if he or she chokes while eating).

[IRS Notice 97-31, 1997-21 I.R.B. 1]

Q 9:12   What is severe cognitive impairment?

The third test for a chronically ill individual (the cognitive impairment trigger) applies to those persons requiring substantial supervision due to severe cognitive impairment. Although the statute contains no definitions, the legislative history indicates that severe cognitive impairment means a deterioration or loss in intellectual capacity that is measured by clinical evidence and standardized tests that reliably measure impairment in short- or long-term memory; orientation to people, places, or time; and deductive or abstract reasoning. In addition, such deterioration or loss in intellectual capacity must place the person in jeopardy of harming himself or herself or others and require substantial supervision by another person. [HIPAA, Conference Report and Statement of the Managers (July 31, 1996)]

For purposes of the cognitive impairment trigger, the IRS has provided the following safe-harbor definitions:

1. Severe cognitive impairment means a loss or deterioration in intellectual capacity that is
   a. Comparable to (and includes) Alzheimer's disease and similar forms of irreversible dementia, and
   b. Measurable by clinical evidence and standardized tests that reliably measure impairment in the individual's (i) short-term or long term memory; (ii) orientation as to people, places, or time; and (iii) deductive or abstract reasoning.

2. Substantial supervision means continual supervision (which may include cuing by verbal prompting, gestures, or other demonstrations by another person that is necessary to protect the severely cognitively impaired individual from threats to his or her health or safety, such as may result from wandering).

[IRS Notice 97-31, 1997-21 I.R.B. 1]

Note. Unlike the ADL trigger, the cognitive impairment trigger is not required to take any ADL into account for purposes of determining whether an individual is a chronically ill individual. [IRS Notice 97-31, 1997-21 I.R.B. 1]

Q 9:13   What are the consumer protections that a long-term care insurance contract must satisfy?

In order to qualify as a long-term care insurance contract for tax purposes, the contract must meet a number of consumer protection requirements contained in the model act and model regulation promulgated by the National Association of Insurance Commissioners (NAIC) as of January 1993. Also, the issuer of the contract must disclose in the contract and in an outline of coverage provided with the contract that the contract is intended to be a qualified long-term care insurance contract under Code Section 7702B(b). If the contract is a level premium contract, the contract must contain a nonforfeiture provision providing a nonforfeiture benefit (e.g., reduced paid-up insurance or extended term insurance) in the event of a default in paying premiums. A state may impose more stringent requirements than those contained in the Code. [I.R.C. § 7702B(g)]

If the issuer of a long-term care insurance contract fails to satisfy a number of specific Code requirements, the issuer can be subject to an excise tax of $100 per insured for each day the Code is violated. The requirements for a long-term care insurance contract issuer include compliance with various provisions of the NAIC model act and model regulations, delivery of a policy or certificate of insurance within 30 days after coverage is approved, and provision of a written explanation of the reasons for a claims denial (including information directly relating to the denial) within 60 days of a written request by the insured or a representative. Again, a state may impose even more stringent requirements. [I.R.C. § 4980C] The IRS has issued interim guidance on a number of issues arising under the consumer protection provisions. [IRS Notice 97-31, 1997-21 I.R.B. 1]

Practice Pointer. It seems advisable for an employer sponsoring a long-term care insurance program to obtain a certification from the insurance carrier that its group contract is in compliance with all applicable federal and state requirements and also to require an indemnification from the insurer should the contract fail to qualify for favorable tax treatment for any reason.

Taxation Issues

Q 9:14   May employers deduct the cost of group long-term care insurance for their employees?

Under Code Section 7702B as enacted by HIPAA, qualified long-term care insurance is treated as accident and health insurance for tax purposes. Therefore, an employer is entitled to deduct its contributions as a business expense under Code Section 162 in the same manner as employer contributions for other accident and health insurance (i.e., medical or disability benefit insurance).

Q 9:15   Are employees taxed on the monthly value of employer-paid group long-term care insurance?

Under HIPAA, group long-term care insurance is treated as accident and health insurance. Therefore, the value of employer-paid coverage is excludable from the covered employee's income under Code Section 106 as contributions to an accident and health plan for employees.

Q 9:16   Can employees deduct premiums they pay for group long-term care insurance?

Yes. HIPAA amended the definition of "medical expenses" in Code Section 213(d) to include an individual's premium payments for qualified long-term care insurance as deductible medical expenses. However, the deduction is subject to annual dollar limitations based on the individual's attained age at the end of the taxable year of payment.

The dollar limits are adjusted annually to reflect increases in the medical care component of the Consumer Price Index. [I.R.C. § 213(d)(1)(D), 213(d)(10); HIPAA § 322] The following limits apply for taxable years beginning in 2010:

Age	Dollar Limit
40 or less	$ 330
40 to 50	620
50 to 60	1,230
60 to 70	3,290
More than 70	4,110

[Rev. Proc. 2009-50, 2009-45 I.R.B. 617]

> **Note.** The Section 213 deduction is available only to the extent that the total of long-term care premiums and other qualifying expenses exceed 7.5 percent of the taxpayer's gross income and have not been compensated for by insurance or otherwise. [IRS Notice 97-31, 1997-21 I.R.B. 1]

Q 9:17 How are employees taxed on benefits received under group long-term care insurance?

Amounts received as benefits under a qualified long-term care insurance contract generally are treated as amounts received for personal injuries and sickness and as reimbursement for expenses incurred for medical care. [I.R.C. § 7702B(a)(2)] As such, they are generally excludable from income. [I.R.C. § 105] However, if the contract pays benefits on a per diem basis (i.e., without regard to the actual costs of the qualified long-term care services), and the insured is not a terminally ill individual, there is a dollar cap on all aggregate per diem contract payments (including amounts received with respect to the chronically ill person under a life insurance contract (see chapter 12)). If the dollar cap is exceeded, then the benefits in excess of the dollar cap are excluded from income only to the extent that actual costs for long-term care services in excess of the dollar cap were incurred. [I.R.C. §§ 7702B(d)(1), 7702B(d)(2)]

The dollar cap is indexed to the medical care component of the Consumer Price Index for years after 1997. [I.R.C. § 7702B(d)(5)] The IRS publishes the inflation-adjusted dollar cap annually. For 2010, the dollar cap is $290 per day ($105,850 on an annual basis). [Rev. Proc. 2009-50, 2009-45 I.R.B. 617]

Availability of deduction under Code Section 213. If amounts paid for qualified long-term care services for the taxpayer, his or her spouse, or his or her dependents are not compensated for by insurance or otherwise, they may be deducted under Code Section 213 as expenses for medical care to the extent that all such expenses exceed 7.5 percent of the taxpayer's gross income. [IRS Notice 97-31, 1997-21 I.R.B. 1]

Q 9:18   Are there any tax reporting requirements for group long-term care insurance plans?

Yes. Any person who pays long-term care benefits is required to file an annual IRS return setting forth:

1. The total amount of benefits paid to any person in the taxable year;

2. Whether or not such benefits are paid in whole or in part on a per diem basis or other periodic basis without regard to actual expenses incurred;

3. The name, address, and taxpayer identification number (TIN) of each payee; and

4. The name, address, and TIN of the chronically ill or terminally ill person on account of whose condition the benefits were paid.

In addition, a written statement must be furnished by January 31 of the following year to each person named in the IRS return, showing the name of the payer and the aggregate amount of long-term care benefits paid to the individual as shown on the IRS return. [I.R.C. § 6050Q, as added by HIPAA § 323(a)]

Form 1099-LTC, Long-Term Care and Accelerated Death Benefits, or an equivalent substitute form, should be used for this purpose.

Characterization Under Other Laws

Q 9:19   Is group long-term care insurance subject to ERISA?

It can be. Despite its hybrid nature, group long-term care insurance does cover, at least in part, "medical, surgical, or hospital care or benefits, or benefits in the event of sickness, accident, disability" within the meaning of Section 3(1) of ERISA. Although long-term care insurance plans typically are offered to employees on an employee-pay-all basis, such a plan will still be considered as maintained by an employer (and hence subject to ERISA) if the employer promotes or endorses the program. [29 C.F.R. § 2510.3-1(j)] Accordingly, ERISA's requirements regarding plan documents, SPDs, Form 5500 annual report filings, summary annual reports, and fiduciary responsibilities would apply.

Q 9:20   Do the COBRA continuation of coverage requirements apply to group long-term care insurance?

No. Prior to the enactment of HIPAA, the answer was unclear, and it appeared that such plans might be subject to COBRA, since they provided at least in part what are considered to be medical care benefits. However, under the HIPAA qualified long-term care provisions, Congress specified that the COBRA rules do not apply to qualified long-term care insurance contract plans. [I.R.C. § 4980B(g)(2); ERISA § 607(1); PHSA § 2208(1), as added by HIPAA § 321(d)]

Treasury regulations provide that a plan is not a group health plan subject to COBRA if substantially all of the coverage provided under the plan is for qualified long-term care services. An employer is permitted to use any reasonable method to determine if substantially all of the coverage provided under the plan is for qualified services. [Treas. Reg. § 54.4980B-2 Q&A-1(e)]

Q 9:21   Does the requirement of the Family and Medical Leave Act to continue health coverage during a period of family and medical leave apply to group long-term care insurance?

During any leave under the Family and Medical Leave Act of 1993 (FMLA), an employer is required to continue an employee's coverage under a group health plan (as defined in the Internal Revenue Code) on the same conditions as coverage would have been provided if the employee had been continuously employed. [29 C.F.R. § 825.209(a)] For this purpose, a group health plan means a plan to provide "health care." [I.R.C. § 5000(b)]

The Department of Labor, which enforces the FMLA, has not specifically stated whether the definition of a group health plan encompasses long-term care insurance. However, because the benefits provided may include "health care" as well as personal care, group long-term care insurance could arguably fall within the definition of a "group health plan." Therefore, the conservative approach would be to continue group long-term care insurance during FMLA leave. The FMLA is discussed in chapter 16.

Inclusion in Cafeteria Plans

Q 9:22   Can long-term care insurance be included under the employer's cafeteria plan?

No. Long-term care insurance cannot be offered as an employer-provided benefit under a Section 125 cafeteria plan, and employer-provided long-term care benefits provided through a flexible spending arrangement are includable in employees' incomes. [I.R.C. §§ 125(f), 106(c), as amended by HIPAA §§ 321(c), 301(d)]

Payroll deduction alternative. Although long-term care coverage cannot be offered as a qualified benefit under a cafeteria plan, the 2010 Health Reform Act enacted in March 2010 creates a new payroll deduction option for offering long-term care coverage to employees. [PPACA § 8001]

The Community Living Assistance Services and Supports (CLASS) Act, which is included as Title VIII of the 2010 Health Reform Act, directs the Secretary of Health and Human Services to establish a national voluntary insurance program for purchasing long-term care coverage starting in 2011. [PHSA § 3203 as added by PPACA § 8001].

Generally any employee or self-employed individual over age 18 can enroll in the program. An individual who enrolls will receive benefits if he or she is certified by a licensed health care practitioner as having a functional limitation that will last for more than 90 days. An individual has a functional limitation if he or she cannot perform a minimum number of activities of daily living without assistance or requires supervision to protect the individual from threats to health and safety due to mental impairment.

The amount of the benefit received cannot be less than an average of $50 per day, and can vary based on a scale of functional ability. The benefit is paid on a daily or weekly basis, and there is no lifetime or aggregate limit.

The Department of Health and Human Services (HHS) will establish yearly premiums based on an actuarial analysis of the 75-year cost of the program that ensures solvency throughout the 75-year period. An individual will not be entitled to benefits until he or she has paid premiums for five years.

Generally, the amount of the monthly premium will remain the same for as long as the individual is an active enrollee. However, the premium may be adjusted if required for the CLASS Act program's solvency. Any resulting increase in such cases will not apply to the monthly premium of any active enrollee who is not actively employed, has attained age 65 and has paid premiums for at least 20 years.

Employers can elect to deduct and withhold premiums for the CLASS Act program from the wages of employees who elect to participate. The new law authorizes HHS and the IRS to set up automatic enrollment procedures for the CLASS Act (much like those that exist for 401(k) plans) that employers may elect to use. Under these procedures, designed to spur participation, new hires would be enrolled automatically in the CLASS Act unless they affirmatively choose to opt out.

For tax purposes, the CLASS Act program is treated in the same manner as qualified long-term care insurance for qualified long-term care services (see Qs 9:16, 9:17). [PHSA § 3210 as added by PPACA § 8002(a)]

Chapter 10

Disability Income Plans

Disability income plans are employer plans, some mandated by state law, that provide full or partial income replacement for employees who become disabled. Employer-provided disability income benefits are generally taxable to employees, and the nondiscrimination requirements of Section 105(h) of the Internal Revenue Code (Code) generally do not apply to disability income benefits. Disability income plans have their own pitfalls, which are reviewed in this chapter. Case law developments under the Americans with Disabilities Act of 1990 regarding differentials in long-term disability benefits for mental and other disabilities are also covered. This chapter also includes a special section on plan design and administration and discusses some of the typical scenarios that arise in day-to-day administration of long-term disability plans.

Basic Concepts

Q 10:1   What is a disability income plan?

A disability income plan is a plan that provides income replacement benefits to employees who are unable to work because of illness or accident. This type of plan does what its name implies: it "replaces" a portion of the income or compensation lost while the employee is disabled. Thus, the level of benefits generally is dependent on the employee's pre-disability income level, not on the nature and extent of his or her particular disability. Typically, the plan benefits consist of a stream of income payments, usually paid on a monthly or weekly basis, although some plans also contain a cash lump-sum feature, such as a cash-out upon retirement of "banked" sick days.

Q 10:2 Does federal law require employers to provide employees with disability income benefits?

No. There is no federal law that requires employers to provide employees with disability income benefits, although several federal laws govern the cost and extent of disability income benefits that are voluntarily provided by employers. In addition, there are numerous state law requirements.

Q 10:3 What state-mandated disability income benefits must employers provide to employees?

Employers must, at a minimum, provide disability income protection for job-related disabilities. All states have workers' compensation laws that require coverage of job-related disabilities. Depending on the laws of the state involved, coverage may be provided through contributions to a state insurance fund, self-insurance, or insurance with an insurance carrier. (See chapter 20 for a discussion of funding issues and chapter 2 for a discussion of Employee Retirement Income Security Act (ERISA) preemption of state workers' compensation laws.)

In addition, California, Hawaii, New Jersey, New York, Rhode Island, and Puerto Rico have temporary-disability laws requiring coverage for disabilities that are not job-related. Here, too, the employer can generally choose from among several options: participating in a state fund, self-insuring, or insuring with a private insurance carrier. (Rhode Island, for example, requires participation in the state fund.) The disability income benefits are limited in amount (generally, one-half to two-thirds of the employee's weekly wage, subject to statutory minimums and maximums) and temporary in nature (52 weeks or less). The benefits are generally funded through employee and employer contributions (except in California and Rhode Island, where the employer is required to provide only an employee-pay-all plan). Many employers provide disability benefits over and above those mandated by state laws.

In each of these states, employers have certain duties in connection with their temporary disability plans, including responsibility for withholding and forwarding employee contributions to the state and filing related reports.

Practice Pointer. To the extent that the employer is required to provide state-mandated temporary disability benefits, its sick-pay and disability plans are typically designed to offset those payments so that the disabled individual does not receive a windfall from two different plans.

The Eighth Circuit Court of Appeals has held that an employer did not violate ERISA when it offset disability benefits by the amount of a beneficiary's workers' compensation. [Leonard v. Southwestern Bell Corp. Disability Income Plan, No. 02-3559, 2003 U.S. App. LEXIS 19747 (8th Cir. Sept. 25, 2003)] Southwestern Bell's plan provided for an offset of benefits of the "same general character" as benefits owed under the plan and gave the plan administrator the discretion to determine which benefits fit that description. According to the court, the plan administrator reasonably concluded that the workers' compensation benefits were of the same general character as the plan's disability benefits because both benefits were intended to provide employees with a minimal level of income or a "safety net" if they became disabled. Moreover, the plan's summary plan description specifically stated that benefits may be reduced by workers' compensation.

> **Practice Pointer.** It may be impossible for a plan to specify all the types of disability income that may be offset against employer-provided disability benefits. Therefore, a catch-all phrase that provides for an offset of benefits "of the same general character" at the discretion of the plan administrator may prove to be the most comprehensive. However, such a phrase should be backed up with a list of the most common benefits, including workers' compensation, that will be offset.

An employee's eligibility for other benefits, such as workers' compensation or Social Security disability, may not kick in at the same time as employer-provided disability benefits. Therefore, some employer plans provide disabled employees with the full amount of disability benefits subject to repayment by the employee when other benefits take effect. However, the ruling in one case calls that practice into question.

After sustaining injuries that rendered her totally disabled, Dale Ogden filed a claim for long-term disability benefits under her employer's plan. The plan approved the claim within three weeks and began paying benefits to Ogden. The plan provided that plan benefits were to be offset by other benefits, including Social Security. The plan gave the administrator two ways to handle the offset. The administrator could estimate the amount of other benefits to be received by the employee and make the offset up front. Alternatively, the plan administrator could pay the full amount of benefits without any offset up front, subject to the employee's agreement to reimburse the plan when the other benefits are received. To reinforce the reimbursement obligation, the employee was required to sign a reimbursement agreement that obligated the employee to cooperate in pursuing benefits from outside sources and to reimburse the plan within 30 days following receipt of any outside benefits.

The plan administrator chose the second option in Ogden's case, and Ogden signed a reimbursement agreement. About two and one-half years after she began receiving benefits under the plan, Ogden was determined to be disabled for Social Security purposes and began receiving Social Security disability benefits. She also received a lump-sum payment of $30,000 for retroactive benefits. At that point, the plan began to set off the Social Security benefits against Ogden's benefits from the plan. It also demanded that Ogden reimburse the plan in the amount of the lump-sum payment. Ogden refused and the plan took her to court.

The Fifth Circuit Court of Appeals concluded that Ogden's reimbursement agreement was not enforceable under ERISA because the law provides only for "equitable relief," not for "legal relief" in the form of money. [Cooperative Benefit Adm'rs, Inc. v. Ogden, 367 F.3d 323 (5th Cir. 2004)]

It should be noted that the employer's plan continued to have the option of recouping its advances by offsetting Ogden's *future* benefits. However, that was not a particularly attractive option for the plan inasmuch as Ogden's benefits were largely offset by the Social Security disability payments.

Q 10:4 What types of disability income plans do employers typically provide?

As might be expected, employers voluntarily offer a wide variety of income-replacement-type disability plans. Types of plans include the following:

1. *Wage continuation or sick pay.* The employer continues payment of all or part of the employee's salary for a specified period of disability. Under some sick-pay arrangements, employees will be granted an annual allotment of sick and paid-time-off days, and unused days will be banked for future use.

2. *Short-term disability income benefits.* These are sometimes referred to as temporary disability benefits (TDI). The employee receives a portion of his or her regular wages under a formal plan of short-term disability benefits (e.g., for 13 or 26 weeks). A TDI plan may be an insured, trusteed, or self-insured arrangement. (See chapter 20 for further discussion of funding.)

3. *Long-term disability income benefits.* This coverage, which usually starts after short-term disability income benefits cease, generally provides a partial income-replacement benefit to employees who are not likely to return to work because of the total and/or permanent nature of their disabilities. The typical benefit formula replaces 50 to 60 percent of base compensation, subject to a maximum monthly or maximum annual limit. This type of plan also frequently will provide for offsets for other disability or retirement-type benefits, such as disability or retirement benefits under Social Security or under a retirement plan.

A federal appeals court has upheld the right of a long-term disability (LTD) plan to reduce the amount of disability payments when the recipient is also receiving Social Security payments. Of course, the plan provisions must provide for such a reduction. [Lake v. Metropolitan Life Ins. Co., 73 F.3d 1372 (6th Cir. 1996)]

Employers should, however, be careful to include the Social Security offset in the terms of the plan. In one case, employees of Prudential Insurance Co. challenged their employer's long-term disability plan's right to reduce their LTD benefits by the amount of their Social Security benefits on the ground that the offset was not provided for under the terms of the employer's plan. At the time the employees became disabled, the only document describing the LTD benefits was a "Program Summary" that was distributed to employees. The summary stated that short-term disability benefits would be offset by state disability benefits and workers' compensation, but said nothing about offsets against LTD benefits. The summary stated that it was for informational purposes only and that the terms of the plan would govern. However, there was no plan in existence at the time; a formal plan document was not finalized until after the employees became disabled. The Second Circuit concluded that during the period when the program summary was the only document describing the benefits, it served as the plan itself. And because the "plan" did not provide for Social Security offsets, no such offsets were permitted. Moreover, the employees' right to LTD benefits without offsets vested at the time they became disabled. [Feifer v. Prudential Ins. Co. of Am., 306 F.3d 1202 (2d Cir. 2002)]

In another decision, the Seventh Circuit upheld a plan's right to reduce LTD benefits by the amount of benefits an employee was receiving under a disability insurance policy she had purchased. Tory Hall, an employee of Diagnostek, was a participant in the company's disability plan, which was underwritten by the Life Insurance Company of North America (LINA). In addition, Hall had purchased a disability insurance policy issued by New York Life through her membership in the Texas Society of Certified Public Accountants. When Hall became disabled, she began receiving benefits under both policies. However, LINA reduced the amount of benefits payable by the amount of Hall's benefits under the New York Life policy. When Hall challenged the reduction, LINA pointed to the terms of its disability plan that provided for a reduction for "other benefits." Other benefits were defined to include Social Security disability benefits and "any amounts which the employee receives on account of disability under any group or franchise insurance or similar plan for persons in a group." According to the LINA, the setoff clearly applied to any insurance obtained through a group. Therefore, it applied to Hall's New York Life policy because it was obtained through the CPA society. The Seventh Circuit agreed with LINA, noting that group insurance includes any arrangement under which a single policy is issued to an entity, such as an employer, an association, or a union, for coverage of individual members. Moreover, even if Hall obtained an individual policy through the CPA society, it would be classified as franchise insurance, which is a variation on group insurance in which all members of the group receive individual policies.

Hall argued that the LINA policy was ambiguous and that ERISA requires ambiguities to be resolved in favor of a plan participant. However, the Seventh Circuit rejected that argument. According to the court, ambiguities are resolved against an insurer to prevent traps for the unwary. However, the court concluded that Hall was not misled by the LINA policy. "Hall did not read the LINA policy, misunderstand a vague passage or veiled allusion, and only then opt into the New York Life policy; she did not read the LINA policy at all until it was too late. That omission led her to pay for coverage under the New York Life policy, which as things have turned out offered her no net benefit, but ERISA does not protect employees against their own imprudence," said the court. [Hall v. Life Ins. Co. of N. Am., 317 F.3d 774 (7th Cir. 2003)]

Q 10:5   Does ERISA apply to disability-income-type plans?

The answer depends on the type of plan at issue. ERISA's definition of a covered "employee welfare benefit plan" includes plans providing benefits in the event of sickness or disability. However, an unfunded short-term disability plan generally is treated as an exempt payroll practice and not as a welfare benefit plan subject to ERISA, although some plans, as discussed below, may not fall within the exemption.

Short-term disability plans. The U.S. Department of Labor (DOL) has ruled that an employer-sponsored, unfunded, short-term disability plan that provides for sick pay for up to 26 weeks of absence is not an ERISA welfare benefit program. [DOL Adv. Op. 93-27A (Oct. 12, 1993)] Rather, the sick-pay plan in question constituted an exempt employer payroll practice under 29 C.F.R. Section 2510.1(b). That regulation exempts from ERISA coverage any plan that merely provides payment of an employee's normal compensation, out of the general assets of the employer, for periods of time during which the employee is physically or mentally unable to perform his or her duties.

A second DOL opinion letter examined a short-term disability plan that paid up to 100 percent of salary for up to 52 weeks of absence due to illness, disability, or injury. The DOL ruled that that plan also appeared to be an exempt payroll practice. [DOL Adv. Op. 93-20A (July 16, 1993); *see also* DOL Adv. Op. Ltr. 94-04A, which concluded that a sick-pay plan for a select group of employees with a two-tier eligibility provision was an exempt payroll practice] A federal district court also determined that a short-term disability program fell within the above exclusion and dismissed the employee's ERISA action for lack of subject matter jurisdiction. [Shuda v. Dobbs Int'l Servs., Inc., 1993 U.S. Dist. LEXIS 13209 (E.D. Pa. Sept. 9, 1993)] However, the DOL intends the exempt payroll practice provision to apply where the individuals remain employees while receiving benefits. Thus, a sick-pay plan under which benefits could be paid to retirees or persons who are employees for limited purposes only was ruled to be an ERISA plan and not an exempt payroll practice. [DOL Adv. Op. 96-16A (Aug. 27, 1996)]

Workers' compensation, unemployment compensation, and state temporary disability plans. ERISA does not cover any plan maintained solely for the purpose of complying with applicable workers' compensation, unemployment compensation, or disability insurance laws. The Supreme Court has interpreted this ERISA exemption to require that plans maintained to comply with state disability laws also must be administered separately in order to qualify for the exemption. Thus, if an employer's plan provides broader benefits than those required to satisfy the state temporary-disability law, ERISA governs the entire plan and the state temporary-disability law cannot regulate it (even if the portion intended to comply with the state disability requirement is deficient). The state can, however, require the employer to maintain a separate plan to satisfy the state temporary-disability law if it determines that the employer's ERISA plan does not do so. [ERISA §§ 3(1), 4(b)(3); Shaw v. Delta Airlines, 463 U.S. 85 (1983); Employee Staffing Servs., Inc. v. Aubry, 20 F.3d 1038 (9th Cir. 1994)] (See chapter 2 for a discussion of ERISA.)

Employee-pay all plans. A plan is generally governed by ERISA if it is established or maintained by an employer, an employee organization, or both. However, DOL regulations provide that employee-pay-all plans are excluded from ERISA coverage if employee participation is completely voluntarily, the employer's involvement with the plan is limited to administrative functions (e.g., collecting premiums through payroll deductions), and the employer does not endorse the plan. (See chapter 2.)

Employer actions that go beyond purely administrative functions can be considered "endorsement" of the plan. In one case, an employee sued the insurer of an employee-pay-all plan for breach of contract under state law. The insurer removed the case to federal court, arguing that the state-law claim was preempted by ERISA. The Sixth Circuit concluded that the plan was subject to ERISA because the employer effectively endorsed the plan. The court noted that the employer served as plan administrator, made coverage available only to salaried employees, and sought advice from its insurance broker to determine the type and extent of coverage. According to the court, the central requirement of the non-endorsement rule is employer neutrality, but the employer "did not act neutrally in the creation of the plan, nor in the selection of plan contents." [Nicholas v. Standard Ins. Co., 48 Fed. Appx. 557 (6th Cir. Oct. 9, 2002)]

Q 10:6   Do employers also provide any dismemberment benefits?

Yes. Some employers also provide dismemberment benefits. This type of plan generally offers a flat payment for loss of a leg, arm, eye, or the like. Such benefits generally are combined with accidental death benefit insurance. (See chapter 12 for a discussion of accidental death and dismemberment benefits.)

Q 10:7   Does the Family and Medical Leave Act apply to disability income and dismemberment benefits?

Yes. See chapter 16 for a detailed discussion of the Family and Medical Leave Act (FMLA), including the FMLA's provisions regarding the employee's and employer's right to substitute sick pay for unpaid FMLA leave.

Q 10:8   Does the Consolidated Omnibus Budget Reconciliation Act apply to disability income or dismemberment plans?

No. The Consolidated Omnibus Budget Reconciliation Act (COBRA) applies only to certain group health plans. (See chapter 6 for a discussion of COBRA.)

Q 10:9   Do any tax or other nondiscrimination rules apply to disability plans?

Generally, the Internal Revenue Code does not impose any nondiscrimination rules on disability plans; however, if a disability plan is funded using a Section 501(c)(9) voluntary employees' beneficiary association (VEBA) trust, then the plan (other than certain collectively bargained plans) must meet the following nondiscrimination rules imposed by Code Section 505(b):

1. Each class of benefits must be provided under a classification of employees that is found by the Internal Revenue Service (IRS) not to discriminate in favor of highly compensated employees and

2. The benefits within each class of benefits must not discriminate in favor of highly compensated employees.

If a disability income benefit funded under a VEBA trust is tied to compensation, there is an annually adjusted limit on compensation that can be taken into account. For 2010, the limit is $245,000. [I.R.C. §§ 505(a), 505(b)(2), 505(b)(7); Notice 2009-94, 2009-50 I.R.B. 848] (See chapter 20 for further discussion of VEBAs.)

> **Practice Pointer.** It is important to note that the compensation limit of Code Section 505(b) applies to the entire plan. It is not permissible to provide benefits based upon higher compensation by, for example, insuring the portion of the plan benefit above the amount funded through the VEBA. In addition, various other federal laws affect these types of employer-provided plans and prohibit discrimination on the basis of pregnancy or other disabilities. (See chapters 16 through 19 for further discussion of these other federal laws.) Specific standards under the federal Age Discrimination in Employment Act of 1967 (ADEA) are discussed in Qs 10:10–10:14.

> **Note.** In enacting changes to the VEBA nondiscrimination rules in the Deficit Reduction Act of 1984, Congress in the legislative history indicated that integration of VEBA disability benefits with Social Security benefits was to be allowed subject to rules comparable to the integration rules in the pension area and that special limits were to apply to the disability income benefits where both the disability pension benefits and the VEBA disability income benefits were integrated with Social Security; however, no Treasury regulations have been issued to implement the congressional intent, and, in view of substantial changes made since 1984 in the pension integration rules, it appears that changes in the Social Security integration procedures of VEBAs are not necessary until Treasury regulations are forthcoming.

Q 10:10 Are disability income plans subject to the ADEA?

Yes. Disability income benefits are part of the terms, conditions, and privileges of employment governed by the ADEA. [ADEA § 4(a); 29 U.S.C. § 623(a) (1988)] (See chapter 17.) Any age-based eligibility, cost, level, and benefit duration provisions will need to comply with the ADEA, as discussed in Qs 10:11–10:14.

Q 10:11 Can an employer limit eligibility for disability income coverage based on age?

No. Eligibility for disability income coverage cannot be denied to older employees. The ADEA would bar such discrimination based on age, at least for individuals within the age group protected by the ADEA (age 40 and older). Anyone falling within a broader group protected by applicable state age discrimination laws (sometimes age 18 and older) will be protected from such age discrimination in a disability plan to the extent that ERISA does not preempt the application of that state law to the plan. For example, an employer subject to the ADEA could not extend disability income coverage to any employee under age 60 or deny coverage to any employee who becomes disabled after age 60. However, under the "benefit package" approach in the Equal Employment Opportunity Commission (EEOC) regulations, a benefit may be eliminated on the basis of age if another benefit of at least equal value is provided instead (see chapter 17). It appears that an employer can, under the ADEA, bar employees from participating in the disability income plan if they fail to enroll for coverage within a designated period from the date of hire. [*See* International Bhd. of Elec. Workers, Local 1439, AFL-CIO v. Union Elec. Co., 761 F. 2d 1257 (8th Cir. 1985), upholding such a restriction under ADEA with respect to a group life insurance plan]

However, employers do have some flexibility under the ADEA to limit the level or duration of disability income benefits (see Q 10:12).

Q 10:12   Can an employer limit the level or duration of disability income benefits based on age?

Yes, provided the employer follows the guidelines contained in the ADEA regulations. Those regulations require that any reduction in the level or duration of disability income benefits be justified on the basis of cost equivalency—that is, the cost of the reduced benefits for older employees must be no less than the cost of benefits provided to younger employees. Two approaches for achieving cost equivalency are provided under the EEOC regulations: the *benefit-by-benefit* approach and the *benefit package* approach. (The specific ADEA rules regarding cost-justified reduction in benefits are discussed in greater detail in chapter 17.)

Q 10:13   May an employer increase an employee's share of the cost of disability income benefits based on age?

No. The employee's share of the cost of disability income benefits cannot increase with age. Essentially, such a practice is viewed as a mandatory reduction in take-home pay in violation of the ADEA. It is permissible, however, for the employer to require that employees bear the same proportion of the cost of the plan. Older employees may be required to make larger absolute dollar contributions than younger employees if the cost of the coverage increases by age, as long as the proportion of the total cost paid by the employee remains constant. For example, the employer might decide to bear 50 percent of the cost of disability income coverage and charge employees 50 percent of the cost. As long as older employees are not charged more than 50 percent of the cost, such an arrangement would not violate the ADEA. (See chapter 17.)

Q 10:14   Are all disability income benefits required to comply with the ADEA as amended in 1990 by the Older Workers Benefits Protection Act?

Generally, yes. However, disability income benefits that commenced before October 16, 1990, and that continue after that date pursuant to an arrangement in effect on that date are not subject to the OWBPA amendments to the ADEA, provided that no substantial modification to the arrangement is made with the intent of evading the purposes of the OWBPA. (For further details, see chapter 17.)

Plan Design and Administration

Q 10:15   May an employer-provided LTD plan provide lesser benefits for mental disabilities than for other disabilities?

This question has been the subject of considerable litigation brought under the Americans with Disabilities Act (ADA). By way of background, LTD plans often provide income replacement benefits for mental and nervous disabilities for a shorter period, typically 24 months, than for other disabilities. This distinction has been heavily litigated, with the EEOC bringing suit against several companies whose plans contain such a distinction.

Two issues arise in these lawsuits. First is the issue of whether a disabled individual even has standing to bring a claim under the ADA, because the ADA covers only individuals with disabilities who can perform the essential functions of the job that they hold or seek. Many of the cases involve the issue of whether the individual's submission of a disability claim for Social Security or workers' compensation purposes should be dispositive of the issue of whether the individual is also disabled for ADA purposes. The EEOC's enforcement position is that it is not. (See chapter 18.)

The Eleventh Circuit Court of Appeals has held that disabled former employees are protected and can sue under the ADA. The court acknowledged that, at first blush, the words "qualified individual" may seem to refer only to job applicants and current employees. However, the court said there was no basis for assuming that Congress intentionally provided ADA protection to future and current employees but denied protection to former employees. According to the Eleventh Circuit, reading the law narrowly to exclude coverage of former employees would deny them access to remedies for discriminatory administration of postemployment benefits and would create a "perverse incentive" for employers to interfere with those benefits. [Johnson v. Kmart Corp., 273 F.3d 1035 (11th Cir. 2001)]

If standing to sue exists, the second issue is whether, under the ADA, an LTD plan may permissibly distinguish between the benefits provided for mental and nervous conditions and for other types of disabilities. A number of federal circuit courts that have ruled on this issue have held that such a difference in benefits is not prohibited discrimination against disabled individuals as opposed to nondisabled individuals, but rather is a permitted discrimination between disabilities. These courts take the position that the ADA requires only that a disabled individual receive the same benefits as a nondisabled individual; it does not prohibit distinctions between mentally and physically disabled individuals (see chapter 18).

The U.S. Court of Appeals for the District of Columbia Circuit ruled that Aramark Corp.'s LTD benefits plan, which capped benefits for mental disabilities at 24 months but continued benefits for physical disabilities up to age 65, did not violate the ADA. [EEOC v. Aramark Corp., 208 F.3d 266 (D.D.C. 2000)]

The court said that Aramark's LTD plan is protected by the ADA's safe harbor provision for bona fide employee benefit plans. Under ADA Section 501c's safe harbor provision, insurers are not prohibited from establishing, sponsoring, observing, or administering the terms of a bona fide benefit plan that is not subject to state laws that regulate insurance. However, the safe harbor provision cannot be used as a subterfuge to evade the purposes of the ADA.

All parties in the lawsuit agreed that the LTD plan was a bona fide employee benefit plan, but the parties disagreed on the meaning of the subterfuge exception. Aramark and Aetna argued that the plan was not a subterfuge because the benefit plan was adopted in 1982, before the enactment of the ADA in 1990. The EEOC asserted that any disability benefit plan is a subterfuge to evade the ADA's purposes if the distinction between mental and physical disabilities is not based on sound actuarial principles. However, the court concluded that, because the company's plan was adopted before the ADA was enacted, it could not have been used as a subterfuge to evade the purposes of the ADA.

The U.S. Court of Appeals for the Second Circuit has also ruled that the ADA does not bar employers from offering LTD plans that provide less coverage for mental and emotional disabilities than for physical disabilities. [EEOC v. Staten Island Sav. Bank, 207 F.3d 144 (2d Cir. 2000)]

Agreeing with six other circuit courts, the court of appeals said that equal coverage of all types of disabilities would destabilize the insurance industry in a manner definitely not intended by Congress when passing the ADA. As long as every employee is offered the same plan regardless of the employee's contemporary or future disability status, no discrimination has occurred, even if the plan offers different coverage for various disabilities, the court said.

The U.S. Supreme Court chose not to review an appeals court decision that an employer-provided LTD benefits plan does not have to provide the same level of benefits for mental and physical disabilities to pass muster under the ADA. The Court of Appeals for the Fourth Circuit had ruled that Kmart Corp.'s provision of an LTD plan that capped benefits for mental disabilities at two years but provided benefits for physical disabilities up to age 65 did not violate Title I's prohibition on employment discrimination. [Lewis v. Kmart Corp., 180 F.3d 166 (4th Cir. 1999), *cert. denied*, 2000 U.S. LEXIS 839 (2000)]

In another case involving Kmart's plan, the Eleventh Circuit had a different view. The court concluded that the ADA demands more than impartial treatment of the disabled. "The essence of disability-based discrimination claim," said the court, "is that an individual has been treated less favorably because of her disability." On its face, Kmart's plan discriminated by providing less favorable treatment for mentally disabled individuals. The Eleventh Circuit remanded the case to the district court to determine whether Kmart's plan was protected by the ADA's safe harbor provision or whether it was knocked out of safe harbor protection because the plan was used as a subterfuge to avoid the ADA. [Johnson v. Kmart Corp., 273 F.3d 1035 (11th Cir. 2001)]

Q 10:16   What are some of the major administrative problems with disability plans?

The typical administrative problems under disability plans concern weeding out the legitimate from the wishful claims.

The essence of an LTD plan is income replacement, an important and legitimate concern to an employee who suddenly loses the ability to perform his or her occupation and earn a paycheck; however, generous income replacement benefits also may present a temptation to a small percentage of employees to commit fraud against the plan in an effort to get easy money by suddenly becoming "disabled" or by failing to return to work after recovering from a disability. This small percentage includes employees who have recently been told that their employment will be terminated or who suspect that they might be in danger of being terminated. Accordingly, the essence of preventive LTD plan drafting and administration is to minimize opportunities for employees to make successful false claims of disability and then sit home collecting income benefits for years of alleged "total disability." Preventive plan management is prudent because a series of bogus disability claims can drain the assets of a self-insured LTD plan and make it financially unsound or drive up the premiums of an insured plan to prohibitive levels, thereby endangering the plan's continuation and, consequently, the future benefits of employees who truly become disabled from working.

> **Practice Pointer.** On the flip side, employers should be prepared to document specific employment-related reasons for an involuntary termination of employment close in time to an application for LTD benefits. [*See* Kinkead v. Southwestern Bell Tel. Co., 49 F.3d 454 (8th Cir. 1995).]

Applicants sometimes lose sight of the fact that the relevant measure of disability is the plan's definition, which may not always match the definition of disability that the treating physician is applying. Treating physicians often are willing to write a brief letter to the plan stating that the employee is "totally disabled." The relevant question from the plan administrator's point of view is, however, whether the individual is "totally disabled" within the meaning of the plan's definition. The plan administrator might find it necessary or helpful to provide the treating physician with a written copy of the plan's disability definition, possibly also with a description of specific job criteria, and request that the treating physician amplify or explain his or her opinion. Treating physicians may respond with detailed letters concerning, for example, inability to engage in heavy activity or heavy lifting but continued ability to engage in light activity or activity while sitting but not involving prolonged standing. It would then fall to the plan administrator to determine whether such documentation satisfies the plan's disability standard.

Another issue of importance is whether the disability was present on or before the date used by the plan. For example, if the employer's sick-pay plan will pay benefits for six months, the LTD plan might provide that individuals who were totally disabled on or before the date sick pay ends are eligible for benefits under the plan and that the last day of the six-month period is the point at which the individual's disability status is examined to determine whether it meets the plan's definition of "total disability." The difficulty occurs when an individual with a progressively worsening condition does not meet the plan's definition of total disability initially but subsequently becomes disabled and claims that he or she has satisfied the plan's definition all along. This issue can be addressed administratively. (See Q 10:37.)

Issues developing in the case law include whether various "designer diseases" (chronic fatigue syndrome, environmental allergy, etc.) are really legitimate disabling conditions and which medical opinion should control when the plan's referral expert disagrees with the opinion of the treating physician. (See further discussion of these issues and other trends in the following questions.)

Q 10:17   What kind of documentation of disability can be required?

Employer-provided LTD plans contain definitions of total and permanent disability that range from very broad (the employee's inability to perform his or her current job as a result of the disability) to very strict (inability to perform any job or occupation for which the individual may be suited by education or training). Frequently, employer-based plans will incorporate a two-step definition of disability. Under such a scheme, for example, the individual may need to demonstrate inability to perform his or her current job for the first two years but may be required to prove a stricter standard for periods beyond two years in order to maintain eligibility for disability income benefits.

Employer-provided long-term disability plans generally require the disabled employee to submit proof of disability meeting the plan's standards. The plan document typically also reserves to the plan administrator the discretion to determine whether the individual is disabled.

To help minimize the administrative burdens associated with such determinations, some plans provide that the plan administrator also has the power to consult its own medical experts or to require the individual to be examined periodically by a specialist of the plan's choosing and at the plan's expense. This is particularly helpful in buttressing the reasonableness of the plan administrator's determination when the plan is faced with relatively newer theories of disability. [*See* Mongeluzo v. Baxter Travenol Long Term Disability Benefit Plan, 46 F.3d 938 (9th Cir. 1995) (chronic fatigue syndrome); Donato v. Metropolitan

Life Ins. Co., 19 F.3d 375 (7th Cir. 1994) (hypersensitivity to common environmental chemicals); Steinmann v. Long Term Disability Plan of May Dep't Stores,
863 F. Supp. 994 (E.D. Mo. 1994) (toxic exposure to unknown substance and
chemical sensitivity); Mitchell v. Eastman Kodak Co., 113 F.3d 433 (3d Cir.
1997) (chronic fatigue syndrome)]

The Supreme Court has held that an employer may deny employee disability
benefits when the plan's physician disagrees with the treating physician on the
issue of the employee's ability to work. In the case of an employee whose own
physician concluded that he was unable to work because of degenerative disk
disease and chronic pain, the Court held that nothing in ERISA requires plan
administrators to accord special deference to the opinions of treating physicians.
[Black & Decker Disability Plan v. Nord, 538 U.S. 822 (2003)]

> **Practice Pointer.** Both the plan document and the summary plan descrip-
> tion (SPD) for the long-term disability plan should clearly disclose the plan
> administrator's power to make determinations of disability and to require
> that upon request the employee be examined by a physician of the plan
> administrator's choosing. In addition, both the plan document and the SPD
> should clearly disclose how frequently the plan may require the disabled
> individual, as a condition of continued receipt of disability income benefits,
> to (1) submit proof of continued disability from his or her own physician(s)
> and/or (2) submit to an examination by a physician or institution selected by
> the plan to verify the existence of continued disability. The SPD should also
> clearly disclose whether the required proof or documentation is to be
> obtained at the individual's or the plan's expense. Additionally, in order to
> avoid a possible prohibited transaction under ERISA, the plan document
> should clearly authorize the plan to pay the fees of experts selected by the
> plan to assist in making disability determinations.

Q 10:18 Is a disability plan required to follow any particular procedures in processing benefit claims?

The DOL has issued final regulations governing health and disability benefit
claims. [DOL Reg. § 2560.503-1(b), (c), (d)] The final regulations require
disability plans to establish and maintain reasonable claims procedures and to
include a description of such procedures in the SPD.

A plan's claims procedures may not contain any provision or be administered
in a way that unduly inhibits the initiation or processing of claims for benefits.
For example, a provision or practice that requires payment of a fee or costs as a
condition for making a claim or appealing an adverse benefit determination
would be considered unduly inhibiting.

The claims procedures must allow an authorized representative to act on
behalf of an employee making a claim.

In addition, the claims procedures must contain administrative processes and
safeguards to ensure and verify that benefit claim determinations are made in

accordance with the governing plan documents and that the plan provisions are applied consistently with respect to similarly situated claimants.

The claims procedures may not contain any provision or be administered in a way that requires a claimant to file more than two appeals of an adverse benefit determination before bringing a lawsuit for benefits. A plan may require mandatory arbitration at one of these levels of appeal; however, the plan may not preclude the claimant from bringing a lawsuit under ERISA to challenge the arbitration decision.

A plan may provide for additional voluntary appeals, including voluntary arbitration or another form of alternative dispute resolution. However, the plan cannot challenge a lawsuit on the basis that a claimant failed to exhaust administrative remedies because he or she did not submit a benefit dispute to a voluntary appeal. Moreover, any statute of limitations or other defense based on timeliness will be tolled during the time a voluntary appeal is pending.

> **Note.** In a case involving a sex discrimination claim, the U.S. Supreme Court held that agreements to resolve employment disputes through binding arbitration are legal and enforceable by employers. [Circuit City Stores v. Adams, 532 U.S. 105 (2001)] The case does not, however, resolve the issue of the DOL's power to limit arbitration under ERISA.

A collectively bargained plan will be deemed to comply with the requirements if the collective bargaining agreement sets forth (or incorporates by reference) provisions concerning the filing of benefit claims and the initial disposition of such claims and a grievance and arbitration procedure for adverse benefit decisions.

Q 10:19   What are disability benefits for purposes of the claims procedures?

A benefit is a "disability benefit" subject to the claims procedures if the plan conditions availability of the benefit on a showing of disability by the claimant. It does not matter how the benefit is characterized by the plan or whether the plan as a whole is a pension plan or a welfare benefit plan. If the claims adjudicator must make a determination of disability in order to decide the claim, the claim must be handled in accordance with the claims procedure regulations.

On the other hand, if a plan provides a benefit that is conditioned on a finding of disability, but that finding is made by a party other than the plan, the special processing rules for disability claims need not be followed. For example, if a pension plan provides that pension benefits will be paid to a person who has been determined to be disabled by the Social Security Administration or under the employer's LTD plan, a claim for pension benefits based on such a determination would be subject to the rules for processing pension benefit claims, not disability claims. [DOL FAQs on Claims Procedure Regulations]

Q 10:20   Do the claims procedure regulations apply to requests for a determination of whether an individual is eligible for coverage under a disability plan?

The claims procedure regulations apply to a coverage determination only if it is part of a claim for benefits. Thus, if an individual asks a question about coverage under a plan without making an actual claim for benefits, the eligibility determination is not governed by the claims procedure rules. On the other hand, if an individual files a claim for benefits under the plan procedures and the claim is denied because he or she is ineligible for coverage under the plan, the coverage determination is part of a claim and must be handled under the claims procedure rules. [DOL FAQs on Claims Procedure Regulations]

Q 10:21   Can a plan set a time limit for submitting a claim for benefits?

The claims procedure regulations do not contain any specific rules governing the period of time that must be given to claimants to file their claims. Therefore, a plan may impose a deadline for the submission of claims.

However, a plan's claims procedure must be reasonable and must not contain any provision, or be administered in any way, that unduly inhibits or hampers the initiation or processing of claims for benefits. Adoption of a period of time for filing claims that serves to unduly limit claimants' reasonable, good faith efforts to make claims for and obtain benefits under the plan would violate this requirement. [29 C.F.R. § 2560.503-1(b)(3)]

Q 10:22   Are disability benefit plans subject to any time limits in making benefit decisions?

The final DOL regulations provide that if a disability claim is wholly or partially denied, the plan administrator must notify the claimant within a reasonable period of time, but not later than 45 days after the plan's receipt of the claim. [DOL Reg. § 2560.503-1(f)(3)]

The 45-day period may be extended by up to 30 days if the plan administrator determines that an extension is necessary for reasons beyond the control of the plan. Before the end of the initial 45-day period, the plan administrator must notify the claimant of the circumstances requiring the extension and the date by which the plan expects to make a decision on the claim.

A second 30-day extension is permitted if the plan administrator determines that, for reasons beyond the control of the plan, a decision cannot be made within the initial 30-day extension period. The plan administrator must notify the claimant of the circumstances requiring the extension and the date on which the plan expects to make a decision before the end of the initial 30-day extension period.

An extension notice must specifically explain the standards on which entitlement to disability benefits is based, the unresolved issues that prevent a decision on the claim, and the additional information needed to resolve those issues. The claimant must be given at least 45 days to provide the additional information.

The period for resolving a disability claim begins at the time the claim is filed in accordance with the reasonable procedures of the plan, whether or not all of the information necessary to decide the claim is submitted at the time of filing. If an extension is necessary as a result of the claimant's failure to submit information necessary to decide the claim, the time for resolving the claim is tolled from the date the claimant is notified of the extension until he or she responds to the request for additional information. In other words, the 30-day extension period does not start to run until the plan has the information it requested to resolve the claim.

Many disability plans require claimants to submit to an examination by an expert chosen by the plan. The DOL makes it clear that the time limit for deciding a claim is not tolled because an examination is required. A plan that requires a physical or other type of examination to evaluate a claim must design a process that provides for decision making within the time frame set by the regulation. [DOL FAQs on Claims Procedure Regulations]

> **Practice Pointer.** The DOL emphasizes that these time limits are maximum periods, not automatic entitlements. If a specific claim presents no problems, it may be unreasonable for a plan to delay a decision until the end of the maximum time period. Similarly, an extended decision-making period is allowed only for reasons beyond the control of the plan. The DOL says it will not view delays caused by cyclical or seasonal fluctuations in claims volume to be matters beyond the control of the plan that would justify an extension. On the other hand, a plan is not required to extend the decision-making period in order to obtain additional information from a claimant. According to the DOL, "a plan may deny claims at any point in the administrative process on the basis that it does not have sufficient information; such a decision would allow the claimant to advance to the next stage of the claims process." [DOL FAQs on the Claims Procedure Regulations]

Q 10:23 Is a plan required to give any explanation when it denies a claim for disability benefits?

ERISA requires employee benefit plans that deny disability benefits to "set forth the specific reasons for such denial, written in a manner calculated to be understood by the participant." [29 U.S.C. § 1133] In addition, DOL regulations provide that, in the case of an adverse benefit determination, the plan administrator must provide a notice setting forth the following information in a manner calculated to be understood by the claimant:

- The specific reason(s) for the adverse determination;
- Reference to the specific plan provision on which the determination is based;
- A description of any additional material or information necessary to perfect the claim and an explanation of why such material or information is necessary;

- A description of the plan's review procedures and the applicable time limits, including a statement of the claimant's right to bring a civil action under ERISA Section 502(a) following an adverse determination on review; and

- A copy of any rule, guideline, protocol, or other similar criterion that was relied on in making the adverse determination or a statement indicating that such a rule was relied on and that a copy will be provided free of charge upon request.

[DOL Reg. § 2560.503-1(g)]

In a case involving termination of an employee's disability benefits, an appeals court concluded that a notice stating that the employee's benefits were being terminated because she no longer fit the plan's definition of "disabled" did not meet those requirements. Most significantly, the plan did not explain why it chose to discount the near-unanimous opinions of the employee's treating physicians that she was indeed disabled. Although it acknowledged that plan administrators do not owe any special deference to the opinions of treating physicians (see Q 2:31), the court cautioned that plan administrators cannot simply ignore physicians' medical conclusions or dismiss those conclusions without explanation. According to the court, "bare conclusions are not a rationale." A plan must provide a reasonable explanation for its determination and must address any reliable, contrary evidence presented by the claimant. [Love v. National City Corp. Welfare Benefits Plan, 574 F.3d 392 (7th Cir. 2009)]

Q 10:24   Is a plan's review of an adverse benefit determination subject to time limits or other restrictions?

The final DOL regulations require every disability benefit plan to establish and maintain a procedure that gives claimants a reasonable opportunity to appeal an adverse decision to an appropriate plan fiduciary. The appeals procedure must provide for a full and fair review of the claim and the adverse determination. [DOL Reg. § 2560.503-1(h)]

Full and fair review. A plan appeals procedure will not be considered to provide a full and fair review unless it meets the following requirements:

1. The procedure gives claimants at least 180 days to appeal the determination, following receipt of notification of an adverse determination.

2. The procedure gives claimants the opportunity to submit written comments, documents, records, and other information relating to the claim.

3. Upon request, the claimant is provided reasonable access to and copies of all documents, records, and other information relevant to the claim. Records and documents must be provided free of charge.

4. The procedure provides for a review that takes into account all comments, documents, and other information submitted by the claimant, without regard to whether such information was submitted or considered in making the initial benefit decision.

A plan may not require more than two levels of review of an adverse benefit decision.

The appeals process cannot give deference to the original adverse decision, and someone other than the individual who made the original decision must make the decision on appeal. The DOL notes that the reviewer may be a supervisor of the individual who made the original decision. However, the reviewer may not give deference to the original decision. That is, the reviewer must consider the full record of the claim and make an independent decision on whether it should be granted. [DOL FAQs on Claims Procedure Regulations]

In deciding the appeal of a decision that was based in whole or in part on medical judgment, the fiduciary handling the appeal must consult with an appropriate health care professional. The health care professional may not be an individual who was consulted in connection with the original adverse decision or a subordinate of that individual. According to the DOL, this requirement is intended to ensure that a fiduciary deciding a claim involving medical issues is adequately informed about the medical issues. The consultation requirement is not intended to prevent the fiduciary from consulting other experts he or she deems appropriate. For example, in connection with an appeal of a denied disability claim, a fiduciary may want to consult with vocational or occupational experts. In all cases, the DOL says a fiduciary must take appropriate steps to resolve the appeal in a prudent manner, including acquiring necessary information and advice, weighing that advice and information, and making an independent decision on the appeal. [DOL FAQs on Claims Procedure Regulations]

> **Practice Pointer.** Privacy regulations, which were authorized by the Health Insurance Portability and Accountability Act (HIPAA), generally require a plan to obtain authorization if a claimant's protected health information (PHI) will be disclosed to outside experts in the course of processing a claim. The privacy regulations are discussed in detail in chapter 5.

The claims procedure regulations require a plan to provide for identification of medical or other experts whose advice was obtained in connection with an adverse benefit determination, even if it did not rely on the advice of those experts in making the determination. A plan is not required to automatically provide the identity of experts in the notice of an adverse determination. However, the plan must disclose the identity of any experts when a claimant requests it. [DOL FAQs on Claims Procedure Regulations]

Notification requirements. A plan administrator must provide a claimant with written or electronic notice of any adverse benefit determination. The notice must be written in a manner reasonably calculated to be understood by the claimant and must contain the following information:

- The specific reason or reasons for the adverse decision
- Reference to the specific plan provision on which the decision was based
- A description of the plan review procedures and time limits, including a statement of the claimant's right to bring a civil action following an adverse determination on review

- Information about any internal rule, guideline, protocol, or similar criterion that was relied upon by the plan in making the adverse determination

Time limit. A decision on appeal of an adverse determination must be made within 45 days. However, a plan may have one extension of 45 days if required by special circumstances. If an extension is required, the plan must provide the participant with a notice specifying the special circumstances before the end of the initial 45-day period.

Q 10:25   Can a claimant agree to an extension of the time period for deciding a claim?

Yes. The time limits in the regulations are imposed on the plan. A claimant can voluntarily agree to give a plan extra time to decide a claim, although the plan may not unilaterally extend the time period. [DOL FAQs on Claims Procedure Regulations]

Q 10:26   Can a plan offer claimants additional appeals beyond what the regulations require?

While the regulations limit a plan's claim procedure to two *mandatory* appeals, a plan can offer *voluntary* additional levels of appeal, including arbitration or some other form of alternative dispute resolution. However, the plan must meet certain conditions to ensure than the additional appeals are truly voluntary. If a plan wishes to offer additional levels of appeal, the plan's claim procedure must provide the following:

1. The plan will not charge that a claimant who takes his or her case to court instead of going through the voluntary appeals process failed to exhaust administrative remedies (see Q 10:31).
2. The plan agrees that any statute of limitations on filing a claim in court will be tolled during the voluntary appeals process.
3. The voluntary appeal is available only after the claimant has gone through all appeals required by the regulations.
4. The plan will give the claimant enough information to make an informed judgment about whether to use the voluntary appeals process.
5. No fees or costs will be imposed on a claimant who uses the voluntary appeals process.

Q 10:27   Do the claims regulations specify a time limit for paying claims?

No. While the regulation establishes time frames within which claims must be decided, the regulation does not address the periods within which payments that have been granted must be actually paid. However, failure to provide benefit payments within reasonable periods of time following plan approval may present fiduciary responsibility issues under ERISA. [DOL FAQs on Claims Procedure Regulations]

Q 10:28　Can claimants authorize someone else to act on their behalf with respect to a claim?

Yes. The regulations provide that a reasonable claims procedure cannot prevent an authorized representative from acting on behalf of a claimant with respect to an initial claim or appeal of an adverse benefit determination. However, the plan may establish reasonable procedures for determining whether an individual has been authorized to act on behalf of a claimant. The DOL says that requiring completion of a form by the claimant identifying the authorized representative would be a reasonable procedure. [DOL FAQs on Claims Procedure Regulations]

Q 10:29　If a plan terminates disability benefits, must the plan treat the termination as an adverse benefit determination?

Under the claims procedure regulations, an adverse benefit determination includes any denial, reduction, or termination of a benefit. Therefore, when a plan terminates the payment of disability benefits because it has determined that the claimant is no longer disabled, the plan must provide the claimant with notice of its determination and the right to appeal that determination. On the other hand, if a plan provides for the payment of disability benefits for a predetermined, fixed period (e.g., a specified number of weeks or months or until a specified date), the termination of benefits at the end of the period is not treated as an adverse benefit determination. Therefore, a request by a claimant for payment of disability benefits beyond the specified period would constitute a new claim. [29 C.F.R. § 2560.503-1(f)(3)]

Q 10:30　If a claimant has designated an authorized representative, is the plan required to provide benefit determinations and other notifications to the representative, to the claimant, or to both?

Nothing would prevent a plan from communicating with both the claimant and the representative. However, it is the view of the DOL that when a claimant has clearly designated an authorized representative, all information and notifications should be directed to the representative unless the claimant directs otherwise. [DOL FAQs on Claims Procedure Regulations]

Q 10:31　Must a participant exhaust all administrative remedies under ERISA before filing a lawsuit to recover LTD benefits?

Generally, yes. Despite the fact that ERISA does not explicitly command exhaustion, the law in most circuits requires a participant to exhaust his or her administrative remedies before commencing suit. Note, however, that final DOL regulations provide that a plan cannot claim that failure to pursue a voluntary review of an adverse disability benefit determination constitutes a failure to exhaust administrative remedies. [29 C.F.R. § 2560.503-1 (c), (d)]

The Court of Appeals for the Sixth Circuit has ruled that a beneficiary seeking to recover long-term disability benefits was precluded from pursuing a lawsuit against an insurance company because the beneficiary failed to exhaust his administrative remedies under ERISA. A pharmacist filed his claim for long-term disability benefits because of a knee replacement and a serious potential for the same operation on the other knee. His employer, insured through UNUM, denied his claim more than 90 days after the date it was filed. UNUM's letter denying the pharmacist's claim included language advising him that he could submit additional information and that he could request a review of the denial within 60 days. Instead of submitting new information, the pharmacist filed suit against UNUM in the Kentucky state court.

The Sixth Circuit ruled that the plaintiff failed to show that the review procedures are insufficient or unfair or that an available remedy is inadequate. He failed to meet his burden to show futility so as to excuse the usual exhaustion requirement. [Ravencraft v. UNUM Life Ins. Co. of Am., 212 F.3d 341 (6th Cir. 2000)]

Q 10:32 If the plan administrator or its medical consultant disagrees with the treating physician, whose opinion controls?

In the past, the federal courts of appeal split on this issue. Some federal appeals courts adopted the so-called *treating physician rule* for making disability determinations in connection with employer-provided disability plans. Under this rule, a determination by an employee's treating physician that the employee is disabled is presumed to be correct. Therefore, in order to deny benefits, the plan administrator must have specific legitimate reasons based on substantial evidence. [Regula v. Delta Family-Care Disability Survivorship Plan, 266 F.3d 1130 (9th Cir. 2001), *overruled in part by* Black & Decker Disability Plan v. Nord, 538 U.S. 822 (2003)] Other appellate courts rejected the treating physician rule, holding that the opinion of an individual's treating physician is entitled to no greater deference than the opinion of any other physician who has examined the individual.

In 2003, the United State Supreme Court resolved the conflict among the circuit courts by holding that the treating physician rule does not apply to disability determinations under ERISA. In reaching its decision, the Court noted that the treating physician rule was originally developed by the courts in reviewing Social Security disability determinations and was eventually included in Social Security regulations. However, neither ERISA nor its regulations, including the claims regulations, mention the treating physician rule. Moreover, the Department of Labor (DOL) filed a brief with the Court opposing the rule.

The Court also noted that whereas the large size of the Social Security program and the fact that it is federally mandated dictates the use of certain presumptions for the uniform and efficient administration of the program, an individual's claim to ERISA benefits is likely to turn on interpretation of the provisions of a specific plan.

The Court questioned whether adoption of the treating physician rule would result in more accurate disability determinations, noting that both the consulting physicians hired by the plan and the individual's treating physician may have an incentive to reach a conclusion favorable to their respective client.

On the other hand, the Court cautioned that plan administrators cannot arbitrarily refuse to acknowledge reliable evidence presented by a claimant, including the opinions of his or her treating physician. [Black & Decker Disability Plan v. Nord, 296 F.3d 823 (9th Cir. 2002), *vacated and remanded*, 538 U.S. 822 (2003)]

In a case decided after the Supreme Court's decision, the Ninth Circuit concluded that a plan administrator did not abuse its discretion in concluding that an employee who suffered from fibromyalgia was not disabled as a result of her condition. According to the court, which had previously adopted the treating physician rule, the plan administrator acted reasonably in rejecting "conclusory statements" from the employee's doctors that she was disabled and relying on "the relatively more thorough and careful opinions" from the plan's doctors that she was not entirely disabled from working. [Jordan v. Northrop Grumman Corp. Welfare Benefit Plan, 370 F.3d 869 (9th Cir. 2004)]

In another case involving "a contest of competing medical opinions," the Seventh Circuit Court of Appeals held that a plan's insurer did not abuse its discretion by unreasonably deferring to its own consulting physicians rather than the employee's treating physicians in concluding that the employee's blood pressure condition did not rise to the level of disability. The court concluded that the insurer acted reasonably in relying on five consulting physicians who each concluded that the employee's condition was not disabling. [Black v. Long Term Disability Ins., 582 F.3d. 738 (7th Cir. 2009)]

Bear in mind, however, that a plan administrator's denial of a claim—and its reliance on the plan's own doctors—may be subject to greater scrutiny if the administrator is also ultimately responsible for payment of benefit claims.

In a 2008 decision, the Supreme Court acknowledged that even when a plan administrator has discretionary authority over benefit claims, an inherent conflict of interest exists if the plan administrator both evaluates and pays claims because the administrator stands to gain financially by denying the claims. For example, in the case before the Court, the Court concluded that an insurance company that both reviewed a participant's claim for disability benefits under an ERISA plan and was responsible for paying the benefits was operating under a conflict of interest. Moreover, the Court ruled the same would hold true for an employer that operated as plan administrator under a self-insured plan. [Metropolitan Life Ins. Co. v. Glenn, 128 S. Ct. 2343 (2008)] According to the Court, that conflict of interest is a "factor" that must be considered in determining whether there is an abuse of discretion in denying the claim. The Court did not specify the weight to be given to the conflict of interest in any given case, indicating that the conflict will be more important where there is a higher likelihood that it influenced the benefits decision (where the administrator has a history of biased claims administration) and less important "where the administrator has taken active steps to reduce potential bias and to promote accuracy, for example, by walling off claims administrators from those interested in firms finances." [Metropolitan Life Ins. Co. v. Glenn, 128 S. Ct. 2343 (2008)]

In the wake of the decision in *Metropolitan Life*, a number of circuit courts addressed the standard of review in similar conflict of interest cases, concluding that a conflict of interest should be analyzed as a factor in determining whether there was an abuse of discretion in denying benefits. [*See* McCauley v. First Unum Life Ins. Co., 551 F.3d 126 (2d Cir. 2008); Champion v. Black & Decker (USA), Inc., 550 F.3d 353 (4th Cir. 2008); Doyle v. Liberty Life Assurance Co. of Boston, 542 F.3d 1352 (11th Cir. 2008); Burke v. Pitney Bowes Inc. Long-Term Disability Plan, 544 F.3d 1016 (9th Cir. 2008)]

In a case involving a denial of disability benefits, the Ninth Circuit concluded that an insurer/administrator's "bias infiltrated that entire administrative decisionmaking process," and ordered the disability benefits to be reinstated. Significantly, one indicator of the administrator's bias was its reliance on a "pure paper" review of medical evidence by its own medical experts. While it acknowledged that the administrator was not bound by the conclusions of the employee's treating physicians, the court concluded that its decision to hire doctors to simply review the employee's files rather than to conduct an in-person medical examination raised questions about the thoroughness and accuracy of the benefits determination. [Montour v. Hartford Life & Accident Ins. Co., 582 F.3d 933 (9th Cir. 2009)]

For a further discussion of judicial review of benefit claim denials, see chapter 2.

Q 10:33   What if the employee does not submit evidence of disability?

Evidence of the existence or continuing existence of a qualifying disability is key to the prudent administration of an LTD plan. Without it, eligibility for plan benefits cannot always be determined reliably. Plan administrators should therefore be firm in enforcing plan requirements for submitting documentation in support of a claim of disability.

Proper management of an LTD plan focuses on obtaining two types of evidence. The first type of evidence is required at the benefit initiation stage. The employee is asked to submit evidence to document that he or she has become totally disabled within the meaning of the particular plan's disability definition and by the time limit specified in the plan. If the employee fails to prove that he or she has satisfied these initial requirements, entitlement to plan benefit payments has not occurred, and income replacement benefits do not commence.

The Seventh Circuit has ruled that a claimant does not make a proper "claim" for benefits under an LTD plan unless he or she satisfies all of the plan's conditions for making a proper claim under the plan, including a requirement that the individual submit a doctor's written certification of disability. The case concerned an employee who had been informed that she was to be terminated. Before her last day of employment, she claimed to have a disabling condition and submitted a claim under the employer's LTD plan; however, the plan required a certified statement from the physician that the employee was disabled, and her doctor refused to certify that she was totally disabled. The plan informed her that it could not process her claim until she submitted the required documentation. She then filed an ERISA lawsuit alleging that her claim for LTD benefits was improperly denied. The Seventh Circuit rejected her argument. The appellate court reasoned that a claim denial actually must occur before there can be an appeal of the denied claim pursuant to ERISA Section 503. Because the former employee failed to satisfy all of the plan's conditions for making a proper claim under the plan, the plan was not required to afford her an opportunity to participate in the ERISA-mandated claim appeal process. The appellate court concluded that an ERISA plan's duty to comply with ERISA's claim appeal requirements is not triggered until the beneficiary first makes a proper benefit claim under the terms of the plan. [Tolle v. Carroll Touch Inc., 23 F.3d 174 (7th Cir. 1994)]

> **Practice Pointer.** The plan's SPD should list every document that the employee is required to submit along with his or her claim form (including by whom the particular document must be signed if that fact is important to the plan's acceptance or rejection of the document). Note, however, that under DOL regulations a claim is considered to be filed when it is submitted in accordance with the reasonable procedures of the plan, whether or not all of the information necessary to decide the claim is submitted at the time of filing. Therefore, the plan administrator must respond to an incomplete claim within the time limits specified in DOL regulations (see Q 10:22).

The second type of evidence is requested only from individuals who have satisfactorily proved initial disability and have commenced receiving plan benefits. The former employee is asked to submit evidence (usually in the form of a doctor's written certification) that he or she has remained continuously disabled and continues to satisfy the plan's disability definition. Frequently, the plan document will provide that the plan administrator may terminate the disability income benefit payments if satisfactory proof of ongoing disability is not submitted on a timely basis. (See Q 10:38.)

> **Practice Pointer.** Plan participants may argue that the plan administrator is being unreasonable in requiring repeated proof of disability. This argument has some appeal only if the facts are utterly indisputable (e.g., as a result of a traffic accident, the former employee has been in a coma for several years). Almost always, the facts will not be that clear-cut. To avoid disputes about whether the plan administrator's request for continued documentation is unreasonable, too frequent, or too onerous, the SPD should specify how often the participant can be required to submit evidence of continued disability (e.g., once each calendar year) as a condition of continued receipt of plan benefits.

The SPD should also warn plan participants that their disability income benefits will be terminated if they fail to submit satisfactory proof of continued disability upon request.

Permanent nature of disability. Plan administrators must take care not to interpret the disability plan's provisions too restrictively. A 1994 federal district court case held that a plan administrator acted arbitrarily and capriciously in refusing to grant an employee's application for LTD benefits because the employee failed to demonstrate with medical certainty that his disability was permanent. The employee suffered from chronic fatigue syndrome (CFS) and submitted the opinions of experts on that disease that he was totally disabled. The court noted that there is currently no method of determining whether a person will ever recover from CFS, nor is there any treatment that has proven effective in overcoming it. In addition, the court noted that the plan also expressly provided that disability benefits would end if the individual is found to be no longer totally and permanently disabled. Thus, the court concluded, the plan contemplated that applicants might recover from their disabilities and did not contain any requirement that a disability would be covered only if there was a medical certainty of lifelong duration. [Sansevera v. E.I. Du Pont de Nemours & Co., 859 F. Supp. 106 (S.D.N.Y. 1994)] In another case in which an employer was held to have wrongfully denied LTD benefits, the court noted that CFS is a combination of mental and physical disorders and is not provable by "dipstick" laboratory tests. [Friedrich v. Intel Corp., 181 F.3d 1105 (9th Cir. 1999)]

After-acquired evidence. One of the most difficult issues is that of after-acquired evidence. In *Mongeluzo v. Baxter Travenol Long Term Disability Benefit Plan* [46 F.3d 938 (9th Cir. 1995)], the employee, who had suffered a variety of symptoms and ailments, had already had his LTD claim appeal denied and had commenced a lawsuit when he received a new medical evaluation stating that his symptoms all along had resulted from CFS. The court reviewed the split among the circuits on the issue of whether after-acquired evidence should be reviewed by the court or whether the court should limit its review to the evidence before the plan administrator at the time the claim was denied. The court held that the new evidence changed the nature of the case and should be considered.

Q 10:34   Must evidence of disability be strictly medical in nature?

The type and quality of the proof of disability that must be submitted to the plan will depend on the terms of the particular plan and the underlying insurance policy, if any. Typically, medical evidence of disability, in the form of a doctor's written certification that the individual is disabled, will be specified as a required part of the initial claim for plan benefits. Often, a plan administrator lacking particular medical expertise will have the claimant's application reviewed by a medical consultant.

Some plans (particularly self-insured disability plans) are not as restrictively drafted and may require only "evidence" of disability. In such a situation, the plan administrator would fail to administer the plan according to the governing instruments (thus committing an ERISA fiduciary violation) if it insisted on receiving only "medical evidence." Evidence of disability is a broader standard that would encompass whatever nonmedical evidence of disability the former employee might wish to submit, such as the opinions of coworkers. [Wolfe v. J.C. Penney Co., 710 F.2d 388 (7th Cir. 1983)] A federal district court held that a disability insurer had abused its discretion by relying only on "objective medical evidence" regarding a participant with a long history of back pain even though the participant's coworkers and supervisor believed that she was in pain and by failing to consider her credibility. [Palmer v. University Med. Group, 994 F. Supp 1221 (D. Or. 1998)]

> **Practice Pointer.** The plan's terms should contain sufficient authority for the plan administrator to use creative methods of documenting the existence or nonexistence of a disability. In *Patterson v. Caterpillar, Inc.* [40 F.3d 938 (7th Cir. 1995)], the Seventh Circuit upheld an employer's use of video surveillance to terminate an employee's disability income benefits when it showed that he used his cane when visiting doctors and lawyers but not when frequenting bars, restaurants, a bowling alley, and the local racetrack.

Plan administrators should be careful not to get too creative, however. A decision by the Ninth Circuit Court of Appeals makes it clear that a plan administrator or insurance company can be sued under state law if an investigation goes too far. Although ERISA preempts state laws that relate to employee benefit plans, it offers no protection from state law liability for invasion of an employee's privacy.

The employee in the case, John Dishman, resigned from his law firm and successfully applied for LTD benefits from UNUM, the firm's insurer. However, after initially approving the benefits, UNUM assigned Dishman's claim to its "complex claim unit" for further investigation. The unit hired several private investigators to do spot checks—and when one of those checks revealed that Dishman might be working for a company in another state, UNUM terminated his benefits. Despite subsequently receiving two other reports stating that he was not employed by the other company, UNUM refused to reinstate his benefits. Dishman retained an attorney and began a lengthy correspondence with UNUM to get back his benefits. When those efforts were unsuccessful, he filed a lawsuit against the insurer. In addition to a claim for nonpayment of disability benefits, Dishman's lawsuit alleged that UNUM was liable under state law for invasion of his privacy. According to Dishman, an investigator hired by UNUM elicited information about his employment status by falsely claiming to be a bank loan officer. He also charged that the investigators obtained personal information about him from neighbors and acquaintances by falsely claiming that he had volunteered to coach a basketball team; sought and obtained personal credit card information and travel itineraries by impersonating him; falsely identified themselves when they were caught photographing his home; and repeatedly called his home and either hung up or "dunned" the person answering the phone for personal information about him.

Dishman prevailed on his claim for disability benefits. However, a district court dismissed his state-law claim for invasion of privacy on the grounds that it was preempted by ERISA. Dishman appealed to the Ninth Circuit, which reversed the district court's decision and reinstated Dishman's invasion of privacy claim.

In reaching its decision, the Ninth Circuit noted that federal courts have had no trouble determining that ERISA preempts state laws that mandate employee benefit plan structures or administration or that provide alternative enforcement methods. However, Dishman's invasion of privacy allegations did not involve employee benefit administration or enforcement. True, UNUM conducted its investigation in the course of administering the disability plan; however, the Ninth Circuit said that this did not create enough of a relationship to warrant preemption.

The court pointed out that if lawsuits like Dishman's were preempted, a plan administrator could "investigate" a claim in all sorts of devious ways with impunity. "What if one of UNUM's investigators had accidentally rear-ended Dishman's car while surveilling him?" the court asked. "Would the fact that the surveillance was intended to shed light on his claim shield UNUM from liability? What if UNUM had tapped Dishman's phone, put a tracer on his car or trained a video camera into his bedroom in an effort to obtain information? Must that be tolerated simply because it is done purportedly in furtherance of plan administration?" According to the Ninth Circuit, the answer was no. ERISA was not intended to provide plan administrators with immunity from wrongdoing that only peripherally involves daily plan administration. [Dishman v. UNUM Life Ins. Co. of Am., 269 F.3d 974 (9th Cir. 2001)]

Q 10:35 Is the plan administrator bound by a determination of Social Security disability?

Not necessarily. Most plans set forth a definition of "totally disabled." ERISA requires the plan administrator to administer the plan according to its terms, so the plan administrator would have to interpret the language in the disability plan, not incorporate standards from some other plan (including governmental plans).

However, it is possible to design an employer-provided long-term disability plan that uses an award of Social Security disability benefits as the measure of disability under the employer's plan as well. In that case, the Social Security Administration's determination would be controlling for the ERISA plan benefits as well, because the ERISA plan incorporates that standard by reference as its own standard for total disability. However, such a plan design tends to be rare because of the administrative problems with delayed Social Security determinations that might not be retroactive to the day last worked or to the day short-term disability benefits terminated.

The Court of Appeals for the Eighth Circuit addressed the issue of whether a favorable determination of Social Security disability was controlling for purposes of establishing disability under a retirement plan. The appellate court found that the plan's definition of disability differed from the one found in the Social Security Act and that evidence concerning whether the employee had become disabled during his eligibility period was conflicting. The appellate court therefore found that the plan had not abused its discretion in determining that the employee had failed to meet the plan's disability standard within the required time period. [Cox v. Mid-America Dairymen, Inc., 12 F.3d 272 (8th Cir. 1993)]

In a similar decision, the First Circuit Court of Appeals held that an employee's receipt of Social Security disability benefits was not binding on a company's disability benefit plan. [Pari-Fasano v. ITT Hartford Life & Accident Ins. Co., 230 F.3d 415 (1st Cir. 2000)] According to the court, the criteria for determining eligibility for Social Security disability benefits are substantively different from the disability criteria used by many insured company plans, including the plan involved in the case. The court noted, however, that entitlement to Social Security disability benefits may be considered as evidence in making a determination under a company plan.

Social Security disability determination as evidence of disability. As noted by the First Circuit, even when the disability plan contains its own definition of totally disabled (or permanent and total disability), nothing in ERISA would prevent the claimant from submitting his or her Social Security determination letter and medical file to the ERISA plan as evidence to buttress his or her claim of disability. In *Donato v. Metropolitan Life Insurance Co.* [19 F.3d 375 (7th Cir. 1994)], the Court of Appeals for the Seventh Circuit refused to reach the issue of whether it would have been a breach of fiduciary duty for MetLife not to have reviewed the employee's Social Security file if she had actually submitted it in support of her claim under the employer's ERISA plan. The court allowed, however, that MetLife was bound to consider the evidence before it at the time it made its disability determination. This suggests that, since the claimant has the right, upon appeal under ERISA, to submit information in support of his or her claim, the claimant is able to force the claims appeal entity to at least take the Social Security determination of disability into consideration. In other words, the claimant has the right, under the ERISA claim appeal process, to insert the Social Security determination into the claim record as supporting evidence, even if it is not controlling for purposes of the ERISA plan's determination.

In a reverse twist, the Tenth Circuit Court of Appeals held that a plan had improperly relied on a Social Security disability determination in denying an employee's claim for disability benefits. Western Atlas provided disability coverage to its employees under a policy issued by the Life Insurance Company of North America (LINA). Under the policy, LINA was required to pay "own occupation" disability benefits for the first 24 months after a sickness or injury if the employee was unable to perform all the essential duties of his occupation. Rufus Caldwell filed a claim for benefits under the policy, which LINA denied on the grounds that Caldwell failed to establish that he was totally disabled within the meaning of the "own occupation" provision. In reaching its decision, LINA relied on a Social Security determination that Caldwell became totally unable to work more than a year after leaving Western Atlas. However, the court said the relevant inquiry under the plan was whether Caldwell was capable of perform-ing his own job at Western Atlas at the time he left the company, whereas the

Social Security determination turned on whether Caldwell was able to perform any job for which he was qualified. Therefore the court said LINA's reliance on the Social Security determination was arbitrary and capricious because that determination was based on irrelevant standards that conflicted with the plan's definition of disability. [Caldwell v. Life Ins. Co. of N. Am., 287 F.3d 1276 (10th Cir. 2002)]

Q 10:36   Can the employee's claim for long-term disability benefits be denied if the employee had a prior medical condition?

The answer to this question depends on the language of the particular LTD plan and the underlying insurance policy. If the LTD plan excludes disabilities caused by or related to prior infirmities, the plan administrator may, in an appropriate case, deny the claim for benefits. However, the plan administrator must be careful to have evidence linking the current disability to the prior condition before denying a claim for benefits for the current disability.

The U.S. Court of Appeals for the Sixth Circuit examined an accident insurance plan with a lump-sum disability benefit feature. Although the plan was not a disability income plan, it contained such a preexisting-condition exclusion. The plan insured only losses resulting directly and independently of all other causes from bodily injuries caused by accident. The plan administrator, citing this definition, denied disability benefits for two employees who had experienced back problems previously. The appellate court determined that the plan administrator had insufficient information to conclude that the present disability was caused even in part by the prior injuries. One employee's doctor had permitted him to return to work without any restrictions. The other employee's record contained no information showing that the current disability was related to any previous back problems. The appellate court remanded the case to the district court for further proceedings. [Tolley v. Commercial Life Ins. Co., CCH Pension Plan Guide ¶ 23, 894P (6th Cir. 1993)]

The Third Circuit held that a plan's decision to deny LTD benefits based on a preexisting condition was unsupported by the evidence. The employee had visited her doctor for a routine gynecological exam about two weeks before her coverage under the LTD plan became effective. At that time, she told the doctor that she had been experiencing urinary frequency and urgency. The doctor took a urine sample, but told the employee to see a urologist if the test results were negative. The doctor did not give the employee a diagnosis at that time. Several months later, the employee was referred to a urologist due to problems with frequent urination. The doctor suspected that the employee was suffering from a condition known as interstitial cystitis. The employee underwent a medical procedure that confirmed that diagnosis. Following the diagnosis, the employee applied for LTD benefits under the plan. However, the plan excluded coverage for preexisting conditions, which were defined as conditions for which medical treatment or advice was rendered, prescribed or recommended within six months prior to the effective date of an employee's coverage under the plan. The plan denied the employee's claim on the grounds that her disability stemmed from a preexisting condition.

The Third Circuit rejected the plan's argument that it was "self-evident" that the employee was suffering from the same condition all along. According to the court, the employee's symptoms were nonspecific and undiagnosed at the time of the first doctor visit. Moreover, it was the expert opinion of the urologist that it was impossible to determine the date of onset of the employee's interstitial cystitis. [Ceccanecchio v. Continental Cas. Co., 2002 U.S. App. LEXIS 21496 (3d Cir. Oct. 15, 2002)]

By contrast, the Third Circuit Court of Appeals ruled that an employee's claim for disability benefits following a diagnosis of Amyotropic Lateral Sclerosis (ALS), commonly known as Lou Gehrig's disease, was barred by the plan's preexisting-condition exclusion. The terms of the plan defined a preexisting condition as one for which "medical treatment or advice was rendered, prescribed or recommended" within 12 months prior to an employee's effective date of coverage. Although the employee was not diagnosed as having ALS until nearly a year after he became covered by the disability plan, he had consulted his physician regarding his symptoms during the preexisting-conditions exclusion look-back period. At that time, the physician's notes indicated that the employee was suffering from motor neuron disease, but that the disease "was not felt to be ALS." Nonetheless, a majority of the court concluded that the doctor's visit knocked out the employee's claim for disability benefits. According to the majority, the plan's insurer was reasonable in finding that the employee received "advice" regarding ALS during the look-back period, even if he did not receive a definitive diagnosis at the time. A strongly worded dissenting opinion took the majority to task for its "backward-looking" reinterpretation of symptoms under which any prior symptom not inconsistent with the ultimate diagnosis would provide a basis for denial of a claim. [Doroshow v. Hartford Life & Accident Ins. Co., 2009 U.S. App. LEXIS 16820 (3d Cir. July 30, 2009)]

Q 10:37   What if a former employee becomes disabled at a later date?

Typically, employer-sponsored LTD plans require not only that the individual be disabled but also that the disability occur on or before a specified date.

As an unusual case illustrates, the plan document should be very specific about when a terminated employee's disability coverage ends. The Second Circuit Court of Appeals concluded that a terminated employee was covered by a company's disability plan for an injury that occurred after she left work on her last day of employment. The company's plan administrator argued that the employee was not covered by the plan at the time of her injury because the plan covered only "active employees." According to the plan administrator, the employee's active employment ended when she walked out the company's door on her last day of work. The Second Circuit disagreed. Under the terms of the plan, an employee was considered actively employed if he or she worked on a full-time basis for a minimum of 30 hours per week. There was no suggestion that the employee did not meet that test on her last day of work. Therefore, the court said, it was logical to conclude that the employee's coverage continued through the whole of her last day of employment. According to the court, the plan administrator's proposed cutoff was a less reasonable reading of the plan' albeit the one most favorable to the plan. [Lauder v. First UNUM Life Ins. Co., 284 F.3d 375 (2d Cir. 2002)]

In a more typical situation, an employee who is absent from work because of illness may subsequently become disabled. In such a case, the eligibility period under the employer's LTD plan might be coordinated with the payment period (such as three months or six months) under the employer's short-term disability plan. Thus, a typical plan design would provide that if the individual becomes totally disabled on or before the date short-term disability benefits end, LTD benefits will begin at the expiration of a waiting period that exactly overlaps the maximum period of short-term disability benefits.

One of the biggest administrative problems for employers under an LTD plan is employees who stop work because of a claimed disability that does not satisfy the criteria necessary to trigger LTD benefits within the time limit imposed under the plan, but who subsequently become progressively sick enough to meet the plan's disability definition after the time limit imposed by the plan has passed. Several years after having terminated employment and after having finally become sick enough to qualify as disabled, the individual claims that he or she was continuously disabled within the meaning of the plan all along. Although the former employee's present physical and financial circumstances can be heart-wrenching, the plan administrator's duty is to determine whether the particular facts satisfy the plan's express requirements for benefit entitlement. For an excellent discussion of a number of these types of cases, see *Ciulla v. USAble Life* [864 F. Supp. 883 (W.D. Ark. 1994)].

To minimize such factual disputes, the SPD should carefully and clearly state the date on which total disability must have occurred. It should also limit the time for submitting the initial claim for benefits so that the documentation regarding health status will be obtained close in time to the relevant plan date.

Practice Pointer. Interpretive problems and administrative headaches can occur if the employee's claim or claim appeal regarding disability benefits is required to be submitted only long after the date the employee's total disability must have occurred. If a year or two passes before the individual finally submits evidence of total disability, the plan is effectively foreclosed from having the patient examined by a physician of its own choice to determine if the patient really is "totally disabled" within the meaning of the plan, because it is unlikely that the physician will be able to perform an examination now that determines the patient's condition back then. The plan's referral expert effectively would be limited to examining the prior medical documentation and discussing the medical history with treating physicians and institutions without the benefit of a personally conducted contemporaneous physical exam. The treating physicians also may be forced to give an *ex post facto* opinion of total disability if they did not have a copy of the plan's standard when examining the patient during the relevant time period. To foreclose such lengthy delays in documentation and proof of disability within the meaning of the plan's definition, the SPD for the LTD plan should clearly state the deadline by which the employee must submit his or her initial claim for disability benefits. The initial plan deadline for claims should be close in time to the date by which the total disability is required to have occurred, so that the plan receives timely documentation and has a fair chance to have its expert examine the claimant or request clarification from the treating physician.

Note, however, that any time limits specified in the plan must comply with DOL regulations on claims procedures and appeals (see Q 10:21)

After-acquired evidence. Another issue is that of after-acquired evidence. In *Mongeluzo v. Baxter Travenol Long Term Disability Benefit Plan* [46 F.3d 938 (9th Cir. 1995)], the employee, who had suffered a variety of symptoms and ailments, had already had his LTD claim appeal denied and had commenced a lawsuit when he received a new medical evaluation stating that he had been suffering from chronic fatigue syndrome all along. The court, noting that the circuits were split on the issue of whether after-acquired evidence should be reviewed by the court or whether the court should limit its review to the evidence before the plan administrator at the time the claim was denied, decided that the new evidence changed the nature of the case and should be considered.

Q 10:38   Can a plan administrator ever terminate disability benefit payments once the individual has begun receiving them?

Yes. If the plan requires (as most do) that the individual remain continuously disabled to remain eligible for continued disability income benefits, the plan administrator might be able to request reasonable proof that the individual in fact remains totally disabled and to terminate the individual's future plan benefits if such proof is not produced. The plan administrator will not, however, be able to do so if the plan does not authorize such periodic redetermination of disability or does not grant the plan administrator discretionary authority to determine eligibility for benefits.

Surveillance. The savings from periodic review of the disabled individual's medical status can be significant where benefits can be legitimately terminated. Some companies have not limited themselves to requiring submission of medical evidence and have found creative methods of documenting that the disability has ended. In *Patterson v. Caterpillar, Inc.* [70 F.3d 503 (7th Cir. 1995)], the court upheld the employer's termination of disability benefits based in part on videotape surveillance showing that the employee used a cane when visiting doctors and lawyers but not while frequenting bars, restaurants, and a local racetrack. The video surveillance also showed him, in a single evening, going to a bowling alley, the bank, back home, and out again to three different bars without a cane. For another case involving videotape surveillance, see *Kariotis v. Navistar International Transportation Corp.* [131 F.3d 672 (7th Cir. 1997)]

Caution. Plan administrators should be careful not to get too creative, however. Although ERISA preempts state laws that relate to employee benefit plans, it offers no protection from state law liability for invasion of an employee's privacy. (See Q 10:34.)

Periodic review. Typically, the plan will specify an interval, such as once every one or two years, at which the individual can be required to submit medical evidence of continued disability. Any such requirement is a material condition for continued entitlement to the plan benefits and should be clearly and fully spelled out in the plan and disclosed in the plan's SPD. Plan-drafting defects could possibly result in the plan administrator's interpretations not being given deference by a court.

The U.S. Court of Appeals for the Third Circuit ruled that an employer could terminate a former employee's LTD benefits when two physicians concluded that she was no longer totally disabled. Originally diagnosed by her treating physician as totally disabled for any gainful employment, the former employee began to receive disability benefits from the plan. She was required to submit semiannual proof of continued disability. During a review several years later, an independent medical examiner selected by the employer concluded that although the former employee had a severe disability, she was capable of working if she had appropriate transportation to work. At the employer's request, the insurer ordered a second examination by an orthopedic surgeon, who also concluded that she was not totally disabled at that time. The appellate court held that the company's termination of her LTD benefits based on these detailed medical opinions was not arbitrary and capricious. The former employee did not show that the opinions were unreliable or below the standards of the profession, nor, except for a conclusory note from her treating physician, did she submit any medical evidence to substantiate her claim that she was still totally disabled and unable to perform any gainful activities. The court found that she had been given sufficient time to submit such proof and upheld the employer's decision to terminate her disability benefits. [Abnathya v. Hoffmann-La Roche Inc., 2 F.3d 40 (3d Cir. 1993)]

The Eleventh Circuit refused, however, to apply the arbitrary and capricious standard of review (a limited review) to a plan administrator's decision to terminate disability benefits where the language of the LTD plan did not expressly grant the plan administrator the discretionary authority to determine eligibility or interpret the terms of the plan. In that case, the appellate court applied a *de novo* standard of review and determined that the evidence before the plan administrator presented a genuine issue of material fact concerning whether the former employee was still totally disabled. The appellate court overturned a summary judgment for the defendant and remanded the case to the lower court for further proceedings. [Kirwan v. Marriott Corp., 10 F.3d 784 (11th Cir. 1994)]

The Ninth Circuit applied the same approach to reach the opposite conclusion where the LTD plan at issue did, by its terms, grant the plan administrator the discretionary authority to determine eligibility for benefits. As in the *Kirwan* case, the plan administrator had determined that the individual was no longer disabled and had terminated the disability income benefits under the plan; however, the district court then proceeded to review all the evidence on a *de novo* basis and reversed the plan administrator's decision. The court of appeals, in turn, reversed the district court and upheld the plan administrator's decision.

The appellate court determined that because the plan administrator's decision concerning continued entitlement to disability benefits had been made pursuant to an express grant of discretionary authority contained in the plan document, the correct standard to apply in reviewing that determination was the more limited review standard of whether the plan administrator's decision was arbitrary and capricious based on the information that had been submitted to it at that time. [Taft v. Equitable Life Assurance Soc'y, 9 F.3d 1469 (9th Cir. 1993)]

Even under the limited review standard, a decision to discontinue benefits must be supported by substantial evidence. The Eighth Circuit Court of Appeals concluded that a plan administrator abused its discretion when it terminated an individual's LTD benefits on the grounds that she was able to work. Plan specialists had determined that the employee was unable to work less than six months earlier, and the plan administrator's subsequent adverse decision was not based on new medical evidence. [Norris v. Citibank, N.A Disability Plan (501), 308 F.3d 880 (8th Cir. 2002)]

Plan amendments. Welfare benefits, including disability benefits, are not subject to the statutory vesting requirements that ERISA imposes on pension plans. Therefore, an employer can amend the terms of a disability plan to reduce an individual's benefits or cut off benefits entirely by terminating the plan—unless the terms of the plan itself have caused the benefits to vest.

In one case, the Supreme Court let stand an appeals court ruling that—despite a plan administrator's retroactive plan amendment discontinuing the payment of health insurance plan premiums for disabled employees—a class of disability plan participants had a vested right to health insurance coverage. [Barker v. Ceridian Corp., 193 F.3d 976 (8th Cir. 1999), *cert. denied*, 529 U.S. 1109 (2000)]

At issue were three ambiguous clauses in Ceridian Corp.'s LTD plan. One clause described the insurance premium benefits, which provided for payment of health insurance premiums for the duration of an employee's disability. A second clause, known as the termination clause, stated that disability benefits would continue as long as an employee remained totally disabled. A third clause contained a reservation of rights, which broadly gave the employer the right to amend its plans.

The appeals court found abundant evidence that the employer's employee benefit representatives interpreted the reservation of rights as applicable only to those not already on disability. The court pointed to testimony from a benefits manager who had drafted the SPD language at issue that the reservation of rights was not intended to have an effect on those who already were disabled.

On the other hand, the Tenth Circuit concluded that there was nothing to prevent another employer from retroactively amending its plan to impose a limit on benefits for certain disabilities.

Kathy Welch, an employee of the Coleman Company, became disabled as a result of fibromyalgia, a chronic disorder characterized by widespread pain and fatigue. In July 1998, Welch submitted a claim for benefits under her employer's

LTD plan. At the time she submitted her claim, Coleman's plan provided benefits until age 65. However, in August 1998, the plan was amended to impose a 24-month limit on benefits for disabilities that are "primarily based on self-reported symptoms." The amendment was effective retroactively to January 1, 1998. Therefore, the plan administrator advised Welch that her benefits would be cut off after 24 months because her disability was based on self-reported symptoms.

Welch sued, claiming that retroactive application of the plan amendment improperly deprived her of vested benefits. The terms of the plan provided that benefits would vest upon termination of the plan. According to Welch, the amendment amounted to termination of one plan and creation of a new plan. The Tenth Circuit disagreed. According to the court, Coleman Company did not take any steps to terminate the plan. While the plan specified that the employer was required to give written notice to policyholders before terminating the plan, no such notice was given. Moreover, although substantive changes were made that affected particular benefits, the employees' basic coverage under the plan was not disrupted in a way that would indicate termination. Thus, the Tenth Circuit concluded that Coleman's plan was amended, not terminated—and the enactment of the amendment did not cause Welch's benefits to vest. [Welch v. UNUM Life Ins. Co. of Am., 382 F.3d 1078 (10th Cir. 2004)]

Practice Pointer. If an employer wishes to have plan amendments apply to a previously disabled employee, care should be taken in writing both the original plan and the amended plan.

For example, in one case the Ninth Circuit concluded that a plan amendment requiring recertification of disability every two years did not apply to a previously disabled employee. The employee suffered a knee injury in 1999 and began receiving long-term disability benefits. At the time of the employee's injury the employer's plan provided that any amendment to the plan applied only to disabilities commencing on or after the effective date of the amendment. The plan states: "Total Disabilities commencing prior to the effective date of a Plan amendment are provided for under the terms of the Plan in effect at the time those disabilities commenced."

At the time the employee's disability began, the plan did not require recertification of disability. In 2002, the plan was amended and a two-year recertification provision was added. However, the amended plan specifically provided that disabilities commencing before the effective date of a plan amended were governed by the terms of the plan in effect when the disabilities commenced.

In 2003, the plan conducted a recertification of the employee's disability and cut off her benefits on the grounds that she no longer met the plan's definition of total disability. The employee sued to regain her benefits—and won. The Ninth Circuit concluded that the recertification requirement did not apply to the employee because her disability benefits were governed by the plan in effect when her disability commenced in 1999. The court noted that both the original plan and the amended plan contained clear language providing that her disability was to be governed by the plan in effect at the time her disability commenced. [Shane v. Albertson's Inc., 504 F.3d 1166 (9th Cir. 2007)]

Q 10:39   Is a disabled participant who tries to obtain training for a new occupation or who returns to work on a limited schedule disqualified from receiving further LTD benefits?

Not necessarily. Once again, the answer to this question depends on the terms of the particular plan. A common LTD plan design feature is to permit employees to resume work on a limited schedule or to attend educational classes as an interim step toward recovery from the disability and/or adjustment to a different occupation. The prior approval of the plan administrator is generally required. The individual can then engage in such activities without completely forfeiting his or her entitlement to disability income benefits. Typically, the disability benefit would be prorated or reduced to take into consideration other income (if any) generated by the approved activity.

In this manner, the disabled individual can prepare for eventual return to productive work without jeopardizing desperately needed financial support. An LTD plan containing such a feature provides a positive incentive for those who wish to return to productive work to attempt to do so, while helping to reduce and better manage the plan's future exposure to liability for benefit payments.

Q 10:40   Can a former employee be precluded by the terms of his or her former employer's disability insurance policy from continuing to receive long-term disability benefits after beginning employment with another company that paid a higher salary?

Yes, according to the U.S. Court of Appeals for the Ninth Circuit, an employee who takes a higher paying job may have disability benefits terminated. In the Ninth Circuit case, an employee was injured in an automobile accident while working as a salesman. After he told his employer that he intended to take a leave of absence because of his medical condition, the company fired him. Prior to being fired, the employee's doctor diagnosed him as totally disabled and the employee filed for long-term disability benefits. The insurer denied the employee benefits because of his termination. The employee filed an administrative appeal and in the interim began working for another company where he earned more money than at his prior job. Eventually, he was terminated again because his disability interfered with his job performance. The employee sued the insurer. The district court ruled that he was totally disabled as of the date he filed his claim for benefits and awarded him benefits through the date on which he began work for the new employer. The court also determined that the employee was no longer disabled after that date because his earnings at the new job exceeded his pre-disability salary and a benefits termination provision of the policy applied.

The appeals court upheld the district court's ruling stating that the employee did not provide any evidence that he was unable to perform the "substantial and material duties of his regular occupation on the date he began the new job." [Deegan v. Continental Cas. Co., 167 F.3d 502 (9th Cir. 1999)]

Trust Requirement

Q 10:41 Are employee contributions toward LTD coverage required to be held in trust?

If the LTD plan is self-insured, the current DOL enforcement policy requires that employee contributions be held in trust. If the LTD plan is paid solely out of the assets of the employer, is insured (whether contributory or noncontributory), or is part of a cafeteria plan, the DOL is not currently enforcing the trust requirement as long as employee contributions are forwarded to the insurance carrier within 90 days. Final plan asset regulations published by the DOL on August 7, 1996, made no changes in the existing regulations insofar as welfare benefit plans are concerned, so the current DOL enforcement position should continue in the future.

These requirements are discussed in detail in chapter 2.

Benefit Calculations

Q 10:42 How are disability benefits calculated?

The answer depends on the terms of the plan. Typically, LTD benefits are equal to a percentage of the employee's compensation prior to the onset of the disability.

If an employee's compensation includes amounts other than straight salary or wages, the plan should clearly state whether such amounts are to be taken into account in computing disability benefits and how they are to be taken into account.

In one case, for example, a plan provided that benefits were to be based on an employee's covered monthly earnings. Covered monthly earnings were defined as the employee's monthly salary and any commissions, averaged over the preceding 12 months, or bonuses, averaged over the preceding 36 months. However, the plan did not define either what constituted commissions or bonuses.

The employee, who worked as a branch manager for a mortgage company, had a compensation arrangement in which she earned 50 percent of the branch profits in addition to her salary. In determining the employee's disability benefit, the plan treated the branch profits as a bonus and averaged them over a 36-month period to calculate her monthly benefit. However, the employee claimed that the branch profits should be treated as commissions and averaged over 12 months. According to the employee, the branch profits could not be considered bonuses because she was contractually entitled to them. However, the plan countered that the employee's employment agreement characterized the branch profit payments as bonuses and the employee should be bound by the terms of the agreement. The Seventh Circuit agreed and held that the branch profits were properly characterized as bonuses. The court noted that the employment agreement characterized the payments as bonuses. Moreover, the branch profits are unlike ordinary commissions because, although they were calculated as a percentage of sales, they were not based on the employee's personal sales, but rather on the sales of the branch as a whole. [Perugini-Christen v. Homestead Mortgage Co., 287 F.3d 624 (7th Cir. 2002)]

Tax Treatment of Employers

Q 10:43   Are employer contributions to, or payments under, a disability income plan deductible for federal income tax purposes?

Yes, generally they are, provided that they are an ordinary and necessary business expense. [I.R.C. § 162(a); Treas. Reg. § 1.162-10] However, if the disability income benefits are provided through a welfare benefit fund such as a Code Section 501(c)(9) VEBA trust, the employer contributions must also satisfy the requirements of Code Sections 419 and 419A in order to be deductible by the employer. (See chapter 20 for further discussion of Code Sections 419 and 419A.)

Tax Treatment of Employees

Q 10:44   Are employees taxed on the cost of monthly employer-provided disability coverage?

No. The tax law provides an income exclusion for the cost of the monthly disability insurance coverage received from the employer. This is true for both income-replacement-type disability plans and dismemberment plans. [I.R.C. §§ 61(a)(1), 104(a)(3), 105(a), 106]

Practice Pointer. An employer may, however, include the amounts of its premium payments for disability insurance coverage in employee's taxable wages for the year. Whether this is done unilaterally by the employer or at the employee's election, the inclusion of premium payments in the employees' incomes will affect the income tax treatment of disability benefits paid to the employees. (Taxation of the benefits actually received from the plan is discussed in Qs 10:45–10:55.)

Q 10:45   Are benefits paid under a dismemberment-type plan taxable to the employee?

No. Code Section 105 contains a blanket exclusion from federal gross income for benefit payments received by employees under an employer-provided dismemberment-type plan. Benefit payments derived from employer contributions will not be taxable to the employee or other recipient if they:

1. Constitute payment for the permanent loss, or loss of use, of a member or function of the body; and

2. Are computed with reference to the nature of the injury without regard to the period the employee is absent from work.

[I.R.C. §§ 104(a)(3), 105(c)]

The portion of dismemberment-type benefit payments attributable to employee contributions is excluded from federal gross income under Code Section 104.

Occasionally, former employees attempt to claim that their disability pension payments should be excluded from taxation under Code Section 105(c) but almost invariably lose. The U.S. Tax Court rejected such a claim by a former police officer who claimed that he had permanently lost the use of his foot and ankle because he could no longer stand for long periods of time, walk up and down stairs without difficulty, or dance. He also claimed that he suffered the loss of a bodily function because he had a heart valve that was not functioning properly. The court rejected his claims, observing that the partial loss of the use of an ankle and foot did not prevent him from working in jobs requiring less strenuous activity, and that loss of the use of a portion of the heart muscle does not equal loss of a member or a bodily function. [King v. Commissioner, T.C. Memo 1996-52 (1996)]

In another decision, the Tax Court acknowledged that the employee, who suffered from a severe neurological impairment that made it impossible for him to work, received the payments on account of a disability resulting from personal injury or sickness. However, the court concluded that the employee's disability payments did not qualify for the exclusion because they were not computed by reference to the nature of his injury without regard to the period of his absence from work. According to the court, under the terms of the disability policy, "an employee who was disabled because he had lost a leg was entitled to the same benefits as one who was disabled because he had lost both legs, another limb, or his sight, suffered kidney failure, or had a heart attack or stroke." Moreover, the employee's benefits were calculated by reference to his pre-disability monthly salary (subject to minimum and maximum limits), and was not affected by the severity or nature of the employee's disability. [Hayden v. Commissioner, T.C. Memo 2003-184 (2003), aff'd, 127 Fed. Appx. 975 (9th Cir. Apr. 18, 2005)]

Q 10:46   Are benefits paid under a disability income plan taxable to the employee?

The taxability of disability income benefits received by an employee depends on who pays the premium. To the extent that the disability income benefits are attributable to employer contributions or payments, they are taxable. However, to the extent that the disability income benefits are attributable to the employee's own contributions, they are not taxed. [I.R.C. §§ 104(a)(3), 105(a)]

If both the employer and the employee contribute toward the cost of the coverage, the portion of the disability benefits attributable to employer contributions is taxable, while the portion attributable to employee contributions is tax free. The taxable and tax-free portions of the benefits are determined by applying a three-year look-back rule. Benefits are generally taxable to the employee to the extent that premiums were paid by the employer within three years preceding the disability (see Qs 10:48, 10:49, Q 10:50).

> **Practice Pointer.** In the past, it was assumed that this three-year look-back rule also applied when a plan switched from an employer-paid to an employee-paid arrangement. However, IRS private letter rulings make it clear that the three-year look-back rule applies only when both the employer and the employee contribute to the cost of coverage in the year in which the employee becomes disabled. According to the rulings, LTD benefits payable to an employee who pays the premiums for coverage *for the plan year in which he or she becomes disabled* are excludable from income, even if the employer paid the premiums in prior years. [Priv. Ltr. Ruls. 200146012, 200146011, 200146010] Revenue Ruling 2004-55 [2004-34 I.R.B. 343] confirms that result. The ruling considered a situation in which an employer-paid plan was amended to allow employees to elect either employer-paid or employee-paid contributions on a year-by-year basis, and concluded that the amendment created a new plan in which, with respect to each employee, benefits are financed either solely by the employer or solely by the employee. Therefore, the amended plan is not subject to the three-year look-back rule.

Revenue Ruling 2004-55 also makes it clear that when an employee elects to have disability coverage paid for by the employer on a pretax basis (i.e., the premiums paid by the employer are excluded from the employee's income), the premiums are treated as paid by the employer and disability benefits received by the employee are includable in the employee's gross income. On the other hand, if an employee elects to have disability coverage paid for by the employer on an after-tax basis (i.e., the premiums paid by the employer are taxed to the employee), the premiums are treated as paid by the employee and disability benefits received by the employee are excludable from the employee's gross income.

Income-replacement-type benefits received under workers' compensation laws as compensation for personal injuries or sickness are fully tax free, even though they are attributable to employer contributions. [I.R.C. § 104(a)(1)] However, benefits received pursuant to state temporary disability laws (see Q 10:3) for non-job-related disabilities are not exempt insofar as they are attributable to employer contributions. [Treas. Reg. § 1.104-1(b)]

The IRS examined a situation in which an employee sustained an injury at work. During his absence from work because of the injury, the employee was paid benefits under a policy limited to payments for work-related injuries. Based on those facts, the IRS ruled that the benefits were not temporary disability benefits but were more in the nature of workers' compensation benefits, and therefore they were not includable in the injured employee's income. [Priv. Ltr. Rul. 9330026]

Q 10:47   When are disability premiums considered paid by the employee?

If premiums are paid directly by the employee or through salary reductions, they are generally considered paid by the employee and, therefore, benefits paid to the employee will be tax free. However, if the employee contributions are made by means of salary reduction under a cafeteria plan, they are treated as employer contributions, and the disability income benefits attributable to such contributions are therefore taxable. (See chapter 7.)

In addition, if an employer grosses up the tax on an employee's contributions, the benefit might be characterized as having become employer-provided; thus, the income-replacement payments would be taxable. [Jamison, Money, Farmer & Co., P.C. v. Standeffer, 678 So. 2d 1061 (Ala. 1996)]

In addition, the IRS has ruled that premium payments made by an employer will be treated as employee contributions if the amount of the payments is included in the employee's taxable wages for the year. In the ruling, an employer paid the entire premium for group LTD insurance coverage for its employees and did not include the cost of the coverage in an employee's gross income (i.e., the premiums were paid on a pretax basis). The employer amended the plan to allow employees to make an irrevocable election at the beginning of each plan year to either continue to have the employer pay the premiums on a pretax basis or to have the employer pay the premiums on an after-tax basis by including the cost of the coverage in taxable wages for the year. For an employee who elects after-tax treatment, the employer allocates a portion of the annual group premium to the employee and includes that amount in the employee's gross income for the year.

The IRS ruled that employees whose LTD premiums are paid by the employer but included in taxable wages are to be treated as having paid for the LTD coverage. Therefore, benefit payments to those employees are excludable from income. However, employees who elect to have the employer's premiums excluded from gross income are treated as having employer-paid coverage. Therefore, benefits paid to those employees are taxable. In either case, the premiums are treated as either fully paid by the employer or the employee. Therefore, the rules for plans financed by both the employer and the employee do not apply. [Rev. Rul. 2004-55, 2004-34 I.R.B. 343]

In addition, the Tax Court has ruled that where an employer paid the premium for an employee's LTD coverage and the employee reimbursed the employer, the payments were attributable to the employee. The disability policy stated that the employer was "nothing more than an agent or conduit which paid the premiums nominally and then collected the premium payments from the employees themselves." Moreover, the employees signed agreements to repay the employer for the disbursements. [Bouquet v. Commissioner, T.C. Memo 1994-212, 67 T.C.M. (CCH) 2959 (1994)]

However, in a reported decision, the Tax Court held that a collectively bargained disability plan is not considered employee-paid, even though employees may have exchanged wage increases for the plan. [Tuka v. Commissioner, 120 T.C. 1 (2003)]

Thomas Tuka was employed as an airline pilot for U.S. Airways until he left work because of carpal tunnel syndrome. Tuka's disability benefits plan was established through collective bargaining negotiations between the Airline Pilots Association and U.S. Airways. Tuka contended that disability benefits paid under the plan were not taxable because the coverage was financed by the pilots, not by U.S. Airways. U.S. Airways pilots made wage concessions of approximately $20 million in exchange for the pilot disability plan.

The Tax Court rejected Tuka's argument that his benefits were paid for by U.S. Airways employees, including himself. The court said that to accept Tuka's position would essentially qualify any negotiated disability package for exclusion because it could be construed as a substitute for wages that employees might otherwise receive. The court did not believe that Congress intended the exclusion to be so broad as to cover all benefits attributable to wage concessions made in a negotiated bargaining process.

The court acknowledged that the Code is not explicit on this point. However, the court felt that the exclusion of benefits depends on whether contributions to an accident and health insurance plan involve after-tax dollars. If an employee is to exclude disability benefits attributable to employer contributions, those contributions must have been includable in the employee's gross income. Even if wage concessions did constitute employee contributions, they were not taxed to the employees. Thus, benefits attributable to those contributions would not be eligible for the exclusion.

Q 10:48   How does an employer calculate the amount that is taxable to an employee receiving disability income payments under a plan involving both employer and employee contributions?

If both the employer and the employee contributed to the cost of coverage in the year the employee became disabled, the employee is taxed on the benefits that are attributable to employer contributions (including contributions made by means of salary reduction under a cafeteria plan). The actual method of allocating employer contributions varies, depending on whether the plan is insured or uninsured and, if insured, whether individual or group policies are used to fund the disability income benefits. (See Qs 10:50 *et seq.*)

Q 10:49   What if the employer contributes a different amount for each class of employees under the disability income plan?

If the ratio of employer to employee contributions differs by class of employees (for example, salaried and hourly), the employer must determine the ratio of employer to employee contributions for the employee class to which the recipient belongs. [Treas. Reg. § 1.105-1(c)(2)]

In a private letter ruling, the IRS considered an employer LTD plan that offered two options. Option A provided a benefit of 40 percent of earnings and was fully employer-paid. Option B provided a benefit of 60 percent of earnings, with the employer paying the cost for 40 percent of earnings, and the employees electing option B paying the cost for 20 percent of earnings. The IRS ruled that the Option A participants and Option B participants were separate classes. Therefore, the Option A benefits were fully taxable, and the Option B benefits were taxable in part based on the ratio of employer and employee contributions under option B. [Priv. Ltr. Rul. 9709051]

Q 10:50   What if the plan contains other types of benefits besides disability income benefits?

If the disability income benefits are part of a larger plan providing multiple benefits and the contributions of the employer and employees for the disability income coverage are not separately identified, the employer must determine the employer-provided portion of each disability income benefit payment based on the respective employer and employee contributions to the overall plan. [Treas. Reg. § 1.105-1(c)(3)]

Q 10:51   How is the taxable amount determined if a group insurance policy is used to fund the disability income plan?

If the disability income benefits are funded using a group insurance policy, the determination of what portion of each disability income payment is deemed attributable to employer contributions, and thus taxable to the employee, is quite complex. The premium cost attributable to an individual employee under a group insurance policy is not readily determinable. Once the employee class is determined, if required (see Q 10:49), the employer calculates the income amount of the payment by multiplying the total payment by a fraction whose numerator is the net employer-paid premiums for the appropriate *experience period* and whose denominator is the total net premiums for the appropriate experience period.

Net premiums are premiums paid, less policy dividends and experience-rating credits. [Treas. Reg. § 1.105-1(d)(2)]

Experience period. If the net premiums for three or more prior policy years are known at the beginning of the calendar year, the three prior years are the appropriate experience period (referred to as the three-year look-back period). If the three prior policy years' net premiums are not known at the beginning of the calendar year, two years' net premiums may be used. If two years' net premiums are not known, one year's net premiums may be used. If not even one prior policy year's net premiums are known, the computation may be made by using either:

1. A reasonable estimate of the net premiums for the first policy year or
2. The net premiums for the current policy year, if they are ascertained during the calendar year.

Example. An employer adopts a new contributory disability income plan on January 1, 2010, and funds the plan with an experience-rated group insurance policy. The policy year is the same as the calendar year. For 2010, the employer will not know the net premiums for the year, because the policy dividend for the year will not be determined until some time in 2011. Thus, the employer must make a reasonable estimate of the net premiums for that year to determine the disability income amounts attributable to employer contributions for 2010. As of January 1, 2011, the net premiums for the year 2010 still will not be known; therefore, the employer may continue to use a reasonable estimate of the net premiums for the year 2010 to determine the taxable benefits for 2011. Alternatively, the employer may wait until the insurer declares the 2010 policy year dividend and use the actual net premiums for 2010 to determine the portion of 2011 disability income payments attributable to employer contributions. [Treas. Reg. § 1.105-1(d)(2)]

Q 10:52   How is the taxable amount determined if the disability income plan is self-insured?

If the disability income plan is self-insured, the determination of what portion of each disability income payment is deemed attributable to employer contributions, and thus taxable to the employee, is similar to that for plans funded with group insurance (see Q 10:51). A ratio of employer contributions to all contributions is applied to the payment, using the appropriate employee class (see Q 10:49) and experience period. [Treas. Reg. § 1.105-1(e)]

Experience period. If the plan has been in effect for at least three years before the calendar year, the employer contributions and total contributions for those three years are used for the allocation. If the plan has existed for only two prior years or one prior year, those periods are used. If the uninsured plan has not been in effect for one full year at the beginning of the calendar year, the determination of the taxable amount may be made on the basis of the portion of the year preceding the determination, or the determination may be made periodically (such as monthly or quarterly) and used for the succeeding period. [Treas. Reg. § 1.105-1(e)]

Example. Harry's employer adopts a new contributory plan in 2010. Harry receives disability income benefits early in 2011 and then leaves his job on April 15, 2011. His employer may determine the taxable portion of Harry's benefits based on contributions during the period January 1 to April 15, 2011, on contributions for the month of March 2011, or on contributions for the first quarter of 2011.

Q 10:53   How is the taxable amount determined if individual insurance policies are used to fund a disability income plan?

If individual insurance policies are used to fund a disability income plan, the portion of each disability income payment deemed attributable to employer contributions, and thus taxable to the employee, is determined by multiplying the total payment by a fraction whose numerator is the employer-paid premiums under the individual policy for the current policy year and whose denominator is the total premiums (employer- and employee-paid) under the individual policy for the current policy year. The calculation may be expressed by the following formula:

$$\text{Taxable amount} = \frac{\text{payment} \times \text{employer-paid premiums}}{\text{all premiums}}$$

[Treas. Reg. § 1.105-1(d)(1)]

Q 10:54   How is the taxable amount of disability income payments determined if each employee is given the option of contributing to the disability income coverage on a pretax salary reduction basis or on an after-tax basis?

The IRS has ruled that premium payments made by an employer will be treated as employee contributions if the amount of the payments is included in the employee's taxable wages for the year. In the ruling, an employer paid the entire premium for group LTD insurance coverage for its employees and did not include the cost of the coverage in an employee's gross income (i.e., the premiums were paid on a pretax basis). The employer amended the plan to allow employees to make an irrevocable election at the beginning of each plan year to either continue to have the employer pay the premiums on a pretax basis or to have the employer pay the premiums on an after-tax basis by including the cost of the coverage in taxable wages for the year. For an employee who elects after-tax treatment, the employer allocates a portion of the annual group premium to the employee and includes that amount in the employee's gross income for the year.

The IRS ruled that employees whose LTD premiums are paid by the employer but included in taxable wages are to be treated as having paid for the LTD coverage. Therefore, benefit payments to those employees are excludable from income. However, employees who elect to have the employer's premiums excluded from gross income are treated as having employer-paid coverage. Therefore, benefits paid to those employees are taxable. In either case, the premiums are treated as either fully paid by the employer or the employee. Therefore, the rules for plans financed by both the employer and the employee do not apply. [Rev. Rul. 2004-55, 2004-34 I.R.B. 343]

Note. For this purpose, disability premiums paid on a pretax basis through a cafeteria plan are treated as *employer-paid premiums*.

Q 10:55   Are taxable disability income benefits subject to mandatory wage withholding?

Whether mandatory withholding (that is, wage payroll withholding required by the Code) applies depends on who is paying the benefits.

Employer payments. Withholding is mandatory if the employer—or an agent of the employer—makes the payments. [I.R.C. §§ 3401, 3402; Treas. Reg. § 31.3401(a)-1(b)(8)] This means that if, for example, the employer maintains a self-insured plan and retains an insurance company or other claims administrator to handle claims payments, the payments will be subject to mandatory wage withholding. The IRS has indicated that withholding is not mandatory if the employer is handling the disability income payments but is acting on behalf of a third-party payer, that is, a trust that has assumed the insurance risk. [Priv. Ltr. Rul. 8532035]

Third-party payer. Withholding is not required if the payments are made by an insurer under an insured plan or by a trust that has assumed the insurance risk for payment of the benefits. [I.R.C. § 3402(o); Treas. Reg. § 31.3402(o)-3]

Q 10:56   Can the employee make a third-party payer withhold?

Yes. An employee who wants to have federal income tax withheld from his or her disability income payments may generally do so by making a request of the payer on IRS Form W-4S or a form of the payer identical to the IRS form, unless the plan is exempted (see Q 10:57) or is governed by a contrary provision in a collective bargaining agreement (see Q 10:60). This is called voluntary withholding, because the Code does not require it absent a request from the employee. This rule applies to temporary disability or sick pay. [I.R.C. §§ 3402(o)(1)(C), 3402(o)(2)(C), 3402(o)(3), 3402(o)(4)]

The amount requested to be withheld must generally be a whole-dollar amount and at least $20 on a weekly basis. If a payment covers only part of a week, the amount to be withheld is prorated.

Example. The amount to be withheld is $20 per week. A final payment upon the employee's return to work consists of 40 percent of a workweek (that is, two nonworking days in a five-day workweek). The amount to be withheld from the final payment is $8.

The third-party payer may permit the employee to elect withholding on a percentage basis (for example, 20 percent) rather than on a whole-dollar-amount basis. The percentage elected must be at least 10 percent.

If the withholding amount elected would reduce the net payment to the employee to below $10, no income tax withholding applies. [I.R.C. § 3402(o)(3); Treas. Reg. §§ 31.3402(o)-3(a), 31.3402(o)-3(b), 31.3402(o)-3(c)]

Q 10:57   Are all recipients of long-term disability income benefits entitled to demand that a third-party payer withhold?

No. The voluntary withholding provision applies to "sick pay" or "temporary" benefits. [I.R.C. §§ 3402(o)(1)(C), 3402(o)(2)(C)] The regulations interpret this exception as exempting the plan from all voluntary withholding if all amounts paid under the plan are paid to individuals who are totally and permanently disabled. The totally and permanently disabled standard requires that the employee be unable to engage in any substantial gainful activity because of a medically determinable physical or mental impairment that either (1) can be expected to result in death or (2) has lasted or can be expected to last for a continuous period of at least 12 months. [Treas. Reg. § 31.3402(o)-3(h)(1)(i)]

Practice Pointer. Many total and permanent disability plans have definitions of disability that are somewhat more liberal than the tax law definition. Therefore, this exemption from the application of the voluntary withholding requirements has quite limited application.

Q 10:58   When does a valid request for voluntary withholding by a third-party payer take effect?

The third-party payer must honor the request for all disability income payments made more than seven days after it receives the request. The payer may choose to honor the request sooner. [Treas. Reg. § 31.3402(o)-3(d)]

Q 10:59   May an employee change or withdraw a voluntary withholding request?

Yes. The employee may change or terminate the request for voluntary withholding at any time. The third-party payer must honor a written request to change or terminate voluntary withholding by the eighth day after receipt. [Treas. Reg. §§ 31.3402(o)-3(d), 31.3402(o)-3(e)]

Q 10:60   Can a collective bargaining agreement override the voluntary withholding rules?

Yes. If third-party payer disability income is paid pursuant to a collective bargaining agreement, and the agreement provides for withholding in specified amounts, the agreement will determine the amount to be withheld, and individual elections will not be valid. For this exception to apply, the payer must be furnished with payees' Social Security numbers and sufficient information for it to determine the amount to be withheld. The payer, however, does not withhold from employees who have filed withholding exemption statements with the employer to the effect that they had no income tax liability in the prior year and expect to incur no income tax liability in the current year. [I.R.C. § 3402(o)(5); Treas. Reg. § 31.3402(o)-3(i)]

Q 10:61   Are taxable disability income payments subject to Social Security withholding?

Some, but not all, of the payments are taxable. Disability income payments attributable to employer contributions or payments (including salary reduction contributions made under a cafeteria plan) are subject to FICA withholding only for benefits paid in the month of disability or in the first six months following the month of disability. [I.R.C. § 3121(a)(4)]

Q 10:62   Who is responsible for Social Security withholding?

The employer is responsible for Social Security withholding. However, if benefits are paid by a third-party payer, the third-party payer is treated as the "employer" and is liable for the employer's share of the FICA tax and for withholding the employee's share of the FICA tax. The third-party payer can avoid liability for the employer's share of the tax—and shift liability to the employer—provided that it:

1. Withholds the employee's portion of the FICA tax;
2. Deposits the withheld tax by the required due date; and
3. Lets the employer know, on or before the due date of the employer deposit, the amount of taxable payments made on which it has withheld and deposited FICA tax.

Upon receiving such a notification from the third-party payer, the employer is then obliged to pay the employer's share of the FICA tax. [I.R.C. § 3121(a)(4); Treas. Reg. § 31.3121(a)(2)-2]

Q 10:63   How are disability income payments required to be reported?

The third-party payer must, by January 15 of the year following the payments, provide the employer with a written statement containing the following information:

1. The payee's name and, if there is voluntary withholding (see Qs 10:58–10:62), the payee's Social Security number;
2. The total amount of sick pay paid to the payee; and
3. The total amount, if any, withheld.

[Treas. Reg. § 31.6051-3]

An employer receiving a third-party payer statement must furnish the information to the IRS and to the payee. The report must include a breakdown of the total payment into the portion, if any, attributable to employee contributions (and therefore nontaxable) and the taxable portion (see Qs 10:46–10:53). The employer may use the same Form W-2 that it uses for regular wages, or it may provide a separate Form W-2 for the disability income payments. [Treas. Reg. § 31.6051-3]

Alternatively, the third-party payer and the employer may enter into an agency agreement whereby the third-party payer files the Form W-2 in lieu of the employer. [Treas. Reg. § 31.6051-3]

Tax Treatment of Self-Employed Persons and Subchapter S Corporation Shareholder-Employees

Q 10:64   What is the income tax treatment of insurance premiums paid by a sole proprietor for disability income insurance coverage?

It has been held that premiums paid for disability income insurance coverage by a sole proprietor are a personal expense and thus not deductible. [I.R.C. § 262; Rev. Rul. 58-90, 1958-1 C.B. 8; Marvin v. Blaess, 28 T.C. 710 (1957)]

Q 10:65   What is the income tax treatment of disability income benefits received by a sole proprietor under an insured plan maintained by the sole proprietorship?

The benefits received from an insured disability income benefit plan are excludable from gross income under Code Section 104(a)(3). [Rev. Rul. 58-90, 1958-1 C.B. 88]

Q 10:66   What is the income tax treatment of disability income benefits received by a sole proprietor under a self-insured plan maintained by the sole proprietorship?

Benefits paid under an accident or health plan—or an arrangement having the effect of an accident or health plan, including a disability income plan—to an individual who is self-employed in the business with respect to which the plan is established are not treated as received through accident and health insurance for purposes of Code Sections 104(a)(3) and 105.

Thus, the exclusion under Code Section 104(a)(3) is not applicable, and the benefits are not excludable from the sole proprietor's gross income. In order to qualify for exclusion of the payments from income, the arrangement must be insurance (e.g., there must be adequate risk shifting) and not merely a reimbursement arrangement. [I.R.C. § 104(a)(3), as amended by HIPAA § 3111(b); Treas. Reg. § 1.105(b)]

Q 10:67   What is the income tax treatment of insurance premiums paid by a partnership for disability income insurance coverage of its partners?

Based on the position the IRS has taken concerning medical insurance premiums (see chapter 3), it appears that if the premium payments are made without regard to partnership income, the premium payments will be treated as guaranteed payments by the partnership under Code Section 707(c), deductible by the partnership on the partnership tax return and includable in each partner's income.

Since the partners are not employees, the guaranteed payments are not subject to withholding at source by the partnership. [Treas. Reg. § 1.707-1(c)]

Alternatively, the partnership may choose to account for the payment of the disability insurance premiums as a reduction in distributions to the partners. In such event, the premiums are not deductible by the partnership, and distributable shares of partnership income and deductions and other items are not affected by payment of the premiums. [Rev. Rul. 91-26, 1991-1 C.B. 184]

Q 10:68 What is the income tax treatment of disability income benefits received by a partner from an insured disability income plan maintained by the partnership?

The disability income benefits are excludable from gross income under Code Section 104(a)(3).

Q 10:69 What is the income tax treatment of disability income benefits received by a partner under a self-insured disability income plan maintained by the partnership?

There is no clear and direct authority as to how a partnership's self-insured disability income benefit plan will be treated for income tax purposes. Based on the IRS position in Revenue Ruling 91-26 (see Q 10:67), it appears possible that the IRS would apply similar rules to a self-insured plan. Thus, if the disability income payments were payable without regard to partnership income, the payments presumably would be viewed as guaranteed payments deductible at the partnership level and includable in the income of the partner receiving the disability income benefits.

Alternatively, the partnership presumably could choose to account for the disability income payments to a partner as a reduction in distributions to the partner that (1) is not deductible by the partnership and (2) does not affect distributive shares of partnership income and deductions and other items. [Rev. Rul. 91-26, 1991-1 C.B. 184]

Note. It appears that the partnership agreement should be able to provide for allocating the disability payments ratably among all the partners in accordance with their partnership shares (see chapter 3).

The disability income benefits received by a partner will be excluded from income provided the amounts are received under an agreement having the effect of accident or health insurance. (See Q 10:66.)

Q 10:70   What is the income tax treatment of insurance premiums paid by a Subchapter S corporation for insured disability income coverage maintained for shareholder-employees of the corporation and the benefits received by the shareholder-employees?

If the shareholder-employee of the Subchapter S corporation is not a more-than-2-percent shareholder, the premiums paid by the employer for services as an employee normally will be excludable from the shareholder-employee's income under Code Section 106, and the disability income insurance benefits will be taxable to the extent they are attributable to employer contributions.

However, if the shareholder-employee is a more-than-2-percent shareholder of the Subchapter S corporation, the shareholder-employee is treated as a partner in a partnership. [I.R.C. § 1373]

Based on Revenue Ruling 91-26 (1991-1 C.B. 184), the premiums will be deductible by the Subchapter S corporation as a business expense and that the more-than-2-percent shareholder-employee must include the premiums paid for the coverage in gross income.

Q 10:71   What is the income tax treatment of disability income benefits received by shareholder-employees of a Subchapter S corporation under an insured disability income plan maintained by the corporation?

Based on Revenue Ruling 91-26 (1991-1 C.B. 184), any benefits received under insured disability income coverage maintained by a Subchapter S corporation will be exempt from the income of the more-than-2-percent shareholders under Code Section 104(a)(3).

Q 10:72   What is the income tax treatment of disability income benefits received by a shareholder-employee of a Subchapter S corporation from self-insured disability income coverage maintained by the corporation?

There is no direct authority on the question. If the shareholder-employee is not a more-than-2-percent shareholder, disability income benefits should be subject to tax under Code Section 105(a). If the shareholder-employee is a more-than-2-percent shareholder, based on Revenue Ruling 91-26 (1991-1 C.B. 184), the disability income payments are deductible by the Subchapter S corporation and includable in the gross income of the shareholder-employee receiving the benefits. The Section 104(a)(3) exclusion from income applies, provided the amounts are received under an arrangement having the effect of accident and health insurance (see Q 10:66).

Chapter 11

Group Term Life Insurance Plans

Group term life insurance plans continue to be a highly valued part of employee benefit programs. Although group term life insurance coverage may be taxable to the employee to some extent, it is entitled to special treatment under Section 79 of the Internal Revenue Code (Code) if the plan conforms to the requirements of that section. This chapter discusses the ground rules and the federal income, estate, and gift tax implications of some of the more common scenarios that arise in the day-to-day administration of group term life insurance plans.

Basic Concepts

Q 11:1   What is a group term life insurance plan?

A *group term life insurance plan* is an insurance arrangement whereby an employer provides term life insurance coverage to a class of employees (the group).

Q 11:2   What is term life insurance for Code Section 79 purposes?

Life insurance is not group term life insurance for purposes of Code Section 79 unless it meets the following conditions:

1. It provides a general death benefit that is excludable from gross income under Code Section 101(a).
2. It is provided to a group of employees.
3. It is provided under a policy carried directly or indirectly by the employer in which the amount of insurance provided to each employee is computed using a formula that precludes individual selection. This formula must be based on factors such as age, years of service, compensation, or position.

The third condition may be satisfied even if the amount of insurance provided is determined under a limited number of alternative schedules that are based on the amount each employee elects to contribute. However, the amount of insurance provided under each schedule must be computed under a formula that precludes individual selection. [Treas. Reg. § 1.79-1(a)]

Q 11:3   May group term life insurance be combined with other benefits?

Group life insurance may not be combined with other benefits unless the policy or the employer designates in writing the part of the death benefit provided to each employee that is group term life insurance, and the part of the death benefit that is provided to an employee and designated as the group term life insurance benefit for any policy year is not less than the difference between the total death benefit provided under the policy and the employee's deemed death benefit at the end of the policy year. [Treas. Reg. § 1.79-1(b)]

Q 11:4   Are employer-provided group term life insurance plans eligible for favorable tax treatment?

Yes. An employer generally may deduct its contribution to a group term life insurance plan. In addition, if a plan meets the definition of group term life insurance contained in Code Section 79 and the regulations issued under that Code section (see Q 11:5), the cost of up to $50,000 of employer-provided coverage is excludable from an employee's income. The cost of coverage in excess of $50,000 is treated as income to the employee. The cost of the excess coverage is determined according to a Premium Table (referred to as "Table I") promulgated by the Internal Revenue Service (IRS) (see Qs 11:80–11:81).

If the plan discriminates in favor of any key employee (see Q 11:42), all key employees lose the favorable tax treatment granted under Code Section 79. Key employees under a discriminatory group term life insurance plan are denied the benefit of the $50,000 exclusion and are taxed on all coverage on the basis of cost determined under Table I in the Treasury regulations (see Q 11:81) or actual cost, whichever is higher. [I.R.C. § 79(d)(1)] In addition, certain "grandfathered" employees (see Q 11:49) who retire under a discriminatory plan lose the benefit of a complete exemption from tax on their group term life insurance coverage. (The applicable discrimination rules are discussed in Qs 11:41–11:49, and the tax consequences of a discriminatory plan are discussed in Qs 11:85–11:87.)

Q 11:5   How does an employer-provided group term life insurance plan qualify for favorable tax treatment under Code Section 79?

To qualify for favorable tax treatment under Code Section 79, the employer-provided group term life insurance coverage for employees must meet each of the following four conditions:

1. The coverage must provide a general death benefit that is fully excludable from income in the hands of the beneficiary under Code Section 101(a) (see Qs 11:14–11:15);

2. The coverage must be provided to a group of employees (see Qs 11:16–11:25);

3. The coverage must be provided under a policy that is "carried directly or indirectly by the employer" (see Qs 11:26–11:38); and

4. The amount of coverage provided to each employee must be computed under a formula that precludes individual selection (see Qs 11:39–11:40).

Q 11:6   Does Code Section 79 apply only to term life insurance policies?

Generally, Code Section 79 does not apply to a policy containing a permanent value. That is, the policy may not have a cash value, paid-up value, or other value extending beyond one year. However, under limited circumstances, a policy containing a permanent benefit may qualify under Code Section 79 if an allocation that meets IRS requirements is made between the term and permanent elements and the value of the permanent benefit is taken into account in determining the employee's taxable income (see Qs 11:32–11:33).

Q 11:7   Can an employer provide group term life insurance coverage for its employees under Code Section 79 by purchasing a group policy from its wholly owned life insurance subsidiary?

Yes. The IRS has ruled that where a parent corporation carries insurance on its employees' lives under a group term life insurance policy purchased from a wholly owned life insurance subsidiary, the coverage qualifies as group term life insurance for Section 79 purposes, and the premiums are deductible by the parent to the extent they constitute reasonable compensation for services rendered. [Rev. Rul. 92-93, 1992-2 C.B. 45]

Note. The same result should apply in other affiliated corporation situations, such as where a parent life insurance company insures the employees of a wholly owned subsidiary or where a brother-sister corporate relationship exists between the insurer and the employer whose employees are insured. Revenue Ruling 92-93 also indicates that the same favorable treatment is available where a life insurance company insures its own employees.

Caution. An employer considering insuring its Section 79 group term life insurance plan through a "captive" life insurance affiliate should carefully consider the possible application of the prohibited transaction rules of the Employee Retirement Income Security Act of 1974 (ERISA). (See chapter 2.) The DOL has granted a class exemption from the prohibited transaction rules that allows an employer to insure its employee benefit plan risks through an affiliated insurer on a direct basis provided certain conditions are met. [PTE 79-41] However, one condition is that no more than 50 percent of the insurer's business can be "related" to the employer. In addition, reinsurance transactions, in which a company uses a captive insurer to reinsure life insurance benefits, are not covered by the class exemption. Therefore, an employer must obtain an individual prohibited transaction exemption (PTE). In the past, the DOL did not grant such exemptions. In 2000, however, the IRS granted the first exemption in a captive reinsurance situation. Since that time the DOL has granted additional exemptions under a procedure, commonly known as "EXPRO," for expediting the processing of exemption requests that are substantially similar to previously granted exemptions. [PTE 96-62]

Q 11:8   Are spouses and dependents insured under a Section 79 group term life insurance plan?

No. Code Section 79 does not apply to coverage of spouses and dependents under an employer-provided group term life insurance plan. Code Section 79 applies only to coverage of employees. [Treas. Reg. § 1.79-3(f)(2)] (The definition of *employee* for this purpose is discussed in Qs 11:16–11:19. See chapter 12 for a discussion of dependent life insurance and chapter 7 for a discussion of dependent life insurance in cafeteria plans.)

Q 11:9   Can group term life insurance provided under a tax-qualified retirement plan qualify for Section 79 treatment?

No. The Section 79 exemption for the first $50,000 of coverage does not apply to group term life insurance provided under a tax-qualified retirement plan. The imputed cost of group term life insurance provided under a tax qualified retirement plan may be determined in one of two ways:

1. By using an IRS table that has rates substantially in excess of the rates used under Code Section 79; or

2. By using the insurance company's published rates for individual one-year term policies offered to all standard risks.

[I.R.C. §§ 79(b)(3), 72(m)(3)]

Note. In the past, the IRS specified that the rates to be used in determining the imputed cost of group term life insurance were the PS 58 rates found in Revenue Ruling 55-747, 1955-2 C.B. 228. However, under current rules (with a limited exception for arrangements entered into before January 28, 2002, that require use of the PS 58 rates), the cost is determined under a new table (Table 2001), with materially lower premium rates. [Notice 2002-8, 2002-4 I.R.B. 398] (For further details, see chapter 12.)

Q 11:10   Can state law affect the coverage eligible for special treatment under Code Section 79?

Yes. Code Section 79 does not apply to amounts of group term life insurance in excess of the limits imposed under applicable state law. [Treas. Reg. § 1.79-1(e)]

When Code Section 79 first became law in 1964, a number of states had laws that substantially limited the amount of group term life insurance that an employer could provide to its employees under policies within those states' jurisdictions. However, states have eliminated these limits.

Q 11:11   Is an employer-provided group term life insurance plan subject to ERISA?

Yes. (See chapter 2 for a discussion of ERISA.) It is also simultaneously subject to state insurance laws to the extent not preempted by ERISA (see Qs 11:57–11:58).

Q 11:12   Does the Age Discrimination in Employment Act of 1967 apply to employer-provided group term life insurance?

Yes. The Age Discrimination in Employment Act of 1967 (ADEA) [Pub. L. No. 90-202, 81 Stat. 602] prohibits discrimination because of age in all compensation, terms, conditions, and privileges of employment, including all employee benefits. [29 U.S.C. § 630(l)] (For further details, see Qs 11:51–11:55 and chapter 17.)

Q 11:13   What are the reporting and disclosure requirements for group term life insurance?

The Code technically requires reporting by certain fringe benefit plans, including group term life insurance plans. However, the IRS has suspended the filing requirement for group term life insurance plans until further notice. [Notice 90-24, 1990-1 C.B. 335]

The employer must give a summary plan description (SPD) to each participant within 120 days after the plan is established. A new employee must receive the SPD within 90 days after becoming a participant. A copy of the SPD must be filed with the DOL within 120 days after the plan is established. [I.R.C. § 6039D; ERISA § 104(b)(1); 29 C.F.R. § 2520.104b-2(a)(3)]

General Death Benefit Requirement

Q 11:14   What type of benefit must a plan offer to qualify as group term life insurance under Code Section 79?

The first of the four requirements listed in Q 11:5 that must be satisfied in order for insurance to be characterized as group term life insurance under Code Section 79 is that the group term life insurance plan must offer a "general death benefit." This is a benefit that is payable upon death without any special conditions. A life insurance benefit under a travel accident policy or an accidental death double indemnity rider does not qualify as group term life insurance under Code Section 79, because the death benefit is not a general death benefit; however, travel accident insurance and accidental death benefits receive favorable tax treatment under other Code provisions. (See chapter 12 for a discussion of these and other death benefits.)

Q 11:15   What is a survivor monthly income benefit, and can it qualify as a general death benefit?

The typical survivor income group term life insurance benefit is payable in the form of a monthly income benefit to a qualified survivor or survivors (e.g., spouse or children). It is payable when the employee dies only if there is a qualified survivor living at the time of the employee's death. Factors such as a qualified survivor's death, a spouse's remarriage, or a child's attainment of a specified age (e.g., 21) may vary the term (i.e., the duration) or the amount of the survivor income benefit, or both.

The Treasury regulations under Code Section 79 expressly recognize that a survivor income group life insurance benefit qualifies as life insurance. [Treas. Reg. § 1.79-3(b); Ltr. Rul. 8509046; Estate of J. Smead, 78 T.C. 43 (1982); Estate of John Connelly, Sr. v. United States, 551 F.2d 545 (3d Cir. 1977)] One federal district court, in deciding that an uninsured survivor income benefit plan was not life insurance for tax purposes, suggested as one ground for disallowance that treatment as life insurance depends on the existence of a definite death benefit that is payable in any event upon the employee's death. [Davis v. United States, 323 F. Supp. 858 (W.D. W. Va. 1971)] The *Davis* case has not been followed generally or in the authorities cited above, and it does not appear to be a correct interpretation of the law on this point. As long as the survivor income group term life insurance policy qualifies as life insurance under Code Section 7702, it should be treated as group term life insurance for purposes of Code Section 79.

"Group of Employees" Requirement

Q 11:16   What types of employees may a Section 79 group term life insurance plan cover?

The second of the four requirements listed in Q 11:5 that must be satisfied for insurance to be characterized as group term life insurance under Code Section 79 is that coverage must be provided to a group of employees. The "group of employees" required by Code Section 79 consists of either (1) all employees of the employer or (2) fewer than all the employees if membership in the group is determined solely on the basis of age, marital status, or factors related to employment, such as membership in a union, duties performed, compensation received, and length of service.

For Section 79 purposes, a requirement of participation in the employer's pension, profit sharing, or accident and health plan is considered to be a "factor related to employment," even if employee contributions to the plan are required. Ownership of stock is not a factor related to employment; however, a requirement of participation in the employer's stock bonus plan may be a factor related to employment. [Treas. Reg. § 1.79-0]

Q 11:17   Who is an "employee" under a Section 79 group term life insurance plan?

The Section 79 definition of *employee* includes the following:

- Common-law employees
- Full-time life insurance salespersons
- Persons who formerly performed services as employees, such as retired employees

[Treas. Reg. § 1.79-0]

Q 11:18   Are corporate directors and independent contractors employees under Code Section 79?

No. These two classes of individuals are not employees under Code Section 79. Accordingly, coverage provided to independent contractors is not eligible for the $50,000 exclusion granted under Code Section 79. Similarly, coverage provided to corporate directors in their capacity as such also is not eligible, because corporate directors are independent contractors rather than employees. [Enright v. Commissioner, 56 T.C. 1261 (1971)]

Q 11:19   Does stock ownership affect characterization as an employee?

No. Employees who are also shareholders (other than certain S corporation shareholders) may generally be part of a group of employees for Section 79 purposes.

Q 11:20   Would an S corporation shareholder or a partner be treated as an eligible employee?

No. Generally such an individual cannot be an eligible employee. A partner is never eligible as an employee under Code Section 79. A more-than-2-percent direct or indirect shareholder in an S corporation is treated as a partner in a partnership and therefore is not eligible for tax-favored treatment under Code Section 79 either. [I.R.C. § 1372; Treas. Reg. § 1.79-0]

Q 11:21   Does coverage for dependents qualify for favorable tax treatment under Code Section 79?

No. Code Section 79 governs only group term life insurance on the life of the employee. [Treas. Reg. § 1.79-3(f)(2)] (See chapter 12 for a discussion of dependent life insurance.)

Q 11:22   Is there a minimum number of employees an employer-provided group term life insurance plan must cover in order to qualify under Code Section 79?

Yes. Generally, a group term life insurance plan cannot qualify for favorable tax treatment under Code Section 79 unless, at some time during the calendar year, coverage is provided to at least ten full-time employees who are members of the group of employees. All life insurance provided under policies carried directly or indirectly by the employer is taken into account in determining whether the test is met. [Treas. Reg. § 1.79-1(c)(1)]

However, there are two exceptions—one for single-employer plans and one for multiemployer union-type plans. For exceptions to the ten-employee minimum, see Qs 11:23–11:25.

Q 11:23   If a single-employer plan fails the minimum size requirement, can it still qualify under Code Section 79?

A single-employer life insurance plan covering fewer than ten full-time employees may qualify as group term life insurance under Code Section 79 provided that the following requirements are met:

1. The coverage is provided to all full-time employees or, if evidence of insurability affects eligibility, to all full-time employees who provide evidence of insurability satisfactory to the insurer;

2. The amount of insurance provided is computed either as a uniform percentage of compensation or on the basis of coverage brackets established by the insurer; and

3. The required evidence of insurability that affects an employee's eligibility for, or amount of, insurance is limited to a medical questionnaire completed by the employee and does not include a physical examination.

When computing the amount of insurance provided, the amount treated as provided may be reduced in the case of employees who do not provide evidence of insurability satisfactory to the insurer. [Treas. Reg. § 1.79-1(c)(2)]

Coverage brackets. If the amount of insurance coverage under a plan with fewer than ten employees is available in different amounts rather than in a single, uniform amount or single, uniform percentage of compensation, then the insurance must meet the following limitations in order to qualify under Code Section 79:

1. Generally, no coverage bracket may exceed 2 times the next lower bracket, and the lowest bracket must be at least 10 percent of the highest bracket; and

2. The insurer may establish a separate schedule of coverage brackets for employees who are over age 65, but

   (a) No bracket in the over-65 schedule may exceed 2 times the next lower bracket, and

   (b) The lowest bracket in the over-65 schedule must be at least 10 percent of the highest bracket in the under-65 schedule.

[Treas. Reg. § 1.79-1(c)(2)]

The IRS will look at substance, not just form, in considering whether this test is met. For example, a plan covering fewer than ten full-time employees met the coverage bracket requirements of the regulations on its face. But it was held not qualified as a Section 79 plan because, although it contained three coverage brackets, no employee in fact had ever been covered under the middle bracket. Treating the plan as if it had only two coverage brackets, the IRS concluded that the plan failed because the top bracket was more than 2 times the next bracket (the lowest bracket). [Rev. Rul. 80-229, 1980-2 C.B. 133]

Insurability. The IRS also ruled that a plan covering fewer than ten full-time employees failed to qualify as a Code Section 79 plan because, although the insurer determined eligibility for coverage on the basis of a medical question-naire only, the premium rate was three times the standard premium rate unless the insured employee agreed to furnish additional medical information or to undergo a medical examination. [Rev. Rul. 75-528, 1975-2 C.B. 35]

Q 11:24   **If a multiemployer plan fails the minimum size requirement, can it still qualify for Section 79 treatment?**

The second exception to the general rule that a plan subject to Code Section 79 must cover ten or more full-time employees applies if the following requirements are met:

1. The insurance is provided under a common plan to the employees of two or more unrelated employers;

2. The insurance is restricted to, but mandatory for, all employees of the employer who belong to or are represented by an organization (such as a

union) that carries on substantial activities in addition to obtaining insurance; and

3. Evidence of insurability does not affect an employee's eligibility for insurance or the amount of insurance.

[Treas. Reg. § 1.79-1(c)(3)]

Q 11:25   Can any employees be excluded when applying either of the two exceptions to the minimum size rules?

Yes. Employees need not be taken into account when applying the minimum size rules (for example, the rule that "all" employees must be covered) if:

1. They are ineligible for insurance under the terms of the policy because they have not been employed for a waiting period, not to exceed six months, specified in the policy;

2. They are part-time employees, that is, employees whose customary employment is for not more than 20 hours in any week or five months in any calendar year; or

3. They have reached the age of 65.

[Treas. Reg. § 1.79-1(c)(4)]

> **Note.** Since the ADEA generally applies to employers with 20 or more employees, an employer with fewer than 10 employees may exclude employees age 65 or older without violating the ADEA. However, in some situations state age discrimination laws may be applicable unless preempted by ERISA (see Qs 11:57–11:58).

Policy Carried Directly or Indirectly by the Employer

Q 11:26   What is a "policy" under Code Section 79?

The third of the four requirements listed in Q 11:5 that must be satisfied in order for insurance to be characterized as group term life insurance under Code Section 79 is that the policy be "carried directly or indirectly by the employer." For this purpose, a "policy" normally is a single group life insurance contract under which a life insurance company provides group term life insurance coverage to employees of the employer.

Q 11:27   Must two or more policies issued by one insurer be treated as one policy for Section 79 qualification purposes?

Yes. The general rule is that two or more insurance policies or obligations of the same insurer (or its affiliate, such as a subsidiary) must be aggregated and treated as a single insurance policy for Section 79 purposes if they are sold in conjunction. Obligations that are offered or made available to a group of employees are considered sold in conjunction if they are offered or made available because of the employment relationship. [Treas. Reg. § 1.79-0]

In determining whether the obligations are sold in conjunction, neither the actuarial sufficiency of the premium charged for each obligation nor the facts that the obligations (1) are in separate documents; (2) receive separate state insurance department approval; or (3) are independent of one another are taken into account. A group of individual contracts under which life insurance is provided to a group of employees may be a single policy. Also, two benefits provided to a group of employees—one term life insurance and the other a permanent benefit—may be considered a single policy, even if one of the benefits is provided only to employees who decline the other benefit. [Treas. Reg. § 1.79-0]

Q 11:28 May an employer elect to treat two or more term policies issued by the same insurer (or its affiliate) as separate policies?

Yes. An employer may elect to treat two or more policies of the same insurer (or its affiliate) that provide no permanent benefits as separate policies if the premiums are properly allocated among such policies. [Treas. Reg. § 1.79-0]

Q 11:29 Why would an employer want to treat two or more group term obligations as separate policies?

Such an election may be desirable if an employer that provides basic group term life insurance coverage to employees also offers employee-pay-all coverage under a separate supplemental group term life insurance policy with the same insurer.

Electing to treat the supplemental policy as a separate policy may enable the employer to treat the supplemental policy as a policy that it does not carry directly or indirectly (see Q 11:34), thus saving employees from possible imputed income on such coverage. However, if the employer provides basic insurance that is noncontributory, the employer may prefer not to elect to treat the basic and supplemental policies as separate policies, because employee contributions offset the imputed income attributable to amounts of coverage in excess of $50,000. [I.R.C. § 79(a)(2)]

Practice Pointer. In order to treat the policies as separate, the employer, aided by the insurer, must be able to demonstrate that the basic and supplemental policies are truly separate and freestanding and that the premiums are calculated independently and are not interdependent. [Priv. Ltr. Rul. 8638050, 8816031] Significantly, the IRS has, on one occasion, permitted an employer to elect to treat a single insurance policy as three separate policies under Code Section 79. Where an employer provided a basic, employer-provided group term life insurance benefit subject to Code Section 79 and two supplemental, employee-pay-all coverages (one for smokers and a second for nonsmokers), the employer was permitted to treat the two supplemental coverages as separate policies where no part of the supplemental programs was paid for by the employer, each rate was self-supporting and involved no cross-subsidization, and the supplemental coverages, when analyzed separately, did not straddle the Table I rates and would be treated as employee-pay-all plans not subject to Code Section 79. [Priv. Ltr. Rul. 9149033]

Q 11:30   If employees are covered by both term policies and permanent policies issued by the same insurer (or its affiliate), can the employer ever treat them as two separate policies?

Yes. The Code Section 79 regulations recognize that many insurers selling group term life insurance plans also mass market permanent life insurance programs on an employee-pay-all basis and that an employer should not automatically be treated as having a single policy for tax purposes merely because the policies are from the same insurance carrier. Accordingly, the employer may elect to treat the obligation providing the permanent benefits as a policy separate from the term policy if:

1. The insurer sells the permanent obligation directly to the employee, who pays the full cost thereof;

2. The employer's participation with respect to sales of the permanent obligation to employees is limited to selection of the insurer and the type of coverage, to sales assistance activities such as providing employee lists to the insurer or permitting the insurer to use the employer's premises for solicitation, and to the collection of premiums through payroll deduction;

3. The insurer sells the obligation on the same terms and in substantial amounts to individuals who do not purchase (and whose employers do not purchase) any other obligation from the insurer; and

4. No employer-provided benefit is conditioned on purchase of the obligation.

[Treas. Reg. § 1.79-0]

Q 11:31   Why would an employer want to treat a term life insurance policy and a permanent life insurance policy issued by the same insurer (or its affiliate) as two separate policies?

Such an election is desirable for two reasons:

1. The employer would avoid possible disqualification of the group term life insurance policy under Code Section 79 because qualifying group term life insurance generally is not permitted to contain a permanent feature unless restrictive requirements contained in the regulations are met; and

2. Even if the restrictive requirements for permanent benefits are met, the Code Section 79 tax treatment for the employees under the combined plan would be onerous.

(See Qs 11:32–11:33, 11:92.)

Q 11:32 When would Code Section 79 apply to a single insurance policy with both a term and a permanent feature?

Code Section 79 may apply to a policy containing a permanent value (that is, a cash value, paid-up value, or other value extending beyond one year), provided that the policy meets the following requirements:

1. The policy or the employer designates in writing the part of the death benefit provided to each employee that is group term life insurance; and

2. The part of the death benefit that is provided to an employee and designated as the group term life insurance benefit for any policy year is not less than the difference between the total death benefit provided under the policy and the employee's deemed death benefit at the end of the policy year.

[Treas. Reg. § 1.79-1(b)]

This rule is intended, in part, to discourage insurance carriers from packaging permanent life insurance with term life insurance in an attempt to obtain the favorable Section 79 group term life insurance treatment for the entire package. The rule requires the package to be broken down into term and permanent components and results in unfavorable tax treatment for the permanent life insurance portion of the package. (The tax treatment is described in Q 11:92.) The amount of the deemed death benefit (DDB) at the end of any policy year may be expressed by the following equation:

$DDB = R/Y$

R = the greater of

—the net level premium reserve at the end of the policy year for all benefits provided to the employee by the policy

or

—the cash value of the policy at the end of the policy year.

Y = the net single premium for insurance (the premium for one dollar of paid-up, whole life insurance) at the employee's age at the end of the policy year.

The net level premium reserve (R) and the net single premium (Y) are based on the 1958 Insurance Commissioners' Standard Ordinary mortality table, plus 4 percent interest. [Treas. Reg. §§ 1.79-1(d)(3), 1.79-1(d)(4)]

Q 11:33 Should an employer seek Section 79 treatment for a single policy combining term and permanent benefits?

No, generally it should not. Because of the conservative mortality table and interest rate that the regulations use to value the permanent benefit, the cost of the coverage imputed as income to the employee may equal or exceed the actual premium paid. If the coverage is not subject to Code Section 79, the employee is taxed only on the actual premium paid by the employer. [Treas. Reg. § 1.61-2(d)(2)(ii)(a)]

Q 11:34   When is the employer considered to be directly or indirectly carrying a policy for purposes of Code Section 79?

A policy is considered to be "carried directly or indirectly by the employer" if:

1. The employer pays any part of the cost of the life insurance directly or indirectly; or
2. The employer or two or more employers arrange for their employees to pay the cost of the life insurance and charge at least one employee less than the Table I cost of his or her insurance and at least one other employee more than the Table I cost of his or her insurance.

[Treas. Reg. § 1.79-0]

Q 11:35   How is an employee-pay-all plan treated under these rules?

Under the second part of the "carried directly or indirectly" test discussed in Q 11:34, an employee-pay-all group term policy may be treated as employer-provided (and, hence, result in imputed income for some employees) if the premium rates charged to the employees straddle the Table I rates under Code Section 79. A straddle occurs whenever the rates charged to at least one participating employee are above the Table I rates, and the rates charged to at least one other participating employee are below the Table I rates. This "straddling rule" in the regulations has its origin in the legislative history of Code Section 79, which indicates that Congress was concerned that younger employees might be required to subsidize older employees by having to contribute more than the actual cost of coverage for young employees, while older employees would be permitted to contribute less than the actual cost of their coverage. [H.R. Rep. No. 749, 88th Cong., 1st Sess. 40 (1963); S. Rep. No. 830, 88th Cong., 2d Sess. 46 (1964)]

> **Note.** Even if employee-pay-all group term life insurance successfully avoids the straddle issue, the policy still might be treated (and taxed) as employer-provided if it is not clearly separate, including separately rated, from employer-paid coverage (see Qs 11:27–11:29).

Q 11:36   Why can it be undesirable for an employee-pay-all plan to be treated as employer-provided group term life insurance?

If the straddling rule (see Q 11:35) would cause an employee-pay-all group term life insurance plan to be treated as employer-provided, then such coverage would be taxable under the rules of Code Section 79. This could result in some employees' being taxed on amounts of coverage in excess of $50,000 even though they paid for it with after-tax dollars. Because the Table I cost is reduced by employee contributions, as a practical matter only employees with large amounts of employee-pay-all insurance purchased at less than Table I rates might be required to include a portion of the value of such coverage in gross income.

Additionally, because of the Section 79 nondiscrimination rules, the employee-pay-all group term life insurance plan that straddles Table I could raise nondiscrimination and tax issues affecting not only the employee-pay-all coverage but also employer-paid coverage having a common key employee participant. [Temp. Treas. Reg. § 1.79-4T, Q&A-10] (The Section 79 nondiscrimination rules are discussed in Qs 11:41–11:49.) However, there are several ways that an employee-pay-all plan can overcome this obstacle (see Q 11:37).

Q 11:37   How does an employee-pay-all plan avoid the impact of the straddling rule that applies under Code Section 79?

There are several ways. One way to avoid the impact of the straddling rule is to have an entity independent of the employer sponsor the plan. Additionally, the impact can arguably be avoided via the rate structure. If employee-pay-all rates at all ages are at or below the Section 79 Table I rates, no imputed income should result (assuming that the employer is also careful to separate the employee-pay-all coverage from any employer-paid coverage as discussed in Qs 11:27–11:29). [Priv. Ltr. Rul. 8638050]

Nonemployer plan. Several IRS letter rulings have held that employee pay-all group term life insurance plans provided through a trust, such as one maintained by a voluntary employees' beneficiary association (VEBA), are not considered to be carried directly or indirectly by the employer and therefore are not subject to Code Section 79. [Priv. Ltr. Ruls. 8430138, 8223052, 8129070] One IRS letter ruling considered the case of a VEBA providing benefits to employees of governmental employers. The VEBA provided noncontributory basic group term life insurance of one times annual salary. It also provided supplemental group term life insurance of up to five times annual salary on an employee-pay-all basis. The insurer rated and administered the basic and supplemental policies separately. The VEBA selected the insurer and negotiated the cost and other terms of the group policies. The employers were not involved with the establishment of the supplemental coverage. The VEBA charged no fees to the employers, and the employers had no significant costs or burdens as a result of the supplemental coverage. The IRS ruling held that the insurance premiums were properly allocated between the basic and supplemental coverages, and thus the employers could elect to treat the basic and supplemental policies as separate policies. As a result of such election, the supplemental policies would not be considered carried directly or indirectly by the employer, and the employees would have no imputed income under Code Section 79 attributable to the supplemental coverage. [Priv. Ltr. Rul. 9611058]

> **Note.** If an employee-pay-all group term life insurance plan maintained by a VEBA does not fall under Code Section 79, then the Section 505(b) compensation limit applies to the benefits under the plan (see chapter 20).

Another letter ruling held that an employee-pay-all group term life insurance arrangement sponsored by an insurance brokerage and employee benefit consulting firm, under which the sponsor selected a bank trustee to hold the policy and recommended an insurer to the trustee, was not a policy carried directly or indirectly by the employer of the group of employees involved. [Priv. Ltr. Rul. 8431040]

Presumably, in all of the rulings cited above, the straddling rule would have applied—and resulted in imputed income to some employees—if the group policy had been considered carried by the employer.

Q 11:38 Does an employee-pay-all group term life insurance policy that has nonsmoker premium rates at or below Table I rates and smoker premium rates above Table I rates trigger the straddling rule?

It apparently does not. An IRS ruling considered an employee-pay-all group term life insurance policy that had separate premium rates for nonsmokers and smokers. The nonsmoker rates were all below Table I rates, and the smoker rates were all above Table I rates. The premium rates for each group of employees were sufficient to make both the nonsmokers' and smokers' coverages self-supporting and independent of each other and the employer's basic life plan. The IRS ruled that the employer could elect to treat the nonsmoker and smoker coverages as two separate policies for purposes of Code Section 79. Because neither policy straddled the Table I rates, neither policy would be considered as carried directly or indirectly by the employer and thereby subject to Code Section 79. [Priv. Ltr. Rul. 9149003]

Several factors were key to the IRS's ruling:

1. Although the coverage was provided through the same insurer, the rate structure for the basic (employer-paid), smoker (employee-paid), and nonsmoker (employee-paid) programs was self-supporting. None of these rates cross-subsidized any other of them.

2. The basic employer-paid program was an employer-provided plan within the meaning of Code Section 79, and income was required to be imputed for the value of coverage in excess of $50,000.

3. Both supplemental programs, smoker and nonsmoker, were paid for entirely with employee contributions; no part of either coverage was paid for by the employer.

4. When analyzed separately, neither of the two employee-pay-all coverages straddled Table I, and thus neither was treated as offered directly or indirectly by the employer.

Practice Pointer. Although such an arrangement apparently would not present difficulties under Code Section 79, practitioners should be aware that other issues besides the tax impact may need to be addressed before implementing a group term life insurance program with a rate disparity predicated on the employee's status as a smoker or nonsmoker. Such considerations include, but are not limited to (1) the potential impact of the Americans with Disabilities Act of 1990 (ADA); (2) the potential applicability (to the extent not preempted by ERISA) of state laws prohibiting discrimination in the terms, conditions, and privileges of employment on the basis of whether the individual is a smoker or nonsmoker; and (3) the more remote possibility of an issue under the ADEA (if the employees who are smokers are generally older and the employees who are nonsmokers are generally significantly younger) (see Q 11:56).

Benefit Formula Precluding Individual Selection

Q 11:39   How can a benefit formula preclude individual selection so as to satisfy Code Section 79?

The fourth and last of the requirements listed in Q 11:5 that must be satisfied in order for insurance to be characterized as group term life insurance and qualify for favorable tax treatment under Code Section 79 is that the amount of insurance provided to each employee must be computed under a formula that "precludes individual selection" of the amount of coverage. The formula must be based on factors such as age, years of service, compensation, or position. The factors used to determine eligibility for a large amount of coverage cannot be based on position and apply only to one person, such as the corporate president, or the plan will involve individual selection and not qualify for Section 79 treatment. [Treas. Reg. § 1.79-1(a)(4); Towne v. Commissioner, 78 T.C. 791 (1982); *see also* Whitcomb v. Commissioner, 81 T.C. 505 (1983)]

In a letter ruling, the IRS considered an employer's proposal to amend its noncontributory group term life insurance plan. The amendment would permit covered employees to elect to reduce, in increments of 10 percent, the full amount of coverage for which they were eligible. The covered employees also could elect to have a flat $50,000 of coverage. The clear purpose of the amendment was to permit employees who wished to do so to reduce or even completely eliminate any imputed income under Code Section 79. The IRS concluded that the amendment permitting employees to reduce their noncontributory group term life insurance coverage would not constitute prohibited individual selection disqualifying the Section 79 plan. [Priv. Ltr. Rul. 9319026] A later letter ruling reached the same conclusion on essentially the same set of facts. [Priv. Ltr. Rul. 9701027]

Practice Pointer. An amendment of this type requires the consent of the insurance carrier. Some carriers may be unwilling to give employees such a choice of coverage because of concerns about adverse selection. In addition, some state insurance laws may not permit such an option under the state insurance law's definition of group life insurance.

Q 11:40   Can a benefit formula meet the "precludes individual selection" test if coverage varies according to how much an employee elects to contribute?

The amount of insurance provided may be determined under a limited number of alternative schedules based on the amount each employee elects to contribute, without being considered individual selection. However, the amount of insurance provided under each such schedule must be computed under a formula that precludes individual selection. [Treas. Reg. § 1.79-1(a)(4)] There is no official guidance on the maximum number of alternative schedules tied to the amount of employee contributions that can be provided and still be considered as a "limited" number.

Nondiscrimination Rules

Q 11:41   What are the basic nondiscrimination rules under Code Section 79?

Code Section 79 imposes two nondiscrimination requirements on employer-provided group term life insurance plans:

1. *Eligibility to participate.* The group term life insurance plan may not discriminate in favor of "key employees" (see Q 11:42) with regard to eligibility to participate; and

2. *Benefits test.* The group term life insurance plan may not discriminate in favor of participants who are "key employees" with respect to the type and amount of benefits available under the plan.

[I.R.C. § 79(d)(1)]

Q 11:42   Who is a key employee, in whose favor a plan cannot discriminate?

A *key employee* is any employee who meets any of the following four tests at any time during the plan year or has met them at any time during any of the preceding four plan years:

1. The employee is an officer of the employer whose annual compensation from the employer exceeds $130,000 (indexed). The annual compensation limit is $160,000 for 2010. [IR 2009-94 (Oct. 15, 2009)] The number of employees treated as officers is limited to 50, or if fewer, the greater of either three officers or 10 percent of the employees.

2. The employee is a more-than-5-percent direct or indirect owner of the employer.

3. The employee is a more-than-1-percent direct or indirect owner of the employer and receives annual compensation from the employer in excess of $150,000.

[I.R.C. §§ 79(d)(6), 416(i)(1); Treas. Reg. § 1.416-1, Q&A T-12]

If a retiree had key-employee status at the time of retirement or separation from service on or before October 27, 1990, the retiree remains a key employee throughout retirement. Effective on and after October 28, 1990, all former employees (not just retirees) who had key-employee status at the time of retirement or separation from service continue to be classified as key employees. [I.R.C. § 79(d)(6), as amended by OBRA '90 § 11703(e)(1)]

Determination of officer status. The determination of an individual's status as an officer is made on the basis of the facts, not just the employee's title. Thus, an employee who has the title but not the authority of an officer (e.g., an employee designated as assistant secretary for document-signing purposes) is not an officer. Conversely, an employee who does not have the title but has the authority of an officer is an officer for key-employee purposes. [Treas. Reg. § 1.416-1, Q&As T-13, T-14]

Q 11:43   When is eligibility to participate discriminatory under Code Section 79?

A group term life insurance plan discriminates with regard to eligibility to participate unless any one of the following tests is satisfied:

1. The plan benefits 70 percent or more of all employees of the employer;

2. At least 85 percent of all employees who are participants are not key employees;

3. The plan benefits employees who qualify under a classification established by the employer that the IRS has found not to discriminate in favor of key employees; or

4. The plan is part of a cafeteria plan that meets the cafeteria plan requirements of Code Section 125. (See chapter 7 for a discussion of cafeteria plans.)

When applying these eligibility tests, employees with less than three years of service, part-time or seasonal employees, employees covered under a collective bargaining agreement where the plan benefits were the subject of good-faith bargaining, and nonresident aliens with no U.S.-source earned income from the employer may be excluded. [I.R.C. § 79(d)(3)]

Practice Pointer. The 85 percent eligibility test is quite a liberal one. For example, assume that an employer with 500 employees has 15 key employees. If the employer provides group term life insurance only to the 100 highest-paid employees and excludes the 400 lowest-paid employees, the employer's plan would satisfy the 85 percent eligibility test. [Temp. Treas. Reg. § 1.79-4T, Q&A-9] The eligibility tests are applied separately to active and former employees. The plan may provide higher coverage for active employees and lower coverage for retired employees. [Temp. Treas. Reg. § 1.79-4T, Qs&As-7, -8]

Q 11:44   When are benefits discriminatory under Code Section 79?

If the plan covers a key employee, benefits are available on a discriminatory basis unless the plan provides:

1. A fixed amount of insurance that is the same for all covered employees;

2. Coverage as a uniform percentage of total compensation or of basic or regular rate of compensation; or

3. Benefits that are nondiscriminatory based on all the facts and circumstances.

[I.R.C. §§ 79(d)(4), 79(d)(5); Temp. Treas. Reg. § 1.79-4T, Q&A-9]

Q 11:45   Are group term life insurance policies tested separately in determining whether the employer's plan is discriminatory?

The answer depends on whether the policies cover a common key employee.

Mandatory aggregation of active coverage. All policies that provide group term life insurance coverage to a common key employee or common key employees and that are carried directly or indirectly by the employer are a single plan for nondiscrimination testing. [Temp. Treas. Reg. § 1.79-4T, Q&A-5]

> **Example.** A key employee has $50,000 of group term life insurance under one policy and an additional $250,000 of coverage under a separate group policy. The two policies are treated as a single plan for nondiscrimination testing purposes.

Mandatory aggregation of active and retiree coverage. A policy that provides group term life insurance to a key employee and a separate policy that will provide coverage to the same key employee after retirement or separation from service must be treated as a single plan. [Temp. Treas. Reg. § 1.79-4T, Q&A-5]

Permissive aggregation of plans. In order to satisfy the nondiscrimination rules, an employer may choose to treat as a single plan two or more policies that do not provide coverage to a common key employee; for example, the employer has one policy covering non-key employees only and a second policy covering key employees. [Temp. Treas. Reg. § 1.79-4T, Q&A-5]

Q 11:46   Can a plan that provides separate layers of coverage pass these nondiscrimination tests?

Yes. If a plan provides layers of coverage based on percentages of compensation, each layer of coverage is tested separately. For example, suppose an employer with 500 employees and 15 key employees provides coverage of 100 percent of compensation for all 500 employees and an additional 100 percent of compensation coverage for the 100 highest-paid employees. The plan does not discriminate as to the amount of benefits because the additional layer of coverage satisfies the 85 percent eligibility test and the amount of coverage is the same (as a percentage of compensation) for all the members of the 100-employee subgroup.

The determination of the subgroups of employees to be tested can make allowances for reasonable differences in insurance (as a multiple of compensation) because of rounding, the use of compensation brackets, or other similar factors. [I.R.C. § 79(d)(5); Temp. Treas. Reg. § 1.79-4T, Q&A-9]

Q 11:47   How is additional group term life insurance that employees purchase under a Code Section 79 plan treated for nondiscrimination testing purposes?

As long as the option to purchase additional coverage at the employee's own expense (including on a pretax basis under a cafeteria plan) is available on a nondiscriminatory basis, the fact that key employees exercise the option to a greater extent than other employees does not make the plan discriminatory.

However, if additional insurance coverage that is available to any key employee is not available on a nondiscriminatory basis to non-key employees, the plan will be discriminatory, even though the employees are paying the full cost of the coverage. [Temp. Treas. Reg. § 1.79-4T, Q&A-10]

Q 11:48   How are the Section 79 nondiscrimination rules applied to a plan covering both active and retired employees?

A plan that covers both active and former employees will fail the nondiscrimination tests unless both groups satisfy the tests. (See Q 11:49 for certain grandfathered employees who are excluded from these tests.)

However, both the eligibility test and the benefits test are applied separately to active and former employees. If only former employees who have retired are eligible for coverage, the retirees are tested separately.

Example. A plan provides group term life insurance equal to two times compensation for all active employees and one times final compensation (based on average annual compensation for the final five years) for all former employees. It is nondiscriminatory. However, if the coverage for former employees were limited to key employees only, the plan would be considered discriminatory. [Temp. Treas. Reg. § 1.79-4T, Q&A-7, -8]

In applying the coverage tests to former employees, the employer may make reasonable mortality assumptions regarding former employees who are not covered by the plan but must be considered in testing. Also, any former employee who terminated employment before the earliest date of termination of any former employee covered by the plan may be excluded from the testing group. [I.R.C. § 79(d)(8); Temp. Treas. Reg. § 1.79-4T, Q&A-7, -8]

Q 11:49   What is the effect of the grandfather rules under Code Section 79?

The grandfathered group under Code Section 79 consists of two categories. It includes:

1. Employees and retired employees who
   a. Attained age 55 on or before January 1, 1984,
   b. Were employed by the employer or a predecessor employer at any time in 1983, and
   c. Are covered by the employer under a group term life insurance plan "in existence" on January 1, 1984, or a "comparable successor" to the plan in existence on January 1, 1984; and
2. Employees who retired on or before January 1, 1984, and who, when they retired, were covered under the plan "in existence" on January 1, 1984, or a predecessor plan.

Plan in existence on January 1, 1984. A plan in existence on January 1, 1984, is a plan that had executed the group policy or policies providing the benefits under the plan on or before that date and had not terminated them before that date. [Temp. Treas. Reg. § 1.79-4T, Q&A-2]

Comparable successor plan. A comparable successor plan is a plan maintained by the employer or a successor employer that does not increase the benefits for a particular employee. Thus, increases in coverage for nongrandfathered employees will not cause the grandfathered employees to lose their favored status. [TRA '86 § 1827(b)(3)] If caused by an increase in compensation, an increase in the amount of life insurance coverage based on a percentage of compensation will not be considered an increase in benefits causing loss of grandfathered status. [Temp. Treas. Reg. § 1.79-4T, Q&A-3] (This temporary regulation does not reflect the statutory changes clarifying the grandfather rules made by the Tax Reform Act of 1986 (TRA '86) and is overly broad in defining what is not a comparable successor plan.)

Effect on discrimination testing. If the conditions for grandfathered status continue to be met, the entire amount of group term life insurance coverage on the grandfathered employees may be disregarded when performing the Section 79 nondiscrimination tests. [TRA '84 § 223(d)(2), as amended by TRA '86 § 1827(b)(2); Priv. Ltr. Rul. 9149010 (Aug. 30, 1991)]

Effect of plan discrimination. If, after disregarding the coverage of the grandfathered group, the plan fails the nondiscrimination tests for other reasons (for example, the coverage of nongrandfathered employees is discriminatory), grandfathered employees who retire on or after January 1, 1987, lose the benefit of grandfathered status (see Q 11:86).

Retirement before 1987. The IRS, in a private letter ruling, took the position that in order for an employee to be considered retired before 1987, the employee had to have both actually retired and attained "retirement age" (generally, the earliest age at which the employee could retire with an actuarially unreduced pension benefit) before 1987. [Priv. Ltr. Rul. 9043041 (July 31, 1990)] It is arguable, however, that actual retirement before 1987 is all the statute requires.

Other Plan Design Limitations

Q 11:50 If a discriminatory group term life insurance benefit is included in a cafeteria plan, will it disqualify the cafeteria plan?

A proposed Treasury regulation on cafeteria plans states that the mere failure of any "qualified benefit" (see chapter 7) to satisfy the discrimination requirements of other applicable Code sections, such as Code Section 79 for group term life insurance plans, will cause the benefits to be included in the incomes of key employees. However, the failure will not disqualify the entire cafeteria plan. [Prop. Treas. Reg. § 1.125-1(j)]

Significantly, Code Section 79 imposes a lesser discrimination standard on employer-provided group term life insurance offered under cafeteria plans. In this case, the group term life insurance option need only pass the nondiscriminatory benefit requirement imposed by Code Section 79(d)(2)(B). With respect to eligibility requirements, Code Section 79 specifically states that satisfaction of the Section 125 requirements will constitute satisfaction of the Section 79(d)(2)(A) nondiscriminatory eligibility requirement. [I.R.C. § 79(d)(3)(A)(iv)]

Q 11:51 Is an employer subject to the ADEA allowed to limit eligibility for group term life insurance benefits based on age?

No. Eligibility for group term life insurance coverage cannot be denied based on age, at least for individuals within the age group protected by the ADEA (age 40 and older) and the age group protected by the applicable state law (sometimes age 18 and older). For example, an employer subject to the ADEA could not extend group term life insurance coverage to its employees under age 60 and deny coverage to anyone over age 60.

Q 11:52 Is an employer subject to the ADEA allowed to limit the amount of group term life insurance benefits based on age?

Yes, provided that the employer follows the guidelines contained in the ADEA regulations. Those regulations require that any reduction in the amount of group term life insurance benefits be justified on the basis of cost equivalency; that is, the cost of the reduced benefits for older employees must be no less than the cost of benefits provided to younger employees. Two approaches for achieving cost equivalency are provided under the Equal Employment Opportunity Commission (EEOC) regulations: the "benefit-by-benefit" approach and the "benefit package" approach. The specific rules regarding cost-justified reduction in benefits are discussed in greater detail in chapter 17.

Q 11:53   Can an employer subject to the ADEA increase the employees' share of the cost of group term life insurance based on age?

No. The employee's share of the cost of group term life insurance benefits cannot increase with age. Essentially, such a practice is viewed as a mandatory reduction in take-home pay in violation of the ADEA. It is permissible, however, for the employer to require that employees bear the same proportion of the cost of the plan. Older employees may be required to make larger absolute-dollar contributions than younger employees if the cost of group term life insurance coverage increases by age, as long as the proportion of the total cost paid by the employee remains constant. For example, the employer might decide to bear 50 percent of the cost of group term life insurance coverage and charge the employees 50 percent of the cost. As long as older employees were not charged more than 50 percent of the cost applicable to their age bracket, such an arrangement would not violate the ADEA (see chapter 17).

Q 11:54   Can an employer subject to the ADEA limit eligibility, based on age, for extension of group term life insurance during disability?

Some group term life insurance plans contain a provision that extends coverage to an employee who becomes disabled for the duration of the disability without premium cost (referred to as a *disability waiver* benefit). Typically, such a provision would apply only in the case of disabilities occurring before a specified age, such as age 60. The EEOC says a disability waiver provision will not be considered discriminatory as long as the cost of the group term life insurance without the disability waiver is at least equal to the cost of the group term life insurance with the disability waiver at the next lower age bracket, for example, ages 55 to 59. [EEOC Notice N-915.023 (Mar. 21, 1988)]

Q 11:55   Can employer-provided group term life insurance be reduced or eliminated at retirement?

Yes. Once an older employee has retired or otherwise terminated employment, the employer can reduce or eliminate group term life insurance benefits without violating the ADEA. [ADEA §§ 2, 4, 11(f); 29 U.S.C. §§ 621, 623, 630(f); EEOC Reg. § 1625.10(f)(1)(i)] (See chapter 17.)

In a precedent-setting opinion, the Third Circuit Court of Appeals held that the ADEA protects retirees from age discrimination. [Erie County Retirees Ass'n v. County of Erie, 220 F.3d 193 (3d Cir. 2000)] In the case, a county provided retiree health benefits under two different plans. Retirees who had reached age 65 and were eligible for Medicare were covered by a health maintenance organization (HMO) that required preauthorization for services by a primary care physician. A group of Medicare-eligible retirees sued, claiming that their plan provided inferior coverage compared to the plan offered to younger retirees.

In reaching its decision that the provision of two different plans was discriminatory, the Third Circuit noted that there are indications in the legislative history of the ADEA that some members of Congress viewed the law as inapplicable to retirees. However, the court said the language of the law clearly applies to retirees. The law protects any "individuals" who have been treated differently by their employer, including a former employer, because of age.

The Third Circuit's decision would not, however, prevent the provision of different benefits to active and retired employees based on their employment status. Therefore, a reduction or elimination of group life insurance benefits at retirement, regardless of age, would not appear to violate the ADEA.

Q 11:56 Does the ADA prohibit charging more for employees who are smokers?

There is no definitive answer to this question yet. A number of employers previously have implemented employee-pay-all group term life insurance programs that have separate premium rates for nonsmokers and smokers, with the rates for smokers being higher. Both the ADA and the guidance issued under the ADA (discussed in detail in chapter 18) generally are silent on whether smoking constitutes a disability or a potentially protected drug addiction under the ADA, although the EEOC has indicated that plan sponsors would have to justify differential rates for smokers and nonsmokers on an actuarial basis. Although the Food and Drug Administration (FDA) has in the past concluded that nicotine addiction is a disease, this view has yet to be adopted or reflected in any official EEOC announcement, notice, or regulation under the ADA. Further, a case in the Fourth Circuit concluding that the FDA has no authority to regulate tobacco products places the precedential value of the FDA's interpretation in question. [Brown & Williamson Tobacco Corp. v. FDA, 161 F.3d 764 (4th Cir. 1998)]

Preemption of State Insurance Laws

Q 11:57 Why are state insurance laws important?

The employer's obligations under a group term life insurance plan are defined by federal and state law taken together.

On the federal level, ERISA does not preempt other federal laws, so the Internal Revenue Code, the ADEA, and other federal laws affecting employee benefits must be consulted.

On the state level, the McCarran-Ferguson Act's reservation to the states of regulatory power regarding life insurance remains largely intact under ERISA. Although ERISA contains a general provision preempting state laws directly or indirectly regulating employee benefit plans from applying to plans governed by ERISA, that provision does not bar the application of state laws regulating insurance. [ERISA § 514(b)(2)(A)] As a result, states may regulate the content of a policy insuring an ERISA plan, thereby effectively dictating the benefit content of the plan. However, notwithstanding this statutory exclusion, ERISA has been held to preempt claims otherwise available under state insurance laws on the basis that ERISA's carefully integrated remedies were intended by Congress to be the exclusive remedies for claims relating to ERISA plans. [Pilot Life Ins. Co. v. Dedeaux, 481 U.S. 41 (1987)] Thus, while the content of an ERISA-covered group term life insurance plan may be affected by state insurance laws governing the plan's insurance policy, the legal remedies relating to the plan's benefits are exclusively federal.

Q 11:58　How does ERISA's "saving clause" preserve state regulation of group term life insurance policies insuring ERISA plans?

In general, ERISA preempts any state law relating to ERISA-covered employee benefit plans. However, ERISA's preemption provisions do not apply to properly drafted state insurance laws. To qualify for this exception from ERISA preemption (which is referred to as the saving clause), the state law must be confined to regulating the "business of insurance."

Business of insurance. The Supreme Court has held that a state law will be treated as regulating the business of insurance, and thus be "saved" from ERISA preemption, if it regulates a practice that (1) has the effect of transferring or spreading a policyholder's risk; (2) is an integral part of the policy relationship between the insurer and the insured; and (3) is limited to entities within the insurance industry. [ERISA § 514; Metropolitan Life Ins. Co. v. Massachusetts, 471 U.S. 724 (1985)] Thus, a law that is nominally a state insurance law nonetheless could be preempted from applying to an ERISA-covered plan if it exceeds these boundaries. For example, a law contained in a state's insurance code which requires employers to provide group term life insurance to all employees age 70 or under would be preempted because it is not limited to entities within the insurance industry and instead attempts to regulate an employer's relationship with its employees. On the other hand, a law contained in a state's insurance code requiring all insurers licensed to do business in that state to cover employees age 70 and under in any policy of group term life insurance issued or delivered in that state would be more likely to pass muster and not be preempted by ERISA.

Exception. ERISA also contains an exception to the exception. Even though state insurance laws that are confined to regulating the business of insurance are saved from being preempted from ERISA, a state insurance law cannot attempt to regulate a self-insured plan or its trust by deeming it to be an insurer or engaged in the business of insurance. Thus, ERISA preempts state insurance laws from applying to self-insured plans. However, this "exception to the exception" would rarely be invoked in the group term life insurance context, because such plans typically are fully insured.

Note. Before determining that ERISA preempts a state insurance law from applying to a particular group term life insurance plan, the employer should consult ERISA counsel. Whether a law "relates to" an ERISA plan and other issues are not always as obvious as they might at first seem, and much conflicting case law exists. ERISA preemption is discussed in further detail in chapter 2.

Plan Administration Issues

Q 11:59   Can an employer keep policy dividends and premium rebates if the group term life insurance is contributory?

Yes, depending on the language of the documents and instruments governing the group term life insurance plan. The DOL takes the position that experience-rating dividends, refunds, and credits under a group insurance policy are plan assets to the extent they are attributable to employee contributions. A memorandum by the DOL's Office of the Solicitor sets forth several plan design scenarios and analyzes each for when the employer may keep the dividends, refunds, and credits and when all or a portion of them become plan assets that must be credited to employees. See chapter 2 for a detailed discussion of the DOL memorandum.

Q 11:60   What if a deceased employee did not properly enroll for life insurance benefits?

As a general rule, an employee must satisfy all the conditions to qualify for benefits, including properly enrolling for those benefits. However, there have been cases where an employee's survivors have claimed that the employee's failure to enroll for life insurance was caused by a lapse on the part of the employer, such as failure to provide the employee with a required summary plan description (SPD) setting forth the enrollment requirements.

In one case, an employee's widow claimed she was entitled to life insurance benefits even though her deceased husband never properly registered for life insurance coverage. According to the widow, her husband's failure to register did not preclude her claim for benefits because the employer never created or distributed an SPD setting forth the registration requirement.

The court acknowledged that an SPD was required by ERISA. However, the court noted that failure to provide an SPD may be a harmless error if an employee is otherwise apprised of his or her rights and obligations under the plan. In this case, the employer made several attempts—albeit unsuccessfully—to secure the employee's completion of the enrollment form, thus putting the employee on actual notice of the enrollment requirement. Therefore, the employee's failure to enroll precluded payment of benefits to his widow. [Weinreb v. Hospital for Joint Diseases Orthopaedic Inst., 404 F.3d 167 (2d Cir. 2005)]

In another case, helpful company employees attempted to make a retroactive life insurance election for an employee who died in a car accident less than a week after beginning work for the company. When the employee started work, he automatically became entitled to life insurance equal to 200 percent of his base salary plus basic accidental death (AD&D) coverage—a total of $628,000 in benefits payable to his two grown children. He was also eligible for up to $785,000 of supplemental group life insurance coverage and $1.256 million of voluntary AD&D benefits, but had not elected those benefits at the time of his death. After learning of the employee's death, a company benefits supervisor and corporate attorney attempted to retroactively elect the maximum supplemental life insurance coverage and AD&D benefits on behalf of the employee. However, the company's insurer refused to pay the claims. The company plan administrator sent a letter to the employee's children stating that the employee was not entitled to the extra benefits because he had not signed an election form. The children sued, arguing that the company employees had made a binding retroactive election on behalf of the employee. However, the First Circuit Court of Appeals backed up the denial of benefits. The court said nothing in the plan allowed someone other than the employee (except an assignee) to make an election for the employee, let alone to do so after an accident occurred. Moreover, while the helpful company employees exercised discretion in matters concerning benefits, that does not mean their discretion extended to making a postaccident election for an employee who had not made an election or committed himself to paying premiums—an action the court called "an eyebrow-raising event in the administration of an ERISA plan." [Green v. ExxonMobil Corp., 470 F.3d 415 (1st Cir. 2006)]

In another case before the First Circuit, a widow claimed she was entitled to $88,000 of supplemental life insurance benefits even though her late husband did not fill out a statement of health form as required by the plan to enroll for supplemental benefits. The widow claimed that she was entitled to the benefits because her husband was informed by a company representative that he could add supplemental life insurance benefits during open enrollment without submitting a health statement. However, the First Circuit rejected her claim. The plan terms expressly provided that supplemental life insurance could not be added without a health statement. Therefore, the benefits the widow sought were not authorized by the terms of the plan. Moreover, although ERISA authorizes equitable relief in certain cases, the $88,000 sought by the widow constituted compensatory money damages, which are not permitted by ERISA. [Todisco v. Verizon Commc'ns, Inc., 497 F.3d 95 (1st Cir. 2007)]

Q 11:61   What happens if an employee dies before a valid beneficiary designation under the group term life insurance plan?

Typically, the ERISA plan would incorporate the terms of the policy, which sometimes contains a default procedure (called a *facility of payment* clause) for instances where a beneficiary designation was never executed and filed with the plan administrator or insurer or where the beneficiary designation that was filed is invalid for some reason. The facility of payment clause may require or permit, in the insurer's discretion, payment of the death benefits to one or more specified legal or blood relatives, a guardian or conservator of the same, or to the estate, provided that the insurer has not received notice of a competing claim.

Practice Pointer. An employer may wish to include this procedure in the SPD. It may also wish to include, both in the ERISA plan document and the SPD, a statement that the plan administrator may request the submission of sufficient legal documentation (such as a marriage certificate or letters testamentary) as a condition of making payment of plan benefits.

Q 11:62 What if a beneficiary designation form is not properly completed?

In two cases, the Seventh Circuit Court of Appeals concluded that employees' beneficiary changes were effective despite errors on the designation forms. In each case, the court applied the doctrine of substantial compliance, under which a beneficiary designation will be deemed effective if the insured evidenced his or her intent to name a beneficiary and attempted to effectuate that intent by taking positive actions.

In the first case, Jimmie Johnson, an employee of General Electric Company (GE), initially designated his then-wife Mildred as sole beneficiary of his employer-sponsored life insurance policy, which was issued by Metropolitan Life Insurance Company. After the Johnsons were divorced several years later, Jimmie completed a new beneficiary designation form, naming his two children and a friend as co-beneficiaries. However, he made a number of errors on the form, including checking the box for the wrong life insurance plan, listing an incorrect address, and indicating that he and his wife were separated rather than divorced. GE sent Johnson a letter confirming receipt of the form.

When Johnson died, GE informed his former wife that she was the beneficiary of Johnson's life insurance and she filed a claim for benefits. However, soon after the claim was filed, Johnson's daughter sent GE a letter stating that she was a beneficiary of her father's insurance and asking how to claim the benefits. MetLife claimed to have no record of a change of beneficiary designation, so Johnson's daughter sent the insurer a copy of the change of beneficiary form.

MetLife asked a district court to resolve the competing claims, and the district court ruled in favor of Johnson's children and friend. On appeal, the Seventh Circuit affirmed that decision. "Under these circumstances," said the court, "we conclude that Johnson clearly evidenced an intent to change his beneficiary designation, that he took positive action to effectuate that intent, and checking the wrong box does not serve to negate that intent. It is true that Johnson made some errors, but the doctrine of substantial compliance by its very nature contemplates something less than actual compliance." [Metropolitan Life Ins. Co. v. Johnson, 297 F.3d 558 (7th Cir. 2002)]

In the second case, an employee removed her husband and daughter as beneficiaries of her employer-sponsored life insurance and named her sister as beneficiary on the form that was submitted to the employer. The employer accepted the form, entered the change in its records, and sent the employee a written confirmation. However, the employee had not signed or dated the form, although the insurance policy specifically required a signature to effect a beneficiary change. After the employee's death, her sister claimed the life insurance benefits. The employee's husband challenged the claim on the grounds that the change in beneficiaries was ineffective because of the lack of a signature. The insurer asked a district court to resolve the competing claims. The district court awarded the benefits to the employee's husband and daughter, but the Seventh Circuit reversed that decision. The Seventh Circuit concluded that the beneficiary change was effective under the doctrine of substantial compliance. The employee evidenced her intent and took positive action to effect that intent. She requested the beneficiary change form from her employer, completed the form (except for the signature and date), and returned it to her employer, who accepted it without indicating that it was incomplete or ineffective. In addition, the court noted that the employee made similar changes with respect to other non-ERISA policies at the same time. [Davis v. Combes, 294 F.3d 931 (7th Cir. 2002)]

In another case, the Third Circuit Court of Appeals held that because a plan participant did not complete the proper forms to change the beneficiary of his life insurance coverage, the benefits were payable to the original beneficiary. [Metropolitan Life Ins. Co. v. Kubichek, 83 Fed. Appx. 425 (3d Cir. Dec. 20, 2003)] The participant elected basic and supplemental coverage under his employer's life insurance plan, naming his mother as beneficiary. The plan provided that the beneficiary could be changed by filing a designated form with the plan. After the participant married, he used that form to name his wife as beneficiary of the basic coverage, but the supplemental coverage was not listed on the form. When the participant died, his widow and his mother both claimed the proceeds of the supplemental coverage. The participant's widow could not produce a copy of the form designated by the plan showing a change of beneficiary for the supplemental coverage. However, as proof of her claim, she produced a letter allegedly sent by the participant several years before his death to his employer, in which the participant complained about not receiving confirmation from the employer that his wife was his sole beneficiary. According to the widow, the letter showed that the participant had intended to name his wife as beneficiary of the supplemental coverage, but the employer had no record of receiving the letter.

The Third Circuit concluded that the participant's mother was the designated beneficiary of the proceeds of the supplemental coverage. The court was skeptical of the authenticity of the letter produced by the participant's widow. However, even if the letter were authentic, it did not constitute proof that the participant substantially complied with the plan's requirement to change his beneficiary. According to the court, proof of substantial compliance requires a showing that the participant made every reasonable effort to effect a change of beneficiary, including a showing that the participant completed and submitted the proper form or tried to do so.

Practice Pointer. Errors on a beneficiary designation form generally don't present a problem when there are no competing claimants for an employee's life insurance benefits. That's especially true if the employee's designated beneficiary is a spouse or other relative who would receive the benefits in default of a designation. However, when there are competing claims, an employer's safest course of action is to ask a court to resolve the issue by filing an interpleader action (see Q 11:64). Employers can reduce the incidence of disputes by reviewing employees' beneficiary designation forms for accuracy and asking employees who have made errors to resubmit the forms.

Q 11:63   If the deceased employee designates a beneficiary under the group term life insurance plan but then names a different beneficiary under his or her will, which beneficiary designation controls?

The U.S. Court of Appeals for the Second Circuit indicates that ERISA, not the terms of a deceased employee's will as construed under applicable state law, governs beneficiary designations under an ERISA-covered group term life insurance plan. [Krishna v. Colgate Palmolive Co., 7 F.3d 11 (2d Cir. 1993)]

The Second Circuit noted that the employer's policy clearly provided for the filing of a written designation in order to name a beneficiary or change beneficiaries. The deceased employee's sister-in-law, who had cared for him prior to his death, was the residuary legatee under his will, and the lower court awarded her his group term life insurance benefits under the employer's policy. However, the Second Circuit reversed the lower court's award to her as heir and remanded the case to the lower court for further fact finding on the validity, under the plan, of the existing beneficiary designation. The court noted that it would be counterproductive to require the policy administrator to look beyond the beneficiary designation under the plan into varying state laws concerning wills, trusts and estates, or domestic relations. It concluded that the lower court should have applied federal law, not state law, to the issue.

Q 11:64   What if a deceased employee indicated an intent to change his or her beneficiary designation, but did not complete the necessary forms?

An ERISA plan is governed by the plan documents. Therefore, a plan administrator must follow the plan documents to determine the designated beneficiary of life insurance proceeds, even if an employee indicated a clear intention to change his or her beneficiary before death.

Practice Pointer. Be aware that this rule may cause an employee's life insurance proceeds to be awarded to someone other than the employee's intended beneficiary—especially if there is a delay or mix-up in handling the beneficiary designation change. Plan administrators should caution all employees to handle such paperwork with the utmost care and due diligence.

A case in point arose in the Sixth Circuit. Patricia Hardy-Craig was entitled to $50,000 of group life insurance coverage through her employer. When the policy became effective in January 1999, Patricia Hardy designated her three daughters as beneficiaries. However, when Patricia Hardy married Floyd Craig in May

1999, she changed her beneficiary designation and named her husband as her sole beneficiary. Subsequently, Hardy-Craig, who had been diagnosed with colon cancer, made four telephone calls to the employer's benefits representatives attempting to switch the beneficiary designation back to her daughters. In each conversation, she indicated that she wanted to name her daughters as beneficiaries of her life insurance and that she wanted Floyd Craig "off." In the first conversation, she was told she did not have enough information about her daughters in front of her to generate a change of beneficiary form, and so a form was not sent to her at that time. In the second conversation, she gave the representative the required information about her daughters, and was told she should receive the form in 5 to 10 business days and should sign and return it within 90 days. In the third conversation a month later, Hardy-Craig informed the representative that she never received the change of beneficiary form. The representative told her that she should have received the form, but informed her that a new form could not be generated at that time because Hardy-Craig could not remember her PIN number. The representative sent out a new temporary PIN and told Hardy-Craig to call back when she received it. Hardy-Craig did so, and as a result of that fourth conversation, a new change of beneficiary form was sent to her, naming her daughters as beneficiaries of her life insurance. However, the form was never signed and returned by Hardy-Craig. Hardy-Craig died in November 2000 with Floyd Craig still named as beneficiary of her group term life insurance.

The court acknowledged that there was little doubt that Hardy-Craig intended to change her designated beneficiary from her husband to her daughters. However, Hardy-Craig did not complete all the steps necessary to complete that change. Although the equities might weigh in favor of the daughters, the law requires that the plan documents control—and those documents named the husband as beneficiary. According to the court, the beneficiary designation determines whom the plan administrator must pay, and the court cannot look beyond the plan documents to determine the employee's intent. [Unicare Life & Health Ins. Co. v. Craig, 157 Fed. Appx. 787 (6th Cir. 2005)]

Q 11:65   What is a plan administrator to do when faced with competing claims from more than one individual?

Plan administrators occasionally are faced with disputes among various individuals claiming to be entitled to the proceeds of a deceased employee's group term life insurance coverage.

A typical example is the beneficiary designation of a second wife by a deceased employee being contested by the children of the first marriage who claim that the employee did not mean to leave them out or that the second wife used undue influence or fraud to induce the employee to cut them out. If the beneficiary designation was properly executed and filed with the plan administrator, the plan administrator was unaware of any such circumstances when it was filed, and the disappointed family members fail, after written request and reasonable time to respond, to provide any documentation or proof to back up their assertions, then the plan administrator should follow the clear terms of the plan and pay the beneficiary designated on the deceased employee's beneficiary designation form.

If, however, it is clear under the terms of the plan that a benefit should be paid but a genuine dispute exists as to who should receive the benefit (e.g., two different individuals claim to be "my son, Robert A. Smith," listed on the deceased employee's beneficiary designation), then the resolution of the dispute involves issues outside of the plan which may not be within the expertise or the resources of the plan administrator to resolve. In such a circumstance, the plan administrator could consider commencing an interpleader action. In such actions, the plan administrator would deposit the group term life insurance proceeds with the court and notify the claimants that they should resolve in court their dispute as to who is entitled to the money. In this manner, the plan admits liability for the benefit, but another entity (the court) assumes responsibility for the funds until payment can be made. The plan is thereby relieved of the responsibility of seeing to any further application of the funds, and the court, in effect, "holds the bag" until the dispute is resolved.

Qualified domestic relations orders. In a case with broad implications for welfare benefit plans and group term life insurance plans in particular, the Court of Appeals for the Seventh Circuit has held that ERISA, read literally, does not preempt the application of a qualified domestic relations order (QDRO) to employer-provided life insurance. In that case, a husband and wife who divorced were obligated by the divorce decree to name their children as beneficiaries under each one's employer-provided life insurance. The father then died without having done so; instead, he had named his new wife as sole beneficiary of his employer-provided life insurance. The Seventh Circuit upheld the allocation of benefits specified in the divorce decree. [Metropolitan Life Ins. Co. v. Wheaton, 42 F.3d 1080 (7th Cir. 1994)]

In addition, four other circuit courts have held that the QDRO rules apply to welfare benefit plans. Those circuits are the Second (Connecticut, New York, Vermont), the Fourth (Maryland, North Carolina, South Carolina, Virginia, West Virginia), the Sixth (Kentucky, Michigan, Ohio, Tennessee), and the Tenth (Colorado, Kansas, New Mexico, Oklahoma, Utah, Wisconsin).

For more information on the application of QDROs to welfare benefit plans, see chapter 2.

Q 11:66 What if the plan administrator has already paid the designated beneficiary when it receives notice that another individual claims to be the beneficiary?

A case decided by the U.S. Court of Appeals for the Fourth Circuit indicates that a plan's insurer will be protected from double liability when it makes good-faith payments to a purported beneficiary prior to receiving notice of any competing claims.

The case concerned a group term life insurance plan that began to pay benefits to a woman who apparently had been married to the deceased employee for 21 years and whom the deceased employee had named as his "wife" and designated beneficiary under the plan. After payments to her had begun, the plan received a claim from his legal wife, from whom he had never obtained a divorce. The insurance company then placed all future payments in escrow pending resolution of the competing claims.

The lower court, noting that the policy required the insurer to pay benefits to the deceased employee's legal widow, ruled that the legal widow was entitled to the remainder of the benefits but permitted the apparent wife to retain the payments already paid to her. Upon appeal, the Fourth Circuit affirmed the lower court. It held that the insurer, as plan administrator, had not abused its discretion and had made a reasonable initial determination on the basis of the documentation it had received at the time. Courts can fashion appropriate equitable relief under ERISA, and, in so doing, the Fourth Circuit applied the widely accepted rule that an insurance company that makes good-faith payments to a purported beneficiary in the absence of notice of competing claims will be discharged from all further liability. As a result, the insurer was not required to pay the legal widow any of the amount already paid to the apparent wife. [Crosby v. Crosby, 16 Employee Benefit Cas. (BNA) 1742 (4th Cir. 1993)]

Q 11:67 What if a deceased employee never changed his or her beneficiary designation of a spouse following a divorce?

In a significant decision, the U.S. Supreme Court held that ERISA preempted a state law that provided that designation of a spouse as beneficiary of certain assets, including life insurance and employee benefits, was automatically revoked upon divorce. In the case, an employee had named his second wife as beneficiary of his employer-provided life insurance and pension plan. The couple divorced and the employee was killed in a car accident just two months later without having changed his beneficiary designation. The Supreme Court ruled that the benefits were payable to the ex-spouse under the terms of the plan, rather than to the employee's two minor children, who would have received the benefits under the state law.

In reaching its decision, the Supreme Court concluded that the state law was preempted because it "related to" an ERISA plan. The Court also concluded that the law conflicted with ERISA because it interfered with nationally uniform plan administration. According to the Court, one of the principal goals of ERISA is to establish a uniform administrative scheme to guide processing of claims and disbursement of benefits. "Uniformity is impossible, however," the Court said, "if plans are subject to different legal obligations in different states." [Egelhoff v. Egelhoff, 532 U.S. 141 (2001)]

Plan administrators also are faced with similar problems when determining the appropriate payee if a deceased employee named his or her spouse as the primary beneficiary of group term life insurance proceeds, later divorced, and then remarried, but never changed the beneficiary designation to the new spouse. To some extent, these will be facts and circumstances determinations. A designation of "my wife, Sue" can be interpreted either as intending to designate the employee's legal wife or as intending to designate the individual named Sue (to whom the employee was married at the time).

To the extent that the plan's or policy's procedures do not specify how the issue is to be resolved, at least one ERISA case concluded that the plan administrator of an ERISA plan must apply federal common law to resolve the issue. The difficulty with applying this standard where no interpretive case law exists is illustrated by a recent case decided by the Court of Appeals for the Fifth Circuit. In that case, the plan administrator applied Texas law to determine that the policy's primary beneficiary (the former spouse) was not entitled to death benefit proceeds in the amount of $110,000, because she had waived her right to the plan's benefits under her divorce decree and the employee had not redesignated her as beneficiary following the divorce. Texas state law created a presumption of waiver if a redesignation was not made, and the lower court upheld the plan administrator's decision.

The Fifth Circuit affirmed the lower court's decision, but on different grounds. It held that ERISA preempted the application of Texas law, but determined that federal common law both governed and permitted the result reached by the plan administrator. In applying federal common law, however, the Fifth Circuit looked to state law (in fact, it looked to the same statute it had held to be preempted from applying directly) in concluding that the divorce decree was a bona fide and enforceable waiver of her rights to the policy proceeds. [Brandon v. Travelers Ins. Co., 18 F.3d 1321 (5th Cir. 1994)]

In *Brandon*, the court was not required to follow state law, but nonetheless looked to the state law in fashioning federal common law under ERISA. Another federal appellate court held that a divorced wife was not entitled to group term life insurance proceeds payable upon the death of her former husband. The divorce agreement provided that neither party had any rights in insurance policies owned by the other. The husband died shortly after the divorce without having changed the beneficiary designation from his former wife. The court applied federal common law and held that the divorce agreement divested the wife of her beneficiary interest in the group policy. Therefore, the husband's estate was entitled to the proceeds. [Mohamed v. Kerr, 53 F.3d 911 (8th Cir.), *cert. denied*, 516 U.S. 819 (1995)]

A Sixth Circuit decision reached the opposite result. The insured had designated his wife as beneficiary and did not change the designation following a divorce, even though the divorce decree contained a provision waiving benefits. The court held that, under ERISA, the plan's provisions controlled, and since the ex-wife was still the beneficiary of record she was entitled to the group life insurance benefits upon the death of the employee. [Metropolitan Life Ins. Co. v. Pressley, 82 F.3d 126 (6th Cir. 1996)]

In a converse situation, the Eighth Circuit held that a divorce decree prohibiting a change of beneficiary from the divorced spouse did not violate ERISA. The court pointed out that the antialienation provision of ERISA [ERISA § 206(d)] applies only to pension plans, not to welfare benefit plans. [Equitable Life Assurance Soc'y v. Crysler, 66 F.3d 944 (8th Cir. 1995)]

In another decision, the Fourth Circuit Court of Appeals concluded that an employee's designation of his second wife as beneficiary under his pension had no effect on a prior life insurance beneficiary designation. The employee was covered by his union's benefit plan, which entitled him to $50,000 of life insurance coverage. The employee originally designated his first wife as beneficiary of his life insurance. However, following a divorce, the employee filed a request to change the beneficiary, naming his mother as sole beneficiary of the life insurance. The employee never filed another request to change his life insurance beneficiary.

The employee, who had remarried, subsequently became disabled and applied for a disability retirement pension and death benefit from the union's pension plan. The application named his second wife as beneficiary of the death benefit under the pension plan. The employee died before becoming eligible for the death benefit under the pension plan. However, his second wife claimed that his designation of her as beneficiary on the pension application also changed the beneficiary designation for his life insurance. Faced with competing claims from the employee's mother and his second wife, the union asked the court to decide who was entitled to the benefits.

The Fourth Circuit held that the employee's mother was entitled to the $50,000 life insurance proceeds. According to the court, the life insurance plan and the pension plan provided different benefits and different procedures for designating beneficiaries. Thus, the pension application affected only the death benefit (if any) payable under the pension plan. The disposition of the life insurance proceeds was determined by the documents the employee filed in connection with that plan, which unambiguously named his mother as beneficiary. [Steamship Trade Ass'n Int'l Longshoremen's Ass'n v. Bowman, 247 F.3d 181 (4th Cir. 2001]

> **Practice Pointer.** There is, of course, no way to know with complete certainty whom the employee in *Bowman* may have wanted to receive his life insurance proceeds. However, given that his most recent paperwork named his second wife as beneficiary under the pension plan, he may have simply overlooked the necessity of changing his life insurance beneficiary. One way to avoid such a situation is to develop a checklist of beneficiary designations that may need to be updated when an employee experiences a change in family circumstances.

Q 11:68   What if the beneficiary is the one who caused the insured employee's death?

Although the incidence is rare, employers and insurers occasionally are faced with the issue of whether to pay group term life insurance benefits to a beneficiary who murdered the employee. State insurance laws typically prohibit an individual who is the beneficiary under an insurance policy from profiting from his or her own felonious acts. This is logical and necessary for an orderly society, since otherwise there would be no disincentive to taking out a hefty insurance policy on an individual and then doing away with that individual in order to collect the proceeds. This general policy consideration is frequently expressed as an insurance policy exclusion applicable if the death of the insured is caused by the beneficiary's illegal acts.

The Supreme Court has held that state beneficiary laws that void the designation of an ex-spouse as beneficiary following a divorce are preempted by ERISA (see Q 11:67). However, in reaching its decision, the Court specifically reserved judgment on state "slayer statutes," which prevent murderers from receiving property of their victims. In the ERISA context, such laws could revoke the beneficiary status of someone who murdered a plan participant. However, the Court pointed out that those laws were not involved in the case at hand, and therefore it did not have to decide that issue. In addition, the Court noted that slayer laws have a long history that predates ERISA. Moreover, because such laws are more or less uniform nationwide, the Court said their interference with ERISA is "at least debatable." [Egelhoff v. Egelhoff, 121 S. Ct. 1322 (2001)]

In one case, the Eighth Circuit held that an insurance company properly refused to pay life insurance and accidental death and dismemberment (AD&D) benefits to a beneficiary who was suspected of involvement in an insured employee's death.

The insured, Mark Foster, worked as a pharmacist for Drug Emporium, which had contracted with UNUM Life Insurance Company of America to provide life insurance benefits for its employee. Foster was entitled to basic life insurance of $100,000 and the same amount in AD&D benefits. In addition, Foster had purchased supplementary life insurance of $100,000. Foster named his fiancee, Sarah Phillips (who became Phillips-Foster when she later married Foster), as beneficiary of the basic life and AD&D policies; he named his four children from two prior marriages as beneficiaries of the supplementary policy. Both the AD&D and supplementary policies contained a suicide exclusion, but the basic policy did not.

After being reported missing, Foster was found dead with a .44 caliber gunshot wound in his chest. Investigation revealed that Foster owned a .44 caliber rifle, that he had been videotaped visiting the storage facility where he kept the rifle on the day before his death, and that he had made a video several hours before his death in which he stated that he was "going to the other side." Foster reportedly belonged to a cult that practiced group sex; believed that he was a voodoo priest; and believed that another cult member, Greg Friesner, was the "chosen one" who would kill him and inherit his powers. Both the police and UNUM's claims investigators concluded that Phillips-Foster, Friesner, and another cult member were prime suspects in Foster's death. They also concluded that there was a "high probability" that Foster was involved in his own death.

When Phillips-Foster and Foster's children filed claims, UNUM denied the claims for benefits under the AD&D and supplementary policies based on the suicide exclusions. It denied benefits under the basic life policy based on a Minnesota law that prohibits payment of life insurance benefits to a person who feloniously kills the insured. When Phillips-Foster filed a lawsuit against UNUM and Foster's children, the court upheld the denial of benefits under the AD&D and supplementary policies. In addition, the court discharged UNUM from the lawsuit after the insurer deposited Foster's $100,000 of basic life benefits with the court. The Eighth Circuit affirmed the district court's decision. According to the Eighth Circuit, "By the time UNUM issued its denial of coverage, its plan administrator had numerous pieces of evidence to support the conclusion that Foster had been involved in his own death and that Phillips-Foster had played some role in it."

The court also rejected Phillips-Foster's claim that UNUM had breached its fiduciary duties by withholding the $100,000 in basic life benefits and failing to make a timely determination on her claim. The court noted that within a month after Phillips-Foster filed her claim, the police had notified UNUM that they considered her a suspect in a conspiracy to cause her husband's death. Moreover, the police asked UNUM to delay disbursement of the insurance money to facilitate their investigation. "UNUM's failure to meet claim deadlines was not under these circumstances a breach of its fiduciary duty," said the court. [Phillips-Foster v. UNUM Life Ins. Co. Am., 302 F.3d 785 (8th Cir. 2002)]

Q 11:69   What recourse does a plan administrator have when paying benefits for a minor beneficiary to a parent or guardian who may be unreliable?

Plan administrators typically do not become involved in the personal circumstances of beneficiaries and simply make payment according to the terms of the plan. Frequently, if the designated beneficiary is a minor, the plan and policy will permit payment to the minor's parent as legal guardian of the child. (State law should be consulted to ascertain that this is true in the particular state. In some circumstances, the parent is the guardian only of the body of the child and may need to seek appointment as legal guardian of the child's financial affairs.)

Sometimes, the employer may have knowledge of circumstances that make it reluctant to pay a child's benefits to the parent. For example, if the surviving parent has already received and quickly spent the proceeds of another benefits plan, the employer may worry that the parent will spend the child's money rather than keeping it for the education and welfare of the child. In this circumstance, a well-meaning employer must still adhere to the terms of the plan but may be able to do so in a manner that helps preserve the benefit for the child. It may be possible, for example, to deposit the proceeds in a blocked bank account from which the parent may withdraw funds only to pay the child's expenses.

Q 11:70   What adverse consequences could result from switching to a successor insurance policy or changing insurance carriers?

A number of administrative issues arise when the employer or plan administrator decides to switch to a different group term life insurance policy issued by the same insurance carrier or to change carriers altogether. Some of the typical issues include the effect on any assignments of coverage, whether the new policy will cover individuals who are on disability extension under the prior policy, and conversion rights under the prior policy.

Impact on assignments. Some employer-provided group term life insurance plans permit employees to assign their insurance to another party. If the assignment is done more than three years prior to the employee's death and meets certain requirements, the death benefit proceeds will not be included in the deceased employee's estate for federal estate tax purposes. [I.R.C. §§ 2035, 2042]

The employer contemplating switching policies or insurance carriers may wish to examine the effect of the change on any existing assignments made by its employees. Executives in particular may have made assignments for estate planning purposes that might be invalidated by the proposed change. If the current assignments are not broad enough to encompass successor policies of the same insurer and/or replacement policies of a different insurer, it may be necessary to have the affected employees redo their assignments, and the three-year period would begin to run anew. (See also Q 11:114.) It appears that if the new policy specifically provides that the assignees of the old policy coverage will have the same rights under the new policy, the need for a new assignment and the start of a new three-year period can be avoided.

Practice Pointer. Plans that permit such assignments should be careful to disavow any responsibility for the validity of the assignment under applicable law. In other words, even though the plan may permit an employee to assign his or her benefits to another, it should not inadvertently assume the responsibility of assuring that the employee achieves the desired tax result. Particularly if a standard form assignment is provided by the plan or the insurance carrier, it may be prudent to include a disclaimer as to the validity of the assignment and caution the employee to review the assignment with his or her attorney or other advisors. As a practical matter, the plan administrator should also permit a reasonable period for the employee to obtain such advice prior to submitting the executed assignment to the plan administrator.

(Assignments of group term life insurance and estate planning are discussed further at Qs 11:109–11:118.)

Continuity of coverage for all participants. If a new insurance carrier is being substituted, the proposed new group term life insurance coverage should be examined to determine whether any of the participants under the current policy would be excluded from coverage under the replacement policy. This can be a concern for disabled individuals who are covered under the current policy's disability extension provisions but might be excluded from coverage under the new policy. The employer may wish to clarify the effect of any "actively at work" requirements or other provisions that could inadvertently cause a participant to be excluded from the new coverage when the current coverage is terminated.

Failure to notify participants of policy cancellation. A related issue that may arise in the substitution or replacement of a group term life insurance policy is whether employees participating in the group term life insurance plan should be notified that the policy is being canceled (see Q 11:74).

Q 11:71   Must the plan pay interest on delayed payment of group term life insurance benefits?

Plan administrators may be faced with delaying payment of group term life insurance proceeds for a number of reasons. First, there may be a delay in obtaining the death certificate to submit as proof that the employee has died. Second, the beneficiaries, guardian or conservator, or estate may face various delays such as obtaining copies of birth or marriage certificates, seeking appointment by a court, or other problems with gathering and submitting the appropriate documentation of their status.

Many states require insurance companies to pay interest for the period beginning with the date of the insured employee's death and ending on the date the plan finally makes payment of the life insurance proceeds. Such laws usually also specify the rate of interest to be paid. These laws, to the extent that they are not preempted by ERISA, are controlling. (See chapter 2 for a discussion of cases addressing the application of ERISA to state laws mandating payment of interest on life insurance death benefits.)

Q 11:72   May the plan delay payment of the benefit in order to provide the designated beneficiary or beneficiaries time to select a form of payment?

The answer depends on the availability of the option under the particular group term life insurance plan. Insurers may offer plans the option of a delayed payment while the designated beneficiary is deciding whether to receive payment as a lump sum, annuity, or other form permitted under the policy. During the period from the date of the employee's death until the beneficiary elects a payment method, the insurer agrees to pay interest on the policy proceeds. Some employers who are concerned, for example, about a surviving spouse's possible inability to make quick decisions find this an attractive option and incorporate it into their plans.

Q 11:73   What administrative difficulties can arise when the employer processes group term life insurance claims for distraught surviving family members?

Claims procedures under employer-provided group term life insurance policies may permit participants to file the claim documentation directly with the employer or may require that it be filed with the insurance carrier. Particularly with the latter method, problems can arise if a well-intentioned employer's attempts to help distraught beneficiaries actually do more harm than good.

For very large employers, the insurance carrier may permit the employer to arrange to handle the paperwork associated with filing claims for life insurance benefits. In exchange for assuming part of the administrative duties under the policy, the employer might be able to obtain more favorable premium rates. Under such an arrangement, the employer might be responsible for determining the validity of beneficiary designations and for receiving and reviewing claim documentation such as a death certificate, letters testamentary, proof of guardianship or custodianship, or proof of a valid common-law marriage. If the employer is handling the claims administration, the SPD provided to employees should specify that all claim documentation should be sent to the employer (typically, to the human resources department) and that the claim cannot be processed until the employer has received the appropriate documents.

However, the more typical arrangement is for claims to be filed directly with the insurance company. The SPD in this instance should clearly and unambiguously state that the claim must be filed with the insurance company in order to be valid and include any pertinent filing deadlines. It should also include the address of the insurance carrier's claims-processing unit handling the account or, if claims filing instructions and addresses are printed on the claims form, at the very least the address of the employer or insurance carrier office where claims forms can be readily obtained.

Problems can arise under this latter type of arrangement when a well intentioned in-house benefit specialist at the employer volunteers to handle the paperwork for a grieving and distracted widow, widower, or other surviving relative. The employer's representative may invite the beneficiary to "send everything to me and I'll forward it for you." This may happen if the employer takes a very paternalistic approach to its employees or if a sympathetic benefit administrator believes that the beneficiary is so grief-stricken as to be temporarily unable to handle his or her affairs. The benefit administrator may then fail to prod the beneficiary to send in the required information on a timely basis or fail to forward documents received from the beneficiary to the insurance carrier on a timely basis. Such actions could then cause the claim for death benefits to miss the deadline contained in the policy. This could expose the employer to potential liability outside of the policy for the plan benefit if the employer represented that it would handle the claim.

Practice Pointer. To avoid interjecting employer actions between the beneficiary making the claim and the insurance carrier receiving the claim, benefit administrators working with this type of claims-filing arrangement should be cautioned to have claimants file the required documentation directly with the insurance carrier. A concerned employer could prod beneficiaries to do so by, for example, sending a reminder letter with a copy of the claims procedure contained in the SPD and, if desired, an extra copy of the claims form and any helpful checklist of required documentation provided by the insurance carrier that must be included with the claim.

Q 11:74   If the group term life insurance policy is canceled, is the plan fiduciary required to notify participants of the cancellation?

It would be prudent to do so, especially if the policy being terminated is not being replaced with another. A federal district court case addressed a situation in which an employer failed to notify participants of the cancellation of the policy insuring the group term life insurance plan. The case concluded that the employer would be liable for a breach of fiduciary duty under ERISA for such failure, even though the decision to cancel the insurance was the employer's business decision. [Gallien v. Connecticut Gen. Life Ins. Co., 851 F. Supp. 547 (S.D.N.Y. 1994), *rev'd on other grounds,* 49 F.3d 878 (2d Cir. 1995)]

In the *Gallien* case, the employee participating in the employer's group term life insurance program became disabled and was covered under the group term life insurance plan's disability extension provision. The employee remained disabled until his death. After he died, his executor applied for the group term life insurance benefit. The insurance company denied the claim, however, because the employer had stopped making premium payments on the policy three months before the participant died, and, as a result, the policy had been canceled. The court held that the insurance company was not liable, because the policy had been properly canceled for failure to pay premiums. However, the court found that the employer, which was also the plan administrator of the group term life insurance plan, had violated its ERISA fiduciary duty and was thus liable to the executor. The court pointed out that the fiduciary had a duty to inform the plan participants of the policy cancellation so that each would have the opportunity, if he or she desired, to make a timely election under the policy's conversion privilege to continue the life insurance coverage on an individual (rather than group) basis.

Practice Pointer. A different result might have been reached if a replacement policy were being obtained (e.g., if the plan simply switched from Prudential to Metropolitan Life and the group term life insurance plan coverage continued uninterrupted). In that case, whether the conversion privilege under the prior policy would be triggered may depend on the terms of the prior policy and the particular facts and circumstances, including whether coverage under the replacement policy was less generous, the length of time the prior policy had been in force, and other issues. However, even if the level of plan coverage remains the same and the prior policy's conversion privilege is not triggered, the plan fiduciaries nonetheless would be required to inform participants about the new insurance carrier. The substitution of an insurance carrier is a material change, and participants would need to be provided with the relevant information necessary for them to submit claims under the plan to the new carrier.

Trust Requirement

Q 11:75 Are employee contributions toward coverage under the employer's group term life insurance policy plan assets for ERISA purposes?

Yes. Amounts that an employee pays to his or her employer, or has withheld from his or her wages for contribution to a group term life insurance plan are plan assets as of the earliest date on which the employer contributions can reasonably be segregated from the employer's general assets. [DOL Reg. §§ 2510.3-102, 2510.3-102(a); 61 Fed. Reg. 41,220 (Aug. 7, 1996)]

Q 11:76 Are there any exemptions from ERISA's trust requirement for employee contributions?

Yes. The DOL has suspended enforcement of the trust requirement for employee contributions that are applied only to the payment of premiums for certain insured welfare benefit plans until the adoption of final regulations providing relief from the trust and reporting and disclosure requirements of Title I of ERISA. [ERISA Tech. Rel. 92-01, 57 Fed. Reg. 23,272 (June 2, 1992), as modified by DOL News Rel. 93-363 (Aug. 27, 1993)] To qualify for this exemption, the employee premiums must be paid to the insurer within 90 days of the date they are received or deducted from wages by the employer.

In the final plan asset regulations published on August 7, 1996, the DOL confirmed that ERISA Technical Release 92-01 is not affected by the final regulations and remains in effect until further notice. [61 Fed. Reg. 41,220, 41,222]

Q 11:77 Are pretax contributions for group term life insurance under a cafeteria plan treated as employee contributions for purposes of the trust requirement?

Yes. The DOL has taken the position that elective contributions to an employee benefit plan, whether made pursuant to a salary reduction agreement or otherwise, constitute amounts paid by the employee or withheld from the employee's wages by the employer and thus are participant contributions within the scope of DOL Regulations Section 2510.3-102 without regard to the treatment of such contributions under the Internal Revenue Code. [29 C.F.R. § 2510.3-102] However, the suspension of enforcement of the trust requirement discussed in Q 11:76 also applies to cafeteria plans.

Taxation Issues

Tax Treatment of Employer Contributions

Q 11:78   Are an employer's contributions for group term life insurance coverage for employees tax deductible?

Yes. An employer's contributions for group term life insurance for employees are generally tax deductible as ordinary and necessary business expenses. However, no deduction is allowed if the employer is a direct or indirect beneficiary of the policy. In addition, an employer's deductions for contributions to a welfare benefit fund, such as a VEBA or a retired lives reserve held by an insurer, are subject to the special limitations applicable to welfare benefit funds. (See chapter 20.) [I.R.C. §§ 162(a), 264(a)(1), 419, 419A]

Q 11:79   Does an employer's deduction hinge on compliance with Code Section 79?

No. Code Section 79 deals exclusively with whether the value of employer-provided coverage is taxable to employees and, if so, to what extent.

Income Tax Treatment of Coverage Provided to Employees

Q 11:80   How, generally, are employees taxed for group term life insurance coverage under Code Section 79 when the plan is not discriminatory?

If a Section 79 group term life insurance plan is not discriminatory, an employee who has coverage of $50,000 or less has no imputed income subject to federal income tax. If the coverage exceeds $50,000, the employee has imputed gross income equal to the "cost" of his or her group term life insurance in excess of $50,000 of coverage, less any employee contributions for the coverage (including any contributions toward the first $50,000 of coverage). [I.R.C. §§ 79(a), 79(d); Treas. Reg. § 1.79-3] (Taxation of employees if the plan is discriminatory is discussed in Qs 11:85–11:87.)

Q 11:81   How should the employer calculate the annual amount that is included in the employee's gross income under Code Section 79?

Table I sets forth the cost of $1,000 of group term life insurance provided for one month, computed on the basis of five-year age brackets. For purposes of Table I, the age of the employee is the employee's attained age on the last day of the employee's taxable year (generally, the calendar year). [Treas. Reg. § 1.79-1(d)(2)]

Uniform Premium Table I*

Five-Year Age Bracket for One-Month Period	Cost per $1,000 of Protection
Under 25	$ .05
25 to 29	.06
30 to 34	.08
35 to 39	.09
40 to 44	.10
45 to 49	.15
50 to 54	.23
55 to 59	.43
60 to 64	.66
65 to 69	1.27
70 and above	2.06

---

* Revised by the IRS and the Treasury Department to reflect significant changes in mortality, effective July 1, 1999.

Q 11:82   How are employee contributions toward coverage taken into account when calculating imputed income under Code Section 79?

After the cost of the group term life insurance is determined for the entire taxable year (see Q 11:81 for non-key employees and Q 11:86 for key employees), that amount is reduced by employee contributions, if any, toward the group term life insurance for the entire year, including employee contributions for coverage under $50,000 (but excluding employee salary reduction contributions under a cafeteria plan).

Employee contributions that represent a payment for a different taxable year (other than amounts applicable to regular pay periods extending into the next taxable year) cannot be used to offset the current cost. Thus, a prepayment of postretirement insurance cost would not reduce the taxable cost currently.

Employee contributions toward group term life insurance coverage that is already excludable from imputed income (e.g., coverage while disabled (see Q 11:83) or coverage when a charity is the beneficiary (see Q 11:89)) cannot be used to offset imputed income on coverage that is not excludable.

If employee contributions are made on an unallocated basis for multiple insured benefits, one of which is group term life insurance, the individual employee's contributions for the portion that is the group term life insurance coverage must be determined by ascertaining (1) how much of the amounts all employees covered for the multiple insured benefits have contributed is allocable to the purchase of group term life insurance and (2) the pro rata portion of this allocable amount attributable to the individual employee, based on the ratio of the amount of group term life insurance on the employee to the total amount on all the employees. [I.R.C. § 79(a); Treas. Reg. § 1.79-3(e)]

Q 11:83　Are disabled employees subject to tax under Code Section 79?

No. An employee who has terminated employment with the employer and is disabled has no imputed income under Code Section 79, regardless of whether the group term life insurance plan is discriminatory. For this purpose, employment is considered terminated when the individual no longer renders services to the employer as an employee. An individual is considered disabled when he or she is unable to engage in any substantial gainful activity because of any medically determinable physical or mental impairment that can be expected to result in death or be of indefinite duration. [I.R.C. §§ 79(b)(1), 72(m)(7); Treas. Reg. § 1.79-2(b)]

Each year, the individual must provide proof of qualifying disability with the individual's income tax return. [Treas. Reg. § 1.79-2(b)(4)(ii)]

Practice Pointer. The disability test is a strict one, and an employee may qualify for disability benefits under the employer's disability plan and yet not be considered disabled for purposes of Code Section 79.

Q 11:84　Does an employee who has retired have imputed income under Code Section 79?

Generally, he or she does if coverage exceeds $50,000 or if the retiree is a key employee (see Q 11:42) under a discriminatory plan.

Grandfathered employees. Until 1984, there was a complete exclusion from income for coverage provided after an employee had retired and attained "retirement age" (generally the earliest age at which the employee could retire with an actuarially unreduced pension). Accordingly, individuals who took early retirement would be subject to income tax on the amount of their retiree group term life insurance coverage in excess of $50,000 until they attained retirement age. Upon the retiree's attainment of retirement age, the coverage ceased to be taxable.

Retired individuals who are in the grandfathered group are still eligible for this prior law exclusion. [TRA '84 § 223(d)(2), as amended by TRA '86 § 1827(b); Treas. Reg. § 1.79-2(b)(3)] (The grandfather rules are discussed in Q 11:49) However, any grandfathered employee who retired after 1986 under a plan that is discriminatory loses the benefit of the retiree exemption. For non-key employees, this means that income on coverage in excess of $50,000 in retirement would be taxable at Table I rates. For key employees, the entire amount of retiree group term life insurance coverage would be taxable at the higher of Table I rates (see Q 11:81) or actual cost. (For what constitutes "retirement" prior to 1987, see Q 11:49.)

Q 11:85   What are the tax consequences if the employer's group term life insurance plan fails the Section 79 nondiscrimination tests?

If the group term life insurance plan discriminates in favor of any key employee (see Q 11:42), all key employees are affected. Each key employee under a discriminatory plan loses the $50,000 exemption and is taxed on the full amount of coverage for the entire year, less his or her own contributions, at the greater of Section 79 Table I cost or actual cost. [I.R.C. § 79(d)(1)]

Employees who are not key employees are not affected and continue to qualify for favorable taxation under Code Section 79. [I.R.C. §§ 79(a), 79(d)(1)]

Any grandfathered individuals who did not retire before January 1, 1987, lose grandfather protection if the plan is discriminatory. Those who are nonkey employees and who otherwise would have qualified for the prior law exclusion will then be taxed for the year on the value of their coverage in excess of $50,000. Those who are key employees will lose the benefit of the total exclusion under prior law, lose the benefit of the current $50,000 exclusion, and will be taxed on all coverage for the year, less employee contributions, using the higher of Table I rates (see Q 11:81) or actual cost.

Q 11:86   How is "actual cost" determined under a discriminatory group term life insurance plan?

Actual cost generally is determined by apportioning among covered employees the net premium (the group premium less policy dividends, premium refunds, or experience-rating credits) attributable to the group term life insurance plan during the taxable year. An employer that has multiple coverages with the same insurer must reasonably allocate the total premiums paid to the insurer between the group term life insurance coverage and the other types of coverage.

The portion of the net premium for group term life insurance apportioned to a particular key employee is generally determined by the following steps:

Step 1.   Select a premium table for the entire group (rates in this table are referred to as "tabular premium" rates). For this purpose, the 1960 Basic Group Table published by the Society of Actuaries ordinarily must be used; however, if the group policy contains a reasonable premium rate table (based on recognized mortality assumptions) on an attained-age basis with age brackets not exceeding five years, that table may be used instead to determine the tabular premiums.

Step 2.   Determine the ratio of the net amount of premiums for the entire group to the total amount of tabular premiums for the entire group.

Step 3.   Multiply the tabular premium for the key employee at his or her age by the ratio determined in Step 2.

Example. Kevin, a key employee, has group term life insurance of $100,000 under a discriminatory plan. The tabular premium at Kevin's age is $1 per month per $1,000 of coverage. The tabular annual premium on an attained-age basis for the group is $100,000, and the actual net annual premium for the group is $150,000. Since the ratio of the actual premium to the tabular premium for the group is 1.5 to 1.0, Kevin's actual premium cost would be $1.50 per month per $1,000 of coverage, or $150 per month ($1,800 for the year).

Exception. If the insurer calculates the mortality charge for coverage for a key employee separately (for example, the charge is based on a medical examination), and the mortality charge plus a proportionate share of the loading charge for the coverage for the group is higher than the amount determined under the allocation method above, the actual cost for that key employee is the higher amount. Any cost for key employees calculated under this method is excluded in applying the general allocation method to other key employees. [Temp. Treas. Reg. § 1.79-4T, Q&A-6]

Q 11:87   What if the plan is discriminatory under Code Section 79 for only a part of a taxable year?

If a plan is discriminatory for any part of the key employee's taxable year, it is treated as discriminatory for the entire taxable year. [Temp. Treas. Reg. § 1.79-4T, Q&A-11]

Q 11:88   Are there any planning strategies an employee can use to avoid imputation of income under Code Section 79?

Yes. The employee may, provided certain conditions are met, designate a charity (that is, any organization described in Code Section 170(c)) as the beneficiary of the policy. The employee may also designate the employer as the beneficiary. These strategies may be used by all employees, including key employees under a discriminatory plan.

Q 11:89   When will designating a charity as beneficiary avoid imputed income under Code Section 79?

The charity must be designated as the sole beneficiary for the entire period during the taxable year for which the employee receives the amount of the coverage subject to the designation (although the designation may be revocable). The charity may be designated as beneficiary for a specific amount or for a fractional amount of the total coverage.

Example. Diane has $50,000 of coverage for the first six months of a taxable year. On July 1, her coverage increases to $60,000 because of a salary increase. She designates a charity as beneficiary for $10,000 for the second six months and thereby avoids any imputed income in that year. The following taxable year, she would have to maintain the designation of the charity as the sole beneficiary of $10,000 during the entire taxable year to avoid imputed income. If Diane revoked the charitable beneficiary designation at any time during that taxable year, no charitable beneficiary designation exclusion would apply for any part of that taxable year.

[I.R.C. § 79(b)(2)(B); Treas. Reg. § 1.79-2(c)]

Q 11:90   When will designation of the employer as beneficiary avoid imputed income under Code Section 79?

The requirements are basically the same as those for charitable beneficiary designations. [I.R.C. § 79(b)(2)(A)] However, if the employer is the nominal beneficiary under the policy, but there is an arrangement whereby the employer is required to pay all or a portion of the death proceeds to the employee's estate or beneficiary, the employer is not considered the beneficiary with respect to such amount, and the employee does not avoid imputed income. [Treas. Reg. § 1.79-2(c)(2)]

Practice Pointer. Some state group insurance laws prohibit an employer from being designated as a beneficiary of an employee's group life insurance. Also, designating the employer as beneficiary can jeopardize the tax deductibility of the employer's premium payments. [I.R.C. § 264(a)(1)]

Q 11:91   Can an assignment other than to a charity or to the employer avoid imputed income for an employee under Code Section 79?

No, it cannot, although such assignment may provide estate tax advantages (see Q 11:110). Because the employer provides the group life insurance by reason of the employment of the insured individual, the employee who makes an assignment continues to have imputed income under Code Section 79. When determining the amount of imputed income, any employee contributions made by the assignee are treated as paid by the employee. [Rev. Rul. 73-174, 1973-1 C.B. 43]

Q 11:92   Can an employee deduct his or her contributions for group term life insurance coverage?

No. Premiums that an individual pays for life insurance coverage are considered a nondeductible personal expense. However, employee contributions reduce the taxable cost of group term life insurance (see Q 11:82). [I.R.C. § 262]

Practice Pointer. A group term life insurance plan qualifying under Code Section 79 can be made part of a cafeteria plan, so that employee contributions can be made on a salary reduction basis. (See chapter 7 for a discussion of cafeteria plans.)

Q 11:93   **If a policy contains both term and permanent benefits and is subject to Code Section 79, how is the employee's coverage taxed?**

The employee is taxed on the portion of the policy designated as group term life insurance in accordance with the general rules of Code Section 79. The employee is also taxed on the cost of the permanent coverage, reduced by any amount the employee has paid for the permanent coverage (see Q 11:2 for a definition of permanent coverage).

The cost of the permanent coverage for an employee is no less than the amount that is expressed by the following equation:

Cost of permanent coverage for an employee = X (DDB2 – DDB1)

X = the net single premium for insurance (the premium for $1 of paid-up whole life insurance) at the employee's age at the beginning of the policy year (X is calculated using the 1958 Insurance Commissioners' Standard Ordinary mortality table plus 4 percent interest).

DDB2 = the employee's deemed death benefit at the end of the policy year.

DDB1 = the employee's deemed death benefit at the end of the preceding policy year.

(The definition of *deemed death benefit* is discussed in Q 11:32.)

Q 11:94   **What is the tax treatment under Code Section 79 of policy dividends under a policy including a permanent feature?**

If the employee pays nothing for the permanent coverage, all policy dividends the employee actually or constructively receives are fully taxable. If the employee has contributed to the cost of the permanent coverage, a portion of the dividends is includable in the employee's income. The includable amount is expressed by the following equation:

Includable amount = (D + C) – (PI + DI + AP)

D = the total amount of dividends the employee actually or constructively received under the policy in the employee's current taxable year and all preceding taxable years.

C = the total cost of the permanent coverage for the employee's current taxable year and all preceding taxable years.

PI = the total amount of premium for the permanent coverage included in the employee's income for the employee's current taxable year and all preceding taxable years.

DI = the total amount of dividends included in the employee's income in all the employee's preceding taxable years.

AP = the total amount the employee has paid for permanent coverage in the employee's current taxable year and all preceding taxable years.

[Treas. Reg. § 1.79-1(d)(5)]

Q 11:95   If the policy year and the employee's taxable year are different, how is the cost of the permanent coverage allocated between taxable years?

The cost of permanent coverage for a policy year is allocated first to the employee's taxable year in which the policy year begins and may be expressed by the following equation:

Cost of permanent coverage for taxable year in which policy year begins = $F \times C$

F = the fraction representing that portion of the premium for the policy year that is paid on or before the last day of the employee's taxable year.

C = the cost of permanent benefits for the policy year.

Any part of the cost of the permanent benefit that is not allocated to the employee's taxable year in which the policy year begins is allocated to the employee's following taxable year. [Treas. Reg. § 1.79-1(d)(6)]

Q 11:96   Is imputed income under Code Section 79 subject to federal income tax withholding?

No. However, the employer must report each year's imputed income amount on a Form W-2 filed with the IRS and provide the employee with a copy of the W-2. [Treas. Reg. §§ 1.6052-1, 1.6052-2]

Q 11:97   Is imputed income under Code Section 79 subject to Federal Insurance Contributions Act tax?

Yes. It is subject to the Federal Insurance Contributions Act (FICA) or Social Security and Hospital Insurance (Medicare) tax. Withholding of the employee's share of the FICA tax is required. The IRS allows employers to treat any period not exceeding one year as a payroll period for this purpose. Thus, an employer can elect to withhold on the imputed income under Code Section 79 only once a year. [I.R.C. § 3121(a)(2)(C); IRS Notice 88-82, 1988-2 C.B. 398]

Cafeteria plans. The FICA tax and the resultant withholding requirement apply even if the group term life insurance is provided under a cafeteria plan. [I.R.C. § 3121(a)(5)(G); IRS Notice 88-82, 1988-2 C.B. 398] A benefit that is otherwise subject to FICA taxes does not become nontaxable merely because it is included under a cafeteria plan. Thus, for example, the cost of group term life insurance coverage amounts over $50,000, which is includable in an employee's income and is subject to FICA tax, will not escape such taxes as a result of being offered as a benefit under a cafeteria plan.

Retirees. The FICA tax and withholding requirements for group term life insurance do not apply to individuals who separated from service before 1989 and do not return to work for the same employer or a successor employer thereafter. For persons who retired during 1989 or after and who have imputed income under Code Section 79, the imputed income is subject to FICA tax. An employer is not required to withhold and pay over the retiree's share of the FICA tax with respect to coverage for periods during which an employment relationship no longer exists between the retiree and the employer. However, the employer is required to include on the W-2 statement provided to the former employee the portion of the compensation applicable to the imputed value of the group term life insurance and the amount of FICA tax due on such value. The former employee is required to pay his or her portion of the FICA tax directly to the IRS. [I.R.C. § 3102(d)]

Q 11:98   Is imputed income under Code Section 79 subject to federal unemployment tax (FUTA)?

No. It is not subject to FUTA. [I.R.C. § 3306(b)(2)(C)]

Q 11:99   If employer-provided group term life insurance coverage does not qualify under Code Section 79, what are the tax consequences for employees?

If the policy does not qualify under Code Section 79, and the proceeds are payable to a beneficiary designated by the employee, the premiums paid by the employer are included in the employee's gross income.

However, special rules may apply if the insurance is provided pursuant to a tax-sheltered annuity governed by Code Section 403(b) or if the insurance is provided under a pension or profit sharing plan. [Treas. Reg. § 1.61-2(d)(2)(ii)(a)]

Income Tax Treatment of Death Benefits

Q 11:100   Are death benefits paid under a Section 79 group term life insurance plan subject to federal income tax?

No. Death benefit proceeds paid in a lump sum are not taxable to the beneficiary. The general rule is that all life insurance death benefits (or proceeds) are fully exempt from federal income tax. [I.R.C. § 101(a)] However, if the insurance carrier also pays the beneficiary interest on the proceeds, the interest is fully taxable. [I.R.C. § 101(c)]

Q 11:101   If a death benefit is paid out in installments, or as an annuity, how are the payments taxed?

The amount of the death benefit is prorated over the expected payout period, so that a portion of each payment representing life insurance proceeds is received tax-free, and the remaining portion (deemed to represent investment earnings accruing after death on the death proceeds until all payments are made) is taxable.

If the group term life insurance policy does not provide for a lump-sum benefit as one option under the policy (for example, it is a survivor-income-benefit-only policy), the death proceeds equal the present value of the anticipated future payments at the date of death. [I.R.C. § 101(d)(2); Treas. Reg. § 1.101-4(b)]

The interest rate used to calculate the taxable portion of the payments is the one the insurer uses to calculate the amount of the payments. However, the IRS prescribes the mortality tables used to calculate the present value of death benefits payable in the form of an annuity, the anticipated payout period, and so forth. The mortality tables under Section 72 regulations, which apply to annuities, are used for this purpose. [I.R.C. § 101(d)(2)(B)(i); Treas. Reg. § 1.101-7]

Q 11:102   Are death benefits from a group term life insurance plan payable in the form of a life annuity subject to the Section 72 provisions governing annuities?

No. Life insurance proceeds payable in the form of an annuity are governed by Code Section 101(d) and the regulations thereunder; annuities are governed by Code Section 72 and the regulations thereunder. The income tax treatment is similar, but not identical, and the treatment under Code Section 101(d) is generally more favorable to the recipient.

For example, Code Section 101(d) permits the payee of a life annuity payout to continue to exclude a portion of each payment from income even after the payee has outlived his or her life expectancy and thus recovered the entire death benefit tax-free. [Treas. Reg. § 1.101-4(c)] In contrast, Code Section 72 makes the annuity payments fully taxable once the annuitant has recovered the investment in the contract. [I.R.C. § 72(b)(2)]

Tax Treatment of Premium Rebates

Q 11:103   Does an employer have income when it receives a premium rebate under a group term life insurance policy?

A premium rebate, generally referred to as an experience refund or policy dividend, may be paid by the insurer if the financial experience under the group policy has been favorable.

Assuming the employer has taken a federal income tax deduction for the premium payments it has made (as is normally the case), the employer must include a premium rebate in its federal gross income, unless the prior deduction did not reduce the employer's federal income tax. If the employer did not take a tax deduction for its premium payments or if the deduction did not result in a tax benefit, the premium rebate is not taxable. [I.R.C. § 111]

Q 11:104   In what year is an employer required to take a taxable premium rebate into its federal gross income?

If the employer is on a cash-basis method of accounting, a taxable premium rebate is taken into income in the taxable year in which the premium rebate is actually or constructively received. [Treas. Reg. § 1.451-1(a)]

If the employer is on an accrual-basis method of accounting, a taxable premium rebate is taken into income in the taxable year when (1) all the events have occurred that fix the right to receive the premium rebate and (2) the amount of the premium rebate is fixed with reasonable certainty. [Treas. Reg. § 1.451-1(a)]

A group policy dividend was held not to be subject to accrual for federal income tax purposes until the board of directors of the insurer had declared a dividend out of surplus, and the amount of the dividend had been fixed by a calculation of the insurer's actuaries. [O. Liquidating Corp. v. Commissioner, T.C. Memo 1960-29 (1960), *rev'd on other grounds*, 292 F.2d 225 (3d Cir. 1961)]

> **Note.** If the group insurance policy were deemed to be a welfare benefit fund under Code Section 419(e)(3)(C) and IRS regulations thereunder, then the deductibility of the premiums would be subject to the account limit rules under Code Sections 419 and 419A. The employer can avoid having to treat such a group policy as a welfare benefit fund by satisfying requirements for the Code Section 419(e)(4)(B) exemption for a "qualified nonguaranteed contract," including the requirement that the employer treat any premium rebate payable with respect to the policy year as received or accrued in the taxable year in which such policy year ends. Most group insurance policies generally are not treated as welfare benefit funds under existing IRS regulations, so compliance with the requirements for qualified nonguaranteed contract status does not appear to be necessary to avoid welfare benefit fund treatment (see chapter 20).

Q 11:105   What is the federal income tax treatment of premium rebates paid to employees under a contributory or employee-pay-all group term life insurance plan?

If the employee premiums were paid with after-tax contributions, a premium rebate received by an employee is nontaxable to the extent that it does not exceed the employee's cumulative after-tax contributions. To the extent that the premium rebate exceeds the employee's cumulative after-tax contributions, or if the contributions by the employee were made on a pretax basis under a cafeteria plan, the employee is subject to tax on the rebate. [I.R.C. § 72(e); Treas. Reg. § 1.72-1(d)]

> **Practice Pointer.** Generally, premium rebates paid to employees under employee-pay-all plans are not taxable when employee contributions have been made on an after-tax basis, especially for employees who have contributed under the plan for a number of years. The employer may wish to apportion a premium rebate among covered employees by taking into

account length of participation or cumulative employee contributions, so as to eliminate any reportable taxable income. Such an apportionment may also be desirable in the interests of fairness to the contributing employees.

Q 11:106   Is a taxable premium rebate paid to employees subject to wage withholding for federal income tax, FICA, and FUTA purposes?

Yes. The IRS has ruled privately that a taxable premium rebate to employees constitutes wages for the purpose of federal income tax withholding and for FICA and FUTA purposes. [Priv. Ltr. Rul. 9203033 (Oct. 22, 1991)]

Q 11:107   What is the federal income tax treatment if the employer or insurer, instead of paying employees a premium rebate, waives employee contributions under the group life insurance policy for a limited period?

In order to avoid the administrative complexities of apportioning a premium rebate among the covered employees and paying a cash amount to each employee, it is a common practice to waive future employee contributions for a limited period sufficient to use up the amount of the group policy surplus. While there is no direct authority on the federal income tax treatment of such a waiver program, it appears that the employee would be viewed as constructively receiving cash in the amount of the waived premiums and then would be deemed to have contributed the cash to the group life insurance policy as premiums. As long as the waived premiums do not exceed the employee's cumulative after-tax contributions to the group policy, the employee should have no income for federal income tax purposes.

Q 11:108   What are the federal income tax consequences if the surplus under a group life insurance policy, instead of being paid as a premium rebate, is used to establish or increase the amount of a premium stabilization reserve?

A premium stabilization reserve is a reserve held by the insurance company for the purpose of leveling the costs of the group policy over a number of policy years. As long as the reserve is reasonable in amount, the insurance company obtains a tax deduction for increases in the amount of such a reserve. [I.R.C. § 807(c)(6)] It is common for such a reserve to be established under an employee-pay-all group life insurance policy to avoid having to change the employee contribution rates frequently.

Establishment and maintenance of a premium stabilization reserve by the insurer appears to have no adverse tax consequences for either the employer or the employees covered by the group life insurance policy. [Rev. Rul. 69-382, 1969-2 C.B. 28] However, if the premium stabilization reserve is held by a VEBA, see chapter 20.

Federal Estate and Gift Taxation

Q 11:109　Are group term life insurance death benefits includable in the deceased employee's federal gross estate?

Generally, yes. Life insurance proceeds are includable in the insured employee's gross estate if they are payable to the insured employee's estate. They are also included in the gross estate if they are payable to a beneficiary but the insured possessed "incidents of ownership" in the insurance at the time of death. [I.R.C. § 2042] Generally, the employee will have incidents of ownership because the employee will have the right to designate the beneficiary or beneficiaries. In addition, the employee often has the right to assign the coverage. (Incidents of ownership are discussed further in Q 11:112.)

> **Note.** A provision in the Economic Growth and Tax Relief Reconciliation Act of 2001 (EGTRRA) provides for repeal of the federal estate tax in 2010 as well as a phased-in increase in the unified estate and gift tax credit and a phased-in reduction in the maximum estate and gift tax rate. However, a sunset provision in EGTRRA provides that all provisions in the Act will expire after December 31, 2010, and the Internal Revenue Code will be applied as if the law had never been enacted. Therefore, unless Congress acts to extend the law, estate tax repeal will last for only one year. This uncertainty obviously complicates estate planning and should be taken into account when considering estate planning strategies for group term life insurance.

Q 11:110　Is there anything the employee can do to shelter the death benefit from federal estate tax?

Yes. The employee can assign his or her group term life insurance coverage. Although assignment will not avoid imputed income to the employee on the coverage provided on the employee's life, it may result in the proceeds payable upon the employee's death being excluded from his or her federal gross estate (see Q 11:109). Thus, assignment could be a successful estate planning technique.

Q 11:111　What kind of assignment of group life insurance coverage is necessary to remove it from the employee's gross estate?

The employee must make an absolute assignment of all incidents of ownership under the policy (see Q 11:112), and the group policy and state law must permit such an assignment. [Rev. Rul. 69-54, 1969-1 C.B. 221, as modified by Rev. Rul. 72-307, 1972-1 C.B. 307] Group policies now generally permit assignment by gift, and most states have statutes specifically recognizing the validity of such gifts. Even if a state does not have specific laws on the subject, assignments should be valid under general principles of contract and insurance law.

> **Practice Pointer.** The employee should make the assignment while he or she is healthy, to increase the chances of estate planning success (see Q 11:113).

Q 11:112   What are the incidents of ownership the employee must surrender to make a successful assignment?

The meaning of the term *incidents of ownership* is not limited to ownership in the pure legal sense. Incidents of ownership include the right of the insured or the insured's estate to the economic benefits of the policy. They also include the power to change the beneficiary, to surrender or cancel the policy, to assign the policy, and to revoke an assignment. [Treas. Reg. § 20.2042-1(c)(2)] Additionally, they include any reversionary interest having a value of more than 5 percent of the value of the policy immediately before the insured's death.

The power to select a mode of payment of the death proceeds may, by itself, constitute an incident of ownership. [Estate of James H. Lumpkin, Jr. v. Commissioner, 474 F.2d 1092 (5th Cir. 1973); *cf.* Estate of John Connelly, Sr. v. United States, 551 F.2d 545 (3d Cir. 1977), *nonacq.*, Rev. Rul. 81-128, 1981-1 C.B. 469] However, the privilege to convert to an individual policy of life insurance upon termination of employment has been held not to constitute an incident of ownership. [Estate of J. Smead, 78 T.C. 43 (1982), *acq. in result*, 1984-2 C.B. 2; Rev. Rul. 84-130, 1984-2 C.B. 194] The fact that an employee may in effect cancel the group term life insurance coverage by terminating employment has also been held to be too limited a right to constitute an incident of ownership. [Landorf v. United States, 408 F.2d 461 (Ct. Cl. 1969); Rev. Rul. 72-307, 1972-1 C.B. 221]

Q 11:113   Can an assignment fail to shelter the death benefit from tax because the employee dies too soon after it is made?

Yes. The assignment must be made more than three years before the employee's death; otherwise the proceeds will be includable in the employee's gross estate. [I.R.C. § 2035]

Q 11:114   Must a group term policy be reassigned each year?

No. Generally, a group term life insurance policy is considered a continuing policy as long as premiums are paid to keep it in force. Therefore, once the initial assignment has been in effect for more than three years, the death proceeds will be excluded from the federal gross estate, and a renewal of the assignment each year is not required. [Rev. Rul. 82-13, 1982-1 C.B. 132]

However, some caution should be exercised about changes in carrier and modifications of the policy. The IRS has allowed a broadly worded assignment that purportedly applied to future group term life insurance with the same or a different insurance carrier to carry over when one insurance carrier replaced another but the group term life insurance plan itself was unchanged. [Rev. Rul. 80-289, 1980-2 C.B. 270] The legal result should be the same if the group term life insurance plan is modified somewhat, as long as it can be considered a successor to the original plan.

However, a federal appeals court imposed a new three-year period in a case in which the original assignment did not purport to carry over to a new insurance carrier or successor plan, and the new insurance carrier required a new assignment to be executed. [American Nat'l Bank & Trust Co. v. United States, 832 F.2d 1032 (7th Cir. 1987)]

Q 11:115　Will the estate tax be affected if the assignee pays the employee's share of the premiums under a contributory group term life insurance plan?

It may be. One federal appeals court permitted a portion of the proceeds to be excluded from the insured's gross estate when the assignee of an individual life insurance policy had paid the premiums after the assignment and the insured died within three years of the assignment. The exclusion was based on the ratio that the premiums paid by the assignee bore to the total premiums paid. [Estate of Morris Silverman, 61 T.C. 338 (1973), *aff'd,* 521 F.2d 574 (2d Cir. 1975)] Thus, in a case involving contributory or employee-pay-all group term life coverage, there may be an advantage to having the assignee pay the employee's contributions for the first three years following the assignment. (This will not, however, affect the employee's income tax liability; see Q 11:91.)

Q 11:116　Should employees generally assign their group life insurance to remove it from their federal gross estates?

There is no hard-and-fast rule. A decision must be based on the facts and circumstances of each case. Most estates are entitled to a federal "unified credit" equivalent to a $2 million tax exemption for 2008 (scheduled to increase to $3.5 million in 2009) unless the amount is used up by lifetime gifts. [I.R.C. §§ 2010, 2001] In addition, property passing to a spouse at death is generally eligible for an unlimited marital deduction. [I.R.C. § 2056] Thus, many employees with modest estates need not be concerned about the federal estate tax. However, employees with larger estates may find that an assignment of group term life insurance serves a bona fide estate planning purpose and may result in significant savings in federal estate taxes.

> **Note.** The increases in the unified credit were enacted by the Economic Growth and Tax Relief Reconciliation Act of 2001, which also provides for repeal of the estate tax in 2010. However, a sunset provision in EGTRRA provides that all provisions in the Act will expire after December 31, 2010, and the Internal Revenue Code will be applied as if the law had never been enacted. In that event, the unified credit will revert to its pre-EGTRRA level ($1 million for 2011 and later years).

Q 11:117　Will an assignment result in federal gift tax liability?

The answer again depends on the employee's facts and circumstances. If an employee's assignment of group term life insurance is a gift, federal gift tax rules will apply. However, an assignment of group term life insurance rarely gives rise to a gift tax liability at the time of assignment. The value of the gift at the time of assignment is generally quite small. Thus the gift (unless it is a gift of a future interest) is generally eligible for an annual per-donee exclusion, which can be doubled if the employee's spouse consents to the gift. For 2008, the exclusion is $12,000, or $24,000 if the employee's spouse consents to the gift. The exclusion is adjusted annually for inflation. If the assignment is to the employee's spouse, a 100 percent marital deduction is generally available. Finally, if the gift is not excluded from the gift tax as a result of the annual exclusion or the marital deduction, the gift tax can usually be avoided by claiming the unified tax credit, subject to a phase-out rule for certain wealthy individuals. [I.R.C. §§ 2503(b), 2505, 2515, 2523, 2001]

Q 11:118   How is an assignment valued for federal gift tax purposes?

The IRS has ruled that an assignment of group term life insurance made on the day preceding the date the monthly premium became due has no value for gift tax purposes. If the assignment is made during the month (under a monthly premium policy), presumably the value of the gift would be only a fraction of the monthly premium. For example, if an assignment is made on the 15th day of a 30-day month, the value of the gift would be equal to one half of the monthly premium. [Rev. Rul. 84-147, 1984-2 C.B. 201]

If the group term life insurance plan is discriminatory under Code Section 79, a participating employee who is not a key employee (see Qs 11:41–11:48) may use the Table I rates in the Code Section 79 regulations (see Q 11:81) to determine this premium cost. The non-key employee may instead use the actual cost of the coverage. [Rev. Rul. 84-147, 1984-2 C.B. 201]

The standards for a key employee under a discriminatory plan are somewhat less clear. The IRS has held that actual cost has to be used. [Rev. Rul. 84-147, 1984-2 C.B. 201] However, the ruling was issued before Code Section 79 was amended to provide that key employees under a discriminatory plan would be taxed on the higher of actual cost or Table I "cost." Presumably, the IRS now would contend that a key employee in a discriminatory plan must use the higher of the two cost figures for gift tax valuation purposes.

Retired lives reserve. The presence of a retired lives reserve apparently has no effect on the gift tax value of an assignment, although there is no specific authority on this point. The typical retired lives reserve fund is unallocated; that is, no specific portion of the reserve is allocable to any individual employee. In addition, the insurance company generally does not guarantee that the reserve will be adequate to continue coverage in retirement for any specified period. However, if a specific amount is set aside for the employee-assignee, as may be the case if key employees are covered by the retired lives reserve, the amount set aside may have to be taken into account for gift tax purposes.

Chapter 12

Death Benefits Other Than Employee Group Term Life Insurance

In addition to group term life insurance for employees, employers may choose to offer various death benefit plans. This chapter examines the application of the Internal Revenue Code (Code), the Employee Retirement Income Security Act of 1974 (ERISA), and other regulations to some of the more common types of employer-provided death benefits: dependent group life insurance, accidental death benefits, business travel accident plans, group universal life insurance, uninsured death benefits, split-dollar life insurance, bonus life insurance, and death benefits under qualified retirement plans, as well as accelerated death benefits and living benefits.

Dependent Group Term Life Insurance

Q 12:1   What is a dependent group term life insurance plan?

A *dependent group term life insurance plan* is a plan covering a group of employees that provides the participating employees with group term life insurance coverage on the lives of the employees' dependents, that is, spouses and children. In the event of the death of an employee's covered dependent, the death proceeds generally are payable to the employee.

Q 12:2   Who pays the cost of a dependent group term life insurance plan?

Depending on the terms of the plan, the cost of the dependent group term life insurance coverage may be paid entirely by the employer or shared by the employer and the participating employees, or the participating employees may pay the full cost of the coverage. In a majority of cases, dependent group term life insurance plans provide that the participating employees pay the full cost of the dependent coverage.

Q 12:3   Is a dependent group term life insurance plan subject to ERISA?

It depends. If the employer pays all or part of the cost of the dependent group term life insurance plan, ERISA applies. [ERISA § 3(1)] If the plan is an employee-pay-all plan, ERISA possibly may apply, depending on the extent of the employer's sponsorship or involvement in the plan.

Department of Labor (DOL) regulations *exempt* a group insurance program from treatment as an ERISA employee welfare benefit plan if it satisfies the following four requirements:

1. No contributions are made by the employer;
2. Participation in the program is completely voluntary;
3. The employer's sole functions with respect to the program are, without endorsing the program,
   - to permit the insurer to publicize the program to employees and
   - to collect premiums through payroll deduction and to remit them to the insurer; and
4. The employer receives no consideration in the form of cash or otherwise in connection with the program, other than reasonable compensation (excluding any profit) for administrative services actually rendered in connection with payroll deductions.

[DOL Reg. § 2510.3-1(j)]

Q 12:4   Is a dependent group term life insurance plan subject to the Age Discrimination in Employment Act?

Yes. The Age Discrimination in Employment Act (ADEA) prohibits discrimination because of age in all compensation, terms, conditions, and privileges of employment, including all employee benefits. [29 U.S.C. § 630(l), as amended by § 102 of the Older Workers Benefits Protection Act (OWBPA)] (For detailed discussion of the ADEA, see chapter 17.)

Q 12:5   May an employer deduct its premium payments for dependent group term life insurance?

Generally, yes. If the employer pays premiums for dependent group term life insurance, its premium payments can be deducted, provided they are an ordinary and necessary business expense. [I.R.C. § 162(a); Treas. Reg. § 1.162-10] If, however, the dependent group term life insurance benefits are provided through a welfare benefit fund such as a Section 501(c)(9) voluntary employees' beneficiary association (VEBA) trust, any employer contributions must also satisfy the requirements of Code Sections 419 and 419A to be deductible by the employer (see chapter 20 for a discussion of Code Sections 419 and 419A).

Q 12:6   Are an employee's own contributions toward dependent group term life insurance coverage deductible?

No. Premiums that an employee pays for life insurance coverage for his or her dependents are considered a nondeductible personal expense. [I.R.C. § 262] Therefore, payroll deduction contributions for such coverage are not excluded from an employee's income and are subject to payroll taxes.

Q 12:7   Is the cost or value of dependent group term life insurance coverage provided to an employee by his or her employer included in the employee's gross income for federal income tax purposes?

The answer to this question requires some historical background.

Before 1989, Treasury regulations for many years had provided that when the employer paid part or all of the cost of the coverage on the life of the spouse or child, but that coverage did not exceed $2,000, the coverage was considered incidental and not includable in the employee's gross income. If the employer paid all or a part of the cost of the coverage and the dependent coverage on a spouse or child exceeded $2,000, the cost of the entire coverage (determined using Table I in the Section 79 regulations) less the employee's contributions toward the coverage was includable in the employee's gross income. [Treas. Reg. § 1.61-2(d)(2)(ii)(b); TD 6888, 1966-2 C.B. 23]

In 1989 the Department of the Treasury amended the regulations to provide that the cost (determined under Table I) of group term life insurance on the life of a spouse or dependent provided in connection with the employee's performance of service is fully taxable. The $2,000 incidental coverage rule was eliminated. At the same time, the Treasury Department issued regulations under Code Section 132 (dealing with the tax treatment of fringe benefits) stating that dependent group term life insurance could not qualify as an excludable *de minimis* fringe benefit. [Treas. Reg. §§ 1.61-2(d)(2)(ii)(b), 1.132-6(e)(2)]

In response to widespread objections to this change, the IRS issued Notice 89-110 [1989-2 C.B. 447] stating that, until further notice, the following rules apply:

1. If employer-provided dependent group term life insurance has a face amount of $2,000 or less, it will be deemed to be an excludable *de minimis* fringe benefit under Code Section 132; and

2. In determining whether dependent group life insurance with a face amount higher than $2,000 is a *de minimis* fringe benefit, only the excess, if any, of the cost of such insurance (determined under Table I) over the amount paid by the employee for such insurance will be taken into account.

Practice Pointer. The IRS has not issued any clarifying guidance on the exact point at which the dependent group life insurance coverage becomes so large that it ceases to be *de minimis*. As a result, this issue remains a judgment call on the part of the employer.

Under the current rules, it appears that employee-pay-all group term dependent life insurance coverage ordinarily should not give rise to any taxable income to employees, even if the rates charged straddle Table I in the Section 79 regulations. For purposes of Section 79, if rates straddle Table I (i.e., at least one employee is charged less than the Table I rates and at least one employee is charged more) the coverage will be treated as carried indirectly by the employer, potentially resulting in taxable income for employees who pay less than the Table I rates (see Q 11:81). However, there is no indication that the IRS will apply the same rule to dependent life insurance coverage.

Q 12:8   Is dependent group term life insurance subject to Section 79 income tax treatment?

No. Code Section 79 applies only to group term life insurance coverage on the employee's own life. It does not apply to group term life insurance on the lives of the employee's dependents. [Treas. Reg. § 1.79-3(f)(2)]

Because Code Section 79 does not apply, employee-pay-all dependent life insurance maintained by a VEBA will be subject to the $150,000 compensation limit (indexed), applicable to the entire dependent life insurance plan, contained in Code Section 505(b)(7) (see chapter 20).

Q 12:9 How are the death benefit proceeds under a dependent group term life insurance plan taxed?

Dependent group term life insurance death benefit proceeds are treated as life insurance proceeds for federal income and estate tax purposes. Therefore, the death benefit proceeds are excluded from federal gross income when received by the employee/beneficiary. Because the deceased spouse or child generally has no incidents of ownership in the policy, the proceeds are not includable in the deceased spouse's or child's estate for federal estate tax purposes. [I.R.C. §§ 101(a), 2042; Treas. Reg. § 1.101-1(a)(1)]

Q 12:10 Can dependent group term life insurance be made part of a cafeteria plan?

Again, some historical perspective is in order. Originally, Treasury regulations permitted the inclusion of dependent group term life insurance in a cafeteria plan and also permitted employee contributions for the coverage to be made on a salary reduction—that is, pretax—basis. [Temp. Treas. Reg. § 1.125-2T] Subsequent proposed regulations took the position that, because dependent group term life insurance is a fringe benefit under Code Section 132, it is not treated as a qualified benefit or cash under Code Section 125. That being so, it cannot be a part of a Section 125 cafeteria plan even if the dependent coverage is purchased with after-tax employee contributions. [Prop. Treas. Reg. § 1.125-2, Q&A-4(d); I.R.C. § 125(f)]

Because the application of its new position would have disqualified some existing cafeteria plans that were offering dependent group term life insurance as an option, the IRS announced that for plan years ending before 1992, dependent group term life insurance could be included in a cafeteria plan provided it was treated as cash, regardless of whether it was eligible for exclusion as a *de minimis* fringe benefit under Code Section 132. The IRS notice went on to say that if the dependent group term life insurance was included in the cafeteria plan, the amount includable in the employee's gross income was the greater of the Table I cost or the amount of the employee's contributions for the coverage—a questionable conclusion because there is no statutory authority for the IRS to apply Table I rates to dependent coverage. For plan years ending after 1991, the IRS notice states that dependent group term life insurance cannot be included in a cafeteria plan on either a pretax or an after-tax basis if the benefit would be eligible for exclusion as a *de minimis* fringe benefit under Code Section 132. [Notice 89-110, 1989-2 C.B. 447]

This has left in question whether Notice 89-110 was intended to modify the position taken by the IRS in its proposed regulations that this benefit cannot be included in a cafeteria plan. In other words, did it mean that dependent group life insurance that is NOT *de minimis* could be included in a cafeteria plan? Practitioners differed on this issue, and some took the position that including a large amount of dependent life insurance coverage in a cafeteria plan on at least an after-tax basis was permissible.

Proposed cafeteria plan proposed regulations issued in 2007 laid the issue to rest once and for all. The proposed regulations specifically provide that group-term life insurance on the life of any individual other than an employee (whether includable or excludable from the employee's gross income) is a nonqualified benefit that cannot be offered through a cafeteria plan. [Prop. Treas. Reg. § 1.125-1(q)(viii)] Moreover, the proposed regulations provide that a plan offering any nonqualified benefit is not a cafeteria plan. The regulations are proposed to be effective for plan years beginning after January 1, 2009. However, the IRS says that plan sponsors can rely on the proposed regulations pending the issuance of final regulations.

Accidental Death Benefits

Q 12:11   What is an accidental death benefit plan?

An employer-provided *accidental death benefit plan* provides coverage for death resulting from accidental means. It does not provide benefits for death resulting from illness or natural causes.

The U.S. District Court of Colorado ruled that the administrator of an accident insurance policy properly denied death benefits to the parents of a Down's syndrome child with a pacemaker who died following pacemaker malfunction, because death was partially due to other causes. The child died at the age of five after suffering arrhythmic seizures, despite having had a pacemaker implanted several years earlier. An autopsy initially attributed the death to the failure of a pacemaker; however, after further medical review, the cause of death was determined to be natural instead of accidental. The court said the pacemaker's malfunction was an accident within the meaning of the policy in the sense that it was "unusual and not expected" and it resulted in bodily injury; however, the court concluded that accidental death benefits were properly denied because the pacemaker malfunction was not an independent cause of death. Although pacemaker malfunction may have been the predominant cause of death, the child's death did not occur independent of his arrhythmia, which was certainly another cause of death, the court said. [Pirkheim v. First UNUM Life Ins. Co., 50 F. Supp. 2d 1018 (D. Colo. 1999)]

The U.S. Court of Appeals for the Sixth Circuit ruled that heart disease contributed to the drowning death of a participant in an employer-sponsored accidental death policy, and the plan administrator correctly denied benefits to the participant's estate based on the policy's exclusion for losses in which sickness or disease is a contributing factor. [McGuire v. Reliance Standard Life Ins. Co., 2000 U.S. App. LEXIS 786 (6th Cir. Jan. 18, 2000)]

In a similar case, the Eleventh Circuit held that an employer's accidental death benefit plan was not required to pay benefits to the widow of an employee who died of a heart attack when he was involved in an automobile accident. The employee did not suffer any external injuries as a result of the accident, and the state medical examiner concluded that the cause of death was cardiac arrhythmia due to heart disease. In reaching its decision, the court noted that an overly strict interpretation of the plan's provision, which limited benefits to losses "caused by an accident" and "from no other causes," would provide coverage only to individuals who were in perfect health at the time of an accident. However, the court concluded that the exclusion could reasonably apply where some other cause "substantially contributed" to a loss. Morever, in the employee's case his preexisting heart condition substantially contributed to his death, even if the auto accident triggered his heart attack. [Dixon v. Life Ins. Co. of N. Am., 389 F.3d 1179 (11th Cir. 2004)]

An employee's accidental death while heading home after a business appointment, however, was deemed covered by an accidental death benefit plan. The U.S. District Court of the Western District of Michigan ruled that an insurer violated the terms of its accidental death policy by denying benefits to the beneficiary of a plan participant who died as the result of an automobile accident that occurred while he was returning home after a business appointment.

The insurer relied on the policy term providing coverage to participants "while performing the duties of the insured person's employment." The insurer believed this provision precluded coverage for the participant because the participant became involved in the accident while he was on his way home from a business appointment and because the accident occurred 15 minutes after the end of the employee's normal scheduled workday. The court said the phrase was not defined in the policy, did not have a distinctive legal meaning, and, based on the evidence presented, was ambiguous. [Hardy v. United of Omaha Life Ins. Co., 87 F. Supp. 2d 766 (W.D. Mich. 1999)]

If the accidental death benefit is combined with a dismemberment insurance feature, it is referred to as an accidental death and dismemberment (AD&D) plan. Dismemberment benefits generally cover permanent loss of a body member or function or loss of use of a body member or function (e.g., loss of a limb or loss of eyesight) and usually are paid as a lump sum.

Q 12:12   How does an employer typically provide AD&D coverage?

In many cases, an employer that provides group term life insurance to employees will provide AD&D insurance under the same or an additional group policy.

Q 12:13   Is an AD&D plan subject to ERISA?

Generally, yes. The ERISA definition of a covered "employee welfare benefit plan" includes plans maintained for the purpose of providing benefits in the event of disability, accident, or death. If the AD&D insurance is an adjunct to a group term life insurance plan, the two coverages will ordinarily be treated as part of a single plan for ERISA purposes.

Practice Pointer. This means that the benefits will need to be described in a summary plan description (SPD) for the plan. Care should be taken to reflect in that document the plan's requirement (if any) that the injury or accident from which the injury results must have occurred while plan coverage is in effect.

Q 12:14 Is an AD&D plan subject to the ADEA?

Yes. The ADEA prohibits discrimination because of age in all compensation, terms, conditions, and privileges of employment, specifically including all employee benefits. [29 U.S.C. § 630(l), as amended by § 102 of OWBPA] In particular, this means that any age-rated employee contributions will be required to satisfy the cost-justification requirements of the ADEA regulations and any age-related cutoffs for active employee coverage are not permitted. (For detailed discussion of the ADEA, see chapter 17.)

Q 12:15 Must an employer pay life insurance benefits to the estate of a worker who was wrongfully discharged?

The U.S. Court of Appeals for the Ninth Circuit held that Electronic Data Systems was liable for paying the life insurance benefits to the estate of a former saleswoman who was in the midst of a wrongful discharge action against the company. The employee had a double indemnity coverage for accidental death under an employer-financed life insurance policy when she quit her job alleging sex discrimination and sued for wrongful discharge under the California Fair Housing and Employment Act. While attending her deposition in the case, she died accidentally.

The court reasoned that the remedial purposes of state and federal antidiscrimination laws compelled it to find the company liable because "[t]he employer should bear the economic consequences of its choice to terminate [the employee's] employment and her life insurance policy." The U.S. Supreme Court declined to disturb the ruling. [Sposato v. Electronic Data Sys., 188 F.3d 1146 (9th Cir. 1999), *cert. denied*, 528 U.S. 1189 (2000)]

Q 12:16 May the employer deduct its premium payments for AD&D insurance?

Yes. The premiums attributable to both the accidental death benefit coverage and the dismemberment coverage can be deducted, provided that they are an ordinary and necessary business expense. [I.R.C. § 162(a); Treas. Reg. § 1.162-10] If, however, the AD&D benefits are provided through a welfare benefit fund such as a Section 501(c)(9) VEBA trust, the employer contributions must also satisfy the requirements of Code Sections 419 and 419A in order to be deductible by the employer. (See chapter 20 for a discussion of Code Sections 419 and 419A.)

Q 12:17 Is employer-provided AD&D coverage taxable income to employees?

No. An employee's gross income does not include employer-provided coverage under an accident or health plan. [I.R.C. § 106]

The dismemberment portion of the coverage is clearly excluded from federal gross income under Code Section 106. For a time, IRS letter rulings had been taking the position that employer premiums for the accidental death benefit insurance portion of the AD&D coverage did not qualify for this exclusion and instead constituted taxable death benefit coverage. More recent letter rulings have abandoned that interpretation, however, and appear to concede that the employer premiums for accidental death coverage are excludable under Code Section 106, a position that is a sounder interpretation of the statute. [Priv. Ltr. Ruls. 8801015, 8746024] Such a position is also consistent with the interpretation taken by the IRS and the Treasury Department in the proposed regulations issued under former Code Section 89.

Accidental death benefit insurance coverage is not considered group term life insurance for Section 79 purposes and therefore does not give rise to imputed income under Code Section 79. [Treas. Reg. § 1.79-1(f)(3)]

Q 12:18 How are the death benefit proceeds under an employer-provided accidental death benefit plan taxed?

Accidental death benefit proceeds are treated as life insurance proceeds for federal income and estate tax purposes. The death benefit proceeds are therefore (1) exempt from income tax and (2) includable in the employee's federal gross estate if they are payable to the employee's estate or if the employee had any incidents of ownership in the policy. [I.R.C. §§ 101(a), 2042; Treas. Reg. § 1.101-1(a)(1); Commissioner v. Estate of Noel, 380 U.S. 678 (1965)] (See chapter 11 for a discussion of the federal estate and gift taxation of group term life insurance, which also applies generally to group accidental death insurance.)

Q 12:19 What is the income tax treatment of the dismemberment benefits that are received by an employee under employer-provided AD&D coverage?

Dismemberment benefits received by an employee under an employer provided AD&D plan will be excluded from the gross income of the employee pursuant to Code Section 105(c) to the extent the payments are for the permanent loss or loss of use of a body member or function or for the permanent disfigurement of the employee, and the benefits are computed with reference to the nature of the injury without regard to the period the employee is absent from work. If the dismemberment benefits do not meet those requirements, however, such employer-provided benefits would be taxable under Code Section 105(a).

Business Travel Accident Insurance

Q 12:20   What is business travel accident insurance?

Employers frequently purchase group travel accident insurance policies that cover employees in the event of accidental death or injury while traveling on the employer's business. The amounts of coverage are generally related to compensation (for example, two times a covered employee's salary).

Q 12:21   Is a business travel accident insurance plan subject to ERISA?

Yes. Because a business travel accident insurance plan provides disability and death benefits in the event of an accident while traveling on company business, it is an ERISA plan. [ERISA § 3(1)] (See chapter 2 for a discussion of ERISA.)

Practice Pointer. This benefit sometimes is overlooked when the employer is preparing SPDs for its various benefit plans. Typically, this oversight occurs because travel accident coverage for employees may be provided by the company's general liability insurer and responsibility for maintaining such policies typically rests with a department other than the human resources department. It is, however, an ERISA plan, and plan document, SPD, and other associated reporting and disclosure requirements must be met.

Q 12:22   Are "side visits" made during business travel covered under the terms of a group accidental death benefit policy?

The U.S. Court of Appeals for the Sixth Circuit has ruled that side visits made during business travel were covered because a policy's language did not support the insurer's position that the participant was no longer covered by the accidental death policy after he terminated a business conference he was attending in Chicago. According to the court, the participant had not yet abandoned his business trip at the time of his death or embarked on a vacation under the policy's terms. [Garber v. Provident Life & Accident Ins. Co., 1999 U.S. App. LEXIS 11280 (6th Cir. May 27, 1999)]

Q 12:23   Is a business travel accident plan subject to the ADEA?

Yes. The ADEA covers all compensation, terms, conditions, and privileges of employment, including all employee benefit plans. [29 U.S.C. § 630(l), as amended by § 102 of OWBPA]

This means that any required employee contributions will be subject to the cost-justification rules contained in the ADEA regulations. Typically, however, this coverage is provided on an employer-paid basis. (For an explanation of the ADEA, see chapter 17.)

Q 12:24   Can an employer deduct its premium payments for business travel accident insurance?

Generally, yes. The premiums for business travel accident insurance can be deducted, provided that such insurance is an ordinary and necessary business expense. [I.R.C. § 162(a); Treas. Reg. § 1.162-10]

Q 12:25   Is employer-provided business travel accident insurance coverage taxable to employees?

No. Gross income of an employee does not include employer-provided coverage under an accident or health plan. [I.R.C. § 106]

Q 12:26   How are the proceeds of business travel accident insurance taxed?

The tax treatment of policy proceeds under a business travel accident plan depends on whether the triggering event was the employee's accidental injury or death.

Accidental injury. If the proceeds are paid as a result of the employee having sustained a covered accidental injury, the proceeds relating to such injury are excludable from federal gross income under Code Section 105(c), provided the payment is for the permanent loss or loss of use of a member or function of the body or the permanent disfigurement of the employee and is computed with reference to the nature of the injury without regard to the period the employee is absent from work.

Death. The death benefit proceeds under an employer-provided business travel accident insurance plan are treated as life insurance proceeds for federal income and estate tax purposes; therefore, the death benefit proceeds are (1) exempt from income tax and (2) includable in the employee's federal gross estate if they are payable to the employee's estate or if the employee had any incidents of ownership in the policy. [I.R.C. §§ 101(a), 2042; Treas. Reg. § 1.101-1(a)(1)]

Group Universal Life Insurance

Q 12:27   What is group universal life insurance?

Group universal life (GUL) insurance is an outgrowth of individual universal life insurance. The typical universal life insurance policy is a species of permanent life insurance that provides a savings element in addition to pure insurance protection. The pure insurance portion is also referred to as the "term insurance" element, but should not be confused with group term life insurance.

Under the traditional forms of permanent life insurance (e.g., whole life insurance), the factors an insurance company uses in determining a policy's benefits and cash values, such as amounts at risk, expenses, term insurance protection costs, and interest rates, are not disclosed. The distinguishing characteristic of a GUL policy is that, unlike other forms of permanent life insurance, it "unbundles" the components of a permanent life insurance policy and accounts for them separately. Unbundling the various elements enables employees to see how much of the policy is pure insurance protection and how much money (cash value) is accumulating in the savings element and at what interest or earnings rate. Accordingly, employees can evaluate the merits of the policy both for the level of insurance protection available and for the potential savings that can be achieved.

Interest rates under GUL policies typically reflect—and are adjusted from time to time based on—current market rates. The amount of pure insurance protection under the policy at any time can be either a level amount over the life of the policy or an amount that declines over the life of the policy. In the latter type, the savings element (the cash value) will accumulate faster because the cost of the pure insurance protection portion also declines over the life of the policy.

Q 12:28   What is variable GUL insurance?

Under a type of insurance known as *variable GUL*, the employee can select from a number of investment options for the savings element of the policy, such as equity funds and money market funds, or let some or all of the savings element accumulate at specified interest rates.

Q 12:29   How is GUL insurance typically provided to employees?

GUL insurance is generally offered as an elective employee-pay-all benefit that may supplement the employer's basic group term life insurance coverage. Employee premiums for GUL insurance generally are paid through payroll deduction, although employees may also be able to pay additional amounts directly in cash to the insurer.

Typically, available coverage is based on an employee's compensation, and the employee has a choice regarding the coverage amount, for example, one, two, or three times his or her compensation.

Q 12:30   Is GUL insurance subject to Section 79 group term life insurance treatment?

Generally, no. GUL insurance is considered a single, integrated, permanent insurance policy and not a policy of group term life insurance. [I.R.C. § 7702]

A policy having permanent elements can be subject to Code Section 79 if (1) the policy or the employer separately states in writing the part of the death benefit provided to each employee that is group term life insurance and (2) the designated group term portion of the benefit is at least a certain amount (calculated under a formula contained in the regulations). Because designating an insurance policy with permanent coverage as group term life insurance can produce adverse tax consequences for employees (see chapter 11), it is unlikely that employers would deliberately structure the GUL arrangement or write its employee communications to bring it within Code Section 79.

Even if GUL coverage could be deemed to have met the above conditions (through either deliberate or inadvertent action), Code Section 79 does not apply to employee-pay-all coverage unless it is arranged for by the employer and the term rates paid by the employees straddle the Table I rates in the Section 79 regulations (i.e., at least one employee pays more and at least one pays less than the Table I rates). This result can be avoided by offering the GUL coverage with rates that do not straddle Table I or by having the coverage sponsored by someone other than the employer, such as an independent insurer, a Section 501(c)(9) VEBA trust, an independent consultant, or an independent insurance broker, so that the employer has no part in arranging for the coverage other than providing payroll deductions (see chapter 11 for a discussion of these strategies). [Treas. Reg. §§ 1.79-0, 1.79-1(a), 1.79-1(b)]

Q 12:31   Is a GUL plan an employee benefit plan subject to ERISA?

Despite the fact that GUL insurance generally is an employee-pay-all plan, it may be subject to ERISA, depending on the amount of employer involvement. DOL regulations exempt a group insurance program from treatment as an ERISA employee welfare benefit plan if it satisfies four requirements (see Q 12:3). [DOL Reg. § 2510.3-1(j)]

The first, second, and fourth requirements in the DOL regulation ordinarily can be easily satisfied. The third requirement presents a facts and circumstances issue, however, and in many cases it may be difficult to be sure of the result. A number of DOL opinion letters take the view that the employer's involvement in developing and implementing the group program must be quite limited in order not to constitute employer sponsorship. [DOL Adv. Ops. 83-3A (Jan. 17, 1983), 82-9A (Feb. 1, 1982), 81-56A (June 29, 1981)]

The DOL requirement precluding employer involvement is much stricter than a similar test, under Code Section 79, for determining whether a group permanent insurance policy covering employees of an employer can be treated as a separate policy from a group term insurance policy of the same insurer (or affiliate) also covering employees of the employer. [Treas. Reg. § 1.79-0] That tax regulation does not contain an employer "sponsorship" concept and appears to permit substantial employer involvement in assisting sales of the coverage to employees (see chapter 11).

Q 12:32   Is a GUL plan subject to the ADEA?

Generally, yes. The ADEA prohibits discrimination because of age in all compensation, terms, conditions, and privileges of employment, specifically including all employee benefits. [29 U.S.C. § 630(l), as amended by § 102 of OWBPA] (For an explanation of the ADEA, see chapter 17.)

Q 12:33   Are employer contributions to GUL coverage tax deductible?

GUL coverage is generally an employee-pay-all proposition (see Q 12:27). Nonetheless, employer premium payments would be tax deductible on the same terms and subject to the same limitations as premium payments for other types of employee life insurance discussed in this chapter.

Q 12:34   How are GUL death benefit proceeds treated for federal income tax purposes?

Death benefit proceeds under GUL coverage receive the same favorable income tax treatment as other forms of life insurance proceeds, provided that the GUL policy meets the general tax definition of a life insurance policy contained in Code Section 7702. (The insurance carrier generally monitors compliance with the requirements of Code Section 7702.) Accordingly, the total death benefit under the GUL policy, including the savings element of the policy, is received by the beneficiary free of income tax. [I.R.C. § 101(a)]

If the GUL death benefit proceeds are paid in the form of installment payments or as a life annuity rather than in a single lump sum, the proceeds are treated as received ratably over the payout period. The portion of each payment constituting the ratable portion of the death benefit proceeds is received tax-free, and the balance of each payment representing investment earnings on the death benefit proceeds is taxable. [I.R.C. § 101(d)]

Q 12:35   How are GUL payments to an employee during his or her lifetime treated for federal income tax purposes?

A payment to an employee during his or her lifetime can occur as the result of a total surrender of the GUL policy, a partial withdrawal, or a policy loan. Each of those types of payments is taxed similarly to other forms of permanent life insurance.

Total surrender. The recovery of an employee's tax basis under the GUL policy, usually equal to his or her contributions, is tax-free. The gain under the GUL policy—that is, the amount by which the cash value of the employee's coverage exceeds the employee's tax basis in the policy—is subject to income tax. In addition, if the GUL policy is a modified endowment contract and the surrender is made before age 59½, a penalty tax may apply to the gain (see Q 12:36). [I.R.C. § 72(e)]

If an employee elects no later than 60 days after surrender to receive the surrender proceeds either in installments or as a life annuity, the employee's tax basis is recovered pro rata over the projected payout period, and the balance of each payment is taxable. [I.R.C. § 72(h)] If the employee outlives the projected payout period under a life annuity payout, and thus recovers his or her entire tax basis in the policy, the remaining payments are fully taxable. On the other hand, if the employee dies before his or her tax basis is recovered, a deduction for the unrecovered basis is allowed on the employee's final tax return or to the beneficiary (if there is a death benefit payable upon the death of the employee). [I.R.C. § 72(b)]

Partial withdrawal. Unless the employee's GUL coverage is a modified endowment contract (see Q 12:36), a partial withdrawal is tax-free to the extent that it does not exceed the employee's tax basis in the GUL policy. The portion (if any) of the withdrawal that exceeds the employee's tax basis in the GUL policy is taxable. [I.R.C. § 72(e)(5)]

Policy loan. Unless the employee's GUL coverage is a modified endowment contract (see Q 12:36), receipt of a policy loan has no income tax consequences to the employee. The amount of the loan is not taxable, and it does not affect the employee's tax basis in the policy. [I.R.C. § 72(e)(4)] Interest that the employee pays on the GUL policy loan generally is treated as a nondeductible personal interest expense, unless the proceeds of the policy loan are invested so that the policy loan interest qualifies as investment interest. [I.R.C. §§ 163(d), 163(h)(1), 163(h)(2)]

Q 12:36 What is a modified endowment contract, and how does this characterization affect employee taxation on lifetime payouts under a GUL policy?

A *modified endowment contract* is a contract that meets the general tax law definition of a life insurance contract in Code Section 7702 but that fails a "seven-pay test" (see Qs 12:37–12:40). Generally, the modified endowment contract rules do not apply to life insurance contracts entered into on or before June 20, 1988 (see Q 12:41). [I.R.C. § 7702A] If GUL coverage of an employee constitutes a modified endowment contract, then lifetime distributions, withdrawals, and policy loans will receive less favorable tax treatment than they would under other types of life insurance policies.

Distributions (e.g., withdrawals) under a policy that is a modified endowment contract are taxed on a taxable-income-out-first (before nontaxable principal) basis rather than on the tax-free basis-out-first recovery rules applicable to other life insurance policies (see Q 12:35). If the employee takes out a policy loan, the loan will be treated as a policy distribution and taxed on an income-out-first basis. Similarly, if the employee obtains a loan from a party other than the insurance carrier using the modified endowment contract as security, the loan is treated as triggering a policy distribution taxable on an income-out-first basis. (In contrast, loans relating to other life insurance policies have no tax effect; see Q 12:35.) [I.R.C. § 72(e)(10)]

Furthermore, a 10 percent penalty tax is imposed on the taxable amount of a distribution from a modified endowment policy to an employee who is under age 59½, unless one of the following exceptions applies:

1. The employee is disabled, as defined in Code Section 72(m)(7); or
2. The distribution is part of a series of substantially equal periodic payments made (not less frequently than annually) for the life or life

expectancy of the employee or the joint lives or joint life expectancies of the employee and his or her beneficiary.

[I.R.C. § 72(v)]

Q 12:37   What is the seven-pay test that an employee's GUL coverage must satisfy to avoid the modified endowment contract treatment?

The seven-pay test of Code Section 7702A requires that the amount of premiums paid under the contract at any time during the first seven contract years cannot exceed the total of all the net level premiums that would have been paid on or before that time, if the contract provided for paid-up future benefits after the payment of seven net level annual premiums. The Code provides computational rules for determining the amount of the seven net level premiums. [I.R.C. § 7702A(c)]

If an employee's GUL coverage fails to satisfy the seven-pay test, it is treated as a modified endowment contract, and unfavorable tax consequences follow (see Q 12:36). [I.R.C. § 7702A(b)]

Q 12:38   If GUL coverage satisfies the seven-pay test for the first seven years, is it assured of escaping modified endowment contract treatment thereafter?

No. Assurance of escaping modified endowment contract treatment generally exists only if there is no material change in the coverage. If there is a material change under the contract (apparently including a coverage increase based on increased compensation), the coverage is treated as a new contract subject to a new seven-pay test, with certain adjustments to reflect the cash surrender value of the contract at the time.

Generally, a material change includes any increase in future benefits under the contract *except* the following:

1. An increase attributable to the payment of premiums necessary to fund the lowest level of the death benefit and certain ancillary benefits payable in the first seven contract years;

2. An increase attributable to the crediting of interest or other earnings (including policyholder dividends); or

3. To the extent provided in Treasury regulations, any cost-of-living increase based on an established broad-based index (such as the consumer price index) that is funded ratably over the remaining period during which premiums are required to be paid under the contract.

[I.R.C. § 7702A(c)(3); Conf. Rept. on the Technical and Miscellaneous Revenue Act of 1988 (TAMRA), Pub. L. No. 100-647, 100th Cong., 2d Sess., Vol. II, 104–105 (1988)]

Practice Pointer. GUL coverage that is dependent on changes in compensation may always be subject to seven-pay testing (creating a succession of overlapping seven-pay tests). Thus, the insurer and employee may have to continuously monitor and limit the amount of premium payments if they want to avoid modified endowment contract status.

Q 12:39   If an employee's GUL coverage fails the seven-pay test at any time, can the failure be cured?

Yes. To cure the failure of the seven-pay test, the portion of the premiums paid during the contract year that caused the failure must be returned to the employee with interest no later than 60 days after the end of the contract year. The interest on the returned premiums is taxable. If the premiums are not returned with interest within the specified period, the coverage beginning on the date of failure is considered to be a modified endowment contract. [I.R.C. §§ 7702A(e)(1)(B), 7702A(e)(1)(C)]

Q 12:40   If the failure of the seven-pay test is not cured, will prior distributions (including loans) also become subject to modified endowment contract treatment?

To some extent, yes. Distributions made at any time during the contract year of the failure are affected. In addition, the Code specifies that regulations are to be issued that will provide that prior distributions made in anticipation of the failure to meet the seven-pay test will be affected. The Code also states that any prior distribution made within two years of the failure is to be treated as made in anticipation of the failure. [I.R.C. § 7702A(d)]

Q 12:41   Does the date on which GUL coverage begins affect the application of the modified endowment contract rules?

Yes. The rules generally apply to contracts entered into after June 20, 1988. The date on which an individual employee's coverage commenced is presumably the operative date. [I.R.C. § 7702A(a)(1)]

If, however, the death benefit under an old GUL contract increases by more than $150,000 over the death benefit in effect on October 20, 1988, the coverage will become subject to the seven-pay test if a material change (see Q 12:38) occurs thereafter. [TAMRA § 5012(e)(2)]

Practice Pointer. If the amount of GUL coverage under a pre-June 21, 1988, contract is tied to compensation, the $150,000 death benefit increase limit could be exceeded in time and the coverage thereafter be subject to the seven-pay test.

The safe harbor is also unavailable if (1) the death benefit is increased after June 20, 1988, and (2) the employee did not have a unilateral right under the contract before June 21, 1988, to obtain the increase without producing evidence of insurability. Additionally, the safe harbor for preexisting coverage is not available for any group term life insurance coverage issued before June 21, 1988, that is converted after June 20, 1988, to GUL coverage. [TAMRA § 5012(e)(3)]

Uninsured Death Benefits

Q 12:42   Are employer-provided uninsured death benefits subject to ERISA?

Generally, yes. ERISA's definition of a covered employee welfare benefit plan includes plans providing benefits in the event of death, regardless of whether the plan is insured. [ERISA § 3(1)] (See chapter 2 for a discussion of when a "plan" exists for ERISA purposes.)

This means that ERISA's reporting and disclosure requirements must be met, except to the extent that the plan qualifies for the partial ERISA exemption for top-hat plans. (See chapter 2 for further details.)

Q 12:43   Is an employer-provided uninsured death benefit plan subject to the ADEA?

Yes. The ADEA covers all compensation, terms, conditions, and privileges of employment, including all employee benefits. [29 U.S.C. § 630(l), as amended by § 102 of OWBPA] (For an explanation of the ADEA, see chapter 17.)

Q 12:44   May an employer deduct an uninsured death benefit it pays on behalf of an employee?

Yes. The amount an employer pays for an uninsured death benefit will generally be deductible when paid, assuming the payment represents reasonable compensation for the employee's past services. [I.R.C. § 162] If, however, the benefit is funded using a VEBA, the additional requirements of Code Sections 419 and 419A also must be satisfied (see chapter 20).

Q 12:45   Are employer-provided uninsured death benefits taxable income to the recipient?

Generally, yes. If an employer-provided death benefit is uninsured, the death benefit payment is fully includable in income. For many years the Code provided an exemption from income for the first $5,000 of employer-provided uninsured death benefits; however, that exemption was repealed effective for employees dying after August 20, 1996, by the Small Business Job Protection Act of 1996 (SBJPA). [Pub. L. No. 104-188, § 1402, 110 Stat. 1755 (1996)]

Exceptions. Even though they are not insured with a commercial life insurance carrier, certain state employee life insurance plans may be recognized as life insurance under state law; therefore, the death benefit payments qualify for the Section 101(a) life insurance exemption instead of being treated as uninsured death benefit payments. [I.R.C. § 7702; Ross v. Odom, 401 F.2d 464 (5th Cir. 1968)] In addition, a church self-funded death benefit plan is treated as life insurance even though the plan is not a life insurance contract under state law, provided it otherwise meets the requirements of life insurance contract status under Code Section 7702. Thus, death benefit payments under such a plan also qualify for the Section 101(a) life insurance exemption. [I.R.C. § 7702(j)]

Q 12:46   Is a death benefit funded through a VEBA treated as an uninsured death benefit or as life insurance proceeds?

Apparently, an uninsured death benefit provided through a VEBA would not qualify for exemption of the death benefit proceeds as life insurance proceeds. Exemption from income taxation as a life insurance death benefit hinges upon a contractual arrangement that meets the Code's definition of life insurance under Code Section 7702. That definition requires that the contract be a life insurance contract under state law. [I.R.C. §§ 101(a), 7702(a)] As a general rule, state laws do not appear to recognize a death benefit provided by a VEBA as a life insurance contract.

The IRS issued a private letter ruling stating that general and accidental death benefit payments paid by VEBAs are amounts received under a life insurance contract by reason of the death of the insured and are therefore excludable from income under Code Section 101(a). The IRS found that a VEBA's general death benefit is subject to Code Section 79, but that the accidental death benefit coverage provided by a VEBA does not qualify as group term life insurance under Code Section 79, pursuant to Treasury Regulations Section 1.79-1(a)(1). [Priv. Ltr. Rul. 9921036; 26 Pens. & Ben. Rep. (BNA) 25 (June 21, 1999)]

Split-Dollar Life Insurance

Q 12:47   What is a split-dollar plan?

A *split-dollar plan* is a life insurance plan under which both the employer and the employee have interests in permanent life insurance policy coverage on the employee's life. At the employee's death, the employer receives a specified portion of the death proceeds, and the employee's estate or beneficiary receives the balance of the proceeds.

Under the traditional split-dollar plan first developed many years ago, the employer paid only the portion of the annual policy premium that equaled the increase in the policy's cash value for that year, and the employee paid the remainder of the premium. At the employee's death, the employer received the cash surrender value of the policy (thus recouping most or all of its cost for the policy), and the employee's estate or beneficiary received the remainder of the death proceeds. Many variations of this prototype exist, generally involving the employer's payment of a larger portion, or even all, of the annual premium.

Ownership of the policy generally takes one of two forms. Under the *endorsement method*, the employer is the owner of record of the policy, and an endorsement is added to the policy to identify the employee's beneficial interest in the policy. Under the alternative arrangement, the *collateral assignment method*, the employee is the owner of record of the policy, but a collateral assignment of the policy is made to the employer to evidence the employer's beneficial interest in the life insurance.

Internal Revenue Service (IRS) final regulations generally provide that a life insurance arrangement (other than a tax-free, employer-provided group term insurance plan) will be treated as a split-dollar insurance arrangement if all of the following conditions apply:

1. The arrangement is between an owner of the life insurance contract and a nonowner;
2. Either party to the arrangement pays all or part of the premiums;
3. One of the parties paying the premiums is entitled to recover (either conditionally or unconditionally) all or any portion of those premiums; and
4. The recovery of the premiums is made from, or secured by, the proceeds of the policy.

[Treas. Reg. § 1.61-22(b)]

According to the IRS, this definition is intended to apply broadly. For example, it will cover an arrangement under which the nonowner of a contract provides funds directly to the owner of the contract and the owner uses the funds to pay premiums as long as the nonowner is entitled to recover all or a portion of the funds from the death benefits. In addition, the amount to be recovered by the party paying the premiums need not be determined by reference to the amount of those premiums.

A special rule applies in the case of split-dollar arrangements between employers and employees and corporations and shareholders. Under this special rule, a split-dollar life insurance arrangement also includes any arrangement between an owner and a nonowner of a life insurance contract if the following conditions apply:

1. The employer or corporation pays, directly or indirectly, all or any portion of the premiums, and
2. The beneficiary of the death benefit is either designated by the employee or shareholder or is a person whom the employee or shareholder would reasonably be expected to name as beneficiary.

[Treas. Reg. § 1.61-22(b)]

Q 12:48   Is split-dollar life insurance subject to ERISA?

Generally, yes. ERISA's definition of a covered employee welfare benefit plan includes plans providing benefits in the event of death. [ERISA § 3(1)] (See chapter 2 for a discussion of when a "plan" exists for ERISA purposes.)

Q 12:49   Can an employer deduct its premium payments under a split-dollar plan?

No. An employer cannot deduct premiums on a life insurance policy covering the life of an officer or employee if the employer is a beneficiary, directly or indirectly, under the policy, as it would be under a split-dollar plan. [I.R.C. § 264(a)(1)]

Q 12:50   Are benefits received by an employee under a split-dollar insurance arrangement subject to tax?

Yes. When and how those benefits are taxed depends on when the arrangement was entered into.

Nearly 40 years ago, the IRS laid down the basic ground rules for taxing split-dollar life insurance. In a 1964 ruling, the IRS concluded that all economic benefits conferred on an employee under a split-dollar insurance policy are taxable to the employee. [Rev. Rul. 64-328, 1964-2 C.B. 11] For example, in a traditional split-dollar arrangement, the economic benefit to the employee equals the value of the current pure insurance protection the employee receives because the cash value buildup accrues to the employee. Therefore, that amount, less any portion of the premium the employee pays, is taxable to the employee.

In recent years, the IRS began tinkering with the split-dollar rules. In a series of notices, rulings, and proposed regulations, the IRS changed the rules for valuing the economic benefit an employee receives under a traditional split-dollar arrangement. In addition, the IRS launched an all-out assault on reverse split-dollar arrangements (see Q 12:57) and proposed a new taxing regime for equity split-dollar arrangements (see Qs 12:58, 12:59). The IRS guidance culminated in the issuance of the final regulation governing the federal income, gift, and employment tax treatment of split-dollar life insurance. [Treas. Reg. § 1.61-22]

Treasury Regulations Section 1.61-22 applies only to split-dollar arrangements entered into after September 17, 2003, or to arrangements entered into on or before September 17, 2003, that are materially modified after that date. Earlier guidance continues to apply to arrangements entered into on or before September 17, 2003. Therefore, the precise tax treatment of a split-dollar arrangement depends on the date it was entered into and whether it has been materially modified since that date.

The final regulation contains a nonexclusive list of changes that are *not* considered material modifications that would subject a contract to the final regulation. Those nonmaterial modifications include:

- A change solely in the premium payment method (e.g., a change from monthly to quarterly premiums);
- A change solely in the beneficiary of the life insurance contract, unless the beneficiary is a party to the arrangement;
- A change solely in the interest rate payable under the life insurance contract on a policy loan;
- A change solely necessary to preserve the status of the life insurance contract under Code Section 7702;
- A change solely to the administrative provisions of the life insurance contract (e.g., a change in the address to which payments are sent);
- A change made solely under the terms of any agreement (other than the life insurance contract) that is a part of the split-dollar life insurance arrangement if the change is a non-discretionary change made by the parties and is made pursuant to a binding commitment (whether set forth in the agreement or otherwise) in effect on or before September 17, 2003;
- A change solely in the owner of the life insurance contract as a result of a corporate acquisition covered by Code Section 381(a), in which substantially all the former owner's assets are transferred to the new owner of the policy;
- A change to the policy required by a court or a state insurance commissioner as a result of the insolvency of the insurance company that issued the policy; and
- A change in the insurance company that administers the policy as a result of an assumption reinsurance transaction between the issuing insurance company and the new insurance company to which the owner and the nonowner were not a party.

Bear in mind, however, that existing split-dollar arrangements may be affected by rule changes in earlier IRS guidance even if they are not subject to the final regulations.

Practice Pointer. The IRS has issued a notice that makes it clear that split-dollar life insurance arrangements may also be subject to new tax rules for nonqualified deferred compensation. [IRS Notice 2007-34, 2007-17 I.R.B. 996] For detailed discussion of the new regulations under Code Section 409A regarding nonqualified deferred compensation, see Smith & Downey, *Nonqualified Deferred Compensation Answer Book* (Aspen Publishers, 2010).

Q 12:51 What are the basic tax principles under the final split-dollar regulations?

The final regulations provide two mutually exclusive taxing regimes for split-dollar insurance.

1. *Economic benefit regime.* Under this regime, the owner of the contract is treated as providing economic benefits to the nonowner. The value of the economic benefits provided to the nonowner for any year equals the sum of:

   The tax treatment of economic benefits depends on the relationship between the contract owner and the nonowner. For example, in a split-dollar arrangement in which an employer provides an employee with economic benefits, the benefits are treated as compensation to the employee, which the employee must report on his or her income tax return and the employer must report on employment tax returns.

   a. The cost of current life insurance protection,

   b. The amount of policy cash value to which the nonowner has current access (less any amount taken into account in a prior tax year), and

   c. The value of any other economic benefit provided to the nonowner.

2. *Loan regime.* Under the loan regime, premium payments made either directly or indirectly by the nonowner of the policy are treated as loans to the owner when repayment is to be made from, or is secured by, either the policy's death benefit or its cash surrender value, or both. For example, if a policy is owned by an employee and premiums are paid by the employer, the employer's premium payments are treated as a series of loans to the employee. The loans will either carry an actual interest rate that the employee will pay, or, if no interest or a low interest rate is charged, the interest rate will be imputed under the rules of Code Section 7872.

The amount of interest paid by the employee, or the amount of imputed interest, is taxed as interest income to the employer. The amount of imputed interest that accrues on the total outstanding premium loan each year is treated as compensation income to the employee and is deductible by the employer.

Under the final regulations, the owner of the life insurance policy is generally the person officially named as owner under the policy. If two or more persons are named as owners, the first-named person generally is treated as the owner of the policy. However, the regulations provide that the economic benefit regime will apply to all employer-employee split-dollar arrangements other than equity split-dollar arrangements, regardless of who is named as owner of the policy.

In the case of equity split-dollar arrangements, which regime applies depends on who is the owner of the policy. In an equity arrangement set up under the endorsement method (the employer is the owner), the economic benefit regime applies. If the collateral assignment method is used (the employee is the owner), the loan regime applies. [Treas. Reg. § 1.61-22]

Q 12:52 Does an employer's payment of part or all of the annual premium under a traditional split-dollar insurance arrangement result in taxable income to the employee?

Yes. An employee is taxed on the value of the death benefit coverage provided by his or her employer, based on the cost of one year of term insurance. However, the rules for determining that value have been in a state of flux in recent years.

In 1964, the IRS ruled that the amount of death benefit protection payable to the employee's estate or beneficiary could be valued according to the IRS's PS 58 table, based on the attained age of the employee. [Rev. Rul. 64-328, 1964-2 C.B. 11] The IRS subsequently ruled that if the life insurance company's published one-year term rates for standard risks under newly issued policies were lower than the PS 58 rates, the insurer's rates could be used. After the value of the death benefit coverage for the employee is calculated, the employee-paid portion of the annual premium is subtracted to arrive at the amount taxable to the employee. [Rev. Rul. 64-328, 1964-2 C.B. 11; Rev. Rul. 66-110, 1966-1 C.B. 12]

In 2001, the IRS announced a change in the valuation rules for split-dollar arrangements. The IRS concluded that the PS 58 rates, which are based on mortality tables originally published in 1946, no longer reflect the fair market value of current life insurance protection. Because the rates are too high, employers using those rates to value current life insurance protection under traditional split-dollar arrangements force employees to pay more tax than they should. To remedy this problem, the IRS released a new table (Table 2001) with materially lower rates than the PS 58 table. At that time, the IRS said that use of the Table 2001 rates was optional for tax years ending after January 9, 2001 (e.g., calendar year 2001). However, the IRS said that it would no longer accept the use of the PS 58 rates to value current life insurance protection for tax years ending after December 31, 2001 (e.g., calendar year 2002). [IRS Notice 2001-10, 2001-5 I.R.B. 1]

In early 2002, the IRS retracted that guidance and issued another set of valuation rules. [IRS Notice 2002-8, 2002-4 I.R.B. 398] Under those rules, employers could continue to use the PS 58 rates for split-dollar life insurance arrangements entered into before January 28, 2002, if a contractual arrangement between the employer and the employee provides that those rates will be used to determine the value of the current life insurance protection to the employee (or to the employee and one or more other persons). Alternatively, Table 2001 could be used to value the current life insurance protection under these arrangements.

For arrangements entered into on or after January 28, 2002, and before the effective date of the final split-dollar regulations, employers must use Table 2001 to determine the value of current life insurance protection on a single life (unless they opt to use an insurer's published rates). Employers must make appropriate adjustments to the Table 2001 rates if the life insurance protection covers more than one life.

At the same time, the IRS took aim at the use of unreasonably low substitute rates set by insurers. The IRS said that it would continue to allow the use of an insurer's rates to value the current life insurance protection. In the case of arrangements entered into on or after January 28, 2002, however, an insurer's rates will be accepted for periods after 2003 (e.g., calendar year 2004 and later years) only if

- The insurer generally makes the availability of such rates know to persons who apply for term insurance; and
- The insurer regularly sells term insurance at those rates to individuals who apply for coverage through normal distribution channels.

Notice 2002-8 also gave employers and employees the option of treating the employer's premium payments as loans by the employer to the employee (apparently even in situations where the employer is the owner of the policy) subject to the imputed interest rules of Code Section 7872. All payments by the employer from the inception of the arrangement (reduced by any repayments to the employer) before the first tax year of loan treatment must be treated as loans entered into at the beginning of the first year.

The final IRS regulations issued in 2003 follow the historic approach of the earlier IRS guidance. The economic benefit to the employee equals the value of the current life insurance protection provided by the employer (total death benefit less cash value).

In the case of traditional, nonequity split-dollar arrangements, the final regulations provide that the employer is treated as the owner of the contract and the employee as the nonowner, regardless of the actual ownership arrangement (e.g., endorsement or collateral assignment). Therefore, the economic benefit regime is mandated, and the value of current life insurance protection provided to the employee for any year equals the amount of the current life insurance protection provided to the employee multiplied by the life insurance premium factor designated or permitted in guidance published in the Internal Revenue Bulletin (currently, Table 2001). Subject to an anti-abuse rule, current life insurance protection is determined on the last day of the nonowner's taxable year unless the parties agree to use the policy anniversary date. [Treas. Reg. § 1.61-22]

> **Example.** Ross Company is the owner of a $1 million life insurance contract that is part of a split-dollar arrangement between Ross Company and its employee, John Eagan. Under the arrangement, Ross Company pays all the $10,000 annual premiums and is entitled to receive the greater of its premiums or the cash surrender value of the contract when Eagan dies or the arrangement terminates. Through year 10, Ross Company has paid $100,000 of premiums. In year 10, the cost of term insurance is $1 per $1,000 of insurance and the cash surrender value of the contract is $200,000. Assuming a premium factor of .001, Eagan's compensation income from the arrangement is $800 ($1 million − $200,000 payable to Ross = $800,000 × .001 premium factor).

As a result of the guidance discussed above, the following rules apply for purposes of determining the amount of annual taxable income to an employee under traditional, nonequity split-dollar arrangements.

Arrangements entered into before January 28, 2002. Arrangements that contractually require PS 58 rates be used to calculate the insured employee's economic benefit will be allowed to continue to use PS 58 rates in the future. Arrangements that do not contain such a contractual requirement must use Table 2001 rates. All plans may use the insurer's published rates.

Arrangements entered into on or after January 28, 2002, and before September 18, 2003. All plans must use the Table 2001 rates if they use the economic benefit regime. Plans may use the insurer's published rates, subject to the following conditions for periods after 2003:

- The insurer generally makes the availability of such rates known to persons who apply for term insurance; and
- The insurer regularly sells term insurance at those rates to individuals who apply for coverage through normal distribution channels.

Plans may use the loan regime instead of the economic benefit regime at the option of the employer and employee.

Arrangements entered into after September 17, 2003 (or materially modified after that date). All employer-employee plans are subject to the economic benefit regime. The taxable economic benefit to the employee equals the value of the current life insurance protection provided by the employer (death benefit less cash value).

The cost of current life insurance protection equals the amount of the current life insurance protection multiplied by the life insurance premium factor designated or permitted in guidance published in the Internal Revenue Bulletin (currently, Table 2001). Subject to an anti-abuse rule, current life insurance protection is determined on the last day of the nonowner's taxable year unless the parties agree to use the policy anniversary date.

Q 12:53 When may an employer use an insurer's published premium rate to determine the value of an employee's current life insurance protection under a split-dollar insurance arrangement?

In 1966, the IRS ruled that, as an alternative to the official tables, an employer may determine the value of the current life insurance protection using an insurer's published rate, provided the rate is available to all standard risks for initial-issue one-year term insurance. [Rev. Rul. 66-110, 1966-1 C.B. 12] However, in the case of split-dollar arrangements entered into on or after January 28, 2002, an insurer's rates will be accepted for periods after 2003 only if:

1. The insurer generally makes the availability of such rates known to persons who apply for term insurance; and

2. The insurer regularly sells term insurance at such rates to individuals who apply for coverage through normal distribution channels.

[IRS Notice 2002-8, 2002-4 I.R.B. 398]

Moreover, under the IRS's final split-dollar regulations, the value of current life insurance protection provided to an employee under a traditional, nonequity split-dollar arrangement must be determined under the economic benefit regime. Under that regime, that value equals the amount of the current life insurance protection multiplied by the life insurance premium factor designated or permitted in guidance published in the Internal Revenue Bulletin (currently, Table 2001). The final regulations apply to arrangements entered into after September 17, 2003 (or materially modified after that date). [Treas. Reg. § 1.61-22]

Q 12:54   What is the income tax treatment of death benefit proceeds under a split-dollar plan?

The tax law provides an income tax exemption for life insurance proceeds. [I.R.C. § 101(a)] This exemption generally applies to split-dollar life insurance benefits received by the employer and by the employee's estate or beneficiary. However, the IRS's final split-dollar regulations provide that death benefits paid to a beneficiary (other than the owner of the life insurance policy) are excludable only to the extent they are allocable to current life insurance protection provided to the nonowner under the split-dollar life insurance arrangement, the cost of which was paid by the nonowner, or the value of which the nonowner actually took into account as an economic benefit provided by the owner to the nonowner. [Treas. Reg. § 1.61-22]

In addition, if the employer is subject to the corporate alternative minimum tax, a portion of the death proceeds may be subject to that tax. Earnings on the cash value owned by the employer may also have to be taken into account for corporate alternative minimum tax purposes. [I.R.C. § 56(g); Prop. Treas. Reg. § 1.56(g)-1(c)(5)]

Q 12:55   What is the federal estate tax treatment of death proceeds under a split-dollar insurance plan?

The death benefit proceeds under a split-dollar insurance plan are treated as life insurance proceeds for federal estate tax purposes. Accordingly, the portion of the death benefit proceeds payable to the employee's estate are includable in the employee's federal gross estate. Further, any portion of the proceeds payable to a named beneficiary are also includable in the employee's federal gross estate if the employee possessed any incidents of ownership in the policy at the time of death. Also, if the employee transferred ownership of his or her interest in the policy within three years of death, such interest will be included in his or her federal gross estate. [I.R.C. §§ 2042, 2035]

Q 12:56   What is a split-dollar plan rollout, and what are its tax consequences to the employee and employer?

A *rollout* is the termination of a split-dollar arrangement with regard to a particular employee through the placement by an employer of complete ownership and control of the life insurance policy in the hands of that employee. In return for giving up its interest in the policy, the employer may, depending on the contractual understanding of the parties, withdraw from the policy the cash surrender value amount or some lesser amount, such as an amount equal to its contributions. The employer may even turn over the policy to the employee without receiving anything in return.

For example, suppose the arrangement is a traditional split-dollar plan (see Q 12:47), under which the employer contributes an amount equal to the increase in cash value each year. If the employer gives the employee full ownership at some future time (for example, at the employee's retirement) in return for payment to the employer of an amount equal to the cash value at the time of rollout, there should be no income tax consequences to the employee as a result of the rollout.

If, however, the employer receives less on a rollout than the amount of the cash value attributable to its contributions, the employee will have received an equity interest in the policy that represents an additional economic benefit to the employee. The IRS has announced proposed and interim rules for the taxation of such arrangements. [Notice 2002-8, 2002-4 I.R.B. 398] (See Q 12:59.)

Q 12:57   What is a reverse split-dollar plan, and what are its tax consequences to the employee?

As its name implies, a *reverse split-dollar plan* is the reverse of the traditional split-dollar plan (see Q 12:47). Under a reverse split-dollar plan, the employer is the beneficiary for the term insurance portion of the death proceeds. The employee designates the beneficiary of the balance of the death proceeds and owns the cash value of the policy.

In a reverse split-dollar arrangement, the employer typically pays the entire premium. The employee owes tax on the value of the policy benefits he or she is entitled to.

Just as with traditional split-dollar arrangements, the IRS says that the PS 58 rate table, which has traditionally been used to value current insurance protection, no longer reflects the fair market value of current insurance protection under a reverse split-dollar arrangement. In 2001, the IRS released a new table (Table 2001) with materially lower rates than the PS 58 table. At that time, the IRS said that use of the Table 2001 rates was optional for tax years ending after January 9, 2001 (e.g., calendar year 2001). However, the IRS said that it would no longer accept the use of the PS 58 rates to value current life insurance protection for tax years ending after December 31, 2001 (e.g., calendar year 2002). [Notice 2001-10, 2001-5 I.R.B. 1]

In early 2002, the IRS retracted that guidance and issued another set of valuation rules. [Notice 2002-8, 2002-4 I.R.B. 398] Under these rules, employers may continue to use the PS 58 rates to value split-dollar life insurance arrangements—including reverse split-dollar arrangements—entered into before January 28, 2002, if a contractual arrangement between the employer and the employee provides that those rates will be used to determine the value of the current life insurance protection to the employee (or to the employee and one or more other persons). Alternatively, Table 2001 may be used to value the current life insurance protection under these arrangements.

For arrangements entered into on or after January 28, 2002, and before the effective date of future guidance, employers must use Table 2001 to determine the value of current life insurance protection on a single life (unless they opt to use an insurer's published rates). Employers must make appropriate adjustments to the Table 2001 rates if the life insurance protection covers more than one life.

When the IRS issued the above notices, it was widely assumed that Table 2001 or an insurer's published rates could be used to determine the value of an employee's benefit under a reverse split-dollar arrangement. In other words, it was assumed that the employee owed tax on the employer-paid premium less the value of the employer's current insurance protection as determined using Table 2001 or an insurer's published rates. However, a notice issued in 2002 belies that assumption.

In the notice, the IRS stated that Table 2001 or an insurer's published rates can be used to value current life insurance protection *only* when that protection is conferred as an economic benefit by one party on the other party (e.g., in an endorsement arrangement where the employee is entitled to the current life insurance protection). However, Table 2001 or an insurer's rates *cannot* be used to value the current life insurance protection of a party to a split-dollar arrangement for purposes of determining the value of any policy benefits another party is entitled to. In other words, in a reverse split-dollar arrangement, the annual value of an employee's benefits cannot be determined simply by subtracting the Table 2001 value of the current insurance protection or the insurer's rates for such protection from the total premium paid by the employer.

In its notice, the IRS specifically states that it is intended to address reverse split-dollar arrangements where the party holding the right to current life insurance rates uses inappropriately high current term insurance rates, prepayment of premiums, or other techniques to understate the value of the policy benefits going to the other party. [IRS Notice 2002-59]

Q 12:58 What is an equity split-dollar arrangement?

Under a traditional split-dollar arrangement, death benefits are split between the employer and the employee's beneficiaries, with the employer getting that portion of the benefit which is equal to the policy's cash value and the remainder going to the employee's beneficiaries. Under an *equity split-dollar arrangement*, the death benefit that goes to the employee's beneficiaries is not limited to what is left over after the employer gets the cash value; the beneficiaries get a portion of the cash value as well. The employer generally recovers only an amount equal to the cumulative premiums it paid. The remainder of the death benefit is paid to the beneficiaries. During the life of the policy, when the cash value buildup exceeds the cumulative premiums paid by the employer, the employee is considered to have an equity interest in the policy. If the policy is surrendered, the employee will receive a portion of the cash value.

Q 12:59　　How is an employee taxed under an equity split-dollar arrangement?

Under an equity split-dollar arrangement, the employer generally recovers only an amount equal to the cumulative premiums it paid, with the remainder of the benefit going to the employee's beneficiaries. During the life of the policy, when the cash value buildup exceeds the cumulative premiums paid by the employer, the employee is considered to have an equity interest in the policy. This additional economic benefit, over and above the pure insurance protection, is taxable. *How* it is taxed is complicated.

For example, Code Section 83 governs the transfer of property from an employer to an employee. The employee generally owes tax when he or she receives the property or, if restrictions are imposed, when the restrictions lapse. If an equity split-dollar arrangement involves the transfer of property from an employer to an employee, Code Section 83 will control.

On the other hand, an equity split-dollar arrangement may be viewed as the purchase of life insurance by an employee with the proceeds of loans from the employer. In this situation, Code Section 7872 takes center stage. Code Section 7872 deals with interest-free or low-interest loans between certain parties, including employers and employees. If, for example, an employer lends money to an employee at no interest, Code Section 7872 imputes an interest charge to the loan. The employer is treated as paying the employee an amount equal to the imputed interest, which the employee then pays back to the employer as interest on the loan. The employee has compensation income for the imputed interest. The employer has a compensation deduction for the imputed interest, offset by the imputed interest income received from the employee.

The problem, of course, is determining whether an equity split-dollar arrangement is a transfer of property (subject to Code Section 83) or a series of loans (under Code Section 7872).

In 2002, the IRS issued Notice 2002-8 [2002-4 I.R.B. 398] laying down interim rules for arrangements entered into before the publication of final split-dollar regulations. In 2003, the IRS issued final regulations effective for split-dollar arrangements entered into after September 17, 2003, or to arrangements entered into on or before September 17, 2003, that are materially modified after that date. [Treas. Reg. § 1.61-22] As a result of this developing guidance, the tax treatment of equity split-dollar arrangements will generally depend on the effective date of the arrangement.

Arrangements entered into before January 28, 2002. Any excess cash value accumulation in equity split-dollar plans entered into before January 28, 2002, will avoid annual income taxation if two conditions are met: (1) The arrangement must continue to be treated as a split-dollar arrangement; and (2) the parties involved in the arrangement must continue to report the economic benefit of the pure insurance using either PS 58 rates (if required to do so by contract), the Table 2001 rates, or an insurance company's published rates.

How policy cash value accumulations in excess of premiums advanced by the employer-sponsor will be treated upon termination of the equity split-dollar arrangement depends on whether or not the arrangement remains as it is or takes advantage of one of the two safe harbors offered by the Notice 2002-8 guidelines.

If the arrangement continues as a split-dollar arrangement under which the parties continue to recognize economic benefits, then the annual excess cash value accumulation will not be subject to income taxation. However, upon plan termination, when the employer-sponsor typically is paid back an amount equal only to premiums paid, any excess cash value transferred to the insured will be income taxable to the employee in the year received. Alternatively, to avoid income taxation of excess cash value at plan termination, one of two safe harbors must be chosen:

1. The plan must be terminated before January 1, 2004.
2. The plan must treat employer-advanced premiums as loans for all periods beginning on or after January 1, 2004.

If the plan terminates, excess cash value transferred to the insured employee before January 1, 2004, will escape taxation at transfer and will not be taxed unless withdrawals exceed the insured employee's basis in the policy cash value.

As with nonequity arrangements, loan treatment can be elected. If the plan elects loan treatment, all premiums paid from inception of the arrangement will be subject to either an actual or an imputed interest rate under Code Section 7872 starting in 2004. Instead of paying a premium or recognizing imputed economic benefit income for tax purposes, the insured employee will either actually pay the interest due or recognize imputed loan interest annually.

If employer-advanced premiums are treated as loans, excess cash value will not be income taxable to the insured employee at plan termination simply because the employer is repaid advanced premiums and the insured employee becomes the sole owner of all policy values, including any excess cash value remaining.

Arrangements entered into after January 28, 2002, and before September 18, 2003. There are only two tax options for equity split-dollar arrangements entered into on or after January 28, 2002, but before the issuance of final regulations.

If premiums are treated as loans, the treatment will be the same as for those pre-January 28, 2002, plans that convert to loan treatment prior to January 1,

2004. The insured will pay loan interest or recognize it as imputed interest and pay tax on it; excess cash value will not be income taxable upon termination of the agreement.

If premiums are not treated as loans, the arrangement must continue to be treated as a split-dollar arrangement and the parties involved must continue to recognize economic benefit each year. Upon termination, any excess cash value transferred to the insured will be subject to income taxation in the year of transfer.

Arrangements entered into after September 17, 2003 (or materially modified after that date). The final split-dollar regulations tax equity split-dollar arrangements entered into after September 17, 2003 (or arrangements that are materially modified after that date), under two mutually exclusive regimes: the economic benefit regime and the loan regime (see Q 12:51). If the employer is the owner of the life insurance contract (e.g., an endorsement arrangement), the tax consequences will be determined under the economic benefit regime. If the employee is the owner (e.g., a collateral assignment arrangement), the tax is determined under the loan regime.

Economic benefit regime. Under the final regulations, the value of the economic benefits provided by the employer to the employee for a taxable year equals not only the cost of any current life insurance protection provided to the employee, but also the amount of policy cash value to which the employee has "current access" (to the extent that such amount was not actually taken into account for a prior taxable year).

The employee has current access to any portion of the policy cash value to which he or she has a current or future right and that currently is directly or indirectly accessible by the employee, inaccessible to the employer, or inaccessible to the employer's general creditors. The policy cash value, like the amount of current life insurance protection, is determined as of the last day of the employee's taxable year unless the parties agree to use the policy anniversary date.

The IRS says that "access" is to be construed broadly, and it includes any direct or indirect right of the employee to obtain, use, or realize potential economic value from the policy cash value. Thus, an employee has current access to a policy's cash value if he or she can directly or indirectly make a withdrawal from the policy, borrow from the policy, or effect a total or partial surrender of the policy. Similarly, the employee has current access if he or she can anticipate, assign, pledge, or encumber the cash value or if the cash value is available to the employee's creditors by attachment, garnishment, or levy.

The policy's cash value will be considered inaccessible to the employer if the employer does not have the full rights to policy cash value normally held by an owner of a life insurance contract. The policy's cash value will be considered inaccessible to the employer's general creditors if, under the terms of the arrangement or by operation of law, the creditors cannot, for any reason, effectively reach the full policy cash value in the event of the employer's bankruptcy.

Loan regime. If the split-dollar arrangement is established under the collateral assignment method, then the premiums advanced by the employer are generally treated in one of two ways under the regulations. The treatment depends on whether or not the insured employee is obligated to repay the premiums advanced under the split-dollar arrangement. If employer-advanced premiums are not subject to repayment upon plan termination, then the full value of the annual employer-advanced premium must be included in the employee's gross income for income tax purposes. If the insured employee is obligated to repay the employer for any premium payments that have been advanced, then the annual premium payments are treated as a series of loans. The loans will either carry an actual interest rate the employee will pay or an imputed interest rate under the rules of Code Section 7872.

Under the loan regime, excess policy cash value is not subject to income taxation upon termination of the split-dollar arrangement.

Bonus Life Insurance

Q 12:60   What is a bonus life insurance plan?

A *bonus life insurance plan* is an arrangement under which an employer pays all or a portion of the premium cost for life insurance coverage for one or more employees either to each employee directly or on his or her behalf to the insurance carrier. The employer treats its payments as cash bonuses to the covered employees. Typically, the life insurance selected is a form of permanent life insurance, such as whole life insurance or universal life insurance, and individual policies rather than a group policy ordinarily provide the life insurance coverage. The insurance policy is wholly owned by the employee.

Q 12:61   What is the income tax treatment of a bonus life insurance plan?

Under a bonus life insurance plan, an employer generally treats the bonus payments it makes as compensation payments that are fully tax deductible by the employer. As well, the employer treats the payments as wages to the covered employees, subject to income tax withholding and Federal Insurance Contributions Act (FICA) and Federal Unemployment Tax Act (FUTA) taxation. In some cases, the employer may "gross up" the payments to the covered employees to reimburse the employee for some or all of the income tax liabilities the employee has with respect to the bonus payments.

Practice Pointer. It is generally assumed that the bonus life insurance plan is not a group term life insurance plan for purposes of Code Section 79. Nevertheless, to avoid possible application of, and adverse tax treatment under, Code Section 79 (see chapter 11), it may be advisable for the employer to give the eligible employees the choice of taking the bonus payment in cash instead of receiving the life insurance coverage.

Q 12:62   Is a bonus life insurance plan subject to ERISA?

Whether a bonus life insurance plan is subject to ERISA appears to be an open issue. Inasmuch as the employer treats its payments as current compensation and employee cash wages, it can be argued that no ERISA plan is created. The position that no ERISA plan exists appears to be strengthened considerably if the employees are given the choice of taking the employer payments in cash in lieu of applying them to the cost of the life insurance coverage.

Death Benefits Under Qualified Retirement Plans

Q 12:63   Can a tax-qualified retirement plan provide death benefit coverage for plan participants?

Yes. Under a tax-qualified retirement plan, the employer can provide the employees with death benefit protection, through insurance or otherwise, provided the death benefit coverage is "incidental" to the retirement benefits. [Treas. Reg. § 1.401-1(b)(1)]

Q 12:64   How does the incidental test apply in the case of life insurance coverage provided under a qualified pension plan?

The IRS has developed several tests for determining whether a preretirement death benefit under a pension plan is incidental:

1. A life insurance or uninsured death benefit will be considered incidental if the cost of the death benefit for a participant provided by employer contributions and earnings does not exceed 25 percent of the total cost of all benefits for the participant. [Rev. Rul. 70-611, 1970-2 C.B. 89] This test applies to a term life insurance contract.

2. If the pension plan is funded in part through the purchase of ordinary insurance contracts (for example, whole life insurance), up to, but not including, 50 percent of the employer contributions for a particular participant may be applied to an ordinary insurance contract on the participant's life. [Rev. Rul. 74-307, 1974-2 C.B. 126] This test is deemed to be consistent with the first test (the 25 percent test) because the ordinary insurance contract provides death benefits and retirement benefits.

3. A life insurance death benefit in a qualified pension plan will be considered incidental if the death benefit before retirement does not exceed the greater of 100 times the monthly retirement benefit, or the cash value of the policy.

[Rev. Rul. 68-31, 1968-1 C.B. 151]

Q 12:65   How does the incidental test apply to life insurance coverage provided under a qualified profit sharing plan?

For life insurance coverage provided under a qualified profit sharing plan, the incidental test applies as follows:

1. Not more than 25 percent of the employer's current contributions and forfeitures allocated to the employee's account may be applied to life or accident or health insurance coverage or both.

2. If ordinary life insurance (for example, whole life insurance) is purchased, the percentage is increased up to, but not including, 50 percent. If accident or health insurance is also purchased, the premium for the accident or health insurance plus half of the premium for the ordinary life insurance cannot exceed 25 percent of the employer's contributions plus forfeitures.

3. If the profit sharing plan permits funds accumulated for a specified period to be distributed, funds accumulated for the required period may be applied to life insurance or health insurance coverage without regard to the incidental test. Generally, funds must be accumulated under a profit sharing plan for at least two years before distribution.

[Rev. Rul. 61-164, 1961-2 C.B. 58]

Q 12:66   How does the incidental test apply to life insurance purchased with voluntary employee contributions?

The incidental test has no application to life insurance purchased with voluntary employee contributions, that is, after-tax employee contributions. Thus, the full amount of such contributions may be applied to the purchase of life insurance if the plan so permits. [Rev. Rul. 69-408, 1969-2 C.B. 58]

Q 12:67   What rules apply in determining whether the life insurance is purchased with employer contributions?

If the qualified retirement plan specifies that the life insurance premiums will be paid with employee contributions, the plan provision will apply. If the plan is silent, however, the life insurance premiums will be considered to be paid first from employer contributions and plan earnings. Whether the life insurance coverage is purchased in whole or in part with employer contributions is important in determining the income tax treatment of the life insurance coverage (see Q 12:68). [Rev. Rul. 68-390, 1968-2 C.B. 175]

Q 12:68   Is an employee taxed on life insurance coverage provided under a qualified retirement plan?

Yes. An employee is taxed on life insurance coverage provided under a qualified retirement plan unless the coverage is provided with the employee's own after-tax contributions. If the life insurance coverage is provided through employer contributions or plan earnings or both, the value of the life insurance coverage (that is, the value of the term protection) is taxable income to the employee each year. [I.R.C. § 72(m)(3); Treas. Reg. § 1.72-16(b)(2)]

Q 12:69   How should an employer determine the value of the life insurance protection taxable to an employee under a qualified retirement plan?

The value of the life insurance protection under a qualified retirement plan is determined in the same way as it is for life insurance protection under a split-dollar plan (see Q 12:52). An employer generally is required to use a table promulgated by the IRS to value the life insurance protection. If, however, the life insurance company providing the coverage has published one-year term rates for standard risks under newly issued policies that are lower than the table rates, the insurer's one-year term rates may be used instead. [Rev. Rul. 64-328, 1964-2 C.B. 11; Rev. Rul. 66-110, 1966-1 C.B. 12]

Under current rules, life insurance values must be calculated using IRS Table 2001. [Notice 2001-10, 2001-5 I.R.B. 1]

Q 12:70   How are life insurance death benefits paid to an employee's estate or beneficiary under a qualified retirement plan treated for federal income tax purposes?

If the life insurance policy provided only term life insurance coverage, the entire death benefit is exempt as life insurance proceeds under Code Section 101(a). If, however, the life insurance policy had a cash reserve value (for example, coverage was provided under a whole life insurance policy), only the pure death benefit protection portion of the policy (that is, the difference between the total death benefit and the cash value) is exempt as life insurance proceeds under Code Section 101(a).

The cash value portion is treated as a pension benefit and is taxable in accordance with the rules of Code Section 72. In addition to actual contributions made by the employee, the employee's tax basis, which is recovered tax-free by the estate or beneficiary, includes the value of the term coverage that was taxed to the employee while living. [Treas. Reg. §§ 1.72-8(a), 1.72-16(c), 1.402(a)-1(a)(5), 1.402(a)-1(a)(6)]

Q 12:71   Can tax-qualified retirement plans provide preretirement death benefits to employees other than through the purchase of life insurance?

Yes. Tax-qualified retirement plans can provide preretirement death benefits other than through life insurance, as long as the incidental death benefit test is satisfied.

Generally, qualified pension plans, but not qualified profit sharing plans, are required to offer to participating employees a qualified preretirement survivor annuity death benefit payable to the surviving spouse of a deceased employee. The amount of the qualified preretirement survivor annuity is based on the amount of the employee's vested pension benefit and must fall within a specified minimum and maximum amount. [I.R.C. §§ 401(a)(11), 417]

An employer does not have to absorb the cost of the preretirement survivor annuity and may charge the cost of the benefit through a reduction in the amount of vested pension benefits. Nonetheless, under many plans the employer subsidizes the cost of the qualified preretirement survivor annuity in whole or in part. [Treas. Reg. § 1.401(a)-20, Q&A-21]

Unless the qualified preretirement survivor annuity is fully subsidized by the employer, the employee must be given the opportunity to waive the benefit with the consent of his or her spouse. [Treas. Reg. § 1.401(a)-20, Q&A-37, -38]

Q 12:72 Can tax-qualified retirement plans provide postretirement death benefits?

Yes. Generally, qualified retirement plans are required to pay retirement benefits to a married employee in the form of a qualified joint and survivor annuity for the employee and the employee's spouse, unless the employee, with the consent of his or her spouse, elects to take the retirement benefits in another form of payment provided under the plan. No election need be provided if the benefit is fully subsidized by the employer. [I.R.C. §§ 401(a)(11), 417; Treas. Reg. § 1.401(a)-20, Q&A-37, -38]

A qualified retirement plan may also include death benefit features in other forms of retirement benefit features and options it offers. For example, it may offer a life annuity with ten years' payments guaranteed, or a joint and survivor annuity for the employee and someone other than a spouse. Any distributions must satisfy the minimum distribution requirements of Code Section 401(a)(9) and the extremely detailed regulations thereunder, including the requirement that any death benefits must be incidental to the retirement benefits. [I.R.C. § 401(a)(9)(G); Prop. Treas. Reg. § 1.401(a)(9)-2]

Accelerated Death Benefits

Q 12:73 What is an accelerated death benefit?

An *accelerated death benefit* is an elective benefit under a life insurance policy whereby the insured can, on request, obtain a portion of the face amount of the policy before death if one or more specific health conditions exist. This benefit was first developed in response to the AIDS crisis and generally is provided in recognition of the fact that there are people who incur enormous medical and health-related expenses before death. A prepayment of life insurance death benefits can provide a source of financing to meet those extraordinary needs.

Q 12:74 What kinds of medical or health-related conditions may qualify an insured to elect accelerated death benefits under a life insurance policy?

A variety of accelerated death benefit products are being offered by life insurance companies. Typically, an insured can request and obtain an accelerated death benefit upon the occurrence of one of the following events (some policies cover more than one event):

1. A terminal illness (i.e., a medical condition from which the insured is expected to die within a fairly short specified time period, such as six months or a year);

2. A dread disease or catastrophic illness (e. g., AIDS, heart attack, stroke, cancer, renal failure); or

3. Extended or permanent confinement in a nursing home or similar facility.

Generally, life insurance companies offering accelerated death benefits limit the amount that can be taken out to a percentage of the face amount (e.g., 50 percent). The maximum percentage available generally is specifically regulated under state insurance law.

Q 12:75 Is an accelerated death benefit payable in a lump sum?

Not necessarily. An accelerated death benefit may be payable in a lump sum or in installments. A terminal illness or dread disease benefit is more likely to be paid in a lump sum, while a benefit for a nursing home confinement is more likely to be paid in installments (e.g., 2 percent of the face amount per month for 25 months).

Q 12:76 How is the face amount of the policy reduced?

Methods for reducing the policy's face amount can vary by the type of accelerated death benefit payment and the carrier involved. One method is to reduce the face amount directly by the amount paid. Another is to treat the payment as a loan secured by a lien on the policy for the amount advanced. If the payment is handled as a loan, interest may be charged on the loan from the date of payment of the accelerated death benefit to the date of death.

Q 12:77 If the policy has a cash value, how does payment of an accelerated death benefit affect the cash value?

How an accelerated death benefit affects the cash value depends on how the product is structured by the insurance company in question. The most commonly used method appears to be to reduce the face amount and the cash value by the same percentage. For example, if an employee with a group universal life policy face amount of $100,000 and a cash value of $30,000 received a lump-sum accelerated death benefit of $50,000, the employee would be left with a policy having a face amount of $50,000 and a cash value of $15,000. Some insurance companies follow other methods, which may reduce the cash value to a greater or lesser degree, or not at all.

Q 12:78 What is the federal income tax treatment of an accelerated death benefit received by an employee under a group life insurance policy?

The Code provides an exclusion from gross income for amounts received under a life insurance contract or amounts received from the sale or assignment of a life insurance contract to a qualified viatical settlement provider, where the insured is either (1) terminally ill (see Q 12:79) or (2) chronically ill (see chapter 9). [I.R.C. § 101(g)(1), as added by § 331 of HIPAA]

Q 12:79 Who is a terminally ill insured?

A *terminally ill insured* is a person who has been certified by a physician (as defined under the Social Security Act) as having an illness or physical condition that reasonably can be expected to result in death within 24 months of the date of the certification. [I.R.C. § 101(g)(4)(A)]

Q 12:80 What is the federal income tax treatment of an accelerated death benefit received by an insured employee under a group life insurance policy for medical reasons other than terminal illness?

In the case of a chronically ill insured, the exclusion from income applies to amounts paid under a life insurance contract and to amounts paid in a sale or assignment to a qualified viatical settlement provider (see Q 12:84) if the payment received by the payee is for costs incurred by the payee (not compensated for by insurance or otherwise) for qualified long-term care services. (See chapter 9 for definitions of a chronically ill individual and qualified long-term care services.) The following requirements must also be met:

1. The payment is not for expenses reimbursable by Medicare (except where Medicare is a secondary payer or the payment is on a per diem or other periodic basis unrelated to actual expenses); and

2. The contract complies with the consumer protection provisions applicable to long-term care contracts and issuers, to the extent specified in IRS regulations.

[I.R.C. § 101(g)(3)]

Where the payments on behalf of a chronically ill individual are made on a per diem or other periodic basis without regard to actual expenses, the exclusion is subject to the same annually indexed dollar cap on excludable benefits that applies to per diem–type long-term care insurance contracts (see chapter 9). For 2007, the dollar cap is $260 per day ($94,900 on an annual basis). [Rev. Proc. 2006-53, 2006-48 I.R.B. 996]

The excess over the dollar cap from all such contracts combined is excludable from income only to the extent of actual costs incurred for qualified long-term care services. [I.R.C. §§ 101(g)(3)(D), 7702B(d)]

Q 12:81   Does the exclusion from income for accelerated death benefits apply where the life insurance contract is employer-owned (a COLI contract)?

No. The exclusion does not apply to an amount paid under the contract or by a qualified viatical settlement provider to an employer or other taxpayer other than the insured, if the taxpayer has an insurable interest because the insured is a director, officer, or employee of the employer, or the insured has a financial interest in a trade or business of the taxpayer. [I.R.C. § 101(g)(5)]

Q 12:82   Are employers likely to favor an accelerated death benefit option as a part of their group life insurance programs for employees?

Very possibly. Offering an accelerated death benefit option of the terminal-illness type under a group term life insurance plan or under a GUL plan can be done without major employer cost, and the option generally is well received by employees. As well, providing such an option may relieve employee pressure on an employer to increase catastrophic coverage limits under the employer's medical plan. Further, by providing an accelerated death benefit option tied to permanent nursing home status, the employer may be able to avoid the need to increase medical plan coverage or to institute a program of long-term care coverage.

Living Benefits

Q 12:83   What is a living benefit?

A *living benefit* is similar to an accelerated death benefit, except that it is paid by a third party rather than by the insurance company that issued the life insurance policy. A living benefit allows the insured to receive the proceeds payable upon death while still living, at an actuarially discounted value based upon the expected remaining lifetime of the individual. Living benefits are also known as *viatical settlements*.

Q 12:84   Who is a qualified viatical settlement provider?

A *viatical settlement provider* is a person regularly engaged in the trade or business of purchasing or taking assignments of life insurance contracts on the lives of insured individuals who are terminally ill or chronically ill, provided that the viatical settlement provider is licensed for such purpose by the state where the insured resides or, if licensing is not required in the state, meets certain standards promulgated by the National Association of Insurance Commissioners (see Q 12:91). [I.R.C. § 101(g)(2)(B)]

Q 12:85   How is a living benefit different from an accelerated death benefit?

The terms *accelerated death benefit* and *living benefit* are often used interchangeably, although they should not be. An accelerated death benefit is paid by the insurance company that issued the policy (the second party), and ownership of the policy is not transferred. In contrast, a living benefit is the receipt of proceeds of a life insurance policy through sale of the policy to a third-party company—a living benefits company—or to an investor, with the living benefits company acting as broker.

Q 12:86   How is the living benefit paid?

A living benefits (viatical settlement) company will pay cash, typically 50 percent to 80 percent of the face amount of an individual life insurance policy of a terminally ill individual and sometimes of an individual who has attained a specified age, such as 83 or older. The living benefits company in return typically takes an irrevocable absolute assignment of the policy.

Q 12:87   Why would an insured individual want a living benefit?

A living benefit is attractive to an individual with a catastrophic illness, such as AIDS, or with limited financial resources. If the individual has a catastrophic illness, the cost of medical treatment can be an incredible burden during what is already a difficult time, and a terminally ill patient requiring expensive and extensive care can become destitute, particularly one who has little or no long-term disability insurance. A living benefit allows the individual to access the cash value of the life insurance policy while still living, usually to help pay medical bills.

Q 12:88   Why is a need for living benefits and similar products developing?

Employer-covered group health plans continue to become more "cost-effective" (a term that covers everything from cutting back on expensive care to restricting access to certain types of treatments through gatekeepers and case management), and lower lifetime health benefit limits sometimes are included in the employer's health benefit plan. Such practices can result in less medical coverage being available to terminally ill patients. [*See, e.g.,* Owens v. Storehouse Inc., 984 F.2d 394 (11th Cir. 1993); McGann v. H & H Music Co., 946 F.2d 401 (5th Cir. 1991) (employer's decision to drastically lower the lifetime benefit limit for AIDS but not for other illnesses and conditions upheld)]

Additionally, employer-provided medical plans rarely cover experimental care, which might have the effect of excluding certain courses of treatments for diseases such as AIDS or cancer.

Q 12:89   Are living benefits a ghoulish practice?

It initially may appear repulsive for a third party to purchase a life insurance policy at a discount, pay the insured only a portion of the face amount, and then receive the full proceeds when the individual dies, while the original beneficiaries (usually close family members) receive no life insurance proceeds. Nonetheless, fairly valued living benefits can be viewed as a positive product that fills a critical need within the insurance industry. The patient obtains access to much-needed funds to pay for hospital and doctor bills and for basic living expenses. Additionally, to the extent that treatments given to terminally ill patients are experimental, living benefits provide funds for experimental research and allow such patients to cross-subsidize one another.

To avoid the appearance of cheating beneficiaries out of the insurance proceeds, living benefits companies often require an irrevocable assignment from each of the designated beneficiaries and will not purchase the policy unless all of them so agree. At least one state also requires that the insured individual be certified as mentally competent before making the assignment.

Q 12:90   Do federal securities laws apply to living benefits companies?

Questions have been raised as to whether "brokered" living benefits (i.e., the living benefits company acts as an intermediary that arranges for the sale of the policies to independent investors) are subject to federal or state securities laws. In 2005, the Eleventh Circuit Court of Appeals held that viatical settlement contracts qualify as "investment contracts" subject to the Securities Act of 1933 and the Securities Exchange Act of 1934. [SEC v. Mutual Benefits Corp., 408 F.3d 737 (11th Cir. 2005] In an earlier decision, however, the D.C. Circuit held that viatical settlement contracts are not securities because the value of the contracts depends principally upon the length of the insureds' life, not the efforts of the viatical settlement company. [SEC v. Life Partners, Inc., 1996 U.S. App. LEXIS 16117 (D.C. Cir. Mar. 19, 1996), reh'g denied, 1996 U.S. App. LEXIS 33222 (D.C. Cir. Dec. 20, 1996)] Currently, the SEC has a number of enforcement actions pending against firms that broker viatical settlements.

Q 12:91   Are living benefits companies regulated in any manner?

A number of states, including New York and California, now require viatical settlements companies to be licensed. The National Association of Insurance Commissioners (NAIC) has adopted a model regulation establishing minimum requirements for living benefits companies that purchase life insurance policies from terminally ill persons. They include a payment of a minimum percentage of the face value of the policy, which percentage depends on the number of months the individual is expected to live. The model regulation also would require living benefits companies to be licensed by the states in which they operate. As more states adopt licensing procedures for living benefits companies, they will effectively legitimate this product in the course of regulating the practices of the entities that provide it.

Q 12:92   How does a living benefit differ from traditional life insurance?

The life insurance industry offers various types of life insurance policies that are priced according to life expectancy and mortality rates. If the insured individual dies earlier than anticipated, the insurance company pays more than it planned (because there was less time for investment earnings to grow). If the insured individual dies later than anticipated, the insurance company makes money. Accordingly, traditional life insurance is a financial wager that a group of individuals will live long enough, and pay enough premiums before they die, so that the insurance company will profit.

Living benefits, on the other hand, involve risk up front. The living benefits company pays out the percentage of face value to the sick individual and does not collect any premiums. It thus can never make any more money than the difference between the face value of the policy and the percentage of face value that it has already paid out to the insured. The living benefits company then bears the risk that its profit margin will be eroded (through loss of the time value of money) by various possible developments, such as the following:

- The individual may recover.
- The individual may live longer than expected.
- A life-extending treatment may be developed (as has occurred with AIDS patients who take various new drug combinations).
- A medical breakthrough may occur.
- The future financial viability of the insurance company could be endangered by events not foreseeable at the time of the living benefit payment.

In addition, if a waiver of premiums because of disability is not available, the living benefits company must pay the premiums to keep the policy in force—which will further reduce its ultimate profit.

Q 12:93   When a living benefits company takes an irrevocable assignment of an individual's life insurance policy, does the company have an insurable interest in the individual's life?

Generally, yes. Insurable interest generally is measured at the time the insurance is originally purchased from the insurance company. In other words, the person who purchases the policy from the insurance company must, at that time, have an insurable interest in the life of the insured (and an individual always has an insurable interest in his or her own life). Exceptions to this general rule do exist in a few states, however.

Q 12:94   Is a living benefit option available only from independent, non-insurance companies?

Generally, yes. The living benefit company typically provides the service directly to the individual insureds. Occasionally, it will do so at the request of an insurance carrier that has been asked to provide an accelerated death benefit but that has no formal mechanism in place for doing so.

Q 12:95   Are living benefit payments taxable to the insured?

Under the Code, living benefit payments receive the same favorable tax treatment as do life insurance proceeds paid under a life insurance policy in the case of a terminally ill insured or a chronically ill insured (see Qs 12:78–12:82).

Chapter 13

Fringe Benefits

Many exclusions or partial exclusions from gross income are provided for fringe benefits under Section 132 of the Internal Revenue Code (Code), a catchall covering all manner of employer-provided benefits: no-additional-cost services, qualified employee discounts, working condition fringe benefits, *de minimis* fringe benefits, qualified transportation benefits, and qualified moving expense reimbursements. This chapter gives an overview of the eight major types of fringe benefit expenses governed by Code Section 132 and then provides a more detailed explanation of several specific types of fringe benefits. In addition, this chapter considers such other fringe benefits as meals and lodging furnished for the convenience of the employer, gifts and achievement awards, disaster relief assistance, and group legal services plans.

Overview

Q 13:1   What are fringe benefits under Code Section 132?

Many federal laws regulating employee benefits refer to employer-provided pension and welfare benefit plans generically as fringe benefits. For tax purposes, Code Section 132 serves as a catchall for several categories of benefits that are not excludable from gross income under other Code sections. Fringe benefits that are qualified under Code Section 132 are excluded from the gross income of the employee in whole or in part. [I.R.C. § 132(a)]

Code Section 132 governs any fringe benefit that qualifies as any of the following:

- No-additional-cost service (see Qs 13:2–13:13)
- Qualified employee discount (see Qs 13:14–13:25)
- Working condition fringe benefit (see Qs 13:26–13:67)
- *De minimis* fringe benefit (see Qs 13:68–13:92)
- Qualified transportation fringe benefit (see Qs 13:93–13:118)
- Qualified moving expense reimbursement (see Qs 13:119–13:123)
- Qualified retirement planning services (see Q 13:125)
- Qualified military base realignment and closure fringe benefits

[I.R.C. § 132(a)]

Special rules also apply to on-premises athletic facilities (see Qs 13:87–13:92) and on-premises eating facilities (see Qs 13:72–13:77). [Treas. Reg. § 1.132-1(a)]

No-Additional-Cost Services

Q 13:2   What is a no-additional-cost service?

A *no-additional-cost service* is any service provided by an employer to an employee for the employee's personal use that meets the following requirements:

1. The service is offered for sale to nonemployee customers by the employer in the ordinary course of its line of business;
2. The employee performs substantial services in that same line of business; and
3. No substantial additional cost is incurred by the employer in providing the service to the employee.

The value of a no-additional-cost service is excluded from an employee's gross income under Code Section 132. [I.R.C. §§ 132(a), 132(b); Treas. Reg. §§ 1.132-1(a)(1), 1.132-2(a)(1)]

Q 13:3 What types of services may qualify as no-additional-cost services under Code Section 132?

No-additional-cost services are excess capacity services, such as hotel accommodations provided by an employer that is a hotelier; transportation by aircraft, train, bus, subway, or cruise line if the employer is in one of those lines of business; and telephone services provided by a telephone company. [Treas. Reg. § 1.132-2(a)(2)]

Q 13:4 What types of services do not qualify as no-additional-cost services?

The Section 132 exclusion for no-additional-cost services does not include non-excess capacity services, such as the facilitation by a stock brokerage firm of stock purchases. (Non-excess capacity services may, however, be eligible for a qualified employee discount of up to 20 percent of the value of the service provided; see Q 13:22.) [Treas. Reg. § 1.132-2(a)(2)]

Q 13:5 Do services provided only to employees qualify as no-additional-cost services?

No. A key requirement for services to qualify as no-additional-cost services is that the employer must provide them to the general public as well. Services primarily provided to employees but not to the employer's customers do not qualify. [I.R.C. § 132(b)(1); Treas. Reg. §§ 1.132-2(a)(1)(i), 1.132-4(a)(ii)]

Q 13:6 Must a no-additional-cost service be provided to employees for free?

No. A service need not be provided entirely free to qualify as a no-additional-cost service under Code Section 132. All that is required is that the employer cannot incur substantial additional cost in providing the service to the employee; for example, forgoing revenue because the service is provided to an employee rather than to a nonemployee customer. Any amounts paid by the employee for the service are disregarded in determining the amount of the exclusion.

The Section 132 exclusion for a no-additional-cost service applies regardless of whether the service is provided at no charge or at a reduced price. The benefit may also be provided through a partial or total rebate of the price the employee pays for the service. [I.R.C. § 132(b); Treas. Reg. §§ 1.132-2(a)(1)(ii), 1.132-2(a)(3)]

Q 13:7 May an employee's family members receive no-additional-cost services?

Yes. For purposes of the Section 132 exclusion from an employee's gross income for a no-additional-cost service, the term *employee* is defined broadly to include several categories of individuals, as follows:

1. Current employees in the employer's line of business;

2. Former employees who have separated from service in such line of business by reason of retirement or disability;

3. A widow or widower of an employee who either died while employed in the employer's line of business or separated from service in the employer's line of business as the result of retirement or disability; and

4. The spouse and dependent children of any of the above (a dependent child includes a son, stepson, daughter, or stepdaughter who is also a dependent of the employee or whose parents are both deceased and who has not attained age 25).

[Treas. Reg. § 1.132-1(b); I.R.C. § 132(h)]

Note. All employees who are treated as employed by a single employer under the controlled group rules of Code Sections 414(b), 414(c), 414(m), and 414(o) are treated as employed by a single employer. Also, any partner who performs services for a partnership is treated as employed by the partnership. [Treas. Reg. §§ 1.132-1(b)(1), 1.132-1(c)]

Q 13:8   For purposes of the no-additional-cost rule, how is an employer's cost of providing the service to employees determined?

For the Section 132 exclusion for no-additional-cost services to apply, an employer cannot incur substantial additional cost (including revenue that is forgone because the service is provided to an employee rather than to a nonemployee customer) in providing the service to the employee.

When calculating the cost incurred by an employer, any amount paid for the service by the employee is disregarded.

The employer must include the cost of labor incurred in providing services to employees. Labor costs must be included even if the employer does not incur nonlabor costs in providing the service to the employee. This is the case even if the individuals providing the services otherwise would have been idle and regardless of whether the services were provided outside normal business hours. If, however, the services being provided to the employee are merely incidental to the primary service being provided by the employer, then the employer generally will not be treated as having incurred substantial additional cost.

Regulations promulgated by the Internal Revenue Service (IRS) contain two examples of items that would be considered merely incidental:

1. The in-flight services of a flight attendant and cost of in-flight meals provided to airline employees flying on a space-available basis would be incidental to the primary service that is being provided (that is, air transportation); and

2. Maid service provided to hotel employees renting hotel rooms on a space-available basis would be incidental to the primary service being provided (that is, hotel accommodations).

[Treas. Reg. § 1.132-2(a)(5)]

It should be noted that if airline employees are permitted to take personal flights and receive reserved seats rather than flying on a space-available basis, the employer forgoes potential revenue and the employees receiving such free flights are not eligible for the no-additional-cost exclusion. [Treas. Reg. § 1.132-2(c)]

Q 13:9 What is the line of business limitation?

The exclusion for no-additional-cost services or qualified employee discounts is available only if the service or property is offered for sale to nonemployee customers in a line of business in which the employee/recipient performs substantial services. [Treas. Reg. § 1.132-4(a)(1)]

An employee may exclude from gross income only those no-additional-cost services or qualified employee discounts in the line(s) of business in which he or she performs substantial services. If an employee performs services directly benefiting more than one line of business, he or she is treated as performing substantial services for all such lines of business; thus, the employee could qualify to receive no-additional-cost services or qualified employee discounts from all of them. [Treas. Reg. § 1.132-4(a)(1)]

Q 13:10 How are lines of business determined?

The Section 410(b) line of business rules do not apply under Code Section 132. Instead, an employer's line of business is determined by reference to the Enterprise Standard Industrial Classification (ESIC) Manual prepared by the Statistical Policy Division of the U.S. Office of Management and Budget. An employer will be treated as having more than one line of business if it offers paying customers property or services in more than one ESIC Manual two-digit code classification. [Treas. Reg. § 1.132-4(a)(2)]

Mandatory aggregation of lines of business. Two or more lines of business must be treated as a single line of business under the following circumstances:

1. If it is uncommon in the employer's industry for any of the separate lines of business to be operated without the others;

2. If it is common for a substantial number of employees (excluding those who work at the employer's headquarters or main office) to perform substantial services for more than one of the employer's lines of business, so that determining which employees perform substantial services for particular lines of business would be difficult; or

3. If the employer's retail operations located on the same premises are in separate lines of business but would be considered to be in one line of business if the merchandise were offered for sale at a department store.

[Treas. Reg. § 1.132-4(a)(3)]

Special rules apply for affiliates of commercial airlines and for certain air transportation organizations. Special grandfather rules are provided for certain retail department stores, for affiliated groups operating airlines, and for telephone service provided to predivestiture retirees. [Treas. Reg. § 1.132-4(b)–(g)]

Q 13:11   Can an employee receive a no-additional-cost service from an unrelated employer?

Yes. An employee of one employer can receive tax-free no-additional-cost services from a second, unrelated employer, provided the following three requirements are satisfied:

1. The two unrelated employers must have a written reciprocal agreement permitting each employer's employees performing substantial services in the same line of business to receive no-additional-cost services from the other employer;

2. The service received by the employee from the unrelated employer is the same type of service generally provided to nonemployee customers in the line of business in which the employee works and in the line of business from which the employee receives the service (so that it would be a no-additional-cost service to the employee if provided directly by the employee's own employer); and

3. Neither employer incurs substantial additional cost either in providing such service to the other employer's employees or under the agreement.

If, however, one of the employers receives a substantial payment from the other regarding the reciprocal agreement, the paying employer will be considered to have incurred substantial additional cost. Services performed under the reciprocal agreement would then be disqualified from treatment as no-additional-cost services. [I.R.C. § 132(i); Treas. Reg. § 1.132-2(b)]

Q 13:12   What nondiscrimination requirements apply to no-additional-cost services under Code Section 132?

In order for the value of a no-additional-cost service to be excluded from the gross income of a highly compensated employee (HCE), the benefit must be available on substantially the same terms to all employees of the employer, or to a group of employees under a reasonable classification set up by the employer that does not discriminate in favor of HCEs. [I.R.C. § 132(j)(1); Treas. Reg. § 1.132-8(a)(1)] For this purpose, the definition of *highly compensated employee* contained in Code Sections 414(q), 414(s), and 414(t) is used. [I.R.C. § 132(j)(6); Treas. Reg. § 1.132-8(f)]

Note. The regulations do not reflect the current definition of *highly compensated employee* contained in Code Section 414(q). Nonetheless, it is clear that the statutory definition, and not the obsolete definition in the regulations, applies.

The nondiscrimination test is applied by aggregating the employees of all related employers, except that employees in different lines of business generally are not aggregated. [Treas. Reg. § 1.132-8(b)(1)]

Q 13:13   What happens if a no-additional-cost benefit is discriminatory?

If any portion of the no-additional-cost benefit is discriminatory, highly compensated employees cannot exclude from gross income either (1) any portion of the value of the benefit or (2) the value of any related fringe benefit program. [Treas. Reg. § 1.132-8(a)(2)]

Employee Discounts

Q 13:14   What is an employee discount?

An *employee discount* is the price at which an employer offers property or services for sale to customers minus the price at which the property or service is offered to the employee. [I.R.C. § 132(c)(3); Treas. Reg. § 1.132-3(b)(1)]

Q 13:15   What is a qualified employee discount?

A *qualified employee discount* is a discount that meets certain guidelines (see Qs 13:16–13:25). If those guidelines are met, then Code Section 132 provides that the value of a qualified employee discount is excluded from the employee's gross income. [Treas. Reg. § 1.132-3(a)(1)]

Q 13:16   How large can a qualified employee discount be under Code Section 132?

The portion of an employee discount that qualifies for the Section 132 exclusion from gross income is as follows:

1. *Property.* For property sold to an employee at a discount, the maximum excludable portion of the discount is the price at which the property is being offered to nonemployee customers in the ordinary course of the employer's line of business multiplied by the gross profit percentage (see Q 13:20).
2. *Services.* For services sold to an employee at a discount, the maximum excludable portion of the discount is 20 percent of the price at which the services are being offered to nonemployee customers.

[I.R.C. § 132(c)(1); Treas. Reg. § 1.132-3(a)(1)]

The portion, if any, of the discount exceeding the above limits is required to be included in the gross income of the employee. [Treas. Reg. § 1.132-3(e)]

Q 13:17   What form may a qualified employee discount take?

A qualified employee discount may consist of price reductions, cash rebates from the employer, or cash rebates from a third party. The exclusion will apply regardless of whether the property or service is provided at a reduced charge or at no charge at all. [Treas. Reg. § 1.132-3(a)(4)] Of course, any portion of the discount exceeding the allowable limit must be included in the gross income of the employee. [Treas. Reg. § 1.132-3(e)]

Q 13:18   If an employer offers property or service to its nonemployee customers at a discounted price, how is the amount of the Section 132 qualified employee discount affected?

The price charged to nonemployee customers is the starting point from which a qualified employee discount is calculated. If the employer offers property or service to its nonemployee customers at a discounted price and sales at discounted prices equal at least 35 percent of the employer's gross sales for its prior tax year, the price at which the employer is considered to offer the property or service for sale to its nonemployee customers will be the discounted price. [Treas. Reg. § 1.132-3(b)(2)]

The discounted price for nonemployee customers is calculated by taking the price at which the property or service is being offered to nonemployee customers at the time of the employee's purchase and reducing it by the percentage discount at which the greatest percentage of the employer's discount gross sales was made for the prior tax year. The qualified employee discount is then calculated using this lower price for nonemployee customers. [Treas. Reg. § 1.132-3(b)(2)(iv)]

Q 13:19   What type of property qualifies for a tax-free employee discount?

Any property offered for sale to customers in the ordinary course of an employer's line of business in which an employee performs substantial services is *qualified property* except for real property and personal property (whether tangible or intangible) of a kind commonly held for investment. [Treas. Reg. § 1.132-3(a)(2)] Thus, employee discounts on the purchase of securities, commodities, or currency, or of either residential or commercial real estate, are not qualified employee discounts and are therefore not excludable from gross income under Code Section 132. [I.R.C. § 132(c)(4); Treas. Reg. § 1.132-3(a)(2)(ii)]

Q 13:20   When determining the qualified employee discount on property, how is the employer's gross profit percentage calculated?

The qualified employee discount on property sold to an employee at a discount generally is equal to the employer's gross profit percentage for the prior tax year. The gross profit percentage is calculated by taking the employer's aggregate sales price of such property sold by the employer to nonemployee customers for the prior tax year (determined using generally accepted accounting principles) and subtracting from it the employer's aggregate cost of the property for the prior tax year; the resulting amount is then divided by the aggregate sales price of property sold to nonemployee customers for the prior tax year. [I.R.C. § 132(c)(2); Treas. Reg. § 1.132-3(c)]

If substantial changes in the employer's business make it inappropriate for the prior year's gross profit margin to be used for the current year, the employer must redetermine the gross profit percentage to be used for the remainder of the current year either based on its markup from cost or by reference to an appropriate industry average. [Treas. Reg. § 1.132-3(c)(iv)]

The gross profit percentage required to be aggregated under Code Sections 414(b), 414(c), 414(m), and 414(o) for employers who do not have the same tax year must be calculated on a 12-month period that is selected and used on a consistent basis. [Treas. Reg. § 1.132-3(c)(1)(ii)]

If an employee performs substantial services in more than one line of the employer's business, the applicable gross profit percentage for determining the amount of employee discount that is excludable from the employee's gross income is the one for the line of business in which the property is sold. [Treas. Reg. § 1.132-3(c)(2)]

Special rules apply to the leased sections of department stores. [Treas. Reg. § 1.132-3(d)]

Q 13:21   What amount is taxable to an employee if the goods he or she purchases are damaged, distressed, or returned?

No amount will be taxable to the employee under Code Section 132 for damaged, distressed, or returned goods made available by the employer, as long as the employee pays a price equal to or exceeding the fair market value of the goods in such shape. [Treas. Reg. § 1.132-3(b)(3)]

Q 13:22   How is a qualified discount on services calculated?

Code Section 132 provides that an employee's excludable discount for services may be up to 20 percent of the price at which the employer offers such services to nonemployee customers in the ordinary course of business. The portion of a discount in excess of that limit is treated as taxable employee wages. [I.R.C. §§ 132(c)(1), 132(c)(3); Treas. Reg. § 1.132-3(e)]

Q 13:23   Can an employee's family members also receive a tax-free employee discount?

Yes. For purposes of the qualified employee discount, the term *employee* is broadly defined to include the following:

1. Current employees in the employer's line of business;
2. Former employees who have separated from service in such line of business by reason of retirement or disability;
3. Any widow or widower of an employee who either died while employed in the employer's line of business or separated from service in the employer's line of business as the result of retirement or disability; and
4. The spouse and dependent children of any of the above (a dependent child includes a son, stepson, daughter, or stepdaughter who is also a dependent of the employee or whose parents are both deceased and who has not attained age 25).

[Treas. Reg. § 1.132-1(b)]

Q 13:24   Can qualified employee discounts be provided by a second, unrelated party?

In some cases, yes. Although there is no counterpart to the reciprocal agreement exception regarding no-additional-cost services (see Q 13:11), qualified employee discounts may nonetheless be provided either directly by the employer or indirectly by a third party. For instance, employees of an appliance manufacturer could receive a qualified employee discount on that manufacturer's appliances sold at a retail store, if the retail store also sells the appliances to its nonemployee customers. [Treas. Reg. §§ 1.132-3(a)(3), 1.132-3(a)(5)]

However, a discount provided to an employer's employees on an unrelated company's products or services would not qualify even if there is a special relationship between the two companies. For example, in a Chief Counsel Advice memorandum, the IRS concluded that a company could not treat as a tax-free fringe benefit a discount it offered to employees who bought or leased products made by their employer's former parent company, even though there was a continuing business relationship between the employer and the former parent company. The discount was taxable because it applied to property that was not sold by the employees' employer. [CCA 200923029 (Jan. 30, 2009)]

Q 13:25   What nondiscrimination rules apply to qualified employee discounts?

In order for the value of an employee discount to be excluded from the gross income of a highly compensated employee (HCE), the benefit must be available on substantially the same terms to all employees of the employer, or to a group of employees under a reasonable classification set up by the employer that does not discriminate in favor of HCEs. [I.R.C. § 132(j)(1); Treas. Reg. § 1.132-8] For this purpose, the definition of *highly compensated employee* contained in Code Sections 414(q), 414(s), and 414(t) is used. [I.R.C. § 132(j)(6); Treas. Reg. § 1.132-8(f)]

The nondiscrimination test is applied by aggregating the employees of all related employers, except that employees in different lines of business generally are not aggregated. [Treas. Reg. § 1.132-8(b)(1)]

Working Condition Fringe Benefits

Q 13:26   What is a working condition fringe benefit?

A *working condition fringe benefit* is any property or service provided by an employer to an employee that would be allowable as a business expense deduction under Code Section 162 or as depreciation under Code Section 167 if the employee paid for the property or service. Code Section 132 provides that the fair market value of the property or service is excluded from the employee's gross income if the employee could have deducted it as a business or depreciation expense (disregarding the Section 67(a) minimum required amount for miscellaneous itemized deductions). [I.R.C. § 132(d); Treas. Reg. § 1.132-5(a)]

If other Code sections require substantiation (see Q 13:27) in order for a deduction under Code Section 162 or 167 to be allowable, those substantiation requirements must be met in order for the expense to be excludable under Code Section 132. [Treas. Reg. § 1.132-5(a)(1)(ii)]

If a deduction would be allowable to the employee under a Code Section other than Code Section 162 or 167, the property or service does not qualify as a working condition fringe benefit under Code Section 132. [Treas. Reg. § 1.132-5(a)(1)(iii)]

Q 13:27   What requirements must be met in order for employer-provided property or services to be working condition fringe benefits?

For employer-provided property or services to be working condition fringe benefits, three basic requirements apply, as follows:

1. If the employee had purchased the property or service, he or she would have been entitled to a business expense or depreciation deduction [I.R.C. § 132(d)];

2. The employee's use of the property or service must be related to the employer's trade or business [I.R.C. §§ 162, 167; Treas. Reg. § 1.132-5(a)(2)]; and

3. The employee's use of the property must be substantiated by adequate records or sufficient evidence corroborating the employee's own statement.

[Treas. Reg. § 1.132-5(c)]

Other requirements (see Q 13:28) may also have to be met for a particular benefit to qualify as a working condition fringe benefit.

Q 13:28   What property or services constitute working condition fringe benefits?

Among the employer-provided items whose fair market value may be excluded from gross income as a *working condition fringe benefit* under Code Section 132 (if the detailed requirements applicable to each are satisfied) are the following:

- Cars (business or demonstration use)
- Chauffeur services
- Transportation for security concerns (such as terrorist activity, death threats, and threat of kidnapping or serious bodily harm)
- Airplanes and air transportation
- Bodyguards
- Use of consumer goods for product testing and evaluation
- Travel expenses, including meals and lodging
- Word processors and computers
- Entertainment
- Club dues

It should be noted that the applicable regulations contain detailed requirements related to the exclusion for many of the above items. [Treas. Reg. § 1.132-5] Club dues (see Q 13:66), employer-provided aircraft (see Qs 13:31–13:45), and the special requirements applicable to employer-provided cars (see Qs 13:46–13:65) are discussed below.

Q 13:29   What employer-provided products and services are not working condition fringe benefits?

A physical examination program provided by the employer is an example of an employer-provided service that is not excludable as a working condition fringe benefit. This is the case even if the value of the program might be deductible to the employee under Code Section 213. [Treas. Reg. § 1.132-5(a)(1)(iv)] The expense of the program might, however, be excludable under Code Sections 106 and 105 as an accident and health plan (see chapter 3).

At one time, the IRS took the position that outplacement assistance was not excludable as a working condition fringe benefit. In a reversal of position, the IRS ruled that if the employer derives a substantial business benefit from the provision of outplacement services that is distinct from the benefit of paying additional compensation, such as promoting a positive corporate image, maintaining employee morale, and avoiding wrongful termination suits, the provision of outplacement services generally may be treated as a working condition fringe benefit. If, however, the employee can elect to receive cash or other taxable benefits in lieu of the outplacement services, the outplacement services will not qualify as a working condition fringe benefit and will be taxable as compensation. [Rev. Rul. 92-69, 1992-2 C.B. 51]

The IRS has issued a private letter ruling stating that benefits provided to a survivor of a deceased employee are not excludable as working condition fringe benefits under Code Section 132(a)(3). A professional services firm planned to provide financial counseling services to survivors of deceased employees and to survivors of eligible employees diagnosed with a terminal illness—but not to employees diagnosed with a terminal illness. The free professional services would include meeting with a company financial planner, tax aspects of employee benefit plan distributions, applications for government benefits and employer-provided benefits, budgeting and cash flow, estate settlement process, investing, and estate tax planning. The IRS said that for purposes of working condition fringe benefits, "employee" does not include a surviving spouse or dependents of the employee. The IRS ruled that the fair market value of the benefits provided to a survivor of a deceased employee may not be excluded from income under Code Section 132(a)(3) and must be included in income by the recipients of the services. [Priv. Ltr. Rul. 199929043]

Q 13:30   What nondiscrimination rules apply to working condition fringe benefits?

Except for product testing programs, Code Section 132 does not impose any nondiscrimination rules on the availability of the exclusion for working condition fringe benefits. Therefore, an employer can make working condition fringe benefits available to selected employees if it wishes. [Treas. Reg. § 1.132-5(q)]

Aircraft

Q 13:31   Is an employee's use of a private aircraft owned or leased by his or her employer a working condition fringe benefit?

Use of an employer-provided noncommercial aircraft (e.g., a private airplane or helicopter) is a tax-free working condition fringe benefit when the flight is taken only for business purposes. The amount excludable from income as a working condition fringe benefit is the amount that the employee could deduct as a business expense if the employee had paid for the flight on the aircraft. The cost of a flight that is purely for business purposes is thus totally excludable from income. [Treas. Reg. § 1.132-5(k)]

Q 13:32   If an employee travels by air for both business and personal reasons, what is the tax treatment of the trip?

If an airplane trip is primarily for the employer's business, the employee must include in income the excess value of all the flights that make up the trip over the value of the flights that would have been taken had there been no personal flights but only business flights.

For instance, if an employee flies on a company plane from New York to San Francisco primarily on business but takes some time to sightsee in San Francisco, the trip is fully exempt as a working condition fringe. If, however, the employee headed to San Francisco for business flies on the company plane to Seattle for sightseeing on the way back, the employee must include in income the excess of the value of the three trips (New York to San Francisco, San Francisco to Seattle, and Seattle to New York) over the two trips that would have been taken purely for business (New York to San Francisco and San Francisco to New York). [Treas. Reg. § 1.61-21(g)(4)(ii)]

Q 13:33   What is the result if a trip on a company aircraft is primarily a personal trip, and the business purpose is secondary?

If an employee combines in one trip both personal and business flights on an employer-provided aircraft, and the trip is primarily personal, the employee includes in income the value of the personal flights that would have been taken had there been no business flights but only personal flights.

For example, if an employee flies from New York to Seattle for personal reasons, but stops en route in San Francisco for some incidental business, the employee would be taxed on the value of direct flights from New York to Seattle and Seattle to New York. [Treas. Reg. § 1.61-21(g)(4)(iii)]

Q 13:34   What is the result if members of an employee's family fly in company aircraft along with the employee?

If the trip is primarily a business trip and the employee's spouse is along for business reasons, the trip for both the employee and the spouse is exempt as a working condition fringe benefit. If, however, the spouse is not along for business reasons, or if the employee brings along children for personal reasons, the value of their flights is generally includable in the employee's gross income. [Treas. Reg. § 1.132-5(k)]

Spousal travel. Travel costs for a spouse can qualify in some circumstances as working condition fringe benefits even though the employer is barred from deducting the cost. An employer can deduct the expenses of a spouse, dependent, or other individual traveling with an employee on a business trip only if the spouse, dependent, or other individual is also an employee of the employer. [I.R.C. § 274(m)(3), as added by § 13272(a) of OBRA '93] In order to qualify as a working condition fringe benefit, the spousal expenses cannot be treated as compensation by the employer, but have to qualify as a business expense under Code Section 162 (even though not deductible under Code Section 274). They also have to be substantiated by the employee, and it must be shown that the spouse's presence on the employee's business trip has a bona fide business purpose. [Treas. Reg. § 1.132-5]

Note that the use of air transportation by the parents of an employee is treated as use by the employee.

Q 13:35 What rules apply for valuing taxable trips in an employer-provided aircraft?

The value of a taxable flight on an employer-provided aircraft may be based on the fair market value of the flight. [Treas. Reg. §§ 1.61-21(b)(6), 1.61-21(b)(7)] Alternatively, the value of a flight can be determined under the special rules of the base aircraft valuation formula, also known as the standard industry fare level (SIFL) formula. The SIFL cents-per-mile rate applicable for the period during which the flight was taken is multiplied by the aircraft multiple (based on the takeoff weight of the aircraft); the applicable terminal charge is then added. The SIFL rates and terminal charges are calculated by the Department of Transportation and revised semiannually. [Treas. Reg. § 1.61-21(g)(5)]

Note. The IRS issues semiannual revenue rulings setting forth the SIFL cents-per-mile rates and terminal charges for a six-month period. For example, the rates and terminal charges in effect for the first half of 2010 are set forth in Revenue Ruling 2010-10. [2010-13 I.R.B. 461]

Q 13:36 Are the SIFL valuation rules the same for all employees?

No. The aircraft multiple, which is based on the takeoff weight of the aircraft, is different for a control employee (see Qs 13:37–13:39) and a noncontrol employee. For example, if the company airplane is 25,001 pounds or more, the aircraft multiple is 31.3 percent for a noncontrol employee. For a control employee, however, the aircraft multiple is 400 percent, producing a much higher value for the personal flights of a control employee than for an employee who is not a control employee. [Treas. Reg. § 1.61-21(g)(7)]

Q 13:37 Who is a control employee?

In the case of a nongovernmental employer, a *control employee* is an employee earning $50,000 or more who is one of the following:

1. A board- or shareholder-appointed, confirmed, or elected officer of the employer (limited to the lesser of ten employees or 1 percent of all employees); or

2. Among the top 1 percent most highly paid employees, not in excess of 50 employees.

A control employee also includes an employee who owns a 5 percent or greater equity, capital, or profits interest in the employer, or who is a director of the employer. [Treas. Reg. § 1.61-21(g)(8)]

Q 13:38 Who is a control employee in the case of a governmental employer?

A control employee of a governmental employer is an elected official or an employee whose compensation equals or exceeds the compensation paid to a federal government employee holding an Executive Level V position. [Treas. Reg. § 1.61-21(g)(9)]

Q 13:39   Can a former employee be a control employee?

In some cases, yes. An employee who was a control employee of an employer at any time after reaching age 55, or within three years of separation from the service of the employer, is a control employee with respect to flights taken after separation from the service of the employer. Such an employee, however, is not counted in applying the limitations set out above (see Q 13:37), for example, the 50-employee limit. [Treas. Reg. § 1.61-21(g)(11)]

Q 13:40   Do the higher valuation rules for a control employee also apply to the personal trips on company aircraft by family members of the control employee?

Yes. Because the value of personal trips made by family members of the control employee is taxable to the control employee, the same valuation rules apply in determining the value of those trips. The value of a flight by a child who is younger than two years old is deemed to be zero, however. [Treas. Reg. § 1.61-21(g)(1)]

Q 13:41   What if some passengers on a company-provided aircraft are traveling primarily for business purposes and others are traveling primarily for personal reasons?

Under a special seating capacity rule, if 50 percent or more of the regular passenger seating capacity of an aircraft is occupied by individuals traveling primarily on the employer's business, the value of any flight by an employee who is not traveling primarily on business is valued at zero (i.e., it is tax-free). In such an instance, an employee is deemed to include a retired or disabled employee, the spouse of a deceased employee, and the spouse or dependent child of an employee, as well as a partner of a partnership. It does not include an independent contractor or director of the employer.

> **Example.** Candace, a control employee, goes on a business trip on a seven-seat company plane and brings along her husband, Hans, and her son, Scott, as nonbusiness guests. Candace will be taxed on the value of the trip for Hans and Scott. If three other primarily business travelers are added as passengers, however, Hans and Scott can travel tax-free. [Treas. Reg. § 1.61-21(g)(12)]

Q 13:42   How does the 50 percent seating capacity rule apply when a trip involves multiple flights?

The 50 percent seating capacity rule must be met both at the time the individual whose flight is being valued boards the aircraft and at the time the individual deplanes.

Example. Charles, a control employee, is flying on the company's seven-seat plane from New York to San Francisco on business and takes along his wife, Willow, and his daughter, Denise, as nonbusiness guests. Three other company employees are also aboard on company business. The plane stops in Chicago, where two of the company employees deplane. Charles will be taxed on the value of the flight from New York to San Francisco for Willow and Denise because the 50 percent rule was not met both at the beginning and at the end of the flight from New York to San Francisco. [Treas. Reg. § 1.61-21(g)(12)(ii)]

Q 13:43   Can an employer use either the fair market value rule or the special SIFL rule in valuing employer-provided aircraft usage?

Yes, either rule may be used. However, if the employer uses the special standard industry fare level (SIFL) rule for one employee, it generally must use the rule consistently for all employees in the same calendar year. [Treas. Reg. § 1.61-21(g)(14)(i)]

Key exception. A company's deduction for personal flights taken by certain "specified individuals" is limited to the amount actually included in the employee's income using *either* the fair market value rule or the SIFL rule (see Q 13:35). Proposed reliance regulations permit taxpayers to value the personal use of aircraft by specified individuals under the fair market value rule, but continue to value flights for other employees and for specified individuals not traveling for personal purposes using the SIFL formula. [Prop. Treas. Reg. § 1.61-21(g)(14)(iii); IRS Notice 2005-45, 2005-24 I.R.B. 1228] Specified individuals include, for example, officers, directors, and 10-percent-or-more owners (see Q 13:45).

An employee can use the special SIFL rule only if his or her employer has used it for withholding and reporting purposes. However, the employee is free to use the fair market value rule even if the employer uses the special SIFL rule. [Treas. Reg. § 1.61-21(c)(2)] If the employee chooses to use the fair market value rule, he or she must use it for all flights within the same calendar year. [Treas. Reg. § 1.61-21(g)(14)(ii)]

Q 13:44   Is the amount of taxable employer-provided aircraft travel subject to wage withholding?

Yes. [I.R.C. §§ 3121(a), 3201(b), 3401(a)]

Q 13:45   Can an employer deduct the full cost of an employee's personal trip on a company aircraft?

The amount included in an employee's income on account of a taxable flight on an employer-provided aircraft may be based on the fair market value of the flight. Alternatively, the value of a flight may be determined using the SIFL formula (see Q 13:35). The amount included in the employee's income is not pegged to the employer's costs for providing the flight, even if the employer's cost is greater than the fair market value or the amount determined using the SIFL formula.

Nonetheless, despite IRS arguments to the contrary, the Tax Court held that as long as the value of a flight is reported as compensation to an employee, the costs of providing the flight are fully deductible if they qualify as ordinary and necessary business expenses. Moreover, the court said that was true even if there is a mismatch between an employer's deduction and the employee's income. The Eighth Circuit affirmed the Tax Court's decision. [Sutherland Lumber-Southwest, Inc. v. Commissioner, 255 F.3d 495 (8th Cir. 2001), *aff'g* 114 T.C. 197 (2000)]

The IRS subsequently lost two other Tax Court cases involving the same issue. [Midland Fin. Co. v. Commissioner, T.C. Memo 2001-203 (Aug. 1, 2000); National Bancorp of Alaska, Inc. v. Commissioner, T.C. Memo 2001-202 (Aug. 1, 2001)]

In the wake of those defeats, the IRS announced that it would no longer challenge companies on this issue if they could show that they properly reported the value of the personal use of a plane as income to the employee. In those situations, the IRS said it would permit the company to claim a full deduction for its costs. However, the IRS emphasized that it would continue to seek to limit a company's deduction when the personal use was not properly reported. [A.O.D. 2002-2 (Feb. 11, 2002)]

Despite the IRS's capitulation, Congress was not happy with the potential mismatch between the amount reported in an employee's income and the employer's deduction. The American Jobs Creation Act of 2004 changed the rules, effective beginning October 31, 2004, to limit an employer's deduction for an executive's personal use of an employer-provided aircraft to the amount included in the executive's income. [I.R.C. § 274(e)(2), (e)(9)]

The limitation applies only to "specified individuals," including any officer, director, or more than 10 percent owner of a C corporation, an S corporation, or a personal service corporation. For partnership purposes, a "specified individual" includes any partner that holds a more than 10 percent equity interest in the partnership, a general partner, an officer, or a managing member of a partnership. Thus, an employer can continue to deduct the full cost of a personal flight by a rank-and-file employee, regardless of the amount included in the employee's income.

An IRS notice explains how employers should calculate the costs for personal use of an aircraft that are disallowed, except to the extent they are treated as compensation to a specified individual. [IRS Notice 2005-45, 2005-24 I.R.B. 1228]

In making the calculation, an employer must take into account all expenses of maintaining and operating the aircraft, including (but not limited to):

- Fuel costs;
- Salaries for pilots, maintenance personnel, and other personnel assigned to the aircraft;

- Meal and lodging expenses of flight personnel;
- Take-off and landing fees;
- Costs for maintenance and maintenance flights;
- Costs of on-board refreshments, amenities, or gifts;
- Hangar fees (at home or away);
- Management fees; and
- Depreciation or expensing deductions.

In the case of a chartered aircraft, expenses include all costs billed for the charter, including amounts for flight time, waiting time, fuel, and overnight expenses. In the case of a leased aircraft, all lease payments are taken into account.

The total deductible expenses attributable to the aircraft must be allocated between expenses for personal use of the aircraft by specified individuals and expenses for all other uses. The allocation must be made for each taxable year using either occupied-seat hours or occupied-seat miles flown by the aircraft. Occupied-seat hours or miles is the sum of the hours or miles flown by an aircraft multiplied by the number of seats occupied for each hour or mile. For example, a flight of 6 hours with 3 passengers aboard results in 18 occupied-seat hours.

All fixed and variable expenses must be aggregated to determine the total expenses paid or incurred during the taxable year. Total expenses must then be divided by total occupied-seat hours or occupied-seat miles flown to determine the cost per occupied-seat hour or occupied-seat mile. The cost per occupied-seat hour or occupied-seat mile may be calculated separately for each aircraft or may be aggregated for similar aircraft. However, the costs of different types of aircraft may not be aggregated. For example, the costs of a turboprop plane may not be aggregated with the costs of a jet plane and the costs of a two-engine jet plane may not be aggregated with the costs of a four-engine jet plane.

The amount disallowed as a deduction is the sum of the cost of each occupied-seat hour (or mile) flown by a specified individual for personal purposes, less the sum of the amounts treated as compensation to the specified individual.

Example. During the tax year, Corona Corporation's aircraft is used for three flights of 5 hours, 5 hours, and 4 hours, respectively. On Flight 1, there are four passengers, none of whom is a specified individual or an individual traveling for personal purposes. On Flight 2, Employee A and one other passenger are specified individuals traveling for personal purposes, and the other two passengers are not specified individuals or are not traveling for personal purposes. On Flight 3, all four passengers, including Employee A, are specified individuals traveling for personal purposes. Corona incurs $56,000 in expenses for the operation of the aircraft for the tax year.

The aircraft is operated for a total of 56 occupied-seat hours for the period (4 passengers × 5 hours or 20 occupied-seat hours for Flight 1, plus 4 passengers × 5 hours or 20 occupied-seat hours for Flight 2, plus 4 passengers × 4 hours or 16 occupied-seat hours for Flight 3). The cost per occupied-seat hour is $1,000 ($56,000 ÷ 56 hours). The total personal use of the aircraft by specified individuals subject to disallowance is 26 occupied-seat hours (2 passengers for 5 hours each on Flight 2 and 4 passengers for 4 hours each on Flight 3), and the total cost subject to disallowance is $26,000 (26 occupied-seat hours × $1,000).

Of that amount, $5,000 ($1,000 × 5 hours) is allocable to Employee A for Flight 2, and $4,000 ($1,000 × 4 hours) is allocable to Employee A for Flight 3.

For Flight 2, Corona treats $1,200 (the fair market value of the flight) as compensation to Employee A. Therefore, Corona may deduct $1,200 of the cost of Flight 2 allocable to Employee A. The deduction for the remaining $3,800 cost allocable to personal use by Employee A on Flight 2 is disallowed. For Flight 3, Corona treats $1,300 (the fair market value of the flight) as compensation to Employee A. Therefore, Corona may deduct $1,300 of the cost of Flight 3 allocable to Employee A. The deduction for the remaining $2,700 of cost allocable to personal use by Employee A on Flight 3 is disallowed. Corona's total deduction with respect to Employee A is $2,500, and the total disallowed amount is $6,500. Corona makes the same calculations for other specified individuals who used the aircraft for personal purposes during the tax year.

Cars and Other Vehicles

Q 13:46 Is the use of an employer-provided vehicle excludable as a working condition fringe benefit?

It can be. An employee can exclude the amount that he or she could deduct as a business expense under Code Section 162 or as depreciation under Code Section 167 if he or she had paid for the availability of the vehicle. [Treas. Reg. § 1.132-5(b)(1)(i)] The amount that would not be deductible is a taxable fringe benefit that must be included in the employee's gross income.

Example. Edward, an employee of Zipp, Inc., has an employer-provided vehicle available to him for one year. The total fair market value of the use of the car for a year is $2,000. Edward drives the vehicle 6,000 miles for business and an additional 2,000 miles for personal purposes. To calculate the value of the working condition fringe benefit, the $2,000 is multiplied by a fraction, the numerator of which is the business-use mileage (6,000) and the denominator of which is the total mileage (8,000). The result, $1,500, is the value of the working condition fringe benefit. Accordingly, only $500 of the value of the availability of the car does not qualify as a working condition fringe benefit and is included in Edward's gross income.

If other employees also use the employer-provided vehicle, their use is included in determining the value of the working condition fringe benefit. [Treas. Reg. §§ 1.132-5(b)(1)(i), 1.132-5(b)(1)(v)]

Q 13:47   **What kinds of employer-provided vehicles can qualify as a working condition fringe benefit?**

Qualifying vehicles include any motorized vehicle manufactured primarily for use on public streets, roads, and highways. [Treas. Reg. §§ 1.132-5(b)(1), 1.61-21(e)(2)]

Q 13:48   **Does the value of the employer-provided vehicle affect its treatment as a working condition fringe benefit?**

No. The value of bona fide business use of a car can be excluded from income as a working condition fringe benefit regardless of the value of the car. On the other hand, the working condition fringe benefit exclusion does not apply to the value of personal use by the employee. This is because if the employee had paid for the availability of the vehicle, he or she would not be able to deduct any part of the payment attributable to personal miles under Code Section 162 or 167. It does not matter if the employee would have chosen a less expensive vehicle. Nor does the result change even if the decision to provide an expensive rather than an inexpensive car is made by the employer for bona fide noncompensatory business reasons. [Treas. Reg. § 1.132-5(b)(1)(iii)]

Q 13:49   **What rules apply if an employee uses more than one employer-provided vehicle?**

The working condition fringe benefit exclusion is determined separately for each employer-provided vehicle. [Treas. Reg. § 1.132-5(b)(2)]

Q 13:50   **Is an employee required to substantiate his or her business use of an employer-provided car?**

Yes. The value of the use of a company car provided to an employee for use in the employer's business will be treated as a fully taxable fringe benefit, and not a working condition fringe benefit, unless the employee can substantiate the amount of his or her business use. [Treas. Reg. § 1.132-5(c)(1);Temp. Treas. Reg. § 1.274-5T(a)]

Q 13:51   **How is the business use of an employer-provided car substantiated?**

The business use of an employer-provided car must be substantiated. To do so, the following elements must be documented:

- Amount of each separate expenditure for the car (e.g., cost of purchase, maintenance, repairs)
- Amount of each business use (i.e., mileage)
- Amount of total use during the taxable period

- Date of expenditure relating to the car or date of business use
- Business purpose for the expense or use

[Temp. Treas. Reg. §§ 1.274-5T(b)(6), 1.280F-6T(b)(1)(i)]

Q 13:52   What kinds of records will be considered adequate for substantiation of business use?

A deduction for expenses related to the business use of a car must be substantiated by adequate records. The following items may, singly or in combination, be adequate records: account books, diaries, or logs; trip sheets; statements of expense (for example, expense reports); and receipts, paid bills, or similar documentary evidence. [Temp. Treas. Reg. § 1.274-5T(c)(2)]

Each required element of business use (see Q 13:51) must be substantiated.

Certain vehicles that are likely to be used only a *de minimis* amount for personal purposes are exempt from the substantiation requirements. A list of such vehicles is contained in the Treasury regulations and includes, among others, forklifts, cement mixers, dump trucks, cranes and derricks, certain moving vans, refrigerated trucks, and delivery trucks with seating for the driver only. [Temp. Treas. Reg. § 1.274-5T(k)(2)]

Q 13:53   When must the records used for substantiation of business use be prepared?

Records generally must be made at or near the time of the expenditure or use—at a time when the taxpayer has full present knowledge of each element of the expenditure or use (such as the amount, time and place, business purpose, and business relationship). Expense account statements prepared from account books, diaries, logs, or similar records made at or near the time of the expenditure or use will also be treated as made at or near the time of the expenditure or use if they are submitted to the employer by the employee in the regular course of good business practice. [Temp. Treas. Reg. § 1.274-5T(c)(2)(ii)(A)]

Q 13:54   Is a written record always required for substantiation of business use?

Generally, yes. The record of the business use of an employer-provided car also may be substantiated, however, in a "computer memory device with the aid of a logging program." [Temp. Treas. Reg. § 1.274-5T(c)(2)(ii)(C)]

If an employee fails to keep adequate written records on business expenses relating to the car and use of the car, he or she may be forced to attempt to substantiate the business expense or use in the following ways:

1. By his or her own oral or written statement containing information in detail as to the element in question; and

2. By other corroborative evidence.

[Temp. Treas. Reg. § 1.274-5T(c)(3)]

Q 13:55   What if some of the documentation needed to substantiate the business use of a car is confidential?

If any information concerning the elements of the expense or use (such as place, business purpose, or business relationship) is confidential in nature, it need not be recorded in the account book, diary, log, statement of expense, trip sheet, or similar record, provided that:

1. It is recorded at or near the time of the expense or use; and
2. It is available elsewhere for the IRS district director to substantiate such element of the expense or use.

[Temp. Treas. Reg. § 1.274-5T(c)(2)(ii)(D)]

Q 13:56   Is there a safe harbor for substantiating an employee's use of an employer-provided vehicle for business only?

Yes. The working condition fringe exclusion under Code Section 132 for the value of the use of the vehicle applies only if applicable substantiation requirements are met. A safe-harbor substantiation rule is provided, under which the employer must maintain a written policy statement expressly limiting the use of the vehicle to business use only. [Treas. Reg. § 1.132-5(e)]

Q 13:57   What must be contained in the employer's written policy statement concerning business use only?

Under the safe-harbor substantiation rule for business use only of an employer-provided vehicle, an employer must prohibit all nonbusiness use of the vehicle. Further, an employer's written policy statement must satisfy the following five conditions:

1. The vehicle must be owned or leased by the employer and must be provided to one or more employees for use in connection with the employer's trade or business;
2. When not being used in the employer's trade or business, the vehicle must be kept on the employer's business premises except when it is temporarily located elsewhere (for example, for maintenance or repairs);
3. No employee using the vehicle may live at the employer's business premises;
4. Under the employer's written policy, no employee may use the vehicle for personal purposes except for *de minimis* personal use (for example, stopping for lunch between two business deliveries); and
5. The employer must reasonably believe that employees do not use the vehicle for personal use (except for *de minimis* use).

To avoid lengthy documentation of business use, employees also in fact must not use the vehicle for any personal use except for *de minimis* personal use. Evidence must exist that would enable the Commissioner to determine whether all of the above conditions are met. [Treas. Reg. § 1.132-5(e); Temp. Treas. Reg. 1.274-6T(a)(2)]

Q 13:58 What is the result if an employer makes a vehicle available to an employee for both business use and commuting?

If an employer provides a vehicle to an employee for both business use and commuting use, the amount of the working condition fringe benefit excludable under Code Section 132 is the value of the vehicle's availability to the employee for uses other than commuting purposes, provided that:

1. Applicable substantiation requirements are met (a safe-harbor substantiation rule is provided under which detailed use records will not be required if the employer maintains a written policy statement on commuting use of the vehicle that contains certain specified information; and

2. A special rule for valuing commuter use is used, and such value is either included in the employee's income or reimbursed by the employee.

[Treas. Reg. § 1.132-5(f)]

Q 13:59 What information must be contained in an employer's written policy statement on business and commuting use?

Under the safe-harbor substantiation rule for business and commuting use, the employer's written policy statement must prohibit all personal use of the vehicle other than commuting. The policy statement will be considered to do so if it satisfies the following five conditions:

1. The vehicle must be owned or leased by the employer, provided to one or more employees for use in connection with the employer's trade or business, and be so used;

2. For bona fide noncompensatory business reasons, the employer requires the employee to commute to or from work (or both) in the vehicle;

3. The employer has established a written policy under which neither the employee nor any individual whose use would be taxable to the employee may use the vehicle for personal purposes, other than for commuting or *de minimis* personal use (for example, a stop for a personal errand);

4. The employer reasonably believes that, except for *de minimis* personal use, neither the employee nor any individual whose use would be taxable to the employee uses the vehicle for personal purposes except commuting; and

5. The employee required to use the vehicle is not a control employee (see Q 13:37) required to use an automobile.

[Temp. Treas. Reg. § 1.274-6T(a)(3)(i)]

To avoid lengthy documentation of business and commuting use, the employee must either reimburse the employer for the value of the commuting use or include a commuting value of $1.50 per one-way commute (for example, from home to work or from work to home) in gross income. [Temp. Treas. Reg. §§ 1.61-2T(f)(3), 1.274-6T(a)(3)(ii)]

Also, evidence must exist that would enable the IRS to determine whether the use of the vehicle meets the five conditions set out above. [Temp. Treas. Reg. § 1.274-6T(a)(3)]

Q 13:60 How is the taxable personal use of an employer-provided vehicle calculated?

The taxable value of the personal use or unsubstantiated business use of, or expense relating to, an employer-provided car must be included in the employee's gross income. Several valuation methods are available, including the following:

1. Fair market value method (see Q 13:62);
2. Annual lease value method (see Q 13:63);
3. Cents-per-mile method (see Q 13:64); and
4. Commuting value method (see Q 13:65).

As a general rule, an employee may use a special valuation rule (that is, any method other than the fair market value method) only if the employer also uses it. An employee may also use a special valuation rule in the unusual situation where the employer does not report the value of personal use as wages to the employee, but one of the other conditions for using a special valuation rule is satisfied (see Q 13:61). [Treas. Reg. § 1.61-21(c)(2)(ii)] Once the employer selects one of the special valuation rules, Treasury regulations impose conditions on when and if the employer can switch methods.

Use by more than one employee. When applying a special valuation rule for any vehicle used by more than one employee at the same time (e.g., an employer-sponsored commuting pool), an employer must use the same rule to value the use of the vehicle by each employee who shares the use of it, and the employer must allocate the value of the vehicle's use among the employees based on the relevant facts and circumstances. [Treas. Reg. § 1.61-21(c)(2)(ii)(B)]

Q 13:61 Do any special conditions apply when electing special vehicle valuation rules?

Yes. The IRS regulations provide that neither an employer nor an employee may use a special valuation rule unless one of four conditions is satisfied. The four conditions are as follows:

1. The employer treats the value of the benefit as wages for reporting purposes within the prescribed time;
2. The employee includes the value of the benefit in income within the prescribed time;
3. The employee is not a control employee (see Q 13:37); or

4. The employer demonstrates a good-faith effort to treat the benefit correctly for reporting purposes.

If none of the four conditions is met, both the employer and employee must use the general valuation rules based on facts and circumstances.

Generally, an employee may use a special valuation rule only if the employer has used the rule. Nonetheless, an employee may use a special valuation rule not used by his or her employer if the employer does not treat the value of the benefit as wages for reporting purposes (see condition 1 above) and condition 2, 3, or 4 is met. The employee may always use the general valuation rules based on facts and circumstances. [Treas. Reg. § 1.61-21(c)]

Q 13:62   How is the fair market value of an employer-provided vehicle determined?

Under the fair market value method, the value of an employer-provided vehicle equals the amount that an individual would be required to pay in an arm's-length transaction to lease the same or comparable vehicle, on the same or comparable conditions, in the geographic area in which the vehicle is available for use.

In computing the fair market value of the vehicle, the fair market value of specialized equipment not susceptible to personal use or any telephone added to the vehicle is disregarded if necessitated by, and attributable to, the employer's business needs. The value of the specialized equipment is included, however, if the employee uses it in a trade or business other than that of the employer. [Treas. Reg. § 1.61-21(b)(4)]

Q 13:63   How does the annual lease value method work?

The annual lease value of an automobile is calculated by determining its fair market value as of the first date it is made available to any employee for personal use and then selecting a dollar range from the Annual Lease Value Table contained in Treasury Regulations Section 1.61-21(d)(2)(iii). If the car is available to the employee for only part of a calendar year, the fair market value is either a prorated annual lease value or a daily lease value.

If the employer and employee jointly own the car, the annual lease value is reduced according to a formula contained in the regulations. If the employee contributes toward the price but does not receive any ownership interest in the car, his or her contribution is disregarded. In general, an employee's ownership interest will not be recognized unless it is reflected in the title of the car; even then, it will not be recognized if the title does not reflect the benefits and burdens of ownership. [Treas. Reg. § 1.61-21(d)(2)(ii)]

The value used under this rule must be recalculated every four years. [Treas. Reg. § 1.62-21(d)(2)(iv)]

Fleet-average valuation rule. If an employer has a fleet of 20 or more automobiles and certain requirements are satisfied, the employer may use a fleet-average value for purposes of calculating the annual lease values of the automobiles in the fleet. [Treas. Reg. § 1.61-21(d)(5)(v)]

Q 13:64   How does the cents-per-mile valuation rule work?

The cents-per-mile valuation method may be used to value an employee's personal use of an employer-provided vehicle when the following is the case:

1. The employer reasonably expects the vehicle will be regularly used in the employer's trade or business throughout the calendar year (or a shorter period of ownership); or

2. The vehicle is primarily used by employees during the calendar year and is actually driven at least 10,000 miles in that calendar year.

In order to use the cents-per-mile valuation rule, however, the value of the car at the time it is first made available to the employee cannot exceed a specified amount that is adjusted annually for inflation. The inflation-adjusted figure for vehicles first made available to employees for personal use in 2010 is $15,300 for autos and $16,000 for trucks and vans (passenger autos built on a truck chassis, including minivans and sport-utility vehicles (SUVs) built on a truck chassis). [Rev. Proc. 2010-10, 2010-3 I.R.B. 300]

Under the cents-per-mile rule, the value of the benefit provided in the calendar year is the standard mileage rate (set annually by the IRS), multiplied by the number of personal miles that the employee has driven (that is, for personal purposes). The standard mileage rate is to be applied to personal miles independently of business miles. For such a purpose, personal miles means all miles for which the employee used the automobile except those driven in the employee's trade or business of being an employee of the employer. For 2010, the standard mileage rate is 50 cents per mile. Whether the car or vehicle is regularly used in the employer's trade or business will be determined based on the facts and circumstances. The car will be treated as being used in such a manner if the following is the case:

1. At least 50 percent of the car's total annual mileage is for the employer's business; or

2. The car is generally used each workday to transport at least three of the employer's employees to and from work in an employer-sponsored commuting vehicle pool.

[Treas. Reg. § 1.61-21(e)(1)(iv)]

If, however, the vehicle is used only infrequently for business use, such as for occasional trips to the airport or between the employer's multiple business premises, such use will not constitute use of the vehicle in the employer's trade or business. [Treas. Reg. § 1.61-21(e)(1)(iv)(B)]

Joint ownership. If an employee has contributed toward the purchase price of the car or toward the cost of leasing the car in return for a percentage ownership interest in the vehicle or lease, the value of the vehicle will be reduced according to a formula contained in the Treasury regulations. If the employee's ownership interest is not reflected in the title of the vehicle, however, it will not be recognized. An ownership interest reflected in the title of the vehicle will not be recognized if, under the facts and circumstances, the title does not reflect the benefits and burdens of ownership. [Treas. Reg. § 1.61-21(e)(1)(iii)(B)]

Excluded and included items. When valuing the use of a vehicle using the cents-per-mile method, the fair market value of maintaining and insuring the vehicle is included. If the employer does not provide fuel, however, the cents-per-mile rate can be lowered by up to 5.5 cents or the amount specified in an applicable revenue ruling or revenue procedure. Outside the United States, Canada, or Mexico, fuel provided by the employer may also reduce the cents-per-mile rate. [Treas. Reg. §§ 1.61-21(e)(1), 1.61-21(e)(3)]

Q 13:65   How does the commuting valuation rule work?

Under the commuting valuation rule, an employee's use of a vehicle may be valued at $1.50 per one-way commute (for example, from home to work or from work to home) if the following six conditions are met:

1. The vehicle is owned or leased by the employer;

2. The vehicle is provided to one or more employees for use in connection with the employer's trade or business and is used in the employer's trade or business;

3. The employer requires the employee to commute to or from work (or both) in the vehicle for bona fide noncompensatory business reasons;

4. The employer has established a written policy forbidding use of the vehicle for personal purposes other than commuting or *de minimis* personal use (for example, stopping for a personal errand on the way between a business delivery and the employee's home);

5. The employee does not use the vehicle for any personal purpose other than commuting and *de minimis* personal use; and

6. The employee who is required to use the vehicle for commuting is not a control employee as defined in Treasury Regulations Sections 1.61-21(f)(5) and 1.61-21(f)(6). (This limitation applies only if the vehicle is an automobile.)

[Treas. Reg. § 1.61-21(f)(1)]

For purposes of the six conditions, personal use by an employee is anything not in the employee's trade or business of being an employee of the employer. [Treas. Reg. § 1.61-21(f)(1)]

Club Dues

Q 13:66   When is reimbursement of club dues a working condition fringe benefit?

Employer-provided membership in a club organized for business, pleasure, recreation, or other social purposes may be excluded from the employee's gross income as a working condition fringe benefit to the extent the club is used for business purposes. [Treas. Reg. § 1.132-5(s)] For example, if a club is used 50 percent for business and 50 percent for personal purposes, 50 percent of the annual dues may be excluded from the employee's income. The other 50 percent must be included in the employee's income as wages.

Club dues may not be deducted as business expenses. [I.R.C. § 274(a)(3)] Therefore, the employer may not claim a deduction for that portion of the dues that are treated as a working condition fringe benefit. However, any dues payments that are treated as compensation to the employee are deductible by the employer. [I.R.C. § 274(e)(2); Treas. Reg. § 1.132-5(s)]

De Minimis Fringe Benefits

Q 13:67   What is a de minimis fringe benefit?

A *de minimis* fringe benefit is any property or service provided by an employer to its employees, the value of which is so small as to make accounting for it unreasonable or administratively impracticable (after taking into account the frequency with which similar fringe benefits are provided by the employer to its employees). [Treas. Reg. § 1.132-6(a)] The value of a *de minimis* fringe benefit may be excluded from the employee's gross income under Code Section 132.

Q 13:68   What kinds of property or services constitute de minimis fringe benefits?

Examples of *de minimis* fringe benefits include:

- Occasional typing of personal letters by a company secretary
- Occasional personal use of an employer's copying machine (as long as 85 percent of the use of the machine is for business purposes)
- Occasional cocktail parties, group meals, or picnics for employees and their guests
- Traditional birthday or holiday gifts with a low fair market value
- Occasional theater or sporting event tickets
- Coffee, doughnuts, and soft drinks
- Use of company telephones for personal local calls
- Flowers, fruit, books, or similar property provided to employees under special circumstances (such as on account of illness, outstanding performance, or family crisis)

[Treas. Reg. § 1.132-6(e)]

The following items are also excludable as *de minimis* fringe benefits if they meet detailed guidelines:

- Dependent group term life insurance
- Meals, meal money, and local transportation fare
- Eating facilities

[Treas. Reg. § 1.132-6; IRS Notice 89-110, 1989-2 C.B. 447 (postponing the effective date of Treasury Regulations Section 1.132-6(e)(2) as applied to dependent group term life insurance until further notice and stating that dependent group term life insurance with a face value of $2,000 or less will be deemed to be a *de minimis* fringe benefit under Code Section 132, while amounts in excess of $2,000 will depend upon cost)]

Note that if an employer gives an employee cash for the items listed above, the cash is not excludable from the employee's gross income as a *de minimis* fringe benefit (except for occasional meal money and local transportation fare), even if the value of the in-kind benefit (the item itself) would be (see Q 13:77). This is because it would not be unreasonable or administratively impracticable to account for the cash. [Treas. Reg. § 1.132-6(c)]

The IRS has taken a similar position with respect to gift coupons. For example, many employers have traditionally given employees holiday gifts in the form of hams or turkeys, and such gifts have traditionally been treated as tax-free *de minimis* fringe benefits. These days, however, many employees cannot enjoy such gifts because religious convictions or dietary limitations (e.g., vegetarianism) bar them from eating the food items. One employer thought it had solved this problem by providing employees with $35 gift coupons redeemable at a local grocery store. The employer estimated the $35 coupons to be approximately equal in value to the gifts it had provided in prior years. However, in a technical advice memorandum, the IRS ruled that the coupons were subject to income and employment taxes. According to the IRS, cash and cash equivalent fringe benefits, such as gift certificates, have a readily ascertainable value. Therefore, they do not qualify as *de minimis* fringe benefits because it is not unreasonable or administratively impracticable to account for them. [Tech. Adv. Mem. 200437030]

Tax return preparation. A long-standing IRS ruling provides that fees paid by a corporation for financial counseling and tax return preparation services for executives are taxable compensation to the executives. [Rev. Rul. 73-13, 1973-1 C.B. 42] On the other hand, the IRS has ruled privately that income tax return preparation services furnished to employees by volunteer income tax assistants (VITAs) at a site sponsored by their employer would qualify as *de minimis* fringe benefits. The employer was to provide office space at corporate headquarters to the VITA facility, recruit and train employees as VITA volunteers, and make available computers and other equipment and supplies. The services to be provided to employees included electronic filing of the employees' tax returns. [Priv. Ltr. Rul. 9442003]

For employees working more than 100 miles away from corporate headquarters, the employer was to issue each employee a coupon entitling the employee to the services of an income tax return preparation service clinic. The clinic would submit the coupon to the employer for reimbursement after the employee had used the services. The IRS ruled that the reimbursement would *not* qualify as a *de minimis* fringe benefit. Although the services of a VITA program are free, the services of the tax preparation clinic are not. Also, the services provided by a tax preparation clinic generally are more sophisticated than those provided by a VITA service. Therefore, employees receiving the coupons would be taxed on the value of the services provided. [Priv. Ltr. Rul. 9442003]

In a field service advice memorandum, the IRS stated that the value of employer-provided income tax return preparation services did not qualify as an excludable working condition fringe benefit, even though employees were required to use the services. A company developed a compensation program to equalize housing, living, and income tax costs for employees working abroad with those of their U.S. counterparts. As part of the program, the company calculates an additional amount that the company must pay an employee or that the employee must pay the company to equalize his or her income tax costs as an expatriate with the amount he or she would owe if working in the United States. The company pays a professional services firm to assist expatriate employees in completing their U.S. tax returns and any tax returns required by their host countries and to calculate the tax equalization amounts. Expatriate employees must agree to have the professional service firm prepare their returns. According to the IRS, "requiring an employee to accept a benefit does not automatically transform an otherwise includable income item into an excludable fringe benefit." Therefore, the value of the tax return preparation services was taxable to the employees. The advice memorandum also makes it clear that the value of tax preparation services provided to an employee must be treated as wages for employment tax purposes. [F.S.A. 200137039]

Employee recognition awards. In a legal memorandum, the IRS addressed whether nonmonetary employee recognition awards having a fair market value of $100 could qualify as *de minimis* fringe benefits—and resoundingly concluded that such awards "do NOT qualify" as *de minimis*. A *de minimis* benefit includes only property or services provided to an employee that have so little value that accounting for them would be unreasonable or administratively impracticable. Thus, if an employer distributes turkeys, hams, or other merchandise of nominal value to employees at holidays, the value of the items would not constitute salary or wages. However, nonmonetary achievement awards would not fall into the same category. [I.L.M. 200208042]

Q 13:69   What products and services do not qualify as *de minimis* fringe benefits?

The following benefits cannot be excluded from gross income under Code Section 132 as *de minimis* fringe benefits:

- Season tickets to sporting or theatrical events
- The commuting use of an employer-provided automobile or other vehicle more than one day a month
- Membership in a private country club or athletic facility, regardless of the frequency with which the employee uses the facility
- Use of employer-owned or leased facilities (e.g., an apartment, hunting lodge, or boat) for a weekend

Even if the value of the items listed may not be excluded as *de minimis* fringe benefits, the value of such items may possibly be excluded under other statutory provisions, such as the exclusion for working condition fringe benefits. [Treas. Reg. § 1.132-6(e)(2)]

(For the treatment of employer-provided income tax preparation services, see the discussion in Q 13:68.)

Q 13:70   Do any nondiscrimination requirements apply to *de minimis* fringe benefits?

Except for employer-provided eating facilities, *de minimis* fringe benefits are not subject to any nondiscrimination rules under Code Section 132. IRS regulations provide detailed requirements for employer-provided eating facilities. [Treas. Reg. § 1.132-6(f)]

Employer-Operated Eating Facilities

Q 13:71   What qualifies as an employer-operated eating facility for employees?

An *employer-operated eating facility for employees* is any facility that meets the following conditions:

1. Is owned or leased by the employer;
2. Is operated by the employer;
3. Is located on or near the employer's business premises; and
4. Furnishes meals that are provided before, during, or immediately after the employee's workday.

Meals include food, beverages, and related services provided at the facility. [Treas. Reg. § 1.132-7(a)(2)]

Q 13:72   Do *de minimis* fringe benefits include the value of meals provided to employees at an employer-operated eating facility for employees?

Yes. The value of meals provided to employees in employer-subsidized cafeterias, dining rooms, and other eating facilities is treated as an excludable *de minimis* fringe benefit under Code Section 132, provided that:

1. On an annual basis, the revenue from the facility equals or exceeds the direct operating costs of the facility [Treas. Reg. § 1.132-7(a)(1)(i)]; and
2. In addition, for the exclusion to be available to highly compensated employees, access to the facility must also be available under a reasonable classification set up by the employer that does not discriminate in favor of highly compensated employees. [Treas. Reg. § 1.132-7(a)(1)(ii)]

Employer deduction. The issue of whether meals qualify as *de minimis* fringe benefits is significant for employers as well as employees. As a general rule, an employer's deduction for meals provided to employees is limited to 50 percent of the cost. [I.R.C. § 274(n)(1)] However, an employer can claim a full deduction for meals that qualify as *de minimis* fringe benefits. [I.R.C. § 274(n)(2)(B)]

Q 13:73   How is the revenue/operating-cost test applied?

A key requirement for *de minimis* fringe benefit treatment is that the employer's annual revenue from the eating facility normally equals or exceeds its costs (see Q 13:72). If the employer sells meals to employees at cost, it will clearly meet this test. However, if the employer provides free meals to employees, there is a potential pitfall: the employer will incur a cost for the meal without offsetting revenue. However, in a 1997 decision involving a casino that provided free meals to all of its employees, the Tax Court held that for purposes of the revenue/operating-cost test, an employer can ignore the cost of meals that can be excluded from employees' incomes under Code Section 119 because they are furnished for the convenience of the employer. [Boyd Gaming Corp. v. Commissioner, 106 T.C. 343 (1996)] That decision was subsequently backed up by a 1997 law change that provides that if an employee is eligible for the exclusion, he or she will be treated as having paid an amount for a meal equal to the employer's cost. [I.R.C. § 132(e), as amended by § 970 of TRA '97; Treas. Reg. § 1.119-1(a)(1)]

Another potential pitfall arises if the employer provides free meals to some employees who do not qualify for the Section 119 exclusion. Again, the employer will incur a cost for those meals without any offsetting revenue and will fail the revenue/operating-cost test. However, IRS regulations provide that if an employer had a noncompensatory business reason for providing meals to "substantially all" of the employees who are furnished meals, meals provided to other employees also qualify for the exclusion. [Treas. Reg. § 1.119-1(a)(2)(ii)(e)] Thus, those employees will also be treated as having paid cost for their meals.

In the case involving the casino, the IRS argued that the "substantially all" test is not met unless more than 90 percent of all meals are furnished for noncompensatory business reasons. While it did not specifically accept or reject the IRS's 90 percent test, the Tax Court concluded that the casino had provided meals to more than half of its employees for compensatory reasons. Therefore, the casino did not meet the revenue/operating-cost test, and none of the meals provided for compensatory reasons qualified as *de minimis* fringe benefits. [Boyd Gaming Corp. v. Commissioner, T.C. Memo 1997-445 (Sept. 30, 1997)] Again, Congress stepped in with a law change providing that all meals furnished to employees are excludable if more than half of all meals are provided for the convenience of the employer. [I.R.C. § 119(b)(4)] Moreover, Congress specifically provided that the law change applied for tax years beginning before, on, or after the date of enactment.

Based on the law change, the casino went back to court—and this time it held the winning hand. The Ninth Circuit Court of Appeals reversed the Tax Court's decision that more than 50 percent of the employee meals were provided for compensatory reasons. The Tax Court had concluded that meals are compensatory unless an employee must accept the meals in order to properly perform his or her job duties. However, the appeals court concluded that the casino's policy of requiring employees to stay on the premises, which was adopted for legitimate business reasons, rendered the meals noncompensatory. Thus, all of the meals qualified for the Section 119 exclusion. [Boyd Gaming Corp. v. Commissioner, 177 F.3d 1096 (9th Cir. 1999)] The IRS subsequently announced that it would not appeal the Ninth Circuit's decision and would resolve other pending cases in keeping with the decision. [IRS Ann. 99-77]

(See the discussion of meals and lodging furnished for the convenience of the employer in Qs 13:126–13:143.)

Q 13:74   What items constitute the direct operating costs of an employer-operated eating facility?

For purposes of the Section 132 exclusion for *de minimis* fringe benefits, the direct operating costs of an employer-operated eating facility include the following costs:

- Food and beverages
- Labor for personnel whose services relating to the facility are performed primarily on the premises
- Payment to another with whom the employer has contracted to run the facility, to the extent that the amount would be direct operating costs if the employer operated the facility directly

[Treas. Reg. §§ 1.132-7(b)(1), 1.132-7(b)(3)]

Revenues and direct operating costs may be determined separately for each dining room or cafeteria or on an aggregate basis. [Treas. Reg. § 1.132-7(b)(2)]

Q 13:75   What nondiscrimination rules apply to the exclusion of employer-provided meals as a *de minimis* fringe benefit under Code Section 132?

Highly compensated employees (as defined in Code Section 414(q)) cannot exclude from gross income any portion of the value of meals provided at an employer-operated eating facility, unless the benefit is made available on substantially the same terms to the following:

1. All employees of the employer; or
2. A nondiscriminatory classification of employees (a facts-and-circumstances determination).

[Treas. Reg. §§ 1.132-7(a)(1)(ii), 1.132-8(d)]

The discrimination test is applied by aggregating the employees of related employers under Code Sections 414(b), 414(c), 414(m), and 414(o) to the extent that such employees regularly work at or near the facility. Employees in separate lines of business are not to be aggregated, and the nondiscrimination test is applied separately to each facility. [Treas. Reg. § 1.132-8(b)]

Even if an HCE must include in income the value of the meals provided to him or her at a discriminatory facility, he or she may nonetheless exclude from gross income the value of meals at nondiscriminatory facilities. [Treas. Reg. § 1.132-8(a)(2)(ii)(B)]

Deemed nondiscrimination. Even if access to an employer-operated eating facility is available to a classification of employees that discriminates in favor of HCEs, the classification will not be treated as discriminatory as long as the facility is not used by executive group employees more than a *de minimis* amount. Executive group employees, for this purpose, are defined as in Code Section 414(q), but with "top 1 percent" substituted for "top 10 percent" in the definition of top-paid group contained therein. [Treas. Reg. § 1.132-8(d)(5)]

Q 13:76 How are employees taxed on nonexcludable meals furnished at employer-provided eating facilities?

If the Section 132 *de minimis* fringe benefit exclusion is not available for the value of employer-provided meals, the recipient must include the following in gross income:

1. The fair market value of the meals *minus*
2. The sum of
    a. The amount (if any) paid for the meals, and
    b. The amount specifically excluded under any other Code section.

[Treas. Reg. § 1.132-7(c)]

Valuation. The fair market value of meals to be allocated to an individual is determined in accordance with the rules contained in Treasury Regulations Section 1.61-21(j). Two methods are provided, as follows:

1. *Direct meal subsidy.* The sum of the individual meal subsidies for each meal consumed by the employee during the calendar year, less the amount paid by the employee.
2. *Indirect meal subsidy.* Allocation of the aggregate meal value (deemed to be 150 percent of the total operating costs of the particular facility), less the facility's gross receipts, among employees in any manner reasonable under the circumstances.

[Treas. Reg. § 1.162-21(j)(2)]

Meal Money and Local Transportation Fare

Q 13:77 Are occasional meal money and local transportation fare excludable from gross income under Code Section 132 as *de minimis* fringe benefits?

They can be. To qualify, the meals, meal money, and local transportation fare provided must be reasonable and also must satisfy the following three requirements:

1. They must be provided on an occasional basis, not a regular or routine basis;

2. They must be provided because overtime work necessitates an extension of the employee's normal work schedule (even if the overtime work was reasonably foreseeable); and

3. Meals or meal money must be provided to enable the employee to work overtime.

[Treas. Reg. § 1.132-6(d)(2)]

Meal money and local transportation fare calculated based on the number of hours worked do not qualify as *de minimis* fringe benefits. [Treas. Reg. § 1.132-6(d)(2)]

Meals and meal money that do not qualify as *de minimis* fringe benefits may nevertheless be excludable under Code Section 119 (see Q 13:73).

Special rules apply to taxi fare (see Q 13:78) and commuting under unsafe conditions (see Qs 13:80–13:85; see also Qs 13:92–13:117 regarding qualified transportation fringe benefits).

Employer-Provided Transportation in Unusual Circumstances and Because of Unsafe Conditions

Q 13:78 What special rules apply to employer-provided transportation such as taxi fare?

Ordinarily, employer-provided transportation (such as taxi fare) for commuting to and from work is not excludable as a fringe benefit under Code Section 132 because commuting is a nondeductible personal expense under Code Section 262. If, however, (1) the employer provides transportation to or from work (or both) because of unusual circumstances and (2) it is unsafe, based on the facts and circumstances, for the employee to use other available means of transportation, the amount included in the employee's gross income is limited to $1.50 per one-way commute. The cost of each one-way commute in excess of $1.50 is excluded from gross income. [Treas. Reg. § 1.132-6(d)(2)(iii)(C)] This special value cannot be used by control employees as defined in Treasury Regulations Sections 1.61-21(f)(5) and 1.61-21(f)(6) (see Q 13:37).

Q 13:79   When do unusual circumstances exist?

For purposes of the Section 132 exclusion, the determination of whether unusual circumstances exist regarding the employee in question is based on the facts and circumstances. For instance, being called to work at 2:00 A.M. when the employee's regular work schedule is 9:00 A.M. to 5:00 P.M. would be an unusual circumstance. Another example is a temporary change in the employee's work schedule, such as working late for a two-week period. [Treas. Reg. § 1.132-6(d)(2)(iii)(B)]

Q 13:80   When do unsafe conditions exist?

For purposes of the Section 132 exclusion, factors that indicate whether an employee's use of alternate transportation is unsafe include the history of crime in the geographic area surrounding the employee's workplace or residence and the time of day during which the employee must commute. [Treas. Reg. § 1.132-6(d)(2)(iii)(C)]

Q 13:81   What additional exclusion is available for employer-provided transportation because of unsafe conditions?

Treasury Regulations Section 1.61-21(k) provides a special partial exclusion from gross income for employer-provided transportation meeting the following four conditions:

1. The transportation is provided solely because of unsafe conditions to an employee who would otherwise walk or use public transportation at the time of day he or she must commute;

2. The employer has established a written policy (such as in the employer's personnel manual) stating that the transportation is not provided for any other personal purposes and the employer's practice in fact conforms with the policy;

3. The transportation is not used for any personal purposes except commuting because of unsafe conditions; and

4. The recipient employee is a qualified employee (see Q 13:82).

[Treas. Reg. § 1.61-21(k)(1)]

If the preceding conditions are met, the includable value of each one-way trip to or from work is $1.50, regardless of the actual fair market value of the trip.

Q 13:82   Who is a qualified employee for purposes of receiving transportation solely because of unsafe conditions?

A qualified employee, for the purpose of receiving transportation because of unsafe conditions, is a nonexempt hourly employee in an employment classification eligible to receive overtime pay at least one and one-half times the regular rate. [Treas. Reg. § 1.61-21(k)(6)(i)(A)] Under IRS regulations, employees who received compensation in excess of the Section 414(q)(1)(C) limit are excluded.

[Treas. Reg. § 1.61-21(k)(6)(i)(B)] However, Code Section 414(q)(1)(C) was repealed in 1996, and it is likely that the IRS will look to the $80,000 (indexed) compensation in Code Section 414(q)(1)(B) instead.

Recordkeeping requirement. An employer must be in compliance with the recordkeeping requirements of the Fair Labor Standards Act of 1938 (FLSA), as amended, concerning wages, hours, and other conditions of employment, or else its employees will be disqualified from treatment as qualified employees for purposes of the special transportation exclusion. If so disqualified, no part of such employer-provided transportation will be excludable. [Treas. Reg. §§ 1.61-21(k)(6)(iii), 1.61-21(k)(6)(v)]

Q 13:83 For purposes of the Section 61 exclusion, when are unsafe conditions considered to exist?

Unsafe conditions will be considered to exist if a reasonable person would, under the facts and circumstances, consider it unsafe for the employee to walk to or from home or to use public transportation at that particular time of day. Factors that indicate unsafe conditions include a history of crime in the geographic area surrounding either the employee's workplace or residence at the time of day the employee must commute. [Treas. Reg. § 1.61-21(k)(5)]

Q 13:84 What type of employer-provided transportation counts toward the special exclusion for unsafe conditions?

The employer-provided transportation must consist of a motorized, wheeled vehicle purchased by the employer (or purchased by the employee and reimbursed by the employer) from an unrelated third party for the purpose of transporting the employee to or from work. The vehicle must have been manufactured primarily for use on public streets, roads, and highways (for example, a bus or automobile). [Treas. Reg. §§ 1.61-21(f)(4), 1.61-21(k)(4)]

Q 13:85 How are qualifying trips valued?

If the requirements of Treasury Regulations Section 1.61-21(k) regarding employer-provided transportation for unsafe conditions are met (see Q 13:81), the amount includable in each employee's gross income is $1.50 per one-way commute (from home to work or from work to home). [Treas. Reg. § 1.61-21(k)(3)]

On-Premises Athletic Facilities

Q 13:86 What is an on-premises athletic facility?

An on-premises athletic facility may be a gym, a swimming pool, a golf course, or any other athletic facilities. [Treas. Reg. § 1.132-1(e)(1)]

Q 13:87   Can the value of on-premises athletic facilities be excluded from the employee's gross income?

Yes. An employee's gross income does not include the value of any on-premises athletic facilities that the employer provides to its employees. [Treas. Reg. § 1.132-1(e)(1)]

Q 13:88   What conditions must be satisfied in order for the value of on-premises athletic facilities to be excluded under Code Section 132?

In order for the value of on-premises athletic facilities to be excludable from the employee's gross income, the facility must meet the following three conditions:

1. It must be located on the employer's premises;
2. It must be operated by the employer; and
3. Substantially all of its use during the calendar year must be by the employer's employees and their spouses and dependent children.

The Section 132 exclusion does not apply if the athletic facility is made available to the general public through membership sales, rental, or similar arrangements. [Treas. Reg. § 1.132-1(e)(1)]

Q 13:89   When is an athletic facility considered to be on the premises of an employer?

An athletic facility must be located on the premises of the employer, but need not be located on the employer's business premises. Whether the premises are owned or leased by the employer does not matter; a leasing employer need not even be a named lessee on the lease as long as the employer pays reasonable rent. Athletic facilities that are facilities for residential use (such as a resort with accompanying athletic facilities) do not qualify, however. [Treas. Reg. § 1.132-1(e)(2)]

Health club, country club, and other memberships do not qualify for the on-premises athletic facility exclusion unless the employer owns or leases and operates the facility and substantially all of the facility's use is by the employer's employees and their spouses and dependent children. [Treas. Reg. § 1.132-1(e)(3)]

Q 13:90   When is an employer considered to be operating an on-premises athletic facility?

An employer will be treated as operating an on-premises athletic facility if it does so through its own employees or it contracts with another to operate the facility. If the facility is operated by more than one employer, it is treated as being operated by each employer. [Treas. Reg. § 1.132-1(e)(4)]

The IRS considered the situation where an employer and its affiliated companies leased an athletic facility for use by active and retired employees and their spouses and children. The athletic facility was not open to the general public. It was operated by an agent of the employer, and membership fees were established by the agency operator. The IRS ruled that the arrangement met the requirements for an on-premises athletic facility. Therefore, the fair market value of membership was exempt from income tax withholding and from FICA and FUTA taxes. [Priv. Ltr. Rul. 9430029]

Q 13:91   May an employee's family members also use an employer's on-premises athletic facilities on a tax-free basis?

Yes. An *employee*, for purposes of the exclusion for on-premises athletic facilities, is defined broadly to include the following:

1. Current employees of the employer;

2. Former employees who separated from the employer's service as the result of retirement or disability;

3. Any widow or widower of an employee who either died while employed by the employer or separated from service as the result of retirement or disability; and

4. Any spouse or dependent child of the above, including any son, stepson, daughter, or stepdaughter who is a dependent of the employee or whose parents are both deceased and who has not attained age 25 (if Code Section 152(e), dealing with a child of divorced parents, applies, the child will be treated as a dependent of both parents).

[Treas. Reg. § 1.132-1(b)]

Qualified Transportation Fringe Benefits

Q 13:92   What is a qualified transportation fringe benefit?

A *qualified* transportation fringe benefit includes any of the following provided by an employer to an employee:

- Transportation in a commuter highway vehicle if that transportation is in connection with travel between the employee's residence and the place of employment (also referred to as van pooling)
- A transportation pass
- Qualified parking
- A qualified bicycle commuting reimbursement (for tax years beginning after December 31, 2008)

An employer may simultaneously provide an employee with transportation in a commuter highway vehicle, a transportation pass, and qualified parking.

However, an employee may not receive a bicycle commuting expense reimbursement for any month in which the employee receives any other qualified transportation fringe benefit. [65 Fed. Reg. 4,388 (Jan. 27, 2000); I.R.C. § 132(f), as amended by the Transportation Equity Act for the 21st Century (TEA-21), Pub. L. No. 105-178, 112 Stat. 107 (1998)) and the Renewable Energy and Job Creation Tax Act of 2008, which passed the House on September 26, 2008, Pub. L. No. 110-343; Notice 94-3, 1994-3 I.R.B. 14]

Final regulations under Code Section 132 provide guidance, in question-and-answer form, to employers that provide qualified transportation fringe benefits to employees. [Treas. Reg. § 1.132-9, 66 Fed. Reg. 2,241–2,251] The regulations explain that there are two categories of qualified transportation fringe benefits for purposes of determining the amount that is excludable from gross income. The first category is transportation in a commuter highway vehicle and transit passes. The second category is qualified parking. There is a statutory monthly limit on the value of the benefits in each category that is excludable from gross income.

Q 13:93   Must a qualified transportation fringe benefit plan be in writing?

No. Code Section 132(f) does not require that a qualified transportation fringe benefit plan be in writing. [Treas. Reg. § 1.132-9 Q&A-6]

Q 13:94   What is a commuter highway vehicle?

A *commuter highway vehicle* is defined as any vehicle that has a seating capacity of at least six adults (excluding the driver) and for which at least 80 percent of the mileage use is reasonably expected to be for purposes of transporting employees in connection with travel between their residences and their place of employment. As well, on trips during which employees are transported for such purposes, their number is expected to be at least half of the adult capacity of the vehicle (not including the driver). [I.R.C. § 132(f)(5)(B); Treas. Reg. § 1.132-9, Q&A-2]

Q 13:95   What is a transit pass?

A *transit pass* is any pass, token, fare card, voucher, or similar item entitling a person to free or reduced-price transportation if such transportation:

1. Is on mass transit facilities (public or private); or
2. Is provided by any person in the business of transporting persons for compensation or hire in a highway vehicle that has a seating capacity of at least six adults (excluding the driver).

[I.R.C. § 132(f)(5)(A); Treas. Reg. § 1.132-9, Q&A-3]

Q 13:96   What is qualified parking?

Qualified parking is parking provided to an employee on or near the business premises of an employer or on or near a location from which the employee commutes to work by means of:

- Mass transit facilities;
- A highway vehicle for hire, which has a seating capacity of at least six adults (excluding the driver);
- A commuter highway vehicle; or
- A carpool.

Qualified parking does not include any parking on or near property used by the employee for residential purposes. [I.R.C. § 132(f)(5)(C); Treas. Reg. § 1.132-9, Q&A-4]

> **Example.** Duane, an employee of Fabco, drives from his home to a commuter railway station, parks his car, and takes the train to work. If Fabco pays for the cost of parking at the railway station, it is a qualified transportation fringe benefit.

Qualified parking includes parking on or near a work location at which the employee provides services for the employer. However, it does not include the value of parking that is excludable from gross income as a working condition fringe benefit, nor does it include business expense reimbursements to an employee for parking that are excludable from income as made under an accountable plan. [*See* Treas. Reg. § 1.62-2.] So, for example, reimbursements for parking expenses incurred by an employee on a business trip for the employer are not treated as qualified parking and do not count toward the monthly limit on parking benefits.

Parking is provided by an employer if the parking is on property owned or leased by the employer, the employer pays for the parking, or the employer reimburses the employee for parking expenses.

Q 13:97   What is a *qualified bicycle commuting reimbursement*?

A *qualified bicycle commuting reimbursement* for 2009 or later years is any reimbursement made during the 15-month period beginning with the first day of the year for reasonable expenses incurred by an employee for the purchase and repair of a bicycle, bicycle improvements, and bicycle storage. In order for the reimbursements to be tax-free, the bicycle must be "regularly used" for travel between the employee's residence and place of employment. [I.R.C. § 132(f)(5)(F), as added by the Renewable Energy and Job Creation Tax Act of 2008, Pub. L. No. 110-343]

There is a maximum annual dollar limit on the amount that can be excluded from income for bicycle reimbursements. The limit for a year is equal to $20 multiplied by the number of the employee's qualified bicycle commuting months for the year. A qualified bicycle commuting month means any month during which: (1) the employee does not receive any other qualified transportation fringe benefit, and (2) the employee regularly uses a bicycle for a substantial portion of travel between the employee's residence and place of employment. The bicycle commuting reimbursement limit is not indexed for inflation.

Unlike other transportation fringe benefits, bicycle commuting reimbursements cannot be provided through a salary reduction arrangement.

Q 13:98   Are all qualified transportation fringe benefits exempt from income tax?

No, not in all cases. There are dollar limits on the amounts that can be excluded from an employee's income. If the amount of the qualified transportation fringe benefit exceeds the applicable dollar limit plus any amount paid by the employee, the excess is income to the employee. [I.R.C. § 132(f)(2); Treas. Reg. § 1.132-9, Q&A-8] Employers are required to value such excess benefits according to what an individual would normally pay in an arm's-length transaction. [Notice 94-3, 1994-3 I.R.B. 14]

Q 13:99   Can employers offer employees a choice between cash or qualified transportation benefits?

In general, an employer may offer employees a choice between cash or qualified transportation fringe benefits in lieu of cash. Code Section 132(f) was amended by the Transportation Equity Act for the 21st Century (TEA-21) to provide a shelter from constructive receipt of income; thus, an employee will not have any amount included in gross income *solely because* he or she was provided with such a choice. [I.R.C. § 132(f)(3)] Accordingly, although Section 132 benefits cannot be included as a qualified benefit under a Section 125 cafeteria plan, Code Section 132 now independently provides a cafeteria plan-like protection from inclusion of benefits in gross income merely because the employee was given the choice of receiving qualified transportation fringe benefits or cash. Note, however, that this option does not apply to qualified bicycle commuting reimbursements.

A compensation reduction election to receive qualified transportation fringe benefits in lieu of cash must meet certain requirements specified in the IRS regulations (see Qs 13:109–13:112).

Q 13:100   What are the dollar limits on qualified transportation fringe benefits?

There is a monthly dollar limit (indexed annually for inflation) on the exclusion for transportation in a commuter highway vehicle or transit passes. If an employee receives both benefits, the monthly limit applies to the combined benefits, regardless of whether the benefits are provided separately or are provided together. A separate monthly dollar limit (indexed) applies to qualified parking. [I.R.C. § 132(f)(2)]

The exclusion for qualified parking is limited to $175 per month, indexed for inflation. The indexed limit for qualified parking for 2010 is $230 per month. [Rev. Proc. 2009-50, 2009-45 I.R.B. 619]

As a general rule, the limit for transportation in a commuter highway vehicle and transit passes is $100 per month indexed for inflation. However, the American Recovery and Reinvestment Act of 2009 [Pub. L. No. 111-5, 123 Stat. 115 (Feb. 17, 2009)] (ARRA) increased the monthly exclusion for employer-provided transit passes and vanpooling to the same level as the exclusion for employer-provided parking for months beginning on or after the date of enactment (February 17, 2009) and before January 1, 2011. [I.R.C. § 132(f)(2), as amended by Pub. L. No. 111-5, § 1151(a)] Thus, the monthly limit for 2010 is $230 per month. [Rev. Proc. 2009-50, 2009-45 I.R.B. 619]

> **Example.** In 2010, Greystone, Inc. provides its employee, Bethany, with transportation in a commuter highway vehicle at a cost of $50 a month and with a transit pass costing $75 a month. Bethany's benefits are fully tax free because the combined value does not exceed the limit of $230 per month for 2010.

There is a maximum annual dollar limit on the amount that can be excluded from income for bicycle reimbursements. The limit for a year is equal to $20 multiplied by the number of the employee's qualified bicycle commuting months for the year. A qualified bicycle commuting month means any month during which: (1) the employee does not receive any other qualified transportation fringe benefit, and (2) the employee regularly uses a bicycle for a substantial portion of travel between his or her residence and place of employment. [I.R.C. § 132(f)(5)(F) as added by the Renewable Energy and Job Creation Tax Act of 2008, Pub. L. No. 110-343]. The bicycle commuting reimbursement limit is not indexed for inflation.

It is the employer's responsibility to determine the taxable amount (if any) of qualified transportation fringe benefits. [Notice 94-3, 1994-3 I.R.B. 14] The taxable portion of any reimbursements for parking, van pooling, or mass transit expenses is to be included in the employees' wages at the time the reimbursement is paid.

An employer may provide qualified parking benefits in addition to transportation in a commuter highway vehicle and transit passes. [Treas. Reg. § 1.132-9, Q&A-1(b)] However, a qualified bicycle commuting reimbursement may be provided only for a month during which the employee does not receive any other qualified transportation fringe benefit. [I.R.C. § 132(f)(5)(F) as added by the Renewable Energy and Job Creation Tax Act of 2008, Pub. L. No. 110-343]

Q 13:101   Are the dollar limits on qualified transportation fringe benefits indexed for inflation?

The dollar limits on qualified transportation fringe benefits (other than qualified bicycle commuting reimbursements) are adjusted annually to reflect cost-of-living changes. If an increase is not a multiple of $5, the increase will be rounded to the next lowest multiple of $5. [I.R.C. § 132(f)(6)]

Q 13:102   Can an employer reimburse an employee in cash for the cost of a qualified transportation fringe benefit?

An employer can provide cash reimbursements to an employee for expenses incurred or paid by the employee for transportation in a commuter highway vehicle or qualified parking. Reimbursements for qualified bicycle commuting expenses can be made in cash.

However, despite strenuous objections from employer groups, the final transportation fringe benefit regulations provide that cash reimbursement for transit passes is permitted only if a voucher or similar item that may be exchanged only for a transit pass is not readily available for direct distribution by the employer to the employee (see Q 13:104). [I.R.C. § 132(f)(3); Treas. Reg. § 1.132-9, Q&A-16]

Employers that make cash reimbursements must establish a bona fide reimbursement arrangement to ensure that employees have actually incurred transportation expenses. Any payment made before the date the expense has been incurred or paid is not a reimbursement. In addition, a bona fide reimbursement arrangement does not include any arrangement that is dependent solely on the employee's certifying in advance that he or she will incur expenses at some future date. [Treas. Reg. § 1.132-9, Q&A-16(a)]

The determination of whether reimbursements are made under a bona fide reimbursement arrangement will depend on the facts and circumstances. However, the arrangement must include reasonable procedures to ensure that an amount equal to the reimbursement was incurred for qualified transportation expenses. In addition, the expense must be substantiated within a reasonable period of time. Substantiation within 180 days will be considered reasonable. [Treas. Reg. § 1.132-9, Q&A-16(c)] Reasonable substantiation procedures may include presentation of a parking receipt or a used or unused time-sensitive transit pass (such as a monthly pass). For example, an IRS information letter indicates that it would be acceptable substantiation for an employee to submit a used transit pass to the employer at the end of the month and to certify both that he or she purchased it and that he or she used it for commuting during the month. Similarly, presentation of a transit pass to the employer at the beginning of the month along with a certification that it will be used for commuting during the coming month would be acceptable. [I.R.S. Info. 2001-0090 (Mar. 16, 2001)]

If receipts are not provided in the ordinary course of business (for example, if the employee uses metered parking or transit passes that are not returned to the user), it is reasonable for the employer to accept the employee's certification of the type and amount of expenses incurred, provided the employer has no reason to doubt the employee's certification. [Treas. Reg. § 1.132-9, Q&A-16(d)]

The regulations do not specify how frequently expenses must be substantiated. However, the IRS information letter specifically states that it would not be permissible for an employee to certify once per year that he or she has incurred expenses up to the amount of the reimbursement the employee has already received. [I.R.S. Info. 2001-0090 (Mar. 16, 2001)]

Q 13:103   May an employer offer both a compensation reduction election and cash reimbursements for the same parking expenses?

No. According to an IRS revenue ruling, an employer's "reimbursements" for parking are not excludable from an employee's gross income when the parking has already been paid by the employee on a pretax basis through a compensation reduction election. [Rev. Rul. 2004-98, 2004-42 I.R.B. 664]

Example. Before implementing its parking arrangement, Employer X paid Employee Y monthly wages of $1,500. After income and payroll tax withholding, Y's net pay came to $1,301.45. Following implementation of the parking arrangement, Y's $1,500 monthly wages were reduced by $100 in exchange for the parking. This reduced Y's net pay to $1,221.70 ($1,400 monthly wages less income and payroll tax withholding). However, Employer X then paid Employee Y an additional $79.75 per month, bringing Y's net pay back up to $1,301.45. Employer X characterized the additional payments as tax-free "reimbursements" for parking expenses. However, the IRS disagreed with that characterization of the payments.

According to the IRS, the employer's "reimbursements" did not qualify as excludable fringe benefits because the employee did not have any expenses for parking to be reimbursed. The IRS pointed out that when an employee is given a choice between cash compensation and nontaxable employer-provided parking, the parking is treated as provided directly by the employer rather than purchased by the employee with the amount of the compensation reduction. As a result, there is no expense incurred by the employee for the employer to reimburse, and any "reimbursements" are included in the employee's gross income and are wages subject to employment taxes.

Q 13:104   Are transit passes subject to special rules?

Yes. The final IRS regulations on transportation fringe benefits provide that transit passes must be distributed in kind unless vouchers or similar items that may be redeemed only for passes are not readily available for direct distribution by the employer. If passes or vouchers are readily available, the in-kind distribution requirement is satisfied if distribution is made by the employer or by another person on behalf of the employer. For example, the in-kind distribution requirement will be met if a transit operator credits amounts to employees' fare cards as a result of payments made to the operator by the employer. [Treas. Reg. § 1.132-9, Q&A-16(b)(1)]

A voucher or similar item is readily available for direct distribution unless:

1. The average annual fees that the employer must pay to obtain the vouchers (excluding reasonable and customary delivery charges that do

not exceed $15 per order) are more than 1 percent of the average annual value of the vouchers; or

2. Other nonfinancial restrictions cause vouchers to be not readily available. Nonfinancial restrictions include advance purchase requirements, purchase quantity requirements, or limits on voucher denominations.

Advance purchase requirements cause vouchers to be not readily available if the voucher provider does not offer vouchers at regular intervals or fails to provide vouchers within a reasonable period after receiving payment. For example, a requirement that vouchers may be purchased only once per year may effectively prevent an employer from obtaining vouchers for distribution to employees. However, a requirement that vouchers be purchased no more frequently than monthly does not effectively prevent the employer from obtaining vouchers for direct distribution to employees.

Purchase quantity requirements cause vouchers to be not readily available if the voucher provider does not offer quantities that are reasonably appropriate for the number of employees who use mass transit—for example, if the voucher provider requires a $1,000 minimum purchase and the employer needs only $200 of vouchers.

Limitations on denominations cause vouchers to be not readily available if the voucher provider does not offer denominations that are appropriate for the employer's needs. For example, vouchers in $5 increments up to the monthly limit would not cause a problem for employers. However, vouchers available only in denominations equal to the monthly limit would not be appropriate for an employer who provides employees with a monthly benefit that is less than the limit.

Practice Pointer. An employer's internal administrative cost of providing the vouchers is not taken into account in determining whether vouchers are readily available.

Q 13:105   How does an employer use debit cards to provide transit passes?

The IRS has ruled that debit cards, credit cards, "smartcards," or other electronic media can be used to provide mass transit passes—provided certain requirements are met. [Rev. Rul 2006-57, 2006-47 I.R.B. 911]. The requirements depend on whether the card in question is equivalent to a transit voucher because it can only be used for transit fares or whether it is equivalent to cash because it can be used for other purposes. In the latter case, use of the card is permitted only if transit vouchers are not readily available for distribution to the employee (see Q 13:104)

The rules relating to the use of electronic media were originally scheduled to take effect on January 1, 2008, but have been delayed because certain transit systems continue to experience technology barriers to achieving compatibility with the requirements. The IRS has said that employers can rely on the rules set forth in Revenue Ruling 2006-57 for transactions occurring before 2011. [Notice 2009-94, 2009-50 I.R.B. 848 (Dec. 14, 2009)]

The IRS ruling describes four situations:

Situation 1. Alpha Corp. provides mass transit benefits to employees in amounts that do not exceed the applicable monthly limit. The local transit system provides smartcards that may be used by employers in the area to provide transit fares to employees. The smartcards are plastic cards containing a memory chip that stores certain information, including the card's serial number and the value of the fares stored on the card. The amount stored on the smartcard cannot be used to purchase anything other than transit fares. Alpha makes monthly payments to the transit system on behalf of employees who participate in the transportation benefit program, which the transit system electronically allocates to each employee's smartcard as instructed by Alpha. Alpha does not require its employees to substantiate their use of the smartcards.

Because the amounts stored on the smartcards can be used only for transit fares, the smartcards qualify as transit system vouchers that are distributed in kind by Alpha to its employees. Therefore, the amounts provided by Alpha to its employees through the use of the smartcards is excluded from the employees' gross income as a qualified transportation fringe benefit without requiring the employees to substantiate their use of the smartcards.

Situation 2. Beta Corp. provides mass transit benefits to employees in amounts that do not exceed the applicable monthly limit. A debit card provider offers cards that can be used only at terminals that sell transit fares. Beta makes monthly payments to the debit card provider on behalf of employees who participate in Beta's transportation benefit program, which the provider electronically allocates to each employee's terminal-restricted debit card as instructed by Beta. Beta does not require employees to substantiate use of the debit cards.

The terminal-restricted debit cards qualify as transit system vouchers because they can be used only at terminals that sell transit fares. Therefore, amounts provided by Beta to its employees through the debit cards are excluded from gross income without requiring employees to substantiate their use of the debit cards.

Situation 3. Gamma Corp. provides mass transit benefits to employees in amounts that do not exceed the applicable monthly limit. Transit vouchers or similar items are not readily available for distribution to Gamma's employees. Instead, Gamma arranges with a debit card provider for debit cards that can be used only at merchants that have been assigned a merchant category code (MCC) indicating that the merchant sells transit fares. The merchants may or may not sell other merchandise.

Gamma uses a reimbursement procedure to add amounts to an employee's debit card. For the first month an employee participates in Gamma's transportation benefit program, the employee pays for transit fares with after-tax amounts and substantiates to Gamma the amount of fare expenses incurred during the month. After receiving the employee's substantiation, Gamma pays the debit card provider an amount equal to the employee's substantiated fare expenses for the prior month, which the debit card provider electronically allocates to a debit card assigned to the employee. In later months, Gamma provides additional funds to the debit card provider to be allocated to the employee's debit card equal to the amount of substantiated fare expenses for the prior month. In the case of expenses that were paid using the debit card, this substantiation consists of a statement from the debit card provider on the use of each debit card, including information on the identity of the merchants at which the debit card was used, and the date and amount of the debit card transactions. In addition, for the first month a debit card is used, Gamma requires an employee to certify that the card was used only to purchase transit fares. In later months, Gamma does not require employee certifications for recurring expenses that match expenses previous expenses as to seller and time period (e.g., for an employee who purchases a transit pass on a regular basis from the same seller). However, Gamma requires an employee to recertify at least annually that the debit card was used only to purchase fare media. In the case of fare expenses that were not paid using the debit card, an employee can receive reimbursement via the debit card if he or she substantiates the amount following reasonable procedures. Thus, an employee receiving reimbursements of less than the maximum monthly excludable amount can increase his or her reimbursements for future months by paying for increased fare expenses out of pocket.

In this case, the IRS says the debit cards do not qualify as transit system vouchers because the cards can be used to purchase items other than transit passes. A merchant classified to accept the cards may sell merchandise other than transit passes, and there is nothing in the debit card technology that prevents it from being used to purchase things other than transit passes. On the other hand, because a transit voucher or similar item is not readily available to Gamma for direct distribution to employees, Gamma can provide transit benefits in the form of cash reimbursements if the reimbursements are made under a bona fide reimbursement arrangement. In the case of expenses incurred during the first month an employee participates in the transportation benefit program and with respect to expenses not paid with a debit card, Gamma's reasonable substantiation procedures constitute a bona fide arrangement. Moreover, in the case of expenses paid with debit card, the IRS says that the periodic statements coupled with employee certifications also constitute a bona fide reimbursement arrangement. Therefore, the amounts provided by Gamma to its employees through the use of the debit cards is excluded from its employees' gross income as qualified transportation fringe benefits.

Situation 4. The facts are the same as those in Situation 3, except that Gamma provides employees with the debit cards as soon as they begin working for Gamma. Prior to using the debit cards, employees certify that the card will be used only to buy transit passes. In addition, written on each debit card is the statement that the card is to be used only for transit passes, and, by using the card, the employee certifies that the card is being used only to purchase transit passes. However, Gamma employees are not required to substantiate the amount of fare media expenses they incur.

The debit cards do not qualify as transit system vouchers. Moreover, the system used to provide the cards does not constitute a bona fide reimbursement arrangement because it provides for advances rather than reimbursements and because it relies solely on employee certifications provided before the expense is incurred. Therefore, the amounts provided to employees through the use of the debit cards are included in employees' gross income and wages.

> **Practice Pointer.** Revenue Ruling 2006-57 notes that because terminal-restricted debit cards are equivalent to transit vouchers, the availability of such cards in an employer's area would preclude the use of cash reimbursements (see Q 13:104). However, the IRS says it does not currently have enough information to determine whether such cards are readily available in areas where cash reimbursements are currently permitted. The IRS says it plans to issue guidance on that issue as the use of terminal-restricted debit cards increases in cash-reimbursement areas. Until such guidance is issued, the IRS will not challenge the ability of employers to provide qualified transportation fringes in the form of cash reimbursement for transit passes when the only available voucher or similar item is a terminal-restricted debit card.

Q 13:106   Is a qualified transportation fringe benefit received by an employee subject to income tax withholding or to Social Security and the Federal Unemployment Tax Act?

To the extent that a qualified transportation fringe benefit is excludable from gross income under Code Section 132(f), it is not subject to income tax withholding or to FICA (Social Security) or FUTA (Federal Unemployment Tax Act). To the extent the benefit is taxable (i.e., to the extent the dollar limits are exceeded), income tax withholding and FICA and FUTA apply. [I.R.C. §§ 3401(a)(19), 3121(a)(20), 3306(b)(16)]

Q 13:107   How are excludable qualified transportation fringes calculated?

The value of transportation in a commuter highway vehicle and qualified parking is calculated on a monthly basis to determine whether the value of the benefit has exceeded the applicable statutory monthly limit on qualified transportation fringes. The applicable statutory monthly limit applies to qualified transportation fringes used by the employee in a given month. Monthly exclusion amounts cannot be combined to provide a qualified transportation fringe in any month exceeding the statutory limit. A month is a calendar month or a substantially equivalent period applied consistently. [Treas. Reg. § 1.132-9, Q&A-9(a)] Thus, if an employer reimburses an employee less than the monthly limit for parking in one month and more than the limit the next month, the employee has taxable income in the month the reimbursement exceeds the limit.

Transit passes. The applicable statutory monthly limit applies to the transit passes provided by the employer to the employee in a month for that month or for any previous month in the calendar year. The exclusion is available to the extent passes distributed do not exceed the cumulative monthly limit for the year. [Treas. Reg. § 1.132-9(b)]

> **Example.** In 2010, XYZ Company does not give Employee P any transit passes until the end of March. At that time, XYZ gives P $500 worth of passes. Since the value of the passes does not exceed the monthly limit figured cumulatively (3 months at $230), the passes are tax free. Note, however, that if P did not join the company until February, $40 would be taxable ($500 passes – $460 cumulative limit for two months).

Qualified bicycle commuting reimbursements. There is a maximum annual dollar limit on the amount that can be excluded from income for bicycle reimbursements. The limit for a year is equal to $20 multiplied by the number of the employee's qualified bicycle commuting months for the year. A qualified bicycle commuting month means any month during which (1) the employee does not receive any other qualified transportation fringe benefit and (2) the employee regularly uses a bicycle for a substantial portion of travel between his or her residence and place of employment. [I.R.C. § 132(f)(5)(F) as added by the Renewable Energy and Job Creation Tax Act of 2008, Pub. L. No. 110-343] The bicycle commuting reimbursement limit is not indexed for inflation.

Q 13:108   May employers distribute transit passes in advance?

Yes. Employers may distribute transit passes in advance for more than one month, but not for more than 12 months. [Treas. Reg. § 1.132-9, Q&A-9(b)] The value of the passes is excludable provided it does not exceed the combined monthly limits for all months in which the passes will be used.

If an employee terminates employment after receiving an advance distribution of transit passes, the value of the passes provided for any month following the termination must be reported as wages for income tax purposes. However, where passes are provided in advance for no more than three months (e.g., for a calendar quarter), and the recipient terminates employment before the last month of the period, the employer may exclude the value of the passes from wages for payroll taxes and income tax withholding. This rule does not apply if at the time the passes were distributed there was an established date for the employee's termination of employment (e.g., if the employee had given notice of retirement). If passes are distributed in advance for more than three months, the value of passes provided for all months following an employee's termination of employment must be included in wages for payroll tax purposes. [Treas. Reg. § 1.132-9(c)]

Q 13:109   What is a compensation reduction arrangement?

A *compensation reduction arrangement* is an program under which the employer provides the employee with the right to elect whether he or she will receive either a fixed amount of cash compensation at a specified future date or a fixed amount of qualified transportation fringes (other than qualified bicycle commuting reimbursements) to be provided for a specified future period. Bicycle commuting reimbursements cannot be provided through a compensation reduction arrangement.

The employee's election must be in writing or in another medium (such as electronic) that includes, in a permanent and verifiable form, the information required to be in the election. The election must contain the date of the election, the amount of the compensation to be reduced, and the period for which the benefits will be provided. The reduction election must be in the form of a fixed dollar amount or fixed percentage of compensation. An election to reduce compensation for a period by a set amount for such period may be automatically renewed for subsequent periods. [Treas. Reg. § 1.132-9, Q&A-12]

Q 13:110   Is there a limit to the amount of the compensation reduction?

Yes. Each month, the amount of the compensation reduction may not exceed the combined applicable statutory monthly limits for transportation in a commuter highway vehicle, transit passes, and qualified parking. Bicycle commuting reimbursements cannot be provided through a salary reduction arrangement.

For example, for 2010, an employee may elect to reduce compensation for any month by no more than $460 ($230 for transportation in a commuter highway vehicle and transit passes, plus $230 for qualified parking) with respect to qualified transportation fringes. [Rev. Proc. 2008-66, 2008-45 I.R.B. 1107] If an employee elected to reduce compensation by $475 for a month, the excess $15 ($475 minus $460) would be includable in the employee's wages for income and employment tax purposes. [Treas. Reg. § 1.132-9, Q&A-13]

Q 13:111   When must the employee have made a compensation reduction election, and under what circumstances can the amount be paid in cash to the employee?

The compensation reduction election must be made before the employee is currently able to receive the cash or other taxable amount at the employee's discretion. The determination of whether the employee is currently able to receive the cash does not depend on whether the cash has been constructively received for purposes of Code Section 451. The election must specify that the period (such as a calendar month) for which the qualified transportation fringe will be provided must not begin before the election is made.

For this purpose, the date a qualified transportation fringe is provided is:

1. The date the employee receives a voucher or similar item; or

2. In any other case, the date the employee uses the qualified transportation fringe.

[Treas. Reg. § 1.132-9, Q&A-14]

Q 13:112   Are compensation reduction elections revocable?

Yes, but only before the employee is currently able to receive the cash compensation he or she elected to reduce. The employee may not revoke a compensation reduction election after he or she is currently able to receive the cash or other taxable amount at the employee's discretion. In addition, the election may not be revoked after the beginning of the period for which the qualified transportation fringe will be provided. [Treas. Reg. § 1.132-9, Q&A-14(c)]

Unless an election is revoked, an employee may not subsequently receive the compensation that was reduced (in cash or in any form other than by payment of a qualified transportation fringe benefit). Thus, an employer's qualified transportation fringe benefit plan may not provide that an employee who ceases to participate (such as in the case of termination of employment) is entitled to receive a refund of the amount by which the employee's compensation reductions exceed the actual qualified transportation benefits provided to the employee. [Treas. Reg. § 1.132-9, Q&A-14(d)]

Q 13:113   May an employee whose qualified transportation costs are less than the employee's compensation reduction carry over this excess amount to subsequent periods?

Yes. An employee may carry over unused compensation reduction amounts to subsequent periods under the plan of the employee's employer. [Treas. Reg. § 1.132-9, Q&A-15]

Q 13:114   May an employer provide nontaxable cash reimbursements under Code Section 132(f) for periods longer than one month?

Yes. Qualified transportation fringes include reimbursement to employees for costs incurred for transportation in more than one month, provided the reimbursement for each month is calculated separately and does not exceed the applicable statutory monthly limit for any month. [Treas. Reg. § 1.132-9, Q&A-17]

Q 13:115   How do the qualified transportation fringe benefit rules apply to van pools?

In general, employer- and employee-operated van pools, as well as private or public transit-operated pools, may qualify as qualified transportation fringes. The value of van pool benefits that are qualified transportation fringes may be excluded up to the applicable statutory monthly limit for transportation in a commuter highway vehicle and transit passes, less the value of any transit passes provided by the employer for the month.

Employer-operated van pools. The value of van pool transportation provided by or for an employer to its employees is excludable as a qualified transportation fringe, provided the van qualifies as a commuter highway vehicle. A van pool is operated by or for the employer if the employer purchases or leases vans to enable employees to commute together or the employer contracts with and pays a third party to provide the vans and assumes some or all of the costs of operating the vans, including maintenance, liability insurance, and other operating expenses.

Employee-operated van pools. Cash reimbursements by an employer to employees for expenses incurred for transportation in a van pool operated by employees independent of their employer are excludable as qualified transportation fringes provided that the van qualifies as a commuter highway vehicle.

Private or public transit-operated van pool transit passes. The qualified transportation fringe exclusion for transit passes is available for travel in van pools owned and operated either by public transit authorities or by any person in the business of transporting persons for compensation or hire. [Treas. Reg. § 1.132-9, Q&A-21]

Q 13:116   Can qualified transportation fringe benefits be provided to individuals who are not employees?

No. An employer may provide qualified transportation fringe benefits only to individuals who are currently employees at the time the qualified benefit is provided. For this purpose, the term *employee* includes only common-law employees or statutory employees, such as officers of corporations. [Treas. Reg. § 1.132-9, Q&A-5]

Self-employed individuals are not employees for purposes of qualified transportation fringe benefit rules. Therefore, individuals who are partners, sole proprietors, 2 percent shareholders of S corporations (who are treated as partners for fringe benefit purposes), or independent contractors are not eligible for qualified transportation fringe benefits. [Treas. Reg. § 1.132-9, Q&A-24]

Q 13:117   May an employee receive qualified transportation fringe benefits from more than one employer?

Yes. The statutory monthly limits on qualified transportation benefits apply separately to each employer. So, for example, if an employee works for two employers, each of them can provide the employee with benefits up to the statutory limits. [Treas. Reg. § 1.132-9, Q&A-10] However, entities under common control (as defined Code Section 414(b), (c), (m), or (o)) are combined for purposes of applying the limits.

Qualified Moving Expense Reimbursements

Q 13:118   What is a qualified moving expense reimbursement?

A *qualified moving expense reimbursement* is a tax-free amount that the employee receives (directly or indirectly) from his or her employer as payment for or reimbursement of expenses that would be deductible as moving expenses under Code Section 217 if they had been directly paid or incurred by the employee. It does not include payment for or a reimbursement of an expense that the employee actually deducted in a prior taxable year. [I.R.C. § 132(g)]

Q 13:119   What are deductible moving expenses?

Deductible moving expenses under Code Section 217 are reasonable expenses for the following:

1. Moving household goods and personal effects from the former residence to the new residence (including the cost of storing and insuring household goods and personal effects for up to 30 consecutive days); and

2. Traveling (including lodging but excluding meals) from the former residence to the new place of residence.

In the case of a foreign move, reasonable moving expenses also cover the following:

1. Moving household goods and personal effects to and from storage; and

2. Storing such goods and effects for part or all of the period during which the foreign place of work is the principal place of work.

A foreign move is the commencement of work at a new principal place of work located outside the United States and its possessions. [I.R.C. §§ 217(b), 217(h)]

If an employee uses a car to move to the new home, the cost of the car travel can be figured by determining actual expenses, such as the amount paid for gas and oil for the car, if an accurate record is kept of each expense. Alternatively, the cost can be figured using a flat mileage rate set annually by the IRS. For 2010, the mileage rate is 16.5 cents per mile. [Rev. Proc. 2009-54, 2009-26 I.R.B. 1124 (June 26, 2009)]

Q 13:120   Are any moving expenses not deductible under Code Section 217?

Yes, moving expenses that are not deductible under Code Section 217 include the following:

*   House-hunting expenses
*   Temporary living expenses
*   Expenses for the sale or purchase of a house
*   Expenses to obtain or break a lease
*   Meal expenses

Q 13:121   Is there a minimum-distance requirement that must be met for otherwise deductible moving expenses?

Yes. The new principal place of work must be at least 50 miles farther from the individual's old residence than was the former principal place of work. For example, if the former principal place of work was 10 miles from the old residence, the new principal place of work must be at least 60 miles from the old residence. If an individual had no former principal place of work, the new principal place of work must be at least 50 miles from the old residence. [I.R.C. § 217(c)(1)] In measuring the distance, the shortest of the more commonly traveled routes between the two points is to be used. [I.R.C. § 217(c)]

Q 13:122   Is there a work-time test that must be met for otherwise deductible moving expenses?

Yes. An employee must work full-time for at least 39 weeks during the first 12 months after the employee's arrival in the general area of the new principal place of work. (A somewhat different test applies in the case of self-employment.) Failure to satisfy the work-time test is excused, however, if the individual is unable to satisfy the test because of (1) death or disability; or (2) involuntary separation from employment (other than willful misconduct) or transfer for the benefit of the employer. [I.R.C. §§ 217(c)(2), 217(d)(1)]

Q 13:123   What withholding and reporting requirements apply to moving expense reimbursements?

If the moving expense reimbursements are not qualified moving expense reimbursements, they are wages subject to FICA, FUTA, and federal income tax withholding. [I.R.C. §§ 3121(a)(11), 3306(b)(9), 3401(a)(15)] If the moving expense reimbursements are qualified moving expense reimbursements, they are not wages, but they must be reported on Form W-2. In addition, the employer must provide the employee with an itemized list of moving expense reimbursements. IRS Form 4782 may be used for this purpose.

Practice Pointer. Many employers provide relocating employees with a lump-sum payment to cover both qualified and nonqualified moving expenses. In such as case, only the portion of the reimbursement allocable to qualified expenses will be tax free. Moreover, to qualify for tax-free treatment, reimbursements for the qualified expenses must be made under an accountable plan that requires the employee to substantiate the amount of the expenses. Reimbursements for qualified expenses that do not meet the accountable plan requirements are included in the employee's wages subject to FICA, FUTA, and income tax withholding. The employee, however, may claim a moving expense deduction for the qualified expenses.

Qualified Retirement Planning Services

Q 13:124 Are employer-provided retirement planning services included in an employee's gross income?

No. An employee's gross income does not include qualified retirement planning services. [I.R.C. § 132(a)(7)]

Qualified retirement planning services may include any retirement planning advice or information provided to an employee and his or her spouse by an employer maintaining a qualified employer plan. [I.R.C. § 132(m)(1)] For this purpose, a qualified plan is a plan, contract, pension or account described in Code Section 219(g)(5). [I.R.C. § 132(m)(3)] Thus, qualified plans include pension plans, government plans, Code Section 403(a) and 403(b) annuities, simplified employee pension plans (SEPs), and simplified income match plans for employees (SIMPLEs).

In enacting the exclusion for qualified retirement planning services, Congress made it clear that the exclusion is not limited to providing information about the employer's plan. It also applies to advice and information on retirement income planning for an employee and spouse, and how the employer's plan fits into the individual's overall retirement income plan. However, the exclusion is not intended to apply to services that may be related to tax preparation, accounting, legal or brokerage services. [H. Rep. No. 107-51, Part I]

Nondiscrimination rules apply to the exclusion for qualified retirement planning services. The exclusion applies to a highly compensated employee only if retirement planning services are available on substantially the same terms to each member of the group of employees that is normally provided with education and information about the employer's qualified plan. [I.R.C. § 132(m)(2)]

The Economic Growth and Tax Relief Reconciliation Act of 2001 (EGTRRA) added the exclusion for qualified retirement planning services to the Code, effective for years beginning after 2001. However, tax law changes made by EGTRRA are scheduled to sunset after 2010. Thus, absent congressional action, the exclusion for qualified retirement planning services will not apply in 2011 and later years.

Meals and Lodging Furnished for the Employer's Convenience

Q 13:125 Is the value of meals furnished by an employer to an employee and his or her family included in the employee's gross income?

The value of meals furnished by an employer to an employee, the employee's spouse, or any dependent of the employee can be excluded from the employee's gross income if the following two requirements are met:

1. The meals are furnished on the business premises of the employer; and

2. The meals are furnished for the convenience of the employer.

[I.R.C. § 119(a)]

Q 13:126 Is the value of lodging furnished by an employer to an employee and his or her family included in the employee's gross income?

The value of lodging furnished by an employer to an employee, the employee's spouse, or any dependent of the employee can be excluded from the employee's gross income if the following three requirements are met:

1. The lodging is furnished on the business premises of the employer;

2. The lodging is furnished for the convenience of the employer; and

3. The employee is required to accept the lodging as a condition of employment.

[I.R.C. § 119(a); Treas. Reg. § 1.119-1(b)]

Q 13:127 Does the meals exclusion apply if an employee receives a cash meal allowance?

No. In order for the meals exclusion to apply, the meals must be furnished in kind, not in the form of cash or under an option to take the meals either in kind or in cash. [Treas. Reg. § 1.119-1(e)] The U.S. Supreme Court held that a state trooper who received cash meal allowances from his employer was not entitled to the exclusion because the meals were not provided by the employer in kind. [Kowalski v. United States, 434 U.S. 77 (1977)]

Q 13:128 Does the meals exclusion apply to an employee if the employer provides groceries rather than finished meals?

Authorities are split on this issue. The U.S. Court of Appeals for the Ninth Circuit held that meals do not include groceries. [Tougher v. Commissioner, 441 F.2d 1148 (9th Cir. 1971)] In contrast, the U.S. Court of Appeals for the Third Circuit found that groceries are meals that can qualify for exclusion if the other statutory requirements are met. [Jacob v. United States, 493 F.2d 1294 (3d Cir. 1974)]

Q 13:129 What is considered "business premises of the employer" for purposes of the meals and lodging exclusions?

The *business premises of the employer* generally refers to the employee's place of employment. [Treas. Reg. § 1.119-1(c)(1)] The U.S. Tax Court has stated that the phrase "on the business premises" with respect to lodging means either (1) living quarters that constitute an integral part of the business property or (2) premises on which the employer carries on some of its business activities.

The Tax Court held that a residence a mile away from the employer's mill was not on the business premises. [Gordon S. Dole v. Commissioner, 43 T.C. 697 (1965), *aff'd per curiam*, 351 F.2d 308 (1st Cir. 1965)]

If an employer furnishes an employee with lodging in a camp located in a foreign country, the camp will be treated as the business premises of the employer, provided that the following three conditions apply:

1. The place at which the employee renders services is in a remote area where satisfactory housing is not available on the open market;

2. The camp is located (as near as practicable) in the vicinity of the employee's workplace; and

3. The camp lodging is furnished in a common area (or enclave) that is not available to the public and that normally accommodates ten or more employees.

[I.R.C. § 119(c); Treas. Reg. §§ 1.119-1(c)(2), 1.119-1(d)]

Q 13:130   Is actual physical presence on the business premises of the employer required for the meals and lodging exclusions to be allowed?

Generally, yes. In a decision by the U.S. Court of Appeals for the Sixth Circuit, it was held that meals and lodging provided to an employee in an employer-owned residence only "two short blocks" from the place of employment were not provided on the business premises of the employer. [Commissioner v. Anderson, 371 F.2d 59 (6th Cir. 1966), *cert. denied*, 387 U.S. 906 (1967)] In a later decision by the U.S. Tax Court, however, *Anderson* was held to be not applicable to a situation where lodging was furnished directly across the street from the workplace, and the IRS has acquiesced in the Tax Court decision. [Lindeman v. Commissioner, 60 T.C. 609 (1973), *acq.* 1973-2 C.B. 2]

Q 13:131   When are meals deemed furnished for the convenience of the employer?

The question of whether meals are furnished for the convenience of the employer is one of fact to be determined by analysis of all the facts and circumstances in each case. [Treas. Reg. § 1.119-1(a)(1)]

In determining whether meals are furnished for the convenience of the employer, the fact that a charge is made for such meals and the fact that the employee may accept or decline such meals are factors that are *not* to be taken into account. [I.R.C. § 119(b)(2)]

IRS regulations interpreting the convenience-of-the-employer requirement set out separate guidelines for (1) meals furnished without a charge and (2) meals furnished with a charge. [Treas. Reg. §§ 1.119-1(a)(2), 1.119-1(a)(3)]

Q 13:132   When are meals provided without a charge considered furnished for the convenience of the employer?

Under IRS regulations, meals furnished without a charge will be regarded as furnished for the convenience of the employer if the meals are furnished for a substantial noncompensatory business reason of the employer. If a substantial noncompensatory business reason exists, the meals will be considered furnished for the convenience of the employer even if there is also a compensatory reason for furnishing the meals. The determination of whether a substantial noncompensatory business reason exists will be based on all the surrounding facts and circumstances. A mere declaration by the employer that such a business reason exists is not enough. [Treas. Reg. § 1.119-1(a)(2)(i)]

Q 13:133   What are some substantial noncompensatory business reasons of an employer for providing meals without charge to an employee?

IRS regulations give a number of illustrations of substantial noncompensatory business reasons for providing meals without charge to employee, as follows.

- The meals are furnished to an employee during working hours to have the employee available for emergency calls during the meal period. It must be shown that emergencies have actually occurred, or can reasonably be expected to occur, that have resulted or can expect to result in an employee being called to work during the meal period. [Treas. Reg. § 1.119-1(a)(2)(ii)(A)]

  An example is given of a hospital that maintains a cafeteria on its premises for the hospital staff during their working hours. Each employee is at times called upon to work during the meal period. The employer does not require the employees to remain on the premises during meal periods, but they rarely leave. The meals are considered provided for the convenience of the employer, and the value of the meals is excluded from the employee's federal gross income. [Treas. Reg. § 1.119-1(f), Ex. 9]

- The meals are furnished to an employee during working hours because the employer's business requires that the employee be restricted to a short meal period, such as 30 or 45 minutes, and the employee could not be expected to eat elsewhere in such a short meal period. Meals can qualify under this rule if the employer's peak workload occurs during the normal lunch hours. [Treas. Reg. § 1.119-1(a)(2)(ii)(B)]

- An example is given of a teller working in a bank, in which the peak workload occurs during normal lunch hours, who is given only 30 minutes for lunch. [Treas. Reg. § 1.119-1(f), Ex. 3]

- The meals are furnished to an employee during working hours because the employee could not otherwise secure proper meals within a reasonable meal period, for example, because there are insufficient eating facilities in the vicinity of the employer's premises. [Treas. Reg. § 1.119-1(a)(2)(ii)(C)]

In a significant decision, the Ninth Circuit Court of Appeals concluded that a casino's policy of requiring employees to stay on the premises, which was adopted for legitimate business reasons, rendered the meals noncompensatory. [Boyd Gaming Corp. v. Commissioner, 177 F.3d 1696 (9th Cir. 1999)] The IRS subsequently announced that it would not appeal the Ninth Circuit's decision and would resolve other pending cases in keeping with the decision. [IRS Ann. 99-77, 1999-32 I.R.B. 243]

Although a meal furnished before or after working hours generally will not qualify for exclusion from income, an exception is made for restaurant and food service employees. In the case of such employees, a meal furnished during, immediately before, or immediately after the working hours of the employee will be regarded as furnished for a substantial noncompensatory business reason of the employer. [Treas. Reg. §§ 1.119-1(a)(2)(i), 1.119-1(a)(2)(ii)(D)] A meal given to a restaurant worker or food service employee on the employee's day off would not, however, qualify for exclusion from income. [Treas. Reg. § 1.119-1(f), Ex. 2]

If substantially all the meals for employees who are furnished meals satisfy the convenience-of-the-employer test, meals furnished to other employees will be considered to satisfy the test also. [Treas. Reg. § 1.119-1(a)(2)(ii)(E)]

If an employer would have furnished a meal during working hours for a substantial noncompensatory reason, but the employee's duties prevented him or her from eating during working hours, a meal served immediately after working hours would qualify for exclusion from the employee's gross income. [Treas. Reg. § 1.119-1(a)(2)(ii)(F)]

Q 13:134   When are meals considered to be furnished for a compensatory business reason?

Meals are regarded as furnished for a compensatory business reason when they are provided for one of the following reasons:

1. To promote the morale or goodwill of the employee; or
2. To attract prospective employees.

[Treas. Reg. § 1.119-1(a)(2)(iii)]

Q 13:135   When are meals furnished with a charge considered to be provided for the convenience of the employer?

If an employer provides meals for which a charge is made by the employer, and the employee is given a choice of accepting the meals and paying for them or not paying for them and providing his or her meals in another manner, the meals will not be considered as provided for the convenience of the employer.

If, however, an employee is charged an unvarying amount irrespective of whether he or she accepts the meals, the amount of the flat charge itself is not includable in the employee's compensation, and the value of the meal is excludable if the meal is provided for the convenience of the employer (using the same rules applied to meals provided without a charge).

If the meals furnished for a flat charge do not meet the convenience-of-the-employer test, the employee is required to include the value of the meals in income regardless of whether the value exceeds or is less than the amount charged for the meals. The value of the meals may be deemed to be equal to the amount charged for them, however, in the absence of evidence to the contrary. [Treas. Reg. § 1.119-1(a)(3)]

> **Practice Pointer.** If the value of the meals exceeds the amount charged for them, in some cases the employer-operated eating facilities rules under the fringe benefit rules of Code Section 132 may make the excess amount a nontaxable *de minimis* fringe benefit (see Qs 13:71–13:76).

Q 13:136 When is an employee considered to accept lodging as a condition of employment?

The requirement that an employee accept lodging as a condition of employment means that the employee is required to accept the lodging in order to perform the duties of his or her employment properly. For example, lodging is considered accepted as a condition of employment if the lodging is furnished because the employee is required to be available for duty at all times or because the employee could not perform the services required unless furnished with lodging. [Treas. Reg. § 1.119-1(b)]

If the three requirements for the lodging exclusion are met (see Q 13:126), the exclusion applies whether or not a charge is made and whether or not the lodging is furnished as compensation under an employment contract or statute fixing the terms of employment. [I.R.C. § 119(b)(1); Treas. Reg. § 1.119-1(b)]

A technical advice memorandum issued by the IRS in 1993 considered whether the value of free lodging provided to a group of employees was excludable from the employees' incomes under Code Section 119. Under the facts involved, the employer was a preparatory boarding school with an extremely large campus. The school provided rent-free housing to five categories of its employees: administrative staff, teaching staff, resident dormitory staff, infirmary staff, and maintenance staff.

The administrative staff and teaching staff all (with minor exceptions) lived outside the central campus area and were required to drive or to take other transportation to work. The school contended that both staffs were on 24-hour call and met with students at their (the staff's) homes. Nonetheless, the IRS found that the employees had offices and classrooms provided and were not required to use their homes for business or for teaching. Also, emergencies were infrequent, and the employees were not considered by the IRS to be available for duty at all times.

The resident dormitory staff lived in the same buildings as the students and were on duty after school hours, as well as evenings and weekends. They were expected to respond to emergencies in the dormitories. Of three nursing staff working in the infirmary, only one, the evening shift nurse, lived in an apartment above the infirmary and was in a position to respond to after-hours emergencies. There were nine maintenance employees, eight of whom had lodging outside the central campus area, with one provided with lodging in the administration building. The IRS found that there was no evidence to support the school's position that it needed all nine maintenance workers to be available for duty 24 hours a day.

The IRS concluded that the only school employees who met both tests under Code Section 119 concerning the convenience of the employer and lodging as a condition of employment tests (see Q 13:126) were the resident dormitory staff, the evening shift nurse who lived above the infirmary, and possibly (depending on further facts) the maintenance worker who lived in the administration building. All other employees were required to include the value of the rent-free housing in income. [Priv. Ltr. Rul. 9404005]

Q 13:137   What is the tax treatment if an employee is charged a flat amount for lodging?

If an employer furnishes an employee lodging for which the employee is charged an unchanging amount irrespective of whether the employee accepts the lodging, the amount charged is not, as such, includable in gross income. In addition, if the three-part test for the lodging exclusion is satisfied (see Q 13:127), the value of the lodging is also excludable from the employee's federal gross income.

If the test for exclusion is not met, the value of the lodging is includable in the employee's federal gross income, regardless of whether it exceeds or is less than the amount charged. In the absence of evidence to the contrary, the value of the lodging can be deemed to be equal to the amount charged. [Treas. Reg. § 1.119-1(b)]

There is, however, a special statutory exception in the case of employees of educational institutions who are provided with qualified campus lodging (see Qs 13:140–13:142).

Q 13:138   What special treatment applies to lodging provided to employees of educational institutions?

If the lodging provided to an employee of an educational institution does not qualify for exclusion under the three-part test of Code Section 119 (see Q 13:126), it may qualify for exclusion in whole or in part as qualified campus lodging (see Qs 13:139–13:141). [I.R.C. § 119(d)]

Q 13:139   Which institutions are considered educational institutions for the purposes of special treatment?

An educational institution for the purpose of special treatment is defined as one that normally maintains a regular faculty and curriculum and normally has a regularly enrolled body of pupils or students in attendance at the place where its educational activities are regularly carried on. [I.R.C. §§ 119(d)(4), 170(b)(1)(A)(ii)]

Q 13:140   What lodging is considered to be qualified campus lodging?

Qualified campus lodging is lodging that does not meet the general three-part test for exclusion and that is:

1. Located on or in the proximity of a campus of the educational institution; and

2. Furnished to the employee, his or her spouse, and any of his or her dependents by or on behalf of the educational institution for use as a residence.

[I.R.C. § 119(d)(3)]

Q 13:141   Is the exclusion for qualified campus housing unlimited?

No. The exclusion for qualified campus housing does not apply to the extent that the employee pays an inadequate rent. The amount in excess of the lesser of (1) 5 percent of the appraised value of the qualified campus housing or (2) the average of the rentals paid by persons other than employees or students during the calendar year for comparable lodging provided by the educational institution, over the rent paid by the employee for the qualified housing during the calendar year is includable in the employee's income. [I.R.C. § 119(d)(2)]

For example, assuming that the 5 percent of appraised value limitation applies, the foregoing means that if the rent paid by the employee for qualified campus lodging equals or exceeds 5 percent of appraised value, no amount is includable in the employee's gross income, even if the fair rental value is greater than the rental payments made. If the rent payments in such a case are less than 5 percent of the appraised value of the qualified campus housing, however, the difference is includable in the employee's gross income.

Q 13:142   Is the value of meals and lodging furnished to employees subject to income tax withholding and to FICA and FUTA taxes?

To the extent the value of meals and lodging is excluded from gross income under Code Section 119, it is not subject to income tax withholding or to FICA and FUTA taxes. On the other hand, the value of meals and lodging that is not excludable under Code Section 119 is subject to income tax withholding and to FICA and FUTA taxation. [I.R.C. §§ 3401(a), 3121(a)(19), 3306(b)(14); Treas. Reg. § 31.3401(a)-1(b)(9)]

Employee Gifts and Achievement Awards

Q 13:143 If an employer makes a gift to an employee in cash or in property, how is the gift treated by the employee for federal income tax purposes?

Although a gift generally is not subject to federal income tax, the Code contains a specific exception to the general rule. It provides that, in general, any amount transferred by, or for the benefit of, an employer to, or for the benefit of, an employee is not to be excluded from gross income, even though it is intended as a gift. [I.R.C. § 102(c)(1)]

There are two specific limited exceptions to the rule that employee gifts are includable in gross income. They are (1) employee achievement awards and (2) *de minimis* fringe benefits. [I.R.C. § 102(c)(2)]

Q 13:144 What is an employee achievement award?

An *employee achievement award* is an item of tangible personal property that is:

1. Transferred by the employer to an employee for length-of-service achievement or safety achievement;
2. Awarded as part of a meaningful presentation; and
3. Awarded under conditions and circumstances that do not create a significant likelihood that it is disguised compensation.

[I.R.C. § 274(j)(3)(A)]

Q 13:145 What is not considered tangible personal property for purposes of the employee achievement award rules?

Tangible personal property obviously does not include cash. It also does not include a certificate, other than a nonnegotiable certificate conferring only the right to receive tangible personal property. Also excluded are vacations, meals, lodging, tickets to theatrical and sporting events, and stocks, bonds, and other securities. [Prop. Treas. Reg. § 1.274-8(c)(2)]

Q 13:146 What is a meaningful presentation?

Whether an employee achievement award is presented in a meaningful presentation is determined by a facts and circumstances test. The presentation need not be elaborate, but it must be a ceremonious observance emphasizing the recipient's achievements in the area of safety or length of service. [Prop. Treas. Reg. § 1.274-8(c)(3)]

Q 13:147 When is an award considered payment of disguised compensation?

An award is considered disguised compensation, disqualifying the award as an employee achievement award, if the conditions and circumstances surrounding the award create a significant likelihood that it is payment of compensation. Examples include the following:

- Making the awards at the time of annual salary adjustments;
- Making the awards as a substitute for a prior program of cash bonuses;
- Providing the awards in a manner that discriminates in favor of highly compensated employees; and
- Presenting the awards where the fully deductible cost to the employer is grossly disproportionate to the fair market value of the item.

[Prop. Treas. Reg. § 1.274-8(c)(4)]

Q 13:148 What qualifies as a length-of-service award?

An award presented upon the occasion of a recipient's retirement is a length-of-service award. In some circumstances, however, a traditional retirement award can be treated as a *de minimis* fringe benefit under Code Section 132(e)(1). [I.R.C. § 274(j)(4)(B); Prop. Treas. Reg. § 1.274-8(d)(2)]

An award does not qualify as a length-of-service award if it is presented for fewer than five years' employment with the employer or if the award recipient has already received a length-of-service award during the same year or in any of the four prior calendar years (other than an award that qualifies as a *de minimis* fringe benefit under Code Section 132(e)(1)).

Q 13:149 What qualifies as a safety achievement award?

An award is not treated as an award for safety achievement if awards for safety achievement (other than awards qualifying as *de minimis* fringe benefits) during the same year have previously been awarded to more than 10 percent of the eligible employees, or if the award is to an ineligible employee(i.e., a manager, administrator, clerical employee, or other professional employee). An eligible employee must have worked full time for the employer for at least one year before the safety achievement award is presented. [I.R.C. § 274(j)(4)(C); Prop. Treas. Reg. § 1.274-8(d)(3)]

Q 13:150 May an employer deduct the cost of an employee achievement award?

To a limited extent, yes. The deduction limit varies depending on whether the employee achievement award is a qualified plan award (see Q 13:151).

If the award is not a qualified plan award, the deductible cost of the award, when added to the cost of all other employee achievement awards that are not qualified plan awards and that are made in the same taxable year to the employee, may not exceed $400.

If the award is a qualified plan award, the deductible cost of the award, when added to the cost of all other employee achievement awards (both qualified plan awards and those not qualified) made to the employee in the same taxable year, must not exceed $1,600. [I.R.C. § 274(j)(2); Prop. Treas. Reg. § 1.274-8(b)]

Q 13:151   What is a qualified plan award?

A *qualified plan award* is an employee achievement award that is presented pursuant to an established written plan or program that does not discriminate in terms of eligibility or benefits in favor of highly compensated employees. The following conditions apply:

1. The definition of highly compensated employees in Code Section 414(q) is used for this purpose;

2. Whether an award plan is established is determined from all the facts and circumstances of the case, including the frequency and timing of changes to the plan; and

3. Whether the award plan is discriminatory is determined from all the facts and circumstances of the case, and a plan may be found discriminatory in operation even though the written terms of the plan are nondiscriminatory.

Even if a nondiscriminatory written plan exists, no award presented by the employer in a taxable year will be considered a qualified plan award if the average cost of all employee achievement awards during the taxable year under any qualified plan exceeds $400. The average cost is determined by dividing (1) the sum of the costs of all employee achievement awards (without regard to the deductibility of the costs) by (2) the total number of employee achievement awards presented. In determining the average cost, employee achievement awards of nominal value ($50 or less) are not taken into account. [I.R.C. § 274(j)(3)(B); Prop. Treas. Reg. § 1.274-8(c)(5)]

Q 13:152   Is an employee required to include the value of an employee achievement award in his or her gross income?

An employee is not required to include in gross income the value of an employee achievement award he or she receives if the cost to the employer does not exceed the amount allowable as a deduction to the employer for the cost of the employee achievement award (see Qs 13:150–13:151).

If the cost to the employer of the employee achievement award is allowable as a deduction only in part, the employee must include in gross income the greater of:

1. An amount equal to the portion of the employer's cost that is not allowable as a deduction (but not in excess of the value of the award); or

2. The amount by which the value of the award exceeds the amount allowable as a deduction to the employer.

[I.R.C. § 74(c)(2); Prop. Treas. Reg. §§ 1.74-2(a), 1.74-2(b)]

If an employer is tax-exempt, the amount deductible is determined as if the employer were taxable. [I.R.C. § 74(c)(3); Prop. Treas. Reg. § 1.74-2(d)(2)]

> **Example.** Genco gives its employee, Felix, an employee achievement award costing $425 and having a fair market value of $475. Assuming the deductible limit of $400 applies, Felix would have gross income of $75 because the award's fair market value exceeds the award's cost to the employer. [Prop. Treas. Reg. § 1.74-2(c), Ex. 3]

Q 13:153 How do employee achievement award rules apply to partnerships and sole proprietorships?

In applying the deduction limitations of Code Section 274(j)(2) to employee achievement awards made by a partnership, the limitations apply to the partnership as well as to each member of the partnership. [I.R.C. § 274(j)(4)(A); Prop. Treas. Reg. § 1.274-8(d)(1)]

In applying the deduction rules of Code Section 274(j) and the exclusion from gross income rules of Code Section 74(c), any award made by a sole proprietorship to the sole proprietor will not be treated as an employee achievement award. [Prop. Treas. Reg. §§ 1.274-8(c)(1), 1.74-2(d)(1)]

> **Practice Pointer.** Inasmuch as the proposed regulations bar only sole proprietorships from qualifying for the exclusion, it appears that a partner in a partnership could receive an employee achievement award qualifying for full or partial exclusion from gross income under Code Section 74(c).

Q 13:154 Is an employee achievement award that exceeds the excludable amount under Code Section 74(c) always taxable?

No. Although employee achievement awards in excess of the excludable limits of Code Section 74(c) generally are subject to income tax (see Q 13:152), in very limited circumstances the excess may be eligible for exclusion on the basis that it is a *de minimis* fringe benefit under Code Section 132(e)(1). [Prop. Treas. Reg. § 1.74-2(e)] (See Qs 13:67–13:70 for a discussion of *de minimis* fringe benefits.)

Q 13:155 Is an employee achievement award received by an employee subject to income tax withholding and to FICA and FUTA?

To the extent an employee achievement award is excludable from gross income under Code Section 74(c), it is not subject to income tax withholding, nor to FICA and FUTA. To the extent the award is includable in gross income,

income tax withholding and FICA and FUTA are applicable. [I.R.C. §§ 3401(a)(19), 3121(a)(20), 3306(b)(16)]

Disaster Relief Assistance

Q 13:156   Is employer-provided disaster relief assistance includable in an employee's gross income?

The IRS has ruled that "qualified disaster relief payments" received from an employer are excludable from an employee's gross income under Code Section 139. [Rev. Rul. 2003-12, 2003-1 C.B. 283] The IRS ruling dealt with employer-provided flood relief, but the reasoning of the ruling is equally applicable to other "qualified disasters." (see Q 13:157).

Section 139 was added to the Code by the Victims of Terrorism Tax Relief Act of 2001. [Pub. L. No. 107-134, 115 Stat. 2427 (2002)] Code Section 139 provides that gross income does not include any amount received by an individual as a qualified disaster relief payment. A qualified disaster relief payment means any amount paid to or for the benefit of an individual:

1. To reimburse or pay reasonable and necessary personal, family, living, or funeral expenses incurred as a result of a qualified disaster; or
2. To reimburse or pay reasonable and necessary expenses incurred for the repair or rehabilitation of a personal residence or repair or replacement of its contents to the extent that the need for such repair, rehabilitation, or replacement is attributable to a qualified disaster.

(Qualified disaster relief also includes amounts paid by a federal, state, or local government, or agency or instrumentality thereof, in connection with a disaster to promote the general welfare.)

Because of the extraordinary circumstances surrounding a disaster, individuals are not required to account for actual expenses in order to qualify for the exclusion. However, the amount of disaster relief payments must be reasonably expected to be commensurate with the expenses involved. In addition, the exclusion applies only to the extent an expense compensated by a disaster payment is not otherwise compensated for by insurance or otherwise.

In the IRS ruling, an employer provided grants to employees who were affected by a flood that was a presidentially declared disaster. The grants were to pay or reimburse employees for medical, temporary housing, and transportation expenses they incurred as a result of the flood that were not compensated for by insurance or otherwise. The employer did not require employees to provide proof of actual expenses to receive a grant payment. However, the employer's program contained requirements (described in the program document) to ensure that grant amounts were reasonably expected to be commensurate with the amount of unreimbursed reasonable and necessary medical, temporary housing, and transportation expenses incurred by employees as a result of the flood. The grants were not intended to indemnify all flood-related losses or to reimburse the cost of nonessential, luxury, or decorative items or services. The grants were available to all employees regardless of their length or type of service with the employer.

The IRS ruled that the employer's grants were qualified disaster relief payments that were excludable from employee's gross incomes because grants were reasonably expected to be commensurate with unreimbursed reasonable and necessary personal, living, and family expenses incurred by employees as a result of a qualified disaster. Moreover, the grants were paid to compensate employees for expenses that were not compensated by insurance or otherwise.

Q 13:157   What is a qualified disaster relief payment?

A *qualified disaster relief payment* is payment made in the event of the following:

1. A disaster that results from a terroristic or military action (as defined in Code Section 692(c)(2));
2. A federally declared disaster (as defined in Code Section 165(h)(3)(C)(i)); or
3. A disaster resulting from any event that the Secretary of the Treasury determines to be of a catastrophic nature.

[I.R.C. § 139(c), as amended by Pub. L. No. 110-343]

In addition, federal, state, or local government grants to promote the general welfare may be made in the event of any disaster that is determined by the government authority to warrant assistance.

Group Legal Services Plans

Q 13:158   What is a group legal services plan?

A *group legal services plan* is an employer-funded program to provide personal legal services to employees, their spouses, and their dependents.

Q 13:159   Does ERISA apply to group legal services plans?

Yes. [ERISA § 3(1); DOL Reg. § 2510.3-1 (a)(2)] (See chapter 2 for a discussion of ERISA.)

Q 13:160   Are employees taxed on benefits received from employer-provided group legal services plans?

Yes. Congress has not acted to extend former Code Section 120, which excluded certain contributions and benefits from the employee's gross income. The former exclusion applied to insurance coverage (whether through an insurer or self-insured) with a value of up to $70 each taxable year.

Chapter 14

Educational Assistance

Educational assistance is a form of benefit that employers frequently provide to their employees. This chapter reviews the rules applicable to employer-sponsored educational assistance programs under Section 127 of the Internal Revenue Code (Code), the separate rules under Code Section 117 applicable to qualified scholarship and tuition reductions, and the potential availability of the Code Section 132 fringe benefit exclusion for employer-provided expenses for job-related educational benefits. This chapter also includes a discussion of employer-sponsored education savings plans.

Educational Assistance Programs

Q 14:1   What is an educational assistance program?

An *educational assistance program* is an employer-provided plan to assist employees in furthering their education. The tax treatment of employer-provided educational assistance programs is governed by Code Section 127.

Note. This portion of the chapter discusses only plans subject to Code Section 127. Favorable tax treatment for the employees of a particular employer may be available under Code Section 132 for reimbursement of job-related educational expenses (discussed in Qs 14:37–14:45) and under Code Section 117 for tuition reimbursement and scholarship or fellowship awards (discussed in Qs 14:21–14:35). None of these benefits may be included in a cafeteria plan (see chapter 7).

Q 14:2   Is Code Section 127 in effect and, if so, when is it scheduled to expire?

The Section 127 exclusion from gross income for up to $5,250 of educational assistance has expired nine times since it was enacted in 1978. Most recently it was scheduled to expire for expenses paid with respect to courses beginning after December 31, 2001. The Economic Growth and Tax Relief Reconciliation Act of 2001 (EGTRRA) made the exclusion permanent. However, EGTRRA itself is scheduled to expire for tax years after 2010 unless Congress acts to extend it.

Q 14:3   Does ERISA apply to educational assistance programs?

ERISA does not apply if the educational assistance program is unfunded (that is, if payments are made solely from the general assets of the employer or employee organization). [DOL Reg. § 2510.3-1(k); DOL Adv. Op. 89-10A (July 6, 1989)] (See chapter 2 for a discussion of ERISA.)

The U.S. Court of Appeals for the Eleventh Circuit has ruled that including retiree educational benefits as a benefit under a multibenefit ERISA plan does not transform the educational benefits into an ERISA benefit. The participant's claim for educational benefits therefore did not fall under ERISA (and thus could not be preempted by ERISA) and did not constitute a federal claim. The court concluded that claims regarding non-ERISA benefits under a multibenefit plan should be litigated in state court as a separate plan and remanded the participant's claim for retiree educational benefits to state court. [Kemp v. International Bus. Mach. Corp., 109 F.3d 708 (11th Cir. 1997)]

Q 14:4   Are educational assistance programs required to be funded?

No. Educational assistance programs may be operated on a pay-as-you-go basis and are not required to be funded. [I.R.C. § 127(b)(5)]

Q 14:5   Can educational assistance be offered in a cafeteria or salary reduction plan?

No. The definition of qualified benefits in Code Section 125 does not include benefits under Code Section 127; consequently, a Section 125 cafeteria plan cannot offer eligible employees a choice between Section 127 educational assistance and other remuneration includable in gross income. [I.R.C. §§ 125(f), 127(b)(4); Treas. Reg. § 1.127-2(c)(2)] Proposed cafeteria plan regulations issued in 2007 make it clear that educational assistance is a nonqualified benefit that cannot be included in a cafeteria plan. [Prop. Treas. Reg. § 1.125-1(q)(iii)] A plan that offers a nonqualified benefit is not a cafeteria plan.

Q 14:6   What types of educational assistance can the employer's program cover?

Qualifying educational assistance includes tuition, fees and similar payments, and the cost of books, supplies, and equipment. It does not include the cost of tools or supplies that may be retained after completion of a course; meals, lodging, or transportation; or any payment for any course or other education involving sports, games, or hobbies—unless such education involves the business of the employer or is required as part of a degree program. The phrase *sports, games, or hobbies* does not include education that instructs employees how to maintain and improve health so long as such education does not involve the use of athletic facilities or equipment and is not recreational in nature. [I.R.C. § 127(c)(1); Treas. Reg. § 1.127-2(c)(3)(iii)]

> **Note.** Expenses that do not qualify under a Section 127 program may possibly qualify as a working condition fringe benefit under Code Section 132 or as a qualified scholarship reimbursement under Code Section 117.

Q 14:7   Can the employer's educational assistance program cover graduate courses?

Under current rules, an employer's Section 127 educational assistance program can cover graduate-level courses. The application of Section 127 to graduate-level education was enacted by EGTRRA. Note, however, that EGTRRA is scheduled to sunset for tax years after 2010 unless Congress acts to extend it.

Q 14:8   May partners, S corporation shareholders, and sole proprietors receive tax-favored educational assistance program benefits under an employer-provided plan?

Yes, they may, because they are treated as employees for purposes of Code Section 127, which governs employer-provided educational assistance programs. A sole proprietor is treated as his or her own employer, and a partnership is treated as the employer of each of its partners. [I.R.C. §§ 127(c)(2), 127(c)(3)]

Q 14:9   Can an educational assistance program provide benefits to retired, disabled, or laid-off employees?

Yes. The regulations under Code Section 127 specifically define *employee* to include retired, disabled, and laid-off employees.

In Revenue Ruling 96-41 [1996-2 C.B. 9], the IRS stated that an educational assistance program will not fail to qualify under Code Section 127 merely because the plan covers participants who are no longer working for the employer. In the revenue ruling, the IRS examined an employer-sponsored educational assistance program covering both current and former employees and a second plan covering employees who were laid off due to cutbacks stemming from a corporate downsizing initiative.

Q 14:10   Can an educational assistance program provide benefits to spouses or dependents who are not employees of the employer?

Spouses and dependents who are not employed by the employer cannot be eligible under a plan that qualifies as an educational assistance program for tax purposes. [I.R.C. § 127; Treas. Reg. § 1.127-2(d)]

Q 14:11   What is the exclusive benefit requirement for employer-provided educational assistance programs?

Code Section 127 requires that an employer-provided educational assistance program be for the exclusive benefit of employees. [I.R.C. § 127(b)(1)]

Q 14:12   Does the educational assistance program have to be in writing?

Yes. Even though ERISA (and, hence, ERISA's written plan document requirement) does not apply to an unfunded educational assistance program (see Q 14:3), a separate provision contained in Code Section 127 requires that the employer-provided educational assistance program be set out in a separate written plan in order for the program's benefits to be excludable from income when they are received by employees. [I.R.C. § 127(b)(1)]

Q 14:13   What disclosure of program benefits must be made to eligible employees?

The sponsoring employer must provide reasonable notification of the availability and terms of its educational assistance program to eligible employees. [I.R.C. § 127(b)(6)]

Q 14:14   Are employer-provided educational assistance programs subject to nondiscrimination rules?

Yes. In order for the benefits to be excludable from federal income tax when received by employees, the plan may not discriminate in favor of highly compensated employees (as defined in Code Section 414(q)) or their dependents. To be nondiscriminatory, the plan is required to pass an eligibility test and a 5 percent concentration test.

Q 14:15   What are the nondiscrimination tests?

Code Section 127 imposes two nondiscrimination requirements on employer-provided educational assistance programs:

1. *Eligibility test.* The program must benefit employees who qualify under a classification set up by the employer and found by the IRS not to discriminate in favor of highly compensated employees (as defined in

Code Section 414(q)) or their dependents. A *highly compensated employee* (HCE) is any employee who was a 5 percent owner at any time during the year or the preceding year; or for the preceding year (a) had compensation from the employer in excess of $80,000 (indexed for inflation; $110,000 for 2010), and (b) if the employer elects the application of this rule, was in the top-paid group of employees for the preceding year.

2. *5 percent concentration test.* No more than 5 percent of the amounts paid or incurred by the employer for educational assistance during the year may be provided to more-than-5-percent owners of the stock or of the capital or profits interest of the employer (or to their spouses or dependents).

[I.R.C. §§ 127(b)(2), 127(b)(3)]

Q 14:16   Are employees taxed on receipt of educational assistance benefits?

Under Code Section 127, if a plan meets certain requirements, employer payments up to a specified limit (see Q 14:17) are excludable from an employee's federal gross income. [Treas. Reg. § 1.127-1]

Without the Section 127 exclusion, educational benefits generally are taxable; however, if the educational expense incurred by the employee is job-related, the employer payment for the expense may be excludable from the employee's gross income or the employee's payment may be deductible (see Qs 14:37–14:45).

In a private letter ruling, the IRS considered an educational assistance plan established by a corporation to provide educational benefits to all its full-time employees. The plan reimbursed employees for satisfactorily completed educational courses up to the maximum amount excludable under Code Section 127. The plan was unfunded, and benefits were paid from the employer's general assets. The plan document expressly provided that not more than 5 percent of the benefits could go to more-than-5-percent shareholders of the corporation, thus satisfying the 5 percent concentration test for nondiscrimination (see Q 14:15). The IRS held that the plan qualified as an educational assistance plan under Code Section 127 and that the educational assistance benefits received by the employees would be excludable either as educational assistance benefits under Code Section 127 or as job-related working condition fringe benefits under Code Section 132. [Priv. Ltr. Rul. 9418010 (2004)]

Q 14:17   What is the maximum amount of tax-favored benefits that may be provided by an educational assistance program?

The maximum amount excludable from income in a taxable year under Code Section 127 is $5,250. [I.R.C. § 127(a)(2)] (See Q 14:16.)

Q 14:18   What are the tax consequences if the employer's educational assistance program fails the Section 127 nondiscrimination tests?

If the employer's educational assistance program fails either of the nondiscrimination tests imposed by Code Section 127, it appears that all employees, not just HCEs, would be taxed on the benefits received from the program. [I.R.C. §§ 127(a), 127(b)] However, if the expenses are job-related, they may be deductible by the employee. [Treas. Reg. § 1.162-5]

Q 14:19   Is the employer required to pay FICA or FUTA taxes on, or withhold taxes from, educational assistance program payments?

No. As long as it is reasonable for the employer to believe that payments from its Section 127 educational assistance program are excludable from the employee's gross income, such program payments are not subject to FICA tax, FUTA tax, or federal income tax withholding requirements. [I.R.C. §§ 3121 (a)(18), 3306(b)(13), 3401 (a)(18)]

Q 14:20   Is an employer required to report an educational assistance program to the IRS?

The tax law provides that an annual return for the plan is required to be filed with the IRS. [I.R.C. § 6039D] In the past, the IRS required employers to file Form 5500, Schedule F, "Fringe Benefit Annual Information Return," for Section 127 plans other than plans providing only job-related training that is deductible under Code Section 162. However, on April 4, 2002, the IRS suspended the filing requirement, effective immediately. The suspension of the requirement applied to all unfiled returns, including returns for prior years. [Notice 2002-24]

Qualified Scholarships and Tuition Reductions

Q 14:21   Is an educational assistance program the only way in which an employee can receive tax-free treatment of amounts received for educational expenses?

No. As pointed out in Q 14:6, if the educational expenses are job-related, employer reimbursement of such expenses can qualify as a working condition fringe benefit that is excludable from income under Code Section 132(d).

In addition, in limited circumstances, employees may be able to exclude reimbursed educational expenses on the ground that the amounts received are either qualified scholarships or qualified tuition reductions under Code Section 117. If the payments meet the qualification requirements of Code Section 117, they are excludable from gross income.

Q 14:22   What is a scholarship or fellowship grant?

A *scholarship or fellowship grant* is a cash amount paid or allowed to, or for the benefit of, an individual to aid in the pursuit of study or research. It also may be in the form of a reduction in the amount owed by the recipient to an educational organization for tuition, room and board, or any other fee. The grant may be funded by a governmental agency, college or university, charitable organization, business, or any other source. [Prop. Treas. Reg. § 1.117-6(c)(3)]

Q 14:23   What is the qualified scholarship exclusion from income?

Under Code Section 117(a), gross income does not include any amount received as a qualified scholarship by an individual who is a candidate for a degree at an educational institution described in Code Section 170(b)(1)(A)(ii), except to the extent the amount represents payment for services rendered. [I.R.C. § 117(c)]

A *qualified scholarship* is any amount received by an individual as a scholarship or fellowship grant to the extent the individual establishes that, in accordance with the conditions of the grant, such amount was used for qualified tuition and related purposes. [I.R.C. § 117(b)(1); Prop. Treas. Reg. § 1.117-6(c)(l)]

Q 14:24   What are qualified tuition and related expenses?

Qualified tuition and related expenses are the following:

- Tuition and fees required for enrollment or attendance at the educational institution; and
- Fees, books, supplies, and equipment required for courses of instruction at the educational institution.

[I.R.C. § 117(b)(2)]

Incidental expenses are not treated as related expenses. Incidental expenses include expenses for room and board, travel, research, clerical help, equipment, and other expenses that are not required. [Prop. Treas. Reg. § 1.117-6(c)(2)]

The terms of the scholarship or fellowship grant need not expressly require that the amounts received be used for tuition and related expenses. However, to the extent the terms of the grant (1) specify that the grant cannot be used for tuition and related expenses or (2) designate a portion of the grant for other purposes, such amounts will not qualify for exclusion from income. [Prop. Treas. Reg. § 1.117-6(c)(l)]

Q 14:25   What is an educational organization as described in Code Section 170(b)(1)(A)(ii)?

An *educational organization,* as described in Code Section 170(b)(1)(A)(ii), has as its primary function the presentation of formal instruction, normally maintains a regular faculty and curriculum, and normally has a regularly enrolled body of pupils or students in attendance at the place where its educational activities are regularly carried on. [Prop. Treas. Reg. § 1.117-6(c)(5)]

Q 14:26　Who is a candidate for a degree?

A *candidate for a degree* is any one of the following:

- A primary or secondary school student;
- An undergraduate or graduate student at a college or university who is pursuing studies or conducting research to meet the requirements for an academic or professional degree; or
- A full-time or part-time student at an educational institution described in Code Section 170(b)(1)(A)(ii) that
  - Provides an educational program that is acceptable for full credit toward a bachelor's or higher degree or offers a program of training to prepare the student for gainful employment in a recognized occupation; or
  - Is authorized under federal or state law to provide such a program and is accredited by a nationally recognized accreditation agency.

[Prop. Treas. Reg. § 1.117-11(c)(4)]

Q 14:27　Is a qualified scholarship excludable from gross income if it is provided in return for services?

No. The portion of any amount received as a qualified scholarship that represents payment for teaching, research, or other services required as a condition for receiving the grant is not excluded from income. [I.R.C. § 117(c)]

A requirement of the grant that the recipient pursue studies, research, or other activities primarily for the benefit of the grantor is treated as a requirement to perform services. A grant conditional upon past, present, or future teaching, research, or other services also constitutes payment for services. [Prop. Treas. Reg. § 1.117-6(d)(3)(ii)]

Q 14:28　If only a portion of a scholarship or fellowship grant is a payment for services, how is the exclusion determined?

An allocation must be made based on what is reasonable compensation for the services performed as a condition of the grant. [Prop. Treas. Reg. § 1.117-6(d)(3)]

Q 14:29　How are these rules on payment for services applied?

Following are examples of applications of the scholarship and tuition reduction rules:

Example 1. A qualified scholarship is provided under a requirement that the individual work for the grantor after graduation; the entire amount of the scholarship is includable in the recipient's income as wages. [Prop. Treas. Reg. § 1.117-6(d)(5), Ex. 1, 2]

Example 2. An individual receives a $6,000 scholarship from a university that requires the individual to work as a researcher for the university, and a researcher without a scholarship is paid $2,000 for such services. The individual may exclude $4,000 from gross income and include $2,000 in income as wages. [Prop. Treas. Reg. § 1.117-6(d)(5), Ex. 5]

Example 3. Tuition assistance payments made by a university on behalf of a faculty member to other schools, attended by the faculty member's children, with which the university had no reciprocal agreement, do not qualify as scholarships and are taxable as compensation. [Knapp v. Commissioner, 867 F.2d 749 (2d Cir. 1989)]

Q 14:30   When is a qualified tuition reduction excludable from income?

Gross income does not include any qualified tuition reduction [I.R.C. § 117(d)(1)], except to the extent that the amount of tuition reduction represents payment for services rendered. [I.R.C. § 117(c)]

Q 14:31   What is a qualified tuition reduction?

A *qualified tuition reduction* is the amount of any reduction in tuition provided to an employee of an educational organization described in Code Section 170(b)(1)(A)(ii) for the education, normally below the graduate level at that organization or another such organization, of the following:

- The employee; or
- Any person treated as an employee, or whose use is treated as an employee use, under the fringe benefit rules in Code Section 132(h) (this includes the spouse and dependent children of the employee of the educational institution).

[I.R.C. § 117(d)(2)]

Q 14:32   Can a qualified tuition reduction be provided for graduate-level education?

No. There is a limited exception in the case of the education of an individual who is a graduate student at an educational institution and who is engaged in teaching or research activities for the educational institution. For such individuals, the general requirement that the education be below the graduate level does not apply. [I.R.C. § 117(d)(5)]

The U.S. Tax Court considered the case of a university medical school professor whose wife was a graduate medical student at the same school. The university granted tuition reductions and waivers to the wife because of her husband's status as a professor. The wife was not an employee of the medical school or the university, and she was not required to do any teaching, research, or other services for which she would receive compensation. The Tax Court held that the qualified tuition reduction exclusion is available only to a graduate student who is an employee, and since the wife was not an employee, the exclusion was not allowable. The court pointed out that the rule permitting the spouse or dependent children to stand in the shoes of the employee (see Q 14:31) applies to courses below the graduate level only. [Daniel R. and Theresa M. Wolpaw v. Commissioner, T.C. Memo 1993-322]

Q 14:33 Are there nondiscrimination rules that apply to qualified tuition reduction programs?

Yes. A qualified tuition reduction provided to an HCE is excludable from the individual's gross income only if such reduction is available on substantially the same terms to each member of a group of employees that is defined under a reasonable classification set up by the employer that does not discriminate in favor of HCEs. HCEs are defined in Code Section 414 (q), the definition used for qualified pension plan purposes. [I.R.C. § 117(d)(3)]

Q 14:34 If a qualified tuition reduction program is discriminatory, are the benefits taxable to all participants or only to those in the highly compensated employee category?

If the qualified tuition reduction program is discriminatory in favor of HCEs, these employees lose the entire benefit of the exclusion from gross income. However, employees who are not highly compensated and who received a qualified tuition reduction obtain the benefit of the income exclusion. [Priv. Ltr. Rul. 9041085 (July 19, 1990)]

Q 14:35 Is a qualified scholarship program or a qualified tuition reduction plan subject to ERISA?

No. As long as the program is unfunded, it is not subject to ERISA. The definition of a welfare plan is not considered to include a scholarship program. (A *scholarship program* includes tuition and educational expense refund programs, under which payments are made solely from the general assets of the employer.) [DOL Reg. § 2510.3-1(k)]

Q 14:36 Can an employer provide qualified scholarships to employees' children?

Yes. However, in addition to meeting the requirements for tax exclusion under Code Section 117, the scholarship program must meet the following specific requirements:

    1. The scholarship program is not used to recruit employees or induce them to stay;

2. The scholarships are awarded by an independent committee;

3. There are identifiable minimum requirements for eligibility;

4. There is an objective basis for selecting recipients;

5. Scholarships cannot be terminated because a recipient's parent leaves the company;

6. Scholarships are not limited to a course of study of particular benefit to the employer; and

7. Scholarships are not awarded to more than

   a. 10 percent of the number of employees' children who are eligible to receive them or

   b. 25 percent of employees' children who were eligible and who actually applied for the scholarships and were considered by the selection committee.

[Rev. Rul. 76-47, 1976-2 C.B. 670]

Job-Related Educational Benefits

Q 14:37   How are employer-provided educational benefits treated for federal income tax purposes if the benefits do not qualify for exclusion under Code Section 127 or 117?

If the educational benefits are job-related, they may be excluded from the employee's gross income as a working condition fringe benefit. If the amounts paid by the employer are for education relating to the employee's trade or business so that, if the employee paid for the education, the amount paid could be deducted as a business expense by the employee under Code Section 162, the costs of the education may be excluded as a working condition fringe. [Treas. Reg. § 1.132-1(f)(1)]

If the educational expenses are not job-related and are not eligible for exclusion under Code Section 127 or 117, they are fully taxable to the employee.

Q 14:38   What employer-provided educational benefits are considered deductible as employee business expenses under Code Section 162 and thus excludable from gross income?

An employee may deduct educational expenses as ordinary and necessary business expenses if the education:

- Maintains or improves skills required by the employee in his or her employment; or

- Meets the express requirements of the employer, or the requirements of applicable law or regulation, imposed as a condition of the retention by the employee of an established employment relationship, status, or rate of compensation.

[Treas. Reg. § 1.162-5(a)]

Q 14:39　What kinds of educational expenses are considered expenses incurred to maintain or improve skills required in the employee's job?

Educational expenses incurred to maintain the employee's skills include refresher courses, courses dealing with current developments, and academic or vocational courses (whether or not leading to an academic degree), as long as the expenses are not required to meet minimal educational requirements of the employee's job and do not qualify the employee for a new trade or business. [Treas. Reg. § 1.162-5(c)(l)]

Q 14:40　When is education considered to meet the express requirements of the employer and therefore to be excludable from gross income?

The education must be required for a bona fide business purpose of the employer. In addition, only the minimum education necessary for the employee to retain his or her employment relationship, status, or rate of compensation is considered to be required. Education in excess of that required may qualify as expenses incurred to maintain or improve the employee's skills (see Q 14:39). [Treas. Reg. § 1.162-5(c)(2)]

Q 14:41　What employer-provided educational benefits do not qualify as deductible employee business expenses and therefore are not excludable from gross income?

Employer-provided educational benefits do not qualify as deductible employee business expenses when the education:

1. Is required for the employee to satisfy the minimum educational requirements of his or her position or
2. Is part of a program of study that will qualify the employee for a new trade or business.

Once the employee has met the minimum educational requirements for his or her position, the employee will be treated as continuing to meet those requirements even if they are changed. Thus, educational expenses to meet such changed requirements by an employee who formerly met the old requirements may qualify as expenses to maintain or improve the employee's skills. [Treas. Reg. § 1.162-5(b)(2)(i)]

Q 14:42　What expenses qualify as educational expenses?

Educational expenses include tuition, books, and other incidental expenses, such as laboratory fees.

Reimbursements for travel to and from the educational institution or other location qualify as excludable job-related education expenses only if the costs qualify as deductible business expenses. The cost of local travel between the employee's place of business and the educational institution qualifies as a deductible business expense. Local travel between the employee's home and the educational institution will also qualify as a deductible business expense if the educational assignment is temporary. So, for example, if an employee is assigned to take a three-week business-related course, the costs of travel from the employee's home to the course location qualify as deductible business expenses. For this purpose, "temporary" means one year or less. [Rev. Rul. 99-7, 1999-5 I.R.B. 4] Travel expenses, including those for meals and lodging, incurred while away from home overnight to obtain work-related education are generally deductible as employee business expenses. [Treas. Reg. § 1.162-5(e)]

Q 14:43 Can the employer exclude the cost of the educational benefit from the employee's gross income if the employer reimburses or advances the cost to the employee in cash rather than paying the cost directly to the educational institution?

Yes, provided the reimbursement or advance payment arrangement satisfies IRS requirements for an "accountable plan," which are, in general, that the employer must:

1. Determine that the expenses would be deductible by the employee,
2. Obtain substantiation of the expenses, and
3. Require repayment of excess reimbursements within a reasonable period of time.

[Treas. Reg. § 1.62-2(c)]

Q 14:44 Are employer-provided educational benefits not qualifying under Code Section 127 or 117 subject to income tax withholding?

If the educational expenses are deductible employee business expenses, and if the employer pays the cost directly or reimburses the employee for the cost under an "accountable plan," no income tax withholding is required. [I.R.C. § 3401 (a)(19); Treas. Reg. § 31.3401(a)-4] If the cost of the educational benefits does not qualify as a deductible employee business expense and therefore does not qualify as a working condition fringe under Section 132, income tax withholding is required. [Temp. Treas. Reg. § 31.3401(a)-1T]

Q 14:45 Are employer-provided educational benefits not qualifying under Code Section 127 or 117 subject to FICA and FUTA tax?

If the educational expenses are deductible employee business expenses, and if the employer pays the cost directly or reimburses the employee for the cost under an "accountable plan," no FICA or FUTA tax applies. However, if the cost is not a deductible employee business expense and therefore is not a working condition fringe benefit for Section 132 purposes, FICA and FUTA taxes apply.

[I.R.C. §§ 3121(a)(20), 3306(b)(16); Treas. Reg. §§ 31.3121(a)-3(a), 31. 3306(b)-2(a)]

Education Savings Plans

Q 14:46   How can employers help employees fund the cost of a child's education?

In addition to Section 117 scholarships (see Q 14:36), an employer can help employees accumulate education funds by contributing to a Coverdell education savings account (ESA) for an employee's qualified beneficiary (see Q 14:47) or by sponsoring a Section 529 college saving plan for employees (see Q 14:53).

Q 14:47   What are Coverdell education savings accounts?

Coverdell education savings accounts, formerly known as education IRAs, are trusts or custodial accounts set up to pay qualified education expenses of an eligible beneficiary. [I.R.C. § 530] Contributions to a Coverdell ESA are not deductible by the contributor. However, contributions are not included in the beneficiary's income, and distributions for qualifying purposes are tax-free.

As a general rule, contributions to an account are phased out for higher-income taxpayers and are not permitted once income exceeds a ceiling amount (see Q 14:49). In the past, this income ceiling applied to both individual and corporate taxpayers. Therefore, virtually all corporations were barred from making contributions on behalf of employees' children. EGTRRA changed the law so that the contribution phaseout does not apply to corporations or other entities. Thus, for 2002 and later tax years, a corporation can make a full annual contribution to an education savings account for an employee's child regardless of its income (and regardless of the income of the employee). Note that, absent congressional action, changes made by EGTRRA will sunset for tax years after 2010. In that event, contributions by corporations and other entities will be subject to the same phaseout rules that apply to other contributors.

> **Practice Pointer.** A company's contribution to an education savings account is *not* a tax-free fringe benefit. The contribution will be treated as additional compensation to the employee for both income tax and payroll tax purposes. Nonetheless, company contributions to education savings accounts may prove to be a popular perk, especially for highly paid employees who do not qualify to make their own contributions because their incomes are above the phaseout limits.

Q 14:48   Who is an eligible beneficiary of a Coverdell education savings account?

A Coverdell ESA may be established to pay the education expenses of any beneficiary under age 18. No contributions may be made on behalf of a child after he or she reaches age 18. [I.R.C. § 530(b)(1)(A)(ii)] However, the account may remain in existence to pay qualifying education expenses of the beneficiary until he or she reaches age 30. At that time, the balance in the account must be distributed to the beneficiary, unless the balance is rolled over to an account for another beneficiary. [I.R.C. §§ 530(b)(1)(E), 530(d)(8)] (See Q 14:51)

Special-needs beneficiaries. Under a special rule enacted by EGTRRA, the IRS is authorized to issue regulations that will allow contributions on behalf of a special-needs beneficiary after he or she reaches age 18 and to allow an account to remain in existence after a special-needs beneficiary reaches age 30. [I.R.C. § 530(b)(1)] The law does not define *special-needs beneficiary.* However, the congressional conference committee report on the law indicates that IRS regulations should define the term to include an individual who requires additional time to complete his or her education due to a physical, mental, or emotional condition (including a learning disability).

Q 14:49   What are the limits on contributions to a Coverdell education savings account?

Any individual or entity can make a contribution to a Coverdell education savings account on behalf of an eligible beneficiary. The maximum annual contributions made on behalf of a beneficiary cannot exceed $2,000 for tax years beginning after December 31, 2001. [I.R.C. § 530(b)(1)(A)(iii)]

Individual contributors are subject to a contribution phaseout. For 2002 and later tax years, the maximum allowable contribution is phased out for individuals with an adjusted gross income between $95,000 and $110,000 on a single return or $190,000 and $220,000 on a joint return.

Starting in 2002, the contribution phaseout does not apply to corporations or other entities.

Note. EGTRRA increased the contribution limit for Coverdell ESAs from $500 to $2,000. EGTRRA also increased the contribution phase-out range for joint filers from $150,000 to $160,000 to its current level of $190,000 to $220,000, and eliminated the contribution phaseout for corporations and other entities. Absent congressional action, the changes made by EGTRRA will sunset for tax years after 2010, causing the contribution limit and phaseouts to revert to pre-EGTRRA levels.

Q 14:50   How are distributions from a Coverdell education savings account treated for tax purposes?

Distributions from a Coverdell ESA are excluded from a beneficiary's gross income if they are used to pay qualified education expenses. Distributions for other purposes are taxable to the extent they represent untaxed earnings. Taxable distributions are also generally subject to a 10 percent penalty. However, the penalty does not apply if the distribution is made on account of the death or disability of the account beneficiary or the beneficiary's receipt of a scholarship. [I.R.C. § 530(d)]

Qualified higher education expenses include tuition, fees, books, supplies, equipment, and certain room and board expenses for graduate or undergraduate education. The beneficiary can be enrolled full-time, half-time, or less than half-time. However, room and board expenses are considered qualified expenses only if the beneficiary is enrolled on at least a half-time basis. [I.R.C. §§ 530(b)(2), 530(b)(3)] For 2009 and 2010 only, qualified higher education offenses include the costs of computer equipment and Internet services. [I.R.C § 529(c)(3)(A)(iii)]

For 2002 and later years, EGTRRA expanded the definition of *qualified expenses* to include qualified elementary and secondary school expenses. These include expenses for tuition, fees, books, supplies, and other equipment incurred in connection with a beneficiary's enrollment or attendance at a public, private, or religious school in kindergarten through grade 12. Qualified elementary and secondary school expenses also include the costs of room and board, uniforms, transportation, and supplementary items or services (including extended day programs) required or provided by the school. Expenses for computer equipment or Internet access and related services are qualified expenses if the equipment or services will be used by a beneficiary during any of the years he or she is in school. However, the cost of computer software primarily involving sports, games, and hobbies is not considered a qualified expense unless the software is educational in nature. [I.R.C. §§ 530(b)(2), 530(b)(4)] Note that, absent congressional action, changes made by EGTRRA are scheduled to sunset for tax years after 2010.

Q 14:51   What if a beneficiary completes his or her education before exhausting the funds in a Coverdell education savings account?

Any remaining balance in a Coverdell ESA must generally be distributed to the beneficiary within 30 days after the date he or she turns age 30. If an actual distribution is not made, the account balance will be deemed distributed to the beneficiary on that date. [I.R.C. § 530(d)(8)] The earnings portion of the distributions will be included in the beneficiary's income and subject to a 10 percent penalty tax. (See Q 14:50.) This tax can be avoided, however, by rolling over the remaining funds into an account for the benefit of another family member who has not yet reached age 30. [I.R.C. § 530(d)(5)]

Under a change made by EGTRRA in 2001, this rule does not apply to a special-needs beneficiary. [I.R.C. § 530(b)(1)] Note that, absent congressional action, changes made by EGTRRA are scheduled to sunset for tax years after 2010.

Q 14:52   If an employer makes a contribution to a Coverdell education savings account for an employee's child, how is the contribution treated for tax purposes?

The contribution is not tax-free to the employee. The contribution must be treated as additional compensation deductible by the employer and taxable to the employee. The employer must withhold income tax and withhold and pay payroll taxes (i.e., Social Security and Medicare taxes) from other compensation due the employee to cover the taxes due on the contribution.

> **Practice Pointer.** The tax on employer contributions is not really a drawback for the employee. Because contributions to a Coverdell ESA are not deductible, the employee (if eligible) would have to make his or her contributions with after-tax dollars in any event.

Q 14:53 What is a Section 529 college savings plan?

A *Section 529 college savings plan* allows contributors to save for a designated child's college education on a tax-favored basis. Contributions to the account are not deductible. However, earnings are not taxable while they remain in the account. In addition, amounts withdrawn from the account (including earnings) are not taxable to the extent they are used to pay qualifying higher education expenses of the designated beneficiary. For state-sponsored college savings programs, the exclusion applies for distributions made in tax years beginning after 2001; for private plans, the exclusion applies for distributions made in tax years beginning after 2003.

Qualified higher education expenses include tuition, fees, books, supplies, and equipment required for attendance at a higher educational institution. Qualified expenses also include room and board for a student who is enrolled at least half time. In the case of a special-needs beneficiary, qualified expenses also include other expenses which are necessary in connection with his or her college enrollment. For 2009 and 2010, the American Recovery and Reinvestment Act of 2009 [Pub. L. 111-5, 123 Stat. 115 (Feb. 17, 2009)] (ARRA) expands the definition of qualified higher education expenses to include amounts paid for the purchase of computer software, any computer or related peripheral equipment, fiber optic cable related to computer use, and Internet access (including related services) that are to be used by the beneficiary and the beneficiary's family during any of the years the beneficiary is enrolled at an eligible educational institution.

Unlike Coverdell ESAs, there are no income limits for employee contributors or fixed dollar limits on contributions to Section 529 education savings plans. However, Section 529 requires a plan to establish safeguards to prevent contributions in excess of the amount necessary to fund a child's college expenditures. The IRS says that a plan will meet this requirement if contributions are limited to the amount determined actuarially that will pay tuition, fees, and room and board for five years of undergraduate enrollment at the highest-cost college allowed by the plan. The plan must prohibit additional contributions once that limit is reached.

Distributions from an education savings account are not eligible for tax-free treatment if they are not used for qualifying expenses. In addition, the law imposes a 10 percent penalty tax on the amount of a distribution from a qualified tuition plan that is includable in gross income. However, unused amounts in one child's account can be rolled over to an account for another beneficiary who is a member of the same family.

Q 14:54   What is an employer-sponsored Section 529 college savings plan?

Although employees can set up and contribute to Section 529 plans on their own, employer-sponsored plans are emerging as a popular employee benefit because they permit employees to make contributions to the plan through payroll deductions.

Amounts contributed to a Section 529 plan through payroll deductions are not excludable from income. The amounts are treated as compensation paid to the employee and are subject to payroll taxes.

Practice Pointer. Despite the lack of an income exclusion for contributions, employees express enthusiasm for these plans. For example, a recent survey found that 43 percent of working Americans who were currently saving for college or plan to do so in the future would participate in a payroll deduction Section 529 plan. [Harris Interactive QuickQuery (SM) Survey sponsored by ADP, Inc., 2003]

Section 529 plans were initially sponsored by states, and some states currently offer the option of payroll deduction plans in which the employer remits employee contributions to the state plan. In addition, mutual fund companies, 401(k) providers, and payroll deduction services have begun to offer payroll deduction plans.

Chapter 15

Vacation and Severance Pay Plans

Vacation and severance pay benefit packages can raise trouble-some issues relating to the Employee Retirement Income Security Act of 1974 (ERISA) and other laws. One emerging issue is whether and to what extent employers can require employees to waive discrimination and other claims against the employer in return for severance benefits.

Vacation Pay Plans

Q 15:1 What is a vacation pay plan?

A *vacation pay plan* is an employer plan that provides compensation to employees for specified periods of vacation, including vacation time that has been earned but not actually taken. Such a plan also generally includes compensation for specified holidays, whether or not those days are actually taken. Vacation pay plans, like other employee benefit plans, can take a wide variety of forms; the benefits may be vested or unvested, the plan may be funded or unfunded, and the plan may be a single-employer plan or a multiemployer plan.

Q 15:2 Are funded vacation pay plans subject to ERISA?

Yes. The ERISA definition of an employee welfare benefit plan lists vacation benefits as one of the types of benefits such a plan provides (see chapter 2). [ERISA § 3(1)] In addition, the U.S. Supreme Court has held that a funded vacation pay plan is an ERISA welfare benefit plan. [Mackey v. Lanier Collection Agency & Serv. Inc., 486 U.S. 825 (1988)] ERISA's definition of an employee welfare benefit plan also incorporates, by reference, the benefits listed in Section

302(c) of the Labor Management Relations Act of 1947 (LMRA), which include funded vacation benefits. [ERISA § 3(1); DOL Adv. Op. 79-89A (Dec. 26, 1979)] Vacation pay benefits provided through a Code Section 501(c)(9) trust and contributed to by an employer have been found to be an ERISA plan. [DOL Adv. Op. 89-6A (Apr. 7, 1989)] Moreover, according to the DOL, such a plan will constitute an ERISA welfare benefit plan even if payments are made regardless of whether an employee actually takes a vacation or holiday. [DOL Adv. Op. 2004-03A (Apr. 30, 2004)]

Q 15:3   Are unfunded vacation pay plans subject to ERISA?

No. Most vacation pay plans are unfunded and are paid out of the employer's general assets. Department of Labor (DOL) regulations take the position that payments for vacation and holidays made from an employer's general assets do not constitute an employee welfare benefit plan, but merely a "payroll practice," and thus are not subject to ERISA. [DOL Reg. § 2510.3-1(b)(3)(i)] The Supreme Court has upheld this regulation as a correct interpretation of the law. [Massachusetts v. Morash, 109 S. Ct. 1668 (1989)] The Ninth Circuit Court of Appeals has held that a vacation and sick day plan constituted a payroll practice and was not an ERISA plan because employees were compensated at full pay, payments were made in the employees' normal paychecks, and the plan was funded by the employer's general assets. [Funkhouser v. Wells Fargo Bank, N.A., 289 F.3d 1137 (9th Cir. 2002)]

Q 15:4   Are vacation pay plans subject to state laws?

The answer depends on whether the vacation pay plan is an ERISA plan.

Unfunded vacation plans. Unfunded vacation plans, being "payroll practices" that have been administratively exempted from ERISA under a DOL regulation [29 C.F.R. § 2510.3-1(b)(3)(i)], are subject to regulation under state law. Thus, an employer's requirement that the employee be employed on a particular day of the year in order to become entitled to accrue an additional year's worth of unfunded vacation pay was held to be invalid under the California Payment of Wages Act. The California law required that terminated employees be paid all vested but unused vacation time upon termination of employment and that employer contracts and policies could not provide for forfeiture of vested vacation time upon termination of employment. The employer claimed that its plan's requirement of employment on a particular date was a condition precedent to entitlement to vacation pay, but the California court disagreed. The court held that vacation pay is not an inducement for future services but rather is compensation for past services, so the justification for demanding that employees remain for the entire year disappears. The court concluded that since the right to a paid vacation constitutes deferred wages for services rendered, a proportionate right to a paid vacation "vests" as the labor is rendered. Once vested, the right is protected from forfeiture by California law, and a terminated employee thus must be paid in wages for a pro rata share of his or her unfunded vacation pay. [Suastez v. Plastic Dress-Up Co., 31 Cal. 3d 774 (Cal. 1982)]

Subsequently, another lawsuit was brought by a group of trade associations whose member employers had vacation programs for their employees that forbade payment of prorated vacation pay and forfeited vacation pay of terminated employees who were not actively employed on specified eligibility dates, such as anniversary dates of hire. The plaintiffs sought a declaratory judgment that the DOL regulation was invalid and that unfunded vacation pay plans were indeed ERISA plans unaffected by the California statute. The Court of Appeals for the Ninth Circuit, however, upheld the DOL regulation exempting unfunded vacation plans from ERISA and held that the California law barring vacation pay forfeitures upon employment termination thus was not preempted by ERISA. [California Hosp. Ass'n v. Henning, 770 F.2d 856 (9th Cir. 1985), *cert. denied,* 477 U.S. 904 (1986)] The issue was finally laid to rest when the Supreme Court upheld a criminal enforcement of a similar Massachusetts law requiring the payment of accrued but unused vacation pay upon discharge from employment. In so doing, the Supreme Court upheld the DOL regulation exempting unfunded vacation pay plans from ERISA. [Massachusetts v. Morash, 109 S. Ct. 1668 (1989)]

A California appeals court held that an employer could not force employees to exhaust their accrued vacation balances before their employment contracts terminated. The court ruled that unfunded accrued vacation benefits are wages that cannot be forfeited. Vacation benefit accruals could be restricted prospectively, the court noted. [Kistler v. Redwoods Cmty. Coll. Dist., 15 Cal. App. 4th 1326 (Cal. Ct. App. 1995)]

The Minnesota Supreme Court held that an employer policy requiring forfeiture of earned vacation pay when an employee is terminated for misconduct did not violate the state's wage payment law. [Lee v. Fresenius Med. Care, Inc., 741 N.W. 2d 117 (Minn. Sup. Ct. 2007), *rev'g* 719 N.W. 2d 222 (Minn. Ct. App. 2006)] The employer's vacation pay policy, as spelled out in its employee handbook, provided that employees would generally be paid for earned but unused vacation time upon termination of employment. However, the policy contained an exception when an employee was terminated as a result of misconduct. The employee who was denied payment for earned but unused vacation time under the exception brought suit against the employer and was initially awarded more than $5,000 in back pay, penalties, and costs. However, the employer challenged the award, and the case went to the appeals court, which held that the forfeiture provision violated the state law. However, when that decision was appealed to the state's highest court, the employer came out the winner. Minnesota law provides that wages "actually earned and unpaid" at the time of discharge are immediately due and payable upon demand. However, the Minnesota Supreme Court concluded that the state law is a timing provision that governs *when* wages must be paid to a terminated employee; it does not control *what* wages must be paid. Instead, the wages due to the employee are determined by contract between the employer and the employee. Thus, employers may impose conditions on an employee's right to receive pay for unused vacation time.

Funded vacation plans. If the vacation pay plan is subject to ERISA—that is, funded (see Qs 15:2–15:3)—and the state law or regulation "relates to" the plan, ERISA generally preempts the state law or regulation, and the vacation pay plan is not subject to the state law or regulation. However, the Supreme Court has held that ERISA does not preempt state laws relating to garnishment of vacation benefits provided through a welfare benefit plan, because there is no parallel provision to ERISA Section 206 (which prohibits assignment or alienation of pension benefits) for ERISA welfare benefit plans. [Mackey v. Lanier Collection Agency & Serv. Inc., 108 S. Ct. 2182 (1988)] (See chapter 2 for a discussion of ERISA preemption.)

Q 15:5   Is vacation pay taxable income to employees?

Yes. Vacation pay is taxable and is subject to income tax withholding. [I.R.C. § 61; Treas. Reg. § 31.3401(a)-(1)(b)(3)] Vacation pay is also subject to Social Security (FICA) and federal unemployment (FUTA) taxes. [I.R.C. §§ 3121(a), 3306(b)]

However, the IRS has ruled that unused vacation pay is not taxable to employees (and not subject to FICA and FUTA tax) when the pay is contributed to a 401(k) plan, provided applicable nondiscrimination requirements and contribution limits are met. [Rev. Rul. 2009-31, 2009-39 I.R.B. 395; Rev. Rul. 2009-32, 2009-39 I.R.B. 398] The IRS has also formally ruled that employer contributions of the value of accumulated unused vacation and sick leave to health reimbursement arrangements (HRAs) for retirees are eligible for tax-free treatment, provided payments from the accounts are limited solely to reimbursements of substantiated medical care expenses incurred by the former employees and their spouses and dependents. [Rev. Rul. 2005-24, 2005-16 I.R.B. 892]

Q 15:6   When can the value of unused vacation and other paid time off be contributed to a 401(k) retirement plan?

Two IRS revenue rulings specifically approve contributions of unused paid time off (PTO) to 401(k) retirement plans. [Rev. Rul. 2009-31, 2009-39 I.R.B. 395; Rev. Rul. 2009-32, 2009-39 I.R.B. 398] According to the rulings, requiring or permitting contributions of the dollar equivalent of unused PTO to a qualified plan will not cause the plan to fail to meet the qualification requirements. In addition, no amount will be included in an employee's gross income on account of the contributions until distributions are made to the employee from the 401(k) plan. Moreover, unused PTO that is not contributed to the plan is not included in an employee's gross income until the tax year in which it is paid to the employee.

Under the IRS rulings, contributions of unused PTO to a 401(k) plan may be either mandatory or at the employee's election.

Example 1. Under Alpha Corp.'s PTO plan, all employees are granted up to 240 hours of PTO each January 1, with the number of hours depending solely on the employee's years of service. Under the plan, no unused PTO hours remaining as of the close of business on December 31 may be carried over to the following year.

Alpha also maintains a calendar-year profit-sharing plan that includes a qualified Section 401(k) cash or deferred arrangement that provides for elective employee contributions.

Effective January 1, 2009, Alpha amends the profit sharing plan to provide that the dollar equivalent of an employee's unused PTO as of the close of business on December 31 will be forfeited under the PTO plan and that same dollar amount will be contributed to the employee's 401(k) account as of December 31, to the extent the contribution (in combination with prior annual additions) does not exceed the applicable 401(k) contribution limits. The dollar amount of any remaining PTO will be paid to the employee by February 28 of the following year. Under Alpha's profit sharing plan, the amounts attributable to PTO are in addition to other contributions under the plan and are treated as nonelective contributions.

Ann, an employee of Alpha, has 20 hours of unused PTO remaining as of the close of business on December 31, 2009. Ann earns $25 per hour, so the dollar equivalent of Ann's unused PTO is $500. Because of the contribution limits, Alpha can contribute only $400 of the unused PTO to Ann's profit-sharing account for 2009. Alpha makes that contribution on December 31, 2009, and pays Ann the remaining $100 in cash on February 28, 2010.

Result: The IRS says that the plan amendment will not cause disqualification of Alpha's 401(k) plan, provided contributions of PTO satisfy the 401(k) nondiscrimination requirements and the 401(k) contribution limits. Alpha's contribution of $400 of unused PTO to the plan will be treated as a nonelective employer contribution to the plan. The amount of unused PTO contributed to the 401(k) plan will not be included in Ann's gross income until the amount is distributed to Ann. Moreover, the remaining dollar amount of unused will not be included in her income until it is paid to her in 2010. Because that amount is not set aside or otherwise made available to Ann, she will not be treated as having constructively received the amount in 2009.

Example 2. Beta Corp. maintains a PTO plan, under which all employees are granted up to 240 hours of PTO each January 1, with the number of hours depending solely on the employee's years of service. Under the plan, a specified number of hours of PTO may be carried over to the following year. The dollar amount of unused PTO in excess of the carryover limit is paid to the employee by February 28 of the following year.

Beta also mains a 401(k) plan that allows for elective employee contributions. Beta amends the 401(k) plan effective January 1, 2009, to allow an employee to elect to reduce the amount of PTO that cannot be carried over and have the dollar equivalent contributed to the employee's 401(k) account, subject to the 401(k) contributions limits.

Brendan, a Beta employee, has 15 hours of unused PTO in excess of the carryover limit remaining as of December 31, 2009, with a value of $450. Brendan elects to have 60 percent of his unused PTO ($270) contributed to the 401(k) plan. The contribution does not violate the 401(k) contribution limits. Beta allocates the $270 to Brendan's account on December 31, 2009, and pays the remaining $180 value of the PTO to Brendan on February 28, 2010.

Result: The plan amendment does not cause disqualification of Beta's 401(k) plan, provided the nondiscrimination requirements are met. Because Brendan had the right to elect either a payment of cash or a plan contribution for the unused PTO, the contribution is treated as an elective employee contribution. Since Brendan elected to have the $270 worth of PTO contributed to the plan before it would become available to him in 2010, the amount will not be included in Brendan's gross income until it is distributed from the 401(k) plan. Moreover, the $180 cash payment will not be included in Brendan's gross income until 2010 because that amount was not made available or set aside for Brendan at any time in 2009.

In addition, in each case, the IRS says that the contribution of unused PTO to the 401(k) plan will not cause the PTO plan to fail to qualify as a bona fide sick and vacation leave plan for purposes of the nonqualified deferred compensation rules of Code Section 409A (see Q 15:44).

Q 15:7   When can the value of unused vacation or other paid time off be contributed to a health reimbursement arrangement?

The IRS has ruled that employer contributions of the value of accumulated unused vacation and sick leave to HRAs for retirees are eligible for tax-free treatment, provided payments from the accounts are limited solely to reimbursements of substantiated medical care expenses incurred by the former employees and their spouses and dependents. [Rev. Rul. 2005-24, 2005-16 I.R.B. 892]

Example. Company A sponsors an HRA that reimburses employees solely for medical care expenses that are substantiated before the reimbursements are made. The plan reimburses expenses of both current and former employees, including retirees and their spouses and dependents. The plan also reimburses expenses of the surviving spouse and dependents of a deceased employee. On the death of a deceased employee's surviving spouse and last dependent, any unused reimbursement amount is forfeited.

Company A's plan is paid for solely by the employer. At the end of a plan year, a portion of each employee's unused reimbursement amount is forfeited and the remainder is carried forward. When an employee retires, Company A automatically contributes an amount to the retiree's account equal to the value of all or a portion of his or her unused vacation and sick leave. Such contributions are mandatory, and the retiree may not receive any of the designated amount in cash or other benefits.

Result: The amount contributed to the plan, including the value of unused leave, as well as amounts paid from the plan, are excludable from an employee's income.

Q 15:8   May an employer deduct vacation pay expense?

Yes. An employer generally may deduct vacation pay as reasonable compensation for prior services rendered. [I.R.C. § 162; Treas. Reg. § 1.162-10, Q&A-1] However, special rules apply to accrual-basis employers.

Q 15:9   When may an accrual-basis employer deduct vacation pay?

An accrual-basis employer generally can deduct for a taxable year only (1) vacation pay paid in that taxable year, plus (2) vacation pay (a) earned and vested in that taxable year and (b) paid to employees within two and one half months after the close of the taxable year. [I.R.C. §§ 404(a)(5), 404(a)(11); 461(h); Prop. Treas. Reg. § 1.446-1(e), Ex. 3; Temp. Treas. Reg. § 1.404(b)-1T, Q&A-2]

Practice Pointer. Because of this time limit on an accrual-basis employer's deduction of vacation pay, vacation pay plans that permit carryover of unused vacation days into the next calendar year frequently limit the carryover to no more than this two-and-one-half-month period, so that the employer will get a current deduction for carryover vacation days.

Q 15:10   What are the tax consequences if an employee forgoes a vacation and has the value of the leave donated to charity?

In the aftermath of the September 11 terrorist attacks, a number of employers adopted leave-based donation programs, which allow employees to forgo vacation, sick, or personal leave and have the employer contribute the value of the leave to charity.

Under general tax law principles, if a person renders services, and payment for those services is made to a charitable organization, the amount paid is still taxable to the person rendering the services. [Treas. Reg. § 1.61-2(c)] In addition, when income is made available so that a taxpayer can draw upon it at any time, the income is taxable. [Treas. Reg. § 1.451-2(a)] Thus, an employee would ordinarily owe tax on the value of donated leave.

An IRS notice provided temporary relief for leave donation programs following the September 11 attacks. Under the temporary relief provision, employees were not taxed on leave that was donated before 2003. [Notice 2001-69, 2001-46 I.R.B. 491] The IRS made it clear, however, that the tax relief for donated leave pay was temporary and does not apply to payments made after December 31, 2002. Furthermore, the IRS said that it has reviewed the issue and will not make any permanent change in its regulations to provide an exemption for donated leave pay. [Notice 2003-1, 2003-2, I.R.B. 257]

Q 15:11   What is the tax treatment of employee leave-sharing programs?

The tax treatment of an employee leave-sharing program depends on the circumstances under which leave is contributed by employees. Leave that is donated for use by other employees who have been affected by a major disaster or who suffer medical emergencies is not taxable to the contributing employee. However, leave contributed for other purposes is taxable to the contributor.

Practice Pointer. If contributed leave is not taxable to the contributing employee, it must be treated as compensation to the recipient employee. On the other hand, if the contributing employee is taxed on the contributed leave, there should be no tax consequences to the recipient. Presumably, the recipient of donated leave will be treated as having received a tax-free gift from the contributor.

Major disaster relief leave-sharing plans. According to an IRS notice, the IRS will not assert that an employee who deposits leave in an employer-sponsored leave bank under a major disaster leave sharing plan realizes income with respect to the deposited leave, provided the plan treats the payments to a leave recipient as wages subject to income tax withholding and payroll taxes. [Notice 2006-59, 2006-28 I.R.B. 60] However, a contributing employee may not claim an expense, charitable contribution, or loss deduction for the contributed leave.

A major disaster leave-sharing plan is a written plan of the employer that meets all of the following requirements:

1. The plan allows an employee to deposit accrued leave in an employer-sponsored leave bank for use by other employees who have been adversely affected by a major disaster.

2. The plan does not allow an employee to deposit leave for transfer to a specific leave recipient.

3. The amount of leave that an employee may deposit in the leave bank in any year generally does not exceed the maximum amount of leave the employee normally accrues during the year.

4. A leave recipient may receive paid leave at his or her normal rate of compensation from leave deposited in the leave bank and must use the leave for purposes related to the major disaster.

5. The plan adopts a reasonable limit, based on the severity of a disaster, on the period of time following a disaster during which an employee may deposit leave in the leave bank and during which a leave recipient must use leave received from the leave bank.

6. A leave recipient may not convert leave received from the leave bank into cash in lieu of using the leave, but may use leave received from the leave bank to eliminate a negative leave balance resulting from leave that was advanced to the recipient because of the effects of a major disaster or may substitute leave received from the leave bank for leave without pay that was used because of the major disaster.

7. The employer must make a reasonable determination, based on need, as to how much leave each approved leave recipient may receive.

8. Leave deposited for one major disaster may be used only for employees affected by that disaster.

9. Any leave that is deposited for a major disaster that is not used by leave recipients by the end of the reasonable period specified by the employer (other than an amount so small that is unreasonable or administratively impracticable to account for it) must be returned within a reasonable time to each contributing employee (or, at the employer's option to each employee who is still employed by the employer) in the same proportion that the amount of leave contributed by the employee bears to the total leave contributed for the disaster.

For this purpose, a major disaster generally means a federally declared disaster or emergency. An employee is considered to be adversely affected by a major disaster if the disaster caused severe hardship to the employee or the employee's family member (as defined under the employer's plan) that requires the employee to be absent from work.

Medical emergency leave-sharing plans. Under a long-standing IRS revenue ruling, amounts deposited in a leave bank to be used by employees experiencing medical emergencies are not taxable to contributing employees, but are included in the gross income of the recipients subject to income tax withholding and payroll taxes. [Rev. Rul. 90-29, 1990-1 C.B. 11]

Under the plan described in this IRS ruling, a "medical emergency" is defined as a medical condition of the employee or a family member that will require the prolonged absence of the employee from duty and will result in a substantial loss of income to the employee because the employee will have exhausted all paid leave available apart from the leave-sharing plan. Under the provisions of the plan, a written application describing the medical emergency must be submitted to the employer by or on behalf of the employee requesting additional paid leave under the leave-sharing plan. After the application has been approved and the employee has exhausted all of his or her paid leave, the employee is eligible to receive additional leave (to be paid at his or her normal rate of compensation) from the leave bank. The plan contains restrictions on the amount of leave that may be contributed to the leave bank.

Other leave-sharing plans. The IRS has not granted favorable tax treatment to other leave-sharing plans. Consequently, the value of leave contributed to such plans remains taxable to contributing employees. For example, the IRS ruled privately on a state program to help the surviving families of correctional guards or highway patrol officers who die while in service but not in the line of duty. Under the program, certain state employees may donate accrued vacation or other similar leave to the leave bank of the deceased guard or officer. The state then pays the cash value of the donated leave to the surviving family. The IRS ruled that a state employee's assignment of the right to receive leave will not relieve the employee of the tax liability on the assigned leave. The leave must be reported on the employee's Form W-2 and is subject to FICA, FUTA and income tax withholding. [Priv. Ltr. Rul. 200626036 (June 30, 2006)] Similarly, the IRS ruled privately that an employer's plan to modify its medical leave-sharing program to include employees suffering catastrophic casualty losses would cause donated leave to be included in a donor employee's income. The IRS concluded that the modified program would not qualify as medical leave-sharing plan because it would provide a recipient employee with leave whenever he or she is facing a catastrophic casualty—even if the casualty did not involve a personal or family medical emergency. Moreover, the modified program would not qualify as a major disaster relief leave-sharing program because it would not be limited to aiding victims of a federally declared disaster. [Priv. Ltr. Rul 200720017 (May 18, 2007)]

Severance Pay Plans

Q 15:12   What is a severance pay plan?

A *severance pay plan* is a plan that provides payments to employees upon termination of employment. Generally, the payments are proportionate to length of employment.

The plan may be a permanent program or a limited program (e.g., an "open-window" program that offers a group of employees cash payments, increased pension benefits, or both as inducements to voluntarily retire or to separate from employment within a certain time period).

The plan may cover voluntary separations, involuntary separations, or both, and may place conditions on payment of benefits (e.g., no benefits are provided if the employee goes to work for a competitor or for a successor employer). In addition, the plan may deny benefits if the employee is terminated for cause; that is, it may include a "bad-boy" provision.

Q 15:13   Are funded severance pay plans considered employee benefit plans subject to ERISA?

Yes. Funded severance pay plans are clearly subject to ERISA's definition of employee welfare benefit plans, which includes plans providing benefits in the event of unemployment (see chapter 2). [ERISA § 3(1)]

Q 15:14   Are unfunded severance pay plans subject to ERISA?

Yes. For a time, some employers took the position that an unfunded severance pay plan, particularly one that was maintained on an informal basis, was a payroll practice or fringe benefit and therefore not an ERISA plan (see chapter 2). However, a number of federal appellate courts decided that unfunded severance pay plans do constitute ERISA plans even if they are not established with all the formalities of other welfare plans. [Gilbert v. Burlington Indus. Inc., 765 F.2d 320 (2d Cir. 1985); Holland v. Burlington Indus. Inc., 772

F.2d 1140 (4th Cir. 1985); Blau v. Del Monte Corp., 748 F.2d 1348 (9th Cir. 1985), *cert. denied,* 474 U.S. 865 (1985)] The issue has been resolved by the Supreme Court, which has stated that an unfunded severance pay plan is an ERISA plan. [Firestone Tire & Rubber Co. v. Bruch, 109 S. Ct. 948 (1989)]

Determining whether a "plan" *exists.* Even though severance pay might be paid, the arrangement must constitute a "plan" in order to be subject to ERISA. A voluntary separation plan under which the employee received a one-time lump-sum payment was held not to be an ERISA plan, because there were no continuing payments and thus no need for continuing administration. [Wells v. General Motors Corp., 881 F.2d 1661 (5th Cir. 1989), *cert. denied,* 110 S. Ct. 1959 (1990)] A severance pay agreement with employees who agreed to continue working at the employer's factory was held not to be an ERISA plan where the agreement did not require an ongoing administrative scheme. [Velarde v. PACE Membership Warehouse, 20 Employee Benefits Cas. (BNA) 2479 (9th Cir. 1997)]

The Seventh Circuit Court of Appeals ruled that no ERISA plan existed when an employer stated that "the company will develop and implement an appropriate separation program." The court said that the vagueness of the statement made it impossible for a court to provide any relief to terminated employees. [Brines v. XTRA Corp., 304 F.3d 699 (7th Cir. 2002)]

An employer's severance practices were held not to be subject to ERISA where decisions as to who would receive severance benefits and in what amounts were solely in the discretion of the employer's president. Because the decisions were made on an ad hoc basis, with some employees receiving payments and others not, there was no plan in existence that permitted employees to determine plan benefits, the sources of financing, and the procedures for obtaining benefits. [Spanos v. Continental Publ'g Servs., 1994 U.S. Dist. LEXIS 6695 (N.D. Cal. May 17, 1994)] A series of four separate lump-sum early retirement incentive programs over a four-year period was held not to constitute an ERISA-covered plan, since the employer did not assume an ongoing administrative scheme, and the sheer number of the employer's offers during this four-year period did not change this fact. [Belanger v. Wyman-Gordon Co., 71 F.3d 451 (1st Cir. 1995)]

In another case, an employee filed suit in state court claiming that the employer breached its promise to provide special severance benefits to employees who agreed to stay on with the company during a transition period. The employer argued that the plan was covered by ERISA and that the employees' state-law claims were therefore preempted. The employer moved the case to a federal court, which dismissed the state-law claims. However, on appeal, the Eighth Circuit held that the special "stay-on bonuses" did not constitute an ERISA plan. According to the court, severance benefits are characterized as an ERISA plan only when they require an ongoing administrative program to meet the employer's obligation. One-time lump-sum payments involving no long-term obligations do not constitute an ERISA plan. Moreover, the fact that the company did have an existing severance plan that was subject to ERISA did not change the result. The evidence indicated that the promised stay-on bonuses were freestanding and not premised in any way on the existing plan. [Crews v. General Am. Life Ins. Co., 274 F.2d 502 (8th Cir. 2001)]

Similarly, the Eighth Circuit permitted a group of laid-off employees to sue under state law to enforce an oral promise to pay severance benefits that they claimed had been made by a former employer. The employer sold the division in which the employees worked and, to induce the employees to work for the buyer, allegedly promised them severance benefits if they were laid off by the buyer within one year of the sale. The amount of the benefits was to be calculated by reference to the original employer's ERISA severance pay plan. The Eighth Circuit concluded that the lawsuit brought by the former employees was not preempted by ERISA because the employees were not participants in the former employer's ERISA plan. Instead, the alleged oral promise "constituted a freestanding contract providing severance payments." Moreover, the promise did not create an ERISA plan because it contemplated only one-time severance payments and, therefore, did not establish an "administrative scheme" contemplated by ERISA. [Eide v. Grey Fox Tech. Servs. Corp., 329 F.3d 600 (8th Cir. 2003)]

The Seventh Circuit Court of Appeals held that a severance offer to one employee did not create a "plan" that applied to another employee. [Sandstrom v. Culto Food Science Inc., 214 F.3d 795 (7th Cir. 2000)] Moreover, the severance offer did not constitute an amendment to the company's written severance pay plan. Under ERISA, a written plan may be amended only in writing. Therefore, side agreements and understandings or special offers to individual employees do not change the written plan as it applies to other employees.

On the other hand, a severance agreement was held to constitute an ERISA plan where the agreement required the employer to maintain an ongoing administrative scheme, and the agreement had reasonably ascertainable terms. The agreement provided for payment of severance benefits over a three-year period and payment of medical claims and required the employer to exercise managerial discretion. [Cvelbar v. CBI Ill., 106 F.3d 1368 (7th Cir. 1997)]

Additional case law concerning when a plan exists for ERISA purposes is discussed in chapter 2.

Practice Pointer. Unless it is clear that ERISA does not apply, it appears prudent for an employer to treat an unfunded severance pay program as an ERISA plan and to comply with all ERISA requirements, such as a formal written plan document, summary plan description, and the like.

Q 15:15   What is the effect of an amended severance pay policy when the plan lacks the "magic" words of amendment procedure as required by ERISA Section 402(b)(3)?

According to a federal district court in Pennsylvania, ERISA Section 402(b)(3) requires plans to have an amendment procedure but does not require plans to use words such as *change, amend,* or *revoke* to establish that procedure.

The plan satisfies ERISA when it states that it will keep the policies up-to-date and current with the latest policy developments. [Clark v. Witco Corp., 102 F. Supp. 2d 292 (W.D. Pa. 2000)]

Q 15:16 What if the severance policy has never been communicated to employees?

Keeping a severance policy secret will not keep it from possibly being an ERISA plan. No formal written plan is required for a plan to be subject to ERISA. ERISA covers a welfare benefit plan if it is established or maintained by an employer or an employee organization, or both, that is engaged in any activities or in any industry that affects commerce. [ERISA § 4(a)] If ERISA covers the plan, then ERISA requires that it be established pursuant to a written instrument, but that is the responsibility of the plan administrator and plan fiduciaries rather than a prerequisite to coverage under ERISA. [Blau v. Del Monte Corp., 748 F.2d 1348 (9th Cir. 1985), *cert. denied,* 474 U.S. 865 (1985)]

Q 15:17 What effect does revoking a severance policy have on previously accrued severance benefits?

The Oregon Court of Appeals has determined that revoking a severance policy substantially impaired an employee's entitlement to benefits that were accrued before the revocation. This is so even though the policy was revoked more than one year before the employee left the company.

The company in question, Prepared Media Laboratory, had a severance plan in place that established a schedule for written notice, depending on the length of time the employee had been with the company. A year after the severance policy was revoked, Prepared Media Laboratory terminated an employee with one day's notice.

The employee claimed that she was entitled to the revoked severance pay benefits that had accrued before the revocation of the severance policy. The company said that she had no contractual right to unused severance benefits and that the benefits could be unilaterally eliminated.

The appeals court said that although the company had the right to revoke the severance plan, it could not revoke employees' entitlements to benefits to which they had already become entitled. [Horton v. Prepared Media Lab., Inc., 999 P.2d 864 (Or. Ct. App. 2000)]

Q 15:18 Is an individual contractual arrangement with executives for severance benefits a severance pay plan subject to ERISA?

Such contractual arrangements could possibly constitute an ERISA plan. At least one court has held that a series of individual executive employment contracts providing so-called golden parachute payments upon a change in control constitutes an ERISA severance pay plan. [Purser v. Enron Corp., 10

Employee Benefits Cas. (BNA) 1561 (W.D. Pa. 1988)] (See Qs 15:46–15:65 for a discussion of golden parachute provisions.)

In DOL Advisory Opinion 91-20A (July 2, 1991), the DOL considered a severance arrangement entered into by an employer as consideration for an individual's acceptance of employment as general counsel and the accompanying move across the country. Even though the severance arrangement covered only one individual, the DOL found it to be a severance pay plan governed by ERISA.

However, a federal appellate court held that an employment contract providing severance pay for a specified period, if termination was without cause, was not an ERISA plan because the arrangement did not require an ongoing administrative scheme. There was no discretion concerning the timing, amount, or form of payment of the severance benefits. [Delaye v. Agripac Inc., 39 F.3d 235 (9th Cir. 1994), *cert. denied*, 514 U.S. 1037]

Q 15:19   Under ERISA, is a severance pay plan considered a welfare benefit plan or a pension plan?

Generally, the DOL views a severance pay plan as a welfare benefit plan, not a pension plan, provided the severance pay plan meets the following requirements:

1. Payments are not contingent, directly or indirectly, on the employee's retirement;
2. The total amount of the payments does not exceed the equivalent of twice the employee's annual compensation in the year preceding the termination; and
3. Payments are completed by these deadlines:
   a. In the case of an open-window plan (see Q 15:12), within 24 months after the later of termination or normal retirement age; and
   b. In all other cases, within 24 months after termination.

[DOL Reg. § 2510.3-2(b)]

> **Practice Pointer.** In view of the more onerous ERISA requirements that attach to a pension plan (compared to a welfare benefit plan), strict compliance with the conditions in the DOL regulation is advisable.

Q 15:20   May an employer-provided severance pay plan provide that the amount of severance pay will be determined on a case-by-case basis?

Evidently, yes. The U.S. Court of Appeals for the Third Circuit held that, as long as the plan explicitly states such a limitation, nothing in ERISA prevents an employer from providing its employees with benefits on a case-by-case basis. Accordingly, while the employer was barred from correcting, one day before the employee was terminated, a printer's error accidentally listing more generous severance pay benefits than it had intended to offer, the employee's reduced benefit was nonetheless upheld on the basis of the express statement in the plan that the employer reserved the right to determine benefits on a case-by-case basis. [Hamilton v. Air Jamaica Ltd., 945 F.2d 74 (3d Cir. 1991)]

A plan must, however, clearly provide that severance pay is discretionary. In another case, the Second Circuit Court of Appeals concluded that a plan's statement that severance benefits would be paid "where applicable" was not enough to give the plan administrator the discretion to decide who would receive severance benefits. According to the court, although a plan does not have contain any "magic words" such as "discretion" or "deference," there must be some unambiguous indication that discretion has been conferred on the administrator. The plan in question did not unambiguously confer such discretion. Moreover, the plan specifically identified two situations in which severance pay was not available. Thus, the employee's conclusion that she was eligible for severance because she did not fall into either category was reasonable. [Kosakow v. New Rochelle Radiology Assocs., P. C., 274 F.3d 706 (2d Cir. 2001)]

> **Practice Pointer.** Although the court decision says that "magic words" are not required, a clear statement that the plan administrator has the discretion to interpret the terms of the plan and to decide on severance eligibility can work wonders.

Q 15:21   May an employer condition the payment of severance pay on the employee signing a release of claims against the employer?

Yes. And the release generally will bar any subsequent lawsuit by an employee if the employee's claim is covered by the release and the employee received adequate consideration for the release. [Williams v. Phillips Petroleum Co., 23 F.3d 930 (5th Cir. 1994)] However, special rules apply to releases of discrimination claims under the Age Discrimination in Employment Act of 1967 (see Q 15:27). The Equal Economic Opportunity Commission (EEOC) has released guidance on waivers of discrimination claims in employee severance agreements in general and waivers of ADEA claims in particular. [*See* Understanding Waivers Of Discrimination Claims In Employee Severance Agreements.]

The EEOC guidance makes it clear that, like any contract, a severance agreement must be supported by "consideration." Consideration is something of value to which a person is not already entitled that is given in exchange for an agreement to do, or refrain from doing, something. The consideration offered for the waiver of the right to sue cannot simply be a pension benefit or payment for earned vacation or sick leave to which the employee is already entitled but, rather, must be something of value *in addition* to any of the employee's existing entitlements. An example of consideration would be a lump sum payment of a percentage of the employee's annual salary or periodic payments of the employee's salary for a specified period of time after termination. The employee's signature and retention of the consideration generally indicates acceptance of the terms of the agreement.

A waiver in a severance agreement generally is valid when an employee knowingly and voluntarily consents to the waiver. The rules regarding whether a waiver is knowing and voluntary depend on the statute under which suit has been, or may be, brought. As a general rule, whether a waiver is knowing and voluntary is determined by case law. However, the rules for waivers under the ADEA are defined by statute in the Older Workers Benefit Protection Act (OWBPA) (see Q 15:27).

To determine whether an employee knowingly and voluntarily waived discrimination claims, some courts rely on traditional contract principles and focus primarily on whether the language in the waiver is clear. [*See, e.g.,* Morrison v. Circuit City Stores, 317 F.3d 646 (6th Cir. 2003).] However, courts may look beyond the contract language and consider the totality of the circumstances to determine whether an employee knowingly and voluntarily waived the right to sue. [*See, e.g.,* Wastak v. Lehigh Health Network, 342 F.3d 281 (3d Cir. 2003).] Factors taken into account may include:

- Whether the severance agreement was written in a manner that was clear and specific enough for the employee to understand based on his or her education and business experience;
- Whether the agreement was induced by fraud, duress, undue influence, or other improper conduct by the employer;
- Whether the employee had enough time to read and think about the advantages and disadvantages of the agreement before signing it;
- Whether the employee consulted with an attorney or was encouraged or discouraged by the employer from doing so;
- Whether the employee had any input in negotiating the terms of the agreement; and
- Whether the employer offered the employee consideration (e.g., severance pay, additional benefits) that exceeded what the employee already was entitled to by law or contract and the employee accepted the offered consideration.

In one case involving an employee who was laid off from her position at an automobile assembly plant, the employee agreed to release the employer from all claims in exchange for a $100,000 severance payment. After signing the waiver and cashing the check, she filed a lawsuit alleging that she was harassed and discriminated against by her coworkers during her employment. The court found that the employee's waiver was knowing and voluntary by looking at the totality of circumstances surrounding its execution: the employee was a college graduate and had completed paralegal training that included a course in contracts; she had no difficulty reading; the agreement was clear and unambiguous; she had ample time to consider whether to sign it; she was represented by counsel; the cash payment provided by the employer was fair consideration; and she did not offer to return the payment she received for signing the waiver. [Hampton v. Ford Motor Co., 561 F.3d 709 (7th Cir. 2009)]

In another case, an employee was informed that his company was downsizing and that he had 30 days to elect voluntary or involuntary separation. The employee chose voluntary separation in exchange for severance pay and additional retirement benefits and signed a waiver, which stated: "I . . . hereby release and discharge [my employer] from any and all claims which I have or might have, arising out of or related to my employment or resignation or termination." The employee later filed suit alleging that he was terminated based on his race and national origin. In finding that the employee's waiver was *not* knowing and voluntary, the court noted that although the language of the agreement was "clear and unambiguous," it failed to specifically mention the release of employment discrimination claims. Because the employee had only a high school education and was unfamiliar with the law, his argument that he believed he was only releasing claims arising from his voluntary termination and the benefits package he accepted was "not an unreasonable conclusion." [Torrez v. Public Service Co. of New Mex., 908 F.2d 687 (10th Cir. 1990)]

A case before the Fifth Circuit Court of Appeals concerned the issue of whether the release must specifically address the release of ERISA claims. The employer's severance plan conditioned eligibility for the severance pay on a designation in writing by the employer's human resource director. The plaintiff-employees were laid off after the severance plan had been terminated. The defendant-employer argued that the human resource director's designation could only occur when employees were laid off. Thus, since the severance plan had already been terminated by then, the employees were not eligible because they lacked the human resource director's designation. The plaintiff-employees argued that that "designation" had occurred earlier through other actions by the human resource director. In any case, the employees did sign a release waiving all claims against the employer and received a reduced severance pay package. But they brought a lawsuit against the employer for the more generous benefits provided by the original severance plan, which they claimed they were eligible for.

The employees argued that the release did not bar the lawsuit because the release covered "all claims, suits, demands or other causes of action," but did not specifically mention ERISA claims. In addition, since the severance pay they received was less than what they would have received under the original severance plan, the release was not in exchange for "adequate consideration."

The appeals court rejected both arguments and dismissed the lawsuit. The court said that the release sweeps widely enough to cover ERISA claims. According to the court, "it would be odd public policy that favored settlements and releases, but then forced employers to scour the United States Code and the state statutes and reports to identify every cause of action." The court also ruled that the reduced severance pay did indeed constitute adequate consideration. To receive the more generous benefits from the original severance pay plan the employees would have to go to court and risk losing. Under a bird-in-the-hand approach, the reduced pay with no litigation was considered adequate consideration. [Chaplin v. NationsCredit Corp., 54 Fed. Appx. 415 (5th Cir. 2002)]

Another case dealt with the issue of whether the imposition of a release signing requirement on a longstanding severance pay plan violated the plan's "anticutback" provision. This provision stated that no amendment to the plan could "eliminate or reduce" an employee's right to severance benefits accrued before the amendment's effective date. Following a merger, the plan was amended to provide that employees must execute a release of claims in order to receive severance pay. When an employee refused to sign a release and was denied benefits, he sued the employer claiming that the release amendment violated the plan's anticutback provision.

The Eleventh Circuit Court of Appeals rejected the employee's claim. While acknowledging that the amendment did impose a condition on the employee's receipt of severance pay, the court said that did not constitute an elimination or reduction of benefits. Because the employee was entitled to the same pay both before and after the amendment, there was no "cut-back." [Loskill v. Barnett Banks, Inc., 289 F.3d 734 (11th Cir. 2002)]

A case from the Tenth Circuit Court of Appeals involved the question of how much specificity about the release must be provided employees in advance. In this case, the plan provided that, to receive severance pay, employees would be required to sign a "General Agreement and Release." However, a week before he was terminated, an employee was notified that the release included a nonsolicitation provision that prohibited the employee from soliciting the employer's customers. When he refused to sign the release, the employee was informed he would not be entitled to severance pay.

The employee sued and the Tenth Circuit Court of Appeals ruled that the employee did not have to sign the release to obtain severance benefits. The court noted that a "release" is generally understood to mean a waiver of legal claims and does not cover a nonsolicitation agreement. The court said that "by failing to provide notice to employees that severance benefits would be conditioned on a nonsolicitation provision, the plan administrator's conduct in this case contravenes ERISA's mandate that employee-welfare plans be written so as to provide employees with notice of their rights and obligations under the plan." [Cirulis v. UNUM Corp. Severance Plan, 321 F.3d 1010 (10th Cir. 2003)].

Q 15:22   Can an employee who has signed a waiver of claims against the employer file a discrimination claim with the EEOC?

Yes. Although a severance agreement may use broad language to describe the claims being released, an employee can still file a discrimination charge with the EEOC. In addition, no agreement can limit an employee's right to testify, assist, or participate in an investigation, hearing, or proceeding conducted by the EEOC under the ADEA, Title VII, the Americans with Disabilities Act (ADA), or the Equal Pay Act (EPA). [EEOC Enforcement Guidance on Non-Waivable Employee Rights Under EEOC Enforced Statutes (April 1997)] Note, however, that although the right to file a charge with the EEOC is protected, an agreement can waive the right to recover from the employer either in an individual lawsuit or in any suit brought on the employee's behalf by the EEOC.

An employee cannot be required to return or "tender back" severance pay or other consideration before filing a claim with the EEOC. On the other hand, an employee may—or may not—be required to return severance pay or other consideration before filing an individual lawsuit. The special rules governing waivers of claims under the ADEA specifically provide that an employee is not required to return severance pay or other consideration before bringing an age discrimination lawsuit. However, lawsuits under Title VII, the ADA, or the EPA, may be a different story. Some courts conclude that the validity of the waiver cannot be challenged unless the employee returns the consideration, while other courts apply the ADEA's "no tender back" rule to claims brought under other discrimination laws. For example, the Seventh Circuit held that because no special exception applies in a Title VII case, an employee must return or offer to return the consideration he or she received before challenging the validity of a waiver of claims. [Hampton v. Ford Motor Co., 561 F.3d 709 (7th Cir. 2009)] On the other hand, a district court has held that because the primary purpose of both the ADEA and Title VII is to make it easier for an employee to challenge discrimination, employees bringing claims under Title VII should not have to return their severance pay before filing suit. [Rangel v. El Paso Natural Gas Co., 996 F. Supp. 1093 (D.N.M. 1998)]

Q 15:23   How does the Age Discrimination in Employment Act regulate the content of severance pay plans?

The Older Workers Benefits Protection Act of 1990 (OWBPA) amended the federal Age Discrimination in Employment Act of 1967 (ADEA) to add substantive regulation of severance programs as follows:

1. Reduction of severance pay by certain other benefits is prohibited, with limited exceptions; and

2. A waiver of ADEA claims that is required to be executed as a condition of receipt of severance benefits must be "knowing and voluntary."

The statute contains certain minimum conditions that a waiver of ADEA claims must meet for it to be treated as knowing and voluntary, and the Equal Employment Opportunity Commission (EEOC) has issued regulations and other guidance detailing these requirements. (See Q 15:31.)

Q 15:24   Can an employer subject to the ADEA reduce or deny severance pay if an employee is eligible for, or receives, retirement benefits?

The ADEA prohibits an employer from reducing or eliminating severance pay solely because the employee is eligible for retirement benefits or will receive retirement benefits. However, the statute contains a limited exception: if severance pay is payable as a result of a contingent event that is not related to the employee's age (for example, a plant closing or layoff), the severance pay can be reduced by "pension sweeteners" (that is, additional pension benefits that are payable solely as a result of the contingent event) if the individual is eligible for an immediate and unreduced pension. [ADEA § 4(1)(2)(A)(ii); 29 U.S.C.A. § 623(1)(2)(A)(ii)]

For purposes of this exception, severance pay includes Section 501(c)(17) supplemental unemployment benefits (which may extend to 52 weeks), the primary purpose and effect of which is to continue benefits until the individual becomes eligible for an immediate and unreduced pension, whereupon they cease. [ADEA § 4(1)(2)(C); 29 U.S.C.A. § 623(1)(2)(C)]

Q 15:25 Does a severance plan that is skewed in favor of younger workers automatically violate the ADEA?

No. One case makes it clear that to be in violation of the ADEA a denial of severance benefits must not only be related to a worker's age but also constitute an adverse employment action. [Cooney v. Union Pac. R.R. Co., 258 F.3d 731 (8th Cir. 2001)]

In the case in question, a merger of two railroads required a reduction in force at one railroad. An agreement with the union representing employees at the facility provided that the railroad would offer buyouts of up to $95,000 to a certain number of employees based on seniority. The buyouts were made separately within each of six zones in the facility. Employees of one zone brought suit, claiming that the buyout program violated the ADEA. The employees pointed out that in their zone, in which the employees were 58 to 63 years old, there were 42 buyout requests but only 5 offers. By contrast, in another zone, where the employees ranged from 40 to 56 years old, there were 51 requests and 51 offers.

The Eighth Circuit Court of Appeals concluded that the buyout program did not violate the ADEA. The severance benefits were awarded on the basis of location and seniority, not retirement eligibility. Moreover, the employees did not suffer an adverse employment action as a result of the denial of severance; they continued to work at the facility under the same terms and conditions, with no loss of salary or benefits.

The court noted that the employees claimed that buyouts were made on a zone-by-zone basis "for union political purposes." However, the court pointed out that even if awarding the buyouts on that basis were discriminatory, it would not constitute age discrimination. Employment decisions motivated by factors other than age do not constitute age discrimination, even if those factors correlate with age. "Thus," said the court, "even if things were cooked for Zone 201 because of union politics . . . that does not show age discrimination." [Cooney v. Union Pac. R.R. Co., 258 F.3d 731 (8th Cir. 2001)]

Conversely, an employer is not required to give older workers a greater amount of consideration than is given to younger workers solely because the older workers are protected by the ADEA. [29 C.F.R § 1625.22 (d)(4); Understanding Waivers Of Discrimination Claims In Employee Severance Agreements]

Q 15:26   May an employer subject to the ADEA reduce or deny severance pay if an employee is eligible for, or receives, retiree health benefits?

The ADEA prohibits an employer from reducing or eliminating severance pay solely because the employee is eligible for retiree health benefits or will receive retiree health benefits. However, the statute contains a limited exception: if severance pay is payable as a result of a contingent event that is not related to the employee's age (e.g., a plant closing or layoff), the severance pay can be reduced by the value of retiree health benefits under certain limited circumstances. These circumstances include:

1. The employee's eligibility for an immediate pension;
2. If the employee receives actuarially reduced pension benefits, the value of retiree health benefits that may be subtracted from severance pay must be reduced by the same percentage as the percentage reduction in pension benefits; and
3. The retiree health benefits must have a certain minimum value in order to be subtracted from severance pay.

[ADEA § 4(1)(2); 29 U.S.C.A. § 623(1)(2)]

Minimum required retiree health benefits. For retiree health benefits to be a permitted reduction of severance pay payable as a result of a contingent event unrelated to the employee's age, one of the following conditions must apply:

1. Retiree health benefits for retirees under age 65 must be at least "comparable" to Medicare benefits under Title XVIII of the Social Security Act; or
2. Retiree health benefits for retirees age 65 and above must be "comparable" to 25 percent of Medicare benefits under Title XVIII of the Social Security Act.

The ADEA directs that if the employer's obligation to provide retiree health benefits is of limited duration, the value of each individual's benefit is to be calculated at a rate of $3,000 per year for benefit years before age 65 and $750 per year for benefit years beginning at age 65 and above. However, if the employer's obligation to provide retiree health benefits is of unlimited duration, the value for each individual is to be calculated at a rate of $48,000 for individuals below age 65 and $24,000 for individuals age 65 and above. The age of the individual used for this purpose is his or her age on the date of the contingent event. The above dollar amounts are indexed based on the dollar value of the medical component of the DOL's urban consumer price index. If the retiree health benefits are contributory, the above limits will be reduced by the percentage that the individual is required to pay. [ADEA § 4(1)(2); 29 U.S.C.A. § 623(1)(2)]

Future liability of employer. If the employer has reduced severance pay that is payable due to a contingent event unrelated to age by the permitted value of retiree health benefits, the employer will be subject to an action for specific performance by any "aggrieved individual" if it subsequently fails to fulfill its obligation to provide retiree health benefits. [ADEA § 4(1)(2); 29 U.S.C.A. § 623(1)(2)]

Q 15:27   Can an employer subject to the ADEA require an individual to sign a waiver as a condition of receiving severance benefits?

Yes, it can. However, the ADEA provides that a waiver will not be considered to be "knowing and voluntary" unless the following requirements are met:

1. The waiver is part of an agreement between the individual and the employer that is written in a manner calculated to be understood by the individual or by the average individual eligible to participate;

2. The waiver specifically refers to rights or claims arising under the ADEA;

3. The individual does not waive rights or claims that may arise after the date the waiver is executed;

4. The individual waives rights or claims only in exchange for money or other consideration in addition to anything of value to which the individual already is entitled;

5. The individual is advised in writing to consult with an attorney prior to executing the agreement;

6. The individual is given a period of:

    a. At least 21 days to consider the agreement or

    b. At least 45 days to consider the agreement in the case of an exit incentive or other employment termination program offered to a group or class of employees;

7. The agreement provides that for a period of at least seven days after the date it is executed, the individual may revoke it, and the agreement will not become effective or enforceable until the seven-day period has expired; and

8. If the waiver is requested in connection with an exit incentive or other employment termination program offered to a group or class of employees, the employer must satisfy certain additional statutory disclosure requirements. (See chapter 17.)

[ADEA § 7(f)(1); 29 U.S.C. § 626(f)(1); EEOC Prop. Reg. § 1625.22]

Q 15:28   How must the ADEA waiver be worded?

EEOC rules impose minimum requirements for a waiver of all ADEA rights and claims to be knowing and voluntary, including the following requirements specifically dealing with the wording of the waiver:

1. The entire waiver agreement must be in writing.

2. The waiver agreement must be drafted in plain language geared to the level of understanding of (a) the particular individual who is party to the agreement or (b) the individuals eligible to participate. Employers must take into account such factors as the level of comprehension and

education of typical participants, which usually will require limiting or eliminating technical jargon and long, complex sentences.

Note that a different standard applies to exit incentive and other employment termination programs offered to a group or class of employees, which must be written in a manner calculated to be understood by the average participant.

3. The waiver agreement cannot have the effect of misleading, misinforming, or failing to inform participants and affected individuals. Any advantages or disadvantages described are required to be presented without either exaggerating the benefits or minimizing the limitations.

4. The waiver agreement must refer to the ADEA by name in connection with the waiver of rights and claims.

5. The individual must be advised in writing to consult an attorney in connection with the waiver.

[29 C.F.R. § 1625.22(b)] The waiver of rights and claims under the ADEA that is given by the employee in return for severance benefits will not be treated as knowing and voluntary if it purports to waive any rights to claims that arise following the execution of the waiver; however, the EEOC's final rule provides that the ADEA does not bar the enforcement of agreements to perform future employment-related actions such as the employee's agreement to retire or otherwise terminate employment at a future date. [29 C.F.R. § 1625.22(c)]

Q 15:29   Must an employee receive something of value in return for signing an ADEA waiver?

Yes. A waiver of ADEA rights and claims will not be treated as knowing and voluntary unless it is given in return for something of value in addition to that to which the individual is already entitled in the absence of a waiver. Also, if a benefit or other thing of value was eliminated in violation of law or of an express or implied contract, then subsequently offering that benefit or thing in return for the ADEA waiver will not be treated as an offer of the required consideration (that is, the required thing of value in addition to the item to which the individual was already entitled).

Thus, for example, if the individual is already entitled to severance pay under the employer's severance pay plan, then the employer cannot require the employee to sign a waiver of ADEA rights and claims in order to receive benefits under the plan; however, if the employer implements a new plan that did not exist previously, or adds an enhanced benefit option, a waiver could be required as a condition of receiving benefits under the new plan or enhanced option. An example of an enhanced option would be if the plan provides for a basic benefit of one week's pay for each year of service, and the employer amends the plan to provide an alternative benefit of two weeks' pay for each year of service if the employee executes an ADEA waiver. Employees who did not sign the waiver under the plan would receive the plan's basic benefit only.

Elimination in violation of law or contract. Whether the benefit or thing of value has been eliminated in violation of law or contract will depend on the facts and circumstances of the particular case.

The U.S. Supreme Court considered the case of an employer that increased pension benefits for employees who elected an early retirement plan and executed a waiver of all employment-related claims against the employer. The Court held that conditioning the increased pension benefits on the execution of the waiver did not constitute a prohibited use of pension plan assets for the benefit of the employer; therefore, the waivers were valid. [Lockheed Corp. v. Spink, 517 U.S. 882 (1996)]

No requirement to favor the protected age group. The final EEOC rule clarifies that the employer is not required to offer more to employees in the ADEA's protected age group (that is, age 40 and over) than to younger employees in return for a waiver of ADEA rights and claims. [29 C.F.R. § 1623.22(d)]

Q 15:30   Is the employer required to give a minimum period to consider the waiver agreement or to revoke it after signing it?

Yes. For a waiver of ADEA rights and claims to be knowing and voluntary, the individual must be given a period of at least 21 days to consider the agreement. If the individual is being asked to sign the waiver in connection with a voluntary or involuntary exit incentive or other voluntary or involuntary employment termination program offered to a group or class of employees, then the individual must be given at least a 45-day period to consider the agreement. Once the individual signs the waiver, he or she must be given a seven-day period during which he or she may revoke the waiver.

Counting days for the 21-day and 45-day periods. The date of the employer's final offer starts the running of the 21-day or 45-day period. If material changes to the final offer are made, the 21-day or 45-day period starts running again unless the parties agree otherwise. Changes that are not material do not restart the period. The employee does not have to wait until the end of this consideration period and can sign before the end of the period as long as the employee's decision to accept that shorter period to consider the agreement is knowing and voluntary and is not induced by the employer through fraud, misrepresentation, or threats to withdraw or alter the offer prior to the expiration of the 21-day or 45-day time period, or by providing different terms to employees who sign the release prior to the end of that period.

The seven-day revocation period. Once the employee has signed the waiver of ADEA rights and claims, he or she has a statutory period of seven days in which to change his or her mind and revoke the waiver. The seven-day period starts running even if the employee signs the waiver before the 21-day or 45-day period has expired and he or she could have taken longer to consider the matter. The parties cannot shorten the seven-day revocation period, by agreement or otherwise. The full seven-day period must be given. [29 C.F.R. § 1625.22(e)]

Q 15:31   To require an ADEA waiver of rights and claims, what disclosure must an employer make in connection with an exit incentive or other employment termination program offered to a group or class of employees?

If the employer requests that the employee waive any right or claim under the ADEA in connection with offering an exit incentive or other employment termination program to a group or class of employees, the employer must, as an additional condition of obtaining a knowing and voluntary waiver from the employee, also supply the additional information described below to the eligible employees in the class, unit, group, job classification, or organizational unit asked to sign the waiver, at the beginning of the 45-day election period described in Q 15:30.

Purpose of disclosure requirement. The required disclosure is to provide an employee with enough information regarding the program to allow him or her to make an informed choice as to whether to sign a waiver agreement.

Programs to which this disclosure obligation applies. This required disclosure applies to ADEA waivers requested in connection with two types of group termination programs: exit incentive programs and other termination programs. The EEOC's final rule defines an exit incentive program as a voluntary program under which a thing of value, referred to as additional consideration, is offered to a group or class of employees in addition to anything of value to which they are already entitled in exchange for their decision voluntarily to resign and sign a waiver. Other termination programs generally are the same thing except that the group or class of employees is involuntarily terminated. Whether a program exists will be based on the facts and circumstances of each case. A program is considered to exist when the employer offers additional consideration in return for the signing of a waiver pursuant to an exit incentive or other employment termination program (for example, a reduction in force) offered to two or more employees. An involuntary termination program typically will offer a standardized formula or package of benefits, while a voluntary termination program offers a standardized formula or package of benefits designed to induce employees to sever their employment voluntarily. The terms of a program generally are not subject to negotiation between the parties. The program is not required to be an ERISA plan in order to qualify as a program for purposes of this required ADEA disclosure.

Required information. If a waiver is requested in connection with an exit incentive or other employment termination program offered to a group or class of employees, the waiver is not considered to be knowing and voluntary unless the employer informs the individual in writing, in a manner calculated to be understood by the average individual eligible to participate, as to:

1. Any class, unit, or group of individuals covered by the program, any eligibility factors for the program, and any time limits applicable to the program; and

2. The job titles and ages of all individuals eligible or selected for the program, and the ages of all individuals in the same job classification or organizational unit who are not eligible or selected for the program.

[ADEA § 7(f)(1)(H); 29 U.S.C. § 626(f)(1)(H)] The presentation of this information must conform to certain standards described below, and the information is required to be provided to each individual in a "decisional unit."

Q 15:32   May an employer deny severance pay due to the employee's bad acts?

The answer depends on whether the plan terms permit denial of severance pay in a particular circumstance. The Court of Appeals for the Seventh Circuit upheld the denial of severance benefits to an employee who had repeatedly violated the employer's sexual harassment policy, based on a plan provision permitting denial of severance benefits to individuals who are discharged for gross misconduct. The employee sued, claiming that the decision to deny him benefits was arbitrary and capricious because his conduct was not severe enough to constitute hostile-environment sexual harassment under Title VII of the Civil Rights Act. The Court of Appeals agreed, but stated that the employer was free to take a more stringent stance against sexual harassment, and the real question was whether the employee had notice of the company's policy. The Court of Appeals concluded that he did have notice, because he had been reprimanded previously and forced to attend company training seminars on sexual harassment awareness. [Chalmers v. Quaker Oats Co., 61 F.3d 1340 (7th Cir. 1995); *see also* Moos v. Square D Co., 72 F.2d 39 (6th Cir. 1995) (employer held justified in denying pension benefits to employee with 21 years of service who had falsified company records to show that he had a college degree, a requirement for his position, under a plan provision permitting benefit denial if the employee is discharged for illegal or gross misconduct that is materially and demonstrably injurious to the company, because the plan administrator had the authority under the plan to interpret this provision)]

Q 15:33   Must an employer provide severance pay if the former employee becomes employed by a successor employer?

The answer depends on the terms of the plan. If the severance plan clearly provides that no severance benefits are payable if the former employee goes to work for a successor employer, the plan provisions generally will be given effect. However, if the plan is silent or ambiguous as to whether severance benefits are payable when an employee goes to work for a successor employer, severance benefits may have to be paid. [Barnett v. Petro-Tex Chem. Corp., 893 F.2d 800 (5th Cir. 1990); Flick v. Borg-Warner Corp., 892 F.2d 285 (3d Cir. 1989)] Case law on this subject continues to proliferate as employees spot a potential windfall under allegedly ambiguous severance pay plan provisions.

In one case, the U.S. Court of Appeals for the First Circuit examined a written severance pay plan that provided benefits in the event of termination due to "lack of work." The employer in question had orally advised several employees that they would not receive severance pay if they continued in employment with an acquiring employer. The transferred employees, who did not miss a day of work, sued for severance pay under the former employer's plan and won. The appellate court refused to recognize as valid an attempted oral modification to the former employer's severance pay plan and construed the written plan liberally in favor of the employees. [Bellino v. Schlumberger Techs., Inc., 944 F.2d 26 (1st Cir. 1991)]

The U.S. Court of Appeals for the Eleventh Circuit reached a similar conclusion when it examined a plan that granted severance pay in the event a full-time employee with a minimum of six months' service is discharged "for reasons other than cause." The Eleventh Circuit determined that this language triggered an entitlement to severance benefits regardless of whether the employees continued in employment with the purchasing employer. [Bedinghaus v. Modern Graphic Arts, 15 F.3d 1027 (11th Cir. 1994)]

Similarly, a federal district court in Michigan held that employees who were immediately rehired at the same or similar jobs by the purchasing employer could nonetheless proceed with a lawsuit under the selling employer's severance pay plan because it was ambiguous as applied to these facts, and the selling employer's communications to those employees on other employee benefit matters had expressly referred to their "termination of employment." [Williams v. Manley Bros. of Ind., Inc., 1993 U.S. Dist. LEXIS 13225 (W.D. Mich. Aug. 25, 1993)]

In contrast, the U.S. Court of Appeals for the Eighth Circuit has interpreted a severance pay plan providing benefits to eligible employees who were laid off due to a reduction in force for lack of work as not applying to a sale of a subsidiary where the subsidiary continued to exist and the employees continued in employment with the purchasing employer without interruption under substantially identical terms and conditions. The appellate court reasoned that a change in the subsidiary's corporate ownership did not create a layoff or reduction in force or lack of work within the meaning of the plan. [Schroeder v. Phillips Petroleum Co., 17 F.3d 1147 (8th Cir. 1994)]

Last-minute amendment or termination of severance pay plan. The U.S. Court of Appeals for the Second Circuit upheld an employer's right to amend an ERISA severance plan to deny severance benefits to employees who would retain their positions in a division that was to be sold as a going concern. The appellate court expressly noted that nothing in ERISA creates a continuing obligation on the part of the employer to provide severance benefits and that, as welfare benefits, they do not become vested. Accordingly, the employer has the right to amend or terminate a severance pay plan at any time. [Reichelt v. Emhart Corp., 921 F.2d 425 (2d Cir. 1990)]

In an unpublished opinion, the Sixth Circuit reached a similar result in upholding an employer's denial of severance pay benefits under a newly adopted plan that specifically excluded employees rehired by the purchaser. The newly adopted plan replaced a prior severance pay plan that did not contain such an exclusion. The facts in that case were significant because the replacement plan was adopted after the employees were notified that their employment would be terminated but before the effective date of their employment termination. The employer claimed that the new plan was in effect on their last day of work and denied their claims for severance pay. The Sixth Circuit agreed, noting that ERISA does not require vesting of welfare benefits and the employer had not otherwise committed to vesting the severance benefits. [Correll v. Teledyne Indus., 1993 U.S. App. LEXIS 28131 (6th Cir. Oct. 27, 1993)]

The U.S. Court of Appeals for the Seventh Circuit upheld the right of an employer to terminate a severance benefits plan only days before selling one of its plants. The court held that severance benefits are welfare benefits that can be terminated at any time. The employees' rights could not have vested prior to the sale. At that point, no severance pay plan existed. [O'Connell v. Continental Can Co., Pens. Plan Guide ¶ 23, 8905 (CCH) (7th Cir. 1994)] On the other hand, the Fourth Circuit Court of Appeals found that the employees' rights to severance benefits had vested, and the employer was barred from reducing the severance pay, because the employer had failed to formally amend the severance pay plan prior to closing the facility where the employee worked. While a draft amendment had been prepared, the plan contained no formal plan amendment procedures, and the president of the employer had not signed an amendment prior to the closing of the facility. [Biggers v. Wittek Indus., Inc., 4 F.3d 291 (4th Cir. 1993)]

The Court of Appeals for the Third Circuit has held that a severance pay plan can be terminated prior to a plant shutdown but that the validity of the acts taken to allegedly terminate the plan will depend on whether the procedure in the plan for terminating it has been followed. [Ackerman v. Warnaco, Inc., 55 F.3d 117 (3d Cir. 1995)]

Q 15:34 Is an employee entitled to severance pay if he or she is offered a job with a successor employer but turns it down?

As in the case of an employee who obtains a job with a successor employer (see Q 15:33), the obligation to pay severance to an employee who turns down a job with a successor employer depends on the terms of the plan.

The Eleventh Circuit Court of Appeals held that a plan improperly denied benefits to an employee who turned down a job with a successor employer. The employee, Thomas Yochum, had worked at Barnett Bank for 27 years when the bank was sold to NationsBank. NationsBank offered Yochum the position of regional president of operations. The job would have given Yochum increased responsibilities. However, NationsBank guaranteed Yochum's salary for only one year and did not offer stock options. Yochum turned down the job and took a position with another bank.

Yochum requested the severance due him under the Barnett Bank severance pay plan. However, the bank's employee benefits committee denied the request on the grounds that he had rejected an offer of comparable employment. Under the terms of the plan, an employee was not entitled to severance pay if he or she rejected an offer of comparable employment, which was defined as "equal compensation and benefits."

The Eleventh Circuit concluded that the plan improperly denied Yochum's benefits because the job offer he rejected did not constitute comparable employment under the terms of the plan. The compensation and benefits were not equivalent to Yochum's at Barnett Bank because his salary and benefits package would have decreased after one year. Moreover, the new job did not offer stock options. [Yochum v. Barnett Banks Inc., 234 F.3d 541 (11th Cir. 2000)]

Q 15:35   Is an employee who resigns entitled to severance benefits?

It depends. The obligation to pay benefits in such a case is determined by the precise terms of the employer's plan. Severance pay plans are typically drafted to provide severance benefits only when an employee's employment is terminated involuntarily or a specified change in the terms and conditions of employment triggers an employee's resignation.

> **Example.** Norma J. Curby was employed as vice president and general manager of a division of Solutia, Inc. Solutia entered into a joint venture agreement with another company to combine Curby's division with a division of the other company. The joint venture resulted in the elimination of Curby's position with Solutia, and Curby accepted the position of vice president of the joint venture. Although the new position came with a substantial raise, Curby viewed it as a demotion. Therefore, she submitted a "notice of termination" to Solutia, believing she had a right to severance benefits because she had "good reason" for terminating her employment as was required under a severance agreement with the company. The company responded that Curby was not entitled to severance benefits under the agreement because benefits were triggered only when there was a "change in control" of the company. The Eighth Circuit agreed with Solutia that Curby was not entitled to severance benefits. The court said that the agreement clearly specified that benefits were payable only if employment was terminated within a specified period following a change in control. Moreover, the agreement specifically provided that if employment was terminated either by the employee or the employer before a change of control, the employee would have no further rights under the agreement. Thus, the court concluded that when Curby chose to terminate her employment, she had no reasonable basis for believing she had a right to severance benefit under the agreement. [Curby v. Solutia, Inc., 351 F.3d 868 (8th Cir. 2003)]

Q 15:36   Are employees entitled to severance pay when they are never actually unemployed?

The U.S. Court of Appeals for the Seventh Circuit has decided that employees who were never unemployed as a result of the sale of the employer's assets were entitled to severance benefits under the plan's language.

According to the decision, even though the employees were immediately hired by the new owner, the employees were terminated by their former employer on the day of the asset sale. The court noted that the former employer had treated the employees as being terminated for every purpose other than the determination of eligibility for severance benefits. [Anstett v. Eagle-Picher Indus., 203 F.3d 501 (7th Cir. 2000)]

> **Practice Pointer.** In view of the above decisions, and numerous other decisions concerning whether an acquired employer is obligated to pay severance benefits to employees who continue to work for a successor employer, an employer wishing to deny severance payments in such situations should adopt a formal plan setting out precisely what rules govern payment or nonpayment of severance benefits, particularly in the case of acquisitions or divestitures.

Q 15:37 Will an acquiring employer be required to give severance benefits based on years of service with a prior employer?

At least one court, the U.S. Court of Appeals for the Eighth Circuit, has held that an employer's calculation of severance pay benefits must credit years of service with a prior employer, where the acquiring employer's severance pay plan did not define "service." [Jacobs v. Pickands Mather & Co., 933 F.2d 652 (8th Cir. 1991)]

> **Practice Pointer.** In addition to having a written severance pay plan, the employer will want to consider how its benefit formula will work under various scenarios and then add appropriate exclusions and clarifications. In addition, the prior-service question could arise in another context. It is important for the acquiring employer to examine, before signing the acquisition agreement, its provisions relating to employee benefit plans to determine whether the acquiring employer will be bound to offer the same or comparable benefits to the acquired employees.

Q 15:38 Does an employer have an ERISA fiduciary duty to disclose that it is considering adopting a severance plan?

The answer depends on how far the planning process has proceeded and the nature of the communications between the employer and its employees.

No plan under consideration. If an employer states that it has no plans to offer termination incentives but later does so, it is not liable to employees who terminated their employment in reliance on the employer's prior statements if, at the time the statements were made, the employer had not begun to give serious consideration to the notion of implementing such a program. [Wilson v. Southwestern Bell Tel. Co., 55 F.3d 399 (8th Cir. 1995)] In *Wilson*, the employer's descriptive materials regarding its 1990 severance incentive plan specifically included a statement that the employer did not intend to make any similar, future severance incentive offerings. In 1991, it announced a pension incentive plan for managers. The Eighth Circuit found that the employer's representations were not false at the time they were made.

Plan under consideration. A number of appellate courts have held that when an employer is seriously considering a change in a benefits plan, it has a duty to answer employee inquiries about the proposed changes. However, the courts are generally in agreement that an employer has no duty to inform an employee about proposed changes unless the employee asks.

In a case in which an early retirement plan was already under consideration, the Second Circuit denied an executive's claim that the employer breached its ERISA fiduciary duty in not disclosing that to him at the time he signed his severance agreement. At the time he was negotiating his retirement, the executive never inquired into the possibility that the company would be implementing any new benefit programs. The court determined that permitting an employer to keep secret its preadoption deliberations and discussions in no way frustrates the purposes of ERISA:

> Until a plan is adopted, there is no plan, simply the possibility of one. Insisting on voluntary disclosure during the formulation of a plan and prior to its adoption would, we think, increase the likelihood of confusion on the part of beneficiaries and, at the same time, unduly burden management, which would be faced with continuing uncertainty as to what to disclose and when to disclose it. Moreover, any requirement of pre-adoption disclosure could impair the achievement of legitimate business goals. One commentator has posited the situation where a business seeking to reduce its workforce contemplates a future improvement of an initial early retirement or severance plan if necessary reductions do not occur through retirements or resignations. If fiduciaries were required to disclose such a business strategy, it would necessarily fail. Employees simply would not leave if they were informed that improved benefits were insufficient.

[Pocchia v. Nynex Corp., 81 F.3d 275 (2d Cir. 1996)]

In a case in which an employee, at the time he was contemplating retirement, specifically inquired about rumors that an early retirement incentive plan might be adopted and was told there were no such plans, when in fact the company had already decided to offer such a plan in the future, the First Circuit held that the retiree had standing to sue under ERISA because he would have been a participant in the early retirement incentive plan but for the employer's misrepresentation. [Vartanian v. Monsanto Co., 131 F.3d 264 (1st Cir. 1997)]

In the *Vartanian* case, the First Circuit adopted the "serious consideration" test adopted by the Third Circuit in *Fischer v. Philadelphia Electric Co.* [96 F.3d 1533 (3d Cir. 1996), *cert. denied,* 520 U.S. 1116 (1997) (referred to as *Fischer II*)] The Third Circuit held that the Philadelphia Electric Company had not made unlawful misrepresentations in violation of ERISA when it denied or failed to disclose that it was discussing the possibility of adopting an early retirement incentive plan because the plan was not yet under the "serious consideration" that would trigger a disclosure duty under ERISA. For a disclosure duty to be present, the Third Circuit held, three factors have to be present:

1. A specific proposal for a change in plan benefits has to exist;
2. The proposal is being discussed for purposes of implementation; and
3. The discussion is by senior management with the authority to implement the change.

Subsequently, the Tenth Circuit applied the *Fischer II* three-part "serious consideration" test to find that the Sun Company had not breached its fiduciary duty to an employee when it knowingly failed to disclose to him, when he asked about the availability of an enhanced severance package as he was deciding to retire, that such a package was being discussed in connection with a planned downsizing. The employee subsequently retired and, upon hearing about the enhanced program that would have given him significantly better termination benefits had he not retired at that point, requested that he get those additional benefits and was denied. The company's action was upheld because at the time of the employee's request it was engaged only in preliminary research and discussion about a possible program. The court held that this business deliberation fell within the employer's nonfiduciary "settlor" function. [Hockett v. Sun Co. (R&M), 109 F.3d 1515 (10th Cir. 1997)]

The court of appeals in the *Sun* case described the details of each of the three *Fischer II* requirements. Quoting from that case, it held that although the specific proposal need not be in final form, it must be sufficiently concrete to support consideration by senior management for the purpose of implementation. The second requirement assures that analysis of benefit alternatives or commissioning a comparative study without seriously considering implementing a change in benefits will not trigger a disclosure requirement, and interactions among upper levels of management, company personnel, and outside consultants generally are preliminary stages of company deliberations. The consideration becomes serious when the discussion turns to the practicalities of implementation. The third element requires courts to focus on the proper actors within the corporate hierarchy—the senior management with responsibility over company benefits who ultimately will make recommendations to the board of directors. The court of appeals then concluded that the Sun Company did not seriously consider the program until a meeting that occurred a month after the employee had retired. The court noted that cost-analysis or actuarial work did not occur until after the employee had retired, and that it is unlikely that any specific proposal would be "sufficiently concrete" without some such information.

In another case, the Tenth Circuit held that a company had no duty to inform a retiring employee of an enhanced severance package that was not yet under serious consideration. Moreover, the court said, the company was well within its rights in denying the employee's request to rescind his retirement and return to work so that he could receive the enhanced benefits, which were announced shortly after he left the company. The court said the plan administrator did not have a duty to inform the employee that his retirement decision was irrevocable. Although an administrator may have a fiduciary duty to inform a participant about the irrevocability of elections under the plan, there is no support for the proposition that ERISA imposes a duty on plan administrators to notify plan participants of the irrevocability of employment decisions. Moreover, the decision disallowing the employee's return to work was made by the company in its capacity as an employer. As such, it was a personnel decision that was not subject to any fiduciary duty under ERISA. [Winkel v. Kennecott Holding Corp., 2001 U.S. App. LEXIS 402 (10th Cir. Jan. 10, 2001)]

The Sixth Circuit also applied the *Fischer II* criteria to find that serious consideration of a $25,000 bonus for early retirees had not started by the time a group of retirees retired. [Muse v. IBM, 102 Daily Lab. Rep. (BNA) E-14 (6th Cir. May 28, 1997)]

The *Fischer II* criteria were not applied in *Ballone v. Eastman Kodak Co.* [109 F.3d 117 (2d Cir. 1997)] because the employees claimed in that case that they were affirmatively lied to (rather than that the employer just played possum).

In one case, a three-judge panel of the Ninth Circuit Court of Appeals went a step further and held that an employer has an affirmative duty to disclose changes that are under serious consideration to affected employees—even if employees don't ask any questions. However, the full Court of Appeals for the Ninth Circuit overturned that decision on reconsideration. According to the full court, an employer has a duty to provide complete and truthful information when an employee asks about potential plan changes. However, the employer does not have an affirmative duty to volunteer information in the absence of an employee inquiry. [Bins v. Exxon Co. USA, 189 F.3d 929 (9th Cir. 1999), *rev'd en banc*, 220 F.3d 1042 (9th Cir. 2000)]

Q 15:39   Does an employer have an ERISA fiduciary duty not to terminate a severance pay plan?

No. The U.S. Court of Appeals for the Ninth Circuit has held that an employer is free, under ERISA, to unilaterally amend or eliminate severance benefits without regard to the interests of employees. An employer does not owe any ERISA fiduciary duty to employees when it is amending or terminating a severance plan. ERISA also preempts state law claims of breach of implied-in-fact employment or of breach of the covenant of good faith and fair dealing. [Joanou v. Coca-Cola Co., 26 F.3d 96 (9th Cir. 1994)]

Employees covered by a collective bargaining agreement were held not to be entitled to severance pay benefits upon a plant closing where the severance pay benefits had been bargained away as part of a plant-closing agreement between the employer and the union. Even though the agreement had been negotiated and ratified after the plant had closed, the court pointed out that severance pay benefits ordinarily do not vest. [Adcox v. Teledyne, Indus., Inc., 21 F.3d 1381 (6th Cir. 1994)]

Practice Pointer. Although ERISA does not restrict the employer's ability to freely amend or terminate a severance pay plan, other laws (such as the ADEA) may affect the manner in which it is done. In addition, a collective bargaining agreement or other written instrument may limit the employer's prerogatives in this area. Note also that even though the decision to amend or terminate a severance pay plan may be an employer prerogative as opposed to a plan administration decision to which ERISA fiduciary responsibility would apply, a risk exists that the manner in which the amendment or termination is effectuated could implicate ERISA fiduciary responsibility on the theory that the actual carrying out of the employer's business decision is an item of plan administration. Also, the plan cannot simply be rescinded; the plan's procedure for termination must be followed. [Ackerman v. Warnaco, Inc., 55 F.3d 117 (3d Cir. 1995)]

Q 15:40   Does the employer have a fiduciary duty not to misrepresent the likely future of severance plan benefits?

Yes. Where an ERISA plan already exists, the U.S. Supreme Court has held that an employer that sponsors and administers an ERISA benefits plan acts in a fiduciary capacity if it misrepresents the likely future of the plan or plan benefits. A fiduciary that makes disclosures about an existing plan must be truthful and violates ERISA's duty to act solely in the interest of participants and beneficiaries when it intentionally misrepresents plan information. [Varity Corp. v. Howe, 516 U.S. 489 (1996)]

On the other hand, a case from the Fifth Circuit makes it clear that a fiduciary's representations need be truthful only at the time they are made. The employer in this case had decided to reduce its workforce by offering a voluntary separation pay plan. In the past, the employer had found that employees were reluctant to accept a severance offer because they assumed there might be another, more generous plan in the offing. Therefore, the company decided to adopt a plan that was as generous as possible in order to accomplish the workforce reduction without resorting to involuntary layoffs. The SPD for the severance pay plan specifically stated: "The company is offering this plan in an effort to reduce its expenses due to business conditions. At this time, the company's management has not decided whether there will be any additional voluntary separation plans. However, management decided that if there are any additional plans, the benefits would not be as good as those contained in this plan." However, the company's "best offer" apparently was not. A few years later, the company offered another voluntary separation plan that had better benefits. A number of workers who had taken advantage of the original plan sued the company for breaching its fiduciary duty under ERISA. Specifically, the workers claimed that the company had misled them by representing the original plan as its "best offer," and they demanded benefits under the more generous plan.

The Fifth Circuit acknowledged that providing information to beneficiaries about likely future benefits is a fiduciary act under ERISA. And when an employer or plan administrator speaks about a plan in a fiduciary capacity, it must speak truthfully. The court concluded that the statements in the SPD were truthful—when they were made. Moreover, the company specifically reserved the right to amend or terminate the severance plan at any time for any purpose. Therefore, the employees were not entitled to the enhanced benefits. [McCall v. Burlington Northern/Santa Fe Co., 237 F.3d 506 (5th Cir. 2000)]

Where the employee does not make any inquiries, courts have generally held there is no affirmative duty to disclose benefit changes in advance, even those that have reached the stage of serious consideration. (See Q 15:38.)

Q 15:41   Must an employer provide severance pay to all employees?

No. There is no nondiscrimination requirement applicable to severance pay plans. A federal appeals court held that an employer did not violate ERISA by offering enhanced early retirement benefits to a select group of upper management employees. The benefits were provided in addition to qualified retirement plan benefits and were not part of the qualified plan. The court concluded that "ERISA simply does not prohibit an employer from offering some employees and not others access to separate, additional plans with enhanced benefits." [Piner v. E.I. DuPont de Nemours & Co., 2000 U.S. App. LEXIS 29016 (4th Cir. Nov. 14, 2000)]

Q 15:42   What if state law mandates that employers provide severance pay?

It appears that state laws purporting to require employers to establish and maintain ongoing severance pay plans are preempted by ERISA. [Brunner v. Sun Refining & Marketing Co., 1989 U.S. Dist. LEXIS 5726 (N.D. Ill. May 10, 1989)] However, a one-shot severance pay requirement is not preempted. [Fort Halifax Packing Co. v. Coyne, 482 U.S. 1 (1987)]

Q 15:43   Is severance pay taxable income to the recipient?

Yes. Severance pay is taxable and is subject to wage withholding. [I.R.C. §§ 61, 3401; Treas. Reg. § 3401(a)-1(b)(4)] Courts in the past have also assumed that severance pay is considered "wages" for FICA and FUTA taxes. [I.R.C. §§ 3121(a), 3306(b)] However, a decision by the Court of Federal Claims casts some doubt on this matter.

In the Court of Federal Claims decision, the court ruled that "supplemental unemployment compensation" does not constitute wages for FICA tax purposes (supplemental unemployment compensation is subject to income tax withholding. [*See* I.R.C. § 3402(o).] The court then applied that FICA exemptions to payments made (1) to employees involuntarily laid off as a result of a reduction in force, (2) to employees whose hours were involuntarily reduced, and (3) to employees who voluntarily accepted buyout offers. The court held that the payments made to the latter two groups did not constitute supplemental unemployment compensation and were, thus, subject to FICA. However, the payments made to employees involuntarily laid off did qualify as supplemental unemployment compensation and were exempt from FICA. [CSX Corp. v. United States, 52 Fed. Cl. 208 (2002)] The IRS did not appeal the decision.

On the other hand, the Court of Federal Claims ruled another employer's severance payments could not be treated as nonqualified deferred compensation that was partly exempt from employment taxes under special timing rules. [*See* I.R.C. § 3121(v)(2).] [Kraft Foods N. Am. Inc. v. United States, 58 Fed. Cl. 507 (2003)] Instead, the court ruled, the severance payments were subject to employment taxes in the years they were made to employees.

Other cases and rulings on this area have typically involved the signing of a release in connection with the severance pay. The issue was whether the payments were made as settlements for possible lawsuits or were wage-type payments (which, again, until the Court of Federal Claims decision, were assumed to be FICA taxable).

For example, the IRS ruled that where an employee had accepted an early retirement severance pay package that included an ADEA waiver, the payments were not excludable from income under Section 104(a)(2) of the Internal Revenue Code as amounts received on account of personal injuries because there was no age discrimination claim or lawsuit that had been filed against the employer. [Priv. Ltr. Rul. 9333007 (May 3, 1993)]

Also, a federal appeals court has held that the extra amount in a lump-sum severance payment received by an employee in return for a waiver of any future legal claims against the employer was not excludable from income as a settlement in lieu of a claim for personal injury damages. [Taggi v. United States, 35 F.3d 93 (2d Cir. 1994)]

In addition, the lump-sum severance pay received by an insurance company employee as part of a settlement agreement upon termination is not excludable from gross income as compensation for personal injury but is taxable as severance pay, the U.S. Court of Appeals for the Seventh Circuit ruled. [Pipitone v. United States, 180 F.3d 859 (7th Cir. 1999)] The employee in the case was age 49 and had worked in the claims department of an insurance company for 14 years. As part of his termination, he entered into a settlement agreement with the company under which the firm agreed to pay him 52 weeks' salary and to provide outplacement services and continued coverage under the company's health plan. The employee agreed not to pursue any other legal action against the company. In 1996, the employee amended the tax return he filed the previous year reporting the severance pay as income. In his amended return, he claimed that the amount was excludable under Code Section 104(a)(2) because it constituted a payment made in consideration for his release of any claims he might have against the company for age discrimination or other potential tort claims.

The IRS denied the employee's refund claim, ruling that "back pay and liquidated damages recovered through the settlement of a claim under the Age Discrimination in Employment Act are not excludable from gross income." The appeals court agreed and held that the lump sum paid to the employee does not fall within the exclusions from income set out in Code Section 104(a)(2), which are (1) the existence of a claim based upon tort or tort-type rights and (2) payment on account of personal injuries or sickness. In addition, the court said, the settlement agreement included provisions that the company intended the payment to be severance pay.

In another case, a lump-sum payment to a chairman under a severance agreement in exchange for his relinquishment of all future salary and bonus entitlements in light of an impending sale of the company constitutes wages subject to FICA, says the U.S. District Court for the Southern District of New York. [Greenwald v. United States, No. 98 Civ. 3439, 2000 U.S. Dist. LEXIS 102 (S.D.N.Y. Jan. 10, 2000)] Greenwald wanted a refund of FICA taxes from money that was paid to him when his employment ended. The court said that the lump-sum payment to Greenwald constituted wages or remuneration for employment subject to FICA taxes and that he was not entitled to a refund.

In yet another case on this point, the U.S. District Court of the District of Connecticut has ruled that a severance payment that an employee received from his employer at the time of his layoff, upon signing a standard severance agreement, is subject to employment taxes. [McCorkill v. United States, 32 F. Supp. 2d 46 (D. Conn. 1999)] Again, the court looked at the language of the severance agreement that specifically stated that the severance payment was primarily provided to recognize the value of the employee's past work and to help with any financial loss that might result from losing his job. The court said the provision showed that the payment arose from and was based on the employee's employment relationship and such payment constitutes wages subject to withholding under FICA.

Note. The tax treatment of settlements and judgments in employment termination lawsuits is beyond the scope of this book.

Q 15:44   Are severance pay plans subject to the special rules for nonqualified deferred compensation?

Severance plans may or may not be subject to the special rules for nonqualified deferred compensation, depending on the way the employer's severance pay program is structured.

Nonqualified deferrals of compensation made after December 31, 2004, are subject to Code Section 409A. Section 409A expansively defines *deferred compensation* as any arrangement that gives a service provider a legally binding right during one year to compensation that will or might be paid in a later year, including employment-related agreements for severance.

Under Section 409A, amounts that are deferred under a nonqualified deferred compensation arrangement and that are not subject to a substantial risk of forfeiture must be currently included in the employee's income, unless the plan meets certain requirements. [I.R.C. § 409A(a)(1)(A)(i)]

To avoid immediate inclusion of deferrals, a nonqualified plan must satisfy the following conditions:

1. It must allow distributions no earlier than the date the employee separates from service, becomes disabled, or dies; at a time specified under the plan; or when there is a change in control event.

2. It must not allow acceleration of benefits, except as provided by regulations.

3. It must comply with certain rules limiting the elections available under the plan.

[I.R.C. § 409A(a)(2), (3) and (4)]

IRS regulations under Section 409A specifically provide that a severance pay plan that provides for deferred compensation is subject to the above rules, even though the right to the compensation is conditioned on separation from service. [Treas. Reg. § 1.409A-1(b)] Thus, as a general rule, a vested severance pay plan that provides for payment of deferred compensation must comply with the above requirements to avoid immediate inclusion of deferred amounts in an employee's gross income.

However, there are key exceptions in the regulations under Section 409A that will shield many common severance arrangements from the application of these rules.

Involuntary separations and window programs. The nonqualified deferred compensation rules do not apply to payments made following an employee's involuntary separation from service or separation under a window program. The following rules apply for purposes of this exception:

Payments are exempt from Section 409A only to the extent they do not exceed the lesser of (1) two times the employee's annual compensation for the calendar year preceding the year in which the separation occurs or (2) the maximum amount that may be taken into account as compensation under the qualified plan compensation limit in effect for the calendar year in which the termination occurs ($230,000 for 2008). If payments exceed the limit, only the excess is subject to Section 409A.

The plan requires all payments made by the end of the second taxable year following the year in which the separation occurs.

Involuntary separation. An involuntary separation from service means a separation from service due to the independent exercise of the unilateral authority of the employer to terminate the employee's services without the employee's consent when the employee is willing and able to continue to work. Characterization of the separation from service as voluntary or involuntary by the employer and employee is presumed to characterize properly the nature of the separation from service. However, the presumption may be rebutted. For example, if a separation from service is designated as voluntary, but the facts and circumstances indicate that the employee knew he or she would be terminated by the employer if he or she did not resign, the separation from service will be treated as involuntary.

In some cases, an employee's voluntary separation for "good reason" will be considered involuntary. A "good reason" generally involves actions taken by the employer that result in a material negative change in working conditions for the employee, such as the duties to be performed, the conditions under which duties are to be performed, or the compensation to be received.

Under a special safe harbor rule, a voluntary separation will be treated as involuntary if certain conditions are met. Those conditions include: (1) Severance will be payable only if the employee separates from service within two years following the initial existence of the good reason condition; and (2) the amount, time, and form of payment are identical to the amount, time, and form of payment to be received in the case of an involuntary separation.

For purposes of the safe harbor, the "good reason" conditions include:

- A material diminution in the employee's base compensation;
- A material diminution in the employee's authority, duties, or responsibilities;
- A material diminution in the authority, duties, or responsibilities of the employee's supervisor, including a requirement that an employee report to a corporate officer or employee instead of reporting directly to the board of directors of a corporation;
- A material diminution in the budget over which the employee has authority;
- A material geographic change in employee's work location; or
- Any other action or inaction that constitutes a material breach of the terms of an employment agreement.

To qualify for the safe harbor, the employee must be required to provide notice of a good reason condition within 90 days of its initial existence, and the employer must have at least 30 days to remedy the condition.

Window program. A window program is a severance pay plan that provides incentives to employees who voluntary separate from service during a limited period of no longer than 12 months. The regulations caution, however, that a plan will not be considered a window program if the employer repeatedly provides window programs under similar circumstance for consecutive limited periods of time.

Collectively bargained severance pay plans. A collectively bargained severance pay plan that provides for severance pay only in the case of an involuntary separation from service or under a window program is not subject to Section 409A.

A plan qualifies as a collectively bargained severance pay plan if:

- The plan is spelled out in an agreement that the Secretary of Labor determines to be a collective bargaining agreement.
- The severance pay provided by the collective bargaining agreement was the subject of arm's-length negotiations between employee representatives and one or more employers, and the collective bargaining agreement meets the requirements of Code Section 7701(a)(46).
- The circumstances surrounding the agreement evidence good-faith bargaining between adverse parties over the severance pay to be provided under the agreement.

Short-term deferral rule. Under a special short-term deferral rule, a severance pay plan will not be treated as providing for deferred compensation if payment is made during the 2½-month period after the pay is no longer subject to a substantial risk of forfeiture. The 2½-month period is the period ending on the later of (a) the 15th day of the third month following the end of the employee's first taxable year in which the right to the payment is no longer subject to a substantial risk of forfeiture or (b) the 15th day of the third month following the end of the employer's first taxable year in which the right to the payment is no longer subject to a substantial risk of forfeiture.

> **Practice Pointer.** Obviously, the short-term deferral rule will be of no help if an employee's severance pay is guaranteed—that is, the pay is not subject to a substantial risk of forfeiture. On the other hand, in certain situations where the right to severance is subject to a substantial risk of forfeiture, another exception may apply—for example, where an employee's right to severance is triggered only when and if the employee is fired, the exception for involuntary terminations will apply. However, unlike the exception for involuntary terminations, the short-term deferral rule has no dollar cap. Therefore, it may be advantageous to apply the short-term deferral rule in the case of a large payout to an employee.

Reimbursements and fringe benefits. An employee may receive more than severance pay when he or she separates from service. For example, the employer may reimburse moving costs or fees for outplacement services. In addition, the employer may continue to provide certain employee benefits for a period following the employee's separation from service. The regulations provide that reimbursements or in-kind benefits provided during a limited period following an employee's separation from service will not be treated as deferred compensations subject to the rules of Section 409A.

For example, cash reimbursements for reasonable expense for moving costs (including a loss on the sale of a home) or outplacement services will not be treated as deferred compensation provided they are incurred by the employee no later than the end of the second year following the year in which the separation from service occurs and reimbursement is made by the employer not later than the end of the third year following the separation from service.

If an employer provides in-kind benefits or pays a third party to provide in-kind benefits, the benefits must actually be provided by the end of the second year following the employee's separation from service.

A benefit that is excludable from income is not treated as deferred compensation for purposes of Section 409A. For example, an arrangement to provide health coverage that is excludable from income under Code Section 105 generally would not be treated as deferred compensation, regardless of how long the coverage is provided. On the other hand, taxable reimbursements of medical expenses are exempt from the definition of deferred compensation only if they are made during the period the employee would be eligible for COBRA health care continuation coverage (generally, 18 months following separation from service).

Limited payments. An employee may choose to treat a limited amount of payments that is not otherwise excluded under the above rules as not being deferred compensation. The IRS says the limited payment exception is intended to avoid the application of Section 409A to incidental benefits, often provided upon separation from service, where the parties may not realize that the benefits are nonqualified deferred compensation.

The maximum exclusion for limited payments equals the maximum amount of elective retirement plan deferrals permitted under Code Section 402(g) for the year of the separation from service ($15,500 for 2008).

The exclusion may be applied to any type of severance pay, but may apply only once. Once a right to a payment is treated as excluded, an employee may not treat any other right (such as an additional right to a payment in the second year following the separation from service) as excluded under this limited payment exception.

Q 15:45   May the employer deduct severance pay?

Out-of-pocket severance pay is generally deductible when paid as reasonable compensation for prior services rendered. [I.R.C. § 162; Treas. Reg. § 1.162-10]

However, the IRS has ruled that funded severance pay contributions may not be deducted immediately and must be capitalized unless they are taken into income by employees or contributed to a tax-qualified pension plan. [Rev. Rul. 94-77, 1994-51 I.R.B. 4]

A federal appeals court held that employer contributions to a funded severance pay plan were not deductible when made, because the plan was neither a tax-qualified pension plan nor a welfare plan. The court found the plan to have elements of deferred compensation, and therefore the employer's deduction was subject to the limits of Code Section 404(a)(5), which permitted the deduction only when the amounts contributed were taxable to the employees. [Wellons v. Commissioner, 31 F.3d 569 (7th Cir. 1994)]

Where severance pay is treated as parachute payments, excess parachute payments are not deductible by the employer (see Q 15:48).

In a technical advice memorandum, the IRS ruled that severance payments made to the employees of an acquired corporation who were terminated by the buyer after the acquisition could be deducted by the buyer as ordinary and necessary expenses under Code Section 162 rather than capitalized and added to the basis of the stock purchased. The ruling was fact-specific and contains an excellent review of the relevant law applicable to the tax treatment of severance pay in mergers and acquisitions. [Priv. Ltr. Rul. 9721002 (May 23, 1997)]

Note. Code Section 162(m) generally limits the tax deduction of a publicly held corporation for compensation of the chief executive officer and the four highest-compensated officers whose compensation is required to be reported to shareholders under the Securities Exchange Act to $1 million per year each. In a private ruling, a company asked the IRS for advice on how to handle amounts paid to several officers who were resigning. The company said that although the officers were resigning and had no intention of resuming their duties, their compensation may have to be reported to shareholders for the resignation year. The IRS ruled that the resigning officers' pay will not be subject to the $1 million deduction cap. According to the IRS, in order to be a "covered employee" an individual must be employed as an executive officer on the last day of the year. [Priv. Ltr. Rul. 199910011]

Under a change made by the Emergency Economic Stabilization Act of 2008, the $1 million deduction cap is reduced to $500,000 for certain executives of companies participating in the troubled assets relief program (TARP). [I.R.C. § 162(m)(5) as added by Pub. L. No. 110-343]

Golden Parachute Payments

Q 15:46   What is a golden parachute agreement?

In a golden parachute agreement, a corporate employer states that it will pay a key employee or a number of key employees an amount over and above other compensation in the event of a change in ownership or control of the corporation or a substantial portion of the corporation's assets. A golden parachute agreement or arrangement generally is intended to serve two purposes: (1) to frighten off attempted hostile acquisition of the employer by an outside party and (2) to provide a special layer of severance pay for managers and executives whose employment would be terminated following such an acquisition. It is important to note that the tax consequences applicable to golden parachute payments are triggered merely by the payment of the requisite amount of compensation, and a termination of employment is not literally required. As a practical matter, however, golden parachute payment provisions in an employment agreement or employer's benefits plan usually are designed to be triggered upon loss of employment within a designated period of time following the acquisition of the employer.

All that is required is an "agreement"; the golden parachute agreement is not required to be in writing or to be legally enforceable. [Cline v. Commissioner, 34 F.3d 480 (7th Cir. 1994)]

Q 15:47   Is a golden parachute agreement subject to ERISA?

If a golden parachute program is unfunded and clearly restricted to providing benefits for a select group of management or highly compensated employees only, the arrangement should be exempt from virtually all of the reporting and disclosure requirements of ERISA (see chapter 2).

The Eighth Circuit Court of Appeals held that no ERISA plan existed in the case of a golden parachute arrangement that provided that the employee would be entitled to a lump-sum payment of slightly under three years' compensation if he terminated his employment "for good reason" within one year of a hostile takeover. The agreement also gave the employee the sole decision as to whether there was a good reason for resigning. The appellate court noted that under the U.S. Supreme Court's decision in *Fort Halifax Packing Co. v. Coyne* [482 U.S. 1 (1987)], there is no ERISA plan unless the employer is required to establish an ongoing administrative scheme for the plan. In this case, there was only a lump-sum payment and no employer discretion as to payment. Once the employee resigned, the only duty the employer had was to issue a check for the payment. This simple mechanical task, the court reasoned, did not require the establishment of an ongoing administrative scheme and, accordingly, was not enough to create an ERISA plan. [Kulinski v. Medtronic Bio-Medicus, Inc., 21 F.3d 254 (8th Cir. 1994)]

A similar result was reached in an earlier decision by the U.S. Court of Appeals for the Fifth Circuit. [Fontenot v. NL Indus., Inc., 953 F.2d 960 (5th Cir. 1992)] In that case, the golden parachute agreement provided that if the employee was terminated within two years of a change in control, the employer would continue certain benefits for three years and pay the employee a lump-sum amount. The appellate court concluded that the one-time payment did not require a separate, ongoing administrative scheme and therefore did not establish an ERISA plan (see chapter 2).

The Tenth Circuit has also ruled that a golden parachute arrangement was not subject to ERISA because it was not an ongoing administrative program. The plan was established to provide one-time payments to a group of employees who were laid off in connection with a merger. In reaching its decision, the court acknowledged that the employer had discretion in determining eligibility for benefits, which is a factor in determining whether an administrative scheme for processing claims is necessary. However, even if some administration was necessary, it would not be ongoing because the plan was unfunded, contingent on a one-time event, and expressly limited to a narrow time period. Moreover, the plan involved only nine employees, and benefits were to be paid in a lump sum based on a mathematical formula. [Lettes v. Kinam Gold Inc., 3 Fed. Appx. 783 (10th Cir. Jan. 23, 2001)]

Q 15:48 Do golden parachute payments receive special federal income tax treatment?

Yes. To the extent the amount of the golden parachute payments is deemed to be excessive, there are adverse tax consequences to both the payer and the recipient of the excess parachute payments. The payer is denied a deduction for the excess parachute payments, and the recipient is subject to an excise tax of 20 percent of the amount of the excess parachute payment. [I.R.C. §§ 280G, 4999]

A golden parachute payment was held not to be subject to these adverse tax provisions when the employment agreement was entered into before June 15, 1984, the effective date of these tax provisions, and the employment agreement was not renewed or amended in any significant way on or after that date. [Powell v. Commissioner, 100 T.C. 77 (1993)]

Q 15:49 Has the IRS issued guidance on golden parachute payments?

The IRS originally issued proposed regulations on golden parachute payments in 1989. In response to comments on those regulations, in 2002 the IRS issued a second set of proposed regulations, which contained significant changes. In 2003, the IRS issued final regulations effective for payments contingent on a change of ownership or control occurring on or after January 1, 2004. Taxpayers may rely on either the 2002 proposed regulations or the 1989 proposed regulations for any payment contingent on a change of ownership or control that occurred before January 1, 2004. [Preamble to REG-209114-90 (Feb. 19, 2002)]

Q 15:50 What is the federal income tax definition of a parachute payment?

The term *parachute payment*, in general, means any payment in the nature of compensation to or for the benefit of a "disqualified individual" (see Q 15:51) that

1. Is contingent on a change in the ownership or effective control of the corporation or in the ownership of a substantial portion of the corporation's assets; and

2. Has an aggregate present value for all such payments to the disqualified individual of at least three times the individual's "base amount" (see Q 15:55).

A parachute payment also includes any payment in the nature of compensation to or for the benefit of a disqualified individual if the payment is made pursuant to an agreement that violates any generally enforced securities laws or regulations, whether state or federal. Special rules apply to securities violation parachute payments. [I.R.C. § 280G(b)(2); Prop. Treas. Reg. § 1.280G-1, Q&A-2 (1989); Prop. Treas. Reg. § 1.280G-1, Q&A-2 (2002); Treas. Reg. § 1.280G-1, Q&A-2 (2003)]

The final regulations make it clear that payments in the nature of compensation include cash, the right to receive cash, or a transfer of property. [Treas. Reg. § 1.280G-1, Q&A-11 (2003)]

The regulations also provide that transfers of statutory and nonstatutory stock options are treated as payments in the nature of compensation for purposes of the golden parachute rules. [Treas. Reg. § 1.280G-1, Q&A-13 (2003)] The IRS has also issued guidance on acceptable and administrable methods for valuing stock options. [Rev. Proc. 2002-13, 2002-8 I.R.B. 549]

The Emergency Economic Stabilization Act of 2008 expanded the definition of parachute payment to include certain severance payments made to executives of companies participating in the troubled asset relief program (TARP). [I.R.C. § 280G(e) as added by Pub. L. No. 110-343]

Q 15:51 Who is a disqualified individual?

Under the golden parachute regulations, a *disqualified individual* is an employee, personal service corporation, or independent contractor who is

1. A shareholder owning stock with a fair market value that is 1 percent of the total fair market value of the outstanding stock of the corporation;

2. An officer, limited to no more than 50 officers (or, if fewer than 50 officers, the greater of three officers or 10 percent of the number of employees); or

3. A highly compensated employee, that is, a member of the group consisting of the lesser of

 a. The highest-paid 1 percent of the employees of the corporation or

 b. The highest-paid 250 employees of the corporation, provided the employee's annualized compensation is $100,000 (for 2007, indexed annually for inflation) or more.

The determination of whether an individual is a disqualified individual is based on the 12 months before and ending on the date of the change in ownership or control of the corporation.

[I.R.C. § 280G(c); Treas. Reg. § 1.280G-1, Q&A-15–Q&A-21 (2003)]

The regulations provide that the determination of whether an individual is an officer is based on the facts and circumstances (e.g., the source of the individual's authority, the term for which the individual is elected or appointed, and the nature and extent of the individual's duties). However, the regulations make it clear that any individual who has the title of officer is presumed to be an officer unless the facts and circumstances demonstrate that the individual does not have the authority of an officer. Conversely, an individual who does not have the title of officer may nevertheless be considered an officer if the facts and circumstances demonstrate that the individual should be considered to be an officer.

Q 15:52 Are there certain types of payments that are not considered parachute payments?

Yes. A parachute payment does not include the following:

- A payment with respect to a small business corporation;
- A payment with respect to a corporation whose stock is not readily tradeable on an established securities market, or otherwise, and whose shareholders with more than 75 percent of the voting power of the corporate stock have approved the payment after full disclosure;
- A payment from a qualified plan (e.g., pension plan, profit sharing plan), including a simplified employee pension plan; and
- A payment that the taxpayer can establish by clear and convincing evidence is reasonable compensation for personal services to be rendered by the disqualified individual on or after the date of the change of ownership or control.

[I.R.C. §§ 280G(b)(4)–(6); Treas. Reg. § 1.280G-1, Q&A-5–Q&A-9 (2003)]

The final regulations on golden parachutes make it clear that the exemption for payments by small business corporations applies to a corporation that meets the definition of a small business corporation in the S corporation rules [I.R.C. § 1361(b)], other than meeting the requirement that the corporation not have a nonresident alien shareholder. However, the exemption applies regardless of whether the corporation actually elects S corporation status. In other words, a corporation that could be treated, but does not elect to be treated, as an S corporation may nevertheless use the exemption for any payments to a disqualified individual. On the other hand, the final regulations also make it clear that the exemption applies only to domestic corporations. Although a corporation may qualify for the exemption if it has a nonresident shareholder, the exemption does not apply to foreign corporations.

The regulations also clarify the shareholder approval requirement that must be met for payments with respect to a corporation whose stock is not readily tradeable to qualify for the exemption. The regulations provide that stock held by a disqualified individual who would receive parachute payments if the shareholder approval requirement is not met is disregarded in determining whether the more than 75 percent shareholder approval requirement has been met. [Treas. Reg. § 1.280G-1, Q&A-7 (2003)]

In addition, the final regulations make it clear that only voting stock is counted for purposes of the shareholder approval requirement. Thus, an individual who only holds options, and who generally would not be entitled to vote, will not be considered to hold outstanding stock entitled to vote for purposes of the shareholder approval requirement.

Finally, in its preamble to the final regulations, the IRS notes that while a foreign corporation cannot qualify for the small business corporation exemption, it can qualify for the shareholder approval exemption. [T.D. 9083 (Aug. 1, 2003)]

In Private Letter Ruling 9314034, the IRS considered the case of a bank merger in which the terminated employees received a lump-sum payment conditioned on the terminated employees' refraining from working for another bank in the same area for three years. The IRS held that the portion of the payment that was allocable to the noncompete requirement would be considered payment for services rendered after the date of the change in ownership or control, and thus would not be considered an excess parachute payment subject to excise tax.

Q 15:53   Is the payer of the parachute payment necessarily the corporation for which the disqualified individual provides services?

No. The parachute payment may be paid directly or indirectly by the corporation, by the person acquiring ownership or effective control of the corporation or ownership of a substantial portion of the corporation's assets, or by any person whose relationship to the corporation or other person is such as to require attribution of stock ownership between the parties under Code Section 318(a). [Treas. Reg. § 1.280G-1, Q&A-10 (2003)]

A federal appeals court held that a severance payment to an executive under an agreement with the acquired corporation in a merger and a bonus paid to the executive by the acquiring corporation in the merger were to be combined in determining whether an excess parachute payment had been made. The acquiring corporation had amended the severance pay agreement to reduce the severance pay amount. However, it then paid the executive a bonus roughly equal to the severance pay reduction. The court found that the two payments constituted a single excess parachute payment subjecting the executive to the 20 percent excise tax. [Cline v. Commissioner, 34 F.3d 480, 485 (7th Cir. 1994)]

The IRS ruled that severance payments made to a terminated board member following a corporate restructuring did not constitute excess parachute payments. A corporation's debenture holders acquired 79 percent of the corporation's stock as a result of a debt refinancing. However, the IRS found that the debenture holders had not acted as a group, and, therefore, there had not been a change in ownership or a change in effective control of the corporation. [Priv. Ltr. Rul. 9442010]

Q 15:54   When is a payment contingent on a change in ownership or control?

In general, a payment is treated as contingent on a change in ownership or control if the payment would not have been made had no change in ownership or control taken place. If it is substantially certain, at the time of the change, that the payment would have been made whether or not the change occurred, the payment is not contingent.

However, a payment is treated as contingent in part on a change in ownership or control, even though it would have been made whether or not a change occurred, if the change accelerated the time of payment.

The change need not result in termination of the disqualified individual's services for a payment to be considered contingent on the change. A payment made pursuant to an agreement or an amendment to an agreement entered into within a year of a change in ownership or control is presumed to be contingent on such change, unless there is clear and convincing evidence to the contrary. [I.R.C. § 280G(b)(2)(C); Treas. Reg. § 1.280G-1, Q&A-22–Q&A-26 (2003)] The IRS ruled, for example, that where a supplemental retirement program provided early retirement benefits to executives who were at least age 52 upon termination of employment, additional plan payments made to executives who were under age 52 at the time of a change in control of the corporation were contingent on the change in control for purposes of Code Section 280G. [Priv. Ltr. Rul. 9608020]

The final regulations clarify that a payment is contingent on a change in ownership or control if the payment would not have been made absent the change in ownership or control, even if the payment is also contingent on a second event, such as termination of employment within a specified period following the change in ownership or control. [Treas. Reg. § 1.280G-1, Q&A-22–Q&A-26 (2003)]

The final golden parachute regulations explicitly adopt the "one change" rule that historically has been applied by the IRS. That rule provides that in any transaction involving two corporations, if one corporation has a change in ownership or control, the other corporation does not also have a change in ownership or control. [Treas. Reg. § 1.280G-1, Q&A22–Q&A-26 (2003)]

Q 15:55   What constitutes an excess parachute payment, subject to a 20 percent excise tax imposed on the recipient and not deductible by the payer?

To constitute an excess parachute payment, the total present value of the parachute payment to the disqualified individual must equal or exceed three times the individual's base amount. The base amount for this purpose generally is the individual's average annual compensation from the corporation over the most recent five taxable years of the individual ending before the change in ownership or control, or the period of service for the corporation during the five-year period, if less. When the parachute payments are spread over more than one taxable year, the base amount is allocated based on the present value of each payment. [I.R.C. §§ 280G(b)(2)(A)(ii), 280G(d)]

An excess parachute payment generally does not include any portion of the payment that the taxpayer establishes by clear and convincing evidence is reasonable compensation for personal services actually rendered by the disqualified individual before the date of the change in ownership or control. In addition, amounts that are reasonable compensation for services to be rendered after a change in ownership or control are exempt from the definition of a parachute payment. [I.R.C. § 280G(b)(4); Treas. Reg. § 1.280G-1, Q&A-3, -9, -40–44 (2003)]

The final regulations clarify that clear and convincing evidence that a payment is reasonable compensation for services rendered after a change in ownership or control will exist if the individual's annual compensation after the change is not significantly greater than his or her annual compensation before the change, provided the individual's duties are substantially the same as they were before the change. If the individual's duties have changed, then the clear and convincing evidence must establish that the individual's annual compensation after the change is not significantly greater than the compensation customarily paid by the employer, or by comparable employers to persons performing comparable services.

Payments to an individual under a covenant not to compete or other agreement that requires the individual to refrain from providing services may also be considered reasonable compensation for services to be rendered after the change. Under the final regulations, an agreement is treated as an agreement to refrain from providing services if it is demonstrated with clear and convincing evidence that the agreement substantially constrains the individual's ability to perform services and there is a substantial likelihood that the agreement will be enforced. If the agreement does not meet that requirement, it will be treated as severance pay, which is not exempt from the golden parachute rules. [Treas. Reg. § 1.280G-1, Q&A-44 (2003)].

Q 15:56   When does a change in ownership of the corporation occur?

A change in ownership of the corporation occurs when any one person, or more than one person acting as a group, acquires stock ownership of more than 50 percent of the total fair market value or total voting power of the corporation's stock. [Treas. Reg. § 1.280G-1, Q&A-27 (2003); Priv. Ltr. Rul. 9610022]

The final regulations make it clear that if a person owns stock in both corporations that enter into a merger, consolidation, purchase or acquisition of stock, or similar transaction, the shareholder is considered to be acting as a group with other shareholders in a corporation only to the extent of his or her ownership in that corporation, not with respect to his or her ownership interest in the other corporation.

Q 15:57   When does a change in the effective control of the corporation occur?

A change in effective control is presumed to occur on the date that either:

1. Any one person, or more than one person acting as a group, acquires (or has acquired during the 12-month period preceding the most recent acquisition) ownership of stock possessing 20 percent or more of the total voting power of the corporate stock; or
2. A majority of members of the board of directors is replaced during any 12-month period by directors whose appointment or election is not endorsed by a majority of the members of the prior board.

This presumption may be rebutted by a showing that there was not in fact a transfer of effective control. [Treas. Reg. § 1.280G-1, Q&A-28 (2003)]

Q 15:58   What kind of stock is counted in determining whether there has been a change in ownership or control of a corporation?

As a general rule, the tests for determining whether there has been a change in ownership or control of a corporation are applied with respect to outstanding stock of the corporation. However, certain stock that is not technically outstanding may also be taken into account.

Under IRS regulations, vested stock underlying a vested option is considered owned by the individual who holds the vested option. Thus, vested shares subject to vested options are considered outstanding in determining whether a change in ownership or control has occurred. [Treas. Reg. § 1.280G-1, Q&A-27(c)] In addition, an IRS revenue ruling provides that unvested shares of restricted stock transferred to an employee in connection with the performance of services are treated as outstanding stock if the employee has made an election under Code Section 83(b). However, the revenue ruling makes it clear that restricted stock with respect to which a Code Section 83(b) election has not been made is not counted as outstanding stock. [Rev. Rul. 2005-39, 2005-27 I.R.B. 1]

> **Note.** As a general rule, restricted stock is not taxable to an employee until it becomes substantially vested. However, if the employee makes a Code Section 83(b) election, the employee pays current tax on the excess (if any) of the fair market value of the stock over the amount (if any) paid for the stock. No amount is included in the employee's income when the stock becomes substantially vested, and any future appreciation is taxed as capital gain when and if the stock is sold.

Q 15:59   When does a change in the ownership of a substantial portion of the corporation's assets occur?

A change in the ownership of a substantial portion of the corporation's assets occurs on the date that any one person, or more than one person acting as a group, acquires (or has acquired within the 12-month period ending on the date of the most recent acquisition) assets from the corporation that have a total fair market value equal to or more than one third of the total fair market value of all the assets of the corporation. [Treas. Reg. § 1.280G-1, Q&A-29 (2003)]

In Private Letter Ruling 9608020, the IRS considered whether a proposed merger would cause either a change in ownership of the corporation's stock (see Q 15:54) or a change in ownership of a substantial portion of the corporation's assets so as to trigger the golden parachute tax rules (see Q 15:46). Under the facts of the ruling, Corporation Y would merge into Corporation X, and Y's shareholders would have their Y stock converted into X stock. As a result, the former Y shareholders would own more than 50 percent of X's stock. All of Y's assets were to be transferred to X.

The IRS ruled that because, under the merger, Y's shareholders would own more than 50 percent of the surviving corporation (X), there would be neither a change in ownership of Y nor a change in the ownership of a substantial portion of Y's assets as a result of the merger. Therefore, the golden parachute tax rules would not be triggered. [Priv. Ltr. Rul. 9412015]

Q 15:60   When is a bankruptcy treated as a change in ownership or control that triggers the golden parachute rules?

Whether a company's bankruptcy will be treated as a change in ownership or control depends on how the bankruptcy reorganization is structured and the magnitude of the change in stock ownership. [Rev. Rul. 2004-87, 2004-34 I.R.B. 154]

> **Example 1.** Corporation A's stock is widely held and actively traded on a stock exchange. Corporation A files a voluntary petition in bankruptcy. After negotiations with creditors, a plan of reorganization is presented to and

approved by a bankruptcy court. Under the plan, the existing shares of Corporation A common stock are canceled and new shares are authorized. The corporation's unsecured creditors receive 75 percent of the new common stock while some shareholders receive the remaining 25 percent. No creditor receives 20 percent or more of the outstanding shares after the reorganization.

Result: A change of ownership of a corporation occurs when any one person, or more than one person acting as a group, acquires ownership of more than 50 percent of the total fair market value or total voting power of the corporation's stock (see Q 15:56). However, in this example, the creditors did not act together to force the corporation into bankruptcy and were not acting as a group to acquire stock in the corporation. Therefore, the reorganization did not amount to a change of ownership triggering the golden parachute rules.

Example 2. The facts are the same as those in Example 1, except that the largest creditor of Corporation A receives 25 percent of the outstanding shares of the corporation following the reorganization.

Result: A change in control of a corporation is presumed to occur when one person, or more than one person acting as a group, acquires stock representing more than 20 percent of the corporation's stock during a 12-month period (see Q 15:57).

In this example, a change in control is presumed to have occurred when the largest creditor acquired 25 percent of Corporation A's outstanding shares. However, the presumption can be rebutted by showing that the creditor will not act to control the management and policies of Corporation A.

Example 3. Corporation B common stock is widely held and actively traded on a stock exchange. Corporation B experiences financial difficulties and files a voluntary petition in bankruptcy. Following the filing, the corporation's stock is delisted from the exchange and no longer actively traded on any market. Corporation C subsequently proposes to buy more than one-third of Corporation B's assets. Under an employment contract, such a sale would trigger certain payments to Executive E. The bankruptcy court approves the asset sale and the payments to Executive E as expenses of the bankruptcy estate. Corporation C acquires the assets from Corporation B and the payments are made to Executive E.

Result: A change in ownership of a substantial portion of a corporation's assets occurs when one person, or more than one person acting as a group, acquires more than one-third of the assets of a corporation (see Q 15:59). Therefore, Corporation C's acquisition represents a change in ownership of Corporation B triggering the golden parachute rules.

Note, however, that the payments to Executive E are not treated as parachute payments. Under the golden parachute rules, a parachute payment does not include any payment if (1) immediately before the change in ownership or control, no stock of the corporation was readily traded on an established securities market or otherwise, and (2) the payment was disclosed to and approved by shareholders holding more than 75 percent of the voting power of the corporation (see Q 15:52). In the case of a bankruptcy, the bankruptcy court approval serves to protect the corporation's owners from any unnecessary or excessive payments to executives. Therefore, the shareholder disclosure and approval requirements are deemed to be met.

Example 4. The facts are the same as those in Example 3, except that the stock of Corporation B continues to be tradeable on an over-the-counter securities market following the stock exchange delisting.

Result: As in Example 3, Corporation C's acquisition represents a change in ownership of Corporation B, triggering the golden parachute rules. Moreover, as in Example 3, the payments to Executive E are not treated as parachute payments. Although Corporation B's stock continued to be tradeable on an over-the-counter securities market, the stock was not considered to be "readily traded" because the trading of stock of a debtor in bankruptcy is impaired. Therefore, the payments to Executive E are eligible for the exemption for payments meeting the shareholder disclosure and approval requirements. Moreover, those requirements are deemed to be met as a result of the bankruptcy court approval.

Q 15:61 How does a disqualified individual pay the excise tax on an excess golden parachute payment?

The 20 percent excise tax on an excess golden parachute payment is generally payable for the taxable year in which the payment is received or the year in which the benefit is includable in income. [I.R.C. §§ 280G, 4999; Treas. Reg. § 1.280G-1, Q&A-11 (2003)] However, under the final regulations, a disqualified person has the option of prepaying the excise tax on payments to be received in future years. To take advantage of this option, the payor and the disqualified person must treat the payment of the excise tax consistently, and the payor must satisfy any wage-withholding obligation with respect to the payment. [Treas. Reg. § 1.280G-1, Q&A-11 (2003)]

The prepayment of the excise tax must be based on the present value of the excise tax that would be due in the year the excess parachute payment would actually be paid (calculated using the discount rate equal to 120 percent of the applicable federal rate). The prepayment option is not available for a payment to be made in cash if the present value of the payment is not reasonably ascertainable or to a payment related to health benefits or coverage.

Q 15:62 Is the disqualified individual permitted to deduct the 20 percent excise tax he or she is required to pay upon receipt of an excess parachute payment?

No. The 20 percent excise tax is not deductible on the individual's federal income tax return. [I.R.C. § 275(a)(6)]

Q 15:63   Is the payment of an excess parachute payment to a disqualified individual subject to tax withholding?

If the disqualified individual is an employee and not an independent contractor, an excess parachute payment is subject to income tax withholding and is also subject to withholding for the 20 percent excise tax. [I.R.C. §§ 3401, 4999(c)(1)]

Q 15:64   Is the payment of an excess parachute payment subject to FICA and FUTA tax?

Yes, if the payment is made to an employee. [I.R.C. §§ 3121(a), 3121(v)(2), 3306(b)]

Q 15:65   Do golden parachute payments violate public policy?

Golden parachutes have been roundly criticized for permitting executives to escape from a merger or acquisition unscathed while rank-and-file workers suffer the consequences. Moreover, Congress took dead aim at golden parachutes by imposing an excise tax on excess parachute payments (see Q 15:48). However, at least one appellate court has held that golden parachutes do not violate public policy.

In *Campbell v. Potash Corp. of Saskatechewan, Inc.* [238 F.3d 792 (6th Cir. 2000)], three former executives of a corporation that was merged with Potash Corporation of Saskatchewan, Inc. (PCS) sued PCS for breach of contract for failing to make golden parachute payments that were triggered under the executives' employment contracts as a result of the change in control. PCS argued that golden parachutes violate public policy and that therefore the agreement requiring them was void. In reaching its decision, the Sixth Circuit Court of Appeals noted that PCS made this argument even though it offered golden parachutes to its own top managers. However, putting that "hypocrisy" aside, the court pointed out that PCS cited no authority for the proposition that golden parachute payments are illegal. PCS pointed to a congressional committee report that stated that golden parachutes should be discouraged and to the excise tax on excess parachute payments. However, the court pointed out that while Congress taxed golden parachutes, it did not prohibit them.

PCS also argued that the particular parachutes in question were excessive and had a gross-up feature to compensate the executives for any tax penalty. However, the Sixth Circuit said those features did not make parachutes violative of public policy.

Chapter 16

Family and Medical Leave

The Family and Medical Leave Act of 1993 (FMLA) has been on the books for more than a decade, yet the requirements of the law continue to trouble employers. In response to a recent poll asking "Which federal employment-related law gives you the biggest headache?" nearly half (49 percent) of human resources professionals named the FMLA. This chapter reviews the federal requirements for leave under the FMLA. Details of the act—including what is meant by "family leave" and "medical leave," under what conditions the leave must be granted, when it is discretionary, and when it can be denied; the length of required leave and whether it must be taken all at once or can be spread out; documentation requirements; and business necessity exceptions—are given close attention.

Furthermore, this chapter discusses the first change to the FMLA since the statute was enacted—the new rules that require employers to provide leave for family members of military personnel—as well as new, final regulations that update the FMLA rules for the first time since 1995.

Basic Concepts

Q 16:1   What is the Family and Medical Leave Act of 1993?

The Family and Medical Leave Act of 1993 (FMLA) requires many employers to permit their employees to take leaves of absence for up to 12 weeks in any 12-month period of employment for certain types of family or medical conditions or emergencies. [29 U.S.C. § 2612] The law is intended to allow employees to balance workplace and family needs by permitting them to attend to family emergencies and vital needs at home without being forced to quit their jobs. [29 C.F.R. § 825.101]

Rights under the FMLA are fixed. Employees cannot waive prospective FMLA rights or trade them for other benefits; nor can employers induce employees to waive their FMLA rights. [29 C.F.R. § 825.220(d)] However, final FMLA regulations issued in 2008 make it clear that this non-waiver provision does not prevent the settlement or release of FMLA claims by employees based on past employer conduct.

The FMLA does not preempt state law providing greater family or medical leave rights. [FMLA § 401(b); 29 U.S.C. § 2651(b); 29 C.F.R. § 825.701] To the extent an employer's family leave program fails to constitute an ERISA-covered plan, ERISA (the Employee Retirement Income Security Act of 1974) would not operate to preempt state laws requiring more generous family leave than is required under the FMLA; however, ERISA may preempt a state law requiring ERISA-covered employee benefit plan coverage to be extended during periods of leave in excess of that required under the FMLA or for different reasons than are specified in the FMLA. (See chapter 2 for a discussion of ERISA's coverage and preemption provisions; see also Q 16:2.)

California was the first state to enact a *paid* family leave program—Family Temporary Disability Insurance (FTDI). The program took effect on July 1, 2004. FTDI, an expansion of an existing disability insurance program for employees, provides partial pay when an employee takes time off work to care for a seriously ill child, spouse, parent, or domestic partner, or to bond with a new child. Payments under FTDI are capped at six weeks over a 12-month period and at 55 percent of pay, up to a maximum amount.

Starting July 1, 2009, New Jersey's Temporary Disability Insurance (TDI) program is extended to provide insurance benefits to all workers when they take family disability leave to care for newborn or newly adopted children or sick family members. Employees who qualify for family disability leave (whether or not their leave is job-protected) are entitled to benefits for up to six weeks, equal to the lesser of two-thirds of their weekly pay or a maximum weekly amount ($524 based on 2008 figures).

Effective October 1, 2009, Washington State provides family leave insurance benefits for employees who care for newborn and newly adopted children. The weekly benefit will be $250, and the maximum duration of benefits will be five weeks.

The District of Columbia Accrued Sick and Safe Leave Act of 2008, effective November 13, 2008, requires employers with 100 or more employees to provide seven paid "sick or safe" days for their employees; employers with 25 to 99 employees to provide five days; and employers with 24 or fewer employees to provide three days. Paid "sick or safe" days are available for a variety of reasons, including: (1) illness of the employee or a family member (child, parent, spouse, or domestic partner); (2) routine or preventative medical care for the employee or a family member; or (3) time off for the employee to seek medical care, shelter, counseling, a court order, or other services related to domestic violence.

Q 16:2   Is a family and medical leave policy conforming to the FMLA a welfare benefit plan subject to ERISA?

It appears not. Unpaid leave is not a type of welfare benefit described in Section 3(1) of ERISA or in the Department of Labor (DOL) regulations. The continuation of group benefit health plan coverage during leave is, per the FMLA, a federally mandated part of the group health plan and should not be deemed to create a separate ERISA plan. Likewise, any paid leave required to be taken before the unpaid leave (see Q 16:41) would appear to be either an exempt payroll practice under DOL regulations or part of a separate ERISA plan. [29 C.F.R. § 2510.3-1]

Covered Employers

Q 16:3   Which employers are subject to the FMLA?

Title I of the FMLA applies to employers engaged in commerce or in any industry or activity affecting commerce that employ 50 or more employees for each working day during each of 20 or more calendar workweeks in the current or preceding calendar year, regardless of whether the 20 calendar workweeks are consecutive. [29 C.F.R. § 825.105(e)]

Further, the FMLA applies to state and local government employers as well as to nongovernmental employers. [FMLA § 101(4); 29 U.S.C. § 2611] Titles II and V of the FMLA provide for similar family and medical leave coverage for federal civil service employees and congressional employees. Public agencies and private elementary and secondary schools are also covered employers, regardless of the number of employees they have. [29 C.F.R. §§ 825.104, 825.108(d), 825.109, 825.600] Congress apparently felt that without certain special rules modifying the general rules for employers and employees in other employment, the educational needs of children in school could be adversely affected. Those special rules are contained in Section 108 of the FMLA. [S. Rep. 103-3, 103d Cong., 1st Sess. at 36 (1993); *see also* 29 C.F.R. § 825, Subpart F]

Separate worksites or divisions. Under the FMLA, all of an employer's separate establishments or divisions are considered to be a single employer. In addition, an employer includes (1) any person acting, directly or indirectly, in the interest of a covered employer with respect to any of the employees of the employer; (2) any successor in interest [defined at 29 C.F.R. § 825.107] of a covered employer; and (3) any public agency. [29 C.F.R. § 825.104] Employees of more than one employer will be treated as being employed by a single employer for purposes of the FMLA if the employers meet either an integrated employer test or joint employment test (see Q 16:4).

Joint employers. The DOL regulations contain special rules for determining whether a "joint employment" relationship exists. If one does, the primary employer is responsible for giving the required notices to employees, providing leave, maintaining health benefits, and restoring jobs. The secondary employer with 50 or more employees (including jointly employed employees) is responsible for compliance with the prohibited act provisions with respect to its temporary and leased employees, including provisions barring discharge or discrimination for exercising or attempting to exercise rights under the FMLA. [29 C.F.R. § 825.106] Which employer is primary and which is secondary is a facts-and-circumstances determination based on various factors listed in the regulations. [29 C.F.R. § 825.106(c)]

Q 16:4 When are two or more corporations treated as a single employer for purposes of the FMLA?

When one corporation has an ownership interest in a second corporation, the FMLA treats each as a separate employer unless they meet an integrated employer test or a joint employment test. If either test is met, the employers will be treated as a single employer for all purposes of the FMLA, including employer coverage, employee eligibility, and employer liability under the FMLA's enforcement provisions.

Integrated employer test. This test is subjective rather than objective and appears designed to afford the DOL broad leeway to find that a single integrated employer exists. According to regulations under the FMLA, "[a] determination of whether or not separate entities are an integrated employer is not determined by the application of any single criterion, but rather the entire relationship is to be reviewed in its totality." The factors to be considered include but not limited to the following:

- Common management;
- Interrelation between operations;
- Centralized control of labor relations; and
- Degree of common ownership/financial control.

[29 C.F.R. § 825.104(c)(2)]

The DOL has not specified any minimum percentage of common ownership or financial control for meeting the integrated employer test.

Joint employment test. This test operates to treat two or more businesses that exercise some control over the work or working conditions of the employee as joint employers for purposes of the FMLA. Under this test, even separate and distinct entities with separate owners, managers, and facilities could be deemed to be joint employers for purposes of the FMLA. If a joint employment relationship exists, then additional rules prescribe which of the joint employers has what FMLA duties with respect to shared, leased, and temporary employees and employees in various other employment arrangements (see Q 16:3).

As with the integrated employer test, the determination of whether a joint employment relationship exists is subjectively determined by viewing the entire relationship in its totality, not by the application of any single criterion. [29 C.F.R. § 825.106(a), (b)]

The DOL regulations note that where an employee performs work that simultaneously benefits two or more employers, or works for two or more employers at different times during the workweek, a joint employment relationship will often exist if the following is the case:

1. There is an arrangement between employers to share an employee's services or to interchange employees;

2. One employer, directly or indirectly, acts in the interest of a second employer in relation to the employee; or

3. The employers are not completely disassociated with respect to the employee's employment and may be treated as directly or indirectly sharing control of the employee because one employer controls, is controlled by, or is under common control with the other employer.

Joint employment will ordinarily be found to exist when a temporary placement agency supplies employees to a second employer. [29 C.F.R. §§ 825.106(a), 825.106(c)]

Professional employer organizations. Final FMLA regulations issued in 2008 include new rules governing joint employment in the context of professional employer organizations (PEOs). PEOs, unlike traditional staffing or placement agencies, typically provide payroll and administrative benefit services for the existing employees of an employer/client.

Under the final regulations, a PEO does not enter into a joint employment relationship with the employees of its client companies when it merely performs such functions as payroll and benefits administration, regulatory paperwork, and updating of employment policies. On the other hand, if a PEO has the right to fire, assign, or direct and control the client's employees, or it benefits from the work that the employees perform, those rights may lead to the determination that the PEO is a joint employer with the client employer, depending on all the facts and circumstances. [29 C.F.R. § 825.106(b)(2)]

Q 16:5   For purposes of the 50-employee test, when is an individual deemed to be "employed" by an employer?

When establishing whether an employer employed at least 50 employees for each working day during each of 20 or more calendar workweeks in the current or preceding calendar year, the following rules should be applied to determine whether a particular employee should be counted.

Listing on payroll. If an employee's name appears on the employer's payroll, he or she must be counted as employed on each working day of the calendar week regardless of whether he or she receives any compensation for the week. [29 C.F.R. § 825.105(b)] However, the FMLA applies only to employees who are employed in one of the 50 states, the District of Columbia, or a territory or possession of the United States. Individuals employed outside those areas are not counted. [29 C.F.R. § 825.105(b)]

Part-time employees. For purposes of the 50-employee test, part-time employees are also considered as being employed on each working day of the calendar week, as long as they were maintained on the payroll. [29 C.F.R. § 825.105(c)]

Example 1. Pemberton Market has a seven-day workweek. Several employees work only three days per week, but those part-time employees must be treated as being employed on all seven days of the calendar week for purposes of the 50-employee test.

Midweek commencement or termination of employment. Employees who are hired after the first working day of the calendar week or who terminate employment before the last working day of the calendar week are not treated as employed on every working day of the calendar week. [29 C.F.R. § 825.105(d)]

Jointly employed employees. The DOL regulations indicate that if a joint employment relationship exists, jointly employed employees must be counted by both employers, whether or not maintained on one of the employer's payroll. Thus, an employer that employs workers from a temporary-help agency must count such individuals (whether or not they are maintained on the employer's payroll) when determining employer coverage and employee eligibility under the FMLA. For example, an employer who jointly employs 15 workers from a temporary placement agency and 40 permanent workers is covered by the FMLA. In addition, the leasing or temporary-help agency also must count such individuals. The various duties under the FMLA are then divided between the primary employer and the secondary employer (see Q 16:3). [29 C.F.R. § 825.106]

However, an opinion letter from the DOL indicates that when a temporary worker works less than a full week, there is no continuing employment relationship with the worker and the worker is not counted for FMLA coverage and eligibility purposes. [29 C.F.R. § 825.105(c) and (d)]

Example 2. Assume that Pemberton Market has 42 regular full-time and part-time employees and 5 routine temps who are provided by a temporary service agency. In addition, during one week, the service agency provides the employer with 5 day laborers. The same five day laborers work for the employer all week. Pemberton must count the 42 regular employees, the 5 routine temps, and the 5 day laborers. The day laborers must be counted because they are jointly employed by the employer each working day of the week and there is a continuing employment relationship with the client employer for the week. Therefore, the employer has a total of 52 (42 + 5 + 5) employees for the week, and the week must be counted toward the 20-workweek threshold.

Example 3. The facts are the same as those in Example 2, except that in addition to the 5 routine temps the service agency provides Pemberton with 3 day laborers each day, but not the same three workers. Pemberton must count the 42 regular employees and the 5 routine temps. The day laborers need not be counted, however, because no day laborer worked every day of the week or appeared to have a continuing employment relationship with Pemberton. Therefore, Pemberton Market has a total of 47 employees for the week, and the week does not count toward the 20-workweek threshold.

Example 4. The facts are the same as those in Example 2, except that the service agency provides Pemberton with 6 day laborers one day and 3 each on the following three days. Pemberton must count 42 regular employees and 5 routine temps. The day laborers need not be counted because no day laborer worked every working day of the week or appeared to have a continuing employment relationship with Pemberton. Therefore, Pemberton has a total of 47 employees for the week, and the week is not counted toward the 20-workweek threshold. [DOL Op. Ltr. Apr. 5, 2004]

In cases where a PEO is determined to be a joint employer of a client's employees, the client employer would only be required to count employees of the PEO (or employees of other clients of the PEO) if the client employer jointly employed those employees. [29 C.F.R. § 825.106(d)]

Independent contractors. A New York district court held that an independent contractor did not fit within the meaning of *employee* for FMLA purposes. A worker was denied FMLA coverage because the corporation had no more than 15 employees on its payroll at any time during two calendar years when the worker was associated with the corporation. In addition, the court found that the worker did not fit within the meaning of *employee* under the FMLA because there was substantial and uncontroverted evidence that the worker was an independent contractor: she was not listed on the payroll, did not receive a W-2 form, and had no federal, state, or FICA taxes withheld. [Sousa v. Orient Arts Inc., 1999 U.S. Dist. LEXIS 2934 (S.D.N.Y. Mar. 12, 1999)]

According to DOL regulations, "In general, an employee, as distinguished from an independent contractor who is engaged in a business of his/her own, is one who 'follows the usual path of an employee' and is dependent on the business which he/she serves." [29 C.F.R. § 825.105(a)]

Paid or unpaid leave. An employee who is on paid or unpaid leave, including FMLA leave, leave of absence, or disciplinary suspension, must be counted for purposes of the 50-employee test if the employer has a reasonable expectation that the employee will later return to active employment. [29 C.F.R. § 825.105(c)]

Layoff. Employees on layoff are not counted for purposes of the 50-employee test, regardless of whether the layoff is temporary, long-term, or indefinite. [29 C.F.R. § 825.105(c)]

Q 16:6   Can a business that does not qualify as a covered employer ever be required to provide family or medical leave?

At least one appellate court has held that an employer that is not technically subject to the FMLA can be obligated to provide family and medical leave as a result of its own actions.

Pearle Vision, Inc., operates optometry stores around the country. Its store in Peoria, Illinois, employed only 12 employees, and fewer than 50 employees worked within a 75-mile radius. As a result, the Peoria store was not subject to the FMLA requirements (see Q 16:7). However, Pearle distributed a summary plan description (SPD) of employee benefits to employees at all of its stores. In the section entitled "The Family and Medical Leave Act of 1993," the SPD stated that "all employees with one year of service who worked 1,250 hours with Pearle in the 12 months immediately prior to requesting leave" were eligible for leave under the FMLA. The SPD repeated the same eligibility clause later, stating, "If you have worked for Pearle at least one year, and have worked 1,250 hours or more during the 12 month period prior to requesting leave, you are eligible for Family and Medical leave." In addition, the SPD contained instructions on how to request leave.

Following those directions, Dr. Tina Thomas, an optometrist at the Peoria store, requested and was granted leave for the birth of her first child. However, before her leave was up, Thomas was notified by a message left on her home telephone's answering machine that Pearle had hired another optometrist to replace her and that Pearle had no other positions available for her in the region. Thomas brought suit against Pearle for breach of contract, alleging that Pearle had incorporated the FMLA into her contract through the SPD.

The Seventh Circuit Court of Appeals acknowledged that Pearle's Peoria store was not subject to the FMLA because the location did not meet the 50-employee threshold. However, the court concluded that Pearle's SPD did create an enforceable contract to provide all employees who met the one year of service and 1,250 hours requirements with the benefits of the FMLA. Moreover, the court said, Pearle's actions were further evidence that the company intended to provide Thomas with FMLA benefits. By providing her with FMLA forms to complete, Pearle acted as if the SPD did in fact grant Thomas the right to request leave under the FMLA, despite the fact that she was not eligible under the statute. According to the court, Thomas reasonably relied on those actions, and Pearle's argument that the SPD did not offer Thomas FMLA benefits was "disingenuous at best." [Thomas v. Pearle Vision Inc., 251 F.3d 1132 (7th Cir. 2001)]

Practice Pointer. The *Pearle Vision* case should serve as a wake-up call for employers with multiple locations. If some locations are not subject to the FMLA because of the 50-employee test, that fact should be clearly stated in all benefits materials. The Seventh Circuit noted that if Pearle had wanted to limit its promise of benefits, it could have drafted the SPD accordingly.

On the other hand, another appeals court concluded that an employer's erroneous approval of FMLA leave did not preclude the employer from subsequently challenging an employee's FMLA coverage.

Daniel Dobrowski worked as an engineer for Jay Dee Contractors. When Dobrowski scheduled elective surgery for a health condition, he requested FMLA leave. Jay Dee granted the request indicating that Dobrowski was an "eligible employee." However, when Dobrowski returned from leave after his surgery, he was informed that he was being discharged because Jay Dee no longer needed his services. When Dobrowski sued the company for violating his FMLA rights, the company claimed the FMLA did not apply because the company employed fewer than 50 employees within 75 miles of Dobrowski's worksite. Dobrowski countered that Jay Dee was equitably estopped from denying his FMLA eligibility after confirming his leave.

The Sixth Circuit Court of Appeals made it clear that an employer may be equitably estopped from denying coverage under the FMLA—but only if the employee establishes that (1) the employer made a misrepresentation of a material fact and (2) the employee relied on that misrepresentation to his detriment. And, while the Sixth Circuit concluded that Jay Dee had materially misrepresented Dobrowski's FMLA eligibility, the court found that there was no evidence Dobrowski detrimentally relied on that misrepresentation. The record showed that Dobrowski had already scheduled his surgery before he was informed of his eligibility for FMLA leave. [Dobrowski v. Jay Dee Contractors Inc., No. 08-1806, 2009 WL 1940368 (6th Cir. July 8, 2009)]

> **Practice Pointer.** Bear in mind that an employee's rights and employer's obligation will turn on the specific facts surrounding an erroneous approval of FMLA leave. In reaching its decision in *Dobrowski*, the Sixth Circuit held that the employer would have been barred from contesting the employee's FMLA eligibility if the employee had shown that he changed his behavior after being told he was eligible for leave.

Eligible Employees

Q 16:7   Is an employer subject to the FMLA required to provide family or medical leave to all its employees?

No, the employer is required to provide FMLA leave only to eligible employees. Moreover, an employer is not obligated to provide FMLA leave to an otherwise eligible employee if the employee unequivocally informs the employer that he or she does not have any intention of returning to work, because no FMLA rights exist in that circumstance. [29 C.F.R. § 825.311(b)]

Date of eligibility determination. An employee's eligibility for a family or medical leave under the FMLA is determined as of the date the leave begins. It is not determined as of the date the employee requests the leave. [29 C.F.R. § 825.110(d)]

Eligibility factors. Eligibility is determined based on two factors: (1) service and (2) size of the employing unit. The impact of these two factors can have some seemingly incongruous results. The FMLA's minimum service requirement may cause some short-time and part-time employees to be excluded from eligibility for family and medical leave, even though they are counted for the purpose of determining whether the employer is subject to the FMLA (see Q 16:5). Further, the worksite size requirement can cause some employees of large employers not to be eligible for FMLA leave.

An *eligible employee* is an employee who (1) has been employed by the employer for at least 12 months (the 12 months need not be consecutive), (2) worked for at least 1,250 hours during the 12-month period immediately preceding the date the leave of absence begins, and (3) works at a worksite meeting the size test described below. [FMLA § 101(2)(A); 29 U.S.C. § 2611(2)(A); 29 C.F.R. § 825.110(a)]

12-month service requirement. To satisfy this requirement, an employee need not have worked for the employer for 12 consecutive months. For example, a seasonal employee can meet the 12-month requirement even though there are periods during each year when he or she does not work. Moreover, according to a case of first impression from the First Circuit Court of Appeals, an employer must count periods of prior employment in counting the 12 months. In the case before the court, an employee worked for a company, left the company's employ, then rejoined the company five years later. Seven months after rejoining the company, the employee took medical leave. The employer argued that the employee did not qualify for FMLA leave because he did not meet the 12-month employment requirement. The First Circuit disagreed. According to the court, the statute is ambiguous as to whether periods of previous employment count toward the 12-month requirement, but according to the DOL's regulations, previous periods of employment do count. Moreover, the court said, the regulations are a reasonable exercise of the DOL's regulatory authority. [Rucker v. Lee Holding Co., 471 F.3d 6 (1st Cir. 2006)]

While the First Circuit Court of Appeals refused to place any limit on how long a break in service is too long to be counted, final FMLA regulations limit the lookback period to seven years. [29 C.F.R. § 825.110(b)(1)] However, the seven-year limit does not apply to breaks in service occasioned by an employee's fulfillment of National Guard or Reserve military service or where a written agreement exists concerning the employer's intention to rehire the employee after the break in service (e.g., where the break in service is for educational or child rearing purposes). The final regulations became effective January 16, 2008.

> **Practice Pointer.** The preamble to the final regulations points out that although many employers maintain records for seven years for tax and standard business reasons, the FMLA requires records to be maintained for only three years. Therefore, an employer who maintains records for only the requisite three years may base its initial determination as to an employee's FMLA eligibility on those records. If an employee wants to base eligibility on a longer lookback period, the employee will have to provide sufficient proof

of his or her period of employment in earlier years. Proof may include: W–2 forms; pay stubs; a statement identifying the dates of prior employment, the position the employee held, the name of the employee's supervisor, and the names of coworkers or any similar information that would allow the employer to verify the dates of the employee's prior service.

On the other hand, the final FMLA regulations make it clear that there is nothing to prevent an employer from considering an individual's employment prior to a continuous break in service of more than seven years when determining the employee's eligibility. However, if the employer chooses to recognize such prior employment, it must do so uniformly with respect to all employees with similar breaks in service. [29 C.F.R. § 825.110(b)(4)]

The final regulations also provide that FMLA eligibility can kick in during a non-FMLA leave. According to the DOL, time spent on leave does not count toward the 1,250-hour requirement (see below) because leave is not hours worked—but it does count toward the 12 months of employment because the employment relationship continues during leave.

> **Example.** Amy has worked 11 months for her employer, Bradley Associates, and has met the 1,250-hour requirement when she begins a 12-week maternity leave. While the first month of leave will be non-FMLA leave, once the 12-month mark is reached, the remainder of the leave will fall under the FMLA, entitling Amy to FMLA protections such as continuation of health benefits and job restoration. [29 C.F.R. § 825.110(d)]

1,250-hour requirement. An employee must have worked 1,250 hours in the 12 months *before* starting a protected period of FMLA leave. The fact that the employee no longer meets the 1,250-hour test at the end of the leave is irrelevant.

In one case, an employee claimed that her employer violated the FMLA by terminating her for excessive absenteeism, even though her absences qualified as protected family leave. A district court ruled that the employee was not an eligible employee under the FMLA, and thus was not protected from termination, because she had not worked 1,250 hours in the 12-month period immediately preceding her termination of employment. However, the Sixth Circuit Court of Appeals held that the relevant date for determining FMLA eligibility is the start of the period of FMLA leave. [Butler v. Owens-Brockway Plastic Prods., Inc., 199 F.3d 314 (6th Cir. 1999)] The circuit court said that the district court's determination would lead to "perverse" results. For example, if an employee took 12 weeks of FMLA leave but no longer met the 1,250-hour test on the day he or she returned from leave, the employer would be permitted to terminate the employee for excessive absenteeism based on the protected leave.

Hours of service are determined according to principles established under the Fair Labor Standards Act (FLSA) for determining compensable hours of work. An employer may use any accurate accounting of actual hours worked under the FLSA's principles. If an employer does not maintain accurate records of hours worked, including for employees who are exempt from the FLSA's recordkeeping requirement (that is, bona fide executive, administrative, and professional employees), the employer has the burden of showing that the employee has not worked for the requisite hours. [DOL Reg. § 825.110(c)]

An employee's time card may not tell the whole story, however. Under the FLSA, any time an employee is "suffered or permitted" to work counts as hours worked. Therefore, if an employer knows that an employee is putting in extra hours, the time may count toward the FMLA hours of service requirement. In one case, an employee's time sheets showed that she was paid for 1,186 hours during the 12 months prior to her leave—not enough to qualify for leave under the FMLA. However, the employee, who worked as a radiologic technologist, claimed that she actually worked more hours than were recorded on her time sheets. She claimed she spent 35.5 hours at continuing education classes that should be counted as hours worked. In addition, she argued that because she was required to begin seeing patients immediately at the official start of her day, she had to arrive 15 minutes early to turn on the X-ray processing machine, test the machine, and prepare the office for patients. According to the employee, the extra time, if included in her hours worked for the 12 months prior to her leave, would push her over the 1,250-hour mark for FMLA eligibility. [Kosakow v. New Rochelle Radiology Assocs. P. C., 274 F.3d 706 (2d Cir. 2001)]

The district court held that the employee was not an eligible employee for FMLA purposes. The court conceded that 35.5 hours of continuing education were arguably work hours. However, said the court, the employee did not present enough evidence to allow a jury to reasonably find that she put in an extra 15 minutes every day. Moreover, the court said, the extra time was merely preliminary noncompensable time that could be excluded from the employee's work time as *de minimis*.

The Second Circuit overruled the district court, pointing out that the employee had produced evidence, including her own affidavit, attesting to the extra time, as well as affidavits from two former receptionists stating that the employee and other radiologic technologists would routinely arrive 10 to 20 minutes early each day. Although the evidence was countered by affidavits from other workers, who stated that they were never required to arrive at work earlier than their scheduled shift time, the Second Circuit said there was a real question of fact about the employee's arrival time that should have been decided by a jury.

The Second Circuit also concluded that if the employee in fact spent 15 minutes on preparatory work every morning, that time could not be automatically excluded from her hours worked. Based on the evidence, a jury could reasonably find that the employer had reason to know that the employee arrived at work early every day and permitted her to do so. Therefore, the time would be includable in the employee's hours worked. According to the Second Circuit, activities taking only a small amount of time can be ignored as *de minimis* if they occur only infrequently. However, the employee claimed she put in extra time every day, and, if that was the case, the time could not be excluded as *de minimis*. [Kosakow v. New Rochelle Radiology Assocs. P. C., 274 F.3d 706 (2d Cir. 2001)]

The "suffered or permitted" to work test was also at issue in a First Circuit case. In *Plumley v. Southern Container, Inc.* [303 F.3d 364 (1st Cir. 2002)], the employee was fired but six months later an arbitrator ruled that the firing was too severe a punishment. The arbitrator ordered the employer to reinstate the employee and pay him back wages for the six-month period. A day after returning to work the employee was absent from work due to an illness in the family. When he was fired for the absence, he sued the employer on the grounds that the firing violated the FMLA. The employer countered that the employee was not FMLA-eligible because he had worked only 851 hours during the previous 12 months. The employee, however, argued that the six months during which he was fighting the first firing should also be counted toward the 1,250-hour service requirement because he was paid wages for that period.

The First Circuit Court of Appeals ruled that the employee had not met the FMLA service requirement. Even though he was compensated for the six-month period, those months did not count as "hours of service" under the FMLA. The court found that "the statutory language, in every technical sense, indicates that only those hours that an employer suffers or permits an employee to do work (i.e., to exert effort, either physically or mentally, for which that employee has been hired and is being paid by the employer) can be included as hours of service within the meaning of the FMLA." The court also noted that, in determining which work is compensable, the FLSA specifically excludes "periods for which no work is being performed due to vacation, holiday, illness, failure of the employer to provide sufficient work, or other similar cause." According to the appeals court, these exclusions illustrate that any compensation that is not paid for hours actually worked in the service of the employer is not to be counted as hours of service. [Plumley v. Southern Container, Inc., 303 F.3d 364 (1st Cir. 2002)]

Final DOL regulations specifically provide that the determination of whether an employee has worked the requisite 1,250 hours is not limited by the employer's methods of recordkeeping, or by compensation agreements that do not accurately reflect all the hours an employee has worked for the employer or has been in service to the employer. [29 C.F.R. § 825.110(c)(1)]

Size of worksite requirement. An employee who meets both the 12-month and the 1,250-hours-of-service requirements nonetheless is not eligible under the FMLA if the number of employees employed at the worksite, plus the total number of employees employed by the employer within 75 miles of the worksite, is fewer than 50. [FMLA § 101(2)(B)(ii); 29 U.S.C. § 2611(2)(B)(ii); *see* 29 C.F.R. § 825.111 for the rather complex definition of *worksite.*]

> **Example.** Elsie has worked full-time for three years at a restaurant that is owned by Ron and that employs 35 people. Ron also owns and operates another restaurant that is located 20 miles away from Elsie's worksite and that employs 25 people. Elsie is therefore eligible for family or medical leave.

Worksite size is determined as of the date the employee requests FMLA leave, not as of the date the leave commences. [29 C.F.R. § 825.110(e)] If the employing unit drops below the minimum required size, FMLA benefits must continue to be provided to those employees already on FMLA leave. In addition, FMLA benefits must be provided to any employee who requested and was determined eligible for FMLA leave while the employing unit still met the minimum size requirement, even if the leave does not begin until after the employing unit has dropped below the minimum required size. [29 C.F.R. § 825.110(e)] For example, if an employer employs 60 employees in August, but expects the number of employees to drop to 40 in December, the employer must still grant FMLA benefits to an otherwise eligible employee who gives notice in August for a period of leave to begin in December.

DOL regulations specifically provide that the distance between worksites should be measured "by surface miles, using surface transportation over public streets, roads, highways, and waterways, by the shortest route from the facility where the eligible employee needing leave is employed." [29 C.F.R. § 825. 111(b)] However, in a recent case, an employee argued that the 75-mile distance between her employer's worksites should be measured in linear miles "as the crow flies." The employer claimed the employee was not eligible for FMLA because the employer did not employ 50 or more employees within 75 miles of the employee's worksite. The employer conceded that it employed a total of 47 employees at the employee's worksite and at a second worksite within 75 surface miles of the employee's worksite. The employer did employ three workers at a third worksite, but the third worksite was more than 75 miles from the employee's worksite when measured by road. The employee countered that the three employees did count because the third worksite was merely 67 miles away in linear miles. The Tenth Circuit Court of Appeals sided with the employer, concluding that the DOL's requirement that the 75-mile distance be measured in surface miles was a reasonable interpretation of the FMLA. While acknowledging that the law does not specify how to measure the geographic proximity of two worksites, the court pointed out that one of the purposes of the 50-employee/75-mile requirement was to address small business concerns about relocating employees from one worksite to cover for an employee on FMLA leave. Therefore, it seems likely that lawmakers intended the distance to be measured in surface miles. [Hackworth v. Progressive Cas. Ins. Co., 2006 U.S. App. LEXIS 28179 (10th Cir. Nov. 14, 2006)]

For employees with no fixed worksite, such as construction workers, transportation workers (truck drivers, seamen, pilots, etc.), and salespersons, eligibility is determined based on the "worksite" to which they are assigned as their home base or from which their work is assigned, or to which they report. [29 C.F.R. § 825.111(a)(2)]

Example. The Armstrong Construction Company headquartered in New Jersey opens a construction site in Ohio and sets up a mobile trailer on the site as its onsite office. Some employees are hired locally and report to the mobile trailer office daily for work assignments and the like. Armstrong also sends personnel including superintendents, foremen, engineers, and an office manager from New Jersey to the job site in Ohio. The construction site in Ohio is the worksite for employees hired locally who report to the mobile trailer office; however, those workers sent from New Jersey continue to have

Armstrong's New Jersey headquarters as their worksite. The workers who have New Jersey as their worksite are not counted in determining the FMLA eligibility of employees whose home base is the Ohio worksite, but are counted in determining the eligibility of employees whose home base is New Jersey.

For transportation employees, the worksite is the terminal to which the employees are assigned, report for work, depart from and return to after completion of a work assignment. [29 C.F.R. § 825.111(a)(2)]

Example. An airline pilot works for an airline headquartered in New York. The pilot regularly reports for duty and originates flights from the company's facilities at an airport in Chicago and returns to Chicago at the completion of one or more flights to go off duty. The pilot's worksite is the facility in Chicago.

Although an employee's residence may appear to be his or her "home base," it is not his or her worksite for FMLA purposes. In the case of an employee who works at home under a telecommuting or flexplace arrangement, their worksite is the office to which they report and from which assignments are made. [29 C.F.R. § 825.111(a)(2)]

In the case of joint employers, an employee's worksite is the primary employer's office from which the employee is assigned or reports, unless the employee has physically worked for at least one year at a facility of a secondary employer. If the employee has worked for at least one year at the facility of a secondary employer, the employee's worksite is the facility of the secondary employer. [29 C.F.R. § 825.111(a)(3)]

Successors in interest. The FMLA expressly defines *an employer* to include a successor in interest. [29 U.S.C. § 2611(4)(A)(ii)(II)] In determining whether the length-of-service requirements are met, work for a covered employer includes work performed for the employer from whom leave is requested as well as for any previous employer to whom the current covered employer is a successor in interest.

As a general rule, an employer is a successor in interest if it merged with or acquired the assets of another employer. However, in a case of first impression, the Sixth Circuit Court of Appeals concluded that a merger or acquisition is not required for a new employer to be treated as successor in interest. In *Cobb v. Contract Transport, Inc.* [452 F.3d 543 (6th Cir. 2006)], Contract Transport, Inc. acquired a federal mail delivery contract that had been lost by Byrd Trucking. Contract Transport hired a number of Byrd Trucking employees to perform the same mail delivery jobs they had performed for Byrd, but it did not acquire Byrd or Byrd's assets. When a former Byrd employee requested FMLA leave, Contract Transport denied the request (and fired the employee) on the grounds that the employee had not worked for Contract Transport for a 12-month period. The Sixth Circuit ruled, however, that Contract Transport was a successor in interest to Byrd Trucking. The court held that, therefore, the employee, who had worked for Byrd and Contract Transport for a combined total of three years, had met the 12-month service requirement and was eligible for FMLA leave. According to the court, a merger or acquisition is not always required for an employer to be treated as a successor in interest. Instead, a court must balance the equities to determine if an FMLA obligation applies. In this case, the equities weighed in the employee's favor: Cobb delivered mail on the exact same route for three years; the only change was in management, not his job. Moreover, the court pointed out, declining to apply successor liability to companies competing for government contracts would circumvent the FMLA inasmuch as the government accepts new bids on contracts every two years. [Cobb v. Contract Transport, Inc., 452 F.3d 543 (6th Cir. 2006)]

Q 16:8   How do the FMLA service requirements apply to airline pilots and flight crew members?

The Airline Flight Crew Technical Corrections Act of 2009 [Pub. L. No. 111-119, 123 Stat. 3476 (Dec. 21, 2009)] corrects a technical glitch in the law that had barred airline pilots and flight crew members from qualifying for FMLA leave.

To be eligible for FMLA leave under the general FMLA rules, an employee must have worked for a covered employee for at least 1,250 hours during the 12 months preceding the leave (see Q 16:7), which equates to 60 percent of a standard 40-hour work week.

In the case of airline pilots and flight crew members, courts took the position that only in-flight time (not "reserve" time spent on the ground between flights) counted toward the 1,250 hours of service. [*See, e.g.*, Knapp v. America West Airlines, 207 Fed. Appx. 896 (10th Cir. 2006)] However, because of restrictions on in-flight time, this interpretation effectively precluded many pilots and flight crew members from FMLA coverage. For example, the Federal Aviation Act (FAA) regulations prohibit airline pilots from flying more than 1,000 hours per year.

To address this problem, the new law clarifies that a flight attendant or flight crew member will be considered to have met the hours-of-service requirement if he or she has worked or has been paid for: (1) at least 60 percent of the applicable total monthly guarantee, or the equivalent for the previous 12-month period for or by the employer with respect to whom such leave is requested; and (2) a minimum of 504 hours (not counting personal commuting, time spent on vacation, or on medical or sick leave) during such period. [929 U.S.C. § 2611(2)(D) as amended] The applicable monthly guarantee is generally the minimum number of hours for which the airline employer has agreed to schedule the employee for any given month under a collective bargaining agreement or the employer's policies.

Q 16:9   How do the FMLA service requirements apply in the case of members of the National Guard and Reserve who are called to active duty?

The reemployment rights of returning members of the National Guard and Reserve are protected by the Uniformed Services Employment and Reemployment Rights Act (USERRA). Final FMLA regulations make it clear that an employee returning from fulfilling his or her National Guard or Reserve military obligation must be credited with the hours of service that would have been performed but for the period of military service for purposes of both the 12-month period and the 1,250 hours of service requirement. [29 C.F.R. §§ 825.110(b)(2)(i), 825.110(c)(2)]

According to the DOL's interpretation of USERRA, an individual who is called to active duty and then returns to work within the timeframe required for USERRA protection should have this active duty time counted toward his or her eligibility to take time off from work under the FMLA.

The DOL's questions and answers state that the 12-month minimum work requirement for FMLA eligibility is calculated by giving FMLA eligibility credit for all of the months that an individual serves in the military. So, for example, if an employee is called to active duty after working for an employer for nine months and then serves in the military for nine months, he or she would meet the 12-month FMLA eligibility requirement upon his or her return to work.

The 1,250-hours-of-service requirement is calculated using the employee's preservice work schedule. The hours that the employee would have worked for the employer during the period of military service are added to the hours actually worked during the 12-month period prior to the start of the leave. [USERRA-FMLA Questions and Answers (July 25, 2002); OPA News Release (July 26, 2002)]

Q 16:10   Can an employee who has not met the 1,250-hour test ever qualify for FMLA leave?

Former DOL regulations interpreting the FMLA contained a provision that could turn an ineligible employee into an eligible one. [Former 29 C.F.R. § 825.110(d)] The regulation required an employer to provide notice to an employee who requested leave if he or she did not qualify because of failure to meet the 1,250-hour test. If the notice was not provided in a timely manner, the employer was required to grant the FMLA leave.

However, the DOL regulation was rejected by the Supreme Court as an invalid interpretation of the law because it improperly "deemed" ineligible employees eligible for FMLA leave. [Ragsdale v. Wolverine World Wide, Inc., 535 U.S. 81 (2002)]

New FMLA regulations, which took effect January 16, 2009, remove the "deeming" provision. According to the explanation of the final regulations, the DOL believes it does not have the authority to "deem" employees eligible for FMLA leave, even where an employer does not provide the required eligibility notice or provides incorrect information. However, the DOL cautions that such failures may have the effect of interfering with an employee's rights under the FMLA and may result in harm, in which case the employee may have statutory remedies.

Qualifying Family and Medical Leave

Q 16:11   What kinds of family or medical conditions or emergencies qualify for leave under the FMLA?

The FMLA as originally enacted requires that leave be granted to an eligible employee in the following four circumstances:

1. Because of the birth of a son or daughter of the employee and in order to care for that son or daughter;

2. Because of the placement of a son or daughter with the employee for adoption or foster care;

3. Because of a serious health condition (see Q 16:15) that makes the employee unable to perform the functions of his or her position (see Q 16:18); or

4. In order to care for the spouse or a son, daughter, or parent of the employee, if that spouse, son, daughter, or parent has a serious health condition (see Q 16:19).

[FMLA § 102(a)(1); 29 U.S.C. § 2612(a)(1); 29 C.F.R. § 825.112(a)]

Military family leave. Under the National Defense Authorization Act for Fiscal Year 2008 (NDAA), which was enacted on January 28, 2008, an eligible employee must also be granted leave:

1. Because of any "qualifying exigency" arising out of the fact that the spouse, son, daughter, or parent of the employee is on active duty (or has been notified of an impending call or order to active duty) in the Armed Forces in support of a "contingency operation" (see Q 16:12) or

2. To care for a "covered servicemember" with a serious illness or injury incurred in the line of duty if the employee is the servicemember's spouse, parent, son, daughter, or next of kin (see Q 16:12).

[Pub. L. No. 110-181, 122 Stat. 3 (2008); FMLA §§ 102(a)(1)(E), 102(a)(3); 29 U.S.C. § 2612(a)(1)(E), (a)(3)]

The provision requiring caregiver leave became effective immediately upon enactment. However, the law provided that the provision relating to leave because of "qualifying exigency" would not take effect until the DOL issued regulations defining that term. Final regulations including that definition took effect on January 16, 2009.

FMLA leave rights apply equally to male and female employees. Fathers as well as mothers can take family leave for a child's birth or placement for adoption or foster care. [29 C.F.R. § 825.112(b)]

Son or daughter. For purposes of leave taken for birth or adoption or to care for a family member with a serious health condition, *son or daughter* is defined to include a biological, adopted, or foster child; a stepchild; a legal ward; or a child of a person standing in loco parentis, if the child is either (1) under 18 years of age or (2) 18 years of age or older but incapable of self-care because of a mental or physical disability. [FMLA § 101(12); 29 U.S.C. 2611(12); 29 C.F.R. § 825.122(c)] However, special rules apply in the case of military family leave (see Q 16:40).

Whether an adopted child is placed by a licensed placement agency or otherwise is irrelevant in determining eligibility for leave. [29 C.F.R. § 825.122(e)]

For purposes of the FMLA, an individual is considered to be *incapable of self-care* if he or she requires either supervision or active assistance with regard to three or more activities of daily living (ADLs) or instrumental activities of daily living (IADLs), including personal grooming and hygiene, bathing, dressing, eating, cooking, cleaning, shopping, taking public transportation, paying bills, maintaining a residence, using telephones and directories, using a post office, and so forth. *Physical or mental disability* means a physical or mental impairment that substantially limits one or more of the major life activities of the individual, as defined in the Equal Employment Opportunity Commission (EEOC) regulations under the Americans with Disabilities Act of 1990 (see chapter 18). [29 C.F.R. § 825.122(c)]

The First Circuit Court of Appeals held that an eligible employee was entitled to FMLA leave to care for an adult daughter who was suffering from pregnancy-related high blood pressure and required bed rest in order to carry the pregnancy to term. Acknowledging that the term *disability* generally brings to mind a long-term condition, the First Circuit held that severe temporary impairment may also qualify as a disability for FMLA purposes. The court noted that a worker who seeks FMLA leave often does so in response to a crisis. However, if a hard-and-fast duration requirement were enforced, an employee would be effectively prevented from taking family leave to care for an adult child until it could be established that the child's problem was long-term. "Such a scenario," said the court, "would place an employee with a sick adult child between a rock and a hard place, forcing him or her to choose between employment demands and family needs." [Navarro v. Pfizer Corp., 261 F.3d 90 (1st Cir. 2001)] It should be noted that the First Circuit decision was not unanimous. Calling his colleagues' views "humanly appealing," a dissenting judge said the law was intended to impose a limitation on the class of adult children for whose care FMLA leave is mandated. According to the dissent, the language of the law was intend to limit leave to those situations in which an adult child with a long-term mental or physical disability remains especially dependent on a parent and needs care when he or she becomes seriously ill.

Practice Pointer. Despite the "humanly appealing" reasoning of the First Circuit case, the preamble to final FMLA regulations issued in 2008 points out that under current EEOC regulations interpreting the ADA, whether or not an impairment rises to the level of a disability generally relates to the nature, severity, duration and long-term impact of the impairment. Thus, the DOL concludes, for example, that if an adult child breaks his leg in a car accident and is expected to recover in a short time, he would not generally qualify as incapable of self-care because of a disability. Thus, any leave taken by the parent would not qualify under the FMLA. The DOL's reliance on the current

EEOC regulations should be read with caution, however. The ADA Amendments Act of 2008 [Pub. L. No. 110-325] provides new rules of construction to determine when a substantially limiting impairment exists. Most significantly, the ADA Amendments Act specifically rejects Supreme Court decisions (and corresponding EEOC regulations) that, in Congress's view, imposed inappropriately high standards for coverage under the ADA. [ADA Amendments Act § 2] The EEOC is directed to issue revised regulations in keeping with the amended rules.

Parent. The definition of *a parent* is similarly quite broad. A *parent* is defined as the biological parent of an employee, or an individual who stood in loco parentis to an employee when the employee was a child. [FMLA § 101(7); 29 U.S.C. § 2611(7)] The definition does not include parents-in-law. [29 C.F.R. §§ 825.113(b), 825.113(c)(3)]

Spouse. The definition of *spouse* is limited to a person who is a husband or a wife, as the case may be. [FMLA § 101(13); 29 U.S.C. § 2611(13)] Thus, persons who live together but are not married pursuant to state law would not qualify for spousal medical leave. A common-law marriage qualifies as a marriage for FMLA purposes in those states where such a marriage is recognized. A domestic partner does not qualify as a spouse. [29 C.F.R. § 825.113(a)]

Under the federal Defense of Marriage Act [Pub. L. No. 104-199, 100 Stat. 2419 (1996)], a spouse refers only to a person of the opposite sex. Consequently, an employee who is legally married to a same-sex spouse under Massachusetts law is not entitled to leave under the FMLA to care for the spouse (but is entitled to FMLA leave to care for a child or parent). However, there is nothing in the statute itself to bar an employer from extending its leave program to cover same-sex spouses.

Q 16:12 Is an employee entitled to take leave under the FMLA when a family member is called up for military service or is injured in the line of duty?

The National Defense Authorization Act for Fiscal Year 2008 (NDAA), which was enacted on January 28, 2008, amends the FMLA to require employers to provide leave for military family members in two circumstances:

1. An eligible employee is entitled to up to 12 weeks of leave in a 12-month period because of any "qualifying exigency" arising out of the fact that the spouse, son, daughter, or parent of the employee is on active duty (or has been notified of an impending call or order to active duty) in the Armed Forces. [FMLA § 102(a)(1)(E); 29 U.S.C. § 2612(a)(1)(E)]

2. An eligible employee who is the spouse, son, daughter, parent, or next of kin (i.e., closest blood relative) of a "covered servicemember" with a serious illness or injury incurred in the line of duty is entitled to a total of 26 weeks of leave in a 12-month period to care for the servicemember. [FMLA § 102(a)(3); 29 U.S.C. § 2612(a)(3)]

[Pub. L. No. 110-181, 122 Stat. 3 (2008)]

The requirement to grant leave to care for a covered servicemember became effective immediately upon enactment. However, the law provided that the provision relating to leave because of "qualifying exigency" would not take effect until the DOL issued regulations defining that term. Final FMLA regulations including that definition took effect on January 16, 2009, triggering the requirement to provide such leave.

An otherwise qualified employee can take military caregiver leave if he or she is the spouse, son, daughter, parent, or next of kin of the covered servicemember requiring care. Qualifying exigency leave may be taken by an otherwise qualified employee who is the spouse, son, daughter, or parent of a covered servicemember who is on active duty or has been notified of an impending call to active duty.

In its preamble to the final FMLA regulations, the DOL notes that for FMLA purposes, the terms "son" and "daughter" are generally defined to include only children under age 18 (or children over 18 who are incapable of self-care). However, to use that definition for purposes of military caregiver leave would mean that most would be unable to take leave to care for a parent who is a covered servicemember. Similarly, the DOL points out that using the existing FMLA definitions of son and daughter would eviscerate the qualifying exigency leave provision because the majority of sons and daughters who are activated as members of the National Guard or Reserves are not under age and those over age 18 are unlikely to be incapable of self-care due to a disability. Consequently, for both types of military leave purposes, a son or daughter may be of any age. [29 C.F.R. § 825.122(g), (h); 29 C.F.R. § 825.800] The final regulations also include special rules defining who qualifies as the parent or next of kin of a covered servicemember for purposes of caregiver leave.

Substitution of paid leave. As with other types of FMLA leave, an eligible employee may elect, or an employer may require the employee, to substitute any of the accrued paid vacation leave, personal leave, family leave, or medical or sick leave of the employee for military family leave (see Q 16:42). However, an employer is not required to provide paid sick leave or paid medical leave in any situation in which the employer would not normally provide any such paid leave. [FMLA § 102(d); 29 U.S.C. § 2612(d)]

Q 16:13   When can an employee take military caregiver leave?

To qualify for military caregiver leave, an otherwise eligible employee (i.e., an employee who has worked for a covered employer for the requisite time normally required for FMLA leave) must be the spouse, son, daughter, parent, or next of kin of the covered servicemember requiring care. In its preamble to the final regulations, the DOL notes that for FMLA purposes, the terms "son" and "daughter" are generally defined to include only children under age 18 (or children over 18 who are incapable of self-care). However, to use that definition for purposes of military caregiver leave would mean that most, if not all employees, would be unable to take leave to care for a parent who is a covered servicemember. Therefore, for military caregiver purposes, a son or daughter of any age may qualify. [29 C.F.R. § 825.122(h); 29 C.F.R. § 825.800]

A parent of a covered servicemember means a covered servicemember's biological, adoptive, step or foster father or mother, or any other individual who stood in loco parentis to the covered servicemember. A parent of a covered servicemember does not include a parent "in law." [29 C.F.R. § 825.122(h); 29 C.F.R. § 825.800]

A covered servicemember's "next of kin" is defined as the nearest blood relative, (other than a spouse, parent, son, or daughter) according to an ordering system specified in the regulations—for example, blood relatives with legal custody of the servicemember, followed by brothers and sisters, grandparents, aunts and uncles, and cousins. If there are multiple family members with the same level of relationship to the covered servicemember, all of those family members may take military caregiver leave, either consecutively or simultaneously. A covered servicemember may, however, designate, in writing, a specific blood relative as next of kin for purposes of military caregiver leave. If such a designation is made, that individual is treated as the servicemember's only next of kin. [29 C.F.R. §§ 825(d), 825.800]

Military caregiver leave may be taken only to care for a "covered servicemember." A covered servicemember is a member of the Armed Forces, including a member of the National Guard or Reserves, who is: (1) undergoing medical treatment, recuperation, or therapy for a serious injury or illness; (2) receiving care as an outpatient; or (3) on the temporary disability retired list for a serious injury or illness. Serious injury or illness means an injury or illness incurred in the line of duty that may render the servicemember medically unfit to perform his or her duties. [FMLA § 101(16); 29 U.S.C. § 2611(16); 29 C.F.R. §§ 825.127(a), 825.800] Under the law as originally enacted, military caregiver leave was not available to care for a former member of the Armed Services. However, the 2010 National Defense Authorization Act [Pub. L. No. 111-84, 123 Stat. 2190], which was signed into law on October 28, 2009, extends military caregiver leave to family members of a veteran undergoing medical treatment, recuperation, or therapy for a serious illness or injury and who was a member of the armed forces at any time during the five-year period preceding the date on which the veteran receives treatment, recuperation, or therapy.

An employer may require an employee to provide certification of the covered servicemember's serious illness or injury and need for care. The DOL has developed an optional form WH-385, Certification for Serious Illness or Injury of Covered Servicemember—for Family Military Leave (Family and Medical Leave Act), that can be used for this purpose.

An employee is entitled to 26 weeks of military caregiver leave in a 12-month period, twice the normal 12-week FMLA leave allotment. However, military caregiver leave is subject to its own special rules and restrictions. The final regulations make it clear that military caregiver leave is not an annual entitlement that renews each year; instead, it is a one-shot "per servicemember, per injury entitlement." [29 C.F.R. § 825.127(c)(2)] An employee is not entitled to additional caregiver leave beyond that 12-month period or beyond 26 weeks with respect to the same servicemember and the same injury. However, an additional period of caregiver leave would be available with respect to the same servicemember for a different injury or with respect to a different servicemember.

The 12-month period in which military caregiver leave may be taken begins on the first day the employee takes leave to care for the covered servicemember and ends 12 months after that date, regardless of the method used by the employer to determine the 12-month period for any other FMLA leave. If an employee does not take all of his or her 26 workweeks of leave entitlement to care for a covered servicemember during this single 12-month period, the remaining part of the 26 workweeks is forfeited. [29 C.F.R. § 825.127(c)(1)]

If an employee takes FMLA leave for another purpose during the 12-month period of military caregiver leave, the total leave during the period cannot exceed 26 weeks. [FMLA § 102(a)(4); 29 U.S.C. § 2612(a)(4); 29 C.F.R. § 825.127(c)(3)] In other words, if the military leave during that period exceeds 14 weeks, then the regular allowable FMLA leave may be reduced. For example, if an employee takes 16 weeks of leave during a 12-month period to care for a covered servicemember, leave for another FMLA qualifying purpose is limited to 10 weeks. Conversely, if the employee takes fewer than 14 weeks of leave to care for a covered servicemember, leave for another FMLA qualifying purpose cannot exceed the normal 12 weeks.

If spouses work for the same employer and both take leave to care for a servicemember plus other FMLA-qualifying leave, their leave may be limited to 26 workweeks during a single 12-month period. [FMLA § 102(f); 29 U.S.C. § 2612(a)] If the other FMLA-qualifying leave is for the birth or adoption of a child or to care for a sick parent, the longstanding rule limiting the spouses' combined leave to 12 weeks applies to that leave (see Q 16:23).

Q 16:14   When can an employee take leave on account of a qualifying exigency related to a family member's call to active military duty?

An otherwise eligible employee of a covered employer is entitled to up to 12 weeks of leave in a 12-month period because of any "qualifying exigency" arising out of the fact that the spouse, son or daughter (including an adult son or daughter), or parent of the employee is on active duty (or has been notified of an impending call or order to active duty) in the Armed Forces. [FMLA § 102(a)(1)(E); 29 U.S.C. § 2612(a)(1)(E); 29 C.F.R. § 825.126] Unlike military caregiver leave, qualifying exigency leave is treated as part of an employee's normal, annual 12-week FMLA entitlement.

As originally enacted, qualifying exigency leave applied only in the case of a servicemember in the National Guard or Reserves who is called to active duty in support of a contingency operation. Qualifying exigency leave was not available to family members of individuals in the regular Armed Forces. The 2010 National Defense Authorization Act (Pub. L. No. 111-84), which was signed into law on October 28, 2009, expands qualifying exigency leave to a spouse, parent, son, or daughter of a servicemember in the regular Armed Forces who is deployed to a foreign country.

Final DOL regulations describe the following "qualifying exigencies" that will trigger FMLA leave:

- *Short-notice deployment.* Addressing any issue that arises from the fact that a covered military member is notified of an impending call or order to active duty seven or fewer calendar days prior to the date of deployment. The leave can be used for a period of seven calendar days beginning on the date the member is notified of the call to duty. [29 C.F.R. § 825.126(a)(1)]

- *Military events and related activities.* Attending any official ceremony, program, or event sponsored by the military that is related to the member's active duty status; or attending family support or assistance programs and informational briefings sponsored or promoted by the military, military service organizations, or the American Red Cross that are related to the call to duty. [29 C.F.R. § 825.126(a)(2)]

- *Childcare and school activities.* Attending to childcare and school activity matters involving a biological child, adopted child, foster child, stepchild, or legal ward of a covered military member or a child for whom a covered military member stands in loco parentis, who is either under age 18 or age 18 or older and incapable of self-care. Such matters include arranging a change to existing childcare; providing childcare on an urgent, immediate need basis; enrolling a child in or transferring a child to a new school or day care facility; or meeting with a child's school or day care staff when necessary due to circumstances arising out of the call to active duty. [29 C.F.R. § 825.126(a)(3)]

- *Financial and legal arrangements.* Making or updating financial or legal arrangements to address the covered military member's absence, such as preparing and executing financial and health care powers of attorney, transferring bank account signature authority, or updating a will; or appearing on the member's behalf in obtaining, arranging, or appealing military service benefits. [29 C.F.R. § 825.126(a)(4)]

- *Counseling.* Attending counseling by someone other than a health care provider for the employee, for the covered military member, or for a child (as described above) of the covered military member, when the need arises due to the call to active duty. [29 C.F.R. § 825.126(a)(5)]

- *Rest and recuperation.* Spending time, not to exceed five days, to be with a covered military member who is on short-term, temporary, rest and recuperation leave during the period of deployment. [29 C.F.R. § 825. 126(a)(6)]

- *Post-deployment activities.* Attending official military events such as arrival ceremonies and reintegration briefings during the 90-day period following termination of active duty status; and addressing issues related to the death of the covered military member such as recovery of the member's body and making funeral arrangements. [29 C.F.R. § 825. 126(a)(7)]

- *Additional activities.* Dealing with other events arising from the call to active duty status, provided that the employer and employee both agree that the event is a qualifying exigency and also agree to both the timing and duration of the leave. [29 C.F.R. § 825.126(a)(8)]

In a situation where the employee's need for leave related to a servicemember's active duty is foreseeable, the employee must provide whatever notice to the employer is reasonable and practicable. [FMLA § 102(e)(3); 29 U.S.C. § 2612(e)(e)]

When an employee requests leave in connection with a servicemember's active duty, the employer can request certification from the employee. [FMLA § 103(f); 29 U.S.C. § 2613(f)] The DOL has developed a new form WH-384, Certification of Qualifying Exigency for Family Military Leave (Family and Medical Leave Act), that can be used for this purpose.

Q 16:15   What is a serious health condition under the FMLA?

An employee is entitled to FMLA leave for his or her own or a family member's *serious health condition,* which is defined as meaning an illness, injury, impairment or physical or mental condition that involves:

1. Inpatient care, or
2. Continuing treatment by a health care provider. [29 C.F.R. § 825.113(a)]

Inpatient care means an overnight stay in a hospital, hospice, or residential medical facility, including any period of incapacity or any subsequent treatment in connection with such inpatient care. [29 C.F.R. § 825.114] Incapacity means the inability to work, attend school, or to perform normal daily activities due to a serious health condition or due to treatment or recovery from a serious health condition. [29 C.F.R. § 825.113(b)]

Treatment includes (but is not limited to) examinations to determine if a serious health condition exists and evaluations of the condition. However, treatment does not include routine physical exams, eye exams, or dental exams. A regimen of continuing treatment includes, for example, a course of prescription medication (such as an antibiotic) or therapy requiring special equipment (such as oxygen). A regimen of continuing treatment that includes taking over-the-counter medications, bed rest, drinking fluids, or other activities that can be initiated without a visit to a health care provider is not enough to constitute a regimen of continuing treatment for FMLA purposes. [29 C.F.R. § 825.113(c)] The requirement for treatment by a health care provider means an in-person visit, which must take place within the first seven days of incapacity. [29 C.F.R. § 825.115(a)(3)]

Treatment for substance abuse can be considered a serious health condition if the FMLA requirements are met. FMLA leave may be taken for treatment for substance abuse by a health care provider or a provider of health care services on referral by a health care provider. However, the DOL regulations specifically state that an absence resulting from an employee's actual use of the substance, rather than treatment for the abuse, does not qualify. [FMLA § 101(11); 29 U.S.C. § 2611(11); 29 C.F.R. § 825.114]

Provided that all other requirements under the regulations are met, the following conditions are expressly recognized as serious health conditions:

- Restorative dental surgery after an accident
- Removal of cancerous growths
- Mental illness resulting from allergies or stress
- Substance abuse
- Pregnancy
- Prenatal care

Cosmetic treatments (such as for acne or plastic surgery) are not considered serious health conditions unless inpatient hospital care is required or complications develop. Ordinarily, unless complications arise, the common cold, the flu, ear aches, upset stomach, minor ulcers, headaches other than migraine, routine dental or orthodontia problems, periodontal disease, and the like, are not serious health conditions and do not qualify for family leave. [29 C.F.R. § 825.113(d)]

Q 16:16   Under the FMLA, what constitutes "continuing treatment by a health care provider"?

Continuing treatment by a health care provider includes any one or more of the following:

Incapacity and treatment. A period of incapacity of more than three consecutive, full calendar days, and any subsequent treatment or period of incapacity that involves either: (a) treatment two or more times within 30 days of the first incapacity (unless extenuating circumstances exist) by a health care provider, a nurse under the direction of a health care provider or a health care services provider (e.g., a physical therapist), under direction or referral of a health care provider; or (b) treatment by a health care provider on at least one occasion, which results in a regimen of continuing treatment under the supervision of a health care provider. [29 C.F.R. § 825.115(a)]

Incapacity means the inability to work, attend school, or to perform normal daily activities due to a serious health condition or due to treatment or recovery from a serious health condition. [29 C.F.R. § 825.113(b)]

Pregnancy and prenatal care. Any period of incapacity due to pregnancy or prenatal care. [29 C.F.R. § 825.115(b)] An absence for this reason qualifies for FMLA leave, even if an employee or family member does not receive treatment from a health care provider during the absence. [29 C.F.R. § 825.115(f)] For example, an employee who is pregnant may be unable to report for work because of severe morning sickness.

Chronic conditions. Any period of incapacity due to a chronic serious health condition that (a) requires periodic visits for treatment by a health care provider or a nurse under the supervision of a health care provider; (b) continues over an extended period of time (including recurring episodes of a single underlying condition); and (c) may cause episodic rather than a continuing period of incapacity. [29 C.F.R. § 825.115(d)] Examples include asthma, diabetes, and epilepsy. An absence for this reason qualifies for FMLA leave, even if an employee or family member does not receive treatment from a health care provider during the absence. [29 C.F.R. § 825.115(f)] For example, an employee with asthma may be unable to report to work due to the onset of an asthma attack, even though the employee can deal with the attack on his or her own.

Like the prior rules, the final regulations issued in 2008 provide that the FMLA applies to incapacity due to a serious chronic health condition that continues over a period of time, involves episodic rather than continuing periods of incapacity, and requires "periodic visits" for treatment. However, the final regulations impose a new limit: "Periodic visits" for treatment must take place at least twice a year. Thus, an employee could not see a doctor once and then claim FMLA protection for absences over a period of years. [29 C.F.R. § 825.115(c)(1)]

Permanent or long-term conditions. A period of incapacity that is permanent or long-term due to a condition for which treatment may not be effective. [29 C.F.R. § 825.115(d)] In this case, the employee or family member must be under the continuing supervision of a health care provider, but need not be receiving active treatment. Examples include Alzheimer's disease, a severe stroke, or the terminal stages of a disease.

Conditions requiring multiple treatments. Any period of absence to receive multiple treatments (including any recovery period) by a health care provider or a provider of health care services under the orders of or referral by a health care provider for (a) restorative surgery after an accident or injury or (b) a condition that would likely result in a period of incapacity of more than three consecutive, full calendar days in the absence of medical intervention or treatment. [29 C.F.R. § 825.115(e)] Examples include absences to receive chemotherapy or radiation for cancer, physical therapy for severe arthritis, or dialysis for kidney disease.

The term *health care provider* is defined as follows:

1. A doctor of medicine or osteopathy who is authorized to practice medicine or surgery (as appropriate) by the state in which the doctor practices; or

2. Any other person determined by the Secretary of Labor to be capable of providing health care services.

[FMLA § 101(6); 29 U.S.C. § 2611(6)]

This latter category includes Christian Science practitioners listed with the First Church of Christ, Scientist, in Boston, Massachusetts. It also includes the following individuals, if authorized to practice under state law and performing within the scope of their practice under state law: nurse practitioners, nurse-midwives, clinical social workers, physician assistants, podiatrists, dentists, clinical psychologists, optometrists, and chiropractors (limited to treatment consisting of manual manipulation of the spine to correct a subluxation shown by X-ray to exist). It also includes any health care provider from whom an employer or the employer's group health plan's benefits manager will accept certification of the existence of a serious health condition to substantiate a claim for benefits. Listed individuals authorized to practice in a country other than the United States are also included. [29 C.F.R. § 825.125]

Q 16:17   How have the courts interpreted the phrase *serious health condition* under the FMLA?

The federal courts have issued several opinions relating to the phrase *serious medical condition.*

When seriousness is to be determined. The medical condition must be currently serious. A federal district court has held that it is not enough for FMLA purposes that the condition, if left untreated, could become serious at some point in the future. In this case, a child had a fever that lasted for only 24 hours. [Seidle v. Provident Mut. Life Ins. Co., 871 F. Supp. 238 (E.D. Pa. 1994)] Note, however, that the FMLA regulations specifically provide that a serious health condition includes a condition that would likely result in a period of incapacity of more than three consecutive, full calendar days in the absence of medical intervention or treatment. [29 C.F.R. § 825.115(e)] (See Q 16:16.)

Eligible conditions. A federal district court ruled that an employee who sought medical care on only one occasion for rectal bleeding, possibly caused by hemorrhoids, did not have a serious health condition of the type contemplated by the FMLA. [Bauer v. Dayton Walther Corp., 910 F. Supp. 306 (E.D. Ky. 1996)] Another federal district court has ruled that although the FMLA clearly protects the jobs of workers who take time off to care for a sick family member, a worker's failure to return to work after the relative dies causes the worker to lose the FMLA's job protections. The case involved an employee who took a 12-week leave to care for his terminally ill father but did not return to work until almost a month after his father died. The employee claimed that he was still caring for his father posthumously. When he returned, the employee was offered a transfer to another position. He rejected the new job, and the company terminated him. The employee sued, claiming that he was entitled under the FMLA to be restored to his old job or a job of equal stature. The court rejected his claim, stating that the FMLA required only restoration to an equivalent job and that, in any event, there is no support in the FMLA for the position that a serious health condition continues to exist after the person has died. [Brown v. J.C. Penney Corp., 924 F. Supp. 1158 (S.D. Fla. 1996)]

Food poisoning was held not to be a serious health condition where the employee visited the doctor once and did not require inpatient treatment at a hospital, hospice, or residential care facility or continuing medical treatment by a health provider. [Oswalt v. Sara Lee Corp., 889 F. Supp 253 (N.D. Miss. 1995), *aff'd*, 74 F.3d 91 (5th Cir. 1996)] A child's ear infection also was not a serious health condition justifying FMLA leave for the mother, where the child's fever lasted for only 24 hours. The child saw the doctor once to receive a prescription for antibiotics and never complained of ear pain, and the child was absent from day care for only three days. The employee failed to show that the child was under continuing treatment by a health care provider. [Seidle v. Provident Mut. Life Ins. Co., 871 F. Supp. 238 (E.D. Pa. 1994)]

A case involving illness of both parent and child suggests that the employee's testimony regarding his or her own condition must be bolstered by a physician, although the parent evidently can be competent to testify to the physical manifestations of the child's condition. In that case, the employee had gastro-enteritis and an upper respiratory infection, but the court found that there was no proof that she was incapacitated for more than three calendar days, and her physician never advised her to remain off work. On the other hand, the employee's child had throat and upper respiratory infections, and a court found it to be a serious health condition because, among other things, the parents were competent to testify that the child had a fever for four days and the pediatrician testified that the child should remain out of day care on the third and fourth days. [Brannon v. Oshkosh B'Gosh Inc., 897 F. Supp. 1028 (M.D. Tenn. 1995)]

A shipping department worker who was fired after taking several days off due to a stomach ulcer had a "serious health condition." A court of appeals affirmed that the firing violated the FMLA. [Thorson v. Gemini., Inc., 205 F.3d 370 (8th Cir. 2000)] The Eighth Circuit Court of Appeals upheld the lower court's judgment against the employer, finding that the "continuing treatment" the employee received for her illness qualified it as a serious health condition under the objective tests set forth in the DOL Regulations. The court found that all of the definitional requirements of *serious health condition* were met.

The court said that subjectively the employee's condition was not serious in the usual sense of the word. Nevertheless, her physician believed she could have a potentially serious condition, and it was not until after she had been terminated from her job that a diagnosis definitively ruled out her physician's initial suspicions. The employee was sufficiently ill to see a physician two times in a period of just a few days, and that is all that the plain language of the final rule requires for continuing treatment, the court said.

Even that annual menace the flu can qualify an employee for FMLA leave. In one case, the Fourth Circuit Court of Appeals noted that DOL Regulations specifically provide that "Ordinarily, unless complications arise, the common cold, the flu . . . etc., are examples of conditions that do not meet the definition of a serious health condition, and do not qualify for family leave." However, the court said, that regulation does not mean that all flu-related absences are automatically barred from FMLA coverage if they meet the basic regulatory requirements. Instead, the regulation is intended to clarify that some common illnesses generally will not meet the requirements because they normally do not result in an inability to work for three or more consecutive days and do not require continuing treatment by a health care provider. On the other hand, when those requirements are met, a flu-related absence is protected by the FMLA. [Miller v. AT&T Corp., 250 F.3d 820 (4th Cir. 2001)]

The Fourth Circuit's viewpoint may be catching. In another case, the Eighth Circuit also held that an employee's bout with the flu may qualify for FMLA protection. According to the Eighth Circuit, "the fact that an employee is sufficiently ill to see a physician two times in a period of just a few days is all that the FMLA requires for continuing treatment." [Rankin v. Seagate Techs., Inc., 246 F.3d 1145 (8th Cir. 2001)]

> **Practice Pointer.** As a general rule, most employees will have enough sick days or other leave time available to cover absences for the flu or other garden-variety illness. Thus, disputes involving FMLA coverage for routine illnesses are likely to crop up only when an employee has a poor attendance record, as was the case in these two decisions. However, as these cases illustrate, by denying the leave and firing the employee an employer could end up on the losing end of a lawsuit. The safest course is to allow the leave if the employee presents evidence of continuing treatment.

Q 16:18   When is an employee unable to perform the functions of his or her position?

For FMLA purposes, an employee is considered to be unable to perform the functions of his or her position when a health care provider finds that the employee (1) is unable to work at all or (2) is unable to perform any one of the essential functions of the employee's position within the meaning of the ADA and the regulations thereunder (see chapter 18). An employee who must be absent from work to receive medical treatment for a serious health condition is considered to be unable to perform the essential functions of the position during the absence for treatment. [29 C.F.R. § 825.123]

In connection with obtaining medical certification of an employee's serious health condition (see Q 16:36), an employer may provide the employee's health care provider with a statement of the essential functions of the employee's position for the health care provider to review. A sufficient medical certification must specify what functions of the employee's position the employee is unable to perform. [29 C.F.R. § 825.123(b)]

Q 16:19   When is an employee needed to care for a family member or covered servicemember?

The medical certification that an employee is needed to care for a family member or covered servicemember covers both physical and psychological care. It thus includes providing psychological comfort and reassurance beneficial to a family member with a serious health condition who is receiving inpatient or home care. It also includes the need for transportation to a medical provider. [29 C.F.R. § 825.124(a)]

An employee may also be needed to substitute for others who normally care for a family member or covered servicemember or to make arrangements for care, such as transfer to a nursing home. [29 C.F.R. § 825.124(b)]

However, a court ruled that neither the FMLA nor California state law required a county hospital to provide five weeks of leave to an employee who sent her son to live with relatives overseas out of concern for his well-being. [Marchisheck v. San Mateo County, 199 F.3d 1068 (9th Cir. 1999), *cert. denied*, 530 U.S. 1214 (2000)] Even though the mother's desire to move her son to a more wholesome environment was laudable, the act of taking him to a foreign country to leave him with relatives could not be considered "caring for" a family member for purposes of the statutes, the court said. The FMLA regulations suggest that caring for a child with a serious health condition involves some level of participation in ongoing treatment of that condition, the court added. The mother did not have plans to seek medical attention for her son once he was overseas; therefore, she could not "care for" her son under the FMLA by removing him to a place where he would not receive medical treatment.

The Ninth Circuit also ruled that while the FMLA encompasses both physical and psychological care, caring for a family member necessarily involves close and continuing proximity to the ill family member. [Tellis v. Alaska Airlines, 414 F.3d 1045 (9th Cir. 2005)]. The employee involved in the case requested FMLA leave to attend to his pregnant wife. However, one day after he made the request, his car broke down and he took a cross-country trip to retrieve a second vehicle that he owned. His wife, who was left in the care of a sister-in-law, gave birth during his absence. When the employer was unable to contact the employee, a decision was made to terminate his employment. The employee argued that his absence was protected by the FMLA because his trip to retrieve the second vehicle provided psychological reassurance to his wife that she would soon have reliable transportation, and his phone calls to her provided moral support and psychological comfort. The court concluded that the employee was not caring for his wife during his cross-country trip, and his termination did not violate the provisions of the FMLA. According to the court, the employee's having a working vehicle may have provided psychological reassurance to his wife, but that was merely an indirect benefit of the unprotected activity of traveling away from the person needing care.

Intermittent leave or a reduced leave schedule to care for a family member includes both the situation where the condition of the family member or covered servicemember is intermittent as well as the situation where the employee is needed only intermittently (such as where other care is normally available or care responsibilities are shared with others). [29 C.F.R. § 825.124(c)]

Q 16:20   How long a period of FMLA leave must an employer provide to an eligible employee?

An eligible employee is generally entitled to a total of 12 workweeks of family or medical leave during any 12-month period. [FMLA § 102(a)(1); 29 U.S.C. § 2612(a)(1)] An employer has several options for defining the 12-month period during which leave must be taken (see Q 16:21).

Special rules apply to the birth or adoption of a child (see Q 16:22) and where a husband and wife work for the same employer (see Q 16:23).

Military family leave. Under the National Defense Authorization Act for Fiscal Year 2008 (NDAA), which was enacted on January 28, 2008, an eligible employee is entitled to up to 12 weeks of leave in a 12-month period because of any "qualifying exigency" arising out of the fact that the spouse, son, daughter, or parent of the employee is on active duty (or has been notified of an impending call or order to active duty) in the Armed Forces in support of a "contingency operation." However, an eligible employee who is the spouse, son, daughter, parent, or next of kin of a "covered servicemember" with a serious illness or injury incurred in the line of duty is entitled to a total of *26 weeks* of leave in a 12-month period to care for the servicemember.

If a military family member requires leave to care for a servicemember as well as leave for another FMLA-qualifying purpose (including leave for a "qualifying exigency" related to a servicemember's active duty), the combined leave is limited to a total of 26 weeks. [Pub. L. No. 110-181, 122 Stat. 3 (2008); FMLA §§ 102(a)(1)(E), 102(a)(3), 102(a)(4); 29 U.S.C. § 2612(a)(1)(E), (a)(3), (a)(4)] (See Qs 16:12–16:14 for details on the military family leave requirements.)

The requirement to grant leave to care for a covered servicemember became effective immediately upon enactment. However, the law provided that the provision relating to leave because of "qualifying exigency" would not take effect until the DOL issued regulations defining that term. Final FMLA regulations including that definition took effect on January 16, 2009, triggering the requirement to provide such leave.

An otherwise qualified employee can take military caregiver leave if he or she is the spouse, son, daughter, parent, or next of kin of the covered servicemember requiring care. Qualifying exigency leave may be taken by an otherwise qualified employee who is the spouse, son, daughter, or parent of a covered servicemember who is on active duty or has been notified of an impending call to active duty.

Q 16:21 May an employer select the 12-month period in which an employee's 12-week FMLA leave entitlement occurs?

Yes. The DOL Regulations provide four different methods of determining the 12-month period during which employees may take their FMLA leave. Whichever method an employer selects must be applied consistently and uniformly to all the employer's employees. If the employer wishes to switch methods, it must give at least 60 days' notice to all employees, and transition to the new method must provide that employees will retain the full benefit of 12 workweeks of leave under whichever method affords the greatest benefit to the employee. Employers are prohibited from switching to a new method in a manner designed to avoid the FMLA's leave requirements. [29 C.F.R. § 825.200(d)]

The four methods for determining the 12-month period during which the 12 workweeks of leave entitlement occurs are as follows:

1. The calendar year. Under this method, employees would be entitled to their FMLA leave at any time during the calendar year.

2. Any fixed 12-month period (such as a fiscal year, a year starting on the yearly anniversary of the employee's date of hire, or a year required by state law). Under this method, employees would be entitled to take their FMLA leave at any time in the fixed 12-month period.

3. The 12-month period measured forward from the date the employee's first FMLA leave begins.

4. A "rolling" 12-month period measured backward from the date an employee takes FMLA leave. Under this method, the employee's entitlement to FMLA leave is the balance of the 12 weeks that have not been taken during the immediately preceding 12 months. For example, if the employee has taken only 3 weeks of FMLA leave in the past 12 months, the employee is entitled to up to 9 weeks of additional leave.

[29 C.F.R. §§ 825.200(b), 825.200(c)]

Note. Under the first and second methods, employees might be able to "bunch" two years' worth of FMLA leave and take 24 weeks off at one time. For example, with a calendar-year period, an employee could take 12 workweeks of FMLA leave in October, November, and December of one calendar year and an additional 12 workweeks of FMLA leave in January, February, and March of the next calendar year (assuming all other FMLA requirements are satisfied). The third and fourth methods prevent such bunching of FMLA leave, but are more administratively complex.

Example 1. Sigma Corp. determines eligibility for FMLA leave based on the calendar year. A Sigma employee, Jane, begins 12 weeks of FMLA leave on October 8, 2007, to care for her newborn child. Her 12-week leave ends on December 31, 2007. Jane does not have to return to work after the New Year's holiday. Under Sigma's calendar-year plan, she can take another 12 weeks of FMLA leave beginning January 1, 2008.

Example 2. The facts are the same as those in Example 1, except that Sigma pegs eligibility for FMLA leave based on an individually determined period measured forward. Jane's initial 12-month FMLA leave period begins October 8, 2007, and ends on October 7, 2008. Therefore, Jane will not be eligible for additional FMLA leave until October 8, 2008.

Example 3. Delphi Corp. measures FMLA leave using a calendar year. John, who has a chronic serious health condition, took four weeks of leave beginning February 1, 2007, four weeks beginning June 1, 2007, and four weeks beginning December 1, 2007. Under Delphi's calendar-year plan, John is eligible for an additional 12 weeks of leave beginning January 1, 2008.

Example 4. The facts are the same as those in Example 3, except that Delphi uses a rolling 12-month leave period measured backward. As of the end of 2007, John is not entitled to additional leave until February 1, 2008. Moreover, under the rolling method, an employee's leave is limited to the balance of the 12-week entitlement that has not been used during the immediately preceding 12 months. Therefore, John will be entitled to only four weeks of additional leave on February 1, 2008, another four weeks on June 1, 2008, and so on.

Practice Pointer. It is important for an employer to select one method for determining a 12-month period and clearly communicate it to its employees. If an employer does not do so, it will be required to use the method most favorable to the particular employee—which could result in numerous measuring periods.

A federal district court refused to dismiss a lawsuit charging that the employee was dismissed in violation of the FMLA. Because the employer had never selected which period it was using and notified employees of its selection, the court found that the employee was entitled to back-to-back 12-week entitlements because of the date on which the anniversary of his employment occurred. Thus, the employee would have had unused FMLA leave at the time the employer terminated him. [McKeirnan v. Smith-Edwards-Dunlap Co., 1995 U.S. Dist. LEXIS 6822 (E.D. Pa. May 17, 1995)] In a similar case, the Ninth Circuit Court of Appeals held that an employer must give employees advance notice of the 12-month period used to calculate FMLA leave entitlement. If the employer does not provide notice, the method that provides the best result for the employee will be used. [Bachelder v. America West Airlines Inc., 259 F.3d 1112 (9th Cir. 2001)]

Q 16:22   What special requirements apply to leave for birth or adoption of a child?

For the birth of a child, an expectant mother may take FMLA leave before the delivery date for prenatal care or if her condition makes her unable to work. [29 C.F.R. § 825.120(a)(4)] The mother is entitled to leave for incapacity due to pregnancy even though she does not receive treatment from a health care provider during the absence, and even if the absence does not last for more than three consecutive days. For example, a pregnant employee may be unable to report to work because of severe morning sickness.

FMLA leave can also begin before actual placement or adoption of a child if the employee must be absent for the placement for adoption or foster care to proceed (for example, for required attendance at counseling sessions, court appearances, consultations with attorneys and doctors, and physical examinations, or to travel to another country to complete an adoption). [29 C.F.R. § 825.121(a)(1)]

Q 16:23   What special limit applies to a husband and wife working for the same employer?

If a husband and wife work for the same employer, and each is entitled to leave for birth of a child or care for a newborn, for placement for adoption or foster care or care for the child after placement, or for care for a sick parent with a serious health condition, the *aggregate* leave taken by the couple for the same event may be limited to 12 workweeks during any 12-month period (even if the husband and wife are employed at different worksites of the employer). Personal medical leave taken by one or both of the spouses is not subject to the aggregate limit. Thus, part of the wife's leave to give birth does not count against this combined 12-week maximum because it is treated as a medical leave for her own serious illness. [FMLA § 102 (f); 29 U.S.C. § 2612(f); 29 C.F.R. §§ 825. 120(a)(3), 825.121(a)(3), 825.201(b)]

> **Example.** Bill and Mary are married, and both work for XYZ, Inc. Mary gives birth to a daughter via an emergency cesarean and spends four weeks recovering. She requests a family leave to care for her newborn. Bill also applies for a family leave to care for his newborn daughter. XYZ can limit the two leaves for the birth of their daughter to a combined maximum of 12 workweeks because of the husband-wife relationship. Bill decides to take four workweeks, and Mary takes eight additional workweeks. Neither is entitled to any further FMLA leave for the birth of their daughter.

> Note that each spouse is entitled to the difference between the leave he or she took for a particular event and the 12-workweek limit for FMLA leave for any other purpose. Thus, Mary could take an additional four workweeks for another type of FMLA leave (her own serious medical condition), and Bill could take up to an additional eight workweeks for a separate FMLA event. [29 C.F.R. § 825.202(c)]

Another type of *combined* leave is also available to an expectant mother who takes an FMLA pregnancy disability leave qualifying as a serious health condition, gives birth, and then takes an FMLA leave for care of the newborn child. The mother could take combined leaves of up to as much as 12 weeks in such a case. [29 C.F.R. §§ 825.120]

For notice requirements applicable to the birth or adoption of a child, see Q 16:29. For the special 12-month limit on FMLA leaves for the birth or adoption of a child, see Q 16:28. For the ability to take part-time FMLA leave to care for a newborn or adopted child, see Q 16:24.

Q 16:24   Must FMLA leave be taken on a continuous and full-time basis?

No. The statute does not require that family or medical leave always be taken on a continuous, full-time basis. Provided certain conditions are met, an employee may take FMLA leave on an intermittent or reduced-leave (i.e., part-time) basis. A *reduced-leave schedule* is a change in the employee's schedule for a period of time that reduces the employee's usual number of hours per workweek or workday (such as from full-time to part-time). *Intermittent leave* is leave taken because of a single illness or injury in separate blocks of time rather than one continuous period. Such leave may include periods from one hour or more to several weeks.

Eligible employees may take FMLA leave on an intermittent or reduced schedule basis when medically necessary due to the serious health condition of a family member or of the employee or the serious injury or illness of a covered servicemember. Intermittent or reduced schedule leave may also be taken when necessary because of a qualifying exigency related to a family member's military duty. If an employee needs leave intermittently or a reduced schedule for a planned medical treatment, the employee must make reasonable efforts to schedule the treatment so as not to unduly disrupt the employer's operations. [29 C.F.R. § 825.203]

If FMLA leave is taken for the birth of a child or the placement of a child for adoption or foster care, the employee cannot take the leave intermittently or a reduced-leave schedule unless the employer agrees to such a leave schedule. [29 C.F.R. §§ 825.120(b), 825.121(b)]

Example 1. Naomi gives birth to a daughter. She requests that she be allowed to take family leave in half days, so that she can work part-time for 24 weeks rather than take full-time leave for 12 weeks. Naomi's employer will not agree to this schedule. As a result, Naomi may not take her leave in half days.

Example 2. Carlos and Nancy adopt a baby. Carlos requests that he be allowed to take his family leave on Fridays to help out at home. His employer does not agree to this intermittent leave; therefore, Carlos may not take his family leave in that manner.

Example 3. Jeannette adopts a baby girl. She can arrange for a babysitter for five days a week, but the babysitter cannot work Monday mornings. Jeannette requests that she be given family leave on Monday mornings only. Her employer agrees to this schedule, even though it is not obligated to do so; Jeannette therefore can take her family leave on an intermittent basis.

It should be noted that entitlement to FMLA leave for birth or placement for adoption or foster care expires at the end of the 12-month period beginning on the date of birth or placement; the balance of any FMLA leave available but not taken for this purpose will be forfeited (see Q 16:26). [29 C.F.R. §§ 825. 120(a)(2), 825.121(a)(2)]

If FMLA leave is taken for care of a spouse, child, or parent with a serious health condition or because of the employee's own serious health condition, the leave may be taken intermittently or a reduced-leave schedule when medically necessary, even if the sick child is a newborn. To satisfy that requirement, there must be a medical need for leave that can be best accommodated through an intermittent or reduced-leave schedule. [29 C.F.R. §§ 825.120(b), 825.202(b)]

Example. John works a 40-hour week and takes a leave of 4 hours each week for chemotherapy treatment for a cancerous condition. Each 4-hour absence by John is treated as one tenth of a workweek in applying the 12-workweek leave limit.

Q 16:25   May an employer temporarily transfer an employee who requests FMLA leave that is foreseeably intermittent or a reduced-leave schedule?

Yes. If an employee requests intermittent or reduced schedule leave that is foreseeable based on planned medical treatment for the employee, a family member, or a covered servicemember (including during a period of recovery from a serious health condition), the employer can require the employee to transfer temporarily to an available alternative position for which the employee is qualified and that better accommodates the recurring periods of leave than the employee's regular position. The employer can also require such a transfer if the employer agrees to intermittent or reduced schedule leave for the birth of a child or for placement of a child for adoption or foster care. [FMLA § 102(b)(2); 29 U.S.C. § 2612(b)(2); 29 C.F.R. § 825.204(a)]

The alternative position must have equivalent pay and benefits to the employee's regular job, but need not have equivalent duties. [29 C.F.R. § 825.204(c)] The employer may increase the pay and benefits of an existing alternative position to make them equivalent to the employee's regular job.

The employer may also transfer the employee to a part-time job with the same hourly rate of pay and benefits, provided the employee is not required to take more leave than is medically necessary. In so transferring an employee, the employer may not eliminate benefits that are provided to full-time employees but not to part-time employees, although the FMLA does not bar an employer from proportionately reducing benefits (such as vacation leave) where the employer's normal practice is to base such benefits on the number of hours worked. [29 C.F.R. § 825.204(c)]

An employer may not transfer an employee to an alternative position in order to discourage the employee from taking FMLA leave or to otherwise work a hardship on the employee. For example, a white collar employee cannot be assigned to perform laborer's work; an employee working the day shift cannot be assigned to graveyard shift; and an employee working at headquarters cannot be assigned to a branch office a significant distance away.

When an employee on intermittent or reduced schedule leave who has been transferred to an alternative position is able to return to full-time work, the employee must be placed in the same or equivalent job as he or she held when the leave began. An employee cannot be required to take more leave than necessary to address the circumstances that precipitated the need for leave.

Q 16:26 How is the amount of FMLA leave used for reduced or intermittent leave determined?

For reduced leave or intermittent leave, only the time actually taken as leave may be charged against the 12-workweek maximum annual leave limitation. [FMLA § 102(b)(1); 29 U.S.C. § 2612(b)(1)] Thus, an employee normally working a five-day workweek who takes off one day would be treated as using one-fifth of a week of FMLA leave. If a full-time employee who normally works eight-hour days works four-hour days on a reduced-leave schedule, he or she is treated as using one half of a week of FMLA leave each week. [29 C.F.R. § 825.205(b)]

The amount of leave credited to an employee who normally works a part-time schedule or variable hours is determined on a pro rata or proportional basis. For example, if an employee who normally works 25 hours per week works 10 hours per week under a reduced-leave schedule, the employee's 15 hours of leave would constitute three-fifths of a week of FMLA leave for each week the employee works the reduced leave schedule. For variable hours (that is, when the number of hours worked by the employee varies from week to week), the employee's normal workweek is calculated by determining the weekly average of hours worked during the 12 weeks immediately before the beginning of the leave period.

When an employee who does not punch a time clock is taking leave intermittently or a reduced-leave schedule, the employer and employee must agree on the employee's normal schedule or average hours worked each week and record their agreement in writing. [29 C.F.R. §§ 825.205, 825.500(f)(2)]

If an employee works at home while on intermittent leave, the worked hours cannot be charged against the 12-week FMLA leave. [Parker v. Sony Pictures Entertainment Inc., 19 F. Supp. 2d 141 (S.D.N.Y. 1998)]

When employees take FMLA leave on an intermittent basis or work a reduced schedule, final regulations retain the rule that the leave must be counted using the shortest time period used to account for other types of leave, but not more than one hour. The final regulations make it clear that an employer can use a smaller time period to account for FMLA leave than is used for other leave, but cannot use a larger time period—and an employer cannot use a time period of more than one hour even if that period is used for other types of leave.

The final regulations ease the rules by recognizing policies that account for the use of leave in different increments at different times—for example, a policy that requires leave to be taken only in a one-hour increment during the first hour of a shift in order to discourage tardy arrivals. Under the final regulations an employer can count FMLA leave using such a policy, provided the employee does not work during the time period. [29 C.F.R. § 825.205(a)(1)]

As a general rule, if an employee qualifies for intermittent leave, an employer cannot force an employee to take more leave than is necessary. For example, if an employee with a serious health condition needs only half a day off for a medically necessary treatment, he or she cannot be required to take a full day off. However, the final regulations carve out a special exception for situations where it is impossible for an employee using intermittent or reduced schedule leave to begin or end work mid-way through a shift. The final regulations provide that the entire period the employee is forced to be off work can be counted against the employee's FMLA allotment. [29 C.F.R. § 825.205(a)(2)] This marks a shift of position on the part of the DOL. In an opinion letter issued in 1994, the Wage-Hour Division took the position that when a flight attendant's need for three hours of intermittent FMLA leave caused her to miss a full flight assignment, only the three hours could be charged against her FMLA leave allotment. [WH Op. Ltr. FMLA-42 (Aug. 23, 1994)]

The final regulations also contain a new provision regarding overtime hours. Under the final rules, overtime not worked is counted against an employee's FMLA allotment when an employee would have been required to work overtime but for the FMLA leave. [29 C.F.R. § 825.205(c)] The DOL cautions, however, that employers cannot discriminate in the assignment of mandatory overtime between employees who take FMLA leave and those who do not. For example, an employer cannot schedule only FMLA leave-takers for mandatory overtime in order to deplete their FMLA allotments while allowing other employees to volunteer for overtime.

Special rules for school employees. Special rules apply to employees of schools whose intermittent or reduced-leave schedule would cause them to be on leave for more than 20 percent of the total number of working days during the period of the leave, or who begin leave close to the beginning or end of an academic term. Such employees may be required, under certain circumstances, to take leave for a particular duration (even if they are willing to return to work earlier) or to transfer to an available alternative position. [29 C.F.R. §§ 825.600–825.604]

Q 16:27   Do salary deductions for unpaid FMLA leave cause an executive, administrative, or professional employee to lose such designation under the FLSA?

No. To qualify for exemption from the overtime requirements of the federal Fair Labor Standards Act (FLSA), an employee must be paid his or her full salary for each weekly or less frequent pay period, regardless of the number of hours actually worked. However, deductions from an executive, administrative, or professional employee's salary for any hours taken as an intermittent or reduced-leave schedule within a workweek, provided such leave is FMLA leave, have no effect on the employee's exempt status under the FLSA. [29 C.F.R. § 825.206] If, however, the employee's salary is reduced for any additional leave that does not qualify as FMLA leave (such as more generous leave required by state law or permitted under the employer's policy), the employee may possibly lose exempt status under the FLSA unless such salary reduction is permitted under FLSA regulations. [29 C.F.R. § 825.206(c)]

In one case, the Fifth Circuit Court of Appeals held that unpaid time off granted to an injured employee did not alter her status under the FLSA. The employee had argued that the FMLA did not apply because her time off had not been formally designated as FMLA leave. However, the court noted that although the time off had not been designated as FMLA leave, it was nonetheless *FMLA-qualifying* leave. Therefore, the employer was entitled to the continued protection of the FLSA exemption. [Rowe v. Laidlaw Transit, Inc., 244 F.3d 1115 (9th Cir. 2001)]

Q 16:28   Is there any lifetime maximum on the amount of FMLA leave that can be taken for a particular event or condition?

With two exceptions, there is no limit on the number of years that an employee can take FMLA leave for the same event or condition. The exceptions to this general rule occur in the case of the birth of a child or the placement of a child for adoption or foster care. Entitlement to FMLA leave for the birth of a child or the placement for adoption or foster care expires at the end of the 12-month period beginning on the date of the birth or placement. Any unused FMLA leave as of that date relating to the birth or placement for adoption or foster care of that particular child is forfeited. [FMLA § 102(a)(2); 29 U.S.C. § 2612(a)(2); 29 C.F.R. §§ 825.120, 825.121]

Example 1. William's father has Alzheimer's disease. Assuming that William satisfies all of the requirements for FMLA leave, he may use 12 workweeks of FMLA leave during each 12-month period to care for his father.

Example 2. Susan's employer runs its FMLA leave program on a calendar-year basis. In year 1, Susan has a baby on May 1 and uses her 12 workweeks of FMLA leave as maternity leave. In year 2, Susan takes no FMLA leave until June 1, when she wants to take additional leave to care for her baby (who does not have a serious health condition). Susan is entitled to up to 12 workweeks of FMLA leave in year 2, but her entitlement to FMLA leave as the result of the birth of her child expired on April 30 of year 2, which date was the end of the 12-month period beginning on the date of her child's birth. Although she could have used part or all of her FMLA leave in year 2 to care for her baby provided that she took such leave before May 1 (that is, still within a year from the date her child was born), Susan failed to do so and now cannot take any further FMLA leave because of the birth of that particular baby. Susan may still take her 12 workweeks of FMLA leave in year 2 for any other event or condition for which FMLA leave must be granted (e.g., if her baby develops a serious health condition or if she gives birth to another child, or if a child is placed with her for adoption or foster care).

Q 16:29   Can an employer require an employee to provide notice that FMLA leave will be taken?

Yes. An employee must give at least 30 days' notice when the need for FMLA leave is foreseeable at least 30 days in advance. Final regulations make it clear that foreseeable leave includes expected birth of a child, placement of a child for adoption or foster care, planned medical treatment for a serious health condition of an employee or family member, or planned medical treatment for a serious injury or illness of a covered servicemember. If 30 days' notice is not practicable, such as because of lack of knowledge of approximately when leave will need to begin or a change in circumstances, notice must be given as soon as practicable, taking into account all the facts and circumstances. [29 C.F.R. § 825.302(a)] For example, an employee's health condition may require leave to begin earlier than anticipated before the birth of a child. Similarly, little opportunity for notice may be given before a placement for adoption. According to the DOL regulations, in most cases it should be practicable for notice to be provided on the day the need for leave becomes known or on the next business day.

If an employee does not provide 30 days' notice of the need for foreseeable FMLA leave, the final regulations provide that the employer can request and the employee must provide an explanation of why such notice was not practicable.

In the case of a foreseeable family military leave due to a qualifying exigency leave, notice must be provided as soon as practicable no matter how far in advance the need for leave is foreseeable.

Practice Pointer. An employer's FMLA compliance procedure should include the ability to identify a situation in which an employee is giving advance notice of leave even when he or she does not specifically mention the FMLA. The Court of Appeals for the Fifth Circuit ruled that employees who take time off for situations covered by the FMLA are not required to mention the act expressly or refer to a specific statute when notifying their employers of the need for leave. Noting that no other federal statute requires employees to refer to the specific statute, the court stated that "[we] do not believe Congress intended to depart from this practice and require employees to consult attorneys before notifying their employer of their need for FMLA leave." [Manuel v. Westlake Polymers Corp., 66 F.3d 758 (5th Cir. 1995)] Moreover, the final FMLA regulations make it clear that an employee is not required to expressly assert FMLA rights or even mention the FMLA to qualify for FMLA leave. The regulations indicate that, in all cases, the employer should inquire further of the employee if it is necessary to have more information about whether FMLA leave is being sought by the employee. The regulations also make it clear that an employee has an obligation to respond to an employer's questions to determine whether an absence is potentially FMLA-qualifying and that failure to respond to reasonable employer inquiries may result in denial of FMLA protections. [29 C.F.R. § 825.302(c)]

The final regulations do specify one situation in which an employee must clearly indicate that FMLA leave is being requested. When an employee seeks leave due to an FMLA-qualifying reason for which the employer has previously provided FMLA-protected leave, the employee must specifically reference the qualifying reason or the need for FMLA leave. [29 C.F.R. § 825.302(c)]

Notice procedures. An employer may require an employee to comply with the employer's usual and customary procedures for requesting leave, absent unusual circumstances. [29 C.F.R. § 825.302(c)] For example, an employer may require a written notice spelling out the reasons for the requested leave, the duration of the leave, and the anticipated start date. An employee may also be required to contact a specific individual to request leave. Where an employee does not comply with the employer's procedures, and no unusual circumstances exist, FMLA-protected leave may be delayed or denied. However, FMLA leave cannot be delayed or denied if the employer's procedures require notice sooner than required under the regulations and the employee complied with the regulatory requirements.

Scheduling leave. When scheduling planned medical treatments, employees must consult with their employers and make reasonable efforts to schedule the treatments so as not to disrupt the employer's operations, subject to the approval of their health care providers. Similarly, employees seeking intermittent or reduced schedule leave must attempt to work out a schedule that meets their needs without unduly disrupting the employer's operations. [29 C.F.R. §§ 825.302(e), 825.303(f)]

Unforeseeable leave. If the need for leave is not foreseeable, notice is to be given as soon as practicable under the circumstances. [29 C.F.R. § 825.303(a)]

Final regulations issued in 2008 remove a longstanding—and controversial—provision that had been interpreted to allow an employee to notify the employer of a need for FMLA leave up to two full business days after an unforeseeable absence, even if the employee could have provided notice sooner. Instead, under the final regulations, an employee will be deemed to have given notice "as soon as practicable" only if the employee followed the employer's normal and customary call-in procedures for absences. Absent unusual circumstances, FMLA-protected leave may be delayed or denied for failure to follow call-in procedures. However, leave may not be denied in the case of emergency medical treatment if circumstances did not allow the employee to contact the employer. [29 C.F.R. § 825.303]

Here again, an employee is not required to specifically request FMLA leave or even mention the FMLA when providing notice to the employer. However, the regulations make it clear that calling in "sick" without further information will not be considered sufficient notice to trigger an employer's obligations under the FMLA.

Q 16:30   Can an employer terminate an employee while the employee is on FMLA leave?

According to the Court of Appeals for the Seventh Circuit, an employer may terminate an employee who is on FMLA leave, provided the employer is able to prove, by a preponderance of the evidence, that it would have terminated that employee even if he or she had not taken leave. [Rice v. Sunrise Express Inc., 209 F.3d 1008 (7th Cir.), *reh'g en banc denied*, 217 F.3d 492 (7th Cir.), *cert. denied*, 531 U.S. 1012 (2000)]

In another case, an employee with mental health problems was asked to take FMLA when her illness manifested itself in disruptive workplace behavior and poor work performance. During the leave, the employee returned to the workplace without permission and disrupted the activities of other workers. When the employee was fired because of the disruptive behavior and poor performance, she sued under the FMLA. An appellate court held that the employer did not violate the FMLA in terminating the employee because it would have terminated the employee for her actions even if she were not taking FMLA leave. [Throneberry v. McGehee Desha County Hosp., 403 F.3d 972 (8th Cir. 2005)]

Q 16:31   How may the employer treat an employee's failure to give notice of the need for FMLA leave?

An employee's failure to give notice of the need for FMLA leave can have adverse consequences for the employee—but only if the employee has been properly alerted by the employer to the FMLA notice requirements. The employer will meet this requirement by posting the proper FMLA notice in the workplace and distributing the required notice to employees (see Q 16:64). [29 C.F.R. §§ 825.300, 825.304(a)]

If the need for FMLA leave is foreseeable at least 30 days in advance and an employee, with no reasonable excuse, fails to give at least 30 days' notice of the need for leave, the employer may delay FMLA coverage until 30 days after the date the employee provides notice. [29 C.F.R. § 825.304(b)]

If the need for leave is foreseeable fewer than 30 days in advance and an employee fails to give notice as soon as practicable under the circumstances, the extent to which the employer can delay FMLA coverage depends on the facts of the particular case. [29 C.F.R. § 825.304(c)] For example, if an employee reasonably should have given the employer two weeks' notice but provided only one week's notice, the employer may delay FMLA-protected leave for one week. Thus, if the employee nonetheless began the leave one week after providing the notice, the leave would not be FMLA-protected.

When the need for leave is not foreseeable and an employee fails to give proper notice, the extent to which the employer can delay FMLA coverage depends on the facts and circumstances. [29 C.F.R. § 825.304(d)] For example, if it would have been practicable for an employee to give the employer notice soon after the need for leave arose consistent with the employer's call-in policy, but the employee waited to give notice until two days after the leave began, the employer may delay FMLA coverage by two days.

An employer can waive employees' FMLA notice obligations or the employer's internal leave notice rules. Absent such a waiver, the employer may take appropriate action under its internal procedures for failure to follow its usual and customary notification rules as long as the actions are taken in a manner that does not discriminate against employees taking FMLA leave. [29 C.F.R. § 825.304(e)]

Q 16:32   How specific must an employee's request for FMLA leave be?

An employer need not play a guessing game about the true nature of the employee's reason for requesting FMLA leave. A U.S. district court held that an employee was not entitled to claim that leave time he took was protected FMLA leave when he failed to inform his employer that the leave was taken because of the illness of his child. The employee asked for time off for family matters or matters of financial importance. The court held that although an employee does not specifically have to invoke his or her FMLA rights, the employee must give sufficient notice of a medical need within a period of time to obtain FMLA protection. [Johnson v. Primerica Life Ins. Co., 1996 U.S. Dist. LEXIS 869 (S.D.N.Y. Jan. 30, 1996)]

A decision from the Seventh Circuit Court of Appeals indicates that an employee may not need to specifically request leave to trigger FMLA rights if the employer is adequately apprised of a medical reason for the employee's absence from work. The employee in the case, John Byrne, worked the night shift as an engineer for Avon Products, Inc. Byrne was said to have been a model employee until November 1998, when security videos showed he was frequently asleep on the job. When his supervisor went to confront Byrne about the problem, it was discovered that Byrne had left work early. The supervisor tried to contact Byrne by phone, but was told by Byrne's sister that he was "very sick." Byrne was eventually contacted and agreed to a meeting, but never showed up. Avon terminated Byrne for skipping the meeting and sleeping on the job. As it turned out, Byrne was suffering from severe depression, hallucinations, and panic attacks and had attempted suicide.

When Byrne recovered and was ready to return to work after two months of treatment, Avon refused to rehire him. Byrne filed suit against Avon for violating the FMLA. A district court ruled in favor of Avon, but the Seventh Circuit reversed that decision. According to the Seventh Circuit, Byrne's sister's statement that Byrne was "very sick" was sufficient notice to trigger FMLA leave. Moreover, since Byrne had been a model employee, his sudden change in behavior may also have been sufficient notice. In either case, the Seventh Circuit held that Byrne was entitled to reinstatement under the FMLA. [Byrne v. Avon Prods., Inc., 328 F.3d 379 (N.D. Ill. 2002), *remanded and vacated by* 2003 U.S. App. LEXIS 8755 (7th Cir. May 9, 2003), *cert. denied by* Avon Prods. v. Byrne, 124 S. Ct. 327 (2003)]

Another Seventh Circuit decision indicates that an employee's behavior alone may give an employer constructive notice of the employee's need for FMLA leave. After encountering a stray dog in her workplace, Beverly Stevenson, an employee with an unblemished record, had an extreme physical and emotional reaction. Immediately after the incident, Stevenson's supervisor found her extremely agitated, spraying room deodorizer and yelling and screaming. Stevenson left work and did not return for several days, and when she did return her behavior was erratic and she was unable to work. Stevenson finally visited a hospital emergency room and was diagnosed with "anxiety and stress" and medication was prescribed. Following the hospital visit, Stevenson returned to work but continued to exhibit erratic behavior, including yelling and swearing. Subsequently, Stevenson repeatedly called in to say that she "wouldn't be in today" because she was "ill." Eventually, Stevenson's employer fired her on account of her absences. Stevenson, however, sued, claiming she was protected by the FMLA.

The Seventh Circuit acknowledged that Stevenson did not give her employer specific notice of her need for FMLA leave. However, the court said that direct notice is not always necessary. In Stevenson's case, the court said a trier of fact could find that the plaintiff's behavior was so bizarre that it amounted to constructive notice of the need for leave. The court remanded the case to the district court for a trial on the merits. [Stevenson v. Hyre Elec. Co., 2006 U.S. Dist. LEXIS 64043 (N.D. Ill. Aug. 24, 2006), *rev'd and remanded,* Stevenson v. Hyre Elec. Co., 2007 U.S. App. LEXIS 24197 (7th Cir. Oct. 16, 2007)]

Final FMLA regulations issued in 2008 make it clear that an employee is not required to expressly assert FMLA rights or even mention the FMLA to qualify for FMLA leave. However, the regulations also make it clear that calling in "sick" without further information will not be considered sufficient notice to trigger an employer's obligations under the FMLA.

According to the regulations, the employer should inquire further of the employee if it is necessary to have more information about whether FMLA leave is being sought by the employee. The regulations also state that an employee has an obligation to respond to an employer's questions to determine whether an absence is potentially FMLA-qualifying and that failure to respond to reasonable employer inquiries may result in denial of FMLA protections. [29 C.F.R. §§ 825.302(c), 825.303]

The final regulations do specify one situation in which an employee must clearly indicate that FMLA leave is being requested. When an employee seeks leave due to an FMLA-qualifying reason for which the employer has previously provided FMLA-protected leave, the employee must specifically reference the qualifying reason or the need for FMLA leave. [29 C.F.R. §§ 825.302(c), 825.303]

Q 16:33   How soon must an employer respond to an employee's request for FMLA leave?

The DOL's FMLA regulation requires an employer to determine whether the employee requesting leave will be eligible for FMLA leave (e.g., whether the employee will have worked for the employer for at least 1,250 hours in the past 12 months) as of the date the leave will commence.

Eligibility notice. Once the employer has received notice from the employee regarding the leave, the regulation requires that the employer advise the employee of his or her eligibility for FMLA leave within five business days, absent extenuating circumstances. [DOL Reg. § 825.300(b)]

Practice Pointer. This represents an increase in the time for employers to respond to FMLA requests. Under longstanding FMLA regulations, employers had only two days to respond. Final regulations increasing the time limit to five days became effective on January 16, 2008.

The eligibility notice must state whether the employee is eligible for FMLA leave. If the employee is not eligible for FMLA leave, the notice must state at least one reason why the employee is not eligible, including the number of months the employee has been employed, the employee's hours of service during the prior 12-month period, or whether the employee is employed at a worksite meeting the minimum size requirement.

A rights and responsibilities notice must be provided at the same time as an eligibility notice. The rights and responsibilities notice must detail the specific expectations and obligations imposed upon the employee and any consequences for failure to meet those expectations and obligations. [29 C.F.R. § 825.300(c)] For example, the notice must explain how the leave will be counted against the employee's FMLA entitlement, any requirements for submitting certification of the need for leave (e.g., medical certification of a health condition or certification of a qualifying exigency in case of family military leave), any rules relating to substitution of paid leave, and any requirements related to payment of health care premiums or maintenance of other employee benefits during leave.

Failure of employer to make timely response. Former DOL regulations stated that an employer that received notice from an ineligible employee regarding an impending FMLA leave but failed to respond with a determination of eligibility before the commencement of the leave was barred from challenging the employee's eligibility based on failure to meet the statutory service requirement. [29 C.F.R. § 825.110(d)] However, the DOL regulation was rejected by the Supreme Court as an invalid interpretation of the law because it improperly "deemed" ineligible employees eligible for FMLA leave. [Ragsdale v. Wolverine World Wide, Inc., 535 U.S. 81 (2002)]

New FMLA regulations, which took effect on January 16, 2009, remove the "deeming" provision. According to the explanation of the final regulations, the DOL believes it does not have the authority to "deem" employees eligible for FMLA leave, even where an employer does not provide the required eligibility notice or provides incorrect information. However, the DOL cautions that such failures may have the effect of interfering with an employee's rights under the FMLA and may result in harm, in which case the employee may have statutory remedies. According to the final regulations, if an employer fails to follow the notice requirements, the employer may be liable for compensation and benefits lost by reason of the violation, for other actual monetary losses, and for equitable relief, including employment, reinstatement, promotion, or any other relief tailored to the harm suffered by the employee. [29 C.F.R. § 825.300(e)]

Designation notice. The employer must also notify the employee whether the requested leave will be designated and counted as FMLA leave. If an employer has enough information to designate the leave as FMLA leave immediately after receiving notice of the employee's need for leave, the employer must provide the employee with the designation notice at that time. However, the employer may need additional information, such as medical certification of a serious health condition of the employee or a family member or certification of the need for family military leave, before it can determine if the leave is FMLA-qualifying. In such a case, the designation notice must be provided within five business days of the time the employer has enough information to determine whether the leave is being taken for an FMLA-qualifying reason. [29 C.F.R. § 825.300(d)]

If the employer determines that the leave will not be FMLA-qualifying (for example, because the leave is for a reason not covered by the FMLA or the employee has exhausted his or her FMLA entitlement), the employer must notify the employee of that determination.

The employer must notify the employee of the amount of leave counted against the employee's FMLA entitlement. If that amount is known at the time the employer designates the leave as FMLA-qualifying, the employer must notify the employee of the number of hours, days, or weeks that will be counted against the employee's FMLA entitlement. If that amount is not known at the time of designation (for example, in the case of unforeseeable intermittent leave), the employer must provide notice of the amount of leave counted against an employee's FMLA entitlement on request by the employee, but no more often than once in a 30-day period and only if leave was taken in that period. This notice may be oral, but must be confirmed in writing no later than the following payday (or the next following payday if the following payday is less than one week after the oral notice). The written notice may be in any form including a notation on the employee's paystub.

Optional forms. The DOL has developed Form WH-381, Notice of Eligibility and Rights & Responsibilities (Family and Medical Leave Act), a form that an employer may opt to use to respond to an employee's request for FMLA leave. Form WH-382, Designation Notice (Family and Medical Leave Act), may be used to designate leave as FMLA-qualifying. These forms may be downloaded from the Wage and Hour Division section of the DOL's Web site at *www.wagehour.dol.gov.*

If the requested leave is not designated as FMLA leave because it does not meet the requirements of the FMLA, the designation notice to the employee may be in the form of simple written statement.

Q 16:34 Can an employee be required to waive his or her rights under the FMLA?

No. Employers are prohibited from inducing an employee to waive his or her FMLA rights. In addition, employees (or their collective bargaining representatives) are barred from "trading off" the right to take FMLA leave against another benefit offered by the employer. [29 C.F.R. § 825.220(d)]

Many employers routinely provide severance or other benefits to terminated employees in exchange for a release of claims against the employer—including claims under the FMLA. However, in a pivotal decision, the Fourth Circuit Court of Appeals held such a release is unenforceable because DOL regulations bar both the prospective and retroactive waiver or settlement of rights under the FMLA without prior approval by the DOL. [29 C.F.R. § 825.220(d); Taylor v. Progress Energy, Inc., 415 F.3d 364 (4th Cir. 2005)] The court vacated the decision in order to hear further arguments, but subsequently reinstated it. [*See* Taylor v. Progress Energy, Inc., 493 F.3d 454, 2007 U.S. App. LEXIS 15846 (4th Cir. July 3, 2007).]

By contrast, the Fifth Circuit Court of Appeals ruled that the DOL's regulations only prohibit the waiver of an employee's prospective substantive right (i.e., the right to the leave itself and the right to reinstatement), not the right to sue or recover damages. [Faris v. Williams WPC-1, Inc., 332 F.3d 316 (5th Cir. 2003)] According to the Fifth Circuit, a waiver of FMLA claims would not be prohibited.

Final FMLA regulations issued in 2008 make it clear that employees and employers can voluntarily agree to a settlement of past FMLA claims without first obtaining permission or approval of either the DOL or the courts. [Prop. 29 C.F.R. § 825.220(d)]

Certification of FMLA Leave Eligibility

Q 16:35 When can an employer require proof of an employee's eligibility for FMLA leave?

An employer may require that an employee's leave to care for a covered family member with a serious health condition or leave for the employee's own serious health condition be supported by a certification from the health care provider. [29 C.F.R. § 825.305(a)]

If the employee's need for leave in connection with a serious health condition of the employee or a family member lasts beyond a single leave year, the employer may require the employee to provide a new medical certification in each subsequent leave year. [29 C.F.R. § 305(e)]

An employer may also require certification of eligibility for family military leave to care for a covered servicemember or in the event of a qualifying exigency related to a servicemember's call to active duty. [29 C.F.R. § 825.305(a)] Recertification does not apply to family military leave. [DOL Reg. § 825.313(c)]

An employer must notify the employee each time a certification is required.

As a general rule, the employer should request certification at the time the employee gives notice of the need for leave or within five business days after the leave begins. However, the employer can request certification at a later date if the employer has reason to question the appropriateness of the leave or its duration. The employee must provide the certification within 15 days after it is requested, unless it is not practicable to do so or the employer gives the employee more than 15 days to provide the certification. [29 C.F.R. § 825.305(b)]

An employee is required to provide complete and sufficient certification. A certification is considered incomplete if the employer receives the certification, but one or more of the applicable entries have not been completed. A certificate is considered insufficient if the employer receives a complete certification, but the information provided is vague, ambiguous, or non-responsive. [29 C.F.R. § 825.305(c)] A certification that is not returned to the employee is not considered incomplete or insufficient; it is treated as a failure to provide certification.

If an employer determines that a certification is incomplete or insufficient, the employer must advise the employee in writing, stating what additional information is required. The employer must provide the employee with seven calendar days to cure any deficiency (unless seven days is not practicable despite the employee's good-faith efforts).

If the employee fails to provide the employer with a complete and sufficient certification, the employer can deny the FMLA leave. [29 C.F.R. § 825.305(c)]

In the case of foreseeable leave, if the employee does not provide certification in a timely manner, the employer may deny FMLA coverage until the certification is provided. [29 C.F.R. § 825.313(a)] For example, if an employee has 15 days to provide certification but does not provide it for 45 days with no excuse for the delay, the employer can deny FMLA protection for the 30 days following the expiration of the 15-day time period allowed for providing the certification.

In the case of unforeseeable leave, absent extenuating circumstances such as a medical emergency, if an employee fails to timely provide certification, the employer can deny FMLA protections following the expiration of the 15-day time period until the employee provides sufficient certification. If the employee never produces the certification, the leave is not FMLA leave. [DOL Reg. § 825.313(b)]

When an employer requests recertification, it must be provided within the time frame provided by the employer or as soon as practicable under the circumstances. However, the employer must allow the employee at least 15 calendar days to provide the recertification. If the employee does not provide recertification within the appropriate time frame, the employer may deny continuation of FMLA protections until the employee produces a sufficient recertification. If the employee never provides the recertification, the leave is not FMLA leave. [29 C.F.R. § 825.313(c)]

According to the Fifth Circuit Court of Appeals, the onus is on the employee to submit the certification on time. The court held that an employer did not violate the FMLA when it terminated an employee who failed to provide medical certification of her need for leave. When the employee requested medical leave for carpal tunnel surgery, the employer informed her that it was tentatively designating the time off as FMLA leave but that she would have to provide medical certification from her doctor. The employee requested and received an extension of time to provide the certification—but the employer did not receive the certification by the extended deadline. Consequently, the employer informed the employee that her employment was being terminated because her absence was unauthorized.

The employee sued the employer for violating the FMLA. The employee pointed out that the FMLA regulations required an employee to be given a "reasonable opportunity" to fix any defects in a medical certification. Moreover, since the employee did not know that her doctor had not sent the certification, she claimed that providing her with that "reasonable opportunity" required the employer to notify her that the certification had not been received. However, the appeals court concluded that the employer did not have such a duty. Noting that the FMLA is intended to balance the needs of employees and the legitimate interests of employers, the Fifth Circuit said "it would seem illogical to require an employer to continually notify an employee who failed to submit medical certification within a specified deadline." [Urban v. Dolgencorp of Tex., Inc., 2005 U.S. App. LEXIS 1339 (5th Cir. Jan. 27, 2005)]

Q 16:36   What proof of entitlement to FMLA leave on the basis of a serious medical condition may an employer require an employee to provide?

An employer may require that an employee's leave to care for a covered family member with a serious health condition or leave for the employee's own serious health condition be supported by a certification from the health care provider. [29 C.F.R. § 825.305(a)]

If the employee's need for leave in connection with a serious health condition of the employee or a family member lasts beyond a single leave year, the employer may require the employee to provide a new medical certification in each subsequent leave year. [29 C.F.R. § 305(e)]

Required content of the certification. The certification of the health care provider must include the following:

- The name, address, telephone number, and fax number of the health care provider and the provider's type of medical practice or specialization.
- The approximate date on which the serious health condition commenced and its probable duration.
- A statement or description of appropriate medical facts regarding the patient's health condition for which FMLA is requested. The medical facts must be sufficient to support the need for leave and may, but are not required to, include information on symptoms, diagnosis, hospitalization, doctor visits, whether medication has been prescribed, any referrals for evaluation or treatment, or any other regimen of continuing treatment. [29 C.F.R. § 825.306(a)(1)-(3)]

Practice Pointer. In its preamble to the final FMLA regulations, the DOL notes that the determination of what medical facts are appropriate for inclusion in the certification will vary depending on the nature of the serious health condition at issue, and is appropriately left to the health care provider. Therefore, the list of medical facts included in the regulation is not mandatory. Moreover, the DOL concluded that it would not be appropriate to require a diagnosis as part of an FMLA certification; whether a diagnosis is included is left to the discretion of the health care provider and an employer may not reject an otherwise complete and sufficient certification because it lacks a diagnosis.

Most significantly, the medical certification must back up the medical necessity for FMLA leave, as follows:

1. In the case of a leave for the employee's own serious health condition, the certification must contain information sufficient to establish that the employee cannot perform the essential functions of the employee's job as well as the nature of any other work restrictions and the likely duration of such inability. [29 C.F.R. § 825.306(a)(4)] When requesting medical certification, an employer has the option of providing a list or statement of the essential functions of the employee's position for the health care provider to review. [29 C.F.R. § 825.123(b)]

Practice Pointer. In the preamble to the final FMLA regulations, the DOL suggests that it would be in the best interests of both the employer and the employee to provide such a list so the health care provider can assess the ability of the employee to perform his or her job based on the most complete description of the employee's duties. However, there is no legal requirement that an employer provide such a list. Therefore, in the absence of an employer-provided list, the health care provider can assess the employee's ability to perform his or her job based on the employee's own description of his or her job functions.

2. In the case of leave to care for a family member with a serious health condition, the certification must provide information sufficient to show that the family member is in need of care and an estimate of the frequency and duration of the leave required to care for the family member. [29 C.F.R. § 825.306(a)(5)]

Practice Pointer. In assessing such certifications, the employer should bear in mind that, according to the final FMLA regulations, the medical certification that an employee needs to care for a family member encompasses both physical and psychological care. [29 C.F.R. § 825.124(a)] (See Q 16:19.)

3. In the case of intermittent leave or leave on a reduced-leave schedule for planned medical treatment of the employee or a family member, the certification must provide information to establish the medical necessity for taking leave on an intermittent or reduced schedule and an estimate of the dates and duration of treatments and any periods of recovery. [29 C.F.R. § 825.306(a)(6)]

4. If an employee requests leave on an intermittent or reduced schedule basis for the employee's own serious health condition, including pregnancy, that may result in unforeseeable episodes of incapacity, the certification must contain information showing the medical necessity for intermittent or reduced schedule leave and an estimate of the frequency and duration of the episodes. [29 C.F.R. § 825.306(a)(7)]

5. If an employee requests leave on an intermittent or reduced schedule to care for a family member with a serious health condition, the certification must contain a statement that the leave is medically necessary to care for the family member and an estimate of the frequency and duration of the required leave. [29 C.F.R. § 825.306(a)(8)]

Practice Pointer. The requirement to certify the medical necessity for leave to be taken on an intermittent or reduced schedule basis represents a new addition to the certification requirements by the final FMLA regulations.

Form for certifications. The DOL has developed two optional forms for medical certifications: Form WH-380-E, Certification of Serious Health Condition—Employee's Own Condition, and Form WH-380-F, Certification of Serious Health Condition—Employee's Family Member's Condition. Employers may use their own forms; however, employers may not seek information beyond what is specified in the DOL's regulations. [FMLA § 103(b); 29 U.S.C. § 2613(b); 29 C.F.R. § 825.306(b)] These forms may be downloaded from the Wage and Hour Division section of the DOL's Web site at *www.wagehour.dol.gov*.

Employer-health care provider communications. An employee may choose to comply with the certification requirement by providing the employer with an authorization, release, or waiver allowing the employer to communicate directly with the health care provider. However, the employee may not be required to provide such authorization. [29 C.F.R. § 825.306(e)]

If an employee submits a sufficient medical certification signed by a health care provider, the employer may not request additional information from the provider. However, the employer may contact the provider for purposes of authentication and clarification only. [29 C.F.R. § 825.307(a)]

Authentication means providing the health care provider with a copy of the certification and requesting verification that the information on the certification was completed or authorized by the provider. Clarification means contacting the health provider to understand the handwriting on the certification or the meaning of a response.

If an employer seeks authentication or clarification of a certification, the contact must be made by a health care provider, a human resources professional, a leave administrator, or a management official. The FMLA regulations stress that, under no circumstances, may the employee's direct supervisor contact the employee's health care provider.

Second and third opinions. If an employer has reason to doubt the validity of the health care provider's certification, it may require, at its own expense, that the employee obtain a second opinion of a health care provider designated or approved by the employer (but not a health care provider regularly employed by the employer or regularly called upon by the employer, with certain exceptions in rural areas). [FMLA § 103(c); 29 U.S.C. § 2613(c); 29 C.F.R. § 825.307(b)]

If there is a conflict between the first and second opinions, an employer may require, again at its own expense, the opinion of a third health care provider designated or approved jointly by the employee and the employer. The opinion of the third health care provider is final and binding on both the employer and employee; however, when the employee fails to attempt in good faith to reach agreement on selection of a third opinion provider, he or she will be bound by the second certification, and an employer failing to attempt in good faith to reach agreement on selection of a third opinion provider will be bound by the first certification. [FMLA § 103(d); 29 U.S.C. § 2613(d); 29 C.F.R. § 825.307(c)]

Pending receipt of a second or third opinion, an employee is provisionally entitled to the benefits of the FMLA, including maintenance of group health benefits. If the certifications do not ultimately establish the employee's entitlement to FMLA leave, the leave will not be designated as FMLA leave and may be treated as paid or unpaid leave under the employer's normal leave policies. [29 C.F.R. § 825.307(b)]

If an employer requires an employee to obtain either a second or third opinion, the employer must reimburse the employee or family member for any reasonable "out of pocket" travel expense incurred to obtain the opinions. The employer may not require the employee or family member to travel outside normal commuting distance to obtain a second or third opinion except in very unusual circumstances. [29 C.F.R. § 825.307(e)]

Q 16:37   Once a health care provider has certified the need for leave because of a serious medical condition, must an employee provide additional certifications?

Yes. Additional certifications must be provided if they are requested by the employer. If the leave has been granted on the basis of a serious medical condition of the employee or his or her spouse, child, or parent, the employer can require the eligible employee to obtain subsequent recertification on a reasonable basis. The FMLA does not define what constitutes a "reasonable basis." [FMLA § 103(e); 29 U.S.C. § 2613(e)]

Permitted frequency of employer requests for recertification. Under the final DOL regulations, the employer may require an eligible employee to obtain subsequent recertification no more frequently than every 30 days and only in connection with an absence by the employee, unless the employee requests an extension of leave, the circumstances described in the original certification have changed significantly, or the employer receives information casting doubt upon the continuing validity of the certification.

If the initial certification specifies a period of more than 30 days for a period of incapacity or for a leave on an intermittent or reduced-leave basis, recertification generally cannot be required before the end of the period, except for the above three situations. However, in all cases, an employer may request recertification of a medical condition every six months in connection with an absence by the employee. [FMLA § 103(e); 29 U.S.C. § 2613(e); 29 C.F.R. § 825.308] For example, if a medical certification says that an employee will be unable to work, whether continuously or on an intermittent basis, for 40 days, the employer must wait 40 days before requesting recertification. However, even if a medical certification indicates that an employee will need intermittent or reduced schedule leave for more than six months (for example, for a lifetime condition), the employer is permitted to request recertification every six months in connection with an absence by the employee.

An example in the final regulations suggests that if an employee who is on leave for four weeks due to knee surgery and recuperation plays in the company softball league games during the employee's third week of FMLA leave, that information might be enough to cast doubt on the continuing validity of the employee's medical certification and allow the employer to request recertification in less than 30 days.

According to a DOL opinion letter, one fact that might cast doubt on an employee's original certification—and justify recertification more frequently than 30 days—is a pattern of Monday and Friday absences. In that situation, a request for recertification within 30 days would be appropriate because the employer has no evidence that provides a medical reason for the timing of absences, and the request for recertification is made in conjunction with an actual absence. The DOL says recertification could be justified, for example, if a medical certification indicated the need for intermittent leave for two or three days a month due to migraine headaches, and the employee took leave every

Monday or Friday (the first and last days of the employee's workweek). [DOL Op. Ltr. May 25, 2004]

This DOL opinion letter also makes it clear that nothing in the FMLA prohibits an employer from including a record of an employee's absences along with the medical certification form or from asking, as part of the recertification process, whether the likely duration and frequency of the employee's incapacity due to the chronic condition is limited to Mondays and Fridays. [DOL Op. Ltr. May 25, 2004]

Recertification in a new leave year. According to a DOL opinion letter, when an employee has requested intermittent FMLA leave for a serious medical condition, the employer can restart the medical certification process with the employee's first absence in a new 12-month leave year. A second and third medical opinion, as appropriate, may also be requested in any case in which the employer has reason to doubt the validity of the new medical certification. Moreover, the DOL says this recertification may be performed even if the employer requested recertification in the previous 12-month leave year. [DOL Op. Ltr. FMLA 2005-2-A]

Final FMLA regulations specifically permit an employer to request a new medical certification for each year of leave. [29 C.F.R. § 825.305(e)]

Effect of state law. If state law requires only one recertification, the employer cannot require additional certifications unless they are for leave in excess of that mandated by the state law. [29 C.F.R. § 825.701(a)(2)]

Q 16:38   What proof of entitlement to family or medical leave on the basis of a child's birth or placement for adoption or foster care may an employer require an employee to provide?

In the case of the birth of a child, or the placement of a child for adoption or foster care, there is no statutory or regulatory guidance as to proof of entitlement. Nevertheless, presumably an employer can require the employee to provide reasonable proof that the event has in fact occurred.

Q 16:39   What certification is required when an employee requests leave because of a qualifying exigency related to a family member's military duty?

An eligible employee is entitled to up to 12 weeks of leave in a 12-month period because of any "qualifying exigency" arising out of the fact that the spouse, son, daughter, or parent of the employee is on active duty (or has been notified of an impending call or order to active duty) in the Armed Forces. [FMLA § 102(a)(1)(E); 29 U.S.C. § 2612(a)(1)(E)]

The first time an employee requests leave because of a qualifying exigency relating to a family member's military duty, the employer may require the employee to provide a copy of the family member's active duty orders or other documentation issued by the military indicating that the family member is on active duty or call to active duty status in support of a contingency operation, and the dates of the family member's active duty service. This information is generally required to be provided only once. However, new documentation may be required if an employee's need for leave arises out of a different active duty or call to active duty status of a different family member. [29 C.F.R. § 825.309(a)]

In addition, the employer may require that leave for any qualifying exigency be supported by a certification from the employee that contains the following information:

- A statement or description, signed by the employee, of the facts regarding the qualifying exigency. This should include information on the type of qualifying exigency (see Q 16:14) and any available documentation that supports the need for leave. For example, if leave is being requested to attend military events or activities, documentation may include an announcement of an informational briefing, while leave to attend to childcare and school activities may be backed up by a document confirming an appointment with a school counselor or official.

- The approximate date on which the qualifying exigency commenced or will commence.

- If the employee is requesting leave for a single, continuous period of time, the beginning and end dates of the absence.

- If the employee is requesting leave on an intermittent or reduced schedule basis, an estimate of the frequency and duration of the qualifying exigency.

- If the qualifying exigency involves meeting with a third party, appropriate contact information for the individual with whom the employee is meeting (e.g., name, title, organization, address, telephone number, fax number, and e-mail address) and a brief description of the purpose of the meeting. [29 C.F.R. § 825.309(b)]

If the employee submits a complete and sufficient verification, the employer cannot request further information from the employee. However, if the qualifying exigency involves meeting with a third party, the employer may contact the third party to verify a meeting or appointment schedule and the nature of the meeting. The employee's permission is not required for such verification, but the employer may not request additional information from the third party. The employer may also contact an appropriate unit of the Department of Defense to verify that the employee's family member is on active duty or call to active duty status. Again, the employee's permission is not required, but the employer may not request additional information. [29 C.F.R. § 825.309(d)]

Optional form. The DOL has developed an optional form that can be used to certify an qualifying exigency. Form WH-384, Certification of Qualifying Exigency, can be downloaded from the Wage and Hour Division section of the DOL's Web site at *www.wagehour.dol.gov.*

Q 16:40   What certification is required when an employee requests military caregiver leave?

An eligible employee who is the spouse, son, daughter, parent, or next of kin (i.e., closest blood relative) of a covered servicemember with a serious illness or injury incurred in the line of duty is entitled to a total of 26 weeks of leave in a 12-month period to care for the servicemember. [FMLA § 102(a)(3); 29 U.S.C. § 2612(a)(3)]

When an employee requests military caregiver leave, the employer may request certification from the employee and from the covered servicemember's health care provider. [29 C.F.R. § 825.310]

Information that may be requested from the employee includes:

- The name of the covered servicemember for whom the employee is providing care;
- The relationship of the employee to the covered servicemember;
- Whether the covered servicemember is a current member of the Armed Forces, the National Guard or Reserves, and the servicemembers' military branch, rank, and unit assignment;
- Whether the servicemember is assigned to a military medical facility as an outpatient;
- Whether the servicemember is on the temporary disability retired list; and
- A description of the care to provided to the servicemember and an estimate of the leave needed to provide the care. [29 C.F.R. § 825.310(c)]
- An employer may require the employee to provide confirmation of a covered relationship to the servicemember. [29 C.F.R. § 825.310(d)]

Medical certification in connection with military caregiver leave may be provided a Department of Defense (DOD) or Department of Veterans Affairs (VA) health care providers or by certain DOD authorized health care providers. [29 C.F.R. § 825.310(a)] An employer may request that the health care provider provide the following information:

- Identifying information about the health care provider.
- Whether the covered servicemember's illness or injury was incurred in the line of duty.
- The approximate date the illness or injury commenced and its expected duration.
- A statement or description of appropriate medical facts about the covered servicemember medical condition for which the leave is requested.
- Information sufficient to establish that the covered servicemember is in need of care and the expected duration of that need.
- If leave is requested on an intermittent or reduced schedule basis for planned medical treatments, whether there is a medical necessity for the periodic care and an estimate of the treatment schedule.

- If leave is requested on an intermittent or reduced schedule basis other than for planned medical treatments (for example, for episodic flare-ups of a medical condition), whether there is a medical necessity for such periodic care and the estimated frequency and duration of such care. [29 C.F.R. § 825.310(b)]

An employer may seek authentication or verification of the medical certification, but second and third opinions are not permitted nor are recertifications. [29 C.F.R. § 825.310(d)]

Optional form. The DOL has developed Form WH-385, Certification for Serious Illness or Injury of Covered Servicemember. The form can be downloaded from the Wage and Hour Division section of the DOL's Web site at *www.wagehour.dol.gov.* An employer can use its own form provided it does not request information beyond that specified in the FMLA regulations. [29 C.F.R. § 825.310(d)]

ITOs and ITAs. In lieu of the DOL form or the employer's own form, an employer must accept "invitational travel orders" (ITOs) or "invitational travel authorizations" (ITAs) issued to any family member to join an injured or ill servicemember at his or her bedside. An ITO or ITA is sufficient certification for the period of time specified in the ITO or ITA. During that time, an eligible employee may take leave to care for the covered servicemember in a continuous block of time or on an intermittent basis. An employee who submits an ITO or ITA cannot be required to provide any additional certification. However, an employer may require the employee to provide confirmation of a covered family relationship to the seriously ill or injured servicemember. [29 C.F.R. § 825. 310(e)]

Substitution of Paid Leave

Q 16:41   Is an employee entitled to be paid by his or her employer while on FMLA leave?

No. An employer is not required to pay an employee any wages or salary while the employee is on family or medical leave pursuant to the FMLA. Generally, FMLA leave is unpaid. [FMLA § 102(c); 29 U.S.C. § 2612(c); 29 C.F.R. § 825.207(a)]

Q 16:42   What if the employee is also eligible for paid leave?

If an employee is eligible for paid leave, such as for accrued vacation, his or her employer may require, or the employee may request, that such paid leave be substituted for FMLA leave. In such a case, the paid leave runs concurrently with and counts against the employee's FMLA entitlement. [FMLA § 102(d); 29 U.S.C. § 2612(d); 29 C.F.R. § 825.207(a)]

The final DOL regulations provide that the employer must inform the employee that the employee must satisfy the procedural requirements of the paid leave policy only in connection with the receipt of payment. If the employee does not comply with the additional requirements of the employer's paid leave policy, the employee is not entitled to substitute paid leave, but the employee remains entitled to take unpaid FMLA leave. [29 C.F.R. § 825.207]

An employee's use of his or her paid leave for non-FMLA purposes does not count against the employee's FMLA entitlement, and the employer cannot dock the employee an equivalent number of days of FMLA leave. Examples of non-FMLA purposes include using vacation days to go to Disney World or using paid sick leave for a medical condition that is not a serious health condition under the FMLA. [29 C.F.R. § 825.207(c)]

If neither the employee nor the employer chooses to substitute paid leave for unpaid FMLA leave (see Qs 16:37, 16:39), the employee remains entitled to all paid leave that is earned or accrued under the terms of the employer's plan. [29 C.F.R. § 825.207(b)]

A worker sued his former employer for improperly firing him after he left his job site because he was suffering from a diabetic attack. According to the worker, his condition qualified him for FMLA leave. A U.S. district court dismissed the worker's lawsuit on the grounds that the worker's absence did not qualify for FMLA protection because the employer's sick leave policy required employees to use paid leave as a substitute for FMLA leave and the worker had not used all of the paid sick leave available to him. The U.S. Court of Appeals for the Eleventh Circuit reversed the district court's decision and reinstated the worker's lawsuit. According to the Eleventh Circuit, the district court misinterpreted the FMLA as permitting employers with paid sick leave policies to choose whether an employee's FMLA-qualifying absence will be either unpaid but protected by the FMLA or paid but unprotected. The Eleventh Circuit acknowledged that the district court's misinterpretation was understandable, given the "unartful and unfortunate use of language in the FMLA . . . indicating that paid leave may be used as a 'substitute' for unpaid FMLA."

According to the Eleventh Circuit, an employer who is subject to the FMLA and also offers a paid sick leave policy has two options when an employee's leave qualifies under both the leave policy and the FMLA: The employer may either (1) permit employees to use their FMLA leave and paid sick leave sequentially or (2) require employees to use their FMLA leave and paid sick leave concurrently. However, Congress did not intend, by using the substitution language, to allow employers to evade the FMLA by providing paid sick leave benefits. Otherwise, said the court, when an employee misses work for an illness that qualifies under both his employer's paid sick leave policy and the FMLA, his employer could elect to have the absence count as paid sick leave rather than FMLA leave and would then be free to discharge him without running afoul of the Strickland Act. [Strickland v. Water Works & Sewer Bd., 239 F.3d 1199 (11th Cir. 2001)]

Q 16:43   Is an employee who uses paid leave as a "substitute" for family or medical leave protected by the FMLA?

In addition to requiring covered employers to grant leave to qualifying employees, the FMLA provides other protections for employees, including the maintenance of health benefits during the leave and the right to reinstatement in the same or an equivalent job following the leave (see Qs 16:44, Q 16:49).

If it is determined that an employer violated the FMLA by denying leave or firing an employee for taking leave, the employee can recover damages from the employer (see Q 16:74). Depending on the circumstances, damages may include lost wages or benefits or other monetary losses suffered by the employee. For example, if an employer wrongfully denied an employee's request for time off to care for an ill family member, the employer may be required to pay the cost of providing alternative care. An employee may also be entitled to an equal amount as liquidated damages, unless the court decides the employer acted in good faith and had reasonable grounds for believing the employee was not entitled to leave. When appropriate, an employee may be entitled to equitable relief, such as reinstatement to his or her job. Finally, an employer who is on the losing end of an FMLA court battle may be required to pay the employee's attorneys' fees, expert witness fees, and other costs incurred in bringing the lawsuits.

In *Strickland v. Water Works and Sewer Board* [239 F.3d 1199 (11th Cir. 2001)], an appellate court raised the key question of whether an employee who qualifies for paid leave under an employer's policies is entitled to the protections of the FMLA. In the case, an employee who left work during a diabetic attack was fired by his employer. The employee sued the employer for violating his rights under the FMLA, including his right to reinstatement following the leave. The employer argued that the employee had no FMLA job protections because he had not exhausted the paid sick leave available to him under the employer's policy. A U.S. district court agreed with the employer and dismissed the employee's lawsuit. According to the district court, paid sick leave or any other paid leave is not protected by the FMLA. However, the Eleventh Circuit Court of Appeals disagreed.

The Eleventh Circuit acknowledged that some of the language in the FMLA might suggest that an eligible employee whose leave qualifies as paid sick leave under the employer's sick leave policy is not protected by the law. However, the court said such a reading would be inconsistent with the purposes of the law.

The FMLA provides that an eligible employee is entitled to a total of 12 workweeks of leave during any 12-month period for specified reasons, including a serious health condition that makes the employee unable to perform his or her job. The FMLA explicitly permits employers to provide FMLA leave on an unpaid basis. However, the law also provides that "an eligible employee may elect, or an employer may require the employee, to substitute any of the accrued paid vacation leave, personal leave, or medical or sick leave of the employee . . . for any part of the 12-week period" of FMLA leave.

According to the Eleventh Circuit, the lower court interpreted the FMLA as permitting an employer to choose whether an employee's FMLA-qualifying absence will be either unpaid but protected by the FMLA or paid but unprotected. The appeals court said that this interpretation was understandable given the FMLA's "unartful and unfortunate" language indicating that paid leave may be used as a "substitute" for unpaid FMLA leave. The use of the term "substitute" could be read to mean that paid sick leave and unpaid FMLA leave are mutually exclusive and that the employer or employee must choose one or the other. However, the court said that such a reading was a misinterpretation.

The appeals court pointed out that the FMLA provides that if an employee is eligible for fewer than 12 weeks of paid leave, the employer can provide the additional time off on an unpaid basis. Moreover, the law says that if neither the employer nor the employee elects to substitute paid leave for unpaid FMLA leave, the employee remains entitled to all the paid leave that he or she has accrued under the employer's plan.

These provisions make it clear that an employer has two options when an employee's leave qualifies under both the FMLA and the employer's sick leave policy: The employer may (1) permit the employee to use his or her FMLA leave and paid sick leave sequentially or (2) require the employee to use the FMLA leave and paid sick leave concurrently. However, the use of the term "substitute" was not intended to allow employers to evade the FMLA by providing their employees with paid sick leave benefits.

Instead, according to the court, the logical purpose of the substitution provision is to protect employers that offer paid sick leave from having to provide both the 12 weeks of leave required by the FMLA and the paid leave benefits separately. To balance the needs of employers and sick employees, Congress intended the FMLA to provide employees with a minimum entitlement of 12 weeks of leave while protecting employers against employees' adding their FMLA entitlement to any paid leave offered by the employer. [Strickland v. Water Works & Sewer Bd., 239 F.3d 1199 (11th Cir. 2001)]

Employee Benefits During Leave

Q 16:44   Is an employee on FMLA leave entitled to continued coverage under the employer's health benefit plans?

Yes. An employee on family or medical leave authorized by the FMLA must continue to receive group health plan coverage for the duration of the leave at the level and under the conditions coverage would have been provided if the employee had continued in employment continuously for the duration of the leave. [FMLA § 104(e)(1); 29 C.F.R. § 825.209]

Group health plan. For this purpose, the FMLA defines *group health plan* by reference to Internal Revenue Code Section 5000(b)(1). The regulations state this definition as any plan of, or contributed to by, an employer (including a self-insured plan) to provide health care, directly or otherwise, to the employer's employees, former employees, or the families of such employees or former employees. [FMLA § 104(c)(1); 29 U.S.C. § 2614(c)(1); 29 C.F.R. §§ 825.209, 825.800; I.R.C. § 5000, as amended by § 13561 of OBRA '93]

Practice Pointer. Employers should be alert to the fact that the FMLA requires continuation of any coverage that falls within the broad definition of a group health plan: the continuation requirement is not limited to major medical plans. For example, the DOL concluded that an employer was required to provide continued coverage under a group dental plan because it qualified as a plan to provide health care to employees. The employer who requested the ruling took the position that continued coverage was not required because the dental plan was neither part of nor a supplement to the employer's major medical plan (which was subject to the FMLA). [DOL Op. Ltr. FMLA 2006-6-A (Oct. 5, 2006)]

Requirements for continued group health plan coverage. The type of coverage provided during FMLA leave must be the same as the employee would have received if working (for example, an employee who has family medical coverage must be permitted to maintain that coverage during the leave). Health benefit coverage must be maintained during the leave regardless of whether it is provided in a base medical plan, supplemental medical plan, flexible spending account (FSA), or any other component of a cafeteria plan. A new health plan or any benefit increases (and, presumably, benefit decreases) as well as premium increases or decreases made under the plan must be provided to employees on FMLA leave.

In addition, employees on FMLA leave retain the right, if available under the applicable group health plan provisions, to add or drop family members or to switch plan coverage options during the period of FMLA leave. Notices of any such opportunity must also be provided to employees on FMLA leave. [29 C.F.R. § 825.209]

Q 16:45 How are employee contributions toward group health plan coverage paid during FMLA leave?

If the group health plan requires contributions by active employees, the employee on leave must continue to make the required contributions. The employer may not add any additional charge for administrative expenses. The COBRA rate, which includes a charge for administrative expenses, may not be charged because the employee is treated as not having experienced a COBRA-qualifying event until he or she fails to return from the leave. [29 C.F.R. § 825.210] (See Q 16:54 regarding the impact of COBRA.)

For paid leave being counted as FMLA leave, contributions must be made by the method normally used (such as by payroll deduction).

For unpaid FMLA leave, the employer may require the employee contributions to be paid to it or directly to an insurance carrier. The DOL regulations provide that the employer may require employees to pay their share of premiums in any of the following ways: (1) at the same time as they would be due if made by payroll deduction; (2) on the same schedule as COBRA payments;

(3) by prepayment, at the employee's option, under a cafeteria plan; (4) under the employer's existing rules for payment by employees on "leave without pay" (except that prepayment cannot be required); or (5) by any other method voluntarily agreed to between the employer and the employee. (This last item may include prepayment of premiums through increased payroll deductions or otherwise when the need for FMLA leave is foreseeable.) [29 C.F.R. § 825.210] If the employee had been making contributions on a pretax basis under a cafeteria plan and does not choose to prepay them, the contributions during the unpaid leave may have to be made on an after-tax basis. [29 C.F.R. § 825.210] (See Qs 16:54–16:62 for special rules relating to cafeteria plans.)

An employer must provide employees with advance written notice of the terms and conditions under which health premiums must be paid. Those terms and conditions cannot require more of an employee using FMLA leave than the employer requires of other employees who are on leave without pay.

Special rule for multiemployer health plans. Employers are required to continue to make contributions on behalf of employees on FMLA leave as though they had continued to be employed, unless the multiemployer health plan expressly contains an alternate procedure for maintaining such coverage. Employees cannot be required to use banked hours or to pay greater premiums than they would have been required to had they been continuously employed. [29 C.F.R. § 825.211]

Employer-provided coverage. The FMLA provides that an employer must maintain an employee's group health plan coverage during FMLA leave at the level and under the conditions coverage would have been provided if the employee had continued in employment continuously for the duration of such leave. [29 U.S.C. § 2614(c)(1)] Consequently, if an employer pays for all or part of an employee's coverage, the employer must continue to do so during the employee's FMLA leave. In Opinion Letter FMLA 2006-3-A, the DOL concluded that an employer that contributes monthly amounts to a cafeteria plan to be used by employees for group health plan coverage is required to continue that practice for employees on FMLA leave, even though employees on other types of unpaid leave are required to pay for their group health plan coverage. Moreover, because the employer provides the money for the group health insurance coverage when employees are working, it may not recover such payments for periods of FMLA leave. [DOL Op. Ltr. FMLA 2006-3-A (Jan. 1, 2006)]

Q 16:46   When does an employer's obligation to continue health plan coverage during FMLA leave end?

An employer may cease providing group health plan coverage during FMLA leave when:

1. The employee informs the employer of his or her intent not to return to work;

2. The employee's employment would have been terminated but for the leave (for example, because of a reduction in force); or

3. The employee fails to return from leave (see Q 16:52).

[29 C.F.R. § 825.209(f)]

Q 16:47   What if the employee's group health coverage ceases during FMLA leave?

If the employee's premium payment for health insurance coverage is more than 30 days late and the employer does not have a longer grace period policy, the employer's obligation to maintain health insurance coverage during the FMLA leave ceases. In order to terminate coverage, notice of the late premium must be given at least 15 days in advance of the termination. [29 C.F.R. § 825.212(a)(1)] If, on the other hand, the employer paid the employee's missed contribution in order to maintain the employee's health coverage, the employer may recover that "makeup" payment from the employee. [29 C.F.R. § 825. 212(b)] In either case, the employer's other obligations under the FMLA continue, including the obligation to restore the employee's health insurance coverage upon his or her return from FMLA leave (see Q 16:51). [29 C.F.R. §§ 825.212(a)(3), 825.212(c)]

Right to reinstatement. If the employee either chooses not to maintain health coverage during FMLA leave or loses health insurance coverage during FMLA leave because of the failure to make timely premium payments, he or she nonetheless is entitled, upon return from FMLA leave, to be reinstated in the group health plan on the same terms as before taking the leave, without any qualifying period, physical examination, exclusion for preexisting conditions, and so forth. [29 C.F.R. §§ 825.209(e), 825.212(c)]

Final FMLA regulations make it clear that if an employer fails to restore the employee's health coverage upon the employee's return to work, the employer may be liable for benefits lost by reason of the violation, for other actual monetary losses sustained as a result of the failure, and for appropriate equitable relief. [29 C.F.R. § 825.212(c)]

Q 16:48   Does the FMLA require an employee on FMLA leave to be provided with continued coverage under his or her employer's other benefit plans?

Generally not. An employee generally is not entitled to continued coverage under his or her employer's other benefit plans. Benefit coverage that has not accrued generally can be canceled or suspended during an FMLA leave period. Thus, group life insurance coverage, for example, can be terminated without violating the FMLA. An employee taking family or medical leave authorized by the FMLA cannot, however, lose any employment benefit that was accrued before the date on which the leave begins. [FMLA § 104(a)(2); 29 U.S.C. § 2614(a)(2)]

Seniority and benefit accruals. It should be especially noted that employees are not entitled to accrue any seniority or employment benefits during the leave period. [FMLA § 104(a)(3)(A); 29 U.S.C. § 2614(a)(3)(A)] This means, for example, that an employee is not required to be given pension credits or vacation credits for the period of leave (although benefits such as paid vacation, sick leave, or personal leave accrued at the time the leave began must be available to the employee upon his or her return from the leave to the extent not substituted for FMLA leave).

In Opinion Letter FMLA 2006-4-A, the DOL examined a situation where a company's collective bargaining agreement with an employee union provided that, in order to be eligible for group health benefits for a calendar year, an employee must have worked a specified number of hours in the preceding year. The company asked whether it was required to count FMLA time toward the required number of hours for group health benefits eligibility for the following year. The DOL's answer was "No." According to the DOL, the FMLA regulations specifically provide that if a benefit plan is predicated on a pre-established number of hours worked each year and the employee does not have sufficient hours as a result of taking unpaid FMLA leave, the benefit is lost. [29 C.F.R. § 825.215(d)(5)] Therefore, the DOL concluded that the company generally would not be required to provide group health insurance coverage to an employee who does not meet the hours requirement due to FMLA leave taken in the prior year. However, the DOL cautioned that a different rule would apply if other types of leave, paid or unpaid, count as hours worked for purposes of determining eligibility for health insurance in the following year. In that case, FMLA leave of an equivalent type would need to be counted. [DOL Op. Ltr. FMLA 2006-4-A (Feb. 13, 2006)]

Key exception. An employee's entitlement to benefits other than group health benefits during a period of FMLA leave is to be determined by the employer's established policy for providing such benefits when the employee is on other forms of leave (whether paid or unpaid, as appropriate). [29 C.F.R. § 825. 209(h)] Moreover, the FMLA contains a general nondiscrimination rule prohibiting an employer from discriminating or retaliating against an employee for having exercised FMLA rights. Thus, the FMLA regulations make it clear that if, under an employer's policy, an employee on leave without pay receives full benefits while on leave, the same benefits must be provided to an employee on unpaid FMLA leave. [29 C.F.R. § 825.220(c)]

Rights upon Return from FMLA Leave

Q 16:49   Does an employee who has taken FMLA leave have a right to be reinstated when the leave period has expired?

Yes. Generally, an employee on a family or medical leave who elects to return to work after the leave is over must be reinstated in his or her former position or an equivalent position with equivalent benefits, pay, and other terms and conditions of employment. [FMLA § 104(a)(1); 29 U.S.C. § 2614(a)(1); 29 C.F.R. §§ 825.100(c), 825.214, 825.215] (See Q 16:57 for a discussion of reinstatement in a cafeteria plan.) However, an employee has no greater right to reinstatement or to other benefits and conditions of employment than if the employee had not taken FMLA leave.

The DOL regulations provide that if reinstatement is denied, the employer has the burden of showing that employment would have been terminated without regard to the leave. [29 C.F.R. § 825.216(a)] However, the Seventh Circuit Court of Appeals held that it is an *employee's* job to prove that he or she is entitled to the benefits of the FMLA. If the employer presents evidence that a benefit would not have been available even if the employee had not taken FMLA leave, then the employee has to overcome that evidence.

So, for example, when an employer claims that the employee would have been discharged even if he or she had not taken leave, the employee must provide enough evidence to convince the jury that he or she would not have been discharged but for the leave. [Rice v. Sunrise Express, Inc., 209 F. 3d 1008 (7th Cir. 2000)]

In another case, a U.S. district court ruled that an employer may have violated the FMLA by failing to notify employees that taking a leave period longer than the required FMLA leave period would result in forfeiture of FMLA reinstatement rights. An employee of the employer took a family leave of 16 weeks for the birth of a child. The employer's policy was that employees who took more than the FMLA-authorized 12 weeks of leave forfeited their FMLA reinstatement rights. The court found, however, that the employer's handbook failed to contain essential information regarding the forfeiture of reinstatement rights and ordered a trial to determine if the employee had received adequate information when requesting leave. [Fry v. First Fidelity Bancorp., No. 95-6019, 1996 U.S. Dist. LEXIS 875 (E.D. Pa. Jan. 30, 1996)]

The U.S. Court of Appeals for the Fifth Circuit upheld a verdict for a plant manager fired shortly after he suffered a heart attack. Upon returning to work, the plant manager was given the option of staying as a shift supervisor but at half the salary of a plant supervisor, or working as a shift supervisor at full plant manager salary for 90 days while he looked for another job. Later, the company offered to terminate him with two months of severance pay. The company claimed the plant manager was not entitled to be restored to his job because it had decided to terminate him before he had the heart attack. The court held that there was insufficient evidence to suggest the company was about to fire the plant manager and that under the FMLA, he was entitled to be restored to his job when he returned from his qualified medical leave or to an equivalent position with equivalent benefits. [Nero v. Industrial Molding Corp., 167 F.3d 921 (5th Cir.), *reh'g denied*, 1999 U.S. App. LEXIS 7939 (5th Cir. Apr. 5, 1999)]

Proof of fitness to work. If the FMLA leave was the result of the employee's serious health condition, the employer may, pursuant to a uniformly applied policy, require that the individual first submit a certification of fitness to return to work that relates to the health condition that caused his or her absence. The employer also may refuse to restore to employment any individual who fails to submit such certification. [29 C.F.R. §§ 825.100(d), 825.312, 825.313(d)]

According to the Sixth Circuit Court of Appeals, the employer's duty to reinstate an employee is triggered once an employee submits a "simple statement" from his or her health care provider indicating that the employee may return to work. While the employer may require more information related to the employee's ability to perform the essential function of his or her job, the employer cannot delay reinstating the employee simply because the employer is obtaining further information or clarification from the employee's health care provider. [Brumbalough v. Camelot Care Ctrs., Inc., 2005 U.S. App. LEXIS 29217 (6th Cir. Dec. 30, 2005)]

Final FMLA regulations provide that an employer may require that the certification specifically address the employee's ability to perform the essential functions of the employee's job. However, in order to require such a certification the employer must provide the employee with a list of those essential functions no later than the time the employer provides the employee with notice designating the leave as FMLA leave and must indicate in the designation notice that the certification must address the employee's fitness to perform the essential functions. [29 C.F.R. § 825.312(b)] The employer may delay restoration to employment until the employee submits the required certification unless the employer has failed to provide the required notice. [29 C.F.R. § 825.312(e)]

Key employee exception. An employer may deny reinstatement to a salaried eligible employee (*key employee*) who is among the highest-paid 10 percent of the employees employed by the employer within 75 miles of the facility at which the employee is employed, if the following requirements are met:

1. The employer's denial of reinstatement is necessary to prevent substantial and grievous economic injury to the operations of the employer (as defined in DOL Regulations Section 825.218); and

2. The employer notifies the employee, in person or by certified mail, of the employer's intent to deny reinstatement on that basis at the time the employer determines that substantial and grievous economic injury will occur (in accordance with the procedure contained in DOL Regulations Section 825.219).

If the key employee, after receiving the notice, requests reinstatement at the end of the leave, the employer must again determine whether there will be substantial and grievous economic injury to the operations of the employer at that time. If so, reinstatement can be denied. [FMLA § 104(b); 29 U.S.C. § 2614(b); DOL Regs. § 825.219(d)] The methodology for determining the highest-paid 10 percent of employees is set forth in DOL Regulations Section 825.217(c).

If an employer invokes the key employee exception and the highly paid employee elects, after receiving notice that the reinstatement will be denied, to take or continue the leave, the employee is entitled to continuation of health benefits during the leave, and the employer cannot recoup any of its cost of the coverage from the highly compensated employee. [DOL Regs. §§ 825.219(c), 825.213(a)(2)] (See Q 16:52 for a discussion of an employer's right generally to recoup its premium payments.)

A district court case makes it clear that the notice provided to the employee invoking the key employee exception is not tantamount to termination of employment.

An employee on FMLA leave received a notice from her employer informing her that she was a key employee under the terms of the FMLA, and, consequently, her position might be filled during her leave. The notice stated that the employee was welcome to request reinstatement at the end of her leave but that the employer could not guarantee that her original position would be available. The employee took this to mean that she had been fired. She wrote to the employer, demanding the severance benefits she was entitled to under her employment contract. The employer replied by both letter and telephone, explaining to the employee that she had not been terminated.

As it turned out, the employer ultimately invited the employee to return to her original position at the end of her FMLA leave. The employee declined the offer and brought a lawsuit against the employer, claiming that she had been terminated and was entitled to severance benefits.

The U.S. district court concluded that, by sending the notice, the employer had properly invoked the key employee exception. However, the notice did not constitute a termination of employment that entitled the employee to severance benefits. [Kelley v. Decisionone Corp., 2000 U.S. Dist. LEXIS 17508 (E.D. Pa. Dec. 6, 2000)]

Q 16:50 When is an employee considered to have been reinstated to the same or an equivalent position?

On return from FMLA leave, an employee is entitled to be returned to the same position he or she held when leave commenced or to an equivalent position with equivalent benefits, pay, and other terms and conditions of employment. [29 C.F.R. § 825.214] An employee is entitled to reinstatement even if the employee has been replaced or the employee's position has been restructured to accommodate the employee's absence.

Two appellate court cases discuss what is required for an employee to be considered to have been returned to the same or an equivalent position.

In one case, an employee worked as a locomotive engineer for the crew that ran an intraplant locomotive. The crew had three members: a locomotive engineer, a conductor, and a switch tender. When one of the three crew members was absent, the other two members filled in as required.

The employee began suffering from depression and took a series of leaves of absence on the advice of her physician and a counselor. During that period, she was treated with various prescription medications. Eventually, the health providers cleared the employee to return to work. Despite that clearance, however, the employer's medical director refused to return the employee to her job as a locomotive engineer until he was confident that she could safely drive the train. The employee was assigned to office work answering phones, although she received the pay and benefits of her locomotive job and retained her job title. The employee subsequently produced a letter from her physician releasing her to return to her position as a locomotive engineer without restriction. However, the employer's medical director again prohibited the employee's return to operating the locomotive. The employee sued the employer for violating her right to job restoration following FMLA leave. However, a U.S. district court threw out her claim.

On appeal, the Eighth Circuit Court of Appeals noted that, before restoring an employee to his or her job, an employer may require certification from the employee's health care provider that the employee is able to resume work. A health care provider employed by the employer may, with the employee's permission, contact the employee's health care provider for clarification of the certification. However, the employer may not delay the employee's return to work while this contact is being made. [29 C.F.R. § 825.310]

The employer argued that the employee was properly restored to her position within the meaning of the FMLA because her pay and benefits were the same as before her leave. Moreover, the employer claimed that it could properly restrict her duties while evaluating her fitness to drive the locomotive. The employee acknowledged that her job title, classification, pay, and benefits did not change when she returned to work. However, because the duties and functions of her office assignment were so different from those of a locomotive engineer, she had not been reinstated to the same or an equivalent position within the meaning of the FMLA.

The court concluded that restoring an employee to an equivalent position requires both that the new position come with equivalent benefits and terms and that it be equivalent in terms of job duties and functions. Thus, the district court should have determined whether the employee's office position was equivalent to her job as a locomotive engineer in terms of duties and job functions. The Eighth Circuit acknowledged that the employer was permitted to ask the employee for medical certification of her fitness to return to work and to seek clarification from her health care providers. However, once the certification was provided, the employee was entitled to be restored to her former position or an equivalent position. [Cooper v. Olin Corp., 246 F.3d 1083 (8th Cir. 2001)]

In another case, a registered nurse who took FMLA leave to recover from injuries sustained in an auto accident was reassigned from a full-time day shift position in the cardiac care unit (CCU) to a full-time night shift position following her leave. The night shift position had the same rate of pay and same duties as the day shift position. The nurse turned down the night shift position on the basis of her family situation: as a single parent, she had to be home at night. The nurse asked to be assigned to a variable staffing pool, which permitted her to work the day shift in the CCU on a part-time, as-needed basis. Although other full-time day shift positions subsequently became available in other departments, the nurse did not apply for them because she preferred to remain in the CCU. The nurse sued the hospital under the FMLA on the grounds that she was not restored to an equivalent position following her leave.

The Fifth Circuit Court of Appeals noted that the DOL regulations do not treat different shifts involving the same duties and pay as equivalent jobs. The regulations state that an employee is "ordinarily entitled to return to the same shift or the same or an equivalent work schedule." [29 C.F.R. § 825.215(e)(2)] In addition, the hospital's shift supervisor acknowledged the lack of equivalence when he testified that most hospital employees found day shift positions more desirable than night shift positions. [Hunt v. Rapides Healthcare Sys. LLC, 277 F.3d 757 (5th Cir. 2001)]

Q 16:51   What benefit plan rights does an employee have upon return from FMLA leave?

At the end of the employee's FMLA leave, the employee is entitled to be returned to the same position with the same benefits or to an equivalent position with equivalent benefits (see Q 16:49), including all benefits provided or made available to employees by the employer (regardless of whether provided via an ERISA plan), such as group life insurance, health insurance, disability insurance, sick leave, annual leave, educational benefits, and pensions. Benefits must be resumed in the same manner and at the same levels as before the leave, except that benefit changes made during the period of leave and affecting the entire workforce also must be provided to the employee unless the changes are dependent upon seniority or accrual. In particular, employees returning from FMLA leave cannot be required to requalify for any benefits they enjoyed before the FMLA leave started. [29 C.F.R. § 825.215]

> **Practice Pointer.** In view of the short leave period (maximum 12 work-weeks) and the possible application of state insurance law requirements for continuance and conversion of group life insurance coverage during a family or medical leave, terminating group life coverage may not be desirable in most instances. Some employers may decide that it is easier to avoid a lapse of the employee's coverage (such as life or disability insurance) by simply paying the employee's share of premiums during the period of FMLA leave. If an employer does so, it may recover such payments in the same manner as its own contributions toward health insurance (see Q 16:52). [29 C.F.R. § 824.213(f)]

Failure to Return from FMLA Leave

Q 16:52   If an employee on FMLA leave does not return to work upon the expiration of the leave, can the employer recover from the employee the employer's cost of providing group health plan coverage during the leave?

With certain exceptions, yes. If an employee on family or medical leave fails to return to work (defined for this purpose as returning to work for at least 30 calendar days) after his or her leave entitlement expires or has been exhausted, the employer can, with two exceptions discussed later, attempt to recoup the employer's cost of group health plan coverage for the unpaid portion (if any) of the FMLA leave period. For self-insured plans, this amount is limited to the employer's share of allowable COBRA premiums, excluding the 2 percent administrative fee. The health premiums that are permitted to be recovered are treated as a debt owed by the nonreturning employee. The employer's responsibility to provide health coverage (and, for self-insured plans, to pay claims incurred) during the period of FMLA leave does not change. [29 C.F.R. § 825.213]

If, however, the employee's failure to return to work is the result of (1) the continuation, recurrence, or onset of a serious health condition of the employee or the employee's family member, or a serious illness or injury of a covered servicemember; or (2) other circumstances beyond the control of the employee, no recoupment of the employer's cost for group health plan coverage during the leave is permitted. [FMLA § 104(c)(2); 29 U.S.C. § 2614(c)(2); 29 C.F.R. § 825. 213(a)] In addition, the employer cannot recover its cost of group health plan coverage from certain key employees who are not reinstated following FMLA leave (see Q 16:49).

Failure to return because of a serious health condition. If the employee claims that he or she is unable to return to work because of a serious health condition affecting the employee or a family member or because of a serious illness or injury of a covered servicemember, the employer is entitled to receive from the employee a certification by a health care provider. [FMLA § 104(c)(3); 29 U.S.C. § 2614(c)(3)] If the employee does not provide the certification within 30 days of the employer's request, the employer may recover the health benefit contributions paid by it during the period of unpaid FMLA leave. [29 C.F.R. § 825. 213(a)(3)]

Failure to return because of circumstances beyond the employee's control. The DOL regulations give several examples of circumstances that qualify as *other circumstances beyond the employee's control,* including a parent's choice to stay home with a newborn with a serious health condition, an unexpected transfer of the employee's spouse to a job location more than 75 miles from the employee's worksite; a need for the employee to provide care to a relative or other individual who is not an immediate family member who has a serious medical condition; a layoff of the employee while on leave; or the employee's status as a key employee who, after having been notified of the employer's intention to deny restoration because of substantial and grievous economic injury to the employer's operations, decides not to return to work and is not reinstated. According to the DOL, other circumstances beyond the employee's control do not include an employee's desire to stay in a distant city with a parent who no longer requires the employee's care or a parent's decision to stay home with a healthy newborn child rather than return to work. [29 C.F.R. § 825.213(a)(2)]

Permitted methods of recovery. If recovery of the cost of group health plan coverage is allowed, the employer may recover it by deducting its share of health insurance premiums from any sums owed to the employee, such as wages, vacation pay, or profit sharing distributions, provided that such deductions are otherwise permitted under applicable federal or state wage payment laws or other laws. Employers may also commence legal action to recover such amounts. [29 C.F.R. § 825.213(f)]

Q 16:53 If an employer has paid the premiums for coverage other than health insurance during an unpaid FMLA leave, may the employer recover the payments if the employee fails to return from the leave?

If an employer chooses to pay the premiums to maintain coverage other than health insurance, such as life insurance or disability insurance, to avoid, for example, a lapse in coverage, at the conclusion of leave the employer may recover only the costs incurred for paying the employee's share of premium payments whether or not the employee returns to work (see Q 16:50). [29 C.F.R. §§ 825.213(b), 825.213(f)]

Relationship to Group Health Plan Rules

Q 16:54 Is the group health plan coverage during FMLA leave considered to be continuation coverage for COBRA purposes?

No. The legislative history of the FMLA indicates that commencement of family or medical leave is not considered a qualifying event for COBRA purposes because it does not result in a loss of group health coverage. [S. Rep. No. 103-3, 103d Cong., 1st Sess., at 32 (1993)]

The taking of FMLA leave does not constitute a COBRA-qualifying event. [Treas. Reg. § 54.4980B-4, Q&A-1(a) (Feb. 3, 1999); Notice 94-103, 1994-51 I.R.B. 10] Instead, the qualifying event occurs when the employee does not return to employment at the end of the FMLA leave period and there is or has been a loss of health care coverage. This is true even if, during the FMLA leave, the employee failed to pay the employee portion of the premiums for coverage or declined coverage under the employer's group health plan. These employee acts are disregarded in determining whether a loss of coverage for COBRA purposes has occurred. [Notice 94-103, 1994-51 I.R.B. 10, Q&A-3; Treas. Reg. § 54.4980B-10, Q&A 3 (Jan. 10, 2001)]

A qualifying event will occur in the FMLA context when (1) the employee (or the employee's spouse or dependent child) is covered under the employer's group health plan on the day before the first day of FMLA leave (or becomes covered during the FMLA leave); (2) the employee does not return to employment with the employer at the end of the FMLA leave; and (3) the employee (or the employee's spouse or dependent child) would, in the absence of COBRA coverage, lose group health plan coverage before the end of the maximum coverage period. [Treas. Reg. § 54.4980B-10, Q&A-1(a) (Jan. 10, 2001)] For this purpose, any termination of group health coverage during the FMLA leave for failure to pay premiums is disregarded. [Notice 94-103, 1994-51 I.R.B. 10, Q&A-3; Treas. Reg. § 54.4980B-10, Q&A-3 (Jan. 10, 2001)]

As a general rule, the COBRA-qualifying event for an employee who fails to return to work at the conclusion of his or her FMLA leave occurs on the last day of FMLA leave. [Notice 94-103, 1994-51 I.R.B. 10, Q&A-2; Treas. Reg. § 54. 4980B-10, Q&A-2 (Jan. 10, 2001)] Based on the legislative history under FMLA and the interim regulations issued by the DOL and the IRS interpreting FMLA, the last day of FMLA leave is "when it becomes known that an employee is not returning to work and therefore ceases to be entitled to leave" under FMLA. [139 Cong. Rec. S978 (1993); 29 C.F.R. § 825.209(f)]

If coverage is not lost until a later date, the plan may provide that the maximum period of COBRA coverage will be measured from the date coverage is lost, rather than from the last day of family leave.

An employee's failure to return from FMLA leave will not be a qualifying event if the employer eliminates group health coverage for the class of employees to which the employee would have belonged if he or she had not taken leave. The employer must continue to employ that class of employees, and the elimination of coverage must occur before the last day of the employee's FMLA leave. [Treas. Reg. § 54.4980B-10]

> **Practice Pointer.** An employer cannot condition COBRA coverage on reimbursement of premiums it paid to continue health coverage during FMLA leave. The DOL has published rules describing the circumstances in which an employer may recover premiums it pays to maintain coverage, including family coverage, from an employee who fails to returns from leave (see Q 16:52). [29 C.F.R. § 825.213] However, even if recovery is permitted, the right to COBRA coverage cannot be conditioned upon the employee's reimbursement. [Treas. Reg. § 54.4980B-10, Q&A-5]

Relationship to Cafeteria Plan Rules

Q 16:55   How does the FMLA affect cafeteria plans?

The FMLA requires covered employers to maintain an employee's health coverage during FMLA leave or, if the employee chooses to drop coverage, to restore benefits when the employee returns from leave.

In many cases, health coverage is provided under a company cafeteria plan, which permits employees to choose between cash compensation and taxable and nontaxable compensation. In that case, the employer must comply with both the FMLA and the tax law rules governing cafeteria plans. For example, IRS regulations make it clear that an employee on FMLA leave has the same cafeteria plan rights as employees participating in the cafeteria plan who are not on FMLA leave. Therefore, employees on leave must be given the same opportunities as active employees to enroll in the plan or change their health coverage elections. In addition, an employee on FMLA leave may have the right to discontinue health coverage during the period of FMLA leave and reinstate coverage on returning from leave (see Qs 16:56–16:63).

Q 16:56   Can an employee taking FMLA leave revoke an existing election of group health plan coverage under a cafeteria plan?

Under final IRS regulations, an employer must either (1) allow an employee on unpaid FMLA leave to revoke his or her health coverage (including coverage under a health care FSA) or (2) continue the employee's coverage but allow the employee to discontinue payment of his or her share of the premiums. According to the final regulations, the FMLA does not require an employer to allow an employee to revoke coverage if the employer pays the employee's share of the premiums. [29 C.F.R. § 825.209(e); Treas. Reg. § 1.125-3, Q&A-1] If the employer continues an employee's coverage during FMLA leave, the employer can recover the employee's share of the premiums when the employee returns to work (see Q 16:59).

Practice Pointer. The best option for an employer may depend on a number of factors. For example, depending on the terms of the plan, it may be administratively easier to continue an employee's coverage than to reinstate coverage once an employee has dropped it. On the other hand, if the employer pays the employee's share of the premiums, it may be difficult to recoup those premium payments from an employee who does not return from FMLA leave. The DOL regulations permit an employer to recover the cost of the premiums, including both employer and employee shares, through deduction from any sums due the employee (unpaid wages, vacation pay, etc.), as long as the deductions do not otherwise violate applicable federal or state wage payment or other laws. Alternatively, the employer may sue the employee to recover such costs. However, the DOL regulations preclude recovery if the employee fails to return to work because of his or her own serious health condition or circumstances beyond the employee's control. Such circumstances might include a serious health condition of a newborn, a spouse's job transfer, a serious health condition of a relative other than an immediate family member, or a layoff during FMLA leave. [29 C.F.R. § 825.213]

Q 16:57   If an employee's group health plan coverage under a cafeteria plan terminated during an FMLA leave, must the employee be permitted to choose to be reinstated upon his or her return from leave?

Yes. An employee returning from an FMLA leave must be permitted to choose to be reinstated in the employer's group health plan coverage if the employee's coverage under a cafeteria plan (including a health care FSA) terminated during the leave. This is the case whether the coverage was terminated by the employee's revocation or as a result of nonpayment of employee premiums.

Generally, reinstatement must be on the same terms as before the leave and under the same terms and conditions as before the leave (including family or dependent coverage), subject to any changes in benefit levels that may have taken place during the FMLA leave. In addition, an employee has the right to revoke or change elections (e.g., because of changes in status, cost, or coverage) under the same terms and conditions as employees participating in the cafeteria plan who are not on FMLA leave. Thus, an employee reinstated after FMLA leave could change elections based on a change in family status to the same extent as other employees. Special rules (see chapter 7) are applicable to reinstatement in a health care FSA, however. [29 C.F.R. §§ 825.209(e), 825.215(d); Treas. Reg. § 1.125-3, Q&A-1; Prop. Treas. Reg. § 1.125-3, Q&A-1]

Q 16:58   When an employee on FMLA leave elects to continue group health plan coverage under a cafeteria plan, who is responsible for making premium payments?

The answer to this question depends on who was paying premiums in the first place. If an employee chooses to continue group health plan coverage (including a health care FSA) while on FMLA leave, he or she can be required to pay the same share of the premiums that he or she was paying while at work. The employer must continue to pay its share of the premium cost that it was paying while the employee was working. [29 C.F.R. §§ 825.100(b), 825.210(a); Treas. Reg. § 1.125-3, Q&A-2; Prop. Treas. Reg. § 1.125-3, Q&A-2]

For example, in Opinion Letter FMLA 2006-3-A, the DOL concluded that an employer that contributes monthly amounts to a cafeteria plan to be used by employees for group health plan coverage is required to continue that practice for employees on FMLA leave, even though employees on other types of unpaid leave are required to pay for their group health plan coverage. Moreover, because the employer provides the money for the group health insurance coverage when employees are working, it may not recover such payments for periods of FMLA leave. [DOL Op. Ltr. FMLA 2006-3-A (Jan. 1, 2006)]

Q 16:59   What payment options are required or permitted when an employee on unpaid FMLA leave elects to continue group health plan coverage under a cafeteria plan?

A cafeteria plan may offer three types of payment options, or a combination of options, to an employee who elects to continue group health plan coverage under a cafeteria plan. They are referred to as the prepay option, the pay-as-you-go option, and the catch-up option. (Payment options for paid FMLA leave are discussed in Q 16:63.)

Prepay option. Under this option, the cafeteria plan may allow employees taking FMLA leave to prepay their premiums for the leave period. The payment can be made on either a pretax or an after-tax basis. Pretax contributions can be made from any taxable compensation the employee receives, such as cashed-out vacation or sick days. However, use of pretax salary reduction contributions is restricted if an employee's FMLA leave spans two cafeteria plan years (see Q 16:62).

Pay-as-you-go option. Under this option, an employee can choose to pay health plan premiums while on FMLA leave. That can be done by following a COBRA premium-type schedule, by using the same method as employees on non-FMLA leave, or by any other method agreed to by the employer and employee. Generally, such contributions will have to be made on an after-tax basis, unless the employee on FMLA leave has taxable compensation during the FMLA leave period from which pretax reductions can be taken.

Catch-up option. This option is available only if the employer and employee agree before the FMLA leave that the employer will pay the employee's health premiums for health coverage the employee elects to continue during the FMLA period and the employee will repay the employer for the FMLA leave premiums when the employee returns to work. The catch-up contributions can be made on either a pretax or an after-tax basis, but contributions on a pretax basis must comply with all of the cafeteria plan requirements. The catch-up option can be the sole FMLA premium payment option if it is also the sole payment option for employees on unpaid non-FMLA leave.

Payment ground rules. The final IRS regulations lay down the following ground rules for payment options:

1. Whatever payment options are offered to employees on non-FMLA leave must be offered to employees on FMLA leave. However, a cafeteria plan may include pre-payment as an option for employees on FMLA leave, even if that option is not offered to employees on unpaid non-FMLA leave.

2. The catch-up option may be the sole option offered to employees on FMLA leave only if catch-up payments are the only option offered to employees on unpaid non-FMLA leave.

3. If the pay-as-you-go option is offered to employees on unpaid non-FMLA leave, that option must also be offered to employees on FMLA leave. In this situation, the employer may also offer employees on FMLA leave the pre-pay or catch-up options.

No-pay alternative. In lieu of offering any of the three options, the employer may choose to waive the employee's contributions for FMLA leave health plan coverage, provided this is done on a nondiscriminatory basis.

Q 16:60　What happens when an employee chooses to continue health coverage on a pay-as-you-go basis, but does not make the required premium payments?

If an employee fails to make payments under the pay-as-you go option (see Q 16:59), the employer has two choices: (1) terminate the employee's coverage or (2) continue the employee's coverage by paying both the employer's and the employee's share of the premiums. Under final IRS regulations, effective for plan years beginning on or after January 1, 2002, an employee on FMLA leave cannot require the employer to terminate coverage. However, an employee who chooses to discontinue premium payments cannot be required to make contributions after the FMLA leave ends.

If an employer continues coverage despite the employee's nonpayment of premiums, the employer can use the catch-up option to recover the employee's share of the premiums when the employee returns from leave. No prior agreement with the employee is required to use the catch-up option in this situation.

Q 16:61　What rules apply to health care FSA coverage for employees on FMLA leave?

Generally, health care FSAs are subject to the same rules as other group health plans for employees on FMLA leave. An employer must permit an employee taking FMLA leave to continue coverage under a health care FSA. In the case of an employee on FMLA leave, the employer may allow the employee either to terminate coverage or to continue participation in a health care FSA but may discontinue paying the employee's share of the premiums. An employee returning from FMLA leave must be permitted to elect back into health care FSA coverage that had been terminated. In addition, under final IRS regulations, an employer may require an employee to resume FSA coverage on returning from FMLA leave, provided employees who return from unpaid non-FMLA leave are required to resume coverage.

An employee who continues health care FSA coverage while on FMLA leave is subject to the normal uniform coverage rules regardless of the premium payment method selected. The full FSA coverage amount, less reimbursements, must be available at all times during the FMLA leave period.

Special rule. If an employee terminates his or her health care FSA coverage while on FMLA leave, the employee cannot be reimbursed for any expenses incurred during the period of termination. If an employee who terminated coverage elects to rejoin the health care FSA when FMLA leave is over or if the employer requires the employee to resume coverage, the employee may not retroactively elect health care FSA coverage for claims incurred while the coverage was terminated. Under the final FMLA regulations, an employee must be given the choice of either (1) resuming his or her original level of coverage and making up any unpaid premium payments or (2) resuming coverage at a reduced level without making up the unpaid premiums. If the employee chooses the second option, the employer cannot require the employee to pay any more than the remaining amounts due, even if the plan has already paid out an amount to the employee that exceeds the total premium payments that will be made for the year.

Example 1. Anthony elects an annual $1,200 health care FSA benefit and makes pretax contributions of $100 a month. On April 1, Anthony takes a three-month FMLA leave of absence and elects to terminate health care FSA coverage. He has had no medical expenses at that point but has made three months of FSA contributions totaling $300. Anthony's FSA coverage ceases during the FMLA leave, and he makes no premium payments for April, May, or June. On July 1, Anthony returns to work and requests reinstatement in the health care FSA. Anthony must be given the option of resuming coverage at the $1,200 level in effect before his leave and making up the $300 of premiums due during his three-month leave. Alternatively, he may choose to resume FSA coverage at a level that is reduced to reflect the period during which no premiums were paid. [Treas. Reg. § 1.125-3, Q&A-6]

If Anthony chooses the first option, his coverage for the remainder of the year will be $1,200 and his premiums for the remaining six months of the year will be increased to $150 per month to make up the $300 of missed premiums. If he chooses prorated coverage, his coverage for the remainder of the plan year will be $900, and he will resume making premium payments of $100 per month for the remainder of the plan year. In neither event will Anthony be entitled to submit claims or receive reimbursements for expenses incurred during his three-month FMLA leave.

Example 2. The facts are the same as those in Example 1, except that Anthony incurred medical expenses totaling $200 in February and obtained reimbursement of those expenses. If Anthony chooses to resume coverage at the level in effect before his FMLA leave, Anthony's coverage for the remainder of the year will be $1,000 ($1,200 less the $200 of reimbursements), and his monthly premiums for the remainder of the year will increase to $150 per month to make up the $300 of missed premiums. If Anthony chooses prorated coverage, his coverage for the remainder of the year will be $700 ($1,200 prorated for three months, reduced by $200 of reimbursements), and his monthly premiums for the remainder of the year will be $100.

Q 16:62 What restrictions apply to employee contributions during an FMLA leave that spans two cafeteria plan years?

A cafeteria plan cannot operate in a way that permits a participant to defer compensation from one plan year to a later plan year. Therefore, if an FMLA leave spans two cafeteria plan years, a participant cannot use the prepay option on a pretax basis to pay the later year's employee contributions.

Example. Bonnie contributes $100 a month to a cafeteria plan on a pretax basis. She takes a three-month FMLA leave for the last two months of the current plan year and the first month of the next plan year and elects to continue plan participation. Although Bonnie can prepay the first two months' contributions on a pretax basis, she cannot prepay the third month's contribution on a pretax basis in the first year because it falls in a later plan year. Bonnie must either prepay for the third month on an after-tax basis or use another plan option, such as pay-as-you-go or catch-up, to pay the third month's contribution. [Treas. Reg. § 1.125-3, Q&A-5]

Q 16:63 What payment options are available to an employee who is on paid FMLA leave?

If an employee is on paid FMLA leave, and the employer mandates that the employee continue group health plan coverage during the leave, the employee's share of the premiums must be paid by the method normally used during any other paid leave. Thus, if the employee is contributing from salary on a pretax basis, that method normally would be continued during the paid FMLA leave period. If the FMLA leave extends beyond the paid leave period and becomes unpaid leave, the options described in Q 16:59 would then become applicable, to the extent provided under the cafeteria plan. [Treas. Reg. § 1.125-3, Q&A-4]

Notice, Disclosure, and Recordkeeping Requirements

Q 16:64   What posting requirement must employers satisfy under the FMLA?

All employers subject to the FMLA must post a notice, in conspicuous places on their premises where it can be readily seen by employees and applicants for employment, that explains the FMLA's provisions and provides information concerning the procedures for filing complaints of FMLA violations with the U.S. Department of Labor's Wage and Hour Division.

In locations where a significant portion of the employer's workers are not literate in English, an employer must provide the general notice in a language in which the employees are literate. [29 C.F.R. § 300] English and Spanish versions of the required FMLA poster can be found on the Wage and Hour Division portion of the DOL's Web site at *www.wagehour.dol.gov/*.

If an employer fails to post the required notice, it cannot take any adverse action against an employee, including denying FMLA leave, for failing to furnish advance notice of a need to take FMLA leave. The employer also can be assessed a $110 penalty for each separate offense. [29 C.F.R. § 825.300]

Q 16:65   How must an employer provide written guidance to employees concerning FMLA entitlements and employee obligations under the FMLA?

An employer must provide FMLA information (1) in any written guidance to employees concerning benefits or leave rights (such as in employee handbooks or other documents) and (2) at the time an employee provides notice of the need for FMLA leave.

The information that employers must provide is quite detailed and specific:

1. The fact that leave will be counted against an employee's annual FMLA entitlement;

2. Requirements (if any) for the employee to furnish medical certifications and the consequences of failing to do so;

3. The employee's right to substitute paid leave and whether the employer requires substitution of paid leave, as well as the conditions related to any substitution;

4. Requirements about any premium payments that must be made to maintain health benefits, the procedure for making the payments, and the possible consequences of failure to make such payments on a timely basis;

5. Any requirement for the employee to present a fitness-for-duty certificate in order to be restored to employment;

6. The employee's right to be restored to the same or an equivalent job;

7. The conditions under which restoration of employment might be denied if the employee is a key employee; and

8. The employee's potential liability to refund group health plan contributions paid by the employer during the leave if he or she fails to return to work at the conclusion of the FMLA leave.

[29 C.F.R. § 825.300]

Q 16:66   What records are employers required to maintain under the FMLA?

Employers are required to make, keep, and preserve records regarding their obligations under the FMLA in accordance with the recordkeeping requirements of both the FMLA and Section 11(c) of the FLSA. [29 C.F.R. § 825.500(a)]

Under the FMLA, employers must keep the following records:

1. Basic payroll and employee data (including name, address, occupation, rate of pay and terms of compensation, daily and weekly hours worked per pay period, wage deductions and additions, and total compensation paid);

2. Dates FMLA leave is taken by employees (the employer's records must expressly designate FMLA leave as such);

3. The hours of leave, if taken in increments of less than one full day;

4. Copies of all general and specific notices provided to employees under the FMLA and copies of employee notices of leave given to the employer under the FMLA;

5. All documents, whether written or electronic, describing employee benefits or employer policies and practices concerning taking paid and unpaid leave;

6. Employee benefit premium payments; and

7. Records of any dispute over designation of leave and FMLA leave, including any written statement from the employer about the reasons for the designation and for the disagreement.

All records and documents relating to medical certifications, recertifications, or medical histories of employees or their family members must be maintained in separate files or records. They are to be treated as confidential medical records, although supervisors and managers may be informed concerning any necessary restrictions on, and accommodations for, the employee's work or duties; first aid and safety personnel may be informed (when appropriate) if the employee's physical or medical condition might require emergency treatment; and government officials investigating FMLA compliance are to be provided relevant information upon request. [29 C.F.R. §§ 825.500(c), 825.500(g)]

Q 16:67   In what form are FMLA records required to be kept?

No particular order or form of records is required. Records must be kept for at least three years and must be made available for inspection, copying, and transcription by representatives of the DOL upon request. Records may be kept on microfilm or other basic source document of an automated data processing memory if adequate viewing equipment is kept available and the reproductions are clear and may be identified by date or pay period and if transcriptions or extensions are made available upon request. Computer records must be made available for copying or transcription. [29 C.F.R. § 825.500(b)]

Relationship to State Laws

Q 16:68   Does the FMLA supersede all state and local laws requiring employers to provide family or medical leave?

No. The FMLA does not supersede any provision of any state or local law that provides greater family or medical leave rights than the rights under the FMLA. [FMLA § 401(b); 29 U.S.C. § 2651(b)]

Practice Pointer. A number of state laws currently provide for greater rights in some respects, and employers must take state and local laws into account in establishing a leave policy under the FMLA. ERISA might preempt the application of such state laws to a particular ERISA employee benefit plan (see chapter 2). [Shaw v. Delta Airlines Inc., 463 U.S. 85 at n.22 (1983)]

To the extent a state's family or medical leave law is applicable, it runs concurrently with the federal FMLA. [29 C.F.R. § 825.701(a)]

A discussion of the interplay between the FMLA and state family leave laws, which omits mention of the possible application of ERISA preemption, is contained in 29 C.F.R. Section 825.701.

Penalties and Enforcement

Q 16:69   Is an employee who exercises his or her rights under the FMLA protected from discrimination by his or her employer?

Yes. Under the FMLA, an employer may not interfere with, restrain, or deny any exercise or attempted exercise of FMLA rights. Nor may an employer discharge or otherwise discriminate against any person for opposing or complaining about unlawful practices under the FMLA or for filing any charge, commencing any proceeding, giving information, or testifying in connection with any FMLA right. All individuals, not just employees, are protected from retaliation for opposing any unlawful practice under the FMLA or any practice that they reasonably believe to be a violation. [29 C.F.R. § 825.220]

Q 16:70   What federal agency is responsible for the interpretation and enforcement of the FMLA?

The DOL is the federal agency charged with implementation of the law. [FMLA §§ 101(10), 106, 107, 404; 29 U.S.C. §§ 2611(10), 2626, 2627, 2654] On November 17, 2008, the DOL published final regulations under the FMLA. The final regulations took effect on January 16, 2009. [73 Fed. Reg. 222]

The DOL also has broad investigative authority over employee compliance and the power to investigate and attempt to resolve complaints of violations of the FMLA. [FMLA §§ 106, 107(b)(1); 29 U.S.C. § 2616, 2617(b)(1); 29 C.F.R. §§ 825.400, 825.401]

Q 16:71   Can the DOL bring suit for violations of the FMLA?

Yes. The DOL has the authority to bring a suit for damages on behalf of one or more employees and to bring an action for injunctive relief and other equitable relief against the employer. [FMLA §§ 107(b)(2), 107(d); 29 U.S.C. §§ 2617(b)(2), 2617(d)]

Q 16:72   Can an employee bring a lawsuit against an employer for violations of the FMLA?

Yes. An employee may sue his or her employer for FMLA violations, except when the DOL already has such a lawsuit pending. An action may be brought in federal or state court for damages or equitable relief on behalf of the employee or employees suing and other employees similarly situated. [FMLA § 107(a); 29 U.S.C. § 2617(a)]

In *Smith v. BellSouth Telecommunications, Inc.* [273 F.3d 1303 (11th Cir. 2001)], the Eleventh Circuit Court of Appeals concluded that the right to sue also extends to prospective and former employees. In the case before the court, an employee brought suit against a former employer under the FMLA's anti-retaliation provision. The employee, who terminated his employment and subsequently applied for a new position with the employer, claimed that the employer improperly refused to rehire him because he had used FMLA leave during his previous term of employment. A federal district court threw out the employee's lawsuit on the grounds that he was not protected by the FMLA because he was no longer employed by the employer when it refused to rehire him. According to the district court, only an "employee" has a right to bring a lawsuit under the FMLA.

On appeal, the Eleventh Circuit held that an ex-employee who claims that a former employer refused to hire him based on his past use of FMLA leave qualifies as an employee for purposes of the FMLA's anti-retaliation rule. Therefore, the employee's lawsuit could proceed to trial. The court noted that the FMLA defines the term "employee" as "any individual employed by an employer." However, the court said, that definition does not necessarily exclude an ex-employee because it could be read as referring to someone who previously had been employed by an employer as well as someone who is currently employed. Moreover, the court noted that, in other contexts, the courts have interpreted that definition broadly to include former employees.

The employer argued that the right to sue under the FMLA's anti-retaliation rules was specifically limited to "eligible" employees—that is, current employees who are eligible for leave under the FMLA. However, the court noted that the anti-retaliation rules specifically provide that employees may sue for equitable relief, including "employment, reinstatement, and promotion.""If Congress intended to limit the right to bring suit under the FMLA to current employees," the court said, "the inclusion of 'employment' as an equitable remedy is puzzling."

The court also noted that DOL regulations interpreting the FMLA prohibit an employer from discriminating against "employees or prospective employees" and from using "the taking of FMLA leave as a negative factor in employment actions, such as hiring . . ."—another indication that the anti-retaliation rules are not limited to current employees.

Finally, the court said that a broad reading of the term "employee" was in keeping with the purpose of the FMLA. The law was intended to balance the demands of the workplace with the needs of families by ensuring the availability of reasonable leave for employees who need time off for health or family reasons. "If former employees . . . knew that they would have no remedy if their former employer retaliated against them for their past use of FMLA leave, it would tend to chill employees' willingness to exercise their protected leave rights and would work against the purpose of the FMLA," the court said.

The First Circuit, which is the only other appellate court to address this issue, has also ruled that former employees who are not rehired because of prior leave-taking have a right to sue under the FMLA. [Duckworth v. Pratt & Whitney Inc., 152 F.3d 1 (1st Cir. 1998)] According to the First Circuit, defining "employee" narrowly to include only current employees would frustrate the purposes of the FMLA. "That interpretation would permit an employer to evade the Act by blacklisting employees who used leave in the past or by refusing to hire prospective employees if the employer suspects they might take advantage of the Act," said the First Circuit.

The Eleventh Circuit covers the states of Alabama, Georgia, and Florida. The First Circuit has jurisdiction in Maine, New Hampshire, Massachusetts, and Rhode Island.

A federal district judge has interpreted the FMLA as permitting employees a right to jury trial on their FMLA claims. [Helmly v. Stone Container Corp., 957 F. Supp. 1274 (S.D. Ga. 1997)]

Recently, the U.S. Supreme Court held that employees of a state also have the right to sue their employers for FMLA violations. According to the Court, the FMLA clearly requires states, as well as private employers, to provide equal protections and to be subject to the same federal penalties under the statute. [Nevada Dep't of Human Res. v. Hibbs, 538 U.S. 721 (2003)]

Q 16:73 What damages and penalties can an employer be liable for if it violates the FMLA?

An employer is subject to a $110 penalty per violation of the FMLA notice posting requirement. It is also barred from taking adverse action against an employee or denying FMLA leave because of the employee's failure to furnish the employer with advance notice of a need to take FMLA leave (see Q 16:29).

In addition, the employer can be held liable for the following:

1. Any wages, salary, employment benefits, or other compensation denied or lost to the employee by reason of the violation or, in a case in which wages, salary, employment benefits, or other compensation have not been denied or lost to the employee (for example, the employee does not go on leave), any actual monetary losses sustained as a direct result of the violation, such as the cost of providing care up to a sum equal to 12 weeks of wages or salary for the employee (26 weeks in a case of leave involving care for a covered servicemember);

2. Interest on the above damages at the prevailing rate;

3. Liquidated damages equal to the actual damages above plus interest, unless the employer proves to the satisfaction of the court that the act or omission causing the violation was in good faith and that the employer had reasonable grounds for believing that the act or omission was not a violation; and

4. Such equitable relief as may be appropriate, including employment, reinstatement, and promotion.

[FMLA §§ 107(a)(1)(A), 107(b)(2); 29 U.S.C. §§ 2617(a)(1)(A), 2617(b)(2); 29 C.F.R. § 825.400(c)]

Note. The term *employer* includes any person who acts directly or indirectly in the interest of an employer to any of the employer's employees. According to the DOL regulations, individuals such as corporate officers, who act in the interest of an employer, would be individually liable for FMLA violations. [29 C.F.R. § 825.104(d)]

Q 16:74 Can an employer be held liable for costs and fees in a successful lawsuit brought by an employee?

Yes. In addition to a judgment in favor of the plaintiff employee (or employees), the court may allow reasonable attorney and expert witness fees and other costs of the lawsuit to be paid by the employer. [FMLA § 107(a)(3); 29 U.S.C. § 2617(a)(3)]

Q 16:75   What is the statute of limitations for a lawsuit claiming a violation of the FMLA?

In general, a lawsuit must be brought not later than two years after the date of the last event constituting the alleged violation of the FMLA for which the action is brought. [FMLA § 107(c)(1); 29 U.S.C. § 2617(c)(1)] In the case of a willful violation, however, the lawsuit may be brought within three years of the date of the last event constituting the alleged violation. [FMLA § 107(c)(2); 29 U.S.C. § 2617(c)(2)]

Q 16:76   How are employees who request leave or otherwise assert FMLA rights protected?

The FMLA prohibits interfering with an employee's rights under the law and with legal proceedings relating to an employee's rights. [29 C.F.R. § 825.220(a)] Individuals, and not just employees, are protected from retaliation for opposing any practice that is unlawful under the FMLA. [29 C.F.R. § 825.220(e)]

In one case, an employee asked her supervisors for help in staffing the store she was managing. The employee thought she was making a reasonable request under the FMLA. She wanted help so she could reduce her 60-hour workweek to recuperate from radiation treatments for throat cancer. The employee had missed two weeks of work earlier in the year for surgery and had taken a few hours of intermittent leave following the surgery for the treatments. Her employer apparently had a problem with her request and fired her a week later. The employee sued her employer. The jury found that the reasons for discharge were pretextual and carried out in retaliation against the employee for exercising her rights under the FMLA. [Churchill v. Star Enters., 3 F. Supp. 2d 622 (E.D. Pa. 1998)]

In another case, which involved an employee who was fired after requesting FMLA leave, the Third Circuit Court of Appeals held that an employee does not need to actually begin leave to be protected by the FMLA. According to the court, firing an employee for a valid request for FMLA leave may constitute interference with the employee's FMLA rights as well as retaliation against the employee. The court said, "[I]t would be patently absurd if an employer who wished to punish an employee for taking FMLA leave could avoid liability simply by firing the employee before the leave begins." [Erdman v. Nationwide Ins. Co., No. 07-3796, 2009 U.S. App. LEXIS 20979 (3d Cir. Sept. 23, 2009)]

On the other hand, the Eleventh Circuit concluded that an employee must actually have rights under the FMLA to be protected from retaliation. In *Walker v. Elmore County Board of Education* [379 F.3d 1249 (11th Cir. 2004)], the court determined that a pregnant school teacher did not have a claim of retaliation against the school board that decided not to renew her contract following her request for maternity leave under the FMLA. Pivotal to the court's decision was the fact that the teacher was not yet eligible for FMLA leave at the time she made her request and would not have become eligible until several days after her leave would begin. According to the court, "There can be no doubt that the request—made by an ineligible employee for leave that would begin when she would still have been ineligible—is not protected by the FMLA." Significantly, the court did not address the question of whether an advance request for leave by an employee who would become eligible by the time the leave began would be protected. "We leave for another day the question of whether the FMLA protects a pre-eligibility request for post-eligibility maternity leave," said the court.

> **Practice Pointer.** Despite the Eleventh Circuit's refusal to address the status of pre-eligibility requests for post-eligibility leave, the FMLA regulations clearly contemplate such requests. For example, in the case of a birth or adoption that is expected or foreseeable, an employee may be required to give at least 30 days' notice before leave is to begin (see Q 16:29). Presumably, that advance notice may be required even if the employee has not yet become eligible for FMLA leave at the time the notice is required to be given. The regulations further specify that an employer who receives a leave request from an employee who has not yet satisfied the eligibility requirements can either confirm the employee's eligibility based on a projection that the employee will have met the requirements on the date the leave is to begin or wait to respond at the time the employee has met the requirements (see Q 16:33).

Chapter 17

Age Discrimination in Employment Act of 1967

The federal Age Discrimination in Employment Act of 1967 (ADEA) places significant restrictions on the content of employee benefit plans. This chapter examines the scope of the ADEA, including which employers are subject to the law and which employees are protected under the law, as well as what does and does not constitute prohibited age discrimination in employee benefits.

Basic Concepts

Q 17:1 What is the federal law that prohibits employment discrimination on the basis of age?

The federal Age Discrimination in Employment Act of 1967 (ADEA) [Pub. L. No. 90-202, 81 Stat. 602 (1967)], as amended, prohibits discrimination by an employer against employees age 40 or older in hiring and firing, in compensation, and in the terms, conditions, and privileges of employment. [ADEA § 4(a); 29 U.S.C. § 623(a)]

In 1990, the Older Workers Benefit Protection Act (OWBPA) added major provisions to the ADEA's age discrimination rules aimed specifically at employer-provided pension and welfare benefit plans. [Pub. L. No. 101-433, 100 Stat. 978 (1990), as amended by Pub. L. No. 101-521, 104 Stat. 2287 (1990)]

Q 17:2   What is the scope of the "protected class" of employees under the ADEA?

Although the ADEA protects employees age 40 and older from employment-based discrimination based on age, the question is "discriminated against compared to whom?" Can an employee point to favorable treatment of any younger employee as possible age discrimination, or must the younger employee who is treated more favorably be outside the protected class (that is, younger than age 40)? The Supreme Court resolved this interpretive issue when it ruled that the ADEA prohibits discrimination against employees in the protected class on the basis of age, not class membership. As a result, it is irrelevant that the individual who allegedly was treated more favorably due to age is also a member of the protected class (that is, also age 40 or older). Rather, the key issue is simply whether the individual who allegedly was treated more favorably due to age is younger than the claimant. Thus, an older worker within the ADEA's protected age group can claim age discrimination when compared to a younger worker even if that younger worker also is within the ADEA's protected age group. The Supreme Court ruled that the ADEA's lower age limit is merely a limit on the class of workers that can sue under the ADEA. [O'Connor v. Consolidated Coin Caterers Corp., 116 S. Ct. 1307 (1996)]

Q 17:3   Does the ADEA preempt state age discrimination laws?

No. Accordingly, state laws prohibiting discrimination based on age which are broader than the federal ADEA (for example, a state law that prohibits age discrimination against employees younger than 40) are enforceable against the employer to the extent that they do not conflict with the ADEA. However, the ADEA's failure to preempt such laws does not affect the issue of whether Section 514 of the Employee Retirement Income Security Act of 1974 (ERISA) preempts state laws that relate to employee benefit plans. [29 C.F.R. § 1625.10(g)] The application of a state age discrimination law to an ERISA employee benefit plan probably would be preempted by ERISA. (See chapter 2.)

Q 17:4   Which federal agency has the power to administer and enforce the ADEA?

Administrative and enforcement powers under the ADEA are vested in the Equal Employment Opportunity Commission (EEOC).

Q 17:5   Does an employer practice that disadvantages older workers always violate the ADEA?

Not necessarily. The United States Supreme Court has held that an employer can be subject to an age discrimination claim if its employment actions have a "disparate impact" on older workers—even if those actions are not specifically tied to age. [Smith v. City of Jackson, 544 U.S. 228 (2005)]

In this case, the city of Jackson, Mississippi, was charged with age discrimination because its pay plan gave larger raises to police officers with fewer than five years of tenure to make their salaries competitive with comparable positions in the market. Police officers who brought suit against the city argued that even though the salary plan was age neutral on its face, it adversely affected older officers.

The Supreme Court concluded that such "disparate impact" claims can be brought under the ADEA. However, the Court also pointed out that an employer can avoid liability if its policy was based on reasonable factors other than age. In the case of the police officers, the Court found the city was not responsible for age discrimination because the decision to grant a larger raise to lower-echelon employees for the purpose of bringing salaries in line with those of police forces in surrounding areas was a decision based on a reasonable factor other than age.

In another case, the Supreme Court held that a state retirement plan's provisions that increases disability pension benefits for workers who become disabled before reaching the plan's normal retirement age did not violate the ADEA. [Kentucky Ret. Sys. v. EEOC, 128 S. Ct. 2361 (2008)] According to the Court, the differences were not "actually motivated" by age. The purpose of the rule is to treat a disabled worker as though he or she had become disabled after, rather than before, becoming eligible for normal retirement benefits. Thus, age factors into the disability calculation only because the normal retirement rules permissibly consider age. The Court emphasized that the rule does not rely on the sorts of stereotypical assumptions, such as the work capacity of "older" workers relative to "younger" workers, that the ADEA sought to eradicate.

In a 2009 decision, the Supreme Court significantly toughened the rules for employees seeking to prove age discrimination when an employer has "mixed motives" for an adverse employment action. The Court held that an employee bringing an ADEA disparate-treatment claim must prove, by a preponderance of the evidence, that age was the "but-for" cause of the adverse employment action. The burden of persuasion does not shift to the employer to show that it would have taken the action regardless of age, even when a plaintiff has produced some evidence that age was one motivating factor in that decision. [Gross v. FBL Fin. Servs., Inc., 526 F.3d 356 (8th Cir.), *vacated & remanded*, 550 U.S. ___ (2009)]

Practice Pointer. The proof rule laid down by the Supreme Court for ADEA stands in stark contrast to the rules governing discrimination claims under Title VII of the Civil Rights Act (see chapter 19). The Court noted that in 1991 Congress amended Title VII to allow employees to prove discrimination in mixed-motive cases by establishing that an improper consideration was a "motivating factor" for an adverse employment action, at which point the burden shifts to the employer to prove that it would have taken the adverse action regardless of the improper consideration. [42 U.S.C. §§ 2000e–2(m) and 2000e–5(g)(2)(B); *see also* Price Waterhouse v. Hopkins, 490 U. S. 228 (1989)]

Covered Employers

Q 17:6 Which employers are subject to the ADEA?

An employer is subject to the ADEA if it is engaged in an industry affecting interstate commerce and has 20 or more employees for each working day in each of 20 or more weeks in the current or preceding calendar year. [ADEA § 11(b); 29 U.S.C. § 630(b)] For this purpose, regular part-time employees are included in the number of employees. [Cohen v. S.U.P.A. Inc., 814 F. Supp. 251 (N.D.N.Y. 1993)] State and local governments, agencies, and instrumentalities, as well as interstate agencies, are also covered employers. [ADEA § 11(b); 29 U.S.C. § 630(b)] Special provisions also apply to personnel actions affecting certain categories of federal employees. [ADEA § 15; 29 U.S.C. § 633(a)] Labor unions having 25 or more members are also covered by the ADEA. [29 U.S.C. § 630(e)]

The EEOC has issued enforcement guidance on how the 20-or-more-employees test is to be applied in a close case, usually by looking at the employer's payroll records to determine that an employment relationship existed. [EEOC Notice 915.002 (May 2, 1997)]

Q 17:7 Do controlled-group rules apply when defining the employer for purposes of the ADEA's 20-employee test?

For purposes of applying the 20-employee test discussed in Q 17:6, the ADEA's definition of a covered employer does not expressly contain any controlled-group rules that would require certain related employers to be treated as a single employer for ADEA purposes. However, a body of case law has developed under the ADEA that imposes a fact-based test that looks at the degree of interrelated operations, common management, centralized control of labor relations and personnel, and common ownership to determine whether separate business entities are considered to be a single employer when counting employees under the 20-employee test. [*See* Rogers v. Sugar Tree Prods., Inc., 7 F.3d 577 (7th Cir. 1993); Frishberg v. Esprit de Corp Inc., 778 F. Supp. 793 (S.D.N.Y.), *aff'd*, 969 F.2d 1042 (1991).]

Covered Employees

Q 17:8   Does the ADEA cover independent contractors?

No. The ADEA only covers employees. [Strange v. Nationwide Mut. Ins. Co., 867 F. Supp. 1209 (E.D. Pa. 1994)] The U.S. Court of Appeals for the Eleventh Circuit held that the question of whether a doctor was an independent contractor or an employee was a factual question to be decided by a jury, and not by the trial court, on a motion to dismiss the action. [Garcia v. Copenhaver, Bell & Assoc., 104 F.3d 1256 (11th Cir. 1997)] In another appeals decision, the Fourth Circuit held that a trainee for an automobile dealership was not an employee of the auto manufacturer for ADEA purposes. [Mangram v. GMC, 108 F.3d 61 (4th Cir.1997)]

Q 17:9   Is a partner an employee for ADEA purposes?

Yes. Under some circumstances a partner in a partnership can be treated as an employee for ADEA purposes. A federal appeals court has ruled that a former partner in a national accounting firm qualified as an employee protected by the ADEA. The court noted that the individual was not required to make a true capital contribution to the firm and that neither his salary nor his bonuses were linked to the firm's profits. The court also determined that the individual's partnership voting rights were illusory. The former partner, who claimed that he was fired in a nationwide attempt to rid the firm of older partners, won a jury award of $3.7 million against the accounting firm. [Simpson v. Ernst & Young, 20 Employee Benefits Cas. (BNA) 2088 (6th Cir. 1996)]

Q 17:10   Does the ADEA apply to welfare benefits for retirees?

Yes, it does. However, under EEOC regulations that were finalized in 2007, a special exemption applies to retiree health plans that coordinate with Medicare.

The issue of coordinating retiree health benefits with Medicare has been the subject of protracted litigation. In 2001, in a case dealing with retiree health benefits, the Third Circuit Court of Appeals handed down a precedent-setting opinion in which it held that the ADEA protects retirees from age discrimination. The Supreme Court refused to review the Third Circuit's decision. [Erie County Retirees Ass'n v. County of Erie, Pa., 220 F.3d 193 (3d Cir. 2000), *cert. denied*, 121 S. Ct. 1247 (2001)]

In the case, Erie County provided retiree health benefits under two different plans. Retirees who had reached age 65 and were eligible for Medicare were covered by a health maintenance organization (HMO) that required preauthorization for services by a primary care physician. Medicare-eligible retirees were required to enroll in Medicare Part B. Retirees under age 65 who were not eligible for Medicare were covered by a point-of-service plan that combined the features of an HMO and a traditional indemnity plan. A group of Medicare-eligible retirees sued, claiming that their plan provided inferior coverage compared to the plan offered to younger retirees.

In reaching its decision, the Third Circuit noted that there were indications in the legislative history of the ADEA that some members of Congress viewed the law as inapplicable to retirees. However, the court said the language of the law clearly applies to retirees. The law protects any "individuals" who have been treated differently by their employer, including a former employer, because of age.

The county argued that its decision to place the Medicare-eligible retirees in the HMO plan was motivated by factors other than age. According to the county, it placed each retiree in the least expensive plan for which he or she was eligible. However, the court concluded that the county's health benefit choices were made on the basis of age. According to the court, Medicare eligibility "follows ineluctably upon attaining age 65. Thus, Medicare status is a direct proxy for age."

> **Practice Pointer.** The ADEA does address the fact that benefits for older workers or retirees may be more expensive. The law says that an employer must either provide equal benefits for older and younger individuals or incur the same costs on behalf of both (see Q 17:16). Thus, providing different benefits for Medicare-eligible retirees would not violate the ADEA if the benefit costs were the same as those for younger retirees. However, it may be impossible for an employer to meet the equal-cost requirement if its retiree health plan is integrated with Medicare.

In the *Erie County* case, the Third Circuit left open the possibility that the county's plan might be protected by the equal benefit-equal cost safe harbor. However, on remand, a district court ruled that the county's retiree medical plan did not qualify for safe harbor protection because the plan that was offered to the Medicare-eligible retirees provided lesser benefits and cost less than the plan offered to younger retirees. [Erie County Retirees Ass'n v. County of Erie, Pa., 140 F. Supp. 2d 466 (W.D. Pa. 2001)] In particular, the court ruled that only costs actually incurred by the county could be taken into account; costs incurred by Medicare in providing benefits to the older retirees could not be counted.

EEOC response. In the wake of the decision in *Erie County*, the EEOC revised its compliance manual to enforce the decision. The EEOC stated that "if an employer eliminates health coverage for retirees who are eligible for Medicare—or if it refuses to continue to cover its older retirees for the benefits it provides that are not offered by Medicare—older retirees will get less coverage than younger retirees on the basis of their age. Unless the employer can meet the equal cost defense, the law does not permit this age discrimination."

However, the revision was short-lived. By a unanimous vote taken on August 17, 2001, the EEOC rescinded that portion of the manual that dealt with retiree health benefits. An EEOC notice announcing the rescission stated that "Medicare carve-out" plans—that is, those that simply deduct Medicare benefits from the benefits provided to Medicare-eligible retirees—do not violate the ADEA. However, the EEOC notice also stated that "additional review is needed to assess other types of retiree health plan practices."

In 2003, the EEOC proposed regulations to allow employers to alter, reduce, or eliminate employer-sponsored retiree health benefits when an employee becomes eligible for Medicare or a comparable state-sponsored health plan. The EEOC derived its regulatory authority from an ADEA provision that allows it to establish an exemption from any ADEA rule if it is "necessary and proper in the public interest." [ADEA § 9] According to the EEOC, "Because the *Erie County* decision was contributing to a continuing decline in the availability of employer-provided retiree health benefits, the Commission concluded that it would be in the best interest of employers, employees, and retirees to permit employers to offer these benefits to the greatest extent possible."

However, the American Association of Retired Persons (AARP) challenged the EEOC's authority to grant the exemption.

In the case brought by the AARP, the U.S. District Court for the Eastern District of Pennsylvania issued an order blocking the EEOC regulations. Relying on the Third Circuit's original decision, the court held that the ADEA prohibits the reduction of benefits based on age. Therefore, the court said, the EEOC does not have the authority to issue regulations taking a contrary position. The court issued an injunction barring the EEOC from issuing the controversial regulations. [AARP v. EEOC, 383 F. Supp. 2d 705 (E.D. Pa. 2005)]

However, that decision, too, was short-lived. The district court subsequently lifted its injunction against the EEOC regulations. The court relied on a new Supreme Court decision, which held that a court's interpretation of a law bars an agency from interpreting the law differently from the court only if the court has determined the *only permissible* meaning of the law. [National Cable & Telecomms. Ass'n v. Brand X Internet Servs., 125 S. Ct. 2688 (2005)] Because the Third Circuit's original *Erie County* decision was *not* the *only permissible* meaning of the ADEA, the EEOC regulations were not automatically barred. The district court barred the EEOC from implementing the regulations pending review by the Third Circuit. In 2007, the Third Circuit affirmed the district court (and the Supreme Court declined to review that decision), allowing the regulations to proceed. [AARP v. EEOC, 390 F. Supp. 2d 437 (E.D. Pa. 2005), *aff'd*, 2007 U.S. App. LEXIS 12869 (3d Cir. 2007)]

The final EEOC regulations took effect on December 26, 2007. [29 C.F.R. § 1625.32] The final regulations permit employers to continue two practices that are commonly used to coordinate retiree health benefits with Medicare:

1. Providing health benefits only to retirees under age 65. These types of plans, called "Medicare bridge plans," are often used to provide health benefits to workers who retire before they become eligible for Medicare.

2. Providing supplemental health benefits to Medicare-eligible retirees (age 65 and older) without having to show that the benefits are identical to any benefits provided to early retirees who cannot receive Medicare benefits. In many cases, these plans, sometimes called "Medicare wraparound or supplement policies," provide retirees with prescription drug coverage.

Q 17:11   Does the ADEA apply to U.S. citizens working abroad?

Yes. The ADEA also covers U.S. citizens who are employed by a U.S. corporation or subsidiary and who work abroad (called "extraterritorial employees"). [29 U.S.C. § 630(f)]

Providing Lesser Benefits to Older Workers

Q 17:12   Why was the OWBPA enacted?

Prior to the OWBPA (see Q 17:14), an employer generally could reduce or even eliminate welfare benefits for older employees without violating the ADEA. Previously, it was not a violation of the ADEA for an employer to observe the terms of a bona fide employee benefit plan that was not a subterfuge to evade the purposes of the ADEA, provided that no such employee benefit plan could be used to refuse to hire someone because of age or to retire someone involuntarily on the basis of age (except for certain executive and high policy-making employees who may be required to retire at age 65). [ADEA §§ 4(f)(2), 12(c); 29 U.S.C. §§ 623(f)(2), 631(c)]

The Supreme Court held that this "bona fide employee benefit plan" exception under the ADEA permitted reductions in benefits for older employees, unless the older employees claiming discrimination on the basis of age could show that the benefits coverage was intended to serve the purpose of discriminating in some aspect of the employment relationship other than fringe benefits. [Public Employees Ret. Sys. of Ohio v. Betts, 492 U.S. 158 (1989)]

The enactment of the OWBPA in 1990 was a swift and direct legislative rejection of the result reached in the *Betts* case.

Q 17:13   What are the requirements of the OWBPA?

The OWBPA amendments to the ADEA legislatively overturned the U.S. Supreme Court decision in the *Betts* case on a prospective basis. The provisions of the OWBPA are as follows:

1. Age discrimination in employee benefits and employee benefit plans is prohibited;
2. The employer is required to bear the burden of proof in order to justify a reduction in benefits for older employees on a cost-equivalency basis;
3. The "subterfuge" wording in the law has been eliminated, and the ADEA applies to an employee benefit plan regardless of whether it, or any of its discriminatory provisions, predated the enactment of the ADEA; and
4. The circumstances under which employees can waive their rights under the ADEA are expressly restricted.

However, a U.S. Court of Appeals has held that there was no ADEA violation where a pension plan provided greater benefits for early retirees than it did for normal retirees. The plan provided that employees who had 20 years of service or who were age 60 with five years of service could retire early and receive the same benefits as employees who retired at normal retirement age. The court ruled that an ADEA violation does not occur if the employer is motivated by a factor other than age. In this case, the motivation was to reduce the employer's costs. Thus, the factor causing the disparate treatment was not age, but cost. [Lyon v. Ohio Educ. Ass'n, 53 F.3d 135 (6th Cir. 1995)] In other words, the case stands for the proposition that disparate treatment on the basis of age is not enough to establish an ADEA violation, there must also be evidence that the employer was motivated by a discriminatory animus against older people.

More recently, however, the Sixth Circuit Court of Appeals held that a prima facie case of age discrimination exists when a benefits provision facially discriminates on the basis of age; no evidence of discriminatory intent is required. [EEOC v. Jefferson County Sheriff's Dep't, 424 F.3d 467 (6th Cir. 2006)]

Q 17:14   What is the effective date of the OWBPA amendments to the ADEA?

In the case of any employee benefit established or modified on or after October 16, 1990, the OWBPA amendments apply as of the date of establishment or modification.

With respect to employee benefits that existed on October 16, 1990, and that have not been modified, the general effective date was the 181st day after the date of enactment, or April 15, 1991. In other words, plans must have been brought into compliance by no later than April 14, 1991.

However, in the case of a collective bargaining agreement that was in effect on October 16, 1990, the effective date for application of the OWBPA amendments was the earlier of (1) the date of termination of the collective bargaining agreement or (2) June 1, 1992.

Where the employer is a state, a political subdivision of a state, or an agency or instrumentality of either, and the employer maintained an employee benefit plan at any time between June 23, 1989, and October 16, 1990, that can be modified only through a change in applicable state or local law, the effective date was October 16, 1992.

If a series of benefit payments to an individual or an individual's representative began prior to October 16, 1990, and continued after that date pursuant to an arrangement that was in effect on October 16, 1990, those benefits are not subject to the OWBPA amendments. However, no substantial modification to such an arrangement could be made after October 16, 1990, if the intent of the modification was to evade the purposes of the OWBPA. [Pub. L. No. 101-433, § 105, 100 Stat. 978 (Oct. 16, 1990)]

Bona Fide Plan Requirements

Q 17:15　What initial requirements must a welfare benefit plan meet in order to qualify for the differences in cost or the latitude in benefit design permitted under the ADEA regulations?

To qualify for the differences in cost or the latitude in benefit design permitted by the ADEA, an employee benefit plan must be "bona fide," the plan's terms must have been accurately described in writing to all employees, and the plan must actually provide benefits in accordance with the terms of the plan. In addition, employees must be notified promptly of the plan's provisions and any changes thereto so that they will know how the plan affects them. For this purpose, satisfaction of ERISA's disclosure requirements is sufficient. [ADEA § 4(f)(2); 29 U.S.C. § 623(f)(2); EEOC Reg. § 1625.10(b)] (See chapter 2 for a discussion of ERISA disclosure requirements.)

Cost-Equivalency Rule

Q 17:16　What is the cost-equivalency rule under the ADEA?

The EEOC regulations state that, in general, an employer violates the ADEA unless:

1. Older employees are provided with the same benefits as younger employees; or
2. Older employees are provided with benefits that are reduced only to the extent that the cost of the benefits for older employees is at least equal to the cost of the benefits for younger employees.

This is the *cost-equivalency rule.* [EEOC Reg. § 1625.10(a)]

Q 17:17　What is the rationale for the cost-equivalency rule under the ADEA?

The purpose of the cost-equivalency rule is to permit age-based reductions in bona fide employee benefit plans where such reductions are justified by significant cost considerations. If the benefits plan satisfies certain specified conditions, then benefit levels for older workers may be reduced to the extent necessary to achieve approximate equivalency in cost for older and younger workers. A benefits plan will be treated as complying with the ADEA where the actual amount of payment made (or cost incurred) on behalf of an older worker is equal to that made (or incurred) on behalf of a younger worker. [EEOC Reg. § 1625.10(a)(1)]

Q 17:18   Under the ADEA's cost-equivalency rule, what methods of cost comparison and adjustment are permitted?

The EEOC regulations provide two methods for making cost comparisons and adjustments: the benefit-by-benefit approach (see Q 17:19) and the benefit package approach (see Q 17:29).

Q 17:19   What is the benefit-by-benefit approach?

The *benefit-by-benefit approach* is a technique whereby an employer may adjust the amount or level of a specific form of benefit for a specific event or contingency. The adjustment must be on a cost-equivalent basis.

For example, under the benefit-by-benefit approach, an employer may not substitute one form of benefit for another, even if both forms of benefit are designed for the same contingency (e.g., death). [EEOC Reg. § 1625.10(d)(2)(i)] An employer may not reduce paid vacations and uninsured paid sick leave based on age, since reductions in such benefits would not be justified by significant cost considerations. [EEOC Reg. § 1625.10(a)(1)]

Q 17:20   What kind of cost data may be used under the ADEA to support a reduction in benefits?

Cost data that is used to justify a reduction in benefits for older employees must be valid and reasonable. This standard is met where an employer has cost data that shows the actual cost to the employer of providing the particular benefit (or benefits) in question over a representative period of years. An employer may rely on:

1. Cost data for its own employees over such a period; or
2. Cost data for a larger group of similarly situated employees.

However, an employer may not rely on cost data for a similarly situated group of employees if:

1. Due to experience rating or other causes, the employer incurs costs that differ significantly from costs for a group of similarly situated employees; and
2. Such reliance would result in significantly lower benefits for its own older employees.

If reliable cost information is not available, reasonable projections made from existing cost data meeting the standards set forth above will be considered acceptable. [EEOC Reg. § 1625.10(d)(1)]

Q 17:21   Must the cost of coverage for older workers be compared on a year-by-year age basis?

No. An employer is permitted to compare the increased cost of providing a benefit on the basis of age brackets encompassing up to five years. Thus, under the benefit-by-benefit approach, a particular benefit may be reduced for employees of any age within the ADEA's protected age group (age 40 and older) by an amount no greater than the additional cost of providing them with the same level of benefit as younger employees within the immediately preceding five-year age group.

> **Example.** If the employer desires to reduce the amount of group term life insurance for employees beginning at age 60, the group term life insurance benefits provided to employees age 60 to 64 can be reduced only to the extent necessary to achieve approximate equivalency in costs with employees age 55 to 59. Similarly, if the employer also desires a further reduction in the benefit levels for employees age 65 to 69, such a further reduction cannot exceed an amount that is proportional to the additional costs for that age group's coverage over that of the group age 60 to 64.

[EEOC Reg § 1625.10(d)(3)]

Q 17:22   If an employer reduces benefits based on age, must it do so for all age brackets?

No. The employer remains free to offer level coverage up to a particular age and then begin reducing coverage. For example, the employer may decide to reduce coverage beginning at age 70. However, reductions at that or any later age cannot exceed the amount that is proportional to the additional costs for that five-year age bracket over that of the preceding five-year age bracket. [EEOC Reg. § 1625.10(d)(3)]

Q 17:23   Can an older employee be required to make greater contributions to an employee benefit plan than a younger employee as a condition of employment?

No. Such a requirement would be, in effect, a mandatory reduction in take-home pay based on age and would discourage employment of older employees. [EEOC Reg. § 1625.10(d)(4)(i)]

Q 17:24   Can older employees be required to make greater contributions than younger employees to a voluntary employee benefit plan as a condition of participation in such a plan?

Yes. As long as participation in the plan is voluntary, no mandatory reduction in take-home pay based on age is being imposed. However, the older employee cannot be required to bear a greater proportion of the total premium cost (both employer-paid and employee-paid) than the younger employee. Requiring an older employee to bear a greater proportion of the premium cost would make compensation in the form of an employer contribution available on less favorable terms than for the younger employee and would have the effect of denying that compensation altogether to older employees unwilling or unable to meet the less favorable terms. [EEOC Reg. § 1625.10(d)(4)(ii)]

Employer-pay-all plans. If younger employees are not required to contribute any portion of the premium cost, older employees may not be required to do so either. [EEOC Reg. § 1625.10(d)(4)(ii)(B)]

Employee-pay-all plans. All employees, young and old alike, may be required to contribute as a condition of participation up to the full premium costs for their ages. [EEOC Reg. § 1625.10(d)(4)(ii)(A)]

Contributory plans. If the employer and the participating employees share the premium costs, the required participant contributions may increase with age provided that the proportion of the total premium that participants are required to pay does not increase with age. For example, all participants could be required to bear 25 percent of the cost of the plan at each age bracket, but the employer could not require employees under age 60 to contribute 25 percent of the cost and require employees age 60 and above to contribute 50 percent of the cost.

Q 17:25   Can older employees be given the option to pay more in order to receive full, unreduced benefits?

Yes. If the employer's plan reduces coverage by age on a cost-justified basis in accordance with the EEOC regulations, the employer may voluntarily offer older employees the choice of paying extra to purchase full, unreduced coverage (but not more than such unreduced coverage actually costs at that age bracket). [EEOC Reg. § 1625.10(d)(4)(iii)]

Q 17:26   How is the benefit-by-benefit approach applied to life insurance?

It is common practice for employer-provided life insurance to remain constant until a specified age, such as age 65 or 70, and then be reduced thereafter. This practice will not violate the ADEA as long as the reduction for an employee of a particular age is justified by the increased cost of coverage for that employee's specific age bracket encompassing no more than five years. [EEOC Reg. § 1625.10(f)(1)(i)]

A total denial of life insurance at any age cannot be justified on a benefit by-benefit basis. It is permissible, however, to cease life insurance coverage upon retirement or other separation from service. [EEOC Reg. § 1625. 10(f)(1)(i)] A denial of life insurance benefits can be imposed, however, on employees who fail to enroll in the plan within a designated time period. The Court of Appeals for the Eighth Circuit has held that an age ban for employees who failed to enroll in the employer's group life insurance plan within 60 days of their date of hire did not violate the ADEA. [International Bd. of Elec. Workers, Local. 1439, AFL-CIO v. Union Elec. Co., 761 F.2d 1257 (8th Cir. 1985)]

Q 17:27   How is the benefit-by-benefit approach applied to long-term disability insurance?

Under the benefit-by-benefit approach (see Q 17:19), an employer providing long-term disability coverage to all employees may avoid any cost increases that such coverage for older employees would entail by reducing the level of benefits available to older employees. An employer may also avoid such cost increases by reducing the duration of the long-term disability benefits available to employees who become disabled at older ages, without reducing the level of benefits. (Any such reduction in the level or duration of benefits must be justified on the basis of the permitted age-based cost considerations set forth in Qs 17:16–17:25.)

The EEOC regulations contain a safe-harbor provision for long-term disability plan designs. No ADEA violation will be asserted by the EEOC if the level of benefits is not reduced, and the duration of benefits is reduced according to the following:

1. For disabilities that occur at or before age 60, the long-term disability benefits may cease at age 65.
2. For disabilities that occur after age 60, the long-term disability benefits may cease five years after disablement. Cost data may be produced to support other patterns of reduction as well.

Of course, it is also permissible to cut off long-term disability benefits and coverage on the basis of recovery from disability or because of some other factor unrelated to age. However, a total denial of long-term disability benefits at any age cannot be justified on a benefit-by-benefit basis. [EEOC Reg. § 1625.10(f)(1)(ii)]

Note. In the rare case where long-term disability payments began prior to October 16, 1990, under an arrangement in existence on that date, such an arrangement is grandfathered unless it is modified with the intent to evade the purposes of the OWBPA (see Q 17:14).

Q 17:28   Can an employer's employee welfare benefit plan coordinate with government-provided benefits?

Yes. With the important exception noted in the following paragraph, an employer's plan can "wrap around" government-provided benefits as long as, taking the employer-provided and government-provided benefits together, an older employee is entitled to a benefit (including coverage for family and/or dependents) that is no less than that provided to a similarly situated younger employee. [EEOC Reg. § 1625.10(e)]

One very important exception to this rule involves the coordination of employer-provided benefits with Medicare benefits. The EEOC regulations contain outdated language permitting employer group health plans for active employees to wrap around Medicare. Those regulations were never updated to reflect subsequent amendments to the ADEA that expressly prohibited reduction of group health benefits of an active employee or spouse due to attainment of age 65 (referred to as the *working-aged* provisions). Furthermore, ADEA's working-aged provisions have since been legislatively deleted from the ADEA and moved to Section 5000 of the Internal Revenue Code, which generally does not allow employer group health plans to wrap around Medicare benefits for active employees. (See chapter 3 for the rules on group health plan coordination with Medicare.)

Q 17:29   What is the benefit package approach?

As an alternative to the benefit-by-benefit approach, the EEOC regulations also permit employers to reduce the level or duration of benefits by using a second method, the *benefit package approach.* Under this method, the employer justifies the age-related cost reduction under one benefit by aggregating the costs of two or more benefits. Essentially, if the employer reduces a benefit more than is justified by a benefit-by-benefit approach, it must give an offsetting benefit so that the overall effect yields neither lesser benefits nor greater cost to employees on the basis of age. No employees may be deprived of one benefit because of age unless an offsetting benefit is made available to them.

> **Example.** Suppose an employer could make age-based, cost-justified reductions in benefits under Plan A and Plan B on a benefit-by-benefit basis. Assume that benefits under each plan could be reduced by 10 percent. If the reduction under both plans costs the same, the employer could, under the benefit package approach, leave benefits under Plan A at 100 percent and reduce benefits under Plan B by 20 percent instead. However, if the permitted reduction on a benefit-by-benefit basis under Plan A costs one-half of the permitted reduction under Plan B, the benefit package approach would reduce benefits under Plan B by only 15 percent.

In other words, the benefit package approach consists of calculating the permissible age-based, cost-justified reductions benefit-by-benefit, totaling them, and applying them all to one plan or, by splitting them among plans, applying them on an aggregate basis. However, under the benefit package approach, employees cannot be deprived of one benefit because of age unless an offsetting benefit is made available to them. [EEOC Reg. §§ 1625.10(d)(2)(ii), 1625.10(f)(2)(iv), 1625.10(f)(2)(v)]

Q 17:30   May the benefit package approach be used for any kind of employee benefit plan?

Under the EEOC regulations, pension or retirement benefits may not be used to justify reductions in other benefits such as employee welfare benefits. In addition, reductions in health benefits may be justified only on the basis of the health benefits standing alone; the cost of other coverage cannot be used to justify reductions in health benefits. On the other hand, health benefits may be included in a benefit package to justify age-based reductions in other benefits. [EEOC Reg. §§ 1625.10(f)(2)(ii), 1625.10(f)(2)(iii)]

However, the EEOC regulations do not reflect the ADEA amendments added by the OWBPA. The OWBPA amendments contain two statutory exceptions to the rule that pension or retirement benefits may not be used to justify reductions in employee welfare benefits (see Qs 17:31, 17:32).

Using Retirement Benefits to Reduce Other Benefits

Q 17:31　Does the ADEA permit retirement benefits to be used to reduce long-term disability benefits?

Yes. The OWBPA amendments to the ADEA provide that long-term disability benefits may be offset by pension benefits (other than those attributable to the individual's own contributions), provided that:

1. The individual has voluntarily elected to receive the pension benefits; or

2. The individual has attained the later of age 62 or normal retirement age and is eligible for pension benefits.

[ADEA § 4(1)(3); 29 U.S.C. § 623(1)(3)(1992 Supp.)]

This permitted integration of pension benefits with long-term disability benefits avoids "double dipping" by employees while permitting the benefits to be integrated in such a way that the employee receives combined payments at the level of the greater of either pension or disability benefits. Accordingly, the income payments to the employee do not decrease, but the source of payments may shift. [136 Cong. Rec. S13606 (Sept. 24, 1990)] (See Q 17:14 for the grandfather rule applicable to long-term disability payments commencing before October 16, 1990.)

> **Practice Pointer.** The statute does not discuss how the amount of pension benefits attributable to the employee's contributions is to be calculated. Presumably, until the EEOC promulgates regulations, it should be permissible to follow the pension accrual rules under ERISA and the Internal Revenue Code.

Q 17:32　Can severance pay be denied or reduced because of eligibility for, or receipt of, retirement benefits?

In general, the ADEA, as amended by the OWBPA, prohibits an employer from reducing or eliminating severance pay solely because the employee is eligible for, or will receive, retirement plan benefits. However, a limited statutory exception exists.

Where the severance pay is payable as a result of a contingent event unrelated to the employee's age, such as a plant closing or layoff, the severance pay may be reduced by *additional* pension benefits (called "pension sweeteners") that are payable solely as a result of the contingent event, provided that the individual is eligible for an immediate and unreduced pension. [ADEA § 4(1)(2)(A)(ii); 29 U.S.C. § 623(1)(2)(A)(ii)]

For this purpose, severance pay includes supplemental unemployment benefits under Code Section 501(c)(17) for up to 52 weeks, having the primary purpose and effect of continuing benefits until the individual becomes eligible for an immediate and unreduced pension and ceasing once the individual becomes eligible for the immediate and unreduced pension. [ADEA § 4(1)(2)(C); 29 U.S.C. § 623(1)(2)(C)]

Q 17:33   May severance pay be denied or reduced because of receipt of retiree health benefits?

Generally, the ADEA, as amended by the OWBPA, also prohibits reduction or elimination of severance pay solely because the employee is eligible for or receives retiree health benefits. The ADEA does, however, contain a carefully circumscribed exception to this general rule.

Where the severance pay is payable as a result of a contingent event unrelated to the employee's age, such as a plant shutdown or layoff, the value of retiree health benefits may be subtracted from severance benefits (including supplemental unemployment benefits as described in Q 17:32) if the following conditions are satisfied:

1. The employee must be eligible for an immediate pension;
2. If the employee receives immediate pension benefits that are actuarially reduced, the value of retiree health benefits that may be subtracted is reduced by the same percentage as the reduction in pension benefits; and
3. Retiree health benefits must have a certain minimum value in order to be subtracted from severance pay benefits (see Q 17:34 to determine this minimum value).

[ADEA §§ 4(1)(2)(A)(i), 4(1)(2)(D); 29 U.S.C. §§ 623(1)(2)(A)(i), 623(1)(2)(D)]

Under this exception, a federal district court has upheld an employer's reduction of severance benefits based on an employee's eligibility for retiree health benefits regardless of whether the employee actually enrolled for and received such benefits. [McCambridge v. Bethlehem Steel Corp., 873 F. Supp. 919 (E.D. Pa. 1994)]

Q 17:34   For purposes of calculating the permitted reduction of severance pay by the value of retiree health benefits, how is the value of the retiree health benefits determined?

The OWBPA amendments to the ADEA contain explicit rules concerning the value of retiree health benefits which can be used to reduce severance pay that is payable as a result of a contingent event unrelated to the employee's age, as follows:

1. The retiree health benefits provided to retirees below age 65 must be at least "comparable" to Medicare benefits under Title XVIII of the Social Security Act. [ADEA § 4(1)(2)(D)(i); 29 U.S.C. § 623(1)(2)(D)(i)]

2. The retiree health benefits provided to retirees age 65 and above must be at least "comparable" to 25 percent of Medicare benefits under Title XVIII of the Social Security Act. [ADEA § 4(1)(2)(D)(ii); 29 U.S.C. § 623(1)(2)(D)(ii)]

If the employer's obligation to provide retiree health benefits is of limited duration, the value for each individual is to be calculated at a rate of $3,000 per year for benefit years before age 65 and $750 per year for benefit years beginning at age 65 and above. [ADEA § 4(1)(2)(E)(i); 29 U.S.C. § 623(1)(2)(E)(i)]

If the employer's obligation to provide retiree health benefits is of unlimited duration, the value for each individual is to be calculated at a rate of $48,000 for individuals below age 65 and $24,000 for individuals age 65 and above. [ADEA § 4(1)(2)(E)(ii); 29 U.S.C. § 623(1)(2)(E)(ii)]

The age of the individual which is used for this purpose is his or her age as of the date of the contingent event unrelated to age. The dollar values described in the preceding paragraphs are adjusted annually based on the medical component of the DOL's all-urban consumer price index. [ADEA § 4(1)(2)(E)(iii); 29 U.S.C. § 623(1)(2)(E)(iii)]

Contributory plans. If the individual is required to pay a premium for the retiree health benefits, the value calculated under the rules in the preceding paragraphs must be reduced by whatever percentage of the overall premium the individual is required to pay. [ADEA § 4(1)(2)(E)(iv); 29 U.S.C. § 623(1)(2)(E)(iv)]

Q 17:35   Must the employer make retiree health benefits available to all retirees regardless of age in order to be entitled under the ADEA to use the value of such benefits to reduce severance pay?

No. A technical amendment in the Older Workers Benefit Protection Amendment Act [Pub. L. No. 101-521, 104 Stat. 2267 (Nov. 5, 1990)] clarified that point. The employer is not required to offer health benefits to retirees both above and below age 65 in order to offset severance pay by the value of retiree health benefits. An employer may offer health benefits only to retirees under age 65 and still make the offset described in the ADEA, as amended by the OWBPA. [ADEA § 4(1)(2)(D)(iii); 29 U.S.C. § 623(1)(2)(D)(iii)]

Q 17:36   Does the ADEA permit employers to reduce severance pay by the value of both pension benefits and retiree health benefits?

Yes. In the case of a contingent event unrelated to age, an employer providing both pension sweeteners (see Q 17:32) and retiree health benefits (see Q 17:33) may reduce the severance pay payable as a result of such contingent event by either or both. [ADEA § 4(1)(2)(A); 29 U.S.C. § 623(1)(2)(A)]

Q 17:37   If the employer reduces severance pay by the value of retiree medical benefits, as permitted under the ADEA, what recourse do retirees have in the event the employer fails to fulfill its obligation to provide retiree medical benefits?

If the employer has availed itself of the limited ADEA exemption allowing severance pay that is payable due to a contingent event unrelated to age to be reduced by the value of retiree health benefits, the employer is subject to an action for specific performance by any "aggrieved individual" for failing to fulfill its obligation to provide retiree health benefits. This relief is in addition to any other remedies provided under federal or state law. [ADEA § 4(1)(2)(F); 29 U.S.C. § 623(1)(2)(F)]

Providing Greater Benefits to Older Workers

Q 17:38   May an employee benefit plan provide greater benefits to older employees on the basis of age without violating the ADEA?

The U.S. Supreme Court resolved a split among the circuit courts on this issue, concluding that the ADEA does not protect workers from "reverse" age discrimination. "[T]he statute does not mean to stop an employer from favoring an older employee over a younger one," said the Court.

Reversing a Sixth Circuit decision, the Court held that a group of workers aged 40 to 49 could not sue under the ADEA on the ground that their employer discriminated against them in favor of older workers. The workers who brought the lawsuit claimed that the employer had violated the ADEA by restricting its retiree health plan to retirees who were age 50 or over by a specified date. [General Dynamics Land Sys. v. Cline, 296 F.3d 466 (6th Cir. 2002), *rev'd*, 540 U.S. 581 (2004)]

According to the Court, the legislative history of the ADEA makes it clear that the law was concerned with protecting relatively old workers against discrimination. "One commonplace conception of American society in recent decades is its character as a 'youth culture,'" said the Court, "and in a world where younger is better, talk about discrimination because of age is naturally understood to refer to discrimination against the older."

The Court also noted that restriction of the ADEA's protected class to workers age 40 and older also indicates that Congress was concerned about age discrimination against older workers in favor of younger workers. According to the Court, if Congress had been worrying about protecting younger workers against older workers, it would not have ignored people under age 40. "The enemy of 40 is 30, not 50," said the Court.

In 2007, the EEOC finalized an amendment to the regulations governing the ADEA, which specifically provides that: "Favoring an older individual over a younger individual because of age is not unlawful discrimination under the

ADEA, even if the younger individual is at least 40 years old. However, the ADEA does not require employers to prefer older individuals and does not affect applicable state, municipal, or local laws that prohibit such preferences." [EEOC Reg. § 1625.2]

Q 17:39   Is an employee required to file a complaint with the Equal Employment Opportunity Commission before filing a lawsuit under the ADEA?

Yes, an employee must file a complaint with the EEOC before the initiation of any ADEA action. After allowing the EEOC 60 days to notify the employer of the charge and to attempt to conciliate the alleged unlawful practice, the individual may file suit (provided the EEOC has not brought suit on his or her behalf). [29 U.S.C. § 626(d); Shikles v. Sprint/United Mgmt. Co., 426 F.3d 1304 (10th Cir. 2005)]

Q 17:40   Are there time limits for filing an age discrimination complaint?

Yes. An employee generally is required to file a complaint with the EEOC within a specified number of days after an unlawful employment practice occurred. The time limit depends on whether the alleged violation occurred in a jurisdiction that has a state or local fair employment practices agency (FEPA) with the authority to grant or seek relief. The deadline is 180 days in a state or locality that *does not* have a FEPA and 300 days in a state or locality that *does* have a FEPA. However, because most jurisdictions have FEPAs, the limitations period is usually 300 days.

The timeliness of a complaint depends on whether the complaint involves a discrete act or a hostile work environment. [Nat'l R.R. Passenger Corp. v. Morgan, 536 U.S. 101 (2002)] A discrete act—such as failure to hire or promote, termination, or denial of transfer—must be challenged within 180 (or 300) days of the date that the employee received unequivocal written or oral notification of the action, regardless of the action's effective date. Repeated occurrences of the same discriminatory employment action, such as discriminatory employee benefits, can be challenged as long as one discriminatory act occurred within the filing period. However, because each occurrence is a discrete discriminatory act, relief usually will be limited to occurrences within the filing period.

On the other hand, because the incidents that make up a hostile work environment claim collectively constitute a single unlawful employment practice, the entire claim is actionable as long as at least one incident that is part of the claim occurred within the filing period. If a discrete act that occurred before the filing period is part of a timely hostile work environment claim, the employee may only challenge the act as part of the hostile work environment claim. For example, if an employee claims that an employer's denial of benefits during the pre-filing period is related to a pattern of abusive conduct that continued into the filing period, then the denial of benefits may be considered in assessing whether the employee was subjected to a hostile work environment and determining the appropriate remedy for that violation. However, because no timely challenge was made to the benefits discrimination, the denial of benefits is not independently actionable, and the employee would not be entitled to separate relief, such as restitution of the denied benefits. [EEOC Compliance Manual, Section 2, Threshold Issues]

Waiver of ADEA Rights and Claims

Q 17:41   May an individual waive all rights and claims under the ADEA?

Yes. An individual may waive all of his or her rights and claims under the ADEA. However, any waiver must be "knowing and voluntary" under the ADEA, as amended by the OWBPA. [ADEA § 7(f)(1); 29 U.S.C. § 626(f)(1)]

Q 17:42   What statutory requirements must be met in order for a waiver to be considered "knowing and voluntary"?

The statute provides that a waiver of ADEA rights and claims will not be considered to be "knowing and voluntary" unless the following requirements are met:

1. The waiver is part of an agreement between the individual and the employer that is written in a manner calculated to be understood by the individual or by the average individual eligible to participate;
2. The waiver specifically refers to rights or claims arising under the ADEA;
3. The individual does not waive rights or claims that may arise after the date the waiver is executed;
4. The individual waives rights or claims only in exchange for money or other consideration in addition to anything of value to which the individual already is entitled;
5. The individual is advised in writing to consult with an attorney prior to executing the agreement;
6. The individual is given a period of:
   a. At least 21 days to consider the agreement or
   b. At least 45 days to consider the agreement in the case of an exit incentive or other employment-termination program offered to a group or class of employees;
7. The agreement provides that, for a period of at least seven days after the date it is executed, the individual may revoke it, and the agreement will not become effective or enforceable until the seven-day period has expired; and
8. If the waiver is requested in connection with an exit incentive or other employment termination program offered to a group or class of

employees, the employer must satisfy certain additional statutory disclosure requirements (see Q 17:51).

[ADEA § 7(f)(1); 29 U.S.C. § 626(f)(1); EEOC Prop. Reg. § 1625.22]

Q 17:43   What specific requirements apply to the wording of an ADEA waiver?

The EEOC's final rule [63 Fed. Reg. 30,624 (June 5, 1998)] imposes minimum
requirements for a waiver of all ADEA rights and claims to be knowing and
voluntary, including the following requirements specifically dealing with the
wording of the waiver:

1. The entire waiver agreement must be in writing;

2. The waiver agreement must be drafted in plain language geared to the
    level of understanding of (a) the particular individual who is party to the
    agreement or (b) the individuals eligible to participate. Employers are
    directed to take into account such factors as the level of comprehension
    and education of typical participants. This usually will require limiting or
    eliminating technical jargon and long, complex sentences. Note that exit
    incentive and other employment termination programs offered to a group
    or class of employees also must be written in a manner calculated to be
    understood by the average participant;

3. The waiver agreement cannot have the effect of misleading, misinform-
    ing, or failing to inform participants and affected individuals. Any advan-
    tages or disadvantages described must be presented without either
    exaggerating the benefits or minimizing the limitations;

4. The waiver agreement must refer to the ADEA by name in connection
    with the waiver of rights and claims; and

5. The individual must be advised in writing to consult with an attorney in
    connection with the waiver.

[29 C.F.R. § 1625.22(b)]

In one case, a laid-off employee brought suit against his former employer,
claiming that the ADEA waiver he signed was invalid because it was not written
in an understandable manner. In particular, the employee claimed that the
language in different paragraphs of the agreement was contradictory. The Eighth
Circuit Court of Appeals upheld the waiver and threw out the employee's
lawsuit. According to the court, the paragraphs pointed to by the employee were
not contradictory; instead, they were intended to serve different purposes.
Moreover, the court pointed out, legal documents are typically detailed and
complex because of the need to address a host of variable and specific
requirements. Therefore, while the employer's attempts to comply with the
waiver requirements made the agreement "nuanced," the agreement was
nonetheless written in a manner that was understandable to the average
participant. [Parsons v. Pioneer Seed Hi-Bred Int'l, Inc., 447 F.3d 1102 (8th Cir.
2006)]

A release stating "I have had reasonable and sufficient time and opportunity to consult with an independent legal representative of my own choosing before signing this Complete Release of All Claims" did not comply with OWBPA's requirement that an individual be *advised* to consult with an attorney. Although the voluntary early retirement agreement advised employees to consult financial and tax advisors, to seek advice from local personnel representatives, and to attend retirement seminars, it said nothing about seeking independent legal advice prior to making the election to retire and accepting the agreement. [American Airlines, Inc. v. Cardoza-Rodriguez, 133 F.3d 111 (1st Cir. 1998)]

Q 17:44   Can future rights and claims under the ADEA be waived?

No. A waiver of rights and claims under the ADEA is not treated as knowing and voluntary if it purports to waive any rights or claims that arise following the execution of the waiver. The EEOC's final rule provides, however, that the ADEA does not bar the enforcement of agreements to perform future employment-related actions such as the employee's agreement to retire or otherwise terminate employment at a future date. [29 C.F.R. § 1625.22(c)]

Q 17:45   Must an employee receive something of value in return for signing an ADEA waiver?

Yes. A waiver of ADEA rights and claims will not be treated as knowing and voluntary unless it is given in return for something of value (i.e., consideration) in addition to that which the individual is already entitled in the absence of a waiver. Also, if a benefit or other thing of value was eliminated in violation of law or of an express or implied contract, then subsequently offering that benefit or thing in return for the ADEA waiver will not be treated as an offer of the required consideration.

Elimination in violation of law or contract. Whether the benefit or thing of value has been eliminated in violation of law or contract will depend on the facts and circumstances of the particular case.

The U.S. Supreme Court considered the case of an employer who increased pension benefits for employees who elected an early retirement plan and executed a waiver of all employment-related claims against the employer. The Court held that conditioning the increased pension benefits on the execution of the waiver did not constitute a prohibited use of pension plan assets for the benefit of the employer; therefore, the waivers were valid. [Lockheed Corp. v. Spink, 517 U.S. 882 (1996)]

No requirement to favor the protected age group. The final EEOC rule clarifies that the employer is not required to offer more to employees in the ADEA's protected age group (that is, age 40 and over) than to younger employees in return for a waiver of ADEA rights and claims. [29 C.F.R. § 1623.22(d)]

Q 17:46 Is an individual required to tender back consideration received in connection with an ADEA waiver before bringing a discrimination claim?

When employers terminate employees, usually by conducting a reduction in force or layoffs, they may ask their employees to waive any legal rights they have against the employer in exchange for additional benefits, such as severance pay or early retirement benefits. These additional benefits are called *consideration.* The law permits employers to ask for waivers but imposes rules to ensure that the process is a fair one. In particular, the ADEA regulates the use of waivers for employees over the age of 40.

Under general principles of contract law, an individual who believes a waiver or other legal agreement is invalid must return, or *tender back,* any consideration received for the waiver or agreement before challenging it in court. Under contract law, an individual who fails to return consideration received is treated as having "ratified" the waiver or agreement, even if it was invalid at the outset.

In 1998, the EEOC issued an interpretive regulation under the OWBPA that prohibits any requirement that an older worker tender back severance pay or other benefits before filing an administrative charge of age discrimination. [29 C.F.R. § 1625.22] That regulation did not address the tender-back requirement with respect to private lawsuits under the ADEA. However, the U.S. Supreme Court resolved that issue in favor of workers.

The Supreme Court ruled that a former employee is not required to tender back consideration for a waiver in order to allege a violation of the ADEA. The facts in *Oubre v. Entergy Operations, Inc.* [112 F.3d 787 (5th Cir. 1996), *rev'd,* 522 U.S. 422 (1998)] involved an employee who, upon her termination, signed an agreement waiving all claims against her employer in exchange for cash payments. The waiver agreement failed to comply with at least three of the requirements of Section 7(f)(1) of the ADEA. After the employee received all of the consideration for the waiver, she filed an ADEA suit against the employer without tendering back the consideration. The lower courts ruled that she could not proceed with her lawsuit because she had not offered to return the consideration to the employer, agreeing with the employer's arguments under state contract and common law. The Supreme Court reversed the Fifth Circuit's decision stating that the release did not comply with the ADEA, and the plaintiff's retention of the consideration did not constitute a ratification that made the release valid. In addition, the employer could not invoke the employee's failure to tender back consideration as a way of excusing its own failure to comply with the statute.

Final EEOC regulations provide that an individual alleging that a waiver agreement or other equivalent arrangement was not knowing or voluntary under the ADEA is not required to tender back the consideration given for the agreement before filing either a lawsuit or a charge of discrimination with the EEOC or with any state or local fair employment agency acting as an EEOC referral agency. [29 C.F.R. § 1625.23] According to the regulations, retention of the consideration does not constitute ratification of the waiver or agreement.

The final EEOC regulations also provide that an employer may not avoid the "no tender back" rule by using other means to limit an older worker's right to challenge a waiver or by penalizing an older worker for challenging a waiver. For example, an employer may not require an older worker to agree to pay damages to the employer or to pay the employer's legal fees in connection with a lawsuit.

Practice Pointer. The regulations provide that tender-back provisions are not valid under the ADEA, but they do not specifically bar the inclusion of such clauses in a waiver agreement. However, the EEOC has cautioned that there is a strong argument that inclusion of an invalid provision in an ADEA waiver agreement—such as a tender-back or damages provision—could invalidate the entire waiver. According to the EEOC, inclusion of such a provision could make the agreement misleading in a material sense, which would violate the OWBPA's requirement that waivers be understandable by the average individual.

Q 17:47   Can an employer require a laid-off worker to sign a covenant not to sue in order to receive early retirement benefits, severance pay, or other benefits?

In some agreements, commonly called *covenants not to sue,* an older worker's receipt of benefits depends on the worker's agreement that (1) he or she will not bring a lawsuit against the employer for age discrimination and (2) if a lawsuit is brought, he or she will pay damages and attorney's fees to the employer.

The EEOC takes the position that covenants not to sue and other agreements are functionally the same as waivers. In other words, older workers give up their ADEA right to sue for age discrimination. Therefore, EEOC regulations provide that covenants not to sue and similar agreements are subject to the requirements and restrictions of the OWBPA, just like any other waiver.

Under those rules, a covenant not to sue, if valid, can serve as a defense to an ADEA lawsuit. However, monetary remedies, such as a requirement to pay damages or legal costs, traditionally associated with covenants not to sue are prohibited. According to the EEOC, such monetary remedies would prevent workers from challenging a covenant in the same manner as a tender-back requirement, even if the covenant is invalid under the OWBPA.

Practice Pointer. The EEOC says that while covenants not to sue are functionally equivalent to waivers, they carry a higher risk of violating the OWBPA. An employee could read a covenant not to sue as giving up not only the right to challenge a past employment practice as age discrimination, but also the right to challenge the agreement itself. Therefore, the EEOC says employers should take precautions in drafting covenants not to sue so that employees understand that such covenants do not affect their right to challenge the knowing and voluntary nature of their agreements in court.

Q 17:48   If a former employee challenges an ADEA waiver, can the employer withhold any consideration it has not yet paid?

No. The EEOC regulations provide that an employer may not abrogate its duties under a waiver agreement, covenant not to sue, or similar agreement, even if an employee challenges the validity of the agreement. [29 C.F.R. § 1625.23(d)] The EEOC takes the position that permitting an employer to stop making payments due under the agreement would make it difficult for older workers to exercise their right to contest the validity of the waiver.

A company eliminated almost all of its direct sales positions and offered terminated employees six months of severance benefits in exchange for signing a waiver. In response to the employees' suit alleging age discrimination, the company indicated that it was suspending any further severance payments and was discontinuing other benefits provided under the waiver agreement. The district court held that the company could not cut off severance payments or demand repayment of benefits because the employees filed suit challenging the validity of the waiver. [Butcher v. Gerber Prods. Co., 8 F. Supp. 2d 307 (S.D.N.Y. 1998)]

Q 17:49   If a former employee successfully challenges an ADEA waiver, can the employer recover the consideration paid for the waiver?

The EEOC regulations provide that when an employee successfully challenges a waiver or similar agreement and prevails on the merits of an ADEA discrimination claim, the courts have the discretion to determine whether the employer is entitled to recovery or setoff. In other words, a court may (but is not required to) order the employee to return the consideration paid for the waiver or reduce the amount of the employee's damage award by the amount of the consideration. However, the employer's recovery or setoff cannot exceed the consideration paid for the waiver or the amount of the employee's damage award, if less. [29 C.F.R. § 1625.23(c)]

> **Example.** Marty, who is age 50, received benefits valued at $15,000 in exchange for an ADEA waiver and obtained $10,000 in damages after proving age discrimination. A court could reduce Marty's damage award by up to $10,000. If Marty had obtained $30,000 in damages, the court could not reduce the award by more than the $15,000 Marty received in return for the waiver.

Q 17:50   Is an employer required to give an employee a minimum period to consider the waiver agreement or to revoke it after signing it?

Yes. The statute requires that, for a waiver of ADEA rights and claims to be "knowing and voluntary," the individual must be given a period of at least 21 days to consider the agreement. If the individual is being asked to sign the waiver in connection with a voluntary or involuntary exit incentive or other voluntary or involuntary employment termination program offered to a group or class of employees, then the individual must be given at least a 45-day period to consider the agreement. Once the individual signs the waiver, he or she must be given a 7-day period during which he or she may revoke the waiver.

Counting days for the 21-day and 45-day periods. The 21-day or 45-day period begins to run from the date of the employer's final offer. If material changes to the final offer are made, the 21-day or 45-day period starts running again unless the parties agree otherwise. Changes that are not material do not restart the period. The employee does not have to wait until the end of this consideration period and can sign before the end of the period as long as the employee's decision to accept that shorter period to consider the agreement is knowing and voluntary and is not induced by the employer through fraud, misrepresentation, or threats to withdraw or alter the offer prior to the expiration of the 21-day or 45-day time period, or by providing different terms to employees who sign the release prior to the end of such period.

The 7-day revocation period. Once the employee has signed the waiver of ADEA rights and claims, he or she has a statutory period of 7 days in which to change his or her mind and revoke the waiver. The 7-day period starts running even if the employee signs the waiver before the 21-day or 45-day period has expired and he or she could have taken longer to consider the matter. The parties cannot shorten the 7-day revocation period, by agreement or otherwise. The full 7-day period must be given. [29 C.F.R. § 1625.22(e)]

Q 17:51 What disclosure must an employer make in connection with an exit incentive or other employment termination program offered to a group or class of employees?

If the employer offers an exit incentive or other employment termination program to a group or class of employees and, in connection with such a program, requests that the employee waive any right or claim under the ADEA, the employer must, as an additional condition of obtaining a knowing and voluntary waiver from the employee, also supply certain additional information described below to the eligible employees in the class, unit, group, job classification, or organizational unit asked to sign the waiver, at the beginning of the 45-day election period (see Q 17:50).

Purpose of disclosure requirement. The required disclosure provides an employee with enough information regarding the program to allow him or her to make an informed choice as to whether to sign a waiver agreement.

Programs to which this disclosure obligation applies. The ADEA refers to two types of group termination programs: exit incentive programs and other termination programs. The EEOC's final rule defines an exit incentive program as a voluntary program under which a thing of value, referred to as "additional consideration," is offered to a group or class of employees in addition to anything of value to which they are already entitled in exchange for their decision to voluntarily resign and sign a waiver. "Other termination programs" generally are the same thing except that the group or class of employees is involuntarily terminated. Whether a "program" exists will be based on the facts and circumstances of each case. A program is considered to exist when the employer offers additional consideration in return for the signing of a waiver pursuant to an exit incentive or other employment termination program (for example, a reduction in force) offered to two or more employees. An involuntary termination program typically will offer a standardized formula or package of benefits, while a voluntary termination program offers a standardized formula or package of benefits designed to induce employees to sever their employment voluntarily. The terms of a program generally are not subject to negotiation between the parties. The program is not required to be an ERISA plan in order to qualify as a program for ADEA purposes.

What information must be provided. If a waiver is requested in connection with an exit incentive or other employment termination program offered to a group or class of employees, the waiver is not considered to be knowing and voluntary unless the employer informs the individual in writing, in a manner calculated to be understood by the average individual eligible to participate, as to:

1. Any class, unit, or group of individuals covered by the program, any eligibility factors for the program, and any time limits applicable to the program; and

2. The job titles and ages of all individuals eligible or selected for the program, and the ages of all individuals in the same job classification or organizational unit who are not eligible or selected for the program.

[ADEA § 7(f)(1)(H); 29 U.S.C. § 626(f)(1)(H)]

The presentation of this information must conform to certain standards, and the information is required to be provided to each individual in a "decisional unit."

A decision by the Tenth Circuit Court of Appeals held that employers must also disclose the selection criteria used to pick employees for the program. [Kruchowski v. Weyerhauser Co., 423 F.3d 1139 (10th Cir. 2005)] However, that decision was short-lived. The Tenth Circuit subsequently withdrew the decision and held that the waiver agreements at issue in the case were invalid—but did not address the requirement to disclose selection criteria. [Kruchowski v. Weyerhauser Co., 446 F.3d 1090 (10th Cir. 2006)]

In reaching its original decision, the Tenth Circuit relied on an earlier decision from the Massachusetts federal district court, which held an ADEA waiver invalid for a variety of reasons, including the fact that selection criteria were not disclosed. [Commonwealth v. Bull HN Info Sys., Inc., 143 F. Supp. 2d 134, 147 (D. Mass. 2001)] No other court has addressed the issue.

The decisional unit. Each employee in the class, unit, group, job classification, or organizational unit asked to sign a waiver is to be given the information.

Q 17:52   Who must prove that a waiver under the ADEA is knowing and voluntary—the employer or the employee?

The party asserting the validity of a waiver of rights and claims under the ADEA (usually the employer) has the burden of proving that the waiver occurred under circumstances meeting the ADEA's requirements in order to be considered knowing and voluntary. [ADEA § 7(f)(3); 29 U.S.C. § 626(f)(3)]

Q 17:53   Does a waiver that is knowing and voluntary under the ADEA restrict the EEOC's powers to investigate and enforce the ADEA?

No. Even if a waiver of all rights and claims under the ADEA meets all of the statutory requirements necessary to be considered knowing and voluntary, the EEOC remains free to pursue its rights and responsibilities to enforce the ADEA. In addition, no waiver may be used to justify interfering with the employee's protected right to file a charge or participate in an investigation or proceeding conducted by the EEOC. [ADEA § 7(f)(4); 29 U.S.C. § 626(f)(4)]

The EEOC has issued enforcement guidance stressing that an individual cannot waive the right to file a charge of ADEA discrimination or waive the right to testify, assist, or participate in an EEOC proceeding. [EEOC Notice (Mar. 19, 1997); EEOC News Rel. (Apr. 11, 1997)]

Q 17:54   If the employee chooses termination rather than continuing to work under intolerable conditions, does this constitute a waiver of ADEA claims?

No. The Eighth Circuit Court of Appeals held that an employee faced with the choice of taking a retirement or termination package or continuing in employment under a threat of termination without benefits and of working under intolerable conditions does not forfeit the ability to claim that he or she was constructively discharged in violation of the ADEA. In that case, the employee's new supervisor was clearly planning to build a file and turn the screws on the employee. The employer could not assert that the employee was estopped from bringing an ADEA claim, because a claim of equitable estoppel required "clean hands" on the employer's part. [Smith v. World Ins. Co., 38 F.3d 1456 (8th Cir. 1994)]

Arbitration of ADEA Claims

Q 17:55   Can an employer require an employee to agree to binding arbitration of employment disputes, including discrimination claims under the ADEA?

It is a rare employer that has not been the target of a lawsuit by a disgruntled employee who claims to have been treated unfairly in terms of compensation, benefits, or other terms and conditions of employment. In some cases, the employee's claims are legitimate; in other cases, they are not. In either event, a lawsuit is a costly proposition for an employer, even if the employer ultimately wins. Moreover, an employer runs the risk of losing at trial even if the employee's charges are groundless, since juries are notoriously unpredictable and often favor the "little guy."

As a result, employers have been looking for alternative ways to resolve employment disputes. One approach is to require employees as a condition of being hired to agree to resolve disputes through binding arbitration. The validity of such agreements has been challenged, however.

Several years ago, the U.S. Supreme Court handed employers a major victory by ruling that mandatory arbitration agreements are legal and enforceable by employers. [Circuit City Stores, Inc. v. Adams, 532 U.S. 105 (2001)] The case involved a claim of employment discrimination under state law. However, the arbitration agreement signed by the employee specifically provided for mandatory arbitration of all claims arising under state and local statutes or common law, including the ADEA, Title VII, and the ADA.

The Supreme Court held that the agreement was enforceable under the Federal Arbitration Act (FAA), which validates and provides for enforcement of arbitration agreements. In reaching its decision, the Court made it clear that binding arbitration agreements can be enforced under the FAA even when the dispute involves statutes such as federal discrimination laws that give employees special protections. "By agreeing to arbitrate a statutory claim, a party does not forgo the substantive rights afforded by the statute; it only submits to their resolution in an arbitral, rather than judicial, forum," the Court said.

Despite the Supreme Court decision, other issues regarding arbitration agreements remain to be resolved. For example, many arbitration agreements cap the amount of damages an employee can receive or do not provide for recovery of costs. The Supreme Court did not address the issue of whether such provisions are enforceable if they conflict with the remedies provided by law.

Moreover, another Supreme Court decision makes it clear that a private arbitration agreement between an employee and an employer does not prevent the EEOC from filing a lawsuit against the employer and recovering monetary damages for the employee. The Supreme Court reversed a lower court decision that had prevented the EEOC from recovering monetary damages for discrimination on behalf of an employee who had previously agreed with his employer to arbitrate discrimination claims. The Supreme Court rejected the argument that the EEOC is a mere proxy for the individuals for whom it seeks relief, ruling that the EEOC is the "master of its own case" and can decide to bring a claim for monetary damages in court even though the employee for whom the EEOC seeks relief would be required to pursue his or her own claim through arbitration. [EEOC v. Waffle House, Inc., 122 S. Ct. 754 (2002), *rev'g* 193 F.3d 805 (4th Cir. 1999)]

More recently, the U.S. Supreme Court held that a provision in a collective-bargaining agreement that clearly and unmistakably requires union members to arbitrate ADEA claims is enforceable as a matter of federal law. [Penn Plaza LLC v. Pyett, 129 S. Ct. 1456 (2009)]

Penalties

Q 17:56   What are the penalties for violating the ADEA?

The ADEA incorporates by reference the remedies of the federal Fair Labor Standards Act of 1938 (FLSA). In general, complainants may obtain attorneys' fees, back pay, and either (1) equitable relief such as a judgment compelling employment, reinstatement, or promotion, or enforcing liabilities for amounts held to be owing or (2) "front pay" equal to the pay the plaintiff would have received from the date of judgment to the date he or she would have left the defendant's employ had there been no discrimination. The employee must mitigate (that is, try to reduce) damages by seeking other employment. Liquidated damages equal to the back-pay liability are payable only in cases of a willful violation of the ADEA. [ADEA § 7; 29 U.S.C. § 626]

The U.S. Court of Appeals for the Eleventh Circuit has held that a back-pay award under the ADEA does not have to be reduced by Social Security benefits received after termination of employment. [Dominguez v. Tom James Co., 113 F.3d 1188 (11th Cir. 1997)]

The OWBPA amendments to the ADEA also give an individual whose severance pay was offset by the value of retiree health benefits a right to compel specific performance of the employer's obligation to provide such retiree health benefits. [ADEA § 4(1)(2)(F); 29 U.S.C. § 623(1)(2)(F)]

Q 17:57   What is the federal income tax treatment of cash awards and settlements made as a result of the ADEA?

The U.S. Supreme Court has held that ADEA cash awards and settlements are fully taxable. [Commissioner v. Schleier, 515 U.S. 323 (1995)] In that case, a discharged employee received a cash settlement in an ADEA lawsuit, half of which was designated as back pay and half as liquidated damages. The former employee took the position that the entire amount was free from income tax by reason of Code Section 104(a)(2) as "damages received on account of personal injuries or sickness." A majority of the court found that to be exempt from income tax, the cash settlement had to meet two requirements:

1. The amount had to be received through a legal suit or action based on tort or tort-type rights; and
2. The amount had to be received "on account of personal injuries or sickness."

The Court concluded that the ADEA cash settlement failed to meet both of these requirements. As a result, the cash settlement was held to be fully taxable.

Relationship to State Laws

Q 17:58   Does the ADEA preempt state age discrimination laws purporting to regulate welfare benefit plans?

No. State age discrimination laws generally are not preempted by the ADEA and often also protect young workers (between age 18 through age 39) from discrimination on the basis of age. [ADEA § 14; 29 U.S.C. § 633] However, ERISA generally preempts state age discrimination laws that affect benefits plans that are ERISA plans. [Shaw v. Delta Airlines Inc., 463 U.S. 85, n. 22 (1983); *but see* Drescher v. Union Underwear Co., 858 F. Supp. 653 (W.D. Ky. 1994) (holding that ERISA did not preempt a state age discrimination law where the claim of age discrimination had only an incidental effect on the ERISA plan)]

Chapter 18

Americans with Disabilities Act of 1990

The Americans with Disabilities Act of 1990 (ADA) prohibits employers from discriminating against disabled employees and requires employers to make reasonable accommodation for an employee's disability. The rules sound simple enough—and sometimes they are. If an employee is permanently confined to a wheelchair, the employee is clearly disabled and certain reasonable accommodations, such as providing stairway ramps, quickly spring to mind. However, other cases are not as simple. Employers and employees frequently disagree on whether an employee has a disability that is protected by the ADA and whether a requested accommodation is reasonable. To address these situations, the Americans with Disabilities Act Amendments Act of 2008 (ADAAA) amended the ADA to more clearly define the term *disability* and to provide rules of construction for interpreting the law. This chapter highlights the regulatory guidance under, and case law interpretation of, the ADA and the new rules laid down by the ADAAA.

Basic Concepts

Q 18:1   What does the Americans with Disabilities Act of 1990 cover?

The ADA prohibits covered employers from discriminating against a disabled individual in regard to any of the following aspects of employment:

- Recruitment, advertising, and job application procedures
- Hiring, advancement, or discharge (including upgrading, promotion, award of tenure, demotion, transfer, layoff, termination, right of return from layoff, and rehiring)
- Compensation (including rates of pay or any other form of compensation and changes in compensation)
- Job assignments, job classifications, organizational structures, position descriptions, lines of progression, and seniority lists
- Leaves of absence, sick leave, or any other leave
- Fringe benefits available by virtue of employment, whether or not administered by the covered employer
- Job training (including selection and financial support for training), such as apprenticeships, professional meetings, conferences, and other related activities and selection for leaves of absence to pursue training
- Activities sponsored by a covered employer (including social and recreational programs)
- Any other term, condition, or privilege of employment

[ADA § 102(a); 42 U.S.C. § 12112(a); EEOC Reg. § 1630.4]

Practice Pointer. The fact that an employee has covered disability does not automatically mean that the employee has a legitimate claim for discrimination under the ADA. The fact that an adverse employment action may have been based on a disability does not necessarily mean that an employer has engaged in unlawful discrimination. For example, an individual still needs to be "qualified" for the job he or she holds or desires. Additionally, in some instances, an employer may have a defense to an action taken on the basis of a disability, such as where a particular individual would pose a direct threat or where the employer's action was based on another federal law (e.g., a law that prohibits individuals with certain impairments from holding certain kinds of jobs). [EEOC Questions and Answers on the Notice of Proposed Rulemaking for the ADA Amendments Act of 2008, Q&A 20]

Covered Employers

Q 18:2   What employers are covered by the ADA?

An employer engaged in an industry affecting commerce, and any agent of such employer, is covered by the ADA, if the employer employed 15 or more employees for each working day in each of 20 or more calendar weeks in the current or preceding calendar year. [ADA § 101(5); 42 U.S.C. § 12111(5); EEOC Reg. § 1630.2(e)(1)]

Covered employers include state and local governments (but not the United States or a corporation wholly owned by the United States, or a Native American tribe). [EEOC Reg. § 1630.2(e)(2)]

Aggregation rules. The ADA does not contain a specific controlled-group rule that would aggregate separate entities and treat them as a single employer for purposes of meeting the ADA's 15-employee jurisdictional requirement. However, case law developments indicate that courts will use a fact-based inquiry to determine when a "single employer" might exist. A district court ruled that a law firm with only ten employees actually served as the legal department of a larger firm and, as a result, was covered by the ADA. The court examined the integrated nature of the companies and the representations of the law firm to the public in making its determination. [Doe v. Shapiro, 852 F. Supp. 124 (E.D. Pa. 1994)] Another district court looked at whether two different entities had substantially overlapping management, substantially interrelated operations, common ownership, and common control of labor relations. [EEOC v. Chemtech Int'l Corp., 890 F. Supp. 623 (S.D. Tex. 1995)] A similar fact-based inquiry in another case led to the conclusion that the two entities were not a single employer for purposes of the ADA's minimum employee requirement. [Switalski v. International Ass'n of Bridge, Structural & Ornamental Iron Workers, Local Union No. 3, 881 F. Supp. 205 (W.D. Pa. 1995)]

Employee benefits plans as employers or agents of the employer. As noted, the ADA applies to agents of covered employers. Case law indicates that employee benefit plans could be considered employers or agents of the employer for ADA purposes. A district court ruled that a union-sponsored welfare fund is a covered entity subject to the ADA. [Mason Tenders Dist. Council Welfare Fund v. Donaghey, No. 93-CIV-1154, Daily Labor Rep. (BNA) No. 223 (S.D.N.Y. Nov. 19, 1993)] The Court of Appeals for the First Circuit ruled that both a health plan and its sponsoring association may be employers under the ADA if they exercise control over an important aspect of the individual's employment. Factors to be considered in making this determination include whether the sponsor and the plan have the authority to determine the level of benefits and whether the employer shares plan administration duties. [Carparts Distrib. Ctr., Inc. v. Automotive Wholesaler's Ass'n, 37 F.3d 12 (1st Cir. 1994)]

Covered Employees

Q 18:3   Which employees are covered by the ADA?

In order to be protected by the ADA, an employee must be a "qualified individual with a disability." This means an individual with a disability who, with or without reasonable accommodation, can perform the essential functions of the employment position that he or she has or desires. [42 U.S.C. § 12111(8)]

Thus, both employees and prospective employees have the right to sue for discrimination under the ADA. In addition, at least one appellate court has held that a former employee with a disability is also protected by the ADA (see Q 18:4).

Q 18:4   Are former employees protected by the ADA?

The U.S. Court of Appeals for the Eleventh Circuit concluded that a former employee can sue for discrimination under the ADA. [Johnson v. Kmart Corp., 273 F.3d 1035 (11th Cir. 2001)]

James Johnson worked for Kmart Corp. for 30 years until his doctor advised him to stop working because of severe depression and mental illness. At that time, Johnson applied for and received long-term disability benefits from Kmart. Under Kmart's plan, employees who were physically disabled received salary replacement benefits until age 65, while employees disabled due to mental illness received salary replacement benefits for only two years. Johnson brought a lawsuit in federal court claiming that the cap on mental health-related disability benefits violated the ADA. However, Kmart argued that, as a former employee, Johnson was not eligible to sue under the ADA.

The ADA prohibits discrimination against any "qualified individual with a disability." And the Eleventh Circuit acknowledged that at first blush, "qualified individual" might seem to refer only to job applicants and current employees. However, the court said there was no basis for assuming that Congress intentionally provided ADA protection to future and current employees but denied protection for former employees. Moreover, the Eleventh Circuit said, other language in the ADA clearly contemplates that former employees will make use of the ADA's remedial mechanism. For example, the law specifically prohibits the discriminatory discharge of an employee based on disability and provides a remedy of reinstatement.

According to the Eleventh Circuit, reading the law narrowly to exclude coverage for former employees would deny them access to remedies for discriminatory administration of postemployment benefits and would create a "perverse incentive" for employers to interfere with those benefits. Moreover, the court emphasized that barring former employees from suing under the ADA would nullify those portions of the law that prohibit discriminatory discharge.

Covered Disabilities

Q 18:5   What is a covered disability under the ADA?

A *covered disability* is any of the following:

- A physical or mental impairment that substantially limits one or more of the major life activities of such individual

- A record of such an impairment
- Being regarded as having such an impairment

[ADA § 3(2); 42 U.S.C. § 12102(2)]

While this basic definition of a covered disability has remained unchanged since the ADA was enacted in 1990, the interpretation of the definition has recently undergone a radical revision. The Americans With Disabilities Act Amendments Act of 2008 [Pub. L. No. 110-325, 122 Stat. 3553] (ADAAA) amends the ADA to more clearly define the term *disability* and to provide rules of construction for interpreting the law. Most significantly, the ADAAA specifically rejects Supreme Court decisions (and corresponding Equal Employment Opportunity Commission regulations) that, in Congress's view, imposed inappropriately high standards for coverage under the ADA. [ADAAA § 2] The EEOC has issued proposed regulations and a series of Questions and Answers that reflect the ADAA changes. [Regulations to Implement the Equal Employment Provisions of the Americans with Disabilities Act, 74 Fed. Reg. 48,431 (Prop. 29 C.F.R. Pt. 1630); EEOC Questions and Answers on the Notice of Proposed Rulemaking for the ADA Amendments Act of 2008]

Q 18:6   When do the changes made by the ADA Amendments Act apply?

The ADAAA went into effect on January 1, 2009. The ADAAA does not apply retroactively. So, for example, the ADAAA would not apply to a situation in which an employer allegedly failed to hire someone or terminated or denied a reasonable accommodation to someone with a disability in December 2008, even if the person did not file a charge with the EEOC until after January 1, 2009. The original ADA definition of disability would be applied to such a charge. However, the ADAAA would apply to denials of reasonable accommodations where a request was made, or an earlier request was renewed, on or after January 1, 2009.

Q 18:7   Why does the ADA also cover the perception of disability, even if no disability in fact exists?

The ADA covers persons regarded as having a substantially limiting impairment even if they do not in fact have a disability. Congress recognized that the reactions of others to an impairment or a perceived impairment can be just as disabling as the limitations caused by an actual impairment. [EEOC Compliance Manual § 915.002, "Definition of Term Disability," pp. 902–43, reprinted at 51 Daily Lab. Rep. (BNA) E-1 (Mar. 16, 1995)]

The EEOC Compliance Manual sets forth the following rationale for this aspect of the definition of the term *disability* under the ADA:

> This aspect of the definition of the term "disability" . . . is designed to protect against myths, fears, stereotypes, and other attitudinal barriers about disability. Common attitudinal barriers include, but are not

limited to, concerns about productivity, safety, insurance, liability, attendance, cost of accommodation and accessibility by co-workers and customers. Quite often, employers will assume, without any objective evidence, that a person's physical or mental condition will cause problems in these areas. The ADA is designed to prevent employment discrimination based on mere speculation and unfounded fears about disability. Thus, the third part of the definition is designed to protect individuals who experience employment discrimination because of myths, fears, and stereotypes associated with disabilities, even if the individuals' physical or mental conditions do not meet the criteria of the first or second part of the definition. (citations omitted)

Despite the broad reach of the "regarded as" prong of the ADA as expressed in the EEOC Compliance Manual, the Supreme Court and other courts subsequently narrowed that reach, taking the position that the ADA applied only if an individual was regarded as having an impairment that substantially limits a major life activity. [*See, e.g.,* Sutton v. United Air Lines, Inc., 527 U.S. 471 (1999)] In other words, as the courts interpreted the law, it was not enough that an individual was subject to an adverse action because of "myths, fears, or stereotypes" about a real or perceived impairment. The individual had to show that an adverse action was taken because the actor regarded the individual as having an impairment that substantially limited a major life activity.

In enacting the ADA Amendments Act of 2008, Congress announced its purpose to specifically reject that line of reasoning and to "reinstate . . . a broad view of the third prong . . . ." [ADAAA § 2(b)(3)] In keeping with that purpose, the ADA Amendments Act adds a new definition of disability for purposes of the "regarded as" prong. The new definition provides that:

> An individual meets the requirement of 'being regarded as having such an impairment' if the individual establishes that he or she has been subject to an action prohibited under this Act because of an actual or perceived physical or mental impairment whether or not the impairment limits or is perceived to limit a major life activity. [42 U.S.C. § 12102(3)(A) as amended by Pub. L. No. 110-325]

However, the new definition does not apply to impairments that are "transitory and minor." A transitory impairment is one with an actual or expected duration of six months or less.

Q 18:8 When is an individual "regarded as" having a disability under the ADAAA rule?

The proposed EEOC regulations provide that an individual is "regarded as" having a disability if the individual is subjected to a prohibited employment action (including non-selection, demotion, termination, or denial of any other term, condition, or privilege of employment) based on an actual or perceived physical or mental impairment. Evidence that the employer believes the individual is substantially limited in any major life activity is not required. [Prop. EEOC Reg. § 1.1630(l)(1)]

"Regarded as" coverage under the ADA can apply if an employer takes a prohibited employment action based on an individual's use of a mitigating measure for, or the symptoms of, an impairment, even if the employer is unaware of the underlying impairment. [Prop. EEOC Reg. § 1.1630(l)(2)] For example, the proposed regulations provide that an individual who is not hired for a driving job because he takes anti-seizure medication is regarded as having a disability, even if the employer does not know why the individual is taking the medication. Similarly, an employer who refuses to hire an individual with a facial tic regards the individual as having a disability, even if the employer does not know the facial tic is caused by Tourette's syndrome.

On the other hand, an employer is not required to entirely ignore a perceived disability. For example, the EEOC Qs&As make it clear that asking if an employee who appears to be having difficulty performing a job because of an impairment needs a reasonable accommodation would not violate the ADA. [EEOC Questions and Answers on the Notice of Proposed Rulemaking for the ADA Amendments Act of 2008, Q&A 22] However, employers have no obligation to provide reasonable accommodation to an individual who only meets the "regarded as" definition of disability, and not one of the other definitions. [Prop. EEOC Reg. § 1.1630(o)(4)]

In addition, an adverse employment action is an impairment that is both transitory (lasting or expected to last for six months or less) and minor. [Prop. EEOC Reg. § 1.1630(l)(3)] For example, an individual who is not hired for a data entry position because she will be unable to type for three weeks due to a sprained wrist is not "regarded as" disabled, because a sprained wrist is transitory and minor. Similarly, an individual who is placed on involuntary leave because of a broken leg that is expected to heal normally is not "regarded as" disabled because a broken leg is transitory and minor. On the other hand, an individual who is not hired for an assembly line job because the employer believes the individual has carpal tunnel syndrome is "regarded as" disabled because carpal tunnel syndrome is neither transitory nor minor. The same holds true for an employee who is fired from a food service job because the employer believes the employee has Hepatitis C. Finally, the regulations say an employee who is terminated from employment because the employer believes that symptoms of a virus are actually symptoms of heart disease, even though the employee does not actually have heart disease, is "regarded as" disabled because the impairment the employer believes the employee has is neither transitory nor minor.

Q 18:9   What is a physical or mental impairment under the ADA?

For purposes of the ADA, as amended by the ADAAA, a *physical or mental impairment* is defined as:

1. Any physiological disorder or condition, cosmetic disfigurement, or anatomical loss affecting one or more specified body systems: neurological, musculoskeletal, special sense organs, respiratory (including speech

organs), cardiovascular, reproductive, digestive, genitourinary, hemic and lymphatic, skin, and endocrine systems; or

2. Any mental or psychological disorder, such as an intellectual disability (formerly termed mental retardation), organic brain syndrome, emotional or mental illness, and specific learning disabilities.

[Prop. EEOC Reg. § 1630.2(h)]

Note. The existence of an impairment is not enough to trigger coverage under the ADA. The impairment rises to the level of a protected disability under the ADA only when it substantially limits one or more major life activities. However, the ADAAA significantly lowers the bar in this regard. According to Congress, one purpose of the ADAAA is "to convey congressional intent that the standard created by the Supreme Court . . . and applied by lower courts in numerous decisions, has created an inappropriately high level of limitation necessary to obtain coverage under the ADA. . . ." [ADAAA § 2(b)(5)] (See Q 18:10.)

Q 18:10 What major life activities must the physical or mental impairment affect?

The ADAAA [Pub. L. No. 110-325], which took effect on January 1, 2009, adds a nonexclusive list of major life activities to the ADA. Under the new law, major life activities include, but are not limited to:

- Caring for oneself
- Performing manual tasks
- Seeing
- Hearing
- Eating
- Sleeping
- Walking
- Standing
- Sitting
- Reaching
- Lifting
- Bending
- Speaking
- Breathing
- Learning
- Reading
- Concentrating
- Thinking
- Communicating

- Interacting with others
- Working

[42 U.S.C. § 12102(2)(A), as amended by Pub. L. No. 110-325; Prop. EEOC Reg. § 1.1630.2(i) (1)]

The ADAAA and the EEOC proposed regulations also clarify that major life activities include the operation of major bodily functions such as functions of the immune system, special sense organs and skin; normal cell growth; and digestive, genitorurinary, bowel, bladder, neurological, brain, respiratory, circulatory, cardiovascular, endocrine, hemic, lymphatic, musculoskeletal, and reproductive functions. [42 U.S.C. § 12102(2)(A), as amended by Pub. L. No. 110-325; Prop. EEOC Reg. § 1.1630(1)(2)]

> **Practice Pointer.** The ADAAA list of major life activities is more expansive than the list contained in pre-ADAAA regulations, with the addition of eating, sleeping, standing, lifting, bending, reading, concentrating, thinking, and communicating and the operation of bodily functions to the list of major life activities. Moreover, the proposed EEOC regulations specifically provide that the list of examples of major life activities is not exhaustive. [Prop. EEOC Reg. § 1.1630(1)(3)]

The Supreme Court has held that reproduction is a major life activity. In *Bragdon v. Abbott* [524 U.S. 624 (1998)], a woman with the human immuno-deficiency virus (HIV) was denied dental services. The Supreme Court determined that HIV is a physical impairment and that it affects the "major life activity" of reproduction and that the impairment had a substantial limitation on that major life activity because it controlled her decision not to have a child. Thus, the issue of whether reproduction is a major life activity was not decided in the context of a plan exclusion for infertility treatment (as might have been the expected route) but in the course of deciding the impact of HIV on a woman who apparently was not far along in the course of the disease.

A divided U.S. Court of Appeals for the Ninth Circuit has concluded that "other activities—specifically, sleeping, engaging in sexual relations, and inter-acting with others—are major life activities within the meaning of the ADA." [McAlindin v. County of San Diego, 192 F.3d 1226 (9th Cir. 1999)] The court held that an employee whose anxiety disorder became paralyzing and who took medications that made him drowsy and sexually impotent produced sufficient evidence of substantial limitations on major life activities to proceed with a discrimination claim under the ADA. Judge Dorothy W. Nelson said the court was following to its logical conclusion the Supreme Court's holding in *Bragdon* that reproduction is a major life activity under the ADA. "The number of people who engage in sexual relations is plainly larger than the number who choose to have children," she said. [184 Daily Lab. Rep. (BNA) A-3 (Sept. 23, 1999)]

> **Practice Pointer.** Although the cases mentioned above were decided prior to the ADAAA, they are in keeping with broadened definition of disability and the mandate that the definition of disability be construed broadly. [Prop. EEOC Reg. § 1.1630.1(a)(4)]

Q 18:11   When is a major life activity substantially limited by the physical or mental impairment?

An impairment rises to the level of a protected disability when it *substantially limits* one or more major life activities. The Americans with Disabilities Act Amendments Act of 2008 [Pub. L. No. 110-325] does not change that requirement. However, the ADAAA lays down rules of construction for determining when a protected disability exists. And, according to the statement of purposes of the Act, the rules are intended to convey Congress' intent that the standards created by the Supreme Court and applied by the lower courts for "substantially limits" has created an inappropriately high level of limitation necessary to obtain coverage under the ADA. [ADAAA § 2(b)(5)] In particular, Congress specifically rejected the reasoning of *Toyota Motor Manufacturing, Kentucky, Inc. v. Williams* [534 U.S. 184 (2002)], in which the Court held that the definition of disability should be interpreted strictly and that an impairment rises to level of a disability only if it substantially interferes with activities that are of central importance to most people's daily lives.

Under the rules of construction laid down by the ADAAA, the definition of disability is to be construed in favor of broad coverage of individuals to the maximum extent permitted under the ADA and the term "substantially limits" is to be construed in keeping with that purpose. Specifically, an impairment that substantially limits a major life activity need not limit other major life activities in order to be considered a disability. An impairment that is episodic or in remission is a disability if it would substantially limit a major life activity when active. [42 U.S.C. 12102(4), as amended by Pub. L. No. 110-325]

In *Toyota Motor Manufacturing Kentucky, Inc. v. Williams*, the Supreme Court held that an impairment must be permanent and long term to rise to the level of a disability. The proposed EEOC regulations provide that temporary, nonchronic impairments of short duration with little or no residual effects (such as the common cold, seasonal or common influenza, a sprained joint, minor and non-chronic gastrointestinal disorders, or a broken bone that is expected to heal completely) usually will not be considered disabilities. [Prop. EEOC Reg. § 1.1630(j)(8)] On the other hand, the "transitory and minor" exception for conditions lasting six months or less that applies for purposes of the "regarded as" prong of the definition of disability does not establish a durational minimum in the case of an actual disability. An impairment may substantially limit a major life activity even if it lasts, or is expected to last, for fewer than six months. [Prop. EEOC Reg. § 1.1630.2(l)(2)(v)]

According to the EEOC proposed regulations, interpreting the definition of disability broadly, as required under the ADAAA, means that some impairments will consistently meet the definition of disability. In addition to conditions such as deafness, blindness, intellectual disability (formerly termed mental retardation), partially or completely missing limbs, and mobility impairments requiring the use of a wheelchair, other examples of impairments that will consistently meet the definition include:

- Autism, which substantially limits major life activities such as communicating, interacting with others, or learning;
- Cancer, which substantially limits major life activities such as normal cell growth;
- Cerebral palsy, which substantially limits major life activities such as walking, performing manual tasks, speaking, or functions of the brain;
- Diabetes, which substantially limits major life activities such as functions of the endocrine system (e.g., the production of insulin);
- Epilepsy, which substantially limits major life activities such as functions of the brain or, during a seizure, seeing, hearing, speaking, walking, or thinking;
- HIV or AIDS, which substantially limit functions of the immune system;
- Multiple sclerosis and muscular dystrophy, which substantially limit major life activities including neurological functions, walking, performing manual tasks, seeing, speaking, or thinking;
- Major depression, bipolar disorder, post-traumatic stress disorder, obsessive compulsive disorder, or schizophrenia, which substantially limit major life activities including functions of the brain, thinking, concentrating, interacting with others, sleeping, or caring for oneself.

[Prop. EEOC Reg. § 1630.2(j)(5)]

The proposed regulations emphasize that the list is merely intended to illustrate some of the types of impairments that are consistently substantially limiting. Other types of impairments not specifically identified may also consistently be substantially limiting, such as some forms of depression other than major depression and seizure disorders other than epilepsy.

The regulations also provide that other types of conditions may be substantially limiting for some individuals but not for others. Those types of impairments, which include asthma, back and leg impairments, and learning disabilities, may require further analysis to determine whether they are substantially limiting for a particular individual, although the level of analysis required still should not be extensive. [Prop. EEOC Reg. § 1630.2(j)(5) and (6)]

Q 18:12   Does mitigation of a disability affect ADA disability status?

In two separate decisions, the Supreme Court held that an individual claiming a disability under the ADA should be assessed with regard to any mitigating or corrective measures employed. In *Sutton v. United Airlines* [527 U.S. 471 (1999)], the Court held that the plaintiffs—two nearsighted pilots, whose vision is normal when wearing corrective lenses—were not actually disabled under 42 U.S.C. Section 12102(2)(A) because they could fully correct their visual impairments. In addition, the Court said, three separate ADA provisions, read in concert, lead to the conclusion that the determination as to whether an individual is disabled should be made with reference to measures, such as eyeglasses and contact lenses, that mitigate the individual's impairment.

In a second case, *Murphy v. United Parcel Service, Inc.* [527 U.S. 516 (1999)], the Court affirmed a Tenth Circuit decision that held that a truck mechanic with high blood pressure was not actually disabled or regarded as disabled for the purposes of the ADA because his high blood pressure was controlled somewhat by medication. In fact, the Court said, it was undisputed that he was generally employable as a mechanic, and there was uncontroverted evidence that he could perform a number of mechanic jobs. He was unqualified to work as a UPS mechanic because he was unable to obtain DOT health certification, the Court said.

However, the ADAAA specifically provides that a purpose of the Act is to "reject the requirement enunciated by the Supreme Court in *Sutton* . . . and its companion cases that whether an impairment substantially limits a major life activity is to be determined with reference to the ameliorative effects of mitigating measures. . . ." [ADAAA § 2(b)(2)] The rules of construction laid down by the ADAAA provide that the determination of whether an impairment substantially limits a major life activity (and thus rises to level of a disability) is to be made without regard to the ameliorative effects of mitigating measures such as:

- Medication, medical supplies, equipment, or appliances, low-vision devices (other than ordinary eyeglasses or contact lenses), prosthetics including limbs and devices, hearing aids and cochlear implants or other implantable hearing devices, mobility devices, or oxygen therapy equipment and supplies;

- Use of assistive technology;

- Reasonable accommodations or auxiliary aids or services; or

- Learned behavioral or adaptive neurological modifications. [Prop. EEOC Reg. § 1630.2(h)(3)

The ameliorative effects of ordinary eyeglasses or contacts lenses are to be considered in determining whether an impairment substantially limits a major life activity. [42 U.S.C. § 12102(4), as amended by Pub. L. No. 110-325; Prop. EEOC Reg. § 1630.2(h)(3)(iv)] In addition, the ADAAA provides that an employer or other entity covered by the ADA cannot use qualification standards, employment tests, or other selection criteria based on an individual's uncorrected vision unless the standard, test, or other criteria is shown to be job-related and consistent with business necessity. [Prop. EEOC Reg. § 1630.10(b)]

For these purposes, ordinary eyeglasses or contact lenses refer to lenses that are intended to fully correct visual acuity or eliminate refractive error. Low-vision devices means devices that magnify, enhance, or otherwise augment a visual image. Auxiliary aids and services include qualified interpreter or other methods of making aurally delivered materials available to individuals with hearing impairments; qualified readers, taped texts, or other effective methods of making visually delivered materials available to individuals with visual impairments; and other similar services and actions.

Practice Pointer. While the positive effects of mitigating measures cannot be taken into account in determining whether an individual has a disability, the negative effects can be. The ADAAA allows consideration of the negative effects from use of a mitigating measure in determining if a disability exists. For example, the side effects that an individual experiences from use of medication for hypertension may be considered in determining whether the individual is substantially limited in a major life activity. In addition, both the positive and negative effects of a mitigating measure can be considered in determining whether an individual requires reasonable accommodation for a disability. [EEOC Questions and Answers on the Notice of Proposed Rule-making for the ADA Amendments Act of 2008, Q&As 10 & 11]

Q 18:13   Are there physical or mental conditions that do not constitute impairments protected by the ADA?

Yes. The term *impairment* as used in the ADA does not include physical characteristics such as eye color, hair color, left-handedness, or height, weight, or muscle tone that are within normal range and are not the result of a physiological disorder.

Characteristic predisposition to illness or disease is not an impairment. Other conditions such as pregnancy that are not the result of a physiological disorder are not impairments, either. Complications from pregnancy are, however, an impairment under the ADA (see Q 18:19).

Common personality traits such as poor judgment or a quick temper, which are not symptoms of a mental or psychological disorder, are not protected, nor are environmental, cultural, or economic disadvantages such as poverty, lack of education, or a prison record.

Advanced age, in and of itself, is not an impairment, but medical conditions commonly associated with advanced age, such as hearing loss, osteoporosis, or arthritis would be protected impairments. [Appendix to EEOC Reg. Part 1630—Interpretive Guidance on § 1630.2(h)]

Transitory conditions such as common colds, influenza, and most broken bones and sprains generally are not substantially limiting impairments, even though the individual may have required absolute bed rest or hospitalization for such conditions. [EEOC Compliance Manual § 915.002, "Definition of Term Disability," pp. 902–29, reprinted at 51 Daily Lab. Rep. E-1 (BNA) (Mar. 16, 1995)] The EEOC's proposed regulation provides several examples of temporary, nonchronic impairments of short duration with little or no residual effects that are usually not disabilities, including (but not limited to) the common cold, seasonal or common influenza, a sprained joint, minor and nonchronic gastrointestinal disorders, or a broken bone that is expected to heal completely. The appendix to the proposed regulation also states that appendicitis and seasonal allergies that do not substantially limit a person's major life activities even when active are not disabilities. Additionally, the fact that an impairment is permanent or of long duration or chronic in nature would not automatically make it a disability if it otherwise does not substantially limit a major life activity. [Prop. EEOC Reg. § 1630.2(j)(8) and corresponding Appendix § 1630.2(j)]

The highest state court of Maine has concluded that sexual addiction is not a disability under the ADA. [Winston v. Maine Tech. Coll. Sys., 631 A.2d 70 (Me. 1993), *cert. denied*, 511 U.S. 1069 (1994)]

Q 18:14   What conditions are excluded from coverage under the ADA?

Homosexuality and bisexuality are not considered to be impairments and are not disabilities for purposes of the ADA. [ADA § 511(a); 42 U.S.C. § 12211(a); EEOC Reg. § 1630.3(e)]

In addition, covered disabilities under the ADA do not include transvestitism, transsexualism, pedophilia, exhibitionism, voyeurism, gender identity disorders not resulting from physical impairments, or other sexual behavior disorders; compulsive gambling, kleptomania, or pyromania; or psychoactive substance use disorders resulting from current illegal use of drugs. [ADA § 511(b); 42 U.S.C. § 12211(b); EEOC Reg. § 1630.3(d)]

Q 18:15   Is illegal drug use an impairment protected under the ADA?

The ADA generally does not protect persons engaging in the illegal use of drugs, but it does cover individuals who are erroneously regarded as engaging in the illegal use of drugs or who are participating in a supervised rehabilitation program (or have in the past or were otherwise rehabilitated successfully) and are no longer engaging in such use. [ADA § 510; 42 U.S.C. § 12210; EEOC Reg. §§ 1630.3(a), 1630.3(b)]

The EEOC's compliance manual indicates that the record or perception must be that the individual is or was addicted to a controlled substance and that a record or perception of occasional or casual use of drugs does not constitute a disability. [EEOC Compliance Manual § 915.002, "Definition of Term Disability," p. 3, reprinted at 51 Daily Lab. Rep. (BNA) E-1 (Mar. 16, 1995)]

Case law developments have clarified that once a substance abuser ceases to engage in his or her illegal drug use and begins to participate in a drug rehabilitation program (or is otherwise rehabilitated), the individual becomes protected by the ADA. [McDaniel v. Mississippi Baptist Med. Ctr., 869 F. Supp. 445 (S.D. Miss. 1994)]

An employer was held to have violated the ADA by requiring that its employees disclose what prescription medicines they were taking. The court ruled that disclosure of the prescriptions would force the employees to reveal their disabilities or perceived disabilities to the employer. However, the court pointed out that the employer could test the employee for illegal drug use and could prohibit employees from using illegal drugs. [Roe v. Cheyenne Mountain Conference Resort, Inc., 920 F. Supp. 1153 (D. Colo. 1996)]

Q 18:16   Are contagious diseases an impairment protected under the ADA?

The mere fact that a disease is contagious does not remove it from the protection of the ADA. The Supreme Court has refused to draw a distinction between the effects of a condition on the carrier and the effects of a condition on others. [EEOC Compliance Manual § 915.002, "Definition of Term Disability," pp. 902–43, reprinted at 51 Daily Lab. Rep. (BNA) E-1 (Mar. 16, 1995), citing the Supreme Court's decision in School Bd. of Nassau County v. Arline, 480 U.S. 273 (1987)]

The U.S. Supreme Court held that HIV infection is a physical impairment from the very beginning of the infection because of the impact on the body's blood cells. [Bragdon v. Abbott, 524 U.S. 624 (1998)] The decision was fact-based and stopped short of stating that HIV is a covered disability across the board. (See Q 18:17.)

Q 18:17   Is HIV an impairment protected under the ADA?

Yes. The EEOC's compliance manual clarifies that HIV is an impairment under the ADA: "An individual who has HIV infection, including asymptomatic HIV infection, has a disability covered under the ADA." [EEOC Compliance Manual § 915.002, "Definition of Term Disability," pp. 902–13 and n.18 at p. 902, reprinted at 51 Daily Lab. Rep. (BNA) E-1 (Mar. 16, 1995)] A federal district court has also confirmed that an individual who was infected with HIV and who had physical and mental impairment that substantially limited one of his major life activities (procreation, because of the risk of transmitting the infection to a partner or child), had a disability under the ADA. [Doe v. Kohn Nast & Graf, PD, 862 F. Supp. 1310 (E.D. Pa. 1994)]

More recently, the U.S. Supreme Court held that HIV is an impairment that substantially limited one of the major life activities of a female, that of procreation. Significantly, the woman was of childbearing years and felt that she could not have a child because of the high risk of transmitting the disease to the child. [Bragdon v. Abbott, 524 U.S. 624 (1998)] The decision stopped short of saying that HIV was always an impairment to procreation, leaving open the question of whether an adult of nonchildbearing age or an individual with a same-sex partner could claim that HIV impaired this particular life activity of procreation.

The proposed EEOC regulations implementing the ADAAA specifically in-clude HIV or AIDS in the list of impairments that will consistently meet the definition of a disability. [Prop. EEOC Reg. § 1630.2(j)(5)]

Q 18:18   Is smoking an impairment protected under the ADA?

The ADA itself does not contain any references to smoking, and the lengthy EEOC guidance issued to date is silent on this issue. In 1994, the EEOC stated that it was "looking into" whether it is permissible under the ADA for plan sponsors to charge higher medical and life insurance premiums for employees who smoke. The EEOC indicated, however, that plan sponsors would have to justify such action on an actuarial basis. [21 Pens. & Ben. Rep. (BNA) 956 (May 15, 1994)]

Significantly, the EEOC's own working definition of disability under the ADA distinguishes between smoking and conditions that the individual may develop as a result of smoking. In discussing the issue of whether voluntary action disqualifies an impairment from ADA coverage, the EEOC used smoking as an example. It stated that voluntariness is irrelevant when determining whether a condition constitutes an impairment for ADA purposes. It noted, by way of example, that "an individual who develops lung cancer as a result of smoking has an impairment notwithstanding that some apparently volitional act of the individual may have caused the impairment." The EEOC thus stopped short of characterizing smoking as an addiction.

Although the Food and Drug Administration (FDA) has in the past concluded that nicotine addiction is a disease, this view has yet to be adopted or elected in any official EEOC announcement, notice, or regulation under the ADA. Further, the U.S. Court of Appeals for the Fourth Circuit's decision concluding that the FDA has no authority to regulate tobacco products places the precedential value of the FDA's interpretation in question. [Brown & Williamson Tobacco Corp. v. FDA, 153 F.3d 155 (4th Cir. 1998)]

The proposed regulations under the ADAAA do not address this issue.

Q 18:19   Is pregnancy an impairment protected under the ADA?

No. Pregnancy is not a disability for purposes of the ADA; however, claims of employment discrimination based on pregnancy are covered by Title VII of the Civil Rights Act of 1964 (see chapter 19). [EEOC Compliance Manual § 915.002, "Definition of Term Disability," pp. 902–09, reprinted at 51 Daily Lab. Rep. (BNA) E-1 (Mar. 16, 1995)]

Note, however, that complications resulting from pregnancy are impairments under the ADA. Whether such an impairment rises to the level of a disability for ADA purposes will turn on whether the impairment substantially limits, or is regarded as substantially limiting, a major life activity. [EEOC Compliance Manual, § 915.002, "Definition of Term Disability," pp. 902–09, reprinted at 51 Daily Lab. Rep. (BNA) E-1 (Mar. 16, 1995)]

If a woman of childbearing years is unable to procreate, the Supreme Court has held that such inability is a protected impairment under the ADA. (see Qs 18:10–18:11.)

Q 18:20   Is obesity an impairment protected under the ADA?

In an amicus brief filed in an ADA case, the EEOC took the position that morbid obesity should be considered a protected disability under the ADA. [EEOC Amicus Brief, Cook v. Department of Mental Health, Retardation & Hosps., 10 F.3d 17 (1st Cir. 1993), *quoted in* 20 Pens. & Ben. Rep. (BNA) 1977 (Aug. 23, 1993)]

Subsequently, the EEOC has issued guidelines on the definition of disability under the ADA which appear to adopt a bright-line test. Being overweight is not by itself an impairment under the ADA. However, severe obesity, which the EEOC compliance manual defines as body weight more than 100 percent over the norm, "is clearly an impairment." [EEOC Compliance Manual § 915.002, "Definition of Term Disability," pp. 902–912, reprinted at 51 Daily Lab. Rep. (BNA) E-1 (Mar. 16, 1995)]

Q 18:21   Is total disability an impairment protected under the ADA?

There is a split of opinion on this issue. Several developments illustrate the limitations of the ADA in this circumstance.

First is the issue of an individual who is either totally disabled or who has made that claim in another context (such as in an application for Social Security disability benefits or in a claim under the employer's long-term disability plan). This is because the ADA protects only qualified individuals with a disability who are able to perform the essential functions of the job with or without reasonable accommodation. The circuit courts are split as to whether these prior statements cause the individual to be estopped from claiming that he or she is a qualified individual with a disability for purposes of the ADA. [*See* McNemar v. Disney Stores Inc., 91 F.3d 610 (3d Cir. 1996), *cert. denied,* 117 S. Ct. 958 (1997) (prior statements in applications made under penalty of perjury) *and* Simon v. Safelite Glass Corp., 128 F.3d 68 (2d Cir. 1997) (prior statements in Social Security application); *cf.* Swanks v. Washington Metro. Area Transit Auth., 116 F.3d 582 (D.C. Cir. 1997) (receipt of disability benefits) *and* Griffith v. Wal-Mart Stores Inc., 135 F.3d 376 (6th Cir. 1998) (prior statements relevant but do not bar suit under ADA); Johnson v. Oregon, 141 F.3d 1361 (9th Cir. 1998) (receipt of both Social Security disability benefits and long-term disability benefits is not an automatic bar to ADA suit where differing definitions of disability apply; courts have discretion to apply judicial estoppel to bar individual from playing fast and loose with the courts); Rascon v. U.S. West Commc'ns, Inc., 143 F.3d 1324 (10th Cir. 1998) (prior statements concerning disability are relevant, but not determinative, under ADA); Talavera v. School Bd., 129 F.3d 1214 (11th Cir. 1997) (statements for Social Security benefits not determinative for ADA purposes because Social Security does not inquire whether individual can work with accommodation); Ford v. Shering-Plough Corp., 145 F.3d 601 (3d Cir. 1998) (former employee who is disabled may sue under ADA; those eligible to sue are not limited to current employees); Butler v. Round Lake Police Dep't, 2009 U.S. App. LEXIS 23602 (7th Cir. Oct. 27, 2009) (sworn testimony of complete disability in application for disability pension barred ADA claim).]

> **Note.** The EEOC issued "Enforcement Guidance on Disability Representations" [Feb. 12, 1997, available at *http://www.eeoc.gov/docs*] to its agency investigators stating that allegations of total disability when applying for benefits under the Social Security Act, workers' compensation laws, or disability insurance plans are relevant but not determinative under the ADA and do not absolutely bar claims under the ADA.

Second, even if the individual has standing to sue, he or she might not be able to prove discrimination based on disability. This issue frequently arises in a challenge to the employer's long-term disability plan's benefit formula, which typically will grant only 24 months' benefits for mental and nervous disorders and have no time limit or a longer time limit for benefits for physical disorders. In *Parker v. Metropolitan Life Insurance Co.*, the employee was totally disabled because of depression and covered under the employer's long-term disability plan. The plan's benefits for mental and nervous disorders ceased after 24 months, but no time limit applied to benefits for other covered disabilities. When the employee's plan benefits were terminated after 24 months, she sued, claiming that the plan's denial of further benefits to her was discriminatory and violated the ADA. The Sixth Circuit Court of Appeals held that the ADA does not prohibit an insurer from providing lower benefits for mental and nervous disorders and the Supreme Court declined to review the decision. [121 F.3d 1006 (6th Cir. 1997), *cert. denied*, 522 U.S. 1084 (1998)] The U.S. Supreme Court also let stand a Third Circuit Court of Appeals decision that a disabled employee receiving disability benefit payments was "judicially estopped" from pursuing an ADA claim. [McNemar v. Disney Stores, 91 F.3d 610 (3d Cir. 1996), *cert. denied*, 519 U.S. 1115 (1997)]

Q 18:22 Is epilepsy an impairment protected by the ADA?

Epilepsy is a disability when it substantially limits one or more major life activities. Epilepsy may be a disability because of limitations that occur as the result of seizures or because of side effects or complications that can result from medications used to control the condition.

Example 1. Margaret underwent brain surgery to control seizures, but continued to experience two or three seizures per month. She is disabled because she is substantially limited in several major life activities such as walking, seeing, hearing, speaking, and working while having a seizure. She is limited in caring for herself (sometimes for more than a day) following particularly severe seizures.

Example 2. Bob takes medication to control his seizures, but the drugs make him drowsy, unable to concentrate, or unable to sleep. He has a disability under the ADA if he is substantially limited in major life activities such as sleeping, thinking, concentrating, and caring for himself as a result of the seizures.

Epilepsy also may be a disability because it substantially limited the individual in the past (i.e., before seizures were controlled).

Example 3. Carl has had epilepsy for five years. For the past three years he has not had a seizure, but before then he experienced severe and unpredictable seizures. As a result, he had to move back home with his parents because he could not live alone, could not drive, and rarely socialized with friends because he feared having a seizure in public. Even if Carl's epilepsy is not now substantially limiting, in the past it substantially limited his major life activities, such as caring for himself and interacting with others. Carl has a *record* of a disability.

Finally, epilepsy is a disability when the disease does not significantly affect the person's everyday activities, but the person's employer treats the person as though it does.

Example 4. Britt refuses to hire an individual with epilepsy because he assumes an epileptic is incapable of working without hurting himself or herself and others; he perceives an epileptic as having a disability.

For more information about epilepsy, see the EEOC Fact Sheet, *Questions and Answers About Epilepsy in the Workplace and the Americans With Disabilities Act (ADA)*.

The proposed EEOC regulations implementing the ADAAA specifically include epilepsy in the list of impairments that will consistently meet the definition of a disability. [Prop. EEOC Reg. § 1630.2(j)(5)]

Q 18:23 Is diabetes an impairment protected by the ADA?

According to the EEOC, diabetes is a disability when it substantially limits one or more of a person's major life activities or when its side effects or complications substantially limit a person's major life activities. Even if diabetes is not currently substantially limiting, because it is controlled by diet, exercise, oral medication, and/or insulin, and there are no serious side effects, the condition may be a disability because it was substantially limiting in the past (i.e., before the condition was diagnosed and adequately treated). Finally, diabetes is a disability when it does not significantly affect the everyday activities of the person who is diabetic, but the diabetic's employer treats him or her as if it does (e.g., assuming that the diabetic person is totally unable to work).

For more information about diabetes, see the EEOC Fact Sheet, *Questions and Answers About Diabetes in the Workplace and the Americans With Disabilities Act (ADA)*.

The proposed EEOC regulations implementing the ADAAA specifically include diabetes in the list of impairments that will consistently meet the definition of a disability. [Prop. EEOC Reg. § 1630.2(j)(5)]

Q 18:24 When is an intellectual impairment a disability for purposes of the ADA?

An individual is considered to have an intellectual disability when (1) the person's intellectual functioning level (IQ) is below 70–75, (2) the person has significant limitations in adaptive skill areas, and (3) the disability originated before the age of 18. "Adaptive skill areas " refers to basic skills needed for everyday life. They include communication, self-care, home living, social skills, leisure, health and safety, self-direction, functional academics (reading, writing, basic math), and work. Intellectual disabilities vary in degree and effect from person to person, just as individual capabilities vary considerably among people who do not have an intellectual disability.

Not everyone with an intellectual impairment is covered by the ADA. A person may meet the ADA's definition of "disability" in one of the following ways:

1. The individual's impairment substantially limits one or more major life activities.

Example 1. Arnold is capable of living on his own, but requires frequent assistance from family, friends, and neighbors with cleaning his apartment, shopping for groceries, getting to doctors' appointments, and cooking. He is unable to read at a level higher than third grade, and so needs someone to read his mail and help him pay bills. Arnold is substantially limited in caring for himself and, therefore, has a disability under the ADA.

2. A person may have two or more impairments that are not substantially limiting by themselves, but that taken together substantially limit one or more major life activities.

Example 2. Joe has a mild intellectual disability and a mild form of ADHD. Neither impairment, by itself, would significantly restrict any major life activity. Together, however, the two impairments substantially limit Joe's ability to concentrate, learn, and work. Joe is a person with a disability.

3. Even if an impairment does not *currently* substantially limit a major life activity, if the person has a past record or history of a substantially limiting intellectual disability, the person is covered under the ADA.

Example 3. During high school, Lisa was erroneously diagnosed as having an intellectual disability that substantially limited her ability to learn. Lisa has a past record or history of a disability and is protected under the ADA.

4. The ADA also protects individuals who, although they do not have a substantially limiting intellectual disability, are treated by an employer as if they do.

Example 4. Carol, who has a facial deformity that affects her speech, applies for a position as a secretary. She is denied employment because the interviewer believes she has an intellectual disability and that the condition will make Carol unable to communicate with clients effectively. The employer regards Carol as a person with a disability.

5. Finally, an individual who has a family member with an intellectual disability may be protected under the ADA. The ADA's protections extend to people who do not themselves have disabilities but are discriminated against on the basis of their association with a person with a disability. The association may be with family members, friends, or any other person. A person who experiences discrimination based on association has a right to protection under the ADA, but is not entitled to reasonable accommodation.

Example 5. Mike has a child with an intellectual disability. He applies for a position as an attorney at a law firm and mentions during a discussion with one of the interviewers that he has a child with an intellectual disability. Mike is denied employment because the firm believes his child's disability will cause him to be absent from work and will affect his productivity. Mike is protected under the ADA.

For more information about intellectual disabilities, see the EEOC Fact Sheet, *Questions and Answers About Persons With Intellectual Disabilities in the Workplace and the Americans With Disabilities Act (ADA)*.

The proposed EEOC regulations implementing the ADAAA specifically include intellectual disability in the list of impairments that will consistently meet the definition of a disability. [Prop. EEOC Reg. § 1630.2(j)(5)]

Q 18:25   When is a vision impairment a disability under the ADA?

A vision impairment is a disability if (1) it substantially limits a major life activity; (2) it was substantially limiting in the past (i.e., if an individual has a "record of" a substantially limiting impairment); or (3) an employer "regards" or treats an individual as having a substantially limiting vision impairment. Major life activities are those basic activities, including seeing, that an average person can perform with little or no difficulty.

Whether vision impairment substantially limits a major life activity depends on how significant the visual loss is. Whereas a person who has no sight at all is obviously substantially limited in seeing, the assessment of most vision impairments requires a more individualized approach. Although mitigating measures, such as corrective lenses and compensatory strategies that the body has developed, must be taken into account, they do not automatically exclude a person from coverage under the ADA.

Example 1. Harold wears eyeglasses, but they improve his poor vision only slightly. Even with eyeglasses, he cannot drive and needs strong magnification to read standard-sized print. Harold is substantially limited in seeing.

Mitigating measures do not include devices, reasonable accommodations, or compensatory strategies that simply compensate for the fact that an individual is substantially limited in seeing. For example, a totally blind person still meets the ADA's definition of disability even if he or she can move about freely with the use of a white cane or service animal, can work with assistive technology or a reader, and can use hearing to do what persons without vision impairment can do (e.g., cross a street).

Individuals with monocular vision in only one eye also may meet the ADA's definition of disability.

Example 2. Keith lost all sight in one eye as the result of an accident several years ago. He has learned some compensatory strategies, such as turning his head slightly to adjust for his loss of visual field and using shadows, highlights, and other visual cues to judge longer distances. However, he has lost both peripheral vision and stereopsis (the ability to combine two retinal images into one, which people with vision in both eyes accomplish easily). The loss of peripheral vision means that he is limited in seeing people or objects on his blind side and must position himself accordingly in meetings, theaters, or while walking down the street. Because he cannot see people approaching or standing on that side, he must rely on his hearing to detect that someone is near him and then must turn his head to see the person. The loss of stereopsis means that he has difficulty judging distances within a six-foot range, and thus cannot use his vision to guide him in reaching for objects or putting objects down on a table or other surface. Because of his lack of stereopsis, Keith must rely on memory or the sense of touch rather than vision to guide him in picking up and placing objects such as tools, pots and pans, books, and pens. Similarly, he must rely on memory and tactile clues to negotiate stairs and step on and off curbs. These tasks are more difficult for him because of his loss of vision and take him longer to perform than they take the average person. Keith is substantially limited in seeing, despite the use of compensatory strategies such as using hearing, touch, or memory to substitute for his lack of vision in one eye.

Some individuals with monocular vision have learned to compensate (e.g., by turning their head or using cues, such as shadows and highlights, to judge distances) effectively enough that they no longer are substantially limited. These individuals (as well as many others), however, may still be disabled for purposes of the ADA. A person who has a record of an impairment that substantially limited a major life activity in the past or who is regarded by his employer as having such an impairment also has a disability and, therefore, is covered by the ADA.

For more information about vision disabilities, see the EEOC Fact Sheet, *Questions and Answers About Blindness and Vision Impairments in the Workplace and the Americans with Disabilities Act (ADA)*.

Although mitigating measures generally are not taken into account in determining whether an impairment rises to the level of a disability, "ordinary eyeglasses or contact lenses"—defined in the ADAAA and the proposed regulation as lenses that are "intended to fully correct visual acuity or eliminate refractive error"—are considered when determining whether a person has a disability. [Prop. EEOC Reg. § 1630.2(j)(3) and corresponding Appendix § 1630.2(j)]

Effect on Welfare Benefits Plan Design

Q 18:26   Is a benefits plan discriminatory under the ADA if it adversely affects individuals with disabilities?

Not necessarily. An employer's uniformly applied leave policies or benefits plans will not be considered to violate the EEOC's ADA regulations merely because they do not address the special needs of every individual with a disability. Thus, for example, an employer may reduce the number of paid sick days that it provides to all employees, or reduce the amount of medical coverage that it provides to all employees, without violating the EEOC's regulations even if the reduction has an impact on employees with disabilities in need of greater sick leave and medical coverage. However, if the benefit reduction is adopted for discriminatory reasons, it will violate the EEOC's regulations. [Appendix to EEOC Reg. Part 1630—Interpretive Guidance on § 1630.5]

An EEOC release holds that an employer can provide a lower level of benefits under its disability retirement plan than under its service-related retirement plan without violating the ADA. No discrimination occurs as long as each plan treats disabled persons equally with nondisabled persons. However, if a disabled person qualified for both a disability pension and a service pension, he or she could not be required to take the less favorable benefit. [EEOC Rel. No. 915.002, CCH Pension Plan Guide ¶ 23909H]

A case from the Eleventh Circuit Court of Appeals held that a health plan did not violate the ADA when the plan was amended to limit coverage for treatments for a plan participant's disability. The plan participant, Sonia Chaudhry, was covered under her mother's health plan, which was administered by an HMO. Chaudhry suffered from a lung ailment that required her to undergo daily chest physiotherapy treatments to prevent mucus buildup. The plan as originally written imposed a limit of 60 visits for physical, occupational, and speech therapy. The HMO interpreted the limit to apply to Chaudhry's chest therapy and advised her that no further benefits were available after she had received 60 treatments. However, Chaudhry appealed the denial of further benefits to a state agency, which ruled that chest physiotherapy was not covered by the 60-treatment limit. As a result, the HMO resumed providing Chaudhry with daily treatments. However, the plan was subsequently amended to include chest physiotherapy in the 60-treatment limit, effective when the plan came up for renewal. Following the renewal date, the HMO provided Chaudhry with 60 treatments and then notified her that no further treatments were available. Chaudhry sued on the grounds that the plan amendment violated ERISA and the ADA. According to the Eleventh Circuit, the amended plan did not discriminate against Chaudhry because of her disability. The plan limited all beneficiaries who needed physical therapy, chest physiotherapy and similar procedures to 60 visits, regardless of the disease or disorder they suffered from and regardless of whether or not they were disabled. Chaudhry was not treated differently from any other beneficiary who might need recurring therapy, regardless of the underlying illness or condition. [Chaudhry v. Neighborhood Health Partnership, Inc., 178 Fed. Appx. 900 (11th Cir. 2006)]

Q 18:27   Does the ADA prohibit an employer from including a preexisting-condition clause in its health insurance plan?

No. The ADA's prohibition against limiting, segregating, and classifying employees on the basis of disability does not bar an employer from including a preexisting-condition clause in its health insurance plan, as long as the clause applies uniformly to all employees and is not used as a subterfuge to evade the purposes of the ADA (regardless of whether the provision was adopted before the ADA became effective with respect to the plan). The intent of the EEOC regulations is that employees with disabilities should be accorded equal access to whatever health insurance coverage the employer provides to other employees. The regulations state that they are not intended to affect preexisting condition clauses in employer-provided health insurance policies. A blanket preexisting-condition clause that excludes coverage for treatment of conditions that arose prior to the individual's eligibility for plan benefits is not a disability-based distinction and does not violate the ADA.

Accordingly, employers may continue to include such clauses in their plans, even if such clauses would adversely affect individuals with disabilities. [Appendix to EEOC Reg. Part 1630—Interpretive Guidance on § 1630.5; EEOC Interim Guidance on Application of ADA to Health Insurance, reprinted at 109 Daily Lab. Rep. (BNA) E-1 (June 9, 1993)]

> **Caution.** It is important to note that such clauses nonetheless must comply with the restrictions on preexisting-condition exclusions imposed by the Health Insurance Portability and Accountability Act of 1996 (HIPAA) and the 2010 Health Reform Act, to the extent they are applicable to the plan or insurance policy in question. The details of the HIPAA and 2010 Health Reform Act requirements are discussed in chapter 5.

Q 18:28 Does the ADA prohibit an employer from limiting plan coverage on a uniform basis for certain treatments or procedures?

No. An employer's welfare benefit plan may include one or more limits on covered benefits if such limits apply equally to all insured employees, regardless of whether they have a protected disability. The EEOC regulations also permit employer-provided health insurance plans to limit coverage for certain procedures or treatments to a specified number per year. The appendix to the EEOC regulations gives the following example of a permissible way to limit health plan coverage:

> If a health insurance plan provided coverage for five blood transfusions a year to all covered employees, it would not be discriminatory to offer this plan simply because a hemophiliac employee may require more than five blood transfusions annually. However, it would not be permissible to limit or deny the hemophiliac employee coverage for other procedures, such as heart surgery or the setting of a broken leg, even though the plan would not have to provide coverage for the additional blood transfusions that may be involved in these procedures. Likewise, limits may be placed on reimbursements for certain procedures or on the types of drugs or procedures covered (for example, limits on the number of permitted X-rays or noncoverage of experimental drugs or procedures), but each limitation must be applied equally to individuals with and without disabilities. [Appendix to EEOC Reg. Part 1630—Interpretive Guidance on § 1630.5]

The EEOC's Interim Guidance provides further examples of plan limits that pass muster under the ADA because they apply to all individuals on a uniform basis. Any universal limit or broad distinction that applies to individuals both with and without disabilities is not a disability-based distinction under the ADA. Additionally, a coverage limit on medical procedures that are not exclusively, or nearly exclusively, utilized for the treatment of a particular disability is not considered to be a disability-based distinction under the ADA.

The Interim Guidance also gives several examples of common health plan limits that it does not consider to be disability-based distinctions, because they apply to numerous conditions that affect individuals with and without disabilities: universal limits on, or universal exclusions for, treatment for mental/ nervous conditions, eye care, experimental drugs, experimental treatments, elective surgery, or the number of blood transfusions or X-rays. Even though such distinctions may have a greater impact on certain individuals with disabilities, the EEOC has stated that such provisions do not intentionally discriminate on the basis of disability and consequently do not violate the ADA. [EEOC Interim Guidance on Application of ADA to Health Insurance, reprinted at 109 Daily Lab. Rep. (BNA) E-1 (June 9, 1993)]

In contrast, a health-related insurance distinction that is disability-based (see Q 18:29) will violate the ADA unless it falls under one of the ADA's exceptions (see Qs 18:30, 18:31).

The Supreme Court let stand the Court of Appeals for the Fourth Circuit decision that Kmart Corp.'s provision of a long-term disability plan that capped benefits for mental disabilities at two years but provided benefits for physical disabilities up to age 65 did not violate Title I's prohibition on employment discrimination. [Lewis v. Kmart Corp., 180 F.3d 166 (4th Cir. 1999), *cert. denied*, 528 U.S. 1136 (2000)]

The employee claimed that Kmart's long-term disability plan discriminates against persons disabled by mental illness by providing inferior coverage without any actuarial or medical justification. Kmart argued that the Mental Health Parity Act, passed by Congress in September 1996, requires parity in the annual and lifetime limits of health insurance benefits but not disability benefits. [27 Pens. & Ben. Rep. (BNA) 5 (Feb. 1, 2000)]

The Second Circuit Court of Appeals also has ruled that the ADA does not prohibit employers from offering long-term disability benefit plans that provide less coverage for mental and emotional disabilities than for physical disabilities. [EEOC v. Staten Island Sav. Bank, 207 F.3d 144 (2d Cir. 2000)] By contrast, in another case involving Kmart's plan, the Court of Appeals for the Eleventh Circuit noted that other courts have held that offering different benefits for mental and physical disabilities does not violate the ADA because the law prohibits only discrimination between the disabled and the nondisabled; it does not prohibit distinctions between the mentally and physically disabled. However, the Eleventh Circuit concluded that the ADA demands more than impartial treatment of the disabled. "The essence of a disability-based discrimination claim," said the court, "is that an individual has been treated less favorably because of her disability. Thus, on its face, Kmart's plan discriminated by providing less favorable treatment for mentally disabled individuals."

Kmart argued that it was protected by a safe harbor provision in the ADA that exempts an employer from liability for distinctions made under a bona fide benefit plan. However, the court pointed out that an employer is not protected from discrimination claims if the benefit plan is used as a subterfuge to avoid the ADA (see Q 18:31). Therefore, the Eleventh Circuit sent the case back to the district court to determine if Kmart's plan was such a subterfuge—that is, whether the company specifically intended to discriminate on the basis of disability or whether it had some other benign intent. [Johnson v. Kmart Corp., 273 F.3d 1035 (11th Cir. 2001)]

A contentious issue has been whether infertility limits or exclusions are permissible in group health plans. As noted previously (see Qs 18:10 and 18:11), at least one court has held that such a restriction would not be disability-based, because it affects both infertile young women who are disabled and older women who became infertile because of their age. It also held that reproduction is not a "major life activity" because it is not engaged in with the same frequency as the EEOC-listed activities, sparking a strongly worded reply from another court to the effect that quality, not quantity, is what counts. The Second Circuit Court of Appeals held that procreation is an integral part of life and thus infertility is a disability under the ADA. [Krauel v. Iowa Methodist Med. Ctr., 915 F. Supp. 102 (S.D. Iowa 1995); Pacourek v. Inland Steel Co., 916 F. Supp. 797 (N.D. Ill. 1996)] The issue has been resolved by the Supreme Court, which held in *Bragdon v. Abbott* [524 U.S. 624 (1998)] that reproduction is a major life activity.

Courts have also taken the position that employer-provided health plans may limit or exclude coverage for certain medical procedures without violating the ADA. For example, the Sixth Circuit Court of Appeals considered a group health plan that excluded organ transplants other than cornea, bone marrow, kidney, and liver. The plan refused to pay for a member's successful heart transplant. It held that the ADA was not violated by covering some organ transplants but not heart transplants, stating that no impermissible disability-based distinction existed. [Lenox v. Healthwise of Ky., 149 F.3d 453 (6th Cir. 1998)]

Caution. Although a coverage limitation may not rise to the level of a disability-based distinction that violates the ADA, such a limitation must comply with requirements and restrictions imposed by HIPAA and the 2010 Health Reform Act, to the extent they are applicable to the plan or insurance policy in question. The details of the HIPAA and 2010 Health Reform Act requirements are discussed in chapter 5.

Q 18:29   What is a disability-based distinction?

According to the EEOC, a *disability-based distinction* singles out:

1. A particular disability (e.g., AIDS, deafness, or schizophrenia);

2. A discrete group of disabilities (e.g., cancers, muscular dystrophies, or kidney diseases); or

3. Disability in general (e.g., all conditions that substantially limit a major life activity).

[EEOC Interim Guidance on Application of ADA to Health Insurance, reprinted at 109 Daily Lab. Rep. (BNA) E-1 (June 9, 1993)]

Thus, a group health plan's refusal to cover high-dosage chemotherapy treatment for breast cancer has been held to be a prohibited disability-based distinction if it is likely that the claimant will be able to prove at trial that it is an accepted treatment for breast cancer and the plan does cover high-dosage chemotherapy for other conditions for which it is an accepted treatment. [Henderson v. Bodine Aluminum, 70 F.3d 958 (8th Cir. 1995)]

Q 18:30   Does the ADA prohibit an employer from excluding or limiting coverage for a particular disability (such as AIDS) or group of disabilities?

Such discrimination generally is prohibited. However, provided that such provisions are not a subterfuge to evade the purposes of the ADA, the ADA does not prohibit or restrict:

1. An insurer, hospital, medical service company, health maintenance organization (HMO), any agent or entity that administers benefits plans, or similar organizations from underwriting risks, classifying risks, or administering such risks that are based on, or not inconsistent with, state laws that regulate insurance;

2. A covered employer from establishing, sponsoring, observing, or administering the terms of a bona fide benefit plan that are based on underwriting risks, classifying risks, or administering such risks that are based on, or not inconsistent with, state laws that regulate insurance; or

3. A covered employer from establishing, sponsoring, observing, or administering the terms of a bona fide benefit plan that is not subject to state laws that regulate insurance.

[ADA § 501(c); 42 U.S.C. § 12201(c); EEOC Reg. § 1630.16(f)]

The burden will be on the employer to demonstrate that a disability-based provision complies with the ADA. [EEOC Interim Guidance on Application of ADA to Health Insurance, reprinted at 109 Daily Lab. Rep. (BNA) E-1 (June 9, 1993)]

The Appendix to the EEOC regulations notes that the purpose of these provisions is to permit the development and administration of benefit plans in accordance with accepted principles of risk assessment. These provisions are not intended to disrupt the current regulatory structure for self-insured employers, nor, according to the Appendix to the EEOC regulations, are they intended to disrupt the current nature of insurance underwriting or current insurance industry practices in sales, underwriting, pricing, administrative and other services, claims, and similar insurance-related activities based on classification of risks as regulated by the states. The permitted activities do not violate the EEOC regulations even if they result in limitations on individuals with disabilities, unless used as a subterfuge to evade the purposes of the regulations. The question of subterfuge will be determined without regard to the date that the insurance plan or employee benefit plan was adopted. (See Q 18:31.)

The Appendix to the EEOC regulations cautions (without distinguishing the different treatment accorded self-insured plans under the ADA) that an employer or other covered entity cannot deny a qualified individual with a disability equal access to insurance or subject a qualified individual with a disability to different terms or conditions of insurance based on disability alone, unless the disability poses increased risks. Decisions not based on risk classification must conform to nondiscrimination requirements. [Appendix to EEOC Reg. Part 1630—Interpretive Guidance on § 1630.16(f)]

The EEOC issued Interim Guidance expanding on the preceding explanation and clarifying what is required to demonstrate that a challenged disability-based health plan provision complies with the ADA.

Insured plans. If the disability-based provision is contained in an insured health plan, the respondent must show that (1) the provision is not a subterfuge to evade the purposes of the ADA (see Q 18:31) and (2) the plan is a bona fide insured health insurance plan that is not inconsistent with state law. The plan will be treated as bona fide if it exists and pays benefits and its terms have been accurately communicated to eligible employees. It will be treated as consistent with state law if it is not inconsistent with state law as interpreted by the appropriate state authorities.

Self-insured plans. A self-insured health plan need prove only that the plan is bona fide (that is, it exists, pays benefits, and its terms have been accurately communicated to covered employees) and that the disability-based provision is not being used as a subterfuge to evade the purposes of the ADA (see Q 18:31). [EEOC Interim Guidance on Application of ADA to Health Insurance, reprinted at 109 Daily Lab. Rep. (BNA) E-1 (June 9, 1993)]

The courts have also upheld the proposition that the ADA does not generally regulate the content of an employer-sponsored health plan. The Fifth Circuit Court of Appeals affirmed a district court's decision that the ADA antidiscrimination provision does not regulate the terms and content of goods and services, including health insurance policies. The insurance company that issued a policy containing an AIDS limit of $10,000 was found not to be liable for the $400,000 in hospital bills for AIDS treatments. [McNeil v. Time Ins. Co., 224 F.3d 767 (5th Cir. 2000)]

In a similar decision, the Sixth Circuit held that an employer-sponsored plan's denial of benefits for speech therapy did not violate the ADA. According to the court, employer-sponsored health plans are not goods offered by a place of accommodation and, therefore, the contents of such plans are not governed by the ADA. [Kolling v. Blue Cross Blue Shield of Mich., 318 F.3d 715 (6th Cir. 2003)]

Caution. Although a coverage limitation may not violate the ADA, such a limitation must comply with requirements and restrictions imposed by HIPAA and the 2010 Health Reform Act to the extent they are applicable to the plan or insurance policy in question. The details of the HIPAA and 2010 Health Reform Act requirements are discussed in chapter 5.

Q 18:31   When is a disability-based distinction in a health insurance plan considered to be a subterfuge to evade the purposes of the ADA?

A disability-based provision contained in a health insurance plan (regardless of whether the plan is insured or self-insured) might be viewed as a subterfuge to evade the purposes of the ADA. It is irrelevant whether the provision was adopted prior to the effective date of the ADA, as the ADA does not contain a safe harbor for preexisting plans.

For purposes of the ADA, a subterfuge exists when the disability-based disparate treatment is not justified by the risks or costs associated with the disability. This will be determined on a case-by-case basis, taking into account the totality of the circumstances.

The employer bears the burden of proving that a challenged disability-based distinction contained in a health insurance plan is not a subterfuge to evade the purposes of the ADA. The EEOC's Interim Guidance on Application of ADA to Health Insurance provides five possible business/insurance justifications for health plan provisions and states that other methods also may be used. The five methods relating to health plans are the following:

1. The employer may prove that the provision actually is not disability-based (for example, an annual dollar limit on benefits that applies to all conditions in the same way).

2. The employer may prove that the provision is justified by legitimate actuarial data or by actual or reasonably anticipated experience and that conditions with comparable actuarial data are treated in the same fashion. In other words, it may prove that such disparate treatment results from the application of legitimate risk classification and underwriting procedures to the increased risks of the disability (with increased cost to the health plan) and is not a result of the disability per se. For this purpose, seriously outdated and/or inaccurate actuarial data does not suffice. The respondent may not rely on actuarial data about a disability which is based on myths, fears, stereotypes, or false assumptions (or assumptions that are no longer true) about a disability.

3. The employer may prove that the disparate treatment is necessary to ensure that the plan satisfies commonly accepted or legally required standards for the fiscal soundness of the plan. (However, the Interim Guidance narrowly defines *necessary* to mean that there is no nondisability-based health insurance plan change that could be made.)

4. The employer may prove that the provision is necessary (again, *necessary* is used to mean that there is no nondisability-based change that could be made) to prevent an unacceptable change in the coverage of the health insurance plan or an unacceptable change in the premiums charged for such coverage. For this purpose, an "unacceptable" change means a drastic increase in premium payments, copayments, or deductibles, or a drastic alteration to the scope of coverage or level of benefits provided, which would make the health insurance plan effectively unavailable to a significant number of other employees, or so unattractive as to result in significant adverse selection, or so unattractive that the employer cannot compete with other employers in the community in recruiting and maintaining qualified workers due to the superiority of their health insurance plans.

5. If a denial, under the disability-based provision, of coverage for a particular treatment is being challenged, the employer may prove by reliable scientific evidence that the particular treatment has no medical value (that is, that it does not cure the condition, slow the degeneration/deterioration or harm resulting from the condition, alleviate the condition's symptoms, or maintain the disabled individual's current health status).

[EEOC Interim Guidance on Application of ADA to Health Insurance, reprinted at 109 Daily Lab. Rep. (BNA) E-1 (June 9, 1993)]

Q 18:32   Does the ADA prohibit an employer from excluding or limiting coverage under an employee benefit plan because of concerns about the impact on the plan of the disability of someone else with whom the employee has a relationship?

Yes. The ADA prohibits employers, or others acting on their behalf, from denying employment opportunities to job applicants or employees who are otherwise qualified individuals with a disability because of the known disability of an individual with whom he or she is known to have a relationship or association.

In the case of employee benefits, this "association" provision is most likely to crop up in the context of group health coverage. The EEOC has taken the position that the association provision prohibits an employer from making employment decisions about any person, whether or not that person has a disability, because of concerns about the impact on the employer's health insurance plan of the disability of someone else with whom that person has a relationship.

For example, an employer would violate the ADA if it denied employment to a qualified individual because that individual had a seriously ill dependent who would be eligible for enrollment in the employer's health plan. Similarly, if a person with whom an employee has a relationship has a disability (such as AIDS), coverage for the employee cannot be denied or limited on the basis of a suspicion or worry that the employee may have it as well and will incur significant expenses under the employee's health insurance plan. This is because the ADA's broad definition of disabled individuals also includes any employee who is perceived as having a disability even if he or she actually does not. [ADA §§ 3(2)(C), 102(4); 42 U.S.C. §§ 12102(2)(C), 12112(4); EEOC Interim Guidance on Application of ADA to Health Insurance, reprinted at 109 Daily Lab. Rep. (BNA) E-1 (June 9, 1993)]

The EEOC has reiterated that position in Questions and Answers About the Association Provision of the Americans with Disabilities Act, available online at *http://www.eeoc.gov/facts/association_ada.html*.

According to the EEOC, an employer may not deny an employee health care coverage that is available to other employees because of the disability of a person with whom the employee has a relationship or association.

Example 1. Employer X, who provides health insurance to the dependents of its employees, learns that Jaime, an applicant for a management position, has a spouse with a disability. X determines that providing insurance to Jaime's spouse will lead to increased health insurance costs. X violates the ADA if it decides not to hire Jaime based on the increased health insurance costs that will be caused by his wife's disability. It would also violate the ADA for X to offer Jaime the position without the benefit of health insurance for his dependents. X may not reduce the level of health insurance benefits it offers Jaime because his wife has a disability; nor may it subject Jaime to different terms or conditions of insurance than it offers to other employees.

On the other hand, the ADA only requires employers to provide employees with dependents who have disabilities equal access to whatever health insurance coverage is offered to other employees. An employer is not required to provide *additional* health insurance coverage to such employees.

Example 2. Employer Y's health insurance plan will pay for only a certain number of days of inpatient care for employees' dependents each year. Karen, an employee, informs Y that her husband's disability will require more time in the hospital than the plan covers. The ADA does not require Y to provide additional health insurance coverage to meet Karen's husband's needs.

A health insurance plan provision that limits the number of days of inpatient care for employees' dependents affects individuals with many kinds of conditions, only some of which are disabilities. Consequently, the limitation is not a disability-based distinction and would not violate the ADA.

If, however, an employer's health insurance plan has terms or provisions that make disability-based distinctions (e.g., provisions that single out specific disabilities, groups of disabilities, or disability generally), the plan itself may violate the ADA unless the employer can demonstrate that the plan provision is not a subterfuge to evade the purposes of the ADA.

Terminating an employee who enrolls a disabled dependent in a group health plan may also violate the ADA. In one case, an appellate court ruled that an employer may have violated the law by terminating an employee shortly after she gave birth to a disabled child and enrolled the child in the employer's group health plan. The employer claimed that the employee's position was eliminated as part of a reorganization of the employer's management structure. However, the court said the short two-month period between the birth of the child and the termination coupled with the employee's unblemished employment record, which spanned more than a decade, cast genuine doubt on the employer's stated reason for the termination. Therefore, whether the termination was a pretext for discrimination should be decided at trial. [Strate v. Midwest Bank-centre, Inc., 398 F.3d 1011 (8th Cir. 2005)]

> **Caution.** Although a limitation on eligibility or coverage under a plan may not violate the ADA, such a limitation must comply with requirements and restrictions imposed by HIPAA and the 2010 Health Reform Act, to the extent they are applicable to the plan or insurance policy in question. The details of the HIPAA and 2010 Health Reform Act requirements are discussed in chapter 5.

Q 18:33   Does the ADA require that dependent coverage under a health insurance plan be the same as employee coverage?

No. The ADA does not require that dependent coverage under a health insurance plan be the same in scope as employee coverage. Thus, for example, a plan could limit a particular benefit to $100,000 for employees and $50,000 for dependents or could cover prescription drugs for employees only. However, the EEOC takes the position that dependent coverage is a benefit available to the employee by virtue of employment, so all insurance terms, provisions, and conditions concerning dependent coverage are subject to the same ADA standards (including standards regarding disability-based distinctions) that apply to employee coverage (see Qs 18:31–18:32).

> **Caution.** Although a coverage limitation may not violate the ADA, such a limitation must comply with requirements and restrictions imposed by HIPAA and the 2010 Health Reform Act, to the extent they are applicable to the plan or insurance policy in question. The details of the HIPAA and the 2010 Health Reform Act requirements are discussed in chapter 5.

Q 18:34   Can employees demand more leave than is provided under an employer's benefit plans as a reasonable accommodation for a disability?

The ADA requires covered employers to make whatever "reasonable accommodation" is necessary to permit an employee with a disability to perform his or her job. And, although it may seem like a paradox, the EEOC and the courts have concluded that a period of time off from the job may be a required reasonable accommodation.

The First Circuit Court of Appeals held that a medical leave of absence may be a reasonable accommodation in some situations. [Garcia-Ayala v. Lederle Parenterals Inc., 212 F.3d 638 (1st Cir. 2000)] An employee who was being treated for breast cancer began receiving benefits under her company's short-term disability plan. The employer's policy was to reserve an employee's job for one year when an employee was absent from work on short-term disability. Therefore, when the employee in question had not returned to work after one year the employer terminated her employment. The employee requested additional leave until her treatment was completed, but the employer refused the request. The employee sued the employer for violating the ADA by failing to make reasonable accommodation for her disability.

In reaching its decision, the First Circuit noted that to be protected by the ADA an employee must show that he or she is able to perform the essential functions of the job with or without reasonable accommodation. Moreover, the court acknowledged that an essential function of any job is the ability to appear for work. Nonetheless, the court said a medical leave of absence can be a reasonable accommodation in some cases. In the instant case, the court said the additional leave was reasonable accommodation because the requested leave was for less than two months, the employee's job was filled by temporary employees, and the employer had no pressing business need to hire a permanent replacement. Therefore, granting the additional leave would not have imposed a hardship on the employer.

On the other hand, the Seventh Circuit Court of Appeals held that an employer was not required by the ADA to accommodate an employee's request for unlimited sick days. According to the court, an employee is protected by the ADA if he or she is a "qualified individual with a disability" who can perform the essential functions of the job either with or without reasonable accommodation. However, the employee in question was unable to perform a very essential job function—regular attendance—with reasonable accommodation. In fact, the court said the accommodation the employee requested—unlimited sick days without penalty—was unreasonable as a matter of law. Employers are not obligated to tolerate erratic, unreliable attendance or to provide an accommodation that would impose a hardship on the business. [EEOC v. Yellow Freight Sys., 253 F.3d 943 (7th Cir. 2001)]

In a similar case, the Eighth Circuit concluded that an individual who worked two days a week administering dialysis to seriously ill patients was not a "qualified individual with a disability." The individual, who suffered from depression, was repeatedly absent without notice and admitted that she could not come to work on a regular and reliable basis, which was essential for her position. [Rask v. Fresenius Med. Care N. Am., 509 F.3d 466 (8th Cir. 2007)]

In addition, EEOC guidance on the ADA makes it clear that permitting the use of paid or unpaid leave is a form of reasonable accommodation when necessitated by an employee's disability. The EEOC guidance emphasizes, however, that an employer is not required to provide paid leave beyond what is provided to other similarly situated employees. For example, if employees normally get 10 days of paid leave and an employee with a disability needs 15 days, the employee should be allowed to use 10 days of paid leave and 5 days of unpaid leave. [EEOC Enforcement Guidance: Reasonable Accommodation and Undue Hardship Under the Americans With Disabilities Act, Mar. 1, 1999]

The EEOC guidance suggests that leave would be a reasonable accommodation in the following circumstances:

- Obtaining medical treatment (e.g., surgery, psychotherapy, substance abuse treatment, or dialysis), rehabilitation services, or physical or occupational therapy
- Recuperating from an illness or episodic manifestation of a disability
- Obtaining repairs on a wheelchair, accessible van, or prosthetic device
- Avoiding temporary adverse conditions in the work environment (such as an air conditioning breakdown causing unusually warm temperature that could seriously harm an employee with multiple sclerosis)
- Training a service animal (e.g., a guide dog)
- Receiving training in the use of Braille or sign language

Practice Pointer. The EEOC guidance makes it clear that leave may not be the only reasonable accommodation. The ADA does not require an employer to provide an employee's preferred accommodation. Therefore, an employer may provide an alternative accommodation as long as it is effective and eliminates the need for leave.

Disability Inquiries and Confidentiality

Q 18:35 May an employer make inquiries regarding an employee's or prospective employee's disability?

An employer may not ask questions about disability or require medical examinations until *after* it makes a conditional job offer to the applicant. [42 U.S.C. § 12112(d)(2)]

Once a job offer has been made, an employer may make medical inquiries and require a medical examination, provided all entering employees in the same job category are subjected to the same inquiries and examinations regardless of disability. [42 U.S.C. § 12112 (d)(2)]

In addition, an employer may make medical inquiries or require medical examinations of existing employees, provided they are job-related and required by business necessity. Inquiries may include questions about the ability of an employee to perform job-related functions. [29 C.F.R. § 1630.14]

Q 18:36 Can an employer disclose medical information about an employee to others?

Any confidential medical information about a job applicant or employee must be kept strictly confidential and should not be maintained with regular personnel files. Medical information should be obtained on separate forms and maintained in a separate medical file that is accessible only to designated individuals. [29 C.F.R. § 1630.14]

Medical information can be confidential even if it contains no medical diagnosis or treatment information and even if it is not generated by a health care professional. For example, an employee's request for reasonable accommodation necessarily includes information about an employee's disability and, therefore, is considered medical information subject to the ADA's confidentiality requirements.

However, the ADA recognizes that employers may need to disclose medical information in certain circumstances. Information that is otherwise confidential under the ADA may be disclosed:

- to supervisors and managers when they need medical information to provide a reasonable accommodation or to meet an employee's work restrictions;

- to first aid and safety personnel if an employee would need emergency treatment or require some other assistance (such as help during an emergency evacuation) because of a medical condition;

- to individuals investigating compliance with the ADA and with similar state and local laws; and

- to appropriate personnel pursuant to workers' compensation laws (e.g., to a state workers' compensation office to evaluate a claim) or for insurance purposes.

Q 18:37   May an employer make disability-related inquiries when an employee uses sick leave?

According to the EEOC, an employer is entitled to know why an employee is requesting sick leave. Therefore, an employer may ask an employee to justify his or her use of sick leave by providing a doctor's note or other explanation—as long as the employer has a policy of requiring all employees, with and without disabilities, to do so. [EEOC Enforcement Guidance on Disability-Related Inquiries and Medical Examinations of Employees Under the Americans with Disabilities Act (ADA), Q&A 15]

If the employee's leave request does not specify a return date, or if the employee needs continued leave beyond the period originally granted, the employer may require the employee to provide periodic updates on his or her condition and possible date of return. However, if the employer has granted a fixed period, and the employee has not requested additional leave, the employer cannot require the employee to provide periodic updates. This does not, however, bar an employer from calling an employee on extended leave to check on the employee's progress or express concern for the employee's health. [EEOC Enforcement Guidance on Disability-Related Inquiries and Medical Examinations of Employees Under the Americans with Disabilities Act (ADA), Q&A 15]

When an employee who has been on leave for a medical condition seeks to return to work, the employer can make disability-related inquiries or require the employee to submit to a medical examination if the employer has reasonable concerns that the condition continues to impair the employee's ability to perform the job or that the employee's condition poses a direct threat to the health and safety of others. Such inquiries must be limited in scope to what is necessary to make an assessment of the employee's ability to work. The employer may not use an employee's leave as justification for making far-ranging disability-related inquiries or requiring an unrelated medical examination. [EEOC Enforcement Guidance on Disability-Related Inquiries and Medical Examinations of Employees Under the Americans with Disabilities Act (ADA), Q&A 17]

Q 18:38   Do the ADA confidentiality rules protect information obtained in connection with other employment laws, such as the FMLA?

At least one court has held that inappropriate disclosure of medical information provided on an FMLA request form will violate the medical privacy protections of the ADA [Doe v. U.S. Postal Serv., 317 F.3d 339 (D.C. Cir. 2003)]

The employee in the case, John Doe, was a maintenance worker for the U.S. Postal Service. After missing several weeks of work due to an AIDS-related illness, Doe was informed that he had to submit an administrative form and a medical certificate containing an explanation of the nature of his illness. The letter warned that if he failed to submit the forms he would face potential disciplinary action for being absent without leave. The letter also informed Doe that his condition might qualify for leave under the FMLA. The letter included the forms to be used to apply for FMLA leave.

Doe decided to apply for FMLA and completed the necessary forms. One portion of the medical form required a health care provider to certify that the employee suffers from a serious health condition and to describe the medical facts supporting that certification. On that form, Doe's physician stated that Doe had "AIDS related complex" and "chronic HIV infection." FMLA forms are generally submitted to an employee's direct supervisor. However, Doe had never told anyone at the Postal Service about his HIV status and was reluctant to reveal that sensitive information to his supervisor. Therefore, he submitted the form to a Postal Service administrative assistant.

The Postal Service ultimately denied Doe's request for leave and Doe returned to work. On his return, he discovered that his HIV status had become common knowledge among his coworkers, many of whom commented to him about it. Several coworkers identified Doe's supervisor as the source of the information.

Doe initially filed a complaint with the EEOC, but later withdrew the complaint and filed a lawsuit alleging that Postal Service officials had improperly disclosed medical information contained in his FMLA certification form. The lawsuit claimed that the disclosure violated medical confidentiality provisions of the ADA. (Although the ADA does not apply directly to federal government employers, the ADA's medical confidentiality rules are incorporated by reference into the Rehabilitation Act, which prohibits federal employers from discriminating on the basis of disability.)

The Postal Service sought to have Doe's lawsuit dismissed on the grounds that Doe had not produced enough evidence to support his claim that a Postal Service employee had disclosed medical information obtained from his FMLA form. In addition, the Postal Service claimed that such a disclosure—if, indeed, it happened—would not violate the ADA because that law only prohibits disclosure of medical information obtained in response to an employer's "inquiry" regarding the ability of an employee to perform job-related functions. According to the Postal Service, there was no "inquiry" into Doe's medical condition because Doe submitted the FMLA form voluntarily.

Although it did not decide the merits of Doe's claim, the United States Court of Appeals ruled that Doe's lawsuit could continue. Most significantly, the court concluded that if Postal Service officials did disclose information from Doe's FMLA form, that disclosure would be in violation of the ADA. According to the court, even if Doe can be said to have submitted the FMLA form voluntarily, that doesn't mean he volunteered his medical diagnosis. The Postal Service conditioned Doe's receipt of FMLA leave on submission of medical documentation. Therefore, it was the Postal Service, not Doe, that initiated the inquiry into his medical condition by asking for medical certification. Moreover, as required for protection under the ADA, that inquiry related to Doe's ability to perform his job because the FMLA provides for medical leave only when an employee suffers from a serious health condition that makes the employee unable to work.

The Postal Service argued that Doe could have avoided disclosing his medical condition by forgoing FMLA leave. However, the court said that reasoning would force employees to choose between waiving their right to avoid being publicly identified as having a disability and exercising their legal rights, including the right to FMLA leave and the right to "reasonable accommodation" under the ADA, which may depend on disclosure of their medical conditions. And, according to the court, Congress did not intend to require such a choice. Instead, the ADA's confidentiality requirement strikes a balance by ensuring that information disclosed in response to an employer's medical inquiry spreads no farther than necessary to satisfy the legitimate needs of both the employer and the employee.

Q 18:39 Can an employer identify employees who will need assistance in the event of an emergency?

In the wake of terrorist attacks on the World Trade Center and the Pentagon on September 11, 2001, employers have become increasingly concerned about evacuating employees in the event of an emergency. Of particular concern are employees who would need assistance during an evacuation.

However, identifying those employees can be tricky. Some employees may need assistance because of medical conditions that are not visually apparent. Others may have obvious disabilities or medical conditions, but may not need assistance. Consequently, the EEOC says that employers are permitted to ask employees to self-identify whether they will require assistance because of a disability or medical condition.

There are three ways that an employer may obtain the necessary information:

1. After making a job offer, but before employment begins, an employer may ask all individuals whether they will need assistance during an emergency.

2. An employer may periodically survey all of its current employees to determine whether they will require assistance in an emergency, as long as the employer makes it clear that self-identification is voluntary and explains the purpose for requesting the information.

3. Whether or not all employees are surveyed, an employer may ask employees with known disabilities whether they will require assistance in the event of an emergency.

An employer should not assume that every individual with an obvious disability will need assistance during an evacuation. Some blind individuals may prefer to walk down flights of stairs unassisted. People with disabilities are generally in the best position to assess their particular needs.

The EEOC has made it clear that employers may ask individuals who indicate a need for assistance to describe the type of assistance they think will be needed. One way that this can be done is to distribute a memo with an attached form requesting information. The employer also may have a follow-up conversation with disabled employees to obtain more detailed information—for example, whether an individual who uses a wheelchair because of limited mobility can, in an emergency, walk with or without crutches or a cane; whether an individual will need special medication or equipment (such as a carrier strap for a wheelchair or a mask for a respiratory condition) in the event of an emergency.

However, an employer is entitled only to the information necessary for it to be prepared to provide assistance. This means that, in most instances, an employer does not need to know the details of an employee's medical condition. Furthermore, the employer should inform employees who are asked about their need for emergency assistance that any information they provide will be kept confidential and shared only with those persons who have responsibility for implementing emergency evacuation plans.

The ADA requires employers to keep medical information about job applicants and employees confidential. However, the ADA rules contain an exception that allows employers to share medical information with first aid and safety personnel (see Q 18:36). According to the EEOC, medical professionals, emergency coordinators, floor captains, colleagues who have volunteered to act as "buddies," building security officers, and other nonmedical personnel who are responsible for ensuring safe evacuation are entitled to the information that they need to fulfill their responsibilities under the employer's emergency evacuation plan. [EEOC Fact Sheet on Obtaining and Using Employee Medical Information as Part of Emergency Evacuation Procedures (Oct. 27, 2005)]

Q 18:40 May a counselor in an employee assistance program ask an employee seeking help for personal problems about any physical or mental conditions the employee may have?

Yes, but only if certain conditions are met. The EEOC says an employee assistance program (EAP) counselor may ask employees about their medical conditions if (1) the counselor does not act for or on behalf of the employer, (2) the counselor is obligated to shield any information he or she receives from employment decision makers, and (3) the counselor has no power to affect employment decisions. [EEOC Enforcement Guidance on Disability-Related Inquiries and Medical Examinations of Employees Under the Americans with Disabilities Act (ADA), Q&A 20]

Q 18:41 May an employer make disability-related inquiries in connection with a voluntary wellness program?

Yes, but employers should exercise caution in setting up such programs to make sure they are strictly voluntary.

The ADA allows employers to conduct voluntary medical examinations and activities, including voluntary medical histories, as part of an employee health program as long as any medical records acquired as part of the wellness program are kept confidential and separate from personnel records. [EEOC Enforcement Guidance on Disability-Related Inquiries and Medical Examinations of Employees Under the Americans with Disabilities Act (ADA), Q&A 22]

Voluntary wellness programs often include blood pressure screening, cholesterol testing, glaucoma testing, and cancer detection screening. Programs that simply promote a healthier life style but do not ask for disability-related information or require medical examinations are not subject to the ADA requirements. For example, a smoking cessation program that is available to anyone who smokes and only asks participants to disclose how much they smoke does not implicate the ADA.

A wellness program is voluntary as long as the employer neither requires participation nor penalizes employees who do not participate. A wellness program with strings attached will violate the ADA. In two recent opinion letters, the EEOC considered—and rejected—employer programs that required employees to participate in a health risk assessment as a prerequisite for obtaining health benefits.

In one case, the employer implemented a clinical heath risk assessment as a requirement for obtaining coverage under its self-funded group health plans. The health risk assessment included a health-related questionnaire, a blood pressure test, and drawing of blood for a blood panel screen. Individual information from the assessment was provided directly to employees, with the employer receiving only aggregate results. Employees declining to participate and members of their families became ineligible for coverage under the employer's health plan. Although the EEOC noted that it has not taken a formal position on this issue, it concluded that requiring all employees to take a health risk assessment that includes disability-related inquiries and medical examinations as a prerequisite to obtaining health insurance violates the ADA. Such a program is not a voluntary wellness program because employees who do not participate are denied a benefit, and hence are penalized for nonparticipation. [ADA: Disability-Related Inquiries and Medical Examinations; Health Risk Assessment (Mar. 6, 1009)]

In a second case, the EEOC examined an employer's requirement that employees complete a health risk assessment in order to receive monies from an employer-funded health reimbursement arrangement. The assessment consisted of more than 100 questions in several categories, including family health history, self care, personal health, women's health, older adult health, and "health choices" regarding nutrition, physical activity, alcohol and tobacco, and safety. Here again, the EEOC concluded that the assessment violated the ADA. Even if it could be considered part of a wellness program, the program is not voluntary because it penalizes any employee who does not complete the questionnaire by making him or her ineligible to receive reimbursement for health expenses. [ADA: Health Risk Assessments (Aug. 10, 2009)] In reaching its conclusion the EEOC noted that many of the questions on the assessment questionnaire constituted disability-related inquires (e.g., questions about how often employees feel depressed; whether they have been told they have certain conditions such as asthma, cancer, heart disease, or diabetes; how many prescription medications they take; and how much alcohol they drink). On the other hand, the EEOC acknowledged that some questions are not likely to elicit information about disability and, therefore, are not subject to the ADA restrictions. Those questions asked employees whether they see a doctor for routine care and asked about "health choices," such as how many servings of fruits or vegetables they eat and how much they exercise.

Caution. The 2010 Health Reform imposes new requirements for employer wellness programs. For a discussion of these requirements see chapter 5.

Procedures for ADA Claims

Q 18:42 Is an employee required to file a complaint with the Equal Employment Opportunity Commission before filing a lawsuit under the ADA?

Yes, an employee must file a complaint with the EEOC before the initiation of a federal lawsuit under the ADA. [EEOC Compliance Manual, Section 2, Threshold Issues]

Q 18:43 What are the time limits for filing a complaint under the ADA?

An employee is generally required to file a complaint with the EEOC within a specified number of days after an unlawful employment practice occurred. The time limit depends on whether the violation occurred in a jurisdiction that has a state or local fair employment practices agency (FEPA) with the authority to grant or seek relief. The deadline is 180 days in a state or locality that *does not* have a FEPA and 300 days in a state or locality that *does* have a FEPA. However, because most jurisdictions have FEPAs, the limitations period is usually 300 days. (See further discussion in chapter 17.)

Q 18:44 Can an employee who has claimed disability benefits also claim protection under the ADA?

In a recent case, the Seventh Circuit Court of Appeals held that a police officer who applied for and received a disability pension was barred from suing for reasonable accommodation of his disability under the ADA. In seeking his disability pension, the police officer swore before the pension board that he was unable to perform the essential functions of his job, thus creating a record inimical to his ADA claim that he could perform, but was denied, light duty assignments.

According to the court, "[C]laiming disability benefits and asserting ADA claims are not always mutually exclusive, but a plaintiff's sworn assertion in an application for disability benefit that she is, for example, 'unable to work' will appear to negate an essential element of her ADA case—at least if she does not offer a sufficient explanation." Also, in the police officer's case, the court found no satisfactory explanation for the inconsistency. [Butler v. Round Lake Police Dep't, 2009 U.S. App. LEXIS 23602 (7th Cir. Oct. 27, 2009); *see also* Cleveland v. Policy Mgmt. Syst. Corp., 526 U.S 795 (1999), dealing with the tension between the ADA and Social Security disability claims).]

Q 18:45 Can an employer require an employee to agree to binding arbitration of employment disputes, including discrimination claims under the ADA?

It is a rare employer that has not been the target of a lawsuit by a disgruntled employee who claims to have been treated unfairly in terms of compensation, benefits, or other terms and conditions of employment. In some cases, the employee's claims are legitimate; in other cases, they are not. In either event, a lawsuit is a costly proposition for an employer, even if the employer ultimately wins. Moreover, an employer runs the risk of losing at trial even if the employee's charges are groundless, since juries are notoriously unpredictable and often favor the "little guy."

As a result, employers have been looking for alternative ways to resolve employment disputes. One approach is to require employees as a condition of being hired to agree to resolve disputes through binding arbitration. However, employees have challenged the validity of such agreements.

The U.S. Supreme Court recently handed employers a major victory by ruling that mandatory arbitration agreements are legal and enforceable by employers. [Circuit City Stores v. Adams, 532 U.S. 105 (2001)] The case involved a claim of employment discrimination under state law. However, the arbitration agreement signed by the employee specifically provided for mandatory arbitration of all claims arising under state and local statutes or common law, including the Age Discrimination in Employment Act (ADEA), Title VII, and the ADA.

The Supreme Court held that the agreement was enforceable under the Federal Arbitration Act (FAA), which validates and provides for enforcement of arbitration agreements. In reaching its decision, the Court made it clear that binding arbitration agreements can be enforced under the FAA even when the dispute involves statutes such as federal discrimination laws that give employees special protections. "By agreeing to arbitrate a statutory claim, a party does not forgo the substantive rights afforded by the statute; it only submits to their resolution in an arbitral, rather than judicial, forum," the Court said.

Despite the Supreme Court decision, other issues regarding arbitration agreements remain to be resolved. For example, many arbitration agreements cap the amount of damages an employee can receive or do not provide for recovery of costs. The Supreme Court did not address the issue of whether such provisions are enforceable if they conflict with the remedies provided by law.

Moreover, another Supreme Court decision makes it clear that a private arbitration agreement between an employee and an employer does not prevent the EEOC from filing a lawsuit against the employer and recovering monetary damages for the employee. The Supreme Court reversed a lower court decision that had prevented the EEOC from recovering monetary damages for discrimination on behalf of an employee who had previously agreed with his employer to arbitrate discrimination claims. The Supreme Court rejected the argument that the EEOC is a mere proxy for the individuals for whom it seeks relief, ruling that the EEOC is the "master of its own case" and can decide to bring a claim for monetary damages in court even though the employee for whom the EEOC seeks relief would be required to pursue his or her own claim through arbitration. [EEOC v. Waffle House, Inc., 122 S. Ct. 754 (2002), *rev'g* 193 F.3d 805 (4th Cir. 1999)]

Penalties

Q 18:46   What sanctions apply to an employer that violates the ADA?

The remedies under the ADA are the same as those under Title VII of the Civil Rights Act of 1964 (see chapter 19). [ADA § 107(a); 42 U.S.C. § 12117(a)]

Q 18:47   Is an employer liable under the ADA for discrimination by an insurance company, third-party administrator, HMO, or other entity with which it has a contract?

Yes, it can be. The EEOC Interim Guidance on Application of ADA to Health Insurance expressly puts employers on notice of this potential liability and explains how it could occur in the health insurance context.

The Interim Guidance explains that the ADA prohibits employers from indirectly discriminating on the basis of disability in the provision of health insurance. Any contractual or other arrangement or relationship, including a contractual or other relationship with an organization that provides fringe benefits to employees, will violate the ADA if the contract or relationship has the effect of discriminating against the employer's own qualified applicants or employees with disabilities. If prohibited discrimination results from a contract or agreement with an insurance company, HMO, third-party administrator, stop-loss carrier, or other organization to provide or administer a health insurance plan on behalf of its employees, the employer will be liable under the ADA. [EEOC Interim Guidance on Application of ADA to Health Insurance, reprinted at 109 Daily Lab. Rep. (BNA) E-1 (June 9, 1993)]

Relationship to State Laws

Q 18:48   Does the ADA preempt state laws or other federal laws?

No. If a state or local government has a nondiscrimination law providing greater protections for individuals with disabilities, that law is not invalidated. [ADA § 501(b)] The law directs the agencies with enforcement authority under the ADA and the Rehabilitation Act of 1973 to develop procedures to avoid duplication of effort and inconsistent standards for the same requirements under each act. [ADA § 107(b); 42 U.S.C. § 12117(b)]

ERISA, on the other hand, does preempt the application of most state laws to ERISA-covered employee benefit plans. Although ERISA does not preempt other federal laws, the fact that the ADA (which does not preempt state nondiscrimination laws) also applies to ERISA plans does not nullify ERISA's preemption of state wage and labor laws. ERISA's preemption generally cannot be evaded by attempting to characterize a state nondiscrimination law as part of the "federal scheme" under another federal law. The Supreme Court has rejected an attempt to "bootstrap" state nondiscrimination laws into the "federal scheme" of Title VII of the Civil Rights Act of 1964 in an attempt to avoid ERISA's state-law preemption provisions. [Shaw v. Delta Air Lines, 463 U.S. 85 (1983)]

Chapter 19

Other Federal Laws

In addition to the major employment laws discussed in the previous chapters, various other federal laws can directly or indirectly affect the content of employee welfare benefit plans. This chapter highlights some of those laws.

Labor Laws and Collective Bargaining

Q 19:1 Must an employer bargain with a labor union representing its employees concerning welfare benefits?

Yes. An employer is generally required to bargain in good faith with a union representing its employees regarding "wages, hours, and other terms and conditions of employment." [National Labor Relations Act of 1935, as amended (NLRA) § 8(d); 29 U.S.C. § 158(d)] Employee pension and welfare benefits are within the scope of this requirement. [Inland Steel Co. v. NLRB, 170 F.2d 247 (7th Cir. 1948), *cert. denied*, 336 U.S. 960 (1949)] Note that the subject of when a union represents the employees is beyond the scope of this book.

Q 19:2   Must an employer bargain with respect to welfare benefits for retired employees?

Retirees are not considered employees under the NLRA, and therefore an employer need not bargain over their welfare benefits, although it may agree to do so. [Allied Chem. & Alkali Workers of Am. Local Union No. 1 v. Pittsburgh Plate Glass Co. Chem. Div., 404 U.S. 157 (1971)] However, an employer is required to bargain with a union about the benefits active employees will receive when they retire.

Q 19:3   Can temporary or contract employees be part of a collective bargaining unit?

The National Labor Relations Board (NLRB) has ruled that a unit consisting of both a "user" employer's own employees and employees who are jointly employed by a user employer and a "supplier" employer constitutes a multiemployer unit that is permitted only if both the user and supplier employers agree. [H.S. Care LLC, 343 NLRB No. 76 (2004)]

In 2000, the NLRB reversed a long-standing ban on such units. [M.B. Sturgis, Inc., 331 N.L.R.B. 1298 (2000)] However, the NLRB's latest action overrules and returns to the long-standing prior precedent.

Q 19:4   May an employer contribute to a welfare benefit fund administered by a labor union?

Generally, no. It is unlawful for an employer to contribute to a union-administered plan. The plan must be jointly administered by the employer and the union and satisfy the conditions listed in Q 19:5. [Labor Management Relations Act of 1947 (LMRA) § 302(c); 29 U.S.C. § 186]

Q 19:5   May an employer contribute to a trust fund it does not control that provides welfare benefits to employees in a collective bargaining unit?

Yes, provided the following conditions are met:

1. A written agreement specifies in detail the basis on which payments are to be made to the employees.

2. The employer and employees are equally represented in the administration of the plan; that is, each must appoint an equal number of trustees. The parties may also agree on the appointment of additional, neutral trustees.

3. The agreement provides that in the event of a deadlock among the trustees, the two sides will agree on an impartial umpire, or a federal court will appoint one.

4. The agreement provides for an annual audit of the trust fund, the results of which will be available for inspection by interested persons.

[LMRA § 302; 29 U.S.C. § 186(c)]

Q 19:6   May the employer unilaterally change welfare benefits for employees covered by a collective bargaining agreement?

No, generally, it may not. Even if the changes are improvements in benefits, the employer must notify and bargain the changes with the union. An employer was found to have violated the NLRA by unilaterally increasing union employees' contributions for health benefit coverage and was required to reimburse the union employees for the additional contributions made. [North Star Steel Co. v. NLRB, 974 F.2d 68 (8th Cir. 1992)]

Q 19:7   Must the employer bargain over a change in insurance carriers or another change in the method of funding the plan?

At least one federal appeals court has held that a mere change in insurance carriers does not substantially affect the terms and conditions of employment and that therefore the employer could change insurance carriers without union consultation or approval. [Connecticut Light & Power Co. v. NLRB, 476 F.2d 1079 (2d Cir. 1973)] However, if the terms of the agreement specify a particular carrier, the employer might have to consult with the union.

Additionally, an employer under a contributory plan should not unilaterally switch from an insured to a self-insured arrangement or modify the plan benefits. [Bastian-Blessing, Div. of Golconda Corp. v. NLRB, 474 F.2d 49 (6th Cir. 1973)]

The NLRB has ruled that employers could not unilaterally replace a comprehensive medical benefits plan for union employees with a managed care health benefits plan, even though the collective bargaining agreement gave the employers the right to amend or modify the existing plan. The NLRB found that the managed care plan was not merely an amendment or modification of the existing comprehensive plan, but instead constituted a new health care delivery system for the union employees. The new plan eliminated a health maintenance organization (HMO) option, took away the employees' choice of doctors, and imposed new benefit limitations. Thus, the employers were required to bargain with the union before replacing the old plan with the new plan. [Loral Defense Sys., 320 N.L.R.B. 755 (1996)]

Two employers that unilaterally replaced their jointly administered Taft-Hartley benefits plans with employer-sponsored plans, after the union had rejected the change and called a strike, were found to have violated the LMRA. [Grondorf, Field, Black & Co. v. NLRB, 107 F. 3d 882 (D.C. Cir. 1997)]

Q 19:8 May an employer terminate welfare benefit plan coverage for striking employees?

Generally, yes. [International Union of Elec. & Mach, Workers v. General Elec. Co., 337 F. Supp. 817 (S.D.N.Y. 1972)] However, if the contract is ambiguous, the issue is one for arbitration. [Viggiano v. Shenango China Div. of Anchor Hocking Corp., 750 F.2d 276 (3d Cir. 1984)] Additionally, the striking employees may have COBRA continuation of coverage rights regarding their health coverage. (See chapter 6 for a discussion of COBRA.)

Q 19:9 May an employer terminate welfare benefit plan coverage for union employees when a collective bargaining agreement expires?

Generally, no. The employer must bargain with the union and cannot drop the benefits unilaterally unless and until the two sides reach an impasse or the employer can demonstrate that the union no longer represents a majority of the employees in the collective bargaining unit. [Stone Boat Yard v. NLRB, 715 F.2d 441 (9th Cir. 1983)]

The Court of Appeals for the Ninth Circuit held that an employer, following the expiration of a collective bargaining agreement, was not entitled to unilaterally discontinue pension contributions without giving prior notice to the union and giving the union the opportunity to bargain, in a case where the parties had not reached an impasse. [NLRB v. Unbelievable Inc., 71 F.3d 1434 (9th Cir. 1995)]

Another federal appeals court held that an employer violated the LMRA when it denied accrued vacation benefits to former employees who were fired following a strike, when the employer had no business reasons for denying the benefits. [NLRB v. Swift Adhesives, 110 F.3d 632 (8th Cir. 1997)]

Q 19:10 May an employer offer or provide welfare plan benefits as an inducement to discourage union activity?

Ordinarily, no. The employer's action may constitute an unfair labor practice if the employer's motivation is to discourage a vote in favor of unionization, to reward employees who vote against unionization, to penalize employees who have joined a union, or the like. [NLRB v. Great Dane Trailers Inc., 388 U.S. 26 (1967); NLRB v. Exchange Parts Co., 375 U.S. 405 (1964)]

Q 19:11 May an employer terminate coverage of health or life insurance benefits for retirees required under a collective bargaining agreement once the collective bargaining agreement expires?

It depends on the terms of the collective bargaining agreement. If the agreement clearly provides that the obligation to provide the retiree coverage is limited to the period of the agreement, the courts will recognize it. However, if the collective bargaining agreement does not clearly limit the employer's obligation to the period of the agreement, a number of courts have found the employer to be obligated to continue the retiree coverage for the lifetimes of the retirees. [UAW Local 134 v. Yard-Man Inc., 716 F.2d 1476 (6th Cir. 1983), *cert. denied*, 104 S. Ct. 1002 (1984); UAW Local 784 v. Cadillac Malleable Iron Co., 728 F.2d 807 (6th Cir. 1984); Weimer v. Kurz-Kasch Inc., 773 F.2d 669 (6th Cir. 1985); Policy v. Powell Pressed Steel Co., 770 F.2d 609 (6th Cir. 1985), *cert. denied,* 106 S. Ct. 1202 (1986)]

In August 1987, UAW Local 284 approved a plan providing health insurance coverage to former officers, staff, and agents of the union. According to the plan, an employee becomes eligible for health and life insurance coverage when the employee (1) is at least 57 years old and has at least ten years of service with Local 284 or (2) becomes totally and permanently disabled while a full-time officer, agent, or employee without respect to his or her length of service with Local 284. For plan purposes, permanent disability occurs when employees are eligible to receive disability benefits from the Social Security Administration (SSA).

Local 284's plan states that coverage for former employees shall be the same as the coverage for active employees. The plan also provides that coverage ceases when the employee reaches age 65, dies, or becomes eligible for active medical insurance coverage by returning to employment of any kind.

In September 1987, an employee, age 56, retired due to disability. In December 1987, the SSA awarded disability benefits to the individual beginning in March 1988. Local 284 began providing retiree benefits to him and his wife in February 1988. These benefits consisted of paying the couple's health and life insurance premiums. In June 1992, Local 284 reduced his coverage so that his retiree benefits were substantially less than those provided to active employees. In addition, he was notified that he would be required to pay a monthly premium to continue receiving retiree benefits.

Active employees were not required to pay a monthly premium for their health and life insurance benefits. The retiree did not pay the premium and sued Local 284 under ERISA, seeking restoration of benefits.

The Sixth Circuit Court of Appeals looked to the expressed text of the document. Under the clear terms of the plan, the court said, the benefits expired upon the individual's reaching age 65. However, because Local 284 filed its motion for recovery of the insurance premiums two years after the retiree reached the age of 65, the court found the delay was excessive and refused reimbursement for premiums paid after he reached age 65.

If the retirement plan's language is clearly expressed, courts will look to the clear language of the document when determining duration of retiree benefits. [Linville v. Teamsters Misc. & Indus. Workers Union, 206 F.3d 648 (6th Cir. 2000)]

Q 19:12   Is an employee entitled to a jury trial in hybrid LMRA/ERISA actions?

Yes. Although ERISA ordinarily does not afford claimants the right to a jury trial, jury trials are available under LMRA Section 301. A joinder of essentially identical claims under both acts will not deprive claimants of the right to a jury trial. [Senn v. United Dominion Indus. Inc., 951 F.2d 806 (7th Cir. 1992); Stewart v. KHD Deutz of Am. Corp., 980 F.2d 698 (11th Cir. 1993)]

Title VI of the Civil Rights Act of 1964

Q 19:13   What does Title VI of the Civil Rights Act of 1964 provide?

Title VI of the Civil Rights Act of 1964, unlike Title VII of the same Act, applies only to recipients of federal financial aid where the primary purpose of the federal financial aid is to provide employment. Such employers cannot discriminate on the basis of race, color, or national origin. [42 U.S.C. §§ 2000d–2000d-6]

Q 19:14   What penalties apply if an employer violates Title VI?

If an employer violates Title VI, its federal funds may be withdrawn. In addition, individual employees have a private right of action for intentional acts of discrimination and may obtain prospective relief. [42 U.S.C. § 2000d]

Title VII of the Civil Rights Act of 1964

Q 19:15   What does Title VII of the Civil Rights Act of 1964 provide?

Title VII of the Civil Rights Act prohibits discrimination in employment practices based on race, color, religion, sex, or national origin. [42 U.S.C. §§ 2000e–2000e-17]

Q 19:16   Which employers are subject to Title VII?

Title VII applies to employers in industries affecting commerce with 15 or more employees in at least 20 weeks in the current or preceding year. State and local government employers, but not the federal government or corporations wholly owned by the federal government, are also covered. [42 U.S.C. § 2000e(b)]

Q 19:17   Does Title VII cover persons who are not common-law employees?

No. Title VII applies to employees only. A doctor working for a hospital was barred from suing the hospital under Title VII because the doctor was an independent contractor, not an employee. [Cileck v. Inova Health Sys. Servs., 115 F.3d 256 (4th Cir. 1997)] Another federal appeals court held that lawyers who controlled a law firm that was organized as a professional corporation were not employees for Title VII purposes. The court looked to the substance rather than the form of the arrangement and concluded that because the lawyers owned and managed the law firm and set firm policy, they were not common-law employees. [Devine v. Stone, Leyton & Gershman, P. C., 100 F.3d 78 (8th Cir. 1996)]

Q 19:18   Does discrimination on the basis of sex include discrimination based on pregnancy?

Yes. The Pregnancy Discrimination Act of 1978 (PDA) amended Title VII to specifically prohibit employment discrimination based on pregnancy, childbirth, or related medical conditions. [42 U.S.C. § 2000e]

In addition, the Supreme Court has held that the PDA protects women from discrimination because they have the ability to become pregnant, not just because they are already pregnant. [International Union, UAW v. Johnson Controls, 499 U.S. 187 (1991)]

Moreover, the EEOC has concluded that because contraception is a means by which a woman controls her ability to become pregnant, the PDA's prohibition on pregnancy discrimination necessarily includes a prohibition on discrimination related to a woman's use of contraceptives. Therefore, the EEOC ruled that an employer's health plan must provide the same coverage for prescription contraceptives that it provides for other drugs, devices, or services that are used to prevent the occurrence of medical conditions other than pregnancy. [EEOC Decision on Contraception (Dec. 14, 2000)] (See Q 19:22.)

Q 19:19   What is a pregnancy disability under Title VII?

A pregnancy disability protected under Title VII is a disability caused or contributed to by pregnancy, childbirth, or related medical conditions. This includes disability related to abortion where the life of the mother would be endangered if the fetus were carried to term and medical complications arising from abortion. [42 U.S.C. § 2000e(k); EEOC Reg. § 1604.10; 29 C.F.R. § 1604.10]

Q 19:20   What employment benefits are affected by the pregnancy disability provisions of Title VII?

Formal and informal health or disability insurance and sick-leave plans must cover disabilities caused or contributed to by pregnancy, childbirth, or related medical conditions in the same manner as disabilities caused or contributed to by other medical conditions. [EEOC Reg. § 1604.10(b)]

Q 19:21   Does Title VII require that welfare benefits be provided for abortion?

With the exception of health insurance benefits, all other fringe benefits (including sick leave) provided for other medical conditions must also be provided for abortions. Health insurance benefits must be provided only when the life of the woman would be endangered if the fetus were carried to term and for medical complications arising from abortion, such as excessive hemorrhaging. Employers are not precluded from providing benefits for abortion either directly or through a collective bargaining agreement; but if they do so, then it must be done in the same manner and to the same degree as other medical conditions are covered. [EEOC Reg. Pt. 1604 App., Q&A-35–Q&A-37]

Starting in 2014, the 2010 Health Reform Law [(Patient Protection and Affordable Care Act, Pub. L. No. 111-148 (Mar. 23, 2010) (PPACA)] as amended by the Health Care and Education Affordability Reconciliation Act of 2010 [Pub. L. No. 111-152 (Mar. 30, 2010)] provides for the establishment of exchanges in each state through which individuals and small employers with up to 100 employees can purchase coverage under a qualified health plan (QHP) that provides certain essential benefits (see chapter 3). [PPACA § 1311(b)] Lower-income individuals obtaining health coverage through the exchanges may qualify for federal assistance in the form of tax credits or cost-sharing reductions. [PPACA § 1411] The health reform law specifically provides that a QHP offered through an exchange cannot be required to provide coverage for abortion services, and that federal assistance cannot be used to pay for abortion services (except in cases of rape or incest, or when the life of the woman would be endangered). If a plan offered through an exchange does cover abortion services, the cost of that coverage must be paid with segregated non-federal funds. [PPACA § 1303; *see also* Executive Order—Patient Protection and Affordable Care Act's Consistency with Longstanding Restrictions on the Use of Federal Funds for Abortion (Mar. 24, 2010)]

Q 19:22   Does Title VII require health plans to provide coverage for prescription contraceptives?

Although it has not issued regulations on this issue, the EEOC has ruled that an employer's health plan violated Title VII because it failed to provide coverage for prescription contraceptives while covering other preventive drugs, devices, and services. The EEOC concluded that because contraception is a means by which a woman controls her ability to become pregnant, the PDA's prohibition on pregnancy discrimination necessarily includes a prohibition on discrimination related to a woman's use of contraceptives.

The EEOC decision noted that oral contraceptives are also used to treat certain medical conditions that exclusively affect women, such as dysmenorrhea (menstrual cramps) and premenstrual syndrome. Therefore, the EEOC concluded that the employer's exclusion of prescription contraception constituted sex discrimination, regardless of whether the contraceptives were used for birth control or other medical purposes. Because oral contraceptives are available only for women, 100 percent of those affected by the exclusion were women. Thus, the exclusion, by definition, constituted sex discrimination.

The employer advanced four reasons as to why the exclusion of prescription contraceptives did not violate the law:

1. The employer argued that the plan covered only abnormal physical or mental conditions and therefore had no obligation to cover contraceptives. However, the EEOC noted that the plan did cover numerous preventive drugs and services. In addition, it covered surgical sterilizations and Viagra.

2. The employer argued that exclusion was permissible because it was based on cost considerations. However, the EEOC noted that Congress had explicitly rejected a cost defense for pregnancy and sex discrimination.

3. The employer argued that the exclusion did not specifically discriminate on the basis of sex. However, the EEOC said that because prescription contraceptives are available only to women, the exclusion amounted, by definition, to sex discrimination.

4. Finally, the employer argued that the claims of sex or pregnancy discrimination were preempted by ERISA. However, the EEOC said that while ERISA does preempt certain state laws that regulate insurance, it explicitly exempts federal laws from preemption.

[EEOC Decision on Contraception (Dec. 14, 2000)]

Since the EEOC ruling, at least two courts have held that an employer's selective exclusion of contraceptives, while covering other preventive medications, violated the PDA. In Washington State, a district court ruled that an employer's selective exclusion of contraceptives from coverage under its health plan violated the federal Civil Rights Acts, as amended by the Pregnancy Discrimination Act of 1978 (PDA). The court concluded that the plan, by excluding contraceptives while covering other preventive drugs and devices, illegally discriminated against female employees on the basis of their childbearing ability. [Erickson v. Bartell Drug Co., 141 F. Supp. 2d 1226 (W.D. Wash. 2001)] Similarly, a Nebraska district court held that a railroad employer's policy of excluding prescription contraceptives and related outpatient services from its plans violated the PDA because it treated the medical care women need to prevent pregnancy less favorably than the medical care needed to prevent other medical conditions that pose no greater threat to employees' health than does pregnancy. [*In re* Union Pac. R.R. Employment Practices Litig., 391 F. Supp. 2d 789 (D. Neb. 2005)] However, the Nebraska case was subsequently overturned on appeal by the Eighth Circuit. The Eighth Circuit held that the PDA does not require employers to provide coverage for contraception because contraception is not "related to" pregnancy for PDA purposes and is gender-neutral. [*In re* Union Pac. R.R. Employment Practices Litig., 479 F.3d 936 (8th Cir. 2007)]

Practice Pointer. Employers should review their plans carefully to determine whether they are vulnerable to such claims of discrimination. Employer plans that cover other preventive drugs and services may want to conduct a cost-benefit analysis on the advisability of adding contraceptive coverage. A study by human resources consultants William M. Mercer, Inc., reports that coverage of the five major types of prescription contraceptives—oral drugs, injectable drugs, implants, diaphragms, and intrauterine devices (IUDs)—costs, on average, about $17 per employee per year, or $1.42 per employee per month.

Employers should also check state law. More than 30 states have passed legislation mandating some level of coverage for contraceptives. Most of these states require health insurance policies that cover prescription drugs to also cover prescription contraceptives. A number of states include exemptions for employers who object to contraceptive coverage for religious reasons. Other states exempt "religious employers." However, religious employers do not necessarily include every organization with a religious connection.

California's Women's Contraception Equity Act, which requires group health plans that provide coverage for prescription drugs to also cover female contraceptives, exempts religious employers. Under the law, religious employers are defined as:

> any entity that (1) includes religious values, (2) primarily employs persons who share the same religious tenets, (3) primarily serves persons who share the religious tenets of the entity, and (4) is a nonprofit organization.

However, according to the California Supreme Court, that definition does not encompass Catholic Charities, which challenged the law. The court concluded that Catholic Charities of Sacramento, Inc. did not satisfy any of the exemption criteria and was essentially a "secular" organization. Most of the organization's employees are not Catholic and their work primarily involves providing food, shelter, and clothing to the poor rather than promoting religious tenets. The U.S. Supreme Court declined to review the state court's decision. [Catholic Charities of Sacramento, Inc. v. Superior Court, 32 Cal. 4th 527 (Cal. Sup. Ct.), *cert. denied by* Catholic Charities of Sacramento, Inc. v. California, 125 S. Ct. 53 (2004)]

Q 19:23   Does Title VII require health plans to provide coverage for infertility treatments?

One federal appeals court has held that a health plan's exclusion of coverage for certain infertility treatments did not violate the PDA and did not constitute illegal sex discrimination under Title VII. [Saks v. Franklin Covey Co., 316 F.3d 337 (2d Cir. 2003)]

The health plan in question excluded coverage for "surgical impregnation procedures," including artificial insemination, in-vitro fertilization, and embryo or fetal implants. The plan did, however, cover other infertility treatments for both men and women, including oral fertility drugs and penile prosthetic treatments. A female plan participant argued that the exclusion violated the PDA because the benefits for infertility treatments were inferior to benefits for nonpregnancy-related illnesses. In addition, she argued that the exclusion discriminated on the basis of sex because it provided incomplete coverage for female infertility treatments but provided complete coverage for male infertility treatments.

Addressing the PDA claim, the court concluded that infertility is not a condition that is unique to women and, therefore, the plan's limited coverage for infertility treatments did not violate the PDA. Moreover, the court held that the exclusion did not constitute sex discrimination because of the exclusion of procedures that are used to treat both male and female infertility. The court acknowledged that the excluded procedures are performed only on women. However, the need for such procedures "may be traced to male, female, or couple infertility with equal frequency." Therefore, the exclusion disadvantaged both men and women equally.

Q 19:24 Must an employer provide the same benefits to an employee on leave for pregnancy-related conditions as it does for employees on leave for other reasons?

Yes. This would include installment purchase disability insurance; payment of premiums for health, life, or other insurance; and continued payments into pension, savings, or profit sharing plans. [EEOC Reg. Pt. 1604 App., Q&A-17]

Q 19:25 May employees who are absent due to pregnancy-related disabilities be required to exhaust vacation benefits prior to receiving sick pay or disability benefits?

No, not unless employees who are absent because of other disabilities are also required to first exhaust vacation benefits. [EEOC Reg. Pt. 1604 App., Q&A-18]

Q 19:26 Can a pregnant employee be discharged for excessive absenteeism?

According to the Fifth Circuit Court of Appeals, the PDA does not protect a pregnant employee from being discharged for excessive absences, as long as the same discharge policy applies to employees who are absent for other reasons. [Stout v. Baxter Healthcare Corp., 282 F.3d 856 (5th Cir. 2002)]

The plaintiff in the case, Wilma Stout, was hired by Baxter Healthcare Corporation as a material handler. Under Baxter's standard policy, Stout was a probationary employee for the first 90 days of her employment. Probationary employees are subject to a strict attendance policy: any employee who misses more than three days of work during the probationary period is terminated. Baxter does not provide vacation time or medical leave for probationary employees.

Stout, who was pregnant during the probationary period, received positive performance reviews and maintained a perfect attendance record during her first two months of employment. However, during the third month, she suffered a miscarriage that rendered her medically unable to work for more than two weeks. Stout notified her supervisor of her condition and provided a medical excuse. Nonetheless, Baxter terminated Stout's employment because her absences exceeded the three days permitted during the probationary period. Stout sued Baxter for pregnancy discrimination under the PDA. Stout's lawsuit claimed that she was fired "because of" her pregnancy and that Baxter's probationary attendance policy had a disparate impact on pregnant employees.

The Fifth Circuit rejected Baxter's claim that she was fired because of her pregnancy. According to the court, all of the evidence indicated that she was fired because of her absenteeism, not because of her pregnancy. There was no evidence that she would have been treated differently if her absences had been due to some reason other than pregnancy. Baxter's policy does not mention or focus on pregnancy, childbirth, or any related medical condition; it merely limits permissible absences, on any basis, of all probationary employees. "The PDA does not protect a pregnant employee from being discharged for being absent from work even if her absence is due to pregnancy or to complications of pregnancy, unless the absences of nonpregnant employees are overlooked," said the court.

The court also rejected Stout's argument that Baxter's policy violated the PDA because it negatively impacted all pregnant probationary employees who gave birth during the probationary period and had to take more than three days' leave. According to the court, the PDA requires only that women affected by pregnancy be treated the same as nonpregnant workers. By contrast, Stout's argument boiled down to a claim that she should have been granted more generous medical leave than that granted to nonpregnant employees. "This," the court said, "the PDA does not require." [Stout v. Baxter Healthcare Corp., 282 F.3d 856 (5th Cir. 2002)]

The U.S. Court of Appeals for the Eleventh Circuit has also held that the Pregnancy Discrimination Act is not violated by an employer that fires an employee for excessive absences, even if those absences were the result of the pregnancy, unless the employer overlooks the comparable absences of nonpregnant employees. [Armindo v. Padlocker Inc., 209 F.3d 1319 (11th Cir. 2000)]

Q 19:27   May time spent on leave for pregnancy-related reasons be treated differently from time spent on leave for other reasons when calculating credit toward vacations and pay increases?

No. Leave for pregnancy-related reasons cannot be treated less favorably than leave for other disabilities. Accordingly, the time spent on pregnancy-related leave would count on the same basis as other disabilities toward accrual of vacation pay and toward pay increases, which would affect the level of pay-related welfare benefits such as group term life insurance, accidental death and dismemberment benefits, and long-term disability benefits. [EEOC Reg. Pt. 1604 App., Q&A-11]

In a 2009 decision, the United States Supreme Court held that an employer did not violate the Pregnancy Discrimination Act (PDA) by calculating pension benefits using an accrual rule for periods of pre-PDA service that gave less retirement credit for pregnancy leaves than for other types of medical leaves. The Court said the PDA was not intended to be retroactive and that the employer was not required to change the past crediting practices in calculating current pension benefits. [AT&T Corp. v. Hulteen, No. 07–543, 566 U.S. ___ (2009)] Although the case dealt with pension benefits, the decision could potentially impact welfare benefits that accrue on the basis of periods of service.

Q 19:28   If the employer provides benefits for long-term or permanent disabilities, must such benefits be provided for pregnancy-related conditions?

Yes, they must. [EEOC Reg. Pt. 1604 App., Q&A-16]

Q 19:29   Can the employer limit pregnancy disability benefits to married employees?

No, it cannot. [EEOC Reg. Pt. 1604 App., Q&A-13]

Q 19:30   Can pregnancy disability benefits be limited to employees only?

If the employer's plan does not cover dependents, Title VII does not require that pregnancy disability benefits for dependents be offered. Similarly, the employer need not provide pregnancy-related benefits to dependents other than spouses, as long as both male and female dependents other than spouses are equally excluded. If the employer's insurance program covers medical expenses of the spouses of female employees, then it cannot exclude medical expenses for spouses of male employees, including those arising from pregnancy-related conditions. [EEOC Reg. Pt. 1604 App., Q&A-21] However, if the employer's plan distinguishes between the level of benefits available to employees and the level available to spouses (for example, employees get 100 percent reimbursement, and spouses, both male and female, get 50 percent reimbursement), then female spouses of male employees may be reimbursed for pregnancy-related benefits at the level applicable to spouses (in this example, at 50 percent). [EEOC Guidelines, Q&A-29]

Q 19:31   Can a female employee be required to purchase dependent or family coverage to receive coverage for her own pregnancy-related condition?

No. A female employee with single coverage cannot be forced to pay for more expensive dependent or family coverage to have her own pregnancy-related condition covered. A female employee is entitled to personal coverage, regardless of marital status. [EEOC Reg. Pt. 1604 App., Q&A-24]

Q 19:32 Can the employer offer an employee-pay-all optional coverage that excludes pregnancy-related conditions or provides less coverage for them than for other medical conditions?

No. Regardless of who pays the premiums, pregnancy-related conditions must be treated the same as all other medical conditions under any sick leave plan, health insurance, or disability insurance available in connection with employment. [EEOC Reg. Pt. 1604 App., Q&A-23]

Q 19:33 May an employer exclude pregnancy-related conditions from one or more health insurance plans or options as long as it offers such coverage under at least one plan or option?

No. If employees have a choice among several health insurance plans or options, pregnancy-related conditions must be covered in all of them on the same basis as other medical conditions. [EEOC Reg. Pt. 1604 App., Q&A-24]

Q 19:34 On what basis must pregnancy-related conditions be reimbursed?

The EEOC guidelines contain the following rules for reimbursement of pregnancy-related conditions:

1. Deductible amounts must be the same for both pregnancy-related and nonpregnancy-related conditions. Employers may not impose a separate deductible on pregnancy-related conditions, nor may they impose a higher deductible applicable only to pregnancy-related conditions.

2. Maximum recoverable amounts, such as annual limits or lifetime limits, must be the same for both pregnancy-related and nonpregnancy-related conditions.

3. Pregnancy-related expenses must be reimbursed in the same manner (for example, through a fixed dollar amount or a percentage of the reasonable and customary charge) as nonpregnancy-related expenses.

4. The percentage of reimbursement (e.g., 80 percent after a uniform annual deductible amount) for pregnancy-related conditions must be the same as for nonpregnancy-related conditions, so that the plan pays the same proportion of actual costs.

5. Pregnancy-related expenses must be eligible under any otherwise covered benefits. For example, a plan must cover the cost of a private hospital room for pregnancy-related conditions if a private room is covered for other expenses. Similarly, if the plan covers physician office visits, prenatal and postnatal office visits must be covered.

6. Preexisting-condition limitations, which exclude conditions existing at the time the insured's coverage becomes effective, may exclude benefits for preexisting pregnancies, if other preexisting conditions are excluded in the same manner.

7. If the plan provides an extension of benefits after coverage stops (usually due to termination of employment), pregnancy-related benefits cannot be treated less favorably than benefits for other medical conditions.

[EEOC Reg. Pt. 1604 App., Q&A-24–Q&A-30]

Q 19:35 Does Title VII encompass discrimination for failure to grant parental leave?

A district court case suggests that discrimination for failure to grant parental leave in order to provide medical care to a baby might not be actionable under Title VII. In concluding that Title VII does not prohibit discrimination on the basis of family leave, the court concluded that giving medical care to a baby was a gender-neutral activity that could be performed by a parent of either sex. [Barnes v. Hewlett-Packard Co., 846 F. Supp. 442 (D. Md. 1994)]

However, the EEOC has made it clear that while employers are permitted by Title VII to provide women with leave specifically for the period that they are incapacitated because of pregnancy, childbirth, and related medical conditions, employers may not treat either sex more favorably with respect to other kinds of leave, such as leave for child care purposes. To avoid a potential Title VII violation, employers should carefully distinguish between pregnancy-related leave and other forms of leave, ensuring that any leave specifically provided only to women is limited to the period when they are incapacitated by pregnancy and childbirth. [EEOC Enforcement Guidance: Unlawful Disparate Treatment of Workers With Caregiving Responsibilities] The EEOC gave the following example.

Example. Eric, an elementary school teacher, requests unpaid leave for the upcoming school year to care for his newborn son. Although the school has a collective bargaining agreement that allows up to one year of unpaid leave for various personal reasons, including to care for a newborn, the school's Personnel Director denies Eric's request. When Eric points out that women are granted childcare leave, the Director says, "That's different. We have to give childcare leave to women." He suggests that Eric request unpaid emergency leave instead, although such leave is limited to 90 days.

According to the EEOC, this is an example of a violation of Title VII because the employer is denying a male employee a type of leave, unrelated to pregnancy, that it grants female employees.

Bear in mind also that employers subject to the Family and Medical Leave Act (FMLA) must provide parental leave as required by that law. (See chapter 16.)

Q 19:36   May an employer impose a "head of household" requirement for medical plan eligibility?

Yes. An employer may impose a head of household requirement for medical plan eligibility under certain circumstances. A *head of household* is defined as the principal (or highest-paid) wage earner. Such a rule would prevent an employee from enrolling his or her spouse unless the spouse earns less than the employee. An employment practice does not violate Title VII if the employment practice satisfies any one of the four affirmative defenses to the Equal Pay Act of 1963, which were incorporated by reference into Title VII. One of these defenses is payment made pursuant to a differential based on any factor other than sex. A U.S. Court of Appeals case upheld a head of household eligibility requirement where the employer desired to provide the greatest benefits for the people who needed coverage (that is, employees who did not have a more highly paid spouse) and wished to avoid covering spouses likely to have coverage from their own employers. The court found that the employer adopted the provision because it "wanted the biggest bang' for the buck with its benefit package," a reason the court found to be a legitimate business reason. [EEOC v. J.C. Penney Co., 843 F.2d 249 (6th Cir. 1988)]

However, employers should check state law. Some states prohibit so-called spousal carve-outs, which deny coverage to spouses who are eligible for coverage from their own employers.

Q 19:37   What penalties apply if Title VII is violated?

Under Title VII, an employer may be liable for back benefits for a period of not more than two years before the filing of a discrimination charge with the EEOC, for attorneys' fees, and for injunctive relief. [42 U.S.C. § 2000e-5]

In addition, the employer may be liable for compensatory and punitive damages if it engages in unlawful, intentional discrimination. To recover punitive damages, the complaining party must demonstrate that the employer engaged in the discrimination with malice or reckless indifference to the federally protected rights of the individual. There is a limit on the sum of compensatory and punitive damages based on the number of employees of the employer, as follows:

15–100 employees	$ 50,000
101–200 employees	100,000
201–500 employees	200,000
501 employees or more	300,000

If there is more than one complaining party, the dollar limits are applied individually, not collectively. Thus, if ten employees allege Title VII intentional discrimination and are successful in obtaining compensatory and/or punitive damages, an employer with over 500 employees could be liable for up to $3 million in damages. [42 U.S.C. § 2000-e]

The Court of Appeals for the Eighth Circuit has held that in order to obtain punitive damages under Title VII, a plaintiff must show something more than intentional discrimination. [Karcher v. Emerson Elec. Co., 94 F.3d 502 (8th Cir. 1996)]

A restaurant violated Title VII by forcing three waitresses out of their jobs after their fifth month of pregnancy because management thought they were "too fat." The court upheld a $300,000 punitive award. [EEOC v. W&O, Inc., 213 F.3d 600 (11th Cir. 2000)]

Almost all of the federal courts of appeal (with one exception) have held that individual employees are not personally liable for damages under Title VII. [*See* Wathen v. General Elec. Co., 115 F. 3d 400 (6th Cir. 1997).]

Q 19:38 Can an employer require an employee to agree to binding arbitration of employment disputes, including discrimination claims under Title VII?

Owing to the increase in lawsuits by employees, employers have been looking for alternative ways to resolve employment disputes. One approach is to require employees, as a condition of being hired, to agree to resolve disputes through binding arbitration. However, employees have challenged the validity of such agreements.

The U.S. Supreme Court handed employers a major victory by ruling that mandatory arbitration agreements are legal and enforceable by employers. [Circuit City Stores v. Adams, 532 U.S. 105 (2001)] The case involved a claim of employment discrimination under state law. However, the arbitration agreement signed by the employee specifically provided for mandatory arbitration of all claims arising under state and local statutes or common law, including the ADEA, Title VII, and the Americans with Disabilities Act (ADA).

The Supreme Court held that the agreement was enforceable under the Federal Arbitration Act (FAA), which validates and provides for enforcement of arbitration agreements. In reaching its decision, the Court made it clear that binding arbitration agreements can be enforced under the FAA even when the dispute involves statutes such as federal discrimination laws that give employees special protections. "By agreeing to arbitrate a statutory claim, a party does not forgo the substantive rights afforded by the statute; it only submits to their resolution in an arbitral, rather than judicial, forum," the Court said.

Despite the Supreme Court decision, other issues regarding arbitration agreements remain to be resolved. For example, many arbitration agreements cap the amount of damages an employee can receive or do not provide for recovery of costs. The Court did not address whether such provisions are enforceable if they conflict with the remedies provided by law.

Another Supreme Court decision makes it clear that a private arbitration agreement between an employee and an employer does not prevent the EEOC from filing a lawsuit against the employer and recovering monetary damages for the employee. The Court reversed a lower court decision that had prevented the

EEOC from recovering monetary damages for discrimination on behalf of an employee who had previously agreed with his employer to arbitrate discrimination claims. The Court rejected the argument that the EEOC is a mere proxy for the individuals for whom it seeks relief, ruling that the EEOC is the "master of its own case" and can decide to bring a claim for monetary damages in court, even though the employee for whom the EEOC seeks relief would be required to pursue his or her own claim through arbitration. [EEOC v. Waffle House, Inc., 122 S. Ct. 754 (2002)]

Equal Pay Act of 1963

Q 19:39   What does the Equal Pay Act provide?

The Equal Pay Act of 1963 prohibits employers from discriminating on the basis of sex by paying lower wages to employees of one sex than to employees of the other sex for equal work on jobs in the same facility, performed under similar circumstances, and requiring equal skill, effort, and responsibility. Exceptions are provided for pay practices based on a seniority system, merit system, or system that measures earnings by quantity or quality of production, or a wage differential based on factors other than sex. [29 U.S.C. § 206(d)]

For this purpose, wages include all remuneration for employment, including fringe benefits such as medical, hospital, accident, life insurance, and retirement benefits; profit sharing and bonus plans; and leave practices. Additionally, differences in the application of fringe benefit plans that are derived from sex-based actuarial studies are not considered to be based on a factor other than sex. [EEOC Reg. § 1620.11]

Q 19:40   Which employers are subject to the Equal Pay Act?

All employers engaged in interstate commerce or in the production of goods for interstate commerce are subject to the Equal Pay Act, as are state and local governments (with certain exceptions). [29 U.S.C. § 206(d); EEOC Reg. § 1620.1]

Q 19:41   What penalties apply if the Equal Pay Act is violated?

If an employer violates the Equal Pay Act, it can be liable for back pay (including any wrongfully denied benefits), liquidated damages equal to the back pay, and attorneys' fees. Complainants may also obtain injunctive relief against the employer. In addition, the Equal Pay Act contains criminal penalties for willful violations. Employers may be subject to a fine of up to $10,000 or imprisonment for up to six months, or both. [29 U.S.C. § 216]

Q 19:42   When does an act of pay discrimination take place?

In 2007, the Supreme Court concluded that under the Equal Pay Act, an unlawful employment practice occurs when a discriminatory compensation decision or other practice is first adopted, and the employee first becomes subject to a discriminatory decision or practice, or an employee is first affected by a discriminatory decision or practice. [Ledbetter v. Goodyear Tire & Rubber Co., 550 U.S. 618 (2007)]

Under the Equal Pay Act, a claim of discrimination must be filed with the Equal Employment Opportunity Commission (EEOC) within 180 days of an alleged unlawful employment practice. Consequently, as a result of the Court's conclusion, a discrimination claim would be barred if an employee did not file within 180 days of the initial act of discrimination—even if the employee did not become aware of the discrimination until some later date. For example, in the Supreme Court case, the employee claimed that she had been paid less than her male counterparts for many years. However the court ruled that only claims related to any discriminatory pay decisions within the prior 180 days were allowable.

In 2008, Congress enacted the Lilly Ledbetter Fair Pay Act of 2009 [Pub. L. No. 111-2, 123 Stat. 5 (Jan. 29, 2009)] to expand the time period in which employees can sue their employer for pay discrimination. The Act clarifies that unlawful discrimination occurs each time compensation is paid pursuant to a discriminatory pay decision.

The Lilly Ledbetter Fair Pay Act provides that, in addition to other relief provided, an employee may obtain back pay for up to two years preceding the filing of the claim if the unlawful employment practices occurring during the claim filing period are similar or related to the unlawful employment practice occurring outside the time for filing a charge.

Rehabilitation Act of 1973

Q 19:43   What does the Rehabilitation Act of 1973 provide?

The Rehabilitation Act provides that a covered employer cannot exclude an otherwise qualified individual with handicaps from participation in, or deny the individual the benefits of, or subject the individual to discrimination under, a federally funded program or activity. [Rehabilitation Act § 504; 29 U.S.C. § 794]

Q 19:44   Which employers are covered by the Rehabilitation Act?

Section 504 of the Rehabilitation Act covers any program or activity receiving federal financial assistance. It is not limited to the particular branch or department of the employer covered by the financial assistance; rather, the protections of the Rehabilitation Act apply company-wide. [29 U.S.C. § 794; Civil Rights

Restoration Act of 1988, Pub. L. No. 100-259, 102 Stat. 29 (1988), codified as amended at 20 U.S.C. § 1687 (2000)]

Q 19:45　Who is a handicapped individual under the Rehabilitation Act?

Under the Rehabilitation Act, a *handicapped individual* is an individual who:

1. Has a physical or mental impairment that substantially limits one or more of the major life activities;
2. Has a record of such impairment; or
3. Is regarded as having such an impairment.

However, this definition does not include an individual who has a currently contagious disease or infection and who, by reason of such infection, would constitute a direct threat to the health or safety of other individuals. It also does not include an individual who, because of an impairment, is unable to perform the essential functions of the job that he or she holds or desires. [29 U.S.C. § 706(8)(B); 41 C.F.R. § 660-741.3(c)(1)] In addition, under some circumstances detailed at length in the statute, the definition does not include an individual who is engaging in the illegal use of drugs, when a covered employer acts on the basis of such use. [29 U.S.C. § 706(8), as amended by ADA § 512]

Practice Pointer. The Department of Labor (DOL) issued final rules under the Rehabilitation Act which generally conform the terms and guidance under this act to similar terms and requirements under the ADA. Moreover, the DOL has stated that the Interpretive Guidance on Title I of the ADA set out as an appendix to 29 C.F.R. Part 1630 issued pursuant to that title may be relied on for guidance in interpreting the parallel provisions of the DOL's regulation under the Rehabilitation Act. [41 C.F.R. § 60-741.2(c)(1)]

Q 19:46　To qualify for coverage under the Rehabilitation Act, must the employee's handicap be so severe as to render the employee unable to perform his or her job?

No. An individual can be qualified as handicapped under the Rehabilitation Act if he or she:

1. Actually suffers from a disabling handicap;
2. Has recovered from a previous such condition;
3. Was previously misclassified as having the condition; or
4. Is thought to have the condition regardless of whether he or she actually has the condition.

[41 C.F.R. §§ 60-741.2(n)(1), 60-741.2(r), 60-741.2(s)]

In other words, the Rehabilitation Act protects individuals with present, past, or perceived handicaps. [Memorandum from Arthur B. Culvahouse Jr., counsel to the President (Sept. 27, 1988), *reprinted in* 195 Daily Lab. Rep. (BNA) D-1 (Oct. 7, 1988)]

Q 19:47   Is acquired immune deficiency syndrome a covered handicap under the Rehabilitation Act?

Yes. Under the Rehabilitation Act, acquired immune deficiency syndrome (AIDS) is a covered handicap until the individual is no longer able to perform the duties of the job or until the individual constitutes a direct threat to the health or safety of other individuals. An HIV-positive individual will be covered regardless of whether he or she exhibits symptoms of AIDS.

Q 19:48   Does the Rehabilitation Act permit an employer to exclude or limit coverage of AIDS under an employee welfare benefit plan?

Probably not. The Rehabilitation Act calls into question the validity of exclusions for handicaps such as AIDS from a covered employer's medical plan. The final regulations issued by the DOL prohibit contractors from denying an individual with a disability equal access to insurance or subjecting such an individual to different terms or conditions of insurance based on disability alone, if the disability does not pose increased risks. Although it might be said that AIDs imposes increased risks, it is not clear that particular disability-based distinctions such as a limitation based on AIDS (as opposed to across-the-board limitations) would pass muster under the Rehabilitation Act.

The DOL regulations do permit insurers, hospitals, medical service companies, HMOs, and their agents or entities that administer benefits plans to underwrite, classify, or administer risks that are based on or not inconsistent with state law. Furthermore, a contractor may establish, sponsor, observe, or administer the terms of a bona fide benefits plan which are based on underwriting, classifying, or administering such risks that are based on or not inconsistent with state law. A contractor is also permitted to establish sponsor, observe, or administer the terms of a bona fide benefits plan that is subject to state laws that regulate insurance. These requirements mirror the requirements under the ADA, and the EEOC's supplementary guidance under the ADA rendered these exceptions exceedingly difficult to qualify for. It remains to be seen whether the DOL will take a similarly restrictive approach.

Worker Adjustment and Retraining Notification Act of 1988

Q 19:49   What does the Worker Adjustment and Retraining Notification Act provide?

The Worker Adjustment and Retraining Notification (WARN) Act provides that an employer cannot order a plant closing or mass layoff that would result in a loss of employment by at least 50 full-time employees at a single employment site during any 30-day period, unless the employer gives at least 60 days' advance notice to affected employees (or their representatives), the state dislocated worker unit, and the chief elected local governmental official. In other words, compensation and employee benefits must be continued during the 60-day period. Smaller employment losses over a 90-day period will be aggregated for purposes of determining whether this 50-employee threshold has been reached, unless the employer can demonstrate that they result from separate and distinct actions and causes and are not an attempt to evade the WARN requirements. [29 U.S.C. §§ 2102(a), 2102(d)]

The first and each subsequent group of terminated employees are entitled to a full 60 days' notice. [DOL Regs. § 639.5(a)]

Notice may be given less than 60 days from the plant closing or mass layoff in the case of a faltering company, unforeseeable business circumstances, natural disaster, or when a layoff of six months or less is extended beyond six months as a result of business circumstances that were not reasonably foreseeable at the time of the initial layoff. [29 U.S.C. § 2102(b); DOL Regs. §§ 639.4(b), 639.9]

Q 19:50   Which employers are subject to the requirements of the WARN Act?

Compliance with the WARN Act is required of any employer having:

1. 100 or more employees, excluding part-time employees; or
2. 100 or more employees, including part-time employees who in the aggregate work at least 4,000 hours per week (not including overtime).

[29 U.S.C. § 2101(a)(1)]

For purposes of determining whether the employer is covered by the WARN Act, workers on temporary layoff or on leave who have a reasonable expectation of recall are counted as employees. [DOL Regs. § 630.3(a)(1)]

Q 19:51   What is a plant closing under the WARN Act?

Under the WARN Act, a *plant closing* is a permanent or temporary shutdown of (1) a single employment site or (2) one or more facilities or operating units within a single employment site, provided that the shutdown results in employment loss at such site for at least 50 full-time employees during a 30-day period. [29 U.S.C. § 2101(a)(2)]

Employment losses for two or more groups of employees within a 90-day period may be aggregated unless the employer demonstrates that the employment losses were the result of separate and distinct actions and causes and are not an attempt by the employer to evade the WARN Act.

Under this aggregation rule, the shutdown of a hospital was determined to be a covered plant closing even though it affected fewer than 50 employees. The Fifth Circuit Court of Appeals said that layoffs during the 90-day period should be aggregated because they were caused by a continuing and accelerating economic demise and were not the result of separate and distinct causes. [Hollowell v. Orleans Reg'l Hosp. LLC, 217 F.3d 375 (5th Cir. 2000)]

Q 19:52   What is a mass layoff under the WARN Act?

Under the WARN Act, a *mass layoff* is a reduction in force that does not result from a plant closing and that causes, during any 30-day period, employment loss at that employment site for either:

1. 33 percent of the full-time employees, which must be at least 50 employees; or

2. 500 full-time employees.

[29 U.S.C. § 2101(a)(3)]

No mass layoff was found to have occurred where a plant closing involved fewer than 50 employees, who had been transferred from another plant months earlier. The court refused to aggregate the current and former workplaces for purposes of the 50-employees rule. [McClain v. Laurel St. Art Club, Inc., 1997 U.S. App. LEXIS 1116 (6th Cir. Jan. 22, 1997)]

In a split decision, the Sixth Circuit Court of Appeals held that no mass layoff occurred when a titanium metal products company laid off 87 workers—two workers short of the number needed to make the action a mass layoff under WARN. [Oil, Chem. & Atomic Workers Int'l Union Local 7-629 v. RMI Titanium Co., 199 F.3d 881 (6th Cir. 2000)] The court said that the union employees' return to layoff status after being recalled temporarily could not be considered layoffs contributing to a mass layoff because there was no elimination of positions.

Q 19:53   What constitutes employment loss under the WARN Act?

For purposes of triggering the employer's obligation to provide the WARN notice, *employment loss* means:

1. Termination of employment for reasons other than discharge for cause, voluntary departure, or retirement;

2. A layoff exceeding six months; or

3. A greater-than-50-percent reduction in the employee's hours of work for each month of any six-month period.

[29 §U.S.C. 2101(a)(6)]

However, an employee is not considered to have experienced an employment loss if the closing or layoff results from relocation or consolidation of all or a part of the employer's business, and prior to the closing or layoff, the employer offers either of the following:

1. To transfer the employee to a different site of employment within a reasonable commuting distance with no more than a six-month break in employment; or

2. To transfer the employee to any other site of employment regardless of distance, and the employee accepts within 30 days of the offer or of the closing or layoff, whichever is later.

[29 U.S.C. § 2101(b)(2)]

In *Rifkin v. McDonnell Douglas Corp.* [78 F.3d 1227 (8th Cir. 1996)], the U.S. Court of Appeals for the Eighth Circuit ruled on the issue of what constitutes a mass layoff and employment loss for WARN purposes. McDonnell Douglas dismissed 557 full-time employees from two plants located in the same metropolitan area. However, 35 of the dismissed employees were rehired within six months. In addition, 31 of the dismissed employees elected early retirement. The court held that no mass layoff had occurred. For purposes of the 500 full-time employees rule, the court determined that there were two employment sites involved, not one, and they could not be aggregated. In addition, the Eighth Circuit concluded that the employees who were rehired within six months or who took early retirement could not be counted toward the 500 full-time employees requirement, because they had not suffered an employment loss.

Q 19:54   Who is responsible for providing the WARN notice?

The employer is responsible for giving the WARN notice. The employer is permitted to decide who is the most appropriate person within its organization to prepare and deliver the notice. That person may be the local site plant manager, the local personnel director, or a labor relations officer. [DOL Regs. § 639.4(a)]

In the case of the sale of a part or all of a business, the seller is responsible for providing notice of any plant closing or mass layoff that takes place up to and including the effective date of the sale. The buyer is responsible for providing notice of any plant closing or mass layoff that takes place after the date of the sale. [29 U.S.C. § 2101(b)]

Q 19:55   To whom must the WARN notice be given?

The 60-day advance notice of a plant closing or a mass layoff must be given to:

- All affected employees
- The state dislocated worker unit
- The chief elected local governmental official

[29 U.S.C. § 2902(a)]

Affected employees who must receive the WARN notice are employees who may reasonably be expected to experience an employment loss, including employees who are likely to lose their jobs because of "bumping" rights or other factors, if such factors can be identified at that time. Part-time employees, who are not counted in determining whether plant closing or mass layoff trigger points have been reached, are nonetheless required to be given the WARN notice. For union employees, the notice is to be given to the chief elected officer of the exclusive representative(s) or bargaining agent(s) of the employees. [DOL Regs. § 639.6(a)]

Q 19:56 When must notice be served?

With three exceptions (see Q 19:57), notice must be timed to reach the required parties at least 60 days before a closing or layoff. When the individual employment separations for a closing or layoff occur on more than one day, the notices are due to the representative's state dislocated worker unit and local government at least 60 days before each separation. If the workers are not represented, each worker's notice is due at least 60 days before that worker's separation.

Q 19:57 Are there any exceptions to the 60-day notice?

Yes, there are three exceptions:

1. *Faltering company.* This exception, to be narrowly construed, covers situations where a company has sought new capital or business to stay open and where giving notice would ruin the opportunity to get the new capital or business, and applies only to plant closings.
2. *Unforeseeable business circumstances.* This exception applies to closings and layoffs that are caused by business circumstances that were not reasonably foreseeable at the time notice would otherwise have been required.
3. *Natural disaster.* This applies where a closing or layoff is the direct result of a natural disaster, such as a flood, earthquake, drought, or storm.

If an employer provides less than 60 days' advance notice of a closing or layoff and relies on one of these three exceptions, the employer bears the burden of proof that the conditions for the exception have been met. The employer also must give as much notice as is practicable. When notices are given, they must include a brief statement of the reason for reducing the notice period in addition to other required information. [DOL Regs. § 639.9]

Q 19:58 Are there any exceptions to the WARN Act notice requirement?

Yes. The WARN Act does not require notice to be given if a temporary facility is being closed or if the closing or layoff results from the completion of a particular project or undertaking, and the affected employees were hired with the clear understanding that their employment was limited to the duration of the facility, project, or undertaking. [DOL Regs. § 639.5(c)]

Notice also is not required in certain cases involving employment transfers and for strikes and lockouts that are not intended to evade the requirements of the WARN Act. [DOL Regs. §§ 639.5(b), 639.5(d)]

Q 19:59 May an employer dispense with the 60-day notice requirement for employees who lose their jobs more than 30 days before the actual plant closing?

No. A roof fall at an underground coal mine in August 1995 prompted the mine operator employer, after evaluating the mine's economic viability, to suspend operations. On October 2, 1995, the employer gave the 300 employees at the site notice that the mine would be closed permanently on December 5, 1995. The next day, the employer laid off 89 miners, leaving the rest on the payroll to undertake closing operations until December. Three of the 89 miners and their union sued the employer under the WARN Act for not giving them proper notice.

The court said that the WARN Act guarantees protected employees 60 days' notice of an impending layoff, even if they are to be laid off outside the 30-day aggregation period that statutorily defines a plant closing. [United Mine Workers v. Martinka Coal Co., 202 F.3d 717 (4th Cir. 2000)]

Q 19:60 Must employers provide notice under the WARN Act when union members approve severance?

Apparently not. Mexican Airlines did not violate WARN by terminating machinists with less than 60 days' notice because the workers approved a severance package and signed valid releases. [International Ass'n of Machinists v. Compania Mexicana de Aviacion SA de CV, 199 F.3d 796 (5th Cir. 2000)]

The court found that the severance package, approved by the workers against the advice of the International Association of Machinists, contained more severance benefits than were owed under the bargaining contract and therefore constituted valid consideration in return for the releases.

Q 19:61 What penalties apply to WARN Act violations?

An employer that fails to comply with the WARN Act requirements will be liable for back pay and benefits for up to 60 days. This liability includes the cost of medical expenses incurred during the employment loss that otherwise would have been covered under an employee benefit plan. In addition, failure to give notice to the chief elected official of the local governmental unit is punishable by a penalty of up to $500 per day. [29 U.S.C. § 2104]

The WARN Act provides that an employee who has not received proper notice of a shutdown or layoff must receive back pay for each day of the violation at a rate not less than the higher of (1) the average regular rate received by the employee during the last three years of employment or (2) the final regular rate received by the employee. However, the WARN Act does not specifically define what types of compensation must be included in a back pay award.

In one case, the Ninth Circuit Court of Appeals held that a back pay award under the WARN Act must take into account both tips and holiday pay that would have been earned by employees during the period of a WARN Act violation. According to the court, the WARN Act is a wage worker's equivalent of business interruption insurance that protects a worker from being told on payday that the plant is closing that afternoon and his or her stream of income will be shut off. Therefore, whether an employee's income is paid by the employer or by tipping customers, or whether it is regular or holiday pay, it is all part of the employee's stream of income.

The Ninth Circuit emphasized, however, that the burden is on employees to prove the amount of tips they would have received during the period of the violation. Moreover, they must prove that they would have worked on a holiday before holiday pay will be factored into the equation. "Both are matters to be proved rather than assumed," said the court. [Local Joint Exec. Bd. of Culinary/Bartender Trust Fund v. Las Vegas Sands, Inc., 2001 U.S. App. LEXIS 7603 (9th Cir. Apr. 11, 2001)]

Employee Benefits of Bankrupt Companies

Q 19:62   How are employee benefit obligations treated when an employer declares bankruptcy?

Under the Bankruptcy Abuse Prevention and Consumer Protection Act of 2005, funds withheld or received by an employer from employee wages for payment as contributions to an employee benefit plan are excluded from the employer's bankruptcy estate. [11 U.S.C. § 541(b), as amended by Pub. L. No. 109-8, § 323, 119 Stat. 23 (2005)] Therefore, these funds are protected from the claims of the employer's creditors. Plans covered by the exclusion include benefit plans subject to ERISA and health insurance plans regulated by state law.

The Bankruptcy Act increases the maximum amount of unpaid wages and benefits earned before the employer's bankruptcy that can be treated as a high-priority claim to $10,000 per employee (up from $4,925). In addition, the Bankruptcy Act increases the time limit for high-priority claim treatment to include wages and benefits earned within 180 days (up from 90 days) before the earlier of the employer's bankruptcy filing or cessation of business. [11 U.S.C. 507(a), as amended by Pub. L. No. 109-8, § 1401]

Q 19:63   Can bankrupt companies avoid the obligation to pay benefits to retirees and their dependents?

The federal Retiree Benefits Bankruptcy Protection Act of 1988 does not permit companies that have filed for Title 11 bankruptcy protection to cut back or terminate health and certain other benefits for retirees and their spouses and dependents, except under specified circumstances. [Retiree Benefits Bankruptcy Protection Act of 1988, Pub. L. No. 100-334, 102 Stat. 610 (1988), adding 11 U.S.C. § 1114] The Bankruptcy Abuse Prevention and Consumer Protection Act of 2005 expands the law to prohibit an employer from cutting back on retiree benefits *before* filing for bankruptcy. The law requires reinstatement of retiree benefits that were modified within 180 days before the filing for bankruptcy protection, unless a court finds that the balance of the equities clearly favors the modification. [11 U.S.C. § 1114, as amended by Pub. L. No. 109-8, § 1403, 119 Stat. 23 (2005)]

It appears that in order for the Retiree Benefits Bankruptcy Protection Act to apply, there must be a legally binding obligation on the employer to provide the retiree benefits, absent the Title 11 reorganization filing.

In a decision by the U.S. Court of Appeals for the Second Circuit, it was held that a debtor-employer in a Title 11 reorganization was not required to continue collectively bargained retiree health benefits after the wage agreement expired because it no longer had any legal obligation to continue the benefits. [*In re* Chateaugay Corp., 945 F.2d 1205 (2d Cir. 1991)]

In a U.S. bankruptcy court decision, a debtor-employer in a Title 11 reorganization was held not to be subject to the requirements of the Retiree Benefits Bankruptcy Protection Act with respect to future reduction or elimination of salaried retiree health and life insurance coverage because the plan documents gave the employer the right to amend, modify, or terminate the retirees' coverage at any time on a prospective basis. [*In re* Doskocil Cos., 130 B.R. 858 (Bankr. D. Kan. 1991)]

Q 19:64   Which benefits are protected?

The Retiree Benefits Bankruptcy Protection Act covers medical, surgical, and hospital benefits. It also covers benefits provided in the event of sickness, accident, disability, or death. [11 U.S.C. § 1114(a)]

Q 19:65   Which plans are covered by the bankruptcy restrictions?

Any plan established before filing of the bankruptcy petition is covered. [11 U.S.C. § 1114(a)]

Q 19:66   Are all retirees protected?

No. A retiree is not protected if his or her gross income for the 12 months preceding the filing of the bankruptcy petition exceeded $250,000, unless the retiree demonstrates to the bankruptcy court's satisfaction that he or she is unable to obtain insurance coverage comparable to that provided by the employer on the day before the bankruptcy petition was filed. When retirees are excluded from the act's protection, so are their spouses and dependents. [11 U.S.C. § 1114(l)]

Q 19:67   May retiree benefits covered under the act be modified or terminated while the bankruptcy case is pending?

Yes. The employer, or trustee if one has been appointed, may do this by negotiating with the authorized representative of the retirees. The employer or trustee must propose modifications needed to permit the reorganization and at the same time assure that all parties are treated fairly and equitably. Then the employer or trustee must engage in good-faith negotiations. Retiree benefits must continue to be paid during the negotiation period. [11 U.S.C. §§ 1114(e), 1114(i)]

Q 19:68   Who is authorized to represent the retirees in negotiations about discontinuance?

The union is the authorized representative of unionized retirees receiving benefits covered by a collective bargaining agreement, unless the union refuses to serve or the bankruptcy court appoints a committee of retirees. The bankruptcy court always appoints such a committee to represent nonunion retirees. [11 U.S.C. §§ 1114(b)–1114(d)]

Q 19:69   What happens if the negotiations do not lead to a resolution?

The bankruptcy court has the power to approve a modification of the retiree benefits if:

1. The authorized representative of the retirees refuses the modification without good cause;

2. The modification is necessary to permit the company to be reorganized; and

3. The modification is clearly favored by the balance of the equities and treats all affected parties fairly and equitably.

[11 U.S.C. § 1114(g)]

Q 19:70   Can the bankruptcy court later make further modifications of the retiree health benefits?

Yes. The bankruptcy court may approve additional modifications, including restoring benefits to their prebankruptcy levels. [11 U.S.C. § 1114(g)]

Q 19:71   Can the employer stop paying benefits once the reorganization plan is approved?

Not necessarily. All reorganization plans must include a provision to the effect that the employer must continue the retiree benefits, at the level established during the bankruptcy proceeding, for the duration of the period the employer has obligated itself to pay such benefits. [11 U.S.C. § 1129(a)(13)] Note, however, the case law indicating that a bankruptcy court is apparently powerless to affect retiree benefits that the employer has no binding legal obligation to provide (see Q 19:62).

Veterans' Health Care Amendments of 1986

Q 19:72   How do the Veterans' Health Care Amendments of 1986 affect health plan contracts?

The Veterans' Health Care Amendments of 1986 [Pub. L. No. 99-272, 100 Stat. 382 (1986)] provide that exclusions in a "health plan contract" for expenses incurred for care furnished by a department or agency of the United States, such as for treatment in a Veterans Administration (VA) hospital or nursing home related to treatment of a veteran's non-service-connected disability, are inapplicable. They also authorize the VA to recover the reasonable cost of such care from any third-party payer if the health plan contract would otherwise cover the care or services had they not been furnished by a department or agency of the United States. [38 U.S.C. § 629]

Q 19:73   Who is a third-party payer from whom the Administrator of Veterans Affairs may recover expenses?

A third-party payer for these purposes generally includes:

- An employer
- The employer's insurance carrier
- Persons obligated to provide or pay expenses of health services under a health plan contract

[38 U.S.C. § 629(i)(3)]

Q 19:74   What health plan contracts are covered?

A covered health plan contract generally includes insurance policies or contracts, medical or hospital service agreements, membership or subscription contracts, or similar arrangements under which the expenses for health services incurred by individuals are paid or under which the services are provided to individuals. [38 U.S.C. § 629(i)(1)(A)]

Q 19:75   What are the health services for which the VA may recover expenses?

Expenses for health care and services that are incurred for a military veteran's non-service-related disabilities can be recovered under covered health plan contracts. Recovery is permitted regardless of any exclusion under the contract concerning care or services furnished by a department or agency of the United States, if the care or services would otherwise be covered under the health care contract. [38 U.S.C. § 629(a)]

Q 19:76   How much is the VA authorized to recover?

The VA may recover the reasonable cost of such services determined pursuant to regulations issued by the Administrator of Veterans Affairs, reduced by any applicable plan deductible and copayment amounts. This amount cannot exceed the amount that the third party demonstrates to the Administrator's satisfaction would be payable under a comparable health plan contract to a nongovernmental facility. [38 U.S.C. § 629(c)(2)(B)]

Q 19:77   How does Title II of COBRA affect the health plan contracts of military retirees?

Title II of COBRA provides that exclusions in health plan contracts for inpatient care received by military retirees and their dependents from military hospitals are inapplicable if the contract would otherwise cover such care. Title II authorizes the Secretary of Defense to recover the reasonable cost of such services from third-party payers. [Pub. L. No. 99-272 § 2001(a)(1); 10 U.S.C. § 1095]

The legislative history clarifies that this provision is to apply to both insurance underwriters and private employers that offer health insurance plans that are either self-insured or partially self-insured and partially underwritten. [H.R. Rep. No. 300, 99th Cong., 1st Sess. at 8 (1985)]

Q 19:78   What is a covered health plan contract?

A *covered health plan contract* generally includes insurance policies or contracts, medical or hospital service agreements, membership or subscription contracts, or similar arrangements under which the expenses for health services for individuals are paid or under which the services are provided to individuals. [10 U.S.C. § 1095(b)]

Q 19:79   What are the health services for which the Secretary of Defense may recover expenses?

Expenses for health care and services that are incurred for inpatient care received by military retirees and their dependents from military hospitals can be recovered. Recovery is permitted, regardless of any exclusion under the health care contract concerning care or services furnished by a department or agency of the United States, if the care or services would otherwise be covered under the health care contract. [10 U.S.C. § 1095(a)(1)]

Uniformed Services Employment and Reemployment Rights Act of 1994

Q 19:80   What does the Uniformed Services Employment and Reemployment Rights Act of 1994 provide?

The Uniformed Services Employment and Reemployment Rights Act of 1994 (USERRA) [codified in Title 38 U.S.C. §§ 4301–4333] generally prohibits employers from discriminating or taking acts of reprisal against persons who serve in the uniformed services. Among other things, such persons cannot be denied initial employment, reemployment, retention in employment, promotion, or any benefit of employment because of membership in the uniformed services, performance or application for service, or obligation to perform service in the uniformed services. [38 U.S.C. § 4311]

The USERRA requires employers to provide employees with certain broad employee benefit and compensation rights while employees are engaged in uniformed service and when they return to employment or seek reemployment. An employer does not have a "right of refusal" for a military leave of absence, as long as the employee has not exceeded the cumulative five years of service provided by the USERRA (see Q 19:88).

If there is an acute need for the employee's services or the leave is cumulatively burdensome in light of previous military leave taken by the same employee, the employer may contact the commander of the employee's military unit to request that the employee's military duty be rescheduled or performed by someone else. However, if the commander determines that rescheduling or replacement is impossible, the employer must grant the employee leave.

Reemployment and other rights granted by USERRA apply to all persons who are absent from work because of "service in the uniformed services." Service in the uniformed services includes active duty in:

- The Army, Navy, Marine Corps, Air Force, or Coast Guard;
- The Army, Navy, Marine Corps, Air Force, or Coast Guard Reserves;
- The Army or Air Force National Guard; and
- The Commissioned Corps of the Public Health Service.

USERRA rights also apply to any other category of persons designated by the President during a time of war or national emergency.

The USERRA applies to service members who volunteer for active duty, as well as those who are called up. The law does not apply when a state calls up members of the National Guard for relief during disasters, riots, or other emergencies. However, state laws generally provide comparable reemployment rights in those cases.

Final USERRA regulations provide that service in the uniformed services includes active duty, active and inactive duty for training, federal National Guard duty, absence from employment for an examination to determine the fitness for duty, and absence to perform funeral honors. In addition, service under the Public Health Security and Bioterrorism Preparedness and Response Act of 2002 [Pub. L. No. 107-188, 116 Stat. 594 (2002)] as an intermittent disaster-response appointee or as a participant in an authorized training program is deemed to be service in the uniformed services. [DOL Regs. §§ 1002.5(l), 1002.5(o), 1002.6, 1002.54-1002.62; 70 Fed. Reg. 75,246 (Dec. 19, 2005)]

Q 19:81   Which employers are covered by the USERRA?

The USERRA covers any employer that pays a salary or wages or has control over employment opportunities. There is no minimum number of employees required for the law to apply, and it covers both public and private employers. [38 U.S.C. § 4303(4)]

The definition of *employer* includes a person, institution, organization, or other entity to whom or to which the employer has delegated employment-related responsibilities—such as administration of employee health and welfare benefit plans—unless those responsibilities are purely ministerial in nature. [DOL Regs. § 1002.5(d), 70 Fed. Reg. 75,246 (Dec. 19, 2005)] For example, a third party that makes substantive decisions on plan benefits would be considered an "employer" for USERRA purposes and would be held accountable for USERRA compliance, whereas a third party whose duties are strictly limited to preparation and maintenance of benefit plan forms would not be. The DOL points out that this broad definition of employer encompasses insurance companies that administer employers' life insurance, long-term disability, or health plans, so that the companies cannot refuse to modify their policies in order for the employers to comply with the USERRA.

The USERRA applies to all public employers in the United States, regardless of size. For example, an employer with only one employee is covered by the law. In addition, DOL regulations make it clear that the USERRA applies to foreign employers operating in the United States as well as to U.S. employers operating overseas (unless compliance would violate the law of the foreign country in which the U.S. employer's workplace is located). [DOL Regs. § 1002.34, 70 Fed. Reg. 75,246 (Dec. 19, 2005)]

An *employer* also includes a successor in interest to a service member's former employer. [DOL Regs. § 1002.35, 70 Fed. Reg. 75,246 (Dec. 19, 2005)] Moreover, the DOL regulations provide that a successor in interest can be liable to provide reemployment rights and benefits to a returning service member, even if the successor in interest was unaware of the employee's potential claim at the time of a merger, acquisition, or other succession. [DOL Regs. § 1002.36, 70 Fed. Reg. 75,246 (Dec. 19, 2005)]

Practice Pointer. Given the increasing number of reservists being called up for active duty, companies that are considering a merger or an acquisition should ascertain whether the company to be acquired has any employees who are absent on military duty.

The DOL regulations provide that whether an employer is a successor in interest is to be decided on a case-by-case basis. In one case [Coffman v.

Chugach Support Servs., 411 F.3d 1231 (11th Cir. 2005)], the appellate court ruled that a defense contractor was not a successor in interest to the company that a returning service member had previously worked for because the two companies had not merged or transferred assets. Charles Coffman, at the time of his deployment, held a managerial position at Del-Jen Inc., which held a contract to provide base support services at an Air Force base in Florida. During Coffman's tour of active duty, the base support services contract was awarded to Chugach Support Services, Inc., with Del-Jen as the subcontractor. On his return from military service, Coffman began working for Del-Jen in a position where the pay was comparable to that of his old job, but was not a managerial position. Coffman wanted to be reinstated in his former managerial job, which was being performed by Chugach, so he wrote to Chugach requesting the position. Chugach denied Coffman's request, claiming that Del-Jen's rehiring of Coffman in a comparable position satisfied the USERRA requirements. The Eleventh Circuit Court of Appeals agreed with Chugach—it had no reemployment responsibilities with respect to Coffman. The court concluded that Chugach was not a successor in interest to Del-Jen, even though Chugach was performing services previously performed by Del-Jen. Note, however, that the Eleventh Circuit's analysis might not be followed in other circuits. In a case involving the FMLA, the Sixth Circuit held that a company that took over a federal mail delivery contract was a successor in interest to the company that previously held the contract even though the two had not merged or transferred assets. [Cobb v. Contract Transp., Inc., 452 F.3d 543 (6th Cir. 2006)]

Q 19:82   What protected status is accorded to employees who perform service in the uniformed services?

Individuals who are absent from a position of employment by reason of service in the uniformed services are considered to be on furlough or leave of absence while performing such service, regardless of the employer's personnel policies. [38 U.S.C. § 4316(b)(1)] Moreover, the legislative history indicates that if the employer treats various types of nonmilitary leave of absence differently, it is the intent of Congress that the most favorable treatment the employer accords to any other type of paid or unpaid leave should be given to military leave. [H.R. Rep. No. 103-65, at 33]

An employee absent for military duty is entitled to the non-seniority rights and benefits generally provided to other employees with similar seniority, status, and pay who are away on furlough or leave of absence. Entitlement to non-seniority rights and benefits is not dependent on how the employer characterizes the employee's status during the period of service. For example, an employer cannot characterize an employee as "terminated" during the period of service to avoid complying with USERRA requirements. [DOL Regs. § 1002. 149, 70 Fed. Reg. 75,246 (Dec. 19, 2005)]

Effect on employers. Employers cannot define military service as they wish in their personnel policies. The treatment of military service is a matter of federal law. Employers may not unilaterally determine whether employees in military service will receive paid or unpaid leave, be terminated from employment, or receive less favorable treatment than employees taking other types of leaves of absence or furlough.

However, the DOL regulations make it clear that the USERRA sets a floor, not a ceiling, on reemployment rights and benefits for protected employees. In other words, an employer may provide greater rights and benefits than the USERRA provides, but an employer cannot refuse to provide any right or benefit guaranteed by the USERRA. [DOL Regs. § 1002.7(a), 70 Fed. Reg. 75,246 (Dec. 19, 2005)] In addition, if an employer provides a benefit or right that exceeds USERRA requirements, it cannot cut back on other rights or benefits guaranteed by the USERRA. For example, even though not required by the USERRA, an employer can provide a fixed number of days of paid military leave per year for employees who are members of the National Guard or reserves. However, provision of that benefit does not permit the employer to refuse to provide required unpaid leave in addition to the days of paid leave. [DOL Regs. § 1002.7(d), 70 Fed. Reg. 75,246 (Dec. 19, 2005)] Similarly, if an employer provides full or partial pay when an employee performs military service, the employer is not excused from providing other rights and benefits required by the USERRA. [DOL Regs. § 1002.151, 70 Fed. Reg. 75,246 (Dec. 19, 2005)]

Q 19:83   Does an employee have any special right to use accrued leave when he or she is called up for military service?

If the employee interrupts his or her employment because of a period of military service, the employer must allow the employee to take any vacation, annual leave, or similar leave with pay that he or she has accrued before the military service begins. [38 U.S.C. § 4316(d)]

DOL regulations make it clear that an employee must be permitted, upon request, to use any accrued vacation, annual leave, or similar leave with pay during the period of military service in order to continue his or her civilian pay. However, an employee is not entitled to use accrued sick leave unless the employer generally allows employees to use sick leave for any reason or allows other similarly situated individuals on furlough or leave of absence to use accrued sick leave. [38 U.S.C. § 4316(d); DOL Regs. § 1002.153(a), 70 Fed. Reg. 75,246 (Dec. 19, 2005)]

However, an employer may not *require* an employee to use accrued leave during a period of military service. [38 U.S.C. § 4316(d); DOL Regs. § 1002. 153(b), 70 Fed. Reg. 75,246 (Dec. 19, 2005)]

Q 19:84   What employee benefits must the employee receive while he or she is on deemed furlough or leave of absence?

The answer to this question depends on the individual employer. The USERRA requires that, as a general rule, the employee receive all rights and benefits not determined by seniority that the employer generally provides to employees with similar seniority, status, and pay who are on furlough or leave of absence. [38 U.S.C. § 4316(a)] Thus, it is the employer's general policies for furloughs or leaves of absence that determine what must be done. This rule applies to all contracts, agreements, policies, practices, and plans in effect when the individual's service in the uniformed services begins and those that are established while that individual is performing such military service. [38 U.S.C. § 4316(b)(1)(B)] Also, as noted in Q 19:81, if the employer's practices differ for various types of leaves, the military leave is to be accorded the most favorable treatment.

Example 1. Big Company's life insurance program coverage continues uninterrupted for 90 days for any employee who is on a paid or unpaid leave of absence. Bob voluntarily leaves employment for 12 weeks to perform military service. After the eighth week of his absence, he dies of a heart attack. Since Big Company was required to treat Bob in the same manner as any other individual on leave of absence or furlough, Bob was covered by the insurance program on his date of death.

Example 2. Big Company permits employees on paid leave of absence to continue long-term disability plan coverage for up to 90 days. It does not permit employees on unpaid leave to continue LTD coverage during their leave. Big Company must permit employees absent due to the performance of military service to continue long-term disability plan coverage, even if the military leave is unpaid. Where the employer has different policies for different types of leave, the military leave is to be treated according to the most favorable policy.

On the other hand, an employee who "knowingly" states in writing that he or she will not return to an employment position after a tour of duty will lose those rights and benefits that are not determined by seniority. However, USERRA regulations provide that such a notice does not waive the employee's reemployment rights or seniority-based rights and benefits upon reemployment. [DOL Regs. § 1002.152, 70 Fed. Reg. 75,246 (Dec. 19, 2005)]

Vacation leave. The DOL regulations make it clear that accrual of vacation leave is considered a non-seniority benefit that must be provided to an employee on military leave, but only if the employer provides for accrual of vacation leave for similarly situated employees on comparable leaves of absence. [DOL Regs. § 1002.150(c), 70 Fed. Reg. 75,246 (Dec. 19, 2005)]

Medical coverage. The USERRA contains special rules for continuation of group health plan coverage (see Q 19:85).

Pension plans. The USERRA also contains special provisions relating to pension plan coverage for the period of absence due to service in the uniformed services. These provisions are beyond the scope of this book.

Q 19:85   Can the employee be required to pay the employee cost, if any, of benefits continued during a military leave?

Yes. The employer can require an employee on military leave to pay the employee cost, if any, of benefits continued during the leave, but only to the extent the employer would also require employees on furlough or leave of absence to do so. [38 U.S.C. § 4316(4)]

For special rules that apply to payments for health plan coverage during military leave, see Q 19:87.

Q 19:86   What special rules apply to continuation of health plan coverage during military leave?

The USERRA imposes COBRA-like extension of coverage requirements on health plans. In the past, this continuation coverage was available for up to 18 months following an employee's departure for military service. However, the Veterans Benefits Improvement Act [Pub. L. No. 108-454, 118 Stat. 3598 (2004)] extended the continuation coverage period to 24 months for coverage elections made on or after December 10, 2004.

Unlike COBRA, USERRA does not have a 20-employee minimum employer size requirement. Accordingly, the extension of the medical plan coverage provision under the USERRA applies even to employers that are exempt from COBRA.

The continuation coverage period begins on the date the employee's absence for the purpose of performing military service begins. Continuation coverage ends on the expiration of the 24-month period or, if earlier, on the date the employee fails to return from military service or apply for reemployment. [38 U.S.C. § 4317; DOL Regs. § 1002.164, 70 Fed. Reg. 75,246 (Dec. 19, 2005)]

During a period of continuation coverage, an employer can generally charge up to 102 percent of the full premium under the plan (i.e., the employer's share plus the employee's share as well as 2 percent for administrative costs). However, if an employee's period of military service is less than 31 days, the employee can be required to pay only the employee share (if any) for the coverage. [DOL Regs. § 1002.166, 70 Fed. Reg. 75,246 (Dec. 19, 2005)]

The USERRA *does not* require an employer to establish a health plan if it does not have one or to provide any particular type of coverage. [DOL Regs. § 1002.164(b), 70 Fed. Reg. 75,246 (Dec. 19, 2005)] In addition, USERRA only requires an employer to continue the health coverage in effect for the employee at the beginning of his or her period of service. It *does not* require an employer to permit an employee to initiate new health plan coverage at the beginning of a period of service if he or she did not previously have such coverage. [DOL Regs. § 1002.164(c), 70 Fed. Reg. 75,246 (Dec. 19, 2005)]

Health plan. The term *health plan* for this purpose includes insurance policies or contracts, medical or hospital service agreements, membership or subscription contracts, or other arrangements under which health services for individuals are provided or the expenses of such services are paid. [38 U.S.C. § 4303(7)] The term also includes group health plans as defined under ERISA's COBRA provisions. [38 U.S.C. § 4317(a)(1)(A)]

> **Practice Pointer.** As an alternative to electing continuation coverage, an employee and his or her dependents may be entitled to special enrollment rights in another group health plan. For example, if an employee loses coverage under an employer's plan as a result of being called to military service, the employee may be entitled to special enrollment in a plan maintained by his or her spouse's employer. (See chapter 5 for a complete discussion of special enrollment rights.)

If an employee's health plan coverage terminates by reason of military service, the coverage must be reinstated upon reemployment (see Q 19:91).

Q 19:87   How does an employee elect and pay for continuation coverage under the USERRA?

The USERRA does not specify requirements for electing continuation coverage. A health plan administrator may develop reasonable rules for electing continuation coverage, provided those rules are consistent with USERRA requirements. However, an employee cannot be barred from electing continuation coverage where it is unreasonable or impossible for the employee to give advance notice of a period of military service or to make a timely election of continuation coverage. [DOL Regs. § 1002.165, 70 Fed. Reg. 75,246 (Dec. 19, 2005)]

The USERRA provides that an employee can be required to pay 102 percent of the full premium during a period of continuation coverage unless theemployee's period of service is for fewer than 31 days, in which case the employee can be required to pay only the employee share of the premium. However, the USERRA does not specify any required methods for paying for continuation coverage. Health plan administrators may develop reasonable procedures for payment. [DOL Regs. § 1002.166, 70 Fed. Reg. 75,246 (Dec. 19, 2005)]

> **Practice Pointer.** If an employer's plan is subject to the COBRA continuation coverage requirements, it may be reasonable for an employer to adopt COBRA-compliant election rules, provided those rules do not conflict with the USERRA requirements. [DOL Regs. § 1002.167(b)] For details on the COBRA election and payment rules, see chapter 6.

The consequences of an employee's failure to elect continuation coverage depend on whether the employer has established reasonable election rules and whether the employee gave advance notice of the military service.

If an employee leaves for military service without giving advance notice (and, consequently, without electing continuation coverage), the employee's health coverage can be cancelled as of the date of his or her departure. However, if the employee's failure to give notice was excused under the USERRA, the coverage must be reinstated retroactively if and when the employee elects continuation coverage and pays all unpaid amounts due. The plan may not charge any administrative reinstatement costs. As a general rule, an employee's failure to give advance notice of a period of military service is excused if giving notice was impossible, unreasonable, or precluded by military necessity. [DOL Regs. § 1002.167(a), 70 Fed. Reg. 75,246 (Dec. 19, 2005)]

If, in a situation where the period of military service is longer than 30 days, the employee gives advance notice but does not elect COBRA coverage before his or her departure, the employee's coverage can be cancelled as of the date of his or her departure. The requirements for reinstating the employee's coverage depend on whether or not the plan has developed reasonable rules for electing continuation coverage. If such rules have been developed, the plan must permit retroactive reinstatement of uninterrupted coverage in the event the employee elects continuation coverage and pays all unpaid premiums with the period set by the plan. If such rules have not been developed, the plan must permit retroactive reinstatement of uninterrupted coverage in the event the employee elects and pays all unpaid premiums before the end of the continuation coverage period. [DOL Regs. § 1002.167(b), 70 Fed. Reg. 75,246 (Dec. 19, 2005)]

> **Practice Pointer.** Although coverage during a period of service shorter than 31 days is technically continuation coverage, the DOL regulations do not address the election and termination requirements for such periods. This omission suggests that that the DOL anticipates employers will not require a specific election of continuation coverage for short periods of service and will simply continue an employee's coverage as long as the employee pays his or her share of the premium.

In cases where an employee elects continuation coverage but does not pay the required premiums, health plans may establish reasonable rules allowing cancellation of coverage for nonpayment. Here again, if a plan is subject to COBRA, it may be reasonable to adopt COBRA-compliant rules to the extent they do not conflict with USERRA's. [DOL Regs. § 1002.167, 70 Fed. Reg. 75,246 (Dec. 19, 2005)]

Q 19:88   How does a multiemployer health plan handle continuation coverage required by the USERRA?

Under a multiemployer health plan, liability for employer contributions and benefits in connection with USERRA health plan provisions must either be allocated to the employee's last employer before the period of service or otherwise as the health plan provides. If the last employer is no longer in operation, liability for continuation coverage is allocated to the health plan. [DOL Regs. § 1002.178, 70 Fed. Reg. 75,246 (Dec. 19, 2005)]

Some multiemployer plans use a health benefits account system in which an employee accumulates amounts for future health benefit eligibility. These plans are often called "dollar bank" plans, "credit bank" plans, or "hour bank" plans.

If an employee with a positive health benefits account balance elects to continue coverage during a period of military service, the employee must be offered two options:

1. The employee may use his or her health account balance to cover the cost of continuation coverage. If the account balance is used up during the period of continuation coverage, the employee must be permitted to continue coverage on a pay-as-you-go basis. Upon the employee's reemployment, the plan must provide for immediate reinstatement of the employee's coverage, but may require the employee to pay the cost of coverage until he or she has earned enough credits to pay for coverage under the plan.

2. The employee may pay for continuation coverage out of pocket so as to maintain his or her account balance intact. Upon reemployment, the employee may resume usage of the account balance. [DOL Regs. § 1002. 171, 70 Fed. Reg. 75,246 (Dec. 19, 2005)]

Q 19:89   When is an employer obligated to reemploy a person who has been absent due to performance of uniformed service?

In general, a reservist or National Guard member can be on active duty for a cumulative period of five years (not including required drill and annual training) without losing his or her right to reemployment. [38 U.S.C. § 4312] DOL regulations clarify that the five-year period includes only the cumulative period of uniformed service by an employee with respect to one particular employer, and does not include periods of service while employed by a different employer. [DOL Regs. § 1002.101, 70 Fed. Reg. 75,246 (Dec. 19, 2005)] Therefore, an employee is entitled to be absent from a particular position of employment because of service in the uniformed services for up to five years and still retain reemployment rights with that employer. The five-year period starts anew with each new employer.

The five-year limit will be extended for service required to complete an initial period of required service or if the employee is unable to obtain release within the five-year period. The five-year limit also does not apply to service under an order to active duty or to remain on active duty during a war or national emergency declared by the President or Congress. Under DOL regulations, certain other periods of service, including service to fulfill periodic National Guard and Reserve training requirements, do not count against the five-year limit. [See DOL Regs. § 1002.103.] In addition, DOL regulations make it clear that the five-year period includes only the time the employee spends actually performing military service. For example, after an employee completes a period of service, he or she is given a certain amount of time to report back to work and submit an application for reemployment (see below). That time, however, is not counted against the five-year limit. [DOL Regs. § 1110.100, 70 Fed. Reg. 75,246 (Dec. 19, 2005)]

On the other hand, separation from service with a dishonorable or bad conduct discharge or under "other than honorable conditions" will terminate an employee's right to reemployment. Similarly, an individual who is dropped from the military rolls because he or she is absent without leave for more than three months or has been imprisoned by a civilian court is not entitled to reemployment. A commissioned officer who is dismissed under circumstances involving a court martial or by order of the President in time of war is not required to be reemployed. [DOL Regs. § 1002.135, 70 Fed. Reg. 75,246 (Dec.19, 2005)]

The law requires the employee (or an official of the military service) to give the employer written or oral advance notice of the employee's call to service. Notice is not required if it is precluded by military necessity or giving notice is otherwise unreasonable or impossible.

The law does not specify how much notice is required, but the Department of Defense advises members of the National Guard and Reserve to give their employers as much advance notice as possible.

The USERRA regulations make it explicit that an employee is *not* required to obtain the employer's permission before departing for uniformed service in order to protect his or her reemployment rights. [DOL Regs. § 1002.87, 70 Fed. Reg. 75,246 (Dec. 19, 2005)] According to the preamble to the regulations, imposing a prior consent requirement would improperly grant the employer veto authority over the employee's performance of military service. On the other hand, the regulations recommend that an employer contact the appropriate military authority to discuss any concerns over the timing, frequency, and duration of an employee's military service. [DOL Regs. § 1002.104, 70 Fed. Reg. 75,246 (Dec. 19, 2005)]

The regulations also make it clear that an employee departing for service is not required to decide at that time whether he or she intends to return to work for the same employer following the tour of duty. The employee may defer that decision until after he or she concludes the period of service, and an employer may not press the employee for any assurances about his or her plans. [DOL Regs. § 1002.88, 70 Fed. Reg. 75,246 (Dec. 19, 2005)] Moreover, even if the employee tells the employer that he or she does not intend to seek reemployment after completing the military service, the employee does not forfeit the right to reemployment. In other words, an employee cannot waive his or her right to reemployment.

To be eligible for full reemployment rights, an employee is required to return to work within a specified time. For periods of service of up to 30 days, the employee must report back to work on the first regularly scheduled workday following the completion of service and safe transportation home, plus an eight-hour period of rest.

If the employee's military service lasts for 31 to 180 days, he or she must submit a written or verbal application for reemployment no later than 14 days after the completion of the period of service. If the employee's military service lasts for 181 days or longer, he or she must submit an application for reemployment not later than 90 days after completion of the period of service. [DOL Regs. § 1002.117, 70 Fed. Reg. 75,246 (Dec. 19, 2005)]

If the deadline for applying for reemployment falls on a day when the employer's offices are not open, or when no one is available to accept the application, the deadline is extended to the next business day. In addition, the deadlines for reporting to work or applying for reemployment can be extended for up to two years if the employee is hospitalized for or convalescing from an injury or illness that occurred or was aggravated during the period of military service.

Bear in mind, however, that an employee does not automatically lose the right to reemployment if he or she fails to report to work or apply for reemployment by the required deadline. Instead, the employee's rights will be governed by the employer's rules for unexcused absences.

When an employee is returning from a period of service of 31 days or more, the employer may ask the employee to provide documentation that will allow the employer to check the length of the employee's service and whether the employee made a timely application for reemployment. The employer may also ask for documentation showing that the employee's separation from military service was not under circumstances that would disqualify the employee for reemployment (e.g., the employee did not receive a dishonorable or bad conduct discharge). [DOL Regs. § 1002.121, 70 Fed. Reg. 75,246 (Dec. 19, 2005)]

If an employee cannot provide such documentation because it is not readily available, the employer may not delay the employee's return to work. If it later turns out the employee was not eligible for reemployment, he or she may be terminated. [DOL Regs. § 1002.122, 70 Fed. Reg. 75,246 (Dec. 19, 2005)]

An employee returning from military service is entitled to "prompt" reemployment. [DOL Regs. § 1002.180, 70 Fed. Reg. 75,246 (Dec. 19, 2005)]

As a rule, an employee must be reinstated to the job he or she held before leaving for military service. In some cases, however, an employee may be entitled to a better job.

In the case of service of less than 90 days, the employee is entitled to the job he or she would have attained without the break for military service, as long as he or she is qualified for the job or can become qualified with reasonable efforts. If service lasted more than 90 days, the employee must be reemployed in (1) the position he or she would have attained without the break for service, or (2) a position of equivalent seniority, status, and pay. [DOL Regs. § 1002.196-197, 70 Fed. Reg. 75,246 (Dec. 19, 2005)]

Practice Pointer. There's an "escalator principle" at work here. The absent employee must continue to move up the corporate ladder while he or she is absent for military service. If the employee is not initially qualified for the position he or she would have attained, the employer must make reasonable efforts to update the employee's skills or provide training the employee would have received on the job.

As noted above, when a returning service member cannot be reemployed in the position he or she would have attained but for the break for service, the employer must provide a position that is equivalent in seniority, status, and pay. Whether a job is equivalent in seniority and pay is relatively easy to determine.

But what makes a job equivalent in status? According to the proposed USERRA regulations, job status generally refers to the incidents or attributes attached to, and inherent in, a particular job. Examples of status may be the exclusive right to a sales territory; the opportunity to advance in a position; eligibility for possible election to a position with the employee representative organization; greater availability of work where piece rates apply; the opportunity to work additional hours and to advance in a job; the opportunity to withdraw from a union; the opportunity to obtain a license; or, the opportunity to work a particular shift. [Prop. DOL Regs. §§ 1002.193-194, 69 Fed. Reg. 56,265 (Sept.20, 2004)]

The law provides that a returning service member must be "promptly reemployed." However, what constitutes prompt reemployment will depend on the circumstances. For example, when an employee returns from a weekend of National Guard duty, prompt reemployment will generally mean the next regularly scheduled workday. On the other hand, prompt reemployment after several years of active duty may require some time because the employer may have to reassign or give notice to another employee who is filling the returning employee's former position. Absent unusual circumstances, reemployment must occur within two weeks of the application for reemployment. [DOL Regs. § 1002.181, 70 Fed. Reg. 75,246 (Dec. 19, 2005)]

An employee who is reemployed after a period of service of more than 180 days cannot be discharged, except for cause, within one year after the date of reemployment. An employee whose service lasted more than 30 days but less than 181 days, cannot be discharged for 180 days. Employees who serve 30 or fewer days are not protected from discharge. However, they are protected from discrimination because of their military service. [DOL Regs. § 1002.247, 70 Fed. Reg. 75,246 (Dec. 19, 2005)]

Disabled veterans. Like other returning service members, a disabled veteran is entitled to the position he or she would have attained but for military service. Moreover, if the disability limits the service member's ability to perform the job, the employer is required to make reasonable efforts to accommodate the disability. [38 U.S.C. § 4313(a)(3)]

If, despite the employer's reasonable efforts to accommodate the disability, a returning disabled service member cannot become qualified for his or her escalator position, he or she is entitled to be reemployed in any other position that is equivalent in seniority, status, and pay that he or she is qualified to perform or can become qualified to perform with reasonable efforts by the employer. [38 U.S.C. § 4313(a)(3)(A)] If no equivalent position exists, the returning service member is entitled to reemployment in an appropriate job that is the nearest approximation in terms of seniority, status, and pay. [38 U.S.C. § 4313(a)(3)(B)]

In the case of a disability that is not permanent, a returning service member may be entitled to interim reemployment in an alternate position that he or she is qualified for and can perform despite the disability. If no such alternate position exists, 'the disabled service member would be entitled to reinstatement on "sick leave" or "light duty"' status until he or she completely recovers.

Reemployment exceptions. Reemployment of a returning service member is not required if the employer's circumstances have changed so that reemployment is impossible or unreasonable. A reduction-in-force that would have included the returning service member is an example of such a change in circumstances. In addition, reemployment is not required if it would cause "undue hardship" for an employer.

In addition, reemployment is not required if the employee was employed for only a brief, nonrecurrent period before military service, and there was no reasonable expectation that such employment would continue indefinitely or for a significant period. [38 U.S.C. § 4311(d)(1)]

For this purpose, "undue hardship" means employer actions requiring significant difficulty or expense when considered in light of a number of factors: the nature and cost of the actions required by the USERRA; the overall financial resources of the facility or facilities involved (including the effect on expenses and resources or the impact of such action on the operation of the facility); and the employer's overall financial resources, size (in terms of employees), and the number, type, and location of its facilities. Also considered are the type of operation or operations of the employer, including the composition, structure, and functions of its workforce, and the geographic separateness and administrative or fiscal relationship of the facility or facilities to the employer. [38 U.S.C. § 4303(15)]

Q 19:90   If an employee welfare benefit plan provides benefits based on length of service, is an employee who returns from military service entitled to have such military service counted for purposes of the benefit?

Yes. If the employee meets the statutory requirements for reemployment, he or she is entitled to seniority and other rights and benefits determined by seniority that he or she had when his or her military leave started and whatever additional seniority, rights, and benefits he or she would have attained if he or she had remained continuously employed. [38 U.S.C. § 4316]

Example 1. Atex Company grants two weeks' vacation to employees with up to nine years of service and three weeks' vacation to employees having ten or more years of service. Jane, an eight-year employee of Atex Company, is absent for three years due to performance of uniformed service and then applies for reemployment in accordance with the USERRA. Atex must treat Jane as if she had completed 11 years of employment for purposes of its vacation policy. Jane will thus be entitled to three weeks of vacation per year from now on.

Example 2. The facts are the same as those in Example 1, except that while Jane is performing military service, Atex amends its vacation policy to grant employees with ten years of service four weeks of vacation. When Jane returns, she will have to be given the benefit of this plan amendment because she would have received the increase had she remained continuously employed.

Example 3. Atex Company's long-term disability plan requires ten years of service as a condition of eligibility. When Jane returns from her three-year period of service, her three years of military service must be credited toward her eligibility under the long-term disability plan.

DOL regulations make it clear that USERRA is not a statutory mandate to impose seniority systems on employers. Rather, the law requires only that those employers who do provide benefits based on seniority restore a returning service member to his or her proper place on the seniority ladder. [DOL Regs. § 1002.211, 70 Fed. Reg. 75, 246 (Dec. 19, 2005)]

Under the regulations, a benefit is subject to the USERRA requirements if the benefit is provided as a reward for length of service rather than a form of short-term compensation for services rendered, and the service member's receipt of the benefit, but for his or her absence due to service, was reasonably certain. The regulation describes a benefit as "reasonably certain" if there was a "high probability" (but not necessarily an "absolute certainty") that the returning service member would have obtained the seniority-based benefit if continuously employed. [DOL Regs. § 1002.213, 70 Fed. Reg. 75,246 (Dec. 19, 2005)]

Q 19:91   If an employee's health coverage terminates during a period of military service, does the coverage have to be reinstated upon reemployment?

If health plan coverage for the employee or a dependent was terminated because of his or her military service, the coverage must be reinstated upon reemployment. [DOL Regs. § 1002.168, 70 Fed. Reg. 75,246 (Dec. 19, 2005)] The reason for the termination of coverage is irrelevant. Thus, an employee who does not elect continuation coverage is entitled to reinstatement on the same footing as an employee who elects continuation coverage but whose period of service lasts beyond the 24-month continuation coverage period. Similarly, an employee who elects continuation coverage but whose coverage is terminated for nonpayment is also entitled to reinstatement of coverage.

No exclusion or waiting period for coverage can be imposed if the exclusion or waiting period would not have been imposed if coverage had not been terminated by reason of military service. However, the USERRA does permit a health plan to impose an exclusion or waiting period with respect to illnesses or injuries that were incurred in or aggravated during the period of military service. A determination that the illness or injury is service-connected must be made by the Secretary of Veterans Affairs. [DOL Regs. § 1002.168, 70 Fed. Reg. 75,246 (Dec. 19, 2005)]

The USERRA requires an employer to reinstate health plan coverage at the time of reemployment. However, the law permits—but does not require—the employer to allow an employee to delay reinstatement of health coverage until a later date. [DOL Regs. § 1002.168] For example, an employee may request a delay if he or she has been covered by a spouse's health plan and wants to wait until the next open enrollment period to drop that coverage.

Q 19:92   Does a period of military service count toward FMLA eligibility?

The Family and Medical Leave Act allows employees of a covered employer to take up to 12 weeks of unpaid, job-protected leave during a 12-month period for certain family and medical reasons. To be eligible for leave, an employee must have worked for the employer for at least (1) 12 months (whether or not consecutive) and (2) 1,250 hours during the 12-month period immediately preceding the start of the leave.

The DOL has indicated that the 12-month employment requirement must be calculated by including all months that an employee serves on military duty. So, for example, if an employee is called to active duty after working for the employer for 9 months and serves on active duty for 4 months, he or she will have met the 12-month employment requirement upon return to work.

In addition, the 1,250-hour requirement must be calculated using the employee's pre-service work schedule. Thus, the hours the employee would normally have worked for the employer but for the military service are added to the hours actually worked in determining whether the employee worked 1,250 hours in the 12-month period immediately preceding the leave. [USERRA-FMLA Questions and Answers, 7/25/02] The DOL regulations make it clear that an employee who is denied family leave for failing to satisfy the FMLA requirements because of a work absence necessitated by military service may have a cause of action against the employer under the USERRA, but not under the FMLA itself. [DOL Regs. § 1002.210, 70 Fed. Reg. 75,246 (Dec. 19, 2005)]

For a detailed discussion of the FMLA, see chapter 16.

Q 19:93   What penalties apply if an employee's USERRA rights are violated?

The USERRA provides several enforcement mechanisms. An employee may file a complaint with the Secretary of Labor (through the Veterans' Employment and Training Service) if the employer has failed or refused, or is about to fail or refuse, to comply with the USERRA. The Secretary will investigate the complaint and attempt to resolve it with the employer. In the event the Secretary is unsuccessful in resolving the complaint, the employee or the employer may request that the Secretary refer the complaint to the Attorney General of the United States for possible follow-up. The employee may also bring an action in U.S. district court (whether or not he or she files a complaint with the Secretary) to require the employer to comply with the law and to compensate for any loss of wages or benefits. The court may award the prevailing party reasonable attorneys' fees, expert witness fees, and other litigation expenses. [38 U.S.C. § 3424]

The Veterans' Benefits Improvements Act of 2008 [Pub. L. No. 110-389, 122 Stat. 4145 (Oct. 23, 2008)] makes it clear that there is no limit on the period for filing a complaint or claim under USERRA. While the Department of Labor has consistently taken the position that no federal statute of limitation applies to USERRA actions, a number of federal courts had held that USERRA claims were subject to the general four-year statute of limitations on federal causes of action not governed by a specific statute of limitations. [See Rogers v. City of San Antonio, 392 F.3d 758 (5th Cir. 2003), *cert.denied*, 545 U.S. 1129 (2005); O'Neil v. Putnam Retail Mgmt., 407 F. Supp. 2d 310 (D. Mass. 2005); Nino v. Haynes Int'l, Inc., 2005 U.S. Dist. LEXIS 43971 (S.D. Ind. Aug. 19, 2005).] In a case decided subsequent to the Veterans' Benefits Improvements Act (VBIA), the Seventh Circuit Court of Appeals ruled that a USERRA action brought 13 years after the alleged USERRA violation occurred was untimely. The court concluded that, at the time of the violation, the general four-year statute of limitations applied. According to the court, there was no evidence that it was the intent of Congress to apply the VBIA retroactively. [Middleton v. City of Chicago, 2009 U.S. App. LEXIS 18979 (7th Cir. Aug. 24, 2009)]

Q 19:94   What is the effective date of the USERRA and its implementing regulations?

The USERRA is generally effective with respect to reemployments initiated on or after the first day after the 60-day period beginning on October 13, 1994 (i.e., December 12, 1994), although the law's general nondiscrimination requirements became effective on October 13, 1994, the date of enactment. Final DOL regulations interpreting the USERRA requirements became effective January 18, 2006. [70 Fed. Reg. 75,246 (Dec. 19, 2005)]

Q 19:95   Is an employer required to give employees notice of their rights under USERRA?

Yes. The Veterans Benefits Improvement Act [Pub. L. No. 108-454, 118 Stat. 3598 (2004)] requires employers to provide employees entering military service with a notice of the rights, benefits, and obligations of employees and employers under USERRA. The law specifies that the requirement can be satisfied by posting a notice in locations where notices to employees are customarily posted. The DOL has developed a workplace poster that can be used to satisfy the notice requirement. The poster for private employers is available at *www.dol.gov/vets/ programs/userra/poster.pdf*.

Q 19:96   Does USERRA provide leave rights for family members of military personnel?

No, it does not. However, in 2008, a new law, dubbed the Wounded Warriors Act [Pub. L. No. 110-181, 122 Stat. 3 (Jan. 28, 2008)], amended the FMLA to allow otherwise eligible employees to take leave related to a family member's military service. The family military leave rights were subsequently expanded by the National Defense Authorization Act for Fiscal Year 2010. [Pub. L. No. 111-84, 123 Stat. 2190 (Oct. 22, 2009)]

The law requires employers to provide leave for military family members in two circumstances:

1. An eligible employee is entitled to up to 12 weeks of leave in a 12-month period because of any "qualifying exigency" arising out of the fact that the spouse, son, daughter, or parent of the employee is called to active duty (or has been notified of an impending call or order to active duty) in the Armed Forces. Qualifying exigency leave is also available when a family member in the Armed Forces is deployed to a foreign country. [FMLA § 102(a)(1)(E)]; 29 U.S.C. § 2612(a)(1)(E)]

2. An eligible employee who is the spouse, son, daughter, parent, or next of kin (i.e., closest blood relative) of a "covered servicemember" with a serious illness or injury incurred in the line of duty is entitled to a total of 26 weeks of leave in a 12-month period to care for the servicemember. Caregiver leave also applies when a family member is called on to care for a veteran who is undergoing medical treatment, recuperation, or therapy for a serious illness or injury and who was a member of the Armed Forces at any time during the 5-year period preceding the date on which the veteran receives treatment. [FMLA § 102(a)(3); 29 U.S.C. § 2612(a)(3)]

For details concerning the FMLA rules, see chapter 16.

Employers should also check state law. A growing number of states have passed legislation mandating leave rights for family members of military personnel.

Genetic Information Nondiscrimination Act of 2008

Q 19:97   What is the Genetic Information Nondiscrimination Act?

The Genetic Information Nondiscrimination Act of 2008 (GINA) [Pub. L. No. 110-223, 122 Stat. 881 (May 21, 2008)] prohibits genetic discrimination in employment and in health insurance. GINA's prohibitions against genetic discrimination in employment took effect November 21, 2009.

Title I of GINA amends the Employee Retirement Income Security Act of 1974 (ERISA), the Public Health Service Act (PHSA), the Internal Revenue Code of 1986 (Code), and the Social Security Act (SSA) to prohibit discrimination in health coverage based on genetic information. For details on these rules, see chapter 5.

Title II of GINA expands Title VII of the Civil Rights Act of 1964 to impose new restrictions on an employer's collection, use, and disclosure of genetic information.

GINA provides that is an unlawful employment practice for an employer:

- To fail or refuse to hire, or to discharge, an employee, or otherwise to discriminate against any employee with respect to the compensation, terms, conditions, or privileges of employment of the employee, because of genetic information with respect to the employee; or

- To limit, segregate, or classify employees in any way that would deprive or tend to deprive any employee of employment opportunities or otherwise adversely affect the status of any employee because of genetic information with respect to the employee.

[GINA § 202(a)]

GINA also provides that it is an unlawful employment practice to request, require, or purchase genetic information about an employee or a family member of an employee, except in certain circumstances. [GINA § 202(b)]

Genetic information obtained by an employer must be treated as a confidential medical record and may not be disclosed except in limited circumstances. [GINA § 206]

GINA applies to "covered entities," including private and public employers with 15 or more employees, employing offices, employment agencies, labor organizations, and joint labor-management committees. The protections of GINA extend to current and former employees, as well as job applicants, apprentices and trainees, and labor union members.

The Equal Employment Opportunity Commission has issued proposed regulations interpreting Title II of GINA. [Prop. 29 C.F.R. §§ 1.635.1–1.635.12]

Q 19:98   What is genetic information?

For purposes of Title II of GINA, genetic information includes information about an individual's genetic tests, the genetic tests of an individual's family members, and the manifestation of a disease or disorder in an individual's family members. Genetic information also includes an individual's request for, or receipt of, genetic services, but does not include information about the sex or age of any individual. Genetic information about an individual includes the genetic information about a fetus carried by a pregnant woman or an embryo legally held by an individual utilizing an assisted reproductive technology.

Genetic tests involve analysis of human DNA, RNA, chromosomes, proteins, or metabolites that detects genotypes, mutations or chromosomal changes. For example, tests to determine whether an individual has a genetic variant linked to a predispostion for breast cancer or colorectal cancer are genetic tests. A test for the presence of a virus that does not detect genotypes, mutations or chromosomal changes is not a genetic test. Genetic tests do not include alcohol or drug tests. [Prop. 29 C.F.R. § 1635.3(f)] The EEOC's preamble to the proposed regulations makes it clear that routine tests such as blood counts, cholesterol tests, and liver-function tests, as well as tests for communicable diseases, are not genetic tests.

GINA and the proposed regulations make it clear that information about an actual manifested disease, disorder or pathological condition of an employee is not genetic information, even if the condition has a genetic basis or component. [GINA § 210; Prop. 29 C.F.R. § 1635.12] However, the acquisition and disclosure of such information is subject to limitation under the ADA. Moreover, any genetic component of such information (such as the results of a genetic test) is subject to GINA.

Q 19:99   Are there circumstances in which an employer can request or obtain genetic information about an employee?

Despite the general prohibition on an employer's acquisition of genetic information about an employee or family members, the law and regulations recognize that there are situations in which an employer legitimately acquires genetic information.

The proposed regulations address the "water cooler problem" in which an employer unwittingly receives protected genetic information in the course of casual conservation with an employee or by overhearing conversations among co-workers. The regulations provide that GINA does not apply where an employer inadvertently requests or requires genetic information about an employee or family member. This exception applies when a supervisor or other official of the employer receives genetic information in response to a general inquiry about the well-being of an employee (e.g., "How are you?" or "How's your son feeling today?"). It also applies when a supervisor or other official overhears a conversation in which an employee relays such information to a co-worker (e.g., an employee tells a co-worker that her mother underwent genetic testing for a predisposition to breast cancer).

Caution. The inadvertent *acquisition* of genetic information does not violate GINA; improper *use* of that information will violate the law. In its preamble to the proposed regulations, the EEOC cautions employers that the use of genetic information to discriminate, no matter how that information may have been acquired, is prohibited.

A number of key exceptions to the prohibition on acquisition of genetic information are particularly significant in the employee benefits context.

Wellness programs. Where an employer provides health or genetic services through a wellness program offered as an employee benefit program, collection of genetic information is excepted if the following conditions are met:

- The employee provides prior knowing, voluntary written authorization;

- Only the employee (or the employee's family member, if the family member is receiving genetic services) and the licensed health care professional or board-certified genetic counselor providing the services may receive individually identifiable genetic information; and

- The results of genetic services may be disclosed only to the employer in the aggregate and individually identifiable genetic information may not be included.

The proposed regulations make it clear that an authorization form must be written in a way that (1) the person from whom the genetic information is being obtained is reasonably likely to understand the form; (2) describes the type of genetic information that will be obtained and the general purposes for which it will be used; and (3) describes the restrictions on disclosure of the genetic information. [Prop. 29 C.F.R. § 1635.8(b)(2)]

In addition, the preamble to the proposed regulations makes it clear that an employer that receives only "aggregate" genetic information may nonetheless be in violation of the rules if the small number of participants in a wellness program makes an individual's genetic information readily identifiable.

Caution. Employers should exercise particular care in crafting wellness programs. In addition to complying with Title II of GINA, such programs are subject to strict restrictions under Title I of GINA on the genetic information that group health plans may request or require. Those requirements are discussed in detail in chapter 5. Moreover, other laws including the HIPAA medical privacy rules and the ADA may come into play. For example, the ADA requires that wellness programs be "voluntary," with the employer neither requiring participation nor penalizing employees who do not participate. Furthermore, in an informal discussion letter, the EEOC opined that certain questions in a wellness questionnaire that was required for participation in an employer's health reimbursement arrangement (HRA) constituted impermissible "disability-related inquiries" under the ADA. [ADA: Health Risk Assessments] For information on the HIPAA privacy rules, see chapter 5; for the ADA requirements, see chapter 18.

FMLA certification. Collection of genetic information is excepted where an employer requests or requires family medical history from an employee or with respect to a family member, including information about manifested diseases and disorders, to comply with the certification provisions of the FMLA or a state equivalent. The preamble to the EEOC proposed regulations notes, however, that such information is still subject to GINA's confidentiality requirements and must be treated as a confidential medical record.

Other exceptions include circumstances where genetic information is to be used by the employer for monitoring of the effects of toxic substances in the workplace, for law enforcement purposes, for purposes of identifying human remains, or for quality control purposes (e.g., to detect sample contamination). The law also creates exceptions for inadvertent acquisition of genetic information when an employer purchases commercially available documents, such as periodicals or news publications, that include family medical histories.

Special accommodation and leave requests. The exception for inadvertent acquisition of genetic information applies when an employer requires medical information to support a request for reasonable accommodation under a federal, state or local law or leave that is not governed by the FMLA or other law. If an individual provides genetic information in response to such a request, the employer's acquisition of that information will not violate GINA. However, employers are cautioned that a violation may occur if a request for medical information is overbroad—for example, a request for an employee's entire medical record would likely include the employee's family medical history or other genetic information. The EEOC suggests that employers take proactive steps to avoid even inadvertent acquisition of such information. For example, if an employer asks an employee to have a health care professional provide information about a disability in support of a request for accommodation, the health care professional should indicate that the employee's family medical history or other genetic information cannot be provided.

Genetic information collected by the employer must be treated as a confidential medical record. The employer must maintain such information on separate forms and in separate files and must restrict access to the information.

Miscellaneous

Q 19:100   Do any other federal laws regulate employee welfare benefit plans?

Yes. The other primary federal laws affecting employee welfare benefits are discussed in chapter 2 (ERISA), chapter 5 (group Health plans: Mandated Benefits and standards), chapter 6 (COBRA and Other Continuation Coverage Requirements), chapter 16 (FMLA), chapter 17 (ADEA), and chapter 18 (ADA). In addition, several other federal laws concerning governmental contracts directly or indirectly affect welfare benefit plans. These laws may be specific, such as the Davis-Bacon Act, which is concerned with federal contracts to construct, alter, or repair federal public buildings or public works [40 U.S.C. § 276(a)], or general in nature, such as the Walsh-Healey Public Contracts Act, which governs federal contracts in amounts exceeding $10,000. [41 U.S.C. § 35] Employers with federal contracts should be aware that various federal labor laws applicable to federal contractors may affect their welfare benefit plans.

The 2010 Health Reform Act imposes new requirements on group health plans, including rules prohibiting such plans from establishing discriminatory rules for eligibility or coverage under the plan (see chapter 5). The law specifically provides that these new requirements must not invalidate or limit the rights, remedies, procedures, or legal standards available to individuals under various other laws, including Title VI of the Civil Rights Act of 1964, Title VII of the Civil Rights Act of 1964, and the Rehabilitation Act of 1973. [PPACA § 1557]

Q 19:101   May individuals sue under RICO in health benefits fraud claims?

Yes. The U.S. Supreme Court has expanded the remedies available to private individuals by ruling that litigants may use the Racketeer Influenced and Corrupt Organizations Act (RICO) in health benefits fraud claims. [Humana, Inc. v. Forsyth, 525 U.S. 299 (1999), *aff'g* Forsyth v. Humana, Inc., 114 F.3d 1467 (9th Cir. 1997); 26 Pens. & Ben. Rep. 4 (Jan. 25, 1999)] Previously, the federal circuit courts had been split over whether RICO's remedies were barred because they impaired the operation of state insurance laws, a violation of the McCarran-Ferguson Act. The decision means that individuals can seek treble damages and attorneys' fees under RICO.

In *Humana*, a group of 84,000 beneficiaries of group health policies sued for overpayment of millions of dollars in medical copayments. The beneficiaries alleged that Humana sold group health policies that provided that beneficiaries would be responsible for a 20 percent copayment on medical bills, while Humana would pay the remaining 80 percent. The class suit alleged that Humana secretly negotiated a discount with a hospital it owned that entitled the managed care provider to substantial discounts that were not passed on to the beneficiaries.

According to the Court, the McCarran-Ferguson Act, which bans the use of federal laws that "invalidate, impair, or supersede" state insurance laws, was no bar. "Because RICO advances the State's interest in combating insurance fraud, and does not frustrate any articulated [state] policy, we hold that the McCarran-Ferguson Act does not block the respondent policy beneficiaries' recourse to RICO in this case," the Court said.

Chapter 20

Funding and Financing Welfare Benefits

Many of the rules that can come into play in benefit funding and financing are discussed in this chapter. So, too, are related considerations such as tax rules that apply if the funding method chosen is a voluntary employees' beneficiary association or other welfare benefit fund and the requirements and limitations on funding postretirement medical benefits under a pension plan or annuity. Also covered is the use of corporate-owned life insurance as a method of financing welfare benefits.

Overview of Funding Alternatives

Q 20:1   Does ERISA require that all welfare benefit plans be funded?

No. ERISA (the Employee Retirement Income Security Act of 1974) only imposes advance funding requirements on pension plans. Accordingly, employers are permitted to pay for the benefits under a welfare benefit plan out of their general assets.

Q 20:2   What funding alternatives does an employer have for a welfare benefit plan?

An employer may choose among the following alternatives for funding a welfare benefit plan:

- Fully insuring the benefits by purchasing an insurance policy
- Self-insuring the benefits under the plan by paying for them out of its general assets
- Self-insuring and funding the benefits by setting aside money in trust to pay benefits (sometimes referred to as self-funding)
- Partially insuring the benefits by self-insuring or self-funding them up to a certain point and insuring them above that point under either a minimum premium or stop-loss arrangement

A plan may also use a combination of these funding methods.

(See chapter 2 for a discussion of the ERISA trust requirement as it relates to employee contributions.)

Q 20:3   What is full insurance coverage?

Under a fully insured plan, the promised benefits are paid pursuant to the terms of an insurance contract between the insurance carrier and the policyholder (the employer or trust), which provides insurance coverage for employees and their eligible dependents as third-party beneficiaries of the contract. The insurance company promises to pay for the benefits described in the contract and is at risk for the degree to which the benefits are used. That is, the annual premiums paid for the insurance may or may not be sufficient to pay for the cost of covered benefits incurred by the insured employees together with administrative costs. Usually, the insurance company also performs the claims-paying function under the insurance contract.

Q 20:4   What are the advantages of the purchase of full insurance coverage?

By purchasing full insurance coverage, an employer can protect itself during the policy year against a higher-than-expected overall rate of claims and against individual claims that are extremely expensive. The employer's liability under full insurance is generally limited to the premiums paid to the insurer; it is the insurer that is liable for all plan benefits, within the plan's limits, regardless of the volume of claims or the amounts of such claims.

Another advantage of full insurance is that an employer can budget its costs by paying regular premiums. However, the employer may be subject to increased premiums for future periods to cover expected utilization based on historical patterns of utilization in the insured population or in a population of similar size or makeup. In some cases, the contract may provide for a "retrospective" premium to offset a portion of the prior adverse experience. The insurance policy typically provides for a dividend or experience-rating credit if premiums paid exceed benefit payments plus the insurer's charge for expenses and profit.

In addition, an employer has the assurance that the plan's claims (and often also claim appeals) will be handled by insurance company professionals.

Furthermore, the insurer provides an impartial buffer between the employer and its employees in the handling of the claims (and claim appeals, if applicable).

Tax benefits. The premiums for an insured plan, which include amounts needed to cover incurred but unpaid claims, are generally deductible by the employer when paid or accrued. [I.R.C. §§ 162(a), 461(h)] In addition, because life insurance death benefit proceeds are taxed more favorably than self-insured death benefit proceeds (see chapter 12), plans providing substantial amounts of death benefits are usually fully insured. [I.R.C. § 101(a)] As well, an insured medical plan is not subject to any nondiscrimination rules (unless the policy is held in a voluntary employees' benefits association (VEBA), in which case Section 505 of the Internal Revenue Code would apply). A self-insured medical plan, on the other hand, must meet the nondiscrimination requirements of Code Section 105(h) to obtain fully favorable tax treatment for all participants (see chapter 3). It should be noted that medical plans within cafeteria plans are subject to additional cafeteria plan rules (see chapter 7).

ERISA trust requirement. An insured welfare benefit plan qualifies for the suspension of the ERISA trust requirement as long as employee contributions are paid to the insurer within 90 days (see chapter 9). [ERISA Tech. Rel. 92-01, 57 Fed. Reg. 23, 272 (June 2, 1992)]

Q 20:5   Are there any disadvantages to purchasing full insurance for a plan?

Yes. The disadvantages of a fully insured plan include the extra costs attributable to the insurer's profit margins built into the premium rates as well as the cost attributable to state premium taxes. All states impose premium taxes on insurance companies; they are measured by the insurance premiums the insurance companies receive (for example, a tax of 2 percent of life or health insurance premiums). Typically, an insurer passes on the cost of the premium tax to the employer or trustee purchasing the insurance.

Further, the portion of the investment earnings an insurer earns on moneys received under the policy that it passes to the employer through dividends or experience-rating credits may be less than what the employer could earn by investing the funds directly or in trust.

An insured plan also is subject to state insurance laws, including those mandating certain types of benefits, whereas a self-insured or trusteed plan is not. [Metropolitan Life Ins. Co. v. Massachusetts, 471 U.S. 724 (1985)] (See chapter 2 for a discussion of ERISA preemption.)

Q 20:6   What is self-insurance?

Under *self-insurance,* an employer obligates itself to pay for all of the covered plan benefits incurred by participants during the plan year. Although the plan may contain maximum limits on the frequency or cost of particular benefits, the employer is fully at risk for the benefits that are represented as being covered under the plan. In other words, within the plan's limits, the employer bears the full brunt of higher-than-expected utilization of benefits or of individual claims that turn out to be quite expensive.

Self-insured plans usually are unfunded; that is, benefits are paid out of the employer's general assets. They can also be funded (sometimes referred to as self-funded); that means that the employer sets aside moneys in trust to pay for all or a part of the benefits under the plan.

In some cases, an employer may also require employee contributions to help defray the cost of benefits and associated administrative costs. A trust may be required to hold such employee contributions (see chapter 2).

Q 20:7 What are the advantages of unfunded self-insurance?

There are four main advantages associated with unfunded self-insurance:

1. The employer must satisfy benefit claims only as they actually become payable. Thus, amounts needed for future benefits, which would be collected as premiums and held by an insurance company under an insured plan, can be kept in the employer's business, perhaps earning more than they would if such amounts were turned over to an insurer or trust.
2. A self-insured plan does not incur the state premium tax cost (see Q 20:5) that an insured plan would incur.
3. An unfunded self-insured plan may lead to savings in administrative costs and expenses.
4. A self-insured plan is exempt under ERISA from a variety of state insurance laws mandating types of benefits, as well as from state laws generally (see chapter 2).

Q 20:8 Are there any disadvantages to self-insurance?

Yes. There are several major disadvantages associated with self-insurance:

1. The employer bears the full brunt of the economic risk that benefit costs may substantially exceed the employer's estimates.
2. Benefit payments may vary greatly during the plan year, making budgeting difficult.
3. The employer may find it difficult to maintain a claims administration operation that functions smoothly and objectively.
4. The employer can deduct only amounts actually used to pay benefits under a self-insured plan in the taxable year. No deduction is allowed for claims incurred but unreported, and perhaps not for claims reported but unpaid.
5. A self-insured, contributory welfare benefit plan is not covered by the DOL's announcement suspending the ERISA trust requirement until further notice.

[ERISA Tech. Rel. 92-01, 57 Fed. Reg. 23, 272 (June 2, 1992)]

Because of such difficulties, small employers generally do not find self-insurance attractive, and they usually prefer to purchase full insurance (see Qs 20:3–20:4). Large employers, on the other hand, are better able to handle the problems, finding that the advantages of self-insurance (see Q 20:7) can outweigh its drawbacks.

Tax disadvantages. A death benefit under a self-insured death benefit plan is not exempt from income tax, whereas a fully insured death benefit plan provides a full death benefit exclusion regardless of amount. [I.R.C. §§ 101(a), 101(b)] In addition, a self-insured medical plan must meet the nondiscrimination requirements of Code Section 105(h), while a fully insured medical plan is not subject to any nondiscrimination rules.

Q 20:9   How is a trust used to self-fund benefits under a welfare benefit plan?

Under a self-insured plan that is also funded, an employer contributes moneys to a trust to be used for the payment of plan benefits and, if the trust document permits, for the payment of related administrative expenses. Generally, the trust will be set up as a tax-exempt irrevocable trust under Code Section 501(c)(9), that is, a VEBA trust (see Qs 20:53–20:73). Once the funds are held irrevocably in trust, they are segregated from the general assets of the employer and are not subject to the claims of the employer's creditors. They are also protected in the event of the employer's insolvency or bankruptcy.

If the self-insured welfare benefit plan is also contributory, a trust is required under ERISA for the employee contributions, which are plan assets. The DOL's announcement suspending the trust requirement for welfare benefit plans does not apply to this category of plans. [ERISA Tech. Rel. 92-01, 57 Fed. Reg. 23, 272 (June 2, 1992)]

Investment earnings on the moneys in trust are also used to pay benefits and, if authorized, administrative costs. A trust may be required in any event, if the employer requires employee contributions toward the cost of coverage.

Q 20:10   What is the difference between self-insurance and self-funding?

With self-insurance, the full economic risk for payment of benefits under the plan lies with the employer, and the employer pays such amounts out of its general assets.

Under self-funding, the economic risk for payment of benefits still lies with the employer, but the employer sets aside funds in trust to meet its obligation under the plan. Sometimes, the employer includes a statement in the plan document and employee communications to the effect that, regardless of the benefits described as covered, the employer's liability is limited to the amounts in the trust. Practically speaking, however, an employer with an ongoing plan often simply will contribute more to the trust to make up any shortfall rather than incur employee dissatisfaction.

Both self-insurance and self-funding usually are referred to generically as self-insurance whenever the key issue is whether the employer bears the economic risk (such as when determining whether ERISA preempts state insurance laws).

Q 20:11   What are the advantages of self-funding a plan using a trust?

If a trust is used to fund benefits payable under a self-insured plan, plan costs can be budgeted through regular contributions to the trust.

In addition, because funded and unfunded self-insured plans are not considered to be in the business of insurance, state insurance laws relating to premium taxes and other state laws mandating the inclusion of particular benefits are, for such plans, preempted by ERISA. (It may not always be possible to avoid state insurance law regulation if the trust is part of a multiple-employer welfare arrangement (MEWA) (see Qs 2:189, 2:190).) Further, the trust can be established on a tax-free basis, and tax deductions can be taken for contributions for both incurred and paid claims. Still another advantage of using a trust to fund a plan is that the plan gets the benefit of investment earnings on trust funds held for future claims.

Q 20:12   Are there any disadvantages to funding a self-insured plan using a trust?

Yes. There are four major disadvantages to funding a self-insured plan using a trust, as follows:

Once funds are contributed to the trust, they generally cannot be recovered by the employer.

1. Trustees' fees, legal fees, and other administrative costs of maintaining the trust may be substantial.
2. Compliance by the trust with VEBA requirements established by the Internal Revenue Service and ERISA fiduciary responsibility requirements may prove difficult.
3. Although the trust approach can limit the employer's liability for higher-than-anticipated benefits to the amount of funds in the trust, as a practical matter an employer with an ongoing plan will voluntarily provide the trust with the money needed to pay for all of the benefits due under the terms of the plan.

Q 20:13   What is a minimum premium insurance arrangement?

A *minimum premium insurance arrangement* is an arrangement under which an employer self-insures plan benefits up to a specified amount (the trigger point), and an insurer agrees to be liable to employees and their beneficiaries for all benefits in excess of the trigger point. The trigger point frequently is set at the level of expected claims under the plan, but it can be a negotiated amount that is higher or lower than the level of expected claims.

Typically, the insurance company performs the administrative services relating to claims payment for the plan as a whole, drawing funds for payment of the self-insured portion of the arrangement out of a checking account set up by the employer specifically to cover benefit payments. The employer is responsible for keeping sufficient moneys in the checking account to cover its obligation under the self-insured portion of the minimum premium arrangement. Usually, the employer has only a short grace period in which to remedy any underfunding of the checking account, such as two or three business days, or the arrangement will abruptly terminate.

In many but not all cases, the minimum premium contract provides that in the event the arrangement terminates, the insurer becomes liable to pay all claims incurred but unpaid before the effective date of the termination. Thus, unlike stop-loss insurance (see Q 20:14), the insurance company under the traditional type of minimum premium arrangement may "drop down" and assume the employer's portion of the economic risk if the employer reneges on its obligation under the arrangement.

At that point, the employer usually must pay an additional premium to the insurer for the additional protection. Also at that time, under the traditional method of setting up a minimum premium arrangement, such an arrangement would then revert to full insurance, and the employer would be required to pay premiums for the full insurance coverage. That happens because, under the traditional method, the minimum premium arrangement is created by a rider to an insurance policy that makes the policy an excess risk policy (with a correspondingly smaller premium, hence the name "minimum premium") rather than a full insurance policy. The rider self-destructs if the employer fails to keep up the funding on its share of the economic risk, leaving the underlying insurance policy in full force. In some cases, however, the minimum premium setup may not revert to full insurance or obligate the insurance company to drop down and cover the employer's liability for claims incurred but unpaid before the date the minimum premium arrangement terminates.

State premium tax costs. Minimum premium plans generally are not subject to state premium taxes on the self-insured portion of the plans—that is, amounts below the trigger point—but are for the actual premiums received by the insurance carrier. However, the state of California imposes premium taxes on amounts below the trigger point under certain employer-maintained minimum premium plans, and it has been held that ERISA does not preempt California's taxation of such amounts. [Metropolitan Life Ins. Co. v. State Bd. of Equalization, 32 Cal. 3d 649 (1982); General Motors Corp. v. California State Bd. of Equalization, 815 F.2d 1305 (9th Cir. 1987), *cert. denied*, 108 S. Ct. 1122 (1988)] The court viewed the plan as essentially an insured plan with a large deductible.

Yet, in a California appellate court decision involving a minimum premium plan, the court found that the facts in *Metropolitan Life* were distinguishable and therefore the earlier case was not controlling. Under the minimum premium plan involved in the later case, the insurer had no contractual obligation to pay pre-trigger-point claims the employer failed to pay, the coverage did not revert to full insurance coverage if the employer failed to pay pretrigger-point claims, and there was no obligation to pay an additional premium to the insurer upon termination. The fact that the insurer was obligated to pay plan benefits in excess of the agreed-upon trigger point was held to be not enough to justify the imposition of state premium tax based on the amount of pretrigger-point benefits paid by the employer. [Aetna Life Ins. Co. v. State Bd. of Equalization, 15 Cal. Rptr. 2d 26 (Ct. App. 1992)]

Note that the characterization of the plan as insured or self-insured for ERISA purposes can be tricky in these cases; however, it is potentially important to the question of whether a trust will be required for participant contributions toward the plan. (See chapter 2.)

Q 20:14　What is a stop-loss insurance arrangement?

Under a *stop-loss insurance arrangement*, an employer fully self-insures the plan benefits. The insurer, however, agrees to reimburse the employer (but not the employees) to the extent that plan benefits paid or incurred by the employer exceed a specified level (e.g., 120 percent of expected claims). If the policy proceeds are payable to the employer, they become part of the employer's general assets and are not specifically earmarked for payment of benefits under the particular plan. Accordingly, stop-loss insurance payable to an employer can be viewed as a hedging technique against the potential adverse impact of plan costs on the employer's cash flow.

Occasionally, a plan trustee purchases stop-loss insurance under which the policy proceeds are payable to the plan or trust. In such a case, the proceeds payable to the trust become plan assets.

State premium costs. Stop-loss insurance plans generally are not subject to state premium taxes except with respect to the actual stop-loss premium paid to the insurer. California does not extend its taxation of benefits paid under certain minimum premium plans (see Q 20:13) to benefits paid under plans with stop-loss coverage.

Q 20:15　Are minimum premium and stop-loss arrangements ever considered to be insured?

The characterization of the minimum premium and stop-loss "in-between" arrangements as insurance depends on the particular statute at issue.

ERISA preemption. If the in-between arrangements are characterized as insured, ERISA will not preempt attempted state regulation of the content of the plan. The ability of multistate employers to maintain a single, uniform benefit plan for all of their geographic locations thus hinges on how the plan is characterized. Further, the characterization of the welfare benefit plan as insured means that it will qualify for the DOL's suspension of the ERISA trust requirement provided that employee contributions are paid to the insurer within 90 days. (See chapter 2.)

The federal common-law cases under ERISA evidence confusion in some instances over which of the two types of arrangements is at issue. Stop-loss arrangements generally have been held to be self-insured for ERISA purposes. [United Food & Commercial Workers v. Pacyga, 801 F.2d 1157 (9th Cir. 1986); *see also* Moore v. Provident Life & Accident Ins. Co., 786 F.2d 922 (9th Cir. 1986); Rasmussen v. Metropolitan Life Ins. Co., 675 F. Supp. 1497 (W.D. La. 1987)] *Moore* and *Rasmussen* involve plans characterized as stop-loss insurance arrangements that in fact appear to be minimum premium plans. Nevertheless, a district court case concluded that, for ERISA purposes, the type of minimum premium arrangement at issue in the case before it was more analogous to an insured plan with a large deductible. [Hall v. Pennwalt Group Comprehensive Med. Expense Benefits Plan, 1989 U.S. Dist. LEXIS. 16893 (E.D. Pa. Aug. 3, 1989)] Similarly, in *Michigan United Food & Commercial Workers Unions v. Baerwaldt* [767 F.2d 308 (6th Cir. 1985), *cert. denied*, 474 U.S. 1059 (1986)], the court stated that ERISA did not preempt the application of state insurance law to a stop-loss arrangement that appeared in truth to be a minimum premium arrangement. It should be noted that if stop-loss policy proceeds are payable to the employer rather than to employees or to the plan, the arrangement should not be characterized as insured for ERISA purposes. That is so because the payment of policy proceeds is merely triggered by a particular benefit expense level under the plan, but the proceeds themselves are not committed for the payment of such benefit expenses. The case law does not follow that theory so neatly.

State insurance law. Whether an in-between arrangement is considered to be insured for state-law purposes initially depends on the individual state's law and the state-law regulator's interpretation; it is then subject to court decisions on ERISA preemption.

Q 20:16   What is an administrative-services-only arrangement?

Under an *administrative-services-only* (ASO) *arrangement,* an employer fully self-insures the plan benefits. An insurance company or other third-party administrator agrees, however, to administer claims and provide other administrative services for a fee. ASO arrangements are not subject to state premium taxes.

Q 20:17   What are some other funding alternatives for welfare benefit plans?

Other funding alternatives for the provision of health benefits include the use of health maintenance organizations (HMOs) and preferred provider organizations (PPOs) (see chapter 3). Special arrangements are also available for restricted funding of postretirement life insurance and health benefits (see Qs 20:39–20:43).

Q 20:18   Does the method of funding affect the amount of an employer's tax deduction for welfare benefit plan contributions?

Yes. First, an employer's contributions will be deductible only to the extent that they constitute ordinary and necessary business expenses of the employer under Code Section 162(a).

Second, if employer contributions are made to a welfare benefit fund, those contributions (1) must be within the deductible limits specifically applicable to welfare benefit funds and (2) actually must be paid, whether the employer is on an accrual or a cash basis of tax accounting. [I.R.C. § 419(a)]

The amount of an excess contribution by an employer in one taxable year may be treated as "carried over" for tax deduction purposes and deemed paid by the employer to the fund in the succeeding taxable year (subject, of course, to the deduction limits for that succeeding year). [I.R.C. § 419(d)]

There are special rules applicable to VEBAs and Code Section 401(h) medical accounts in pension and annuity plans (see Qs 20:53–20:101).

Q 20:19   How do the deduction limits for contributions to welfare benefit plans apply to insured and self-insured plans?

The following rules apply to deduction limits for contributions to insured and self-insured plans.

Insured plans. If a plan is insured, the welfare benefit fund limits generally do not apply. (IRS regulations apply the welfare benefit rules only to certain narrow categories of employer arrangements with insurance companies; see Qs 20:21–20:25.) An employer can generally deduct the actual premiums charged by the insurer, including the portion of the premiums that the insurer needs to establish reserves for incurred but unpaid claims. [I.R.C. § 162(a); Rev. Rul. 56-632, 1956-2 C.B. 1010]

Self-insured plans that are unfunded. If a self-insured plan is unfunded, the welfare benefit fund limits on deductibility do not apply. An employer can deduct amounts actually used to pay benefits in the taxable year. No deduction is allowed for claims incurred but unreported, however, and perhaps not for claims reported but unpaid. [I.R.C. § 461(h); United States v. General Dynamics Corp., 107 S. Ct. 1732 (1987)]

Self-insured plans that are funded. If a self-insured plan is funded through a welfare benefit trust, the limits on the deductibility of an employer's contributions to a welfare benefit fund apply (see Qs 20:20–20:52). The employer generally can deduct amounts contributed to the trust, except to the extent they exceed the maximum deductible amounts applicable to welfare benefit funds. [I.R.C. §§ 419, 419A]

Welfare Benefit Fund Rules

Q 20:20   What is a welfare benefit fund under the Internal Revenue Code?

A *welfare benefit fund* is any "fund" that is part of a plan through which an employer provides welfare benefits to employees or their beneficiaries. [I.R.C. § 419(e)(1)] If a welfare benefit fund exists, then the employer's tax deduction for the amount it contributes to the welfare benefit fund cannot exceed the limits contained in Code Sections 419 and 419A.

A *fund* is defined as follows:

1. A tax-exempt trust or other tax-exempt organization described in Code Section 501(c)(7), 501(c)(9), 501(c)(17), or 501(c)(20). This encompasses a nonprofit social club [I.R.C. § 501(c)(7)]; a VEBA providing life, sickness, accident, or other benefits [I.R.C. § 501(c)(9)]; a trust providing supplemental unemployment compensation benefits [I.R.C. § 501(c)(17)]; and a trust or other organization that is part of a group legal services plan. [I.R.C. § 501(c)(20)] Most welfare benefit funds are formed as trusts pursuant to Code Section 501(c)(9) and are commonly referred to as 501(c)(9) trusts or VEBAs.

2. Any trust, corporation, or other organization not exempt from tax. Thus, a taxable trust or taxable corporation that is maintained for the purpose of providing welfare benefits is a welfare benefit fund.

3. To the extent provided in regulations, any account held for an employer by any person.

[I.R.C. § 419(e)(3); Temp. Treas. Reg. § 1.419-1T, Q&A-3]

Caution. In late 2007, the IRS cautioned taxpayers about certain trust arrangements being sold to professional corporations and other small businesses as welfare benefit funds. In Notice 2007-83 [2007-45 I.R.B. 960], the IRS identified certain trust arrangements involving cash value life insurance policies and substantially similar arrangements as "listed transactions." If a transaction is designated as a listed transaction, affected persons have disclosure obligations and may be subject to applicable penalties. In Notice 2007-84 [2007-45 I.R.B. 963], the IRS cautioned taxpayers that the tax treatment of trusts that, in form, provide postretirement medical and life insurance benefits to owners and other key employees may vary from the treatment claimed. The Service indicated that it may issue further guidance to address these arrangements, and taxpayers should not assume that the guidance will be applied prospectively only. The Service also issued a revenue ruling dealing with situations in which an arrangement is a welfare benefit fund but the employer's deduction for contributions to the fund is denied in whole or in part for premiums paid by the trust on cash value life insurance policies. [Rev. Rul. 2007-65, 2007-45 I.R.B. 949] (See Q 20:31.)

Q 20:21　Do any employer arrangements with insurance companies constitute welfare benefit funds?

Under temporary regulations issued by the Treasury and supplemented by IRS Announcement 86-45 [1986-15 I.R.B. 52], only the following employer arrangements with insurance companies are considered funds:

1. Certain retired lives reserves held for postretirement life insurance or medical benefits. The reference to "certain" reserves suggests that retired lives reserves established from employee contributions only are not funds.

2. Certain ASO arrangements. Again, the reference to "certain" arrangements suggests that some ASO arrangements are not funds for this purpose. In most ASO arrangements, the insurer holds no plan funds, and benefits are paid from the employer's or trustee's bank account.

3. Certain arrangements under which an employer (a) makes deductible contributions and (b) has, on or before the later of the end of the policy year to which such contributions relate or the time such contracts are made, a contractual right to a dividend, refund, credit, or additional benefit based on the benefit or claims experience, administrative cost experience, or investment experience attributable solely to the employer.

Most group experience-rated policies do not contain a contractual right to a dividend or refund and do not base the dividend or refund solely on the single employer's plan experience. Instead, the contract typically provides for a dividend or refund at the insurance company's discretion. Any such dividend or refund generally is reduced to reflect risk charges and pooling charges under the policy and thus is not based solely on that particular employer's plan experience. (A *risk charge* generally is an across-the-board charge made by the insurance carrier to all of its group policyholders. A *pooling charge* is an additional charge the insurance company makes for high amounts of insurance coverage or extraordinary risks that are pooled rather than charged to that particular employer's experience, so that they do not skew the premiums on the group.)

The Department of the Treasury has indicated that at some time in the future it may issue additional regulations expanding the types of insurance company arrangements that will be treated as funds. Any such regulations will not have retroactive effect, however. Moreover, Congress has provided that, except for the arrangements described in items 1 and 3 of the preceding list, any regulations expanding the definition of a fund will not become effective until six months after final regulations are issued. [Temp. Treas. Reg. § 1.419-1T, Q&A-3, *as modified by* Ann. 86-45, 1986-15 I.R.B. 52; TRA '86 § 185(a)(8)(B)]

Q 20:22   Are experience-rated group insurance contracts treated as welfare benefit funds?

Generally, no. The temporary Treasury regulations, as modified by IRS Announcement 86-45, include a narrow group of insurance company arrangements within the Section 419 definition of a welfare benefit fund. Congress subsequently indicated that typical group insurance arrangements should not be subject to the welfare benefit fund rules because the economic risk of benefit payments is transferred to the insurance company. [Ann. 86-45, 1986-15 I.R.B. 52; Conf. Rep. to TRA '86, H.R. Rep. No. 841, 99th Cong., 2d Sess., Vol. II, at 850 (1986)]

Q 20:23   Are insurance contracts paid for solely by employee contributions considered welfare benefit funds?

Under the temporary Treasury regulations (see Q 20:21), only certain insurance arrangements involving employer contributions (and related tax deductions) are treated as funds. Therefore, unless future regulations further expand the term *fund*, insurance contracts paid for solely by employee contributions are not welfare benefit funds.

Q 20:24   Besides experience-rated group insurance contracts, what other types of employer arrangements with insurance companies are not welfare benefit funds?

The Code's definition of *fund* also excludes a life insurance contract under which the employer is directly or indirectly the beneficiary. Thus, corporate-owned life insurance and insurance used to fund split-dollar plans (see Qs 12:47–12:55) do not constitute a fund subject to the deduction limits of Code Sections 419 and 419A. [I.R.C. § 419(e)(4)(A)(i)]

In addition, the Code's definition of *fund* specifically excludes from fund status a "qualified nonguaranteed contract." [I.R.C. § 419(e)(4)(A)(ii)]

Q 20:25   What is a qualified nonguaranteed contract?

Under an exclusion from fund status contained in Code Section 419, a *qualified nonguaranteed contract* is any insurance contract (including a reasonable reserve held thereunder to cover higher-than-expected future costs, called a *premium stabilization reserve*) if the following applies:

1. There is no guarantee of a renewal of the contract (at guaranteed renewal rates); and
2. The only payments (other than those for insurance protection) to which the employer or employees are entitled are experience-rated refunds or policy dividends that are not guaranteed and that are determined by factors (for example, risk charges and pooling charges) other than the amount of welfare benefits paid to or on behalf of the employees or their beneficiaries.

In addition, in order to have the Section 419 exclusion apply, an employer must treat any experience-rated refund or policy dividend attributable to a policy year as received or accrued for tax purposes in the taxable year in which the policy year to which it relates ends. [I.R.C. § 419(e)(4)(B)]

Practice Pointer. The legislative history of the amendments effected by the Tax Reform Act of 1986 expresses Congress's intent that the definition of *fund* avoid encompassing true insurance arrangements. Accordingly, an employer with an experience-rated group policy that does not fit the definition of fund in the temporary Treasury regulations and IRS Announcement 86-45 apparently does not have to attempt to fit within the statutory exclusion for qualified nonguaranteed contracts in order to avoid welfare benefit fund tax treatment. That situation may change, however, if further regulations are issued expanding the classes of insurance contract arrangements that are to be treated as funds. Any such expansion of the definition of *fund* will be applied on a prospective basis only.

Q 20:26 Is a fund maintained for more than one employer a welfare benefit fund?

Generally, yes. The welfare benefit fund rules do not, however, apply to a ten-or-more-employer plan. A *ten-or-more-employer plan* is a plan under which:

1. No employer normally contributes more than 10 percent of the total contributions to the plan; and

2. The experience rating, if any, does not apply to individual employers; that is, the experience of the group is pooled.

This last point is extremely important. In 1995, the IRS issued a notice warning that significant tax problems may be raised by programs being promoted as ten-or-more-employer plans that insulate participating employers from the experience of the group. [IRS Notice 95-34, 1995-1 C.B. 309]

In 2003, the IRS followed up on its 1995 notice by issuing final regulations that spell out the requirements for a welfare benefit fund that is part of a ten-or-more-employer plan. [Treas. Reg. § 1.419A(f)(6)-1] In particular, the regulations clarify when a plan has an experience-rating arrangement with respect to individual employers. According to the IRS, the regulations respond to a proliferation of tax shelter arrangements that promise unlimited current deductions for employer contributions by purporting to qualify for the ten-or-more-employer plan exception but, in practice, pass through favorable experience to individual employers.

As a general rule, the final regulations provide that a plan maintains an experience-rating arrangement with respect to an individual employer—making the plan ineligible for the exception—if any employer's cost of coverage for any period is based, in whole or in part, either on the benefits experience or overall experience of that employer or one or more employees of that employer.

In addition, the final regulations provide that all agreements and understandings (including promotional materials and policy illustrations) will be taken into account in determining whether the requirements are satisfied in form and in operation. For example, if promotional materials indicate that an employer or its employees can be expected to receive a future benefit based on the employer's accumulated contributions, the plan will be treated as maintaining experience-rating arrangements with respect to individual employers, even if the formal plan does not specifically provide for experience rating.

The final regulations also identify five characteristics that are indications that an arrangement does *not* qualify as a ten-or-more-employer plan.

1. Assets of the plan or fund are allocated to a specific employer or employers through separate accounting of contributions and expenditures.

2. The amount charged under the plan is not the same for all the participating employers and the differences are not merely reflective of differences in current risk or rating factors that are commonly taken into account in manual rates used by insurers.

3. The plan does not provide for fixed welfare benefits for a fixed coverage period for a fixed cost.

4. The plan provides for fixed welfare benefits for a fixed coverage period for a fixed cost, but the cost is unreasonably high for the covered risk for the plan as a whole.

5. Benefits or other amounts can be paid, distributed from the plan by reason of an event other than the illness, personal injury, or death of an employee or family member, or the employee's involuntary separation from employment (such as the employer's withdrawal from the plan).

The IRS notes that the presence of some of these characteristics suggests that there are multiple plans present instead of a single plan, while the presence of other characteristics tend to indicate that an employer's cost of coverage is (or will be) based on that employer's benefits experience or that the plan is expected to accumulate a surplus that ultimately will be used for the benefit of the individual employers (or their employees). Therefore, the regulations provide that a plan exhibiting any of the characteristics is not a ten-or-more-employer plan unless it is established to the satisfaction of the IRS that the requirements of tax law and regulations have been met. On the other hand, the fact that a plan has none of the above characteristics does not create an inference that it is a ten-or-more-employer plan.

The final regulations generally became effective for contributions paid or incurred in taxable years of an employer beginning on or after July 11, 2002.

Q 20:27   Must there be a formal welfare benefit plan in order for the welfare benefit fund rules to apply?

No. If there is no welfare benefit plan as such, but there is a method or arrangement of employer contributions or benefits that has the effect of such a plan, the welfare benefit fund rules will apply to a fund maintained under the informal arrangement. [I.R.C. § 419(f)]

Q 20:28   Must there be an employer-employee relationship for the welfare benefit fund rules to apply?

No. An employer-employee relationship is not necessary for the welfare benefit fund rules to come into play. If an arrangement would be a welfare benefit fund, except that the person providing services is an independent contractor and not an employee, the welfare benefit fund rules apply. [I.R.C. § 419(g)]

Q 20:29   What are the limits on an employer's tax deduction for contributions to a welfare benefit fund?

If a welfare benefit fund exists, an employer's deduction for a taxable year generally is limited to the fund's "qualified cost" for the year. [I.R.C. § 419(b)] The limits do not apply, however, to employer contributions to a collectively bargained plan (see Q 20:37) or to a ten-or-more-employer plan (see Q 20:26).

Q 20:30   What is a welfare benefit fund's qualified cost?

A welfare benefit fund's *qualified cost* is

- The sum of the qualified direct cost (see Q 20:31) plus permitted additions (within limits) to a qualified asset account (see Qs 20:32–20:43) for the taxable year, less
- The fund's after-tax income for the taxable year (see Q 20:44).

[I.R.C. § 419(c)]

Q 20:31   What is a welfare benefit fund's qualified direct cost?

When calculating the qualified cost that an employer can deduct, the first element is the welfare benefit fund's qualified direct cost. The fund's *qualified direct cost* is the aggregate expenditure for benefits and administrative expenses that would have been allowed as a deduction under Code Section 162 by a cash-basis employer if they had been provided directly by the employer rather than through a fund.

A benefit is treated as provided when it would be includable in the employee's gross income (if there were no statutory exclusion). Special rules are provided for amortization of the cost of a child care facility. [I.R.C. § 419(c)(3)]

In a 2007 revenue ruling, the IRS held that if the benefit provided through a fund is life insurance coverage, premiums paid on cash value life insurance policies by the fund are not included in the fund's qualified direct cost whenever the fund is directly or indirectly a beneficiary under the policy. If the benefit provided through the fund is something other than life insurance coverage, premiums paid on cash value life insurance policies by the fund are not included in the fund's qualified direct cost whenever the fund is directly or indirectly a beneficiary under the policy. However, the fund's qualified direct cost does include amounts paid as welfare benefits by the fund during the taxable year for claims incurred during the year. [Rev. Rul. 2007-65, 2007-45 I.R.B. 949] According to the IRS, if the cash value insurance was held directly by the employer, the employer would have retained ownership rights which would have precluded a deduction for the premiums it paid. Therefore, because they would *not* be deductible if paid directly by the employer, the premium payments cannot be included in the fund's qualified direct cost.

Q 20:32   What is a qualified asset account?

The second element that needs to be known when calculating the amount of an employer's qualified cost is the permitted amount under the qualified asset account. A *qualified asset account* is an account consisting of assets set aside to provide for the payment of the following benefits:

- Disability
- Medical
- Supplemental unemployment compensation or severance pay
- Life insurance

[I.R.C § 419A(a)]

Q 20:33   What limits apply to a qualified asset account?

The overall limit on a qualified asset account is the amount reasonably and actuarially necessary to fund benefit claims incurred and unpaid as of the end of the taxable year, together with related administrative costs. [I.R.C. § 420A(c)(1)]

Disability benefits. The qualified asset account may not, in any event, include disability benefits to the extent that they are payable at an annual rate exceeding the lesser of:

1. 75 percent of the employee's average compensation for his or her three most highly compensated years; or
2. The amount of the Section 415 limit applicable to benefits payable under defined benefit pension plans ($185,000 for 2008).

Supplemental unemployment compensation or severance pay benefits. The qualified asset account also may not, in any event, include supplemental unemployment compensation or severance pay benefits to the extent that they are payable at an annual rate in excess of 150 percent of the Section 415 dollar limitation in effect for defined contribution retirement plans (in 2008, the limit is 150 percent of $46,000, or $69,000). [I.R.C. § 420A(c)(4)]

Q 20:34 How does an employer establish that the amount it contributes to a qualified asset account is reasonably and actuarially necessary and thus deductible?

Two alternatives for establishing that an amount an employer contributes is reasonably and actuarially necessary are available for a taxable year:

1. If the employer chooses not to obtain an actuarial certification, it must be able to justify that the reserve for incurred but unpaid claims is reasonable, and the account limit cannot exceed certain safe harbor limits (see Q 20:35); or

2. The employer may obtain a certification from an actuary that the entire amount of the account (not just the amount exceeding the safe-harbor limits) is actuarially justified.

[I.R.C. § 419A(c)(5); Conf. Rep. 861, 98th Cong., 2d Sess., at 1158 (1984)]

In a technical advice memorandum, the IRS addressed the issue of whether a reserve for incurred but unpaid claims was reasonable and actuarially necessary. The IRS was investigating a VEBA that claimed a reserve for incurred but not reported (IBNR) claims equal to almost 50 percent of the claims paid by the VEBA for the year. The plan administrator described the method that was used to determine the amount of the IBNR reserve as being based on claims-lag studies using the employer's historical workforce and claims experience patterns. Such a method, known as the completion factor method, is typically used for non-life coverages that do not involve long payout periods. The plan administrator stated that the method was in accordance with generally accepted actuarial principles. After comparing the reserves of the VEBA with claims paid for a period of years, the IRS agreed that the high IBNR reserve was reasonable and actuarially necessary for this particular VEBA; therefore, the VEBA could take that IBNR reserve into account when calculating the VEBA's account limit for the year, so that employer contributions made to fund the reserve for the IBNRs were deductible for that plan year.

The technical advice memorandum also stated that, for purposes of the Section 419 and 419A deduction limits, a VEBA's total assets are to be valued using the VEBA's accounting method. Thus, cash-basis VEBAs cannot take receivables and payables into account when calculating the value of the VEBA's assets for the year, but VEBAs using the accrual method of accounting should do so. The VEBA in question used the accrual method of accounting; thus, it was required to include receivables, but subtract payables, when valuing its assets as of the last day of the plan year. [Priv. Ltr. Rul. 9446002]

The U.S. Tax Court has held that a welfare benefit plan is not automatically entitled to claim the safe-harbor limits under Code Section 419 when computing its annual addition to its qualified asset account for medical, dental, and short-term disability benefits that are incurred but unpaid as of the end of the plan year. A taxpayer is not entitled to use these limits unless they are reasonable. [Square D Co. v. Commissioner, 109 T.C. 9 (1997)]

Q 20:35   What are the safe-harbor limits for qualified asset accounts?

The safe-harbor limits for qualified asset accounts vary according to the type of benefit being funded, as follows:

- *Medical benefits:* 35 percent of qualified direct costs (other than insurance premiums) for the immediately preceding taxable year
- *Life insurance and death benefits:* to be prescribed in Treasury regulations
- *Short-term (up to 12 months) disability benefits:* 17.5 percent of qualified direct costs (other than insurance premiums) for the immediately preceding taxable year
- *Long-term disability:* to be prescribed in Treasury regulations
- *Supplemental unemployment compensation and severance pay benefits:* 75 percent of the average annual qualified direct costs for any two of the immediately preceding seven taxable years

[I.R.C. § 419A(c)(5)]

Practice Pointer. Use of the term *safe harbor* is somewhat misleading: the legislative history indicates that the reserve is also required to be reasonable in amount. Thus, if in a particular case a reasonable incurred claims reserve for medical benefits would be only 20 percent of qualified direct costs for the preceding year, a reserve equal to the 35 percent safe harbor would exceed the permissible limit.

In a U.S. Tax Court decision, the court held that the 35 percent safe harbor for medical benefits merely set the outside limit in the absence of an actuarial certification for a medical benefits reserve for incurred but unpaid claims. It is not an automatic entitlement; the employer must show that the reserve amount claimed as a deduction is reasonable. The court allowed reserves of 27 and 28 percent for the two taxable years in issue, which the parties had stipulated were reasonable amounts if the safe-harbor limit did not apply. [General Signal Corp. v. Commissioner, 103 T.C. 14 (1994)] Subsequently, the Tax Court reaffirmed its adherence to its reasoning in *General Signal.* [Square D Co. v. Commissioner, 109 T.C. 9 (1997)]

The IRS adopted the Tax Court's position. [Priv. Ltr. Rul. 9446002] The IRS stated that if the employer does not obtain an actuarial certification, the account limit is still the amount reasonably and actuarially necessary to provide the benefits. Additionally, it cannot exceed the Section 419A(c)(5) safe-harbor account limits. The reasonable and actuarially necessary requirement applies regardless of the size of the reserve and whether or not the reserve exceeds the safe-harbor limits, the IRS explained.

Q 20:36   Can a qualified asset account include a premium or cost stabilization reserve?

No. A premium or cost stabilization reserve is not a reserve held to pay claims incurred but unpaid and thus is not an allowable reserve. In Private Letter Ruling 9145003 the IRS indicated that reserves set aside to pay level dividends or to stabilize premium rates are not allowable reserves. They thus can trigger an unrelated business income tax if maintained by a VEBA.

Practice Pointer. If a VEBA is being used by an employer to provide group term life insurance coverage through an insurance carrier, and a premium stabilization reserve is desired, it generally is preferable for the insurance company to hold the premium stabilization reserve because the group policy ordinarily will not be subject to the welfare benefit fund limitations (see Qs 20:21–20:25). If a VEBA is being used to fund a collectively bargained plan or an employee-pay-all plan, however, the VEBA is not subject to the qualified asset account limits (see Q 20:37) and thus can hold a premium or cost stabilization reserve without triggering an unrelated business income tax.

Q 20:37   Are all welfare benefit funds subject to the qualified asset account limits?

No. The qualified asset account limits do not apply to a collectively bargained plan. They also do not apply to an employee-pay-all plan funded through a Section 501(c)(9) trust (VEBA) if (1) the plan has at least 50 employees (determined without relying on the plan aggregation rules), and (2) no employee in the plan is entitled to a refund other than one based on the experience of the entire fund. [I.R.C. § 420A(f)(5)]

Under temporary IRS regulations, a *collectively bargained welfare fund* is a fund that is maintained pursuant to an agreement that the Secretary of Labor determines to be a collective bargaining agreement and that meets certain additional requirements, as follows:

- Regardless of the DOL's determination that an agreement is a collective bargaining agreement, the benefits provided through the fund must have been the subject of arm's-length negotiations between the employee representatives and one or more employers, and the agreement must satisfy Code Section 7701(a)(46).

- The circumstances surrounding the agreement must evidence good-faith bargaining between adverse parties over the welfare benefits to be provided through the fund.

- At least 90 percent of the employees eligible to receive benefits under the fund must be covered by the collective bargaining agreement (for funds in existence on July 1, 1985, this figure is 50 percent).

- Only the portion of the fund attributable to employees covered by a collective bargaining agreement, and from which benefits for such employees are provided, is considered to be maintained pursuant to a collective bargaining agreement.

- The number of employees who are not covered by the collective bargaining agreement and are eligible to receive benefits under the fund cannot increase by reason of an amendment, merger, or other action of the employer or the fund.

The IRS applied the preceding criteria to determine that two out of four subtrusts under a VEBA were welfare benefit funds maintained pursuant to collective bargaining agreements within the meaning of Code Section 420A(f)(5). [Priv. Ltr. Rul. 9617041] It also applied the preceding criteria to determine that a formal settlement agreement approved by a bankruptcy court, under which a retiree committee was to establish the terms and conditions of a VEBA, was a collective bargaining agreement; thus, the VEBA was a welfare benefit fund maintained pursuant to a collective bargaining agreement within the meaning of Code Section 420(f)(5). [Priv. Ltr. Rul. 9606009]

Importantly, the DOL has investigated so-called bogus collectively bargained plans that have been structured to take advantage of tax and ERISA exemptions but that in reality were not collectively bargained. A signature on a "collective bargaining agreement" was, for some of these arrangements, a condition for obtaining the benefit (such as a dental plan) only on its face. Small employers in particular have participated in these arrangements only to be hurt by the fund's adverse financial performance.

The DOL has proposed a regulation setting forth specific criteria that, if met and if certain other specified factors are not present, would constitute a finding that a plan is established or maintained under or pursuant to one or more collective bargaining agreements for purposes of ERISA. Employee welfare benefit plans that meet the requirements of the proposed regulation would be excluded from the definition of multiple-employer welfare arrangements and consequently would not be subject to state regulation. The DOL has also proposed regulations that set forth a procedure for obtaining a determination by the Secretary as to whether a particular employee welfare benefit plan is established or maintained under or pursuant to one or more agreements that are collective bargaining agreements for purposes of ERISA. The procedure would be available only in situations where the jurisdiction or law of a state has been asserted against a plan or other arrangement that contends it meets the exception for plans established or maintained under or pursuant to one or more collective bargaining agreements. [65 Fed. Reg. 209 (Oct. 27, 2000)]

In a 2003 notice, the IRS warned business owners about arrangements that are promoted as collectively bargained welfare benefit funds that are excepted from the account limits. [Notice 2003-24, 2003-18 I.R.B. 1] The notice alerts taxpayers and their representatives that the tax benefits purportedly generated by the transactions are not allowable for federal income tax purposes.

According to the IRS, business owners have been approached about arrangements that supposedly allow the business owner to take current tax deductions for all contributions to the welfare benefit fund. Before the contact, these businesses typically have had no involvement with labor organizations or other aspects of the collective bargaining process. The individual or the company promoting the arrangement typically arranges for an organization to act on behalf of the business in bargaining with an employee representative over benefits to be provided to some or all of the employees of the business (including the owners of the business). The arrangements usually require large employer contributions relative to the amount needed to provide the benefits. Moreover, benefits for owner-employees are more favorable than those for nonowners. According to the IRS, these arrangements generally do not satisfy the requirements for welfare benefit funds and do not provide the tax deductions claimed by the promoters. The IRS says it has disallowed deductions for contributions to these types of arrangements in the past and intends to do so in the future.

Q 20:38   If an employer has more than one welfare benefit fund, may the funds be aggregated in applying the asset account limits?

An employer generally may elect to treat two or more welfare benefit funds as a single fund. [I.R.C. § 419A(h)(1)] Furthermore, the tax rules in the pension plan area treating related employers as a single employer also apply to welfare benefit funds. [I.R.C. § 419A(h)(2)]

Q 20:39   Can a welfare benefit fund's qualified asset account include a reserve for future medical or life insurance benefits?

Yes. A welfare benefit fund's qualified asset account limit can include a reserve for postretirement medical or life insurance benefits. That means that an employer can make advance, deductible contributions to build up a reserve fund to pay for retiree medical or life insurance benefits in future years. The reserve must be funded over the working lives of the covered employees and must be actuarially determined on a level basis using assumptions that are reasonable in the aggregate.

Postretirement medical benefits. In funding for postretirement medical benefits, no increase in current medical costs can be assumed, even if some assumption of future increases in medical costs could be actuarially justified. In other words, the amount that an employer contributes to a reserve cannot include any amount to cover anticipated inflation in medical costs. [I.R.C. § 419A(c)(2)]

Postretirement life insurance benefits. Postretirement life insurance (including uninsured death benefits) may be funded only for amounts not in excess of $50,000. There is, however, an exception for grandfathered employees and retirees (see chapter 11), who continue to enjoy the full exclusion from income for group term life insurance coverage following actual retirement and attainment of retirement age as long as they retain grandfathered group status. For those individuals, the full amount of their postretirement group term life insurance may be prefunded. [I.R.C. § 419A(e)(2); TRA '86 § 1851(a)(3)(B)]

A U.S. Tax Court case considered the situation of an employer that made extremely large contributions to a VEBA, sufficient to fund not only reserves for incurred but unpaid claims, but also to fund postretirement medical and life insurance benefits. The employer's records showed, however, that it had the clear intention to use the amounts contributed at year-end to pay for benefits in the following year. That intention was in fact carried out over several years. In addition, the employer showed no postretirement reserves on its financial statements and made no disclosure of any such reserves to its employees or to their union representatives. The court held that, in order to have a valid postretirement reserve, Congress intended that funds must be accumulated for the purpose of providing postretirement benefits. It rejected the employer's argument that the term *reserve* in the law meant no more than a "liability." The court held that there must be actual funding. Inasmuch as the employer clearly intended to use the funds contributed for medical benefits for active employees in the following year, no valid postretirement reserves had been established. As a result, the court disallowed almost 90 percent of the employer's contributions to the VEBA for the years in issue. [General Signal Corp. v. Commissioner, 103 T.C. 14 (1994)]

In a letter ruling, the IRS examined an employer's method of funding an additional reserve for postretirement medical benefits over the remaining working lives of covered employees and found it satisfactory under Code Sections 419 and 419A. The employer used an aggregate funding method, recalculated annually to include the experience of the plan and trust, under which the amount of the annual contribution for postretirement medical benefits equaled a specified annual cost per participant (derived under a special formula set forth in the ruling) multiplied by the number of currently employed participants. The IRS determined that the employer's method, which in essence spread the unfunded estimated future cost of covered retirees over the remaining working lives of the employees, formed the basis for a reasonable addition to a reserve for postretirement medical benefits. [Priv. Ltr. Rul. 9710033]

> **Note.** The Pension Protection Act of 2006 (PPA) amended the Code to allow a reserve for future medical benefits of welfare benefit plans sponsored by bona fide associations (as defined in Section 2791(d)(3) of the Public Health Service Act). The reserve cannot exceed 35 percent of the sum of (1) qualified direct costs for a tax year, plus (2) the change in claims incurred but unpaid for that year for medical benefits (other than postretirement medical benefits). [I.R.C. § 419A(c)(6), as added by Pub. L. No, 109-280, 120 Stat. 780 (2006)] The PPA rule is effective for tax years beginning after 2006.

Q 20:40   Can an employer fund postretirement medical or life insurance benefits for individuals who have already retired?

According to the legislative history of the welfare benefit fund rules, no advance deduction is allowed with respect to a plan providing benefits exclusively for retirees, because such a plan is considered a plan of deferred compensation subject to the rules of Code Section 404. [Conf. Rep. to TRA '84, H.R. Rep. No. 861, 98th Cong., 2d Sess., at 1157 (1984)] If, however, the retiree plan is a continuation of a plan covering active employees, the welfare benefit fund rules do apply.

In a letter ruling, the IRS considered the case of an employer with three separate medical plans, one plan for active employees and the other two plans for retirees. Both of the retiree plans required, as a condition of eligibility, prior coverage under the active plan for a period of up to ten years immediately before retirement. The IRS held that the benefits under the retiree plans were a continuation of the active plan benefits, and therefore the employer's deductions were governed by Code Section 419 rather than by Code Section 404. [Priv. Ltr. Rul. 9151027]

Q 20:41 When can an employer fund and deduct reserves to fund postretirement benefits?

As a general rule, a reserve for postretirement benefits is funded and deducted on a level basis each year beginning in the year the reserve is created and ending with the year the employee is expected to retire. To take a simplified example, if it is actuarially determined that $10,000 will be needed to fund postretirement benefits for an employee with 10 years to go until retirement, the employer may contribute and deduct a reserve contribution of $1,000 each year.

However, the Tax Court has held that the rules are different when a reserve is created for employees who are already retired. In the case, the employer established a trust in 1991 to fund its retiree medical benefits. The employer's actuary calculated the present value of retiree benefits for active employees to be about $14 million and the present value of benefits for retirees to be $27,759,057. Based on these calculations, the actuary determined that the employer could make a 1991 contribution of about $3 million to fund retiree medical benefits for current employees, but could contribute the full $27,759,057 for current retirees. The employer contributed the full amount determined by the actuary and claimed a deduction for the entire contribution.

The employer backed up its deduction by pointing out that the tax law allows a deduction for contributions to a reserve "funded over the working lives of the covered employees and actuarially determined on a level basis (using assumptions that are reasonable in the aggregate)." [I.R.C. § 419A(c)(2)] According to the employer, because the current retirees had exhausted their working lives, the full amount needed to fund their benefits could be contributed and deducted in the year the reserve was created.

The IRS argued that the law requires the cost of the postretirement benefits to be spread over the *remaining* working lives of the covered employees. Moreover, because retirees have no *remaining* working lives, the cost for their benefits must be spread over the remaining working lives of the active employees.

In a reported decision, a unanimous Tax Court held that the employer was entitled to fund and deduct the full amount for retiree benefits in the year the reserve was created. According to the court, a "reserve funded over the working lives of the covered employees" means that assets necessary to satisfy the employer's liability may be accumulated no more rapidly than over the working lives of the covered employees so that the reserve for an employee can be fully funded no earlier than the employee's retirement. However, when the year in which the reserve is created falls after the employee has retired, there are no future years to which the benefits may be allocated and the entire present value of the projected benefit is properly allocated to the first year. [Wells Fargo & Co., v. Commissioner, 120 T.C. 5 (1993)]

Practice Pointer. The Tax Court decision paves the way for employers to claim significant tax deductions by prefunding the present value of retiree medical benefits for current retirees.

Of course, any amount intended as reserves to fund postretirement medical and/or life insurance benefits must actually be accumulated and used for such benefits. Accordingly, an employer was denied a deduction when it depleted its reserve by paying current claims for benefits made by active employees. [General Signal Corp. v. Commissioner, 142 F.3d 546 (2d Cir. 1998)]

Q 20:42 Do any nondiscrimination rules apply to the funding of postretirement medical and life insurance benefits for employees?

Yes. An employer may not deduct its contributions to a reserve for postretirement life insurance or medical benefits unless the plan under which the reserve is maintained does not discriminate in favor of the highly compensated. To make a determination regarding nondiscrimination, the nondiscrimination tests of Code Section 79 apply to group term life insurance (see chapter 11); the nondiscrimination rules of Code Section 105(h) apply to self-insured medical benefit plans (see chapter 3); and the nondiscrimination rules of Code Section 505(b) apply to insured medical benefits. The nondiscrimination rules do not, however, apply to a collectively bargained plan if the retiree benefits were the subject of good-faith bargaining. [I.R.C. §§ 419A(e)(1), 505(b)(3)]

Q 20:43 Besides nondiscrimination rules, what other special rule applies to funding postretirement medical and life insurance benefits for key employees?

If the reserve for postretirement medical and life insurance benefits is maintained for the benefit of one or more key employees, a separate account must be established for each key employee so covered, and postretirement benefits for the key employee may be paid only from his or her separate account. [I.R.C. § 419A(d)(1)] A *key employee* in this context is defined as any employee who, during the plan year or any preceding plan year, was a key employee as defined under the rules for top-heavy qualified retirement plan purposes. [I.R.C. §§ 416(i), 419A(d)(3)]

Effect on tax-qualified retirement plans. Any amount to be used for postretirement medical benefits that is allocated to a key employee's separate account is treated as an annual addition to a defined contribution plan for purposes of the dollar limitation on contributions to defined contribution plans under Code Section 415. [I.R.C. § 419A(d)(2)] The effect of the rule is to discourage funding of retiree medical benefits for key employees because it can reduce their retirement plan benefits.

Q 20:44   How is a welfare benefit fund's after-tax income determined?

The last element that needs to be known when calculating an employer's deductible amount of qualified cost is the amount of the welfare benefit fund's after-tax income for the taxable year. That after-tax income is subtracted from the sum of the qualified direct cost and the permitted additions to the qualified asset account in order to arrive at the employer's qualified cost.

When calculating the amount of the fund's after-tax income, the starting point is the fund's gross income for income tax purposes. Employee contributions, if any, then are added to the gross income, but employer contributions are not. Gross income (including employee contributions) is then reduced by expenses directly connected with the production of the gross income and by any income or unrelated business income taxes imposed on the fund. [I.R.C. § 419(c)(4)]

Q 20:45   What are the tax consequences if an employer contributes more to a welfare benefit plan than can be deducted under the welfare benefit fund rules?

An employer cannot take a current deduction for contribution amounts made (or deemed to be made) to the extent that they collectively exceed the qualified cost limit of Code Section 419, although the excess can be carried over to a later tax year. [I.R.C. § 419A(b)]

In addition, the net investment income of the fund will be taxed as so-called unrelated business taxable income (UBTI) if a VEBA or other tax-exempt trust is involved or taxed as "deemed unrelated income" if a taxable trust or fund held by an insurance company is involved to the extent that the fund exceeds the Section 419A qualified asset account limit. [I.R.C. §§ 419A(g), 512(a)(3)]

According to a technical advice memorandum issued by the IRS, the amount of UBTI is to be calculated using the same accounting method as the VEBA uses (cash or accrual basis). [Priv. Ltr. Rul. 9446002]

Q 20:46   Does investment income on a reserve for postretirement medical benefits accumulate tax-free?

Generally, no. The net investment income from a reserve for postretirement medical benefits is not treated as part of the qualified asset account when applying the unrelated business income or deemed unrelated income tax rules. The Code provides that net investment income earned on reserves held for postretirement medical benefits accumulates on an after-tax basis. [I.R.C. § 512(a)(3)(E)(i)]

If the welfare benefit fund is a separate fund established under a collective bargaining agreement, no account limits apply to the qualified asset account of the fund; therefore, it should have no tax on its postretirement medical benefits reserve. [I.R.C. § 419A(f)(5)(A)]

Further, no account limits apply to the qualified asset account of a separate fund that is an employee-pay-all plan established under Code Section 501(c)(9) (that is, a VEBA), if:

1. The plan has at least 50 employees (determined without relying on the plan aggregation rules); and

2. No employee in the plan is entitled to a refund other than one based on the experience of the entire fund.

Because there are no account limits in such a case, the postretirement medical benefits reserve can earn income tax-free. [I.R.C. § 419A(f)(5)(B)]

It should also be noted that the unrelated-business income tax does not apply to a welfare fund where substantially all of the contributions to the fund are made by employers that were tax-exempt organizations throughout the five-taxable-year period ending with the taxable year in which the contributions are made. Such employers can fund a postretirement medical benefits reserve free of tax. [I.R.C. § 512(a)(3)(E)(iii)]

Q 20:47   What are other circumstances where the income on a reserve held for postretirement medical benefits is not subject to tax?

Income on a reserve held for postretirement medical benefits is not subject to tax if the income itself is not gross income under the Code. For example, if a VEBA maintains a reserve for postretirement medical benefits and invests the funds in tax-exempt municipal obligations, it will have no gross income and thus no unrelated business income. [I.R.C. § 512(a)(3)] Of course, it will generally receive a lower return on tax-exempt obligations than it would pretax on fully taxable obligations.

A VEBA apparently can avoid the unrelated-business income tax by purchasing life insurance on the lives of the employees covered with the VEBA as owner and beneficiary and maintaining the insurance coverage until the employee's death. Some insurers have developed a group universal life insurance policy (fixed or variable) specifically for such a market. The product is commonly referred to as *trust-owned life insurance* (TOLI). One issue that may be raised by a TOLI is whether the VEBA will be considered to have an insurable interest in the lives of the employees involved. A number of state laws defining insurable interest have been liberalized to cover TOLIs and similar situations.

Q 20:48   Are reserves established to fund postretirement medical and life insurance benefits required to be maintained separately from other benefit funds?

At this time, there is conflicting authority on whether a separate account must be maintained for funding of postretirement medical or life insurance benefits in order to receive favorable tax treatment of the funding.

Some practitioners have contended that a retiree medical or life insurance reserve could be established within a VEBA and that the amounts, once set aside, could be used at any time thereafter for any benefits the VEBA was authorized to provide (e.g., medical benefits for active employees). A letter ruling, however, strongly suggests that the IRS will require that the retiree reserve be used solely for its intended purpose, at least as long as there are employees and retirees in the covered group still alive.

In Private Letter Ruling 9206030, the IRS considered the proposed transfer of retiree group term life insurance reserves from three life insurance companies to a VEBA. The reserves were held by the insurers under contractual arrangements that met the requirements of Revenue Ruling 69-382 [1969-2 C.B. 28], the ruling that spelled out the requirements for favorable tax treatment on retired lives reserves before the enactment of the statutory provisions governing such reserves in the Deficit Reduction Act of 1984.

The letter ruling first held that the reserves could be transferred from the insurers to the VEBA without resulting in gross income to the employer or triggering a 100 percent excise tax under Code Section 4976, if both the VEBA trust agreement and the plan document were amended to provide that the amounts transferred are to be credited to a separate account for postretirement life insurance benefits. Second, the letter ruling held that the funds in the separate account were to be used exclusively for the payment of postretirement life insurance benefits.

Nevertheless, another letter ruling permitted an overfunded retired lives reserve to be used for coverage of active as well as retired employees. Under the facts of the ruling, the amount of a retired lives reserve held for retiree group life insurance far exceeded the anticipated premiums needed to fund the retiree group life insurance. It was unlikely that the retired lives reserve would ever be depleted if it continued to be used solely for payment of retiree group life insurance premiums. The employer asked the IRS to permit the transfer of the retired lives reserve from the insurer to a VEBA, and to permit the VEBA to use the reserve to pay premiums for both retired and active employees.

The IRS ruled that the reserve transfer to the VEBA would not be a reversion to the employer subject to the 100 percent excise tax on reversions from a welfare benefit fund. The IRS also ruled that the VEBA's payments from the reserve for both retired and active coverage was permissible. [Priv. Ltr. Rul. 9437016] If the retired lives reserve had not been grossly overfunded, it is doubtful that the IRS would have ruled favorably on use of the retired lives reserve to pay premiums for active employee coverage.

A U.S. Tax Court decision found that there was no requirement in the law for the establishment of a separate account for a postretirement reserve and that it appeared to be sufficient if the VEBA had been funded with the purpose of funding the postretirement benefits and the funds in the VEBA were adequate for that purpose. [General Signal Corp., v. Commissioner, 103 T.C. 14 (1994)]

If an employer wishes to take the amount of the retired lives reserve into account as a reduction in its postretirement benefit liabilities under Financial Accounting Standard 106, it appears necessary to maintain a separate account to be used exclusively to provide postretirement benefits (see chapter 21).

Q 20:49   Who pays the taxes, if any, on a welfare benefit fund's investment income?

If a VEBA or other tax-exempt trust holds the welfare benefit fund, the trust pays the unrelated-business income tax at trust income tax rates. If the tax-exempt entity is organized in corporate form, the corporate entity pays the tax at corporate income tax rates. If the fund is held by a taxable trust or other entity or by an insurance company, the fund's deemed unrelated income is taxable to the employer; it is taxed at whatever corporate income tax rates apply to the employer. [I.R.C. §§ 511, 419A(g)]

If a trust pays the UBTI, the moneys in the trust are reduced, possibly enabling further deductible employer contributions before the applicable limit is reached. To achieve an equivalent result, the tax paid by the employer on any deemed unrelated income is treated as an employer contribution to the fund on the last day of the taxable year when calculating the employer deduction; in determining the fund's after-tax income, the tax paid is treated as if it were imposed on the fund. [I.R.C. § 419A(g)(3)]

Q 20:50   What federal excise taxes can apply to an employer maintaining a welfare benefit fund?

If an employer maintains a welfare benefit fund and disqualified benefits (see Q 20:51) are provided, an excise tax of 100 percent of the disqualified benefit is imposed on the employer. [I.R.C. § 4976]

Q 20:51   What disqualified benefits trigger the 100 percent excise tax?

Disqualified benefits that trigger the 100 percent excise tax are defined as follows:

1. Any postretirement medical benefit or life insurance benefit provided by a welfare benefit fund with respect to a key employee if a separate account is required to be established for the key employee, but the payment is not made from the separate account;

2. Any postretirement medical benefit or life insurance benefit that a discriminatory plan provides with respect to an individual in whose favor discrimination is prohibited (this provision does not apply to a collectively bargained plan in which the postretirement benefits were the subject of good-faith bargaining); or

3. Any portion of a welfare benefit fund reverting to the benefit of the employer (this provision does not apply to a return of contributions that were not deductible for the current taxable year or any prior year).

[I.R.C. § 4976(b)]

Q 20:52   How can the 100 percent excise tax triggered by a disqualified benefit be avoided?

The answer depends on why the benefit is disqualified.

Failure to pay from a separate account when required. Because of the need to establish separate accounts for key employees and the necessity of taking additions to separate accounts into consideration when applying the dollar limitation for defined contribution plans, some employers have taken steps to avoid penalties by excluding key employees from coverage under retired lives reserves arrangements. In such cases, the separate account requirement does not apply, and the retiree benefits for key employees can be paid out of current employer funds during the period of retirement.

In addition, it should be noted that the excise tax provisions do not apply to grandfathered retired lives reserves that were in existence in 1984. [I.R.C. § 4976(b)(4)]

Discriminatory plan. There is no way to avoid the excise tax, other than to maintain a nondiscriminatory plan. Still, the grandfathered portion of the reserve will not be subject to the nondiscrimination rules and hence the excise tax.

Surplus funds reverting to the employer. A direct return of deductible contributions or fund earnings to an employer apparently will trigger the 100 percent excise tax plus regular income tax, even if all liabilities to employees and retirees under the plan have been fully satisfied. Presumably, any surplus remaining in the fund must be used to provide additional employee benefits, must be distributed in cash to the participants in a nondiscriminatory manner, or must be donated to charity.

However, application of such a surplus to employer contributions under another existing welfare benefit plan should not be viewed as an indirect reversion. [Gen. Couns. Mem. 39, 774 (Aug. 1, 1988)] For example, if there is a surplus remaining in a retired lives reserve held under a medical benefit plan after all plan obligations have been fully satisfied, the employer should be able to use the surplus to pay for the benefits under a disability plan. It may be desirable to apply for an IRS letter ruling in such a case.

Voluntary Employees' Beneficiary Associations

Q 20:53   What is a VEBA?

A voluntary employees' beneficiary association (VEBA) is a tax-exempt organization, described in Code Section 501(c)(9), that provides for the payment of life, sickness, accident, or other benefits to its members or their dependents or designated beneficiaries. No part of the VEBA's net earnings may inure (other than through benefit payments) to the benefit of any private shareholder or individual.

A VEBA is a separate organization, usually set up as a trust because of ERISA requirements. The employer makes tax-deductible contributions to a VEBA, which uses the money to pay the benefits. [ERISA § 403]

Q 20:54   Why are VEBAs useful?

VEBAs offer a number of advantages:

1. A VEBA trust may be used to satisfy an employer's obligation to hold employee contributions under an ERISA plan in trust (see Qs 2:99–2:103).

2. Some employers try, in the VEBA plan document and trust, to limit their economic risk for payment of plan benefits to the moneys held by the trust.

3. The investment income on funds set aside in the VEBA trust (other than reserves for postretirement medical benefits) generally can accumulate tax-free, within limits.

4. Disability income payments made from a VEBA can avoid mandatory income tax withholding requirements if the risk of payment is shifted from the employer to a third-party payer (the VEBA trust).

5. In the case of employee-pay-all group term life insurance, imputed income under Code Section 79 may be avoided entirely because the coverage is not carried directly or indirectly by the employer (see Qs 11:34–11:38).

Q 20:55   How is a VEBA organized?

A VEBA may be organized in the legal form of a trust or a nonprofit corporation. In practice, the trust form is almost always used. The trust may be established by the employer or by the employees themselves. In most cases, however, the employer establishes the VEBA.

Q 20:56   Who can join a VEBA?

Membership of a VEBA must consist of individuals who become entitled to participate by reason of their being employees and whose eligibility for membership is defined by reference to objective standards that constitute an employment-related common bond. The employment-related common bond can include a common employer or affiliated employers, coverage under the same collective bargaining agreement or agreements, membership in a labor union, or membership in one or more locals of a national or international union.

The Treasury regulations consider employees of one or more employers engaged in the same lines of business in the same geographic locale to share an employment-related bond. [Treas. Reg. § 1.501(c)(9)-2(a)(1)] In administering that requirement, the IRS has taken the position that the same geographic locale requirement covered only a single state or a single standard metropolitan statistical area as defined by the Bureau of the Census. However, a federal appeals court has held the same geographic locale requirement of the regulations is invalid. [Water Quality Ass'n Employees' Benefit Corp. v. United States, 795 F.2d 1303 (7th Cir. 1986)]

The IRS has since proposed a regulatory definition of a single geographic locale as one that cannot exceed the boundaries of three contiguous states; that is, three states each of which shares a land or river border with at least one of the others. In addition, Alaska and Hawaii are deemed to be contiguous with each other and with the states of Washington, Oregon, and California. [Prop. Treas. Reg. § 1.501(c)(9)-2(d)(1)]

The proposed regulation would give the IRS discretionary authority to recognize an even larger geographic area as a single geographic area if:

1. It would not be economically feasible to cover employees of employers engaged in that line of business in that area under two or more separate VEBAs, each extending over fewer states; and

2. Employment characteristics in that line of business, population characteristics, or other regional factors support the particular states included (this requirement is deemed satisfied if the states included are contiguous).

[Prop. Treas. Reg. § 1.501(c)(9)-2(d)(2)]

Q 20:57   Do all of the members of a VEBA have to be employees?

No. Treasury regulations do stipulate, however, that, at a minimum, 90 percent of the total membership of the association must be employees on one day of each quarter of the association's taxable year. [Treas. Reg. § 1.501(c)(9)-2(a)(1)]

Q 20:58   Can nonemployees be VEBA members?

Yes. Some nonemployees—that is, independent contractors—may be members of a VEBA, as long as 90 percent of the members are employees. [Treas. Reg. § 1.501(c)(9)-2(a)(1); Water Quality Ass'n Employees' Benefit Corp. v. United States, 795 F.2d 1303 (7th Cir. 1986)]

Q 20:59   Can retirees and other former employees be VEBA members?

Yes. Retirees and other former employees can be members of a VEBA and count as employees for purposes of the requirement that 90 percent of the total membership of the association must be employees. [Treas. Reg. § 1.501(c)(9)-2(b)(2)]

Q 20:60   Can spouses and dependents be VEBA members?

Spouses and dependents of active employees cannot be VEBA members, but they can participate in the VEBA's employee benefit plans. Surviving spouses and dependents of deceased participants can be treated as employees for purposes of the 90 percent rule, however. [Treas. Reg. § 1.501(c)(9)-2(b)(3)]

Q 20:61   How is the requirement that VEBA membership be voluntary met?

Membership is regarded as voluntary if an affirmative act on the part of an employee to become a member of a VEBA is necessary. In addition, membership will be treated as voluntary (even if no affirmative act by the employee is necessary) if the employee does not incur a detriment, such as a deduction from pay, as a result of membership. [Treas. Reg. § 1.501(c)(9)-2(c)(2)]

Q 20:62   May an employer control a VEBA?

No. Treasury regulations provide that a VEBA must be controlled by any of the following: (1) the VEBA membership; (2) an independent trustee or trustees (e.g., a bank); or (3) trustees or other fiduciaries (at least some of whom are designated by or on behalf of the membership). The requirement of control by an independent trustee is deemed satisfied if the VEBA is an employee welfare benefit plan subject to ERISA. [Treas. Reg. § 1.501(c)(9)-2(c)(3)] It was widely assumed that as long as the VEBA was a welfare benefit plan subject to ERISA, the employer could exercise substantial control, as a fiduciary, over the VEBA. However, a U.S. Court of Federal Claims decision suggests that substantial employer control over the VEBA could jeopardize its tax-exempt status. [Lima Surgical Assoc. Inc. Voluntary Employees' Beneficiary Ass'n Plan Trust v. United States, 20 Cl. Ct. 674 (1990), *aff'd on other grounds,* 944 F.2d 885 (Fed. Cir. 1991)]

Q 20:63   What benefits may a VEBA provide?

A VEBA may provide the following benefits:

1. Life benefits, payable on the death of a member or dependent. The death benefit may be provided directly or through insurance. Pensions, annuities, and similar benefits are not included, except for a death benefit payable in the form of an annuity.
2. Sickness and accident benefits, which include medical benefits and disability income benefits, whether insured or uninsured. This category also contains benefits in noncash form, such as clinical care by visiting nurses and medical care transportation.

Other benefits that are similar to life, sickness, and accident benefits. A welfare benefit is treated in a manner similar to life, sickness, and accident benefits if it is intended to safeguard or improve the health of the member or dependents or if it protects against a contingency that interrupts or impairs a member's earning power. [Treas. Reg. § 1.501(c)(9)-3(d)]

Other welfare benefits that may be provided by a VEBA include:

- Vacation benefits, vacation facilities, and reimbursement of vacation expenses
- Subsidies for recreational activities, such as athletic leagues
- Child care facilities for preschool and school-age dependents
- Job readjustment allowances
- Income maintenance payments in the event of economic dislocation
- Temporary living expense loans and grants at times of disasters, such as fire or flood
- Supplemental unemployment compensation benefits as defined in Code Section 501(c)(17)(D)(i)
- Education or training benefits or courses, including apprentice training programs
- Legal services through a qualified legal services plan
- Benefits permitted under Code Section 302c(5) of the Labor Management Relations Act of 1947
- Holiday pay and paid personal days
- Social, recreational, and cultural benefits for retirees
- Free membership in recreational organizations
- Severance benefits under a severance pay plan within the meaning of 29 C.F.R. § 2510.3-2(b)

[29 U.S.C. § 186c; TAM 9126004; Priv. Ltr. Ruls. 9820038, 9815058, 9815057; Treas. Reg. § 1.501(c)(9)-3]

Not included in the category of "other benefits" provided by VEBAs are commuting expenses, property insurance (e.g., auto or homeowner's insurance), loans other than disaster loans, savings facilities, and pensions and other deferred compensation-type benefits. Where a severance plan provided benefits for termination of employment for any reason other than death, including retirement, the benefits were held to be pension-type benefits rather than severance benefits, and the VEBA was held not to be tax exempt. [Lima Surgical Assoc. Inc. Voluntary Employees' Beneficiary Ass'n Plan Trust v. United States, 20 Cl. Ct. 674 (1990), *aff'd on other grounds,* 944 F.2d 885 (Fed. Cir. 1991)]

The IRS took the position that income maintenance benefits payable when an employee's monthly compensation dropped, for any reason, below 80 percent of the average over a three-year period did not qualify as a VEBA benefit because the payments were not the result of an unanticipated event similar in nature to death, sickness, or accident, and the payments could result from the employee's own decision to work fewer hours. [Gen. Couns. Mem. 39,879 (Jan. 6, 1986)]

Q 20:64 What is prohibited inurement to a private shareholder or individual?

No part of a VEBA's net earnings may inure (other than through benefit payments) to the benefit of any private shareholder or individual. *Prohibited inurement* is defined by Treasury regulations to include the following:

1. Disposition of VEBA property to, or performance of services for, a person for less than adequate consideration (other than as benefits);

2. Payment of unreasonable compensation to the trustees or employees of the VEBA; and

3. The purchase of insurance or services at more than fair market value from a company in which one or more of the VEBA's trustees, officers, or fiduciaries has an interest.

[Treas. Reg. § 1.501(c)(9)-4(a)]

Also, payment to highly compensated employees (HCEs) of benefits that are disproportionately high in relation to the benefits of other members may constitute prohibited inurement, unless the benefits are based on objective and reasonable standards. A VEBA plan that based termination benefits on a formula that took into account both compensation and length of service, and under which 95 percent of the benefits were attributable to the highly compensated stockholder-employees, was held to violate the prohibited inurement restriction. [Treas. Reg. § 1.501(c)(9)-4(b); Lima Surgical Assoc. Inc. Voluntary Employees' Beneficiary Ass'n Plan Trust v. United States, 20 Cl. Ct. 674 (1990), *aff'd on other grounds*, 944 F.2d 885 (Fed. Cir. 1991)]

Contingent compensation. Fees paid to a VEBA's administrator and general counsel that were based on a percentage of employer contributions, without any ceiling placed upon the amount, probably would constitute prohibited inurement. A contingent compensation arrangement is disfavored and would, at the least, have to satisfy a five-factor test and be "girded with the proper safeguards." [Gen. Couns. Mem. 38,322 (Mar. 24, 1980)]

Rebates of premiums. Rebates of excess insurance premiums, based on the mortality or morbidity experience of the insurer, to the person or persons who paid the premiums, is not prohibited inurement. Thus, if an employer pays the premiums on an insurance policy owned by a VEBA, the employer can receive dividends or experience-rating credits from the insurer without violating the prohibited inurement restriction. [Treas. Reg. § 1.501(c)(9)-4(c)]

Q 20:65 Do any special restrictions apply to the disposition of VEBA assets on termination?

Yes. The prohibited inurement rule (see Q 20:64) affects how VEBA assets may be disbursed when a plan maintained by the VEBA, or the VEBA itself, terminates.

On termination of a plan maintained by a VEBA, the prohibited inurement rule will not be violated if any assets remaining after satisfaction of all liabilities are used to provide additional life, sickness, accident, or other benefits to employees using criteria that avoid disproportionate benefits to officers, shareholders, or highly compensated employees of the employer.

Similarly, the prohibited inurement rule is not violated if, on termination of the VEBA, the assets are distributed to members on the basis of objective and reasonable standards that do not result in either unequal payments to similarly situated members or disproportionate payments to officers, shareholders, or highly compensated employees. If the VEBA's governing document or applicable state law provides that any assets remaining will be returned to the employer or employers that contributed to it, the VEBA will fail to qualify for tax exemption under Code Section 501(c)(9). [Treas. Reg. § 1.501(c)(9)-4]

The IRS reviewed a situation where, because of industry changes, a VEBA wanted to transfer assets directly to another VEBA without any distribution of assets to participating employers. The amount to be transferred would be calculated based on the employee's share of the distribution and the amount of time that their participating employer had been in the plan. The IRS ruled that the VEBA's exempt status would not be harmed and that the transfer and continuing payments did not constitute a prohibited reversion. [Priv. Ltr. Rul. 9551007]

Q 20:66   What is the tax status of a VEBA?

A tax-qualified VEBA is exempt from regular income tax, but the employer generally is subject to the deductible contribution limits under Code Sections 419 and 419A (see Q 20:29). As discussed in connection with the welfare benefit fund rules (see Qs 20:45–20:46), however, a VEBA may be subject to unrelated business income tax (see Q 20:49) on some or all of its income if:

1. It holds reserves in excess of the limits permitted by Code Sections 419 and 419A; or

2. It holds a reserve for postretirement medical benefits.

[I.R.C. § 512(a)(3)(E)(i)]

The Second Circuit denied a company's deduction for its contribution to a VEBA because the contribution was not made to a reserve intended to fund postretirement benefits. The court, affirming the U.S. Tax Court, concluded that Code Section 419(c) requires actual accumulation of funds in a reserve. [General Signal Corp. v. Commissioner, 142 F.3d 546 (2d Cir. 1998)]

The Third Circuit denied deductions claimed by three medical corporations for excess VEBA contributions made to purchase life insurance policies for doctor-owners. The court determined that the amounts paid exceeded the conventional life insurance premiums by nearly 500 percent and were part of a plan to obtain tax benefits and return the excess contributions as tax-free cash distributions. Thus, although the contributions were required by the VEBA plan document, the court concluded that the contributions were not ordinary and necessary business expenses of the corporations and were not deductible.

Instead, the court concluded that the excess contributions were taxable dividends to the doctor-owners. The three corporations were among 19 consolidated cases that agreed to be bound by the court's decision. [Neonatology Assocs., P.A. v. Commissioner, 299 F.3d 221 (3d Cir. 2002)]

Q 20:67   What are the tax consequences to the employee when employer contributions are made to a VEBA?

An employee is not ordinarily taxed when contributions are made to the VEBA. There is one exception. An employee is taxed if (1) the amounts contributed are fully vested and not subject to a substantial risk of forfeiture, and (2) there is no statutory exclusion from gross income for the benefits for which the contributions are made (e.g., severance and vacation pay benefits).

In most cases, there is a statutory exclusion from gross income. For example, contributions to fund accident and health benefits, funded through insurance or otherwise, are excluded from gross income under Code Section 106. Contributions to purchase group term life insurance up to $50,000 are excluded from gross income under Code Section 79. Contributions to pay premiums on additional term insurance or whole life insurance on the life of the employee are not currently taxable if the VEBA is the policy owner.

Contributions to fund supplemental unemployment compensation, disaster loans, and job readjustment allowances are not taxable because the employee does not have a vested right to receive the benefit until he or she becomes unemployed, suffers a disaster, or otherwise qualifies for the benefit. [Treas. Reg. § 1.83-3(e)]

Q 20:68   What are the tax consequences to the employee when distributions are made from a VEBA?

A member is taxed upon receipt of benefits under a VEBA unless there is a specific statutory exclusion. The tax consequences are the same as if the employer provided the benefit directly to the member rather than through the VEBA. The availability of an exclusion from income depends on the section of the Code dealing with the type of benefit received and not on whether the person is eligible for membership in the VEBA. [Treas. Reg. § 1.501(c)(9)-6]

Q 20:69   May an employee deduct contributions to a VEBA?

An employee may not deduct contributions to a VEBA—with one exception. Contributions to pay for medical insurance are deductible to the extent such contributions and other itemized medical expenses exceed 7.5 percent of the employee's adjusted gross income. [Priv. Ltr. Ruls. 8040050, 7949046]

Q 20:70 May a VEBA provide benefits that discriminate in favor of highly compensated employees?

Generally, if a VEBA discriminates in favor of HCEs, it will lose its tax qualification. [I.R.C. §§ 505(a)(1), 505(b)] The nondiscrimination rules do not apply, however, in the case of collectively bargained plans where there was good-faith bargaining. [I.R.C. § 505(a)(2)]

Q 20:71 What are the nondiscrimination requirements for a VEBA?

The general nondiscrimination requirements for a VEBA are as follows:

1. Each class of benefits under the plan must be provided under a classification of employees set forth in the plan that does not discriminate in favor of highly compensated individuals; and

2. No class of benefits can discriminate in favor of highly compensated individuals.

Life insurance, disability benefits, severance pay, and supplemental unemployment compensation benefits do not violate the second requirement merely because the benefits bear a uniform relationship to total compensation or to a basic or regular rate of compensation. [I.R.C. § 505(b)] In applying the Section 505(b) nondiscrimination requirements, an employer may disregard employees with less than three years of service, employees under age 21, seasonal employees, less-than-half-time employees, employees covered by a collective bargaining agreement, and nonresident aliens with no U.S.-source earned income from the employer.

If the benefit is subject to nondiscrimination rules contained in some other provision of the Code, those other nondiscrimination rules supersede the general rules in Code Section 505(b)(1). [I.R.C. § 505(b)(3)] Thus, if the nondiscrimination rules of Code Section 79 (group term life insurance), Code Section 105(h) (self-insured medical plans), Code Section 125 (cafeteria plans), or Code Section 129 (dependent care assistance) apply, the nondiscrimination rules of Code Section 505(b)(1) do not apply.

Q 20:72 Is there a limit on the amount of compensation that may be used as a base for VEBA benefits?

Yes. Compensation for VEBA purposes is defined in the same manner as for qualified retirement plan purposes. Compensation taken into account cannot exceed $200,000, indexed to the cost of living. [I.R.C. §§ 414(s), 505(b)(6), 505(b)(7)] For 2008, the indexed compensation limit is $230,000.

Effect of limit on specific types of plans. The compensation limit does not apply to a group term life insurance plan subject to Code Section 79. [I.R.C. § 505(b)(7)] If the plan is not governed by Code Section 79 (e.g., it is a disability income plan or an employee-pay-all group term life insurance plan not subject to Code Section 79), it is subject to the compensation limit. If the plan fails to comply with this compensation limit, it appears that the VEBA will lose its tax exemption.

Q 20:73   Must a VEBA file a notice with the IRS in order to be tax-exempt?

Yes. A VEBA should file an application for exemption on IRS Form 1024, generally within 15 months of the month of its organization. [I.R.C. § 505(c); Temp. Treas. Reg. § 1.505(c)-1T]

Q 20:74   Are there any other reporting and recordkeeping requirements for VEBAs?

A VEBA must maintain records indicating the amounts contributed by each member and contributing employer and the amounts and types of benefits paid by the VEBA to or on behalf of each member. [Treas. Reg. § 1.50(c)(9)-5] The employer must provide members with a summary plan description because the VEBA is a welfare benefit plan. In addition, the VEBA must file an annual return with the DOL on Form 5500. A VEBA must also file Form 990 in any year in which total gross receipts exceed $25,000 and Form 990-T if it has unrelated business income.

Funding Postretirement Medical Benefits Under a Pension Plan

Q 20:75   May postretirement medical benefits be funded other than through a welfare benefit fund (including a VEBA or a retired lives reserve)?

Yes. A pension plan or annuity plan may provide for the payment of benefits for sickness, accident, hospitalization, and medical expenses of retired employees and their spouses and dependents, provided that certain requirements are met. [I.R.C. § 401(h)]

Q 20:76   What requirements apply to the funding of retirement medical benefits through a pension plan or annuity plan?

To fund retirement medical plans through a pension plan or an annuity plan, the following seven requirements must be satisfied:

1. The benefits must be subordinate to the retirement benefits under the plan (see Q 20:77);

2. A postretirement medical benefit account separate from the pension account must be established and maintained for the benefits;

3. The employer's contributions to the separate account must be reasonable and ascertainable;

4. Before all liabilities for the postretirement medical benefits are satisfied, it must be impossible to use the separate account funds for any other purpose;

5. The plan must require, by its terms, that once all liabilities for postretirement medical benefits are satisfied, any surplus will be returned to the employer;

6. Individual separate accounts (within the overall retiree medical benefit separate account) must be established for retiree medical benefits payable to each key employee covered for medical benefits; and

7. Retiree medical benefits for the key employee and his or her spouse and dependents may be paid only from the key employee's individual separate account.

[I.R.C. § 401(h)]

The accounts just referred to are not subject to the Section 419 welfare benefit fund rules.

In addition, a new rule added by the Pension Protection Act of 2006 [Pub. L. No. 109-280, 120 Stat. 780 (2006)] permits an exclusion from gross income of up to $3,000 per year for retirement plan distributions paid directly to an insurer to purchase accident or health insurance or qualified long-term care insurance for an eligible retired public safety officer and his or her spouse and dependents. [I.R.C. § 402(*l*); Prop. Treas. Reg. § 1.402(a)-1(e)(2)] In anticipation of a proposed technical correction, the IRS has made it clear that the exclusion for qualifying distributions from pension plans of public safety officers also applies to premiums paid to an accident or health plan that is self-insured. [Notice 2007-99, 2007-52 I.R.B. 1243] The Worker, Retiree, and Employer Recovery Act of 2008 (WRERA) [Pub. L. No. 110-458, 122 Stat. 5092 (Dec. 24, 2008)] officially amended the exclusion to apply to premiums for coverage under an "accident or health plan." [I.R.C. § 402(l)(4)(D), as amended by WRERA § 108(j)(1)(B)(ii)] Thus, under the WRERA, the exclusion applies to self-insured plans as well as to insurance issued by an insurance company. The amendment applies retroactively to distributions in tax years beginning after December 31, 2006.

Q 20:77   When do the retiree medical benefits qualify as subordinate to the retirement benefits under a pension or annuity plan?

Retiree medical benefits are considered subordinate to the pension benefits if at all times the total contributions for retiree medical benefits (plus any contributions for life insurance protection) made after the date on which the plan first provides retiree medical benefits do not exceed 25 percent of the total contributions (for pensions *and* retiree medical *and* any life insurance) made after that date (excluding contributions made to fund past service pension credits). [Treas. Reg. § 1.401-14(c)(1)] This limit translates to one third of the cumulative current service pension contributions since the date the Section 401(h) account was established under the pension plan. For example, if an employer establishes a Section 401(h) retiree medical separate account on

January 1 of a taxable year and the employer's current service pension contribution for the year is $3 million, the employer can contribute $1 million to the Section 401(h) account for that year.

That regulatory interpretation of the statutory *subordinate* test was widely criticized because it meant that, in the case of a well-funded pension plan, little or no contribution could be made to a Section 401(h) medical benefit separate account to fund retiree medical benefits.

For a brief time in 1989, the IRS permitted employers with a pension plan that was fully funded or close to fully funded to use the cost of pension benefit accruals for current service, rather than actual contributions, in applying the subordinate test in the regulations. [Gen. Couns. Mem. 39, 785 (Mar. 23, 1989)] Concerned over the revenue loss implications of the liberalized IRS position, however, Congress reinstated the more restrictive test, applicable generally to contributions after October 3, 1989. [I.R.C. § 401(h); OBRA '89 § 7311]

Q 20:78   May a Section 401(h) account be maintained under a defined contribution money purchase pension plan?

It appears that it can. Traditionally, Section 401(h) accounts have been maintained in connection with defined benefit plans. However, the Code provision merely refers to a "pension or annuity plan." Because a defined contribution money purchase plan is a type of pension plan, such a plan should be able to establish a Section 401(h) account.

Q 20:79   May a Section 401(h) account be maintained under a profit sharing plan?

No. A profit sharing plan is not a pension or annuity plan under the Code; therefore, a profit sharing plan cannot have a Section 401(h) account associated with it. [I.R.C. §§ 401(a), 403(a)(1)]

In addition, the IRS has ruled that a profit-sharing plan that provided each participant with a separate profit-sharing account and medical reimbursement account was not tax-qualified. The plan provided that payments from the medical reimbursement account could be used only to reimburse substantiated medical expenses of the plan participant, or the participant's spouse or dependent. Consequently, the plan violated the rule under Code Section 411 requiring that a participant's accrued benefit under a profit sharing plan be nonforfeitable. [Rev. Rul. 2005-55, 2005-33 I.R.B. 284]

Q 20:80   Does the Section 401(h) separate account requirement require a physical segregation of assets?

No. The separation between pension and medical benefits is required for recordkeeping purposes only. The funds attributable to the medical benefit separate account need not be invested separately from the pension funds. If the investment properties are not allocated separately, the earnings on the plan investments must be allocated between the pension and medical benefits account in a reasonable manner. [Treas. Reg. § 1.401-14(c)(2)] It appears that the individual separate accounts required for key employees covered for the retiree medical benefits are also recordkeeping accounts only, with no physical separation of plan assets required.

Q 20:81   What deductibility limits apply to employer contributions to fund retiree medical benefits under Code Section 401(h)?

When an employer makes a contribution to a welfare benefit plan, it must designate the portion of the contribution allocable to the retiree medical benefit account. The deductible contributions made to fund the retiree medical benefit account cannot exceed the total cost of providing the medical benefits. The total cost of providing the medical benefits is to be determined in accordance with any generally accepted actuarial method that is reasonable in view of the provisions and coverage of the plan, the funding medium, and other applicable considerations.

The amount deductible for any taxable year cannot exceed the greater of:

1. An amount determined by distributing the remaining unfunded costs of past and current service credits as a level amount, or as a level percentage of compensation, over the remaining future service of each employee (assuming future service of at least one year); or

2. 10 percent of the cost that would be necessary to completely fund or purchase the retiree medical benefits.

Contributions in excess of the amount deductible may be carried over and deducted in later years, subject to the limits applicable in those years. Making a nondeductible contribution, however, will subject the employer to a 10 percent excise tax. [I.R.C. § 4972; Treas. Reg. §§ 1.401-14(c)(3), 1.404(a)-3(f)]

Q 20:82   What must a Section 401(h) account do with employee forfeitures of retiree medical benefit accounts?

A pension plan must expressly provide that in the event an individual's interest in the Section 401(h) medical benefit account is forfeited, the amount of the forfeiture must be applied as soon as possible to reduce employer contributions to fund the medical benefits. [Treas. Reg. § 1.401-14(c)(6)]

Q 20:83   May the funds in a Section 401(h) account be used to pay pension benefits under the plan?

No. The prohibition against diversion of retiree medical benefit funds for any other purpose includes using the funds for pension objectives. Conversely, excess assets under the pension portion of the plan generally cannot be transferred to the retiree medical benefit account without causing the plan to lose its tax-qualified status. [Treas. Reg. § 1.401-14(c)(4)]

There are a number of key exceptions, however. Under Code Section 420, the following transfers of *excess* pension assets to a Section 401(h) account are permitted:

- Qualified transfers to fund current retiree health liabilities (see Qs 20:85–20:98);

- Qualified future transfers (see Q 20:99); and

- Collectively bargained transfers to fund collectively bargained retiree health liabilities (see Q 20:100).

Q 20:84   Are payments from a Section 401(h) account used to pay for retiree health coverage costs or benefits subject to income tax?

No. If amounts are withdrawn from a Section 401(h) account to pay for the costs of medical care coverage for a retiree (for example, to pay premiums for medical care insurance), the amounts are excluded from the retiree's income under Code Section 106. If amounts are withdrawn from a Section 401(h) account to provide retiree medical care benefits directly, the amounts are excludable from the retiree's income under Code Section 105(b), or under Code Section 104(a)(3) if the payments are attributable to employee contributions to the Section 401(h) account.

Q 20:85   Under what type of plan can a qualified transfer of excess pension assets be made to a Section 401(h) account?

A qualified transfer of excess pension assets can be made to a Section 401(h) account only under a defined benefit pension plan. Thus, a qualified transfer cannot be made under a defined contribution money purchase pension plan.

For tax years beginning on or after January 1, 2007, the PPA provides that a defined benefit plan that is a multiemployer plan is eligible for a qualified transfer. [I.R.C. § 420(a), as amended by Pub. L. No. 109-280 § 114, 120 Stat. 780 (2006)] For tax years beginning before 2007, a multiemployer plan could not make a qualified transfer of excess pension assets from a defined benefit plan to a Section 401(h) account.

Q 20:86   How does an employer determine the amount of excess pension assets that can be transferred in a qualified transfer to a Section 401(h) account?

The PPA modified the definition of excess pension assets eligible for a qualified transfer to reflect new pension plan funding rules in Code Section 430.

Under the PPA definition, *excess pension assets* are equal to the excess (if any) of:

1. The lesser of (a) the fair market value of the plan's assets (reduced by the prefunding balance and the funding standard carryover balance as determined under Code Section. 430(f)) or (b) the value of plan assets as determined under Code Section 430(g)(3) (after reduction under Code Section 430(f)) over

2. 125 percent of the sum of the funding shortfall and the target normal cost determined under Code Section 430 for the plan year.

[I.R.C. § 420(e)(2), as amended by Pub. L. No. 109-280, 120 Stat. 780 (2006)]

> **Note.** The new rule for determining excess pension assets is tied to the funding rules for single-employer plans. In the case of multiemployer plans, the IRS is directed to apply the Code Section 420 rules, as appropriate, to reflect the fact that the plan is not maintained by a single employer. [I.R.C. § 420(e)(5), as amended by Pub. L. No. 109-280, 120 Stat. 780 (2006)]

Under pre-PPA rules, the amount of the excess pension assets that can be transferred in a qualified transfer is determined pursuant to the full-funding limitation rules of Code Section 412(c)(7). Under those rules, *excess pension assets* (if any) are equal to:

1. The value of the plan's assets (determined under Code Section 412(c)(7)(A)(ii)), minus

2. The greater of (a) the lesser of 150 percent of current liability or the accrued liability (including normal cost) or (b) 125 percent of current liability.

[I.R.C. § 420(e)(2), prior to amendment by Pub. L. No.109-280 (Aug. 17, 2006)]

Q 20:87   What is a qualified transfer of excess pension assets to a Section 401(h) account?

In order to be considered a qualified transfer, a transfer of excess pension assets to a Section 401(h) account must satisfy the following six requirements:

1. A transfer may be made only once in any taxable year of the employer and may be made only in taxable years beginning before 2014.

2. The assets transferred (and the income of such assets) must be used to pay qualified current retiree health liabilities other than liabilities of key employees as defined in Code Section 416(i)(1) (see Q 20:88).

3. Certain vesting requirements under the pension plan must be satisfied (see Q 20:89).

4. The employer must meet a minimum cost requirement for retiree health benefits in the year of transfer and in the following four years (see Q 20:90).

5. The amount transferred cannot exceed specified limits (see Q 20:91).

6. The transfer cannot contravene any other provision of law (see Q 20:92).

Q 20:88   What are qualified current retiree health liabilities?

A transfer of excess pension assets can be used only for qualified current retiree health liabilities. The term *qualified current retiree health liabilities* means, with respect to any taxable year, the aggregate amounts (including administrative expenses) that would have been allowable as a deduction to the employer for the taxable year with respect to health benefits for existing retirees entitled to the health benefits as well as to pension benefits under the plan, and health benefits for their spouses and dependents, if:

1. The health benefits were provided directly by the employer; and
2. The employer was a cash-basis taxpayer.

The amount of qualified retiree health liabilities must be reduced by any amount previously contributed to a Section 401(h) account or to a Section 419 welfare benefit fund to pay for the qualified current retiree health liabilities.

Q 20:89   What vesting requirements apply in order to have a qualified transfer to a Section 401(h) account?

In order to have a qualified transfer, a pension plan must provide that the accrued benefits of any plan participant or beneficiary become nonforfeitable as if the plan had terminated immediately before the qualified transfer. For a participant who separated from service during the one-year period ending on the date of the qualified transfer, benefits must become nonforfeitable as if the plan had terminated immediately before the separation from service. [I.R.C. § 420(c)(2)]

Practice Pointer. Because of the substantial cost of full vesting of accrued benefits to an employer, any employer with an overfunded defined benefit pension plan should carefully consider the pros and cons before entering into a qualified transfer.

Q 20:90   What is the minimum cost requirement for retiree health benefits that an employer must satisfy in order to have a qualified transfer?

An employer will not incur taxes or penalties on the transfer of excess pension assets to fund retiree health benefits if the employer satisfies a minimum cost requirement. The tax law provides that the minimum cost requirement will be met if the average per capita cost for retiree health benefits is maintained at a minimum dollar level for a five-year *cost-maintenance period*, including the year of the transfer and the four years following the transfer. However, Congress recognized that because the minimum cost requirement is expressed in terms of per capita cost, an employer could satisfy the requirement by maintaining the average per-person cost at the minimum level while reducing the number of people covered by the plan. Therefore, in the Tax Relief Extension Act of 1999 [Pub. L. No. 106-170, 113 Stat. 1869 (1999)], Congress authorized the IRS to develop regulations to prevent an employer that significantly reduces retiree health coverage during the cost-maintenance period from meeting the minimum cost requirement. The IRS has issued final regulations implementing this new "maintenance of effort" requirement. [Treas. Reg. § 1.420-1]

Minimum cost requirement. The minimum cost requirement is met if each group health plan or arrangement under which retiree health benefits are furnished provides that the applicable employer cost for each taxable year during the cost-maintenance period (the taxable year of the qualified transfer and the succeeding four taxable years) cannot be lower than the higher of the applicable employer costs in either of the two taxable years immediately preceding the taxable year of the qualified transfer.

In applying the minimum cost requirement, the term *applicable employer cost* means, for any taxable year, the amount determined by dividing:

1. The qualified current retiree health liabilities of the employer for the taxable year (determined by excluding any reduction for prior contributions to the Section 401(h) account or to a Section 419 welfare benefit fund—and, if there was no qualified transfer in the taxable year, by assuming that such a transfer occurred at year-end) by

2. The number of individuals (retirees, spouses, and dependents) to whom retiree health coverage was provided during the taxable year.

An employer may elect to determine the applicable employer cost separately for Medicare-eligible individuals and for those individuals not eligible for Medicare. [I.R.C. § 420(c)(3)]

The IRS has ruled that when computing the applicable employer cost for Medicare eligible retirees, the retiree prescription drug subsidy is not taken into account. (For details on the retiree prescription drug subsidy, see chapter 4.)

Example. Magma Corp. maintains a defined benefit pension plan for its employees. Magma also maintains a retiree health plan. In 2007, Magma transferred a portion of the defined benefit plan assets to a Section 401(h) account to provide for benefits under the retiree health plan. Magma's applicable employer cost was $3,600 for 2005, $3,800 for 2006, and $4,000 for 2007. In 2006, Magma receives a retiree prescription drug subsidy of $600 per covered retiree. For 2007, Magma's cost for retiree health benefits, without regard to the retiree drug subsidy, is $4,300 per covered employee. Magma's applicable employer cost is not reduced by the retiree prescription drug subsidy. Therefore, Magma's applicable employee cost for 2007 is $4,300. Magma satisfies the maintenance of cost requirement because its applicable employer cost of $4,300 is not less than $3,800 (the higher of its applicable employer costs for 2005 and 2006, the two years preceding the transfer).

In a private letter ruling, the IRS held that in calculating the minimum cost requirement for current retiree health liabilities under Code Section 420(c)(3), an employer could make the computation based on the weighted average number of individuals to whom coverage was provided during the taxable year. The IRS noted that the Code does not specify a method for making the calculation, and the employer's method was reasonable and consistent with the intent of the law. [Priv. Ltr. Rul. 9419037]

Practice Pointer. Assuming a steady continuation of medical cost inflation, an employer continuing to provide the same level of retiree health coverage should have no problem with the minimum cost requirement.

Maintenance of effort requirement. The final IRS regulations measure whether an employer has significantly reduced coverage by looking at the number of individuals (retirees, spouses, and dependents) who lose coverage during the period as a result of employer actions.

Under the regulations, the number of individuals losing coverage due to employer actions is expressed as an employer-initiated reduction percentage. This percentage is calculated by dividing the number of individuals losing coverage under the plan during a tax year by the total number of individuals receiving coverage under the plan as of the last day of the prior tax year. For example, if 400 individuals were covered on the last day of the prior year and 40 individuals lost coverage during the year as a result of employer actions, the employer-initiated reduction percentage is 10 percent.

For any tax year beginning on or after January 1, 2002, that is included in the cost-maintenance period, an employer is deemed to have significantly reduced coverage if either:

1. The employer-initiated reduction percentage for the tax year exceeds 10 percent or
2. The sum of the employer-initiated reduction percentages for the tax year and all prior tax years in the period exceeds 20 percent.

However, under a special rule enacted by the American Jobs Creation Act of 2004 [Pub. L. No. 108-357, 118 Stat. 1418 (2004)], an eligible employer will not fail the minimum cost requirement if, in lieu of any reduction in the number of covered retirees permitted by the regulations, the employer reduces its cost by an amount not in excess of the cost reduction that would have occurred if the employer had made the maximum permissible reduction in retiree health coverage allowed under the regulations. An employer is an eligible employer if, for the preceding taxable year, the qualified current retiree health liabilities of the employer were at least 5 percent of gross receipts.

In other words, instead of looking at the number of retirees who lose coverage, this test looks at the amount of the reduction in dollars spent by the employer. Therefore, an employer has the option of cutting costs by reducing benefits for a group of retirees rather than cutting off benefits for some retirees altogether.

In applying the regulations to a subsequent taxable year, any reduction in an employer's cost is treated as if it were an equivalent reduction in the number of covered retirees.

The special rule applies for taxable years ending October 22, 2004.

Employer-initiated loss of coverage. A loss of coverage is considered employer-initiated if the individual's coverage ends during the tax year as a result of a plan amendment or any other action of the employer (e.g., sale of all or part of the employer's business) that has the effect of ending the individual's eligibility for coverage. An employer action is taken into account regardless of when it occurred. In other words, plan amendments or other actions taken before the asset transfer are taken into account if they result in a loss of coverage during the maintenance-of-effort period. An individual's loss of coverage is not considered employer-initiated if coverage ends under plan terms that were adopted contemporaneously with the provision under which the individual became eligible for retiree health coverage. For example, if a plan is set up to provide coverage only for a certain period of time, individuals who lose coverage at the end of that period will not be treated as having lost coverage as a result of the employer's action.

The final regulations also carve out a special rule for business sales. Under this rule, an employer may, but is not required to, treat retiree health coverage as not having ended for individuals whose health coverage is provided by the buyer. However, the employer must continue to include those individuals and amounts spent by the buyer in its calculations for determining if the minimum cost requirement is met. In addition, actions by the buyer will be attributed to the employer for purposes of determining whether individuals lose coverage as a result of employer action. For example, if a buyer initially provides coverage to individuals affected by a sale but later amends its plans to stop providing coverage to those individuals, the employer must treat them as having lost coverage as a result of employer action.

The IRS has ruled that a loss of coverage will be considered employer-initiated if a covered retiree accepts an offer from the employer to waive such coverage in exchange for enhanced pension benefits. According to the IRS, the employer's action is considered an employer action under the regulations. [Rev. Rul. 2004-65, 2004-27 I.R.B.1]

Q 20:91   Is there a limit on the amount of excess pension assets that can be transferred in a qualified transfer?

Yes. The amount of excess pension assets that may be transferred in a qualified transfer cannot exceed the amount reasonably estimated to be what the employer will pay (directly or through reimbursement out of the Section 401(h) account) during the taxable year of the transfer for qualified *current* retiree health liabilities. [I.R.C. § 420(b)(3)] Therefore, qualified transfers cannot be used to prefund future retiree health liabilities. However, rules enacted by the Pension Protection Act of 2006 permit qualified future transfer and collectively bargained transfers to prefund future liabilities (see Qs 20:99, 20:100).

Q 20:92   What is the significance of the provision that a transfer of excess pension assets to a Section 401(h) account cannot contravene any other provision of law?

The legislative history indicates that the amendments made to the Code and to ERISA to authorize qualified transfers of excess pension assets do not supersede any legal restrictions that may prevent an employer from using pension benefits to satisfy preexisting corporate retiree health benefit liabilities. As one example, such a transfer might be in violation of a collective bargaining agreement. Also, a transfer might violate laws applicable to government contractors. [I.R.C. § 420(b)(1)(B); Conf. Rep. 101-964, 101st Cong., 2d Sess., at 1147 (1990)]

Q 20:93   What limits apply to employer contributions where a qualified transfer is made?

An employer may not contribute any amount to a Section 401(h) account or Section 419 welfare benefit fund with regard to qualified current retiree health liabilities for which transferred assets are required to be used. Any amount paid out of a Section 401(h) account is treated as paid first out of the transferred assets and the income thereon. [I.R.C. § 420(d)(2)]

Q 20:94   What limits apply to employer tax deductions where a qualified transfer is made?

No employer deduction is allowed for the amount of any qualified transfer or for any qualified current retiree health liabilities paid out of the transferred assets (and the income thereon). In addition, no deduction is allowed for an employer's payment of current liabilities to the extent there are unspent transferred amounts in the 401(h) account [I.R.C. § 420(d)(1)]

Q 20:95   What happens if the amount of the qualified transfer exceeds the qualified current retiree health benefits?

If the amount of the qualified transfer exceeds the qualified current retiree health benefits, it must be transferred back to the pension portion of the plan from the Section 401(h) account. In such cases, the amount transferred is not includable in the employer's income but is treated as an employer reversion for purposes of the 20 percent excise tax under Code Section 4980(a) on pension plan reversions (but not for purposes of the 50 percent tax on certain reversions under Code Section 4980(d)). [I.R.C. § 420(c)(1)(B)]

Q 20:96   If a qualified transfer is planned, are there special notice requirements under ERISA that must be followed?

Yes. The pension plan administrator must notify each participant and beneficiary under the plan of a qualified transfer at least 60 days before the date of the transfer. The notice is to include information regarding the amount of excess pension assets, the portion to be transferred, the amount of retiree health benefits expected to be provided by the transferred assets, and the amount of pension benefits of the participant that will be nonforfeitable following the transfer.

In addition, the statute requires that employer notice be given to the Department of Labor (DOL), the IRS, the pension plan administrator, and each employee organization representing participants in the plan at least 60 days before the date of the transfer. By agreement between the IRS and the DOL, the employer's filing with the DOL will be considered to satisfy the IRS filing requirement as well. Accordingly, an employer need not make a separate filing with the IRS. [ERISA Tech. Rel. 91-1, 56 Fed. Reg. 10, 927 (Mar. 14, 1991); I.R.S. Ann. 92-54, 1992-13 I.R.B. 35]

The employer notice must identify the following:

1. The plan from which the qualified transfer is being made;
2. The amount of the transfer;
3. A detailed accounting of assets projected to be held by the plan immediately before and immediately after the transfer; and
4. The current liabilities under the plan at the time of the transfer.

[ERISA § 101(e); 29 U.S.C. § 1021(e), as added by OBRA '90 § 12012]

Q 20:97 What effect does a qualified transfer have on the minimum funding rules for a pension plan?

Under the rules enacted by the PPA, any assets transferred in a qualified transfer to a retiree health account will *not* be treated as plan assets for purposes of the Code Section 420 funding rules. [I.R.C. § 420(e)(4), as amended by Pub. L. No. 109-280, 120 Stat. 780 (2006)]

Under prior law, for purposes of the minimum funding rules of Code Section 412, the assets transferred in a plan year on or before the valuation date for the year (and any income allocable thereto) are treated as assets in the plan as of the valuation date, and the plan is treated as having a net experience loss in the amount of the transfer, amortizable over ten years. [I.R.C. § 420(e)(4), prior to amendment by Pub. L. No. 109-280, 120 Stat. 780 (2006)]

Q 20:98 Does a qualified transfer violate the exclusive benefit requirement or the prohibited transaction and prohibited reversion rules of ERISA and the Code?

No. Both ERISA and the Code provide that a qualified transfer does not violate the exclusive benefit rule or give rise to a prohibited transaction or a reversion to the employer. [I.R.C. § 420(a); ERISA §§ 403(c)(1), 408(b)(13); 29 U.S.C. §§ 1103(c)(1), 1108(b)(13)]

Q 20:99   What is a qualified future transfer?

A *qualified future transfer* is a transfer that meets all of the requirements for a qualified transfer except that special rules apply to:

- the determination of excess pension assets.
- the limitation on the amount transferred; and
- the minimum cost requirements.

[I.R.C. § 420(f)(1), as added by Pub. L. No. 109-280, 120 Stat. 780 (2006)]

Under the rules enacted by the PPA, a single-employer defined benefit plan (but not a multiemployer plan) can make a qualified future transfer of excess pension assets to a Section 401(h) account to fund future retiree health benefit liabilities for up to 10 years. A qualified future transfer is made in lieu of, not in addition to, a regular qualified transfer. If specific requirements are met a qualified future transfer is treated as a qualified transfer. [I.R.C. § 420(f)(1), as added by Pub. L. No. 109-280, 120 Stat. 780 (2006)]

A qualified future transfer can be made for a transfer period (of not less than two consecutive tax years) that ends during the 10-taxable-year period beginning with the tax year of the transfer. [I.R.C. § 420(f)(5), as added by Pub. L. No. 109-280, 120 Stat. 780 (2006)] Thus, a qualified future transfer can be made to fund retiree health liabilities for up to 10 tax years, including the year of the transfer. However, the year of the transfer is not required to be included in the transfer period.

Excess pension assets. The amount of excess pension assets eligible for a qualified future transfer is generally determined in the same manner as for a qualified transfer (see Q 20:86).

However, the excess is equal to the value of the plan assets less 120 percent rather than 125 percent, of the pension plan's current liability (as determined under Code Section 420(e)(2)). [I.R.C. § 420(f)(2)(B)(i), as added by Pub. L. No. 109-280, 120 Stat. 780 (2006)] Consequently, the amount eligible for a qualified future transfer may be slightly larger than that for a qualified transfer.

On the other hand, in the case of a qualified future transfer, the employer is required to maintain the funded status of the pension plan throughout the transfer period (i.e., a period up to 10 years for which future liabilities can be funded). If, as of any valuation date in the transfer period, the plan's assets are less than 120 percent of the plan's current liability (as determined under Code Section 420(e)(2)), either the employer must make additional contributions or an amount must be transferred from the health benefits account to eliminate the shortfall. [I.R.C. § 420(f)(2)(B)(ii), as added by Pub. L. No. 109-280, 120 Stat. 780 (2006)]

Limitation on amount transferred. The amount of excess pension assets that can be transferred in a qualified future transfer is equal to the sum of:

1. The amount of estimated current retiree health liabilities (as determined under Code Section 420(f)(2)) for the tax year of the transfer (if the transfer period includes the year of the transfer), plus

2. The sum of the current retiree health liabilities (as determined under IRS regulations) that the plan reasonably estimates will be incurred for all other tax years in the transfer period.

[I.R.C. § 420(f)(2)(C)(i), as added by Pub. L. No. 109-280, 120 Stat. 780 (2006)]

If the employer subsequently decides to make a regular qualified transfer to fund current liabilities for any year in the transfer period, current liabilities for that year must be reduced by the amount taken into account for purposes of the qualified future transfer.

Minimum cost requirement. In the case of a qualified future transfer, the employer must meet the minimum cost requirement for each of the taxable years in the transfer period and for the four years following the end of the transfer period. [I.R.C. § 420(f)(2)(D)(i)(I), as added by Pub. L. No. 109-280, 120 Stat. 780 (2006)]

As an alternative, in the case of a qualified future transfer (but not other types of transfers) an employer can choose to apply a minimum benefit requirement for the applicable period. [I.R.C. § 420(f)(2)(D)(ii), as added by Pub. L. No. 109-280, 120 Stat. 780 (2006)] For this purpose, the PPA revives the benefit maintenance rule that was in effect before changes made by the Tax Relief Extension Act of 1999. Under that rule, an employer was required to provide substantially the same level of health benefits (or coverage) in each year of the maintenance period as it provided during the tax year that immediately preceded the year of the transfer. [I.R.C. § 420(c)(3), prior to amendment by Pub. L. No. 109-280, 120 Stat. 780 (2006)]

The PPA rules for qualified future transfers became effective August 18, 2006.

A clarifying amendment made by the Worker, Retiree, and Employer Recovery Act of 2008 [Pub. L. No. 110-458] provides that any assets transferred pursuant to a qualified future transfer or a collectively bargained transfer may be used to pay the expected cost of future retiree health liabilities without violating the current-use requirement. [I.R.C. § 420(c)(1)(A), as amended by the WRERA § 108(i)(1)] The amendment is effective as if it were included in PPA 2006.

Q 20:100   What is a collectively bargained transfer?

Under the rules enacted by the PPA, a single-employer defined benefit plan (but not a multiemployer plan) can make a collectively bargained transfer of excess pension assets to a Section 401(h) account to fund retiree health benefit liabilities. A collectively bargained transfer is made in lieu of, not in addition to, a regular qualified transfer. If specific requirements are met a collectively bargained transfer is treated as a qualified transfer. [I.R.C. § 420(f)(1), as added by Pub. L. No. 109-280, 120 Stat. 780 (2006)]

A *collectively bargained transfer* is a transfer that meets the following requirements:

1. The transfer is made in accordance with a collective bargaining agreement;

2. Before the transfer, the employer designates the transfer as a collectively bargained transfer in a written notice delivered to each employee organization that it is a party to the collective bargaining agreement; and

3. The transfer involves a plan maintained by an employer (or a successor), which in its tax year ending 2005, provided health benefits or coverage to retirees and their spouses and dependents under all of its benefit plans and the aggregate cost (including administrative expenses) of benefits or coverage that would have been an allowable employer deduction (under the cash method of accounting) if provided directly by the employer was at least 5 percent of the employer's gross receipts.

[I.R.C. § 420(f)(2)(E)(i), as added by Pub. L. No. 109-280, 120 Stat. 780 (2006)]

In addition, a collectively bargained transfer must generally meet the requirements for a qualified transfer, subject to the following special rules.

Excess pension assets. The amount of excess pension assets eligible for a collectively bargained transfer is generally determined in the same manner as for a qualified transfer (see Q 20:86).

However, the excess is equal to the value of the plan assets less than 120 percent, rather than 125 percent, of the pension plan's current liability (as determined under Code Section 420(e)(2)). [I.R.C. § 420(f)(2)(B)(i), as added by Pub. L. No. 109-280, 120 Stat. 780 (2006)] Consequently, the amount eligible for a collectively transfer may be slightly larger than that for a qualified transfer.

On the other hand, in the case of a collectively bargained transfer, the employer is required to maintain the funded status of the pension plan throughout the transfer period (i.e., the up to 10 year period for which future liabilities can be funded). If, as of any valuation date in the transfer period, the plan's assets are less than 120 percent of the plan's current liability (as determined under Code Section 420(e)(2)), either the employer must make additional contributions or an amount must be transferred from the health benefits account to eliminate the shortfall. [I.R.C. § 420(f)(2)(B)(ii), as added by Pub. L. No. 109-280, 120 Stat. 780 (2006)]

Limitation on amount transferred. The amount of excess pension assets that can be transferred in a collectively bargained transfer must not exceed the estimated amount the employer maintaining the plan will pay (directly or through reimbursement) out of the account for collectively bargained retiree health liabilities (other than liabilities for key employees as determined under Code Section 416(i)(1)) during the collectively bargained cost maintenance period (see following paragraph). The estimated amount is reduced by amounts in all accounts or funds to pay collectively bargained retiree health liabilities.

Collectively bargained cost maintenance period. The collectively bargained cost maintenance period for each covered retiree, covered spouse, and dependents, is the shorter of:

- The remaining lifetime of the covered retiree and his covered spouse and dependents; or
- The coverage period of the collectively bargained health plan determined the date of the collectively bargained transfer.

[I.R.C. § 420(f)(6)(A), as added by Pub. L. No. 109-280, 120 Stat. 780 (2006)]

Minimum cost requirement. To meet the minimum cost requirement for a collectively bargained transfer, each collectively bargained group health plan under which collectively bargained health benefits are provided must provide that the collectively bargained employer cost for each tax year during the collectively bargained cost maintenance period cannot be less than the amount specified by the collective bargaining agreement. [I.R.C. § 420(f)(2)(D)(i)(II), as added by Pub. L. No. 109-280, 120 Stat. 780 (2006)]

Use of assets. Any assets transferred to a health benefits account in a collectively bargained transfer, can only be used to pay collectively bargained health liabilities for the tax year of the transfer or for any other tax year during the collectively bargained cost maintenance period. [I.R.C. § 420(f)(2)(E)(ii), as added by Pub. L. No. 109-280, 120 Stat. 780 (2006)]

Employer deductions. As with a regular qualified transfer, no employer deduction is allowed for the amount of any collectively bargained transfer or for any qualified current retiree health liabilities paid out of the transferred assets (and the income thereon). However, the rule that prohibits a deduction to the extent of unspent transferred funds does not apply. In addition, the rule that bars employer contributions to a Section 401(h) account or Section 419 welfare benefit fund with regard to qualified current retiree health liabilities for which transferred assets are required to be used does not apply. [I.R.C. § 420(f)(4), as added by Pub. L. No. 109-280, 120 Stat. 780 (2006)]

The IRS is directed to provide rules to ensure that the Code Section 420 rules do not result in a deduction being allowed more than once for the same contribution; or for two or more contributions or expenditures relating to the same collectively bargained retiree health liabilities.

The Pension Protection Act rules for qualified future transfers became effective August 18, 2006.

A clarifying amendment made by the Worker, Retiree, and Employer Recovery Act of 2008 [Pub. L. No. 110-458] provides that any assets transferred pursuant to a qualified future transfer or a collectively bargained transfer may be used to pay the expected cost of future retiree health liabilities without violating the current-use requirement. [I.R.C. § 420(c)(1)(A), as amended by the WRERA § 108(i)(1)] The amendment is effective as if it were included in the PPA 2006.

Q 20:101   Is the investment income of a Section 401(h) account subject to tax?

No. As part of a tax-exempt pension or annuity plan, the earnings on a Section 401(h) account are tax-free. In that respect, funding postretirement medical benefits through a Section 401(h) account has a major advantage over funding retiree medical benefits through a VEBA or a retired lives reserve held by an insurance company. In those cases, the investment earnings are subject to unrelated business income tax (or deemed unrelated income tax) (see Q 20:46).

Financing Welfare Benefits with Life Insurance

Q 20:102   How can an employer's cost of welfare benefits be financed through the purchase of life insurance?

It formerly was fairly common for employers seeking to minimize the cost of employee welfare benefits, particularly benefits that are not prefunded (such as uninsured death benefit plans, retiree health benefits, and executive plans of various types), to consider the purchase of life insurance on employees' lives as a financing mechanism for meeting the cost of such benefits. Such arrangements generally are referred to as *corporate-owned life insurance* (COLI). However, recent tax crackdowns have reduced the attractiveness of such arrangements as a financing mechanism.

Under a typical arrangement, the employer is the owner and beneficiary of life insurance policies on the lives of certain of its employees. The policies are purchased to cover the employer's liability for benefits under the plan, but the policy proceeds are not committed to pay any particular plan's benefits. The insurance does not constitute a funding method for the welfare plan because the policies are wholly owned by the employer and are subject to the claims of its creditors. The employees have no rights or interest in the insurance policies on their lives.

Q 20:103   How is employer-owned life insurance treated for income tax purposes?

Because the employer is the owner and beneficiary of the policies, it cannot take an income tax deduction for the premiums it pays. [I.R.C. § 264(a)(1)]

In the past, the proceeds from an employer-owned life insurance policy generally received the same income tax treatment as other types of life insurance. Thus, if the employer kept the coverage in force until the employee's death, the policy proceeds were received free of income tax. [I.R.C. § 101(a)]

However, effective for life insurance policies issued after August 17, 2006, the Pension Protection Act of 2006 provides that the income exclusion for the proceeds of employer-owned life insurance contracts is limited to the amount of premiums and other costs paid by the employer. The remainder of the policy proceeds are includable in the employer's gross income. [I.R.C. § 101(j), as added by Pub. L. No. 109-280, 120 Stat. 780 (2006)]

The full amount of the proceeds from a policy are excludable from an employer's income only if both of the following conditions are met:

1. Notice and consent requirements are met, *and*

2. A special exception applies.

Preexisting contracts. The limited exclusion applies only to employer-owned life insurance contracts issued after August 17, 2006. Contracts issued before that date remain eligible for full exclusion of the proceeds payable on the employee's death. However, any material increase in the death benefit or other material change will cause a preexisting contract to be treated as a new contract subject to the limited exclusion rules.

In the case of a master contract, the addition of covered lives is treated as a new contract only with respect to the additional covered lives.

In addition, the following changes are not considered material changes for purposes of determining whether an existing contract is treated as a new contract:

- Increases in the death benefit that occur because of operation of the life insurance rules in Code Section 7702 or under the terms of the contract (provided the insurer's consent to the increase is not required);
- Administrative changes;
- Accounting changes; or
- Changes as a result of the exercise of an option or right granted under the contract as originally issued.

For example, a death benefit increase will not cause a contract to be treated as a new contract if the increase results from the application of policyholder dividends to purchase paid-up additions, or if the increase is a result of market performance or contract design in the case of a variable contract. [Notice 2009-48, Q&A-14, 2009-24 I.R.B. 1085]

Code Section 1035 allows one life insurance contract to be exchanged for another without recognition of gain or loss. If a preexisting contract is exchanged for another in a tax-free exchange, the contract received in the exchange will generally not be treated as a new contract. However, an exchange that results in a material increase in the death benefit or other material change (other than a change in issuer) will be treated as the issuance of a new contract. [Notice 2009-48, Q&A-15, 2009-24 I.R.B. 1085]

Q 20:104　　What is employer-owned life insurance?

Under the tax law rules, the term *employer-owned life insurance contract* means a life insurance contract that (1) is owned by a person engaged in a trade or business and under which such person (or a related person) is directly or indirectly a beneficiary under the contract, and (2) covers the life of an insured who is an employee of the "applicable policyholder" on the date the contract is issued. [I.R.C. § 101(j)(3)] The applicable policyholder is generally the person who owns the contract, but also includes certain related persons or persons engaged in trades or businesses with the owner that are under common control.

A contract is not considered an employer-owned life insurance contract if it is owned by a related person who is not engaged in a trade or business. For example, a contract owned by the owner of a business or by a qualified plan or VEBA that is sponsored by a business is not an employer-owned life insurance contract. However, a contract owned by a grantor trust whose assets are treated as the assets of a grantor engaged in a trade or business is an employer-owned life insurance contract if the above requirements are met. [Notice 2009-48, Q&A-1, 2009-24 I.R.B. 1085]

A contract that is subject to a split-dollar life insurance arrangement is an employer-owned life insurance contract if the contract is owned by a person engaged in a trade or business and the above requirements are met. [Notice 2009-48, Q&A-2, 2009-24 I.R.B. 1085]

A contract that is owned by a partnership or a sole proprietorship on the life of an employee is an employer-owned life insurance contract if the applicable requirements are met. However, a contract owned by a sole proprietor on his or her own life is not an employer-owned life insurance contract. [Notice 2009-48, Q&A-3, 2009-24 I.R.B. 1085]

For purposes of the employer-owned life insurance rules, the term *employee* is not limited to common-law employees. The term includes a director of a corporation, even though a director is an independent contractor in his or her capacity as a director. The term *employee* also includes officers and highly compensated employees. [Notice 2009-48, Q&A-5, 2009-24 I.R.B. 1085]

Q 20:105   What are the special exceptions to the income exclusion limits for employer-owned life insurance?

There are two types of exceptions to the rule limiting the income exclusion for the proceeds of an employer-owned life insurance contract: exceptions based on the insured's status and exceptions for amounts paid to the insured's heirs.

1. Exceptions based on insured's status. If notice and consent requirements are met, the income exclusion limitation does not apply to any amount received by reason of the death of an insured who was:
   - an employee of the employer at any time during the 12-month period before his or her death; or
   - a director; highly compensated employee (HCE), or a highly compensated individual with respect to the employer at the time the contract was issued.

For this purpose, the determination of who is an HCE is made under Code Section 414(q), without regard to the employer's election to include an employee in the top-paid group of employees for the preceding year. The determination of who is an HCE is made under Code Section 105(h)(5), except that 35 percent is substituted for 25 percent in calculating the highest-paid percentage.

For purposes of determining whether an insured was a director, HCE, or highly compensated individual at the time the contract was issued, an employer-owned life insurance contract is treated as issued on the later of (1) the date of the application for coverage, (2) the effective date of coverage, or (3) the formal issuance of the contract. [Notice 2009-48, Q&A-4, 2009-24 I.R.B. 1085] However, an employer-owned contract may be treated as a new contract, and thus newly "issued," if there is a material increase in the death benefit or other material change in the contract.

2. Exceptions for amounts paid to the insured's heirs. If notice and consent requirements are met, the income-exclusion limitation does not apply to any amount received by reason of the death of an insured that is paid to any of the following:

   - A member of the insured's family (within the meaning of Code Section 267(c)(4), relating to the constructive ownership of stock);
   - An individual who is the designated beneficiary of the insured under the contract (other than the employer);
   - A trust established for the benefit of any member of the insured's family or designated beneficiary; or
   - The estate of the insured.

The limitation is also inapplicable to any amount that is used to purchase an equity (or capital or profits) interest in the employer from the insured's heirs, a trust, or the insured's estate. For example, the limitation would not apply to insurance-funded buy-sell arrangements if the notice and consent requirements are met. To qualify for this exception, the purchase must made by the due date, including extensions, of the tax return for the tax year of the applicable policyholder in which the policyholder is treated as receiving the death benefit under the contract. [Notice 2009-48, Q&A-6, 2009-24 I.R.B. 1085]

Q 20:106 What are the notice and consent requirements for employer-owned life insurance contracts?

To qualify for any of the special exceptions to the employer-owned life insurance rules, the following notice and consent requirements must be met before the issuance of the policy:

1. The employee must be notified in writing that the employer (or other applicable policyholder) intends to insure the employee's life and of the maximum face amount for which the employee could be insured at the time the contract is issued;

2. The employee must provide written consent to being insured under the contract and to continuation of the coverage after termination of employment; and

3. The employee must be informed in writing that that employer (or other applicable policyholder) will be a beneficiary of any proceeds payable on death of the employee.

[I.R.C. § 101(j)(4)]

These notice and consent requirements apply even in the case of an owner-employee of a wholly-owned corporation. Actual knowledge of the arrangement will not substitute for the statutory requirement that notice and consent be written. [Notice 2009-48, Q&A-7, 2009-24 I.R.B. 1085] On the other hand, notice and consent is not required if an employee irrevocably transfers an existing insurance contract to an employer. The actual transfer of an existing contract by an employee to an employer is sufficient to satisfy the requirements that (1) the employee be notified in writing of the intention to insure and the maximum face amount of the insurance, (2) the employee give written consent, and (3) the employee be notified that the employer will be the beneficiary of the policy on the employee's death. However, if the employer subsequently increases the face amount of the contract, written notice and consent will be required for the new face amount. [Notice 2009-48, Q&A-8, 2009-24 I.R.B. 1085]

A single consent can apply to more than one employer-owned life insurance contract. For example, if an employee is properly notified that the employer intends to insure the employee's life for a maximum of $1 million, and the employee consents in writing, the employer may purchase two employer-owned life insurance contracts with a face amount of $500,000 each. [Notice 2009-48, Q&A-10, 2009-24 I.R.B. 1085]

However, an employer cannot simply notify an employee that it will obtain the maximum amount of insurance for which the employee can be insured. The employee must be notified in writing of the maximum face amount of insurance either in dollars or as a multiple of salary that the employer reasonably expects to purchase on the employee's life. [Notice 2009-48, Q&A-12, 2009-24 I.R.B. 1085]

To meet the notice and consent requirements, the insurance must be issued before the earlier of (1) the expiration of the one-year period beginning on the date the employee's written consent was executed or (2) termination of the employee's employment with the trade or business of the employer (or other applicable policyholder). Once the requirements are met, no further notice or renewal of the employee's consent is required unless the total face amount of employer-owned life insurance contracts on the employee's life exceeds the amount of which the employee was notified and to which the employee consented. [Notice 2009-48, Q&A-9, 2009-24 I.R.B. 1085]

A life insurance contract is considered issued on the later of (1) the date of the application for coverage, (2) the effective date of the coverage, or (3) the formal issuance of the contract. Thus, if a contract is effective for a limited time before formal issuance of the contract (e.g., to secure underwriting), the notice and consent requirements may be satisfied during the period between the effective date of coverage and the formal issuance of the contract. [Notice 2009-48, Q&A-4, 2009-24 I.R.B. 1085]

The "written" notice and consent requirements may be satisfied electronically as long as the electronic system includes all the required elements (notice of intent to insure and maximum face amount, employee consent to insurance and continuation after termination, and notification that the employer will be the death beneficiary). In addition, the electronic system must:

- Ensure that the information received by the employee is the same as the information sent by the employer;
- Make it reasonably certain that the person accessing the system is the employee for whom notice and consent is required;
- Include a process for electronic signature or other means of formally recording the employee's consent; and
- Permit the production of a hard copy of the electronic notice and consent on request by the IRS and a statement that, to the best of the employer's knowledge, the required notice was provided to the employee and the employee consented to being insured.

[Notice 2009-48, Q&A-11, 2009-24 I.R.B. 1085]

The Internal Revenue Code does not contain any exceptions to the notice and consent requirements or provide a mechanism for correcting inadvertent failures to meet the requirements. However, the IRS will not challenge the applicability of a special exception based on an inadvertent failure to meet the notice and consent requirements if all of the following conditions are met:

- The employer (or other applicable policyholder) made a good faith effort to satisfy the requirements (for example, by maintaining a formal system for providing notice and securing consents from new employees);
- The failure to satisfy the requirements was inadvertent; and
- The failure was discovered and corrected no later than the due date of the tax return of the employer (or other applicable policyholder) for the tax year in which the employer-owned life insurance contract was issued.

However, because the employee's consent must be written, a failure to obtain consent cannot be corrected if the employee has died. [Notice 2009-48, Q&A-13, 2009-24 I.R.B. 1085]

Return and recordkeeping requirements. An employer or related policyholder owning one or more employer-owned life insurance contracts issued after August 17, 2006, must file a return showing for each year that the contracts are owned:

- The number of employees of the applicable policyholder at the end of the year;
- The number of those employees insured under employer-owned life insurance contracts at the end of the year;
- The total amount of insurance in force at the end of the year under those contracts;

- The name, address, and taxpayer identification number (TIN) of the applicable policyholder, and the type of business in which the policyholder is engaged; and

- The applicable policyholder has a valid consent for each insured employee (or, if all required consents were not obtained, the number of insured employees for whom consent was not obtained).

[I.R.C. § 6039I(a) as added by Pub. L. No. 109-280, 120 Stat. 780 (2006)]

In addition, the employer or related policyholder must keep whatever records may be necessary for purposes of determining whether the requirements for such policies are met.

Temporary Treasury regulations authorize the IRS to prescribe the form and manner of satisfying the reporting requirements imposed by Section 6039I on applicable policyholders owning one or more employer-owned life insurance contracts issued after August 17, 2006. [Temp. Treas. Reg. § 1.6039I-1T] The regulations became effective on November 13, 2007, and apply to taxable years ending after that date. [Temp. Reg. § 1.6039I-1T] The IRS has issued new Form 8925, *Report of Employer-Owned Life Insurance Contracts*, which will be used to satisfy the reporting requirement.

Effective date. The rules apply to life insurance contracts issued after August 17, 2006. However, the rules generally would not apply to any contract issued after that date under a tax-free Code Section 1035 exchange for a contract issued on or before that date. In the case of a master contract (within the meaning of Code Section 264(f)(4)(E), relating to the deduction for amounts paid in connection with insurance contracts), the addition of covered lives will be treated as a new contract only for the additional covered lives.

On the other hand, any material increase in the death benefit, or other material change, will cause a contract to be treated as a new contract. Increases in the death benefit that occur as a result of the operation of Code Section 7702 or the terms of the existing contract will not cause a contract to be treated as a new contract. In addition, certain changes to a contract will not be considered material changes so as to cause a contract to be treated as a new contract. These changes include administrative changes, changes from general to separate account, or changes as a result of the exercise of an option or right granted under the contract as originally issued.

Q 20:107   What is leveraged COLI?

In a *leveraged COLI* arrangement, the corporate policyholder borrows against the policy cash value to pay current premiums. The key to a leveraged COLI arrangement is the ability of the corporate policyholder to deduct interest paid on the policy loan and thus achieve positive cash flow. However, that ability has been significantly eroded in recent years.

Interest paid or accrued on business indebtedness is generally deductible under Code Section 163. However, in 1964, Congress began to craft special rules for leveraged COLI. In that year, Congress enacted a provision that denied an interest deduction for debt used to purchase multi-premium life insurance if the debt is part of "a plan of purchase which contemplates the systematic direct or indirect borrowing of all or part of the increases in the cash value of such contract." [I.R.C. § 264(a)(3)] The no-deduction rule was eased by a rule that provided that if four of the first seven annual premiums are paid with unborrowed funds, then interest on the three borrowed premiums were deductible. [I.R.C. § 264(c)(1)] Thus, subject to the four-out-of-seven test, corporations were able to take out policies on their employees and pay premiums by borrowing against the policies' cash values.

These leveraged COLI arrangements generally involved large insurance policies on key executives and employees. However, Congress tightened the rules again in 1986 by capping the contract debt eligible for interest deductions at $50,000 per insured. [former I.R.C. § 264(a)(4), as amended by the Internal Revenue Code of 1986]

The 1986 law change spurred the development of leveraged COLI arrangements involving life insurance policies on large numbers of rank-and-file employees (sometimes called "dead peasant" or "dead janitor" insurance).

However, in 1995 Congress cracked down again. The Health Insurance Portability and Accountability Act (HIPAA) amended the law to generally eliminate all deductions for interest paid on COLI loans, with a small exception for certain "key person" coverage (see Q 20:108). [I.R.C. § 264(a)(4)] The HIPAA provision took effect for debt incurred after December 31, 1995, with a transition rule for existing debt. The transition rule permitted a three-year phase-out of deductions, subject to an interest rate cap and a limit on the number of insurance contracts that could be leveraged.

The leveraged COLI crackdown was not confined to Congress. The IRS launched an all-out attack on broad-based leveraged COLI plans involving large numbers of employees.

The IRS scored its first victory in 1999, when the Tax Court disallowed all interest deductions for a broad-based COLI program set up by Winn-Dixie Stores in 1993. The program, which involved whole life insurance policies on 36, 000 employees, was structured to meet the $50,000 per employee debt limit and the four-out-of-seven test, which were then in effect. The plan called for Winn-Dixie to borrow to pay the premiums in years one through three and to use accumulated cash values to pay the premiums in years four through seven. According to Winn-Dixie's insurer, the plan would generate a pretax loss each year, but would result in after-tax profits. In fact, those profits were projected to exceed more than $2.2 billion over the 60-year estimated life span of the plan (although those profits were never realized because the plan was discontinued following the enactment of HIPAA). Despite its technical compliance with the law, the Tax Court held that the interest paid by Winn-Dixie on the COLI loans was not deductible because the COLI transactions lacked economic substance and did not serve a business purpose. In 2001, the Eleventh Circuit Court of Appeals affirmed the Tax Court's decision and the Supreme Court declined to hear the case. [Winn-Dixie Stores, Inc. v. Commissioner, 113 T.C. 254, *aff'd*, 254 F.3d 1313 (11th Cir. 2001), *cert. denied*, 122 S. Ct. 1537 (2002)] The IRS also scored victories in two similar cases involving broad-based leveraged COLI plans in 2001. In each of those cases, the courts denied the claimed interest deductions on the ground that the COLI plans lacked economic substance. [I.R.S. v. CM Holdings, Inc., 301 F.3d 96 (3d Cir. 2002); American Elec. Power v. United States, 136 F. Supp. 2d (S.D. Ohio 2001)]

In August 2001, the IRS offered to settle other broad-based COLI cases if the taxpayers agreed to concede 80 percent of the interest deductions claimed with respect to their COLI plans. However, in late 2002, the IRS gave taxpayers 45 days to agree to a settlement and then withdrew the settlement offer. The IRS says it will "vigorously defend or prosecute all future COLI litigation." [IRS Ann. 2002-96, 2002-43 I.R.B. 756]

Q 20:108   Under what circumstances is interest on COLI policy loans deductible?

Under current rules, a deduction is allowed for interest paid or incurred on indebtedness with respect to policies or contracts covering up to 20 "key persons" to the extent the aggregate indebtedness with respect to policies or contracts covering an individual does not exceed $50,000. [I.R.C. § 264(d)(2)] The deduction is also subject to an interest rate limitation. Under that limitation, no deduction is allowed to the extent interest paid or accrued for any month exceeds the applicable rate of interest for that month. [I.R.C. § 264(d)(2)(A)] For this purpose, the applicable rate of interest for any month is the "Moody's rate" for the month (i.e., the rate published in Moody's Corporate Bond Yield Average-Monthly Average Corporates, Moody's Investors Services, Inc., or a successor). [I.R.C. § 264(d)(2)(B)]

A *key person* is an officer or 20-percent-or-more owner of the employer. The number of persons who can be treated as key persons is limited to the greater of (1) five persons or (2) the lesser of 5 percent of the number of officers and employees of the employer or 20 persons.

If loans with respect to "key person" policies are part of a plan of systematic borrowing, the loans must meet the four-out-of-seven test. That is, interest on the loans will be deductible only if four of the first seven annual premiums are paid with unborrowed funds. [I.R.C. §§ 264(a)(3), (c)(1)]

Q 20:109   If COLI is used to finance the benefits payable under an ERISA plan, is the COLI policy a plan asset for ERISA purposes?

No. If the arrangement is structured properly, a COLI policy remains an employer asset rather than a plan asset. The DOL concluded that a COLI policy purchased to finance a noncontributory death benefit plan for employees, where the corporation owned the policy and proceeds were payable directly to the corporation as beneficiary, was not a plan asset. [DOL Adv. Op. 81-11A (Jan. 16, 1981)]

Chapter 21

Financial Accounting Rules for Nonpension Retiree and Postemployment Benefits

The Financial Accounting Standards Board (FASB) is the designated organization in the private sector for establishing standards of financial accounting and reporting. Those standards govern the preparation of financial reports and are officially recognized as authoritative by the Securities and Exchange Commission and the American Institute of Certified Public Accountants. This chapter examines the FASB's major pronouncement regarding employer provided welfare benefits for retirees or other former employees.

In July 2009, the FASB reorganized its accounting standards into a topic-based FASB Accounting Standards Codification (ASC). The following discussion includes references to the new ASC citations followed by the original accounting standards citations.

Postretirement Welfare Benefits

Q 21:1 What financial accounting considerations apply to postretirement welfare benefits?

For employees, postretirement health and other benefits are a form of deferred compensation for services rendered. (See Q 21:2.) Historically, employers were not required to disclose postretirement health and welfare benefits on their financial statements; employers simply accounted for retiree benefits on a pay-as-you-go basis (that is, showing them as an expense when paid). Because of this practice, many employers had no idea of the magnitude of liability for promised future benefits under their retiree medical and welfare benefit plans, which in some cases was shockingly high. Similarly, investors were largely in the dark about the extent of such liability.

To remedy these situations the FASB released its Statement of Financial Accounting Standards No. 106, *Employers' Accounting for Postretirement Benefits Other Than Pensions* (FAS 106). FAS 106 requires employers to estimate the future cost of their liability for future retiree medical benefits and other retiree welfare benefits using specified assumptions and methodology and to recognize a portion of that amount as an expense on their financial statements each year. The accounting treatment specified by FAS 106 forces an awareness of the true cost of retiree benefit promises and a disclosure of the substantial future financial impact they can have. The disclosure provisions of FAS 106 were subsequently amended by FAS 132, *Employers' Disclosures About Pensions and Other Postretirement Benefits*. The standards set forth in FAS 106 and FAS 132 are codified in ASC Codification Topic 715, *Compensation-Retirement Benefits*.

For publicly traded companies, the Securities and Exchange Commission (SEC) requires employers to disclose the impact of postretirement benefits on current financial statements.

Note. Financial accounting standards do not apply to governmental plans. [FAS 106, ¶ 108]

Q 21:2   What is the FASB's position on how postretirement nonpension benefits should be treated for accounting purposes?

According to the FASB, a postretirement benefit is part of the compensation paid to an employee for services rendered. [ASC 715-60-05-3] The accounting standards are derived from the basic idea that a benefit plan is an exchange between the employer and the employee. In exchange for services provided by the employee, the employer promises to provide, in addition to current wages and other benefits, an amount of retirement income or benefit. It follows from that basic view that benefits are not gratuities but instead are part of an employee's compensation, and because payment is deferred the benefit plan is a type of deferred compensation. It also follows that the employer's obligation for that compensation is incurred when the services are rendered. Because the obligation to provide benefits arises as employees render the services necessary to earn the benefits under the terms of the employer's plan, the accounting standards provide guidance on when the cost of providing the benefits should be recognized over the employees' periods of service. [ASC 715-10-05]

The FASB views a postretirement benefit plan as a deferred compensation arrangement. In the FASB's view, the employer promises to exchange future benefits for an employee's current services, and the benefit obligation accrues as an employee renders the services necessary to earn benefits according to the plan's terms. Even though a legal liability to provide retiree medical benefits and other retiree welfare benefits may not exist, an accounting liability nonetheless may. [FAS 106, Appendix A, Basis for Conclusions, ¶¶ 154, 155]

Case law has not been unequivocal about the legal enforceability of promises to provide postretirement benefits, although legal enforceability of certain claims has been demonstrated. The FASB, however, has looked beyond the legal status of the promise to consider whether the liability is effectively binding on the employer because of past practices, social or moral sanctions, or customs.

Q 21:3   What benefits are subject to the FASB accounting standards for postretirement benefit plans?

The accounting standards apply to all postretirement benefits expected to be provided by the employer to current and former employees (including retirees, disabled employees, and other former employees who are expected to receive postretirement benefits) and their beneficiaries and dependents, other than pensions and life insurance provided through a pension plan. Postretirement benefits include health care, life insurance (outside a pension plan), and other welfare benefits such as tuition assistance, day care, legal services, and housing subsidies provided after retirement. [ASC 715-60-15; FAS 106, ¶¶ 6, 11]

Postretirement benefits are divided into two general types of retiree welfare benefit plans: (1) defined contribution plans and (2) defined benefit plans. [ASC 715-60; ASC 715-70; FAS 106, ¶¶ 10, 16]

Note. Postemployment benefits other than retirement benefits are the subject of a separate accounting standard issued by the FASB (ASC 712; FAS 112) (see Qs 21:24–21:26).

Q 21:4   Do the postretirement benefit accounting standards apply if an employer is not legally obligated to provide retiree benefits?

Yes. [FAS 106, Appendix A, Basis for Conclusions, ¶ 156] The Employee Retirement Income Security Act of 1974 (ERISA) status of a retiree welfare plan as not being "vested" and as subject to amendment or termination under a reservation of rights clause is irrelevant for accounting purposes.

No legally enforceable obligation is required. The standards apply to any arrangement that is in substance a postretirement benefit plan, regardless of its form or the means or timing of its funding. The standards apply to written plans and to unwritten plans whose existence is based on a practice of paying postretirement benefits or on oral representations made to current or former employees. In the absence of evidence to the contrary, FASB presumes that an employer that has provided postretirement benefits in the past or is currently promising such benefits to employees and will continue to provide retiree benefits in the future. [ASC 715-10-15; FAS 106, ¶ 8]

FAS 106 also applies to funded and unfunded retiree welfare benefits. [ASC 715-10-15-7; FAS 106, ¶ 8]

Q 21:5   What are the requirements for retiree medical plans?

An employer's liability for postretirement medical benefits must be shown on the employer's balance sheet and profit and loss statement. The liability must be accounted for on an accrual basis rather than on a cash (pay-as-you-go) basis. That means that the cost of the benefit must be shown when the employees are deemed to be "earning" the benefits, rather than at the time the benefits are in fact paid. The liability for postretirement medical benefits is not required to be funded, however.

For calculating the amount of the employer's postretirement liability, retiree medical plans are divided into two broad categories: defined contribution plans and defined benefit plans (see Qs 21:6–21:9). The main impact of the accounting standards is on employers' maintenance of defined benefit plans—plans that list specific covered benefits and limits thereon—because the ultimate cost of such plans will depend on factors such as future utilization, longevity of participants, and medical cost inflation. Certain uniform assumptions must be used when calculating the cost effect of those and other factors. The cost of such future benefits is then allocated to the employee's service period (generally, the employee's date of hire to his or her date of initial eligibility for retiree medical benefits, whether or not he or she elects early retirement) and must be accrued by the employer and shown on its financial statements during those years.

Q 21:6   What is a defined contribution postretirement plan?

A *defined contribution postretirement plan* is a plan that provides postretirement benefits in return for services rendered, establishes an individual account for each participant, and has terms that specify how contributions to the individual's account are determined (rather than the amount of postretirement benefits to be received). The individual's postretirement benefits under such a plan are limited by the amounts in the individual's account (derived from contributions, investment earnings, and allocation of forfeitures by other employees, if any). [ASC 715-70-05; FAS 106, ¶ 104]

> **Practice Pointer.** In the past, defined contribution welfare benefit plans for retirees were relatively rare. In order to control costs and to limit the amount of accounting liabilities, however, many employers have switched from defined benefit plans to defined contribution plans.

Q 21:7   What are the accounting requirements for a defined contribution postretirement plan?

For a defined contribution postretirement plan, to the extent that the defined contributions are to be made to an employee's account during the periods in which the employee is providing services, the FASB requires that the contribution for a period be the cost to be charged as an expense for that period. If the plan provides for contributions for periods *after* the employee retires or terminates, the estimated cost is to be accrued during the employee's service period. [ASC 715-70-35; FAS 106, ¶ 105]

Q 21:8   What is a defined benefit postretirement plan?

A *defined benefit postretirement plan* is a plan that specifies the postretirement benefits in terms of the following:

- Monetary amounts (e.g., $100,000 of life insurance) and
- Benefit coverage to be provided (e.g., up to $200 per day for hospitalization or 80 percent of surgical fees).

Generally, the amount of benefits depends on a benefit formula (which may include factors such as the number of years of service rendered or the employee's compensation before retirement), the longevity of the retiree and any beneficiaries and covered dependents, and the incidence of events requiring benefit payments. [ASC 715-60-05; FAS 106, ¶¶ 16, 17]

Q 21:9   What are the accounting requirements for a defined benefit postretirement plan?

For a defined benefit postretirement plan, the accounting standards require accounting on an actuarial cost basis similar to the accounting standards required and in use for defined benefit pension plans (*see* ASC FAS 87, *Employers' Accounting for Pensions*). The computations must take into account the following components:

- Service cost
- Interest cost
- Actual return on plan assets (if any)
- Amortization of prior service cost
- Recognized gain or loss (including changes in assumptions)
- Amortization of any transitional obligation or asset existing at the date that the standards first apply.

[ASC 715-60-35; FAS 106, ¶¶ 19–22]

Q 21:10   Is the accounting liability determined solely by the written terms of the postretirement plan?

Generally, yes. If an employer has a cost-sharing policy, however, the written plan may be modified to take that employer's policy into account if the cost-sharing policy meets either of the following conditions:

1. The employer has a past practice of:
   a. Maintaining a consistent level of cost-sharing between itself and its retirees through changes in deductibles, coinsurance provisions, or retiree contributions; or
   b. Consistently increasing or reducing the employer's share of the cost of covered benefits through changes in retired or active plan participants' contributions toward their retiree health care benefits, deductibles,

coinsurance provisions, out-of-pocket limitations, and so forth in accordance with the employer's established cost-sharing policy; or

2. The employer has the ability to institute different cost-sharing provisions at a specified time or when certain conditions exist (e.g., when health care cost increases exceed a certain level) and has communicated its intent to do so to affected plan participants.

[ASC 715-60-35-51; FAS 106, ¶¶ 23–28]

Q 21:11   What special actuarial assumptions are required in the case of postretirement health care benefits?

FAS 106 requires the use of several assumptions unique to health care benefits, including the following:

- Consideration of historical per capita claims cost by age (and perhaps also by sex and geographical location)
- Health care cost trend rates, if the plan provides benefits-in-kind
- Medical coverage to be paid by governmental authorities (e.g., Medicare) and other providers of health care benefits

[ASC 715-60-35-90; FAS 106, ¶¶ 34–42]

Q 21:12   Does the FASB require that an employer fund its employees' postretirement welfare benefits?

No. The FASB has no authority to require funding of benefits or to regulate the content of benefit plans in any way.

Q 21:13   If an employer has funded its postretirement benefits, do the fund assets offset the employer's liabilities?

Yes. Fund assets offset an employer's accounting liabilities, provided the assets are segregated in a trust or otherwise effectively restricted (such as in a retired-lives reserve held by an insurance company) so that they can be used to provide postretirement benefits only. [ASC 715-60-55-26; FAS 106, ¶¶ 63–66]

Practice Pointer. Some employers have purchased corporate-owned life insurance (COLI) policies on their employees with the intention of using policy proceeds to pay for postretirement benefit costs. Because such policies are general assets of an employer and subject to the claims of the employer's creditors, they cannot be considered plan assets and cannot be used to offset the employer's liabilities for postretirement benefits. In addition, COLI policies are now subject to notice and consent requirements as well as limits on the exclusion of policy proceeds that may affect the viability of such policies as a financing mechanism for postretirement benefits (see chapter 20).

Q 21:14   How are postretirement benefits that are insured under an insurance contract treated for financial accounting purposes?

To the extent that postretirement benefits are covered by insurance contracts, the benefits are excluded from the employer's postretirement benefit obligation. For this purpose, an insurance contract is a contract in which an insurance company undertakes an unconditional legal obligation to provide specified benefits to specific individuals in return for a fixed consideration or premium. The contract must be irrevocable and involve the transfer of significant risk from the employer or plan to the insurance company. If the insurer does business primarily with the employer and related parties (i.e., is a captive insurer) or if there is any reasonable doubt that the insurer will meet its obligations, the contract is not treated as an insurance contract.

> **Note.** As a practical matter, insurance coverage that guarantees payment of all postretirement medical benefits is generally unavailable except at a cost employers find unacceptable. An insurer, however, may be willing to insure a portion of the benefits, such as benefits not exceeding a specified cap.

Insurance contracts that qualify as such are not treated as plan assets. If the insurance contract is a participating contract that shares in the experience of the insurer, however, then the participation right is considered a plan asset. [ASC 715-60-35-109; FAS 106, ¶¶ 67–71]

Disclosure Requirements

Q 21:15   What disclosure requirements for postretirement benefits must be included in financial statements?

Both defined benefit and defined contribution postretirement plans must satisfy disclosure requirements. Those requirements are designed to make an employer's financial statements more useful to investors by disclosing information about the magnitude of the employer's benefit obligations and their associated costs. Disclosures must be presented for plans providing postretirement health care benefits as well as for plans primarily providing other postretirement benefits (if the obligations are significant). Information must be provided for plans both inside and outside the United States (if the obligations for non-U.S. plans are significant).

Required disclosures may be aggregated for all of the employer's defined benefit postretirement plans or may be disaggregated in groups if that is considered to provide the most useful information, except in certain cases of combining disclosures about plans outside the United States with those for U.S. plans. Disclosures about plans with assets in excess of the accumulated benefit obligation generally can be aggregated with those of plans with accumulated benefit obligations in excess of plan assets. If those disclosures are combined, the employer must disclose the aggregate benefit obligation and aggregate fair value of plan assets for plans with benefit obligations in excess of plan assets. Disclosures about postretirement benefit plans outside the United States may be combined with those for U.S. plans, unless the benefit obligations of the plans outside the United States are significant relative to the total benefit obligation and those plans use significantly different assumptions. [ASC 715-20-50-3; ASC 715-20-50-4; FAS 106, ¶¶ 74–78; FAS 132, ¶¶ 6–7]

Additional disclosures describing the types of plan assets, investment strategy, measurement dates, plan obligations, cash flows, and components of net periodic benefit cost recognized during interim periods are also required. Effective for fiscal years ending after December 15, 2009, a reconciliation of the beginning and ending balances of the benefit obligation for the reporting period is required. This reconciliation must separately state service costs, interest costs, participant contributions, and other data. [FASB Action Alert No. 08-40, Oct. 2, 2008; ASC 715-20-65-2]

Q 21:16   What disclosure requirements apply to defined benefit postretirement plans?

Any employer that sponsors one or more defined benefit postretirement plans or defined benefit pension plans must disclose separately for each type of plan the following information:

1. A reconciliation of beginning and ending balances of the benefit obligation showing separately, if applicable, the effects during the period attributable to each of the following: service cost, interest cost, contributions by plan participants, actuarial gains and losses, foreign currency exchange rate changes, benefits paid, plan amendments, business combinations, divestitures, curtailments, settlements, and special termination benefits. For this purpose, the benefit obligation is the accumulated postretirement benefit obligation—the present value of benefits attributed to employee service rendered to a particular date.

2. A reconciliation of beginning and ending balances of the fair value of plan assets showing separately, if applicable, the effects during the period attributable to each of the following: actual return on plan assets, foreign currency exchange rate changes, contributions by the employer, contributions by plan participants, benefits business combinations, divestitures, and settlements.

3. The funded status of the plan and the amounts recognized in financial statements, separately showing assets and current and noncurrent liabilities recognized.

4. Information about plan assets, including fair value of total plan assets, a description of investment policies and strategies, a description of the basis used to determine the overall expected long-term rate of return on assets assumption, and additional information expected to be useful in understanding risk and return characteristics.

5. The benefits expected to be paid in each of the next five fiscal years, and in the aggregate for the following five fiscal years.

6. The employer's best estimate of contributions expected to be paid to the plan during the next fiscal year.

7. The amount of net benefit cost recognized, showing separately the service cost component, the interest cost component, the expected return on plan assets for the period, the gain or loss component, the prior service cost or credit component, the transition asset or obligation component, and the gain or loss due to settlements or curtailments.

8. Net gain or loss and net prior service cost or credit recognized in other comprehensive income for the period.

9. Amounts accumulated in other comprehensive income that have not yet been recognized as components of the net periodic benefit cost.

10. On a weighted average basis, the assumptions used in accounting for the plans, including assumed discount rates, rates of compensation increase for pay-related plans, and expected long-term rates of return on plan assets.

11. The assumed health care cost trend rate(s) for the next year used to measure the expected cost of benefits covered by the plan (gross eligible charges) and a general description of the direction and pattern of change in the assumed trend rate thereafter, together with the ultimate trend rate(s) and when that rate is expected to be achieved.

12. The effect of a 1 percent increase and the effect of a 1 percent decrease in the assumed health care cost trend rates on (a) the aggregate of service and interest cost components of net periodic postretirement health care benefit cost and (b) the accumulated postretirement benefit obligation for health care benefits. For purposes of this disclosure, all other assumptions shall be held constant, and the net effects shall be measured based on the substantive plan that is the basis for the accounting.

13. If applicable, the amounts and types of securities of the employer and related parties included in plan assets, the approximate amount of future annual benefits of plan participants covered by insurance contracts issued by the employer or related parties, and any significant transactions between the employer or related parties and the plan during the period.

14. If applicable, any alternative amortization method used to amortize prior service amounts or unrecognized net gains and losses pursuant to ASC 715-30-35-13 and 715-30-35-25 or 715-60-35-18 and 715-60-35-31 (FAS 87 ¶¶ 26 and 33 or FAS 106 ¶¶ 53 and 60).

15. If applicable, any substantive commitment, such as past practice or a history of regular benefit increases, used as the basis for accounting for the benefit obligation.

16. If applicable, the cost of providing special or contractual termination benefits recognized during the period and a description of the nature of the event.

17. An explanation of any significant change in the benefit obligation or plan assets not otherwise apparent in other disclosures required by ASC 715 (FAS 132).

18. Amounts in accumulated other comprehensive income expected to be recognized as components of net periodic benefit cost over the following fiscal year.

19. The amount and timing of any plan assets expected to be returned to the employer during the following 12-month period.

Amounts related to the employer's results of operations are to be disclosed for each period for which an income statement is presented, and amounts related to the employer's statement of financial position are to be disclosed for each balance sheet presented. Reduced disclosure requirements are required for nonpublic entities. [ASC ¶¶ 715-20-50-1 *et seq.*; FAS 132, ¶¶ 5, 8]

Q 21:17　What disclosure requirements apply to defined contribution postretirement welfare plans?

An employer that sponsors a defined contribution postretirement plan or plans is required to disclose the amount of cost recognized for them during the period separately from the amount of cost recognized for defined benefit plans. The disclosures must include a description of the nature and effect of any significant changes during the period affecting comparability, such as a change in the rate of employer contributions, a business combination, or a divestiture. [ASC 715-70-50-1; FAS 132, ¶ 9]

Q 21:18　What disclosures are required for multiemployer plans?

Employers are required to disclose the amount of contributions to multiemployer plans during the period. This may be total contributions to multiemployer plans without disaggregating the amounts attributable to pensions and other postretirement benefits. The disclosures are required to include a description of the nature and effect of any changes affecting comparability, such as a change in the rate of employer contributions, a business combination, or a divestiture. [ASC 715-80-50-1; FAS 132, ¶ 10]

Q 21:19　What effect do the accounting requirements have on employers' financial statements?

In almost all cases, employers are required to show greater expenses on the profit and loss statement and greater liabilities on the balance sheet than would otherwise be reported. As a result, the employer's net earnings generally are reduced. The effect depends on the age of the employer's workforce and the comparative size of its current retiree population. Employers with a large retiree population and a mature workforce are most affected, whereas employers with few retirees and a young workforce are less severely affected.

Example 1. Employer X has a mature workforce (average age 50) and a very large retiree population. X will therefore have a large FAS 106 liability in absolute dollar terms. However, because X must pay a high amount on a pay-as-you-go basis for its substantial retiree population, the additional accrued benefits that FAS 106 requires it to disclose may be smaller, as a percentage of what it records on its financial statements as a pay-as-you-go expense.

Example 2. Employer Y has the same number of employees as does Employer X in Example 1. Y's workforce, however, is relatively young (average age 27) and Y has only one retiree to date. Y's current retiree medical expense, on a pay-as-you-go basis, is insignificant. Therefore, Y has a relatively small FAS 106 liability in absolute dollar terms as compared to X, because the required accruals are spread out over the service period (date of hire to date of first eligibility for retiree medical benefits), and the yearly increments for prefunding at such young ages are small. In percentage terms; however, Y's retiree medical expense liability is huge.

Employers that substantially prefund their postretirement welfare benefits are less affected than similarly situated employers that do no prefunding.

Q 21:20   How does the accounting liability affect an employer's ability to conduct its business?

The accounting liability could affect a company in the following ways:

1. The requirement that an employer accrue the cost of postretirement medical coverage over the working lives of employees and disclose how much of this obligation is unfunded can affect the financial ratios required to be maintained under the terms of the company's existing loans.

2. A company's ability to obtain short-term and long-term financing is affected by the amount of liability shown on its balance sheet. Banks scrutinize a company's cash-flow picture over the anticipated period of the loan to gauge the company's ability to repay the loan. The state of a company's finances (including its cash-flow obligations for future benefit payments under a retiree medical plan) will affect whether loans will be obtainable and, if so, how favorable the terms (for example, repayment period, interest rate, and points) will be.

3. A company's annual benefit payment obligation and balance sheet liability could also be a factor in assessing the value of the company in a merger, acquisition, or divestiture situation.

4. The accounting liability could affect the value of a company's stock, since it affects the earnings of the company as well as its surplus.

Reducing or Eliminating the Accounting Liability

Q 21:21 What steps can an employer take to limit or reduce its accounting liability?

There are a number of steps that an employer can take to control its financial accounting liability, including the following:

- Adopting stricter eligibility limits
- Capping the amount of the plan benefits payable during a year or during a retiree's lifetime
- Setting limits on employer contributions
- Instituting or increasing employee or retiree contributions (or both)
- Switching from a defined benefit plan to a defined contribution plan
- Increasing deductible or copayment levels (or both)
- Extending a cafeteria plan to include retirees
- Replacing one form of benefit with another (e.g., dropping postretirement medical coverage and increasing pension benefits)
- Prefunding retiree benefits
- Incorporating managed care features
- Basing the level of retiree benefits on length of service (e.g., full benefits after 30 years of service, half benefits after 15 years of service)
- Integrating the retiree plan with other benefits (e.g., Medicare)
- Discontinuing retiree medical coverage or substituting an employer-sponsored Medicare + Choice plan (see Chapter 4).

Q 21:22 How does funding an employer's liability for retiree medical benefits affect the employer's financial accounting liability?

The amount of a plan asset reduces the liability that must be shown on the employer's balance sheet. Additionally, the income on plan assets reduces the expense that is shown on the profit and loss statement.

To be a plan asset, the asset must be segregated and restricted (usually in a trust) to be used for postretirement benefits. Plan assets ordinarily cannot be withdrawn by the employer except under specified limited circumstances. Assets not segregated in a trust, or otherwise effectively restricted so that they cannot be used by the employer for other purposes, are not plan assets for financial accounting purposes. Under certain circumstances, an insurance contract is not treated as a plan asset (see Q 21:13).

Q 21:23 How do retiree medical plan cutbacks affect an employer's liability?

The accounting liability required to be disclosed by an employer can be reduced, sometimes significantly, by cutting back the employer's retiree medical plan prospectively. (See the discussion of cost containment through plan redesign in Q 21:21.)

Employers with a large retiree population and a mature workforce are affected more severely than are employers with a few retirees and a young workforce.

Postemployment Benefits

Q 21:24   What is the difference between postemployment benefits and postretirement benefits?

Postemployment benefits are benefits provided by an employer to former or inactive employees (and their beneficiaries and covered dependents, if applicable) after employment, but before retirement.

Inactive employees are employees who are not currently rendering service to the employer and who have not been terminated. This category includes employees who have been laid off and those on disability leave, regardless of whether they are expected to return to active status.

Q 21:25   What postemployment benefits are subject to FAS 112?

Accounting Standards Codification Topic 712, *Compensation-Nonretirement Postemployment Benefits* (formerly FAS 112, *Employers' Accounting for Postemployment Benefits*), governs all types of benefits provided to former or inactive employees, their beneficiaries, and their covered dependents. Those benefits include, but are not limited to, termination benefits, salary continuation, supplemental unemployment benefits, severance benefits, disability-related benefits (including workers' compensation), job training and counseling, and continuation of benefits such as health care benefits and life insurance coverage. [ASC 712-10-05; FAS 112, ¶ 1]

Q 21:26   What is the FASB's position on how postemployment benefits should be treated for accounting purposes?

The FASB takes the position that, for accounting purposes, postemployment benefits are part of the compensation provided to an employee in exchange for services.

Nonretirement postemployment benefits offered as special termination benefits (such as severance pay) must be recognized as a liability and a loss when the employees accept the offer and the amount can be reasonably estimated. [ASC 712-10-25-1]

Contractual termination benefits must be recognized as a liability and a loss when it is probable that employees will be entitled to the benefits and the amount can be reasonably estimated. [ASC 712-10-25-2]

Glossary of Terms

Account limit: The maximum addition to a qualified asset account of a welfare benefit fund that an employer is permitted to deduct. It equals the amount reasonably and actuarially necessary to fund benefit claims incurred but unpaid as of the end of the taxable year, plus administrative costs and certain contributions to an additional reserve for postretirement medical or life insurance benefits. Such a limit does not apply to employee-pay-all voluntary employees' beneficiary associations (VEBAs) covering more than 50 employees, none of whom is entitled to a refund that is not based on the experience of the entire fund.

ADA: The Americans with Disabilities Act of 1990.

ADEA: The Age Discrimination in Employment Act (29 U.S.C. §§ 621 *et seq.* [1967]). This statute protects workers over 40 from compulsory retirement because of age; it also protects them from adverse job actions based on age (e.g., refusal to hire, discriminatory layoff) and against benefits discrimination. Employers are subject to ADEA if they engage in an industry affecting interstate commerce and had 20 or more employees in each working day of 20 or more weeks in the current or preceding calendar year.

AD&D plan: A plan providing benefits for accidental death or dismemberment.

AEI: Assistance-eligible individual.

Age Discrimination in Employment Act: See ADEA.

Aggregation: The process of considering separate plans together to see whether they satisfy requirements under ERISA and/or the Internal Revenue Code. Aggregation can be either permissive or mandatory.

ASO arrangement: Administrative-services-only arrangement. A system under which an employer self-insures its welfare benefit plan, but contracts with a third party administrator such as an insurance company that provides claims administration and related services.

Assistance-eligible individual: A COBRA-qualified beneficiary who is eligible for subsidized continuation coverage.

Cafeteria plans: Plans allowing employees to choose from a "menu" of one or more qualified benefits and cash (including nontaxable benefits). Under Code

Section 125, benefits from a properly drafted cafeteria plan are not taxed to the employee who selects them—unless the employee actually chooses taxable benefits (and is not merely entitled to do so).

Capitation fee: The set fee that an employer pays an HMO to provide care for each member employee, regardless of the actual cost of the care.

Captive insurance company: An insurance company that is partially or wholly owned by an employer.

CMS: Centers for Medicare and Medicaid Services (formerly the Health Care Financing Administration (HCFA)) of the U.S. Department of Health and Human Services.

COB: Coordination of benefits. A group health insurance plan's COB provisions apply when more than one plan covers a particular medical expense, in order to cut costs and prevent windfalls to employees. The general rule is that if a person is covered under one plan as an employee and under another as a dependent, the employment-related plan is the primary payor.

COBRA: The Consolidated Omnibus Budget Reconciliation Act of 1985 (Pub. L. No. 99-272). This statute (signed in 1986) requires employers to offer the option of purchasing continuation coverage to qualified beneficiaries who would otherwise lose group health insurance coverage as the result of a qualifying event, such as termination of employment or divorce from an employee.

Code: The Internal Revenue Code of 1986 (26 U.S.C. § 1 *et seq.*), as adopted by TRA 1986 (Pub. L. No. 99-514). ("Former Code" refers to repealed provisions, including those in the previous Internal Revenue Code of 1954.)

COLI: Corporate-owned life insurance; insurance on the lives of employees.

Coinsurance: A cost-sharing mechanism under which the employee is required to pay a percentage (e.g., 10 percent) of medical expenses arising after the deductible has been satisfied; the plan pays the balance.

Common-law employee: A person who performs service(s) for an employer, if the employer has the right to direct both the objective of the services and the manner in which they are performed.

Coordination of benefits: See COB.

Creditable Coverage: Prior group health plan coverage that may be applied to a plan's preexisting condition period. Creditable coverage includes, among other things, group health plan or health insurance coverage, coverage under Medicare Part A or B, state health benefit risk pools, and public health plans. Group health plans and health insurance issuers must provide a written certification of the period of creditable coverage under a plan in order to document this prior coverage.

Deductible: A cost-sharing method under which employees are required to assume part of the cost of health care (e.g., $500 per person per year) before direct payment or reimbursement is available from the plan.

Defense of Marriage Act: See DOMA.

Dependent care assistance plan: A plan under which an employer provides assistance for an employee's employment-related expenses of caring for a child, parent, or other dependent—either directly in the form of dependent care centers or through cash reimbursements for dependent care expenses. Benefits of up to $5,000 ($2,500 for a married employer filing a separate return) from such a plan are not taxable income for the employee, subject to certain income limitations.

Determination period: Under COBRA, a period of 12 consecutive months that is used to calculate the premiums for continuation coverage.

DFVC: Delinquent Filer Voluntary Compliance program.

Disability plan: A plan that provides benefits to employees who are unable to work because of illness or accident. As a general rule, benefits under such a plan are taxable to employees who receive them. State workers' compensation laws compel employers to provide coverage for job-related disabilities. Disability plans include wage continuation (sick pay) plans and plans paying temporary or long-term disability benefits.

Disqualified benefit: In a welfare benefit fund context: (1) a portion of the fund that reverts to the benefit of the employer or (2) a postretirement medical or life insurance benefit provided either (a) under a discriminatory plan or (b) with respect to a key employee but not made from the mandatory separate account. The employer is subject to an excise tax equal to 100 percent of the disqualified benefit.

Diversification rule: An ERISA rule mandating that fiduciaries diversify plan investments to avoid the risk of large losses—unless circumstances make it imprudent to diversify.

DOL: U.S. Department of Labor; the DOL has enforcement authority over the regulatory and administrative (i.e., nontax) provisions of ERISA.

DOMA: Acronym for a federal law of the United States passed on September 21, 1996, as Public Law No. 104-199, 110 Stat. 2419. Its provisions are codified at 1 U.S.C. § 7 and 28 U.S.C. § 1738C.

EAP: See Employee Assistance Program.

EBSA: Employee Benefit Security Administration (formerly the Pension and Welfare Benefits Administration (PWBA)); a division of the Department of Labor that monitors compliance with ERISA and the Code with respect to employee benefit matters.

Educational assistance program: A program under which employers provide tuition assistance for employees' continuing education. Benefits under such programs are not taxable to the employee receiving them.

EEOC: Equal Employment Opportunity Commission; the federal agency that enforces ADA, ADEA, and Title VII of the Civil Rights Act of 1964.

Employee assistance program: An employer-provided benefit that may include counseling, referrals, or treatment for substance abuse and certain personal or family circumstances of employees.

Employee-pay-all plans: Plans that are paid for entirely by the employees, with no financial input from the employer.

Employee welfare benefit plan: Any plan, fund, or program that is established or maintained by an employer and/or an employee organization to provide benefits (e.g., medical, sick pay, and vacation benefits) to plan participants or their beneficiaries. Under DOL regulations, certain severance pay arrangements and supplemental retirement income payments may be treated as welfare plans rather than pension plans.

Employer-provided benefit: A benefit that is provided, directly or via employer contributions, by an employer.

EPA: Equal Pay Act of 1963.

ERISA: Employee Retirement Income Security Act of 1974 (Pub. L. No. 93-406). ERISA is the basic law designed to protect the rights of beneficiaries of employee benefit plans offered by employers, unions, and the like. ERISA imposes various qualification standards and fiduciary responsibilities on both welfare benefit and retirement plans and provides enforcement procedures as well.

ESRD: End-stage renal disease.

Exclusive benefit rule: The ERISA requirement that plans, by their terms and operations, be maintained for the exclusive benefit of employees who are plan participants. Under ERISA, fiduciaries have a duty to administer plans solely in the interest of participants and beneficiaries and are not permitted to allow plan assets to inure to the benefit of the employer.

FASB: Financial Accounting Standards Board; the body that sets uniform standards for treatment of accounting items. In the employee benefits context, FASB has prepared an exposure draft concerning disclosure of unfunded retiree welfare benefit liabilities.

Federally qualified HMO: An HMO that meets the standards set forth in the HMO Act and that can "mandate" an employer to provide HMO coverage to employees in the HMO's service area.

FICA: Federal Insurance Contribution Act; the statute that requires employers and employees to pay Social Security taxes.

Fiduciary: Any person (in the legal sense of an individual, corporation, etc.) that exercises discretionary authority or control over the administration of a plan or the management or disposition of plan assets or that gives investment advice to the plan for a fee or other compensation.

Flexible benefit account: A type of medical or dependent care expense reimbursement option under a cafeteria plan or a type of cafeteria plan standing alone. Coverage is paid for by employer contributions, or salary reduction contributions, or both.

Flexible spending account: A cafeteria plan benefit option (most commonly used for medical expense reimbursement and dependent care costs) that reimburses employees for certain expenses they incur.

Flexplace arrangement: An option that allows an employee to work at home or at another off-site location, for a specified number of hours per week, and for a preset, limited duration. Also known as telecommuting.

FMLA: The Family and Medical Leave Act of 1993.

401(k) plan: An arrangement (defined by Code Section 401(k)) under which a covered employee can elect to defer income by making pretax contributions to a profit sharing or stock bonus plan. A cafeteria plan may provide a 401(k) plan as a qualified benefit option.

FSA: See Flexible spending account.

Funding: Accumulating money or other assets that can be used to pay for plan benefits; for example, by creating a welfare benefit trust or other welfare benefit fund.

General death benefit: A benefit payable under a group term life insurance plan on the death of an employee, without special conditions (e.g., double indemnity for accidental death). This is the type of benefit that can qualify for special tax treatment under a Section 79 group term life insurance policy.

GINA: Genetic Information Nondiscrimination Act of 2008.

Group enrollment period: An annual period of at least ten working days during which employees must be given the option of enrolling in one or more federally qualified HMO or switching from an HMO to another health plan option offered by the employer.

Group health plan: Under ERISA, an employee welfare benefit plan providing medical care to participants and beneficiaries, either directly or indirectly (e.g., through insurance or otherwise). Under the Internal Revenue Code, a plan maintained by an employer to provide medical care, directly or indirectly, to employees, ex-employees, and their families.

Group term life insurance plan: A plan qualifying under Code Section 79 to provide employees with employer-paid life insurance coverage at little or no tax cost. Employees have taxable income only to the extent that (1) the cost of insurance providing a group term general death benefit exceeds the cost of providing $50,000 of coverage, or (2) the plan contains nonqualifying features. Special rules may apply to highly compensated employees or key employees.

Group universal life insurance: A program (usually on an employee-pay-all basis) that provides employees with universal life insurance, giving them a choice between a fixed death benefit or a death benefit that is a multiple of compensation plus the policy's cash value at the time of death. This type of insurance does not qualify for special tax treatment under Code Section 79.

GUL insurance: See Group Universal Life Insurance.

HDHP: A high-deductible health plan; a requirement for contributions to a health savings account (HSA) or medical savings account (MSA).

Health Care Financing Administration: See CMS.

Health reimbursement arrangement: An employer-funded plan for reimbursement of employees' health care expenses.

Health savings account: A tax-favored savings account for employees that is combined with high-deductible health insurance coverage.

HEART Act: The Heroes Earnings Assistance and Relief Tax Act of 2008.

HHS: The U.S. Department of Health and Human Services, which promulgates the regulations issued under the HMO Act.

HICN: Health Insurance Claim Number; the number carried on an individual's Medicare card.

HIPAA: The Health Insurance Portability and Accountability Act of 1996.

HITECH Act: The Health Information Technology for Economic and Clinical Health Act was signed into law on February 17, 2009, as part of the American Recovery and Reinvestment Act (ARRA). Its main goal is to encourage the adoption of electronic health records (EHRs) through incentive payments to physicians.

HMO: Health maintenance organization; an organization of medical care providers that provides a specified range of medical care in return for a set capitation fee, without regard to the actual cost of providing medical care for each HMO member.

HMO Act: The Health Maintenance Organization Act of 1973. This federal statute, as amended, sets the standard for federally qualified HMOs and regulates other HMO matters.

HRA: See Health reimbursement arrangement.

HSA: See Health savings account.

Incidents of ownership: Rights that will result in the inclusion of life insurance policy proceeds in the policyholder's estate for federal estate tax purposes.

Insured plan: A welfare benefit plan that is funded by the employer's purchase of policies from commercial insurers.

Internal Revenue Code: See Code.

I.R.C.: See Code.

IRS: Internal Revenue Service; the federal agency, part of the U.S. Department of the Treasury, that is charged with primary responsibility for administering, interpreting, and enforcing the Code. (Note, however, that the Secretary of the Treasury—not the IRS—issues regulations under the Code.)

Lilly Ledbetter Fair Pay Act of 2009: Named for a plaintiff in a 2007 Supreme Court case that limited the time period for filing a discriminatory pay claim, this law overturns the Supreme Court's ruling and clarifies that unlawful discrimination takes place each time compensation is paid pursuant to a discriminatory pay decision. The law's effective date is retroactive to May 28, 2007 (the day before the Supreme Court's decision).

LMRA: Labor Management Relations Act of 1947.

Medical care: Under the Code definition, diagnosis, cure, mitigation, treatment, or prevention of disease or affecting any structure or function of the body; also traveling for or incidental to medical care. Insurance for medical care is treated as medical care; so is the cost of prescription drugs and insulin.

Medical plan: An arrangement sponsored by an employer that reimburses employees for costs of personal injuries or illness.

Medical savings account: A tax-favored savings account for employees of small employers that is combined with high-deductible health insurance coverage.

MEWA: Multiple employer welfare arrangement; a noncollectively bargained arrangement or plan maintained to benefit employees of two or more employers that are not under common control. ERISA generally does not preempt state law with regard to MEWAs. Small employers participating in MEWAs may be exempt from COBRA's continuation-coverage requirement and other special rules that apply under COBRA.

MHPA: Mental Health Parity Act of 1996.

MHPAEA: The Mental Health Parity and Addiction Equity Act, signed into law on October 3, 2008 as part of the Economic Stabilization Act; it seeks to correct the imbalance between the benefits afforded mental health and substance use disorders under group health plans and general medical and surgical benefits typically afforded under such plans.

Michelle's Law: A law requiring extended health plan coverage for dependent college students in the case of medically necessary leaves of absence.

Minimum-premium insurance arrangement: A method of funding welfare benefit plans under which benefits are self-insured by an employer or trustee up to a set trigger point; a commercial insurer is liable for all benefits above the trigger point.

MSA: See Medical savings account.

NAIC: National Association of Insurance Commissioners.

Named fiduciary: For ERISA purposes, a fiduciary to which the ERISA plan document gives express authority to control plan operations and administration.

National medical-support notice: A uniform method of informing employers about the need to enroll children of noncustodial parents in employer-sponsored health care plans.

NDAA: The National Defense Authorization Act for Fiscal Year 2008; also known as the Wounded Warriors Act. A law amending the Family and Medical Leave Act of 1993 to allow eligible employees to take leave related to a family member's military service.

NLRA: The National Labor Relations Act of 1935.

NLRB: National Labor Relations Board.

NMHPA: The Newborns' and Mothers' Health Protection Act of 1996.

NMSN: See National medical-support notice.

Noncompliance period: Under COBRA, the period beginning on the date a violation first occurs; it is used to compute the penalty excise tax imposed on employers that violate COBRA rules.

Nondiscrimination rules: Rules that deny the employer, the employee, or both certain tax benefits if plans discriminate in favor of certain employees, such as highly compensated employees or key employees.

Open enrollment period: See group enrollment period.

Party-in-interest: A person who stands in a relationship to a plan (e.g., sponsor, fiduciary, provider of services) that is close enough to result in the prohibition of certain transactions (e.g., sales, loans, leases, exchanges of property).

PDA: The Pregnancy Discrimination Act of 1978.

Pension and Welfare Benefits Administration: See EBSA.

Plan administrator: Under ERISA, the plan sponsor (e.g., employer) or person that the plan instrument designates as the plan administrator.

Plan sponsor: The employer or employee organization that establishes or maintains a plan; the association, committee, joint board of trustees, or similar group if the plan is established or maintained by two or more employers and/or employee organizations.

POS plan: Point-of-service health plan; combines traditional indemnity health coverage and a network of participating health care providers.

PPA 2006: The Pension Protection Act of 2006.

PPO: Preferred provider organization; a network of medical care providers organized by an employer or insurer to provide various medical care services to covered employees for specified fees. The covered employees are required or encouraged to go to those preferred providers when they need medical care, on the assumption that the preferred providers will charge less than other providers.

Pregnancy disability: A disability that is caused, or contributed to, by pregnancy, childbirth, or related medical conditions. Under Title VII of the Civil Rights Act of 1964, employers must treat such disabilities the same as other, nonpregnancy-related disabilities.

PDA: The Pregnancy Discrimination Act of 1978.

Prohibited transaction: Specified transactions (e.g., sales and exchanges, leases, and loans) between a plan and a party in interest that are forbidden by ERISA. The Department of Labor has the power to exempt individual transactions or classes of transactions from the restriction.

Prudent man rule: Under ERISA, the standard of care to which fiduciaries are held. That is, the care, skill, diligence, and prudence that a prudent person, acting in a like capacity and familiar with such matters, would use in conducting an enterprise of the same character and aims under similar circumstances.

QDRO: Qualified domestic relations order; a court order requiring payment of plan benefits to an alternate beneficiary that satisfies conditions imposed by ERISA.

QESC: Qualified employer-sponsored coverage; health coverage offered through an employer that qualifies as creditable coverage.

QMCSO: Qualified medical child support order; a court order satisfying certain form and content requirements under which the group health plan must pay plan benefits to the child or children listed as alternate payee.

QRD: A permitted distribution from a health flexible spending account (FSA) to a participant called to active military duty.

Qualified asset account: An account consisting of assets set aside for future payment of benefits by a welfare benefit fund. The Internal Revenue Code sets limits on the deduction employers may take for additions to a qualified asset account.

Qualified beneficiary: A person entitled to COBRA continuation coverage because of his or her status on the day before a qualifying event occurs. Covered employees under a group health plan can be qualified beneficiaries; so can their covered spouses and covered children.

Qualified benefit: A noncash benefit that a cafeteria plan is permitted to offer.

Qualified cash-or-deferred arrangement: See 401(k) plan.

Qualified cost: The limit on an employer's tax deduction for contribution to a welfare benefit fund. It equals the fund's qualified direct cost and permitted additions to a qualified asset account, minus the fund's after-tax income for the taxable year.

Qualified direct cost: The aggregate benefits and administrative expenses of a welfare benefit fund that a cash-basis employer would be entitled to deduct if it paid the expenses directly.

Qualified domestic relations order: See QDRO.

Qualified medical child support order: See QMCSO.

Qualified nonguaranteed contract: An insurance contract that is excluded from the Internal Revenue Code's definition of a welfare benefit fund. All insurance contracts are treated as qualified nonguaranteed contracts unless they provide a guarantee of renewal at set rates and do not provide only insurance protection and nonguaranteed policy dividends or experience-rated refunds determined by factors other than the level of welfare benefits paid.

Qualified reservist distribution: See QRD.

Qualifying event: An event that entitles a person to elect continuation coverage under COBRA (e.g., termination of employment for reasons other than gross misconduct or separation or divorce from a covered employee). The nature of the qualifying event determines whether continuation coverage will be available for 18, 29, or 36 months.

Red flag rules: Federal Trade Commission regulations requiring financial institutions, creditors, and other covered entities to develop and implement identity theft prevention programs by November 1, 2008 as part of the Fair and Accurate Credit Transactions (FACT) Act of 2003.

Retiree medical account: A separate account that is contained in a pension or annuity plan providing health benefits subordinate to the plan's retirement benefits.

Rollout: Termination of a split-dollar life insurance plan by giving the employee complete ownership and control of the life insurance policy.

Salary reduction contribution: A contribution (also called an elective contribution) made to purchase a cafeteria plan benefit under an agreement between employer and employee. Such a contribution is a pretax contribution, which is not included in the employee's taxable income.

Self-insurance: An employer's practice of paying benefits out of its own assets or funds (without involvement of a commercial insurer) to pay benefits.

Service area: The geographic area within which an HMO provides health care.

Severance pay plan: A plan that pays benefits (usually proportionate to length of employment) to employees undergoing a voluntary or involuntary separation from service.

SPD: A summary plan description, required by ERISA to be distributed to plan participants. It explains the material terms of the plan and contains required technical information and a notice of ERISA rights.

Split-dollar plan: A life insurance plan that gives both the employer and the employee an interest in a cash-value life insurance policy on the employee's life. Either (1) the employer owns the policy and the policy is endorsed to show the employee's beneficial interest (endorsement method), or (2) the employee owns the policy and makes a collateral assignment to the employer to evidence the employer's beneficial interest. The employee has taxable income equal to the value of death benefit coverage paid for by the employer.

STD plan: Short-term disability plan; provides benefits for short-term disability of an employee.

Stop-loss insurance arrangement: A funding mechanism for welfare benefit plans under which an employer self-insures the plan benefits but arranges to have an insurance company pay for claims above a specified level, such as 120 percent of expected claims.

Table I: A table, found in the Treasury regulations under Code Section 79, that gives the monthly cost of providing $1,000 of insurance coverage, based on the employee's age. Table I is used to value coverage under Code Section 79.

TARP: The Troubled Asset Relief Program, established under the Emergency Economic Stabilization Act of 2008.

Term life insurance: Insurance that provides death benefit coverage for a specified period without permanent policy benefits such as cash or loan value.

Title VII: The portion of the Civil Rights Act of 1964 that deals with discrimination in employment. Title VII forbids employment discrimination (e.g., in hiring, firing, and promotion) based on criteria such as race, sex, religion, and national origin.

Treasury regulations: Regulations promulgated by the U.S. Department of the Treasury. The IRS is a part of the Treasury Department, and regulations interpreting the Internal Revenue Code are technically Treasury regulations.

Use-it-or-lose-it rule: A rule forbidding cafeteria plans to let participants defer receipt (and taxation) of compensation from year to year by carrying over unused pretax contributions or plan benefits.

USERRA: The Uniformed Services Employment and Reemployment Rights Act of 1994.

VEBA: Voluntary employees' beneficiary association; a tax-exempt welfare benefit fund regulated by Code Section 501 (c) (9) that pays death, sickness, accident, or other benefits to members, their dependents, and/or beneficiaries.

VFCP: Voluntary Fiduciary Correction Program (VFCP), a DOL program that allows plan fiduciaries to voluntarily correct certain types of prohibited financial transactions.

WARN Act: Worker Adjustment and Retraining Notification Act of 1988.

Welfare benefit plan: See Employee welfare benefit plan.

WHCRA: The Women's Health and Cancer Rights Act of 1998.

WRERA: The Worker, Retiree, and Employer Recovery Act of 2008.

ZEBRAs: Zero Balance Cafeteria Plan Accounts; under such accounts participants purchase medical expense reimbursement coverage by making salary reduction contributions only in the amount to be reimbursed. Such arrangements are specifically forbidden in cafeteria plans.

Cases

[References are to question numbers.]

E

H

I

J

K

L

N

O

P

R

S

T

U

V

Department of Labor Regulations and Pronouncements

[References are to question numbers.]

ERISA Sections

[References are to question numbers.]

Internal Revenue Code Sections

[References are to question numbers.]

Index

References are to question numbers.

F

Q